# Fundamentals of Taxation

## 2022

**Ana Cruz**

*Miami Dade College*

**Michael Deschamps**

*MiraCosta College*

**Frederick Niswander**

*East Carolina University*

**Debra Prendergast**

*Governors State University*

**Dan Schisler**

*East Carolina University*

McGraw Hill

FUNDAMENTALS OF TAXATION 2022 EDITION, FIFTEENTH EDITION

Published by McGraw Hill LLC, 1325 Avenue of the Americas, New York, NY 10019. Copyright © 2022 by McGraw Hill LLC. All rights reserved. Printed in the United States of America. Previous editions © 2021, 2020, and 2019. No part of this publication may be reproduced or distributed in any form or by any means, or stored in a database or retrieval system, without the prior written consent of McGraw Hill LLC, including, but not limited to, in any network or other electronic storage or transmission, or broadcast for distance learning.

Some ancillaries, including electronic and print components, may not be available to customers outside the United States.

This book is printed on acid-free paper.

1 2 3 4 5 6 7 8 9 LMN 26 25 24 23 22 21

ISBN 978-1-260-73431-7 (bound edition)
MHID 1-260-73431-5 (bound edition)
ISBN 978-1-264-20940-8 (loose-leaf edition)
MHID 1-264-20940-1 (loose-leaf edition)

Portfolio Manager: *Kathleen Klehr*
Product Developer: *Allie Kukla/Elizabeth Pappas*
Marketing Manager: *Claire McLemore*
Content Project Managers: *Jill Eccher/Emily Windelborn*
Buyer: *Susan K. Culbertson*
Designer: *Matt Diamond*
Content Licensing Specialist: *Melissa Homer*
Cover Image: *(group meeting) Chris Ryan/age fotostock; (family cookout) Blend Images/Image Source; (parents with baby) Mike Kemp/Blend Images/ Brand X/Getty Images; (cars on the street)) art2002/iStock/Getty Images; (working on laptop) Foxy burrow/Shutterstock*
Compositor: *Straive*

All credits appearing on page or at the end of the book are considered to be an extension of the copyright page.

The Internet addresses listed in the text were accurate at the time of publication. The inclusion of a website does not indicate an endorsement by the authors or McGraw Hill LLC, and McGraw Hill LLC does not guarantee the accuracy of the information presented at these sites.

I dedicate this work to my parents.

*– Ana Cruz*

To my lovely wife Shannon for all of her support and encouragement and to my students whose curiosity and enthusiasm greatly enrich this experience.

*– Michael Deschamps*

To my wife Debi, who keeps me grounded.

*– Rick Niswander*

To my family: You are the parts that make me whole. I dedicate this work to you.

*– Debra Prendergast*

I would like to dedicate this text to my wife Debra, and my daughters Jessica and Samantha.

*– Dan Schisler*

©iStockphoto/Getty Images

# Updates to the 2022 Edition

**Chapter-by-chapter enhancements that have been made in the 2022 edition include the following:**

 New for the 15<sup>th</sup> edition, **Enrolled Agent Fast Facts** are included in every chapter. Each Fast Fact highlights a feature of, or benefit to, becoming an Enrolled Agent (EA), a certification awarded by the US Department of the Treasury. Each Fast Fact will also include a link for students to register for free access to Surgent's EA exam review for Part I of the EA exam at https://Surgent.com/McGrawHill/EA. Surgent is a nationwide leader in exam review preparation and a partner with McGraw Hill in promoting the EA certification to students.

## Throughout text

- Updated all tax forms, schedules, and worksheets.

## Chapter 1

- Added text for the $1,400 Recovery Rebate Credit under provisions of the American Rescue Plan Act (ARPA).
- Updated the standard deduction increases to $25,100 for married and $12,550 for single.
- Updated text for new social security limit.
- Revised text for new tax tables and new tax rate schedules.

## Chapter 2

- Updated the standard deduction increases to $25,100 for married, $12,550 for single, and $18,800 for head of household. Additional standard deduction amounts also increase.
- Revised Table 2-1 line-by-line look at Form 1040 and Schedules 1 through 3.
- Revised the introduction to Child Tax Credit to incorporate changes from the ARPA.
- Updated social security wage limit.
- Revised rate of interest on assessments for nonpayment, underpayment, or late payment of tax. Also updated penalty amounts for failure to file.

## Chapter 3

- Updated income thresholds for taxation of dividends and capital gains.
- Updated text related to employer payment of up to $5,250 of employee student loans for extension of time until 2025.
- Adjusted tax-free exclusion amount under dependent care assistance plans.
- Updated inflation-adjusted phaseout amounts for interest income exclusion for savings bonds.

## Chapter 4

- Revised text to reflect increase to $600 for charitable contribution deduction for married-filing-jointly taxpayers who do not itemize.
- Added text indicating that discharged student loan debt is not taxable through 2025.
- Updated the limits for Health Savings Accounts (HSAs).
- Added text for COVID-related personal protective equipment (PPE) expenditures that are permitted for HSA disbursements and the educator expense deduction.
- Removed text on the Tuition and Fees Deduction which expired at the end of 2020.

## Chapter 5

- Adjusted the limitations for long-term care insurance.
- Updated the standard milage allowance amount for medical expense.
- Added language noting that COVID-related PPE expenses qualify as an itemized deduction for medical expenses.
- Noted that the AGI limitation for itemized charitable contributions from 60% to 100% has been extended through 2021.
- Revised text to reflect increase to $600 for charitable contribution deduction for married-filing-jointly taxpayers who do not itemize.
- Noted that the mortgage insurance premium deduction was extended through 2021.
- Added text explaining that taxpayers can take a penalty-free distribution of up to $100,000 from a retirement plan for repair and replacement expenses incurred in a qualified disaster area.

## Chapter 6

- Revised upper limit for Section 179 expense deduction, the standard mileage rate, and self-employment tax income limits.
- Added text related to 100% deductibility for meals provided by a restaurant for 2021 and 2022 under provisions of the Consolidated Appropriations Act of 2021.
- Updated the phaseout ranges for qualified business income deduction limitations.

## Chapter 7

- Modified income thresholds for taxation of dividends and capital gains.

## Chapter 9

- Revised text for the credit for child and dependent care assistance to reflect increased credit amounts, higher expense percentages, modified phaseoutphaseout limits, and the full refundability of the credit for 2021.
- Modified text to reflect that both education credits now have the same phaseout limits.
- Extensively revised coverage of the child tax credit to reflect changes to the maximum credit amount, creation of multiple phaseout amounts and mechanisms, new provisions for advanced payments, and the full refundability of the credit.
- Updated income limitations for retirement savings contribution credit.
- Changed adoption credit maximum deduction as well as AGI phaseout limits.
- Revised income and phaseout limitations for the Earned Income Tax Credit and noted that 2019 earned income can be used for credit calculation.
- Revised poverty level amounts used to calculate the premium tax credit and noted that the 400% household income upper limit is eliminated for 2021 and 2022.

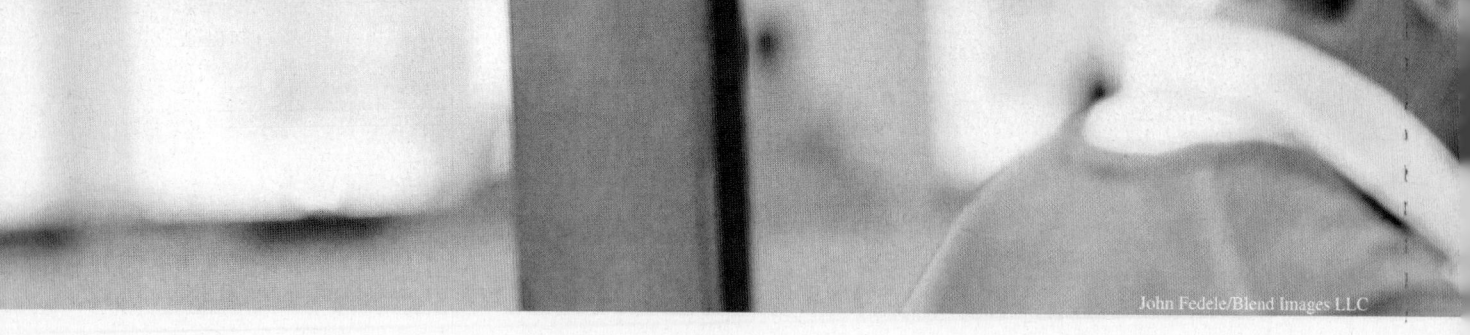

## Chapter 10

- Revised withholding allowances, withholding tables, calculation of withholding amounts and social security wage limit.
- Revised text for the employee retention tax credit to reflect changes from the Taxpayer Certainty and Disaster Tax Relief Act of 2020.
- Revised penalty amounts for filing incorrect or late Form W-2s.

## Chapter 11

- Changed contribution limits for Keogh and SEP defined contribution plans.
- Updated benefit limits for defined benefit plans.
- Revised phaseout thresholds for contributions to traditional IRA and Roth IRA plans.
- Revised examples for starting IRA Required Minimum Distributions (RMD) to further explain the effect of changing starting age from 70½ to 72.
- Updated list of exemptions to 10% withdrawal penalty of retirement plan distributions.

## Chapter 13

- Revised income and exemption thresholds for Alternative Minimum Tax.

## Chapter 15

- Revised text to reflect increase of the limitation on corporate charitable contributions through 2021.
- Noted that business meals provided by a restaurant are fully deductible in 2021 and 2022.

**Remote Proctoring & Browser-Locking Capabilities**

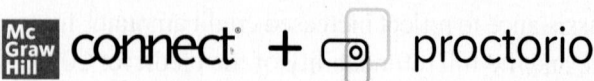

Remote proctoring and browser-locking capabilities, hosted by Proctorio within Connect, provide control of the assessment environment by enabling security options and verifying the identity of the student. Seamlessly integrated within Connect, these services allow instructors to control students' assessment experience by restricting browser activity, recording students' activity, and verifying students are doing their own work. Instant and detailed reporting gives instructors an at-a-glance view of potential academic integrity concerns, thereby avoiding personal bias and supporting evidence-based claims.

# Digital Features

## Tableau Dashboard Activities

Tableau Dashboard Activities allow students to explore live Tableau dashboards directly integrated into Connect through interactive filters and menus as well as auto-graded questions focused on both calculates and analysis. Students can check their understanding and apply what they are learning within the framework of analytics and critical thinking.

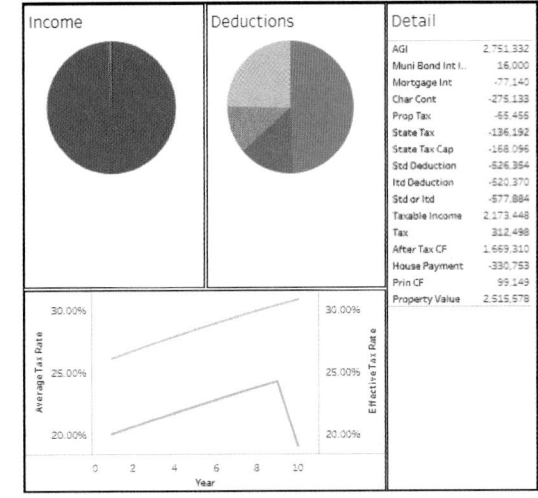

## Writing Assignment

Available within Connect and Connect Master, the Writing Assignment tool delivers a learning experience to help students improve their written communication skills and conceptual understanding. As an instructor you can assign, monitor, grade, and provide feedback on writing more efficiently and effectively.

## Test Builder in Connect

Available within Connect, Test Builder is a cloud-based tool that enables instructors to format tests that can be printed, administered within a Learning Management System, or exported as a Word document of the test bank. Test Builder offers a modern, streamlined interface for easy content configuration that matches course needs, without requiring a download.

Test Builder allows you to

- access all test bank content from a particular title.
- easily pinpoint the most relevant content through robust filtering options.
- manipulate the order of questions or scramble questions and/or answers.
- pin questions to a specific location within a test.
- determine your preferred treatment of algorithmic questions.
- choose the layout and spacing.
- add instructions and configure default settings.

Test Builder provides a secure interface for better protection of content and allows for just-in-time updates to flow directly into assessments.

# Four Primary Teaching Advantages of *Fundamentals of Taxation*

**1** First, we organize the content of *Fundamentals of Taxation* to **closely follow IRS tax forms.** We introduce students to standard IRS forms early and reinforce their use throughout the text. **Actual tax forms are incorporated throughout** giving students the opportunity to understand the principles behind tax law while they learn how to work with clients to obtain the information they will need to complete tax forms.

**2** Second, we **illustrate the proper reporting of tax issues.** We present a tax issue, discuss the legal requirements, illustrate the proper tax form placement, and show the completed form in the text. By effectively leading the student through each issue, we demonstrate how tax form preparation is the result of a careful process that balances legal knowledge with practical experience using tax forms.

**3** Third, we **integrate an individual income tax software package** into the content and refer to its examples. We instruct students how to use the software to complete returns using sample "taxpayers" who appear from chapter to chapter. An important consideration in writing *Fundamentals of Taxation* was to allow instructor flexibility. You can choose to rely heavily on the software, you can incorporate the software only after you cover the law and the reporting, or you can deemphasize the software component. This flexible approach allows you to structure your taxation course the way you want to.

**4** Fourth, we supplement the content with **citations of relevant tax authorities** such as the Internal Revenue Code, Treasury Regulations, Revenue Rulings, Revenue Procedures, and court cases. These citations are almost always provided in **footnotes.** Thus, you and your students can easily use, or not use, the footnote material.

## Ana Cruz

Courtesy of
Ana Cruz

Dr. Ana Cruz is chair of the Business Department at Miami Dade College, Wolfson Campus, where she utilizes her extensive experience in the areas of general business, management, accounting, and taxes. She has worked in the service, retailing, and manufacturing industries, as well as in the federal government sector, where she served as a field examiner for the Internal Revenue Service. Dr. Cruz, a certified public accountant, has published several articles in business journals, has participated in several SACS On-Site Committees, and has received the Southeast Banking Corporation Foundation Endowed Teaching Chair (1998) and the Wolfson Senior Foundation Endowed Teaching Chair (2002). She was also named the Professor of the Year for the State of Florida by the Council for Advancement and Support of Education and the Carnegie Foundation (2005).

# How Does *Fundamentals of Taxation* Provide a Clear Path to Student Success?

## Clear Objectives for Your Students

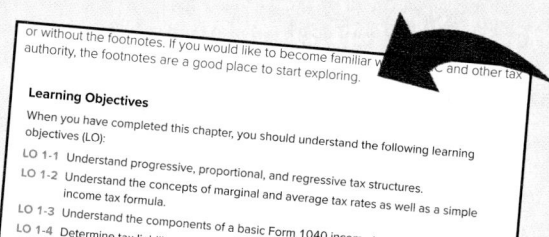

or without the footnotes. If you would like to become familiar w... ...C and other tax authority, the footnotes are a good place to start exploring.

**Learning Objectives**

When you have completed this chapter, you should understand the following learning objectives (LO):

LO 1-1  Understand progressive, proportional, and regressive tax structures.

LO 1-2  Understand the concepts of marginal and average tax rates as well as a simple income tax formula.

LO 1-3  Understand the components of a basic Form 1040 income tax return.

LO 1-4  Determine tax liability in instances when a Form 1040 return is appropriate.

LO 1-5  Understand the types of tax authority and how they interrelate (Appendix A).

LO 1-6  Understand the provisions of IRS Circular 230 for paid tax preparers (Appendix B).

Learning income tax return preparation requires constant reinforcement and practice. The authors have set up *the text* to provide an easy-to-follow format starting with a list of learning objectives, which are then repeated throughout the text where the related material appears.

**Concept Checks** are mini-quizzes that test students' understanding of each objective.

CONCEPT CHECK 2-1— LO 2-1

1. When preparing a tax return, you will seldom use any of the Schedules. True or false?
2. The concept of Adjusted Gross Income (AGI) is important because many deductions and credits reported on the tax return are computed based on the amount shown as AGI. True or false?

LO 12-4: Explain how to exclude a gain on the sale of a personal residence.
- A taxpayer can exclude up to $500,000 ($250,000 i... residence.
- The residence exclusion applies only to the taxpayer...
- The taxpayer must have lived there two of the last fiv...
- Reduced exclusions are available if a move is the res...

LO 12-5: Apply the rules affecting related parties and wash sales.
- A taxpayer cannot deduct any loss from the sale or e...
- Related parties include family members and controlled...
- The wash sale rules disallow a tax loss when the ow...
- A wash sale occurs when a taxpayer sells stock and... the sale) the taxpayer acquires substantially the sam...

A summary of the learning objectives appears at the end of each chapter, providing a quick reference chart for students as they prepare for exams.

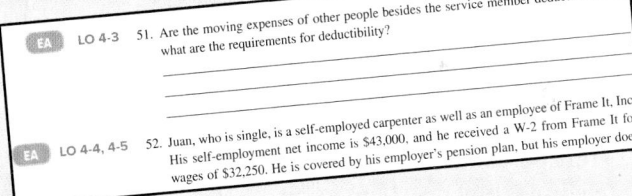

EA  LO 4-3   51. Are the moving expenses of other people besides the service member deductible? If so, what are the requirements for deductibility?

EA  LO 4-4, 4-5   52. Juan, who is single, is a self-employed carpenter as well as an employee of Frame It, Inc. His self-employment net income is $43,000, and he received a W-2 from Frame It for wages of $32,250. He is covered by his employer's pension plan, but his employer does...

The same learning objectives are also referenced in the end-of-chapter material next to each discussion question, multiple-choice question, and problem. Additionally, **marginal EA tags** in the end-of-chapter material help instructors and students identify specific questions that will help prepare students for the Enrolled Agent Exam.

## Debra Prendergast

Courtesy of Debra Prendergast

Dr. Debra Prendergast holds a doctor of philosophy degree in public policy from the University of Illinois at Chicago, a master's of business administration degree from Governors State University, and a bachelor of arts degree in business administration with a concentration in accounting from Saint Xavier University in Chicago. She is a licensed certified public accountant in Illinois. She began her professional career as a management advisory services consultant with Grant Thornton before taking a controller position for an interior resource corporation in Chicago. In 1988, she left the corporate world and began her academic career. She spent 21 years at Northwestern College and in 2010 she became an administrator at Prairie State College. She recently retired as the dean of Mathematics, Natural Sciences, Curriculum and Cooperatives. She also is an adjunct faculty member in the College of Business at Governors' State University.

# Robust and Relevant End-of-Chapter Material

*Fundamentals of Taxation* offers a robust selection of end-of-chapter material.

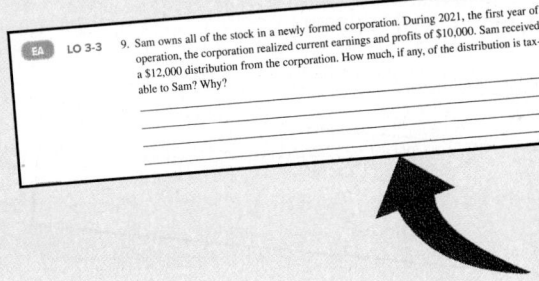

EA  LO 3-3   9. Sam owns all of the stock in a newly formed corporation. During 2021, the first year of operation, the corporation realized current earnings and profits of $10,000. Sam received a $12,000 distribution from the corporation. How much, if any, of the distribution is taxable to Sam? Why?

**Discussion questions** test the basic concepts of each chapter. Students supply short answers to a variety of questions covering each of the major concepts in the chapter.

## Multiple-Choice Questions    connect

All applicable multiple-choice questions are available with *Connect*

EA  LO 2-1   16. A single taxpayer is 26 years old and has wages of $18,350 and interest income of Which Form 1040 Schedule must the taxpayer use?
   a. Schedule 1.
   b. Schedule 2.
   c. Schedule 3.
   d. The taxpayer does not need to use a Schedule.

EA  LO 2-1   17. Which Schedule must the taxpayer use to claim a payment made for alimony if th payer was divorced in 2021?
   a. Schedule 1.
   b. Schedule 2.

**Multiple-choice questions** complement the discussion questions as an alternative way to quickly test a variety of learning objectives. They range from easy to more complex computational multiple choices.

## Tax Return Problems    connect

All applicable tax return problems are available with *Connect*

Use your tax software to complete the following problems. If you are manually preparing the tax returns, you will need to use a Form 1040 and one or more Schedules, depending on the complexity of the problem. *Note to instructors and students:* When using software, certain tax credits may appear on the tax return even though we have not yet discussed those tax credits. This occurs because the taxpayer may be entitled to the credits and the software will automatically include the credit on the final tax return.

For the following tax return problems, assume the taxpayer does NOT wish to contribute to the Presidential Election Fund, unless otherwise stated in the problem. In addition, the taxpayers did not receive, sell, send, exchange, or otherwise acquire any financial interest in any virtual currency during the year.

**Tax Return Problem 1**  Jose and Dora Hernandez are married filing jointly. Their address is 32010 Lake Street, Atlanta, GA 30294. Additional information about Mr. and Mrs. Hernandez is as follows:

Available in Connect, **Auto-graded Tax Return Problems** incorporate the TaxAct software and encourage students to apply a range of concepts they have learned throughout the chapter. All Auto-graded Tax Return Problems can also be done by hand. The authors indicate which forms are needed for each problem.

# Tax Your Brain

The Tax Your Brain feature is designed to work with the examples in the text to reinforce the understanding of key concepts. Students are given information in an example and then asked to apply what they have learned to a different situation.

**TAX YOUR BRAIN**

Assume that Janice's year 2022 wage income will be $50,000 (she worked full time) and she will have $8,300 withheld from her wages. Also assume that she expects to sell a large number of paintings and that she estimates her total 2022 tax liability will be $18,000. To avoid an underpayment penalty, does Janice need to pay estimated payments during 2022 and, if so, how much must she pay?

**ANSWER**

Janice does not need to make any estimated payments. Her required annual payment is $7,854, which is the lower of (a) 90% of $18,000 (the estimate of her 2022 tax liability) or (b) $7,854 (her tax liability for 2021). Because her estimated tax withholdings are $8,300, she is not obligated to make estimated payments. She will need to pay the remaining $9,700 ($18,000 − $8,300) no later than April 15, 2023.

By asking students to think critically about theories and concepts while supplying the answer right after the question, the Tax Your Brain examples provide another opportunity for hands-on experience.

# New Law

The New Law marginal icons in applicable chapters alert students and instructors to key information regarding new tax law that applies to the current year's textbook.

## Frederick Niswander

Dr. Frederick (Rick) Niswander is a professor of accounting after serving for over seven years as Vice Chancellor for Administration and Finance at East Carolina University. He holds a doctor of philosophy degree from Texas A&M University and a bachelor of science in business administration degree from Idaho State University. He has taught introductory financial accounting, international accounting, intermediate accounting, and a graduate accounting course that encompasses taxation, financial, and governmental accounting. Prior to obtaining his doctorate and joining the ECU faculty in 1993, he was the chief financial officer of a privately held real estate company in Phoenix, Arizona, for eight years. Dr. Niswander first became a CPA in 1981 and has been a North Carolina CPA since 1994. He is a member of the North Carolina Association of CPAs, the American Institute of Certified Public Accountants, and the American Accounting Association. He has held leadership roles in the American Institute of CPAs including chair of the Board of Examiners and as a member of the AIPCA Board of Directors.

# How Does *Fundamentals of Taxation* Help Students Better Understand Tax?

## Forms-Based Approach

Examples of completed tax forms demonstrate how tax theory covered in the text translates to real returns.

> **The forms-based approach** to tax concepts in this text gives students the opportunity to apply concepts by completing actual tax forms both manually and through tax software—not only giving them a valuable skill but **ultimately making them more employable in today's workplace.**
>
> —Angela Deaton Mott, Northeast Mississippi Community College

Appendix B includes comprehensive problems for 1040 Schedules A, C, D, and E. These longer problems include both easy and difficult schedules to test students' comprehension of a range of topics covered across multiple chapters.

Incorporation of real-world tax returns into the text for electronic as well as manual preparation forces students to learn hands-on skills.

# Connect Auto-graded Tax Return Problems

**1040 for a Single taxpayer with no dependents.**

| 1040 PG 1 | 1040 PG 2 |

**Form 1040** Department of the Treasury—Internal Revenue Service (99)
**U.S. Individual Income Tax Return** **2021** OMB No. 1545-0074 IRS Use Only—Do not write or staple in this space.

**Filing Status**
Check only one box.
☐ Single ☐ Married filing jointly ☐ Married filing separately (MFS) ☐ Head of household (HOH) ☐ Qualifying widow(er) (QW)
If you checked the MFS box, enter the name of your spouse. If you checked the HOH or QW box, enter the child's name if the qualifying person is a child but not your dependent ▶

| Your first name and middle initial | Last name | Your social security number |
| If joint return, spouse's first name and middle initial | Last name | Spouse's social security number |

Home address (number and street). If you have a P.O. box, see instructions. | Apt. no. | **Presidential Election Campaign** Check here if you, or your spouse if filing jointly, want $3 to go to this fund. Checking a box below will not change your tax or refund.
City, town, or post office. If you have a foreign address, also complete spaces below. | State | ZIP code |
Foreign country name | Foreign province/state/county | Foreign postal code | ☐ You ☐ Spouse

At any time during 2021, did you receive, sell, exchange, or otherwise dispose of any financial interest in any virtual currency? ☐ Yes ☐ No

**Standard Deduction**
Someone can claim: ☐ You as a dependent ☐ Your spouse as a dependent
☐ Spouse itemizes on a separate return or you were a dual-status alien

**Age/Blindness** You: ☐ Were born before January 2, 1957 ☐ Are blind **Spouse:** ☐ Was born before January 2, 1957 ☐ Is blind

**Dependents** (see instructions):
If more than four dependents, see instructions.

| (1) First name   Last name | (2) Social security number | (3) Relationship to you | (4) ✔ if qualifies for (see instructions): |
| | | | Child tax credit | Credit for other dependents |
| | | | ☐ | ☐ |
| | | | ☐ | ☐ |

The **Auto-graded Tax Return Problems,** assignable within *Connect,* provide a much-improved student experience when solving the tax-form-based problems. The **Auto-graded Tax Return Problems** allows students to apply tax concepts by completing the actual tax forms online with automatic feedback and grading for both students and professors.

## Michael P. Deschamps

Courtesy of Michael Deschamps

Michael P. Deschamps received his BS degree in accounting, graduating magna cum laude from the University of San Diego, where he served as the chapter president for Beta Alpha Psi, the accounting honor society. After working in public accounting and obtaining his CPA license, he returned to San Diego State University, where he earned a master's degree in taxation and a certificate in financial planning. In addition, he earned his Enrolled Agent Certificate in 2004 and a Certificate in Online Education from CSU-East Bay in 2017. He is currently a tenured professor and the tax program coordinator at MiraCosta College in Oceanside, CA, where he has developed a highly regarded tax program that leads to the Enrolled Agent Exam and is certified by the State of California for the California Registered Tax Preparer (CRTP) credential. He is an active member of Teachers of Accounting at Two-Year Colleges (TACTYC) and has been a frequent presenter on tax and accounting topics at the organization's national conventions. He has also given presentations on tax and accounting issues to a variety of organizations.

*Fundamentals of Taxation* features an integrated tax software package from TaxAct, one of the leading tax preparation software companies in the market today. Students are instructed in the practical applications of tax software with exercises that teach how software can be used to prepare all types of tax returns.

Sample "taxpayers" are used throughout the book, in varying situations, to give students full exposure to the many types of tax preparation challenges they will face. This exposure allows students to **make the connection** between the **tax law,** the **software inputs,** and the **tax output** on the appropriate tax forms.

*Fundamentals of Taxation* also provides the instructor with the flexibility needed in an individual income tax course. Each chapter can be used **with or without the tax software,** depending on the objectives of an individual instructor's course.

TaxAct features **in-depth form instructions** that supplement *Fundamentals of Taxation,* making it easier than ever to integrate software into the classroom. Students are provided with the latest tax forms via the **Check for Updates from the Online tab in the program,** so that at the start of the semester, each student will be prepared to work with the most up-to-date information available. With over **120 tax forms, schedules, and worksheets,** TaxAct is sure to have the course materials you will need throughout the semester.

**For instructions on how to install the software,** please refer to Chapter 1, Appendix C of this text. You can also visit **www.TaxAct.com** today for more information. Please note, at the time of printing, TaxAct is accessible by PC computers only. To ensure all students are able to access TaxAct, a free-of-charge site license is available to schools permitting downloading of the TaxAct software to school lab computers. Please see the online Instructor Resource site for the site license agreement and instructions for submittal.

> **"** *I currently use* **TaxAct** *for my tax practice, and I like your choice.* **"**
>
> —Natasha Librizzi, Milwaukee Area Technical College

# How Does *Fundamentals of Taxation* Better Prepare My Students?

## From Shoebox to Software

**TaxAct®**
Professional

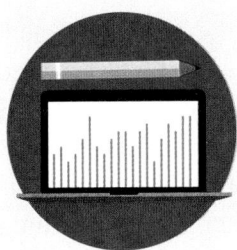

The From Shoebox to Software examples in each chapter help students understand how they start with a mass of paper provided by a client and proceed to a completed tax return using tax software. The student can actually see the jump from the theoretical tax world to practical application.

> *Most importantly, **students learn how to apply** what they learned by preparing tax returns at the end of the chapter, and the bonus is they learn how to use tax software. In 16 weeks, **students would have prepared over 30 tax returns.** This is what attracts students to enroll in the course. It not only meets their requirement for their course of study—they walk away with a life skill.*
>
> —Lolita M. Lockett, Florida Community College at Jacksonville

---

### From Shoebox to Software — Two Comprehensive Examples

We now introduce two new taxpayers.

**YIMING CHOW**

The first taxpayer is Yiming Chow, who is single and lives at 456 Maple Avenue, Ashley, OH 43003. His SSN is 412-34-5670 and date of birth is 10/27/1989. During 2021 Mr. Chow received a W-2 from his employer, a 1099-INT from the local financial institution, and a 1099-DIV associated with a mutual fund investment. He also received a 1099-G from the state of Ohio for a $57 tax refund pertaining to tax year 2020. Mr. Chow did not itemize his deductions in 2020. All these documents are shown in Exhibit 3-8.

Open the tax software. Go to the File pull-down menu and click on New Return. Go through the process to start a new return, and then click on the Forms icon to bring up the list of available forms. Open a Form 1040 to input the basic name, address, and social security number information for Mr. Chow.

Now enter the information from the various tax forms into the tax software using the applicable forms in the Documents Received section. Note that you do not need to enter any information concerning the tax refund. Mr. Chow did not itemize deductions in 2020, so you do not need to report his tax refund as income.

Once you have entered the appropriate information, click on Form 1040. Line 11 should be $41,688. Line 15, taxable income, should be $29,138. Mr. Chow's tax liability on line 16 is $3,284. Because Mr. Chow has wage income and dividend income, you may find it instructive to calculate the tax liability by hand to see if you get the same answer. Because Mr. Chow had $3,750 withheld from his wages, his refund is $466, as shown on lines 34 and 35a. Mr. Chow had qualifying health care coverage at all times during the tax year.

Make sure you save Mr. Chow's return for use in later chapters.

**MR. AND MRS. RAMIREZ**

The second taxpayer is the married couple Jose and Maria Ramirez. They live at 1234 West Street, Ellenwood, GA 30294. They have three children, Arturo, Benito, and Carmen, born in 2008, 2010, and 2012, respectively. The children lived in the household during the entire year. The

SSNs are listed along with the date of birth (in parentheses). The information is as follows:

Jose 412-34-5670 (2/10/1975), Maria 412-34-5671 (4/15/1980), Arturo 412-34-5672 (5/30/2008), Benito 412-34-5673 (8/7/2010), and Carmen 412-34-5674 (1/30/2012).

Mr. Ramirez received a W-2 from his employer, a 1099-INT from the financial institution, and a 1099-DIV from his stockbroker. He also received a 1099-G from the state of Georgia for a $645 tax refund. The taxpayer itemized deductions last year, and you have determined that the entire refund is taxable. All of the Ramirezes' documents are shown in Exhibit 3-9.

Open the tax software. Go to the File pull-down menu and click on New Return. Go through the process to start a new return, and then click on the Forms icon to bring up the list of available forms. Open a blank Form 1040 to input the basic name, address, and social security number information for Mr. and Mrs. Ramirez. Use the Dependent worksheet in the worksheet section to enter information for the children.

For now we will assume that the couple will take the standard deduction.

Now enter the information from the various tax forms into the tax software using the applicable forms in the Documents Received section.

Because you do not have tax return information for tax year 2020, you need to provide information concerning the tax refund. Enter in the system that the full amount of the refund is taxable.

Once you have entered the appropriate information, the total income and the AGI of the taxpayer should be $111,848. After subtracting a standard deduction of $25,100, taxable income should be $86,748.

The tax on line 16 should be $10,376. The tax software automatically calculated a $9,000 child tax credit on line 28. We will discuss this credit in Chapter 9. The credit reduces the Ramirezes' tax liability to $1,376. Because the taxpayer had withholding of $6,418, the Ramirezes' return should show a refund of $5,042 on lines 34 and 35a. Mr. and Mrs. Ramirez had qualifying health care coverage at all times during the tax year.

Make sure you save the Ramirezes' tax return for use in later chapters. These will be running demonstration problems throughout the text.

---

The simulation of real-world situations in each Shoebox example helps students become professional tax preparers. Their first day of work is far less stressful because it is not the first time they have seen a Form 1040 or a Schedule D. They are far more productive because they know where to start and how to complete the work.

# Surgent Enrolled Agent Exam Review Course!

*Surgent*
*EAreview*

Surgent has partnered with McGraw Hill and is making the Enrolled Agent Exam Review Course available to you. The Enrolled Agent credential is awarded by the Internal Revenue Service to tax preparers who pass the three-part IRS Special Enrollment Examination. By earning the Enrolled Agent credential, tax preparers are awarded the same client representation rights as CPAs and attorneys. In addition, Enrolled Agents historically have a higher lifetime earning potential than tax preparers who do not earn the Enrolled Agent credential.

As a student using Cruz, *Fundamentals of Taxation 2022* edition, you are eligible to receive six months of free access to Part One (Individual Taxation) of the Surgent Enrolled Agent Exam Review. To start your free access, please visit **https://Surgent.com/McGrawHill/EA** and complete the registration form. In addition, you are entitled to a discount on the remaining exam sections of our Enrolled Agent Exam Review course. Please see the website above for additional information or to enroll.

## McGraw Hill Customer Experience Group Contact Information

At McGraw Hill, we understand that getting the most from new technology can be challenging. That's why our services don't stop after you purchase our products. You can contact our Product Specialists 24 hours a day to get product training online. Or you can search the knowledge bank of Frequently Asked Questions on our support website. For Customer Support, call **800-331-5094,** or visit **www.mhhe.com/support.** One of our Technical Support Analysts will be able to assist you in a timely fashion.

## Dan Schisler

Courtesy of
Dan Schisler

Dr. Dan Schisler is a professor and research fellow in the Accounting Department at East Carolina University. He holds a doctor of philosophy degree from Memphis State University, a master's degree in accounting—tax concentration from Auburn University, and a bachelor of science degree in accounting from Southeastern Louisiana University. In addition to public accounting experience with Peat Marwick Main & Co., Dr. Schisler has published numerous articles in national academic and practitioner journals such as *Journal of the American Taxation Association, Advances in Taxation,* and *Accounting Horizons.* He teaches tax and accounting at the graduate and undergraduate levels at East Carolina, where he has been recognized for teaching excellence by numerous teaching awards at the department, school, and university levels. Dr. Schisler holds CPA certificates in North Carolina and Louisiana.

# Assurance of Accuracy

Dear Colleague,

As textbook authors, and more importantly, as instructors of taxation, we recognize the great importance placed on accuracy—not only in the book you are now holding but also in the supplements. With this in mind, we have taken the following steps to ensure that *Fundamentals of Taxation* is error-free:

1. We received detailed feedback from dozens of instructor reviews. Each review contributed in significant ways to the accuracy of the content.
2. Each of us wrote, reviewed, and carefully checked the end-of-chapter material.
3. Multiple accuracy checkers reviewed each chapter and its accompanying end-of-chapter material.
4. A copy editor checked the grammar of the final manuscript.
5. A proofreader reviewed each page to ensure that no errors remained.
6. Our Solutions Manual and Testbank were created by the authors and reviewed by independent accuracy checkers.
7. *Connect* content was verified first by independent accuracy checkers and again by the author team.

Given these steps taken, we have the utmost confidence that you and your students will have a great experience using *Fundamentals of Taxation.*

## As We Go to Press

This book is completed in mid-October and printed in early December. We picked that publication date to provide you a book that is as up-to-date as possible. A consequence of using that time frame is that Congress or the IRS may change some aspect of the tax law (especially around year-end or election time) that will affect the material in this book. Thus, it is important that students and instructors utilize *Connect* for information on how tax law changes have affected material in this book.

This book makes liberal use of IRS tax forms to illustrate how the tax law is implemented in practice. In fact, that notion—applying the tax law to practice—is one of the key features of the text.

As noted, we send the book to the printer in late October so we can provide the most up-to-date book as possible to be used for the 2021 tax filing season, which begins in January 2022. When we couple these two notions—using IRS tax forms and an October printing deadline— we must rely on draft tax forms that the IRS releases starting in June and running through the end of the year (see the note about draft tax forms on page 1-9 for more information). Go to the IRS website at www.irs.gov to obtain the final forms.

Sincerely,

*Ana Cruz*
*Mike Deschamps*
*Rick Niswander*
*Debra Prendergast*
*Dan Schisler*

# Instructors: Student Success Starts with You

## Tools to enhance your unique voice

Want to build your own course? No problem. Prefer to use an OLC-aligned, prebuilt course? Easy. Want to make changes throughout the semester? Sure. And you'll save time with Connect's auto-grading too.

# 65%
**Less Time Grading**

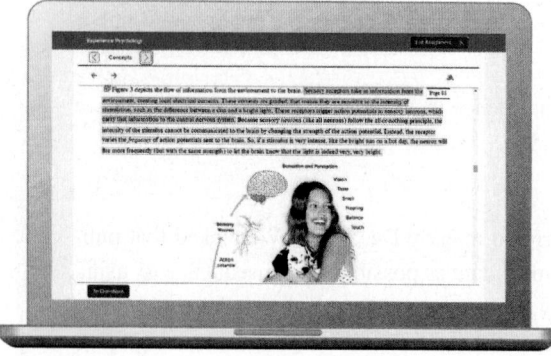

Laptop: McGraw Hill; Woman/dog: George Doyle/Getty Images

## Study made personal

Incorporate adaptive study resources like SmartBook® 2.0 into your course and help your students be better prepared in less time. Learn more about the powerful personalized learning experience available in SmartBook 2.0 at **www.mheducation.com/highered/connect/smartbook**

## Affordable solutions, added value

Make technology work for you with LMS integration for single sign-on access, mobile access to the digital textbook, and reports to quickly show you how each of your students is doing. And with our Inclusive Access program you can provide all these tools at a discount to your students. Ask your McGraw Hill representative for more information.

Padlock: Jobalou/Getty Images

## Solutions for your challenges

A product isn't a solution. Real solutions are affordable, reliable, and come with training and ongoing support when you need it and how you want it. Visit **www.supportateverystep.com** for videos and resources both you and your students can use throughout the semester.

Checkmark: Jobalou/Getty Images

# Students: Get Learning that Fits You

## Effective tools for efficient studying

Connect is designed to help you be more productive with simple, flexible, intuitive tools that maximize your study time and meet your individual learning needs. Get learning that works for you with Connect.

## Study anytime, anywhere

Download the free ReadAnywhere app and access your online eBook, SmartBook 2.0, or Adaptive Learning Assignments when it's convenient, even if you're offline. And since the app automatically syncs with your Connect account, all of your work is available every time you open it. Find out more at **www.mheducation.com/readanywhere**

*"I really liked this app—it made it easy to study when you don't have your text-book in front of you."*

- Jordan Cunningham,
  Eastern Washington University

Calendar: owattaphotos/Getty Images

## Everything you need in one place

Your Connect course has everything you need—whether reading on your digital eBook or completing assignments for class, Connect makes it easy to get your work done.

## Learning for everyone

McGraw Hill works directly with Accessibility Services Departments and faculty to meet the learning needs of all students. Please contact your Accessibility Services Office and ask them to email accessibility@mheducation.com, or visit **www.mheducation.com/about/accessibility** for more information.

Top: Jenner Images/Getty Images, Left: Hero Images/Getty Images, Right: Hero Images/Getty Images

# A Monumental Development Effort

## Acknowledgments

Writing a textbook is always a collaborative effort among authors, the publisher, authors' families, and instructors. The professors listed here contributed their time and insight to help this new edition launch successfully. By attending focus groups, reviewing selected chapters, reading through the whole manuscript, and reviewing page proofs, they contributed careful observations that enabled us to make significant improvements. Each person contributed something different—either a well-deserved criticism or a helpful word of encouragement. We sincerely appreciate their help and professionalism:

Nancy Batch, *Mountain View College*

Margaret Black, *San Jacinto College–North*

Joy Bruce, *Gaston College*

Bernard Bugg, *Shaw University*

Marian Canada, *Ivy Tech Community College*

Amy Chataginer, *Mississippi Gulf Coast Community College–Jefferson Davis*

Amy Conley, *Genesee Community College*

Curtis Crocker, *Central Georgia Technical College*

Geoffrey Danzig, *Miami Dade College–North*

John Daugherty, *Pitt Community College*

Patricia Davis, *Keystone College*

Susan Davis, *Green River Community College*

Peggy DeJong, *Kirkwood Community College*

George DeOrio, *Kaplan Career Institute–ICM Campus Technical College*

Scott Edelman, *Dominican College*

Don Furman, *State University of New York–New Paltz*

Kim W. Gatzke, *Delgado Community College*

Michelle Hayes, *Kalamazoo Valley Community College*

Margaret (Peggy) Helms, *Wayne Community College*

Gary Hollingsworth, *Antonelli College*

Carol Hughes, *Asheville Buncombe Tech Community College*

Norma Hunting, *Chabot College*

Kimberly Hurt, *Central Community College–Grand Island*

Karen Kettelson, *Western Technical College*

Mary Lou Kline, *Reading Area Community College*

Becky Knickel, *Brookhaven College*

Natasha Librizzi, *Milwaukee Area Technical College*

William Lloyd, *Lock Haven University of Pennsylvania*

Susan Logorda, *Lehigh Carbon Community College*

Ivan Lowe, *York Technical College*

Ming Lu, *West LA College*

William Lyle, *Georgia Piedmont Technical College*

Ted Lynch, *Hocking College*

Richard Mandau, *Piedmont Technical College*

Stacie Mayes, *Rose State College*

Mike Metzcar, *Indiana Wesleyan University*

Janelle Montgomery, *Rose State College*

Angela Deaton Mott, *Northeast Mississippi Community College*

Michelle Nickla, *Ivy Tech Community College*

Patricia Diane Nipper, *Southside Virginia Community College–Keysville*

Irene Novikov, *Foothill College*

Chris O'Byrne, *Cuyamaca College*

Cynthia Phipps, *Lake Land College*

Betty Pilchard, *Heartland Community College*

Jennifer Robinson, *Trident Technical College*

Patrick Rogan, *Cosumnes River College*

Dennis Sheridan, *Fayetteville Technical Community College*

Amy Shigley, *Edmonds Community College*

Mark Siegel, *South Texas College of Law*

Bonnie Silbernagel, *Lakeshore Technical College*

Barb Squires, *Corning Community College*

Carolyn Strauch, *Crowder College*

Denise Teixeira, *Chemeketa Community College*

Jerri Tittle, *Rose State College*

Alan Viersen, *MiraCosta College*

Shunda Ware, *Atlanta Technical College*

Kenneth Wise, *Wilkes Community College*

Edwin J. Wu, *Norfolk State University*

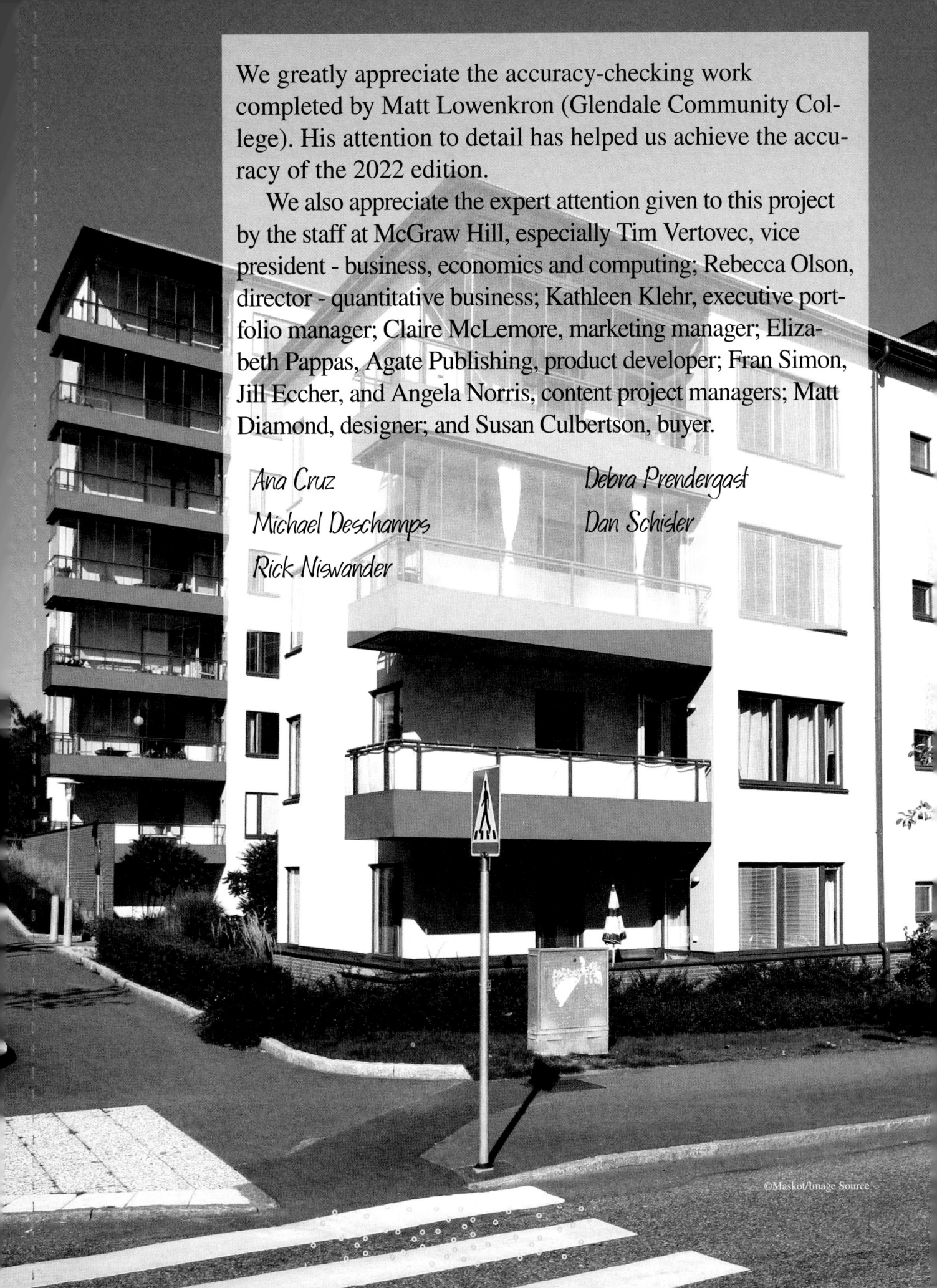

We greatly appreciate the accuracy-checking work completed by Matt Lowenkron (Glendale Community College). His attention to detail has helped us achieve the accuracy of the 2022 edition.

We also appreciate the expert attention given to this project by the staff at McGraw Hill, especially Tim Vertovec, vice president - business, economics and computing; Rebecca Olson, director - quantitative business; Kathleen Klehr, executive portfolio manager; Claire McLemore, marketing manager; Elizabeth Pappas, Agate Publishing, product developer; Fran Simon, Jill Eccher, and Angela Norris, content project managers; Matt Diamond, designer; and Susan Culbertson, buyer.

Ana Cruz                    Debra Prendergast

Michael Deschamps          Dan Schisler

Rick Niswander

# Contents

Caiaimage/Glow Images

## Chapter 7

### Capital Gains and Other Sales of Property (Schedule D and Form 4797)   7-1

©iStockphoto/Getty Images

## Chapter 8

### Rental Property, Royalties, and Income from Flow-Through Entities (Line 5, Schedule 1, and Schedule E)   8-1

kristian sekulic/Getty Images

## Chapter 9

### Tax Credits (Form 1040, Lines 19, 20, 27 through 29, and 31, Schedule 3, Lines 1 through 14)   9-1

Hill Street Studios/Blend Images LLC

## Chapter 10

### Payroll Taxes   10-1

Caia Image/Glow Images

## Chapter 11

### Retirement and Other Tax-Deferred Plans and Annuities   11-1

Maskot/Image Source

## Chapter 12

### Special Property Transactions   12-1

Robert Nicholas/AGE Fotostock

John Fedele/Blend
Images LLC

Chris Ryan/age fotostock

# Fundamentals of Taxation

## 2022

# Chapter One

# Introduction to Taxation, the Income Tax Formula, and Form 1040

This chapter introduces the federal tax system and presents a broad overview of the tax formula. We begin with a wide-angle look at the U.S. tax system and the three types of tax rate structures. We introduce a simplified income tax formula and Form 1040.

Throughout the entire text, the footnotes generally provide citations to the Internal Revenue Code (IRC) and other tax law or regulations. You can read this text either with or without the footnotes. If you would like to become familiar with the IRC and other tax authority, the footnotes are a good place to start exploring.

### Learning Objectives

When you have completed this chapter, you should understand the following learning objectives (LO):

LO 1-1 Understand progressive, proportional, and regressive tax structures.

LO 1-2 Understand the concepts of marginal and average tax rates as well as a simple income tax formula.

LO 1-3 Understand the components of a basic Form 1040 income tax return.

LO 1-4 Determine tax liability in instances when a Form 1040 return is appropriate.

LO 1-5 Understand the types of tax authority and how they interrelate (Appendix A).

LO 1-6 Understand the provisions of IRS Circular 230 for paid tax preparers (Appendix B).

## INTRODUCTION

The federal government enacted the first federal income tax in 1861 as a method to finance the Civil War. Prior to that time, federal tax revenues came primarily from excise taxes and duties on imported goods. Once the war was over, Congress repealed the income tax. Congress again passed a federal income tax in 1894 to broaden the types of taxes and to increase federal revenues. However, in 1895 the Supreme Court held that the federal income tax was unconstitutional. That ruling resulted in the Sixteenth Amendment to the Constitution in 1913:

### Sixteenth Amendment to the Constitution of the United States of America

The Congress shall have power to lay and collect taxes on incomes, from whatever source derived, without apportionment among the several States, and without regard to any census or enumeration.

**TABLE 1-1**

**Type and Number of Individual Tax Returns**

Source: IRS Statistics of Income Division, Industrial Master File Data, IRS Data Warehouse, March 2021, *IRS Publication 1304,* September 2020, and *IRS Statistics of Income Bulletin,* Winter 2019, Spring 2018, Table A.

| Type of Tax Return | 2019 | 2018 | 2017 | 2016 |
|---|---|---|---|---|
| Total returns | 157,682,637 | 153,774,296 | 153,095,659 | 150,315,944 |
| Returns electronically filed (included in above) | 148,496,552 | 137,645,234 | 135,994,623 | 132,409,588 |

The Sixteenth Amendment provides the underlying legal and statutory authority for the administration and enforcement of individual income taxes. Congress has promulgated tax law that is the primary source of information for what is, and is not, permitted. That tax law is the Internal Revenue Code (IRC). The IRC covers taxation of individuals, corporations, and partnerships, as well as other tax rules. Appendix A in this chapter discusses the types of tax laws, regulations, and court cases that compose what we refer to as *tax authority.* The material in Appendix A is of particular importance to students who want to be involved in tax planning, tax research, and other tax-related activities that require an understanding of taxes beyond a fill-in-the-forms level.

Currently the federal government collects revenue from various types of taxes. The largest revenue generators are the individual income tax, social security tax, corporate income tax, federal gift and estate tax, and various excise taxes. This text focuses on the largest revenue generator for the federal government: the individual income tax.[1] In tax year 2019, the most current year available, the federal government collected $1.48 trillion in income tax on $11.3 trillion of gross income ($8.7 trillion of taxable income) as reported on 157.7 million individual tax returns.[2] Table 1-1 presents a breakdown of the number of individual tax returns filed for 2016 through 2019.

One major criticism of the current tax system is the complexity of the law and the length of the forms. Complexity in the tax system is not necessarily bad. Taxpayers often do not realize that many provisions that require use of the more complex tax forms are deduction or credit provisions that actually *benefit* the taxpayer. This text will help you understand the tax system's complexity, the rationale behind some of the complexity, and how to complete a tax return effectively.

Taxpayers report their income and expense to the Internal Revenue Service (IRS) on a Form 1040 plus, if appropriate, various Schedules. For a simple tax return, the taxpayer will use just the Form 1040. As a return gets more complicated, taxpayers can use one or more of three Schedules to provide additional information to properly prepare their tax return. The Schedules are all numbered as Schedule 1, Schedule 2, and Schedule 3. In this chapter, we will introduce the basic Form 1040 and a part of Schedule 1. In future chapters, we will discuss the rest of Schedule 1 and the remaining Schedules.

In tax year 2019, the IRS added Form 1040-SR intended for Seniors. It is substantially the same as a Form 1040, but formatted with a larger type size. We do not discuss the Form 1040-SR in this text.

# TAX RATE STRUCTURES

## LO 1-1

The study of taxation must begin with a basic understanding of rate structures and the tax system. We will discuss three different types of tax rate structures:

1. Progressive rate structure.
2. Proportional rate structure.
3. Regressive rate structure.

Each of these rate structures is present in the tax collection system at the local, state, or federal level. Taxing authorities use one or more of these structures to assess most taxes.

---

[1] The last two chapters are an overview of partnership and corporate taxation.

[2] IRS Statistics of Income Division, Individual Master File Data, IRS Data Warehouse, March 2021.

**TABLE 1-2**
**Individual Income Tax Rate Brackets for Married Taxpayers for Tax Year 2021**

| Taxable Income | Tax Rate |
|---|---|
| Up to $19,900 | 10.0% |
| $19,901–$81,050 | 12.0% |
| $81,051–$172,750 | 22.0% |
| $172,751–$329,850 | 24.0% |
| $329,851–$418,850 | 32.0% |
| $418,851–$628,300 | 35.0% |
| Over $628,300 | 37.0% |

## Progressive Rate Structure

With a *progressive structure,* the tax rate increases as the tax base increases. The tax rate is applied to the tax base to determine the amount of tax. The most obvious progressive tax in the United States, and the focus of this text, is the federal income tax. Table 1-2 illustrates the progressive rate structure of the individual income tax for married taxpayers who file joint returns.

The federal income tax is progressive because the tax rate gets larger as the taxable income (tax base) increases. For very low taxable income, the tax rate is 10% per additional dollar of income, and for very high taxable income, the tax rate is 37% per additional dollar.

**EXAMPLE 1-1**

Mary and George are married, file a joint federal tax return, and have taxable income of $335,000. Their tax liability is

| | |
|---|---:|
| $19,900 × 10% = | $ 1,990.00 |
| ($81,050 − $19,900) × 12% = | 7,338.00 |
| ($172,750 − $81,050) × 22% = | 20,174.00 |
| ($329,850 − $172,750) × 24% = | 37,704.00 |
| ($335,000 − $329,850) × 32% = | 1,648.00 |
| Total tax liability | $68,854.00 |

Note from Example 1-1 that as the tax base (taxable income) increases, the tax rate per dollar of income gets progressively larger, rising from 10% to 32%.

**TAX YOUR BRAIN**

On average, how much income tax did Mary and George pay on their taxable income, and how do you interpret your answer?

**ANSWER**

Mary and George had an average tax rate of about 20.55% calculated as their tax liability of $68,854 divided by their taxable income of $335,000. This means that, on average, for each dollar of taxable income, Mary and George paid 20.55 cents to the federal government for income tax.

Table 1-3 provides some additional evidence of the progressivity of the U.S. tax system. Note that although it appears that taxpayers in the under $15,000 category paid a higher proportion of tax, the group also reported Earned Income Credit much greater than the total tax liability, which means that most taxpayers in this category received a refund greater than they paid in taxes. The Earned Income Credit is a tax credit discussed in Chapter 9 that is intended to support lower income workers to enable them to continue to work. The average tax rates in Table 1-3 confirm that the individual income tax is indeed a progressive tax.

**TAX YOUR BRAIN**

In Table 1-3, compare those taxpayers with incomes less than $100,000 to those taxpayers with incomes greater than $100,000. What does your comparison suggest about income progressivity?

**ANSWER**

Over 124 million taxpayers had adjusted gross income of less than $100,000, and this group paid over $251 billion of individual income tax. There were over 29 million taxpayers with income over $100,000 and they paid tax of almost $1.3 trillion. This is further support for the notion that the U.S. individual income tax system is a progressive system.

**TABLE 1-3** Individual Income Tax Returns from 2019, Number of Tax Returns, Taxable Income (in thousands), Total Tax Liability (in thousands), and Average Tax Rate by Ranges of Adjusted Gross Income

Source: IRS Statistics of Income Division, Individual Master File Data, IRS Data Warehouse, March 2021.

| Item | Ranges of Adjusted Gross Income | | | | | |
|---|---|---|---|---|---|---|
| | Under $15,000 | $15,000 to under $30,000 | $30,000 to under $50,000 | $50,000 to under $100,000 | $100,000 to under $200,000 | $200,000 or more |
| Number of returns | 39,269,402 | 27,369,909 | 27,138,637 | 34,436,449 | 20,908,838 | 8,559,402 |
| Taxable income | $6,938,229 | $192,881,768 | $604,264,808 | $1,753,557,416 | $2,304,350,171 | $3,864,997,623 |
| Total tax liability | $777,332 | $14,769,011 | $50,115,871 | $186,008,777 | $317,634,367 | $906,217,543 |
| Average tax rate* | 11.20% | 7.66% | 8.29% | 10.61% | 13.78% | 23.45% |

*The average tax rate is total tax liability divided by taxable income.

## Proportional Rate Structure

With a proportional tax structure, the tax *rate* remains the same regardless of the tax base. The popular name for a proportional tax is a *flat tax*. The most common flat or proportional taxes in existence in the United States are state and local taxes levied on either property or sales. For example, a local sales tax could be 6% on the purchase of a new car. Regardless of whether the price of the car (the tax base) was $15,000 or $80,000, the tax rate would still be 6% and the taxpayer would pay either $900 or $4,800 in sales tax, depending on the car purchased.

Another proportional tax is the Medicare tax. This tax pays for medical expenses for individuals over age 65. The rate is 2.9% of every dollar of wage income or self-employment income. There is an additional 0.9% tax on income over $250,000 for married taxpayers and $200,000 for most others. We discuss this in Chapter 10. We also discuss an additional 3.8% Medicare tax for high-income taxpayers in Chapter 7. Thus, a doctor will pay Medicare tax of $4,350 on the $150,000 of net income from her medical practice (2.9% × $150,000), and a golf professional will pay $2,900 from his $100,000 tournament winnings (2.9% × $100,000). Although the doctor pays more total tax, the *rate* of tax is the same for both the doctor and the golf professional.

In recent years, there have been political movements to replace the current progressive tax system with a flat tax. One plan called for a 17% flat tax on income. Compared to the current system, the 17% flat tax would result in an increase in tax liability for taxpayers with income of less than $200,000 and a decrease in tax liability for taxpayers with income of more than $200,000 (see Table 1-3).

## Regressive Rate Structure

With a regressive tax, the rate decreases as the tax base increases. The social security tax is the most common regressive tax. The rate for social security taxes is 6.2% (12.4% for self-employed taxpayers) on the first $142,800 of wages in tax year 2021. Once wages exceed the $142,800 ceiling, social security taxes cease. Thus, the rate drops (from 6.2% to 0%) as the tax base increases.

**CONCEPT CHECK 1-1— LO 1-1**

1. The three types of tax rate structures are _____, _____, and _____.
2. The tax rate structure for which the tax rate remains the same for all levels of the tax base is the _____ rate structure.
3. The federal income tax system is an example of a _____ tax structure.

# MARGINAL TAX RATES AND AVERAGE TAX RATES
## LO 1-2

Newspaper and magazine articles often discuss taxes and use the terms *average tax rate* and *marginal tax rate*. These two terms are not interchangeable; they mean very different things.

The average tax rate is the percentage that a taxpayer pays in tax given a certain amount of taxable income. The marginal tax rate represents the proportion of tax that a taxpayer pays on the last dollar (or, more accurately, the *next* dollar) of taxable income.

Let us assume that Ben and Martha have taxable income of $49,775 and file an income tax return as a married couple. Using the tax rates in Table 1-2, they determine that their tax liability is

| | |
|---|---:|
| $19,900 × 10% = | $1,990.00 |
| ($49,775 − $19,900) × 12% = | 3,585.00 |
| Total tax liability | $5,575.00 |

If you refer to Table 1-2, you will learn that, for a married couple, each dollar of taxable income between $19,900 and $81,050 is taxed at a rate of 12%. In other words, if Ben and Martha earned an additional $100 of taxable income, they would owe the federal government an additional $12. Thus, their marginal tax rate (the rate they would pay for an additional dollar of income) is 12%.

Conversely, the average rate is the percentage of total tax paid on the entire amount of taxable income. Ben and Martha have taxable income of $49,775 on which they had a tax liability of $5,575. Their average rate is 11.2% ($5,575/$49,775). The average rate is, in effect, a blended rate. Ben and Martha paid tax at a 10% rate on some of their taxable income and at a 12% rate on the rest of their income. Their average rate is a mixture of 10% and 12% that, in their case, averages out to 11.2%.

---

**TAX YOUR BRAIN**

For Ben and Martha, the marginal rate was larger than the average rate. Is that always the case?

**ANSWER**

No. When taxable income is zero or is within the lowest tax bracket (from $0 to $19,900 for married couples), the marginal rate will be equal to the average rate. When taxable income is more than the lowest tax bracket, the marginal rate will always be larger than the average rate.

---

# A SIMPLE INCOME TAX FORMULA
## LO 1-2

Taxpayers must annually report their taxable income, deductions, and other items to the IRS. Taxpayers do so by filing an income tax return. In its most simplified form, an individual income tax return has the following components:

> Income
> − Permitted deductions from income
>
> = Taxable income
> × Appropriate tax rates
>
> = Tax liability
> − Tax payments and tax credits
>
> = Tax refund or tax due with return

Although many income tax returns are complex, the basic structure of every tax return follows this simplified formula. For many taxpayers, this simplified formula is sufficient.

For example, most individuals who receive all their income from an hourly or salaried job have a tax return that conforms to this basic structure. In later chapters we will expand on this tax formula, and we will provide more information about complexities in our tax laws. However, for this chapter the simplified version is appropriate.

**CONCEPT CHECK 1-2— LO 1-2**

1. The marginal tax rate is the rate of tax imposed on the next dollar of taxable income. True or false?
2. What is the marginal tax rate for a married couple with taxable income of $97,350?
3. Average tax rate and marginal tax rate mean the same thing. True or false?
4. Complex tax returns do not follow the basic (or simplified) income tax formula. True or false?

# THE COMPONENTS OF A BASIC FORM 1040
## LO 1-3

Taxpayers must annually report their income, deductions, tax liability, and other items to the federal government. They do so by filing a tax return called a Form 1040, shown in Exhibit 1-1.

Let us review the components of the simplified tax formula and how they apply to filing Form 1040. We will refer to the line numbers from the form in much of the discussion.

### Filing Status

Taxpayers must determine and declare a filing status. They are single, married filing a joint return with a spouse, married filing separately, head of household, or qualifying widow(er). The filing status is important because income is taxed at different rates depending on the appropriate filing status.

For purposes of this chapter, we will assume the taxpayer is either single or married filing a joint return. We explain the additional categories and expand our discussion of filing status in Chapter 2.

### Wages, Salaries, and Tips (Form 1040, line 1)

Wages, salaries, and tips are the major sources of gross income for most taxpayers. In fact, for millions of Americans, these items are their only source of income. Individuals receive wages, salaries, and tips as "compensation for services."[3] This category is quite broad and encompasses commissions, bonuses, severance pay, sick pay, meals and lodging,[4] vacation trips or prizes given in lieu of cash, fringe benefits, and similar items.[5]

Employees receive wages and related income from their employers. Income received as a self-employed individual (independent contractor) does not meet the definition of wages and is reported on Schedule C. We discuss Schedule C in Chapter 6.

Wages include tips.[6] Employees receiving tip income must report the amount of tips to their employers.[7] They use IRS Form 4070 for that purpose. Large food and beverage establishments (those at which tipping is customary and that employ more than 10 employees on a typical business day) must report certain information to the IRS and to employees.[8] These employers must also allocate tip income to employees who normally receive tips. You can find more information about reporting tip income in IRS Publication 531, available on the IRS website at www.irs.gov.

Taxpayers classified as employees who receive compensation will receive a Form W-2 (see Exhibit 1-2) from their employer indicating the amount of wage income in box 1, "Wages, tips, other compensation." This amount is reported on line 1 of Form 1040.

[3] IRC § 61(a)(1).
[4] Unless excluded under IRC § 119.
[5] Reg. § 1.61-2 and § 1.61-21.
[6] IRC § 3401(f).
[7] IRC § 6053(a).
[8] IRC § 6053(c).

**EXHIBIT 1-1**

Form **1040** Department of the Treasury—Internal Revenue Service (99)
**U.S. Individual Income Tax Return** 2021 OMB No. 1545-0074 IRS Use Only—Do not write or staple in this space.

**Filing Status**
Check only one box.
☐ Single ☐ Married filing jointly ☐ Married filing separately (MFS) ☐ Head of household (HOH) ☐ Qualifying widow(er) (QW)

If you checked the MFS box, enter the name of your spouse. If you checked the HOH or QW box, enter the child's name if the qualifying person is a child but not your dependent ▶

| Your first name and middle initial | Last name | Your social security number |
|---|---|---|
| If joint return, spouse's first name and middle initial | Last name | Spouse's social security number |

Home address (number and street). If you have a P.O. box, see instructions. | Apt. no. |

City, town, or post office. If you have a foreign address, also complete spaces below. | State | ZIP code |

Foreign country name | Foreign province/state/county | Foreign postal code |

**Presidential Election Campaign** Check here if you, or your spouse if filing jointly, want $3 to go to this fund. Checking a box below will not change your tax or refund.
☐ You ☐ Spouse

At any time during 2021, did you receive, sell, exchange, or otherwise dispose of any financial interest in any virtual currency? ☐ Yes ☐ No

**Standard Deduction**
Someone can claim: ☐ You as a dependent ☐ Your spouse as a dependent
☐ Spouse itemizes on a separate return or you were a dual-status alien

**Age/Blindness** You: ☐ Were born before January 2, 1957 ☐ Are blind   Spouse: ☐ Was born before January 2, 1957 ☐ Is blind

**Dependents** (see instructions):
If more than four dependents, see instructions and check here ▶ ☐

| (1) First name  Last name | (2) Social security number | (3) Relationship to you | (4) ✔ if qualifies for (see instructions): Child tax credit | Credit for other dependents |
|---|---|---|---|---|
| | | | ☐ | ☐ |
| | | | ☐ | ☐ |
| | | | ☐ | ☐ |
| | | | ☐ | ☐ |

Attach Sch. B if required.

| 1 | Wages, salaries, tips, etc. Attach Form(s) W-2 | | | 1 | |
| 2a | Tax-exempt interest | 2a | b Taxable interest | 2b | |
| 3a | Qualified dividends | 3a | b Ordinary dividends | 3b | |
| 4a | IRA distributions | 4a | b Taxable amount | 4b | |
| 5a | Pensions and annuities | 5a | b Taxable amount | 5b | |
| 6a | Social security benefits | 6a | b Taxable amount | 6b | |
| 7 | Capital gain or (loss). Attach Schedule D if required. If not required, check here ▶ ☐ | | | 7 | |
| 8 | Other income from Schedule 1, line 10 | | | 8 | |
| 9 | Add lines 1, 2b, 3b, 4b, 5b, 6b, 7, and 8. This is your **total income** ▶ | | | 9 | |
| 10 | Adjustments to income from Schedule 1, line 26 | | | 10 | |
| 11 | Subtract line 10 from line 9. This is your **adjusted gross income** ▶ | | | 11 | |
| 12a | Standard deduction or itemized deductions (from Schedule A) | 12a | | | |
| b | Charitable contributions if you take the standard deduction (see instructions) | 12b | | | |
| c | Add lines 12a and 12b | | | 12c | |
| 13 | Qualified business income deduction from Form 8995 or Form 8995-A | | | 13 | |
| 14 | Add lines 12c and 13 | | | 14 | |
| 15 | **Taxable income.** Subtract line 14 from line 11. If zero or less, enter -0- | | | 15 | |

**Standard Deduction for—**
• Single or Married filing separately, $12,550
• Married filing jointly or Qualifying widow(er), $25,100
• Head of household, $18,800
• If you checked any box under *Standard Deduction,* see instructions.

For Disclosure, Privacy Act, and Paperwork Reduction Act Notice, see separate instructions. Cat. No. 11320B Form **1040** (2021)

Form 1040 (2021) Page **2**

| | | | |
|---|---|---|---|
| 16 | **Tax** (see instructions). Check if any from Form(s): **1** ☐ 8814 **2** ☐ 4972 **3** ☐ | 16 | |
| 17 | Amount from Schedule 2, line 3 | 17 | |
| 18 | Add lines 16 and 17 | 18 | |
| 19 | Nonrefundable child tax credit or credit for other dependents from Schedule 8812 | 19 | |
| 20 | Amount from Schedule 3, line 8 | 20 | |
| 21 | Add lines 19 and 20 | 21 | |
| 22 | Subtract line 21 from line 18. If zero or less, enter -0- | 22 | |
| 23 | Other taxes, including self-employment tax, from Schedule 2, line 21 | 23 | |
| 24 | Add lines 22 and 23. This is your **total tax** ▶ | 24 | |
| 25 | Federal income tax withheld from: | | |
| a | Form(s) W-2 | 25a | |
| b | Form(s) 1099 | 25b | |
| c | Other forms (see instructions) | 25c | |
| d | Add lines 25a through 25c | 25d | |

If you have a qualifying child, attach Sch. EIC.

| | | | |
|---|---|---|---|
| 26 | 2021 estimated tax payments and amount applied from 2020 return | 26 | |
| 27a | Earned income credit (EIC) | 27a | |
| | Check here if you had not reached the age of 19 by December 31, 2021, and satisfy all other requirements for claiming the EIC. See instructions ▶ ☐ | | |
| b | Nontaxable combat pay election | 27b | |
| c | Prior year (2019) earned income | 27c | |
| 28 | Refundable child tax credit or additional child tax credit from Schedule 8812 | 28 | |
| 29 | American opportunity credit from Form 8863, line 8 | 29 | |
| 30 | Recovery rebate credit. See instructions | 30 | |
| 31 | Amount from Schedule 3, line 15 | 31 | |
| 32 | Add lines 27a and 28 through 31. These are your **total other payments and refundable credits** ▶ | 32 | |
| 33 | Add lines 25d, 26, and 32. These are your **total payments** ▶ | 33 | |

**Refund**

| | | | |
|---|---|---|---|
| 34 | If line 33 is more than line 24, subtract line 24 from line 33. This is the amount you **overpaid** | 34 | |
| 35a | Amount of line 34 you want **refunded to you.** If Form 8888 is attached, check here ▶ ☐ | 35a | |

Direct deposit? See instructions.

▶ b Routing number ▶ c Type: ☐ Checking ☐ Savings
▶ d Account number

| 36 | Amount of line 34 you want **applied to your 2022 estimated tax** ▶ | 36 | |

**Amount You Owe**

| 37 | **Amount you owe.** Subtract line 33 from line 24. For details on how to pay, see instructions ▶ | 37 | |
| 38 | Estimated tax penalty (see instructions) ▶ | 38 | |

**Third Party Designee**

Do you want to allow another person to discuss this return with the IRS? See instructions ▶ ☐ **Yes.** Complete below. ☐ **No**

Designee's name ▶ Phone no. ▶ Personal identification number (PIN) ▶

**Sign Here**

Under penalties of perjury, I declare that I have examined this return and accompanying schedules and statements, and to the best of my knowledge and belief, they are true, correct, and complete. Declaration of preparer (other than taxpayer) is based on all information of which preparer has any knowledge.

Joint return? See instructions. Keep a copy for your records.

| Your signature | Date | Your occupation | If the IRS sent you an Identity Protection PIN, enter it here (see inst.) ▶ |
| Spouse's signature. If a joint return, **both** must sign. | Date | Spouse's occupation | If the IRS sent your spouse an Identity Protection PIN, enter it here (see inst.) ▶ |

Phone no. | Email address

**Paid Preparer Use Only**

| Preparer's name | Preparer's signature | Date | PTIN | Check if: ☐ Self-employed |
| Firm's name ▶ | | | Phone no. | |
| Firm's address ▶ | | | Firm's EIN ▶ | |

Go to *www.irs.gov/Form1040* for instructions and the latest information. Form **1040** (2021)

Source: U.S. Department of the Treasury, Internal Revenue Service, Form 1040. Washington, DC: 2021.

# A Note about Draft Tax Forms

Many of the IRS tax forms used throughout the text have the word "Draft" and a date printed across the form (see Exhibit 1-1). The IRS creates and modifies tax forms during the tax year. These forms are in draft form until they have obtained final approval within the IRS and by the federal Office of Management and Budget. The IRS distributes the draft forms internally, to tax professionals, and to tax software companies. By doing so, the IRS seeks comments to catch errors or to improve the forms. Final approval usually occurs on a rolling basis between mid-October and mid-December. Once the form has received final approval, the "Draft" label is removed and taxpayers can use the final form as they prepare their tax returns.

This text went to press in late October, when most IRS forms were available only in draft form. By the time you read this, final forms will be available on the IRS website (www.irs.gov) and in your tax software after you have updated it.

## Taxable Interest (Form 1040, line 2b)

Interest is compensation for the use of money with respect to a bona fide debt or obligation imposed by law (such as loans, judgments, or installment sales). Interest received by or credited to a taxpayer is taxable unless specifically exempt.[9] Interest paid is often deductible.[10] This section covers interest received.

For individuals, interest income is most often earned in conjunction with savings accounts, certificates of deposit, U.S. savings bonds, corporate bonds owned, seller-financed mortgages, loans made to others, and similar activities.

Generally, interest income is determined based on the interest rate stated in the documents associated with the transaction. Some exceptions exist, and some interest income is nontaxable. These items are discussed in the Appendix to Chapter 3.

Normally, taxpayers will receive a Form 1099-INT that will report the amount of interest earned (see Exhibit 1-3). The amount in box 1 is reported on Form 1040, line 2b.

## Other Income (Form 1040, lines 3 through 6)

The 1040 has lines for dividends (line 3), taxable income from pension and retirement plans (lines 4 and 5), and taxable income from social security (line 6). We discuss these income items in future chapters.

## Additional Income (Form 1040, lines 7 and 8)

The income items listed on lines 1 through 6 are some of the most common. Many other sources of income can be taxable. One type is a capital gain or loss, reported on line 7. We discuss capital gains and losses in Chapter 7. The IRS has placed less-common income items on a separate Schedule, in this case, Schedule 1 (see Exhibit 1-4). Lines 1–9 of Schedule 1 list these additional income items; we will discuss many of these items in future chapters.

## Unemployment Compensation (Form 1040, Schedule 1, line 7)

Federal and state unemployment compensation benefits are taxable.[11] The rationale behind taxing these payments is that they are a substitute for taxable wages. Unemployment benefits are reported to recipients on Form 1099-G in box 1 (see Exhibit 1-5). The amount in box 1 is reported on line 7 of Schedule 1.

Citizens of Alaska also report any Alaska Permanent Fund dividends they receive on line 8f of Schedule 1.

## Standard deduction or itemized deductions (Form 1040, line 12a)

Taxpayers are permitted a standard deduction from income, or they can itemize their deductions, if larger. We discuss itemized deductions in Chapter 5. For purposes of this chapter, the line 12a deduction is either $12,550 if the taxpayer is single or $25,100 if the taxpayer is filing a return as married. These dollar amounts represent the amount of income that is not taxed.

---

[9] IRC § 61(a)(4).

[10] Interest paid in conjunction with a trade or business is covered in Chapter 6. Personal interest paid is in Chapters 4 and 5.

[11] IRC § 85(a).

## EXHIBIT 1-2

| | | |
|---|---|---|
| **a** Employee's social security number | | |

OMB No. 1545-0008 — Safe, accurate, FAST! Use — IRS e-file — Visit the IRS website at www.irs.gov/efile

**b** Employer identification number (EIN)

**1** Wages, tips, other compensation | **2** Federal income tax withheld

**c** Employer's name, address, and ZIP code

**3** Social security wages | **4** Social security tax withheld
**5** Medicare wages and tips | **6** Medicare tax withheld
**7** Social security tips | **8** Allocated tips

**d** Control number

**9** | **10** Dependent care benefits

**e** Employee's first name and initial   Last name   Suff.

**11** Nonqualified plans | **12a** See instructions for box 12
**13** Statutory employee / Retirement plan / Third-party sick pay | **12b**
**14** Other | **12c**
| **12d**

**f** Employee's address and ZIP code

**15** State | Employer's state ID number | **16** State wages, tips, etc. | **17** State income tax | **18** Local wages, tips, etc. | **19** Local income tax | **20** Locality name

Form **W-2** Wage and Tax Statement   **2021**   Department of the Treasury—Internal Revenue Service

Copy B—To Be Filed With Employee's FEDERAL Tax Return.
This information is being furnished to the Internal Revenue Service.

Source: U.S. Department of the Treasury, Internal Revenue Service, Form W-2 Wage and Tax Statement. Washington, DC: 2021.

## EXHIBIT 1-3

☐ CORRECTED (if checked)

PAYER'S name, street address, city or town, state or province, country, ZIP or foreign postal code, and telephone no.

Payer's RTN (optional)

OMB No. 1545-0112

**2021**   Form **1099-INT**

**Interest Income**

**1** Interest income $

**2** Early withdrawal penalty $

**3** Interest on U.S. Savings Bonds and Treas. obligations $

PAYER'S TIN | RECIPIENT'S TIN

Copy B
For Recipient

RECIPIENT'S name

**4** Federal income tax withheld $ | **5** Investment expenses $

**6** Foreign tax paid $ | **7** Foreign country or U.S. possession

Street address (including apt. no.)

**8** Tax-exempt interest $ | **9** Specified private activity bond interest $

City or town, state or province, country, and ZIP or foreign postal code

**10** Market discount $ | **11** Bond premium $

FATCA filing requirement ☐

**12** Bond premium on Treasury obligations $ | **13** Bond premium on tax-exempt bond $

This is important tax information and is being furnished to the IRS. If you are required to file a return, a negligence penalty or other sanction may be imposed on you if this income is taxable and the IRS determines that it has not been reported.

Account number (see instructions)

**14** Tax-exempt and tax credit bond CUSIP no. | **15** State | **16** State identification no. | **17** State tax withheld $ $

Form **1099-INT**   (keep for your records)   www.irs.gov/Form1099INT   Department of the Treasury - Internal Revenue Service

Source: U.S. Department of the Treasury, Internal Revenue Service, Form 1099-INT. Washington, DC: 2021.

**EXHIBIT 1-4**

| SCHEDULE 1 (Form 1040) Department of the Treasury Internal Revenue Service | **Additional Income and Adjustments to Income**  ▶ **Attach to Form 1040, 1040-SR, or 1040-NR.**  ▶ **Go to** *www.irs.gov/Form1040* **for instructions and the latest information.** | OMB No. 1545-0074  **2021**  Attachment Sequence No. **01** |
|---|---|---|

Name(s) shown on Form 1040, 1040-SR, or 1040-NR | Your social security number

### Part I Additional Income

| 1 | Taxable refunds, credits, or offsets of state and local income taxes . . . . . . | **1** | |
|---|---|---|---|
| 2a | Alimony received . . . . . . . . . . . . . . . . . . . | **2a** | |
| b | Date of original divorce or separation agreement (see instructions) ▶ _____ | | |
| 3 | Business income or (loss). Attach Schedule C . . . . . . . . . . | **3** | |
| 4 | Other gains or (losses). Attach Form 4797 . . . . . . . . . | **4** | |
| 5 | Rental real estate, royalties, partnerships, S corporations, trusts, etc. Attach Schedule E . . . . . . . . . . . . . . . . | **5** | |
| 6 | Farm income or (loss). Attach Schedule F . . . . . . . . . . | **6** | |
| 7 | Unemployment compensation . . . . . . . . . . . . . | **7** | |
| 8 | Other income: | | |
| a | Net operating loss . . . . . . . . . . | **8a** | ( ) |
| b | Gambling income . . . . . . . . . . . | **8b** | |
| c | Cancellation of debt . . . . . . . . . . | **8c** | |
| d | Foreign earned income exclusion from Form 2555 . . . . | **8d** | ( ) |
| e | Taxable Health Savings Account distribution . . . . . . . | **8e** | |
| f | Alaska Permanent Fund dividends . . . . . . . . | **8f** | |
| g | Jury duty pay . . . . . . . . . . . . | **8g** | |
| h | Prizes and awards . . . . . . . . . . | **8h** | |
| i | Activity not engaged in for profit income . . . . . . . | **8i** | |
| j | Stock options . . . . . . . . . . . . | **8j** | |
| k | Income from the rental of personal property if you engaged in the rental for profit but were not in the business of renting such property . . . . . . . . . . . . . . | **8k** | |
| l | Olympic and Paralympic medals and USOC prize money (see instructions) . . . . . . . . . . . . . | **8l** | |
| m | Section 951(a) inclusion (see instructions) . . . . . . . . | **8m** | |
| n | Section 951A(a) inclusion (see instructions) . . . . . . . | **8n** | |
| o | Section 461(l) excess business loss adjustment . . . . . . . | **8o** | |
| p | Taxable distributions from an ABLE account (see instructions) . | **8p** | |
| z | Other income. List type and amount ▶ _____ _____ | **8z** | |
| 9 | Total other income. Add lines 8a through 8z . . . . . . . . . | **9** | |
| 10 | Combine lines 1 through 7 and 9. Enter here and on Form 1040, 1040-SR, or 1040-NR, line 8 . . . . . . . . . . . . . . . . . . | **10** | |

| For Paperwork Reduction Act Notice, see your tax return instructions. | Cat. No. 71479F | Schedule 1 (Form 1040) 2021 |
|---|---|---|

Source: U.S. Department of the Treasury, Internal Revenue Service, Schedule 1. Washington, DC: 2021.

**Part II** | **Adjustments to Income**

| | | |
|---|---|---|
| 11 | Educator expenses | 11 |
| 12 | Certain business expenses of reservists, performing artists, and fee-basis government officials. Attach Form 2106 | 12 |
| 13 | Health savings account deduction. Attach Form 8889 | 13 |
| 14 | Moving expenses for members of the Armed Forces. Attach Form 3903 | 14 |
| 15 | Deductible part of self-employment tax. Attach Schedule SE | 15 |
| 16 | Self-employed SEP, SIMPLE, and qualified plans | 16 |
| 17 | Self-employed health insurance deduction | 17 |
| 18 | Penalty on early withdrawal of savings | 18 |
| 19a | Alimony paid | 19a |
| b | Recipient's SSN ▶ | |
| c | Date of original divorce or separation agreement (see instructions) ▶ | |
| 20 | IRA deduction | 20 |
| 21 | Student loan interest deduction | 21 |
| 22 | Reserved for future use | 22 |
| 23 | Archer MSA deduction | 23 |
| 24 | Other adjustments: | |
| a | Jury duty pay (see instructions) | 24a |
| b | Deductible expenses related to income reported on line 8k from the rental of personal property engaged in for profit | 24b |
| c | Nontaxable amount of the value of Olympic and Paralympic medals and USOC prize money reported on line 8l | 24c |
| d | Reforestation amortization and expenses | 24d |
| e | Repayment of supplemental unemployment benefits under the Trade Act of 1974 | 24e |
| f | Contributions to section 501(c)(18)(D) pension plans | 24f |
| g | Contributions by certain chaplains to section 403(b) plans | 24g |
| h | Attorney fees and court costs for actions involving certain unlawful discrimination claims (see instructions) | 24h |
| i | Attorney fees and court costs you paid in connection with an award from the IRS for information you provided that helped the IRS detect tax law violations | 24i |
| j | Housing deduction from Form 2555 | 24j |
| k | Excess deductions of section 67(e) expenses from Schedule K-1 (Form 1041) | 24k |
| z | Other adjustments. List type and amount ▶ | 24z |
| 25 | Total other adjustments. Add lines 24a through 24z | 25 |
| 26 | Add lines 11 through 23 and 25. These are your **adjustments to income.** Enter here and on Form 1040 or 1040-SR, line 10, or Form 1040-NR, line 10a | 26 |

**EXHIBIT 1-5**

| | | |
|---|---|---|
| ☐ **CORRECTED (if checked)** | | |

| PAYER'S name, street address, city or town, state or province, country, ZIP or foreign postal code, and telephone no. | **1** Unemployment compensation $ | OMB No. 1545-0120 **20**21 Form **1099-G** | **Certain Government Payments** |
| | **2** State or local income tax refunds, credits, or offsets $ | | |
| PAYER'S TIN | RECIPIENT'S TIN | **3** Box 2 amount is for tax year | **4** Federal income tax withheld $ | **Copy B For Recipient** |
| RECIPIENT'S name | | **5** RTAA payments $ | **6** Taxable grants $ | This is important tax information and is being furnished to the IRS. If you are required to file a return, a negligence penalty or other sanction may be imposed on you if this income is taxable and the IRS determines that it has not been reported. |
| Street address (including apt. no.) | | **7** Agriculture payments $ | **8** If checked, box 2 is trade or business income ▶ ☐ | |
| City or town, state or province, country, and ZIP or foreign postal code | | **9** Market gain $ | | |
| Account number (see instructions) | | **10a** State | **10b** State identification no. | **11** State income tax withheld $ $ |

Form **1099-G**   (keep for your records)   www.irs.gov/Form1099G   Department of the Treasury - Internal Revenue Service

Source: U.S. Department of the Treasury, Internal Revenue Service, Form 1099-G. Washington, DC: 2021.

### Taxable Income (Form 1040, line 15)

*Taxable income* refers to the wages, interest, and other items on lines 1–8, minus the adjustments to income on line 10, the standard deduction on line 12a, the charitable contribution for those who do not itemize on line 12b, and the Qualified Business Income deduction on line 13.[12] Taxable income is the tax base used to determine the amount of tax.

---

**CONCEPT CHECK 1-3— LO 1-3**

1. Only certain types of income are reported directly on the face of Form 1040. They are _____

2. Unemployment compensation is reported to the taxpayer on a Form _____.

## CALCULATION OF INCOME TAX (FORM 1040, LINE 16) AND HEALTH CARE TAX
**LO 1-4**

### Income Tax (Form 1040, Line 16)

The total amount of tax liability on line 16 of Form 1040 is determined based on the amount of taxable income (line 15). Taxpayers could calculate their tax using the tax rate schedule shown in Table 1-2 (or a similar one if the taxpayer were single). However, that method can be a bit complicated and can result in calculation errors. To make things easier, the IRS has prepared tax tables that predetermine the amount of tax liability for taxable incomes of up to $100,000.

The tax tables applicable for tax year 2021 are printed in Appendix D of this text. Please refer to the 2021 tax tables when reviewing the examples and when working the problems at the end of this chapter unless you are told otherwise.

---

[12] We discuss the qualified business income deduction in Chapter 6.

**EXAMPLE 1-2**

Dembe is a single taxpayer and has taxable income of $42,787. Referring to the tax table, his income is between $42,750 and $42,800. Reading across the table to the Single column gives a tax of $5,159.

**EXAMPLE 1-3**

Jie and Min are married and are filing a joint tax return. They have taxable income of $45,059. In the tax table, their income is between $45,050 and $45,100. Their corresponding tax liability is $5,011.

Notice the effect of a differing filing status. Dembe had lower taxable income than did Jie and Min, but Dembe's tax liability was higher. All other things being equal, for equivalent amounts of taxable income, the highest tax will be paid by married persons filing separately, followed by single persons, then heads of household, and finally by married persons filing jointly. There are two exceptions to this general observation. The first is that, for taxable income up to $9,950, tax liability will be the same for all groups. The second is that married persons filing separately and single persons will have equal tax liability at taxable income levels up to $314,150.

In the preceding examples, we used the tax tables in Appendix D of this text to determine the amount of tax liability. If we calculated the amount of tax using the tax rate schedules provided in Appendix F of this text (or in Table 1-2 for married taxpayers), we would have computed a slightly different number.

**EXAMPLE 1-4**

Bill and Andrea Chappell, a married couple, have taxable income of $48,305. Using the tax tables in Appendix D, their tax liability is $5,401. Using the tax rate schedule in Table 1-2 (and printed in Appendix F of this text), their tax liability is

| | |
|---|---|
| Tax on $19,900 × 10% | $1,990.00 |
| Tax on ($48,305 − $19,900) × 12% | $3,408.60 |
| Total tax | $5,398.60 |

Here the difference between the two tax numbers is $2.40. There will usually be a slight difference between the amount of tax calculated using the tax tables and the amount calculated using the tax rate schedules. The reason is that the tax rate schedules are precise, whereas the tax tables in Appendix D determine tax liability in $50 increments (except for taxable income less than $3,000 where the increments are $25). In fact, the amount of tax liability shown in the tax tables represents the tax due on taxable income exactly in the middle of the $50 increment. The tax tables calculated Bill and Andrea's tax based on taxable income of $48,325 (the middle of the range of $48,300 to $48,350). So, the tax tables added $20 to their taxable income. $20 × 12% marginal rate = $2.40 difference. Thus, a taxpayer with taxable income in the lower half of the increment (like Bill and Andrea in the example) will pay a little more in tax while someone in the upper half of the increment will pay a little less.

Again, unless instructed otherwise, for taxable income under $100,000, use the tax tables in Appendix D when you calculate tax liability.

**TAX YOUR BRAIN**

Determine the precise tax liability using the tax rate schedules in Appendix F for Dembe in Example 1-2 and for Jie and Min in Example 1-3.

**ANSWER**

Using the tax rate schedules, Dembe's tax liability is $5,161.64. The tax liability of Jie and Min is $5,009.08.

### Health Care Tax

The Affordable Care Act requires all individuals to either have health care coverage, or qualify for a health coverage exemption, or make a shared responsibility payment with their tax return. Effective January 1, 2019, the shared responsibility payment is zero. Thus, unlike past tax years, there are no additional calculations and no additional tax in 2021.

### Total Tax (Form 1040, line 24)

Line 24 is the tax from line 16, minus tax credits from Schedule 3 (we discuss these credits in Chapters 2 and 9), plus other taxes from Schedule 2 (we discuss these in Chapters 6, 9, and 10). The amount represents the total amount the taxpayer must pay to the government for the tax year. As we will learn, the taxpayer has likely already paid all or most of this liability.

**CONCEPT CHECK 1-4—**

**LO 1-4**

1. Taxpayers with taxable income under $100,000 *must* calculate their tax liability using the tax tables. True or false?
2. Refer to the tax tables. What is the tax liability of a married couple with taxable income of $91,262? _____
3. Using the tax rate schedule in Table 1-2 (or Appendix F), determine the tax liability (to the nearest penny) for a married couple with taxable income of $91,262. _____

## TAX PAYMENTS (FORM 1040, LINES 25d, 26, AND 32)

**LO 1-3**

Usually, taxpayers pay most of their tax liability prior to the due date of the tax return. Commonly, taxpayers pay through income tax withholding or quarterly estimated tax payments.

When certain taxable payments are made to individuals, the law requires the payer to retain (withhold) a portion of the payment otherwise due and to remit the amount withheld to the Treasury.[13] The withheld amount represents an approximation of the amount of income tax that would be due for the year on the taxable payment. Withholding, credited to the account of the taxpayer, reduces the amount of tax otherwise due to the government on the due date of the return.

Taxpayers have taxes withheld from their wages. When an employer pays a salary or wages to an employee, the employer is required to retain part of the amount otherwise due the employee. The amount retained is payroll tax withholding and is a part of virtually every pay stub in the country. The total amount of individual income tax withheld from the earnings of an employee is shown in box 2 of the Form W-2 given to each employee shortly after the end of the calendar year. The amount in box 2 is transferred to line 25a of Form 1040.

### Earned Income Credit (Form 1040, line 27a)

An Earned Income Credit (EIC) is available for certain low-income taxpayers. The EIC is a percentage of earned income with a phaseout of the credit at higher earned income amounts. For purposes of this chapter, we will assume the EIC is zero. We discuss the EIC in more detail in Chapter 9.

### Total Payments (Form 1040, line 33)

Line 33 is the sum of the tax withholding from line 25d, estimated payments on line 26, and the credits summarized on line 32.

[13] See Chapter 10 for discussion of the rules associated with withholding and remitting payroll taxes.

# From Shoebox to Software An Introduction

Throughout this text, we provide a series of features called From Shoebox to Software. These sections explain how a tax preparer goes about putting together all or part of a tax return. Because this is the first time we have presented a From Shoebox to Software feature, we will explain what it is and how it works.

The majority of the information that appears on a tax return comes from some sort of source document. The most common document is an IRS form. Almost all taxpayers receive source documents provided on standardized IRS forms. These documents include a W-2 for wages, a 1099-INT for interest payments, a 1099-B for stock brokerage transactions, and many others. These documents serve a dual purpose. First, they provide taxpayers information necessary to prepare a portion of their tax returns in a standardized and easy-to-use format. Second, the IRS receives a copy of each document and uses the information to check whether individual taxpayers have properly reported items on their tax returns.

The second type of document used for tax return preparation is a nonstandardized, free-form document. It could be a charge card receipt from a restaurant meal with a business customer, a bill from a hospital for medical care, or a written record (such as a journal) of business car expenses.

Taxpayers accumulate documents during the tax year and then use them when the tax return is prepared. Tax return preparers have a standard joke about clients coming to their office with a pile of documents—some useful, some not. This pile of documents is often called a "shoebox" because many times that's what the documents are kept in during the year. Virtually every tax preparer has a story (often many) about a client who drops a shoebox full of documents on the preparer's desk—often on April 14, the day before the individual income tax return filing deadline.

The tax return preparer must then make sense of the shoebox full of documents. One challenge is to separate the documents useful in the preparation of the return (W-2s,

medical receipts, etc.) from documents that do not matter (the receipt for a new gas grill used by the taxpayer at home). The series of From Shoebox to Software explanations (and your future understanding of tax rules and regulations) will help you extract the valuable documents from the rest of the papers.

From Shoebox to Software explanations will also help you determine how the information from the document is "put into" tax software so the completed return is accurate. It is one thing to have the correct data and quite another to be able to efficiently, effectively, and correctly use them in the software. Many tax software products are available for use. Some are very simple, and others are extremely complex. In this book we use TaxAct software, produced by 2nd Story Software. However, it doesn't matter what software product you use because almost all tax software has a similar structure: Source document information is entered into a series of input forms that then feed into a tax return form that is then assembled with other tax return forms into a final completed tax return. The drawing below illustrates the process.

When you use the tax software, you initially record the information from the source document on a source document input form. For example, you record information from a W-2 source document on a W-2 input form in the tax software. You record most tax information in a similar manner.

Sometimes you record source document data directly on a tax return form. This occurs if the item is unusual or does not "flow" to another form.

The From Shoebox to Software text boxes will show you how to take raw data and enter them correctly on the tax forms. Before you start to use the software, you should take a few minutes to read Appendix C of this chapter, where we provide some basic information and guidelines concerning the TaxAct software that is included with this text.

Source document ⟹ Source document input form ⟹ Tax return form

Source document ⟹ Source document input form ⟹ Tax return form ⟹ Completed tax return

Source document ⟹ Source document input form ⟹ Tax return form

### Tax Refund (line 35a) or Tax Due with Return (line 37)

Compare the amount owed (line 24) with the total amount already paid (line 33). Excess payment results in a refund; remaining tax liability means the taxpayer must pay the remaining amount owed when filing the return.

*(text continues on page 1-18)*

# From Shoebox to Software A Comprehensive Example

This comprehensive example allows you to use what you have learned. Use your tax software and follow along as we explain the procedure. When you have finished, you will have prepared a 1040 using the information in the example.

Your clients are Ed and Betty Davidson, a married couple, both age 52. They live at 456 Main Street, Greenville, NC 27858. Ed's social security number is 412-34-5670 and Betty's is 412-34-5671.[14]

Betty worked at Brenden Manufacturing and received a W-2 from the company. Ed performed volunteer work during the year and received no compensation. They received $372.33 in interest income from First Savings Bank during the year.

You received the following documents (see below and the next page) from the Davidsons.

Open TaxAct. Click on Forms on the toolbar at the top of the page. This will open the Forms Explorer and allow you to select the form you wish to work on. You will use the Forms method to input information into the TaxAct software. We realize that the software has a mode, called Q&A, that will ask the user a series of questions and will create a tax return based on the answers. Tax practitioners seldom use this mode. If you plan to become a tax practitioner (or even if you just want to do your own return yourself), you will need to get in the habit of using the Forms mode to become

more familiar with the various IRS forms used when filing a return.

The Forms Explorer has three primary categories of forms from which to choose:

**Forms and schedules:** This section includes all of the IRS forms that you need to complete a tax return. At this point, we care about only one form—the 1040.

**Documents received:** Earlier we mentioned that the Shoebox contains two types of source documents. One type of source document is an IRS form. In the Documents Received section, you will find input screens for many IRS forms received by taxpayers. When you properly input the IRS form information on the appropriate screen, the data will automatically flow to all other applicable forms. For the Davidsons, we are interested in the input forms for their W-2 and the 1099-INT.

**Worksheets:** This section contains worksheets for you to input information that the software will summarize and then show on the appropriate tax form. These worksheets are helpful to collect supporting information in one place. The software worksheets also help the tax practitioner have consistent work paper files and procedures. For this example, we will not use any of the worksheets.

| a Employee's social security number 412-34-5671 | OMB No. 1545-0008 | Safe, accurate, FAST! Use IRS e-file | Visit the IRS website at www.irs.gov/efile |
|---|---|---|---|

| b Employer identification number (EIN) | 1 Wages, tips, other compensation 52,766.00 | 2 Federal income tax withheld 3,191.12 |
|---|---|---|

| c Employer's name, address, and ZIP code | 3 Social security wages 52,766.00 | 4 Social security tax withheld 3,271.49 |
|---|---|---|
| Brenden Manufacturing 6789 Main Street Greenville, NC 27858 | 5 Medicare wages and tips 52,766.00 | 6 Medicare tax withheld 765.11 |
| | 7 Social security tips | 8 Allocated tips |

| d Control number | 9 | 10 Dependent care benefits |
|---|---|---|

| e Employee's first name and initial    Last name                    Suff. | 11 Nonqualified plans | 12a See instructions for box 12 |
|---|---|---|
| Betty Davidson 456 Main Street Greenville, NC 27858 | 13 Statutory employee ☐   Retirement plan ☐   Third-party sick pay ☐ | 12b |
| | 14 Other | 12c |
| | | 12d |
| f Employee's address and ZIP code | | |

| 15 State  Employer's state ID number NC | 16 State wages, tips, etc. 52,766.00 | 17 State income tax 1,005.91 | 18 Local wages, tips, etc. | 19 Local income tax | 20 Locality name |
|---|---|---|---|---|---|

Form **W-2** Wage and Tax Statement **2021** Department of the Treasury—Internal Revenue Service

**Copy B—To Be Filed With Employee's FEDERAL Tax Return.**
This information is being furnished to the Internal Revenue Service.

Source: U.S. Department of the Treasury, Internal Revenue Service, Form W-2 Wage and Tax Statement. Washington, DC: 2021.

[14] Throughout the text we use common fictional social security numbers for all our fictional taxpayers.

☐ CORRECTED (if checked)

| PAYER'S name, street address, city or town, state or province, country, ZIP or foreign postal code, and telephone no. | Payer's RTN (optional) | OMB No. 1545-0112 | Interest Income |
|---|---|---|---|
| First Savings Bank 123 Main Street Greenville, NC 27858 | **1** Interest income $ 372.33 | 20**21** Form **1099-INT** | |

| | | **2** Early withdrawal penalty $ | | **Copy B** |
|---|---|---|---|---|
| PAYER'S TIN | RECIPIENT'S TIN | **3** Interest on U.S. Savings Bonds and Treas. obligations $ | | **For Recipient** |
| 33-1234500 | 412-34-5670 | | | |

RECIPIENT'S name

**Ed Davidson**

Street address (including apt. no.)

**456 Main Street**

City or town, state or province, country, and ZIP or foreign postal code

**Greenville, NC 27858**

| **4** Federal income tax withheld $ | **5** Investment expenses $ |
|---|---|
| **6** Foreign tax paid $ | **7** Foreign country or U.S. possession |
| **8** Tax-exempt interest $ | **9** Specified private activity bond interest $ |
| **10** Market discount $ | **11** Bond premium $ |
| **12** Bond premium on Treasury obligations $ | **13** Bond premium on tax-exempt bond $ |

FATCA filing requirement ☐

This is important tax information and is being furnished to the IRS. If you are required to file a return, a negligence penalty or other sanction may be imposed on you if this income is taxable and the IRS determines that it has not been reported.

| Account number (see instructions) | **14** Tax-exempt and tax credit bond CUSIP no. | **15** State | **16** State identification no. | **17** State tax withheld $ $ |
|---|---|---|---|---|

Form **1099-INT**     (keep for your records)     www.irs.gov/Form1099INT     Department of the Treasury - Internal Revenue Service

Source: U.S. Department of the Treasury, Internal Revenue Service, Form 1099-INT. Washington, DC: 2021.

To start, you must input the basic information about the Davidsons. Go to the File menu (upper left) and click on New Return. The system will then give you the opportunity to import data from a prior year's tax return. For all examples in this text, there is no prior year information.

You will now be at the main TaxAct screen in the Q&A mode. Click on the Forms icon on the taskbar. This will take you to a split screen with a Basic Information Worksheet on the right and a list of worksheets, forms, and documents received on the left. As you work through preparation of a tax return, TaxAct will create the appropriate return and schedules depending on the data provided.

You now need to input basic name and address information for the Davidsons. You do so on the Basic Information Worksheet. After you have filled in name, address, and SSN, click the plus sign beside Forms and Schedules on the left side of the split screen. This will allow you to select and view a 1040 for the Davidsons. Check to see that the information is correct. If not, go back to Form 1040 and correct it.

We now need to input the W-2 and 1099-INT information. Click on the Forms icon and then click on Documents Received toward the bottom of the left column. Input the W-2 first. Double-click on Federal Form W-2. This will bring up a W-2 input form. You now need to input the information from Betty's W-2 from Brenden Manufacturing. Fill in all appropriate boxes, including the employer name and address. Make sure you input the correct social security number and name for Betty. When you have completed the W-2 for Brenden Manufacturing, click the Back button at the bottom. You will be back at the Forms Explorer.

Now input the information from the 1099-INT.

You have now input the tax information for the Davidsons. Let's look at the result. Go to Forms, click on Forms and Schedules, and double-click on Federal Form 1040. This will bring up the completed 1040 of the Davidsons.

Your completed 1040 should look like the form shown on the next page.

Line 1, wages, salaries, and tips, is $52,766. This is the wage information from the W-2 of Betty.

Line 2b, taxable interest, shows the $372 of interest income from First Savings Bank. When you typed in the information, you put in $372.33, yet line 2b only shows $372. What happened to the 33 cents? When you input information, you use dollars and cents. When the software completes the forms, it will round all numbers to the nearest dollar (the IRS says we need to round down amounts below 50 cents and round up amounts of 50 cents or more).

Line 11, Adjusted Gross Income, is the summation of lines 1 and 2. Line 12a is the $25,100 deduction for a married couple. Taxable income, line 15, is $28,038.

Line 24 is the total tax liability of $2,965. You can check this figure with reference to the 2021 tax tables.

Line 25a, federal income tax withheld, is the amount from box 2 from Betty's W-2.

When you compare the Davidsons' total liability of $2,965 to the $3,191 they have already paid in withholding and credits, you see that the Davidsons will receive a refund of $226. This amount is on line 35a.

Form **1040** Department of the Treasury—Internal Revenue Service (99)
**U.S. Individual Income Tax Return** **2021** OMB No. 1545-0074 IRS Use Only—Do not write or staple in this space.

| **Filing Status** Check only one box. | ☐ Single  ☑ Married filing jointly  ☐ Married filing separately (MFS)  ☐ Head of household (HOH)  ☐ Qualifying widow(er) (QW) |
|---|---|

If you checked the MFS box, enter the name of your spouse. If you checked the HOH or QW box, enter the child's name if the qualifying person is a child but not your dependent ▶

| Your first name and middle initial | Last name | Your social security number |
|---|---|---|
| Davidson | Ed | 4 1 2 3 4 5 6 7 0 |

| If joint return, spouse's first name and middle initial | Last name | Spouse's social security number |
|---|---|---|
| Betty | Davidson | 4 1 2 3 4 5 6 7 1 |

| Home address (number and street). If you have a P.O. box, see instructions. | Apt. no. | **Presidential Election Campaign** |
|---|---|---|
| 456 Main Street | | Check here if you, or your spouse if filing jointly, want $3 to go to this fund. Checking a box below will not change your tax or refund. |

| City, town, or post office. If you have a foreign address, also complete spaces below. | State | ZIP code |
|---|---|---|
| Greenville | NC | 27858 |

| Foreign country name | Foreign province/state/county | Foreign postal code |
|---|---|---|
| | | |

☐ You ☐ Spouse

At any time during 2021, did you receive, sell, exchange, or otherwise dispose of any financial interest in any virtual currency? ☐ Yes ☑ No

**Standard Deduction** Someone can claim: ☐ You as a dependent ☐ Your spouse as a dependent
☐ Spouse itemizes on a separate return or you were a dual-status alien

**Age/Blindness** **You:** ☐ Were born before January 2, 1957 ☐ Are blind **Spouse:** ☐ Was born before January 2, 1957 ☐ Is blind

**Dependents** (see instructions):

| (1) First name    Last name | (2) Social security number | (3) Relationship to you | (4) ✔ if qualifies for (see instructions): Child tax credit | Credit for other dependents |
|---|---|---|---|---|
| | | | ☐ | ☐ |
| | | | ☐ | ☐ |
| | | | ☐ | ☐ |
| | | | ☐ | ☐ |

If more than four dependents, see instructions and check here ▶ ☐

Attach Sch. B if required.

| | | | | |
|---|---|---|---|---|
| **1** | Wages, salaries, tips, etc. Attach Form(s) W-2 | | **1** | 52,766 |
| **2a** | Tax-exempt interest . . . **2a** | **b** Taxable interest . . . . | **2b** | 372 |
| **3a** | Qualified dividends . . . **3a** | **b** Ordinary dividends . . . . . | **3b** | |
| **4a** | IRA distributions . . . . **4a** | **b** Taxable amount . . . . . | **4b** | |
| **5a** | Pensions and annuities . . **5a** | **b** Taxable amount . . . . . | **5b** | |
| **6a** | Social security benefits . . **6a** | **b** Taxable amount . . . . . | **6b** | |
| **7** | Capital gain or (loss). Attach Schedule D if required. If not required, check here . . . . ▶ ☐ | | **7** | |
| **8** | Other income from Schedule 1, line 10 . . . . . . . . . | | **8** | |
| **9** | Add lines 1, 2b, 3b, 4b, 5b, 6b, 7, and 8. This is your **total income** . . . . . . . ▶ | | **9** | 53,138 |
| **10** | Adjustments to income from Schedule 1, line 26 . . . . . . . . | | **10** | |
| **11** | Subtract line 10 from line 9. This is your **adjusted gross income** . . . . . . . ▶ | | **11** | 53,138 |
| **12a** | Standard deduction or itemized deductions (from Schedule A) . . **12a** 25,100 | | | |
| **b** | Charitable contributions if you take the standard deduction (see instructions) **12b** | | | |
| **c** | Add lines 12a and 12b . . . . . . . . . . . . . . . . . | | **12c** | 25,100 |
| **13** | Qualified business income deduction from Form 8995 or Form 8995-A . . . . . . | | **13** | |
| **14** | Add lines 12c and 13 . . . . . . . . . . . . . . . . . . | | **14** | 25,100 |
| **15** | **Taxable income.** Subtract line 14 from line 11. If zero or less, enter -0- . . . . . . | | **15** | 28,038 |

**Standard Deduction for—**
• Single or Married filing separately, $12,550
• Married filing jointly or Qualifying widow(er), $25,100
• Head of household, $18,800
• If you checked any box under *Standard Deduction,* see instructions.

For Disclosure, Privacy Act, and Paperwork Reduction Act Notice, see separate instructions. Cat. No. 11320B Form **1040** (2021)

Form 1040 (2021)      Page **2**

| | | | | |
|---|---|---|---|---|
| 16 | **Tax** (see instructions). Check if any from Form(s): 1 ☐ 8814  2 ☐ 4972  3 ☐ _____ | 16 | 2,965 |
| 17 | Amount from Schedule 2, line 3 | 17 | |
| 18 | Add lines 16 and 17 | 18 | 2,965 |
| 19 | Nonrefundable child tax credit or credit for other dependents from Schedule 8812 | 19 | |
| 20 | Amount from Schedule 3, line 8 | 20 | |
| 21 | Add lines 19 and 20 | 21 | 0 |
| 22 | Subtract line 21 from line 18. If zero or less, enter -0- | 22 | 2,965 |
| 23 | Other taxes, including self-employment tax, from Schedule 2, line 21 | 23 | |
| 24 | Add lines 22 and 23. This is your **total tax** ▶ | 24 | 2,965 |
| 25 | Federal income tax withheld from: | | |
| a | Form(s) W-2    25a   3,191 | | |
| b | Form(s) 1099    25b | | |
| c | Other forms (see instructions)    25c | | |
| d | Add lines 25a through 25c | 25d | 3,191 |
| 26 | 2021 estimated tax payments and amount applied from 2020 return | 26 | |

If you have a qualifying child, attach Sch. EIC.

| | | | |
|---|---|---|---|
| 27a | Earned income credit (EIC)    27a | | |
| | Check here if you had not reached the age of 19 by December 31, 2021, and satisfy all other requirements for claiming the EIC. See instructions ▶ ☐ | | |
| b | Nontaxable combat pay election    27b | | |
| c | Prior year (2019) earned income    27c | | |
| 28 | Refundable child tax credit or additional child tax credit from Schedule 8812    28 | | |
| 29 | American opportunity credit from Form 8863, line 8    29 | | |
| 30 | Recovery rebate credit. See instructions    30 | | |
| 31 | Amount from Schedule 3, line 15    31 | | |
| 32 | Add lines 27a and 28 through 31. These are your **total other payments and refundable credits** ▶ | 32 | 0 |
| 33 | Add lines 25d, 26, and 32. These are your **total payments** ▶ | 33 | 3,191 |

**Refund**

Direct deposit? See instructions.

| | | | |
|---|---|---|---|
| 34 | If line 33 is more than line 24, subtract line 24 from line 33. This is the amount you **overpaid** | 34 | 226 |
| 35a | Amount of line 34 you want **refunded to you.** If Form 8888 is attached, check here ▶ ☐ | 35a | 226 |
| ▶ b | Routing number _____   ▶ c Type: ☐ Checking ☐ Savings | | |
| ▶ d | Account number _____ | | |
| 36 | Amount of line 34 you want **applied to your 2022 estimated tax** ▶ 36 | | |

**Amount You Owe**

| | | | |
|---|---|---|---|
| 37 | **Amount you owe.** Subtract line 33 from line 24. For details on how to pay, see instructions ▶ | 37 | |
| 38 | Estimated tax penalty (see instructions) ▶ 38 | | |

**Third Party Designee**

Do you want to allow another person to discuss this return with the IRS? See instructions ▶ ☐ **Yes.** Complete below. ☐ **No**

| Designee's name ▶ | Phone no. ▶ | Personal identification number (PIN) ▶ |
|---|---|---|

**Sign Here**

Joint return? See instructions. Keep a copy for your records.

Under penalties of perjury, I declare that I have examined this return and accompanying schedules and statements, and to the best of my knowledge and belief, they are true, correct, and complete. Declaration of preparer (other than taxpayer) is based on all information of which preparer has any knowledge.

| Your signature | Date | Your occupation | If the IRS sent you an Identity Protection PIN, enter it here (see inst.) ▶ |
|---|---|---|---|
| Spouse's signature. If a joint return, **both** must sign. | Date | Spouse's occupation | If the IRS sent your spouse an Identity Protection PIN, enter it here (see inst.) ▶ |
| Phone no. | | Email address | |

**Paid Preparer Use Only**

| Preparer's name | Preparer's signature | Date | PTIN | Check if: ☐ Self-employed |
|---|---|---|---|---|
| Firm's name ▶ | | | Phone no. | |
| Firm's address ▶ | | | Firm's EIN ▶ | |

Go to *www.irs.gov/Form1040* for instructions and the latest information.      Form **1040** (2021)

Source: U.S. Department of the Treasury, Internal Revenue Service, Form 1040. Washington, DC: 2021.

A taxpayer who is entitled to a refund can elect to (a) receive a check or (b) have the refund deposited directly in the taxpayer's bank account by supplying account information on lines 35b, c, and d.

In many ways, a tax return is the document a taxpayer uses to "settle up" with the IRS after a tax year is over. On it, the taxpayer reports income and deductions, the amount of tax, and the tax already paid. The refund (line 35a) or tax due (line 37) is simply the balancing figure required to make total net payments equal to the amount of total tax liability.

Individual income tax returns must be filed with the IRS no later than April 15 of the following year. Thus, tax returns for calendar year 2021 must be filed (postmarked) no later than April 15, 2022. If April 15 falls on a weekend, taxpayers must file by the following Monday. Taxpayers can receive a six-month extension to file their returns if they file Form 4868 no later than April 15. Any remaining tax liability is still due by April 15—the extension of time pertains only to the tax return, not the tax due.

| **EXAMPLE 1-5** | Nora, who is single, has determined that her total tax liability is $4,486. Her employer withheld $4,392 from Nora's paychecks. When Nora files her return, she will need to enclose a check for $94. Thus, Nora's total payment is $4,486 ($4,392 withholdings plus $94 paid with her return), which is equal to her total liability. |
|---|---|

| **EXAMPLE 1-6** | Hector and Juanita, a married couple, determined that their total tax liability is $8,859. Juanita's employer withheld $5,278 from her paycheck and Hector's employer withheld $3,691. Hector and Juanita will receive a refund of $110 ($5,278 + $3,691 − $8,859). Thus, Hector and Juanita's total payment is $8,859 ($5,278 and $3,691 of withholdings minus the $110 refund), which is equal to their total liability. |
|---|---|

| **CONCEPT CHECK 1-5—** LO 1-3  | 1. Taxpayers pay all of their tax liability when they file their tax returns. True or false? <br> 2. Bret's tax liability is $15,759. His employer withheld $15,367 from his wages. When Bret files his tax return, will he be required to pay or will he get a refund? _____ What will be the amount of payment or refund? _____ <br> 3. An Earned Income Credit will increase the amount of tax liability. True or false? |
|---|---|

## Recovery Rebate Credit

In response to the COVID-19 pandemic, Congress passed three Acts which were signed into law. Each of these Acts provided assistance to individuals and businesses to address the economic impact of the pandemic. A provision in each Act that affected a significant majority of taxpayers was payment of a Recovery Rebate Credit (RRC) to individuals.

The first Act was the CARES Act passed in March 2020. It provided an RRC of $1,200 per qualified person. The second Act was the Consolidated Appropriations Act passed in December 2020 which provided an RRC of $600 per qualified person. These two credits were reported on tax returns for tax year 2020 and are not considered here.

In March 2021, the American Rescue Plan Act (ARPA) was passed and signed into law. It provided an additional RRC for tax year 2021. The 2021 RRC is an advance refundable tax credit of $1,400 per qualified person. A qualified person is the taxpayer, spouse, and any eligible dependent. Unlike the 2020 RRC payments, any dependent, regardless of age, is deemed to be a qualified person (see Chapter 2 for details as to how a dependent is determined). Generally, recipients must have a social security number.

The credit amount may be limited based on the Adjusted Gross Income (AGI) of the taxpayer as noted on Form 1040, line 11. The full credit is allowed for AGI up to $75,000 (single), $150,000 (married filing jointly), or $112,500 (head of household). Above those levels, the credit amount is reduced proportionally and is completely eliminated at AGI of $80,000 for single ($5,000 phaseout range), $160,000 MFJ ($10,000 phaseout range), or $120,000 for HoH ($7,500 phaseout range). For AGI in the phaseout range, the credit is phased out proportionately. For example, if AGI for a married couple was $164,000, they would have "used up" 40% of the phaseout range ($4,000 of a $10,000 range). Thus, the total credit would be reduced by 40%.

---

**EXAMPLE 1-7**

Consider the following independent cases:

Carla is single with AGI of $52,000. She would be entitled to an RRC of $1,400.

Tomas and Gizelle have one dependent child and AGI of $118,290. They are entitled to an RRC of $1,400 per person, or $4,200 in total. If their AGI were $167,000, they would be 70% into their $10,000 phaseout range and their credit would be reduced by 70% to $1,260 [$4,200 − ($4,200 × 70%)].

Antonio is single with AGI of $82,000. His regular RRC would be $1,400, but his AGI exceeds $80,000 so he would not be eligible for any RRC.

---

As was the case with the first two RRC bills, Congress wanted to get funds into the hands of taxpayers quickly, so the IRS sent checks or electronic payments to eligible taxpayers starting in March 2020. To determine the proper RRC amount, the IRS used the AGI and dependent information reported on the most recent tax return filed by the taxpayer. Normally, the most recent tax return would have been for tax year 2019 (although by mid-March some taxpayers would have filed their returns for tax year 2020).

The credit will be reconciled on the 2021 tax return. On that return, taxpayers eligible for a larger rebate will receive the additional credit as part of the return process. Taxpayers who should have received less will NOT have to pay back the excess.

---

**EXAMPLE 1-8**

Consider the following independent cases. Assume the taxpayers have filed a 2019 tax return but not a 2020 tax return.

A single taxpayer had 2019 AGI of $89,000. The taxpayer would not have received an RRC in early 2021. However, if the actual AGI of the taxpayer for 2021 was $68,000 the taxpayer would be entitled to the full $1,400 credit and would report the credit on line 30 of Form 1040.

A single taxpayer has 2019 AGI of $60,000 so the taxpayer would have received a RRC of $1,400. If that taxpayer actually had 2021 AGI of $110,000 the taxpayer would not be otherwise qualified to receive a rebate check. However, the taxpayer is not required to pay back the excess when the 2021 return is filed.

---

*In this textbook, unless otherwise noted, we assume that example taxpayers (such as the Davidson's in the comprehensive example) received the correct amount of RRC.  Thus, they will not be entitled to any additional credit.*

## Appendix A

### TAX AUTHORITY
### LO 1-5

Throughout this text, there are many references to "tax authority." As a beginning tax student, you need to understand what tax authority is. The best definition of *tax authority* is that the term refers to the guidelines that give the taxpayer not only guidance to report taxable income correctly but also guidelines and precedent for judicial decisions concerning conflicts between the IRS and the taxpayer. There are three types of primary tax authority:

Statutory sources
Administrative sources
Judicial sources

## Statutory Sources of Tax Authority

The ultimate statutory tax authority is the Sixteenth Amendment to the U.S. Constitution. By far the most commonly relied-upon statutory authority is the IRC. Congress writes the IRC. Changes to it must pass through the entire legislative process to become law. Table 1-4 shows the legislative process for tax laws.

**TABLE 1-4**
**Legislative Process for U.S. Tax Laws**

- U.S. House of Representatives Ways and Means Committee.
- Voted on by the House of Representatives.
- U.S. Senate Finance Committee.
- Voted on by the Senate.
- Joint Conference Committee (if differences between the House and Senate versions).
- Joint Conference bill voted on by the House of Representatives and the Senate.
- If the bill passes the House and Senate—signed or vetoed by the president of the United States.
- If signed—incorporated into the Internal Revenue Code.

**TABLE 1-5**
**Subtitles of the Internal Revenue Code**

| Subtitle | Subject |
|---|---|
| A | Income taxes |
| B | Estate and gift taxes |
| C | Employment taxes |
| D | Excise taxes |
| E | Alcohol and tobacco taxes |
| F | Procedure and administration |
| G | Joint Committee on Taxation |
| H | Presidential election campaign financing |
| I | Trust funds |

Typically, federal tax legislation begins in the Ways and Means Committee of the House of Representatives (although bills can start in the Senate Finance Committee). A tax bill passed by the House is sent to the Senate for consideration. If the Senate agrees to the bill with no changes, it sends the bill to the president for a signature or veto. If, as is more likely, the Senate passes a bill different from the House version, both houses of Congress select some of their members to be on a Joint Conference Committee. The committee's goal is to resolve the conflict(s) between the House and Senate versions of the bill. Once conflicts are resolved in the Conference Committee, both the House and the Senate vote on the common bill. If passed by both bodies, the bill goes to the president and, if signed, becomes law and part of the IRC.

Each enacted law receives a public law number. For example, Public Law 99-272 means the enacted legislation was the 272nd bill of the 99th Congress (the January 2021 to January 2023 legislative years of the Congress will be the 117th Congress).

Throughout the legislative process, each taxation committee (House Ways and Means, Senate Finance, and the Joint Conference Committee) generates one or more committee reports that note the "intent of Congress" in developing legislation. These committee reports can provide courts, the IRS, and tax professionals guidance as to the proper application of enacted tax law. The public law number of the bill is used to reference committee reports. Public Law 99-272 would have a House Ways and Means Committee report, a Senate Finance Committee report, and possibly a Joint Conference Committee report.[15]

---

[15] Not all bills have committee reports from each house of Congress. If there are no conflicts between the House and Senate, additional committee reports are not necessary. Such an outcome is unusual.

The IRS publishes the congressional reports in the *IRS Cumulative Bulletin. Cumulative Bulletins* are in most libraries in the government documents section. The reports are also on various governmental Internet sites. Use an Internet search engine to help you find these sites. *Cumulative Bulletins* for the last five years are available on the IRS website (www.irs.gov).

The IRC is organized by subtitle, as shown in Table 1-5.

Most of this text pertains to subtitle A of the IRC (income taxes). The IRC is hundreds of pages in length. An excerpt from the IRC follows:

IRC § 61. Gross Income Defined
(a) General Definition—Except as otherwise provided in this subtitle, gross income means all income from whatever source derived, including (but not limited to) the following items:
    (1) Compensation for services, including fees, commissions, fringe benefits, and similar items;
    (2) Gross income derived from business;
    (3) Gains derived from dealings in property;
    (4) Interest;
    (5) Rents;
    (6) Royalties;
    (7) Dividends;
    (8) Annuities;
    (9) Income from life insurance and endowment contracts;
    (10) Pensions;
    (11) Income from discharge of indebtedness;
    (12) Distributive share of partnership gross income;
    (13) Income in respect of a decedent; and
    (14) Income from an interest in an estate or trust.

The major national tax publishers such as Research Institute of America (RIA) and Commerce Clearing House (CCH) publish the IRC in bound versions and on their respective websites. The IRC can also be located on numerous tax Internet sites, although students are cautioned that the content of most generic websites is often not up to date (RIA and CCH are current).

---

**CONCEPT CHECK 1-6—**
**LO 1-5**

1. The committee charged with considering tax legislation in the House of Representatives is called the _____ Committee.
2. The most commonly relied-on statutory authority is _____.
3. All tax legislation must pass both the House of Representatives and the Senate and be signed by the president of the United States in order to become law. True or false?

---

As authorized by Congress, the president of the United States enters into tax treaties. Thus, treaties between the United States and other countries are also statutory tax authority.

A problem with the IRC is that it is usually extremely broad and sometimes difficult to apply to specific tax situations. Because of this limitation, administrative and judicial tax authorities have evolved.

## Administrative Tax Authority

The IRS, a division of the U.S. Treasury Department, develops administrative tax authority. The tax authority created by the IRS is, in effect, the IRS's interpretation of the IRC. Table 1-6 presents a list of the major IRS administrative authorities. These are the rulings or interpretations of the IRS at the national level. Each region of the IRS also publishes several authoritative guidelines.

**TABLE 1-6**

**Examples of Administrative Authority (in order of strength of authority, from highest to lowest)**

| Type of Administrative Authority | Example of Typical Research Citation |
|---|---|
| IRS Regulations (Treasury Regulations) | Reg. § 1.351-1 |
| Revenue Rulings | Rev. Rul. 80-198, 1980-2 CB 113 |
| Revenue Procedures | Rev. Proc. 87-32, 1987-2 CB 396 |
| Private Letter Rulings | PLR 8922063 |
| IRS Notices | Notice 97-69, 1997-2 CB 331 |

## Treasury Regulations

IRS Regulations are by far the strongest administrative authority. Regulations are the IRS's direct interpretation of the IRC. There are four types of IRS Regulations (listed in order of strength of authority, high to low):

**Legislative Regulations:** The IRS writes these regulations under a direct mandate by Congress. Legislative Regulations actually take the place of the IRC and have the full effect of law.

**General or Final Regulations:** The IRS writes these regulations under its general legislative authority to interpret the IRC. Most sections of the IRC have General Regulations to help interpret the law.

**Temporary Regulations:** These regulations have the same authority as General Regulations until they expire three years after issuance. The IRS issues Temporary Regulations to give taxpayers immediate guidance related to a new law. Temporary Regulations are noted with a "T" in the citation (for example, Reg. § 1.671-2T).

**Proposed Regulations:** These regulations do not have the effect of law. The IRS writes Proposed Regulations during the hearing process leading up to the promulgation of General Regulations. The purpose of the Proposed Regulations is to generate discussion and critical evaluation of the IRS's interpretation of the IRC.

Regulations are referred to (or cited) by using an IRC subtitle prefix, the referring code section, and the regulation number. For example, Reg. § 1.162-5 refers to the prefix (1) denoting the income tax subtitle, IRC section 162, and regulation number 5. Here are some examples of regulation subtitle prefixes:

1. Income Taxes (Reg. § 1.162-5).
20. Estate Tax (Reg. § 20.2032-1).
25. Gift Tax (Reg. § 25.2503-4).
31. Employment Taxes (Reg. § 31.3301-1).
301. Procedural Matters (Reg. § 301.7701-1).[16]

Like the IRS, the national publishers (RIA and CCH) publish and sell paperback and hardbound versions of IRS Regulations. You can also find regulations on a number of tax Internet sites including the IRS website (www.irs.gov).

## Revenue Rulings and Revenue Procedures

Revenue Rulings (Rev. Rul.) and Revenue Procedures (Rev. Proc.) are excellent sources of information for taxpayers and tax preparers. When issuing a Revenue Ruling, the IRS is reacting to an area of the tax law that is confusing to many taxpayers or that has substantive tax implications for numerous taxpayers. After many taxpayers have requested additional guidance on a given situation, the IRS may issue a Rev. Rul. The Rev. Rul. lists a factual situation, the relevant tax authority, and the IRS's conclusion as to the manner in which taxpayers should treat the issue.

---

[16] Various other prefixes are used in specific situations. When dealing with income taxes, however, the first (1) is used most often.

Revenue Procedures, on the other hand, are primarily proactive. Through a Rev. Proc., the IRS illustrates how it wants something reported. Often, the IRS provides guidelines or safe harbors to help taxpayers follow the law as interpreted by the IRS. For example, after the Tax Reform Act of 1986, the allowable depreciation methods were drastically changed. The IRS issued Rev. Proc. 87-56 and 87-57 to help taxpayers and preparers properly calculate and report depreciation expense under the new rules.

The citations for Revenue Rulings and Revenue Procedures indicate the year of the ruling or procedure and a consecutive number (reset to 1 at the beginning of each year). For example, Rev. Proc. 87-56 was the 56th Revenue Procedure issued in 1987. Revenue Rulings and Procedures are in the *Cumulative Bulletins* published by the IRS and available on its website.

## Other IRS Pronouncements

Other pronouncements issued by the IRS include Private Letter Rulings (PLRs) and IRS Notices. Each of these has limited authority. The IRS issues PLRs when a taxpayer requests a ruling on a certain tax situation. The PLR is tax authority only to the taxpayer to whom it is issued, although it does indicate the thinking of the IRS.

When there is a change in a rate or allowance, the IRS issues an IRS Notice. For example, if there is a change to the standard mileage rate for business travel from 55 cents a mile to 50 cents a mile, the IRS will issue an IRS Notice to publicize the change.

In addition to the administrative authority discussed in this section, the IRS also publishes various other sources of information that can benefit taxpayers, such as Technical Advice Memorandums and Determination Letters.

---

**CONCEPT CHECK 1-7— LO 1-5**

1. Administrative tax authority takes precedence over statutory tax authority. True or false?
2. IRS Revenue Procedures are applicable only to the taxpayer to whom issued. True or false?
3. The administrative tax authority with the most strength of authority is _____.

## Judicial Tax Authority

The tax laws and regulations are complex. There can be differences of opinion as to how a taxpayer should report certain income or whether an item is a permitted deduction on a tax return. When conflict occurs between the IRS and taxpayers, it is the job of the court system to settle the dispute. The rulings of the various courts that hear tax cases are the third primary tax authority.

Figure 1-1 depicts the court system with regard to tax disputes. Three different trial courts hear tax cases: (1) the U.S. Tax Court, (2) the U.S. District Court, and (3) the U.S. Court of Federal Claims. Decisions by the Tax Court and the district courts may be appealed to the

**FIGURE 1-1**
**Court System for Tax Disputes**

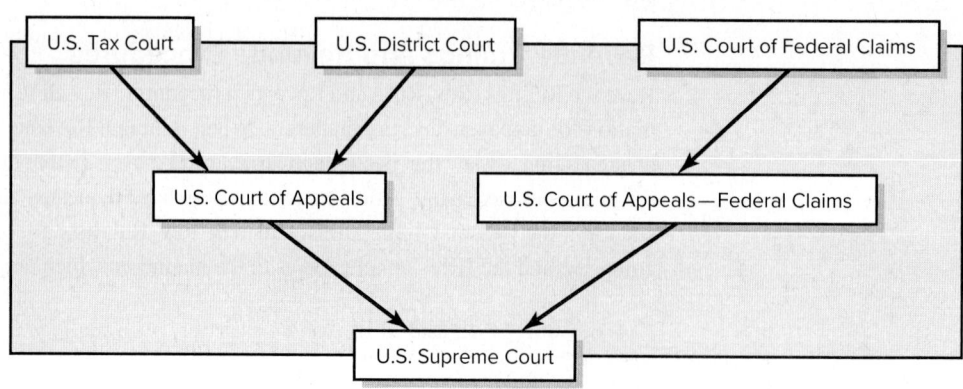

U.S. Court of Appeals and then to the Supreme Court. U.S. Court of Federal Claims cases are appealed to the U.S. Court of Appeals—Federal Claims, and then to the Supreme Court.

The Tax Court hears most litigated tax disputes between the IRS and taxpayers. The Tax Court is a national court with judges who travel throughout the nation to hear cases. Judges are tax law specialists and hear tax cases in major cities several times a year.

The court system becomes involved when a taxpayer and the IRS do not agree. Typically the IRS assesses the taxpayer for the tax the IRS believes is due. The taxpayer then needs to decide whether to go to court to contest the IRS's position and, if so, determine a court venue. One major advantage the taxpayer has when filing a petition with the Tax Court is that the taxpayer does not need to pay the IRS's proposed tax assessment prior to trial. With the other two judicial outlets (the district court and the Court of Federal Claims), the taxpayer must pay the government and then sue for a refund.

---

**CONCEPT CHECK 1-8— LO 1-5**

1. The U.S. Supreme Court does not accept appeals of tax cases. True or false?
2. A taxpayer who does not agree with an assessment of tax by the IRS has no recourse. True or false?
3. A taxpayer who does not want to pay the tax assessed by the IRS prior to filing a legal proceeding must use the _____ Court.

## Appendix B

# IRS RULES FOR PAID TAX PREPARERS
## LO 1-6

Anyone can prepare a tax return; in fact each year, millions of Americans do so. It is also the case that millions benefit from the services of a paid tax preparer. The IRS has established rules that must be followed by any person who receives compensation to prepare a tax return or provide tax advice. These rules are found in Circular 230. You can download Circular 230 from the IRS website at www.irs.gov.

The provisions of Circular 230 apply to Certified Public Accountants (CPAs), attorneys, enrolled agents, registered tax return preparers, or any other person who, for compensation, prepares a tax return, provides tax advice, or practices before the IRS. Practicing before the IRS includes all communications with the IRS with respect to a client. Failure to comply with the provisions can subject the practitioner to suspension, disbarment from practice before the IRS, a public censure, fines, and civil or criminal penalties

The rules are far-reaching and complex. They affect not only tax return preparation but also tax opinions, marketing and advertising, client records, fees, tax preparer registration, and other matters.

A paid preparer is someone who, for compensation, prepares all or substantially all of a tax return or tax form submitted to the IRS or a claim for refund. There is an exemption for individuals who do not sign the tax return and who are supervised by a CPA, attorney, or enrolled agent.

Paid preparers must register with the IRS and obtain a preparer tax identification number (PTIN). Preparers who are not CPAs, attorneys, or enrolled agents must also pass a competency examination and fulfill continuing education requirements of at least 15 hours annually (including 2 hours of ethics or professional conduct). Enrolled agents must obtain 72 hours of continuing education every three years (including 2 hours of ethics or professional conduct). CPAs and attorneys are subject to continuing education requirements under the rules of each state. Paid preparers must renew their PTIN annually.

Under the provisions of Circular 230, paid preparers or individuals giving tax advice must

- Sign all tax returns they prepare.
- Provide a copy of the returns to clients.
- Return records to clients.
- Exercise due diligence.
- Exercise best practices in preparing submissions to the IRS.
- Disclose all nonfrivolous tax positions when such disclosure is required to avoid penalties.
- Promptly notify clients of any error or omission on a client tax return.
- Provide records and information requested by the IRS unless the records or information is privileged.
- Inform a client if the client has made an error or omission in a document submitted to the IRS.

Paid preparers or individuals giving tax advice must *not*

- Take a tax position on a return unless there is a "realistic possibility" of the position being sustained.
- Charge a fee contingent on the outcome of the return or any position, except in certain limited situations.
- Charge an "unconscionable fee."
- Unreasonably delay the prompt disposition of any matter before the IRS.
- Cash an IRS check for a client for whom the return was prepared.
- Represent a client before the IRS if the representation involves a conflict of interest.
- Make false, fraudulent, or coercive statements or claims or make misleading or deceptive statements or claims. In part, this item pertains to claims made with respect to advertising or marketing.

Circular 230 contains detailed requirements associated with providing clients with a tax opinion that the client can rely upon to avoid a potential penalty related to a tax position. These opinions are called "covered opinions."

Paid preparers who are in willful violation of the provisions of Circular 230 may be censured, suspended, or disbarred. They may also be subject to monetary penalty or to civil or criminal penalties.

## Appendix C

## GETTING STARTED WITH TAXACT

This text includes an online version of the TaxAct tax preparation software for individual income tax returns. Throughout this text, we provide examples and end-of-chapter questions and problems that you can solve using tax software.

The tax return problems can be completed either by hand using the tax forms available in this text and on the IRS website or by using the TaxAct software. Your instructor will tell you how to prepare the problems. If you are using the tax software, this section will help you get started.

Many tax software products are on the market. They are all similar. Because of that, except for this chapter, we have purposefully written the text in a "software-neutral" manner. What we discuss for TaxAct will generally apply to any individual income tax product you would be likely to use.

The following information will help you get started using the TaxAct software:

- Visit the *Connect* Library and select TaxAct Program under Course-wide content.
- Select each TaxAct program you wish to download and follow the prompts to complete installation.
- Once download is complete, TaxAct will automatically open. The program may ask you a number of questions that you will skip or respond with "Cancel." Subsequent times you start the software, it may ask about state tax software. Respond with "Cancel."
- You will eventually arrive at the Home screen.

The TaxAct software allows the user to input tax information in two formats. One is the Interview Method (called Q&A). With this method, the computer asks a series of questions that guide users through the issues pertaining to their tax returns. This method is active when the program starts and is sometimes helpful for individuals preparing a tax return who know very little about taxes.

The second method is the Forms Method. With it, the user selects the appropriate tax form or input form and types the correct information onto the appropriate line or lines. This method is suited to those who have some familiarity with the tax forms and how they interact. Using this text, you will quickly reach the necessary level of familiarity.

We will exclusively use the Forms Method throughout the text. We do this for three reasons. First, we strongly believe that when preparing taxes, the user needs to understand the forms that are needed, how they interact, and where the numbers come from and go to. Otherwise it is like memorizing only one way to get to work—if something changes, the individual is totally lost. Second, in the text, we often focus on one or two forms at a time, not an entire tax return (except for the comprehensive examples). The Q&A method is not designed to zero in on a form or two—instead it guides a user through an entire return. Third, the Q&A method makes assumptions that are sometimes difficult to change.

Other tax software uses similar Q&A (interview) or Forms approaches. No matter what software you end up using after you graduate from school, the basic approach and input methodology found in TaxAct will be the same from program to program.

To get the program into the proper input method and to get it ready to accept data, you need to click on the Forms icon on the toolbar, toward the top left of the page.

When you want to start a new "client," perform the following steps:

1. Click on the File pull-down menu at the upper left.
2. Click on New Return.
3. The system may ask you whether you want to order a state tax product. Click Continue.

Now click on the Forms icon to get to the Forms Method.

The TaxAct program is a highly complex computer program. The software recognizes that information "starts" on a certain form or schedule and then is carried forward to other forms or schedules. For example, the name and address of the taxpayer are initially entered on a Basic Information Worksheet and then transferred to Form 1040. TaxAct automatically transfers these data to other forms that require the information.

As you use the TaxAct software, you will notice that most numerical information is in either a green or blue color. Green numbers are numbers that you can enter directly on the form you are working on. Blue numbers are calculated on (or derived from) another form or worksheet. If you click on a blue number, you can then click on the Folder icon and go to the supporting form or worksheet.

If you click on a blue number and try to enter a figure, the software will warn you that you are trying to alter a calculated value. You can then choose to go to the supporting schedule, or you can choose to override the value. The software strongly advises you *not* to enter information directly but to go to the appropriate supporting form. We concur. Until you have a much better understanding of how tax software works (or unless we specifically tell you otherwise), you should use the supporting schedules. If you fail to do so, you can get unanticipated results that may create an erroneous return. This can occur, for example, when the software transfers a number to two or more follow-up forms. If you change the number on one of the follow-up forms but not on the other(s), you will have an erroneous return.

**Important note:** Preliminary versions of tax software are generally issued in October or November with final versions coming out around January. Software vendors want to make sure you are using the most up-to-date versions of their software and tax forms. This text comes with a preliminary version of the software, and the vendors require you to get an updated version before you can print any tax forms. **Before TaxAct will allow you to print out a tax return, you need to update your software.** To confirm you have the latest version, go to your TaxAct home screen and complete the following:

1. Click on Online in the upper menu of TaxAct program.
2. Click on Check for Updates.
3. Click the program you wish to update.
4. Follow the instructions to choose the federal or state update required to complete the update.

Finally, we use a number of example "taxpayers" who may reappear off and on throughout the text (the Davidsons introduced in this chapter are an example). Note two important things about these taxpayers. First, they are entirely fictional. They are constructed for illustrative purposes only and do not represent any existing taxpayers. Second, because we will also use the example taxpayers in later chapters (some more often than others), it is important that you save the tax return information in the TaxAct software. That way, you do not have to rekey the data later.

## Summary

**LO 1-1:** Understand progressive, proportional, and regressive tax structures.

- Taxes are levied by multiplying a tax rate (the rate of tax) by a tax base (the amount taxed).
- Progressive: The tax rate increases as the tax base increases.
- Proportional: The tax rate remains the same regardless of the tax base.
- Regressive: The tax rate decreases as the tax base increases.

**LO 1-2:** Understand the concepts of marginal and average tax rates as well as a simple income tax formula.

- The marginal tax rate is the proportion of tax paid on the next dollar of income.
- The average tax rate is the percentage of total tax paid on the amount of taxable income.
- The simple tax formula is

    Income
    − Permitted deductions from income
    _____
    = Taxable income
    × Appropriate tax rates
    _____
    = Tax liability
    − Tax payments and tax credits
    _____
    = Tax refund or tax due with return

**LO 1-3:** Understand the components of a basic Form 1040 income tax return.

- Major components of the Form 1040 return are filing status, wage income, taxable interest income, standard or itemized deduction, taxable income, tax liability, tax payments, earned income credit, and amount owed or refund.

**LO 1-4:** Determine tax liability in instances when a Form 1040 return is appropriate.

- Tax liability is determined with reference to the tax tables issued by the IRS (and printed in Appendix D of this text).
- Tax liability can also be determined by using the tax rate schedules printed in Appendix F.

| | |
|---|---|
| **LO 1-5:** Understand the types of tax authority and how they interrelate (Appendix A). | • Statutory tax authority is the Internal Revenue Code and committee reports from appropriate congressional committees.<br>• Administrative tax authority is issued by the IRS. It includes<br>  • IRS Regulations.<br>  • Revenue Rulings.<br>  • Revenue Procedures.<br>  • Private Letter Rulings.<br>  • IRS Notices.<br>• Judicial tax authority is developed by the courts as a result of court cases between taxpayers and the IRS. |
| **LO 1-6:** Understand the provisions of IRS Circular 230 for paid tax preparers (Appendix B). | • Circular 230 covers individuals who are compensated for preparing a tax return, providing tax advice, or practicing before the IRS.<br>• Paid tax preparers include CPAs, attorneys, enrolled agents, registered tax preparers, and others.<br>• Paid tax preparers must register with the IRS and receive a preparer tax identification number (PTIN).<br>• Circular 230 sets forth actions paid preparers must do and must not do. |

## *EA Fast Fact*

What is an Enrolled Agent? An Enrolled Agent (EA) is a federally-authorized tax practitioner who has technical expertise in the field of taxation and who is empowered by the U.S. Department of the Treasury to represent taxpayers before all administrative levels of the Internal Revenue Service for audits, collections, and appeals. "Enrolled" means to be certified to practice by the federal government, and "Agent" means authorized to appear in the place of the taxpayer at the IRS. At present, only Enrolled Agents, attorneys, and CPAs may represent taxpayers before the IRS.

### IMPORTANT

You are eligible to receive absolutely free, the Surgent Enrolled Agent review program for Part I of the EA exam as a result of purchasing this text. To activate your free access, go to https://Surgent.com/McGrawHill/EA.

## Discussion Questions

All applicable discussion questions are available with *Connect*

LO 1-1    1. (Introduction) Give a brief history of the income tax in the United States.

_____

_____

_____

LO 1-1    2. (Introduction) For tax year 2019, what proportion of individual income tax returns was electronically filed?

_____

_____

_____

LO 1-1    3. Name the three types of tax rate structures and give an example of each.

_____

_____

_____

LO 1-1    4. What is a *progressive tax?* Why do you think the government believes it is a more equitable tax than, say, a regressive tax or proportional tax?

_____

_____

_____

LO 1-1    5. What type of tax is a sales tax? Explain your answer.

_____

_____

_____

LO 1-1    6. What is the definition of *tax base,* and how does it affect the amount of tax levied?

_____

_____

_____

LO 1-1    7. What type of tax rate structure is the U.S. federal income tax? Explain your answer.

_____

_____

_____

LO 1-1    8. A change to a 17% flat tax could cause a considerable increase in many taxpayers' taxes and a considerable decrease in the case of others. Explain this statement in light of the statistics in Table 1-3.

_____

_____

_____

LO 1-1    9. Explain what is meant by *regressive tax.* Why is the social security tax considered a regressive tax?

_____

_____

_____

LO 1-2   10. Define and compare these terms: *average tax rate* and *marginal tax rate.*

_____

_____

_____

**EA**  LO 1-3   11. What is meant by *compensation for services?* Give some examples.

_____

_____

_____

Chapter 1   *Introduction to Taxation, the Income Tax Formula, and Form 1040*   **1-33**

**EA**   LO 1-3   12. What is the definition of *interest?*

_____

_____

_____

**EA**   LO 1-3   13. What federal tax forms do taxpayers normally receive to inform them of the amount of wages and interest they earned during the year?

_____

_____

_____

**EA**   LO 1-3   14. Explain why unemployment compensation is taxable.

_____

_____

_____

**EA**   LO 1-3   15. What is the amount of the standard deduction for single and married taxpayers who use Form 1040?

_____

_____

_____

LO 1-3, 1-4   16. What is the most common way taxpayers pay their income tax liability during the year?

_____

_____

_____

## Multiple-Choice Questions   McGraw Hill **connect**

All applicable multiple-choice questions are available with **Connect**©

LO 1-1   17. A tax rate that decreases as the tax base increases is an example of what kind of tax rate structure?
   *a.* Progressive.
   *b.* Proportional.
   *c.* Regressive.
   *d.* Recessive.

LO 1-1   18. A tax rate that decreases as the tax base decreases is an example of what kind of tax rate structure?
   *a.* Progressive.
   *b.* Proportional.
   *c.* Regressive.
   *d.* Recessive.

LO 1-1   19. Jake earned $15,000 and paid $1,500 of income tax; Jill earned $40,000 and paid $4,000 of income tax. The tax rate structure they are subject to is
   *a.* Progressive.
   *b.* Proportional.
   *c.* Regressive.
   *d.* Recessive.

LO 1-1    20. Margaret earned $15,000 and paid $1,500 of income tax; Mike earned $50,000 and paid $4,000 of income tax. The tax rate structure they are subject to is

     *a.* Progressive.

     *b.* Proportional.

     *c.* Regressive.

     *d.* Recessive.

LO 1-1    21. Which of the following is an example of a regressive tax?

     *a.* Federal income tax.

     *b.* State and local taxes levied on property.

     *c.* Sales tax.

     *d.* Social security tax.

LO 1-1    22. Which of the following is an example of a progressive tax?

     *a.* Federal income tax.

     *b.* State and local taxes levied on property.

     *c.* Sales tax.

     *d.* Social security tax.

LO 1-2    23. Jennifer and Paul, who file a joint return, have taxable income of $94,475 and the following tax liability:

| | |
|---|---:|
| $19,900 × 10% = | $ 1,990.00 |
| ($81,050 − $19,900) × 12% = | 7,338.00 |
| ($94,475 − $81,050) × 22% = | 2,953.50 |
| Total tax liability | $12,281.50 |

Their marginal tax rate is

     *a.* 10%.

     *b.* 12%.

     *c.* 13%.

     *d.* 22%.

LO 1-2    24. Jennifer and Paul, who file a joint return, have taxable income of $94,475 and the following tax liability:

| | |
|---|---:|
| $19,900 × 10% = | $ 1,990.00 |
| ($81,050 − $19,900) × 12% = | 7,338.00 |
| ($94,475 − $81,050) × 22% = | 2,953.50 |
| Total tax liability | $12,281.50 |

Their average tax rate is

     *a.* 10%.

     *b.* 12%.

     *c.* 13%.

     *d.* 22%.

EA   LO 1-3    25. Which of the following is not a permitted filing status?

     *a.* Married filing jointly.

     *b.* Single filing jointly.

     *c.* Head of household.

     *d.* Qualifying widow.

**EA**  LO 1-3  26. Individual taxpayers with only wage income must file a Form
- *a.* 1040.
- *b.* 1040W.
- *c.* 1099W.
- *d.* W-2.

**EA**  LO 1-3  27. Wage income is reported to a taxpayer on a Form
- *a.* W-2.
- *b.* 1099-G.
- *c.* 1099-W.
- *d.* 1099-INT.

**EA**  LO 1-3  28. Interest income is reported to a taxpayer on a Form
- *a.* W-2.
- *b.* W-2-INT.
- *c.* 1099-G.
- *d.* 1099-INT.

**EA**  LO 1-3  29. On Form 1040, the amount of the standard deduction from income for taxpayers filing a joint return is
- *a.* $1,500.
- *b.* $12,550.
- *c.* $25,100.
- *d.* $37,650.

**EA**  LO 1-3  30. Elizabeth determined that her tax liability was $3,492. Her employer withheld $3,942 from her paychecks during the year. Elizabeth's tax return would show
- *a.* A refund of $450.
- *b.* A refund of $3,942.
- *c.* Tax due of $450.
- *d.* Tax due of $3,492.

**EA**  LO 1-4  31. Sandra, a single taxpayer, has taxable income of $79,293. Using the tax tables, she has determined that her tax liability is
- *a.* $9,115.
- *b.* $11,737.
- *c.* $13,189.
- *d.* $11,193.

LO 1-4  32. A married taxpayer has taxable income of $52,759. You have calculated tax liability using the tax tables and using the tax rate schedules. What can you say about the two figures?
- *a.* Tax liability determined using the tax tables will be more than tax liability determined using the tax rate schedules.
- *b.* Tax liability determined using the tax tables will be less than tax liability determined using the tax rate schedules.
- *c.* Tax liability determined using the tax tables will be the same as tax liability determined using the tax rate schedules.
- *d.* The answer cannot be determined with the information provided.

EA LO 1-3, 1-4    33. Eddie, a single taxpayer, has W-2 income of $40,841. Using the tax tables, he has determined that his tax liability is

       *a.* $2,995.

       *b.* $3,194.

       *c.* $4,501.

       *d.* $4,730.

EA LO 1-3, 1-4    34. Arno and Bridgette are married and have combined W-2 income of $72,441. They paid an additional $538 when they filed their taxes. How much income tax did their employers withhold during the year?

       *a.* $4,743.

       *b.* $5,281.

       *c.* $5,819.

       *d.* The answer cannot be determined with the information provided.

## Problems   Mc Graw Hill **connect**

All applicable problems are available with *Connect*©

LO 1-1    35. Using the information in Table 1-3, determine the average amount of taxable income per tax return, rounded to the nearest dollar, for each of the ranges of taxable income provided.

LO 1-1    36. Using the information in Table 1-3, determine the amount of average income tax liability per tax return, rounded to the nearest dollar, for each income range provided.

LO 1-1    37. Use the information in Table 1-3. If the federal tax system was changed to a proportional tax rate structure with a tax rate of 17%, calculate the amount of tax liability for 2019 for all taxpayers. How does this amount differ from the actual liability?

EA LO 1-2    38. What is the income tax formula in simplified form?

EA LO 1-3    39. What are the five filing statuses that are permitted on a Form 1040?

**EA** LO 1-3 40. When taxpayers file a tax return, they will either pay an additional amount or receive a refund of excess taxes paid. Briefly explain how this "settling up" process works. Why might a taxpayer pay too much during the year?

_____
_____
_____

**EA** LO 1-4 41. Miremba is single and has taxable income of $92,616. For that income, determine tax liability using the tax tables and using the tax rate schedule. Why is there a difference between the two amounts?

_____
_____
_____

**EA** LO 1-4 42. Havel and Petra are married and will file a joint tax return. Havel has W-2 income of $38,588, and Petra has W-2 income of $49,381. What is their tax liability? Determine their tax liability using both the tax tables and the tax rate schedule.

_____
_____
_____

**EA** LO 1-2, 1-4 43. Determine the tax liability, marginal tax rate, and average tax rate (rounded to two decimal places) in each of the following cases. Use the tax tables to determine tax liability.
   a. Single taxpayer, taxable income of $35,562:
      Liability = _____ Marginal = _____ Average = _____
   b. Single taxpayer, taxable income of $89,889:
      Liability = _____ Marginal = _____ Average = _____

**EA** LO 1-2, 1-4 44. Determine the tax liability, marginal tax rate, and average tax rate (rounded to two decimal places) in each of the following cases. Use the tax tables to determine tax liability.
   a. Married taxpayers, taxable income of $89,889:
      Liability = _____ Marginal = _____ Average = _____
   b. Married taxpayers, taxable income of $66,829:
      Liability = _____ Marginal = _____ Average = _____

**EA** LO 1-2, 1-4 45. Determine the tax liability, marginal tax rate, and average tax rate (rounded to two decimal places) in each of the following cases. Use the tax tables to determine tax liability.
   a. Married taxpayers, taxable income of $35,562:
      Liability = _____ Marginal = _____ Average = _____
   b. Single taxpayer, taxable income of $66,829:
      Liability = _____ Marginal = _____ Average = _____

**EA** LO 1-4 46. Use the tax rate schedules to determine the tax liability for each of the cases in Problems 43, 44, and 45.
   a. Liability for 43a = _____ 43b = _____
   b. Liability for 44a = _____ 44b = _____
   c. Liability for 45a = _____ 45b = _____

**EA** LO 1-3, 1-4 47. The W-2 income of Sandra, a single taxpayer, was $77,243. Using the tax tables, determine Sandra's tax liability.

_____
_____

**EA** LO 1-3, 1-4    48. The W-2 incomes of Betty and her husband Ronald were $47,117 and $41,539, respectively. If Betty and Ronald use a filing status of married filing jointly, determine their tax liability using the tax tables.

_____

_____

**EA** LO 1-3, 1-4    49. Sheniqua, a single taxpayer, had taxable income of $91,431. Her employer withheld $15,882 in federal income tax from her paychecks throughout the year. Using the tax tables, would Sheniqua receive a refund or would she be required to pay additional tax? What is the amount?

_____

_____

**EA** LO 1-3, 1-4    50. Xavier and his wife Maria have total W-2 income of $95,102. They will file their tax return as married filing jointly. They had a total of $7,910 withheld from their paychecks for federal income tax. Using the tax tables, determine the amount of refund or additional tax due upon filing their tax return. Indicate whether the amount is a refund or additional tax.

_____

_____

## Discussion Questions Pertaining to Appendix A (LO 1-5)

51. Discuss the concept of *tax authority*. How does tax authority help taxpayers and tax preparers report tax items properly?

_____

_____

_____

52. What are the three types of tax authority? Who issues each type?

_____

_____

_____

53. Discuss the concept of *statutory tax authority*. Why is there a need for additional types of authority when statutory authority is the law?

_____

_____

_____

54. What is the legislative process concerning tax laws? Where does tax legislation often begin?

_____

_____

_____

55. What are committee reports, and how can they help the taxpayer or tax preparer?

_____

_____

_____

56. What is the purpose of a Joint Conference Committee? Its reports are considered more important or are more authoritative. Why?

_____

_____

_____

57. Explain what is meant by *Public Law 100-14.*

_____

_____

_____

58. What is administrative authority, and who publishes it?

_____

_____

_____

59. What is a Proposed Regulation? Can a taxpayer rely on a Proposed Regulation as authority on how to treat a certain tax item?

_____

_____

_____

60. Can a taxpayer rely on a Temporary Regulation as authority on how to treat a certain tax item? If so, how long is a Temporary Regulation valid?

_____

_____

_____

61. Differentiate between a General Regulation and a Legislative Regulation. Which one is the stronger tax authority?

_____

_____

_____

62. Where are Revenue Rulings and Revenue Procedures found? When might a Revenue Ruling be useful to a taxpayer? When might a Revenue Procedure be useful to a taxpayer?

_____

_____

_____

63. In what courts are disputes between the IRS and a taxpayer heard?

_____

_____

_____

64. What are the advantages of petitioning the Tax Court versus other trial courts?

_____

_____

_____

65. When would a taxpayer want to sue the government in a district court versus the Tax Court?

_____

_____

_____

66. If a taxpayer loses a case against the IRS in one of the three trial courts, does the taxpayer have any avenue for appeals?

_____

_____

_____

67. After the Court of Appeals, does a taxpayer have any additional avenue for appeals? If so, what are the taxpayer's probabilities of receiving an appeal after the Court of Appeals? Why?

_____

_____

_____

68. Why might a district court's opinion regarding a tax decision be more likely to be reversed on appeal?

_____

_____

_____

69. (Longer answer) What is a Treasury Regulation? What are the four types of regulations and how do they differ?

_____

_____

_____

70. (Longer answer) What is the difference between a Revenue Ruling and a Revenue Procedure? How does the level of authority of a ruling or procedure compare with regulations and statutory authority?

_____

_____

_____

## Multiple-Choice Questions Pertaining to Appendix A (LO 1-5)

All applicable multiple-choice questions are available with **Connect**©

71. Which of the following is (are) primary sources of tax authority?
    a. Statutory sources.
    b. Administrative sources.
    c. Judicial sources.
    d. All of the above.

72. Which of the following is a statutory source of tax authority?
    a. Internal Revenue Code.
    b. Regulations.
    c. Revenue Rulings.
    d. Tax Court decision.

73. Which of the following types of IRS Regulations have the greatest strength of authority?

    *a.* General or Final Regulations.

    *b.* Legislative Regulations.

    *c.* Proposed Regulations.

    *d.* Temporary Regulations.

74. Which of the following refers to an income tax regulation?

    *a.* Reg. § 1.162-5.

    *b.* Reg. § 20.2032-1.

    *c.* Reg. § 25.2503-4.

    *d.* Reg. § 31.3301-1.

75. Which of the following trial court(s) hear(s) tax cases?

    *a.* U.S. Tax Court.

    *b.* U.S. district courts.

    *c.* U.S. Court of Federal Claims.

    *d.* All of the above.

## Discussion Questions Pertaining to Appendix B (LO 1-6)

**EA** 76. IRS rules for paid tax preparers apply to what types of tax professionals?

_____

_____

**EA** 77. Who must obtain a preparer tax identification number?

_____

_____

**EA** 78. List at least five items that paid preparers must do to comply with Circular 230.

_____

_____

**EA** 79. List at least five items that paid preparers must *not* do to comply with Circular 230.

_____

_____

## Multiple-Choice Questions Pertaining to Appendix B (LO 1-6)

All applicable multiple-choice questions are available with **Connect**©

**EA** 80. A preparer tax identification number must be obtained by

    *a.* Only CPAs, attorneys, and enrolled agents.

    *b.* Only individuals who are not CPAs, attorneys, or enrolled agents.

    *c.* Any individual who is paid to prepare a tax return.

    *d.* Only individuals who prepare a Form 1040.

**EA** 81. A paid preparer must *not*

    *a.* Cash a client's IRS check.

    *b.* Charge a reasonable fee.

c. Inform a client if the preparer makes a mistake on the client's tax return.

d. Provide a client with a copy of their return.

 82. A paid preparer must

a. Ignore a conflict of interest when representing a client before the IRS.

b. Charge a contingent fee.

c. Sign all tax returns prepared.

d. Provide records requested by the IRS in all circumstances.

## Tax Return Problems

All applicable tax return problems are available with *Connect*©

Use your tax software to complete the following problems. If you are manually preparing the tax returns, you will need a Form 1040 for each problem.

For the following tax return problems, assume the taxpayer does NOT wish to contribute to the Presidential Election Fund, unless otherwise stated in the problem. In addition, the taxpayers did not receive, sell, send, exchange, or otherwise acquire any financial interest in any virtual currency during the year.

**Tax Return Problem 1**

Alex Montgomery is single and lives at 3344 Bayview Drive, Richmond Hill, GA 31324. His SSN is 412-34-5670. He recently graduated from the Savannah College of Art and Design and works as a video game developer. His Form W-2 contained the following information.

Wages (box 1) = $72,288.22

Federal W/H (box 2) = $ 9,137.20

Social security wages (box 3) = $72,288.22

Social security W/H (box 4) = $ 4,481.87

Medicare wages (box 5) = $72,288.22

Medicare W/H (box 6) = $ 1,048.18

Alex had qualifying health care coverage at all times during the year.
Prepare a Form 1040 for Alex.

**Tax Return Problem 2**

Brenda Peterson is single and lives at 567 East Street, Marshfield, MA 02043. Her SSN is 412-34-5670. She worked the entire year for Applebee Consulting in Marshfield. Her Form W-2 contained information in the following boxes:

Wages (box 1) = $67,155.75

Federal W/H (box 2) = $ 8,366.12

Social security wages (box 3) = $67,155.75

Social security W/H (box 4) = $ 4,163.66

Medicare wages (box 5) = $67,155.75

Medicare W/H (box 6) = $ 973.76

She also received two Forms 1099-INT. One was from First National Bank of Marshfield and showed interest income of $537.39 in box 1. The other Form 1099-INT was from Baystate Savings and Loan and showed interest income of $329.31 in box 1.

Brenda had qualifying health care coverage at all times during the tax year.
Prepare a Form 1040 for Brenda.

**Tax Return Problem 3**

Jin Xiang is single and lives at 2468 North Lake Road in Deerwood, MN 56444. Her SSN is 412-34-5670. She worked the entire year for Lakeland Automotive. The Form W-2 from Lakeland contained information in the following boxes:

Wages (box 1) = $42,851.89

Federal W/H (box 2) = $ 4,583.91

Social security wages (box 3) = $42,851.89

Social security W/H (box 4) = $ 2,656.82

Medicare wages (box 5) = $42,851.89

Medicare W/H (box 6) = $ 621.35

On the weekends, Jin worked at Parts-Galore, a local auto parts store. The Form W-2 from Parts-Galore contained information in the following boxes:

Wages (box 1) = $11,591.87

Federal W/H (box 2) = $ 548.82

Social security wages (box 3) = $11,591.87

Social security W/H (box 4) = $ 718.70

Medicare wages (box 5) = $11,591.87

Medicare W/H (box 6) = $ 168.08

Jin also received a Form 1099-INT from Minnesota Savings and Loan. The amount of interest income in box 1 of the Form 1099-INT was $51.92.

Jin had qualifying health care coverage at all times during the tax year.

Prepare a Form 1040 for Jin.

**Tax Return Problem 4**

Jose and Maria Suarez are married and live at 9876 Main Street, Denver, CO 80205. Jose's SSN is 412-34-5670 and Maria's SSN is 412-34-5671.

For the first five months of the year, Jose was employed by Mountain Mortgage Company. The Form W-2 from Mountain Mortgage contained information in the following boxes:

Wages (box 1) = $35,028.52

Federal W/H (box 2) = $ 3,746.89

Social security wages (box 3) = $35,028.52

Social security W/H (box 4) = $ 2,171.77

Medicare wages (box 5) = $35,028.52

Medicare W/H (box 6) = $ 507.91

Jose was laid off from his job at Mountain Mortgage and was unemployed for three months. He received $1,000 of unemployment insurance payments. The Form 1099-G Jose received from the state of Colorado contained $1,000 of unemployment compensation in box 1 and $100 of federal income tax withholding in box 4.

During the last four months of the year, Jose was employed by First Mountain Bank in Denver. The Form W-2 Jose received from the bank contained information in the following boxes:

Wages (box 1) = $19,244.72

Federal W/H (box 2) = $ 1,767.89

Social security wages (box 3) = $19,244.72

Social security W/H (box 4) = $ 1,193.17

Medicare wages (box 5) = $19,244.72

Medicare W/H (box 6) = $ 279.05

Maria was employed the entire year by Blue Sky Properties in Denver. The Form W-2 Maria received from Blue Sky contained information in the following boxes:

Wages (box 1) = $59,181.12
Federal W/H (box 2) = $ 5,922.80
Social security wages (box 3) = $59,181.12
Social security W/H (box 4) = $ 3,669.23
Medicare wages (box 5) = $59,181.12
Medicare W/H (box 6) = $    858.13

The Suarezes also received two Forms 1099-INT showing interest they received on two savings accounts. One Form 1099-INT, from the First National Bank of Northeastern Denver, showed interest income of $59.36 in box 1. The other Form 1099-INT, from Second National Bank of Northwestern Denver, showed interest income of $82.45 in box 1.

Jose and Maria had qualifying health care coverage at all times during the tax year.

Prepare a Form 1040 for Mr. and Mrs. Suarez.

We have provided selected filled-in source documents that are available in the *Connect Library.*

# Chapter Two

# Expanded Tax Formula, Form 1040, and Basic Concepts

This chapter expands the basic tax formula introduced in the previous chapter. We also expand our discussion of Form 1040, and tax situations common to most taxpayers including determination of filing status, dependents, and the standard deduction.

### Learning Objectives

When you have completed this chapter, you should understand the following learning objectives (LO):

LO 2-1  Describe the expanded tax formula and the components of the major sections of Form 1040.

LO 2-2  Determine the proper filing status.

LO 2-3  Determine dependents.

LO 2-4  Determine the standard deduction.

LO 2-5  Compute the amount of tax due to the Internal Revenue Service (IRS).

LO 2-6  Determine what interest and penalties the IRS can assess and in what instances certain penalties are applicable.

## INTRODUCTION

This chapter expands our discussion of Form 1040. It is important to familiarize yourself with the concept of and the difference between the standard deduction and itemized deductions. This will enable you to determine which form is the most appropriate for a taxpayer to use.

Furthermore, our discussion takes you through the body of the forms to arrive at the amount due to the IRS or the refund due. The last section of the chapter presents some of the possible penalties the IRS can assess a taxpayer for failure to file and pay, failure to pay estimated tax, accuracy-related errors, and fraud.

# THE INCOME TAX FORMULA AND FORM 1040
## LO 2-1

In Chapter 1 we introduced a very simple tax formula:

| |
|---|
| Income |
| – Permitted deductions from income |
| = Taxable income |
| × Appropriate tax rates |
| = Tax liability |
| – Tax payments and tax credits |
| = Tax refund or tax due with return |

This simple formula is applicable to a basic Form 1040. Most taxpayers, however, have a more complex tax situation. In this chapter, we begin to explore the intricacies of a tax return.

An expanded tax formula, for a more complex return (Form 1040 including one or more Schedules), is as follows:

| |
|---|
| Gross income (GI) |
| – Permitted deductions from gross income |
| = Adjusted Gross Income (AGI) |
| – Standard deduction or itemized deductions |
| = Taxable income (TI) |
| × Appropriate tax rates |
| = Tax liability |
| – Tax credits |
| + Other taxes |
| – Tax payments and refundable credits |
| = Tax refund or tax due with return |

The basic Form 1040 in Exhibit 2-1 contains lines for items most commonly used by taxpayers. Some individuals will be able to file a return using only the basic 1040. However, many taxpayers have a more-complex tax situation. As we mentioned in Chapter 1, the basic Form 1040 is supplemented by three Schedules (Schedule 1, Schedule 2, and Schedule 3). These Schedules provide much more detail to cover almost any tax situation. We provide copies of Schedule 1 through Schedule 3 in Exhibit 2-2.

There are many details on the Schedules. To aid you in understanding where we discuss each of the tax form lines, we have provided Table 2-1, which lists each line on the Form 1040 and the Schedules along with the chapter in which we introduce the item.

**EXHIBIT 2-1**

Form **1040** Department of the Treasury—Internal Revenue Service (99)
**U.S. Individual Income Tax Return** **2021** OMB No. 1545-0074 IRS Use Only—Do not write or staple in this space.

| Filing Status Check only one box. | ☐ Single ☐ Married filing jointly ☐ Married filing separately (MFS) ☐ Head of household (HOH) ☐ Qualifying widow(er) (QW) |
|---|---|

If you checked the MFS box, enter the name of your spouse. If you checked the HOH or QW box, enter the child's name if the qualifying person is a child but not your dependent ▶

| Your first name and middle initial | Last name | Your social security number |
|---|---|---|
| If joint return, spouse's first name and middle initial | Last name | Spouse's social security number |

| Home address (number and street). If you have a P.O. box, see instructions. | Apt. no. | **Presidential Election Campaign** Check here if you, or your spouse if filing jointly, want $3 to go to this fund. Checking a box below will not change your tax or refund. ☐ You ☐ Spouse |
|---|---|---|
| City, town, or post office. If you have a foreign address, also complete spaces below. | State | ZIP code |
| Foreign country name | Foreign province/state/county | Foreign postal code |

At any time during 2021, did you receive, sell, exchange, or otherwise dispose of any financial interest in any virtual currency? ☐ Yes ☐ No

**Standard Deduction**
Someone can claim: ☐ You as a dependent ☐ Your spouse as a dependent
☐ Spouse itemizes on a separate return or you were a dual-status alien

Age/Blindness You: ☐ Were born before January 2, 1957 ☐ Are blind Spouse: ☐ Was born before January 2, 1957 ☐ Is blind

**Dependents** (see instructions):

| (1) First name  Last name | (2) Social security number | (3) Relationship to you | (4) ✔ if qualifies for (see instructions): Child tax credit / Credit for other dependents |
|---|---|---|---|
If more than four dependents, see instructions and check here ▶ ☐

| Attach Sch. B if required. | 1 | Wages, salaries, tips, etc. Attach Form(s) W-2 | | 1 | |
|---|---|---|---|---|---|
| | 2a | Tax-exempt interest | 2a | b Taxable interest | 2b |
| | 3a | Qualified dividends | 3a | b Ordinary dividends | 3b |
| | 4a | IRA distributions | 4a | b Taxable amount | 4b |
| | 5a | Pensions and annuities | 5a | b Taxable amount | 5b |
| | 6a | Social security benefits | 6a | b Taxable amount | 6b |

**Standard Deduction for—**
- Single or Married filing separately, $12,550
- Married filing jointly or Qualifying widow(er), $25,100
- Head of household, $18,800
- If you checked any box under Standard Deduction, see instructions.

| 7 | Capital gain or (loss). Attach Schedule D if required. If not required, check here ▶ ☐ | 7 |
|---|---|---|
| 8 | Other income from Schedule 1, line 10 | 8 |
| 9 | Add lines 1, 2b, 3b, 4b, 5b, 6b, 7, and 8. This is your **total income** ▶ | 9 |
| 10 | Adjustments to income from Schedule 1, line 26 | 10 |
| 11 | Subtract line 10 from line 9. This is your **adjusted gross income** ▶ | 11 |
| 12a | **Standard deduction or itemized deductions** (from Schedule A) | 12a | |
| b | Charitable contributions if you take the standard deduction (see instructions) | 12b | |
| c | Add lines 12a and 12b | | 12c |
| 13 | Qualified business income deduction from Form 8995 or Form 8995-A | | 13 |
| 14 | Add lines 12c and 13 | | 14 |
| 15 | **Taxable income.** Subtract line 14 from line 11. If zero or less, enter -0- | | 15 |

For Disclosure, Privacy Act, and Paperwork Reduction Act Notice, see separate instructions. Cat. No. 11320B Form **1040** (2021)

---

Form 1040 (2021) Page **2**

| 16 | **Tax** (see instructions). Check if any from Form(s): 1 ☐ 8814 2 ☐ 4972 3 ☐ ___ | 16 |
|---|---|---|
| 17 | Amount from Schedule 2, line 3 | 17 |
| 18 | Add lines 16 and 17 | 18 |
| 19 | Nonrefundable child tax credit or credit for other dependents from Schedule 8812 | 19 |
| 20 | Amount from Schedule 3, line 8 | 20 |
| 21 | Add lines 19 and 20 | 21 |
| 22 | Subtract line 21 from line 18. If zero or less, enter -0- | 22 |
| 23 | Other taxes, including self-employment tax, from Schedule 2, line 21 | 23 |
| 24 | Add lines 22 and 23. This is your **total tax** | 24 |
| 25 | Federal income tax withheld from: | |
| a | Form(s) W-2 | 25a | |
| b | Form(s) 1099 | 25b | |
| c | Other forms (see instructions) | 25c | |
| d | Add lines 25a through 25c | | 25d |
| 26 | 2021 estimated tax payments and amount applied from 2020 return | | 26 |

If you have a qualifying child, attach Sch. EIC.

| 27a | Earned income credit (EIC) | 27a | |
|---|---|---|---|

Check here if you had not reached the age of 19 by December 31, 2021, and satisfy all other requirements for claiming the EIC. See instructions ▶ ☐

| b | Nontaxable combat pay election | 27b | |
|---|---|---|---|
| c | Prior year (2019) earned income | 27c | |
| 28 | Refundable child tax credit or additional child tax credit from Schedule 8812 | 28 | |
| 29 | American opportunity credit from Form 8863, line 8 | 29 | |
| 30 | Recovery rebate credit. See instructions | 30 | |
| 31 | Amount from Schedule 3, line 15 | 31 | |
| 32 | Add lines 27a and 28 through 31. These are your **total other payments and refundable credits** ▶ | 32 |
| 33 | Add lines 25d, 26, and 32. These are your **total payments** ▶ | 33 |

**Refund**

| 34 | If line 33 is more than line 24, subtract line 24 from line 33. This is the amount you **overpaid** | 34 |
|---|---|---|
| 35a | Amount of line 34 you want **refunded to you.** If Form 8888 is attached, check here ▶ ☐ | 35a |

Direct deposit? See instructions.
▶ b Routing number ___ ▶ c Type: ☐ Checking ☐ Savings
▶ d Account number ___

| 36 | Amount of line 34 you want applied to your 2022 estimated tax ▶ | 36 | |
|---|---|---|---|

**Amount You Owe**

| 37 | **Amount you owe.** Subtract line 33 from line 24. For details on how to pay, see instructions ▶ | 37 |
|---|---|---|
| 38 | Estimated tax penalty (see instructions) | 38 | |

**Third Party Designee**
Do you want to allow another person to discuss this return with the IRS? See instructions ▶ ☐ Yes. Complete below. ☐ No
Designee's name ▶ ___ Phone no. ▶ ___ Personal identification number (PIN) ▶ ___

**Sign Here**
Under penalties of perjury, I declare that I have examined this return and accompanying schedules and statements, and to the best of my knowledge and belief, they are true, correct, and complete. Declaration of preparer (other than taxpayer) is based on all information of which preparer has any knowledge.

Your signature | Date | Your occupation | If the IRS sent you an Identity Protection PIN, enter it here (see inst.) ▶

Joint return? See instructions. Keep a copy for your records.

Spouse's signature. If a joint return, **both** must sign. | Date | Spouse's occupation | If the IRS sent your spouse an Identity Protection PIN, enter it here (see inst.) ▶

Phone no. ___ Email address ___

**Paid Preparer Use Only**

| Preparer's name | Preparer's signature | Date | PTIN | Check if: ☐ Self-employed |
|---|---|---|---|---|
| Firm's name ▶ | | | Phone no. | |
| Firm's address ▶ | | | Firm's EIN | |

Go to *www.irs.gov/Form1040* for instructions and the latest information. Form **1040** (2021)

Source: U.S. Department of the Treasury, Internal Revenue Service, Form 1040. Washington, DC: 2021.

**EXHIBIT 2-2**

| SCHEDULE 1<br>(Form 1040)<br><br>Department of the Treasury<br>Internal Revenue Service | **Additional Income and Adjustments to Income**<br><br>▶ Attach to Form 1040, 1040-SR, or 1040-NR.<br>▶ Go to *www.irs.gov/Form1040* for instructions and the latest information. | OMB No. 1545-0074<br><br>2021<br><br>Attachment<br>Sequence No. 01 |
|---|---|---|

Name(s) shown on Form 1040, 1040-SR, or 1040-NR | Your social security number

### Part I   Additional Income

| | | | |
|---|---|---|---|
| 1 | Taxable refunds, credits, or offsets of state and local income taxes . . . . . . | **1** | |
| 2a | Alimony received . . . . . . . . . . . . . . . . . . . . | **2a** | |
| b | Date of original divorce or separation agreement (see instructions) ▶ _____ | | |
| 3 | Business income or (loss). Attach Schedule C . . . . . . . . . . | **3** | |
| 4 | Other gains or (losses). Attach Form 4797 . . . . . . . . . . | **4** | |
| 5 | Rental real estate, royalties, partnerships, S corporations, trusts, etc. Attach Schedule E . . . . . . . . . . . . . . . . . | **5** | |
| 6 | Farm income or (loss). Attach Schedule F . . . . . . . . . . | **6** | |
| 7 | Unemployment compensation . . . . . . . . . . . . . . | **7** | |
| 8 | Other income: | | |
| a | Net operating loss . . . . . . . . . . . . . | **8a** ( ) | |
| b | Gambling income . . . . . . . . . . . . | **8b** | |
| c | Cancellation of debt . . . . . . . . . . . | **8c** | |
| d | Foreign earned income exclusion from Form 2555 . . . . . | **8d** ( ) | |
| e | Taxable Health Savings Account distribution . . . . . . | **8e** | |
| f | Alaska Permanent Fund dividends . . . . . . . . | **8f** | |
| g | Jury duty pay . . . . . . . . . . . . | **8g** | |
| h | Prizes and awards . . . . . . . . . . . | **8h** | |
| i | Activity not engaged in for profit income . . . . . . . | **8i** | |
| j | Stock options . . . . . . . . . . . . | **8j** | |
| k | Income from the rental of personal property if you engaged in the rental for profit but were not in the business of renting such property . . . . . . . . . . . . | **8k** | |
| l | Olympic and Paralympic medals and USOC prize money (see instructions) . . . . . . . . . . . . . | **8l** | |
| m | Section 951(a) inclusion (see instructions) . . . . . . . | **8m** | |
| n | Section 951A(a) inclusion (see instructions) . . . . . . | **8n** | |
| o | Section 461(l) excess business loss adjustment . . . . . . | **8o** | |
| p | Taxable distributions from an ABLE account (see instructions) . | **8p** | |
| z | Other income. List type and amount ▶ _____<br>_____ | **8z** | |
| 9 | Total other income. Add lines 8a through 8z . . . . . . . . . . | **9** | |
| 10 | Combine lines 1 through 7 and 9. Enter here and on Form 1040, 1040-SR, or 1040-NR, line 8 . . . . . . . . . . . . . | **10** | |

For Paperwork Reduction Act Notice, see your tax return instructions.     Cat. No. 71479F     Schedule 1 (Form 1040) 2021

Schedule 1 (Form 1040) 2021 Page **2**

| **Part II** | **Adjustments to Income** | | |
|---|---|---|---|
| **11** | Educator expenses | **11** | |
| **12** | Certain business expenses of reservists, performing artists, and fee-basis government officials. Attach Form 2106 | **12** | |
| **13** | Health savings account deduction. Attach Form 8889 | **13** | |
| **14** | Moving expenses for members of the Armed Forces. Attach Form 3903 | **14** | |
| **15** | Deductible part of self-employment tax. Attach Schedule SE | **15** | |
| **16** | Self-employed SEP, SIMPLE, and qualified plans | **16** | |
| **17** | Self-employed health insurance deduction | **17** | |
| **18** | Penalty on early withdrawal of savings | **18** | |
| **19a** | Alimony paid | **19a** | |
| **b** | Recipient's SSN ▶ | | |
| **c** | Date of original divorce or separation agreement (see instructions) ▶ | | |
| **20** | IRA deduction | **20** | |
| **21** | Student loan interest deduction | **21** | |
| **22** | Reserved for future use | **22** | |
| **23** | Archer MSA deduction | **23** | |
| **24** | Other adjustments: | | |
| **a** | Jury duty pay (see instructions) | **24a** | |
| **b** | Deductible expenses related to income reported on line 8k from the rental of personal property engaged in for profit | **24b** | |
| **c** | Nontaxable amount of the value of Olympic and Paralympic medals and USOC prize money reported on line 8l | **24c** | |
| **d** | Reforestation amortization and expenses | **24d** | |
| **e** | Repayment of supplemental unemployment benefits under the Trade Act of 1974 | **24e** | |
| **f** | Contributions to section 501(c)(18)(D) pension plans | **24f** | |
| **g** | Contributions by certain chaplains to section 403(b) plans | **24g** | |
| **h** | Attorney fees and court costs for actions involving certain unlawful discrimination claims (see instructions) | **24h** | |
| **i** | Attorney fees and court costs you paid in connection with an award from the IRS for information you provided that helped the IRS detect tax law violations | **24i** | |
| **j** | Housing deduction from Form 2555 | **24j** | |
| **k** | Excess deductions of section 67(e) expenses from Schedule K-1 (Form 1041) | **24k** | |
| **z** | Other adjustments. List type and amount ▶ _____ | **24z** | |
| **25** | Total other adjustments. Add lines 24a through 24z | **25** | |
| **26** | Add lines 11 through 23 and 25. These are your **adjustments to income.** Enter here and on Form 1040 or 1040-SR, line 10, or Form 1040-NR, line 10a | **26** | |

Schedule 1 (Form 1040) 2021

| | | | |
|---|---|---|---|
| **SCHEDULE 2**<br>**(Form 1040)**<br><br>Department of the Treasury<br>Internal Revenue Service | **Additional Taxes**<br>▶ Attach to Form 1040, 1040-SR, or 1040-NR.<br>▶ Go to *www.irs.gov/Form1040* for instructions and the latest information. | OMB No. 1545-0074<br><br>2021<br><br>Attachment<br>Sequence No. 02 | |

Name(s) shown on Form 1040, 1040-SR, or 1040-NR | Your social security number

### Part I  Tax

| | | |
|---|---|---|
| **1** | Alternative minimum tax. Attach Form 6251 . . . . . . . . . . . . . | **1** |
| **2** | Excess advance premium tax credit repayment. Attach Form 8962 . . . . . | **2** |
| **3** | Add lines 1 and 2. Enter here and on Form 1040, 1040-SR, or 1040-NR, line 17 . . | **3** |

### Part II  Other Taxes

| | | |
|---|---|---|
| **4** | Self-employment tax. Attach Schedule SE . . . . . . . . . . . . . | **4** |
| **5** | Social security and Medicare tax on unreported tip income. Attach Form 4137 . . . . . . . . . . . . . . . **5** | |
| **6** | Uncollected social security and Medicare tax on wages. Attach Form 8919 . . . . . . . . . . . . . . . . **6** | |
| **7** | Total additional social security and Medicare tax. Add lines 5 and 6 . . | **7** |
| **8** | Additional tax on IRAs or other tax-favored accounts. Attach Form 5329 if required | **8** |
| **9** | Household employment taxes. Attach Schedule H . . . . . . . . . | **9** |
| **10** | Repayment of first-time homebuyer credit. Attach Form 5405 if required . . . . . | **10** |
| **11** | Additional Medicare Tax. Attach Form 8959 . . . . . . . . . . . | **11** |
| **12** | Net investment income tax. Attach Form 8960 . . . . . . . . . . | **12** |
| **13** | Uncollected social security and Medicare or RRTA tax on tips or group-term life insurance from Form W-2, box 12 . . . . . . . . . . . . . . | **13** |
| **14** | Interest on tax due on installment income from the sale of certain residential lots and timeshares . . . . . . . . . . . . . . . . . . . . | **14** |
| **15** | Interest on the deferred tax on gain from certain installment sales with a sales price over $150,000 . . . . . . . . . . . . . . . . . . . . | **15** |
| **16** | Recapture of low-income housing credit. Attach Form 8611 . . . . . . . . | **16** |

*(continued on page 2)*

For Paperwork Reduction Act Notice, see your tax return instructions. | Cat. No. 71478U | Schedule 2 (Form 1040) 2021

Schedule 2 (Form 1040) 2021

Page **2**

## Part II  Other Taxes *(continued)*

| | | | |
|---|---|---|---|
| **17** | Other additional taxes: | | |
| **a** | Recapture of other credits. List type, form number, and amount ▶ _____ | **17a** | |
| **b** | Recapture of federal mortgage subsidy. If you sold your home in 2021, see instructions . . . . . . . . . . . . . | **17b** | |
| **c** | Additional tax on HSA distributions. Attach Form 8889 . . . | **17c** | |
| **d** | Additional tax on an HSA because you didn't remain an eligible individual. Attach Form 8889 . . . . . . . . . . . | **17d** | |
| **e** | Additional tax on Archer MSA distributions. Attach Form 8853 . | **17e** | |
| **f** | Additional tax on Medicare Advantage MSA distributions. Attach Form 8853 . . . . . . . . . . . . . . | **17f** | |
| **g** | Recapture of a charitable contribution deduction related to a fractional interest in tangible personal property . . . . . . | **17g** | |
| **h** | Income you received from a nonqualified deferred compensation plan that fails to meet the requirements of section 409A . . . | **17h** | |
| **i** | Compensation you received from a nonqualified deferred compensation plan described in section 457A . . . . . . . | **17i** | |
| **j** | Section 72(m)(5) excess benefits tax . . . . . . . . . . | **17j** | |
| **k** | Golden parachute payments . . . . . . . . . . . . | **17k** | |
| **l** | Tax on accumulation distribution of trusts . . . . . . . | **17l** | |
| **m** | Excise tax on insider stock compensation from an expatriated corporation . . . . . . . . . . . . . . . . . | **17m** | |
| **n** | Look-back interest under section 167(g) or 460(b) from Form 8697 or 8866 . . . . . . . . . . . . . . . . | **17n** | |
| **o** | Tax on non-effectively connected income for any part of the year you were a nonresident alien from Form 1040-NR . . . . | **17o** | |
| **p** | Any interest from Form 8621, line 16f, relating to distributions from, and dispositions of, stock of a section 1291 fund . . . . | **17p** | |
| **q** | Any interest from Form 8621, line 24 . . . . . . . . . | **17q** | |
| **z** | Any other taxes. List type and amount ▶ _____ | **17z** | |
| **18** | Total additional taxes. Add lines 17a through 17z . . . . . . . . . | | **18** | |
| **19** | Additional tax from Schedule 8812 . . . . . . . . . . . . . . | | **19** | |
| **20** | Section 965 net tax liability installment from Form 965-A . . . | **20** | |
| **21** | Add lines 4, 7 through 16, 18, and 19. These are your **total other taxes.** Enter here and on Form 1040 or 1040-SR, line 23, or Form 1040-NR, line 23b . . . . . . . | | **21** | |

Schedule 2 (Form 1040) 2021

**SCHEDULE 3**
**(Form 1040)**

Department of the Treasury
Internal Revenue Service

**Additional Credits and Payments**

▶ Attach to Form 1040, 1040-SR, or 1040-NR.
▶ Go to *www.irs.gov/Form1040* for instructions and the latest information.

OMB No. 1545-0074

**2021**

Attachment
Sequence No. **03**

Name(s) shown on Form 1040, 1040-SR, or 1040-NR | Your social security number

### Part I  Nonrefundable Credits

| | | | |
|---|---|---|---|
| **1** | Foreign tax credit. Attach Form 1116 if required . . . . . . . . | **1** | |
| **2** | Credit for child and dependent care expenses from Form 2441, line 11. Attach Form 2441 . . . . . . . . . . . . . . . . . | **2** | |
| **3** | Education credits from Form 8863, line 19 . . . . . . . . . . | **3** | |
| **4** | Retirement savings contributions credit. Attach Form 8880 . . . . | **4** | |
| **5** | Residential energy credits. Attach Form 5695 . . . . . . . . | **5** | |
| **6** | Other nonrefundable credits: | | |
| **a** | General business credit. Attach Form 3800 . . . . . | **6a** | |
| **b** | Credit for prior year minimum tax. Attach Form 8801 . . . | **6b** | |
| **c** | Adoption credit. Attach Form 8839 . . . . . . . | **6c** | |
| **d** | Credit for the elderly or disabled. Attach Schedule R . . . . | **6d** | |
| **e** | Alternative motor vehicle credit. Attach Form 8910 . . . . | **6e** | |
| **f** | Qualified plug-in motor vehicle credit. Attach Form 8936 . . . | **6f** | |
| **g** | Mortgage interest credit. Attach Form 8396 . . . . . . | **6g** | |
| **h** | District of Columbia first-time homebuyer credit. Attach Form 8859 | **6h** | |
| **i** | Qualified electric vehicle credit. Attach Form 8834 . . . . . | **6i** | |
| **j** | Alternative fuel vehicle refueling property credit. Attach Form 8911 | **6j** | |
| **k** | Credit to holders of tax credit bonds. Attach Form 8912 . . . | **6k** | |
| **l** | Amount on Form 8978, line 14. See instructions . . . . . . | **6l** | |
| **z** | Other nonrefundable credits. List type and amount ▶ _____ | **6z** | |
| **7** | Total other nonrefundable credits. Add lines 6a through 6z . . . . . . . . . | **7** | |
| **8** | Add lines 1 through 5 and 7. Enter here and on Form 1040, 1040-SR, or 1040-NR, line 20 . . . . . . . . . . . . . . . . . . . . . . . . | **8** | |

*(continued on page 2)*

For Paperwork Reduction Act Notice, see your tax return instructions.  Cat. No. 71480G  Schedule 3 (Form 1040) 2021

---

Schedule 3 (Form 1040) 2021  Page **2**

### Part II  Other Payments and Refundable Credits

| | | | |
|---|---|---|---|
| **9** | Net premium tax credit. Attach Form 8962 . . . . . . . . . | **9** | |
| **10** | Amount paid with request for extension to file (see instructions) . . . . . . . | **10** | |
| **11** | Excess social security and tier 1 RRTA tax withheld . . . . . . . . . . | **11** | |
| **12** | Credit for federal tax on fuels. Attach Form 4136 . . . . . . . . . . | **12** | |
| **13** | Other payments or refundable credits: | | |
| **a** | Form 2439 . . . . . . . . . . . . . . . . . | **13a** | |
| **b** | Qualified sick and family leave credits from Schedule(s) H and Form(s) 7202 for leave taken before April 1, 2021 . . . . | **13b** | |
| **c** | Health coverage tax credit from Form 8885 . . . . . | **13c** | |
| **d** | Credit for repayment of amounts included in income from earlier years . . . . . . . . . . . . . . . . | **13d** | |
| **e** | Reserved for future use . . . . . . . . . . . | **13e** | |
| **f** | Net section 965 inclusions . . . . . . . . . . | **13f** | |
| **g** | Credit for child and dependent care expenses from Form 2441, line 10. Attach Form 2441 . . . . . . . . . . | **13g** | |
| **h** | Qualified sick and family leave credits from Schedule(s) H and Form(s) 7202 for leave taken after March 31, 2021 . . . . . | **13h** | |
| **z** | Other payments or refundable credits. List type and amount ▶ _____ | **13z** | |
| **14** | Total other payments or refundable credits. Add lines 13a through 13z . . . . . | **14** | |
| **15** | Add lines 9 through 12 and 14. Enter here and on Form 1040, 1040-SR, or 1040-NR, line 31 . . . . . . . . . . . . . . . . . . . . . . . | **15** | |

Schedule 3 (Form 1040) 2021

Source: U.S. Department of the Treasury, Internal Revenue Service, Schedules 1–3. Washington, DC: 2021.

**TABLE 2-1**
Line-by-line look
at Form 1040 and
Schedules 1 through 3

| Description | Line Location | Chapter(s) Where Discussed |
|---|---|---|
| Form 1040 | | |
| Filing Status | page 1 | 1, 2 |
| Dependents | page 1 | 2 |
| Wages, Salaries, and Tips | 1 | 1, 3 |
| Taxable and nontaxable interest | 2a/b | 1, 3 |
| Ordinary and qualified dividends | 3a/b | 3 |
| IRA distributions | 4a/b | 11 |
| Pensions and annuities | 5a/b | 11 |
| Social security benefits | 6a/b | 3 |
| Capital gain or loss | 7 | 7 |
| Other income | 8 and Sch 1 | |
| Adjustments to income from Schedule 1 | 10a and Sch 1 | |
| Adjusted gross income | 11 | |
| Standard or itemized deduction | 12a | 1, 2, 5 |
| Adjustments to income - charitable contributions | 12b | 5 |
| Qualified business income deduction | 13 | 6 |
| Taxable income | 15 | |
| Tax | 16 | 1, 2 |
| Nonrefundable child tax credit or credit for other dependents | 19 | 2, 9 |
| Other nonrefundable credits | 20 and Sch 3 | |
| Other taxes | 23 and Sch 2 | |
| Total tax | 24 | |
| Federal income tax withheld | 25a/b/c | 1, 2, 10 |
| Estimated tax payments and prior overpayments | 26 | 2, 10 |
| Earned income credit | 27a | 9 |
| Refundable child tax credit or additional child tax credit | 28 and Sch 8812 | 9 |
| American opportunity credit | 29 | 9 |
| Recovery rebate credit | 30 | 1 |
| Other credits | 31 and Sch 3 | |
| Overpayment | 34 | |
| Amount of refund | 35a | 1, 2 |
| Amount owed | 37 | 1, 2 |
| Estimated tax penalty | 38 | 2 |
| Schedule 1 | | |
| Additional Income | | |
| Taxable refunds of state and local taxes | 1 | 3 |
| Alimony received | 2a | 4 |
| Business income or loss (Schedule C) | 3 | 6 |
| Other gains or losses (Form 4797) | 4 | 7 |
| Rentals, partnerships, etc. (Schedule E) | 5 | 8, 13 |
| Farm income | 6 | — |
| Unemployment compensation | 7 | 1, 3 |
| Other income | 8a to z | 3 |
| Adjustments to Income | | |
| Educator expenses | 11 | 4 |
| Certain business expenses | 12 | -- |
| Health savings account deduction | 13 | 4 |
| Moving expenses for members of armed forces | 14 | 4 |
| Deductible part of self-employment tax | 15 | 4, 6 |
| SEP, SIMPLE, and other retirement plans | 16 | 11 |
| Self-employed health insurance deduction | 17 | 4 |
| Penalty on early withdrawal of savings | 18 | 4 |

| | | |
|---|---|---|
| Alimony paid | 19a | 4 |
| IRA deduction | 20 | 11 |
| Student loan interest deduction | 21 | 4 |
| **Schedule 2** | | |
| Alternative minimum tax | 1 | 13 |
| Excess advance premium tax credit | 2 | 9 |
| Self-employment tax | 4 | 6 |
| Unreported social security and Medicare tax | 7 | -- |
| Additional tax on retirement plans | 8 | 11 |
| Household employment taxes (Sch H) | 9 | 10 |
| Repayment of first-time homebuyer credit | 10 | -- |
| Additional Medicare tax | 11 | 7 |
| Net invetment income tax | 12 | 7 |
| Other taxes | 17a to z | -- |
| Section 965 tax | 20 | -- |
| **Schedule 3** | | |
| Foreign tax credit | 1 | 9 |
| Credit for child and dependent care | 2 | 9 |
| Education credits | 3 | 9 |
| Retirement savings contribution credit | 4 | 9 |
| Residential energy credit | 5 | -- |
| Other credits | 6a to z | 9, 13 |
| Net premium tax credit | 9 | 9 |
| Amount paid with extension to file | 10 | 2 |
| Excess social security tax | 11 | 2 |
| Credit for federal tax on fuels | 12 | 2 |
| Other credits | 13a to z | 2, 9 |

### Adjusted Gross Income (Form 1040, Line 11)

Before we begin to discuss some of the items introduced on Form 1040, we need to introduce the concept of *Adjusted Gross Income* (AGI). The tax code defines AGI as gross income minus a list of permitted deductions.[1] In practice, calculation of AGI is simple: Just subtract all of the *for* AGI deductions (summarized on Schedule 1, line 26) from total income (Form 1040, lines 1–9, plus Schedule 1, line 10). AGI is also shown on Form 1040, line 11. *For* AGI deductions are deductions that a taxpayer can take prior to calculating AGI.

AGI is an extremely important concept. Many deductions and credits are determined with reference to it. Furthermore, when a taxpayer's AGI exceeds certain levels, certain tax benefits are reduced or eliminated. We will refer to AGI throughout this text.

**CONCEPT CHECK 2-1— LO 2-1**

1. When preparing a tax return, you will seldom use any of the Schedules. True or false?
2. The concept of Adjusted Gross Income (AGI) is important because many deductions and credits reported on the tax return are computed based on the amount shown as AGI. True or false?

[1] The permitted deductions are given in IRC § 62(a).

# FILING STATUS (FORM 1040, FIRST PAGE)
## LO 2-2

The amount of tax liability depends on many factors, including the filing status of the taxpayer(s). Because of individual circumstances, taxpayers file their returns as one of the following: (1) single, (2) married filing jointly, (3) married filing separately, (4) head of household, or (5) qualifying widow(er) with dependent child. Taxpayers must choose the filing status that is appropriate for them. We discuss each of these filing statuses next.

### Single

Individuals use a filing status of single if they are not married and if they do not qualify as either head of household or qualifying widow(er). Marital status is determined on the last day of the tax year.

For purposes of this section, individuals also are single if a divorce or separate maintenance decree was legally executed on or before December 31 of the tax year.

### Married Filing Jointly

A couple that is legally married on the last day of the tax year can file one joint tax return that combines all income, deductions, and credits of both spouses.[2] It does not matter if only one spouse earns all of the income. The marital status of a couple is determined under the laws of the state in which they reside. If a spouse dies during the year, the surviving taxpayer can file a joint return if the couple was married on the date of death and the surviving spouse has not remarried as of December 31 of the tax year.

As stated in the section for single status, a person who is legally separated from their spouse under a decree of divorce or separate maintenance is not considered married.[3] However, couples in the process of obtaining a divorce (that is not yet final) can file a joint return.

If either spouse is a nonresident alien at any time during the year, generally that person cannot file a joint return. This is because the non-U.S. income of a nonresident spouse is not taxable in the United States. However, if both spouses agree to subject their worldwide income to U.S. taxation, they can file a joint return.

### Married Filing Separately

A married couple can elect to file two separate returns rather than one joint return.[4] Only in unusual circumstances is it advantageous for a married couple to file separate returns rather than a joint return.

A taxpayer who files as married filing separately must show the name and social security number of their spouse on Form 1040 (see Exhibit 2-1). Additionally, if one taxpayer itemizes deductions, the other spouse must also itemize even if these itemized deductions are less than the standard deduction. The standard deduction can be taken only if both of them choose the standard deduction. For a more detailed discussion of this topic, see the sections about standard deductions later in this chapter and about itemized deductions in Chapter 5.

### Head of Household

To qualify as head of household, a taxpayer must be unmarried at the end of the tax year, be a U.S. citizen or resident throughout the year, not be a qualifying widow(er), and maintain a household that is the principal place of abode of a *qualifying person* for more than half of the year. Temporary absences, such as attending school, do not disqualify the person under this section.

---

[2] IRC § 7703(a)(1), § 6013(a).

[3] IRC § 7703(a)(2).

[4] IRC § 1(d).

**EXHIBIT 2-3**  Who Is a Qualifying Person for Filing as Head of Household?[1]

**Caution:** See the text of this chapter for the other requirements you must meet to claim head of household filing status.

**Note:** The references to "chapter 3" noted below are to Chapter 3 in Publication 17, not Chapter 3 in this book.

Source: IRS Publication 17.

---

**Table 2-1. Who Is a Qualifying Person Qualifying You to File as Head of Household?[1]**

> **Caution.** See the text of this chapter for the other requirements you must meet to claim head of household filing status.

| IF the person is your . . . | AND . . . | THEN that person is . . . |
|---|---|---|
| qualifying child (such as a son, daughter, or grandchild who lived with you more than half the year and meets certain other tests)[2] | he or she is single | a qualifying person, whether or not the child meets the *Citizen or Resident Test*. See chapter 3. |
| | he or she is married **and** you can claim him or her as a dependent | a qualifying person. |
| | he or she is married **and** you can't claim him or her as a dependent | not a qualifying person.[3] |
| qualifying relative[4] who is your father or mother | you can claim him or her as a dependent[5] | a qualifying person.[6] |
| | you can't claim him or her as a dependent | not a qualifying person. |
| qualifying relative[4] other than your father or mother (such as a grandparent, brother, or sister who meets certain tests) | he or she lived with you more than half the year, **and** he or she is related to you in one of the ways listed under *Relatives who don't have to live with you* in chapter 3 **and** you can claim him or her as a dependent[5] | a qualifying person. |
| | he or she didn't live with you more than half the year | not a qualifying person. |
| | he or she isn't related to you in one of the ways listed under *Relatives who don't have to live with you* in chapter 3 **and** is your qualifying relative only because he or she lived with you all year as a member of your household | not a qualifying person. |
| | you can't claim him or her as a dependent | not a qualifying person. |

[1] A person can't qualify more than one taxpayer to use the head of household filing status for the year.

[2] The term qualifying child is defined in chapter 3. **Note.** If you are a noncustodial parent, the term "qualifying child" for head of household filing status doesn't include a child who is your qualifying child only because of the rules described under *Children of divorced or separated parents (or parents who live apart)* under *Qualifying Child* in chapter 3. If you are the custodial parent and those rules apply, the child generally is your qualifying child for head of household filing status even though the child isn't a qualifying child you can claim as a dependent.

[3] This person is a qualifying person if the only reason you can't claim them as a dependent is that you, or your spouse if filing jointly, can be claimed as a dependent on someone else's return.

[4] The term qualifying relative is defined in chapter 3.

[5] If you can claim a person as a dependent only because of a multiple support agreement, that person isn't a qualifying person. See *Multiple Support Agreement* in chapter 3.

[6] See *Special rule for parent* under *Qualifying Person*, earlier.

---

Also to qualify as maintaining a household, a taxpayer must pay for more than half the cost of keeping up a home for the year. These costs include rent or mortgage payments, real estate taxes, home insurance, utilities, maintenance and repair, and food eaten in the home. Nonqualifying costs are personal expenditures such as clothing, medical costs, transportation costs, and the like.[5]

A special rule allows a taxpayer's parents to live in a household separate from that of the taxpayer and still permits the taxpayer to qualify for head of household status. However, the taxpayer must pay for more than half of the cost of the household where the parents live.

[5] Reg. § 1.2-2(d).

To understand the definition of a qualifying person for head of household filing status, refer to Exhibit 2-3, from IRS Publication 17. Notice that a *qualifying relative* who is a dependent only because this person lived with the taxpayer for the entire year is not a qualifying person for head of household. In addition, married individuals who live apart from their spouses for at least the last six months of the year can qualify as head of household.

### Qualifying Widow(er) with Dependent Child

If a spouse dies during the tax year, the surviving spouse usually can file a joint return. For the two tax years following the death of a spouse, the surviving spouse may be eligible to file as a qualifying widow(er) if all the following conditions are satisfied:

- The taxpayer was eligible to file a joint return in the year the spouse died.
- The taxpayer did not remarry before the end of the tax year in question.
- The taxpayer paid more than half the cost of keeping up a household (see the "Head of Household" section for costs that qualify).
- The household was the principal place of abode for the entire year (except for temporary absences) of both the taxpayer and a child, stepchild, or adopted child who can be claimed as a dependent by the taxpayer (see the rules concerning dependents given later).

This filing status is also called *surviving spouse.*[6]

On the top of the first page of Form 1040, there are check boxes for each filing status (single, married filing jointly, married filing separately, qualifying widow(er), and head of household). The taxpayer needs to check the box corresponding to the appropriate filing status.

---

**CONCEPT CHECK 2-2— LO 2-2**

1. Even though you are in the process of getting a divorce, you can file as married filing jointly. True or false?
2. The social security number of the taxpayer's spouse must be shown on the taxpayer's tax return when filing as married filing separately. True or false?
3. A surviving spouse who qualified as married filing jointly when the spouse died can file as a qualifying widow(er) for the next two years as long as the surviving spouse pays for more than half the cost of keeping up a household and does not remarry. True or false?

## DEPENDENTS (FORM 1040, PAGE 1)

**LO 2-3**

Taxpayers may have related individuals living with them and/or they may provide financial support for a related individual. As we will see in this section, these individuals may qualify as dependents if they meet certain tests. The existence of dependents is important for determination of child credits, filing status, and other matters.

Dependents are listed in the middle of page 1 of Form 1040.

A taxpayer can claim a dependent if the person is *a qualifying child or a qualifying relative* and the person meets all of the following tests:

1. Dependent taxpayer test.
2. Joint return test.
3. Citizen or resident test.

The dependent taxpayer test means that if an individual can be claimed as a dependent by someone else, then the taxpayer cannot claim that person as a dependent. This is the case even if the person is a qualifying child or qualifying relative of the taxpayer.

[6] IRC § 2(a).

For the joint return test, the taxpayer cannot claim as a dependent someone who files a joint return with their spouse.[7] However, if the dependent files a joint return simply to claim a refund (that is, if there is no tax liability on the joint return and there would be no tax liability on separate returns), then a dependent claim is allowed.[8]

---

**EXAMPLE 2-1**

Lucia is the daughter of Michael and Iris Wilson. Lucia married Peter Young in January 2021. The Youngs are both 18 years old, are full-time students at State University, and have lived, for the entire year, with the Wilsons, who paid for all the living expenses of both Lucia and Peter. Lucia and Peter both work part time at the university, and each earned $1,000 during the year, from which their employer withheld income taxes. The Youngs had no other sources of income, and they filed a joint tax return for 2021. Assume that, in all respects other than the joint return test, the Wilsons can claim Lucia and Peter as dependents. In this case, Lucia and Peter are dependents of the Wilsons. Even though Lucia and Peter filed a joint return, it was solely to claim a refund. The tax liability on a joint return would be zero, and if they filed separate returns, there would still be no liability.

---

**TAX YOUR BRAIN**

Use the information in Example 2-1, but assume that Lucia and Peter each earned $20,000 from their university employment. Who can claim them as a dependent?

**ANSWER**

No one. The joint tax return of Lucia and Peter would show a tax liability. Thus, the Wilsons cannot claim them as dependents because Lucia and Peter do not meet the joint return test. Lucia and Peter would not receive the dependency claim either. The IRS deems that the person or persons filing a tax return are not dependents. Note that the answer would be the same even if Lucia and Peter filed separate returns.

---

An individual meets the citizen or resident test if the person is (a) a U.S. citizen, resident, or national; (b) a resident of Canada or Mexico; or (c) an adopted child of the taxpayer if the child is a member of the taxpayer's household all year and the taxpayer is a U.S. citizen or national.[9]

Recall that to claim someone as a dependent, the individual must meet the three tests just noted, *and* the individual must be either a qualifying child or a qualifying relative. We will define those terms next.

## Qualifying Child

A qualifying child meets *all five* of the following tests:

1. Relationship test.
2. Age test.
3. Residency test.
4. Support test.
5. Special test for qualifying child of more than one taxpayer.

---

[7] IRC § 152(b)(2).
[8] Rev. Rul. 54-567, 1954-2 CB 108; Rev. Rul. 65-34, 1965-1 CB 86.
[9] IRC § 152(b)(3).

### Relationship Test

The relationship test is met if the dependent is *one* of the following:

- Child or descendant of child (grandchild or great-grandchild).
- Stepchild.
- Eligible foster child.
- Brother, sister, half-brother, half-sister, stepbrother, or stepsister, or a descendant of them.[10]

A child includes an adopted child and includes a child placed for adoption in the taxpayer's household by an authorized adoption agency even if the adoption is not finalized.[11] Cousins are not included in the definition of qualifying child.

### Age Test

At the end of the tax year, the child must be *one* of the following:

- Under the age of 19.
- Under the age of 24 and a full-time student. A full-time student is a person who was in school full time during any part of each of five calendar months during the calendar year.
- Totally and permanently disabled regardless of age.

For years after 2008, the child must be younger than the person claiming the dependency.

### Residency Test

The child must live with the taxpayer for more than half of the year to meet this requirement. Temporary absences are exceptions to this rule if the absences are due to education, vacation, illness, or military service.

### Support Test

The child must not provide more than half of their support. The definition of *support* is broad. It "includes food, shelter, clothing, medical and dental care, education, and the like."[12] Items such as medical insurance premiums, child care, toys, gifts, and vacations have been found to be includable in support, whereas life insurance premiums have been excluded. A scholarship is not counted as support if it is received by, and used in support of, a child (including stepchild, foster child, adopted child, or child placed for adoption) who is a full-time student at an educational institution.[13]

For items paid for in cash, support is the amount paid. For noncash items such as lodging, use the fair market value of the item to determine the amount of support.

### Special Test for Qualifying Child of More Than One Taxpayer

If a child meets the other four tests and can be a qualifying child for more than one taxpayer, only one individual can claim the exemption. The IRS lets you decide who the taxpayer claiming the dependent should be. However, if you cannot make a decision, the IRS will use the tie-breaker rule shown in Exhibit 2-4 (from IRS Publication 17).

---

[10] IRC § 152(c)(2).

[11] Reg. § 1.152-2(c)(2).

[12] Reg. § 1.152-1(a)(2)(i).

[13] IRC § 152(f)(5).

**EXHIBIT 2-4**
**When More Than One Person Files a Return Claiming the Same Qualifying Child (Tie-Breaker Rule)**

Source: IRS Publication 17.

| IF more than one person files a return claiming the same qualifying child and . . . | THEN the child will be treated as the qualifying child of the. . . |
|---|---|
| only one of the persons is the child's parent, | parent. |
| two of the persons are parents of the child and they do not file a joint return together, | parent with whom the child lived for the longer period of time during the year. |
| two of the persons are parents of the child, they do not file a joint return together, and the child lived with each parent the same amount of time during the year, | parent with the highest adjusted gross income (AGI). |
| none of the persons are the child's parent, | person with the highest AGI. |

## Child of Divorced or Separated Parents

In most cases, a child of divorced or separated parents will be the qualifying child of the parent with custody. However, the child will be deemed to be the qualifying child of the noncustodial parent if *all* the following tests are met:

- The child has been in the custody of either or both parents for more than half of the year.
- Either or both parents provided more than half the child's support.
- The parents are (a) divorced or legally separated, (b) separated under a written separation agreement, or (c) living apart at all times during the last six months of the year.
- The decree or separation agreement for 2021 states that the noncustodial parent can claim the child as a dependent, or the custodial parent signs a written document specifying that the child will not be claimed as a dependent.

Form 8332 must be used to revoke a release of claim to exemption that was previously released to the noncustodial parent and be attached to the tax return of the parent claiming the qualifying child. Additionally, if the custodial parent gives notice of revocation in 2021, the revocation takes effect in tax year 2022.

**CONCEPT CHECK 2-3—**
**LO 2-3**

1. What are the five specific tests you need to meet to claim someone as a qualifying child? _____

2. To meet the age test, a child who is not disabled must be _____ or _____ if a full-time student.

## Qualifying Relative

Persons are a qualifying relatives if they meet *all four* of the following tests:

1. Not a qualifying child test.
2. Relationship or member of household test.
3. Gross income test.
4. Support test.

The four tests are discussed in the next paragraphs.

### *Not a Qualifying Child Test*

If a child is your qualifying child or the qualifying child of another taxpayer, that child cannot be your qualifying relative.

### *Relationship or Member of Household Test*

The person either must be a member of the taxpayer's household for the entire year *or* must be related to the taxpayer in *one* of the following ways:

- Child or descendant of child (grandchild or great-grandchild).
- Stepchild.
- Eligible foster child.
- Brother, sister, half-brother, half-sister, or a descendant of them.
- Stepbrother or stepsister.
- Father or mother.
- Brother or sister of parents.
- Son-in-law, daughter-in-law, father-in-law, mother-in-law, brother-in-law, or sister-in-law.

Note that if someone is related to the taxpayer (as indicated in the preceding list), it is not necessary that the person live with the taxpayer for the entire year or, actually, any part of the year. But it may be difficult to meet the support test if the individual does not live in the household.

### *Gross Income Test*

The dependent must *not* have gross income equal to or greater than $4,300.

For purposes of this test, gross income does not include certain items such as tax-exempt interest, the nontaxable portion of social security benefits, and the nontaxable portion of a scholarship or fellowship.

### *Support Test*

The taxpayer must provide over 50% of the dependent's support.[14] Recall that the definition of support was explained in the "Qualifying Child" section.

In practice, a taxpayer must determine how much was paid for the support of the dependent (regardless of who paid it) and then determine whether the taxpayer provided over half of that support.

If several dependents receive the benefits of an item of support, allocate the cost of the item to the dependents on a pro rata basis unless the taxpayer can show that a different allocation is appropriate.[15] Money received and spent by a dependent counts as support. Examples include wages from a part-time job or social security benefits paid to a dependent.

Do not confuse the issue of what expenditures qualify for support with the issue of who paid for the expenditures. These are different but related concepts. Confusion can arise because sometimes it is easier to determine the total amount of support by reference to where the money came from rather than by creating an itemized list of support paid on behalf of an individual.

The support test has two exceptions. The first occurs when several persons provide for more than half the support of someone, but no one person meets the 50% threshold.[16] If each person in the group would be able to claim the individual as a dependent (absent the support test) and no one person in the group furnished more than half of the individual's support, then one of the persons in the group who provided more than 10% of the support can claim the dependent with the agreement of the other persons in the group. Such a multiple support agreement must be in writing; taxpayers use Form 2120 for this purpose. Each person who meets the 10% test but who will not be claiming the dependent must fill out Form 2120. The taxpayer who will claim the dependent must file all the Forms 2120 with the return.

If someone is the subject of a multiple support agreement over a number of years, it is not necessary that the same individual claim the dependent each year.

---

[14] IRC § 152(d)(1)(C).

[15] Rev. Rul. 64-222, 1964-2 CB 47.

[16] IRC § 152(d)(3).

**EXAMPLE 2-2**

Martha, Monique, Terry, Robert, and Angie provided all the support for George in the following percentages:

| | |
|---|---|
| Martha (friend) | 30% |
| Monique (neighbor) | 5% |
| Terry (son) | 40% |
| Robert (son) | 10% |
| Angie (daughter) | 15% |

Initially you need to determine the members of the group who could claim George as a dependent, absent the support test. These are Terry, Robert, and Angie, who are George's children (Martha and Monique cannot claim George because he does not meet the relationship test). Next determine whether Terry, Robert, and Angie (as a group) contributed more than 50% of George's support. In this case, they contributed 65%. If a multiple support agreement is prepared, either Terry or Angie would be entitled to claim George as a dependent. Robert is not entitled to the dependent because he did not contribute *more* than 10% of George's support.

**TAX YOUR BRAIN**

Using Example 2-2, assume that George had a part-time job that provided 25% of his support. The other five people provided the remaining 75% of George's support in the same proportions given. Which person(s) would be entitled to claim George as a dependent for purposes of a multiple support agreement?

**ANSWER**

No one would be entitled to claim George. We previously determined that only Terry, Robert, and Angie would have been entitled to claim George as a dependent, absent the support test. These three people must supply over half of George's support. Here the three individuals contributed only 48.75% of George's support (65% of the 75% not paid by George). Thus, no one can claim George as a dependent.

The second exception to the 50% support test is the case of a child of divorced or separated parents. If the child is not a qualifying child, the child can be treated as a qualifying relative of the noncustodial parent if the following are true:

- The child has been in the custody of either or both parents for more than half the year.
- Either or both parents provided more than half the child's support.
- The parents are (1) divorced or legally separated, (2) separated under a written separation agreement, or (3) living apart at all times during the last six months of the year.
- The decree or separation agreement for 2021 states that the noncustodial parent can claim the child as a dependent, or the custodial parent relinquishes the dependent claim to the noncustodial parent by signing a written agreement to that effect.[17] However, the agreement is not binding on future tax years.

The preceding tests do not apply if the support of the child is determined based on a multiple support agreement.

**CONCEPT CHECK 2-4—**

**LO 2-3**

1. You must meet one of these four tests to be a qualifying relative: not a qualifying child test, relationship or member of household test, gross income test, and support test. True or false?
2. A qualifying relative can earn up to $12,550 for the year 2021. True or false?

---

[17] IRC § 152(e)(2).

# STANDARD DEDUCTION (FORM 1040, LINE 12a)

## LO 2-4

The Tax Cuts and Jobs Act of 2017 eliminated the personal exemption beginning with tax year 2018. This amount is built into the standard deduction. Taxpayers can subtract a standard deduction from AGI.[18] Taxpayers may alternatively elect to subtract itemized deductions and should do so if their itemized deductions are larger than the standard deduction amount.[19]

The standard deduction is the sum of the basic standard deduction and the additional standard deduction.[20] Both components depend on filing status and are subject to annual adjustment for inflation. The basic standard deduction for tax year 2021 is as follows:

 **NEW LAW**

For 2021, the standard deduction for each filing status has increased.

| Filing Status | Basic Standard Deduction |
| --- | --- |
| Single | $12,550 |
| Married filing jointly | $25,100 |
| Married filing separately | $12,550 |
| Head of household | $18,800 |
| Qualifying widow(er) | $25,100 |

Taxpayers who either are 65 or older or are blind can claim an additional standard deduction. Taxpayers who are both 65 or older and blind get two additional standard deductions. Note that blind taxpayers are entitled to the additional standard deduction regardless of their age. The additional standard deductions for taxpayers who are 65 or older or blind are

| Filing Status | Tax Year 2021 |
| --- | --- |
| Single | $1,700 |
| Married filing jointly | $1,350 |
| Married filing separately | $1,350 |
| Head of household | $1,700 |
| Qualifying widow(er) | $1,350 |

**EXAMPLE 2-3**

Flora is 56 years old, single, and blind. She is entitled to a standard deduction of $14,250 ($12,550 + $1,700). If she were 70 instead of 56, she would have a standard deduction of $15,950 ($12,550 + $1,700 + 1,700).

**EXAMPLE 2-4**

Peter and Jessica are married and have an 8-year-old dependent child who is blind. Peter and Jessica are entitled to a standard deduction of $25,100. This example illustrates that the additional standard deduction applies only to the taxpayer and the spouse, if any. Dependents do not affect the standard deduction computation.

The standard deduction is zero in any of the following instances:

- A married couple files separate returns and one spouse itemizes deductions. In this case, the other spouse must also itemize.
- A taxpayer is a nonresident alien.
- A taxpayer files a return for a period of less than 12 months because of a change in accounting period.

[18] IRC § 63(c).

[19] We discuss itemized deductions in Chapter 5.

[20] IRC § 63(c)(1).

When a taxpayer can be claimed as a dependent on the tax return of another individual, the basic standard deduction for the taxpayer is limited to the greater of (1) $1,100 or (2) the taxpayer's earned income plus $350.[21] Earned income is generally income from work or the efforts of the taxpayer. Salaries and wages are the most common type of earned income.

Congress enacted the preceding rule to prevent taxpayers from shifting income to their children or other dependents. For example, a couple could give a child a bond that pays interest of $3,500 per year. Without the rule, the entire $3,500 interest income would be tax-free because the basic standard deduction for any filing status exceeds the amount of income. With the rule in place, the standard deduction for the child would be $1,100.

The standard deduction increases, in effect, for the wages of the dependent person. This permits children, for example, to work a part-time summer job for some extra spending money but not have to pay income taxes.

---

**EXAMPLE 2-5**

Sherry's parents can claim her as a dependent on their tax return. In 2021 her only source of income was a part-time job in a local store where she earned $2,500 during the year. Sherry's standard deduction is $2,850, which is the greater of (a) $1,100 or (b) $2,500 + $350. As a result, Sherry would owe no income tax on her wages.

---

**EXAMPLE 2-6**

In 2021 Joji received $1,425 of interest income from a local bank. The interest was his only source of income for the year. His standard deduction is $1,100, which is the greater of (a) $1,100 or (b) $0 + $350.

---

**CONCEPT CHECK 2-5—**

**LO 2-4**

1. What is the amount of the standard deduction in each of the following cases?
   a. The taxpayer is single, 42 years of age, and blind. _____
   b. The taxpayer is head of household, 37 years of age, and not blind. _____
   c. The taxpayers are married filing jointly, one spouse is 67 and the other one is 61 years of age, and neither is blind. _____

# TAX DUE TO IRS
## LO 2-5

It is important to learn how to compute the amount of tax and arrive at the total liability amount. We illustrate some steps to help you determine these two items before we discuss tax payments.

### Amount of Tax (Form 1040, Line 16)

Most taxpayers determine the amount of tax by looking up the applicable tax due in a tax table.

The tax tables used in the preparation of Form 1040 are in Appendix D of this text. As you can see, there are columns for (1) single, (2) married filing jointly, (3) married filing separately, and (4) head of household. The qualifying widow(er) filing status uses the same column as married filing jointly.

---

**EXAMPLE 2-7**

A taxpayer has taxable income of $71,330. Referring to the tax tables, we can see that the amount of tax for line 15 would be $11,440 for a single person, $8,161 for a married couple filing jointly or a qualifying widow(er), $9,988 for a head of household, or $11,440 for a married couple filing separately.

---

The tax tables stop at taxable income of less than $100,000. Taxpayers with taxable income of $100,000 or more must use the tax rate schedules provided in Appendix F of this text. Recall that the IRS uses tax rate schedules to create the tax tables according to the midpoint of each $50 range.

---

[21] IRC § 63(c)(5). The dollar value given in (1) is for tax year 2021.

**NEW LAW**

For 2021, the standard deduction for each filing status has increased.

## Child Tax Credit (Form 1040, Lines 19 and 28)

In this chapter we briefly introduce the child tax credit, a credit used by many taxpayers. A credit will reduce tax liability in the amount of the credit. We discuss this credit in more detail in Chapter 9.

Taxpayers are allowed a $3,000 refundable tax credit for each qualifying child who is 6 to 17 years of age, and $3,600 for children under age 6.[22] The definition of a qualifying child is the same as a qualifying child for exemption purposes. The qualifying child must also be a U.S. citizen or resident,[23] be younger than the person claiming the credit for the child, and be unmarried. A $500 nonrefundable credit is also provided for qualifying dependents other than qualifying children.

The new law increased the credit from $2,000 to $3,000 (or to $3,600 for children under age 6). The $1,000 (or $1,600) increase is phased out beginning at modified AGI of $75,000 (single), $112,500 (head of household), and $150,000 (married jointly). Any remaining credit is reduced by $50 for each $1,000, or fraction thereof, of modified AGI in excess of $400,000 for taxpayers who are married filing jointly, and $200,000 for all other taxpayers.[24] *Modified AGI* is AGI plus income earned abroad or in certain U.S. territories or possessions. See Chapter 9 for further details on this credit.

## Total Tax Liability (Form 1040, Line 24)

This line represents the total amount the taxpayer must pay to the government for the tax year.

## Tax Payments (Form 1040, Lines 25–32)

Taxpayers must pay the amount of tax indicated on the total tax line (line 24). Normally taxpayers pay some or all of their tax liability prior to the due date of the tax return. Most commonly, taxpayers make payment through income tax withholding and quarterly estimated tax payments, although other payment methods are also possible.

## Income Tax Withholding (Form 1040, Line 25a to 25d)

When certain taxable payments are made to individuals, the payer must retain (withhold) a proportion of the payment otherwise due and remit the amount withheld to the U.S. Treasury. The withheld amount represents an estimate of the amount of income tax that would be due for the year on the taxable payment. The IRS credits withholding to the account of the appropriate taxpayer. Withholding reduces the amount otherwise due the IRS on the due date of the return.

For most taxpayers, withholding comes from two sources. First, when an employer pays a salary or wages to an employee, the employer is required to retain part of the amount otherwise due the employee and to pay the retained amount, for the benefit of the employee, to the federal government. The amount retained is the payroll tax withholding, which is a part of virtually every pay stub in the country.[25] Employers report the total amount withheld from the earnings of an employee on a Form W-2 given to each employee shortly after the end of the calendar year.

Second, income tax withholding can also occur when a taxpayer receives interest, dividends, rents, royalties, pension plan distributions, and similar payments. In certain circumstances, payers are required to withhold a portion of the payment and remit it to the government. The concept is similar to that used for wage payments. Payers report the amount of the total payment and the amount withheld on the applicable Form 1099 provided to the taxpayer. Pension plan distributions are the most common payments requiring or permitting withholding.

[22] IRC § 24(a).

[23] IRC § 24(c).

[24] IRC § 24(b).

[25] Chapter 10 discusses payer rules associated with determining and remitting withholding taxes, social security tax, and Medicare tax.

## Estimated Tax Payments (Form 1040, Line 26)

Taxpayers must pay their tax liability throughout the tax year, not at the time they file their tax return. If taxes withheld approximate the total tax liability for the year (the situation for most taxpayers), no estimated payments are due. However, a taxpayer who has income that is not subject to withholding may be required to make estimated payments during the year.[26] Failure to do so may subject the taxpayer to an underpayment penalty.[27]

Taxpayers must make periodic payments based on the *required annual payment,* which is defined as the lesser of 90% of the tax shown on the return or 100% of the tax shown on the return for the preceding year.[28] Payments are equal to 25% of the required annual payment and are due on April 15, June 15, September 15 in the current year, and January 15 of the next calendar year (January 18 for 2022). For taxpayers with prior-year AGI over $150,000, the 100% figure increases to 110%.

As noted previously, failure to make required estimated payments will subject the taxpayer to a potential underpayment penalty plus interest. However, taxpayers are not assessed a penalty if the difference between the tax shown on the return and the amount of tax withheld for wages is less than $1,000.[29]

Exhibit 2-5 is a flowchart from IRS Publication 17 that illustrates the decision process associated with determining whether estimated payments are required.

**EXHIBIT 2-5** **Do You Have to Pay Estimated Tax?**

Source: IRS Publication 17.

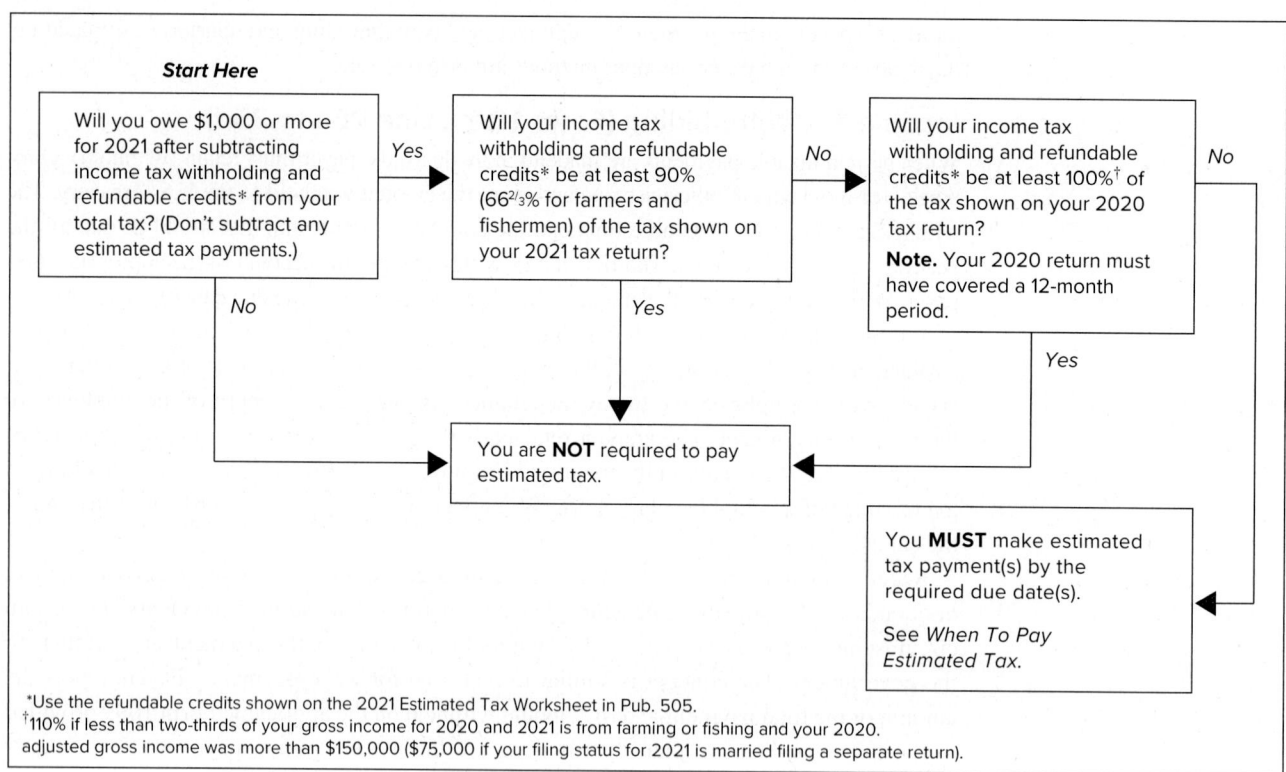

*Use the refundable credits shown on the 2021 Estimated Tax Worksheet in Pub. 505.
†110% if less than two-thirds of your gross income for 2020 and 2021 is from farming or fishing and your 2020. adjusted gross income was more than $150,000 ($75,000 if your filing status for 2021 is married filing a separate return).

[26] IRC § 6654(d).
[27] IRC § 6654(a).
[28] IRC § 6654(d)(1)(B).
[29] IRC § 6654(e)(1).

**EXAMPLE 2-8**

Janice, who is single, had taxable income of $55,000 in 2021 and had a total tax liability for the year of $7,854. During 2022 she will work only part-time, earn $25,000, and have income tax withholding of $4,100. She receives additional income from selling paintings. Based on her expected painting sales and wage earnings, she expects her tax liability for 2022 will be $5,764. To avoid an underpayment penalty, Janice must make estimated tax payments during 2022. Janice's required annual payment is $5,188, which is the lower of (a) 90% of $5,764 (the tax expected to show on her 2022 return) or (b) $7,854 (the amount of her 2021 liability). Because she expects to have taxes of $4,100 withheld from her paycheck, she must pay the remaining $1,088 ($5,188 − $4,100) in estimated payments during 2022. She must pay the amount in four equal installments of $272 on the dates indicated previously. Note that if Janice's 2022 tax liability actually turns out to be exactly $5,764, she will still owe $576 ($5,764 liability minus withholding of $4,100 minus estimated payments of $1,088) when she files her 2022 tax return.

**TAX YOUR BRAIN**

Assume that Janice's year 2022 wage income will be $50,000 (she worked full time) and she will have $8,300 withheld from her wages. Also assume that she expects to sell a large number of paintings and that she estimates her total 2022 tax liability will be $18,000. To avoid an underpayment penalty, does Janice need to pay estimated payments during 2022 and, if so, how much must she pay?

**ANSWER**

Janice does not need to make any estimated payments. Her required annual payment is $7,854, which is the lower of (a) 90% of $18,000 (the estimate of her 2022 tax liability) or (b) $7,854 (her tax liability for 2021). Because her estimated tax withholdings are $8,300, she is not obligated to make estimated payments. She will need to pay the remaining $9,700 ($18,000 − $8,300) no later than April 15, 2023.

**NEW LAW**

Social Security wage limitation increased to $142,800.

## Other Payments (Form 1040, Line 32, and Schedule 3)

Taxpayers with earned income (wages, salaries, tips, or earnings from self-employment) below certain limits are entitled to a tax credit.[30] Usually credits are shown on Schedule 3, but the earned income credit is reported on Form 1040. The amount of this credit is calculated on Schedule EIC and is reported on line 27a. We cover the EIC in Chapter 9.

Employers are required to withhold FICA (social security and Medicare) taxes from wages paid to employees. However, once wages paid to an individual employee exceed a certain limit ($142,800 in 2021), social security withholding ceases.[31] Each employer calculates the FICA withholding without regard to other employers. However, the employee simply needs to reach the limit during the calendar year. Thus, an employee can have excess social security taxes withheld from paychecks when working for more than one employer. Excess social security taxes are a payment toward income taxes due and are reported on Schedule 3, line 11. Note that the $142,800 wage limitation is determined per taxpayer, not per tax return.

Qualifying taxpayers can receive a child tax credit. This credit is reported on line 28 of Form 1040. We discuss the child tax credit in Chapter 9.

---

[30] IRC § 32.

[31] The limitation amount is adjusted annually based on the national average wage index. Go to www.ssa.gov for future limitation amounts. This applies only to social security, not to Medicare, which has no limit on the amount of earnings.

A taxpayer may request an automatic six-month extension of time to file a tax return.[32] Extending the time to file the return does not extend the time to pay the applicable tax. As a result, if taxpayers filing an extension determine that they owe additional tax, the payment must accompany the extension request (Form 4868). The additional payment is on Schedule 3, line 10.

Taxpayers can use Schedule 3, lines 12 and 13, to claim certain other payments. Farmers and fishermen may be entitled to a refund of federal fuel taxes paid on fuel that was not used in a motor vehicle on the highway (such as fuel used in a farm tractor or a commercial fishing boat). The total from Form 4136 is on line 12. Certain undistributed long-term capital gains (Form 2439), and other credits are reported on line 13a.

### Tax Refund (Form 1040, Line 35a) or Tax Due with Return (Form 1040, Line 37)

Compare the amount owed with the total amount paid (Form 1040, line 24 versus line 33). Excess payment results in a refund; excess remaining tax liability means the taxpayer must pay the remaining amount owed when filing the return.

A taxpayer who is entitled to a refund can elect to (1) receive a check, (2) have the refund deposited directly in a bank account, or (3) apply the excess to next year's tax return. The taxpayer who selects the direct deposit option must supply account information on lines 35a through d on Form 1040.

The estimated tax penalty shown on Form 1040, line 38, comes from Form 2210 and is a result of paying insufficient tax amounts throughout the year. We discuss the penalty in the following section.

---

**CONCEPT CHECK 2-6—**

**LO 2-5**

1. Use the tables in Appendix D of the text to determine the tax amounts for the following situations:

    a.  Single taxpayer with taxable income of $34,640. _____

    b.  Married taxpayers filing jointly with taxable income of $67,706. _____

2. What is the limit on the FICA (social security) amount for 2021? _____

## INTEREST AND TAX PENALTIES

**LO 2-6**

Failure to adhere to the tax law can subject a taxpayer to IRS assessments for penalties and interest. Although the IRS can assess a number of different penalties, it assesses only a few to individual taxpayers. In this section, we discuss the most common civil and criminal penalties applicable to individuals. We provide details on the following penalties:

- Interest charged on assessments.
- Failure to file a tax return.
- Failure to pay tax.
- Failure to pay estimated taxes.
- Substantial understatement of tax liability (accuracy-related penalties).
- Fraud penalties.
- Erroneous claim for refund or credit penalty.

[32] IRC § 6081.

# From Shoebox to Software

The amount of federal tax withholding is the amount in box 2 of Form W-2 plus the amount in box 4 of all Forms 1099 received (1099-MISC, 1099-B, 1099-INT, etc.). Taxpayers may have multiple W-2 and 1099 forms. Information from W-2s and 1099s is entered into the appropriate forms in the Documents Received section of the tax return software. The software will automatically sum the various documents and will place the total on line 25d. The tax preparer should check the amount on line 25d to ensure that all appropriate documentation was correctly entered.

Amounts for estimated payments will come from canceled checks or worksheets prepared when determining the appropriate payment amounts. You enter appropriate amounts in the tax software on a supporting schedule. The software utilizes this supporting schedule to record amounts paid during the year for federal and state estimated tax payments.

The Earned Income Credit comes from Schedule EIC.

A taxpayer who files Form 4868, Application for Automatic Extension of Time to File U.S. Individual Income Tax Return, must pay any additional tax owed with that form. The amount paid should be included on Schedule 3, line 10. If the tax software is used to prepare Form 4868, the amount on line 10 (amount paid) will normally be transferred to Schedule 3, line 10. Retain the canceled check or other evidence of payment.

Tax preparers should determine whether excess social security taxes have been withheld when total wages (Form 1040, line 1) exceed the social security limit ($142,800 in 2021) and the taxpayer has received multiple Forms W-2. The tax software will automatically calculate this amount from W-2s entered into the W-2 worksheets.

Entries on Schedule 3, lines 12 and 13, are relatively unusual.

## Interest Charged on All Assessments

Many taxpayers are under the false impression that filing a tax return extension also delays the payment of any remaining tax liability. An extension is an extension of time to file, *not* an extension of time to pay. The amount of unpaid tax liability is still due on April 15 for individual taxpayers unless the IRS announces an extension of the date. If the taxpayer still owes tax after April 15, the IRS assesses interest based on the remaining amount owed. The IRS charges interest on all nonpayments, underpayments, and late payments of tax. The rate charged is the federal short-term rate plus 3 percentage points.[33] Rates are set quarterly. Here are the annualized rates of interest on assessments for the past several years:

| Time Period | Percentage Rate |
| --- | --- |
| July 1, 2020, to June 30, 2021 | 3% |
| July 1, 2019, to June 30, 2020 | 5 |
| Jan. 1, 2019, to June 30, 2019 | 6 |
| Apr. 1, 2018, to Dec. 31, 2018 | 5 |
| Jan. 1, 2017, to Mar. 31, 2018 | 4 |
| Apr. 1, 2016, to Dec. 31, 2016 | 4 |
| July 1, 2015, to Mar. 31, 2016 | 3 |
| Oct. 1, 2011, to June 30, 2015 | 3 |
| Apr. 1, 2011, to Sept. 30, 2011 | 4 |
| Jan. 1, 2011, to Mar. 31, 2011 | 3 |
| Apr. 1, 2009, to Dec. 31, 2010 | 4 |
| Jan. 1, 2009, to Mar. 31, 2009 | 5 |
| Oct. 1, 2008, to Dec. 31, 2008 | 6 |
| July 1, 2008, to Sept. 30, 2008 | 5 |
| Apr. 1, 2008, to June 30, 2008 | 6 |
| Jan. 1, 2008, to Mar. 31, 2008 | 7 |
| July 1, 2007, to Dec. 31, 2007 | 8 |
| July 1, 2006, to June 30, 2007 | 8 |

[33] IRC § 6621(a)(2).

## Failure to File a Tax Return

A taxpayer who does not file a tax return by the due date of the return, plus extensions, must pay a failure to file penalty. The penalty for failure to file is 5% of the amount of tax due on the return if the failure is less than one month. For each additional month or fraction of a month, the IRS adds an additional 5% penalty, up to a maximum of 25%. Any income tax return not filed within 60 days of its due date is subject to a minimum penalty of the lesser of $435 or the amount of tax required on the return. If failure to file is due to fraud, the penalty is 15% per month, up to a maximum of 75%.[34] The IRS calculates the penalty on the tax liability shown on the return reduced by any payments made by withholding, estimated payments, or credits.

| | |
|---|---|
| **EXAMPLE 2-9** | Ernest was extremely busy during April and forgot to file his tax return by April 15. He did not file an extension. Ernest finally filed his tax return on June 1 and had a remaining tax liability of $2,000. Ernest has a $200 failure to file penalty, calculated as follows: |

| | |
|---|---:|
| Underpayment | $2,000 |
| Penalty per month or fraction thereof (2 months × 5%) | 10% |
| Failure to file penalty | $ 200 |

If a taxpayer can show the delay in filing was due to a reasonable cause, the IRS could agree to abate (forgive) the penalty. If after showing that ordinary business care and prudence were exercised in providing payment of the liability, the taxpayer was nevertheless unable to pay the tax or would suffer an undue hardship if paid on the due date, reasonable cause occurs.[35]

The IRS makes the abatement determination case by case based on the facts and circumstances of the particular situation.

## Failure to Pay Tax

The failure to pay and the failure to file penalties are interrelated. The failure to pay penalty is 0.5% of the tax shown on the return for each month (or fraction of a month) the tax is unpaid, up to a maximum of 25%.[36]

However, the failure to file penalty (discussed earlier) is reduced by the failure to pay penalty when both apply. This means that the maximum monthly penalty is 5% when both penalties apply. The IRS will also abate the failure to pay penalty if the taxpayer can show a reasonable cause for not paying. If the taxpayer filed a proper extension to file the tax return, the IRS will presume a reasonable cause exists when both of the following conditions apply:

- The amount due with the tax return is less than 10% of the amount of tax shown on the tax return.

- Any balance due shown on the tax return is paid with the return.

| | |
|---|---|
| **EXAMPLE 2-10** | Assume the same facts as in Example 2-9. However, Ernest filed a proper automatic six-month extension to file his return. Thus, his new due date is October 15. If the $2,000 owed by Ernest is less than 10% of the amount of tax on the return, then there is no failure to pay penalty. There is also not a failure to file penalty because Ernest obtained an extension of time to file. |

[34] IRC § 6651(f).

[35] Reg. § 301.6651-1(c).

[36] IRC § 6651(a)(2).

**EXAMPLE 2-11**

Assume the same facts as in Example 2-10 except that Ernest does not file his tax return until December 1 and the $2,000 tax due is more than 10% of his total tax shown on the return. In this case, Ernest would be subject to both the failure to file penalty and the failure to pay penalty. Because the return was due on October 15, the failure to *file* penalty runs from October 15 to December 1 (two months of penalty). Because the $2,000 is more than 10% of the total tax, the failure to pay penalty runs from April 15 to December 1 (eight months of penalty).

The calculations are as follows:

| | | |
|---|---|---|
| Failure to pay | Underpayment | $2,000 |
| | 0.5% for 8 months | 4% |
| | Failure to pay penalty | $ 80 |
| Failure to file | Underpayment | $2,000 |
| | 5% for 2 months | 10% |
| | Failure to file penalty | $ 200 |
| Less failure to pay penalty for the months when both apply (2 months × 0.5% × $2,000) | | ($20) |
| | Adjusted failure to file | $ 180 |

Ernest must pay $2,260 ($2,000 + $80 + $180) in taxes and penalties (plus interest) when the return is filed.

## Penalty for Failure to Pay Estimated Income Tax

Normally individuals pay income taxes throughout the tax year, not just in April when they file their returns. Taxpayers whose primary income is wages or salary make tax payments through employer withholding. However, taxpayers who earn a large portion of their income from sources other than wages may have little or no income tax withheld.[37]

These taxpayers must pay estimated tax payments throughout the year on a quarterly basis. The quarterly payments are due on April 15, June 15, September 15 in the current year, and January 15 of the next calendar year. The IRS will impose an estimated tax penalty on taxpayers who do not pay enough estimated tax.[38]

To avoid this penalty, the taxpayer must pay during the year, either through withholding or estimated payments, a minimum of the following:

- 90% of the current year's tax liability.
- 100% of the prior year's tax liability if the taxpayer's AGI in the prior year is less than $150,000.

If the taxpayer's prior-year AGI is more than $150,000, the percentage for the prior year rule increases to 110%.[39]

No estimated tax penalty applies if the tax due after withholding or estimated payments is less than $1,000. The IRS calculates the penalty on a per quarter basis using the same rate at which it charges interest (the short-term federal rate plus 3 percentage points).

Taxpayers use Form 2210 to calculate the failure to pay estimated tax penalty. The tax software automatically calculates the amount of underpayment penalty, if any.

## Accuracy-Related Penalties

On a return when negligence or any substantial understatement of income occurs, the IRS will assess a penalty equal to 20% of the tax due.[40]

*Negligence* includes any failure to make a reasonable attempt to comply with the provisions of the IRC. Negligence also includes any careless, reckless, or intentional disregard for tax

---

[37] Self-employment and investment income are discussed in Chapters 6 and 3, respectively.

[38] Even taxpayers subject to withholding may be required to make estimated payments if nonwage income is sufficiently large.

[39] IRC § 6654(d)(1)(C).

[40] IRC § 6662(a).

authority. The IRS may waive the negligence penalty if the taxpayer makes a good-faith effort to comply with the IRC. If the taxpayer were to take a position contrary to established law, the filing of Form 8275R (the form used to disclose a contrary position) can help avoid the negligence penalty. The 20% penalty also applies when the taxpayer has substantially understated income tax. *Substantial understatement* occurs when the understatement is either

- More than 10% of the tax required to be shown on the return.
- $5,000 or more.[41]

The IRS may reduce the amount of the understatement subject to the 20% penalty if the taxpayer has substantial tax authority for the tax treatment.[42] Substantial authority exists only if the weight of tax authority supporting the taxpayer's treatment is substantial in relation to the tax authority supporting the IRS's position.

## Fraud Penalties

The IRS can impose a 75% penalty on any portion of understatement of tax that is attributable to fraud.[43] Although the IRC does not define *fraud,* the courts provide a comprehensive definition. One court defined it as intentional wrongdoing with the purpose of evading tax.[44] Another court said it is the intent to conceal, mislead, or otherwise prevent the collection of tax.[45] If any underpayment is due to fraud, the IRS assesses the 75% penalty.[46]

Fraud on a tax return can also lead to criminal charges. Criminal penalties apply only to tax evasion (attempt to evade or defeat tax), willful failure to collect or pay tax, and willful failure to file a return. The IRS can assess criminal penalties in addition to civil penalties. Possible criminal penalties include the following:

- **Any person who willfully attempts to evade or defeat any tax:** The charge is a felony punishable by fines of not more than $100,000 or imprisonment of not more than five years or both.[47]
- **Any person who fails to collect, account for, and pay over any tax:** The charge is a felony punishable by fines of not more than $10,000 or imprisonment of not more than five years or both.[48]
- **Any person who willfully fails to pay estimated tax or other tax and file a return:** The charge is a misdemeanor punishable by fines of not more than $25,000 or imprisonment of not more than one year or both.[49]

## Penalty for Erroneous Claim for Refund or Credit

A 20% penalty could be assessed by the IRS on the disallowed amount of the claim if the claim for refund or credit of income filed is found to be excessive. An amount for a claim is classified as "excessive" if the claim amount exceeds the amount of the allowable claim. This penalty does not apply if the fraud or the accuracy-related penalty has been assessed.

---

**CONCEPT CHECK 2-7— LO 2-6**

1. A taxpayer filed an automatic extension before April 15 but sent no money to the IRS. He then filed his return by June 2 and paid the amount due of $3,000. What are the amounts for the failure to file a tax return penalty and the failure to pay penalty? _____
2. Fraud on a tax return can also lead to criminal charges. True or false?

---

[41] IRC § 6662(d)(1)(A).
[42] IRC § 6662(d)(2)(B).
[43] IRC § 6663.
[44] *Mitchell v. Comm'r,* 118 F.2d 308 (5th Cir. 1941).
[45] *Stoltzfus v. United States,* 398 F.2d 1002 (3d Cir. 1968).
[46] IRC § 6663(a).
[47] IRC § 7201.
[48] IRC § 7202.
[49] IRC § 7203.

# Summary

**LO 2-1:** Describe the expanded tax formula and the components of the major sections of Form 1040.

- The taxpayer must use the appropriate Form 1040 Schedules.
- Adjusted Gross Income (AGI) is gross income minus a list of permitted deductions.
- Many deductions and credits are determined with reference to AGI.

**LO 2-2:** Determine the proper filing status.

- There are five filing statuses.
  - Single: not married as of the last day of the year.
  - Married filing jointly: legally married on the last day of the year; the marital status is determined by state law.
  - Married filing separately: married but elect to file separately. The standard deduction can be taken only if both take it.
  - Head of household: unmarried at the end of the year and must maintain a household for a qualifying person for more than half the year.
  - Qualifying widow(er) with dependent child: eligible to file a joint return the year the spouse died, unmarried, and paying more than half the cost of a household that was the principal place of residence of the taxpayer and child for the year.

**LO 2-3:** Determine dependents.

- A dependent must meet the following: dependent taxpayer test, joint return test, and citizen or resident test.
- A dependent must be a qualifying child or a qualifying relative.
- A qualifying child must meet five tests: relationship test, age test, residency test, support test, and special test for qualifying child of more than one taxpayer.
- A qualifying relative must meet four tests: not a qualifying child test, relationship or member of household test, gross income test, and support test.

**LO 2-4:** Determine the standard deduction.

- Standard deduction for each filing status: single—$12,550; married filing jointly—$25,100; married filing separately—$12,550; head of household—$18,800; and qualifying widow(er)—$25,100.
- The amount of the standard deduction increases for people who are age 65 and/or blind.
- Dependent taxpayers are limited to the higher of $1,100 or the taxpayer's earned income plus $350.

**LO 2-5:** Compute the amount of tax due to the Internal Revenue Service (IRS).

- The tax liability is computed by using the tables or the tax rate schedule.
- Tax payments (withholding by the employer and estimated payments sent to IRS) and tax credits reduce the tax due to IRS.
- Excess payment results in a refund; excess remaining tax liability means an amount is owed to IRS.

**LO 2-6:** Determine what interest and penalties the IRS can assess and in what instances certain penalties are applicable.

- Interest on assessments: The rate charged is the federal short-term rate plus 3 percentage points.
- The failure to file a tax return penalty is 5% per month or fraction of a month, not to exceed 25%.
- The failure to pay tax penalty is 0.5% per month or fraction of a month, not to exceed 25%. If an income tax return is filed more than 60 days after its due date, the minimum penalty is $435 or 100% of the unpaid tax.
- The maximum amount is 5% per month or fraction of a month, not to exceed 25% when both penalties, failure to file a tax return and failure to pay tax, apply.
- The failure to pay estimated income tax penalty applies if a taxpayer fails to pay during the year a minimum of 90% of the current year's tax liability or 100% of the prior year's tax liability. If AGI is more than $150,000, the percentage increases to 110%.
- The accuracy-related penalty applies when negligence or any substantial understatement occurs. The rate is 20% of the tax due.
- Fraud penalties are 75% on any portion of the understatement of tax that is attributable to fraud.
- A 20% penalty for erroneous claim for refund or credit could be assessed by the IRS if the amount is found to be excessive.

## EA Fast Fact

Enrolled Agents specialize in taxation. They advise, represent, and prepare tax returns for individuals, partnerships, corporations, estates, trusts, and any entities with tax-reporting requirements. Because EAs hold a federal certification, they have an unrestricted right to represent any taxpayer in any state. What that means is the Enrolled Certification is completely portable, allowing you to practice anywhere you want in the United States, and its territories, without having to meet any state requirements.

**IMPORTANT**

You are eligible to receive absolutely free, the Surgent Enrolled Agent review program for Part I of the EA exam as a result of purchasing this text. To activate your free access, go to https://Surgent.com/McGrawHill/EA.

## Discussion Questions  Mc Graw Hill connect

All applicable discussion questions are available with **Connect**©

**EA**  **LO 2-1**  1. What is a *for* AGI deduction? Give three examples.

_____

_____

_____

**EA**  **LO 2-2**  2. What are the five types of filing status?

_____

_____

_____

**EA**  **LO 2-2**  3. What qualifications are necessary to file as head of household?

_____

_____

_____

**EA**  **LO 2-2**  4. George and Debbie were legally married on December 31, 2021. Can they file their 2021 income tax return using the status of married filing jointly? Why or why not? What other filing status choices do they have, if any?

_____

_____

_____

**EA**  **LO 2-3**  5. Why is it important to determine if the taxpayer has dependents to be claimed on the income tax return?

_____

_____

_____

**EA** LO 2-3  6. What are the three general tests that a qualifying person must meet to be a dependent of the taxpayer?

_____
_____
_____

**EA** LO 2-3  7. What are the five specific tests necessary to be a qualifying child of the taxpayer?

_____
_____
_____

**EA** LO 2-3  8. What age must a child be at the end of the year to meet the age test under the qualifying child rules?

_____
_____
_____

**EA** LO 2-3  9. What are the four specific tests necessary to be a qualifying relative of the taxpayer?

_____
_____
_____

**EA** LO 2-3  10. What is a multiple support agreement, and what is its purpose?

_____
_____
_____

**EA** LO 2-3  11. Mimi is 22 years old and is a full-time student at Ocean County Community College. She lives with her parents, who provide all of her support. During the summer, she put her Web design skills to work and earned $5,125. Can Mimi's parents claim her as a dependent on their joint tax return? Why or why not? Assume that all five tests under qualifying child are met.

_____
_____
_____

**EA** LO 2-4  12. What is the standard deduction for each filing status?

_____
_____
_____

**EA** LO 2-5  13. Under what circumstances must a taxpayer use a tax rate schedule rather than using a tax table?

_____
_____
_____

**EA** LO 2-6  14. When and at what rate is interest calculated on amounts owed to the IRS?

_____
_____
_____

EA  LO 2-6  15. Prepare a table of the possible IRS penalties listed in the text and give a brief summary of the purpose of each penalty.

| IRS Penalties | Purpose of Penalty |
|---|---|
| | |
| | |
| | |
| | |
| | |
| | |

## Multiple-Choice Questions Mc Graw Hill connect®

All applicable multiple-choice questions are available with *Connect*©

EA  LO 2-1  16. A single taxpayer is 26 years old and has wages of $18,350 and interest income of $450. Which Form 1040 Schedule must the taxpayer use?
  a. Schedule 1.
  b. Schedule 2.
  c. Schedule 3.
  d. The taxpayer does not need to use a Schedule.

EA  LO 2-1  17. Which Schedule must the taxpayer use to claim a payment made for alimony if the taxpayer was divorced in 2021?
  a. Schedule 1.
  b. Schedule 2.
  c. Schedule 3.
  d. The taxpayer does not need to use a Schedule.

EA  LO 2-2  18. A taxpayer is married with a qualifying child (dependent), but she has been living separately from her spouse for the last eight months of the year. However, she paid for more than half of the cost of keeping up the household. Her spouse does not want to file jointly. What filing status must she use when filing her tax return? She wants to obtain the maximum legal benefit.
  a. Married filing separately.
  b. Head of household.
  c. Qualifying widow(er).
  d. Single.

EA  LO 2-2  19. A taxpayer's spouse died on December 31, 2020. He has no qualifying child. Which status should the taxpayer select when filing his 2021 tax return?
  a. Qualifying widow(er).
  b. Married filing jointly.
  c. Single.
  d. Married filing separately.

**EA**   LO 2-3   20. Esmeralda is 20 years of age and a full-time student living with her parents. She had wages of $545 ($50 of income tax withholding) for 2021. Can Esmeralda file a tax return to claim her $50 of income tax withholding even though she is a dependent of her parents?

    *a.* Yes, Esmeralda can file a tax return.

    *b.* No, Esmeralda cannot file a tax return.

    *c.* Esmeralda's parents can report her wages on their tax return.

    *d.* No, Esmeralda is a dependent of her parents.

**EA**   LO 2-3   21. A taxpayer can claim a dependent if the person is a qualifying child or a qualifying relative and the person meets all of the following tests.

    *a.* Citizen or resident, dependent taxpayer, and age tests.

    *b.* Dependent taxpayer, joint return, and support tests.

    *c.* Joint return, citizen or resident, and support tests.

    *d.* Dependent taxpayer, joint return, and citizen or resident tests.

**EA**   LO 2-3   22. To be a qualifying child, the taxpayer must meet three general tests and five specific tests. Which of the following is *not* part of the five specific tests?

    *a.* Support test.

    *b.* Age test.

    *c.* Gross income test.

    *d.* Relationship test.

**EA**   LO 2-3   23. To be a qualifying relative, who has to live in the home of the taxpayer for the entire year?

    *a.* Child.

    *b.* Cousin.

    *c.* Stepchild.

    *d.* Father.

**EA**   LO 2-4   24. Which amount represents the standard deduction for a taxpayer who is 44 years old and claims head of household status?

    *a.* $12,550.

    *b.* $18,800.

    *c.* $18,350.

    *d.* $18,650.

**EA**   LO 2-4   25. A married couple, both of whom are under 65 years old, decided to file as married filing separately. One of the spouses is going to itemize deductions instead of taking the standard deduction. What is the standard deduction permitted to the other spouse when she files her tax return?

    *a.* $12,550.

    *b.* $13,900.

    *c.* $18,800.

    *d.* $0.

**EA**   LO 2-5   26. Employers are required to withhold social security taxes from wages paid to employees. What is the amount of the social security wage limitation for 2021?

    *a.* $142,800.

    *b.* $118,500.

    *c.* $137,700.

    *d.* $128,400.

**EA** **LO 2-5** 27. What is the amount of the tax liability for a married couple filing jointly with taxable income of $135,500?

    *a.* $29,810.

    *b.* $21,307.

    *c.* $25,158.

    *d.* $20,325.

**EA** **LO 2-6** 28. What is the percentage of interest the IRS was charging on assessment (amount of unpaid tax liability) during March 2021? You might want to do this research by going to the IRS Web site (www.irs.gov).

    *a.* 5%.

    *b.* 6%.

    *c.* 3%.

    *d.* 4%.

**EA** **LO 2-6** 29. When there is negligence on a return, the IRS charges a penalty of _____ of the tax due.

    *a.* 25%.

    *b.* 20%.

    *c.* 18%.

    *d.* 10%.

**EA** **LO 2-6** 30. When there is fraud on a return, the IRS charges a penalty of _____ on any portion of understatement of tax that is attributable to the fraud.

    *a.* 20%.

    *b.* 25%.

    *c.* 75%.

    *d.* 100%.

## Problems Mc Graw Hill connect

All applicable problems are available with *Connect*©

**EA** **LO 2-1** 31. The benefits of many deductions, credits, or other benefits are limited to taxpayers with Adjusted Gross Income below certain limits.

    *a.* Explain how the limitation (phaseout) process works.

    *b.* Give two examples of deductions, credits, or other benefits that are limited.

    *c.* Why would Congress wish to limit the benefits of these items?

**EA** **LO 2-2** 32. List the five types of filing status and briefly explain the requirements for the use of each one.

EA   LO 2-2   33. In which of the following cases may the taxpayer claim head of household filing status?

a. The taxpayer is single and maintains a household that is the principal place of abode of her infant son.

_____

b. The taxpayer is single, maintains a household for herself, and maintains a separate household that is the principal place of abode of her dependent widowed mother.

_____

c. The taxpayer was married from January to October and lived with his spouse from January to May. From June 1 to December 31, the taxpayer maintained a household that was the principal place of abode of his married son and daughter-in-law, whom the taxpayer can claim as dependents.

_____

d. Same as (c) except the taxpayer lived with his ex-spouse until August and maintained the household from September 1 to the end of the year.

_____

EA   LO 2-3   34. What are the three tests a qualifying child or qualifying relative must meet to be claimed as a dependent?

_____

_____

_____

_____

EA   LO 2-3   35. Roberta is widowed and lives in an apartment complex. She receives $8,000 of social security income that she uses to pay for rent and other household expenses. The remainder of her living expenses is paid by relatives and neighbors. The total amount of support paid by Roberta and the others totals $22,000. Amounts paid for support during the year are as follows:

| | |
|---|---|
| Roberta | $8,000 |
| Ed (neighbor) | 4,000 |
| Bill (son) | 5,000 |
| Jose (neighbor) | 2,000 |
| Alicia (niece) | 3,000 |

a. Which of these persons is entitled to claim Roberta as a dependent absent a multiple support agreement?

_____

b. Under a multiple support agreement, which of these persons is entitled to claim Roberta as a dependent? Explain your answer.

_____

c. If Roberta saved all of her social security income and the other persons paid for the shortfall in the same proportions as shown, which of these persons would be entitled to claim Roberta as a dependent under a multiple support agreement? Explain your answer.

_____

_____

**EA** LO 2-3 36. Akiko is a U.S. citizen and is the 68-year-old widowed mother of Janet. After retirement, Akiko decided to fulfill a lifelong dream and move to Paris. Akiko receives $1,000 of interest income, but all of her other living expenses (including rent on her Paris apartment with spectacular views of the Eiffel Tower) are paid by Janet. Janet resides in Chicago. Can Janet claim Akiko as a dependent? Explain your answer.

_____

_____

_____

**EA** LO 2-4 37. Donald is a 21-year-old full-time college student. During 2021 he earned $2,550 from a part-time job and $1,150 in interest income. If Donald is a dependent of his parents, what is his standard deduction amount? If Donald supports himself and is not a dependent of someone else, what is his standard deduction amount?

_____

_____

**EA** LO 2-4 38. Raphael and Martina are engaged and are planning to travel to Las Vegas during the 2021 Christmas season and get married around the end of the year. In 2021 Raphael expects to earn $45,000 and Martina expects to earn $15,000. Their employers have deducted the appropriate amount of withholding from their paychecks throughout the year. Neither Raphael nor Martina has any itemized deductions. They are trying to decide whether they should get married on December 31, 2021, or on January 1, 2022. What do you recommend? Explain your answer.

_____

_____

_____

_____

_____

**EA** LO 2-4 39. Determine the amount of the standard deduction for each of the following taxpayers for tax year 2021:

*a.* Christina, who is single.

_____

*b.* Adrian and Carol, who are filing a joint return. Their son is blind.

_____

*c.* Peter and Elizabeth, who are married and file separate tax returns. Elizabeth will itemize her deductions.

_____

*d.* Karen, who earned $1,100 working a part-time job. She can be claimed as a dependent by her parents.

_____

*e.* Rodolfo, who is over 65 and is single.

_____

*f.* Bernard, who is a nonresident alien with U.S. income.

_____

*g.* Manuel, who is 70, and Esther, who is 63 and blind, will file a joint return.

_____

*h.* Herman, who is 75 and a qualifying widower with a dependent child.

_____

**EA**   LO 2-5   40. Using the appropriate tax tables or tax rate schedules, determine the amount of tax liability in each of the following instances:

    *a.* A married couple filing jointly with taxable income of $32,991.

    *b.* A married couple filing jointly with taxable income of $192,257.

    *c.* A married couple filing separately, one spouse with taxable income of $43,885 and the other with $56,218.

    *d.* A single person with taxable income of $79,436.

    *e.* A single person with taxable income of $297,784.

    *f.* A head of household with taxable income of $96,592.

    *g.* A qualifying widow with taxable income of $14,019.

    *h.* A married couple filing jointly with taxable income of $11,216.

**EA**   LO 2-5   41. Determine the average tax rate and the marginal tax rate for each instance in question 40.

    *a.* Average = _____ Marginal = _____
    *b.* Average = _____ Marginal = _____
    *c.* Average = _____ Marginal = _____
    *d.* Average = _____ Marginal = _____
    *e.* Average = _____ Marginal = _____
    *f.* Average = _____ Marginal = _____
    *g.* Average = _____ Marginal = _____
    *h.* Average = _____ Marginal = _____

**EA**   LO 2-5   42. Using the appropriate tax tables or tax rate schedules, determine the tax liability for tax year 2021 in each of the following instances. In each case, assume the taxpayer can take only the standard deduction.

    *a.* A single taxpayer, not head of household, with AGI of $23,493 and one dependent.

    *b.* A single taxpayer, not head of household, with AGI of $169,783 and no dependents.

    *c.* A married couple filing jointly with AGI of $39,945 and two dependents.

    *d.* A married couple filing jointly with AGI of $162,288 and three dependents.

    *e.* A married couple filing jointly with AGI of $301,947 and one dependent.

    *f.* A taxpayer filing married filing separately with AGI of $68,996 and one dependent.

g.  A qualifying widow, age 66, with AGI of $49,240 and one dependent.

_____

h.  A head of household with AGI of $14,392 and two dependents.

_____

i.  A head of household with AGI of $59,226 and one dependent.

_____

**EA**   **LO 2-6**   43.  Victoria's 2021 tax return was due on April 15, 2022, but she did not file it until June 12, 2022. Victoria did not file an extension. The tax due on the tax return when filed was $8,500. In 2021, Victoria paid in $12,000 through withholding. Her 2020 tax liability was $11,500. Victoria's AGI for 2021 is less than $150,000. How much penalty will Victoria have to pay (disregard interest)?

_____

_____

_____

_____

_____

**EA**   **LO 2-6**   44.  Vinitpaul has the following information:

| | |
|---|---|
| AGI for 2021 | $155,000 |
| Withholding for 2021 | 24,000 |
| Total tax for 2020 | 29,000 |
| Total tax for 2021 | 28,304 |

a.  How much must Vinitpaul pay in estimated taxes to avoid a penalty?

_____

_____

_____

b.  If Vinitpaul had paid $1,000 per quarter, would he have avoided the estimated tax penalty?

_____

_____

**EA**   **LO 2-6**   45.  Charles and Joan Thompson file a joint return. In 2020 they had taxable income of $92,370 and paid tax of $11,903. Charles is an advertising executive, and Joan is a college professor. During the fall 2021 semester, Joan is planning to take a leave of absence without pay. The Thompsons expect their taxable income to drop to $70,000 in 2021. They expect their 2021 tax liability will be $8,005, which will be the approximate amount of their withholding. Joan anticipates that she will work on academic research during the fall semester.

During September, Joan decides to perform consulting services for some local businesses. Charles and Joan had not anticipated this development. Joan is paid a total of $35,000 during October, November, and December for her work.

What estimated tax payments are Charles and Joan required to make, if any, for tax year 2021? Do you anticipate that the Thompsons will be required to pay an underpayment penalty when they file their 2021 tax return? Explain your answer.

_____

_____

_____

_____

_____

**LO 2-5**  46. Many tax items are subject to annual adjustments for inflation. These include tax brackets, retirement contributions, standard deductions, and many others. What effect do certain inflation adjustments have on tax liability from year-to-year?

A married couple has combined W-2 income of $68,220.

*a.* For tax year 2021, determine their tax liability.

_____

*b.* In tax year 2020, the tax tables and amount of standard deduction were different from tax year 2021. Locate the 2020 tax tables and determine the 2020 standard deduction amount. The web is a good place to start your search. If the couple had $68,220 of W-2 income in tax year 2020, what would have been their tax liability?

_____

*c.* What is the difference between 2020 tax liability and 2021 tax liability?

_____

*d.* How much of that difference is the result of changes to the tax tables? How much of that difference is the result of the change to the standard deduction?

_____

## Tax Return Problems

All applicable tax return problems are available with **Connect**©

Use your tax software to complete the following problems. If you are manually preparing the tax returns, you will need to use a Form 1040 and one or more Schedules, depending on the complexity of the problem. *Note to instructors and students:* When using software, certain tax credits may appear on the tax return even though we have not yet discussed those tax credits. This occurs because the taxpayer may be entitled to the credits and the software will automatically include the credit on the final tax return.

For the following tax return problems, assume the taxpayer does NOT wish to contribute to the Presidential Election Fund, unless otherwise stated in the problem. In addition, the taxpayers did not receive, sell, send, exchange, or otherwise acquire any financial interest in any virtual currency during the year. For any Tax Return Problems for which the taxpayers are entitled to a child tax credit, assume that the taxpayers did NOT receive any advance child tax credit payments during 2021. Thus, the entire child tax credit (if permitted) will be claimed on the 2021 tax return.

**Tax Return Problem 1**

Jose and Dora Hernandez are married filing jointly. They are 50 and 45 years old, respectively. Their address is 32010 Lake Street, Atlanta, GA 30294. Additional information about Mr. and Mrs. Hernandez is as follows:

Social security numbers:

| | |
|---|---|
| Jose: 412-34-5670 | Dora: 412-34-5671 |
| Date of birth: 4/23/1971 | Date of birth: 7/12/1976 |
| W-2 for Jose shows these amounts: | W-2 for Dora shows these amounts: |
| Wages (box 1) = $45,800.00 | Wages (box 1) = $31,000.00 |
| Federal W/H (box 2) = $ 4,038.00 | Federal W/H (box 2) = $ 2,290.00 |
| Social security wages (box 3) = $45,800.00 | Social security wages (box 3) = $31,000.00 |
| Social security W/H (box 4) = $ 2,839.60 | Social security W/H (box 4) = $ 1,922.00 |
| Medicare wages (box 5) = $45,800.00 | Medicare wages (box 5) = $31,000.00 |
| Medicare W/H (box 6) = $ 664.10 | Medicare W/H (box 6) = $ 449.50 |

Form 1099-INT for Jose and Dora shows this amount:

Box 1 = $300.00 from City Bank.

Dependent: Daughter Adela is 5 years old. Her date of birth is 3/15/2016. Her social security number is 412-34-5672.

Jose is a store manager, and Dora is a receptionist.

Prepare Form 1040 plus all the appropriate Schedules and worksheets for Mr. and Mrs. Hernandez for 2021. They are entitled to the child tax credit (this credit is discussed in more detail in Chapter 9). For now, enter the credit on the appropriate line of the form. They want to contribute to the presidential election campaign. Mr. and Mrs. Hernandez had qualifying health care coverage at all times during the tax year.

**Tax Return Problem 2**

Marie Lincoln is a head of household. She is 37 years old and her address is 4110 N.E. 13th Street, Miami, FL 33127. Additional information about Ms. Lincoln is as follows:

Social security number: 412-34-5670

Date of birth: 1/14/1984

W-2 for Marie shows these amounts:

Wages (box 1) = $43,600.00

Federal W/H (box 2) = $ 2,488.00

Social security wages (box 3) = $43,600.00

Social security W/H (box 4) = $ 2,703.20

Medicare wages (box 5) = $43,600.00

Medicare W/H (box 6) = $ 632.20

Form 1099-INT for Marie shows this amount:

Box 1 = $556 from A & D Bank.

Dependent: Son Steven is 10 years old. His date of birth is 5/11/2011. His social security number is 412-34-5672.

Marie is a retail store manager.

Prepare Form 1040 plus all the appropriate Schedules and worksheets for Ms. Lincoln for 2021. She is entitled to the child tax credit (this credit is discussed in more detail in Chapter 9). For now, enter the credit on the appropriate line of the form. She wants to contribute to the presidential election campaign. Ms. Lincoln had qualifying health care coverage at all times during the tax year.

**Tax Return Problem 3**

Margaret O'Hara has been divorced for about two years. She is 28 years old, and her address is 979 Adams Street, Jacksonville, FL 32202. Additional information about Ms. O'Hara is as follows:

Social security number: 412-34-5670

Date of birth: 6/17/1993

W-2 for Margaret shows these amounts:

Wages (box 1) = $38,000.00

Federal W/H (box 2) = $ 4,820.00

Social security wages (box 3) = $38,000.00

Social security W/H (box 4) = $ 2,356.00

Medicare wages (box 5) = $38,000.00

Medicare W/H (box 6) = $ 551.00

Margaret is a research assistant.

Prepare Form 1040 plus all the appropriate Schedules and worksheets for Ms. O'Hara for 2021. She does not want to contribute to the presidential election campaign. Ms. O'Hara had qualifying health care coverage at all times during the tax year.

We have provided selected filled-in source documents that are available in the *Connect Library*.

Design elements icons: (Tax Your Brain Icon; Brain Teaser Icon; Checkmark Icon; Laptop Icon; New Law Icon) ©McGraw-Hill Education

# Chapter **Three**

# Gross Income: Inclusions and Exclusions

We now explore the details associated with a tax return. This chapter covers many of the items that compose *gross income*. These items are reported on lines 1–7 on Form 1040 and line 9 on Schedule 1.

### Learning Objectives

When you have completed this chapter, you should understand the following learning objectives (LO):

**LO 3-1** Describe when and how to record income for tax purposes.

**LO 3-2** Apply the cash method of accounting to income taxes.

**LO 3-3** Explain the taxability of components of gross income, including interest, dividends, tax refunds, and social security benefits.

**LO 3-4** Apply the rules concerning items excluded from gross income.

**LO 3-5** Apply the rules associated with tax accounting for savings bond interest used for education expenses, below-market interest loans, gift loans, and original issue discount debt (Appendix).

## INTRODUCTION

This chapter encompasses major components of income and many types of nontaxable income.

You will recall that gross income is "all income from whatever source derived."[1] Obviously, gross income is an extremely broad, all-encompassing concept. Much of this book is devoted to the discussion of various components of gross income and taxable income.

Not all income is subject to tax. In practice, all income is gross income unless the Internal Revenue Code (IRC) specifically excludes it from taxation. In this chapter, you will learn about many gross income exclusions.

## WHEN AND HOW TO RECORD INCOME
## LO 3-1

Accountants record (recognize) income for financial statement purposes when it is both realized and earned (the *accrual method of accounting*). *Realization* is the process of converting a noncash resource into cash or a right to cash. Conversion occurs when a company or person

[1] IRC § 61(a).

exchanges a noncash asset or resource for cash or a receivable in a transaction with a third party. Although the most commonly used example is selling inventory for cash or an account receivable, the realization concept applies to professional services (exchanging knowledge for cash), asset sales (exchanging a building for cash or a right to cash), licensing a patent (exchanging an idea for cash or a right to cash), or wages (exchanging time, knowledge, and effort for cash).

Income has been earned when companies or persons have performed all actions necessary to complete the transaction. When a grocery store sells you a can of beans, it has earned the income because it has done everything it needs to do to complete the transaction. The store does not need to open the can, heat the contents, and serve you at the dinner table.

For tax purposes, income recognition follows similar rules with a few twists. In general, an individual must recognize income on a tax return if a transaction meets *all* of the following three conditions:

1. There must be an economic benefit. If a person is economically better off because of a transaction, the person must normally record income. If someone works for an employer and receives cash for that work, the person has income. If a person sells a car to a friend for a note receivable, the person has income.[2] It is important to note that the benefit may be indirect. If an accountant performs some tax work for a client and the client agrees to pay a $500 debt the accountant owes to a local bank, the accountant has $500 of income because an economic benefit (less debt) was received even if the $500 cash was never in the possession of the accountant.

2. A transaction must actually have reached a conclusion. Two factors are at work here. First, a transaction must occur. Simply owning an asset that has increased in value does not create income (even though there may be an economic benefit). If an individual owns 100 shares of IBM common stock and the stock increases in price by $1 per share, no income will result because no transaction has occurred. The second factor is that the transaction process must be complete. Often a time gap occurs between the agreement to enter into a transaction and the completion of the transaction. In general, the completion date is the date when income is recognized.

3. Finally, the income cannot be tax-exempt. Certain income is statutorily excluded from taxation and will not be included in gross income even if the preceding two conditions are met.

---

**EXAMPLE 3-1**

On December 29, 2020, Raul agreed to repair a damaged roof and started to work on that date. On January 6, 2021, he completed the job and received payment. Raul would record income in 2021, not 2020.

---

**CONCEPT CHECK 3-1— LO 3-1**

1. An individual must recognize income on a tax return if the transaction meets three conditions. Name the three conditions: _____,

_____,

_____.

2. An individual can exclude certain income from taxation even though a transaction that has economic benefits has occurred. True or false?

---

[2] Taxpayers likely have a "cost" or "basis" that can be subtracted from the proceeds to arrive at the net amount of income that must be reported.

# CASH METHOD OF ACCOUNTING

**LO 3-2**

Almost all individuals use the cash receipts and disbursements method of accounting.[3] Unincorporated businesses without inventories often use the cash method as well. Under the *cash method,* taxpayers report income in the year they receive or constructively receive the income rather than the year in which the taxpayer earns the income. *Constructive receipt* means that the income is available to or in the control of the taxpayer regardless of whether the taxpayer chooses to utilize the income. Thus, interest credited to a taxpayer's savings account on December 31 is income in the year credited, not the year withdrawn.

Income can be "realized in any form, whether in money, property, or services."[4] Note that even cash basis taxpayers do not actually have to receive cash before they record income (although that is quite often the case). Receipt of property or services triggers income recognition. Furthermore, taxpayers recognize income even if they receive it indirectly.

| | |
|---|---|
| **EXAMPLE 3-2** | If a lawyer agrees to give legal advice to a neighbor in exchange for the neighbor agreeing to paint the lawyer's house, both parties will have income equal to the fair market value of the services received by them. |

| | |
|---|---|
| **EXAMPLE 3-3** | Heather owns an unincorporated cash basis architectural firm. She performs architectural services for a client during December 2020. She completed the work in 2020 (so the income was earned), but she did not receive payment by the end of the year. Heather received payment for her services on January 23, 2021, and recognizes income in 2021. |

| | |
|---|---|
| **EXAMPLE 3-4** | Antonio provided golf lessons worth $300 to Arturo in December 2020. Antonio owed Millie $300, and he asked Arturo to pay the $300 to Millie. In January 2021 Arturo paid Millie $300. Antonio recognizes income of $300 in 2021. |

In some instances, cash basis taxpayers can report income as though they were accrual basis taxpayers. For instance, in the case of interest income on Series EE and Series I U.S. savings bonds, taxpayers can defer the income until the maturity of the bond or can elect to report the interest annually.[5] Special rules also apply to farmers and ranchers, who can elect to average their income over a three-year period and can elect to defer certain insurance proceeds and federal disaster payments.[6]

| | |
|---|---|
| **CONCEPT CHECK 3-2—** **LO 3-2**  | 1. Income may be realized in any form, whether in money, property, or services. True or false?<br>2. If you provide consulting services to your friend and, in exchange, he fixes your car, you and your friend must report on both tax returns the fair market value of the services provided. True or false? |

[3] The method of accounting (cash or accrual) used for an individual taxpayer's first tax return effectively establishes that person's accounting method. See Reg. § 1.446-1(e)(1). Thus, although it is possible that an individual can use the accrual method of accounting, it is unlikely that the individual uses the accrual method for the first return.

[4] Reg. § 1.61-1(a).

[5] IRC § 454.

[6] IRC § 1301, § 451(f).

# TAXABILITY OF COMPONENTS OF GROSS INCOME
## LO 3-3

This section discusses the taxability of various types of gross income, including interest, dividends, tax refunds, and social security benefits.

### Interest Income (Form 1040, Line 2)

Recall that interest is compensation for the use of money with respect to a bona fide debt or obligation imposed by law. For most individuals, interest income comes from interest-earning deposits at financial institutions—banks, savings and loans, or credit unions. These institutions report interest income to taxpayers on Form 1099-INT. Taxpayers can also earn interest income in other ways not reported on an IRS form. An example is a creditor–debtor arrangement between two individuals in which taxpayer A lends some money to taxpayer B and taxpayer A receives $50 in interest. In this instance, taxpayer A would earn interest income, but no IRS document would be required to record the interest income.

Some tax issues pertaining to interest income are complex and less common. These include below-market interest rate loans, gifts, shareholder and similar loans, and interest from original issue discount (OID). The Appendix to this chapter provides further details about these subjects. Next we discuss common types of interest income.

#### Interest on U.S. Savings Bonds

Individuals purchased Series EE and Series E (before July 1980) U.S. savings bonds at a discount from face value. The owners of the bonds do not receive a periodic cash interest payment. Instead, the face value of the bond increases over the period to maturity, and that increase represents the amount of interest earned. The owner of such bonds can defer reporting any interest (that is, the increase in bond value) until the bonds mature, are redeemed, or are otherwise disposed of, whichever comes first. Alternatively, the owner can elect to report the annual increase in face value as interest income on each year's income tax return (on an accrual basis).[7] Such election applies to all bonds owned at the time of the election and to any bonds subsequently acquired.

---

**EXAMPLE 3-5**

Alina purchased a $1,000 face value Series EE U.S. savings bond for $500 on January 1, 2021. The bond earned interest at a rate of 6% throughout 2021 so that at year-end, the bond had a face value of $530. If Alina does nothing, she does not need to report the $30 interest income for 2021 until she cashes the bond upon maturity. Alternatively, Alina can elect to report the $30 as interest income in 2021. If she does, she must report all future interest income on the bond in the same manner.

---

Until August 2004, the U.S. Treasury sold Series HH bonds at face value. Interest on these bonds is paid by check semiannually and is included in income in the year received.

#### Tax-Exempt Interest

Certain interest income is exempt from taxation. Taxpayers can exclude from gross income any interest earned on bonds issued by any state, any possession of the United States, any political subdivision of either of the foregoing, or the District of Columbia (such as municipal bonds).[8] However, interest is taxable if received from state or local bonds issued for private activities such as convention centers, industrial parks, or stadiums.[9]

[7] IRC § 454(a).
[8] IRC § 103(a), (c).
[9] IRC § 103(b)(1).

# From Shoebox to Software   Interest Income

Taxable interest income is on line 2b of Form 1040. Tax-exempt interest is on line 2a. If any of the following is true, the taxpayer must complete and file Schedule B:

- Had more than $1,500 of interest income.
- Received seller-financed mortgage interest.
- Received tax-exempt interest in any amount.
- Received interest as a nominee.
- Claimed an exclusion for interest on Series EE U.S. savings bonds issued after 1989 or Series I bonds.
- Reported any adjustments for accrued interest, amortizable bond premium, or original issue discount (see the Appendix at the end of this chapter).
- Had a foreign account; received a distribution from or was the grantor of or a transferor to a foreign trust.

Schedule B is shown in Exhibit 3-1. The total from line 4 of the applicable schedule is reported on line 2b of Form 1040.

Information concerning interest income comes from a number of sources:

- If interest is received from a financial institution, corporation, or branch of government, the taxpayer will receive Form 1099-INT that will indicate, in box 1, the amount of interest received or credited to the taxpayer's account during the year. Form 1099-INT is shown in Exhibit 3-2.
- Taxpayers who are partners of a partnership or who are shareholders of a Subchapter S corporation will receive Schedule K-1, which will reflect the taxpayer's proportionate share of interest income. We discuss partnerships

and Subchapter S corporations in Chapters 14 and 15, respectively.

- If the taxpayer owns bonds that were purchased at a discount (see the Appendix to this chapter), the taxpayer should receive Form 1099-OID showing, in box 1, the amount of original issue discount that must be reported as income in the current year. A Form 1099-OID is shown in Exhibit 3-3.
- Taxpayers who receive interest from other sources will need to calculate the appropriate amount of interest to include on Schedule B. Other sources of interest income include

  - Payments received from seller-financed mortgages.
  - Receipts from installment sale receivables or other receivables received over time.
  - Imputed interest on loans made at a below-market interest rate (see the chapter Appendix).
  - Interest on bonds sold between interest dates.

When using the tax software, you record the information from all Forms 1099 received onto the appropriate input form in the Documents Received section.

Taxpayers who are eligible to exclude U.S. savings bond interest because they paid qualified higher education expenses (see the Appendix to this chapter) must complete Form 8815 and attach it to their tax return. With the tax software, you enter the required information directly on Form 8815.

Self-employed individuals who receive interest income as a part of their business report the amounts on Schedule C (see Chapter 6).

## Dividends (Form 1040, Line 3)

*Dividends* are distributions of property by a corporation to its shareholders. Dividends are generally taxed at capital gains rates to the extent they are made from either a corporation's current earnings and profits or its accumulated earnings and profits.[10] Distributions in excess of earnings and profits represent a nontaxable return of capital that reduces the taxpayer's cost basis in the stock. If the distribution is greater than the basis of the stock, the excess is a capital gain.[11]

[10] IRC § 316(a). Earnings and profits are similar, but not identical, to retained earnings for financial statement purposes. Earnings and profits are beyond the scope of this book.

[11] IRC § 301(c).

**EXHIBIT 3-1**

| | |
|---|---|
| **SCHEDULE B**<br>(Form 1040)<br><br>Department of the Treasury<br>Internal Revenue Service (99) | **Interest and Ordinary Dividends**<br>▶ Go to *www.irs.gov/ScheduleB* for instructions and the latest information.<br>▶ Attach to Form 1040 or 1040-SR. |

OMB No. 1545-0074

**2021**

Attachment Sequence No. **08**

Name(s) shown on return

Your social security number

~~DRAFT AS OF June 22, 2021 DO NOT FILE~~

**Part I**

**Interest**

(See instructions and the instructions for Forms 1040 and 1040-SR, line 2b.)

**Note:** If you received a Form 1099-INT, Form 1099-OID, or substitute statement from a brokerage firm, list the firm's name as the payer and enter the total interest shown on that form.

**1** List name of payer. If any interest is from a seller-financed mortgage and the buyer used the property as a personal residence, see the instructions and list this interest first. Also, show that buyer's social security number and address ▶

**Amount**

**1**

**2** Add the amounts on line 1 . . . . . . . . . . . . . . . . . . **2**

**3** Excludable interest on series EE and I U.S. savings bonds issued after 1989. Attach Form 8815 . . . . . . . . . . . . . . . . **3**

**4** Subtract line 3 from line 2. Enter the result here and on Form 1040 or 1040-SR, line 2b . . . . . . . . . . . . . . . . . . . . ▶ **4**

**Note:** If line 4 is over $1,500, you must complete Part III.

**Part II**

**Ordinary Dividends**

(See instructions and the instructions for Forms 1040 and 1040-SR, line 3b.)

**Note:** If you received a Form 1099-DIV or substitute statement from a brokerage firm, list the firm's name as the payer and enter the ordinary dividends shown on that form.

**5** List name of payer ▶

**Amount**

**5**

**6** Add the amounts on line 5. Enter the total here and on Form 1040 or 1040-SR, line 3b . . . . . . . . . . . . . . . . . . . ▶ **6**

**Note:** If line 6 is over $1,500, you must complete Part III.

**Part III**

**Foreign Accounts and Trusts**

**Caution:** If required, failure to file FinCEN Form 114 may result in substantial penalties. See instructions.

You must complete this part if you **(a)** had over $1,500 of taxable interest or ordinary dividends; **(b)** had a foreign account; or **(c)** received a distribution from, or were a grantor of, or a transferor to, a foreign trust.

| | | Yes | No |
|---|---|---|---|
| **7a** | At any time during 2021, did you have a financial interest in or signature authority over a financial account (such as a bank account, securities account, or brokerage account) located in a foreign country? See instructions . . . . . . . . . . . | | |
| | If "Yes," are you required to file FinCEN Form 114, Report of Foreign Bank and Financial Accounts (FBAR), to report that financial interest or signature authority? See FinCEN Form 114 and its instructions for filing requirements and exceptions to those requirements . . . . . . | | |
| **b** | If you are required to file FinCEN Form 114, enter the name of the foreign country where the financial account is located ▶ | | |
| **8** | During 2021, did you receive a distribution from, or were you the grantor of, or transferor to, a foreign trust? If "Yes," you may have to file Form 3520. See instructions . . . . . . . . . | | |

For Paperwork Reduction Act Notice, see your tax return instructions.          Cat. No. 17146N          **Schedule B (Form 1040) 2021**

Source: U.S. Department of the Treasury, Internal Revenue Service, Schedule B (Form 1040). Washington, DC: 2021.

**EXHIBIT 3-2**

| | | |
|---|---|---|
| | ☐ CORRECTED (if checked) | |

| PAYER'S name, street address, city or town, state or province, country, ZIP or foreign postal code, and telephone no. | Payer's RTN (optional) | OMB No. 1545-0112 | **Interest Income** |
| | **1** Interest income $ | 20**21** Form **1099-INT** | |
| PAYER'S TIN / RECIPIENT'S TIN | **2** Early withdrawal penalty $ | | **Copy B** |
| | **3** Interest on U.S. Savings Bonds and Treas. obligations $ | | **For Recipient** |
| RECIPIENT'S name | **4** Federal income tax withheld $ | **5** Investment expenses $ | This is important tax information and is being furnished to the IRS. If you are required to file a return, a negligence penalty or other sanction may be imposed on you if this income is taxable and the IRS determines that it has not been reported. |
| | **6** Foreign tax paid $ | **7** Foreign country or U.S. possession | |
| Street address (including apt. no.) | **8** Tax-exempt interest $ | **9** Specified private activity bond interest $ | |
| City or town, state or province, country, and ZIP or foreign postal code | **10** Market discount $ | **11** Bond premium $ | |
| FATCA filing requirement ☐ | **12** Bond premium on Treasury obligations $ | **13** Bond premium on tax-exempt bond $ | |
| Account number (see instructions) | **14** Tax-exempt and tax credit bond CUSIP no. | **15** State **16** State identification no. **17** State tax withheld $ $ | |

Form **1099-INT**     (keep for your records)     www.irs.gov/Form1099INT     Department of the Treasury - Internal Revenue Service

Source: U.S. Department of the Treasury, Internal Revenue Service, Form 1099-INT. Washington, DC: 2021.

**EXHIBIT 3-3**

| | | |
|---|---|---|
| | ☐ CORRECTED (if checked) | |

| PAYER'S name, street address, city or town, state or province, country, ZIP or foreign postal code, and telephone no. | **1** Original issue discount for the year* $ * This may not be the correct figure to report on your income tax return. See instructions on the back. | OMB No. 1545-0117 Form **1099-OID** (Rev. October 2019) | **Original Issue Discount** |
| | **2** Other periodic interest $ | For calendar year 20___ | |
| PAYER'S TIN / RECIPIENT'S TIN | **3** Early withdrawal penalty $ | **4** Federal income tax withheld $ | **Copy B** |
| | **5** Market discount $ | **6** Acquisition premium $ | **For Recipient** |
| RECIPIENT'S name | **7** Description | | |
| Street address (including apt. no.) | | | This is important tax information and is being furnished to the IRS. If you are required to file a return, a negligence penalty or other sanction may be imposed on you if this income is taxable and the IRS determines that it has not been reported. |
| City or town, state or province, country, and ZIP or foreign postal code | **8** Original issue discount on U.S. Treasury obligations* $ | **9** Investment expenses $ | |
| FATCA filing requirement ☐ | **10** Bond premium $ | **11** Tax-exempt OID $ | |
| Account number (see instructions) | **12** State **13** State identification no. **14** State tax withheld $ $ | | |

Form **1099-OID** (Rev. 10-2019)     (keep for your records)     www.irs.gov/Form1099OID     Department of the Treasury - Internal Revenue Service

Source: U.S. Department of the Treasury, Internal Revenue Service, Form 1099-OID. Washington, DC: 2021.

Corporations normally pay dividends in the form of cash, but they may pay them in property or anything of economic value. The basis of the property received as a dividend in the hands of the shareholder is the property's fair market value at the date of distribution.[12]

A *stock dividend* is a distribution of shares of the corporation's own stock to shareholders. Stock dividends (and stock splits) are generally not taxable to a shareholder.[13] Shareholders allocate the basis of the stock originally held between the old and the new stock in proportion to the fair market value of each on the date of the distribution. Certain stock dividends are taxable, including these:

- Stock dividends in which a shareholder has the option to receive stock or cash or other property.
- Disproportionate dividends in which some shareholders receive property and other shareholders receive an increase in their stock interest in the corporation.
- Distributions of preferred stock to some common shareholders and common stock to other common shareholders.
- Distributions made on preferred stock.[14]

*Mutual funds* (known as *regulated investment companies*) are entities that pool the financial resources of thousands of individuals to purchase stocks or bonds. Mutual funds are required to distribute the income they receive, whether in the form of dividends from holding stocks or capital gains and losses from sales of a portion of the portfolio. Real estate investment trusts make similar distributions.

## Taxation of Dividends

**NEW LAW**

For 2021, the taxability of qualified dividends is based on increased income thresholds.

To this point in the text, all income is the same for purposes of determining the amount of tax. However, certain types of income are taxed at different rates.

Prior to passage of the 2003 Jobs and Growth Act (the 2003 Act) in June 2003, dividends and ordinary income were taxed at the same rate. The 2003 Act states that qualified dividends received in 2003 or later may receive preferential treatment.[15] The Tax Cuts and Jobs Act of 2017 provides for taxability of qualified dividends based on taxable income thresholds. The thresholds increased for 2021. In 2021, for married filing jointly with taxable income of less than $80,800, head of household with taxable income of less than $54,100, and married filing separately or single with taxable income of less than $40,400, the dividends are taxed at 0%. Thereafter, dividends are taxed at 15% for income up to $501,600 for married filing jointly, $250,800 for married filing separately, $473,750 for head of household, and $445,850 for single taxpayers. A 20% tax rate on dividends applies for taxable income above those amounts.

*Qualified dividends* (1) are made from the earnings and profits of the payer corporation and (2) are from domestic corporations or qualified foreign corporations.[16]

---

**EXAMPLE 3-6**

Refer to the tax rate schedules in Appendix F. A single individual who has taxable income of $110,000 before dividends will be in the 24% marginal tax bracket. If that individual then receives a qualified dividend of $1,000, the tax rate applied to the dividend would be 15%. The tax liability of the individual would be determined as follows:

| | |
|---|---:|
| Taxable income (before dividend) | $110,000 |
| Less lower bracket amount | 86,375 |
| Income taxed at 24% | 23,625 |
| Tax rate | × 24% |
| Tax at highest bracket | 5,670 |
| Plus tax on first $86,375 | 14,751 |
| Tax before dividend | 20,421 |
| Tax on dividend ($1,000 × 15%) | 150 |
| Total tax liability | $ 20,571 |

---

[12] IRC § 301(d).

[13] IRC § 305(a).

[14] Reg § 1.305-5(a).

[15] IRC § 1(h)(11)(A).

[16] IRC § 1(h)(11)(B)(i).

Dividends are reported on line 3b of Form 1040. A taxpayer who receives more than $1,500 of dividend income must complete and file Schedule B. Refer to Exhibit 3-1 for Schedule B. Note that Schedule B contains information about both interest and dividends. The total from line 6 of Schedule B is reported on line 3b of Form 1040.

Corporate and mutual fund payers are required to provide shareholders a Form 1099-DIV (see Exhibit 3-4), which indicates the amount of dividends in box 1a. Note that the amount in box 1b represents how much of box 1a is *qualified*

dividends. If all dividends received by an individual are qualified dividends, the amount in box 1a will be the same as the amount in box 1b. The total amount of qualified dividends is reported on line 3a of Form 1040.

Most taxpayers will have no other sources of dividend income other than that reported on Form 1099-DIV.

As was the case with interest payments reported on Form 1099-INT, any dividend income from Form 1099-DIV should be recorded in the tax software using the appropriate supporting form located in the Documents Received section of the software.

The example also illustrates that taxpayers add the dividend income "at the end" no matter when in the tax year they earned the dividend. In other words, tax is computed first on the nondividend income and then on the dividend income.

**CONCEPT CHECK 3-4—**

**LO 3-3**

1. Qualified dividends arise from the earnings and profits of the payer corporation. True or false?
2. A corporation can pay only cash dividends to its shareholders. True or false?

## EXHIBIT 3-4

| | | |
|---|---|---|
| ☐ CORRECTED (if checked) | | |

| PAYER'S name, street address, city or town, state or province, country, ZIP or foreign postal code, and telephone no. | **1a** Total ordinary dividends $ | OMB No. 1545-0110 20**21** Form **1099-DIV** | **Dividends and Distributions** |
|---|---|---|---|
| | **1b** Qualified dividends $ | | |
| | **2a** Total capital gain distr. $ | **2b** Unrecap. Sec. 1250 gain $ | **Copy B** **For Recipient** |
| PAYER'S TIN          RECIPIENT'S TIN | **2c** Section 1202 gain $ | **2d** Collectibles (28%) gain $ | |
| | **2e** Section 897 ordinary dividends $ | **2f** Section 897 capital gain $ | |
| RECIPIENT'S name | **3** Nondividend distributions $ | **4** Federal income tax withheld $ | This is important tax information and is being furnished to the IRS. If you are required to file a return, a negligence penalty or other sanction may be imposed on you if this income is taxable and the IRS determines that it has not been reported. |
| | **5** Section 199A dividends $ | **6** Investment expenses $ | |
| Street address (including apt. no.) | **7** Foreign tax paid $ | **8** Foreign country or U.S. possession | |
| City or town, state or province, country, and ZIP or foreign postal code | **9** Cash liquidation distributions $ | **10** Noncash liquidation distributions $ | |
| FATCA filing requirement ☐ | **11** Exempt-interest dividends $ | **12** Specified private activity bond interest dividends $ | |
| Account number (see instructions) | **13** State  **14** State identification no. | **15** State tax withheld $ $ | |

| Form **1099-DIV** | (keep for your records) | www.irs.gov/Form1099DIV | Department of the Treasury - Internal Revenue Service |
|---|---|---|---|

Source: U.S. Department of the Treasury, Internal Revenue Service, Form 1099-DIV. Washington, DC: 2021.

## State and Local Tax Refunds (Schedule 1, Line 1)

Taxpayers may receive a refund of state or local taxes paid in a prior year. If a taxpayer deducted state or local taxes as an itemized deduction on Schedule A (see Chapter 5) in the prior year, the taxpayer must report the refund as income in the year in which it was received. The taxable amount is the lesser of (a) the amount received, (b) the amount deducted on Schedule A, or (c) the amount by which the itemized deductions exceed the standard deduction. If the taxpayer did not itemize deductions in the prior year (that is, the taxpayer took the standard deduction), no amount of the refund is taxable.[17]

**EXAMPLE 3-7**

Leila, who is single, reported itemized deductions of $14,500 on her 2020 tax return. Her itemized deductions included $1,150 of state taxes paid. In 2021 she received a $120 refund of state taxes paid in 2020. She must include the entire $120 in income in 2021.

**EXAMPLE 3-8**

Assume that Leila reported itemized deductions of $12,440 in 2020. Only $40 of her $120 tax refund would be taxable in 2021 because her itemized deductions exceeded her standard deduction by only $40 (in 2020, the standard deduction for single individuals was $12,400).

State and local tax refunds are reported to taxpayers on Form 1099-G, box 2 (see Exhibit 3-5). The applicable amount of the refund is reported on line 1 of Schedule 1.

**TAX YOUR BRAIN**

Steve received a state tax refund of $200 from the state of California and, at the end of the year, received a Form 1099-G showing the payment in box 2. Must Steve report the refund on his Form 1040?

**ANSWER**

Not necessarily. Just because Steve received a 1099-G does not mean that the amount indicated in box 2 is actually taxable to him. Steve must determine whether he itemized deductions in the prior year and, if so, how much of the $200 is taxable based on how much tax benefit he received in the prior year, if any.

## Unemployment Compensation (Schedule 1, Line 7)

Federal and state unemployment compensation benefits are taxable.[18] The rationale behind taxing these payments is that they are a substitute for taxable wages. There was an exception created by the American Rescue Plan Act of 2021 exempting some of that money from federal income taxes on tax returns for the year 2020. Unemployment benefits are reported to recipients on Form 1099-G in box 1 (see Exhibit 3-5).

A taxpayer who repays some or all of the unemployment compensation received subtracts the repayment from the amount otherwise received. The repayment is reported by indicating, on Schedule 1, line 7, the net amount of unemployment compensation received (amount received minus amount repaid) and, on the dotted line, writing *repaid* followed by the amount repaid.

[17] IRC § 111(a).
[18] IRC § 85(a), (b).

**EXHIBIT 3-5**

| | | | |
|---|---|---|---|
| ☐ CORRECTED (if checked) | | | |

| PAYER'S name, street address, city or town, state or province, country, ZIP or foreign postal code, and telephone no. | **1** Unemployment compensation<br>$ | OMB No. 1545-0120<br>**2021**<br>Form **1099-G** | **Certain Government Payments** |
|---|---|---|---|
| | **2** State or local income tax refunds, credits, or offsets<br>$ | | |
| PAYER'S TIN | RECIPIENT'S TIN | **3** Box 2 amount is for tax year | **4** Federal income tax withheld<br>$ | **Copy B**<br>**For Recipient** |
| RECIPIENT'S name | **5** RTAA payments<br>$ | **6** Taxable grants<br>$ | This is important tax information and is being furnished to the IRS. If you are required to file a return, a negligence penalty or other sanction may be imposed on you if this income is taxable and the IRS determines that it has not been reported. |
| Street address (including apt. no.) | **7** Agriculture payments<br>$ | **8** If checked, box 2 is trade or business income ▶ ☐ | |
| City or town, state or province, country, and ZIP or foreign postal code | **9** Market gain<br>$ | | |
| | **10a** State | **10b** State identification no. | **11** State income tax withheld<br>$<br>$ | |
| Account number (see instructions) | | | |

Form **1099-G**          (keep for your records)          www.irs.gov/Form1099G          Department of the Treasury - Internal Revenue Service

Source: U.S. Department of the Treasury, Internal Revenue Service, Form 1099-G. Washington, DC: 2021.

## Social Security Benefits (Form 1040, Line 6)

The taxability of social security benefits depends on the provisional income and filing status of the taxpayer.[19] The effect of the rules is to exclude social security benefits from taxation for lower-income individuals but tax up to 85% of benefits for taxpayers with higher income. You can find additional information concerning the tax treatment of social security benefits in IRS Publication 915.

*Provisional income* (also called *modified Adjusted Gross Income*) is calculated as follows:[20]

---

Adjusted Gross Income (before social security benefits)

Plus: Interest on U.S. savings bonds excluded for educational purposes[21]

Most tax-exempt interest[22]

Employer-provided adoption benefits[23]

Excluded foreign income[24]

Deducted interest on educational loans[25]

Deducted tuition and fees (Tax Extenders Act of 2008)

50% of social security benefits

---

[19] Social security benefits refer to the monthly retirement and disability benefits payable under social security and to tier-one railroad retirement benefits. They do not include tier-two railroad benefits or supplementary Medicare benefits that cover medical expenses.

[20] IRC § 86(b)(2).

[21] Interest excluded under IRC § 135.

[22] Exclusion under IRC § 103.

[23] IRC § 137.

[24] Under IRC § 911, 931, or 933.

[25] Interest deductible under IRC § 221.

## From Shoebox to Software Social Security Benefits

Taxpayers will receive Form SSA-1099 or RRB-1099 showing the amount of social security benefits or railroad retirement benefits received, respectively. See Exhibit 3-6 for Form SSA-1099.

The amount of benefits to use in taxability calculations is in box 5. As with other 1099 forms, you record the information on the appropriate form within the tax software. Specifically, you record both social security and railroad retirement benefits on the Social Security Benefits worksheet in the worksheet section of the tax software.

If provisional income exceeds certain thresholds, 50% of social security benefits are taxable. As provisional income increases, the proportion of benefits included in taxable income increases to as much as 85%. The thresholds and taxability are shown in the following chart:

|  | **Married, Filing Jointly** | **Single, Head of Household, or Qualifying Widow(er)** |
|---|---|---|
| Lower limit of provisional income | $32,000 | $25,000 |
| Upper limit of provisional income | $44,000 | $34,000 |
| Taxable portion of benefits if provisional income is between the two limits | Lesser of 50% of benefits or 50% of the excess of provisional income over $32,000 | Lesser of 50% of benefits or 50% of the excess of provisional income over $25,000 |
| Taxable portion of benefits if provisional income is above the upper limit | Lesser of (a) 85% of benefits or (b) 85% of the excess of provisional income over $44,000 *plus* the lesser of (1) $6,000 or (2) 50% of benefits | Lesser of (a) 85% of benefits or (b) 85% of the excess of provisional income over $34,000 *plus* the lesser of (1) $4,500 or (2) 50% of benefits |

Taxpayers use the single column if they are married filing separately and have lived apart from their spouse for the entire year. If such persons lived with their spouse at any time during the year, the lower and upper limits are zero. Thus, for these persons, social security benefits are taxable to the extent of the lesser of 85% of social security benefits or 85% of provisional income.

---

**EXAMPLE 3-9**    Robert and Cindy file a joint return. Their AGI before social security was $15,000, and they received $8,000 in benefits. They had no items to add back to AGI. Their provisional income is $19,000 ($15,000 + $4,000). No social security benefits are taxable.

---

**EXAMPLE 3-10**    Khawla files a return as a qualifying widow. She received $7,000 of social security benefits, $19,000 of interest income, and $5,000 of nontaxable municipal bond interest. Her provisional income is $27,500 ($3,500 + $19,000 + $5,000). Khawla will report taxable social security benefits equal to the lesser of 50% of social security benefits ($3,500) or 50% of the excess of provisional income over $25,000 ($1,250). Thus, her taxable benefits total $1,250 (see Exhibit 3-7).

**EXHIBIT 3-6**

## FORM SSA-1099 – SOCIAL SECURITY BENEFIT STATEMENT

**2020** • PART OF YOUR SOCIAL SECURITY BENEFITS SHOWN IN BOX 5 MAY BE TAXABLE INCOME.
• SEE THE REVERSE FOR MORE INFORMATION.

| Box 1. Name | Box 2. Beneficiary's Social Security Number |
|---|---|

| Box 3. Benefits Paid in 2020 | Box 4. Benefits Repaid to SSA in 2020 | Box 5. Net Benefits for 2020 *(Box 3 minus Box 4)* |
|---|---|---|

| DESCRIPTION OF AMOUNT IN BOX 3 | DESCRIPTION OF AMOUNT IN BOX 4 |
|---|---|

SAMPLE

Box 6. Voluntary Federal Income Tax Withheld

Box 7. Address

Box 8. Claim Number *(Use this number if you need to contact SSA.)*

Form **SSA-1099-SM** (1-2021)     **DO NOT RETURN THIS FORM TO SSA OR IRS**

Source: U.S. Department of the Treasury, Internal Revenue Service, Form SSA-1099. Washington, DC:

NOTE: This form is for calendar year 2020. The form for 2021 will be identical to the above except for the year notation.

---

**EXAMPLE 3-11**      Carson and Maureen file a joint return showing interest and dividend income of $46,000, self-employment income for Carson of $31,000, and nontaxable municipal bond interest of $10,000. They excluded $1,000 of interest on educational loans. They received social security benefits of $9,000. Their provisional income is $92,500 ($46,000 + $31,000 + $10,000 + $1,000 + $4,500). They will report taxable social security benefits equal to the lesser of 85% of social security benefits ($7,650) or 85% of the excess of provisional income over $44,000 (which is $41,225) plus the lesser of $6,000 or $4,500 (50% of social security benefits). Thus, their taxable benefits total $7,650.

---

**CONCEPT CHECK 3-5— LO 3-3**

1. Linda and Mason file a joint return. Their AGI before social security was $22,000, social security benefits received were $9,000, and tax-exempt interest was $1,250. What is the amount of their provisional income? _____

**EXHIBIT 3-7**

| | | | |
|---|---|---|---|
| 1. | Enter the total amount from **box 5 of all your Forms SSA-1099** and **RRB-1099.** Also enter this amount on Form 1040 or 1040-SR, line 6a | 1. | 7,000 |
| 2. | Multiply line 1 by 50% (0.50) | 2. | 3,500 |
| 3. | Combine the amounts from Form 1040 or 1040-SR, lines 1, 2b, 3b, 4b, 5b, 7, and 8 | 3. | 19,000 |
| 4. | Enter the amount, if any, from Form 1040 or 1040-SR, line 2a | 4. | 5,000 |
| 5. | Combine lines 2, 3, and 4 | 5. | 27,500 |
| 6. | Enter the total of the amounts from Form 1040 or 1040-SR, line 10b, Schedule 1, lines 10 through 19, plus any write-in adjustments you entered on the dotted line next to Schedule 1, line 22 | 6. | 0 |
| 7. | Is the amount on line 6 less than the amount on line 5? | | |
| | ☐ **No.** (STOP) None of your social security benefits are taxable. Enter -0- on Form 1040 or 1040-SR, line 6b. | | |
| | ☒ **Yes.** Subtract line 6 from line 5 | 7. | 27,500 |
| 8. | If you are: • Married filing jointly, enter $32,000 • Single, head of household, qualifying widow(er), or married filing separately and you **lived apart** from your spouse for all of 2020, enter $25,000 • Married filing separately and you lived with your spouse at any time in 2020, skip lines 8 through 15; multiply line 7 by 85% (0.85) and enter the result on line 16. Then, go to line 17 | 8. | 25,000 |
| 9. | Is the amount on line 8 less than the amount on line 7? | | |
| | ☐ **No.** (STOP) None of your social security benefits are taxable. Enter -0- on Form 1040 or 1040-SR, line 6b. If you are married filing separately and you **lived apart** from your spouse for all of 2020, be sure you entered "D" to the right of the word "benefits" on line 6a. | | |
| | ☒ **Yes.** Subtract line 8 from line 7 | 9. | 2,500 |
| 10. | Enter: $12,000 if married filing jointly; $9,000 if single, head of household, qualifying widow(er), or married filing separately and you **lived apart** from your spouse for all of 2020 | 10. | 9,000 |
| 11. | Subtract line 10 from line 9. If zero or less, enter -0- | 11. | 0 |
| 12. | Enter the **smaller** of line 9 or line 10 | 12. | 2,500 |
| 13. | Enter one-half of line 12 | 13. | 1,250 |
| 14. | Enter the **smaller** of line 2 or line 13 | 14. | 1,250 |
| 15. | Multiply line 11 by 85% (0.85). If line 11 is zero, enter -0- | 15. | 0 |
| 16. | Add lines 14 and 15 | 16. | 1,250 |
| 17. | Multiply line 1 by 85% (0.85) | 17. | 5,950 |
| 18. | **Taxable social security benefits.** Enter the **smaller** of line 16 or line 17. Also enter this amount on Form 1040 or 1040-SR, line 6b | 18. | 1,250 |

Source: U.S. Department of the Treasury, Internal Revenue Service, Forms SSA-1099 and RRB-1099. Washington, DC: 2019.

As of the date this text went to print, the 2021 worksheet to calculate the taxable amount of Social Security payments had not been released. The worksheet above is created using the 2020 form. The calculation of taxable Social Security is correct. However, some of the line number references to other tax forms on the worksheet above will be different on the 2021 worksheet. When the 2021 worksheet is released, an updated Exhibit will be posted to Connect.

## Other Income (Schedule 1, Line 8)

Gross income includes ". . . all income from whatever source derived . . .".[26] The concept is broad, and taxpayers often receive income that does not neatly fit into the lines on Form 1040 or Schedule 1. Schedule 1, line 8, is where taxpayers report other taxable gross income. Items that taxpayers must report on line 8 include these:

- **Jury duty pay:** Individuals who serve jury duty receive a small amount of pay for each day served. This pay is included in other income. If the individual is required to remit the payment to an employer, the payment is deductible, the net effect of which is that the taxpayer reports zero.[27]

- **Prizes and awards:** If employees receive a prize or award from their employer, the award is included in W-2 income. Prizes and awards received from other sources are taxable as other income unless specifically excluded (such as a scholarship award).

[26] IRS Publication 17, *Your Federal Income Tax: For Individuals.*
[27] IRC § 62(a)(13).

- **Forgiveness of debt:** If a taxpayer borrows money, it is not taxable income because the taxpayer must repay the loan (that is, the taxpayer does not have a complete, unfettered right to the money). If a lender fully or partially forgives a loan, the taxpayer has income to the extent of the forgiveness.[28] However, a borrower does not report income if payment of the debt would have given rise to a deduction.[29] For example, a lender forgives some interest otherwise due on a loan to a self-employed cash basis taxpayer. A taxpayer who had paid the interest would have recorded a business deduction for the interest paid. Thus, the taxpayer reports no income. Other exceptions to the general forgiveness of debt rule (such as forgiveness during bankruptcy proceedings or when the taxpayer is insolvent) are beyond the scope of this text.[30]

- **Certain insurance proceeds:** Taxpayers receiving insurance proceeds in excess of the adjusted basis of the property insured must report taxable income equal to the excess. This category does not include life insurance or health insurance proceeds.

**CONCEPT CHECK 3-6— LO 3-3**

1. Name a type of income item that is listed on line 8 of Schedule 1.

_____

# ITEMS EXCLUDED FROM GROSS INCOME

**LO 3-4**

Congress has exempted certain income from tax by statute. These exemptions include the following items.

## Nontaxable Employee Fringe Benefits

The general rule is that employee compensation, in whatever form, is taxable to the employee. However, certain types of fringe benefits are tax-free to the employee, and the employer can deduct the cost of providing the benefits.[31] Most benefits are subject to nondiscrimination rules.[32]

The following fringe benefits provided by an employer are not taxable to the employee:

- **No-additional-cost services** provided to an employee, a spouse, or dependent children:[33] The employer must ordinarily offer the services for sale to outside customers, and the employer must incur no substantial additional cost (including forgone revenue) to provide the service. Examples include unsold hotel rooms or airline seats (but not if the benefit bumps a paying customer).

- **Discounts** provided employees for products or services normally sold by the business:[34] Examples are reduced-priced meals in restaurants, discounts on clothing at a retail store, and reduced interest rate loans from a financial institution. In the case of products, the discount cannot exceed the gross profit percentage, and in the case of services, the maximum discount is 20% of the normal selling price.

---

[28] IRC § 61(a)(11).

[29] IRC § 108(e)(2).

[30] These exceptions are found in IRC § 108 and the regulations thereunder.

[31] Employer deductibility is not a focus of this text.

[32] Generally, nondiscrimination rules prohibit or limit the nontaxability of certain benefits if highly compensated employees disproportionately receive the benefits at the expense of lower-paid employees. For example, if discounts (see the text) are given only to employees with salaries over $500,000, it is likely that the nondiscrimination rules would apply and make the discount amount a taxable benefit rather than a tax-free benefit.

[33] IRC § 132(b).

[34] IRC § 132(c).

- **Working condition fringe benefits:** These are services or properties provided to an employee that would have been deductible as a trade or business expense or as depreciation expense had the employee paid for them.[35] Working condition fringes include professional organization dues paid by an employer or the use of an employer-provided vehicle for business purposes.
- **Qualified transportation fringe benefits:** These benefits include transit passes, parking near the employer's business or near a mass transit location, and use of an employer-provided vanpool that holds six or more persons and is used 80% or more for commuting.[36] In 2021 parking benefits cannot exceed $270 per month, and transit passes and vanpool benefits cannot exceed $270 per month.
- *De minimis* **benefits:** (holiday turkeys, company picnics, flowers or fruit sent when an employee is sick, etc.) A *de minimis* benefit is one whose value is so small that keeping track of which employees received the benefit is administratively impractical.[37]

Employees can exclude from income additional employer-provided benefits. Commonly used benefits follow:

- Employers often provide reduced-cost or fully paid accident and health insurance to employees. The value of the premium paid by the employer is not taxable to the employee.[38] Reimbursement for medical care paid by the insurance policy (or paid directly by the employer if no policy exists or if the policy does not cover the cost) is not taxable income to the employee unless the reimbursement exceeds the cost of the care.
- Employers can pay (or reimburse employees) for up to $5,250 per year of educational assistance, whether or not it is job-related.[39] Expenses include, but are not limited to, tuition, fees, books, and supplies.

**NEW LAW**

The benefit of employer payment for employee student loans under the CARES Act has been extended until December 2025.

- Employers can contribute up to $5,250 in payment of employee student loans under the CARES Act employer student loan repayment benefit. The payment is not included in the employee income, and an employee cannot claim a deduction for the interest paid on the loan. This benefit is extended until December 31, 2025. The $5,250 cap applies to both the new student loan repayment benefit as well as other educational assistance (tuition, fees, books, etc.) allowed under current law.
- Employer-paid premiums on group term life insurance are not taxable to employees.[40] Tax-free coverage is limited to $50,000 per person. Coverage in excess of the $50,000 limit is taxable to the employee based on the cost of the excess.[41]
- The costs of employer-paid meals and lodging are tax-exempt if the meals and lodging are furnished for the convenience of the employer and are furnished on the business premises (in the case of meals), or the employee is required to accept the lodging as a condition of employment.[42] Examples meeting these criteria would be lodging for employees on an oil rig, at a lumber camp, or on a ship at sea, or meals provided employees who work at a business location far from eating places.

**NEW LAW**

The exclusion amount under dependent care assistance increased to $10,500 ($5,250 for married filing separately).

- Payments under written dependent care assistance plans are tax-free.[43] The exclusion cannot exceed $10,500 ($5,250 for married filing separately) and cannot exceed earned income (earned income of the lesser-earning spouse for married filing jointly). Dependent care expenses are those that are considered to be employment-related expenses for purposes of the child care credit rules.
- Flexible benefit plans (often referred to as *cafeteria plans* or *flexible spending accounts*) are written plans that permit employees to choose their own benefits (which may include cash

[35] IRC § 132(d).
[36] IRC § 132(f).
[37] IRC § 132(e).
[38] IRC § 106(a).
[39] IRC § 127(a).
[40] IRC § 79(a).
[41] To determine the cost of the excess, see Reg. § 1.79-3(d)(2).
[42] IRC § 119(a).
[43] IRC § 129(a).

payments).[44] Normally the law provides that if a person has an opportunity to receive cash but elects to defer the payment or take payment in a noncash asset, income is still recognized. In the case of cafeteria plans (which by their very nature permit employees to choose), the value of the *benefits* received is not taxed to the employee. However, if employees elect to receive cash, the cash is taxable. The menu of options from which employees can choose often includes many of the fringe benefits discussed earlier (health care insurance, group life insurance, educational expenses, transportation fringe benefits, and the like). Under a cafeteria plan, the employee gets to choose the components that are most beneficial.

## Other Nontaxable Income

Taxpayers can receive certain nontaxable income not directly related to employment. This nontaxable income includes the following items.

### Scholarships and Fellowships

In general, scholarships and fellowships are tax-free.[45] The individual must be a degree-seeking student at an educational institution and must use the proceeds for qualified tuition and related expenses (tuition, fees, books, supplies, and equipment). If the scholarship or fellowship payment exceeds permitted expenses, the excess is taxable income. Benefits under tuition reduction plans provided to employees of educational institutions are not taxable. If a student must perform certain services for the educational institution (such as graduate assistantships), the amount paid for the services is not a scholarship or fellowship but is a taxable wage.

**EXAMPLE 3-12**   Hilda is a graduate student at State University. In 2021 she received a scholarship of $7,000 ($4,000 toward tuition and fees and $3,000 to pay for campus housing) and a graduate assistantship that paid $5,000. Tuition, fees, and books cost $6,000 during the year. Hilda can exclude $4,000 from income. She will be required to report wage income of $5,000 from the graduate assistantship and $3,000 of other income for the housing benefit.

### Qualified Tuition Program Withdrawals

A *Qualified Tuition Program (QTP)* is a state program that, in effect, is a tax-free savings account when used exclusively for educational expenses. Individuals make cash contributions to the QTP, and the state invests the contributions. If the contributor makes withdrawals from the QTP and uses the money to pay for qualified higher education expenses at an eligible educational institution, the withdrawal is tax-free. The term *qualified higher education expense* includes up to $10,000 in annual expenses for tuition in connection with enrollment or attendance at an elementary or secondary public, private, or religious school. For tax years 2009 through 2021, the definition of qualified higher education expenses includes the purchase of computer equipment or Internet access that will be used by the beneficiary while the beneficiary is enrolled at an eligible educational institution.[46] These programs are also called *529 plans* (from the IRC section that created them). We discuss these plans in more detail in Chapter 11.

### Life Insurance Proceeds

Life insurance proceeds, payable because of the death of the insured, are fully excludable from the gross income of the recipient.[47] If proceeds are paid over time (rather than as a lump sum), payments are tax-free except to the extent that the payments exceed the amount payable at the time of death (for example, if there are earnings on the proceeds). The proportion of each payment that is tax-free is the excludable amount divided by the expected number of payments.[48]

[44] IRC § 125(a).
[45] IRC § 117(a), (b).
[46] IRC § 529.
[47] IRC § 101(a)(1).
[48] IRC § 101(d)(1). If payments are made over the life of the recipient, the denominator is determined by reference to appropriate life expectancy tables. Changes are not made to the calculations even if the recipient exceeds the life expectancy.

---

**EXAMPLE 3-13**

Jamie is entitled to receive $50,000 of life insurance payable because of his wife's death. Instead of receiving a lump sum, he agreed to take five annual payments of $12,000 each. The excluded amount is $50,000/5 = $10,000 per payment. Thus, the remaining $2,000 of each payment is interest income.[49]

---

*Accelerated death benefits* are amounts received under a life insurance policy on the life of an individual who is terminally ill or chronically ill. Taxpayers can exclude such payments from gross income.[50] A person is *terminally ill* if a physician certifies that death is likely within 24 months. A *chronically ill* person has a disability requiring long-term care or substantial supervision.[51]

### Gifts and Inheritances

Gifts and inheritances are tax-free to the recipient.[52] *Gifts* are transfers made during the lifetime of the giver; *inheritances* are transfers of property at or after death. An individual can classify a transfer as a tax-free gift only if the giver was motivated by kindness, generosity, affection, or similar emotions.

---

**TAX YOUR BRAIN**

Norma was the 100,000th customer at her local grocery store. Because of that, the store gave Norma a free trip to Australia as a gift. Is the trip taxable or tax-free?

**ANSWER**

The trip to Australia is taxable. The owners did not give Norma the trip because they were motivated by kindness or generosity; they gave it to her for promotional reasons. The fair value of the trip is taxable to Norma.

---

Gifts may be subject to a gift tax that is the responsibility of the giver. Rules concerning gift taxes are beyond the scope of this text.

### Compensation for Sickness or Injury

The following items are exempt from income under the umbrella of compensation for injuries or sickness:[53]

- Payments received under workers' compensation acts.
- Damages (other than punitive damages) received as a result of personal physical injuries or sickness.
- Pensions or annuities received for personal injuries or sickness from active service in the armed forces, Coast Guard, public health service, or foreign service.
- Disability income resulting from a terrorist attack while in the employ of the United States engaged in official duties outside the United States.

### Other

Other nontaxable income includes:

- Child support (nontaxable to the recipient and not deductible by the payer).[54]
- Public assistance payments (such as welfare).
- Employer-provided adoption assistance up to $14,440 per child. In 2021, the amount excludable from an employee's gross income starts to phase out when modified Adjusted Gross Income is in excess of $216,660 and is eliminated when modified Adjusted Gross Income reaches $256,660. We discuss this topic in more detail in Chapter 9.

**NEW LAW**

Employer-provided adoption assistance increased to $14,440. This amount starts to phase out when AGI is in excess of $216,660 and is eliminated at $256,660.

---

[49] Generally, the taxpayer will receive a Form 1099-INT from the insurance company disclosing the amount of interest income.

[50] IRC § 101(g)(1).

[51] IRC § 101(g)(4).

[52] IRC § 102(a).

[53] IRC § 104(a).

[54] IRS Publication 504.

# From Shoebox to Software   Two Comprehensive Examples

We now introduce two new taxpayers.

## YIMING CHOW

The first taxpayer is Yiming Chow, who is single and lives at 456 Maple Avenue, Ashley, OH 43003. His SSN is 412-34-5670 and date of birth is 10/27/1989. During 2021 Mr. Chow received a W-2 from his employer, a 1099-INT from the local financial institution, and a 1099-DIV associated with a mutual fund investment. He also received a 1099-G from the state of Ohio for a $57 tax refund pertaining to tax year 2020. Mr. Chow did not itemize his deductions in 2020. All these documents are shown in Exhibit 3-8.

Open the tax software. Go to the File pull-down menu and click on New Return. Go through the process to start a new return, and then click on the Forms icon to bring up the list of available forms. Open a Form 1040 to input the basic name, address, and social security number information for Mr. Chow.

Now enter the information from the various tax forms into the tax software using the applicable forms in the Documents Received section. Note that you do not need to enter any information concerning the tax refund. Mr. Chow did not itemize deductions in 2020, so you do not need to report his tax refund as income.

Once you have entered the appropriate information, click on Form 1040. Line 11 should be $41,688. Line 15, taxable income, should be $29,138. Mr. Chow's tax liability on line 16 is $3,284. Because Mr. Chow has wage income and dividend income, you may find it instructive to calculate the tax liability by hand to see if you get the same answer. Because Mr. Chow had $3,750 withheld from his wages, his refund is $466, as shown on lines 34 and 35a. Mr. Chow had qualifying health care coverage at all times during the tax year.

Make sure you save Mr. Chow's return for use in later chapters.

## MR. AND MRS. RAMIREZ

The second taxpayer is the married couple Jose and Maria Ramirez. They live at 1234 West Street, Ellenwood, GA 30294. They have three children, Arturo, Benito, and Carmen, born in 2008, 2010, and 2012, respectively. The children lived in the household during the entire year. The

SSNs are listed along with the date of birth (in parentheses). The information is as follows:

Jose 412-34-5670 (2/10/1975), Maria 412-34-5671 (4/15/1980), Arturo 412-34-5672 (5/30/2008), Benito 412-34-5673 (8/7/2010), and Carmen 412-34-5674 (1/30/2012).

Mr. Ramirez received a W-2 from his employer, a 1099-INT from the financial institution, and a 1099-DIV from his stockbroker. He also received a 1099-G from the state of Georgia for a $645 tax refund. The taxpayer itemized deductions last year, and you have determined that the entire refund is taxable. All of the Ramirezes' documents are shown in Exhibit 3-9.

Open the tax software. Go to the File pull-down menu and click on New Return. Go through the process to start a new return, and then click on the Forms icon to bring up the list of available forms. Open a blank Form 1040 to input the basic name, address, and social security number information for Mr. and Mrs. Ramirez. Use the Dependent worksheet in the worksheet section to enter information for the children.

For now we will assume that the couple will take the standard deduction.

Now enter the information from the various tax forms into the tax software using the applicable forms in the Documents Received section.

Because you do not have tax return information for tax year 2020, you need to provide information concerning the tax refund. Enter in the system that the full amount of the refund is taxable.

Once you have entered the appropriate information, the total income and the AGI of the taxpayer should be $111,848. After subtracting a standard deduction of $25,100, taxable income should be $86,748.

The tax on line 16 should be $10,376. The tax software automatically calculated a $9,000 child tax credit on line 28. We will discuss this credit in Chapter 9. The credit reduces the Ramirezes' tax liability to $1,376. Because the taxpayer had withholding of $6,418, the Ramirezes' return should show a refund of $5,042 on lines 34 and 35a. Mr. and Mrs. Ramirez had qualifying health care coverage at all times during the tax year.

Make sure you save the Ramirezes' tax return for use in later chapters. These will be running demonstration problems throughout the text.

---

**CONCEPT CHECK 3-7—**

**LO 3-4**

1. Holiday turkeys given to employees are included in gross income. True or false?
2. In general, scholarships are not taxable if the use of the money is to pay tuition, fees, books, supplies, and equipment. True or false?

**EXHIBIT 3-8**

| | | | |
|---|---|---|---|
| | ☐ CORRECTED (if checked) | | |

| PAYER'S name, street address, city or town, state or province, country, ZIP or foreign postal code, and telephone no.<br><br>Jones Brokerage<br>P.O. Box 500<br>Ashley, OH 43003 | **1a** Total ordinary dividends<br>$ 96.71<br>**1b** Qualified dividends<br>$ 96.71 | OMB No. 1545-0110<br>2021<br>Form **1099-DIV** | **Dividends and Distributions** |

| | | **2a** Total capital gain distr.<br>$ | **2b** Unrecap. Sec. 1250 gain<br>$ | **Copy B**<br>**For Recipient** |
|---|---|---|---|---|
| PAYER'S TIN | RECIPIENT'S TIN | **2c** Section 1202 gain<br>$ | **2d** Collectibles (28%) gain<br>$ | |
| 56-4456789 | 412-34-5670 | **2e** Section 897 ordinary dividends<br>$ | **2f** Section 897 capital gain<br>$ | |

| RECIPIENT'S name<br><br>Yiming Chow | **3** Nondividend distributions<br>$ | **4** **Federal income tax withheld**<br>$ | This is important tax information and is being furnished to the IRS. If you are required to file a return, a negligence penalty or other sanction may be imposed on you if this income is taxable and the IRS determines that it has not been reported. |
|---|---|---|---|
| Street address (including apt. no.)<br><br>456 Maple Ave. | **5** Section 199A dividends<br>$ | **6** Investment expenses<br>$ | |
| City or town, state or province, country, and ZIP or foreign postal code<br><br>Ashley, OH 43003 | **7** Foreign tax paid<br>$ | **8** Foreign country or U.S. possession | |
| | **9** Cash liquidation distributions<br>$ | **10** Noncash liquidation distributions<br>$ | |
| FATCA filing requirement ☐ | **11** Exempt-interest dividends<br>$ | **12** Specified private activity bond interest dividends<br>$ | |

| Account number (see instructions) | **13** State | **14** State identification no. | **15** State tax withheld<br>$<br>$ |
|---|---|---|---|

Form **1099-DIV**   (keep for your records)   www.irs.gov/Form1099DIV   Department of the Treasury - Internal Revenue Service

---

| **a** Employee's social security number<br>412-34-5670 | OMB No. 1545-0008 | Safe, accurate, FAST! Use   IRS e~file | Visit the IRS website at www.irs.gov/efile |
|---|---|---|---|

| **b** Employer identification number (EIN) | **1** Wages, tips, other compensation<br>41,321.34 | **2** Federal income tax withheld<br>3,750.00 |
|---|---|---|
| **c** Employer's name, address, and ZIP code<br><br>Acme Company<br>900 Oak Street<br>Ashley, OH 43003 | **3** Social security wages<br>41,321.34 | **4** Social security tax withheld<br>2,651.92 |
| | **5** Medicare wages and tips<br>41,321.34 | **6** Medicare tax withheld<br>599.16 |
| | **7** Social security tips | **8** Allocated tips |
| **d** Control number | **9** | **10** Dependent care benefits |
| **e** Employee's first name and initial   Last name   Suff.<br><br>Yiming Chow<br>456 Maple Avenue<br>Ashley, OH 43003 | **11** Nonqualified plans | **12a** See instructions for box 12 |
| | **13** Statutory employee ☐  Retirement plan ☐  Third-party sick pay ☐ | **12b** |
| | **14** Other | **12c** |
| | | **12d** |
| **f** Employee's address and ZIP code | | |

| **15** State   Employer's state ID number<br>OH | **16** State wages, tips, etc.<br>41,321.34 | **17** State income tax<br>839.63 | **18** Local wages, tips, etc. | **19** Local income tax | **20** Locality name |
|---|---|---|---|---|---|

Form **W-2**   **Wage and Tax Statement**   2021   Department of the Treasury—Internal Revenue Service

**Copy B—To Be Filed With Employee's FEDERAL Tax Return.**
This information is being furnished to the Internal Revenue Service.

Source: U.S. Department of the Treasury, Internal Revenue Service, Forms 1099-DIV, W-2, 1099-G, and 1099-INT. Washington, DC: 2021.

**EXHIBIT 3-8**   *(concluded)*

☐ CORRECTED (if checked)

| PAYER'S name, street address, city or town, state or province, country, ZIP or foreign postal code, and telephone no.<br><br>**State of Ohio**<br>**P.O. Box 500**<br>**Columbus, OH 45555** | **1** Unemployment compensation<br>$ | OMB No. 1545-0120<br><br>20**21**<br>Form **1099-G** | **Certain Government Payments** |
|---|---|---|---|
| | **2** State or local income tax refunds, credits, or offsets<br>$        57.00 | | Copy B |

| PAYER'S TIN<br>**47-4450000** | RECIPIENT'S TIN<br>**412-34-5670** | **3** Box 2 amount is for tax year<br>**2020** | **4** Federal income tax withheld<br>$ | **Copy B**<br>**For Recipient** |
|---|---|---|---|---|
| RECIPIENT'S name<br><br>**Yiming Chow**<br>Street address (including apt. no.)<br><br>**456 Maple Avenue**<br>City or town, state or province, country, and ZIP or foreign postal code<br><br>**Ashley, OH 43003** | | **5** RTAA payments<br>$ | **6** Taxable grants<br>$ | This is important tax information and is being furnished to the IRS. If you are required to file a return, a negligence penalty or other sanction may be imposed on you if this income is taxable and the IRS determines that it has not been reported. |
| | | **7** Agriculture payments<br>$ | **8** If checked, box 2 is trade or business income ▶ ☐ | |
| | | **9** Market gain<br>$ | | |
| | | **10a** State | **10b** State identification no. | **11** State income tax withheld<br>$<br>$ |
| Account number (see instructions) | | | | |

Form **1099-G**   (keep for your records)   www.irs.gov/Form1099G   Department of the Treasury - Internal Revenue Service

☐ CORRECTED (if checked)

| PAYER'S name, street address, city or town, state or province, country, ZIP or foreign postal code, and telephone no.<br><br>**First National Bank**<br>**125 Main Street**<br>**Ashley, OH 43003** | Payer's RTN (optional) | OMB No. 1545-0112<br><br>20**21**<br>Form **1099-INT** | **Interest Income** |
|---|---|---|---|
| | **1** Interest income<br>$        270.12 | | Copy B |

| PAYER'S TIN<br>**46-6735241** | RECIPIENT'S TIN<br>**412-34-5670** | **2** Early withdrawal penalty<br>$ | **Copy B**<br>**For Recipient** |
|---|---|---|---|
| | | **3** Interest on U.S. Savings Bonds and Treas. obligations<br>$ | |
| RECIPIENT'S name<br><br>**Yiming Chow**<br>Street address (including apt. no.)<br><br>**456 Maple Avenue**<br>City or town, state or province, country, and ZIP or foreign postal code<br><br>**Ashley, OH 43003** | | **4** Federal income tax withheld<br>$ | **5** Investment expenses<br>$ | This is important tax information and is being furnished to the IRS. If you are required to file a return, a negligence penalty or other sanction may be imposed on you if this income is taxable and the IRS determines that it has not been reported. |
| | | **6** Foreign tax paid<br>$ | **7** Foreign country or U.S. possession |
| | | **8** Tax-exempt interest<br>$ | **9** Specified private activity bond interest<br>$ |
| | | **10** Market discount<br>$ | **11** Bond premium<br>$ |
| | FATCA filing requirement ☐ | **12** Bond premium on Treasury obligations<br>$ | **13** Bond premium on tax-exempt bond<br>$ |
| Account number (see instructions) | | **14** Tax-exempt and tax credit bond CUSIP no. | **15** State | **16** State identification no. | **17** State tax withheld<br>$<br>$ |

Form **1099-INT**   (keep for your records)   www.irs.gov/Form1099INT   Department of the Treasury - Internal Revenue Service

**EXHIBIT 3-9**

| | | |
|---|---|---|
| ☐ CORRECTED (if checked) | | |

**PAYER'S name, street address, city or town, state or province, country, ZIP or foreign postal code, and telephone no.**

First National Bank
1000 Main Street
Ellenwood, GA 30294

Payer's RTN (optional)

**1** Interest income
$ 3,150.00

OMB No. 1545-0112

2021

Form **1099-INT**

**Interest Income**

**2** Early withdrawal penalty
$

**Copy B**

**For Recipient**

| PAYER'S TIN | RECIPIENT'S TIN |
|---|---|
| 56-3455667 | 412-34-5670 |

**3** Interest on U.S. Savings Bonds and Treas. obligations
$

**RECIPIENT'S name**

Jose Ramirez

Street address (including apt. no.)

1234 West Street

City or town, state or province, country, and ZIP or foreign postal code

Ellenwood, GA 30294

**4** Federal income tax withheld
$

**5** Investment expenses
$

**6** Foreign tax paid
$

**7** Foreign country or U.S. possession

**8** Tax-exempt interest
$

**9** Specified private activity bond interest
$

**10** Market discount
$

**11** Bond premium
$

FATCA filing requirement ☐

**12** Bond premium on Treasury obligations
$

**13** Bond premium on tax-exempt bond
$

This is important tax information and is being furnished to the IRS. If you are required to file a return, a negligence penalty or other sanction may be imposed on you if this income is taxable and the IRS determines that it has not been reported.

Account number (see instructions)

**14** Tax-exempt and tax credit bond CUSIP no.

**15** State | **16** State identification no. | **17** State tax withheld
$
$

Form **1099-INT** (keep for your records) www.irs.gov/Form1099INT Department of the Treasury - Internal Revenue Service

---

| | | |
|---|---|---|
| ☐ CORRECTED (if checked) | | |

**PAYER'S name, street address, city or town, state or province, country, ZIP or foreign postal code, and telephone no.**

Smith Brokerage
P.O. Box 100
Ellenwood, GA 30294

**1a** Total ordinary dividends
$ 2,916.00

**1b** Qualified dividends
$ 2,916.00

OMB No. 1545-0110

2021

Form **1099-DIV**

**Dividends and Distributions**

**2a** Total capital gain distr.
$

**2b** Unrecap. Sec. 1250 gain
$

**Copy B**

**For Recipient**

| PAYER'S TIN | RECIPIENT'S TIN |
|---|---|
| 56-4456789 | 412-34-5670 |

**2c** Section 1202 gain
$

**2d** Collectibles (28%) gain
$

**2e** Section 897 ordinary dividends
$

**2f** Section 897 capital gain
$

**RECIPIENT'S name**

Jose Ramirez

Street address (including apt. no.)

1234 West Street

City or town, state or province, country, and ZIP or foreign postal code

Ellenwood, GA 30294

**3** Nondividend distributions
$

**4** Federal income tax withheld
$

**5** Section 199A dividends
$

**6** Investment expenses
$

**7** Foreign tax paid
$

**8** Foreign country or U.S. possession

**9** Cash liquidation distributions
$

**10** Noncash liquidation distributions
$

This is important tax information and is being furnished to the IRS. If you are required to file a return, a negligence penalty or other sanction may be imposed on you if this income is taxable and the IRS determines that it has not been reported.

FATCA filing requirement ☐

**11** Exempt-interest dividends
$

**12** Specified private activity bond interest dividends
$

Account number (see instructions)

**13** State | **14** State identification no. | **15** State tax withheld
$
$

Form **1099-DIV** (keep for your records) www.irs.gov/Form1099DIV Department of the Treasury - Internal Revenue Service

Source: U.S. Department of the Treasury, Internal Revenue Service, Forms 1099-INT, 1099-DIV, W-2, and 1099-G. Washington, DC: 2021.

**EXHIBIT 3-9**   *(concluded)*

| | | |
|---|---|---|
| **a** Employee's social security number<br>412-34-5670 | OMB No. 1545-0008 | Safe, accurate, FAST! Use   IRS e-file   Visit the IRS website at www.irs.gov/efile |

| | |
|---|---|
| **b** Employer identification number (EIN)<br>56-8876543 | **1** Wages, tips, other compensation  105,137.10    **2** Federal income tax withheld  6,418.32 |

| | |
|---|---|
| **c** Employer's name, address, and ZIP code<br><br>Beta Tech<br>500 Easy Street<br>Ellenwood, GA  30294 | **3** Social security wages  105,137.10    **4** Social security tax withheld  6,518.50 |
| | **5** Medicare wages and tips  105,137.10    **6** Medicare tax withheld  1,524.49 |
| | **7** Social security tips    **8** Allocated tips |

| | |
|---|---|
| **d** Control number | **9**    **10** Dependent care benefits |

| | |
|---|---|
| **e** Employee's first name and initial   Last name   Suff. | **11** Nonqualified plans    **12a** See instructions for box 12 |
| <br>Jose Ramirez<br>1234 West Street<br>Ellenwood, GA  30294 | **13** Statutory employee □   Retirement plan □   Third-party sick pay □    **12b** |
| | **14** Other    **12c** |
| | **12d** |

| **f** Employee's address and ZIP code |
|---|

| 15 State | Employer's state ID number | 16 State wages, tips, etc. | 17 State income tax | 18 Local wages, tips, etc. | 19 Local income tax | 20 Locality name |
|---|---|---|---|---|---|---|
| GA | | 105,137.10 | 2,469.52 | | | |

Form **W-2** **Wage and Tax Statement**    **2021**    Department of the Treasury—Internal Revenue Service

**Copy B—To Be Filed With Employee's FEDERAL Tax Return.**
This information is being furnished to the Internal Revenue Service.

---

☐ CORRECTED (if checked)

| PAYER'S name, street address, city or town, state or province, country, ZIP or foreign postal code, and telephone no.<br><br>State of Georgia<br>P.O. Box 400<br>Atlanta, GA  34567 | **1** Unemployment compensation<br>$ | OMB No. 1545-0120<br><br>2021<br><br>Form **1099-G** | **Certain Government Payments** |
|---|---|---|---|
| | **2** State or local income tax refunds, credits, or offsets<br>$   645.00 | | |
| PAYER'S TIN   41-3500000    RECIPIENT'S TIN   412-34-5670 | **3** Box 2 amount is for tax year<br>2020 | **4** Federal income tax withheld<br>$ | **Copy B**<br>**For Recipient** |
| RECIPIENT'S name<br><br>**Jose Ramirez**<br>Street address (including apt. no.)<br><br>**1234 West Street**<br>City or town, state or province, country, and ZIP or foreign postal code<br><br>**Ellenwood, GA  30294** | **5** RTAA payments<br>$ | **6** Taxable grants<br>$ | This is important tax information and is being furnished to the IRS. If you are required to file a return, a negligence penalty or other sanction may be imposed on you if this income is taxable and the IRS determines that it has not been reported. |
| | **7** Agriculture payments<br>$ | **8** If checked, box 2 is trade or business income ▶ ☐ | |
| | **9** Market gain<br>$ | | |
| Account number (see instructions) | **10a** State   **10b** State identification no. | **11** State income tax withheld<br>$<br>$ | |

Form **1099-G**    (keep for your records)    www.irs.gov/Form1099G    Department of the Treasury - Internal Revenue Service

## Appendix

# TAX ACCOUNTING FOR SAVINGS BOND INTEREST USED FOR EDUCATION EXPENSES, BELOW-MARKET INTEREST LOANS, GIFT LOANS, AND ORIGINAL ISSUE DISCOUNT DEBT
## LO 3-5

This Appendix covers topics pertaining to interest that are important but less common.

### Savings Bond Interest Exclusion

Interest on Series EE or Series I savings bonds is not taxable if the taxpayer uses the bond proceeds to pay qualified higher education expenses for the taxpayer, a spouse, or their dependent(s).[55] The bonds must have been purchased (not received by gift) after 1989 by an individual at least 24 years old at the time of purchase who is the sole owner of the bonds (or joint owner with a spouse). Qualified higher education expenses are tuition and fees at a qualified educational institution.[56] However, the taxpayer must reduce qualified expenses by tax-exempt scholarships, certain educational assistance allowances, certain benefits under a qualified state tuition program, and expenses used in determining Hope and lifetime learning credits or a Coverdell Education Savings Account distribution exclusion.[57] Married persons living together must file a joint return in the year of exclusion.

Taxpayers can exclude the full amount of interest subject to the phaseout amount only if the amount of qualified higher education expense paid in a year exceeds the redemption proceeds (principal plus interest) for the year. If proceeds exceed expenses, the amount of interest that is excludable is limited to the interest multiplied by a fraction calculated as qualified expenses paid during the year divided by aggregate redemption proceeds.

**EXAMPLE 3-14**

In 2021, Angeline and Albert redeemed $4,000 (principal of $3,000 and interest of $1,000) of Series I savings bonds to pay qualified higher education expenses. Qualified expenses for the year totaled $3,500. Angeline and Albert may exclude interest of $875 from income in 2021 [$1,000 × ($3,500/$4,000)]. The remaining $125 is taxable interest income.

 **NEW LAW**

The phaseout amounts for the savings bond interest exclusion have increased for 2021.

The amount of savings bond interest exempt from tax is further limited if the modified AGI of the taxpayer for tax year 2021 exceeds $124,800 on a joint return or $83,200 on other returns.[58] If modified AGI exceeds those limits, the amount of the reduction is equal to

$$\text{Amount otherwise excludable} \times \frac{\text{Modified AGI} - \text{Limitation amount}}{\$30,000\ (\$15,000\ \text{for single filers})}$$

When modified AGI reaches $154,800 for joint returns and $98,200 for other returns, the amount of exempt interest phases out. Taxpayers calculate the modified AGI limitation after all other limitations.

[55] IRC § 135(a).
[56] IRC § 529(e)(5).
[57] IRC § 135(c)(2), (d).
[58] These amounts are subject to annual adjustment for inflation.

**EXAMPLE 3-15**

Olga, a single taxpayer, has determined that her excludable savings bond interest is $1,400 prior to any modified AGI limitation. Her modified AGI is $84,000. Olga will be able to exclude $1,325 of savings bond interest on her 2021 tax return, calculated as follows: $1,400 × [($84,000 − $83,200)/$15,000] = reduction amount of $75. Thus the excludable savings bond interest will be $1,400 − $75 = $1,325. Olga must report savings bond interest of $75 on her 2021 tax return.

Modified AGI is AGI adjusted as follows:

Adjusted Gross Income

Plus: Deduction for student loan interest[59]

Deduction for tuition and fees (Tax Extenders Act of 2008)

The savings bond interest exclusion itself[60]

Excluded foreign income and allowances[61]

Excluded adoption assistance from an employer[62]

**EXAMPLE 3-16**

Virginia has AGI of $41,000 that includes a student loan interest deduction of $800. Her modified AGI for purposes of the savings bond interest exclusion is $41,800.

## Below-Market Interest Rate Loans

Most interest-bearing instruments carry an interest rate that approximates the market rate of interest for instruments of similar maturity, credit risk, and collateral. For example, if two persons of equal loan-paying ability and credit rating obtain a loan at a financial institution to finance the purchase of a Ford F-150 on a four-year repayment schedule, the interest rates on the two loans should be approximately equal.

In some circumstances, one party in a transaction wishes to charge a low rate of interest rather than a market rate.[63] Assume that an individual is selling a parcel of land for $100,000 and will accept $10,000 down with annual interest-only payments on the balance at an interest rate of 10% with principal due at the end of five years. Total payments would be $100,000 in principal and $45,000 of interest. Because interest income is taxable at a rate up to 37% and capital gains are generally taxed at 15% unless the taxpayer's taxable income is over $445,850, it would be beneficial to the seller if the price were raised to, say, $130,000 while lowering the interest rate to 2.5%. Total payments will still be $145,000 ($130,000 principal and $15,000 interest), but the seller will have, in effect, converted $30,000 of interest income into capital gain income, thereby saving almost $6,600 in tax.[64]

The law limits the ability of taxpayers to create debt instruments with interest rates that materially vary from market rates on the date the instrument is created.[65] Taxpayers are required to "impute interest" on a deferred payment contract for which no interest, or a low rate of interest, is stated. Imputing interest reallocates payments so that more of each payment is interest and less is principal. The imputed interest rules apply to installment transactions that are due more than six months after the date of the sale or exchange of property.

[59] Under IRC § 221.
[60] Under IRC § 135.
[61] Under IRC § 911, § 931, § 933.
[62] Under § 137.
[63] Charging above-market rates is also possible but less likely.
[64] The $30,000 difference is taxed at 15% rather than 37%, so the taxpayer will save 22%, or $6,600.
[65] IRC § 483, § 1274.

An installment obligation arises when a taxpayer sells property and does not receive the entire sales price at the time of sale. The imputed interest rules apply when the gross payments due under an installment contract are greater than the present value of the payments due under the contract, discounted at the applicable federal rate (AFR).[66] In effect, installment contracts with stated interest rates below the AFR will result in the imposition of the imputed interest rules. The AFR is determined monthly, varies with the term of the loan (short-, mid-, or long-term), and is based on the rate paid by the federal government on borrowed funds.

**EXAMPLE 3-17**

In 2021 Lloyd sells land for $40,000, payable with $5,000 down, and the balance in five equal annual installments of $7,642, which include interest at 3%. Lloyd's basis in the land is $30,000. The AFR at the time of sale is 8%. The present value (PV) of the five annual payments discounted at 8% is $30,512. Thus, the sales price is $35,512 (the PV of the payments plus the down payment), and Lloyd's capital gain is $5,512.

Here is the amortization schedule:

| Year | Payment | Principal | Interest | Balance |
|------|---------|-----------|----------|---------|
|      |         |           |          | $30,512 |
| 2021 | $7,642  | $5,201    | $2,441   | 25,311  |
| 2022 | 7,642   | 5,617     | 2,025    | 19,694  |
| 2023 | 7,642   | 6,067     | 1,575    | 13,627  |
| 2024 | 7,642   | 6,552     | 1,090    | 7,075   |
| 2025 | 7,642   | 7,075     | 567      | –0–     |

The preceding calculations illustrate that Lloyd will have a capital gain of $5,512 and interest income of $7,698 rather than a capital gain of $10,000 and $3,210 of interest income.

The imputed interest rules do not apply to the following:[67]

- Debt subject to the original issue discount rules (see the following).
- Sales of property for $3,000 or less.
- Certain carrying charges.[68]
- Sales in which all payments are due in six months or less.
- In the case of sales of patents, any portion of the sales price that is contingent on the productivity, use, or disposition of the patent.

Taxpayers use the accrual basis to calculate imputed interest (even if the taxpayer reports on the cash basis) except in the following instances when cash basis reporting is permitted:[69]

- Sale of a personal residence.
- Sales of farms for $1 million or less.
- Sales in which total payments are $250,000 or less.
- Certain land transfers between related parties.[70]
- Debt in which the stated principal is $2 million or less and the lender and borrower elect to use the cash method (not applicable to accrual method lenders or dealers).

[66] The imputed interest rules in question are in IRC § 483(b). The AFR is determined under IRC § 1274(d).
[67] IRC § 483(d).
[68] Covered in IRC § 163(b).
[69] IRC § 1274(c)(3), § 1274A(c).
[70] Described in IRC § 483(e).

## Gift, Shareholder, and Similar Loans

The concepts associated with imputed interest rules also apply to certain low-interest or interest-free loans involving related parties.[71] Imputed interest rules apply to term loans or demand loans in which the interest rate is less than the AFR and that occur in the following situations:

- Gift loans over $15,000 in which interest forgone is in the form of a gift. An example of a gift loan is a loan from a parent to a child in which no interest rate is stated. The $15,000 limit does not apply if the loan is for acquisition of income-producing assets.[72] However, imputed interest is limited to net investment income if the loan amount is $100,000 or less. No interest imputation is necessary if net investment income is less than $1,000.
- Compensation-related loans over $10,000 between employees and employers or between independent contractors and the corporations for which they work or any shareholder thereof.
- Loans over $10,000 between a corporation and any shareholder.
- Other loans in which the principal purpose is to avoid tax.
- Other loans in which the below-market or interest-free loan would have a significant effect on the tax liability of the borrower or lender.

**EXAMPLE 3-18**

Marty made interest-free loans to his three brothers, Pete, Bob, and Bill, of $8,000, $30,000, and $150,000, respectively. Pete used his $8,000 to buy a boat; Bob purchased IBM bonds with his $30,000 and earned $1,500 of investment income; and Bill bought a personal residence with his $150,000. The imputed interest rules would not apply to Pete because the loan is less than $10,000. The loans to Bob and Bill fall under the imputed interest rules because Bob purchased income-producing property (the interest expense would be limited to the $1,500 of net investment income) and Bill's loan was over $100,000.

Imputed interest is determined in a manner similar to that outlined earlier. The lender is deemed to give the borrower the amount of the calculated imputed interest, which the borrower then repays to the lender. Thus, the transaction results in taxable interest income to the lender and interest expense to the borrower (which may or may not be deductible). For loans between an employer and employee, the deemed payment from the lender to the borrower creates compensation income to the employee. Similarly, deemed payments on loans between a corporation and a shareholder create dividend income to the shareholder.

## Original Issue Discount

If someone purchases a debt instrument (such as a bond) from an issuer for an amount less than par, the transaction creates OID. The initial OID is equal to the difference between the acquisition price and the maturity value.[73]

**EXAMPLE 3-19**

On January 1, 2021, Leonardo purchased $200,000 of Meno Corporation's newly issued bonds for $176,100, to yield 11%. The bonds carry an interest rate of 9% and mature in 10 years. The initial OID on these bonds is $23,900 (the $200,000 face amount less the $176,100 payment).

OID is deemed to be zero if it is less than 0.25% of the maturity value, multiplied by the number of complete years to maturity.[74] In Example 3-19, this *de minimis* threshold is $5,000

[71] IRC § 7872.

[72] In the case of gift loans between individuals that total $100,000 or less, the amount of imputed interest is limited to the borrower's net investment income.

[73] IRC § 1273(a)(1).

[74] IRC § 1273(a)(3).

(0.0025 × 10 years × $200,000). Thus, if Leonardo purchased the bonds for any amount more than $195,000, no OID is recognized.

If OID exists, the holder must include part of the OID in interest income every year, regardless of the holder's method of accounting (that is, the holder accounts for the income under the accrual method).[75] The taxpayer calculates the imputed interest using the constant interest rate method (sometimes referred to as the *effective interest method* that you probably learned in your financial accounting class). In this method, total interest income is equal to the carrying amount (basis) of the bond multiplied by the effective interest rate (the yield to maturity on the date of purchase). The amount of OID is the difference between interest income as calculated using the effective interest method and the amount of cash received. The carrying amount of the bond increases by the amount of OID.

---

**EXAMPLE 3-20**

Using the information from Example 3-19, we see that the effective interest calculations for the first four bond payments are as follows (remember that bond interest is paid semiannually):

| Payment Date | (1)<br>Interest Income | (2)<br>Cash Received | (3)<br>OID | (4)<br>Carrying Amount |
|---|---|---|---|---|
| | | | | $176,100 |
| June 30, 2021 | $9,686 | $9,000 | $686 | 176,786 |
| Dec. 31, 2021 | 9,723 | 9,000 | 723 | 177,509 |
| June 30, 2022 | 9,763 | 9,000 | 763 | 178,272 |
| Dec. 31, 2022 | 9,805 | 9,000 | 805 | 179,077 |

Column (1) is the prior balance in column (4) times 11% divided by 2.
Column (2) is the $200,000 face amount multiplied by the 9% face rate divided by 2.
Column (3) is column (1) minus column (2).
Column (4) is the prior balance in column (4) plus the OID amount in column (3).

---

In 2021 Leonardo would report interest income of $19,409 ($9,686 + $9,723). Leonardo's interest income in 2022 would be $19,568.

OID rules apply to all debt instruments with OID except for[76]

- Tax-exempt debt.
- U.S. savings bonds.
- Debt with a maturity of one year or less on the date of issue.
- Any obligation issued by a natural person before March 2, 1984.
- Nonbusiness loans of $10,000 or less between natural persons.

An individual who sells a debt instrument with OID prior to maturity calculates OID on a daily basis until the date of sale.

The OID rules stated earlier apply to the original purchaser only. The Revenue Reconciliation Act of 1993 extended many of the provisions of the OID rules to market discount bonds,[77] which are bonds purchased in the bond market at a discount. The market discount is the difference between the redemption price (normally par) and the basis (cost) of the bond immediately after purchase.[78] The *de minimis* rule for OID also applies to market discount bonds.

With OID instruments, taxpayers report a portion of the OID as interest income annually. Such is not the case with market discount bonds. Rather, the gain on disposition of the bond, if any, is ordinary income to the extent of the accrued market discount (determined ratably on

[75] IRC § 1272(a)(1).
[76] IRC § 1272(a)(2).
[77] IRC § 1278.
[78] IRC § 1278(a)(2)(A).

a straight-line method computed on a daily basis). If a person holds the bond to maturity, the entire market discount amount is ordinary income.

---

**EXAMPLE 3-21**

Yvonne purchased $100,000 of the seven-year bonds of Ruby Company on July 1, 2021, for $90,000. The bonds were originally issued on January 1, 2019 (so at the time of purchase they had a remaining maturity of 4½ years). One year later, Yvonne sold the bonds for $96,000. Without the market discount bond rules, Yvonne would recognize a capital gain of $6,000. However, her capital gain is reduced (and her ordinary income is increased) by a portion of the market discount. Yvonne spreads the $10,000 discount over the maturity period (as of the date of purchase) on a straight-line basis, resulting in an allocation of $2,222 per year ($10,000/4.5). Thus, Yvonne will recognize a capital gain of $3,778 and ordinary income of $2,222.

---

**CONCEPT
CHECK 3-8—
LO 3-5**

1. An individual is required to impute interest on a deferred payment contract where no interest, or a low rate of interest, is stated. True or false?
2. If someone purchases a debt instrument (such as a bond) from an issuer for an amount less than par value, the transaction creates OID. True or false?

---

# Summary

**LO 3-1:** Describe when and how to record income for tax purposes.

- Recognition of income for accounting takes place when the income has been realized and earned.
- Recognition of income for tax purposes is similar to the recognition of income for accounting, but three additional conditions must be met: the transaction has an economic benefit, the transaction has been concluded, and the income derived from the transaction must not be tax-exempt income.

**LO 3-2:** Apply the cash method of accounting to income taxes.

- Almost all individuals use the cash receipts and disbursements method of accounting for taxes.
- Rather than report income in the year in which income is earned, an individual reports income in the year income is received or constructively received.
- Receipt of property or services will trigger income recognition.
- Special situations exist in which cash basis taxpayers can report income as though they were accrual basis taxpayers.

**LO 3-3:** Explain the taxability of components of gross income, including interest, dividends, tax refunds, and social security benefits.

- If the amount of interest income is over $1,500, use Schedule B.
- Interest from banks, savings and loans, or credit unions is reported on Form 1099-INT and is taxable.
- Interest earned on Series E, EE, and I U.S. savings bonds can be reported gradually on an annual basis or fully at maturity.
- Some interest received is tax-exempt if the debt is issued by a U.S. state, possession, or subdivision thereof (such as municipal bonds).
- Other sources of interest that must be reported: payments received from seller-financed mortgages, receipts from installment sale receivables, imputed interest on loans made with below-market interest rates, and interest on bonds sold between interest dates.
- If the amount of dividend income is over $1,500, use Schedule B.
- Dividends are distributions to shareholders.
- Dividends are taxed at capital gain rates if they are qualified dividends.
- Stock dividends and stock splits are generally not taxable.
- State and local tax refunds are taxable if, in the prior tax year, the tax was deducted as an itemized deduction.
- Unemployment compensation is taxable.
- Part of social security benefits may be taxable. Provisional income must be calculated and compared to the information on the chart (see the text) showing the thresholds and taxability.
- Other income to be reported on the tax return: jury duty pay, prizes and awards, forgiveness of debt, and insurance proceeds in excess of the adjusted basis of the property.

**LO 3-4:** Apply the rules concerning items excluded from gross income.

- Congress has exempted certain income from tax by statute.
- Fringe benefits must be subject to nondiscrimination rules by the employer to qualify.
- Examples of fringe benefits not taxable in most circumstances: no-additional-cost services provided to an employee, discounts provided to employees for products or services normally sold by the business, a working condition fringe benefit, qualified transportation, and *de minimis* benefits.
- Nontaxable fringe benefits with certain limitations: life insurance, educational assistance, dependent care assistance, and cafeteria plans offered to employees.
- Other nontaxable income includes scholarships and fellowships, qualified tuition program (QTP) withdrawals, life insurance proceeds, gifts and inheritances, compensation for sickness or injury, child support, welfare, and employer-provided adoption assistance.

**LO 3-5:** Apply the rules associated with tax accounting for savings bond interest used for education expenses, below-market interest loans, gift loans, and original issue discount debt (Appendix).

- Savings bond interest exclusion can be taken for the full amount if the amount of qualified higher education expense paid in a year exceeds the redemption proceeds (principal plus interest).
- Limitation applies if modified AGI exceeds $124,800 on a joint return or $83,200 on other returns.
- Taxpayers are required to impute interest on a deferred payment contract if no interest, or a low rate of interest, is stated. Certain exceptions apply.
- Original issue discount (OID) is equal to the difference between the acquisition price and the maturity value.
- If OID exists, the holder must report part of the OID as income every year.

---

## *EA Fast Fact*

ADMITTED TO PRACTICE BEFORE THE IRS **ENROLLED AGENT**

Enrolled Agents are often considered America's Tax Experts. They are federally certified tax practitioners who specialize in tax preparation and have unlimited rights to represent taxpayers before the Internal Revenue Service, just as CPAs and attorneys have. If a taxpayer receives a notice letter from the IRS, are audited, or are the target of a collection action, an Enrolled Agent can speak directly to the IRS on behalf of the taxpayer to assist in resolving the issue.

**IMPORTANT**

You are eligible to receive absolutely free, the Surgent Enrolled Agent review program for Part I of the EA exam as a result of purchasing this text. To activate your free access, go to https://Surgent.com/McGrawHill/EA.

---

## Discussion Questions

All applicable Discussion Questions are available with **Connect**©

**EA**    LO 3-2    1. Explain how income is recognized under the cash method of accounting.

_____

_____

_____

_____

**EA**    LO 3-2    2. Are there circumstances in which income is recognized even when a cash basis taxpayer does not receive cash? Explain.

_____

_____

_____

_____

**EA**    LO 3-2    3. What is meant by the concept of *constructive receipt*?

_____

_____

_____

_____

**EA**    LO 3-2    4. Refer to Example 3-4 in the chapter. Explain why Antonio is required to report income even though he did not receive an asset (either cash or property).

_____

_____

_____

_____

**EA**    LO 3-3    5. Your friend John files his own tax returns. He received a computer as a dividend from a closely held corporation. He says that he does not need to report the computer as dividend income because the dividend was not paid in cash. Is he right? Why?

_____

_____

_____

_____

**EA**    LO 3-3    6. Interest on corporate bonds is taxable to the recipient, whereas interest on municipal bonds is tax-free. Would you expect that the interest rate on a corporate bond would be higher or lower than the rate on a municipal bond of comparable quality and term? Why?

_____

_____

_____

_____

LO 3-3    7. What is a *dividend*?

_____

_____

_____

_____

**EA**    LO 3-3    8. How are dividends taxed?

_____

_____

_____

_____

**EA** **LO 3-3** 9. Sam owns all of the stock in a newly formed corporation. During 2021, the first year of operation, the corporation realized current earnings and profits of $10,000. Sam received a $12,000 distribution from the corporation. How much, if any, of the distribution is taxable to Sam? Why?

_____

_____

_____

_____

**EA** **LO 3-3** 10. Under what circumstances is a dividend nontaxable to a shareholder recipient?

_____

_____

_____

**EA** **LO 3-3** 11. How do *dividends* and *earnings and profits* relate to each other?

_____

_____

_____

**EA** **LO 3-3** 12. Under what circumstances is a state or local income tax refund included in the taxable income of a taxpayer?

_____

_____

_____

_____

**EA** **LO 3-3** 13. Under what circumstances are social security benefits taxable to a single taxpayer?

_____

_____

_____

_____

**EA** **LO 3-3** 14. When determining the taxability of social security benefits, the IRC uses the concept of *provisional income.* How is provisional income calculated?

_____

_____

_____

_____

**EA** **LO 3-4** 15. Congress has chosen to exempt certain income from taxation, such as scholarships, gifts, life insurance proceeds, municipal bond interest, and employee fringe benefits. Given that one of the primary purposes of the IRC is to raise revenue for the government, why do you think Congress would provide these and other exemptions?

_____

_____

_____

_____

EA    LO 3-4    16. What is an employer-provided fringe benefit?

EA    LO 3-4    17. Define and give examples of a *de minimis* employee fringe benefit.

EA    LO 3-4    18. Explain the requirements necessary for a scholarship to be tax-free to the recipient.

## Multiple-Choice Questions    Mc Graw Hill **connect**

All applicable multiple-choice questions are available with **Connect**©

EA    LO 3-1    19. Accountants recognize revenue when it is both realized and
  *a.* Recorded.
  *b.* Earned.
  *c.* Collected.
  *d.* Accumulated.

EA    LO 3-1    20. For tax purposes, one of the requirements to recognize income is that
  *a.* There must be an economic benefit.
  *b.* The income must be tax-exempt.
  *c.* The transaction must occur, but completion of the transaction is not necessary.
  *d.* There must be a cash transaction.

EA    LO 3-2    21. Income may be realized in the form of
  *a.* Money or services.
  *b.* Only money.
  *c.* Money, services, or property.
  *d.* None of the above.

EA    LO 3-2    22. When filing their tax returns, almost all individuals use
  *a.* The hybrid method.
  *b.* The accrual method.
  *c.* The recognition method.
  *d.* The cash receipts and disbursements method.

**EA** LO 3-3 23. An individual must complete Schedule B if the following situation occurs
 *a.* Receives interest income over $1,500.
 *b.* Receives child support payments of $1,650.
 *c.* Receives qualified dividends of $1,050.
 *d.* Receives interest income of $1,450.

**EA** LO 3-3 24. The basis of the property received as a dividend by a shareholder of a corporation is
 *a.* The book value at the date of distribution.
 *b.* The original cost at the date of purchase.
 *c.* The accounting value at the date of distribution.
 *d.* The fair market value at the date of distribution.

**EA** LO 3-3 25. When an individual who is single has taxable income of $60,000, the tax rate on qualified dividends is
 *a.* 0%.
 *b.* 25%.
 *c.* 15%.
 *d.* 5%.

**EA** LO 3-3 26. Graciela, who is single, reported itemized deductions of $12,500 on her 2020 tax return. Her itemized deductions included $200 of state taxes paid. In 2021, she received a $150 refund of state taxes paid in 2020. What is the amount that Graciela needs to report on her 2021 tax return? Use the Internet (www.irs.gov) to find out how much the standard deduction was for 2020.
 *a.* $200.
 *b.* $100.
 *c.* $0.
 *d.* She needs to amend her 2020 tax return.

**EA** LO 3-3 27. For purposes of determining taxability of social security benefits, provisional income is calculated by starting with AGI before social security benefits and adding back specific items. One of these items is
 *a.* Employer-provided adoption benefits.
 *b.* Taxable interest income.
 *c.* Wages earned.
 *d.* Qualified dividends.

**EA** LO 3-3 28. Frank, who is single, received $7,000 of social security benefits. His AGI before the social security benefits was $15,750. He also had $100 of tax-exempt interest. What is the amount of taxable social security benefits?
 *a.* $19,350.
 *b.* $7,000.
 *c.* $0.
 *d.* $3,500.

**EA** LO 3-3 29. Items that must be reported on line 8 (other income) of Schedule 1 include
 *a.* Dividend income.
 *b.* Capital gains.
 *c.* Interest income.
 *d.* Jury duty pay.

**EA** **LO 3-4** 30. Which of the following fringe benefits provided by the employer is *not* taxable to the employee?

    *a.* Sick pay.

    *b.* Vacation pay.

    *c.* 10% discount on products sold by the business; the gross profit percentage for the business is 20%.

    *d.* Bonus.

**EA** **LO 3-4** 31. Payments to employees under written dependent care assistance plans are tax-free. The exclusion cannot exceed the earned income of the lesser-earning spouse and cannot exceed _____ for an individual filing as married filing jointly.

    *a.* $5,250.

    *b.* $10,500.

    *c.* $5,150.

    *d.* $5,000.

**EA** **LO 3-4** 32. Employers can pay (or reimburse) employees for up to _____ per year of educational assistance, whether or not the education is job-related.

    *a.* $5,250.

    *b.* $5,150.

    *c.* $5,000.

    *d.* $2,500.

**EA** **LO 3-4** 33. An example of nontaxable income is

    *a.* Wages.

    *b.* Dividend income.

    *c.* Interest income.

    *d.* Child support payment.

## Problems   Mc Graw Hill **connect**

All applicable problems are available with **Connect**

**EA** **LO 3-1** 34. In 2016 Anna borrowed $10,000. In 2021 the debt was forgiven. Anna does not believe she should report the forgiveness of debt as income because she received nothing at the time the debt was forgiven in 2021. Do you agree or disagree? Support your position.

**EA** **LO 3-2** 35. Determine the amount of taxable income that should be reported by a cash basis taxpayer in 2021 in each of the following independent cases:

    *a.* A taxpayer completes $500 of accounting services in December 2021 for a client who pays for the accounting work in January 2022.

    *b.* A taxpayer is in the business of renting computers on a short-term basis. On December 1, 2021, she rents a computer for a $200 rental fee and receives a $500 deposit. The customer returns the computer and is refunded the deposit on December 20, 2021.

c. Same facts as (b) except that the computer is returned on January 5, 2022.

_____

d. On December 18, 2021, a landlord rents an apartment for $700 per month and collects the first and last months' rents up front. It is customary that tenants apply the security deposit to their last month's rent upon moving out.

_____

e. An accountant agrees to perform $500 of tax services for an auto mechanic who has agreed to perform repairs on the car of the accountant's wife. The mechanic repairs the car in December 2021 and the accountant starts and completes the tax work in March 2022.

_____

**EA**  **LO 3-3**  36. A taxpayer who purchases a Series EE U.S. savings bond must report the interest income (i.e., increase in value) on the bond on the date the bond is redeemed, or the taxpayer can elect to report the interest currently in income. Under what circumstances should a taxpayer report income at maturity? Under what circumstances is it more advantageous to report income currently?

_____

_____

_____

_____

**EA**  **LO 3-3**  37. Nancy, who is 59 years old, is the beneficiary of a $200,000 life insurance policy. What amount of the insurance proceeds is taxable under each of the following scenarios?

a. She receives the $200,000 proceeds as a lump-sum payment.

_____

b. She receives the proceeds at the rate of $4,000 a month for five years.

_____

c. She receives the proceeds in monthly payments of $1,300 over her remaining life expectancy (assume she will live 25 years).

_____

d. Use the information from (c). If Nancy lives beyond her 25-year life expectancy, what amount of each monthly payment will be taxable in the 26th year?

_____

**EA**  **LO 3-3**  38. Determine the amount of tax liability in the following situations. In all cases, the taxpayer is using the filing status of married filing jointly.

a. Taxable income of $62,449 that includes a qualified dividend of $560.

_____

b. Taxable income of $12,932 that includes a qualified dividend of $322.

_____

c. Taxable income of $144,290 that includes a qualified dividend of $4,384.

_____

d. Taxable income of $43,297 that includes a qualified dividend of $971.

_____

e. Taxable income of $262,403 that includes a qualified dividend of $12,396.

_____

**EA**  LO 3-3  39. Each of the following taxpayers received a state income tax refund in 2021. In all cases, the taxpayer has a filing status of married filing jointly. What amount of the refund is properly included in 2021 income?

   *a.* Refund of $729; taxpayer did not itemize deductions in 2020.

   _____

   *b.* Refund of $591; taxpayer had $25,391 of itemized deductions in 2020.

   _____

   *c.* Refund of $927; taxpayer had itemized deductions of $25,100 in 2020.

   _____

**EA**  LO 3-3  40. A married couple received $10,000 of social security benefits. Calculate the taxable amount of those benefits if the couple's provisional income is (a) $20,000, (b) $41,000, and (c) $63,000.

   _____

   _____

   _____

**EA**  LO 3-3  41. Carl and Karina file a joint return. Karina earned a salary of $38,000 and received dividends of $3,000, taxable interest income of $2,000, and nontaxable interest of $1,000. Carl received $9,000 of social security benefits and a gift of $6,000 from his brother. What amount of social security benefits is taxable to Carl and Karina?

   _____

   _____

   _____

   _____

**EA**  LO 3-3  42. Sean, who is single, received social security benefits of $8,000, dividend income of $13,000, and interest income of $2,000. Except as noted, those income items are reasonably consistent from year to year. At the end of 2021, Sean is considering selling stock that would result in an immediate gain of $10,000, a reduction in future dividends of $1,000, and an increase in future interest income of $1,500. He has asked you for advice. What course of action do you recommend?

   _____

   _____

   _____

   _____

**EA**  LO 3-4  43. Burger Store is located near many large office buildings, so at lunch it is extremely busy. Burger Store management previously permitted lunchtime employees a half-hour off-premises lunch break. However, employees could not easily return in a timely manner. Thus, a new policy was instituted to allow employees a 20-minute break for free lunch (only on the Burger Store premises). The company's accountant believes that the cost of these meals must be allocated to employees as additional compensation because the meals do not qualify as a nontaxable fringe benefit for employee discounts. In your opinion, should the cost of these meals be taxable or tax-free to employees? Support your answer.

   _____

   _____

   _____

   _____

## Discussion Questions Pertaining to Appendix (LO 3-5)

EA 44. Explain the rules governing the exemption of interest on U.S. savings bonds from taxation if it is used for educational purposes.

_____

_____

_____

_____

EA 45. Define *imputed interest.*

_____

_____

_____

_____

EA 46. Why were the interest imputation rules created?

_____

_____

_____

_____

EA 47. Briefly explain the application of the imputed interest rules.

_____

_____

_____

_____

EA 48. The interest imputation rules indirectly use a market rate of interest. What is meant by a *market rate of interest*?

_____

_____

_____

_____

EA 49. Define *original issue discount* (OID). Under what circumstances are the OID rules applied?

_____

_____

_____

_____

EA 50. Concerning the exemption for U.S. savings bond interest used for education expenses, what are the lower and upper income limitations for married taxpayers, and how is the exemption determined when taxpayer income falls between the limitation amounts?

_____

_____

_____

_____

EA 51. On July 1, 2021, Rene, a cash basis taxpayer, purchased $500,000 of the newly issued bonds of Acce Corporation for $452,260. The 10-year bonds carry an interest rate of 8% and were sold to yield 9.5%. What amount of interest income must Rene report in 2021, 2022, and 2023?

_____

_____

_____

_____

**EA**  52. In 2021, Joseph and Patricia Jefferson redeemed $8,000 of Series EE U.S. savings bonds (principal of $5,500 and interest of $2,500), the proceeds from which were used to pay for qualified higher education expenses of their dependent daughter who is attending a qualified educational institution. For the year, tuition and fees were $8,000 and room and board cost $7,000. The daughter received a $2,000 tax-exempt scholarship during the year that was used to pay tuition and fees. The Jeffersons' modified AGI was $96,000 in 2021. They do not participate in any other higher education–related programs. Calculate the amount of savings bond interest that the Jeffersons can exclude from gross income in 2021.

_____

_____

_____

_____

**EA**  53. Daniel and Alexis, both 28, are interested in saving for the college education of their twin daughters Alie and Amber. They decide to purchase some Series EE U.S. savings bonds because they know that the interest on the bonds is tax-free in certain circumstances. To easily keep track of the savings for each child, they purchase half of the bonds in the names of Daniel and Alie and the other half in the names of Daniel and Amber. Assuming that current tax law does not change, under what circumstances will Daniel and Alexis be permitted to exclude interest on redemption of these bonds?

_____

_____

_____

_____

**EA**  54. A person is selling some property and wishes to obtain payment partially in cash with the remainder in the form of a carryback note receivable.

   *a.* Why might the seller wish to increase the sales price and reduce the interest rate on the carryback note? Assume that the cash down payment and the total amount of payments will not change.

_____

_____

   *b.* Would the buyer likely agree to the increased price and decreased interest rate? Why or why not?

_____

_____

_____

## Multiple-Choice Questions Pertaining to the Appendix (LO 3-5)  **connect**

All applicable multiple-choice questions are available with **Connect**

**EA**  55. The amount of savings bond interest exempt from tax is limited when an individual is single and their AGI reaches
   *a.* $124,800.
   *b.* $83,200.
   *c.* $98,200.
   *d.* $96,100.

EA 56. Original issue discount (OID) is deemed to be zero if it is less than _____ of the maturity value, multiplied by the number of complete years to maturity.

    *a.* 25%.

    *b.* 5%.

    *c.* 0.25%.

    *d.* 15%.

EA 57. An individual with an OID instrument must annually report a portion of the OID as

    *a.* Dividend income.

    *b.* Pension income.

    *c.* Capital gain income.

    *d.* Interest income.

## Tax Return Problems  connect

All applicable tax return problems are available with **Connect**©

Use your tax software to complete the following problems. If you are manually preparing the tax returns, you will need to use a Form 1040.

For the following tax return problems, assume the taxpayer does not wish to contribute to the Presidential Election Fund, unless otherwise stated in the problem. In addition, the taxpayers did not receive, sell, send, exchange, or otherwise acquire any financial interest in any virtual currency during the year. For any Tax Return Problems for which the taxpayers are entitled to a child tax credit, assume that the taxpayers did NOT receive any advance child tax credit payments during 2021. Thus, the entire child tax credit (if permitted) will be claimed on the 2021 tax return.

**Tax Return Problem 1** John and Martha Holloway are married filing jointly. They are 35 and 31 years old, respectively. Their address is 10010 Dove Street, Atlanta, GA 30294. Additional information about Mr. and Mrs. Holloway is as follows:

Social security numbers:

| | |
|---|---|
| John: 412-34-5670 | Martha: 412-34-5671 |
| Date of birth: 3/4/1986 | Date of birth: 8/20/1990 |

W-2 for John shows these amounts:

    Wages (box 1) = $22,000.00

    Federal W/H (box 2) = $ 1,500.00

    Social security wages (box 3) = $22,000.00

    Social security W/H (box 4) = $ 1,364.00

    Medicare wages (box 5) = $22,000.00

    Medicare W/H (box 6) = $ 319.00

W-2 for Martha shows these amounts:

    Wages (box 1) = $35,500.00

    Federal W/H (box 2) = $ 3,100.00

    Social security wages (box 3) = $35,500.00

    Social security W/H (box 4) = $ 2,201.00

    Medicare wages (box 5) = $35,500.00

    Medicare W/H (box 6) = $ 514.75

Form 1099-DIV for Martha shows this amount:
Box 1a and box 1b = $345.00 from MAR Brokerage.

Form 1099-INT for Martha shows these amounts:
Box 1 = $450.00 from ABC Bank.
Box 4 = $35.00.

John is a maintenance worker, and Martha is a human resources manager.

Prepare Form 1040 plus all the appropriate schedules and worksheets for Mr. and Mrs. Holloway for 2021. They want to contribute to the presidential election campaign. Mr. and Mrs. Holloway had qualifying health care coverage at all times during the tax year.

**Tax Return Problem 2**

Carl and Elizabeth Williams are married filing jointly. They are 45 and 40 years old, respectively. Their address is 19010 N.W. 135th Street, Miami, FL 33054. Additional information about Mr. and Mrs. Williams is as follows:

Social security numbers:

| | |
|---|---|
| Carl: 412-34-5670 | Elizabeth: 412-34-5671 |
| Date of birth: 7/13/1976 | Date of birth: 9/19/1981 |

W-2 for Carl shows these amounts:

| | |
|---|---|
| Wages (box 1) = $75,000.00 | |
| Federal W/H (box 2) = $ 6,950.00 | |
| Social security wages (box 3) = $75,000.00 | |
| Social security W/H (box 4) = $ 4,650.00 | |
| Medicare wages (box 5) = $75,000.00 | |
| Medicare W/H (box 6) = $ 1,087.50 | |

W-2 for Elizabeth shows these amounts:

| | |
|---|---|
| Wages (box 1) = $31,000.00 | |
| Federal W/H (box 2) = $ 3,700.00 | |
| Social security wages (box 3) = $31,000.00 | |
| Social security W/H (box 4) = $ 1,922.00 | |
| Medicare wages (box 5) = $31,000.00 | |
| Medicare W/H (box 6) = $ 449.50 | |

Form 1099-INT for Carl and Elizabeth shows this amount:
Box 1 = $2,450.00 from Global Bank.

They also received tax-exempt interest of $500.00, as well as $45.00 for jury duty pay when Carl went to court to serve for a few days.

Carl received two weeks of workers' compensation pay for a total of $3,100.00.

Dependent: Son, Carl Jr., who is 7 years old. His date of birth is 3/25/2014. His social security number is 412-34-5672.

Carl is a sales manager, and Elizabeth is an office clerk.

Prepare Form 1040 plus all the appropriate schedules and worksheets for Mr. and Mrs. Williams for 2021. They are entitled to a $3,000 child tax credit (this credit is discussed in Chapter 9). For now, enter the credit on the appropriate line of the form. They do not want to contribute to the presidential election campaign. Mr. and Mrs. Williams had qualifying health care coverage at all times during the tax year.

**Tax Return Problem 3**

Hiroshi and Mizuki Sakamoto are married filing jointly. They are 68 and 66 years old, respectively. Their address is 1001 N.W. 93rd Street, Miami, FL 33168. Additional information about Mr. and Mrs. Sakamoto, who are retired, is as follows:

Social security numbers:

| | |
|---|---|
| Hiroshi: 412-34-5670 | Mizuki: 412-34-5671 |
| Date of birth: 10/9/1953 | Date of birth: 11/9/1955 |
| SSA-1099 for Hiroshi shows this amount: | SSA-1099 for Mizuki shows this amount: |
| Box 5 = $21,600.00 | Box 5 = $15,600.00 |
| Form 1099-INT for Hiroshi shows this amount: | Form 1099-INT for Mizuki shows this amount: |
| Box 1 = $9,100.00 from CD Bank. | Box 1 = $7,500.00 from CD Bank. |

Prepare Form 1040 plus all the appropriate schedules and worksheets for Mr. and Mrs. Sakamoto for 2021. They want to contribute to the presidential election campaign. Mr. and Mrs. Sakamoto had qualifying health care coverage at all times during the tax year.

We have provided selected filled-in source documents that are available in the *Connect Library.*

# Chapter **Four**

# Adjustments *for* Adjusted Gross Income

Taxpayers can deduct certain items from total income for purposes of computing Adjusted Gross Income (AGI). In this chapter, we introduce you to most of these *for* AGI deductions. This is a key step in determining the actual tax liability of the individual.

## Learning Objectives

When you have completed this chapter, you should understand the following learning objectives (LO):

**LO 4-1**  Describe the tax rules for student loan interest.

**LO 4-2**  Be able to determine eligibility requirements and applicable dollar limits related to the health savings account deduction.

**LO 4-3**  Determine the deduction for military moving expenses.

**LO 4-4**  Explain the deduction for half of self-employment taxes.

**LO 4-5**  Discuss the self-employed health insurance deduction.

**LO 4-6**  Explain the penalty on early withdrawal of savings.

**LO 4-7**  Be able to apply the rules regarding alimony and calculate the deduction for alimony paid, if applicable.

**LO 4-8**  Determine the deduction for educator expenses.

 **NEW LAW**

For tax year 2021, non-itemizers can deduct below-the-line cash charitable contributions up to $600 on a married-filing-joint return ($300 for singles).

## INTRODUCTION

In previous chapters, we primarily discussed tax rules and the presentation of many components of total income (that are compiled on Form 1040 and Schedule 1). Taxpayers can also deduct certain items from total income to arrive at Adjusted Gross Income (AGI). These deductible items are *for* AGI deductions, commonly referred to as *above-the-line* deductions (AGI is considered to be "the line"). AGI is critically important to the calculation of other key items on the tax return. The total of *for* AGI deductions are on Page 1, line 10, of Form 1040.[1] See Exhibit 4-1 for the AGI portion of Schedule 1.

You may recall that certain deductions are also subtracted from AGI to arrive at taxable income. These *from* AGI deductions, or *below-the-line* deductions, are the standard or itemized deductions and personal exemptions. In effect, gross income minus *for* AGI (above-the-line) deductions equals AGI. If you then subtract *from* AGI (below-the-line) deductions, you will get taxable income.

---

[1] We do not discuss all *for* AGI deductions in this chapter. Taxpayers may also take *for* AGI deductions for contributions to Individual Retirement Accounts (Schedule 1, line 20) and to retirement plans for self-employed individuals (Schedule 1, line 16) We discuss these deductions in Chapter 11.

**EXHIBIT 4-1**

Schedule 1 (Form 1040) 2021                                                                                      Page **2**

| | **Part II** **Adjustments to Income** | | |
|---|---|---|---|
| 11 | Educator expenses | 11 | |
| 12 | Certain business expenses of reservists, performing artists, and fee-basis government officials. Attach Form 2106 | 12 | |
| 13 | Health savings account deduction. Attach Form 8889 | 13 | |
| 14 | Moving expenses for members of the Armed Forces. Attach Form 3903 | 14 | |
| 15 | Deductible part of self-employment tax. Attach Schedule SE | 15 | |
| 16 | Self-employed SEP, SIMPLE, and qualified plans | 16 | |
| 17 | Self-employed health insurance deduction | 17 | |
| 18 | Penalty on early withdrawal of savings | 18 | |
| 19a | Alimony paid | 19a | |
| b | Recipient's SSN ▶ | | |
| c | Date of original divorce or separation agreement (see instructions) ▶ | | |
| 20 | IRA deduction | 20 | |
| 21 | Student loan interest deduction | 21 | |
| 22 | Reserved for future use | 22 | |
| 23 | Archer MSA deduction | 23 | |
| 24 | Other adjustments: | | |
| a | Jury duty pay (see instructions) | 24a | |
| b | Deductible expenses related to income reported on line 8k from the rental of personal property engaged in for profit | 24b | |
| c | Nontaxable amount of the value of Olympic and Paralympic medals and USOC prize money reported on line 8l | 24c | |
| d | Reforestation amortization and expenses | 24d | |
| e | Repayment of supplemental unemployment benefits under the Trade Act of 1974 | 24e | |
| f | Contributions to section 501(c)(18)(D) pension plans | 24f | |
| g | Contributions by certain chaplains to section 403(b) plans | 24g | |
| h | Attorney fees and court costs for actions involving certain unlawful discrimination claims (see instructions) | 24h | |
| i | Attorney fees and court costs you paid in connection with an award from the IRS for information you provided that helped the IRS detect tax law violations | 24i | |
| j | Housing deduction from Form 2555 | 24j | |
| k | Excess deductions of section 67(e) expenses from Schedule K-1 (Form 1041) | 24k | |
| z | Other adjustments. List type and amount ▶ _____ | 24z | |
| 25 | Total other adjustments. Add lines 24a through 24z | 25 | |
| 26 | Add lines 11 through 23 and 25. These are your **adjustments to income.** Enter here and on Form 1040 or 1040-SR, line 10, or Form 1040-NR, line 10a | 26 | |

Schedule 1 (Form 1040) 2021

Source: U.S. Department of the Treasury, Internal Revenue Service, Form 1040. Washington, DC: 2021.

# STUDENT LOAN INTEREST (SCHEDULE 1 OF FORM 1040, LINE 21)
## LO 4-1

Tax law provides numerous tax benefits for expenses associated with obtaining education beyond high school. These benefits are available for individuals saving for higher education (Coverdell Education Savings Accounts, state tuition programs, and qualified U.S. savings bonds), for many expenses incurred while attending a qualified educational institution (American opportunity/Hope and lifetime learning credits), and for interest paid on loans incurred for higher education expenses.[2]

[2] Coverdell Education Savings Accounts and the American opportunity (AOTC) and lifetime learning credits are discussed in Chapters 9 and 11, respectively.

Paying higher education expenses often requires students or their parents or guardians to borrow money from lending institutions such as banks or from federal or state student loan programs. An individual can take a deduction for "an amount equal to the interest paid by the taxpayer during the taxable year on any qualified education loan."[3] Only the person legally obligated to make the interest payments can take the deduction.[4] *A person who is claimed as a dependent on another person's return cannot claim the deduction,[5] nor can persons whose filing status is married filing separately.[6]*

| | |
|---|---|
| **EXAMPLE 4-1** | In 2017 Geraldo borrowed $5,000 for higher education expenses on a qualified education loan. In 2021, when he began making payments on the loan, he was still living at home and his parents appropriately claimed his as a dependent. Geraldo cannot claim the student interest deduction. Although he was the person legally obligated to repay the loan, he was claimed on the return of another person. |

The amount of this deduction is limited to $2,500 per year.[7] The deduction may be further limited based on the modified Adjusted Gross Income of the taxpayer. Student loan interest payments will be suspended until September 30, 2021. As with the previous CARES Act suspension, this will be an interest-free suspension and all payments made during this time will be principal only.

## Qualified Education Loan

A *qualified education loan* is one incurred by the taxpayer solely to pay qualified education expenses on behalf of the taxpayer, taxpayer's spouse, or any dependent of the taxpayer at the time the loan was incurred.[8] Note that the loan must be *solely* to pay for educational expenses. Thus, home equity loans or revolving lines of credit often do not qualify. Qualified education expenses must be paid or incurred within a reasonable period before or after the loan date.[9] Expenses meet this test if the proceeds of the loan are disbursed within 90 days of the start or 90 days after the end of the academic period. Federal education loan programs meet this criterion. The expenses also must occur during the period the recipient was carrying at least half the normal full-time workload for the intended course of study.[10] The course of study can be at the undergraduate or graduate level.

## Qualified Education Expenses

Qualified education expenses are the costs of attending an eligible educational institution.[11] These costs include tuition, fees, books, supplies, equipment, room, board, transportation, and other necessary expenses of attendance. However, taxpayers must reduce qualified expenses by the amount of income excluded from gross income in each of the following cases. In each instance, because the income is not included, the item does *not* create a deduction:

- An employer-paid educational assistance program.[12]
- Redemption of U.S. savings bonds used to pay higher education tuition and fees.[13]
- Funds withdrawn from a Coverdell Education Savings Account.[14]
- Qualified tax-free scholarships and fellowships.[15]

[3] IRC § 221(a).
[4] Reg. § 1.221-1(b).
[5] IRC § 221(c).
[6] IRC § 221(e)(2).
[7] IRC § 221(b)(1).
[8] IRC § 221(d)(1)(A).
[9] IRC § 221(d)(1)(B); Reg. § 1.221-1(e)(3)(ii).
[10] IRC § 221(d)(3), § 25A(b)(3).
[11] IRC § 221(d)(2).
[12] IRC § 127.
[13] IRC § 135.
[14] IRC § 530.
[15] IRC § 117.
[16] IRC § 25A(g)(2)(B).
[17] IRC § 25A(g)(2)(C).

- Armed forces' or veterans' educational assistance allowances.[16]
- Any other educational assistance excludable from gross income (not including gifts, bequests, devises, or inheritances).[17] This category includes a state-qualified tuition plan.

---

**EXAMPLE 4-2**

In September Lebron spent $3,000 on qualified educational expenses. He received a loan for $2,800 in the same month as he paid the expenses. During the semester, he received a scholarship of $500 that he properly excluded from income. Lebron's qualified educational expenses are $2,500 ($3,000 − $500). As a result, interest on $2,500 of the $2,800 loan will be eligible for student loan interest treatment, while interest on the remaining $300 is nondeductible personal interest.

---

## Other Provisions and Limitations

As noted earlier, deductible education expenses must occur in conjunction with attendance at an eligible educational institution. An *eligible institution* is generally a postsecondary educational institution that meets the requirements to participate in the federal student loan program.[18] This includes almost all four-year colleges and universities, two-year community colleges, and many trade and technical schools. The classification also incorporates institutions with an internship or residency program leading to a degree or certificate awarded by an institute of higher education, a hospital, or a health care facility that offers postgraduate training.[19] Qualified expenses must be for an academic period during which the student was enrolled at least half-time in one of these qualifying programs.

The deduction for interest on qualified education loans may be limited based on the modified Adjusted Gross Income of the taxpayer.[20] *Modified AGI* is equal to the AGI on the taxpayer's tax return plus (a) any deduction for student loan interest; (b) any foreign, U.S. territories, or Puerto Rican income excluded from taxable income; and (c) any deduction taken for tuition and fees.[21]

The deductible amount of student loan interest is reduced when modified AGI reaches $140,000 on a joint return ($70,000 for a single return) and is totally eliminated when modified AGI reaches $170,000 ($85,000 for single returns).[22] The following formula is used:

Preliminary deduction × Fraction (see below) = Disallowed interest

For married taxpayers, the fraction is (Modified AGI − $140,000)/$30,000.

For single taxpayers, the fraction is (Modified AGI − $70,000)/$15,000.

The denominators in these fractions represent the difference between the beginning and the end of the phaseout range (that is, for married filing jointly, the $30,000 denominator is the difference between $140,000 and $170,000). These fractions represent the disallowed proportion of the preliminary deduction.

Note that the preliminary deduction amount cannot exceed the $2,500 maximum allowed deduction.

---

**EXAMPLE 4-3**

Shannon and Marian borrowed $30,000 on a qualified educational loan to pay for qualified higher education expenses for their two children. During 2021 they paid $1,800 interest on the loan. Shannon and Marian's modified AGI on their joint return was $160,000. They are entitled to deduct $600 as follows:

$$\$1,800 \times \frac{\$160,000 - \$140,000}{\$30,000} = \$1,200 \text{ disallowed}$$

Permitted deduction = $1,800 − $1,200 = $600.

---

[18] IRC § 221(d)(2), § 25A(f)(2).

[19] IRC § 221(d)(2)(B).

[20] IRC § 221(b)(2).

[21] IRC § 221(b)(2)(C)(i).

[22] These limitation amounts are adjusted for inflation under IRC § 221(f).

# From Shoebox to Software

There are generally four critical issues concerning student loan interest:

- Whether the loan was taken out solely for education expenses.
- Whether loan funds were used for education expenses.
- The amount of the interest payment for the year.
- Limitation of the deduction based on AGI phaseouts.

Identifying applicable loans and maintaining (or in some cases obtaining) proper documentation is more difficult because a number of years usually transpire between the date that the loan is created, the date that the expenses are paid, and the date the interest deduction is sought. On many student loans, the student can elect to defer payments while enrolled in college and even after that point for certain economic hardship reasons. Be careful, however; deferral does not prevent interest from accruing.

Loans made through the federal student loan program usually meet the first two critical issues because the U.S. government intends that these loans cover education expenses not paid by student earnings or parental contributions. The federal government provides an annual report to the taxpayer (often a substitute Form 1099-INT) that provides the amount of interest paid during the year.

Loans from financial institutions require a higher level of documentation. The taxpayer should review loan documents and canceled checks to determine whether the loan and the expenditures qualify for favored treatment. Lenders normally provide Form 1098-E (see Exhibit 4-2) indicating the amount of interest paid by the taxpayer in a year.

In both cases, when preparing a return using tax software, you enter applicable information on a Student Loan Interest Deduction worksheet. The Student Loan Interest Deduction worksheet can be found in IRS Publication 970, Tax Benefits for Education (Exhibit 4-3).

## EXHIBIT 4-2

☐ CORRECTED (if checked)

RECIPIENT'S/LENDER'S name, street address, city or town, state or province, country, ZIP or foreign postal code, and telephone number

OMB No. 1545-1576

2021

Form **1098-E**

**Student Loan Interest Statement**

| RECIPIENT'S TIN | BORROWER'S TIN |
|---|---|

**1** Student loan interest received by lender
$

**Copy B
For Borrower**

BORROWER'S name

Street address (including apt. no.)

City or town, state or province, country, and ZIP or foreign postal code

Account number (see instructions)

**2** If checked, box 1 does **not** include loan origination fees and/or capitalized interest for loans made before September 1, 2004 ☐

This is important tax information and is being furnished to the IRS. If you are required to file a return, a negligence penalty or other sanction may be imposed on you if the IRS determines that an underpayment of tax results because you overstated a deduction for student loan interest.

Form **1098-E** (keep for your records) www.irs.gov/Form1098E Department of the Treasury - Internal Revenue Service

Source: U.S. Department of the Treasury, Internal Revenue Service, Form 1098-E. Washington, DC: 2021.

*(continued)*

**TAX YOUR BRAIN**

If Shannon and Marian paid $3,200 interest on the loan in 2021 what is the allowed deduction for student loan interest?

**ANSWER**

Because the interest deduction is limited to a total of $2,500 before the AGI limitation, the couple would be entitled to an $833 deduction as follows:

$$\$2,500 \times \frac{\$160,000 - \$140,000}{\$30,000} = \$1,667 \text{ disallowed}$$

Permitted deduction = $2,500 − $1,667 = $833.

**EXHIBIT 4-3**
Student Load Interest Deduction Worksheet—Schedule 1, Line 21

| **Before you begin:** | ✓ Figure any write-in adjustments to be entered on the dotted line next to Schedule 1, line 22 (see the instructions for Schedule 1, line 22).<br>✓ Be sure you have read the **Exception** in the instructions for this line to see if you can use this worksheet instead of Pub. 970 to figure your deduction. |
|---|---|

1. Enter the total interest you paid in 2020 on qualified student loans (see the instructions for line 20). **Don't** enter more than $2,500 ............................................................ **1.** _____

2. Enter the amount from Form 1040 or 1040-SR, line 9 ...................... **2.** _____

3. Enter the total of the amounts from Form 1040 or 1040-SR, line 10b, and Schedule 1, lines 10 through 19, plus any write-in adjustments you entered on the dotted line next to Schedule 1, line 22 ............................. **3.** _____

4. Subtract line 3 from line 2 .................................... **4.** _____

5. Enter the amount shown below for your filing status.
   - Single, head of household, or qualifying widow(er)—$70,000
   - Married filing jointly—$140,000  } .......... **5.** _____

6. Is the amount on line 4 more than the amount on line 5?

   ☐ **No.** Skip lines 6 and 7, enter -0- on line 8, and go to line 9.

   ☐ **Yes.** Subtract line 5 from line 4 ............................ **6.** _____

7. Divide line 6 by $15,000 ($30,000 if married filing jointly). Enter the result as a decimal (rounded to at least three places). If the result is 1.000 or more, enter 1.000 ...................... **7.** . _____

8. Multiply line 1 by line 7 ............................................ **8.** _____

9. **Student loan interest deduction.** Subtract line 8 from line 1. Enter the result here and on Schedule 1, line 20.
   **Don't** include this amount in figuring any other deduction on your return (such as on Schedule A, C, E, etc.) ............................................. **9.** _____

As of the date this text went to print, the 2021 student loan interest deduction worksheet had not been released by the IRS. The form above is the 2020 worksheet. The deduction calculations for 2020 and 2021 will be exactly the same. However, on the 2021 form, some of the line numbers references to other tax forms will be different than shown on the 2020 form above. When the 2021 form is released, an updated Exhibit will be posted to Connect.

 **NEW LAW**

Student Loan Forgiveness Exclusion—The American Rescue Plan Act of 2021 provides that for tax years 2021 through 2025, any discharge of student loan debt for any reason, including private student loans, may be excluded from taxable income, as long as there is no provision for the student to provide services to the discharging lender.

**CONCEPT CHECK 4-1—**
**LO 4-1**

1. For the interest on a student loan to qualify for the deduction, the student must be enrolled at least _____ .

2. Under the student loan program, qualified educational expenses include _____ and _____ .

3. The deductible amount of student loan interest is reduced when modified AGI for those filing married jointly reaches _____ .

# HEALTH SAVINGS ACCOUNT DEDUCTION (SCHEDULE 1, LINE 13)
## LO 4-2

A health savings account is a tax-exempt savings account used for qualified medical expenses for the account holder, their spouse, and dependents. In general, qualified taxpayers can take a *for* AGI deduction for contributions to the HSA.[23] Contributions grow tax-free, and distributions are not taxable if used for qualified medical expenses.

To be eligible to fund an HSA, a taxpayer, under the age of 65, must be self-employed; an employee (or spouse) of an employer who maintains a high-deductible health plan (HDHP); or an employee of a company that provides no health coverage, and the employee has purchased a high-deductible policy on their own. In addition, the individual cannot have other health insurance except for coverage for accidents, disability, dental care, vision care, long-term care, or workers' compensation.[24] In addition, the taxpayer cannot be enrolled in Medicare and cannot be claimed as a dependent on someone else's return. No permission or authorization from the IRS is required to establish an HSA. In order to set up an HSA, the taxpayer must work with a trustee who serves as custodian of the account.

[23] IRC § 223(a).
[24] IRC § 223(c)(1)(B).

# From Shoebox to Software

Taxpayers who contribute to or withdraw from an HSA during the year must file Form 8889 and attach it to their Form 1040. Form 8889 is shown in Exhibit 4-4.

**EXHIBIT 4-4**

| Form **8889** | **Health Savings Accounts (HSAs)** | OMB No. 1545-0074 |
|---|---|---|
| Department of the Treasury Internal Revenue Service | ▶ **Attach to Form 1040, 1040-SR, or 1040-NR.** ▶ **Go to *www.irs.gov/Form8889* for instructions and the latest information.** | **2021** Attachment Sequence No. **52** |

Name(s) shown on Form 1040, 1040-SR, or 1040-NR | Social security number of HSA beneficiary. If both spouses have HSAs, see instructions ▶

*Before you begin:* Complete Form 8853, Archer MSAs and Long-Term Care Insurance Contracts, if required.

**Part I**   **HSA Contributions and Deduction.** See the instructions before completing this part. If you are filing jointly and both you and your spouse each have separate HSAs, complete a separate Part I for each spouse.

| | | | |
|---|---|---|---|
| **1** | Check the box to indicate your coverage under a high-deductible health plan (HDHP) during 2021. See instructions . . . . . . . . . . . . . . . . . . . . . ▶ | ☐ Self-only   ☐ Family | |
| **2** | HSA contributions you made for 2021 (or those made on your behalf), including those made from January 1, 2022, through April 15, 2022, that were for 2021. **Do not** include employer contributions, contributions through a cafeteria plan, or rollovers. See instructions . . . . . . | **2** | |
| **3** | If you were under age 55 at the end of 2021 and, on the first day of **every** month during 2021, you were, or were considered, an eligible individual with the **same** coverage, enter $3,600 ($7,200 for family coverage). **All others,** see the instructions for the amount to enter . . . . . . | **3** | |
| **4** | Enter the amount you and your employer contributed to your Archer MSAs for 2021 from Form 8853, lines 1 and 2. If you or your spouse had family coverage under an HDHP at any time during 2021, also include any amount contributed to your spouse's Archer MSAs . . . . . . . . | **4** | |
| **5** | Subtract line 4 from line 3. If zero or less, enter -0- . . . . . . . . . . . . | **5** | |
| **6** | Enter the amount from line 5. But if you and your spouse each have separate HSAs and had family coverage under an HDHP at any time during 2021, see the instructions for the amount to enter . . | **6** | |
| **7** | If you were age 55 or older at the end of 2021, married, and you or your spouse had family coverage under an HDHP at any time during 2021, enter your additional contribution amount. See instructions | **7** | |
| **8** | Add lines 6 and 7 . . . . . . . . . . . . . . . . . . . . . . . | **8** | |
| **9** | Employer contributions made to your HSAs for 2021 . . . . . . | **9** | |
| **10** | Qualified HSA funding distributions . . . . . . . . . | **10** | |
| **11** | Add lines 9 and 10 . . . . . . . . . . . . . . . . . . . . . | **11** | |
| **12** | Subtract line 11 from line 8. If zero or less, enter -0- . . . . . . . . . . . | **12** | |
| **13** | **HSA deduction.** Enter the **smaller** of line 2 or line 12 here and on Schedule 1 (Form 1040), Part II, line 13 | **13** | |
| | **Caution:** If line 2 is more than line 13, you may have to pay an additional tax. See instructions. | | |

**Part II**   **HSA Distributions.** If you are filing jointly and both you and your spouse each have separate HSAs, complete a separate Part II for each spouse.

| | | | |
|---|---|---|---|
| **14a** | Total distributions you received in 2021 from all HSAs (see instructions) . . . . . . . | **14a** | |
| **b** | Distributions included on line 14a that you rolled over to another HSA. Also include any excess contributions (and the earnings on those excess contributions) included on line 14a that were withdrawn by the due date of your return. See instructions . . . . . . . . . . | **14b** | |
| **c** | Subtract line 14b from line 14a . . . . . . . . . . . . . . . . . . . | **14c** | |
| **15** | Qualified medical expenses paid using HSA distributions (see instructions) . . . . . . . | **15** | |
| **16** | **Taxable HSA distributions.** Subtract line 15 from line 14c. If zero or less, enter -0-. Also, include this amount in the total on Schedule 1 (Form 1040), Part I, line 8e . . . . . . . . . . | **16** | |
| **17a** | If any of the distributions included on line 16 meet any of the **Exceptions to the Additional 20% Tax** (see instructions), check here . . . . . . . . . . . . . ▶ ☐ | | |
| **b** | **Additional 20% tax** (see instructions). Enter 20% (0.20) of the distributions included on line 16 that are subject to the additional 20% tax. Also, include this amount in the total on Schedule 2 (Form 1040), Part II, line 17c . . . . . . . . . . . . . . . . . . . . | **17b** | |

**Part III**   **Income and Additional Tax for Failure To Maintain HDHP Coverage.** See the instructions before completing this part. If you are filing jointly and both you and your spouse each have separate HSAs, complete a separate Part III for each spouse.

| | | | |
|---|---|---|---|
| **18** | Last-month rule . . . . . . . . . . . . . . . . . . . . . . . | **18** | |
| **19** | Qualified HSA funding distribution . . . . . . . . . . . . . . . . . . | **19** | |
| **20** | **Total income.** Add lines 18 and 19. Include this amount on Schedule 1 (Form 1040), Part I, line 8z, and enter "HSA" and the amount on the dotted line . . . . . . . . . . . . | **20** | |
| **21** | **Additional tax.** Multiply line 20 by 10% (0.10). Include this amount in the total on Schedule 2 (Form 1040), Part II, line 17d . . . . . . . . . . . . . . . . . . | **21** | |

**For Paperwork Reduction Act Notice, see your tax return instructions.**     Cat. No. 37621P     Form **8889** (2021)

Source: U.S. Department of the Treasury, Internal Revenue Service, Form 8889. Washington, DC: 2021.

*(continued)*

A trustee, normally a bank or insurance company, administers the HSA. Trustees are required to provide HSA holders contribution and distribution information. Contributions are reported on Form 5498-SA (see Exhibit 4-5). Taxpayers use contribution information to prepare Part I of Form 8889.

Distributions are reported by the trustee on Form 1099-SA, shown in Exhibit 4-6. The distributions are reported on Part II of Form 8889 (see Exhibit 4-4).

## EXHIBIT 4-5

| ☐ CORRECTED (if checked) | | |
|---|---|---|
| TRUSTEE'S name, street address, city or town, state or province, country, ZIP or foreign postal code, and telephone number | **1** Employee or self-employed person's Archer MSA contributions made in 2021 and 2022 for 2021 $ | OMB No. 1545-1518 **2021** Form **5498-SA** — HSA, Archer MSA, or Medicare Advantage MSA Information |
| | **2** Total contributions made in 2021 $ | |
| TRUSTEE'S TIN        PARTICIPANT'S TIN | **3** Total HSA or Archer MSA contributions made in 2022 for 2021 $ | **Copy B** |
| PARTICIPANT'S name | **4** Rollover contributions $ | **5** Fair market value of HSA, Archer MSA, or MA MSA $ | **For Participant** |
| Street address (including apt. no.) | **6** HSA ☐    Archer MSA ☐ | |
| City or town, state or province, country, and ZIP or foreign postal code | MA MSA ☐ | This information is being furnished to the IRS. |
| Account number (see instructions) | | |
| Form **5498-SA**        (keep for your records) | www.irs.gov/Form5498SA | Department of the Treasury - Internal Revenue Service |

Source: U.S. Department of the Treasury, Internal Revenue Service, Form 5498-SA. Washington, DC: 2021.

## EXHIBIT 4-6

| ☐ CORRECTED (if checked) | | |
|---|---|---|
| TRUSTEE'S/PAYER'S name, street address, city or town, state or province, country, ZIP or foreign postal code, and telephone number | OMB No. 1545-1517 Form **1099-SA** (Rev. November 2019) For calendar year 20 | Distributions From an HSA, Archer MSA, or Medicare Advantage MSA |
| PAYER'S TIN        RECIPIENT'S TIN | **1** Gross distribution $ | **2** Earnings on excess cont. $ | **Copy B** |
| RECIPIENT'S name | **3** Distribution code | **4** FMV on date of death $ | **For Recipient** |
| Street address (including apt. no.) | **5** HSA ☐    Archer MSA ☐ | |
| City or town, state or province, country, and ZIP or foreign postal code | MA MSA ☐ | This information is being furnished to the IRS. |
| Account number (see instructions) | | |
| Form **1099-SA** (Rev. 11-2019)        (keep for your records) | www.irs.gov/Form1099SA | Department of the Treasury - Internal Revenue Service |

Source: U.S. Department of the Treasury, Internal Revenue Service, Form 1099-SA. Washington, DC: 2021.

Any insurance company or any bank (including a similar financial institution as defined in section 408(n)) can be an HSA trustee or custodian. In addition, any other person already approved by the IRS to be a trustee or custodian of IRAs or Archer MSAs is automatically approved to be an HSA trustee or custodian. Other persons may request approval to be a trustee or custodian in accordance with the procedures set forth in Treas. Reg. § 1.408-2(e) (relating to IRA nonbank trustees).

An HDHP is a health plan with specified minimum deductible amounts and a maximum annual deductible and out-of-pocket expense limitation.[25] *Out-of-pocket expense* represents the amount the health plan requires the policyholder to pay for covered benefits (other than the premium). Essentially, an HDHP is a health insurance plan with lower premiums and higher deductibles than a traditional health plan. It is a form of catastrophic coverage. For calendar year 2021, these amounts are as follows:

|  | Minimum Deductible | Maximum Deductible and Annual Out-of-Pocket Expenses |
|---|---|---|
| Individual coverage | $1,400 | $ 7,000 |
| Family coverage | $2,800 | $14,000 |

The employee or employer contributes to the HSA. For individual coverage maximum, the aggregate contribution an individual under age 55 can make to an HSA is $3,600. For family coverage, with a contributor under age 55, the maximum aggregate annual contribution is $7,200.[26]

If the taxpayer is 55 or older, they may contribute an additional $1,000 in 2021. This assumes that only one spouse has an HSA. If both spouses have separate HSAs, see IRS Publication 969 for further information. Individuals are now allowed to make a one-time contribution to an HSA of an amount distributed from their IRA. The contribution must be made in a direct trustee-to-trustee transfer. Amounts distributed from the IRA are not includable in the individual's income to the extent that the distribution would otherwise be includable in income. Such distributions are not subject to the 20% additional tax on early distributions. An individual who becomes covered by a high-deductible plan during the year can make a contribution to an HSA as if they were eligible for the entire year. Contributions for a tax year must be made by the due date of the return.

Contributions made by a qualified individual are a *for* AGI deduction, assuming that the limitations are met. If an employer contributes, the amount is not deductible (because the employee paid nothing), but the payment is not counted as income to the employee. The funds in the account are allowed to accumulate from year to year and the interest or other earnings on the assets in the account are tax free.

Distributions from HSAs are tax free if they are used to pay for qualified medical expenses.[27] Under IRS Announcement 2021-7, COVID-19 PPE expenses are also eligible to be paid or reimbursed under health flexible spending arrangements (health FSAs), Archer medical savings accounts (Archer MSAs), health reimbursement arrangements (HRAs), and health savings accounts (HSAs).

Group health plans may be amended to provide for reimbursement of expenses for COVID-19 PPE incurred for any period beginning on or after January 1, 2020. Group health plans may be amended to include COVID-19 PPE retroactive back to January 1, 2020, if the plan is amended no later than the last day of the first calendar year beginning after the end of the plan year in which the amendment is effective, no amendment with retroactive effect is adopted after December 31, 2022, and the plan is operated consistent with the terms of the amendment, including during the period beginning on the effective date of the amendment through the date the amendment is adopted.

---

**CONCEPT CHECK 4-2— LO 4-2**

1. To be eligible to fund an HSA, a taxpayer must be _____ , an employee (or spouse) of an employer who maintains a high-deductible health plan, or an uninsured employee who has purchased a high-deductible policy on their own.

2. If they are used to pay for qualified medical expenses, distributions from HSAs are _____ .

3. If taxpayers make contributions to or withdrawals from an HSA during the year, they must file Form _____ and attach it to their Form _____ .

[25] IRC § 223(c)(2).
[26] IRC § 223(b).
[27] IRC § 223(d)(2).

Part I of Form 8889, Health Savings Accounts, is used to report the amount of the deduction that is reported on line 13 of the Schedule 1. Form 8889 must be attached to the taxpayer's return. The form is also used to report the taxable and nontaxable amounts of a distribution from an HSA. You can find additional information about HSAs in IRS Publication 969.

Funds contained within an HSA account are exempt from tax. An employee is always 100% vested in their HSA. Amounts that remain in the HSA at the end of the year are carried over to the next year. Earnings on amounts in an HSA are not included in income while held in the HSA.

# MOVING EXPENSES FOR MEMBERS OF THE ARMED FORCES (SCHEDULE 1, LINE 14)
## LO 4-3

The moving expense deduction and the exclusion from income provision are allowed only to members of the U.S. Armed Forces, or their spouse or dependents, on active duty. Form 3903 (Exhibit 4-7) is used to report the deduction.

If members of the U.S. Armed Forces are on active duty and move because of a permanent change of station, they can deduct their unreimbursed moving expenses.

A permanent change of station includes

- A move from their home to their first post of active duty,
- A move from one permanent post of duty to another, and
- A move from their last post of duty to their home or to a nearer point in the United States. The move must occur within one year of ending their active duty or within the period allowed under the Joint Travel Regulations.

### Services or Reimbursements Provided by the Government

Service members would not include in their income the value of moving and storage services provided by the government because of a permanent change of station. Similarly, they would not include in income amounts received as a dislocation allowance, temporary lodging expense, temporary lodging allowance, or move-in housing allowance.

Generally, if the total reimbursements or allowances that service members receive from the government because of the move are more than their actual moving expenses, the excess is included in their wages on Form W-2. However, if any reimbursements or allowances (other than dislocation, temporary lodging, temporary lodging expense, or move-in housing allowances) exceed the cost of moving and the excess is not included in their wages on Form W-2, the excess still must be included in gross income on Form 1040.

### Moving Household Goods and Personal Effects

Service members can deduct the expenses of moving their household goods and personal effects, including expenses for hauling a trailer, packing, crating, in-transit storage, and insurance. They cannot deduct expenses for moving furniture or other goods that were purchased on the way from their old home to their new home.

Service members can include only the cost of storing and insuring their household goods and personal effects within any period of 30 consecutive days after the day these goods and effects are moved from their former home and before they are delivered to their new home.

### Travel

Service members can deduct the expenses of traveling (including lodging but not meals) from their old home to their new home, including car expenses and air fare. They can deduct as car expenses either of the following:

- Their actual out-of-pocket expenses such as gas and oil
- The standard mileage rate for moving expenses in 2021 of 16 cents a mile.

They can add parking fees and tolls to the amount claimed under either method. They cannot deduct any expenses for meals, nor can they deduct the cost of unnecessary side trips or very expensive lodging.

A foreign move is a move from the United States or its territories to a foreign country or from one foreign country to another foreign country. It is not a move from a foreign country to the United States or its territories.

For a foreign move, the deductible moving expenses described earlier are expanded to include the reasonable expenses of

- Moving the service member's household goods and personal effects to and from storage
- Storing these items for part or all of the time the new job location remains the service member's main duty location. The new duty location must be outside the United States.

### Spouse and Dependents

A member of the service member's household is anyone who has both the service member's former home and new home as their main home. It does not include a tenant or employee unless that person can be claimed as a dependent by the service member.

If a member of the Armed Forces dies, is imprisoned, or deserts, a permanent change of station for the spouse or dependent includes a move to any of the following:

- The place of enlistment
- The member's, spouse's, or dependent's home of record
- A nearer point in the United States.

If the military moves the member, spouse, and dependents to or from separate locations, the moves are treated as a single move to the military member's new main job location.

### How to Complete Form 3903 for Members of the Armed Forces

1. Complete lines 1 through 3 of the form, using the member's actual expenses. Do not include any expenses for moving services provided by the government. Also, do not include any expenses that were reimbursed by an allowance that the member does not have to include in their income.

2. Enter on line 4 the total reimbursements and allowances the member received from the government for the expenses claimed on lines 1 and 2. Do not include the value of moving or storage services provided by the government. Also, do not include any part of a dislocation allowance, a temporary lodging allowance, a temporary lodging expense, or a move-in housing allowance.

3. Complete line 5. If line 3 is more than line 4, subtract line 4 from line 3 and enter the result on line 5 and on Schedule 1, line 14. This is the member's moving expense deduction. If line 3 is equal to or less than line 4, the member does not have a moving expense deduction. Subtract line 3 from line 4 and, if the result is more than zero, enter it on Form 1040, line 1.

**CONCEPT
CHECK 4-3—
LO 4-3**

1. For 2021, a service member who incurs moving expenses as a result of a move related to a permanent change of station may deduct any unreimbursed moving expenses subject to prescribed limitations. True or false?

2. A spouse or dependents of an active-duty military member may deduct moving expenses as a result of a military order and incident to a permanent change of station. True or false?

**EXHIBIT 4-7**

| Form **3903** | **Moving Expenses** | OMB No. 1545-0074 |
|---|---|---|
| Department of the Treasury Internal Revenue Service (99) | ▶ Go to www.irs.gov/Form3903 for instructions and the latest information. ▶ Attach to Form 1040, 1040-SR, or 1040-NR. | **2021** Attachment Sequence No. **170** |

Name(s) shown on return / Your social security number

**Before you begin:** You can deduct moving expenses only if you are a **Member of the Armed Forces** on active duty and, due to a military order, you, your spouse, or your dependents move because of a permanent change of station. Check here to certify that you meet these requirements. See the instructions . . . . . . . . . . . ▶ ☐

1. Transportation and storage of household goods and personal effects (see instructions) . . . **1**

2. Travel (including lodging) from your old home to your new home (see instructions). **Do not** include the cost of meals . . . **2**

3. Add lines 1 and 2 . . . **3**

4. Enter the total amount the government paid you for the expenses listed on lines 1 and 2 that is **not** included in box 1 of your Form W-2 (wages). This amount should be shown in box 12 of your Form W-2 with code **P** . . . **4**

5. Is line 3 **more than** line 4?

☐ **No.** You **cannot** deduct your moving expenses. If line 3 is less than line 4, subtract line 3 from line 4 and include the result on Form 1040 or 1040-SR, line 1; or Form 1040-NR, line 1a.

☐ **Yes.** Subtract line 4 from line 3. Enter the result here and on Schedule 1 (Form 1040), line 14. This is your **moving expense deduction** . . . **5**

For Paperwork Reduction Act Notice, see your tax return instructions. Cat. No. 12490K Form **3903** (2021)

Source: U.S. Department of the Treasury, Internal Revenue Service, Form 3903. Washington, DC: 2021.

## DEDUCTION FOR HALF OF SELF-EMPLOYMENT TAX (SCHEDULE 1, LINE 15)
## LO 4-4

Self-employed individuals must normally pay self-employment tax equal to 15.3% of their net earnings from self-employment.[28] The self-employment tax is the FICA tax for social security and Medicare that W-2 employees have deducted from their paychecks at a rate of 7.65% and that employers must match at the same rate. Self-employed individuals are responsible for both halves of the tax, and the tax is calculated on the net earnings of the business. Self-employed persons are allowed a *for* AGI deduction equal to one-half of the self-employment tax imposed.[29] The tax software will automatically calculate the appropriate amount for line 15. Self-employment tax is calculated on Form SE; it is covered in more detail in Chapter 6.

One Affordable Care Act (ACA) provision that is still in effect relates to the portion of FICA taxes pertaining to the Medicare tax. It requires that an additional Medicare tax of 0.9% be assessed for those individuals, according to filing status, whose income exceeds the following threshold amounts:

| Filing Status | Threshold Amount |
|---|---|
| Married filing jointly | $250,000 |
| Married filing separately | $125,000 |
| Single | $200,000 |
| Head of household | $200,000 |
| Qualifying widow(er) | $200,000 |

[28] IRC § 1401.
[29] IRC § 164(f).

An employer is required by law to withhold the additional Medicare tax from wages it pays to individuals in excess of $200,000 in a calendar year. This added tax raises the wage earner's Medicare portion of FICA compensation to 2.35%, above the regular 1.45%.

There can be an additional Medicare tax called the Net Investment Income Tax. Individuals can be accessed an additional 3.8% Medicare tax if they have net investment income and their modified AGI is over the threshold amounts detailed above.

---

**CONCEPT CHECK 4-4—**

**LO 4-4**

1. Self-employment tax is calculated on the _____ earnings of the business.
2. For W-2 employees, for 2021 the total FICA tax is calculated at a rate of _____ of their gross earnings.
3. An employer is required by law to withhold the additional Medicare tax from wages it pays to individuals in excess of $_____ in a calendar year.

# SELF-EMPLOYED HEALTH INSURANCE DEDUCTION (SCHEDULE 1, LINE 17)

## LO 4-5

Payments for health insurance for self-employed individuals, their spouse, and their dependents are not deductible as a business expense on Schedule C.[30] However, applicable taxpayers can deduct, as a *for* AGI deduction, 100% of self-employed health insurance premiums.[31]

The amount of the deduction may be limited in two respects. First, taxpayers cannot take a deduction for any amount in excess of net earnings from self-employment from the trade or business under which coverage is provided.[32] Net earnings from self-employment are determined by reducing gross income by the regular expenses of the business as well as the deduction for one-half of the self-employment tax and any deduction for contributions to qualified retirement plans.

---

**EXAMPLE 4-4**

Dinh had net earnings of $2,800 from self-employment. He paid $160 per month for health insurance ($1,920 per year). Dinh is entitled to a *for* AGI deduction of $1,920 for health insurance. If Dinh's net earnings from self-employment were $1,500, his deduction would have been limited to $1,500.

---

The second limitation pertains to availability of other health insurance coverage. If the taxpayer is entitled to participate in any subsidized health plan maintained by any employer of the taxpayer or of the taxpayer's spouse, a deduction is not allowed.[33] Eligibility for alternative coverage is determined on a monthly basis. A *subsidized health plan* is one in which someone other than the employee pays for part or all of the cost of the plan.

---

**EXAMPLE 4-5**

Sophia is self-employed and had net earnings from self-employment of $17,000 for the year. She has an individual-only health insurance policy through her business for which she pays $145 per month. An unrelated local business employs Miguel, her husband. Miguel's employer provides health insurance coverage for all employees and pays $100 toward the monthly premium of each employee. Miguel can cover Sophia under his policy, but the couple has chosen not to do so because the cost would be higher than Sophia's current policy. In this case, Sophia cannot deduct any of her health insurance premiums because she is entitled to participate under a subsidized plan. The fact that she chooses not to be covered does not matter.

---

[30] IRC § 162(l)(4). Chapter 6 covers the taxation of self-employed individuals.

[31] IRC § 162(l)(1).

[32] Generally, net earnings from self-employment are defined in IRC § 1402(a). For purposes of the health insurance deduction, that definition is modified by IRC § 401(c)(2).

[33] IRC § 162(l)(2)(B).

**TAX YOUR BRAIN**

Using the information from Example 4-5, assume that Miguel did not begin work at the local business until April 1, 2021. Prior to that time, he was an employee of Sophia's business, and both he and Sophia were covered under a group policy that cost $300 per month. On April 1 Sophia changed to an individual policy at $145 per month. How much can Sophia deduct for self-employed health insurance in 2021?

**ANSWER**

$900. Sophia is entitled to deduct the health insurance costs for herself and her spouse for the first three months of the year ($300 × 3 months). After that time, she is eligible under Miguel's policy, so she cannot take any additional deductions.

The alternative coverage rule is applied separately to plans that provide long-term care services or are qualified long-term care insurance contracts and to plans that do not provide such services.[34]

**EXAMPLE 4-6**

Patrick is self-employed and is entitled to participate in a subsidized qualified long-term care insurance plan through his wife Jennifer's employer. The general health care plan offered by Jennifer's employer is not subsidized. Patrick is entitled to participate in both health plans. He chooses to obtain general health care and qualified long-term care insurance through his own business. Patrick will be able to deduct the cost of the general health care plan (subject to the income limitation), but he cannot deduct the cost of the long-term care insurance. The general rule is that if someone else is willing to pay for insurance coverage, fully or partially, the premiums are not deductible.

The self-employed health insurance deduction is also available to a partner in a partnership and to a shareholder in a Subchapter S corporation who owns more than 2% of the stock in the corporation.[35] In the case of a Subchapter S shareholder, wages from the corporation are included in self-employed income for purposes of determining the deduction limitation based on net earnings from self-employment.

**CONCEPT CHECK 4-5— LO 4-5**

1. Self-employed individuals are allowed to take a *for* AGI deduction for up to 80% of the cost of their self-employed health insurance premiums. True or false?
2. One limitation on this deduction is that taxpayers cannot deduct the premium cost that exceeds gross earnings from self-employment. True or false?
3. Another limitation on this deduction is that eligible participation in a health plan subsidized by the employer of either the taxpayer or the taxpayer's spouse will prohibit the deduction. True or false?

# PENALTY ON EARLY WITHDRAWAL OF SAVINGS (SCHEDULE 1, LINE 18)
## LO 4-6

Certificates of deposit (CDs) and time savings accounts normally require holding an investment for a fixed period ranging from three months to five years. Often the rules associated with these financial instruments state that a depositor who withdraws the funds prior to the end of the fixed term will forfeit a certain amount of interest to which they would otherwise be entitled. For example, a two-year CD might state that the depositor will forfeit three months of interest on the CD in the event the depositor withdraws the money before the end of the two-year period. If such a premature withdrawal occurs, the taxpayer will be credited with the entire amount of interest (and that amount must be reported as interest income), but the financial institution will deduct three months of interest as a penalty.

If a taxpayer incurs an early withdrawal of savings penalty, the taxpayer is entitled to report the penalty as a *for* AGI deduction on line 18 of Schedule 1.[36]

[34] IRC § 162(l)(2)(B)(i), (ii).
[35] IRC § 162(l)(5), § 1372(a).
[36] IRC § 62(a)(9).

# From Shoebox to Software

Financial institutions report early withdrawal penalties in box 2 of Form 1099-INT (see Exhibit 4-8). When you record Form 1099-INT, the software automatically carries forward the box 2 amount onto line 18 of Schedule 1.

**EXHIBIT 4-8**

| ☐ CORRECTED (if checked) | | |
|---|---|---|
| PAYER'S name, street address, city or town, state or province, country, ZIP or foreign postal code, and telephone no. | Payer's RTN (optional) | OMB No. 1545-0112 |
| | **1** Interest income $ | **20**21 Form **1099-INT** — **Interest Income** |
| PAYER'S TIN / RECIPIENT'S TIN | **2** Early withdrawal penalty $ | **Copy B For Recipient** |
| | **3** Interest on U.S. Savings Bonds and Treas. obligations $ | |
| RECIPIENT'S name | **4** Federal income tax withheld $ | **5** Investment expenses $ |
| Street address (including apt. no.) | **6** Foreign tax paid $ | **7** Foreign country or U.S. possession |
| | **8** Tax-exempt interest $ | **9** Specified private activity bond interest $ |
| City or town, state or province, country, and ZIP or foreign postal code | **10** Market discount $ | **11** Bond premium $ |
| FATCA filing requirement ☐ | **12** Bond premium on Treasury obligations $ | **13** Bond premium on tax-exempt bond $ |
| Account number (see instructions) | **14** Tax-exempt and tax credit bond CUSIP no. | **15** State **16** State identification no. **17** State tax withheld $ $ |

Form **1099-INT** (keep for your records) www.irs.gov/Form1099INT Department of the Treasury - Internal Revenue Service

This is important tax information and is being furnished to the IRS. If you are required to file a return, a negligence penalty or other sanction may be imposed on you if this income is taxable and the IRS determines that it has not been reported.

Source: U.S. Department of the Treasury, Internal Revenue Service, Form 1099-INT. Washington, DC: 2021.

**EXAMPLE 4-7**

On February 1, 2021, Donnie and Marie deposited $10,000 into a one-year CD earning 2% interest at State Bank and Trust. If the couple withdrew their money prior to the end of the term, they would forfeit one month's interest as a penalty. On October 1, 2021, they withdrew their money. Donnie and Marie would report $133 interest income on line 2b of page 1 of Form 1040 or, if required, on Schedule B ($10,000 × 2% × 8/12). They would also report a *for* AGI deduction of $17 on line 18 of Schedule 1 of the Form 1040 ($10,000 × 2% × 1/12) as a penalty on early withdrawal of savings.

**CONCEPT CHECK 4-6— LO 4-6**

1. The early withdrawal penalty is reported on Schedule 1 of Form 1040 as a(n) _____ deduction.

2. The amount of the penalty is reported to the taxpayer by the financial institution on Form _____.

# ALIMONY PAID (SCHEDULE 1, LINE 19a)
## LO 4-7

In a divorce or legal separation, certain payments may flow from one party to the other. These payments are (a) alimony, (b) child support, or (c) a property settlement. For 2021, only alimony has a potential tax consequence, and it is important to be able to distinguish it from the other two types of payments.

*Child support* is a fixed payment (in terms of dollars or a proportion of the payment) that is payable for the support of children of the payer spouse.[37] A *property settlement* is a division of property of the marital community incident to a divorce.[38] For tax purposes, child support payments and property settlement payments do not result in income to either spouse; nor does either spouse receive a tax deduction.

Only the payment of alimony, however, potentially has tax ramifications.[39] Under the TCJA of 2017, beginning in 2019, alimony is no longer deductible by the payer spouse nor included in income of the recipient spouse. This rule only applies to divorce or separation agreements executed after December 31, 2018, and also affects those agreements executed on or before December 31, 2018, but modified after that date making them subject to the new provisions.

For those agreements that were executed on or before December 31, 2018, and were not subsequently modified after that date, the respective parties will still be able to deduct the payments and be required to include the payments in income until such time that the agreements expire.

Alimony received under a pre-2019 agreement is taxable to the payee (receiving) spouse in the year received.[40] It is income on line 2a of the Schedule 1. Alimony payments are deductible by the payer spouse in the year paid as a *for* AGI deduction.[41]

To qualify as *alimony,* a payment must be cash and must be required under the provisions of a decree of divorce or separate maintenance or the provisions of a written separation agreement or other decree requiring one spouse to make payments to support the other spouse.[42] All payments must occur after the decree or after the execution of the agreement. Any payments made prior to this time would be neither deductible by the payer spouse nor included in the income of the payee spouse.

All payments must end at the payee spouse's death. There can be no provisions to make payments to the estate of the spouse or in any other manner after the death of the spouse. If this rule is not satisfied, then none of the payments are alimony, even those made during the life of the spouse.[43]

Alimony includes payments made to third parties on behalf of the payee spouse under the terms of the divorce decree or separate maintenance agreement.[44] Such payments might include paying the spouse's rent, mortgage, car payment, or property taxes. Payments made to maintain property owned by the payer spouse but used by the payee spouse do not qualify as alimony.[45]

Payments are not alimony if the spouses file a joint return or if they live in the same household when payments occur.[46] However, if a payment is made when the spouses are living

---

[37] IRC § 71(c)(1). For divorce decrees effective before 1/1/2019.

[38] IRC § 1041.

[39] The IRC refers to payments for "alimony or separate maintenance." In general, *separate maintenance* refers to payments made by one spouse to another while separated but still married, whereas *alimony* payments are those made after the divorce becomes final. For purposes of this section, we will refer to these payments simply as *alimony.*

[40] IRC § 71. For divorce decrees effective before 1/1/2019.

[41] IRC § 62(a)(10), § 215(a).

[42] IRC § 71(b)(2). For divorce decrees effective before 1/1/2019.

[43] IRC § 71(b)(1)(D). For divorce decrees effective before 1/1/2019; Reg. § 1.71-1T(b), Q&A-10.

[44] IRC § 71(b)(1). For divorce decrees effective before 1/1/2019.

[45] Reg. § 1.71-1T(b), Q&A-6.

[46] IRC § 71(e), § 71(b)(1)(C). For divorce decrees effective before 1/1/2019.

together and one spouse is preparing to leave the household and does so within one month after the payment, such payment will be considered alimony. Furthermore, if the spouses are not yet legally separated under a decree of divorce and a payment is made under a written separation agreement, such payment will count as alimony even if the spouses are members of the same household when the payment is made.[47]

Finally, if the divorce decree or separate maintenance agreement states that certain payments are not alimony, the agreement will control.[48]

# From Shoebox to Software

Alimony received is reported on line 2a of Schedule 1 and the date of the original divorce or separation agreement is reported on line 2b. Alimony paid is reported on line 19a. Persons making alimony payments must report the taxpayer identification number of the recipient on line 19b and the date of the original divorce or separation agreement is reported on line 19c.

In the tax software, you report information concerning alimony received or paid on a worksheet (Alimony Income

or Alimony Paid Adjustment, as the case may be). The tax software carries the information forward to the appropriate line on Schedule 1.

Canceled checks or other forms of payment provide information about the amount of alimony payments. Whether the payments constitute alimony is determined by reference to the divorce decree or separation agreement. In particularly complex cases, the taxpayer should obtain the advice of an attorney.

**EXAMPLE 4-8**

Akeem and Taylor's divorce decree was final on December 12, 2018. Under terms of the divorce, Akeem transferred title on the couple's house to Taylor's name. The house was worth $100,000 at the time of the transfer. The divorce decree also mandated that, beginning in December 2018, Akeem make payments on the 12th of each month of (a) $200 to Taylor for maintenance of the couple's only child, (b) $400 per month to Taylor, and (c) mortgage payments of $800 to the bank on behalf of Taylor. Payments for the child will continue until she reaches age 18; payments to or on behalf of Taylor will cease upon her death. They file separate returns and no modifications have been made to the original divorce decree. How much can Akeem deduct in 2021 for alimony?

For 2021, Akeem will be able to deduct $1,200 per month ($400 + $800), or $14,400 for the year. Note also that the amount of alimony income that Taylor must report is the same as the amount of alimony deduction calculated by Akeem.

However, if the divorce decree between Akeem and Taylor was materially modified on January 1, 2021, then as a result of the tax law referenced above, Akeem would not be able to deduct the payments and Taylor would not be required to report the payments as income. In that case, the answer for 2021 would be zero for both parties.

**TAX YOUR BRAIN**

Would the answer to Example 4-8 change if the child turned 18 in 2021?

**ANSWER**

No. Child support is never deductible and would have no effect on the alimony deduction.

## Alimony Recapture Rules

For those divorce agreements executed before January 1, 2019, if the alimony payments decrease sharply in the second or third year of payment, the payments may be subject to a recapture provision.[49] This relates to the concept of "substance over form"; the payments may

[49] IRC § 71(f). For divorce decrees effective before 1/1/2019.

[47] Reg. § 1.71-T(b), Q&A-9.

[48] IRC § 71(b)(1)(B). For divorce decrees effective before 1/1/2019.

be called alimony but are, in substance, a property settlement. Note that these recapture rules do not apply after the third year of payment.

The recapture rules effectively reclassify payments from alimony to a property settlement. If recapture is required, the recipient (who previously recorded income) treats the recapture amount as a deduction, and the payer (who previously recorded a deduction) must count the recapture as income. The recapture occurs in the third postseparation year.[50]

**TAX YOUR BRAIN**

Why would the IRS care about the timing and magnitude of alimony payments?

**ANSWER**

Alimony payments create income for one taxpayer and a deduction for another, whereas property settlements have no tax effect on either party. In practice, it is likely that the tax rates of the spouses will differ after the divorce, perhaps significantly. For example, one spouse could be in the 35% bracket while the other one is in the 22% bracket. Taxpayers may try, in effect, to shift income from the high-tax spouse to the low-tax spouse.

**CONCEPT CHECK 4-7—**

**LO 4-7**

1. Alimony may be paid in either cash or property, as long as the payments are made on a regular basis to a non-live-in ex-spouse. True or false?
2. For payments to qualify as alimony, the couple must be legally divorced at the time payments are made. True or false?
3. The goal of the alimony recapture rule is to properly define the substance of payments made to a former spouse to ensure proper tax treatment. True or false?

# EDUCATOR EXPENSES (SCHEDULE 1, LINE 11)
## LO 4-8

Eligible educators may deduct up to $250 of qualified education expenses as an above-the-line AGI deduction.[51] The deduction is taken on line 11 of Schedule 1 of Form 1040. If the taxpayer's filing status is married filing jointly and both individuals are eligible educators, the maximum deduction is $500, but neither spouse can deduct more than $250 of their expenses. Taxpayers must reduce otherwise permitted qualified expenses by any reimbursements received pertaining to the expenses.

An eligible educator is a teacher, instructor, counselor, principal, or aide in a kindergarten through 12th grade school who devotes at least 900 hours in the school year to that job.[52] Qualification under the 900-hour test is measured within the academic year, while the $250 deduction applies to expenses paid for during the calendar year.

Qualified education expenses are those for books, supplies, equipment (including computers and software), and other materials used in the classroom. The expense must also be ordinary (common and accepted in the educational field) and necessary (helpful and appropriate in the taxpayer's educational profession). Expenses for home schooling or for nonathletic supplies for health or physical education courses do not qualify. The Protecting Americans from Tax Hikes (PATH) Act of 2015 further enhanced this deduction by allowing "professional development expenses" to qualify. Professional development expenses cover courses related to the curriculum in which the educator provides instruction.

 **NEW LAW**

The Consolidated Appropriations Act, 2021, states that personal protective equipment, disinfectant, and other supplies (COVID-19 Protective Items) used for the prevention of the spread of COVID-19 in the classroom qualify as eligible expenses for purposes of the $250 educator expense deduction, if paid or incurred after March 12, 2020.

---

[50] IRC § 71(f)(6). For divorce decrees effective before 1/1/2019.

[51] IRC § 62(a)(2)(D).

[52] IRC § 62(d)(1).

Under Rev. Proc. 2021-15, the IRS has released guidance that defines COVID-19 Protective Items as face masks, disinfectant for use against COVID-19, hand soap, hand sanitizer, disposable gloves, tape, paint, or chalk used to guide social distancing, physical barriers such as clear plexiglass, air purifiers, and other items recommended by the Centers for Disease Control and Prevention (CDC) to be used for the prevention of the spread of COVID-19.

| **EXAMPLE 4-9** | William and Lakeisha are married and will file a joint tax return. Both are eligible educators. William spent $420 on eligible expenses for his 4th grade class, and he received a $190 reimbursement from his school. Lakeisha spent $360 pertaining to her 11th grade science class and received no reimbursement. In total, the couple spent $780 and received reimbursement of $190, for a net expense of $590. However, William's deduction is limited to his net expenses of $230 ($420 − $190), and Lakeisha's is limited to a maximum of $250. Thus, the total deduction on their joint tax return is $480. |

## From Shoebox to Software  Comprehensive Examples

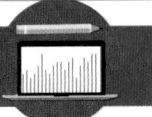

In this section, we will add information to the tax returns of two taxpayers introduced in Chapter 3.

### YIMING CHOW
Open the tax return file of Yiming Chow that you saved from Chapter 3. You are now going to add some information pertaining to the one *for* AGI deduction.

#### Student Loan Interest Deduction
Mr. Chow incurred $622 of interest expense pertaining to a federal student loan incurred while he was a student at State University in Colorado.

You must perform the following steps to report the student loan interest.

Open Mr. Chow's Form 1040, Schedule 1.

Click on line 21. Then click on the yellow folder to open the supporting form. Alternatively, you could have opened the Student Loan Interest Deduction worksheet in the worksheet section.

On line 1 enter the $622 interest payment beside Mr. Chow's name.

Line 16 of the worksheet should now read $622. If you reopen Mr. Chow's Form 1040, Schedule 1, the $622 deduction should be reflected on line 21.

After you have entered the student loan interest data, Mr. Chow's AGI is $41,066 and his taxable income is $28,516. His total tax liability is $3,212. Because his total tax withholdings were $3,750, he should now receive a refund of $538 (rather than having a refund of $466 as determined in Chapter 3).

When you have finished, remember to save Mr. Chow's tax return for use in later chapters.

### JOSE AND MARIA RAMIREZ
Open the tax return file of Mr. and Mrs. Ramirez that you saved from Chapter 3. You will now add some information pertaining to alimony. Remember that for now we are assuming the standard deduction for the Ramirezes.

Mr. Ramirez pays alimony of $150 per month to his former wife (her SSN is 412-34-5666). He paid 12 payments during the year. His divorce agreement was executed in 2014 and there were no modifcations to the agreement post 2018. To record the alimony payments in the tax software, perform the following steps:

Open the Ramirezes' tax return and then open their Form 1040, Schedule 1.

Go to the form's worksheet tab and bring up the Alimony Paid Adjustment worksheet.

On the worksheet, enter $1,800 as the amount of alimony paid by Jose and enter his ex-wife's SSN.

Open the Ramirezes' Form 1040, Schedule 1. The $1,800 alimony payment is on line 19a and the ex-wife's SSN is on the adjacent dotted line 19b.

After you have entered the alimony information, the AGI of the Ramirezes is $110,048. Their taxable income is $84,948, and their total tax liability is $9,980. After the child tax credit of $9,000, and income tax withheld of $6,418, they will receive a refund of $5,438.

When you have finished, make sure you save the Ramirezes' tax return for use in later chapters.

### CONCEPT CHECK 4-8—
### LO 4-8

Please fill in the blanks with the best answer(s).

1. To be eligible for the deduction, an educator must work at least _____ hours in the job.
2. The maximum deduction for a couple who are both eligible educators and married filing jointly is _____ .
3. Expenses for _____ and _____ do not qualify for this deduction.

# Summary

**LO 4-1:** Describe the tax rules for student loan interest.

- Only interest on a *qualified* student loan is potentially deductible.
- A *qualified* loan is one used solely to pay for qualified education expenses.
- The deduction for student loan expense may be limited based on the modified AGI of the taxpayer.
- Student loan interest payments are suspended until September 30, 2021. Payments during the suspension will be for principal only.

**LO 4-2:** Be able to determine eligibility requirements and applicable dollar limits related to the health savings account deduction.

- A health savings account (HSA) is a tax-exempt savings account used to pay for qualified medical expenses.
- To be eligible for an HSA, the taxpayer must be self-employed, an employee (or spouse) of an employer with a high-deductible health plan, or an uninsured employee who has purchased a high-deductible policy on their own.
- Distributions from an HSA are tax-free as long as they are used to pay for qualified medical expenses.

**LO 4-3:** Determine the deduction for military moving expenses.

- The moving expense deduction and the exclusion from income provision are allowed only to members of the Armed Forces, or their spouse or dependents, on active duty.
- If members of the Armed Forces are on active duty and move because of a permanent change of station, they can deduct their unreimbursed moving expenses.
- If the military moves the member, spouse, and dependents to or from separate locations, the moves are treated as a single move to the military member's new main job location.

**LO 4-4:** Explain the deduction for half of self-employment taxes.

- Self-employed individuals pay both halves of the FICA tax. For 2021 self-employed individuals will pay self-employment tax of 15.3%, unless their income is above the threshold for their filing status that requires them to pay the additional 0.9% Medicare tax on their earnings, effectively raising their Medicare tax on earnings from 1.45% to 2.35%.
- The amount related to the employer's portion of the self-employment tax that is a *for* AGI (above-the-line) deduction remains at 7.65% of self-employment income for 2021.
- The tax is based on the *net* earnings from self-employment.

**LO 4-5:** Discuss the self-employed health insurance deduction.

- Self-employed individuals may be able to deduct 100% of self-employed health insurance premiums.
- The amount of the deduction may be limited by two factors:
  - Self-employed individuals cannot take a deduction in excess of the *net* earnings from self-employment.
  - The amount is a function of the availability of other health insurance coverage.

**LO 4-6:** Explain the penalty on early withdrawal of savings.

- A taxpayer who withdraws funds early from a time deposit account may be subject to an early withdrawal penalty.
- The amount of the penalty is reported on Form 1099-INT issued by the financial institution.

**LO 4-7:** Be able to apply the rules regarding alimony and calculate the deduction for alimony paid, if applicable.

- Alimony is one of three potential payments that can exist in a divorce or legal separation.
- Of the three, only alimony potentially has a tax consequence.
- Provided that they relate to divorce agreements executed before 2019, if payments properly qualify as alimony, they are deductible by the payer as a *for* AGI (above-the-line) deduction.
- The recipient (the payee) of the payments must include these payments as income on their tax return.
- Beginning in 2019, alimony is no longer deductible by the payer spouse nor included in income of the recipient spouse.
- This rule applies to divorce or separation agreements executed after December 31, 2018, and those agreements executed on or before December 31, 2018, but modified after that date making them subject to these new provisions.

**LO 4-8:** Determine the deduction for educator expenses.

- Educators may be able to deduct up to $250 of qualified out-of-pocket expenses paid in 2021.
- If both spouses are eligible educators and file a joint return, each may deduct up to $250.
- Qualified educators who work at least 900 hours during the school year are eligible to take the deduction.
- Qualifying expenditures include classroom supplies such as paper, pens, glue, scissors, books, and computers as well as professional development expenses covering courses related to the curriculum in which the educator provides instruction.
- For 2021, personal protective equipment, disinfectant, and other supplies (COVID-19 Protective Items) used for the prevention of the spread of COVID-19 in the classroom qualify as eligible expenses for purposes of the $250 educator expense deduction.

## EA Fast Fact

ADMITTED TO PRACTICE BEFORE THE IRS **ENROLLED AGENT**

What encompasses the Representation Right before the IRS that EAs possess?

- Acting on the taxpayer's behalf
- Protecting the taxpayer's rights
- Communicating with the IRS for the taxpayer regarding their rights or liabilities under law & regulations administered by the IRS
- Preparing and filing necessary documents
- Advising the taxpayer on return positions
- Representing the taxpayer at hearings with the IRS in Examination, Collection, and Appeals

**IMPORTANT**

You are eligible to receive absolutely free, the Surgent Enrolled Agent review program for Part I of the EA exam as a result of purchasing this text. To activate your free access, go to https://Surgent.com/McGrawHill/EA.

## Discussion Questions

All applicable Discussion Questions are available with **Connect**©

**EA** LO 4-1  1. What is a qualified education loan for purposes of the student loan interest deduction?

**EA** LO 4-1  2. What are qualified education expenses for purposes of the student loan interest deduction?

**EA** LO 4-1  3. For purposes of the student loan interest deduction, what is modified AGI, and how is it determined?

**EA** LO 4-1  4. For purposes of the student loan interest deduction, what is an eligible educational institution?

_____

_____

_____

**EA** LO 4-1  5. Explain the limitations associated with the deductibility of student loan interest.

_____

_____

_____

**EA** LO 4-1  6. In 2017, Ming incurred a loan to pay for qualified higher education expenses for her 20-year-old granddaughter, who was a dependent. In 2021, her granddaughter graduated from college, moved away to start a new job, and ceased to be a dependent on Ming's tax return. Ming started making payments on the loan in 2021. Without regard to any modified AGI limitations, is Ming permitted to deduct interest on the loan?

_____

_____

_____

**EA** LO 4-2  7. Explain the purpose of a health savings account (HSA).

_____

_____

_____

**EA** LO 4-2  8. What are the qualifications to be eligible for an HSA deduction?

_____

_____

_____

**EA** LO 4-2  9. What are the consequences of an *employer* contribution to an employee's HSA?

_____

_____

_____

**EA** LO 4-3  10. Explain who qualifies for the deductibility of moving expenses in 2021.

_____

_____

_____

**EA** LO 4-3  11. Define the two key criteria that are necessary for a service member to deduct their moving expenses.

_____

_____

_____

**EA** LO 4-3  12. Which form would a member of the military use to deduct qualifying moving expenses and what key pieces of information should be included there?

_____

_____

_____

**EA**   LO 4-3   13. Jerome, per orders of his military unit, moved from Raleigh, NC, to Portland, ME, and incurred $5,000 of unreimbursed moving expenses. What are some examples of moving costs that are not going to be deductible?

_____

_____

_____

**EA**   LO 4-3   14. How does a change of duty station to a foreign location change the deduction of allowable moving expenses for a service member?

_____

_____

_____

**EA**   LO 4-4   15. Explain why self-employed taxpayers generally pay double the amount of FICA taxes that regular wage earners do.

_____

_____

_____

**EA**   LO 4-4   16. Refer to Question 15. How does the tax code attempt to remedy this seeming inequity?

_____

_____

_____

**EA**   LO 4-5   17. Explain the two limitations associated with the deduction for health insurance by self-employed individuals.

_____

_____

_____

**EA**   LO 4-6   18. What is meant by a *penalty on early withdrawal of savings,* and under what circumstances is it deductible?

_____

_____

_____

**EA**   LO 4-7   19. Define *alimony, child support,* and *property settlement.*

_____

_____

_____

**EA**   LO 4-7   20. Why is it important to distinguish between a property settlement and alimony?

_____

_____

_____

**EA**   LO 4-8   21. Who is eligible to take an above-the-line AGI deduction for educator expenses, and what is the maximum amount of the permitted deduction?

_____

_____

_____

**EA** **LO 4-8** 22. What expenses qualify as deductible educator expenses?

_____

_____

_____

**EA** **LO 4-8** 23. In the case of a joint return, what is the treatment of educator expenses?

_____

_____

_____

**LO 4-9** 24. As a result of the COVID-19 pandemic, are there any special allowances in regard to the types of expenses that qualify for the educator expense deduction?

_____

_____

_____

## Multiple-Choice Questions  Mc Graw Hill connect®

All applicable multiple-choice questions are available with **Connect**©

**EA** 25. (Introduction) *For* AGI, or above-the-line, deductions
   *a.* Are determined by the taxpayer.
   *b.* Are set by statute.
   *c.* Increase tax liability.
   *d.* Are reported in Schedule A.

**EA** 26. (Introduction) *For* AGI, or above-the-line, deductions
   *a.* Increase AGI.
   *b.* Reduce tax credits.
   *c.* Are available only for married filing jointly.
   *d.* Can reduce overall tax liability.

**EA** **LO 4-1** 27. Student loan interest is reported on Form
   *a.* 1098-SA.
   *b.* 1098-E.
   *c.* 1099-S.
   *d.* 1098-GA.

**EA** **LO 4-1** 28. Taxpayers eligible to take the student loan interest deduction do *not* include
   *a.* A student who is claimed as a dependent on another's return.
   *b.* A self-supporting student.
   *c.* The parents of a dependent student who took out the loan on their child's behalf.
   *d.* A married student filing jointly.

**EA** **LO 4-1** 29. For 2017 through 2020, Tanisha, who is single, borrowed a total of $25,000 for higher education expenses on qualified education loans. In 2021, while still living at home and being claimed by her parents as a dependent, she began making payments on the loan. The first year's interest on the loan was reported as $750, and her AGI for the year was less than $70,000. The amount that Tanisha can claim on her 2021 tax return is
   *a.* $750.
   *b.* $540.
   *c.* $425.
   *d.* $0.

**EA**   LO 4-2   30. For 2021 the maximum aggregate annual contribution that a taxpayer, under age 55, can make to an HSA for *family coverage* is

    *a.* $1,400.

    *b.* $3,600.

    *c.* $7,200.

    *d.* $14,000.

**EA**   LO 4-2   31. To be eligible to fund an HSA, a taxpayer must meet which of the following criteria:

    *a.* An employee (or spouse) who works for an employer with a high-deductible health plan.

    *b.* An uninsured employee who has purchased a high-deductible health plan on their own.

    *c.* A self-employed individual.

    *d.* Any of the above.

**EA**   LO 4-3   32. To be eligible to deduct moving expenses, a taxpayer

    *a.* Must be a member of the armed forces.

    *b.* Must be on active duty.

    *c.* Must be undergoing a permanent change of station.

    *d.* Must meet all of the above items.

**EA**   LO 4-3   33. Deductible expenses for a service member's moving do not include

    *a.* The cost of transporting household goods.

    *b.* Hotel costs while moving to the new location.

    *c.* Meals incurred during the move.

    *d.* Storage of household goods for a limited time upon arrival at the new location.

**EA**   LO 4-3   34. If service members move because of a permanent change of station, they can deduct the reasonable unreimbursed expenses of moving themselves and members of their household, including

    *a.* Moving household goods and personal effects.

    *b.* Travel, including auto, bus, train, or air transportation.

    *c.* The cost of storing and insuring their household goods and personal effects for a limited period of time.

    *d.* All of the above.

**EA**   LO 4-4   35. The deduction for half of the self-employment tax is

    *a.* Based on a total of 7.65% of FICA taxes.

    *b.* Based on the gross earnings of the business.

    *c.* Based on filing status.

    *d.* Based on the net earnings of the business.

**EA**   LO 4-5   36. As a *for* AGI deduction, self-employed health insurance premiums are deductible at

    *a.* 50%.

    *b.* 70%.

    *c.* 80%.

    *d.* 100%.

EA LO 4-5 37. Shana is a self-employed carpenter who had net earnings from self-employment of $3,800. She paid $350 per month for health insurance over the last year. Shana is entitled to a *for* AGI deduction for health insurance of

    *a.* $4,200.

    *b.* $3,800.

    *c.* $350.

    *d.* $0.

EA LO 4-6 38. Penalties for the early withdrawal of savings are reported by the financial institution on

    *a.* Box 2 of Form 1099-INT.

    *b.* Form EWIP.

    *c.* A letter of notification.

    *d.* None of the above.

EA LO 4-7 39. Charise is required under a 2018 divorce decree, which has to date remained unchanged, since its inception, to pay $700 of alimony and $350 of child support per month for 12 years. In addition, Charise makes a voluntary payment of $150 per month. How much of each total monthly payment can Charise deduct in 2021?

    *a.* $150.

    *b.* $350.

    *c.* $700.

    *d.* $850.

EA LO 4-7 40. The Renfros were granted a decree of divorce in 2018 that was substantially revised in 2020. In accordance with the decree, Josh Renfro is to pay his ex-wife $24,000 a year until their only child, Evelyn, now 10, turns 18, and then the payments will decrease to $14,000 per year. For 2021, how much can Josh deduct as alimony in total?

    *a.* $10,000.

    *b.* $14,000.

    *c.* $24,000.

    *d.* None of the above.

EA LO 4-7 41. At the beginning of July 2021, Ricardo left his spouse and is currently living in an apartment. The couple has no children. At the end of the current year, no formal proceedings have occurred in relation to the separation or potential divorce. Ricardo has been making a $3,000 a month maintenance payment since moving out. How much can Ricardo deduct in total as alimony for 2021?

    *a.* $0.

    *b.* $3,000.

    *c.* $18,000.

    *d.* $36,000.

EA LO 4-8 42. Which of the following items does not qualify as an educator expense item deduction?

    *a.* Books.

    *b.* Home schooling expenses.

    *c.* Computers and software.

    *d.* Professional development expenses related to the curriculum.

**EA** LO 4-8 43. Under current tax law, the deductible amount for expenses under the educator expense deduction is limited per taxpayer to

a. $100.

b. $150.

c. $200.

d. $250.

**EA** LO 4-8 44. How many hours during the academic year must eligible educators work to qualify for the Educator Expense deduction?

a. 0.

b. 450.

c. 900.

*d.* 1,000.

## Problems ![Mc Graw Hill] **connect**

All applicable problems are available with **Connect**©

**EA** LO 4-1 45. What are some of the limitations concerning deductibility of student loan interest? Be specific and comprehensive.

_____

_____

_____

**EA** LO 4-1 46. Discuss the characteristics of an *eligible educational institution* as it relates to the deductibility of student loan interest.

_____

_____

_____

**EA** LO 4-1 47. Tam attended Brown University during 2016–2020. She lived at home and was claimed by her parents as a dependent during her entire education. She incurred education expenses of $10,000 during college, of which $2,000 was paid for by scholarships. To finance her education, she borrowed $6,000 through a federal student loan program and borrowed another $4,000 from a local lending institution for educational purposes. After graduation, she married and moved with her spouse to a distant city. In 2021 she incurred $600 of interest on the federal loans and $400 on the lending institution loan. She filed a joint return with her spouse showing modified AGI of $132,000. What amount of student loan interest can Tam and her spouse deduct in 2021, if any?

_____

_____

_____

**EA** LO 4-2 48. If an employer contributes to an HSA on behalf of an employee,

a. Is the contribution deductible by the employee?

_____

_____

b. Is the payment considered income to the employee?

_____

_____

**EA** **LO 4-3** 49. Dulari, a single member of the military, was stationed at Camp Pendleton, California. On July 1, 2021, her army company transferred her to Washington, DC, as a permanent duty station. Dulari was active duty for the entire year. During 2021 she incurred and paid the following expenses related to the move:

| | |
|---|---:|
| Pre-move house-hunting costs | $1,800 |
| Lodging and travel expenses (not meals) while moving | 2,150 |
| Cost of moving furniture and personal belongings | 3,200 |

She did not receive reimbursement for any of these expenses from the army; her AGI for the year was $35,500. What amount can Dulari deduct as moving expenses on her 2021 return?

_____

_____

_____

**EA** **LO 4-3** 50. In May 2021 Reginald graduated from the Naval Academy with a degree in aeronautical engineering and was assigned to Pensacola, Florida. as a permanent duty station. In his move to Pensacola, Reginald incurred the following costs:

$450 in gasoline.

$250 for renting a truck from UPayMe rentals.

$100 for a tow trailer for his car.

$85 in food.

$25 in double espressos from Starbucks.

$300 for motel lodging on the way to Pensacola.

$405 for a previous plane trip to Pensacola to look for an apartment.

$175 in temporary storage costs for his collection of sports memorabilia.

If the government reimburses him $900, how much, if any, may Reginald take as a moving expense deduction on his 2021 tax return?

_____

_____

_____

**EA** **LO 4-3** 51. Are the moving expenses of other people besides the service member deductible? If so, what are the requirements for deductibility?

_____

_____

_____

**EA** **LO 4-4, 4-5** 52. Juan, who is single, is a self-employed carpenter as well as an employee of Frame It, Inc. His self-employment net income is $43,000, and he received a W-2 from Frame It for wages of $32,250. He is covered by his employer's pension plan, but his employer does not offer a health plan in which he could participate.

a. Up to how much of his self-employed health insurance premiums could he deduct for this year, if any? Why?

_____

_____

_____

    *b.* How much of Juan's self-employment taxes would be deductible?

_____

_____

_____

**EA**   **LO 4-6**   53. Sebastian has received a 1099-INT from his financial institution showing $167 in box 2 of the form. How should she handle this on his 2021 tax return and why?

_____

_____

_____

**EA**   **LO 4-7**   54. Three types of potential payments are associated with a decree of separation or a divorce.

    *a.* What are those three payments?

_____

_____

    *b.* Which one potentially has a tax consequence?

_____

_____

    *c.* What is the timing rule regarding the recapture period of those payments?

_____

_____

**EA**   **LO 4-7**   55. Under the terms of a divorce decree executed May 1, 2018, and which has not been amended since, Ahmed transferred a house worth $650,000 to his ex-wife, Farah, and was to make alimony payments of $3,000 per month. The property has a tax basis to Ahmed of $300,000.

    *a.* How much of this must be reported on Farah's 2021 tax return?

_____

_____

    *b.* Of that amount, how much is taxable gain or loss that Farah must recognize related to the transfer of the house?

_____

_____

_____

**EA**   **LO 4-7**   56. Under the alimony recapture rules, what amounts are designated for recapture reclassification, and what are the tax consequences for those agreements executed before 2019 that remain unchanged post 2018?

_____

_____

_____

**EA**   **LO 4-1–4-7**   57. Indicate whether each of the following items is considered a *for* AGI (above-the-line) deduction for the 2021 tax year:

    *a.* Student loan interest.

    *b.* Gambling losses.

    *c.* Early withdrawal penalty.

    *d.* Child support payments.

  *e.* Charitable contributions up to $300 in cash.

  *f.* One-half of self-employment taxes.

  *g.* Alimony.

  *h.* Scholarships for tuition and books.

  *i.* Moving expenses for service members.

  *j.* Property taxes.

  *k.* Self-employed health insurance premiums.

_____

_____

_____

## Tax Return Problems  

All applicable tax return problems are available with **Connect**©

Use your tax software to complete the following problems. If you are manually preparing the tax returns, you will need a Form 1040 and associated schedules for each problem.

For the following tax return problems, assume the taxpayer does *not* wish to contribute to the Presidential Election Fund, unless otherwise stated in the problem. In addition, the taxpayers did not receive, sell, send, exchange, or otherwise acquire any financial interest in any virtual currency during the year. For any Tax Return Problems for which the taxpayers are entitled to a child tax credit, assume that the taxpayers did NOT receive any advance child tax credit payments during 2021. Thus, the entire child tax credit (if permitted) will be claimed on the 2021 tax return.

**Tax Return Problem 1**

Jason Ready attended the University of Akron from 2017 to 2021 under the Army ROTC program. Excluding the school expenses covered by his ROTC scholarship, he incurred additional school expenses of $15,000 in total for his education, and $2,250 of that amount was incurred in 2021 for his last semester. To finance these expenses, he borrowed $10,500 through a federal student loan program and borrowed another $4,500 from Buckeye State Credit Union for educational purposes. After graduation, he received his officer's commission and was ordered to report to the Military Entrance Processing Station in Portland, Oregon, for duty. He lives off base at 4560 Ranch Drive, Portland, OR 97035. His social security number is 412-34-5670 (date of birth 7/10/1999).

 His W-2 contained the following information:

  Wages (box 1) = $67,533.05

  Federal W/H (box 2) = $ 8,204.45

  Social security wages (box 3) = $67,533.05

  Social security W/H (box 4) = $ 4,187.05

  Medicare wages (box 5) = $67,533.05

  Medicare W/H (box 6) = $ 979.23

In moving to Portland, he incurred the following unremibursed moving expenses:

 $475 in gasoline.

 $325 for renting a truck from IGOTYA rentals.

 $135 in food.

 $520 for motel lodging on the way to Portland.

He also received two Forms 1098-E. One was from the federal student loan program, which showed $550 of student loan interest; the other was from Buckeye State Credit Union and showed $160.40 of student loan interest.

Prepare a Form 1040, Schedule 1, and a Form 3903. If manually preparing the return, the Student Loan Interest Deduction worksheet can be found in IRS Publication 970, *Tax Benefits for Education.*

**Tax Return Problem 2**

In July 2021 Kirk and Rasheeda Wallace and their two dependent children, who are both over 17, moved from Chicago to Albuquerque, New Mexico, a distance of 1,327 miles, which they drove in their own car. The children's names are Marcus and Tara and both will be attending the University of New Mexico in the fall, Marcus as a freshman and Tara as a junior. The move was a result of a civilian job transfer for Kirk. The distance from their old home to Kirk's old office was 30 miles. Rasheeda quit her job in Chicago and decided to perform volunteer work for a year before seeking further employment. Their new home is located at 7432 Desert Springs Way, Albuquerque, NM 87101. Kirk, but not Rasheeda, was employed in the new location throughout the year. Kirk's social security number is 412-34-5670 (date of birth 6/12/1978), Rasheeda's is 412-34-5671 (date of birth 8/12/1980), Marcus's is 412-34-5672 (date of birth 2/17/2004), and Tara's is 412-34-5673 (date of birth 9/14/2002).

Kirk is an electrical engineer for a national firm; his W-2 contained the following information:

Wages (box 1) = $110,220.45
Federal W/H (box 2) = $ 5,810.36
Social security wages (box 3) = $110,220.45
Social security W/H (box 4) = $ 6,833.67
Medicare wages (box 5) = $110,220.45
Medicare W/H (box 6) = $ 1,598.20

In addition, both he and Rasheeda received Form 1098-E from the federal student loan program. Kirk had student loan interest of $1,050, and Rasheeda had student loan interest of $750. The children are both eligible for the Credit for Other Dependents and as a result $1,000 will go on line 19 of pg. 2 of Form 1040.

Prepare a Form 1040 and a Schedule 1 for Kirk and Rasheeda. If manually preparing the return, the Student Loan Interest Deduction worksheet can be found in IRS Publication 970, *Tax Benefits for Education.*

**Tax Return Problem 3**

Kathy and Rob Alvarez obtained a divorce effective May 1, 2018, and there have been no revisions to the original agreement since that time. In accordance with the divorce decree, Kathy was required to pay $2,450 per month until their only child turns 18; then the payments would be reduced to $1,500 per month. Rob has full custody of the child and appropriately takes the child credit. Furthermore, Kathy was to transfer title of their house, which had a cost of $250,000 and a fair value of $410,000 on the date of transfer, to Rob and was to continue making the monthly mortgage payments of $1,525 on behalf of Rob. Kathy works for a large oil distributor in Santa Fe, NM, and after the divorce lives at 1132 Northgate Avenue, Santa Fe, NM 87501. Kathy's social security number is 412-34-5671 (date of birth 11/4/1987), and Rob's social security number is 412-34-5670 (date of birth 8/14/1985).

Her W-2 contained the following information:

Wages (box 1) = $85,100.25
Federal W/H (box 2) = $ 4,861.75
Social security wages (box 3) = $85,100.25
Social security W/H (box 4) = $ 5,276.22
Medicare wages (box 5) = $85,100.25
Medicare W/H (box 6) = $ 1,233.95

She also received a Form 1099-INT from First New Mexico Bank with $256 of interest income in box 1. In addition, Kathy made a timely $2,500 contribution to her new HSA account.

Prepare a 2021 Form 1040 and a Schedule 1 as well as a Form 8889 for Kathy.

**Tax Return Problem 4**

Rick and Cindy Davis are married and file a joint return. They live at 3223 Taccone Ave., Apt. 37, Medford, MA 02155. Rick is an elementary school teacher in the Medford Public School system and Cindy is currently unemployed after losing her job in late 2020 due to the pandemic. Cindy's social security number is 412-34-5671 (date of birth 10/11/1982) and Rick's is 412-34-5670 (date of birth 3/19/1980).

Rick's W-2 contained the following information:

Wages (box 1) = $70,245.55
Federal W/H (box 2) = $ 5,272.16
Social security wages (box 3) = $70,245.55
Social security W/H (box 4) = $ 4,355.22
Medicare wages (box 5) = $70,245.55
Medicare W/H (box 6) = $ 1,018.56

Rick and Cindy have interest income of $237 from a savings account at Boston State Bank.

Cindy also owns stock in Microsoft. Cindy received $265 in qualified dividends from Microsoft in 2021. Rick was divorced in 2015 and pays his ex-wife (Mary Tortelli) alimony. Their original divorce decree, which remains unchanged, dictates that Rick pay Mary $525 per month in alimony for 10 years. Mary's social security number is 412-34-5675.

Cindy received unemployment compensation of $3,800 during 2021 and no taxes were withheld from the payments. Additionally, Rick won a $1,100 prize in a nationally sponsored fantasy football league and no income taxes were withheld from his winnings. Rick also spent $355 on supplies for his classroom for which he was not reimbursed.

Prepare a Form 1040 and Schedule 1 for Rick and Cindy Davis.

# Chapter **Five**

# Itemized Deductions

This chapter provides a detailed investigation of Schedule A and itemized deductions. Specifically, we present the new laws and rules regarding the six basic categories of the primarily personal expenditures allowed as tax deductions. In addition to the law and rules for deductibility, we present the practical application of the law on Schedule A and related forms.

### Learning Objectives

When you have completed this chapter, you should understand the following learning objectives (LO):

**LO 5-1** Describe the deductibility and reporting of medical expenses.

**LO 5-2** Be able to explain the state and local tax deductions.

**LO 5-3** Apply the tax rules associated with the interest deduction.

**LO 5-4** Explain the deductibility and reporting of charitable contributions.

**LO 5-5** Discuss the casualty loss deduction.

**LO 5-6** Know how to report other itemized deductions.

## INTRODUCTION

While Internal Revenue Code allows taxpayers to deduct certain items from gross income when determining taxable income, the Tax Cuts and Jobs Act of 2017 (TCJA) made some significant changes in this area. One type of permitted deduction is a *for* (or *above-the-line*) AGI deduction such as moving expenses, student loan interest, and health savings accounts. We discussed these *for* AGI deductions in Chapter 4.

The other type of permitted deduction is a *from* (*below-the-line*) AGI deduction. You are already familiar with one *from* AGI deduction—the standard deduction, discussed in Chapter 2. We now introduce you to another *from* AGI deduction—the itemized deduction— and it is here that some of the most impactful changes occur as a result of the TCJA tax bill.

Itemized deductions are reported on Schedule A (see Exhibit 5-1). If you review Schedule A, you will see that itemized deductions are organized into six major categories:

1. Medical.
2. State and local taxes.
3. Interest.
4. Charitable gifts.
5. Casualty losses.
6. Other itemized deductions, which contain a built-in threshold or limitation for deductibility.

 **NEW LAW**

For 2021, there is a special "below-the-line" deduction for *non-itemizers* of up to $600 on a married-filing-joint return ($300 for singles) for cash charitable contributions.

**EXHIBIT 5-1**

| SCHEDULE A<br>(Form 1040)<br><br>Department of the Treasury<br>Internal Revenue Service (99) | **Itemized Deductions**<br>▶ Go to *www.irs.gov/ScheduleA* for instructions and the latest information.<br>▶ Attach to Form 1040 or 1040-SR.<br>**Caution:** If you are claiming a net qualified disaster loss on Form 4684, see the instructions for line 16. | OMB No. 1545-0074<br>**2021**<br>Attachment<br>Sequence No. **07** |
|---|---|---|

Name(s) shown on Form 1040 or 1040-SR

Your social security number

| | | | |
|---|---|---|---|
| **Medical and Dental Expenses** | **Caution:** Do not include expenses reimbursed or paid by others. | | |
| | 1 Medical and dental expenses (see instructions) | **1** | |
| | 2 Enter amount from Form 1040 or 1040-SR, line 11 **2** | | |
| | 3 Multiply line 2 by 7.5% (0.075) | **3** | |
| | 4 Subtract line 3 from line 1. If line 3 is more than line 1, enter -0- | | **4** |
| **Taxes You Paid** | 5 State and local taxes. | | |
| | **a** State and local income taxes or general sales taxes. You may include either income taxes or general sales taxes on line 5a, but not both. If you elect to include general sales taxes instead of income taxes, check this box ▶ ☐ | **5a** | |
| | **b** State and local real estate taxes (see instructions) | **5b** | |
| | **c** State and local personal property taxes | **5c** | |
| | **d** Add lines 5a through 5c | **5d** | |
| | **e** Enter the smaller of line 5d or $10,000 ($5,000 if married filing separately) | **5e** | |
| | 6 Other taxes. List type and amount ▶ | **6** | |
| | 7 Add lines 5e and 6 | | **7** |
| **Interest You Paid**<br>**Caution:** Your mortgage interest deduction may be limited (see instructions). | 8 Home mortgage interest and points. If you didn't use all of your home mortgage loan(s) to buy, build, or improve your home, see instructions and check this box . . . . . . . . . ▶ ☐ | | |
| | **a** Home mortgage interest and points reported to you on Form 1098. See instructions if limited | **8a** | |
| | **b** Home mortgage interest not reported to you on Form 1098. See instructions if limited. If paid to the person from whom you bought the home, see instructions and show that person's name, identifying no., and address<br>▶ | **8b** | |
| | **c** Points not reported to you on Form 1098. See instructions for special rules | **8c** | |
| | **d** Mortgage insurance premiums (see instructions) | **8d** | |
| | **e** Add lines 8a through 8d | **8e** | |
| | 9 Investment interest. Attach Form 4952 if required. See instructions . | **9** | |
| | 10 Add lines 8e and 9 | | **10** |
| **Gifts to Charity**<br>**Caution:** If you made a gift and got a benefit for it, see instructions. | 11 Gifts by cash or check. If you made any gift of $250 or more, see instructions | **11** | |
| | 12 Other than by cash or check. If you made any gift of $250 or more, see instructions. You **must** attach Form 8283 if over $500. | **12** | |
| | 13 Carryover from prior year | **13** | |
| | 14 Add lines 11 through 13 | | **14** |
| **Casualty and Theft Losses** | 15 Casualty and theft loss(es) from a federally declared disaster (other than net qualified disaster losses). Attach Form 4684 and enter the amount from line 18 of that form. See instructions | | **15** |
| **Other Itemized Deductions** | 16 Other—from list in instructions. List type and amount ▶ | | **16** |
| **Total Itemized Deductions** | 17 Add the amounts in the far right column for lines 4 through 16. Also, enter this amount on Form 1040 or 1040-SR, line 12a | | **17** |
| | 18 If you elect to itemize deductions even though they are less than your standard deduction, check this box . . . . . . . . . . . . . ▶ ☐ | | |

For Paperwork Reduction Act Notice, see the Instructions for Forms 1040 and 1040-SR.    Cat. No. 17145C    **Schedule A (Form 1040) 2021**

Source: U.S. Department of the Treasury, Internal Revenue Service, Form 1040, Schedule A. Washington, DC: 2021.

The six learning objectives of this chapter are tied to these six categories of itemized deductions.

Most itemized deductions are, in effect, personal living expenses: medical expenses, interest expenses, payments for taxes, and the like. Personal living expenses can be deducted only if they are expressly permitted.

Itemized deductions also include investment-related expenses (part of the deductible interest category).

In practice, taxpayers determine their (1) standard deduction and (2) total itemized deductions and use the higher number. In other words, a taxpayer cannot take *both* the standard deduction *and* the itemized deduction but only the higher of the two. Recall, for example, that the standard deduction is $25,100 for a married couple.[1] Thus, a married couple who has itemized deductions of less than $25,100 should claim the standard deduction, but if the itemized deductions total more than $25,100, the couple should consider itemizing the deductions.

# DEDUCTIBLE MEDICAL EXPENSES (SCHEDULE A, LINE 4)
## LO 5-1

Taxpayers can deduct an itemized deduction for medical expenses (net of insurance proceeds) for themselves, their spouse, and dependent(s). The qualifying relationship must exist at the date the taxpayer incurs or pays the expenses. Only the amount in excess of 7.5% of AGI is deductible.[2] Because the threshold is so high, medical expenditures usually must be substantial for the taxpayer(s) to benefit from a medical deduction. A formula for calculating the amount of deductible medical expense is shown in Table 5-1.

Two special rules apply for determining whether an individual qualifies as a dependent for purposes of the medical expense deduction:

1. The dependent child of divorced parents is treated as a dependent of both parents. The parent who pays the child's medical expenses may deduct the expenses even if the parent is not permitted to claim the child's dependency exemption.

**TABLE 5-1**
**Medical Expense Deduction Formula**

**Calculation of Deductible Medical Expenses**

| |
|---|
| Allowable medical expenses |
| minus (insurance reimbursements) |
| Allowable net paid medical expenses |
| minus (7.5% of Adjusted Gross Income) |
| Deductible medical expenses |

**EXAMPLE 5-1**

Alice and Bob are married taxpayers, with AGI of $100,000 in tax year 2021. To benefit from an itemized deduction for medical expenses, Alice and Bob must have medical costs in excess of $7,500 ($100,000 × 7.5% floor).

2. The gross income and the joint return tests for the dependency exemption are waived. A taxpayer who pays the medical expenses of an individual who satisfies the relationship, citizenship, and support tests for the dependency exemption may deduct the medical expenses paid for that person.[3]

A deduction may be claimed only for medical expenses actually paid during the taxable year regardless of when the care was provided and regardless of the taxpayer's method of accounting.[4] A medical expense charged to a credit card is considered paid.

[1] The standard deduction for a qualifying widow(er) is $25,100, for head of household is $18,800, and for a single person as well as married filing separately is $12,550.

[2] IRC § 213.

[3] Reg. § 1.213-1(a)(3)(i).

[4] IRC § 213(a).

The taxpayer may deduct costs for medical care, which includes the following:

1. The diagnosis, cure, mitigation, treatment, or prevention of disease, or for the purpose of affecting any structure or function of the body.
2. Transportation primarily for and essential to medical care.
3. Qualified long-term care services.
4. Insurance for medical care or qualified long-term care services.

**NEW LAW**

In most instances, medical expenses are relatively straightforward and include all costs for licensed medical treatment. Ambiguity occurs when expenditures for personal, living, and family purposes (generally not deductible) are incidental to medical care (generally deductible).

Under IRS Announcement 2021-7, the IRS has ruled that amounts paid for personal protective equipment (PPE), such as face masks, hand sanitizer, and sanitizing wipes, used for the primary purpose of preventing the spread of the Coronavirus Disease 2019 (COVID-19 PPE) are treated as amounts paid for medical care under IRC section 213(d).

Amounts paid by an individual taxpayer for COVID-19 PPE for use by the taxpayer, the taxpayer's spouse, or the taxpayer's dependents that are not compensated for by insurance are deductible as medical expenses under IRC section 213(a) provided that the taxpayer can itemize deductions and total medical expenses exceed 7.5% of AGI.

**TAX YOUR BRAIN**

A physician prescribes a special diet consisting of low-fat, high-fiber foods to lower cholesterol. The physician's bill is definitely deductible. However, is the cost of the food a deductible medical expense?

**ANSWER**

The mere fact that a physician prescribes or recommends a course of action does not automatically qualify the expenditure as a deduction.[5] If an expense item is ordinarily for personal purposes, the excess of the cost of the special items (excess over the ordinary-use goods) qualifies as a medical deduction. For example, the extra cost of a specially designed auto (above the normal cost of the auto) for a taxpayer confined to a wheelchair would qualify as a medical deduction.[6] Therefore, the special food would be deductible only to the extent the food costs exceeded normal food costs. This would be difficult to substantiate. Thus, it is unlikely that the food would qualify as a deductible medical expense.

Taxpayers may *not* deduct expenditures that are merely for the benefit of the general health of an individual.[7] For example, expenditures for cosmetic surgery are normally not deductible. Clearly, any payments made for operations or treatments for any part of the body or function of the body are deductible if they serve a distinct medical need. Plastic surgery to repair a birth defect would be a deductible expense. This includes payments to virtually all health care providers, such as doctors, dentists, ophthalmologists, nurses, and physical therapists as well as many unconventional medical treatments, from acupuncture to treatments by Christian Science practitioners.[8]

---

[5] *Atkinson v. Comm'r*, 44 TC 39 (1965), *acq.*, 1965-2 CB 4.

[6] Rev. Rul. 76-80, 1976-1 CB 71.

[7] Reg. § 1.213-1(e)(1)(ii).

[8] Rev. Rul. 72-593, 1972-2 CB 180; Rev. Rul. 55-261, 1955-1 CB 307. Payments to the following medical providers are specifically included as deductible charges: psychologists, physicians, surgeons, specialists or other medical practitioners, chiropractors, dentists, optometrists, osteopaths, psychiatrists, and Christian Science practitioners.

**TAX YOUR BRAIN**

Can a capital expenditure such as an addition of a swimming pool to a house qualify as a deductible medical expense?

**ANSWER**

If the capital expenditure for the swimming pool is for the primary medical care of the taxpayer, their spouse, or their dependent(s), it may qualify for a deduction.[9] This area has been highly litigated by the IRS. To ensure the deduction for the pool, a physician must prescribe swimming and there can be no recreational element (such as a diving board or slide) to the pool. Other factors used in determining the deductibility of a swimming pool include the availability of other types of exercise and access to a community pool.[10]

For medical capital expenditures that improve the taxpayer's property, the deduction is available only to the extent that the medical expenditure exceeds the increase in the fair market value (FMV) of the residence. Thus, if the cost of a swimming pool for medical purposes was $30,000 and the increase in FMV to the residence was $20,000, the medical deduction would be limited to $10,000 (the excess cost over the FMV increase).

**EXAMPLE 5-2**

Siouxrita suffers from a severe knee condition and is unable to climb steps. Consequently, she installed an elevator in her home at a cost of $7,000. An appraiser indicates that the elevator increased the value of the home by $2,000. The cost of the elevator, $7,000, is a medical expense to the extent that it exceeds the increase in the value of the property, $2,000. Thus, $5,000 of the cost of the elevator is included in the calculation of Siouxrita's medical expense deduction.

Generally, deductible medical costs do not include cosmetic surgery unless the surgery is necessary to correct a deformity arising from a congenital abnormality, personal injury, or disfiguring disease.[11]

**EXAMPLE 5-3**

Tamara was riding her mountain bike on a trail and lost control. Her head and face hit a tree stump, causing damage to the right side of her face. The cost of the cosmetic surgery to repair the damage, the hospital stay, and all physician fees would qualify as a medical deduction.

Medical expenses are *not* deductible if they have been "compensated for by insurance or otherwise."[12] As a result, any insurance reimbursements or partial reimbursements reduce the deductible medical expenses subject to the 7.5% AGI limitation.

## Medicine and Drugs

For the cost of a drug to be deductible, a physician must first prescribe it.[13] This would include payments for birth control pills or drugs to alleviate nicotine withdrawal as long as a prescription was required.[14]

One other limitation to the deductibility of medicine or drug costs is that the taxpayer must obtain the drug legally. Thus, even if a physician prescribes an otherwise illegal drug for medicinal purposes, the cost of acquiring the illegal drug is not deductible.

Prescription drugs obtained from sources outside the United States, such as Canada, are deductible if they are prescribed by a physician for the treatment of a medical condition and the FDA has approved that they can be legally imported. Amounts paid for over-the-counter medications are generally not reimbursable from health saving accounts (HSAs), which were covered in Chapter 4.

[9] Reg. § 1.213-1(e)(1)(iii).
[10] Rev. Rul. 83-33 (1983-1 CB 70) specially addresses the swimming pool issue.
[11] IRC § 213(d)(9).
[12] IRC § 213(a).
[13] IRC § 213(b).
[14] Rev. Rul. 73-200, 1973-1 CB 140; Rev. Rul. 99-28, 1999-25 IRB 6.

A physician prescribes marijuana for pain control purposes for a terminally ill cancer patient. The use of marijuana for medicinal purposes is legal under state law. Can a taxpayer deduct the cost of marijuana?

**ANSWER**

Because marijuana cannot be legally procured under federal law, its cost is not deductible.[15]

## Travel and Transportation for Medical Purposes

Transportation costs for medical purposes could include such items as cab, bus, or train fares, as well as expenses for a personal auto. The cost of the transportation must be primarily for, and essential to, deductible medical care.[16]

**EXAMPLE 5-4**

Jake Avery, who currently lives in New Orleans, must fly to Memphis to see a specialist concerning an inner ear condition. His spouse a big Elvis fan, decides to go along to visit Graceland. The travel costs for Jake, but not his spouse are deductible as a medical expense. If, on the other hand, his spouse's assistance is required on the trip due to problems stemming from the ear condition, the spouse's costs would also be deductible.[17]

There are two ways to calculate the deduction for the use of a personal auto for medical transportation: (1) the *actual cost* of operating the car for medical purposes or (2) the *standard mileage allowance*.[18]

When using the actual costs, the taxpayer must keep documentation for items such as gasoline, oil, repairs, and so on that are directly associated with transportation to and from medical care. However, the taxpayer gets no deduction for general repairs, maintenance, or insurance. The simpler approach for deducting personal auto expense is to use the standard mileage allowance, which in 2021 is 16 cents per mile. The taxpayer can deduct other supplemental costs such as parking and tolls in addition to the applicable mileage rate.

**EXAMPLE 5-5**

Maria has an inoperable brain tumor that requires treatment at University Medical Center in Houston twice a month. It is a 500-mile round trip. She pays a total of $10 in tolls, $20 in parking, and $75 for gasoline on each round trip. Assuming that Maria made the trip six times in the current tax year, what is the maximum transportation expense deduction for medical purposes (*disregarding* the 7.5% AGI floor)?

**ANSWER**

Actual costs follow:

| | |
|---|---|
| Gasoline ($75 × 6) | $450 |
| Tolls ($10 × 6) | 60 |
| Parking ($20 × 6) | 120 |
| Total deduction | $630 |

Use of the standard mileage rate in effect for the year gives this deduction:

| | |
|---|---|
| Mileage (500 miles × $0.16/mile × 6) | $480 |
| Tolls ($10 × 6) | 60 |
| Parking ($20 × 6) | 120 |
| Total deduction | $660 |

Maria would generally choose the standard mileage rate in this situation because it produces a higher deduction. This may not always be the case, however. In reality, the convenience and the lack of receipt substantiation make the standard mileage rate more popular even though the deduction of actual costs could be higher.

---

[15] Reg. § 1.213-1(e)(2); Rev. Rul. 97-9, 1997-1 CB 77.

[16] IRC § 213(d)(1)(B).

[17] *Kelly v. Comm'r,* TC Memo 1969-231, *rev'd on other grounds,* 440 F.2d 307 (7th Cir. 1971).

[18] Rev. Proc. 80-32, 1980-2 CB 767.

In addition to the mileage, the cost of meals and lodging at a hospital or similar institution is deductible if the principal reason for being there is to receive medical care.[19] Lodging near the related medical facility is deductible as long as no significant element of personal pleasure, recreation, or vacation is involved. The lodging expenditures are limited to $50 for each night for each individual, and meals are not deductible.[20] You can include lodging for a person traveling with the person receiving the medical care. For example, if a parent is traveling with a sick child, up to $100 per night can be deducted.

## Long-Term Care

As the population ages, more funds will be spent providing long-term care for senior citizens. *Qualified long-term care services* are medical, maintenance, and personal care services provided to a chronically ill individual pursuant to a plan of care prescribed by a licensed health care practitioner.

The general rule concerning the deductibility of nursing home or other long-term care institution costs provides that amounts spent are deductible if the principal reason for the individual's stay is medical care as opposed to enjoyment or convenience. The entire cost of the long-term institution is deductible as a medical expense if indeed that is the case. If full-time medical care is not required, only the fee allocable to actual medical care is deductible, and costs for food and lodging are nondeductible.[21]

Determining medical expenses is usually quite easy for the individual or client who keeps good records. Generally, medical care providers supply the necessary receipts to document the medical charges incurred in a hospital or doctor's office. Other source documents for medical charges include checkbook registers, bank records, and credit card statements. Be careful, however, in taking a medical deduction for a check made out to a local drugstore that sells items in addition to prescription drugs. The IRS may require an itemized receipt for the prescription drugs. Pharmacy departments usually provide this information. Another major item, which is easy to misclassify, is the payment of health insurance premiums. These are deductible only if the taxpayer pays the premiums with after-tax funds (not in an employer pretax plan).

## Insurance for Medical Care or Long-Term Care

Premiums for medical insurance, such as major medical, hospitalization, dental, and vision insurance, are deductible. This includes Medicare B premiums for voluntary supplemental coverage, but it does not include Medicare A insurance payroll taxes withheld from the taxpayer's paycheck. Premiums for long-term care policies are deductible, subject to dollar limitations. Deductible amounts for 2021[22] follow:

| Age at Close of Taxable Year | 2021 Amount |
| --- | --- |
| 40 and under | $   450 |
| More than 40, but not more than 50 | 850 |
| More than 50, but not more than 60 | 1,690 |
| More than 60, but not more than 70 | 4,520 |
| Age 71 and over | 5,640 |

In the event that the long-term insurance contract pays periodic payments to an individual who is chronically ill, any amount in excess of the per diem limit is in fact taxable. The per diem rate for 2021 is $400.

[19] *Montgomery v. Comm'r,* 428 F.2d 243 (6th Cir. 1970), *aff'g* 51 TC 410 (1968).

[20] IRC § 213(d)(2)(A), (B).

[21] Reg. § 1.213-1(e)(1)(v).

[22] IRS Rev. Proc. 2020-45.

# From Shoebox to Software

**EXAMPLE 5-6**   We will return to Maria and Jose Ramirez in terms of Example 5-5. In Chapter 4, you created and saved a tax file for Jose and Maria Ramirez. They had an AGI of $110,048. For this chapter, you will reopen their return and you will add the following medical costs:

| | |
|---|---:|
| Maria's hospital charges | $13,000 |
| Maria's physician charges | 8,000 |
| Maria's prescription drugs | 3,000 |
| Jose's high blood pressure drugs | 300 |
| Jose's eye surgery | 750 |
| Regular dental visits (4 total) | 280 |
| Jose's regular physician charges | 400 |
| Transportation (from Example 5-5) | 660 |
| Lodging for trips to the University of Texas (for both Jose and Maria—Maria could not drive because the treatments affected her vision—6 nights at $127/night) | 600 |
| High-fiber health food recommended for Jose | 450 |

Assuming that Jose and Maria do not have health insurance, how much is their medical deduction, and how is it presented on Form 1040, Schedule A?

Tax software: Retrieve the Ramirezes' file saved from Chapter 4. Because of the numerous types of medical expenses allowed, it is easier to go directly to Schedule A to enter the medical deductions.

To complete the form, you must understand tax law. All of the expenses qualify for a deduction with the exception of the high-fiber health food. Additionally, the lodging is limited to $50 per person per night. In this case, because Jose was required to drive Maria, expenses for both of them qualify, and lodging would be limited to $100 per night ($50 for Jose, $50 for Maria) for six nights. Thus, the total medical deduction before the 7.5% AGI limitation is $26,990.

The $26,990 deduction could be placed on line 1 of Schedule A; or if you wished to list all of the deductions, you could right-click on line 1 and then list the expenses on the "add line item detail" provided. The taxpayer's AGI ($110,048) would automatically transfer to line 2, and the 7.5% limitation ($8,254) would be calculated. Any changes to other areas of the tax return would automatically update AGI and thus change the allowable medical deduction.

The medical expense presentation on Schedule A (Exhibit 5-2) is as follows:

**EXHIBIT 5-2**

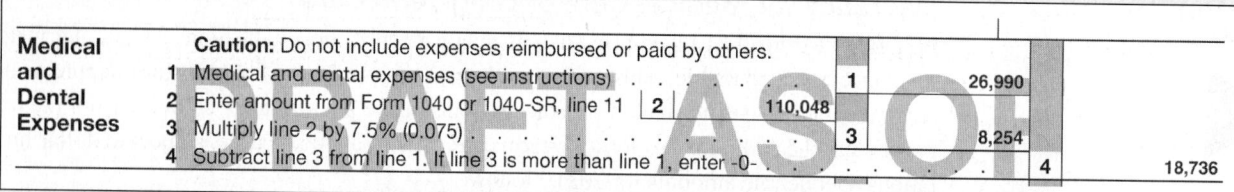

| Medical and Dental Expenses | **Caution:** Do not include expenses reimbursed or paid by others. | | |
|---|---|---:|---:|
| | 1 Medical and dental expenses (see instructions) . . . . . | **1** 26,990 | |
| | 2 Enter amount from Form 1040 or 1040-SR, line 11   **2** 110,048 | | |
| | 3 Multiply line 2 by 7.5% (0.075) . . . . . . . . | **3** 8,254 | |
| | 4 Subtract line 3 from line 1. If line 3 is more than line 1, enter -0- . . . . . | | **4** 18,736 |

Source: U.S. Department of the Treasury, Internal Revenue Service, Form 1040, Schedule A. Washington, DC: 2021.

The net medical expense deduction would be $18,736.

If Jose and Maria had health insurance and received benefits of $14,000, the amount shown on line 1 would be $12,990 ($26,990 − $14,000). You could either directly enter $12,990 on line 1 or show the insurance benefits as a negative on the line item detail. The result would be a deduction of only $4,736 (see Exhibit 5-3). Save the file showing $4,736 in net medical expenses for use later in the text.

**EXHIBIT 5-3**

| Medical and Dental Expenses | **Caution:** Do not include expenses reimbursed or paid by others. | | |
|---|---|---:|---:|
| | 1 Medical and dental expenses (see instructions) . . . . . | **1** 12,990 | |
| | 2 Enter amount from Form 1040 or 1040-SR, line 11   **2** 110,048 | | |
| | 3 Multiply line 2 by 7.5% (0.075) . . . . . . . . | **3** 8,254 | |
| | 4 Subtract line 3 from line 1. If line 3 is more than line 1, enter -0- . . . . . | | **4** 4,736 |

Source: U.S. Department of the Treasury, Internal Revenue Service, Form 1040, Schedule A. Washington, DC: 2021.

**TAX YOUR BRAIN**

Sofia is an elderly woman who does not require any medical or nursing care. However, she has recently become legally blind and needs help with normal living activities such as cooking, cleaning, and bathing. Sofia enters an assisted living facility where she feels she will be happier and more accessible to her children. Does the cost of the facility qualify as a medical deduction?

**ANSWER**

Because medical care is not the principal reason for the woman's stay at the facility, there is no medical deduction.[23] Of course, any actual medical costs, such as doctor visits, are still deductible.

Exhibit 5-3 assumes that Maria and Jose received a $14,000 insurance reimbursement in the year in which they paid the medical expenses. What happens if Maria and Jose receive the insurance benefits in the subsequent year? In this case, the insurance reimbursement would be included in income in the year received to the extent of the tax benefit received in the prior year.

**EXAMPLE 5-7**

Use the same facts as in Exhibit 5-2. If Jose and Maria received the $14,000 medical insurance benefits in the subsequent year, they must include the benefit amount in income to the extent of the tax benefit received. Their medical expense deduction would have been $18,736, so they would have received a tax benefit equal to the entire $14,000. In this case, they would report the $14,000 in income in the tax year received on line 8, Other Income, on Schedule 1 of Form 1040.

One common misconception is that the entire amount of an insurance reimbursement will always be included in income. If the insurance reimbursement caused the itemized deductions to be lower than the standard deduction, only a limited amount of the reimbursement would be included in income. The taxpayer would have to compare the taxable income in the deduction year tax return as it was reported to the taxable income that would have been reported had the insurance reimbursement been received in that year. The difference is the amount of income reported.

**CONCEPT CHECK 5-1—**
**LO 5-1**

1. Medical expenses are generally deductible only to the extent that they exceed _____ of AGI.
2. Medical expenses can be deducted only in the year the expenses are _____ .
3. The deductible amount of medical expense is reduced by _____ for those expenses.
4. The cost of long-term care insurance premiums is deductible, but the extent of the deduction depends on the taxpayer's _____ .

# DEDUCTIBLE STATE AND LOCAL TAXES (SCHEDULE A, LINE 7)
**LO 5-2**

Taxes are deductible in various places on a tax return. In this section, we discuss taxes that are personal; that is, they are not paid in connection with a trade or business or any other activity relating to the production of income. For example, if an individual taxpayer owns rental property, the property taxes relating to the rental property are a *for* AGI deduction and are deducted on Schedule E (see Chapter 8). Likewise, if an individual taxpayer operates a business as a sole proprietorship, any payroll or property taxes paid relating to the business are deductible on Schedule C (see Chapter 6) and thus reduce AGI (*for* AGI deductions).

There are four major categories of deductible taxes on individual returns:

1. Personal property taxes.
2. Local real estate property taxes.
3. Other state and local taxes.
4. Foreign taxes.

[23] *Robinson v. Comm'r*, 51 TC 520 (1968), *aff'd, vacated & remanded*, 422 F.2d 873 (9th Cir. 1970).

The taxes that most individual taxpayers deduct on Schedule A are state and local income taxes and property taxes on real estate and personal property.[24] For cash method taxpayers, deductible taxes are generally deductible in the year paid. For accrual method taxpayers, taxes are generally deductible in the year in which the taxes are accrued. One important note is that federal taxes generally are not deductible on the federal tax return.

The Tax Cuts and Jobs Act (TCJA) of 2017 limited the deduction for income, real estate, and other state and local taxes. The limitation for the deductibility of all state and local taxes is $10,000 ($5,000 for MFS).

## Personal Property Taxes

Personal property taxes paid on personal-use assets, such as the family car, are deductible on Schedule A. Personal property taxes paid on rental property are deducted on Schedule E. Personal property taxes paid on assets used in a proprietor's business are deducted on Schedule C.

State or local property taxes must meet three tests to be deductible:

1. The tax must be levied on personal property.
2. The tax must be an *ad valorem tax*; that is, it must be based on the value of the property.
3. The tax must be imposed, at a minimum, on an annual basis with respect to personal property.

**TAX YOUR BRAIN**

David lives in Johnson County and his brother Joseph lives in Lee County. Johnson County imposes a property tax of 2% of the value of personal vehicles. Lee County, on the other hand, imposes a flat fee of $250 per personal auto. Both counties impose the tax on an annual basis. How should David and Joseph treat these taxes?

**ANSWER**

David may deduct the tax he pays because it is an annual tax based on the value of personal property. Joseph, on the other hand, cannot deduct the property tax because it is a flat fee that is not based on value.

Many counties and states have different names for the taxes they levy. For example, some counties levy vehicle registration fees, which are deductible if they meet the preceding three tests. Usually, the primary determinant is whether the fee is based on the value of the vehicle. If it is, the fee is deductible (assuming that it passes the other two tests).

Property taxes on real estate must meet the three tests as well. Taxes on real property usually are much higher than personal property taxes and may create additional controversy. Problems may develop in the following situations:

1. Jointly owned real property.
2. Sale of property during the tax year.

### *Property Taxes on Property Owned Jointly*

In most states and counties, joint owners of property are jointly and severally liable for property taxes. In other words, if an individual is a part owner of a parcel of real estate and the other owner does not pay the real estate property taxes, that individual is liable for the full payment. In this situation, the owner who pays the tax may deduct the tax amount.[25]

**EXAMPLE 5-8**

Two brothers, Jacob and Rami, own a parcel of real estate with ownership interests of 30% to Jacob and 70% to Rami. Jacob pays the entire $2,300 county real estate tax. If Jacob and Rami live in a state where all joint owners are jointly and severally liable for the tax, then Jacob can deduct the entire $2,300 on Schedule A.[26]

[24] IRC § 164.

[25] Rev. Rul. 72-79, 1972-1 CB 51.

[26] This assumes the real estate is not business or "for the production of income" property. If the property were business use property, the taxes would be *for* AGI deductions and deducted on Schedule C (business), Schedule E (rental property), or Schedule F (farming property). See Chapters 6 and 8.

If local law mandates that co-owners of property do not have joint and several liability for a tax, then only the proportionate share of the taxes can be deducted.

**EXAMPLE 5-9**

Assume the same facts as in Example 5-8. However, Jacob and Rami live in a state that does not have joint and several liability for the tax. In this case, Jacob's deduction is $690 ($2,300 × 30%) even though he paid the entire amount.[27]

### Property Taxes on Property Sold during the Year

When property is sold during the year, both the buyer and the seller receive a deduction for a portion of the real estate tax paid according to the number of days each owner held the property.[28]

**EXAMPLE 5-10**

On March 1, David sold some land to Moesha. The real estate tax of $3,300 was not due until August, and Moesha properly paid it. How much, if anything, can David and Moesha deduct? In this case, the buyer and seller prorate the real estate tax on a daily basis. Therefore, David would deduct $533 ($3,300 × 59/365), and Moesha would deduct the remainder of $2,767 ($3,300 × 306/365). Note that the day of sale is not included in David's holding period, and we are assuming a non–leap year event.

The previous example could raise a question. If Moesha paid the tax, how can David get a deduction? At the time of transfer of ownership, a closing agent (often an attorney) prepares a *closing agreement* that prorates, or divides, the taxes (and other items) between the seller and the buyer. The taxes owed by the seller are withheld from the amount otherwise due to the seller. In effect, David paid the tax at the time of sale instead of at the due date.

### Real Estate Taxes

Real estate property taxes are deductible in the calculation of federal taxable income subject to the aggregate total limit for state and local taxes (SALT) of $10,000. If the tax is paid on personal-use real estate, such as the taxpayer's principal residence, it is an itemized deduction on Schedule A. If it is paid on rental real estate, it is deducted on Schedule E in the calculation of the taxpayer's net income or loss from the rental property. If it is paid on business real estate, such as an office building that the taxpayer owned and used as a proprietor, it is deducted on Schedule C in the calculation of net profit or loss from self-employment.

Many individuals make monthly mortgage payments that include real estate property taxes as well as mortgage principal and interest. Each month, the real estate tax payment is deposited into an escrow account that the mortgage company uses to pay the property taxes when they are due. In this case, the taxpayer deducts the actual amount of property taxes ultimately paid to the local taxing authority from the escrow account, not the amount paid to the mortgage holder. The mortgage company notifies the individual of the amount of the taxes paid on a year-end statement, normally a Form 1098.

**EXAMPLE 5-11**

Miriam's monthly mortgage payment for her principal residence is $1,500, of which $1,250 is mortgage principal and interest and $250 is for real estate property taxes. Every month the mortgage company deposits the $250 tax payment into an escrow account. In November 2021, the mortgage company paid the actual tax bill of $2,800 from the escrow account. Miriam can deduct $2,800 of real estate property taxes on her 2021 Schedule A as long as she is within the $10,000 limit for all of her state and local tax deductions.

### State and Local Taxes

The deduction for state income taxes is one of the largest itemized deductions for many taxpayers. Only seven states in the United States do not have some form of state income tax.[29]

[27] *James v. Comm'r*, TC Memo 1995-562.

[28] IRC § 164(d)(1).

[29] Currently the only states that do *not* have some form of income tax are Alaska, Florida, Nevada, South Dakota, Texas, Washington, and Wyoming.

---

**EXAMPLE 5-12**   Elijah lives in South Carolina and has state taxable income of $120,000. His state income tax is $7,200. If he itemizes, Elijah gets a deduction on Schedule A for that amount in the year the tax is paid as long as he is within the $10,000 limit for all of his state and local tax deductions.

---

In any year, an individual taxpayer can deduct the amount of state income taxes paid, whether through withholding, estimated taxes, or filing the prior year's state tax return. However, if the state tax payments that were deducted result in the taxpayer receiving a refund in the following year, the state tax refund must be included as taxable income in the year of receipt. This is the *tax benefit rule,* which states that if a taxpayer receives a federal tax benefit from an expense when the expense is paid, that taxpayer is taxed on a refund of that expense when the refund is received. If the taxpayer does not receive a tax benefit from the expense when it is paid, they are not taxed on a refund of that expense when it is received.

---

**EXAMPLE 5-13**   In 2020 Ricardo had $4,700 in state income tax withheld from his paycheck. When he filed his 2020 federal tax return in April 2021, he was eligible to itemize and thus deducted the $4,700 in state income taxes paid, thus reducing his 2020 taxable income and federal tax liability. When he filed his 2020 state tax return (also in April 2021), he found that he had overpaid his state taxes and was due a refund of $800. He received the $800 state refund in June 2021. The $800 refund must be included in federal taxable income for the tax year 2021. The reasoning behind the inclusion is that Ricardo received a tax benefit for the entire $4,700 even though, in the end, he paid only $3,900 ($4,700 tax paid less the $800 refund). The inclusion of the $800 in income in the subsequent year corrects the excess deduction. The $800 is included on line 1 of Schedule 1 of Form 1040, Taxable refunds, credits, or offsets of state and local income taxes.

---

Taxpayers who do not itemize deductions (but claim the standard deduction) cannot deduct state income tax. Thus, if they get a refund, it is nontaxable income on their federal return because they received no tax benefit from a nondeductible expense. A refund of that expense is therefore not subject to tax. The same rules apply to taxpayers who are required to pay city or other local income taxes.

Employers may be required to withhold *state disability insurance* (SDI) from the paychecks of their employees in the state of California. California SDI is treated as state income tax for purposes of calculating federal taxable income.

Taxpayers may be able to elect to take an itemized deduction for the amount of either (1) state and local income taxes or (2) state and local general sales taxes paid during the tax year subject to the overall $10,000 limitation for state and local taxes.[30] Taxpayers generally cannot deduct both. In general, taxpayers in states with an income tax will take the income tax deduction, whereas taxpayers in states with no income tax will take the sales tax deduction. In states with both a state income tax and a state sales tax, the taxpayer will take the one with the greater benefit.

The amount of the sales tax deduction is determined by calculating actual sales taxes paid during the year. From a practical perspective, most taxpayers would find it difficult to determine and document actual sales tax payments. Thus, a deduction is permitted using sales tax tables provided by the IRS in the instructions for Schedule A or by using the sales tax deduction calculator the IRS provides at http://apps.irs.gov/app/stdc/. To use the calculator, you can either copy and paste into your browser the URL just provided or go to www.irs.gov and enter "sales tax deduction calculator" in the search box. When using the sales tax tables, taxpayers determine their sales tax deduction based on several factors, including their income. Income is defined as AGI plus any nontaxable items such as tax-exempt interest, workers' compensation, nontaxable social security or retirement income, and similar items. The tool will also ask for information about family size, zip code, and sales tax paid on specific items if applicable.

[30] IRC § 164(b)(5).

**EXAMPLE 5-14**   Lester and Charmaine live in Clearwater, FL 33755, with their two dependent children, which makes a family size of four. Florida does not have a state income tax. The couple had AGI of $79,337 and interest income from a tax-exempt municipal bond of $2,190. Using the IRS sales tax deduction calculator tool for income between $80,000 and $90,000 with a family size of four and their zip code, you can calculate the itemized general sales tax deduction available to Lester and Charmaine.

Taxpayers who purchase an aircraft, boat, or, in most cases, a home or addition to a home can add the amount of sales tax paid on those items to the amount of sales tax determined with reference to the IRS tables.[31]

Taxpayers claim the general sales tax deduction on Schedule A, line 5a. The Schedule A instructions contain a worksheet for calculating the state and local sales tax deduction. The state and local sales tax tables are located in the appendix of the Schedule A instructions.

## Foreign Taxes

Foreign taxes paid are deductible.[32] However, an itemized deduction for foreign property taxes connected with a trade or business is no longer allowed. The taxpayer has the option of taking a credit (discussed in Chapter 9) for foreign taxes paid or deducting them on Schedule A. Individual taxpayers are usually better off utilizing the credit rather than the deduction because the credit is a dollar-for-dollar reduction in taxes, but the deduction reduces only taxable income, and the net tax effect depends on the taxpayer's tax rate.

**EXAMPLE 5-15**   Byung-ho, a U.S. citizen and resident, has several investments in England. The investments produced substantial income, and he had to pay $3,500 in British income taxes. Assume that Byung-ho's effective U.S. federal tax rate is 35%. He has a choice: File Form 1116 and take a $3,500 credit for the British tax, assuming that the foreign tax credit limitation does not apply, or deduct the taxes on Schedule A as an itemized deduction. The credit will reduce Byung-ho's net U.S. tax by $3,500. If he takes the deduction option, his net tax savings is only $1,225 ($3,500 × 35%), and that is only if he is still under the overall $10,000 limitation. Clearly, the better tax option is to file Form 1116 and take the credit.

A taxpayer cannot take both the credit and the deduction for the same foreign taxes paid. In most instances, the credit produces the better tax effect. However, if a taxpayer pays taxes to a country with which the United States has severed diplomatic relations or to a country that supports international terrorism, the credit is not allowed.[33] In this case, the deduction of the tax on Schedule A is the only option.

## Documentation for State, Local, and Foreign Taxes

Generally, the source document for property taxes (both personal and real property) is the receipt from the county or city tax collector. Other sources for property taxes are canceled checks. Many lending institutions escrow the property taxes along with the mortgage payment. If this is the case, the amount of property taxes is listed on the year-end mortgage interest statement (Form 1098) that the lending institution supplies. When real property is sold during the year, the allocation of the property taxes is usually shown on the closing statements signed when title changes hands.

For state income taxes, there are normally three source documents. For the majority of clients, the largest portion of state income taxes paid comes from the taxpayer's W-2 wage statement as state income tax withholding. Taxpayers who are self-employed or have considerable investment income could also pay quarterly estimated payments during the year. Usually, canceled checks to the state's department of revenue or other tax authority suffice as

[31] IRC § 164(b)(5)(H)(i); Schedule A Instructions.
[32] IRC § 164(a)(3).
[33] IRC § 901(j)(2).

documentation. The third source document is the prior year's state tax return. Reviewing the prior year return is crucial because it will show any tax paid with the prior year's return. If there was a refund, the tax preparer will know to include the refund in income for the current year (assuming the taxpayer itemized their return and deducted state taxes in the previous year).

Foreign taxes are sometimes more difficult to locate. The traditional source documents to locate foreign taxes paid include:

1. The prior year's tax return from the foreign country.
2. Mutual fund or stock brokerage statements.
3. Canceled checks.

Some mutual funds or brokerage offices are required to withhold or pay foreign taxes on the sale of stock within the mutual fund. These taxes, in turn, pass through to investors. In addition, if a taxpayer invests in foreign stocks, taxes are often withheld from foreign dividends received. These withholdings are reported to the taxpayer on Form 1099-B.

**Summary of Deductible Taxes**

| Type | Potential Source Documents |
|---|---|
| Personal property | County/city tax collector receipt<br>Checkbook register/canceled check |
| Real estate property taxes | County/city tax collector receipt<br>Checkbook register/canceled check<br>Real estate closing statements<br>Form 1098—Bank Mortgage Interest |
| State/local income tax | W-2 wage statement—State withholding box<br>W-2 wage statement—Local withholding box<br>Quarterly estimated tax payments<br>Prior year's state/local tax return |
| Foreign | Prior year's foreign tax return<br>Mutual fund/stock statements<br>Canceled checks |

**CONCEPT CHECK 5-2— LO 5-2**

1. For personal property taxes to be deductible, they must be based on the value of the property. True or false?
2. When property is sold during the year, only the seller is allowed to take a deduction for taxes paid. True or false?
3. The tax benefit rule states that if a taxpayer receives a tax benefit when an expense is paid, no further action is required on the taxpayer's part if a refund is received in the future as a result of the previous expense deduction. True or false?
4. The overall dollar limitation for the deductibility for state and local taxes is $11,000. True or false?

# DEDUCTIBLE INTEREST (SCHEDULE A, LINE 10)
## LO 5-3

Most taxpayers in the United States do not itemize deductions until they purchase their first residence. The main component of the interest deduction is the home mortgage deduction. In the past, almost all types of personal interest were deductible on Schedule A. However, consumer loan interest deductions (such as auto loan interest and credit card interest) have been virtually eliminated. The only types of personal interest still available as a deduction are mortgage interest on a personal residence and investment interest. Any interest connected with a trade or

# From Shoebox to Software

**EXAMPLE 5-16**    Locate the saved tax file for Jose and Maria Ramirez from earlier in this chapter. They had the following additional information:

| Property or Activity | Tax |
|---|---|
| Jose's state income tax withheld (per W-2) | $2,470 |
| State estimated tax payments ($250 per quarter with the last payment on 12/31/2021) | 1,000 |
| State taxes paid with prior year return | 300 |
| Foreign taxes paid on foreign stock investments | 400 |
| Personal residence real estate property tax | 1,300 |
| Truck | 200 |
| Van | 250 |
| Ski boat | 200 |

Lines 5–7 on Schedule A are the appropriate lines to record deductible personal taxes. Go to Schedule A for the Ramirezes.

1. Note that the state withholding is already on line 5a from the W-2 you entered previously.

2. To enter the state estimated tax payments, double-click on line 5a and identify the location to input state estimated payments. Enter the $250 per quarter payments and the dates they were paid.

3. Enter the $300 paid with last year's return (usually filed in April)* in the location for this item.

4. Enter the personal residence property tax ($1,300) on the real estate tax line (line 5b).

5. Enter the total of the taxes on the truck, van, and boat on line 5c. You can use the line item detail by right-clicking on line 5c and entering each item individually. The total from the worksheet will then be carried forward to line 5c.

When you have completed Schedule A for taxes, it will look like the one in Exhibit 5-4.

The total itemized deduction for state and local taxes equals $5,720. The foreign taxes of $400 could have been placed on line 6, but the Ramirezes would most likely receive a higher tax benefit by filing Form 1116 and taking the $400 as a foreign tax credit.

**EXHIBIT 5-4**

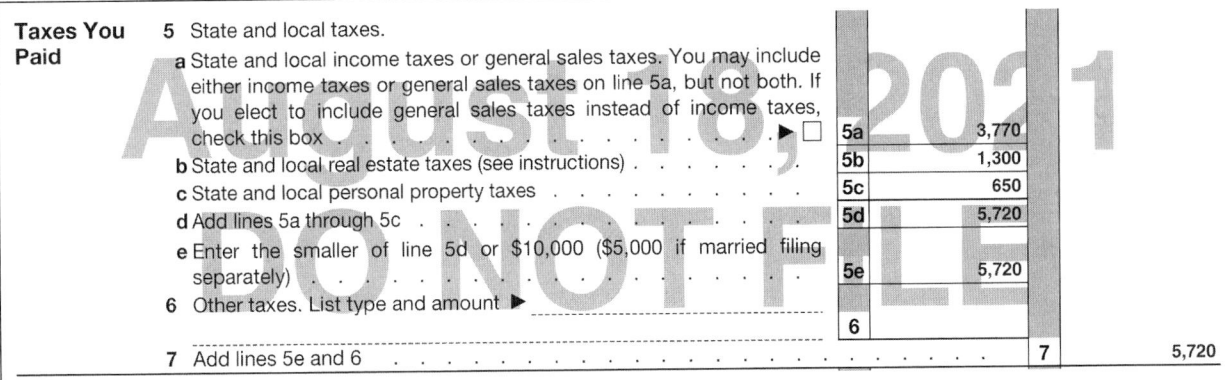

| Taxes You Paid | 5 | State and local taxes. | | |
|---|---|---|---|---|
| | a | State and local income taxes or general sales taxes. You may include either income taxes or general sales taxes on line 5a, but not both. If you elect to include general sales taxes instead of income taxes, check this box . . . . . . . . . . . . . . . ▶ ☐ | 5a | 3,770 |
| | b | State and local real estate taxes (see instructions) . . . . . . | 5b | 1,300 |
| | c | State and local personal property taxes . . . . . . . . | 5c | 650 |
| | d | Add lines 5a through 5c . . . . . . . . . . . . | 5d | 5,720 |
| | e | Enter the smaller of line 5d or $10,000 ($5,000 if married filing separately) . . . . . . . . . . . . . . . | 5e | 5,720 |
| | 6 | Other taxes. List type and amount ▶ _____ | 6 | |
| | 7 | Add lines 5e and 6 . . . . . . . . . . . . . . | 7 | 5,720 |

Source: U.S. Department of the Treasury, Internal Revenue Service, Form 1040, Schedule A. Washington, DC: 2021.

business or for the production of income is still deductible. However, these amounts are *for* AGI deductions and are deducted on the appropriate form (Schedule C, Schedule E, or Schedule F).

## Mortgage Interest and Home Equity Loans

*Interest* is the fee paid by a borrower to a lender for the use or forbearance of money. Congress encourages home ownership by granting an itemized deduction for qualified residence interest, better known as *home mortgage interest*. Qualified residence interest is *interest paid on acquisition indebtedness or a home equity loan secured by a qualified residence*. If the loan is not secured by a qualified residence, the interest is not qualified residence interest. *Acquisition indebtedness* means any debt incurred to acquire, construct, or substantially improve any qualified residence.[34]

[34] IRC § 163(h)(3)(B)(i).

Suppose the taxpayer has a large unsecured personal line of credit with the local lending institution and borrows $35,000 to add another room to the existing residence. Does the interest charged by the institution on the $35,000 qualify as residence interest?

**ANSWER**

No. Because the debt was not secured by the residence, the interest would not be deductible. Had the line of credit been a home equity line, the interest would be deductible as the funds were used specifically for home improvement.

Taxpayers can deduct qualified residence interest on their principal residence and on a second residence selected by the taxpayer.[35] As to the amount of deductible interest, the Tax Cuts and Jobs Act of 2017 made some significant changes here. The aggregate amount treated as acquisition indebtedness for any period beginning in 2018 or later cannot exceed $750,000 ($375,000 for married individuals filing separate returns). The $750,000 limitation refers to the amount of *principal* of the debt, not the interest paid. Taxpayers may have more than one acquisition loan per residence (a first mortgage and a second mortgage).

There are some exceptions to this new limit. First, the old $1,000,000 debt limit will still apply if the taxpayer entered into a binding contract before December 15, 2017, to close purchase of a principal residence before January 1, 2018, and actually purchased the home before April 1, 2018.

The second example is if the taxpayer refinances an acquisition loan (for example, refinances a $1,000,000, 6% loan with a new $1,000,000, 4% loan), incurred before December 15, 2017, that was refinanced on or after December 15, 2017, the new loan continued to qualify as acquisition debt to the extent that the principal does not increase and therefore interest on the full $1,000,000 would still be deductible. There is a worksheet in IRS Publication 936 that can be used to calculate the allowable mortgage deduction.

**EXAMPLE 5-17**

Katrina and Marcus, who are married, incur debt of $580,000 to build their new personal residence. In the following year, they decide to build a vacation home at the beach and borrow an additional $200,000 to build it. Katrina and Marcus's acquisition indebtedness is limited to $750,000. In this case, the additional interest on the excess $30,000 of indebtedness is not allowed.

The 9th Circuit Court of Appeals ruled a few years ago that the mortgage interest deduction debt limits apply to unmarried co-owners *on a per-taxpayer basis, not on a per-residence basis* and the IRS, in AOD (Action on Decision) 2016-02, acquiesced to that decision.

The implication of this ruling is very important. Whereas a married couple filing jointly is seen as effectively being one taxpayer, and thus subject to the overall mortgage interest deduction limit of up to $750,000 in acquisition debt, an unmarried couple that owns a property together would be subject to a mortgage interest deduction of up to $750,000 in acquisition debt per individual.

This would also apply to the home equity interest deduction limitations as well. Assume that a nonmarried couple acquires a new house, owning the home as joint tenants. Also assume the total acquisition mortgage debt is $1,300,000 and the total home equity loan is $200,000, making the total debt $1,500,000. Under this new ruling, each person would potentially be able to deduct the interest on their portion of the total debt, which would be $750,000 per individual. This becomes another example of the "marriage penalty" that we have seen in the past in the tax code.

What is *home equity indebtedness,* how does it differ from acquisition indebtedness, and how does the Tax Cuts and Jobs Act of 2017 impact this category of loan? *Home equity loans* are loans that are secured by a qualified residence in an amount that does not exceed the FMV of the residence less the acquisition debt.

Despite the newly enacted restrictions on home mortgages, taxpayers can often still deduct interest on a home equity loan, a home equity line of credit, or a second mortgage, no matter how the loan is labeled, *as long as the loan is used to buy, build, or substantially improve the taxpayer's home that secures the loan.* The $750,000 limit on acquisition debt applies to the

[35] IRC § 163(h)(4)(A)(i)(II).

combined amount of all loans secured by a qualifying property—whether they are first (your primary mortgage) or second (home equity) mortgages.

For instance, under the TCJA, the interest on a home equity loan for building an addition to an existing house is usually deductible, although interest on the same loan used to pay personal living expenses, such as credit card debts, is not. As under prior law, the loan needs to be secured by the taxpayer's main home or by a second home, known as a qualified residence. But it can't exceed the cost of the home, and the loan also needs to meet some other requirements.

For example, in January 2021, a taxpayer gets a $500,000 mortgage to buy a main home with a fair market value of $800,000. The following month, the taxpayer takes out a $250,000 home equity loan to put an addition on the main home. Both loans are secured by the main home and the total doesn't exceed the home's cost. *Because the total amount of both loans doesn't exceed $750,000, all the interest paid on the loans is deductible.* But if the taxpayer used the home equity loan proceeds for personal expenses, such as paying off student loans and credit cards, then the interest on the home equity loan wouldn't be deductible.

People are sometimes confused about the difference between home equity loans and lines of credit (HELOCs) and, while they are different products, the interest deduction rules are the same. A home equity loan has a fixed interest rate, while HELOCs have an interest rate that is variable and tracks market rates.

---

**EXAMPLE 5-18**

Bryan purchased a house several years ago for $130,000. The acquisition debt still outstanding is $115,000. The house's FMV is now $150,000. Therefore, the net equity in the house is now $35,000 ($150,000 FMV − $115,000 debt). Bryan could borrow as home equity indebtedness up to $35,000, and the interest would still be deductible as the aggregate acquisition debt would still be below the $750,000 limit, as long as the funds were used to substantially improve the residence (most lending institutions, however, will lend only up to 80% or 90% of the net equity in the personal residence).

---

Interest on home equity debt is an adjustment for the Alternative Minimum Tax (AMT).

## Mortgage Points

*Points* are amounts that borrowers pay to obtain a mortgage. The most common names of these charges are "loan origination fees" or "loan processing fees." Each point equals 1% of the loan principal. For example, Marisa pays 2 points on a $300,000 mortgage loan. The points equal $6,000 (0.01 × 2 × $300,000). Typically, taxpayers deduct points ratably over the term of the loan. However, the law allows an exception for points paid in connection with a principal residence. Points are deductible by a cash basis taxpayer as mortgage interest if they meet the following "safe harbor" criteria:

1. The Uniform Settlement Statement must clearly designate the amounts as loan origination fees, loan discount, discount points, or points payable in connection with the loan.
2. The amounts must be computed as a percentage of the stated principal amount of the indebtedness incurred by the taxpayer.
3. The amounts paid must conform to an established business practice of charging points for loans for the acquisition of principal residences in the geographical area.
4. The amounts must be paid in connection with the acquisition of the taxpayer's principal residence, and that residence must secure the loan.
5. The amounts must be paid directly by the taxpayers.[36]

Generally the buyer of the home incurs points when obtaining a loan. As an inducement for the sale, the seller of the residence may actually pay the points for the buyer. If this is the case, the buyer receives the tax benefit if the point amount reduces the basis of the home when the property is sold. Taxpayers can take a deduction for the points paid only if the indebtedness is incurred in connection with the purchase or improvement of their principal residence. Points paid to refinance an existing mortgage are deducted ratably over the life of the loan. If the loan is paid off before it is due, the unamortized points are deductible in the year the debt is paid.

[36] Rev. Proc. 94-27, 1994-1 CB 613.

**EXAMPLE 5-19**

Jaron and his spouse purchased a home in 2007 for $230,000. They borrowed $184,000 with a 30-year, 5.5% note from a local lending institution. In 2021, they decided to make an addition to the house that would cost $75,000. He and his spouse borrowed the $75,000 and paid a 1% loan origination fee. In 2021, the $750 in points could be deducted because the indebtedness was in connection with the improvement of their principal residence.

**EXAMPLE 5-20**

Assume the same initial facts as Example 5-19. However, instead of the $75,000 addition, Jason and his spouse decided to refinance their loan (balance now at $175,000) because the interest rate was now 2.75% for a 30-year loan. The 1% origination fee of $1,750 cannot be fully deducted this year because the new loan was not for the original purchase or improvement of the residence. They can deduct the points ratably over the 30-year loan period, or $58 per year ($1,750/30 years). If the refinancing had occurred on June 1, then the deduction for the current year would be $34 ($1,750/30 years × 7/12).[37]

**NEW LAW**

## Mortgage Insurance Premium Deduction Extended for 2021

Often individuals who purchase a home with a down payment of less than 20% are required to pay a mortgage insurance premium or, as it is sometimes referred to, private mortgage insurance (PMI). In effect, mortgage insurance protects the lender against a loan default. In the past, the mortgage insurance premiums were not always deductible. With the Consolidated Appropriations Act of 2021, for mortgage insurance contracts issued in 2021, the taxpayer may take an itemized deduction for the amount of the premium paid in 2021 on line 8d of Schedule A. For tax years 2019 and 2020, the taxpayer may file an amended return to claim that deduction on their Schedule A if it makes sense to do so.

The deductible amount is reduced by 10% for every $1,000 ($500 if married filing separately) by which Adjusted Gross Income exceeds $100,000 ($50,000 if married filing separately). Thus, the deduction is not allowed when AGI exceeds $110,000 ($55,000 if married filing separately).

## Investment Interest

If a taxpayer borrows money to finance the purchase of investment assets—such as stocks, bonds, or land held strictly for investment—the interest expense is investment interest expense.

*Investment interest expense* is any interest that is paid or accrued on indebtedness properly allocable to property held for investment. The deduction of investment interest expense is limited to the net investment income for the year and is deductible as an itemized deduction on Schedule A.[38] Net investment income is gross investment income less deductible investment expenses. If the investment interest expense exceeds the taxpayer's net investment income, they can carry forward the excess expense to future tax years when net investment income is available. One common example of investment interest expense is interest from a loan whose proceeds the taxpayer uses to purchase stock.

**EXAMPLE 5-21**

Gayle purchased a tract of land that she felt would substantially appreciate over the next several years. She borrowed $20,000 from a local lending institution and signed a 5%, 15-year note. If Gayle's only investment income is interest of $1,000, she could deduct the interest on the lending institution loan up to a maximum of $1,000 in the current year (her net investment income). Any remaining amount of interest would be carried forward to future years and would be deducted when additional net investment income becomes available.

Typical items that qualify as investment income are interest income, ordinary dividends, and short-term capital gains. However, gains and losses from the disposition of several investment properties must first be netted to determine investment income. Income from passive activities and income from rental real estate with active participation are specifically excluded from the definition of investment income, as well as net long-term capital gains and qualified dividend income.[39]

[37] Rev. Proc. 87-15, 1987-1 CB 624.

[38] IRC § 163(d)(1).

[39] IRC § 163(d)(4)(D). Passive activities and rental real estate are discussed in detail in Chapters 8 and 13, respectively.

# From Shoebox to Software

Determining the amount of the total interest deduction usually is not difficult. In most cases, a financial institution sends the taxpayer Form 1098 reporting the interest expense. See Exhibit 5-5 for an example of a common Form 1098 from a financial institution.[40]

**EXAMPLE 5-22**

Assume that the Form 1098 in Exhibit 5-5 was for Jose and Maria Ramirez and had $7,300 on line 1. To enter the $7,300 on line 8a of Schedule A, you must enter the amount on a Form 1098. Enter the $7,300 on line 1, and it will automatically be transferred to Schedule A. Save the Ramirezes' return for future use.

Difficulty can arise when a taxpayer has numerous loans outstanding. Typically, the lending institution labels the interest as related to the principal residence (either acquisition indebtedness or home equity indebtedness). However, if the taxpayer has several loans, some of which are personal loans (like a car loan) and others are investment loans, the tax preparer must question the client to discover which loans are for what activities.

**EXHIBIT 5-5**

| RECIPIENT'S/LENDER'S name, street address, city or town, state or province, country, ZIP or foreign postal code, and telephone no. | *Caution: The amount shown may not be fully deductible by you. Limits based on the loan amount and the cost and value of the secured property may apply. Also, you may only deduct interest to the extent it was incurred by you, actually paid by you, and not reimbursed by another person.* | OMB No. 1545-1380  20**21**  Form **1098** | **Mortgage Interest Statement** |
|---|---|---|---|
| | **1** Mortgage interest received from payer(s)/borrower(s)*  $ | | **Copy B**  **For Payer/ Borrower**  The information in boxes 1 through 9 and 11 is important tax information and is being furnished to the IRS. If you are required to file a return, a negligence penalty or other sanction may be imposed on you if the IRS determines that an underpayment of tax results because you overstated a deduction for this mortgage interest or for these points, reported in boxes 1 and 6; or because you didn't report the refund of interest (box 4); or because you claimed a nondeductible item. |
| RECIPIENT'S/LENDER'S TIN / PAYER'S/BORROWER'S TIN | **2** Outstanding mortgage principal  $ | **3** Mortgage origination date | |
| | **4** Refund of overpaid interest  $ | **5** Mortgage insurance premiums  $ | |
| PAYER'S/BORROWER'S name | **6** Points paid on purchase of principal residence  $ | | |
| Street address (including apt. no.) | **7** ☐ If address of property securing mortgage is the same as PAYER'S/BORROWER'S address, the box is checked, or the address or description is entered in box 8. | | |
| City or town, state or province, country, and ZIP or foreign postal code | **8** Address or description of property securing mortgage | | |
| **9** Number of properties securing the mortgage / **10** Other | | | **11** Mortgage acquisition date |
| Account number (see instructions) | | | |

Form **1098** (Keep for your records) www.irs.gov/Form1098 Department of the Treasury - Internal Revenue Service

☐ CORRECTED (if checked)

Source: U.S. Department of the Treasury, Internal Revenue Service, Form 1098. Washington, DC: 2021.

However, if a taxpayer elects to treat a portion of long-term capital gain or qualified dividend income as investment income, the long-term gain or dividend income is not eligible for the lower tax rate that would otherwise apply.[41] Generally, taxpayers use Form 4952 to calculate and report the amount of deductible investment interest expense. However, Form 4952 does not have to be included with the return if all three of these circumstances apply:

1. Investment interest expense does not exceed investment income from interest and ordinary dividends minus qualified dividends.

[40] Many financial institutions develop their own Form 1098 (labeled Form 1098 Substitute). Therefore, the form may differ somewhat depending on the institution. The form, however, reports the same information.
[41] IRC § 163(d)(4)(B).

2. The taxpayer has no other deductible investment expenses.

3. The taxpayer has no disallowed investment interest expense from 2020.

Net investment income may be subject to a 3.8% Medicare tax for AGI over certain thresholds.

---

**CONCEPT CHECK 5-3— LO 5-3**

1. Acquisition indebtedness means any debt incurred to _____, _____ , or _____ any qualified residence.

2. The aggregate amount treated as acquisition indebtedness, for any period cannot exceed $_____ for married filing jointly.

3. The deduction of investment interest expense is limited to the _____ _____ income for the year.

4. Each point paid to acquire a home loan equals _____ of the loan principal.

---

# DEDUCTIBLE GIFTS TO CHARITY (SCHEDULE A, LINE 14)
## LO 5-4

The government encourages the private sector to support charitable organizations by granting individual taxpayers a charitable contribution deduction, which may be claimed as an itemized deduction on Schedule A. Contributions must be to one of the following five types of organizations:[42]

1. Any governmental unit or subdivision of the United States or its possessions as long as the gift is for exclusively public purposes.

2. Any nonprofit organization that is organized and operated exclusively for religious, charitable, scientific, literary, or educational purposes or to foster international amateur sports competition and is not disqualified from tax-exempt status under IRC § 501(c)(3).

3. A post or organization of war veterans for which no part of the net earnings benefits any private shareholder or individual.

4. A domestic fraternal society or association that uses the contribution only for religious, charitable, scientific, or educational purposes.

5. A cemetery company owned and operated exclusively for the benefit of its members.

If you are uncertain whether an organization is a qualified donee organization, check the IRS Exempt Organization online search tool at www.irs.gov/charities-non-profits/tax-exempt-organization-search.

The amount of the deduction depends on the type of donated property and is subject to AGI limitations. To be deductible, the donation must be cash or other property of value. The government imposes strict documentation requirements for both types of contributions.

A taxpayer receives no deduction for services rendered to a charitable organization.[43] The services do not give rise to taxable income to the taxpayer, so no deduction is permitted.

A taxpayer who travels away from home overnight to attend a convention as a representative of a charitable organization may deduct related transportation and travel expenses, including meals and lodging. If the taxpayer incurs travel expenses as a volunteer for a qualified charity, the expenses are deductible if they have significant duties throughout the course of the trip and no significant amount of personal recreation is attached to the trip.

---

**EXAMPLE 5-23**

Kathy, a local CPA, is an ardent supporter of the Boys and Girls Club in Hickory Hills, AL. Each year she compiles monthly financial statements and prepares the Form 990 tax return for the club. Kathy estimates that she spends 20 hours per year working for the Boys and Girls Club. Her normal rate is $100 per hour. Because Kathy's donation is her services and she has recorded no income for those services, she receives no charitable contribution deduction.

Kathy is able to deduct any out-of-pocket expenses she paid in connection with her service to the Boys and Girls Club. Actual expenditures are deductible for automotive travel, or the taxpayer has the option to deduct 14 cents per mile as a standard rate for charitable contributions.

---

[42] IRC § 170(c).

[43] Reg. § 1.170A-1(g).

## Property Donations: Capital versus Ordinary Income Property

Not all donations to charity are in the form of cash. In fact, many large donations are made with capital gain property (such as stocks, bonds, land, and other investments). Still other donations are made with ordinary income property (inventory and accounts receivable). Generally, if capital gain property is donated to a public charity, the deductible donation amount is the property's FMV.

## Charitable Contribution of Personal Tangible Property Clarification

A key exception to this general rule concerns the contribution of tangible personal property. If the donated property is put to a use that is unrelated to the purpose or function of the charity's tax-exempt status, the contribution must be reduced by the amount of any long-term capital gain that would have been realized if the property had been sold at its FMV at the time of the contribution. For example, if a sculpture is donated to a museum and is put on display for the public, that would be a related purpose. If, however, the museum had simply sold the sculpture without displaying it and used the funds for museum operations, that would be an unrelated purpose and would require this exception. A second exception occurs if the investment property is short-term property (held one year or less). In this case, the deduction is limited to the tax basis of the asset (its cost). The donation of investment/capital gain property is also subject to additional limitations depending on the type of the recipient organization (see the following section on limitations).

| EXAMPLE 5-24 | Kemba donated his old computer to Helping Hands Industries. He had purchased the computer for personal use several years ago at a cost of $1,500. The computer's FMV at the date of donation was $400. The computer is a capital asset held for more than one year, so Kemba may deduct the $400 FMV as a charitable contribution, subject to the overall charitable contribution limits. |
|---|---|

Generally, when ordinary income property (such as inventory and accounts receivable) is donated to charity, the deduction amount is limited to the tax basis of the property donated. The deduction does not depend on the type of recipient organization.

## Percentage Limitations of Charitable Donations

 **NEW LAW**

As a result of recent tax law, there are now four limitations concerning charitable contributions by individual taxpayers for the tax year 2021: These are the 100%, 60%, 30%, and 20% limitations. The new legislation increases the maximum 60% of the AGI charitable contribution limit for cash donations to 100% of the AGI limit for 2021. This means that you can get a charitable contribution deduction for those donations for the full amount of your Adjusted Gross Income. Noncash charitable contributions in excess of this amount can be carried forward for five years subject to the 60% of AGI limit in those years.

*The higher 100% of AGI limit applies only to cash contributions made directly to charitable organizations,* not to contributions to donor advised funds, supporting organizations or private foundations. Cash contributions to those organizations will still be subject to the 60% of AGI limitation.

A contribution in excess of the limitation is carried forward for the next five tax years, subject to the overall 60% limitation in those years. For each category of contributions, the taxpayer must deduct carryover contributions only after deducting all allowable contributions in that same category for the current year. The deduction of amounts from previous years is done on a first-in, first-out basis.

Also, as noted in Chapter 4, for tax year 2021, *non-itemizers* can deduct below-the-line cash charitable contributions up to $600 on a married-filing-joint return ($300 for singles).

| EXAMPLE 5-25 | Doris is a wealthy widow and has $200,000 in AGI from various investments. If she makes a $150,000 cash donation to State University in 2021, her charitable deduction is the entire contribition of $150,000. |
|---|---|

The 30% limitation applies to contributions of long-term tangible capital gain property. When long-term tangible capital gain property is contributed to a public charity, and the property is put to a related use by the charity, the taxpayer can take a deduction for the asset's FMV. However, the deduction is limited to 30% of the taxpayer's AGI.[44] Again, any excess is carried forward for five years.

[44] IRC § 170(b)(1)(C).

**EXAMPLE 5-26**

Assume the same facts as in Example 5-25. However, instead of giving cash of $150,000, Doris contributed a vacation cottage that she has owned for many years. The cottage, which is in a marshland and could be used for research purposes, has an FMV of $150,000. The university uses the cottage as a research station for biology and zoology students, which would be a related use. In this case, Doris's deduction is limited to $60,000 for this year ($200,000 AGI × 30% limitation). The excess $90,000 of the eligible deduction is carried forward for the next five years.

There is one exception to this rule: If the taxpayer elects to reduce the FMV of the contributed property by the amount of long-term capital gain that would have been recognized if the property had been sold at its FMV at the time of the contribution, the 60% limitation would apply to the contribution, rather than the 30% of AGI limitation.[45]

**EXAMPLE 5-27**

Assume the same facts as in Example 5-26. However, Doris elects to reduce the FMV of the cottage by the amount of long-term capital gain she would have recognized if she had sold the cottage. Her adjusted basis in the cottage is $70,000. Her charitable contribution would therefore be $70,000 because 60% of her AGI of $200,000 would be a $120,000 limitation on charitable contributions.

Another exception to this rule concerns the donation of long-term tangible capital gain property to a charity that the charity uses for purposes unrelated to the organization's function.

**EXAMPLE 5-28**

Assume the same facts as in Example 5-26, except that the university promptly sells the cottage. In this case, the deduction would be limited to Doris's adjusted basis in the cottage of $70,000 because the presumption is that the use of the property was unrelated to the university's tax-exempt purpose. In this exception, the 30% limit does not apply, and the deduction would be based on 60% of AGI, as seen in Example 5-27.

The 30% limitation also applies to any contribution (cash or property) to charities that are not 100% limitation charities such as war veterans' organizations, fraternal orders, cemetery companies, and certain nonoperating private foundations.

The 20% limitation refers to the donation of capital gain property to a private foundation. The deduction for cash given to a private foundation is limited to 30% of AGI, whereas capital gain property given to the same organization is limited to 20% of AGI.[46]

Another element of the TCJA is that no charitable deduction is allowed for a payment to an educational institution for which the taxpayer receives a preferential benefit.

**EXAMPLE 5-29**

Samatha, a wealthy business owner, gave the following amounts to State College: $4,500 for 30 season tickets for women's basketball and $10,000 to its athletic foundation for preferential seating location and parking. The $4,500 is not deductible at all because the taxpayer is buying a product, and, under TCJA of 2017, the $10,000 donation is not deductible as well.

## Required Documentation of Charitable Gifts

Recently, the substantiation requirements for charitable contributions have become more stringent. The nonprofit organizations themselves bear most of the increased requirements. They are now required to provide summary receipts to donors. From the taxpayer's perspective, when a gift to a charitable organization is less than $250 in cash, the contributor is required to keep a canceled check, a receipt from the organization, or other written records to substantiate the deduction.[47] If the donation is $250 or more, the taxpayer must have written acknowledgment from the recipient organization stating (1) the date and amount of the contribution, (2) whether the taxpayer received any goods or services from the charity as a result of the contribution, and (3) a description and good-faith estimate of the value of any goods and services

[45] IRC § 170(b)(1)(C)(iii).
[46] IRC § 170(b)(1)(D).
[47] Reg. § 1.170A-13(a)(1)(i)–(iii).

that the taxpayer received. A canceled check does not meet the substantiation requirements for donations of $250 or more.

**EXAMPLE 5-30**  Jamal goes to a church function organized to raise funds for a new youth group building. He pays $500 for a painting that has a $100 FMV. Jamal's charitable contribution to the church is $400. To substantiate the deduction, he must get a receipt from the church and keep his canceled check.

Taxpayers are not required to aggregate multiple contributions they make to a charity during the year for purposes of the $250 limitation. The required documentation is based on the amount of each separate contribution.

**EXAMPLE 5-31**  Every week, Adina donates $50 to her synagogue. In October 2021, she made an additional $500 contribution to the temple building fund. Adina may document each weekly contribution with a canceled check. To take the $500 contribution as a deduction, she must receive a written acknowledgment from the synagogue. It must state the date and amount of the contribution and the fact that Adina received no goods or services from the temple as a result of her donation.

# From Shoebox to Software

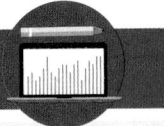

**EXAMPLE 5-32**  Jose and Maria Ramirez gave the following items to their church: (1) cash of $1,000, with no individual contribution greater than $250; (2) a painting with an FMV of $750, basis $500; and (3) three large bags of used clothing. The Ramirezes' charitable contribution would be calculated and placed on Schedule A and Form 8283 as follows:

| | |
|---|---|
| Cash | $1,000 |
| Painting | 750 |
| Clothes (thrift value)[48] | 200 |
| Total | $1,950 |

Open their tax return. Enter the cash contributions directly on line 11 of Schedule A. Form 8283 is required for noncash gifts in excess of $500. Double-click on line 12 or open a Form 8283. Enter the required information as shown on Form 8283 in Exhibit 5-6. Make sure you save your file when you have finished.

**EXHIBIT 5-6**

| Gifts to Charity | | | |
|---|---|---|---|
| | 11 | Gifts by cash or check. If you made any gift of $250 or more, see instructions . . . . . . . . . . | **11** 1,000 |
| **Caution:** If you made a gift and got a benefit for it, see instructions. | 12 | Other than by cash or check. If you made any gift of $250 or more, see instructions. You **must** attach Form 8283 if over $500. . . . | **12** 950 |
| | 13 | Carryover from prior year . . . . . . . . . . | **13** |
| | 14 | Add lines 11 through 13 . . . . . . . . . . . | **14** 1,950 |

Source: U.S. Department of the Treasury, Internal Revenue Service, Form 8283. Washington, DC: 2021.

*(continued)*

The substantiation requirements are the same for noncash gifts. A taxpayer who donates noncash property valued at less than $250 should obtain a receipt or letter from the charity showing the name of the charity, the date and location of the contribution, and a description of the donated property. The charity is not required to value the donated property, but the taxpayer should keep a record of the property's FMV at the date of the donation and how that FMV was determined.

However, if noncash gifts are worth more than $500, the taxpayer must file Form 8283 on which they must list the organization's name, a description of the property, the date acquired, the acquisition method of the property, the cost or basis, and the FMV. If the value of the donated property is more than $5,000, an appraisal is required within 60 days prior to the date of contribution.

[48] *Thrift value* is the value for which the clothes could be sold. In most cases, thrift value is a very subjective value.

**EXHIBIT 5-6**   *(concluded)*

| Form **8283** (Rev. December 2020) Department of the Treasury Internal Revenue Service | **Noncash Charitable Contributions** ▶ Attach one or more Forms 8283 to your tax return if you claimed a total deduction of over $500 for all contributed property. ▶ Go to *www.irs.gov/Form8283* for instructions and the latest information. | OMB No. 1545-0074 Attachment Sequence No. **155** |
|---|---|---|

| Name(s) shown on your income tax return | Identifying number |
|---|---|

**Note:** Figure the amount of your contribution deduction before completing this form. See your tax return instructions.

**Section A.   Donated Property of $5,000 or Less and Publicly Traded Securities**—List in this section **only** an item (or a group of similar items) for which you claimed a deduction of $5,000 or less. Also list publicly traded securities and certain other property even if the deduction is more than $5,000. See instructions.

**Part I**   **Information on Donated Property**—If you need more space, attach a statement.

| 1 | (a) Name and address of the donee organization | (b) If donated property is a vehicle (see instructions), check the box. Also enter the vehicle identification number (unless Form 1098-C is attached). | (c) Description and condition of donated property (For a vehicle, enter the year, make, model, and mileage. For securities and other property, see instructions.) |
|---|---|---|---|
| A | | ☐ | |
| B | | ☐ | |
| C | | ☐ | |
| D | | ☐ | |
| E | | ☐ | |

**Note:** If the amount you claimed as a deduction for an item is $500 or less, you do not have to complete columns (e), (f), and (g).

| | (d) Date of the contribution | (e) Date acquired by donor (mo., yr.) | (f) How acquired by donor | (g) Donor's cost or adjusted basis | (h) Fair market value (see instructions) | (i) Method used to determine the fair market value |
|---|---|---|---|---|---|---|
| A | | | | | | |
| B | | | | | | |
| C | | | | | | |
| D | | | | | | |
| E | | | | | | |

**Section B.   Donated Property Over $5,000 (Except Publicly Traded Securities, Vehicles, Intellectual Property or Inventory Reportable in Section A)**—Complete this section for one item (or a group of similar items) for which you claimed a deduction of more than $5,000 per item or group (except contributions reportable in Section A). Provide a separate form for each item donated unless it is part of a group of similar items. A qualified appraisal is generally required for items reportable in Section B. See instructions.

**Part I**   **Information on Donated Property**

2   Check the box that describes the type of property donated.

| | | | | | |
|---|---|---|---|---|---|
| a ☐ Art* (contribution of $20,000 or more) | | e ☐ Other Real Estate | | i ☐ Vehicles | |
| b ☐ Qualified Conservation Contribution | | f ☐ Securities | | j ☐ Clothing and household items | |
| c ☐ Equipment | | g ☐ Collectibles** | | k ☐ Other | |
| d ☐ Art* (contribution of less than $20,000) | | h ☐ Intellectual Property | | | |

\* Art includes paintings, sculptures, watercolors, prints, drawings, ceramics, antiques, decorative arts, textiles, carpets, silver, rare manuscripts, historical memorabilia, and other similar objects.

\*\* Collectibles include coins, stamps, books, gems, jewelry, sports memorabilia, dolls, etc., but not art as defined above.

**Note:** In certain cases, you must attach a qualified appraisal of the property. See instructions.

| 3 | (a) Description of donated property (if you need more space, attach a separate statement) | (b) If any tangible personal property or real property was donated, give a brief summary of the overall physical condition of the property at the time of the gift. | (c) Appraised fair market value |
|---|---|---|---|
| A | | | |
| B | | | |
| C | | | |

| | (d) Date acquired by donor (mo., yr.) | (e) How acquired by donor | (f) Donor's cost or adjusted basis | (g) For bargain sales, enter amount received and attach a separate statement. | (h) Amount claimed as a deduction (see instructions) | (i) Date of contribution (see instructions) |
|---|---|---|---|---|---|---|
| A | | | | | | |
| B | | | | | | |
| C | | | | | | |

**For Paperwork Reduction Act Notice, see separate instructions.**   Cat. No. 62299J   Form **8283** (Rev. 12-2020)

Source: U.S. Department of the Treasury, Internal Revenue Service, Form 8283. Washington, DC: 2021.

**CONCEPT CHECK 5-4—**
**LO 5-4**

1. Depending on the type and amount of a charitable donation, it can be claimed either as a *for* AGI deduction or as an itemized deduction on Schedule A. True or false?
2. The overall limitation on the deductibility of charitable contributions is 30% of AGI. True or false?
3. If noncash gifts are worth more than $500, the taxpayer must file Form 8283. True or false?

# DEDUCTIBLE CASUALTY AND THEFT LOSSES (SCHEDULE A, LINE 15)
## LO 5-5

The Internal Revenue Code notes three instances in which an individual taxpayer can deduct a loss of property.[49] The first two deal with business or "production of income" property. Such losses are *for* AGI deductions[50] and are treated differently than losses to personal-use property. Losses discussed in this section pertain to losses of personal-use property (such as a personal residence, personal auto, or vacation home).

### What Is a Casualty?

Over the years, court cases and IRS administrative rulings have developed a generally accepted definition of *casualty:* an identifiable event of a sudden, unexpected, or unusual nature.[51] *Sudden* means the event is not gradual or progressive. If a loss is due to progressive deterioration, such as termite damage, it is not deductible as a casualty. A casualty is also an unusual event caused by external forces. Common household accidents, such as accidentally breaking furniture or damage caused by a pet, are not casualties. To claim a deduction, the taxpayer must own the damaged property.

*Under the TCJA, a personal casualty is now deductible only if such a loss is attributable to a federally declared disaster area that is designated as such by the president.*

**EXAMPLE 5-33**

Damage to walls and flooring from the progressive deterioration of a roof is a nondeductible casualty loss because the event was not sudden but gradual and progressive.[52] Likewise, when a patio porch collapses as a result of excessive dry rot, the casualty loss is disallowed.[53]

*Unexpected* refers to an event that is unanticipated and occurs without the intent of the taxpayer. An *unusual* event is one that is extraordinary and nonrecurring.[54]

**TAX YOUR BRAIN**

Since 1995 the North Carolina coast has been hit by a number of hurricanes, each of which caused substantial casualty losses. If a hurricane strikes the North Carolina coast in 2021, is the event still a casualty?

**ANSWER**

With a strict reading of the tax authority concerning casualty losses, the hurricane probably would not qualify as a casualty. The hurricane is not unexpected or unusual in recent history. However, the IRS is very unlikely to challenge a natural disaster if for no other reason than the negative public opinion that would result. A hurricane could provide a sudden loss even if it were not unusual. The Tax Court has held that even if an event is foreseeable, it does not preclude a casualty loss deduction. Further, if as a result of extensive damage, the president declared the North Carolina coast a federal disaster area, the resulting personal losses would be eligible for deduction within the prescribed limits.[55]

[49] IRC § 165(c).
[50] Casualty losses of business property are discussed in Chapters 6 and 8.
[51] Rev. Rul. 76-134, 1976-1 CB 54.
[52] *Whiting v. Comm'r*, 34 TCM 241 (1975).
[53] *Chipman v. Comm'r*, 41 TCM 1318 (1981).
[54] Rev. Rul. 72-592, 1972-2 CB 101.
[55] *Heyn v. Comm'r*, 46 TC 302 (1966), *acq.* 1967-2 CB 2.

| **TABLE 5-2**<br>**Personal Casualty**<br>**Expense Deduction**<br>**Formula** | **Calculation of Deductible Casualty Loss** |
|---|---|
| | Determine: |
| | FMV immediately before the casualty<br>minus (FMV immediately after the casualty) |
| | Amount A: Decline in FMV |
| | Amount B: Adjusted basis of the property |
| | Select the smaller of Amount A or Amount B<br>minus (insurance recovery) |
| | Allowable loss<br>minus ($100 per event) |
| | Eligible loss<br>minus (10% of AGI) |
| | Deductible casualty loss |

The magnitude of the casualty is not the primary factor in deciding whether the event is a casualty. The key factor is the presidential declaration of a federally declared disaster area. Thus, a minor event could qualify as a casualty. A formula that can be used to determine the amount of deductible casualty loss is shown in Table 5-2.

## The Amount of a Casualty Loss and the Year Deductible

The taxpayer may deduct uninsured loss or out-of-pocket loss in a federally declared disaster area subject to certain limits detailed here. The taxpayer's uninsured loss is calculated as follows:

$$\text{Uninsured loss} = \text{Loss due to casualty or theft} - \text{Insurance recovery}$$

In general, the casualty loss is the lower of the following:

1. The FMV immediately before the casualty reduced by the FMV immediately after the casualty.
2. The amount of the adjusted basis for determining the loss from the sale or other disposition of the property involved.[56]

The taxpayer is required to provide proof of the adjusted basis and FMV. *Adjusted basis* is the original cost or basis of the asset minus any depreciation or amortization and plus the cost of any capital improvements. The FMV is normally determined by an appraised value before and after the casualty event. Repair costs can also play an important role in determining the casualty loss. If the property is only partially destroyed, the casualty loss is its decline in value.

---

**EXAMPLE 5-34**

Tracy and Barbara purchased their personal residence in 1997 for $95,000. In March 2021, when the appraised value of the house was $250,000, it and most of their belongings in it were destroyed by a wild fire that consumed hundreds of acres in Southern California. The area was designated by the president a federally declared disaster area. The amount of the casualty loss for the house is $95,000 (the lower of the adjusted basis of $95,000 or the decrease in FMV of $250,000) because Tracy and Barbara received no insurance reimbursement for the damage. Losses for the personal belongings would be calculated on an item-by-item basis (from an inventory list of everything in the house).

---

**EXAMPLE 5-35**

In 2019, Akeem purchased an automobile (used for nonbusiness purposes) for $17,000. In April 2021, he had an accident with another automobile. Akeem auto had an FMV of $14,500 when the accident occurred. The FMV after the accident is difficult to determine. However, the cost to repair the auto to its precasualty condition was $5,000. The $5,000 would be a reasonable amount to deduct as a casualty loss. However, because this was not a result of federally declared disaster, Akeem is not allowed to take any casualty loss for this car accident.

---

[56] Reg. § 1.165-7(b)(1).

Typically, a taxpayer reports a federally declared disaster area casualty loss on the tax return in the tax year it took place. However, casualty losses may be deducted in different tax years depending on the circumstances.

Theft losses that occurred in a federally declared disaster area are deducted in the tax year in which the theft was discovered rather than the year of theft, if different.

---

**EXAMPLE 5-36**

As a hobby, Stefan collects rare coins. He had his collection appraised by an expert in October 2020. In March 2021, when Stefan was reviewing his collection after returning to his home after being evacuated from a federally declared disaster area, he noted that two extremely rare coins had been replaced with forgeries. Stefan would deduct the loss in 2021.[57]

---

In all cases, taxpayers must subtract any insurance reimbursement in determining their loss. Even when the insurance reimbursement has not yet been received, if a reasonable prospect of recovery exists with respect to a claim of insurance, the casualty loss should be adjusted for the anticipated recovery.[58] Should the loss be deducted and recovery occur in the subsequent tax year, the taxpayer must include the reimbursement in income in the year of reimbursement to the extent a tax benefit was gained from the casualty loss.

Individuals are required to file an insurance claim for federally declared disaster area *insured* personal casualty and theft losses to claim a deduction. If no insurance claim is filed, and there was insurance, then no deduction is permitted.

 **NEW LAW**

If the casualty loss occurred as the result of a major event (usually a natural disaster), and the president of the United States declares the area a national disaster area, the taxpayer can elect to deduct the casualty loss against the preceding year's taxable income. Congress added this provision to allow taxpayers suffering major disasters to get immediate assistance from a tax refund. The taxpayer files an amended return (Form 1040X) for the previous tax year including the casualty loss in the calculation. If the preceding year's tax return had not been filed at the time of the casualty, the loss can be deducted on the original return.

The Consolidated Appropriations Act of 2021 permits residents of qualified disaster areas to take a qualified distribution of up $100,000 from a qualified retirement plan without penalty to pay for repairs and replacements related to the event. Amounts taken are to be included in income over a three-year period or may be recontributed to the retirement plan instead.

## Limitation on Personal Casualty Losses from Federally Declared Disaster Areas

The tax law places two general limitations on personal casualty deductions. Each separate casualty is reduced by $100. It is important to note that this is $100 per *casualty*, not $100 per *item of property*.[59] For example, a taxpayer may lose his home, car, and other personal belongings in a tornado. This is one casualty, and only one $100 reduction is necessary. If the events are closely related, they are considered a single casualty. If the taxpayer had a theft loss early in the year and the tornado occurred later in the year, each loss would be reduced by $100.

The second and more substantial limitation is the 10% of AGI limitation. For the taxpayer to obtain any benefit from a casualty loss, the total losses for the year after the $100 per casualty deduction must exceed 10% of AGI. Because of the 10% limitation, most taxpayers do not benefit from casualty losses unless the loss was substantial.

For more information about specific issues related to casualty and theft losses, refer to IRS Publication 547, *Casualties, Disasters, and Thefts.*

---

**EXAMPLE 5-37**

Simone is a single taxpayer with an AGI of $75,000. For her to receive any tax benefit, a casualty loss, in a federally declared disaster area, must exceed $7,600 ($100 per casualty plus 10% of AGI). Recall that the $7,600 is net of any insurance recovery.

---

[57] This loss may be difficult to prove if Stefan did not have adequate documentation noting that he owned the rare coins prior to the theft.

[58] Reg. § 1.165-1(d)(2)(i).

[59] IRC § 165(h).

# From Shoebox to Software

**EXAMPLE 5-38**

Jose and Maria Ramirez (see the saved file) had the following casualties from a large storm during the 2021 tax year. Recall that they had AGI of $110,048. The area has been declared a federal disaster area.

| Asset | Cost or Basis | Decrease in FMV | Date Destroyed or Damaged | Insurance Proceeds |
|---|---|---|---|---|
| Furniture | $ 3,000 | $ 3,000 | 04/11/2021 | $ –0 – |
| Auto | 15,500 | 9,500 | 04/11/2021 | –0 – |
| Personal residence damaged by storm | 225,000 | 55,000 | 04/11/2021 | 50,000 |

| | |
|---|---|
| Casualty loss | |
| Residence (lower of cost or decrease in value) | $ 55,000 |
| Insurance proceeds | (50,000) |
| Furniture | 3,000 |
| Auto (lower of cost or decrease in value) | 9,500 |
| Casualty before limitations | $ 17,500 |
| $100 per event | (100) |
| 10% AGI floor | (11,005) |
| Net casualty loss | $ 6,395 |

Jose and Maria would have a $6,395 casualty loss deduction for the year. Because the area of the damage was declared a national disaster area, they could elect to take the deduction against their 2020 taxable income by filing an amended return.

Open the tax return file you previously saved for the Ramirezes. Report the casualty losses on line 15 of Schedule A. The taxpayers first report the losses on Form 4684. Double-click on line 15 of Schedule A to go to Form 4684 or open Form 4684 directly. Personal casualties are reported on lines 1 through 12. Click on Open Supporting Form and enter the data here. If you open Schedule A, you will see the net casualty loss of $6,395 on line 15.

The completed Form 4684 (Exhibit 5-7) follows on page 5-29.

---

**TAX YOUR BRAIN**

Binh suffered a $40,000 casualty loss in a federally declared disaster area in September 2021. Assuming that she had AGI of $110,000 in 2020 and $200,000 in 2021 (the disaster also affected business), what is the best way to treat the casualty loss?

**ANSWER**

Binh can elect to amend her 2020 tax return and get an immediate refund against her 2020 taxes or can wait until April 2022 and deduct the loss on her 2021 return.

An amendment to the 2020 return is as follows:

| | |
|---|---|
| Disaster loss | $40,000 |
| $100 per casualty | (100) |
| 10% AGI floor | (11,000) |
| Casualty loss deduction | $28,900 |

If she files on her 2021 return, the deduction is as follows:

| | |
|---|---|
| Disaster loss | $40,000 |
| $100 per casualty | (100) |
| 10% AGI floor | ($20,000) |
| Casualty loss deduction | $19,900 |

The advantage to filing an amended return for 2020 is that she will receive a larger refund and receive the funds more quickly.

**EXHIBIT 5-7**

| Form **4684** | **Casualties and Thefts** | OMB No. 1545-0177 |
|---|---|---|
| Department of the Treasury Internal Revenue Service | ▶ Go to *www.irs.gov/Form4684* for instructions and the latest information.<br>▶ Attach to your tax return.<br>▶ Use a separate Form 4684 for each casualty or theft. | 2021<br>Attachment Sequence No. **26** |

| Name(s) shown on tax return | Identifying number |
|---|---|
| Jose and Maria Ramirez | 412-34-5670 |

**SECTION A—Personal Use Property** (Use this section to report casualties and thefts of property **not** used in a trade or business or for income-producing purposes. For tax years 2018 through 2025, if you are an individual, casualty or theft losses of personal-use property are deductible only if the loss is attributable to a federally declared disaster. You must use a separate Form 4684 (through line 12) for each casualty or theft event involving personal-use property. **If reporting a qualified disaster loss, see the instructions for special rules that apply before completing this section.**)

If the casualty or theft loss is attributable to a federally declared disaster, check here ☑ and enter the DR- ___123456 - 123___ or EM- _____ - _____ declaration number assigned by FEMA. (See instructions.)

1  Description of properties (show type, location (city, state, and ZIP code), and date acquired for each property). Use a separate line for each property lost or damaged from the same casualty or theft. If you checked the box and entered the FEMA disaster declaration number above, enter the ZIP code for the property most affected on the line for Property **A**.

| | Type of Property | City and State | ZIP Code | Date Acquired |
|---|---|---|---|---|
| Property **A** | Furniture | Ellenwood, GA | 30294 | 2018 |
| Property **B** | Auto | Ellenwood, GA | 30294 | 2018 |
| Property **C** | Personal Residence | Ellenwood, GA | 30294 | 2006 |
| Property **D** | | | | |

| | | | **Properties** | | | |
|---|---|---|---|---|---|---|
| | | | **A** | **B** | **C** | **D** |
| 2 | Cost or other basis of each property | 2 | 3,000 | 15,500 | 225,000 | |
| 3 | Insurance or other reimbursement (whether or not you filed a claim) (see instructions)<br>**Note:** If line 2 is **more** than line 3, skip line 4. | 3 | | | 50,000 | |
| 4 | Gain from casualty or theft. If line 3 is **more** than line 2, enter the difference here and skip lines 5 through 9 for that column. See instructions if line 3 includes insurance or other reimbursement you did not claim, or you received payment for your loss in a later tax year | 4 | | | | |
| 5 | Fair market value **before** casualty or theft | 5 | 3,000 | 15,500 | 225,000 | |
| 6 | Fair market value **after** casualty or theft | 6 | 0 | 6,000 | 170,000 | |
| 7 | Subtract line 6 from line 5 | 7 | 3,000 | 9,500 | 55,000 | |
| 8 | Enter the **smaller** of line 2 or line 7 | 8 | 3,000 | 9,500 | 55,000 | |
| 9 | Subtract line 3 from line 8. If zero or less, enter -0- | 9 | 3,000 | 9,500 | 5,000 | |

| | | | |
|---|---|---|---|
| 10 | Casualty or theft loss. Add the amounts on line 9 in columns A through D | 10 | 17,500 |
| 11 | Enter $100 ($500 if qualified disaster loss rules apply; see instructions) | 11 | 100 |
| 12 | Subtract line 11 from line 10. If zero or less, enter -0- | 12 | 17,400 |
| | **Caution:** Use only one Form 4684 for lines 13 through 18. | | |
| 13 | Add the amounts on line 4 of all Forms 4684 | 13 | 0 |
| 14 | Add the amounts on line 12 of all Forms 4684. If you have losses not attributable to a federally declared disaster, see the instructions | 14 | 17,400 |
| | **Caution:** See instructions before completing line 15. | | |
| 15 | • If line 13 is **more** than line 14, enter the difference here and on Schedule D. **Do not** complete the rest of this section.<br>• If line 13 is **equal** to line 14, enter -0- here. **Do not** complete the rest of this section.<br>• If line 13 is **less** than line 14, and you have no qualified disaster losses subject to the $500 reduction on line 11 on any Form(s) 4684, enter -0- here and go to line 16. If you have qualified disaster losses subject to the $500 reduction, subtract line 13 from line 14 and enter the smaller of this difference or the amount on line 12 of the Form(s) 4684 reporting those losses. Enter that result here and on Schedule A (Form 1040), line 16; or Schedule A (Form 1040-NR), line 7. If you claim the standard deduction, also include on Schedule A (Form 1040), line 16, the amount of your standard deduction (see the Instructions for Form 1040). Do not complete the rest of this section if all of your casualty or theft losses are subject to the $500 reduction. | 15 | 0 |
| 16 | Add lines 13 and 15. Subtract the result from line 14 | 16 | 17,400 |
| 17 | Enter 10% of your adjusted gross income from Form 1040, 1040-SR, or 1040-NR, line 11. Estates and trusts, see instructions | 17 | 11,005 |
| 18 | Subtract line 17 from line 16. If zero or less, enter -0-. Also, enter the result on Schedule A (Form 1040), line 15; or Schedule A (Form 1040-NR), line 6. Estates and trusts, enter the result on the "Other deductions" line of your tax return | 18 | 6,395 |

**For Paperwork Reduction Act Notice, see instructions.** Cat. No. 12997O Form **4684** (2021)

The taxpayer must be able to prove both the fact of the casualty or theft and the amount of the loss. Newspaper articles, photographs, and police reports are commonly used to document the fact of a casualty or theft. When a casualty results from a sudden, unexpected, or unusual event, the amount of the loss is not always easy to determine. In many instances, an appraisal of the property is required to calculate the loss. Casualty losses are first reported on Form 4684, and the net loss is carried to the appropriate form (Schedule A, line 15, for personal casualties). If the insurance or other reimbursement is more than the basis in the property damaged or destroyed, the reimbursement is a gain. The gain is generally taxable if the taxpayer does not use the reimbursement proceeds to purchase replacement property that is related in service or use. However, in the instance of gain realized on homes in federally declared disaster areas, the gain may escape taxation.

**CONCEPT CHECK 5-5— LO 5-5**

1. A casualty is an identifiable event of a _____ , _____ , or _____ nature.
2. Casualty losses in federally declared disaster areas are first reported on Form _____ .
3. Generally, the tax law places _____ limitations on personal casualty deductions. First, each separate casualty event is reduced by _____ .
4. In general, to obtain any tax benefit from a casualty loss in a federally declared disaster area, the loss must be in excess of _____ of AGI.

# OTHER ITEMIZED DEDUCTIONS (SCHEDULE A, LINE 16)
## LO 5-6

The most common other itemized deductions are the following:

1. Gambling losses (gambling losses include, but aren't limited to, the cost of nonwinning bingo, lottery, and raffle tickets), but only to the extent of gambling winnings reported on Schedule 1 of Form 1040, line 8b.
2. Casualty and theft losses of income-producing property from Form 4684, lines 32 and 38b, or Form 4797, line 18a.

These are items that have a built-in threshold or other restrictions that limit the amount of deduction that is available.

**EXAMPLE 5-39**

Jane likes to visit the casino near her home on a regular basis and play the slot machines. For the year, she had gambling winnings of $12,000 and gambling losses of $15,500. She is allowed to deduct gambling losses as an other itemized deduction on Schedule A only up to the amount of gambling winnings, which would be $12,000. The gambling winnings are reported on line 8b of Schedule 1 for Form 1040.

**CONCEPT CHECK 5-6— LO 5-6**

1. The sum of all other itemized deductions must exceed 2.5% of the taxpayer's AGI before receiving any benefit. True or false?
2. An example of a deductible other itemized deduction would include the total amount of gambling losses without regard to any limitation. True or false?

# From Shoebox to Software   Comprehensive Example

In this example, you will create a return for a new taxpayer. Open the tax software and create a new return.

Alan (SSN 412-34-5670) and Cherie (SSN 412-34-5671) Masters are married filing a joint return and reside at 1483 Tax Street, Highland, MO 63747. They have two children under the age of 17 who are eligible for the child tax credit on line 28 of the 1040:

Scotty (SSN 412-34-5672), born 7/12/2010.

Brittney (SSN 412-34-5673), born 9/16/2012.

The couple had the following 2021 income items that you need to enter in the tax software:

| Alan's W-2 | |
|---|---|
| Wages | $112,505 |
| Federal withholding | 14,056 |
| Social security wages | 112,505 |
| Social security withholding | 6,975 |
| Medicare withholding | 1,631 |
| State withholding | 5,456 |
| Cherie's W-2 | |
| Wages | $37,495 |
| Federal withholding | 5,499 |
| Social security wages | 37,495 |
| Social security withholding | 2,325 |
| Medicare withholding | 544 |
| State withholding | 3,123 |
| Taxable amount on 1099-G from Missouri state tax refund ($7,560 deducted on federal 2020 return) | 897 |
| 1099-INT, New Bank | 2,300 |
| 1099-DIV, Shake Co., Inc. (qualified) | 3,100 |

They also had the following additional itemized deductions:

| | |
|---|---|
| Medical expenses | $6,400 |
| Personal property taxes | 2,000 |
| Real estate property taxes | 3,532 |
| Mortgage interest from line 1 of Form 1098 (total mortgage acquisition debt was $675,000) | 15,055 |
| Charitable contributions (cash) (no individual contribution was more than $250) | 2,750 |

See Exhibit 5-8 for the completed Schedule A for Alan and Cherie.

Notice the following in the tax software:

1. The medical expenses are entered directly on line 1. In Alan and Cherie's case, they get no benefit from their medical expenditures due to the 7.5% AGI floor.

2. Note that the state income tax paid flows through to line 5a when the amounts are entered on the W-2 input form.

3. The real estate property taxes and personal property taxes are entered directly on lines 5b and 5c, respectively.

4. The mortgage interest is entered through the Documents Received section. To enter it, click on Form 1098 and enter $15,055 on line 1. The interest transfers to line 8a of Schedule A.

5. The charitable contributions are entered directly on line 11 of Schedule A.

Make sure you save the return for the Masters.

**EXHIBIT 5-8**

| SCHEDULE A<br>(Form 1040)<br><br>Department of the Treasury<br>Internal Revenue Service (99) | **Itemized Deductions**<br>▶ Go to *www.irs.gov/ScheduleA* for instructions and the latest information.<br>▶ Attach to Form 1040 or 1040-SR.<br>**Caution:** If you are claiming a net qualified disaster loss on Form 4684, see the instructions for line 16. | OMB No. 1545-0074<br><br>2021<br>Attachment<br>Sequence No. **07** |
|---|---|---|

Name(s) shown on Form 1040 or 1040-SR
**Alan and Cherie Masters**

Your social security number
412-34-5670

| | | | |
|---|---|---|---|
| **Medical and Dental Expenses** | **Caution:** Do not include expenses reimbursed or paid by others. | | |
| | **1** Medical and dental expenses (see instructions) . . . . . . . . | **1** 6,400 | |
| | **2** Enter amount from Form 1040 or 1040-SR, line 11 **2** 156,297 | | |
| | **3** Multiply line 2 by 7.5% (0.075) . . . . . . . . . . . . | **3** 11,722 | |
| | **4** Subtract line 3 from line 1. If line 3 is more than line 1, enter -0- . . . | | **4** 0 |
| **Taxes You Paid** | **5** State and local taxes. | | |
| | **a** State and local income taxes or general sales taxes. You may include either income taxes or general sales taxes on line 5a, but not both. If you elect to include general sales taxes instead of income taxes, check this box . . . . . . . . . . . . . . . . ▶ ☐ | **5a** 8,579 | |
| | **b** State and local real estate taxes (see instructions) . . . . . . | **5b** 3,532 | |
| | **c** State and local personal property taxes . . . . . . . . . | **5c** 2,000 | |
| | **d** Add lines 5a through 5c . . . . . . . . . . . . . . | **5d** 14,111 | |
| | **e** Enter the smaller of line 5d or $10,000 ($5,000 if married filing separately) . . . . . . . . . . . . . . . . . . | **5e** 10,000 | |
| | **6** Other taxes. List type and amount ▶ _____ | **6** | |
| | **7** Add lines 5e and 6 . . . . . . . . . . . . . . . . | | **7** 10,000 |
| **Interest You Paid**<br>**Caution:** Your mortgage interest deduction may be limited (see instructions). | **8** Home mortgage interest and points. If you didn't use all of your home mortgage loan(s) to buy, build, or improve your home, see instructions and check this box . . . . . . . . . . . ▶ ☐ | | |
| | **a** Home mortgage interest and points reported to you on Form 1098. See instructions if limited . . . . . . . . . . . . . | **8a** 15,055 | |
| | **b** Home mortgage interest not reported to you on Form 1098. See instructions if limited. If paid to the person from whom you bought the home, see instructions and show that person's name, identifying no., and address . . . . . . . . . . . . . . . . .<br>▶ _____<br>_____ | **8b** | |
| | **c** Points not reported to you on Form 1098. See instructions for special rules . . . . . . . . . . . . . . . . . . . | **8c** | |
| | **d** Mortgage insurance premiums (see instructions) . . . . . . . | **8d** | |
| | **e** Add lines 8a through 8d . . . . . . . . . . . . . . | **8e** 15,055 | |
| | **9** Investment interest. Attach Form 4952 if required. See instructions . | **9** | |
| | **10** Add lines 8e and 9 . . . . . . . . . . . . . . . . | | **10** 15,055 |
| **Gifts to Charity**<br>**Caution:** If you made a gift and got a benefit for it, see instructions. | **11** Gifts by cash or check. If you made any gift of $250 or more, see instructions . . . . . . . . . . . . . . . . . | **11** 2,750 | |
| | **12** Other than by cash or check. If you made any gift of $250 or more, see instructions. You **must** attach Form 8283 if over $500. . . . | **12** | |
| | **13** Carryover from prior year . . . . . . . . . . . . . . | **13** | |
| | **14** Add lines 11 through 13 . . . . . . . . . . . . . . | | **14** 2,7550 |
| **Casualty and Theft Losses** | **15** Casualty and theft loss(es) from a federally declared disaster (other than net qualified disaster losses). Attach Form 4684 and enter the amount from line 18 of that form. See instructions . . . . . . . . . . . . . . . . . . | | **15** |
| **Other Itemized Deductions** | **16** Other—from list in instructions. List type and amount ▶ _____<br>_____ | | **16** |
| **Total Itemized Deductions** | **17** Add the amounts in the far right column for lines 4 through 16. Also, enter this amount on Form 1040 or 1040-SR, line 12a . . . . . . . . . . . . . . | | **17** 27,805 |
| | **18** If you elect to itemize deductions even though they are less than your standard deduction, check this box . . . . . . . . . . . . . . . . . . . . ▶ ☐ | | |

For Paperwork Reduction Act Notice, see the Instructions for Forms 1040 and 1040-SR.   Cat. No. 17145C   **Schedule A (Form 1040) 2021**

Source: U.S. Department of the Treasury, Internal Revenue Service, Form 1040, Schedule A. Washington, DC: 2021.

# Summary

**LO 5-1:** Describe the deductibility and reporting of medical expenses.

- Itemized, or below-the-line, deductions are taken in lieu of the standard deduction. They are reported on Schedule A.
- Medical expenses are deductible to the extent that they exceed 7.5% of AGI.
- Taxpayers may deduct just about all medical expenses that are doctor prescribed. Expenses related to the maintenance of general health are usually not deductible.
- Medical capital expenditures are deductible only to the extent that the expenditures exceed the increase in FMV of the property.
- Premiums for long-term care insurance are deductible, but the extent to which they are depends on the taxpayer's age.

**LO 5-2:** Be able to explain the state and local tax deductions.

- The four major categories of deductible taxes on individual returns are personal property taxes, local real estate taxes, other state and local taxes, and foreign taxes.
- As a result of the TCJA, the limitation for the deductibility of total state and local taxes is now $10,000 ($5,000 for MFS).
- For a property tax to be deductible, it must be based on the value of the property.
- An individual taxpayer can deduct the amount of state income taxes actually paid or has the option of deducting state and local sales taxes paid.
- Taxpayers have the option of taking a credit for foreign taxes or deducting the taxes as an itemized deduction on Schedule A.

**LO 5-3:** Apply the tax rules associated with the interest deduction.

- Interest paid on an acquisition loan, or a home equity loan or second mortgage used to buy, build, or substantially improve the taxpayer's home that secures the loan, is deductible up to certain limits.
- For acquisition indebtedness, including the interest on a home equity loan, or a second mortgage, used to buy, build, or substantially improve the taxpayer's home, the interest is generally deductible only on principal amounts up to $750,000. However, in the case of unmarried co-owners of a property, that limitation is extended to $750,000 per person.
- Points are amounts paid by borrowers to obtain a mortgage. Typically, taxpayers deduct points ratably over the term of the loan; however, there are some exceptions.
- For 2021, PMI or the premiums on mortgage insurance are treated as deductible mortgage interest, subject to applicable phase-out rules.

**LO 5-4:** Explain the deductibility and reporting of charitable contributions.

- For 2021, all charitable contributions in cash to public charities are deductible up to 100% of the individual taxpayer's AGI.
- Depending on the nature of the item contributed for 2021, there are four deduction limitations for charitable contributions by individual taxpayers: 100%, 60%, 30%, and 20%.
- The substantiation requirements for charitable contributions have become more stringent, and the taxpayer is subject to more stringent reporting requirements.
- Contributions above the limitation amounts can be carried forward five years.

**LO 5-5:** Discuss the casualty loss deduction.

- *Casualty* is defined as an identifiable event of a sudden, unexpected, or unusual nature. *Sudden* means the event is not gradual or progressive.
- Under the TCJA, a personal casualty is deductible only if such a loss is attributable to a federally declared disaster area.
- The taxpayer's uninsured loss is calculated as Uninsured loss = Loss due to casualty or theft − Insurance recovery.
- Typically, a taxpayer reports a casualty on the tax return in the tax year the casualty took place; however, there are exceptions.
- The deductible amount is generally limited. First, each separate casualty is reduced by $100. Second, the loss must be in excess of 10% of AGI.
- Residents of qualified disaster areas can take a qualified distribution of up to $100,000 from a retirement plan or account without penalty to pay for repairs and replacements related to the event.

**LO 5-6:** Know how to report other itemized deductions.

- Other itemized deductions are items that have a built-in threshold or other restrictions that limit the amount of deduction that is available.
- Gambling losses (gambling losses include, but aren't limited to, the cost of nonwinning bingo, lottery, and raffle tickets) are an other itemized deduction, but only to the extent of gambling winnings.
- Casualty and theft losses of income-producing property reported on Form 4684, lines 32 and 38b, or Form 4797, line 18a, are another example of other itemized deductions.

## EA Fast Fact

What counts toward becoming an Enrolled Agent is your knowledge of the tax code. This is proven by passing the SEE, or Special Enrollment Exam, which is commonly referred to as the Enrolled Agent exam. While there is no formal educational requirement, it is highly useful to take some classes in taxation that will help you to gain the foundation necessary to pass the exam. In addition, there are review programs offered specific to the Enrolled Agent exam. The pathway to completing the exam, and earning the certification, can often be accomplished in 12 to 18 months.

**IMPORTANT**

You are eligible to receive absolutely free, the Surgent Enrolled Agent review program for Part I of the EA exam as a result of purchasing this text. To activate your free access, go to https://Surgent.com/McGrawHill/EA.

## Discussion Questions

All applicable Discussion Questions are available with **Connect**©

1. (Introduction) What is the difference between deductions *from* AGI and deductions *for* AGI?

2. (Introduction) What are the six types of personal expenses that can be classified as itemized deductions on Schedule A, Form 1040?

**EA** LO 5-1  3. Describe the concept of a 7.5% floor for medical deductions.

**EA** LO 5-1  4. Can an individual take a medical deduction for a capital improvement to their personal residence? If so, how is it calculated?

**EA** LO 5-1  5. What are the general requirements for a medical expense to be considered deductible?

LO 5-1  6. When are travel costs deductible as medical costs? How are medical travel costs calculated?

**EA**   LO 5-1   7. What is the proper tax treatment for prescription drugs obtained outside the United States, such as from Canada?

_____

_____

_____

**EA**   LO 5-1   8. Can a taxpayer take a deduction for premiums paid for health insurance? How do reimbursements from health insurance policies affect the amount of the medical deduction? What happens if an insurance reimbursement for medical expenses is received in a subsequent tax year?

_____

_____

_____

**EA**   LO 5-2   9. What are the four major categories of deductible taxes on individual returns?

_____

_____

_____

**EA**   LO 5-2   10. For a tax to be deductible as an itemized deduction, what three tests are required?

_____

_____

_____

**EA**   LO 5-2   11. If state or local income taxes are deducted on the current year's tax return, what is required if the taxpayer receives a refund in the next year?

_____

_____

_____

**EA**   LO 5-2   12. For 2021, how can the amount of the sales tax deduction be determined?

_____

_____

_____

**EA**   LO 5-2   13. When using the IRS sales tax deduction calculator to assist in determining a sales tax deduction, what information concerning the taxpayer do you need?

_____

_____

_____

**EA**   LO 5-2   14. What options does a taxpayer who paid foreign taxes have when considering their tax treatment? Which option is usually more tax beneficial?

_____

_____

_____

**EA**   LO 5-3   15. What is qualified residence interest? Are there any limits to the deductibility of acquisition loan interest?

_____

_____

_____

EA LO 5-3 16. What is a home equity loan? Is the interest tax deductible? Are there any requirements for the deductibility of home equity loan interest?

_____

_____

_____

EA LO 5-3 17. What is investment interest expense? What are the limits to the deductibility of investment interest expense?

_____

_____

_____

EA LO 5-4 18. Donations to what types of organizations are tax deductible?

_____

_____

_____

EA LO 5-4 19. Distinguish between the tax treatment for donations to charitable organizations of cash, ordinary income property, and capital gain property.

_____

_____

_____

EA LO 5-4 20. What happens to a charitable contribution that is in excess of the AGI limits?

_____

_____

_____

EA LO 5-5 21. Define *personal casualty loss*. Include in your discussion the concepts of sudden, unexpected, and unusual.

_____

_____

_____

EA LO 5-5 22. How is a personal casualty loss determined, and how is the loss calculated? Include in your discussion how the determination of the loss is made and limits or floors that are placed on personal casualties as well as any exceptions to those limits.

_____

_____

_____

EA LO 5-6 23. Give an example of an other itemized deduction. How are other itemized deductions limited?

_____

_____

_____

EA LO 5-6 24. For gambling losses, what is the process for determining their deductibility?

_____

_____

_____

EA
LO Introduction

25. Explain the relationship between the standard deduction and itemized deductions.

_____

_____

_____

## Multiple-Choice Questions   Mc Graw Hill **connect**

All applicable multiple-choice questions are available with **Connect**©

EA

26. (Introduction) Itemized deductions are taken when
    a. The taxpayer wants to.
    b. They are less than the standard deduction.
    c. They are higher than the standard deduction.
    d. The standard deduction is limited by high AGI.

EA

27. (Introduction) The majority of itemized deductions are
    a. Business expenses.
    b. Tax credits.
    c. Personal living expenses.
    d. None of the above.

EA   LO 5-1

28. Generally, a taxpayer may deduct the cost of medical expenses for which of the following?
    a. Marriage counseling.
    b. Health club dues.
    c. Doctor-prescribed birth control pills.
    d. Trips for general health improvement.

EA   LO 5-1

29. The threshold amount for the deductibility of allowable medical expenses ordinarily is:
    a. 7.5% of AGI.
    b. 10% of AGI.
    c. 10% of taxable income.
    d. 15% of taxable income.

EA   LO 5-1

30. During 2021, Raul incurred and paid the following expenses:

| | |
|---|---|
| Prescription drugs | $ 470 |
| Vitamins and over-the-counter cold remedies | 130 |
| Doctor and dentist visits | 700 |
| Health club fee | 250 |
| Hair transplant surgery | 2,400 |

What is the total amount of medical expenses (before considering the limitation based on AGI) that would enter into the calculation of itemized deductions for Raul's 2021 income tax return?
    a. $1,170.
    b. $1,300.
    c. $1,550.
    d. $3,950.

EA   LO 5-1   31. Prescription drugs obtained from sources outside the United States, such as Canada, are
   a. Always deductible no matter how they were obtained.
   b. Deductible only for citizens of Canada living in the United States.
   c. Deductible if prescribed by a physician and approved by the FDA for legal importation.
   d. Never deductible.

EA   LO 5-1   32. For 2021, Perla, who is single and 55 years of age, had AGI of $60,000. During the year, she incurred and paid the following medical costs:

| | |
|---|---|
| Doctor and dentist fees | $4,350 |
| Prescription medicines | 625 |
| Medical care insurance premiums (paid for with after-tax funds) | 380 |
| Long-term care insurance premiums | $1,700 |
| Hearing aid | 150 |

What amount can Perla take as a medical expense deduction (after the AGI limitation) for her 2021 tax return?
   a. $7,205.
   b. $7,195.
   c. $2,705.
   d. $2,695.

EA   LO 5-1   33. Which of the following statements is not true?
   a. A taxpayer can deduct medical expenses incurred for members of their family who are dependents.
   b. The AGI threshold for deductible medical expenses is 10%.
   c. Deductible medical expenses include long-term care services for disabled spouses and dependents.
   d. Transportation costs for medical purposes could include such items as cab, bus, or train fares, as well as expenses for a personal auto.

EA   LO 5-2   34. For 2021, the amount of the sales tax deduction is calculated by
   a. Determining the actual sales tax paid during the year.
   b. Using the IRS sales tax deduction calculator.
   c. Using the sales worksheet and tax tables provided by the IRS in the Schedule A instructions.
   d. All of the above.

EA   LO 5-2   35. Maya, who had significant itemized deductions for 2021 and therefore was eligible to use Schedule A, purchased a new vehicle in 2021 for $50,000 with a state sales tax of 10%. The allocated deduction amount for other purchases made by Maya throughout the year, using the IRS state and local sales tax tables, would be $750. She also paid state income taxes of $4,500 for 2021. Maya's best option to legally maximize her tax savings in 2021, assuming she was under the $10,000 limit for state and local taxes, would be to:
   a. Deduct the amount of state sales tax for the vehicle purchase on Schedule A.
   b. Take the standard deduction.
   c. Take the deduction for the state income taxes paid on Schedule A.
   d. Deduct her total amount of allowable state sales tax deduction on Schedule A.

EA   LO 5-2   36. During 2021, Noriko paid the following taxes related to her home:

| | |
|---|---|
| Real estate property taxes on residence (paid from escrow account) | $1,800 |
| State personal property tax on her automobile (based on value) | 600 |
| Property taxes on land held for long-term appreciation | 400 |

What amount can Noriko deduct as property taxes in calculating itemized deductions, assuming she was under the $10,000 limit for state and local taxes, for 2021?

a. $400.

b. $1,000.

c. $2,400.

d. $2,800.

EA LO 5-2 37. Of the following items, which one does not qualify as an itemized deduction for state and local taxes?

a. Personal property taxes assessed on the value of specific property.

b. State, local, and foreign income taxes.

c. Hotel taxes incurred on personal travel.

d. Real estate taxes on a residence.

EA LO 5-3 38. What is the maximum amount of personal residence *acquisition* debt on which interest is fully deductible on Schedule A?

a. $1,000,000.

b. $750,000.

c. $250,000.

d. $0.

EA LO 5-3 39. For 2021, the deduction by a taxpayer for investment interest expense is

a. Not limited.

b. Limited to the taxpayer's net investment income for 2021.

c. Limited to the investment interest paid in 2021.

d. Limited to the taxpayer's gross investment income for 2021.

EA LO 5-3 40. For 2021, Tarik, a single parent, reported the following amounts relating to his investments:

| | |
|---|---|
| Net investment income | $7,000 |
| Interest expense on a loan to purchase stocks | 2,000 |
| Interest expense on funds borrowed to purchase land for investment | 6,000 |

What is the maximum amount that Tarik could deduct in 2021 as investment interest expense?

a. $7,000.

b. $6,000.

c. $2,000.

d. $1,000.

EA LO 5-3 41. Referring to the previous question, what is the treatment for the interest expense that Tarik could not deduct in 2021?

a. It is lost.

b. It cannot be used except as a carryback to previous years.

c. It can be carried forward and deducted in succeeding years.

d. None of the above.

EA LO 5-4 42. Which of the following organizations qualifies for deductible charitable contributions?

a. A nonprofit educational institution.

b. The Salvation Army.

c. Churches.

d. All of the above.

EA    LO 5-4    43. Which of the following statements is *not* true regarding documentation requirements for charitable contributions?

    *a.* If the total deduction for all noncash contributions for the year is more than $500, Section A of Form 8283, Noncash Charitable Contributions, must be completed.

    *b.* A noncash contribution of less than $250 must be supported by a receipt or other written acknowledgment from the charitable organization.

    *c.* A contribution charged to a credit card is a noncash contribution for purposes of documentation requirements.

    *d.* A deduction of more than $5,000 for one property item generally requires that a written appraisal be obtained and attached to the return.

EA    LO 5-4    44. Lamont Byrd donated stock (capital gain property) to a public charity that he has long supported. He purchased the stock four years ago for $100,000, and on the date of the gift, it had a fair market value of $300,000. What is his maximum charitable contribution deduction for the year on this contribution of stock if his AGI is $500,000?

    *a.* $90,000.

    *b.* $100,000.

    *c.* $150,000.

    *d.* $300,000.

EA    LO 5-5    45. In 2021, the president of the United States declared a federal disaster due to brush fires in the Southwest. Lisa lives in that area and lost her home in the fires. What choice does she have regarding when she can claim the loss on her tax return?

    *a.* It may be claimed in 2020 or 2021.

    *b.* It must be claimed in 2020 if the loss is greater than her modified Adjusted Gross Income.

    *c.* It may be claimed in 2022 if an election is filed with the 2021 return.

    *d.* It must be claimed in 2020 if the return has not been filed by the date of the loss.

EA    LO 5-5    46. In 2021, the Redfeather's vacation cottage was severely damaged by an earthquake in a location that was a presidentially declared disaster area. They had an AGI of $110,000 in 2021, and following is information related to the cottage:

| | |
|---|---|
| Cost basis | $ 95,000 |
| FMV before casualty | 135,000 |
| FMV after casualty | 20,000 |

The Redfeather's had insurance and received an $80,000 insurance settlement. What is the amount of allowable casualty loss deduction for the Redfeather's in 2021 *before* the AGI and event limitation?

    *a.* $45,000.

    *b.* $14,900.

    *c.* $15,000.

    *d.* $3,900.

EA    LO 5-6    47. Which expense, incurred and paid in 2021, can be claimed as an other itemized deduction?

    *a.* Self-employed health insurance.

    *b.* Unreimbursed moving expenses.

    *c.* Gambling losses

    *d.* Self-employment taxes.

**EA**  LO 5-6  48. Raquel, who works in medical sales, drives her own vehicle to various locations for client sales meetings. Her employer reimburses her $400 each month for various business expenses and does not expect Raquel to provide proof of her expenses. Her employer included this $4,800 reimbursement in Raquel's 2021 W-2 as part of her wages. In 2021, Raquel incurred $3,000 in transportation expense, $1,000 in parking and tolls expense, $1,800 in car repair expense, and $600 for expenses while attending a professional association convention. Assume that Raquel uses the vehicle for business purposes only and that she maintains adequate documentation to support all of these expenditures. What amount is Raquel entitled to deduct on her Schedule A for other itemized deductions?

    *a.* $6,400 of expenses subject to the 2% of AGI limitation.

    *b.* $4,800 because her employer follows a nonaccountable plan.

    *c.* $1,600, the difference between her expenditures and her reimbursement.

    *d.* $0 because employee expenses are no longer deductible as an itemized deduction.

**EA**  LO 5-6  49. Which of the following is an other itemized deduction on the Schedule A?

    *a.* Tax preparation fees.

    *b.* Safe deposit box fee.

    *c.* Gambling losses.

    *d.* Union dues and fees.

## Problems Mc Graw Hill connect

All applicable problems are available with *Connect*

**EA**  LO 5-1  50. Mickey is a 12-year-old dialysis patient. Three times a week for the entire year, he and his mother, Sue, drive 20 miles one way to Mickey's dialysis clinic. On the way home, they go 10 miles out of their way to stop at Mickey's favorite restaurant. Their total round trip is 50 miles per day. How many of those miles, if any, can Sue use to calculate an itemized deduction for transportation? Use the medical mileage rate in effect for 2021. Explain your answer.

**EA**  LO 5-1  51. Reggie, who is 55, had AGI of $32,000 in 2021. During the year, he paid the following medical expenses:

| | |
|---|---|
| Drugs (prescribed by physicians) | $ 500 |
| Marijuana (prescribed by physicians) | 1,400 |
| Health insurance premiums—after taxes | 850 |
| Doctors' fees | 1,250 |
| Eyeglasses | 375 |
| Over-the-counter drugs | 200 |

Reggie received $500 in 2021 for a portion of the doctors' fees from his insurance. What is Reggie's medical expense deduction?

**EA** **LO 5-1** 52. Shannon and Rosa, both under 65 and married, have a combined AGI of $45,000 in year 2021. Due to certain heart issues, Shannon has been prescribed Lipitor® by a physician. For year 2021, Shannon spent a total of $3,100 on the medication and $1,750 on doctor's bills. Can Shannon deduct the medical costs as an itemized deduction? Explain your answer.

_____

_____

_____

**EA** **LO 5-3** 53. Leslie and Jason, who are married, paid the following expenses during 2021:

| | |
|---|---|
| Interest on a car loan | $ 100 |
| Interest on lending institution loan (used to purchase municipal bonds) | 3,000 |
| Interest on home mortgage (home mortgage principal is less than $750,000) | 2,100 |

What is the maximum amount that they can use in calculating itemized deductions for 2021?

_____

_____

_____

**EA** **LO 5-2** 54. On April 1, 2021, Farid sold a house to Amy. The property tax on the house, which is based on a calendar year, was due September 1, 2021. Amy paid the full amount of property tax of $2,500. Calculate both Farid's and Amy's allowable deductions for the property tax. Assume a 365-day year.

_____

_____

_____

**EA** **LO 5-2** 55. In 2020, Alondra, a single taxpayer, had $3,750 in state tax withheld from her paycheck. She properly deducted that amount on her 2020 tax return as an itemized deduction that she qualified for, thus reducing her tax liability. After filing her 2020 tax return, Alondra discovered that she had overpaid her state tax by $417. She received her refund in July 2021. What must Alondra do with the $417 refund? Explain your answer.

_____

_____

_____

**EA** **LO 5-3** 56. Eve purchased a personal residence from Adam. To sell the residence, Adam agreed to pay $4,500 in points related to Eve's mortgage. Discuss the tax consequences from the perspectives of both Eve and Adam.

_____

_____

_____

**EA** **LO 5-3** 57. Shelby has net investment income of $18,450 and wage income of $80,500. She paid investment interest expense of $19,000. What is Shelby's deduction for investment interest expense? Explain your answer.

_____

_____

_____

**EA**   LO 5-3   58. Tyrone and Akira, who are married, incurred and paid the following amounts of interest during 2021:

| | |
|---|---|
| Home acquisition debt interest | $15,000 |
| Credit card interest | 5,000 |
| Home equity loan interest (used for home improvement) | 6,500 |
| Investment interest expense | 10,000 |
| Mortgage insurance premiums (PMI) | 1,000 |

With 2021 net investment income of $2,000, calculate the amount of their allowable deduction for investment interest expense and their total deduction for allowable interest. Home acquisition principal and the home equity loan principal combined are less than $750,000.

_____

_____

_____

**EA**   LO 5-4   59. Jinhee purchased a ticket to a concert to raise money for the local university. The ticket cost $350, but the normal cost of a ticket to this concert is $100. How much is deductible as a charitable contribution?

_____

_____

_____

**EA**   LO 5-4   60. Jaylen made a charitable contribution to his church in the current year. He donated common stock valued at $33,000 (acquired as an investment in 2007 for $13,000). Jaylen's AGI in the current year is $75,000. What is his allowable charitable contribution deduction? How are any excess amounts treated?

_____

_____

_____

**EA**   LO 5-4   61. Adrian contributed an antique vase he had owned for 25 years to a museum. At the time of the donation, the vase had a value of $35,000. The museum displayed this vase in the art gallery.
   *a.* Assume that Adrian's AGI is $80,000, and his basis in the vase is $15,000. How much may Adrian deduct?
   *b.* How would your answer to part (*a*) change if, instead of displaying the vase, the museum sold the vase to an antique dealer?

_____

_____

_____

**EA**   LO 5-5   62. In 2021 Amelia's pleasure boat that she purchased in 2014 for $48,500 was destroyed by a hurricane in a part of Florida that was declared a federal disaster area. Her loss was not totally covered by her insurance. On what form(s) will Amelia report this loss?

_____

_____

_____

**EA** **LO 5-5** 63. Reynaldo and Sonya, a married couple, had flood damage in their home due to a dam break near their home in 2021, which was declared a federally designated disaster area. The flood damage ruined the furniture that was stored in their garage. The following items were completely destroyed and not salvageable:

| Damaged Items | FMV Just Prior to Damage | Original Item Cost |
|---|---|---|
| Antique poster bed | $6,000 | $ 5,000 |
| Pool table | 7,000 | 11,000 |
| Large flat-screen TV | 700 | 2,500 |

Their homeowner's insurance policy had a $10,000 deductible for the personal property, which was deducted from their insurance reimbursement of $12,700, resulting in a net payment of $2,700. Their AGI for 2021 was $60,000. What is the amount of casualty loss that Reynaldo and Sonya can claim on their joint return for 2021?

_____

_____

_____

**EA** **LO 5-6** 64. During the year 2021, Ricki, who is not self-employed and does not receive employer reimbursement for business expenses, drove her car 2,500 miles to visit clients, 4,800 miles to get to her office, and 500 miles to attend business-related seminars. All of this mileage was incurred ratably throughout the year. She spent $500 for airfare to another business seminar and $200 for parking at her office. Using the automobile expense rates in effect for 2021, what is her deductible transportation expense?

_____

_____

_____

**EA** **LO 5-6** 65. Hortencia is employed as an accountant for a large firm in Connecticut. For relaxation she likes to go to a nearby casino and play in blackjack tournaments. During 2021, she incurred $6,475 in gambling losses and $5,250 in gambling winnings.

Hortencia plans to itemize her deductions in 2021 because she purchased a home this year and has significant mortgage interest expense; what amount could she claim on her return for other itemized deductions for the year?

_____

_____

_____

## Tax Return Problems   Mc Graw Hill **connect**

All applicable tax return problems are available with *Connect*©

Use your tax software to complete the following problems. If you are manually preparing the tax returns, you will need to prepare Form 1040 with a Schedule 1 and Schedule A for each problem and a Form 8283 for the third problem.

For the following tax return problems, assume the taxpayer does *not* wish to contribute to the Presidential Election Fund, unless otherwise stated in the problem. In addition, the taxpayers did not receive, sell, send, exchange, or otherwise acquire any financial interest in any virtual currency during the year. For any Tax Return Problems for which the taxpayers are entitled to a child tax credit, assume that the taxpayers did NOT receive any advance child tax credit payments during 2021. Thus, the entire child tax credit (if permitted) will be claimed on the 2021 tax return.

**Tax Return Problem 1**

Elise Dubois is single, has no dependents, and lives at 55855 Ridge Drive in Lafayette, LA 70593. Her social security number is 412-34-5670 (date of birth 3/15/1981).

Her W-2 contained the following information:

Wages (box 1) = $48,965.25
Federal W/H (box 2) = $ 5,024.38
Social security wages (box 3) = $48,965.25
Social security W/H (box 4) = $ 3,035.85
Medicare wages (box 5) = $48,965.25
Medicare W/H (box 6) = $ 710.00

She has gambling winnings of $1,050 and the following expenses:

| | |
|---|---|
| State income taxes | $3,200 |
| Real estate property taxes | 1,150 |
| Medical expenses | 6,400 |
| Charitable cash contributions | |
| (no single contribution was more than $250) | 450 |
| Mortgage interest expense | 5,605 |
| Personal property taxes | 720 |
| Gambling losses | 1,235 |

Prepare a Form 1040 with a Schedule 1 and Schedule A for Elise using any appropriate worksheets.

**Tax Return Problem 2**

John and Shannon O'Banion, who live at 3222 Pinon Drive, Mesa, CO 81643, file as married filing jointly. John's social security number is 412-34-5670 (date of birth 5/12/1983), and Shannon's is 412-34-5671 (date of birth 11/3/1985).

John's W-2 contained the following information:

Wages (box 1) = $66,346.74
Federal W/H (box 2) = $ 5,224.75
Social security wages (box 3) = $66,346.74
Social security W/H (box 4) = $ 4,113.50
Medicare wages (box 5) = $66,346.74
Medicare W/H (box 6) = $ 962.03

Shannon did not work for the year due to a medical condition but did receive unemployment compensation of $5,328 for the year with federal withholding of $654.68. In the same year, they had the following medical costs:

| | |
|---|---|
| Shannon's prescribed diabetes medication | $ 4,250 |
| Shannon's hospital charges | 9,350 |
| Shannon's regular physician visits | 835 |
| Shannon's eye doctor | 75 |
| Shannon's diabetes blood testing supplies | 685 |
| Insurance reimbursements | 1,925 |

In addition, they had the following other expenses:

| | |
|---|---|
| State income taxes | $4,950 |
| Real estate property taxes | 4,170 |
| Car loan interest | 500 |
| Personal property taxes | 765 |
| Cash charitable contributions (made ratably throughout the year to their church) | 2,135 |
| Mortgage interest expense | 9,970 |
| Union dues for John | 575 |
| Tax preparation fees | 175 |

Prepare a Form 1040 with a Schedule 1 and Schedule A for the O'Banions using any appropriate worksheets.

**Tax Return Problem 3**

Keisha Sanders, a divorced single taxpayer and practicing attorney, lives at 9551 Oak Lane in Boise, ID 83709. Her social security number is 412-34-5670 (date of birth 2/27/1977).

Her W-2 contained the following information:

Wages (box 1) = $84,601.55

Federal W/H (box 2) = $ 8,898.38

Social security wages (box 3) = $84,601.55

Social security W/H (box 4) = $ 5,245.30

Medicare wages (box 5) = $84,601.55

Medicare W/H (box 6) = $ 1,226.72

In addition, Keisha made alimony payments totaling $10,800 for the year to her former husband Alex, an unemployed mine worker, whose social security number is 412-34-5671. This was in regards to a divorce decree that was completed prior to November 2017 and had not been amended post 2018. She also received a 1099 INT from Idaho State Credit Union in the amount of $254.85.

Keisha also has the following information for her Schedule A itemized deductions:

| | |
|---|---|
| **Interest expense** | |
| Home mortgage (qualified residence interest) | $8,100 |
| MasterCard (used exclusively for personal expenses and purchases) | 675 |
| Car loan (personal use) | 710 |
| Student loan interest | 1,750 |
| **Taxes paid** | |
| State income tax withheld | 2,950 |
| State income tax deficiency (for 2020) | 350 |
| Real estate property taxes—principal residence | 1,700 |
| Personal property taxes—car | 75 |
| Registration fee—car | 125 |
| **Medical expenses** | |
| Doctors' fees | 635 |
| Prescription drugs | 260 |
| Vitamins and over-the-counter drugs | 250 |
| Dental implant to correct a bite problem | 1,600 |
| Health club fee | 400 |

*(continued)*

**Charitable contributions
(all required documentation is maintained)**   *(concluded)*

| | |
|---|---:|
| *Cash:* | |
| Mosque | |
| (made ratably throughout the year and no single | |
| contribution was greater than $250) | 3,100 |
| United Way | 100 |
| PBS annual campaign | 200 |
| *Property:* | |
| Greater Boise Goodwill—used clothing and household items | |
| Date of donation November 15, 2021 | |
| Thrift shop value at date of donation | 550 |
| Actual purchase price of the items | 1,300 |

Prepare a Form 1040, with a Schedule 1, a Schedule A, and a Form 8283 for Keisha using any other appropriate worksheets. If manually preparing the return, the Student Loan Interest Deduction worksheet can be found in IRS Publication 970, Tax Benefits for Education.

We have provided selected filled-in source documents that are available in *Connect.*

**Tax Return Problem 4**

Kofi Allon, who is 32 years old and single, is employed as a technical consultant for a large electronics distributor. He lives at 678 Birch Street, LaMesa, CA 91941. Kofi's social security number is 412-34-5670 (date of birth 5/29/1988).

Kofi's W-2 contained the following information:

Wages (box 1) = $75,350.62

Federal W/H (box 2) = $ 9,605.43

Social security wages (box 3) = $75,350.62

Social security W/H (box 4) = $ 4,671.74

Medicare wages (box 5) = $75,350.62

Medicare W/H (box 6) = $ 1,092.58

Kofi's other income includes interest on a money market account at the San Diego Credit Union of $275 and $265 in interest on a certificate of deposit at the Bank of California. He also made alimony payments of $650 per month to his ex-wife for 10 months for a divorce agreement that was finalized on February 21, 2021. (Marta Tombe, social security number 412-34-5673).

In addition, he had the following other expenses for 2021:

| | |
|---|---:|
| Home mortgage interest | $7,670 |
| Auto loan interest | 1,325 |
| Credit card interest | 730 |
| Property taxes on personal residence | 2,342 |
| State income taxes | 2,050 |
| Unreimbursed hospital bills | 6,300 |
| Doctor bills | 2,760 |
| Other qualifying medical expenses | 725 |
| Income tax preparation fee | 425 |
| Job-hunting expenses | 925 |
| Cash donations to his church (made ratably over the year and no single contribution was greater than $250) | 885 |

In May of 2021, Kofi's house was broken into and his vintage 1961 Fender Stratocaster guitar was stolen. The guitar had a current fair market value of $16,800, and Kofi had paid $7,500 for the instrument in May of 2008. The guitar was uninsured.

**Required:** Prepare a Form 1040 and a Schedule A for Kofi including any appropriate schedules.

Design elements icons: (Tax Your Brain Icon; Brain Teaser Icon; Checkmark Icon; Laptop Icon; New Law Icon) ©McGraw-Hill Education

# Chapter Six

# Self-Employed Business Income (Line 3 of Schedule 1 and Schedule C)

Many taxpayers in the United States attribute a large portion of their taxable income to self-employment trade or businesses. Self-employment status automatically increases the complexity of a taxpayer's tax return. It also increases the importance of understanding applicable tax law to minimize a taxpayer's tax liability. In this chapter, we present and discuss the tax rules for recognizing income and maximizing expenses on Schedule C for self-employed businesses.

## Learning Objectives

When you have completed this chapter, you should understand the following learning objectives (LO):

**LO 6-1** Describe how income and expenses for a self-employed individual are recognized and reported.

**LO 6-2** Explain the concept of ordinary and necessary business expenses.

**LO 6-3** Explain the calculation of depreciation for trade or business assets.

**LO 6-4** Describe travel and entertainment expenses and discuss their deductibility.

**LO 6-5** Apply the rules for deducting the business portion of a residence and business bad debts.

**LO 6-6** Explain the hobby loss rules and the limits on education expense deductibility.

**LO 6-7** Describe the calculation of self-employment taxes.

## INTRODUCTION

This chapter discusses the taxation of self-employed trade or businesses (sole proprietors). In Chapter 4, the concept of a *for* Adjusted Gross Income (AGI) deduction was presented. Chapter 4 discussed several income components of AGI in detail. However, this is the first chapter in which income items and *for* AGI deductions are aggregated to determine the effect on AGI. Simply put, the income from a sole proprietorship is netted with related ordinary and necessary business expenses to determine the increase (or decrease if a net loss results) in AGI. A sole proprietor reports trade or business income or loss on Schedule C of Form 1040. Taxpayers must use Schedule C when the trade or business is neither incorporated nor conducting business as some other entity form (such as a partnership or limited liability company). Schedule C is shown in Exhibit 6-1.

Neither the tax law nor the regulations directly define the term *trade or business*. However, the term is used quite frequently in various code sections, particularly when addressing the deductibility of expenses. The general consensus of the relevant tax authority (mainly Tax Court cases, IRS Publication 334, and the IRS instructions accompanying Schedule C) is that a "trade or business" is any activity that is engaged in for profit.[1] The profit motive is necessary, and the activity should be engaged in with continuity and regularity. Thus, sporadic activity or hobby activities are not considered trade or business activity.

If an activity produces a profit, there is usually no problem with the trade or business classification. However, when substantial losses result from an activity, a profit motive may be questioned. To combat losses from hobbylike activities, Congress developed hobby loss rules.[2] Once the taxpayer can establish that an activity is a trade or business, income and expenses from the activity are reported on Schedule C.[3]

## Schedule C

A review of Schedule C shows that the form is fundamentally an income statement for the trade or business. The first section is primarily information related. The proprietor's name and social security number, business address, business code, and accounting method are required for each business. A separate business name must be listed if it exists. An employer identification number is required only if the business has a Keogh retirement plan or is required to file various other tax returns.[4]

A business code for each business is required in box B.[5] The taxpayer elects the accounting method used in the first year of business.[6] However, because nearly all individual taxpayers are cash method taxpayers, the cash receipts and disbursements method is the norm for sole proprietorships. As a result of the 2017 Tax Act, businesses with gross receipts less than $26 million (three-year average) can use the cash method of accounting even if inventory is a material income-producing factor. Prior to 2018, accrual method of accounting was required for material inventory levels.

Question G in the top section of Schedule C refers to "material participation." If the taxpayer does not materially participate in the business, the income or loss is classified as *passive*. With passive activities, losses can be taken only to the extent of passive income. We discuss the concepts of material participation and passive activities in detail in Chapter 13.

---

[1] *Doggett v. Burnet*, 65 F.2d 191 (D.C. Cir. 1933); *Coffey v. Comm'r*, 141 F.2d 204 (5th Cir. 1944); *Black Dome Corp.*, 5 T.C.M. 455 (1946).

[2] IRC § 183 and Chapter 1 of IRS Publication 535. The hobby loss rules are discussed in detail later in this chapter.

[3] If the business has expenses of $5,000 or less, the taxpayer may be able to file Schedule C-EZ.

[4] The ID number is required if the business must file an employment, excise, estate, trust, or alcohol, tobacco, and firearms tax return. If an ID number is required, the social security number of the owner should not be listed. An ID number can be acquired by filing Form SS-4 with the IRS.

[5] The business codes are located in the instructions for Form 1040, Schedule C. The codes are also usually included with the tax software. To review the business codes in your tax software, you generally open a Schedule C and double-click on box B.

[6] IRC § 446.

**EXHIBIT 6-1**

| SCHEDULE C<br>(Form 1040)<br><br>Department of the Treasury<br>Internal Revenue Service (99) | **Profit or Loss From Business**<br>(Sole Proprietorship)<br>▶ Go to *www.irs.gov/ScheduleC* for instructions and the latest information.<br>▶ **Attach to Form 1040, 1040-SR, 1040-NR, or 1041; partnerships must generally file Form 1065.** | OMB No. 1545-0074<br>**2021**<br>Attachment<br>Sequence No. **09** |
|---|---|---|

Name of proprietor | Social security number (SSN)
---|---

**A** Principal business or profession, including product or service (see instructions) | **B** Enter code from instructions ▶

**C** Business name. If no separate business name, leave blank. | **D** Employer ID number (EIN) (see instr.)

**E** Business address (including suite or room no.) ▶
City, town or post office, state, and ZIP code

**F** Accounting method: **(1)** ☐ Cash **(2)** ☐ Accrual **(3)** ☐ Other (specify) ▶

**G** Did you "materially participate" in the operation of this business during 2021? If "No," see instructions for limit on losses . ☐ Yes ☐ No

**H** If you started or acquired this business during 2021, check here ▶ ☐

**I** Did you make any payments in 2021 that would require you to file Form(s) 1099? See instructions ☐ Yes ☐ No

**J** If "Yes," did you or will you file required Form(s) 1099? . . . . . . . . . . . . ☐ Yes ☐ No

### Part I Income

| | | | |
|---|---|---|---|
| 1 | Gross receipts or sales. See instructions for line 1 and check the box if this income was reported to you on Form W-2 and the "Statutory employee" box on that form was checked . . . . . . ▶ ☐ | **1** | |
| 2 | Returns and allowances . . . . . . . . . . . . . . . . . . . . . . . . | **2** | |
| 3 | Subtract line 2 from line 1 . . . . . . . . . . . . . . . . . . . . . . | **3** | |
| 4 | Cost of goods sold (from line 42) . . . . . . . . . . . . . . . . . . . | **4** | |
| 5 | **Gross profit.** Subtract line 4 from line 3 . . . . . . . . . . . . . . . . | **5** | |
| 6 | Other income, including federal and state gasoline or fuel tax credit or refund (see instructions) . . . | **6** | |
| 7 | **Gross income.** Add lines 5 and 6 . . . . . . . . . . . . . . . . . . ▶ | **7** | |

### Part II Expenses. Enter expenses for business use of your home **only** on line 30.

| | | | | | | | |
|---|---|---|---|---|---|---|---|
| 8 | Advertising . . . . . | **8** | | 18 | Office expense (see instructions) | **18** | |
| 9 | Car and truck expenses (see instructions) . . . . . | **9** | | 19 | Pension and profit-sharing plans . | **19** | |
| 10 | Commissions and fees . | **10** | | 20 | Rent or lease (see instructions): | | |
| 11 | Contract labor (see instructions) | **11** | | a | Vehicles, machinery, and equipment | **20a** | |
| 12 | Depletion . . . . . | **12** | | b | Other business property . . . | **20b** | |
| 13 | Depreciation and section 179 expense deduction (not included in Part III) (see instructions) . . . . | **13** | | 21 | Repairs and maintenance . . . | **21** | |
| | | | | 22 | Supplies (not included in Part III) . | **22** | |
| | | | | 23 | Taxes and licenses . . . . . | **23** | |
| | | | | 24 | Travel and meals: | | |
| 14 | Employee benefit programs (other than on line 19) . . | **14** | | a | Travel . . . . . . . . . | **24a** | |
| 15 | Insurance (other than health) | **15** | | b | Deductible meals (see instructions) . . . . . . . | **24b** | |
| 16 | Interest (see instructions): | | | 25 | Utilities . . . . . . . . | **25** | |
| a | Mortgage (paid to banks, etc.) | **16a** | | 26 | Wages (less employment credits) . | **26** | |
| b | Other . . . . . . | **16b** | | 27a | Other expenses (from line 48) . . | **27a** | |
| 17 | Legal and professional services | **17** | | b | **Reserved for future use** . . . | **27b** | |

| | | | |
|---|---|---|---|
| 28 | **Total expenses** before expenses for business use of home. Add lines 8 through 27a . . . . . ▶ | **28** | |
| 29 | Tentative profit or (loss). Subtract line 28 from line 7 . . . . . . . . . . . . . . | **29** | |
| 30 | Expenses for business use of your home. Do not report these expenses elsewhere. Attach Form 8829 unless using the simplified method. See instructions.<br>**Simplified method filers only:** Enter the total square footage of (a) your home: _____<br>and (b) the part of your home used for business: _____. Use the Simplified Method Worksheet in the instructions to figure the amount to enter on line 30 . . . . . . . . | **30** | |
| 31 | **Net profit or (loss).** Subtract line 30 from line 29.<br>• If a profit, enter on both **Schedule 1 (Form 1040), line 3,** and on **Schedule SE, line 2.** (If you checked the box on line 1, see instructions). Estates and trusts, enter on **Form 1041, line 3.**<br>• If a loss, you **must** go to line 32. | **31** | |
| 32 | If you have a loss, check the box that describes your investment in this activity. See instructions.<br>• If you checked 32a, enter the loss on both **Schedule 1 (Form 1040), line 3,** and on **Schedule SE, line 2.** (If you checked the box on line 1, see the line 31 instructions.) Estates and trusts, enter on **Form 1041, line 3.**<br>• If you checked 32b, you **must** attach **Form 6198.** Your loss may be limited. | 32a ☐ All investment is at risk.<br>32b ☐ Some investment is not at risk. | |

**For Paperwork Reduction Act Notice, see the separate instructions.** Cat. No. 11334P Schedule C (Form 1040) 2021

*(continued)*

**EXHIBIT 6-1** *(concluded)*

Schedule C (Form 1040) 2021      Page **2**

| Part III | Cost of Goods Sold (see instructions) |
|---|---|

33   Method(s) used to value closing inventory:    **a** ☐ Cost    **b** ☐ Lower of cost or market    **c** ☐ Other (attach explanation)

34   Was there any change in determining quantities, costs, or valuations between opening and closing inventory? If "Yes," attach explanation . . . . . . . . . . . . . . . . . . ☐ Yes    ☐ No

35   Inventory at beginning of year. If different from last year's closing inventory, attach explanation . . | **35** |

36   Purchases less cost of items withdrawn for personal use . . . . . . . . . | **36** |

37   Cost of labor. Do not include any amounts paid to yourself . . . . . . . | **37** |

38   Materials and supplies . . . . . . . . . . . . . . . . . | **38** |

39   Other costs . . . . . . . . . . . . . . . . . . . . . | **39** |

40   Add lines 35 through 39 . . . . . . . . . . . . . . . . . | **40** |

41   Inventory at end of year . . . . . . . . . . . . . . . . . | **41** |

42   **Cost of goods sold.** Subtract line 41 from line 40. Enter the result here and on line 4 . . | **42** |

| Part IV | Information on Your Vehicle. Complete this part **only** if you are claiming car or truck expenses on line 9 and are not required to file Form 4562 for this business. See the instructions for line 13 to find out if you must file Form 4562. |
|---|---|

43   When did you place your vehicle in service for business purposes? (month/day/year)   ▶ _____ / _____ / _____

44   Of the total number of miles you drove your vehicle during 2021, enter the number of miles you used your vehicle for:

   **a** Business _____    **b** Commuting (see instructions) _____    **c** Other _____

45   Was your vehicle available for personal use during off-duty hours? . . . . . . . . ☐ **Yes**    ☐ **No**

46   Do you (or your spouse) have another vehicle available for personal use?. . . . . . . ☐ **Yes**    ☐ **No**

47a   Do you have evidence to support your deduction? . . . . . . . . . . . . ☐ **Yes**    ☐ **No**

   **b** If "Yes," is the evidence written? . . . . . . . . . . . . . . . . . ☐ **Yes**    ☐ **No**

| Part V | Other Expenses. List below business expenses not included on lines 8–26 or line 30. |
|---|---|

48   **Total other expenses.** Enter here and on line 27a . . . . . . . . . . . . | **48** |

Schedule C (Form 1040) 2021

# INCOME FOR A SCHEDULE C TRADE OR BUSINESS
## LO 6-1

Taxpayers report the gross receipts from the trade or business on line 1 of Schedule C. Gross receipts include direct sales to customers, work performed for other businesses as an independent contractor,[7] and amounts reported to the taxpayer on a Form W-2 as a "statutory employee."

---

**EXAMPLE 6-1**

Jason owns a drywall business. He contracts with various general contractors to complete drywall work during the construction of numerous personal residences. He is paid directly by the contractors but is not an employee of any one contractor. Jason would report the proceeds from his work on Schedule C (assuming his business is not incorporated). If Jason worked for only one contractor, he would likely be considered an employee and a Schedule C would not be required.

---

Amounts received by an independent contractor are usually reported to the taxpayer on Form 1099-NEC. Businesses that pay a nonemployee for services rendered are required to send a Form 1099-NEC to the independent contractor and to the IRS. A Form 1099-NEC (see Exhibit 6-2) is typically required when more than $600 is paid to an independent contractor in a given tax year.

---

**EXAMPLE 6-2**

Jake is an accounting systems professor at State University. He also has a consulting business through which he performs accounting systems analysis for local industries. Jake consulted with five different corporations and received five Forms 1099-NEC of $2,500 each (in addition to a W-2 from State University). Jake is required to report $12,500 in income on Schedule C, line 1. He reports his wages from State University on line 1 of Form 1040. He does not combine the wages with the gross receipts of his trade or business on Schedule C.

---

**TAX YOUR BRAIN**

Does the amount reported on line 1 of Schedule C always match the Forms 1099-NEC received by the taxpayer?

**ANSWER**

No; recall that a 1099-NEC is not required if the payment is below $600 or if the payments were received from individuals (businesses are required to report payments to the IRS via the 1099-NEC). Thus, if one or more of the consulting jobs in Example 6-2 were for less than $600, the company involved is not required to send a 1099-NEC to Jake. However, he must still report the income on line 1 of Schedule C. If for some reason the amount reported on line 1 is less than the total from the Forms 1099-NEC, the taxpayer is required to attach a statement explaining the difference.

---

[7] *Independent contractor* is a term that is used synonymously with self-employed. An individual is an independent contractor when he or she is not considered an employee of the person or business making the payment for a service.

**EXHIBIT 6-2**

| | | | |
|---|---|---|---|
| ☐ CORRECTED (if checked) | | | |

| PAYER'S name, street address, city or town, state or province, country, ZIP or foreign postal code, and telephone no. | | OMB No. 1545-0116 **2021** Form **1099-NEC** | **Nonemployee Compensation** |
|---|---|---|---|

| PAYER'S TIN | RECIPIENT'S TIN | **1** Nonemployee compensation $ | **Copy B** **For Recipient** |
|---|---|---|---|
| RECIPIENT'S name | | **2** Payer made direct sales totaling $5,000 or more of consumer products to recipient for resale ☐ | This is important tax information and is being furnished to the IRS. If you are required to file a return, a negligence penalty or other sanction may be imposed on you if this income is taxable and the IRS determines that it has not been reported. |
| | | **3** | |
| Street address (including apt. no.) | | **4** Federal income tax withheld $ | |
| City or town, state or province, country, and ZIP or foreign postal code | | | |
| Account number (see instructions) | | **5** State tax withheld $ $ | **6** State/Payer's state no. | **7** State income $ $ |

Form **1099-NEC**    (keep for your records)    www.irs.gov/Form1099NEC    Department of the Treasury - Internal Revenue Service

Source: U.S. Department of the Treasury, Internal Revenue Service, Form 1099-NEC. Washington, DC: 2021.

The final amount reported on line 1 of Schedule C proceeds to "statutory employees." Statutory employees receive a W-2 from their employer, but box 13 (on the W-2) is checked, indicating that the employee is to be treated as a statutory employee. Statutory employees include full-time life insurance agents, certain agents or commission drivers, traveling salespersons, and certain at-home workers. These taxpayers are employees, but their statutory status allows them to reduce their income with *for* AGI expenses.[8]

## Cost of Goods Sold

Recall that if inventory is a material income-producing factor, taxpayers must use the accrual method of accounting (at least for sales, cost of goods sold, and inventory) if gross receipts are greater than $26 million. Inventory must be accounted for at the beginning and the end of each tax year. The inventory can be valued at cost or the lower of cost or market.[9] If the taxpayer's annual gross receipts in each of the three prior tax years exceed $26 million in 2021, the taxpayer must capitalize certain indirect costs in inventory (allocate these costs between cost of goods sold and inventory) under the Uniform Capitalization Rules.[10] These indirect costs consist of costs associated with the production or resale of inventory such as equipment repairs, utilities, rent, supervisory wages, and depreciation.[11] You report cost of goods sold for a Schedule C business on page 2 (Part III). The calculation is similar to the traditional financial accounting calculation:

$$
\begin{array}{l}
\text{Beginning inventory} \\
+\ \text{Purchases} \\
+\ \text{Cost of labor} \\
-\ \text{Ending inventory} \\
=\ \text{Cost of goods sold}
\end{array}
$$

[8] Employers withhold social security and Medicare tax from the earnings of statutory employees. Thus, statutory employees do not owe self-employment tax on these earnings. We discuss the specifics of the self-employment tax later in the chapter.

[9] If the taxpayer uses LIFO valuation, lower of cost or market cannot be used [Reg. § 1.472-2(b)].

[10] IRC § 263A.

[11] See Reg. § 1.263A-1(e)(3)(ii) for a more comprehensive list of costs to be capitalized in inventory under the Uniform Capitalization Rules.

**CONCEPT CHECK 6-1—**
**LO 6-1**

1. Schedule C is used only when an individual is an employee of a company. True or false?
2. The income reported on a Schedule C will always match the amount the individual receives on one or more Forms 1099-NEC. True or false?
3. If inventory is a material income-producing factor, the accrual method of accounting must always be used to account for inventory. True or false?

# ORDINARY AND NECESSARY TRADE OR BUSINESS EXPENSES
**LO 6-2**

For an expense to be deductible, it must be "ordinary" and "necessary." For an expense to be *ordinary,* it must be customary or usual in the taxpayer's particular business. The *necessary* criterion refers to an expense that is appropriate and helpful rather than one that is essential to the taxpayer's business.[12] The courts have added a third standard: "reasonableness."[13] The courts have held that a trade or business expense must not only be ordinary and necessary but also reasonable in amount and reasonable in relation to its purpose. In most situations, making payments to related parties that are larger than normally required when the payee is an unrelated third party violates the reasonableness standard.

**EXAMPLE 6-3**

Minato owns a successful landscaping business and is in the 35% marginal tax bracket. He employs his 17-year-old son, Brian, as a laborer. To reduce his taxable income and provide money to Brian for college in the fall, Martin pays Brian $25 per hour. An unrelated laborer for the business is normally paid $10 per hour. The extra $15 per hour would be disallowed because it is unreasonable.

**TAX YOUR BRAIN**

The wages will be taxable to Brian, so why would the IRS contest Martin paying his son an unreasonable wage?

**ANSWER**
Brian would most likely pay a lower percentage of income tax on his wages than his father (probably 10%). Assuming an excess of $10,000 was paid to Brian, the tax savings for the family would be $2,500 ($10,000 × [35% − 10%]).

In addition to the three criteria of ordinary, necessary, and reasonable, certain other expenditures are expressly forbidden as deductibles. The most common forbidden expenses are

1. Illegal bribes, kickbacks, and other payments.
2. Payments for certain lobbying and political expenses.
3. Payments for fines and penalties.[14]

---

[12] *Welch v. Helvering,* 290 U.S. 111 (1933).

[13] *Comm'r v. Lincoln Elec. Co.,* 176 F.2d 815 (6th Cir. 1949), *cert. denied,* 338 U.S. 949 (1950); *Haskel Eng'g & Supply Co. v. Comm'r,* 380 F.2d 786 (9th Cir. 1967).

[14] IRC § 162(c), (e), (f).

**EXAMPLE 6-4**

Jaze owns a hazardous waste management company. To transport the waste from the refining plant to the approved disposal area, he must cross a public highway with the waste. The state permit for transporting waste on state roads is $2,500 a year. However, the fine for not having the permit is only $50 per offense. Because Jaze must cross the road only once every two weeks, he decides to forgo the permit and pay the penalty if he gets a ticket. Even though he can make an argument that the fines are ordinary, necessary, and reasonable business expenses (and make economic sense), the fine charges are not tax-deductible.

A taxpayer cannot deduct these expenses even if the preceding payments are ordinary, necessary, and reasonable in the taxpayer's trade or business.

On Schedule C, the IRS provides a sample of possible expenses. Many are self-explanatory, but the listed expenses are not exhaustive. If the criteria of ordinary, necessary, and reasonable are met, an expense is deductible. However, many expenses have additional conditions and limits to their deductibility. The remainder of this chapter focuses on these conditions and limits.

**CONCEPT CHECK 6-2— LO 6-2**

1. For an expense to be deductible on Schedule C, the expense must be _____, _____, and _____.

2. Certain types of expenditures are expressly forbidden from being deductible from income on Schedule C. What are two examples of forbidden expenses? _____ and _____.

# DEPRECIATION
## LO 6-3

The depreciation allowance (commonly called *cost recovery*) is the expense allowed for the wear or loss of usefulness of a business asset. Understanding the concept of depreciation is extremely important to comprehending the overall tax system. Why? Depreciation is a material noncash expense on the tax return that provides a large cash flow savings in terms of a tax reduction. Depreciation is allowed for every tangible asset (except land) used in a trade or business or for the production of income.[15] For each activity that uses depreciable assets, a taxpayer must complete Form 4562 to report depreciation.

### Components of Depreciation

For depreciation to be allowed, the property must be used in a business or held for the production of income (such as rental property) and not be inventory or investment property. For property placed in service on or after January 1, 1987, depreciation is calculated under the Modified Accelerated Cost Recovery System (MACRS). For tax purposes, the depreciation calculation has four principal factors:

1. Basis (usually the cost of the asset).
2. Depreciation periods (asset class lives).
3. Depreciation convention (half-year, mid-quarter, or mid-month).
4. Depreciation method (200% or 150% declining balance or straight-line).

---

[15] Thus, depreciation is calculated for Schedule C (trades or businesses—discussed in this chapter), Schedule E (rents and royalties—Chapter 8), and Form 2106 (unreimbursed employee business expenses—Chapter 5).

## Depreciable Basis

*Basis* is a concept similar to book value on a financial accounting balance sheet. Typically, the depreciable basis of property is its initial cost. Cost is equal to the cash paid for the asset plus liabilities created or assumed plus expenses associated with the purchase.

The depreciable basis can differ depending on how the property was acquired. For example, if the property is inherited, the basis is generally fair market value (FMV) at the date of death of the decedent. If the property was converted from personal use property to business use property, the depreciable cost basis is the lower of the FMV or the cost at the date of conversion. Basis can also differ from cost if the property is acquired in a nontaxable exchange (trade-in). Typically, the depreciable basis of an asset received after a trade-in is the cost of the new asset less any deferred gain on the old asset.[16] Table 6-1 summarizes how basis is determined for various acquisition methods. Often the primary tax authorities refer to "adjusted basis," which is the cost basis less any accumulated depreciation. The adjusted basis (cost basis less depreciation) is used to calculate gains and losses when the asset is sold—covered in chapter 7.

**TABLE 6-1**
**Depreciable Basis**

| How Business Asset Was Acquired | Depreciable Basis |
|---|---|
| Purchase | Cost of asset |
| Converted from personal to business use | Lower of cost or FMV at the conversion date |
| Nontaxable exchange | Typically, the asset's cost less the deferred gain on the old asset |
| Inherited | Typically, the FMV at the decedent's death |

**EXAMPLE 6-5**

Ashley purchased a computer for $2,500 to use in her sole proprietorship business. She also inherited land and a building from her father. The land had a basis of $10,000 and an FMV of $18,000 at the death of her father. The building had a $150,000 adjusted basis and a $300,000 FMV at his death. Ashley now uses both the land and building for her office. In this case, the computer has a $2,500 depreciable basis (cost). The building's depreciable basis is $300,000 because it was inherited and its basis is "stepped up" to its FMV. The land's basis would also be the FMV of $18,000 but is not depreciable.

**EXAMPLE 6-6**

Ashley also converted to business use an old van (basis $13,000; FMV $6,000 on the date of conversion) that she had held for personal use. She now plans to use the van 100% for business. The van's depreciable basis is $6,000 (the lower of the adjusted basis or the FMV at conversion). Had the van been used less than 100% for business, its $6,000 basis would be multiplied by the business use percentage to determine the depreciable basis.

**TAX YOUR BRAIN**

If a taxpayer buys an 8-year-old piece of equipment to use in a business for $4,000, can the taxpayer depreciate the $4,000 cost even though the equipment is used and was most likely fully depreciated by the prior owner?

**ANSWER**

Yes, the taxpayer depreciates the $4,000 basis as if it were new. The theory in this case is that the equipment has some useful productive life; otherwise it would not have been purchased. Depreciation is based on the taxpayer's cost; it does not matter whether the asset is new or used.

---

[16] Nontaxable exchanges are discussed in greater detail in Chapter 12. For nontaxable exchanges, the basis is determined under IRC § 1031(d).

**CONCEPT
CHECK 6-3—
LO 6-3**

1. Shelly purchased a laptop computer for her personal use last year for $2,200. This year she started her own business and transferred the computer to business use. The value of the computer at transfer was $1,300. What is Shelly's depreciable basis in her computer? _____

2. Jackson purchased a van for $22,000 and used it 100% for business. In the current year, he deducted $4,400 in depreciation related to the van. What is Jackson's adjusted basis in the van at the end of the current year? _____

## Depreciation Periods (Class Lives of Assets)

The IRS has established class lives and MACRS recovery classes for various types of assets.[17] The MACRS system makes a distinction between personal property and real property. *Personal property* includes equipment, furniture, and fixtures or anything else that is not classified as real property. *Real property* consists of land and buildings as well as any other structural components attached to land. Personal properties usually have shorter useful lives, and thus have recovery periods of three, five, and seven years. Real properties have recovery periods of 27.5 years and 39 years. The other recovery classes (10, 15, and 20 years) could apply to either real or personal property. A summary of recovery periods for various types of assets is provided in Table 6-2.

**TABLE 6-2**
**Summary of Recovery Period and Asset Types Placed in Service on or after January 1, 1987**

Source: IRS Publication 946.

| MACRS Recovery Period | Typical Assets Included in Recovery Period |
|---|---|
| 3-year | Racehorses less than two years old and certain specialized industry tools |
| 5-year | Autos and light trucks; computers and peripheral equipment |
| 7-year | Furniture, fixtures, and equipment |
| 10-year | Vessels, barges, tugs, and fruit- or nut-bearing plants |
| 15-year | Wastewater treatment plants and telephone distribution plants |
| 20-year | Farm buildings |
| 27.5-year | Residential real property (e.g., apartments) |
| 31.5-year | Nonresidential property acquired between January 1, 1987 and May 13, 1993 |
| 39-year | Nonresidential property acquired after May 13, 1993 |

## Depreciation Conventions

Depreciation expense for tax purposes differs from depreciation for financial accounting calculations. With financial accounting, the depreciation calculation depends on the number of months the property was used in a given year. For the tax calculation, certain conventions (assumptions) are established:[18]

1. **Half-year convention:** The half-year convention treats all property placed in service during any taxable year as being placed in service at the midpoint of that taxable year.[19]

---

[17] See IRS Publication 946, *How to Depreciate Property.* Also, Rev. Proc. 87-56, 1987-2 CB 674, contains the class lives for most assets. This Rev. Proc. is essential for tax preparers to have on hand as a quick depreciation reference source.

[18] IRC § 168(d)(4).

[19] IRC § 168(d)(4)(A).

2. **Mid-quarter convention:** The mid-quarter convention treats all property placed in service during any quarter of a taxable year as being placed in service at the midpoint of that quarter.[20]

3. **Mid-month convention:** The mid-month convention treats all property placed in service during any month as being placed in service at the midpoint of that month.[21]

These conventions are built into the depreciation tables issued by the IRS and are shown in the Appendix of this chapter. It is important to determine the convention to use when calculating depreciation expense.

---

**CONCEPT CHECK 6-4— LO 6-3**

1. An auto used in a trade or business would be depreciated over what period of time for MACRS tax purposes?
   a. 3 years.
   b. 5 years.
   c. 7 years.
   d. 10 years.

2. An apartment complex would be depreciated over what period of time for MACRS tax purposes?
   a. 10 years.
   b. 20 years.
   c. 27.5 years.
   d. 39 years.

3. A warehouse would be depreciated over what period of time for MACRS tax purposes?
   a. 10 years.
   b. 20 years.
   c. 27.5 years.
   d. 39 years.

### Half-Year Convention

The convention used most often is the half-year convention. With it, one-half year of depreciation is taken no matter when the asset is purchased during the year. A taxpayer uses the half-year convention for all personal property unless required to use the mid-quarter convention (discussed next).[22]

---

**EXAMPLE 6-7**

Cal purchased the following assets during the tax year for his sole proprietorship:

| January 6 | Equipment | $ 7,400 |
| May 4 | Truck | 20,000 |
| December 1 | Equipment | 2,000 |

Even though he purchased the assets at different times, he takes one-half year of depreciation on each asset. The equipment (both the January and the December purchases) would be 7-year MACRS property; the truck would be 5-year MACRS property.

---

### Mid-Quarter Convention

Taxpayers must use the mid-quarter convention when they place more than 40% of their personal property (not real property) in service during the last three months of the tax year or if the

[20] IRC § 168(d)(4)(C).
[21] IRC § 168(d)(4)(B).
[22] IRC § 168(d)(1).

**TAX YOUR BRAIN**

Mid-quarter convention is mandated when more than 40% of the asset purchases are made in the fourth quarter. How are assets purchased in the first quarter treated when the mid-quarter convention is required?

**ANSWER**

The first-quarter property is treated as being placed in service at the midpoint of the first quarter. The IRS depreciation tables published in Rev. Proc. 87-57 (and reproduced in the chapter Appendix) account for the different quarters by having separate tables for assets placed in service in the first, second, third, and fourth quarters.

**EXAMPLE 6-8**

Assume the same facts as in Example 6-7, but Cal purchased the truck on November 5 instead of May 4. Because he purchased 75% of the assets ($22,000/$29,400) in the fourth quarter, he must use the mid-quarter convention. The January equipment is treated as being placed in service at the midpoint of the first quarter, and the other two assets are treated as being placed in service at the midpoint of the fourth quarter. The taxpayer would use the table used in the first year for each year of the life.

tax year consists of three months or less.[23] The 40% threshold is measured in terms of aggregate bases of the property placed in service and does not include the basis of real property acquired.[24]

### Mid-Month Convention

The final convention is mid-month, which applies only to real property (27.5-year, 31.5-year, and 39-year property). Under the mid-month convention, the property is treated as being placed in service at the midpoint of the month acquired. Thus, real property acquired on March 3 is treated as acquired halfway through the month (9.5 months of depreciation would be taken in the first year).

### Convention for Year of Disposal

Regardless of the convention required for a given asset (half-year, mid-quarter, or mid-month), the property is subject to the same convention in the year of disposal. For example, if a 7-year MACRS asset is disposed of in year 3, a half year of depreciation is taken on the asset regardless of whether the date of disposal was in January or December. Likewise, mid-quarter assets receive half a quarter of depreciation, and mid-month assets receive half a month of depreciation in the month of disposition.

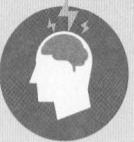

**TAX YOUR BRAIN**

Can the IRS build the percentages for the year of disposal into the depreciation tables?

**ANSWER**

No, the IRS can build the first-year depreciation percentages into the tables because they are known (for example, half a year of depreciation is taken in the first year). However, the IRS does not know in which year every taxpayer will dispose of the property. Thus, in the year of disposal, taxpayers must divide the table percentage by two for the half-year convention and by the appropriate number of months for the mid-quarter and mid-month conventions.

**EXAMPLE 6-9**

Emine purchased a business computer system on November 3, 2019, for $3,000. The computer was subject to the mid-quarter convention because more than 40% of Emine total asset purchases occurred in the fourth quarter. Emine sold the computer on March 5, 2021. Thus, in the 2021 tax year, Emine would take 1.5 months of depreciation on the computer (one-half of the first quarter, or 1.5/12). If she sold the computer in December 2021, Emine would depreciate the computer for 10.5 months (one-half of the final quarter plus the first three quarters, or 10.5/12).

[23] IRC § 168(d)(3).
[24] IRC § 168(d)(3).

**CONCEPT CHECK 6-5—**

**LO 6-3**

1. A taxpayer can choose any depreciation convention as long as she or he is consistent in doing so. True or false?
2. A taxpayer must use the mid-quarter convention for personal property if more than 40% of the property is purchased in the fourth quarter. True or false?
3. The half-year convention is the most-often-used convention for personal property. True or false?
4. To depreciate an apartment complex, a taxpayer should use the half-year convention. True or false?
5. The taxpayer must use the same depreciation convention in the year of disposal as the convention used in the year of acquisition. True or false?

## DEPRECIATION METHODS

Only three depreciation methods are allowed for MACRS property purchased on or after January 1, 1987:

1. 200% declining balance switching to straight-line.
2. 150% declining balance switching to straight-line.
3. Straight-line.[25]

The 200% declining balance method is required for all 3-, 5-, 7-, or 10-year MACRS property (personal property). For 15-year and 20-year property, 150% declining balance is used. In both cases, the depreciation switches to straight-line in the tax year in which straight-line yields a higher depreciation allowance. Straight-line is required for all depreciable real property. In all cases, salvage value is ignored for tax purposes. The taxpayer can make an irrevocable election to use straight-line for any of the classes.[26]

### *Showing the Calculation*

To correctly calculate depreciation, the taxpayer or tax preparer must know only the type of property, the recovery period, and the depreciable basis.

**EXAMPLE 6-10**

In May 2021, Samantha purchased equipment for $8,000, a work truck for $19,000, and an office building for $120,000. The depreciation calculation for each asset follows (numbers may be rounded in the final year):

| Property Type | Recovery Period | Conventions | Depreciation Expense |
|---|---|---|---|
| Equipment | 7-year property | Half-year | $   8,000 basis |
| 2021 | Table 6A-1* | ($8,000 × 14.29%) | 1,143 |
| 2022 | | ($8,000 × 24.49%) | 1,959 |
| 2023 | | ($8,000 × 17.49%) | 1,399 |
| 2024 | | ($8,000 × 12.49%) | 999 |
| 2025 | | ($8,000 × 8.93%) | 714 |
| 2026 | | ($8,000 × 8.92%) | 714 |
| 2027 | | ($8,000 × 8.93%) | 714 |
| 2028 | | ($8,000 × 4.46%) | 358 |
| Truck | 5-year property | Half-year | $ 19,000 basis |
| 2021 | Table 6A-1* | ($19,000 × 20.00%) | 3,800 |
| 2022 | | ($19,000 × 32.00%) | 6,080 |
| 2023 | | ($19,000 × 19.20%) | 3,648 |
| 2024 | | ($19,000 × 11.52%) | 2,189 |

*(continued)*

[25] Depreciation for alternative minimum tax (AMT) purposes is calculated separately for each asset using either 150% declining balance or straight-line. We provide a detailed presentation of AMT depreciation calculations in Chapter 13.

[26] IRC § 168(b)(5).

**EXAMPLE 6-10**

*(concluded)*

| Property Type | Recovery Period | Conventions | Depreciation Expense |
|---|---|---|---|
| 2024 | | ($19,000 × 11.52%) | 2,189 |
| 2025 | | ($19,000 × 5.76%) | 1,094 |
| Building | 39-year property | Mid-month | $120,000 basis |
| 2021 | Table 6A-8* | ($120,000 × 1.605%) | 1,926 |
| 2022–2059 | | ($120,000 × 2.564%) | 3,077 |
| 2060 | | ($120,000 × 0.963%) | 1,148 |

\* In the Appendix to this chapter.

In Example 6-10, if both the equipment and the truck had been purchased in the fourth quarter and exceeded 40% of the aggregate basis of acquired personal property, the mid-quarter convention would be required. In this case, the appropriate table for the two personal property assets would be Table 6A-5 in the Appendix to this chapter. The first-year percentage would be 3.57% for the equipment and 5.00% for the truck.

Table 6-3 summarizes depreciation conventions and methods for various asset types. Table 6-3 also indicates the appropriate depreciation table (located in the Appendix to this chapter) to use for calculations.

**TABLE 6-3**
**Summary of MACRS**
**Depreciation**

Source: IRS Publication 946.

| Asset Type | Convention | Method | Depr. Table† |
|---|---|---|---|
| **Personal property** | | | |
| 3 yr.—racehorses | Half-year/mid-quarter* | 200% double declining balance to straight-line | 6A-1† |
| 5 yr.—cars, trucks, computers | Half-year/mid-quarter* | 200% double declining balance to straight-line | 6A-1 |
| 7 yr.—furniture and equipment | Half-year/mid-quarter* | 200% double declining balance to straight-line | 6A-1 |
| **Real property** | | | |
| 27.5-yr. residential | Mid-month | Straight-line | 6A-6 |
| 31.5-yr. nonresidential: 12/31/86–5/13/93 | Mid-month | Straight-line | 6A-7 |
| 39-yr. nonresidential: 5/14/93 to present | Mid-month | Straight-line | 6A-8 |

\* For mid-quarter conventions, use Tables 6A-2, 6A-3, 6A-4, or 6A-5 (in the Appendix to this chapter), depending on the quarter in which the asset was placed in service.
† Refers to the tables in the Appendix to this chapter.

**CONCEPT CHECK 6-6—**

**LO 6-3**

1. Shu purchased a piece of business equipment for $12,000 on May 3, 2021. This equipment is the only business asset Shu purchased during the year. What is Shu's depreciation expense related to the equipment? _____

2. If Shu sold the equipment on January 5, 2023, what would the depreciation expense be for 2023? _____

3. Davis purchased an apartment complex on March 5, 2021, for $330,000. What is Davis's depreciation expense related to the complex? _____

## IRC § 179 Expense Election

Instead of MACRS depreciation, the taxpayer can elect to expense a certain portion of personal property purchased during the year (real property is excluded). See Table 6-4 for the maximum IRC § 179 amounts. The Tax Cuts and Jobs Act of 2017 increased the maximum Section 179 for 2018 to $1,000,000. The maximum increases to $1,050,000 in 2021.

The § 179 deduction is designed to benefit small businesses by permitting them to expense the cost of the assets in the year of purchase rather than over time. The expense is allowed in

| | | |
|---|---|---|
| **TABLE 6-4** | 2018 | $1,000,000 |
| **Applicable Maximum** | 2019 | 1,020,000 |
| **§ 179 Expense** | 2020 | 1,040,000 |
| | 2021 | 1,050,000 |

full only if the total of personal property purchases is less than $2,620,000 in 2021 in aggregate cost. The expense election is phased out dollar-for-dollar for purchases in excess of $2,620,000. Thus the expense election is completely eliminated when asset purchases reach $3,670,000 ($2,620,000 + $1,050,000). Several other limitations apply to the § 179 expense election:

1. The property must be used in an active trade or business. Purchased property associated with investment or rental property is not eligible for the expense election.

2. The § 179 expense cannot create a net operating loss. However, the total amount of wages, salaries, tips, or other pay earned as an employee is included as income derived from a trade or business. Thus, a taxpayer who is an employee and has an active business on the side can have a loss in the side business caused by the § 179 expense as long as the taxpayer's salary exceeds the loss. Any § 179 expense disallowed by the lack of business income can be carried over indefinitely.

3. The property cannot be acquired from a related party or by gift or inheritance.

4. If the property is acquired with a trade-in, the § 179 expense is limited to the cash paid for the property.

---

**EXAMPLE 6-11**   ABC Co. purchased $1,151,000 of personal property in 2020. The company can elect to expense $1,040,000 under § 179. The remaining $111,000 is depreciated using regular MACRS rates.

---

Taxpayers who purchase several assets during the year can pick the asset(s) they wish to expense under § 179 (up to the yearly limit).

---

**CONCEPT CHECK 6-7— LO 6-3**

1. Assume the same asset purchase as in Concept Check 6-6. Shu purchased a piece of business equipment for $12,000 on May 3, 2021. This equipment was the only business asset purchased during the year, and the business has substantial income. What is Shu's deduction for the equipment, assuming § 179 expense is elected? Would there be any additional MACRS regular depreciation? § 179 expense $_____ additional MACRS _____

2. What if the equipment Shu purchased had cost $1,055,000? What would the total expense deduction be if § 179 were elected? § 179 expense $_____ additional MACRS _____

The Tax Cuts and Jobs Act of 2017 allowed taxpayers to treat qualified real property as Section 179 property. This qualified real property includes improvements to nonresidential real property (buildings) such as roofs, HVAC, fire/alarm systems. These properties are subject to the same Section 179 limits of $1,050,000 and are subject to the same phase-out limitations.

## 100% Bonus Depreciation

In 2021, an accelerated depreciation deduction equal to 100% of the basis of certain property is allowed. Eligible property includes:

1. New or used property with a MACRS recovery period of less than 20 years.

2. Property acquired and placed in service prior to December 31, 2023.

After 2023, the 100% bonus is phased down to 0% over five years from 2024 through 2027.

---

**EXAMPLE 6-12**   Jack purchased a piece of new equipment (7-year MACRS) for $570,000 for his business on March 1, 2021. Jack is allowed to deduct the entire $570,000 by using the 100% bonus depreciation. The taxpayer could use either Section 179 or the bonus.

The increase to the 100% bonus through 2023 limits the importance of the Section 179 deduction and regular depreciation for most non–real property business assets.

## Listed Property

Because of the fear of loss of revenue from the use of accelerated depreciation methods on assets that have both business and personal use components to them, Congress established limitations and restrictions on "listed property." Listed property consists of the following:

- Any passenger automobile.
- Any other property used as a means of transportation (not included are vehicles that constitute a trade or business, such as taxis).
- Any property of a type generally used for entertainment, recreation, or amusement (such as a boat). This includes photographic, phonographic, communication, and video recording equipment.[27]

Computers and peripheral equipment have traditionally been listed property. The 2017 Tax Act removed these items from the listed property classification. Listed property does not include the above items that are used exclusively for business at a regular business establishment.

For the normal MACRS rules discussed earlier to apply, listed property must be used predominantly for business, which means that it is used more than 50% for business. If a taxpayer is an employee (not self-employed), the use of the asset is not business use unless it is both used for the employer's convenience and required as a condition of employment.

---

**EXAMPLE 6-13**

Linda is a public relations officer for her local city government. She purchased a separate cell phone to complete work while she was traveling and working from home. Her phone use is 70% business related, but her employer does not require the phone as a condition of employment, nor is its use for the employer's convenience. Because Linda is an employee and the cell phone does not meet the business use test, no depreciation is allowed.

---

If the listed property does not meet the predominantly business use test, the taxpayer cannot claim an IRC § 179 expense deduction for the property and must use straight-line depreciation (usually over a five-year recovery period).[28]

---

**EXAMPLE 6-14**

Jack purchased a large screen for video conferences for $2,500 for use in his home office (he is self-employed). The screen is used 70% for business and 30% by his children to play computer games. Because the screen is predominantly used for business and is five-year property, the MACRS depreciation for the first year would be $350 ($2,500 × 70% business use × 20% [Table 6A-1]). If the business use were only 30%, straight-line depreciation would be required and the depreciation deduction in the first year would be $75 ($2,500 × 30% × 10%).[29]

---

If in the first year of the asset's life, the 50% test is met, but in subsequent years, the business use falls below the 50% threshold, the depreciation must be calculated using the straight-line method. Additionally, depreciation must be recalculated for all years for which MACRS depreciation was used, and the excess MACRS depreciation (or IRC § 179 expense) must be included in the taxpayer's gross income (recaptured) in the year the business use test is *not* met.[30]

---

[27] IRC § 280F(d)(4).

[28] Chapter 5 of IRS Publication 946 discusses the treatment of listed property.

[29] The 10% is calculated by taking the straight-line rate of 20% (1/5) and applying the half-year convention (1/2).

[30] IRC § 280F(b)(2).

**EXAMPLE 6-15**

Assume the same facts as in Example 6-14, but the business use was 70% in year 1 and 30% in year 2. The depreciation and recapture amounts would be calculated as follows:

|        | MACRS | Straight-Line | Difference |
|--------|-------|---------------|------------|
| Year 1 | $350  | $175          | $175       |
| Year 2 | —     | 150           |            |

The depreciation deduction would be $150 (full-year at 1/5 straight-line) in year 2, and the excess depreciation taken in year 1 ($175) would be included (recaptured) in gross income. The straight-line method would be required for future years even if the business use percentage subsequently increased above 50%.

## Luxury Automobile Limitations

In addition to the business use limitation, the amount of depreciation allowed for luxury automobiles is limited. Passenger autos are defined as four-wheeled vehicles made primarily for use on public streets, roads, and highways with a gross vehicle weight of less than 6,000 pounds.[31] Light trucks do not have a separate limit as they have had in the past.[32] The depreciation expense limits for luxury autos and light trucks placed in service in tax year 2021 follow:

|        |      | Auto Limit |
|--------|------|------------|
| Year 1 | 2021 | $18,200    |
| Year 2 | 2022 | 16,200     |
| Year 3 | 2023 | 9,800      |
| Year 4 | 2024 | 5,860      |

These limits apply to § 179, the 100% bonus, and regular MACRS depreciation. They are reduced further if the business use of the auto is less than 100%. If for some reason the 100% bonus was not taken, the limit for regular depreciation would revert to $10,200.

**EXAMPLE 6-16**

In 2021, Allison purchased a Toyota Camry for $25,000 to be used exclusively for business. The 100% bonus expense deduction would produce a deduction equal to $25,000. Because the maximum depreciation for 2021 is $18,200, the depreciation allowance is limited to $18,200.

**EXAMPLE 6-17**

Jackson purchased a new car for $19,000 on July 7, 2021, and used it 75% for business. The maximum amount of expense for the car in the first year is $13,650 ($18,200 × 75%).

Prior to 2005, many taxpayers circumvented the luxury auto rules by purchasing vehicles with a gross weight of more than 6,000 lb. Thus, if a taxpayer purchased a large SUV, the taxpayer could use § 179 or bonus depreciation to expense the entire purchase amount up to the § 179 limit. For purchases after October 22, 2004, the § 179 deduction is limited to $26,200 in 2021 with inflation adjustments on these large SUVs. However, the regular MACRS depreciation is still unaffected by the luxury ceiling amounts, thus keeping the purchase of these vehicles attractive in terms of depreciation. However, the current bonus depreciation is not limited to $26,200 and with the 100% bonus there will be no limitation in 2018–2023.

**EXAMPLE 6-18**

Javier purchased a new GMC Yukon for $46,000 on May 3, 2021, to be used 100% for business. During 2021, he could deduct a maximum of $26,200 in § 179 expense and $4,020 in MACRS depreciation ([$46,000 − $25,900] × 20% − 5-year/half-year convention). However, with the new 100% bonus Javier could deduct the entire $46,000, which, of course, is the better option.

---

[31] IRC § 280F(d)(5).

[32] Other information concerning the auto limitation can be found in Rev. Proc. 2021–31, 2021–34 IRB.

**CONCEPT CHECK 6-8—**
**LO 6-3**

1. Zachary purchased a Ford Expedition (more than 6,000 lb) for $39,000 in March 2021. What is the maximum depreciation expense allowed, assuming that Zachary is eligible for the IRC § 179 expense election and no bonus is elected?
   a. $7,800.
   b. $26,200.
   c. $28,760.
   d. $39,000.

2. Assume the same facts as in Question 1. However, the Expedition was used only 80% for business. What is the maximum depreciation expense allowed, assuming that Zachary is eligible for the IRC § 179 expense election and no bonus is elected?
   a. $6,240.
   b. $20,960.
   c. $23,008.
   d. $31,200.

### Leased Vehicles

To circumvent the luxury auto depreciation limitations, leasing business vehicles became popular. However, the IRS limited the lease deduction for vehicles by requiring taxpayers to include a certain amount in income to offset the lease deduction. The "lease inclusion amount" is based on the vehicle's FMV and the tax year in which the lease began. The full lease payment is deducted (unless the business use is less than 100%), and the income inclusion reduces the net deduction. The IRS annually provides current lease inclusion amounts in a Revenue Procedure.[33]

### Adequate Records

Taxpayers must have adequate records to document the business use and the time or mileage accumulated. IRS Publication 946 (see Chapter 5) notes that "an account book, diary, log, statement of expense, trip sheet, or similar record" is sufficient to establish an expenditure or use. Adequate records for a portion of the year (which is then annualized) are acceptable if the taxpayer can show that the records represent the use throughout the year.

# TRANSPORTATION AND TRAVEL
## LO 6-4

Ordinary and necessary travel expenses are deductible by a trade or business.[34] A distinction is made between transportation and travel. *Transportation,* in a tax sense, traditionally means the expense of getting from one workplace to another workplace within the taxpayer's home area. *Travel,* on the other hand, generally refers to business travel away from the home area that requires an overnight stay.

### Local Transportation Expenses

Taxpayers may take a deduction for business transportation expenses from one place of work to another as long as the expense is not for commuting (from home to workplace). These costs could include travel by air, rail, bus, taxi, or car. To differentiate between commuting costs and business transportation expenses, taxpayers must first determine their *tax home,* which is the taxpayer's regular place of business, regardless of where the taxpayer actually lives.

---

[33] The 2021 inclusion amounts are published in Rev. Proc. 2021–31.
[34] IRC § 162(a)(2).

# From Shoebox to Software

After completing several tax returns, depreciation calculations become routine. However, for new tax preparers, depreciation calculations and proper placement on the tax return can cause a great deal of stress. In practice, tax software performs most of the calculations. However, the old computer adage "garbage in, garbage out" also holds true for tax software. All current-year software calculations should be checked because the type of property, recovery class, and § 179 expense election must be input into the software. In this section, we calculate the depreciation for a new client in the insurance business. We also show the correct presentation of the depreciation information on Form 4562.

**EXAMPLE 6-19**

Alan Masters, a taxpayer from Chapter 5, started his own insurance agency on July 1, 2021. Later in the chapter, we incorporate business income and other nondepreciation expenses, but now we focus on depreciation. For the tax year 2021, Alan's business acquired the following assets (assume no 100% bonus is elected):

| Asset | Date Purchased | Percentage of Business Use | Cost | Class and Depreciation Method |
|---|---|---|---|---|
| Computer | 07/12/2021 | 100% | $ 2,500 | 5-yr DDB* |
| Phone system | 07/12/2021 | 100 | 2,300 | 5-yr DDB |
| Auto | 07/15/2021 | 90 | 22,000 | 5-yr DDB |
| Furniture | 07/12/2021 | 100 | 23,000 | 7-yr DDB |
| Office building | 07/01/2021 | 100 | 120,000 | 39-yr S/L† |

\* DDB = double declining balance method.
† S/L = straight-line method.

Assume that Alan took no IRC § 179 or bonus depreciation deduction. Because less than 40% of the aggregate basis of the personal property was purchased in the fourth quarter, the mid-quarter convention is not required. The half-year convention is used for these assets.

| Current Year Depreciation | |
|---|---|
| Computer ($2,500 × 20%) | $ 500 |
| Phone system ($2,300 × 20%) | 460 |
| Auto ($22,000 × 90% × 20%) | 3,960* |
| Furniture ($23,000 × 14.29%) | 3,288 |
| Office building ($120,000 × 1.177%) | 1,412 |
| Total depreciation expense | $9,620 |

\* Because the 100% bonus was not taken, the luxury limit would decrease to $9,090 (90% of $10,100 in this case). The depreciation is not limited in this situation.

Open the tax return file of Alan and Cherie Masters and then open Schedule C. Answer the questions at the top of Schedule C. Alan uses the cash method of accounting and does "materially participate" in the business. Most tax software programs have a Form 4562 Asset Depreciation and Vehicle Expenses worksheet. Enter the information for each asset on a separate worksheet. You need to enter the business and personal mileage for the auto to determine the business percentage. In this case, use 9,000 business miles and 1,000 personal miles.

Exhibit 6-3 shows the presentation on Form 4562. Note that the listed property is individually entered on page 2 of Form 4562. The total depreciation deduction is $9,620 under the assumption that no IRC § 179 expense election was made.

If the IRC § 179 election were made, the entire amount of personal property (everything but the building) purchased could be expensed. Because the § 179 expense limit is now $1,050,000, most small businesses will be able to expense all of their non–real property purchases. If § 179 expense or the 100% bonus were taken, which in all likelihood it would be, all of the assets would be listed in Part I of Form 4562 and the total expense shown.

**EXHIBIT 6-3**

| Form **4562** | **Depreciation and Amortization** | OMB No. 1545-0172 |
|---|---|---|
| Department of the Treasury Internal Revenue Service  (99) | **(Including Information on Listed Property)** ▶ **Attach to your tax return.** ▶ Go to *www.irs.gov/Form4562* for instructions and the latest information. | **2021** Attachment Sequence No. **179** |

| Name(s) shown on return | Business or activity to which this form relates | Identifying number |
|---|---|---|
| **Alan Masters** | Insurance | 412-34-5670 |

### Part I    Election To Expense Certain Property Under Section 179
**Note:** If you have any listed property, complete Part V before you complete Part I.

| | | |
|---|---|---|
| 1 | Maximum amount (see instructions) . . . . . . . . . . | **1** |
| 2 | Total cost of section 179 property placed in service (see instructions) . . . | **2** |
| 3 | Threshold cost of section 179 property before reduction in limitation (see instructions) . . . | **3** |
| 4 | Reduction in limitation. Subtract line 3 from line 2. If zero or less, enter -0- . . . . . . . | **4** |
| 5 | Dollar limitation for tax year. Subtract line 4 from line 1. If zero or less, enter -0-. If married filing separately, see instructions | **5** |

| 6 | (a) Description of property | (b) Cost (business use only) | (c) Elected cost |
|---|---|---|---|
| | | | |
| | | | |

| | | |
|---|---|---|
| 7 | Listed property. Enter the amount from line 29 . . . . . . . . . | **7** |
| 8 | Total elected cost of section 179 property. Add amounts in column (c), lines 6 and 7 . . | **8** |
| 9 | Tentative deduction. Enter the **smaller** of line 5 or line 8 . . . . . . . . | **9** |
| 10 | Carryover of disallowed deduction from line 13 of your 2020 Form 4562 . . . . | **10** |
| 11 | Business income limitation. Enter the smaller of business income (not less than zero) or line 5. See instructions | **11** |
| 12 | Section 179 expense deduction. Add lines 9 and 10, but don't enter more than line 11 . . . . . . | **12** |
| 13 | Carryover of disallowed deduction to 2022. Add lines 9 and 10, less line 12 ▶ | **13** | |

**Note:** Don't use Part II or Part III below for listed property. Instead, use Part V.

### Part II    Special Depreciation Allowance and Other Depreciation (Don't include listed property. See instructions.)

| | | |
|---|---|---|
| 14 | Special depreciation allowance for qualified property (other than listed property) placed in service during the tax year. See instructions . . . . . . . . . . . . . . . | **14** |
| 15 | Property subject to section 168(f)(1) election . . . . . . . . . . . . | **15** |
| 16 | Other depreciation (including ACRS) . . . . . . . . . . . . . | **16** |

### Part III    MACRS Depreciation (Don't include listed property. See instructions.)

**Section A**

| | | |
|---|---|---|
| 17 | MACRS deductions for assets placed in service in tax years beginning before 2021 . . . . . . . | **17** |
| 18 | If you are electing to group any assets placed in service during the tax year into one or more general asset accounts, check here . . . . . . . . . . . . . . . ▶ ☐ | |

**Section B—Assets Placed in Service During 2021 Tax Year Using the General Depreciation System**

| (a) Classification of property | (b) Month and year placed in service | (c) Basis for depreciation (business/investment use only—see instructions) | (d) Recovery period | (e) Convention | (f) Method | (g) Depreciation deduction |
|---|---|---|---|---|---|---|
| 19a    3-year property | | | | | | |
| b    5-year property | | 4,800 | 5 yr | HY | DDB | 960 |
| c    7-year property | | 23,000 | 7 yr | HY | DDB | 3,288 |
| d    10-year property | | | | | | |
| e    15-year property | | | | | | |
| f    20-year property | | | | | | |
| g    25-year property | | | 25 yrs. | | S/L | |
| h    Residential rental property | | | 27.5 yrs. | MM | S/L | |
| | | | 27.5 yrs. | MM | S/L | |
| i    Nonresidential real property | 7/21 | 120,000 | 39 yrs. | MM | S/L | 1,412 |
| | | | | MM | S/L | |

**Section C—Assets Placed in Service During 2021 Tax Year Using the Alternative Depreciation System**

| | | | | | | |
|---|---|---|---|---|---|---|
| 20a    Class life | | | | | S/L | |
| b    12-year | | | 12 yrs. | | S/L | |
| c    30-year | | | 30 yrs. | MM | S/L | |
| d    40-year | | | 40 yrs. | MM | S/L | |

### Part IV    Summary (See instructions.)

| | | |
|---|---|---|
| 21 | Listed property. Enter amount from line 28 . . . . . . . . . . . . . | **21** | 3,960 |
| 22 | **Total.** Add amounts from line 12, lines 14 through 17, lines 19 and 20 in column (g), and line 21. Enter here and on the appropriate lines of your return. Partnerships and S corporations—see instructions . | **22** | 9,620 |
| 23 | For assets shown above and placed in service during the current year, enter the portion of the basis attributable to section 263A costs . . . . . . . . .    **23** | | |

**For Paperwork Reduction Act Notice, see separate instructions.**    Cat. No. 12906N    Form **4562** (2021)

Source: U.S. Department of the Treasury, Internal Revenue Service, Form 4562. Washington, DC: 2021.

**EXHIBIT 6-3**   *(concluded)*

Form 4562 (2021)                                                                                                          Page **2**

**Part V**   **Listed Property**   (Include automobiles, certain other vehicles, certain aircraft, and property used for entertainment, recreation, or amusement.)

**Note:** For any vehicle for which you are using the standard mileage rate or deducting lease expense, complete **only** 24a, 24b, columns (a) through (c) of Section A, all of Section B, and Section C if applicable.

**Section A—Depreciation and Other Information (Caution:** See the instructions for limits for passenger automobiles.**)**

**24a** Do you have evidence to support the business/investment use claimed? ☑ **Yes** ☐ **No**   **24b** If "Yes," is the evidence written? ☑ **Yes** ☐ **No**

| (a) Type of property (list vehicles first) | (b) Date placed in service | (c) Business/ investment use percentage | (d) Cost or other basis | (e) Basis for depreciation (business/investment use only) | (f) Recovery period | (g) Method/ Convention | (h) Depreciation deduction | (i) Elected section 179 cost |
|---|---|---|---|---|---|---|---|---|
| **25** Special depreciation allowance for qualified listed property placed in service during the tax year and used more than 50% in a qualified business use. See instructions . **25** | | | | | | | | |
| **26** Property used more than 50% in a qualified business use: | | | | | | | | |
| Auto | 7/15/21 | 90 % | 22,000 | 19,800 | 5 yr | DDB | 3,960 | |
| | | % | | | | | | |
| | | % | | | | | | |
| **27** Property used 50% or less in a qualified business use: | | | | | | | | |
| | | % | | | | S/L – | | |
| | | % | | | | S/L – | | |
| | | % | | | | S/L – | | |
| **28** Add amounts in column (h), lines 25 through 27. Enter here and on line 21, page 1 . **28** | | | | | | | 3,960 | |
| **29** Add amounts in column (i), line 26. Enter here and on line 7, page 1 . **29** | | | | | | | | |

**Section B—Information on Use of Vehicles**

Complete this section for vehicles used by a sole proprietor, partner, or other "more than 5% owner," or related person. If you provided vehicles to your employees, first answer the questions in Section C to see if you meet an exception to completing this section for those vehicles.

| | (a) Vehicle 1 | (b) Vehicle 2 | (c) Vehicle 3 | (d) Vehicle 4 | (e) Vehicle 5 | (f) Vehicle 6 |
|---|---|---|---|---|---|---|
| **30** Total business/investment miles driven during the year (**don't** include commuting miles) . | | | | | | |
| **31** Total commuting miles driven during the year | | | | | | |
| **32** Total other personal (noncommuting) miles driven . . . . . | | | | | | |
| **33** Total miles driven during the year. Add lines 30 through 32 . . . . . . . | | | | | | |
| **34** Was the vehicle available for personal use during off-duty hours? . . . . . | Yes / No | Yes / No | Yes / No | Yes / No | Yes / No | Yes / No |
| **35** Was the vehicle used primarily by a more than 5% owner or related person? . . | | | | | | |
| **36** Is another vehicle available for personal use? | | | | | | |

**Section C—Questions for Employers Who Provide Vehicles for Use by Their Employees**

Answer these questions to determine if you meet an exception to completing Section B for vehicles used by employees who **aren't** more than 5% owners or related persons. See instructions.

| | Yes | No |
|---|---|---|
| **37** Do you maintain a written policy statement that prohibits all personal use of vehicles, including commuting, by your employees? . . . . . . . . . . . . . . . . . . . . . . . | | |
| **38** Do you maintain a written policy statement that prohibits personal use of vehicles, except commuting, by your employees? See the instructions for vehicles used by corporate officers, directors, or 1% or more owners . . | | |
| **39** Do you treat all use of vehicles by employees as personal use? . . . . . . . . . . . | | |
| **40** Do you provide more than five vehicles to your employees, obtain information from your employees about the use of the vehicles, and retain the information received? . . . . . . . . . . . . . . | | |
| **41** Do you meet the requirements concerning qualified automobile demonstration use? See instructions. . . . . | | |

**Note:** If your answer to 37, 38, 39, 40, or 41 is "Yes," don't complete Section B for the covered vehicles.

**Part VI**   **Amortization**

| (a) Description of costs | (b) Date amortization begins | (c) Amortizable amount | (d) Code section | (e) Amortization period or percentage | (f) Amortization for this year |
|---|---|---|---|---|---|
| **42** Amortization of costs that begins during your 2021 tax year (see instructions): | | | | | |
| | | | | | |
| | | | | | |
| **43** Amortization of costs that began before your 2021 tax year . . . . . . . . . . . **43** | | | | | |
| **44** **Total.** Add amounts in column (f). See the instructions for where to report . . . . . . . . **44** | | | | | |

Form **4562** (2021)

**EXHIBIT 6-4**

Source: IRS Publication 463, p. 12.

Figure B. **When Are Transportation Expenses Deductible?**
Most employees and self-employed persons can use this chart.
(Do not use this chart if your home is your principal place of business.
See *Office in the home.*)

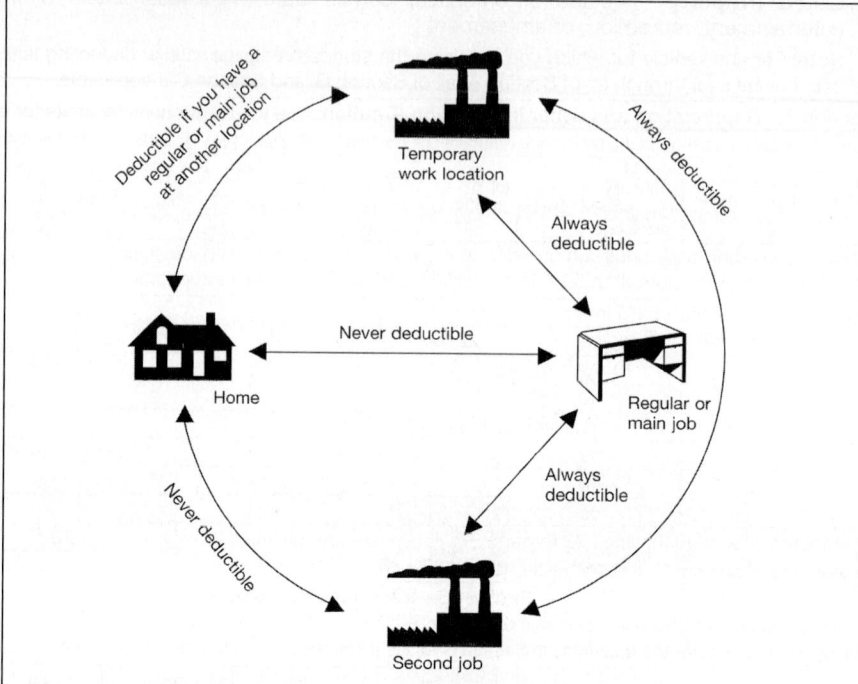

**Home:** The place where you reside. Transportation expenses between your home and your main or regular place of work are personal commuting expenses.

**Regular or main job:** Your principal place of business. If you have more than one job, you must determine which one is your regular or main job. Consider the time you spend at each, the activity you have at each, and the income you earn at each.

**Temporary work location:** A place where your work assignment is realistically expected to last (and does in fact last) one year or less. Unless you have a regular place of business, you can only deduct your transportation expenses to a temporary work location <u>outside</u> your metropolitan area.

**Second job:** If you regularly work at two or more places in one day, whether or not for the same employer, you can deduct your transportation expenses of getting from one workplace to another. If you do not go directly from your first job to your second job, you can only deduct the transportation expenses of going directly from your first job to your second job. You cannot deduct your transportation expenses between your home and a second job on a day off from your main job.

Exhibit 6-4 is an excerpt from IRS Publication 463 that summarizes when transportation costs can be deducted.

Local transportation costs are deductible in the following situations:

- Getting from one workplace to another in the course of conducting a business or profession when traveling within the city or general area of the taxpayer's tax home.
- Visiting clients or customers.
- Going to a business meeting away from the taxpayer's regular workplace.
- Getting from home to a temporary workplace when the taxpayer has one or more regular places of work. These temporary workplaces can be either inside or outside the taxpayer's tax home.[35]

[35] IRS Publication 463, p. 13.

**EXAMPLE 6-20**

Catalina is a self-employed computer analyst in downtown Atlanta. She maintains an office at the downtown location but lives 30 miles out of town. She is currently performing a job that will last approximately a week that is 45 miles on the other side of Atlanta (75-mile one-way trip from her home). Because this is a temporary work location, Catalina can deduct the cost of her transportation from her home to the temporary location.

**EXAMPLE 6-21**

Assume the same facts as in Example 6-20. However, every morning Karen goes to the office for two hours. In this case, only the cost of her trip from her office to the temporary workplace is deductible. The cost of the trip from home to the office is commuting.

If the taxpayer's principal residence is their principal place of business, the cost of transportation between the residence and either a temporary location or a client/customer is deductible.[36]

### Automobile Expenses: Standard Mileage Rate

If an automobile is used as transportation in a trade or business activity, a deduction is allowed for the cost of the auto's use. Taxpayers calculate the auto deduction in one of two ways: Use either the standard mileage rate or the actual expenses of business operation.[37] A taxpayer can use the standard mileage rate if

- The taxpayer owns the vehicle and uses the standard mileage rate for the first year it was placed in service.
- The taxpayer leases the auto and uses the standard mileage rate for the entire lease period.

The standard mileage rate *cannot* be used in the following instances:

- The auto has claimed depreciation (other than straight-line), § 179, or bonus depreciation.
- The taxpayer operates five or more cars *simultaneously* in business operations.

For tax year 2021, the standard mileage rate is 56 cents per mile.[38] If the standard mileage rate is used, the taxpayer cannot deduct any actual car expenses. The mileage rate encompasses depreciation or lease payments, maintenance and repairs, gasoline, oil, insurance, and vehicle registration fees. The taxpayer simply takes the business miles driven and multiplies them by the standard rate to determine the deduction.

Certain vehicle information is required concerning the auto (date placed in service and miles driven). If Form 4562 is not required (for depreciation of other business assets), this auto information is placed in Part IV of Schedule C. Otherwise this information is shown on Form 4562.

**EXAMPLE 6-22**

Marta is a self-employed baker who makes wedding cakes and other pastries for parties. She owns a car for going to meetings with clients and a van that she uses for delivering cakes and pastries. Marta can use the standard mileage rate for both the car and the van.

[36] Rev. Rul. 99-7, 1999-1 CB 361; IRS Publication 463, p. 15.

[37] The standard mileage rate is available to self-employed taxpayers and businesses. Mileage is no longer deductible by employees since miscellaneous itemized deductions are on longer allowed on Schedule A—per the 2017 Tax Act.

[38] IRS Notice 2021-02.

A self-employed taxpayer can still deduct the business portion of any interest paid in acquiring a vehicle even if the standard mileage rate is used for the vehicle. Other permitted deductions include parking fees, tolls, and property taxes on the vehicle. If the vehicle is used less than 100% for business, the business portion of the property taxes should be reported on Schedule C, and the personal portion of the property taxes should be reported on Schedule A as an itemized deduction.

**EXAMPLE 6-23**

Ed purchased a vehicle for business and personal use. In 2021, he used the vehicle 60% for business (14,000 miles incurred ratably through the year) and used the standard mileage rate to calculate his vehicle expenses. He also paid $1,600 in interest and $180 in county property tax on the car. The total business deductions related to Ed's car are calculated as follows:

| | |
|---|---|
| Standard mileage rate (14,000 × 0.56) | $7,840 |
| Interest ($1,600 × 60%) | 960 |
| Property taxes ($180 × 60%) | 108 |
| Total auto deduction on Schedule C | $8,908 |

The 40% personal interest is disallowed, and the remaining $72 of personal property tax is deducted on Schedule A as an itemized deduction.

### *Automobile Expenses: Actual Car Expenses*

The second option for deducting business auto expenses is to use actual car expenses. Actual car expenses include the following:

- Depreciation or lease payments.
- Gas, oil, tires, repairs.
- Insurance, licenses, registration fees.[39]

The expenses must be divided between business and personal use (an allocation based on mileage can be used). Once depreciation on a vehicle has been taken, the taxpayer cannot use the standard mileage rate in future years on that vehicle. A taxpayer who has used the standard mileage rate in the past and decides to switch to the actual expense method must use straight-line depreciation and must reduce the depreciable basis by 26 cents per mile in 2021.[40]

The actual expense method usually results in a larger deduction but also requires receipts for actual expenses as well as a mileage log to determine business use versus personal use. With the standard mileage rate, only mileage documentation is required. Taxpayers can use the standard mileage rate for one vehicle and actual expenses for another vehicle.

### Travel Expenses

Travel expenses are different from transportation expenses because travel involves an overnight stay for business purposes. The basic travel requirement is that the trip requires sleep or rest.[41] The significance of meeting the "travel away from home" standard is that it allows the deduction of meals, lodging, and other incidental expenses such as dry cleaning. All travel expenses can be deducted if the trip was entirely business-related.

[39] IRS Publication No. 463, p. 15.

[40] The rate was 25 cents per mile in 2018. The rate was 26 cents for 2019 and 27 cents for 2020. IRS Notice 2021-2.

[41] *United States v. Correll,* 389 U.S. 299 (1967).

**EXAMPLE 6-24**    Alba is self-employed and has her primary business in New York City. Alba flew to Washington, D.C., in the morning for a business meeting and then flew to Boston for an afternoon meeting with a client. She then took a late flight home that evening. The trip would not qualify as travel because Alba did not require sleep. Thus, only the transportation cost is deductible.

If a temporary work assignment can be expected to last less than one year, travel from the taxpayer's tax home to the work assignment and temporary living costs at the remote location are deductible. If the work assignment is expected to last longer than one year, the position is considered permanent, and meals and lodging are considered nondeductible personal living expenses.[42] Limitations exist if the trip is partly personal or if lavish or extravagant expenditures for meals or lodging are incurred.

### *Limits on Travel Cost: Personal and Luxury*

Tax challenges occur when a trip consists of both personal and business activity. If the trip is primarily a vacation but some business is transacted on the trip, transportation costs are not deductible. Any expenses directly related to business activities, however, are deductible. If the trip was primarily business-related even if some personal vacation was involved, the taxpayer can deduct the transportation expenses.

**EXAMPLE 6-25**    Timothy is currently self-employed in Raleigh, North Carolina, as a personal financial adviser. He flies to New York to visit his parents for seven days. While in New York, Timothy rents a car to meet with a business client one afternoon. The rental car and other costs associated with the business meeting are deductible, but the cost of the flight is not. The trip was primarily personal.

**EXAMPLE 6-26**    Assume the same facts as in Example 6-25. However, in this case, Timothy spends five days in New York conducting business and then drives to his parents' house for the weekend (two days). Because the trip is primarily business, the transportation expenses are deductible in addition to meals and lodging while on business. Expenses incurred while visiting his parents for two days are not deductible.

Additional limitations are placed on foreign business travel.[43] For foreign travel, a trip is considered entirely for business if it meets one of the following four criteria:

- The taxpayer does not have substantial control over arranging the trip.
- The taxpayer is outside the United States no more than seven consecutive days (do not count the days on which the taxpayer leaves or returns).
- The taxpayer spends less than 25% of the time on personal activities (the days on which the trip began and ended are counted).
- Vacation is not a major consideration for the taxpayer.

If one or more of the conditions are met and the trip to the foreign country is considered primarily business, the taxpayer still must allocate travel time between business days and nonbusiness days. To calculate the deductible amount of the round-trip travel expenses, the

[42] Rev. Rul. 93-86, 1993-2 CB 71.
[43] IRC § 274 and related regulations.

taxpayer multiplies total trip costs by the fraction of the number of business days to the total number of travel days outside of the United States. Weekends and holidays that intervene the business days are considered business days.[44] If a vacation is taken beyond the place of business activities, the travel deduction is limited to those expenses to and from the business location.[45]

## Deductibility of Meals and Entertainment

The Tax Cuts and Jobs Act of 2017 repealed any deduction for entertainment expenses. Prior to 2018, these expenses were 50% deductible if directly related or associated with business. The deduction for food and beverages associated with a trade or business has been retained. Traditionally, meals have been limited to 50%. However, The Consolidated Appropriations Act of 2021 increased the business meals deduction to 100% provided by a restaurant for 2021 and 2022 tax years. Club dues and membership fees are expressly denied as deductions.[46]

The taxpayer's meals while away from home on business may be deducted if the taxpayer either keeps track of the actual cost of meals or uses the federal per diem rates. The federal meal and incidental per diem rates vary and depend on the location of the meals and lodging.[47] For the tax year 2021, the continental standard per diem (CONUS) rate is $151 ($96 lodging and $55 for meals and incidentals). These standard amounts are increased for business travel in IRS-designated high-cost areas. Using a per diem rate eliminates the need for detailed recordkeeping.[48]

**CONCEPT CHECK 6-9— LO 6-4**

1. A taxpayer can take depreciation on a business auto and use the standard mileage rate in the same year. True or false?
2. Transportation costs are allowed only when the taxpayer visits a client. True or false?
3. A deduction is allowed for meals, lodging, and incidental expenses when a taxpayer travels away from home and requires sleep. True or false?
4. A taxpayer can deduct $55/day for meals and incidentals without keeping receipts on a business trip. True or false?
5. Taking five clients to a major league baseball game immediately following a substantial business discussion is deductible. True or false?

[44] Reg. § 1.274-4(d)(2)(v).

[45] There are additional limitations concerning luxury water travel. See IRS Publication 463 for more information.

[46] IRC § 274(a)(3).

[47] These limits are subject to adjustment and depend on the location within the continental United States. Go to www.gsa.gov and click on Per Diems for the most recent figures.

[48] The 50% meals deduction is expected to come back in the tax year 2023. The 100% deduction was added to help restaurants during COVID.

# BUSINESS USE OF THE HOME AND BUSINESS BAD DEBTS
## LO 6-5

Typically no deduction is allowed with respect to a taxpayer's residence (except for itemized deductions for mortgage interest, taxes, and casualty losses concerning the primary residence). Difficulties arise when a taxpayer uses the primary residence or a portion of it for business purposes.

A self-employed taxpayer can deduct expenses for the business use of the home if the business use is exclusive, regular, and for the taxpayer's trade or business.[49] The home must be the principal place of business or a place where the taxpayer meets patients, clients, or customers. The exclusive use test is satisfied if a specific area of the home is used *only* for the trade or business (such as a separate room). To meet the regular use test, a taxpayer must use the home office on a continuing basis, not just occasionally or incidentally.[50]

To determine whether the taxpayer's home is the principal place of business, several factors must be considered. First, what is the relative importance of the activities performed at each business location? Second, what amount of time is spent at each business location? Business home use also includes administration or management activities if there is no other fixed location to conduct such business.

**EXAMPLE 6-27**

Rob is a self-employed independent insurance agent who works exclusively from two rooms in his home. He rarely meets clients at his home because most of his client contact occurs over the phone or at the client's home or office. Even though most of Rob's client contact is not in his home, all of the administrative work is completed in the home office. The two rooms qualify as a home office if they are used exclusively for business.

Prior to 2018, an employee could deduct a home office if the use of the home was *for the convenience of his or her employer.* The 2017 Act eliminated this deduction with the elimination of miscellaneous itemized deductions on Schedule A (see Chapter 5).

### Home Office Deduction for Self-Employed Taxpayers

The home office deduction for self-employed individuals is reported on Form 8829 and transferred to Schedule C, line 30. The first objective in determining the home office deduction is to calculate the area (in square footage) used regularly and exclusively for business.

**EXAMPLE 6-28**

The five-room home that Rob owns (see Example 6-27) has 3,000 square feet. According to the floor plan of the house, the two rooms used exclusively for business are 750 square feet each. Thus, one-half (1,500/3,000) of Rob's house is used exclusively for business.

[49] IRC § 280A(c)(1).
[50] IRS Publication No. 587, p. 3.

The next objective in calculating the home office deduction for self-employed individuals is to separate the home expenses into direct and indirect expenses. *Direct expenses* are those that are only for the business part of the home. For example, repairs and painting expenses for the business portion are direct expenses. Direct expenses are deducted in full in column (a) of Form 8829. Indirect expenses are expenses of running the entire household (insurance, utilities, taxes, interest, and so on). The indirect expenses are multiplied by the business percentage calculated in Part I of Form 8829 to derive the deductible portion.

### Deduction Limit

Home office expenses that are not otherwise deductible (such as insurance, utilities, and depreciation) are limited to the gross income from the business use of the home. *Gross income* is first reduced by the amount of regular trade or business expenses (non–home related) and home office expenses that would be deductible in any event (mortgage interest and property taxes). If any positive income remains, the business use portions of insurance, utilities, and depreciation (note that depreciation is last) can be deducted.

| | |
|---|---|
| **EXAMPLE 6-29** | Assume the same facts as in Example 6-28. Rob had $19,000 of gross income from his home trade or business and the following expenses: |

| | |
|---|---:|
| Trade or business expenses | $12,000 |
| Mortgage interest | 9,800 |
| Real estate taxes | 1,200 |
| Utilities | 1,500 |
| Insurance | 1,700 |
| Repairs | 2,000 |
| Depreciation (for business started in January: house basis $200,000 [200,000 × 50% business × 2.461%]) | 2,461 |

Expenses allowed are calculated as follows:

| | |
|---|---:|
| Gross income | $19,000 |
| Trade or business expenses | (12,000) |
| Interest ($9,800 × 50%) | (4,900) |
| Taxes ($1,200 × 50%) | (600) |
| Deduction limit | $ 1,500 |

Even though one-half of the utilities, insurance, repairs, and depreciation are for the exclusive use of the home office, they are limited to $1,500. The excess is indefinitely carried over (assuming continued home office use) to the following tax year and deducted, subject to the limit in that year. Exhibit 6-5 shows the presentation of the preceding example on Form 8829. Beginning for tax years 2013 and forward, taxpayers can use a simplified option for the home office deduction. With this option, taxpayers:

- Use a standard of $5 per square foot for the home office to a maximum of 300 square feet.
- Take mortgage interest and real estate taxes in full on Schedule A as itemized deductions.
- Take no depreciation on the home office.

**EXHIBIT 6-5**

| Form **8829** | **Expenses for Business Use of Your Home** | OMB No. 1545-0074 |
|---|---|---|
| Department of the Treasury Internal Revenue Service (99) | ▶ File only with Schedule C (Form 1040). Use a separate Form 8829 for each home you used for business during the year. ▶ Go to *www.irs.gov/Form8829* for instructions and the latest information. | 2021 Attachment Sequence No. **176** |

| Name(s) of proprietor(s) | Your social security number |
|---|---|
| Rob Taxpayer | 412-34-5670 |

**Part I   Part of Your Home Used for Business**

| | | | |
|---|---|---|---|
| 1 | Area used regularly and exclusively for business, regularly for daycare, or for storage of inventory or product samples (see instructions) | **1** | 1,500 |
| 2 | Total area of home | **2** | 3,000 |
| 3 | Divide line 1 by line 2. Enter the result as a percentage | **3** | 50 % |

**For daycare facilities not used exclusively for business, go to line 4. All others, go to line 7.**

| | | | | |
|---|---|---|---|---|
| 4 | Multiply days used for daycare during year by hours used per day | **4** | | hr. |
| 5 | If you started or stopped using your home for daycare during the year, see instructions; otherwise, enter 8,760 | **5** | | hr. |
| 6 | Divide line 4 by line 5. Enter the result as a decimal amount | **6** | | |
| 7 | Business percentage. For daycare facilities not used exclusively for business, multiply line 6 by line 3 (enter the result as a percentage). All others, enter the amount from line 3 ▶ | **7** | | 50 % |

**Part II   Figure Your Allowable Deduction**

| | | | |
|---|---|---|---|
| 8 | Enter the amount from Schedule C, line 29, **plus** any gain derived from the business use of your home, **minus** any loss from the trade or business not derived from the business use of your home. See instructions. | **8** | 7,000 |

See instructions for columns (a) and (b) before completing lines 9–22.

| | | (a) Direct expenses | (b) Indirect expenses | | |
|---|---|---|---|---|---|
| 9 | Casualty losses (see instructions) | **9** | | | |
| 10 | Deductible mortgage interest (see instructions) | **10** | | 9,800 | |
| 11 | Real estate taxes (see instructions) | **11** | | 1,200 | |
| 12 | Add lines 9, 10, and 11 | **12** | | 11,000 | |
| 13 | Multiply line 12, column (b), by line 7 | | **13** | 5,500 | |
| 14 | Add line 12, column (a), and line 13 | | | **14** | 5,500 |
| 15 | Subtract line 14 from line 8. If zero or less, enter -0- | | | **15** | 1,500 |
| 16 | Excess mortgage interest (see instructions) | **16** | | | |
| 17 | Excess real estate taxes (see instructions) | **17** | | | |
| 18 | Insurance | **18** | | 1,700 | |
| 19 | Rent | **19** | | | |
| 20 | Repairs and maintenance | **20** | | 2,000 | |
| 21 | Utilities | **21** | | 1,500 | |
| 22 | Other expenses (see instructions) | **22** | | | |
| 23 | Add lines 16 through 22 | **23** | | 5,200 | |
| 24 | Multiply line 23, column (b), by line 7 | | **24** | 2,600 | |
| 25 | Carryover of prior year operating expenses (see instructions) | | **25** | | |
| 26 | Add line 23, column (a), line 24, and line 25 | | | **26** | 2,600 |
| 27 | Allowable operating expenses. Enter the **smaller** of line 15 or line 26 | | | **27** | 1,500 |
| 28 | Limit on excess casualty losses and depreciation. Subtract line 27 from line 15 | | | **28** | 0 |
| 29 | Excess casualty losses (see instructions) | | **29** | | |
| 30 | Depreciation of your home from line 42 below | | **30** | 2,461 | |
| 31 | Carryover of prior year excess casualty losses and depreciation (see instructions) | | **31** | | |
| 32 | Add lines 29 through 31 | | | **32** | 2,461 |
| 33 | Allowable excess casualty losses and depreciation. Enter the **smaller** of line 28 or line 32 | | | **33** | 0 |
| 34 | Add lines 14, 27, and 33 | | | **34** | 7,000 |
| 35 | Casualty loss portion, if any, from lines 14 and 33. Carry amount to **Form 4684**. See instructions | | | **35** | |
| 36 | **Allowable expenses for business use of your home.** Subtract line 35 from line 34. Enter here and on Schedule C, line 30. If your home was used for more than one business, see instructions. ▶ | | | **36** | 7,000 |

**Part III   Depreciation of Your Home**

| | | | |
|---|---|---|---|
| 37 | Enter the **smaller** of your home's adjusted basis or its fair market value. See instructions | **37** | 200,000 |
| 38 | Value of land included on line 37 | **38** | 0 |
| 39 | Basis of building. Subtract line 38 from line 37 | **39** | 200,000 |
| 40 | Business basis of building. Multiply line 39 by line 7 | **40** | 100,000 |
| 41 | Depreciation percentage (see instructions) | **41** | 2.461 % |
| 42 | Depreciation allowable (see instructions). Multiply line 40 by line 41. Enter here and on line 30 above | **42** | 2,461 |

**Part IV   Carryover of Unallowed Expenses to 2022**

| | | | |
|---|---|---|---|
| 43 | Operating expenses. Subtract line 27 from line 26. If less than zero, enter -0- | **43** | 1,500 |
| 44 | Excess casualty losses and depreciation. Subtract line 33 from line 32. If less than zero, enter -0- | **44** | 2,461 |

For Paperwork Reduction Act Notice, see your tax return instructions.    Cat. No. 13232M    Form **8829** (2021)

## Business Bad Debts and Business Casualty Losses

Certain bad debt losses can be deducted as ordinary deductions if incurred in a trade or business.[51] Generally, the same rules for deducting trade or business expenses also apply to bad debts. In other words, if a debt is considered a bona fide business bad debt, it must have been ordinary, necessary, and reasonable in the trade or business. The distinction between a business bad debt and a nonbusiness bad debt is extremely important. A *nonbusiness bad debt* is treated as a short-term capital loss and can be deducted only when it becomes completely worthless.[52] *Business bad debts,* on the other hand, can be deducted when either partially worthless or completely worthless and are treated as an ordinary deduction.

### Bona Fide Business Bad Debt

To be a business bad debt, a debt must be a *bona fide debt,* which consists of debt that arises from a debtor–creditor relationship based on a valid and enforceable obligation to pay a fixed sum of money.[53] Additionally, for a note or account receivable to be considered a debt, the receivable must have been previously included in income. Thus, a cash basis taxpayer cannot write off, as a bad debt, any account receivable that is not collected. Because the receivable has not been included in income on Schedule C, it therefore has no basis, and no deduction is allowed.

**EXAMPLE 6-30**   Mateo, a cash basis sole proprietor (consultant), gave advice to a corporate client that he billed $700. Subsequently the corporate client went out of business and filed for bankruptcy. Because the $700 receivable was never included in income, Mateo cannot take a bad debt deduction.

**EXAMPLE 6-31**   In addition to the $700 bill for the consulting services, Mateo lent the corporate client $5,000 (evidenced by a valid note) to help the client pay bills and avoid bankruptcy. The business purpose for the loan was that the corporate officers were a source of many client referrals for Mateo's firm. When the corporate client later went bankrupt, Mike could take an ordinary deduction for the $5,000.

If a bad debt is deducted, any recoveries of the bad debt in subsequent years must be included in gross income.[54]

### Business Casualty Losses

An individual taxpayer reports a loss from a business casualty on page 2 of Form 4684.[55] When business property is lost in a fire, storm, shipwreck, theft, or other casualty, the taxpayer normally receives an ordinary loss deduction for the basis of the property unless the property is only partially destroyed. With partial losses, the loss is the lower of the decrease in FMV before and after the casualty or the adjusted basis. All losses are reduced by insurance proceeds.[56]

[51] IRC § 165(c).

[52] Reg. § 1.166-1(d).

[53] Reg. § 1.166-1(c).

[54] Reg. § 1.166-1(f).

[55] More details on casualty losses are provided in Chapter 5. The limits for casualties of personal use (nonbusiness use) property are discussed there.

[56] The gain can be avoided by the replacement of similar property. Deferrals of gains from involuntary conversions are discussed in Chapter 12.

**TAX YOUR BRAIN**

Can a taxpayer have a casualty gain?

**ANSWER**

Yes. As an example, a business building purchased in 1985 for $55,000 is now worth $200,000. The building is likely to be insured for its replacement cost and to be fully depreciated ($0 adjusted basis). If the building were completely destroyed by fire and the insurance proceeds were $200,000, the taxpayer could have a gain of $200,000 ($200,000 proceeds less the $0 adjusted basis).

**EXAMPLE 6-32**

On September 17, 2021, Duane's office building was destroyed by a tornado. Duane had purchased the building in 1987 for $90,000 but had recently made improvements to it. The adjusted basis (cost less accumulated depreciation) and FMV at the time of the tornado were $80,000 and $110,000, respectively. Duane had not updated his insurance policy in several years and thus received only $70,000 from the insurance company. Because the building was totally destroyed, the business casualty is $10,000 (the adjusted basis of $80,000 less the $70,000 insurance reimbursement). See Exhibit 6-6 for the proper reporting. The $10,000 is transferred from Form 4684, page 2, to Form 4797 and eventually to Form 1040, page 1. Note that although the loss relates to Schedule C, it does not appear on Schedule C but goes directly to Form 1040 as a *for* AGI deduction.

**CONCEPT CHECK 6-10— LO 6-5**

1. Jose uses 20% of his home exclusively for business. He had the entire exterior of the house painted and the interior of one room that he uses for an office painted for $3,000 and $500, respectively. What is the total deduction Jose can take as a home office expense for the painting?
   a. $500.
   b. $3,500.
   c. $700.
   d. $1,100.

2. Which of the following comments is true regarding the home office deduction?
   a. The taxpayer must see clients at home to be allowed a home office deduction.
   b. The home office deduction is limited to income from the Schedule C business.
   c. The taxpayer is allowed to take a § 179 expense election on the business portion of the home itself.
   d. Depreciation on the home is never allowed as a home office deduction.

3. When business property is partially destroyed by a casualty, the loss is calculated using which of the following?
   a. The decrease in the FMV of the property.
   b. The adjusted basis of the property.
   c. The lower of the FMV or the adjusted basis of the property.
   d. The adjusted basis of the property less 10% of AGI.

**EXHIBIT 6-6**

| Form 4684 (2021) | Attachment Sequence No. **26** | | Page **2** |
|---|---|---|---|

Name(s) shown on tax return. Do not enter name and identifying number if shown on other side.
Duane Taxpayer

Identifying number
412-34-5670

## SECTION B—Business and Income-Producing Property

**Part I**  **Casualty or Theft Gain or Loss**  (Use a separate Part I for each casualty or theft.)

19  Description of properties (show type, location, and date acquired for each property). Use a separate line for each property lost or damaged from the same casualty or theft. **See instructions if claiming a loss due to a Ponzi-type investment scheme and Section C is not completed.**

Property A  Office Building, 123 Ally Drive, Anywhere, USA
Property B
Property C
Property D

| | Properties | | | |
|---|---|---|---|---|
| | **A** | **B** | **C** | **D** |
| 20 Cost or adjusted basis of each property | 80,000 | | | |
| 21 Insurance or other reimbursement (whether or not you filed a claim). See the instructions for line 3. **Note:** If line 20 is **more** than line 21, skip line 22. | 70,000 | | | |
| 22 Gain from casualty or theft. If line 21 is **more** than line 20, enter the difference here and on line 29 or line 34, column (c), except as provided in the instructions for line 33. Also, skip lines 23 through 27 for that column. See the instructions for line 4 if line 21 includes insurance or other reimbursement you did not claim, or you received payment for your loss in a later tax year | | | | |
| 23 Fair market value **before** casualty or theft | 110,000 | | | |
| 24 Fair market value **after** casualty or theft | 0 | | | |
| 25 Subtract line 24 from line 23 | 110,000 | | | |
| 26 Enter the **smaller** of line 20 or line 25 | 80,000 | | | |
| **Note:** If the property was totally destroyed by casualty or lost from theft, enter on line 26 the amount from line 20. | | | | |
| 27 Subtract line 21 from line 26. If zero or less, enter -0- | 10,000 | | | |

28  Casualty or theft loss. Add the amounts on line 27. Enter the total here and on line 29 **or** line 34. See instructions ...  **28**  10,000

**Part II**  **Summary of Gains and Losses**  (from separate Parts I)

| (a) Identify casualty or theft | (b) Losses from casualties or thefts | | (c) Gains from casualties or thefts includible in income |
|---|---|---|---|
| | (i) Trade, business, rental, or royalty property | (ii) Income-producing property | |

**Casualty or Theft of Property Held One Year or Less**

| 29 | ( ) | ( ) | |
| | ( ) | ( ) | |
| 30 Totals. Add the amounts on line 29  **30** | ( ) | ( ) | |

31  Combine line 30, columns (b)(i) and (c). Enter the net gain or (loss) here and on Form 4797, line 14. If Form 4797 is not otherwise required, see instructions  **31**

32  Enter the amount from line 30, column (b)(ii), here. Individuals, enter the amount from income-producing property on Schedule A (Form 1040), line 16; or Schedule A (Form 1040-NR), line 7. (Do not include any loss on property used as an employee.) Estates and trusts, partnerships, and S corporations, see instructions  **32**

**Casualty or Theft of Property Held More Than One Year**

33  Casualty or theft gains from Form 4797, line 32  **33**

| 34  **Casualty loss from line 28** | ( 10,000 ) | ( ) | |
| | ( ) | ( ) | |

35  Total losses. Add amounts on line 34, columns (b)(i) and (b)(ii)  **35**  ( 10,000 ) ( )

36  Total gains. Add lines 33 and 34, column (c)  **36**

37  Add amounts on line 35, columns (b)(i) and (b)(ii)  **37**  (10,000)

38  If the loss on line 37 is **more** than the gain on line 36:

  a  Combine line 35, column (b)(i), and line 36, and enter the net gain or (loss) here. Partnerships and S corporations, see the *Note* below. All others, enter this amount on Form 4797, line 14. If Form 4797 is not otherwise required, see instructions  **38a**  (10,000)

  b  Enter the amount from line 35, column (b)(ii), here. Individuals, enter the amount from income-producing property on Schedule A (Form 1040), line 16; or Schedule A (Form 1040-NR), line 7. (Do not include any loss on property used as an employee.) Estates and trusts, enter on the "Other deductions" line of your tax return. Partnerships and S corporations, see the *Note* below  **38b**

39  If the loss on line 37 is **less** than or **equal** to the gain on line 36, combine lines 36 and 37 and enter here. Partnerships, see the *Note* below. All others, enter this amount on Form 4797, line 3  **39**

**Note:** Partnerships, enter the amount from line 38a, 38b, or 39 on Form 1065, Schedule K, line 11. S corporations, enter the amount from line 38a or 38b on Form 1120-S, Schedule K, line 10.

Form **4684** (2021)

# HOBBY LOSS RULES AND EDUCATION EXPENSES
## LO 6-6

To limit deductible losses from activities that are primarily for personal pleasure instead of a trade or business, Congress established the hobby loss rules.[57] The Tax Cuts and Jobs Act of 2017 effectively eliminated the deduction for any activity deemed a hobby. The expenses prior to 2018 were deducted to the extent of hobby income but were treated as miscellaneous itemized deductions.[58] The classification of a hobby is even more important in the tax years 2018 and beyond. If the hobby classification holds, the income is included in income, but the expenses are currently disallowed. Example 6-33 is an example of a potential hobby.

---

**EXAMPLE 6-33**

Alex is a successful CPA who enjoys decorative woodworking. He makes decorative rocking chairs, tables, and other handcrafted furniture. He spends 10 to 15 hours a week (considerably less time during tax season) making the furniture and had gross sales of $3,000. His expenses for the year were $10,000. If this activity is treated as a trade or business, Alex would have a $7,000 loss to deduct against other income. If the woodworking is treated as a hobby, none of the expenses would be allowed.

---

What is the deciding factor in determining whether an activity is a hobby or business? Nine factors are used in the hobby determination:

1. Manner in which the taxpayer carries on the activity.
2. Expertise of the taxpayer or his or her advisers.
3. Time and effort expended by the taxpayer in carrying on the activity.
4. Expectations that assets used in the activity can appreciate in value.
5. Success of the taxpayer in carrying on other similar or dissimilar activities.
6. Taxpayer's history of income or losses with respect to the activity.
7. Amount of occasional profits, if any, that are earned.
8. Taxpayer's financial status.
9. Elements of personal pleasure or recreation.[59]

The regulations note that taxpayers are to take *all* of the facts and circumstances into account and that no one factor is controlling in the hobby determination.[60] If the IRS asserts that an activity is a hobby, the burden to prove that the activity is a trade or business rests with the taxpayer. However, if the taxpayer has shown a profit for three out of five consecutive tax years (two out of seven for horse racing), the burden of proof shifts to the IRS.[61]

After the activity is characterized as a hobby, expenses are not currently allowed in the 2018 tax year and forward.

---

[57] IRC § 183.

[58] As shown in Chapter 5, miscellaneous itemized deductions were eliminated by the 2017 Act.

[59] Reg. § 1.183-2(b).

[60] Reg. § 1.183-2(b).

[61] IRC § 183(d).

### Education Expenses

A major expense for many self-employed individuals is the cost incurred for education. However, with education expenses, it is sometimes difficult to distinguish whether the education is an ordinary and necessary business expense (deductible) or qualifies the taxpayer for a new profession (not deductible). This ambiguity has led to considerable litigation between taxpayers and the IRS. Education expenses are deductible if the education meets either of these criteria:

- Maintains or improves skills required by the individual in his or her employment or other trade or business.
- Meets the express requirements of the individual's employer or the requirements of applicable law or regulation.[62]

However, even if one of the two preceding requirements is met, the education expenses are not deductible if the education is required to meet minimum educational requirements for employment or if the education qualifies the taxpayer for a new trade or business. The definition of what constitutes a new trade or business has been the source of much confusion.

**TAX YOUR BRAIN**

Assume that Leon is a CPA who has been practicing for 10 years in audit. He decides that he would like to start a tax practice. He begins taking classes in a masters of taxation program. Are the expenses for the classes deductible?

**ANSWER**

Yes, they are because the education does not qualify Leon for a new profession. The education only improves his skills in the CPA profession for which he already qualifies.

Eligible education expenses include not only tuition but also books, supplies, fees, and travel.

**CONCEPT CHECK 6-11—**

**LO 6-6**

1. If a taxpayer has shown a net profit for the last three years, the activity is not considered a hobby. True or false?
2. A taxpayer can never take a net loss on an activity considered a hobby. True or false?
3. Expenses that can be deducted elsewhere on the tax return must be the first expenses deducted from hobby income. True or false?
4. Education expenses that help qualify a taxpayer for a new trade or business (or profession) are deductible. True or false?

# SELF-EMPLOYMENT TAX

**LO 6-7**

One of the major disadvantages to being self-employed is the requirement to pay self-employment tax. *Self-employment (SE) tax* consists of two parts: (1) the social security tax and (2) the Medicare tax.[63] Self-employed taxpayers are not discriminated against because every U.S. citizen or resident (with few exceptions) must pay these taxes. However, because most taxpayers are employees, the employer is required to pay half of these taxes,

---

[62] Reg. § 1.162-5.

[63] The social security tax is the old age, survivors, and disability insurance tax (OASDI), and the Medicare tax is a hospital insurance tax.

and the employee pays the other half. The employee's one-half share is commonly reported as FICA on most paychecks. Self-employed taxpayers must pay *both* the employer's and the employee's shares.[64] Any self-employed taxpayer with $400 or more in self-employment income must pay self-employment taxes. Income from Schedule C and as a partner in a partnership are sources of SE income.

The tax base for the social security tax is limited. In tax year 2021, the first $142,800 of wages and self-employment income is subject to the social security tax. The tax base for the Medicare tax, on the other hand, is not limited. Here are the social security tax and Medicare rates:

|                 | Rate (Percent) | Income Limit |
|-----------------|----------------|--------------|
| Social security | 12.4%          | $142,800     |
| Medicare        | 2.9%           | Unlimited    |
| Total SE        | 15.3%[65]      |              |

An additional Medicare tax of 0.9% is imposed on self-employment income in excess of $250,000 for joint returns ($125,000 for MFS, $200,000 for all other returns). The thresholds are reduced by any wages the taxpayers have in addition to SE income.

The total SE rate is multiplied by 92.35% of SE income. The self-employed taxpayer receives a *for* AGI deduction for one-half of the SE tax paid (see Chapter 4).

---

**EXAMPLE 6-34**

In 2021, Linda is employed at a local bank and has wages of $143,000. She also has a Schedule C business of selling jewelry at night and on the weekends. Linda has net income from the Schedule C of $15,000. In this case, Linda owes zero additional social security tax because she is over the $142,800 limit for 2021. She would have to pay the Medicare tax on her Schedule C income:

$$\$15,000 \times 0.9235 \times 2.9\% = \$402$$

Linda paid social security tax and Medicare tax on the first $143,000 (only $142,800 for social security) through withholding from her paycheck at the bank.

---

**EXAMPLE 6-35**

Suppose Linda's wages from the bank (see Example 6-34) were only $79,200. Linda would have to pay SE tax (both parts) on the additional $15,000 from her Schedule C business:

| | |
|---|---|
| Social security $15,000 × 0.9235 × 12.40% = | $1,718 |
| Medicare $15,000 × 0.9235 × 2.90%    = | 402 |
| Total SE tax | $2,120 |

---

**NEW LAW**

Increase to SE limit.

The SE tax is reported on Schedule SE, which must accompany any Schedule C the taxpayer files. If a taxpayer has more than one Schedule C, only one Schedule SE is required. However, if the tax return is a joint return, each spouse is individually subject to the $142,800 limit and must file their own Schedule SE. Exhibit 6-7 illustrates a completed Schedule SE for Linda in Example 6-35. Due to COVID-19 and the 2020 Cares Act, a deferral of self-employment tax is allowed for post-March 26, 2020 income if the taxpayer elects to do so.

---

[64] IRC § 1401.

[65] An employee pays only 7.65% because the employer pays 7.65% (the other half).

**EXHIBIT 6-7**

| SCHEDULE SE<br>(Form 1040)<br><br>Department of the Treasury<br>Internal Revenue Service (99) | **Self-Employment Tax**<br><br>▶ Go to *www.irs.gov/ScheduleSE* for instructions and the latest information.<br>▶ Attach to Form 1040, 1040-SR, or 1040-NR. | OMB No. 1545-0074<br><br>20**21**<br>Attachment<br>Sequence No. **17** |
|---|---|---|

| Name of person with self-employment income (as shown on Form 1040, 1040-SR, or 1040-NR)<br>Linda Taxpayer | Social security number of person<br>with **self-employment** income ▶ | 412-34-5670 |
|---|---|---|

### Part I — Self-Employment Tax

**Note:** If your only income subject to self-employment tax is **church employee income,** see instructions for how to report your income and the definition of church employee income.

**A** If you are a minister, member of a religious order, or Christian Science practitioner **and** you filed Form 4361, but you had $400 or more of **other** net earnings from self-employment, check here and continue with Part I . . . . . . . . . ▶ ☐

Skip lines 1a and 1b if you use the farm optional method in Part II. See instructions.

| | | | |
|---|---|---|---|
| **1a** | Net farm profit or (loss) from Schedule F, line 34, and farm partnerships, Schedule K-1 (Form 1065), box 14, code A . . . | **1a** | |
| **b** | If you received social security retirement or disability benefits, enter the amount of Conservation Reserve Program payments included on Schedule F, line 4b, or listed on Schedule K-1 (Form 1065), box 20, code AH | **1b** | ( ) |

Skip line 2 if you use the nonfarm optional method in Part II. See instructions.

| | | | |
|---|---|---|---|
| **2** | Net profit or (loss) from Schedule C, line 31; and Schedule K-1 (Form 1065), box 14, code A (other than farming). See instructions for other income to report or if you are a minister or member of a religious order | **2** | 15,000 |
| **3** | Combine lines 1a, 1b, and 2 . . . . . . . . . | **3** | 15,000 |
| **4a** | If line 3 is more than zero, multiply line 3 by 92.35% (0.9235). Otherwise, enter amount from line 3 . . . | **4a** | 13,853 |
| | **Note:** If line 4a is less than $400 due to Conservation Reserve Program payments on line 1b, see instructions. | | |
| **b** | If you elect one or both of the optional methods, enter the total of lines 15 and 17 here . . . . . | **4b** | |
| **c** | Combine lines 4a and 4b. If less than $400, **stop;** you don't owe self-employment tax. **Exception:** If less than $400 and you had **church employee income,** enter -0- and continue . . . . . . . ▶ | **4c** | 13,853 |
| **5a** | Enter your **church employee income** from Form W-2. See instructions for definition of church employee income . . . . . . | **5a** | | |
| **b** | Multiply line 5a by 92.35% (0.9235). If less than $100, enter -0- . . | **5b** | |
| **6** | Add lines 4c and 5b . . . . . . . . . | **6** | 13,853 |
| **7** | Maximum amount of combined wages and self-employment earnings subject to social security tax or the 6.2% portion of the 7.65% railroad retirement (tier 1) tax for 2021 . . . . . . . . . | **7** | 142,800 |
| **8a** | Total social security wages and tips (total of boxes 3 and 7 on Form(s) W-2) and railroad retirement (tier 1) compensation. If $142,800 or more, skip lines 8b through 10, and go to line 11 . . . . . . . | **8a** | 79,200 | |
| **b** | Unreported tips subject to social security tax from Form 4137, line 10 . . . | **8b** | |
| **c** | Wages subject to social security tax from Form 8919, line 10 . . . . . | **8c** | |
| **d** | Add lines 8a, 8b, and 8c . . . . . . . . . | **8d** | 79,200 |
| **9** | Subtract line 8d from line 7. If zero or less, enter -0- here and on line 10 and go to line 11 . . . ▶ | **9** | 63,600 |
| **10** | Multiply the **smaller** of line 6 or line 9 by 12.4% (0.124) . . . . . | **10** | 1,718 |
| **11** | Multiply line 6 by 2.9% (0.029) . . . . . . . . . | **11** | 402 |
| **12** | **Self-employment tax.** Add lines 10 and 11. Enter here and on **Schedule 2 (Form 1040), line 4** . . | **12** | 2,120 |
| **13** | **Deduction for one-half of self-employment tax.**<br>Multiply line 12 by 50% (0.50). Enter here and on **Schedule 1 (Form 1040), line 15** . . . . . . . | **13** | 1,060 | |

### Part II — Optional Methods To Figure Net Earnings (see instructions)

**Farm Optional Method.** You may use this method **only** if **(a)** your gross farm income[1] wasn't more than $8,820, **or (b)** your net farm profits[2] were less than $6,367.

| | | | |
|---|---|---|---|
| **14** | Maximum income for optional methods . . . . . . . . . | **14** | 5,880 |
| **15** | Enter the **smaller** of: two-thirds (2/3) of gross farm income[1] (not less than zero) **or** $5,880. Also, include this amount on line 4b above . . . . . . . . . | **15** | |

**Nonfarm Optional Method.** You may use this method **only** if **(a)** your net nonfarm profits[3] were less than $6,367 and also less than 72.189% of your gross nonfarm income,[4] **and (b)** you had net earnings from self-employment of at least $400 in 2 of the prior 3 years. **Caution:** You may use this method no more than five times.

| | | | |
|---|---|---|---|
| **16** | Subtract line 15 from line 14 . . . . . . . . . | **16** | |
| **17** | Enter the **smaller** of: two-thirds (2/3) of gross nonfarm income[4] (not less than zero) **or** the amount on line 16. Also, include this amount on line 4b above . . . . . . . . . | **17** | |

[1] From Sch. F, line 9; and Sch. K-1 (Form 1065), box 14, code B.
[2] From Sch. F, line 34; and Sch. K-1 (Form 1065), box 14, code A—minus the amount you would have entered on line 1b had you not used the optional method.
[3] From Sch. C, line 31; and Sch. K-1 (Form 1065), box 14, code A.
[4] From Sch. C, line 7; and Sch. K-1 (Form 1065), box 14, code C.

| For Paperwork Reduction Act Notice, see your tax return instructions. | Cat. No. 11358Z | Schedule SE (Form 1040) 2021 |
|---|---|---|

Source: U.S. Department of the Treasury, Internal Revenue Service, SCHEDULE SE (Form 1040). Washington, DC: 2021.

# From Shoebox to Software   Schedule C Business Comprehensive Example

Alan Masters (see Example 6-19) left his job and opened his own independent insurance agency on July 1. His business produces the following income and expenses during the year:

### Gross Receipts from Three Insurance Companies

1099-NEC received:

| | |
|---|---:|
| XYZ Insurance | $22,000 |
| All Country Insurance | 21,550 |
| State Wide Insurance | 14,830 |
| Total revenue | 58,380 |
| Advertising | (1,250) |
| Postage | (1,500) |
| Wages | (7,000) |
| Payroll taxes | (535) |
| License fee | (125) |
| Supplies | (2,300) |
| Continuing professional education (registration) | (975) |
| Travel to CPE course | |
| Plane | (385) |
| Taxi | (25) |
| Lodging $91/night × 2 nights | (182) |
| Meals per diem $55 × 2 days | (110) |
| Business asset depreciation (see Example 6-19) | (9,620) |
| Cell phone | (588) |
| Internet service | (780) |

Alan does not elect to use § 179 expenses.

Go to the Schedule C for Alan Masters created earlier.

Open a Form 1099-MISC and enter the amounts from the three Forms 1099-MISC. The total income should equal $58,380.

Enter the expenses directly on Schedule C. If there is not a listed line item, enter the expenses on the Other Expenses section on page 2 of Schedule C.

When you combine numbers on a line, include information about the items combined on the "line item detail" using tax software (for example, combine the payroll tax and license fee on line 23).

Exhibits 6-8, 6-9, and 6-10 show the completed Schedule C, Form 4562, and Schedule SE, respectively. Form 4562 is the same as shown with Example 6-19. Note that travel expenses are on Schedule C as the total of the plane, taxi, and lodging. Also note that Alan had wages of $112,505 from the example in Chapter 5. The taxes and licenses amount on line 23 is the total of the payroll tax and the license fee. It is good practice to clearly note in your working papers when you combine two or more numbers. If you do that, not only will your working papers tie directly to the tax return but also you will be able to see what you did when you work on the tax return in a subsequent year.

---

**TAX YOUR BRAIN**

Why would employers prefer not to treat individuals working for them as employees?

**ANSWER**

If an individual is not an employee, the *payer* does not have to pay the *employer's* share of FICA taxes or withhold income taxes. In essence, the worker is treated as self-employed and must pay SE tax (both shares). Many less-than-ethical employers treat part-time employees as self-employed. The part-time employee enjoys the classification at first because the paycheck is larger (no income tax or FICA is withheld). However, when the employee files his or her tax return the following spring, he or she must pay income tax and SE tax. Sometimes the money is not available then. The individual could also be subject to underpayment penalties.

---

**CONCEPT CHECK 6-12—**

**LO 6-7**

1. Kia had $53,000 of income from a self-employed consulting practice and had no other income during the year. What is Kia's total self-employment tax? _____

2. Assume the same facts as in Question 1. In addition to her $53,000 in self-employment income, Kia received a W-2 from her employer (different from her self-employed business) with $145,000 in wages. What is Kia's self-employment tax in this situation? _____

3. Assume the same facts as in Question 1. In addition to her $53,000 in self-employment income, Kia received a W-2 from her employer (different from her self-employed business) with $105,000 in W-2 wages. What is Kia's self-employment tax in this situation? _____

**EXHIBIT 6-8**

| SCHEDULE C<br>(Form 1040)<br><br>Department of the Treasury<br>Internal Revenue Service (99) | **Profit or Loss From Business**<br>(Sole Proprietorship)<br>▶ Go to *www.irs.gov/ScheduleC* for instructions and the latest information.<br>▶ **Attach to Form 1040, 1040-SR, 1040-NR, or 1041; partnerships must generally file Form 1065.** | OMB No. 1545-0074<br>**2021**<br>Attachment<br>Sequence No. **09** |
|---|---|---|

| Name of proprietor<br>**Alan Masters** | Social security number (SSN)<br>412-34-5670 |
|---|---|

| **A** | Principal business or profession, including product or service (see instructions)<br>**Insurance** | **B** Enter code from instructions<br>▶ 5 2 4 2 1 0 |
|---|---|---|

| **C** | Business name. If no separate business name, leave blank. | **D** Employer ID number (EIN) (see instr.) |
|---|---|---|

**E** Business address (including suite or room no.) ▶
City, town or post office, state, and ZIP code

**F** Accounting method: **(1)** ✓ Cash **(2)** ☐ Accrual **(3)** ☐ Other (specify) ▶

**G** Did you "materially participate" in the operation of this business during 2021? If "No," see instructions for limit on losses . ✓ Yes ☐ No

**H** If you started or acquired this business during 2021, check here . . . . . . . . . . . . . ▶ ☐

**I** Did you make any payments in 2021 that would require you to file Form(s) 1099? See instructions . . ☐ Yes ✓ No

**J** If "Yes," did you or will you file required Form(s) 1099? . . . . . . . . . . . . . . ☐ Yes ☐ No

### Part I  Income

| | | | |
|---|---|---|---|
| 1 | Gross receipts or sales. See instructions for line 1 and check the box if this income was reported to you on Form W-2 and the "Statutory employee" box on that form was checked . . . . . ▶ ☐ | **1** | 58,380 |
| 2 | Returns and allowances . . . . . . . . . . . . . . . . . . . . . . . . | **2** | |
| 3 | Subtract line 2 from line 1 . . . . . . . . . . . . . . . . . . . . . . . | **3** | 58,380 |
| 4 | Cost of goods sold (from line 42) . . . . . . . . . . . . . . . . . . . . | **4** | |
| 5 | **Gross profit.** Subtract line 4 from line 3 . . . . . . . . . . . . . . . . . | **5** | 58,380 |
| 6 | Other income, including federal and state gasoline or fuel tax credit or refund (see instructions) . . . | **6** | |
| 7 | **Gross income.** Add lines 5 and 6 . . . . . . . . . . . . . . . . . . . ▶ | **7** | 58,380 |

### Part II  Expenses. Enter expenses for business use of your home **only** on line 30.

| | | | | | | | |
|---|---|---|---|---|---|---|---|
| 8 | Advertising . . . . . | **8** | 1,250 | 18 | Office expense (see instructions) | **18** | 1,500 |
| 9 | Car and truck expenses (see instructions) . . . . . | **9** | | 19 | Pension and profit-sharing plans . | **19** | |
| 10 | Commissions and fees . | **10** | | 20 | Rent or lease (see instructions): | | |
| 11 | Contract labor (see instructions) | **11** | | a | Vehicles, machinery, and equipment | **20a** | |
| 12 | Depletion . . . . . | **12** | | b | Other business property . . . | **20b** | |
| 13 | Depreciation and section 179 expense deduction (not included in Part III) (see instructions) . . . . . | **13** | 9,620 | 21 | Repairs and maintenance . . . | **21** | |
| | | | | 22 | Supplies (not included in Part III) . | **22** | 2,300 |
| | | | | 23 | Taxes and licenses . . . . . | **23** | 660 |
| | | | | 24 | Travel and meals: | | |
| 14 | Employee benefit programs (other than on line 19) . . | **14** | | a | Travel . . . . . . . . . | **24a** | 592 |
| 15 | Insurance (other than health) | **15** | | b | Deductible meals (see instructions) . . . . . . . | **24b** | 110 |
| 16 | Interest (see instructions): | | | 25 | Utilities . . . . . . . . | **25** | |
| a | Mortgage (paid to banks, etc.) | **16a** | | 26 | Wages (less employment credits) . | **26** | 7,000 |
| b | Other . . . . . . | **16b** | | 27a | Other expenses (from line 48) . . | **27a** | 2,343 |
| 17 | Legal and professional services | **17** | | b | **Reserved for future use** . . . | **27b** | |

| | | | |
|---|---|---|---|
| 28 | **Total expenses** before expenses for business use of home. Add lines 8 through 27a . . . . . . . ▶ | **28** | 25,375 |
| 29 | Tentative profit or (loss). Subtract line 28 from line 7 . . . . . . . . . . . . . . . | **29** | 33,005 |

| 30 | Expenses for business use of your home. Do not report these expenses elsewhere. Attach Form 8829 unless using the simplified method. See instructions.<br>**Simplified method filers only:** Enter the total square footage of (a) your home: _____<br>and (b) the part of your home used for business: _____ . Use the Simplified Method Worksheet in the instructions to figure the amount to enter on line 30 . . . . . . . | **30** | |
|---|---|---|---|

| 31 | **Net profit or (loss).** Subtract line 30 from line 29.<br>• If a profit, enter on both **Schedule 1 (Form 1040), line 3,** and on **Schedule SE, line 2.** (If you checked the box on line 1, see instructions). Estates and trusts, enter on **Form 1041, line 3.**<br>• If a loss, you **must** go to line 32. | **31** | 33,005 |
|---|---|---|---|

| 32 | If you have a loss, check the box that describes your investment in this activity. See instructions.<br>• If you checked 32a, enter the loss on both **Schedule 1 (Form 1040), line 3,** and on **Schedule SE, line 2.** (If you checked the box on line 1, see the line 31 instructions.) Estates and trusts, enter on **Form 1041, line 3.**<br>• If you checked 32b, you **must** attach **Form 6198.** Your loss may be limited. | **32a** ☐ All investment is at risk.<br>**32b** ☐ Some investment is not at risk. |
|---|---|---|

| For Paperwork Reduction Act Notice, see the separate instructions. | Cat. No. 11334P | Schedule C (Form 1040) 2021 |
|---|---|---|

Source: U.S. Department of the Treasury, Internal Revenue Service, Schedule C (Form 1040). Washington, DC: 2021.

**EXHIBIT 6-8**   *(concluded)*

Schedule C (Form 1040) 2021                                                                 Page **2**

| **Part III** | **Cost of Goods Sold** (see instructions) |
|---|---|

**33**   Method(s) used to
value closing inventory:   **a** ☐ Cost      **b** ☐ Lower of cost or market      **c** ☐ Other (attach explanation)

**34**   Was there any change in determining quantities, costs, or valuations between opening and closing inventory?
If "Yes," attach explanation  . . . . . . . . . . . . . . . . . . . . . . . . . . .   ☐ Yes      ☐ No

**35**   Inventory at beginning of year. If different from last year's closing inventory, attach explanation  . .   | **35** |

**36**   Purchases less cost of items withdrawn for personal use  . . . . . . . . . .   | **36** |

**37**   Cost of labor. Do not include any amounts paid to yourself . . . . . . . . . .   | **37** |

**38**   Materials and supplies  . . . . . . . . . . . . . . . . . .   | **38** |

**39**   Other costs . . . . . . . . . . . . . . . . . . . . .   | **39** |

**40**   Add lines 35 through 39 . . . . . . . . . . . . . . . . . .   | **40** |

**41**   Inventory at end of year . . . . . . . . . . . . . . . . .   | **41** |

**42**   **Cost of goods sold.** Subtract line 41 from line 40. Enter the result here and on line 4 . . . . . . .   | **42** |

| **Part IV** | **Information on Your Vehicle.** Complete this part **only** if you are claiming car or truck expenses on line 9 and are not required to file Form 4562 for this business. See the instructions for line 13 to find out if you must file Form 4562. |
|---|---|

**43**   When did you place your vehicle in service for business purposes? (month/day/year)  ▶  _____ / _____ / _____

**44**   Of the total number of miles you drove your vehicle during 2021, enter the number of miles you used your vehicle for:

**a** Business _____   **b** Commuting (see instructions) _____   **c** Other _____

**45**   Was your vehicle available for personal use during off-duty hours?  . . . . . . . . .   ☐ Yes      ☐ No

**46**   Do you (or your spouse) have another vehicle available for personal use?. . . . . . . .   ☐ Yes      ☐ No

**47a**   Do you have evidence to support your deduction?  . . . . . . . . . . . . .   ☐ Yes      ☐ No

**b**   If "Yes," is the evidence written?  . . . . . . . . . . . . . . . . . . .   ☐ Yes      ☐ No

| **Part V** | **Other Expenses.** List below business expenses not included on lines 8–26 or line 30. |
|---|---|

| Continuing Education | 975 |
|---|---|
| Cell Phone | 588 |
| Internet | 780 |
| | |
| | |
| | |
| | |
| | |

**48**   **Total other expenses.** Enter here and on line 27a  . . . . . . . . . . . . . . .   | **48** | 2,343 |

Schedule C (Form 1040) 2021

**EXHIBIT 6-9**

| Form **4562** | **Depreciation and Amortization** (Including Information on Listed Property) ▶ Attach to your tax return. ▶ Go to *www.irs.gov/Form4562* for instructions and the latest information. | OMB No. 1545-0172 **2021** |
|---|---|---|
| Department of the Treasury Internal Revenue Service    (99) | | Attachment Sequence No. **179** |

| Name(s) shown on return **Alan Masters** | Business or activity to which this form relates **Insurance** | Identifying number **412-34-5670** |
|---|---|---|

### Part I    Election To Expense Certain Property Under Section 179
**Note:** If you have any listed property, complete Part V before you complete Part I.

| | | | |
|---|---|---|---|
| 1 | Maximum amount (see instructions) | **1** | |
| 2 | Total cost of section 179 property placed in service (see instructions) | **2** | |
| 3 | Threshold cost of section 179 property before reduction in limitation (see instructions) | **3** | |
| 4 | Reduction in limitation. Subtract line 3 from line 2. If zero or less, enter -0- | **4** | |
| 5 | Dollar limitation for tax year. Subtract line 4 from line 1. If zero or less, enter -0-. If married filing separately, see instructions | **5** | |

| 6 | (a) Description of property | (b) Cost (business use only) | (c) Elected cost |
|---|---|---|---|
| | | | |
| | | | |

| | | | |
|---|---|---|---|
| 7 | Listed property. Enter the amount from line 29 . . . . . . . . **7** | | |
| 8 | Total elected cost of section 179 property. Add amounts in column (c), lines 6 and 7 | **8** | |
| 9 | Tentative deduction. Enter the **smaller** of line 5 or line 8 | **9** | |
| 10 | Carryover of disallowed deduction from line 13 of your 2020 Form 4562 | **10** | |
| 11 | Business income limitation. Enter the smaller of business income (not less than zero) or line 5. See instructions | **11** | |
| 12 | Section 179 expense deduction. Add lines 9 and 10, but don't enter more than line 11 | **12** | |
| 13 | Carryover of disallowed deduction to 2022. Add lines 9 and 10, less line 12 ▶ | **13** | |

**Note:** Don't use Part II or Part III below for listed property. Instead, use Part V.

### Part II    Special Depreciation Allowance and Other Depreciation (Don't include listed property. See instructions.)

| | | | |
|---|---|---|---|
| 14 | Special depreciation allowance for qualified property (other than listed property) placed in service during the tax year. See instructions | **14** | |
| 15 | Property subject to section 168(f)(1) election | **15** | |
| 16 | Other depreciation (including ACRS) | **16** | |

### Part III    MACRS Depreciation (Don't include listed property. See instructions.)

**Section A**

| | | | |
|---|---|---|---|
| 17 | MACRS deductions for assets placed in service in tax years beginning before 2021 | **17** | |
| 18 | If you are electing to group any assets placed in service during the tax year into one or more general asset accounts, check here ▶ ☐ | | |

**Section B—Assets Placed in Service During 2021 Tax Year Using the General Depreciation System**

| (a) Classification of property | (b) Month and year placed in service | (c) Basis for depreciation (business/investment use only—see instructions) | (d) Recovery period | (e) Convention | (f) Method | (g) Depreciation deduction |
|---|---|---|---|---|---|---|
| 19a   3-year property | | | | | | |
| b   5-year property | | 4,800 | 5 yr | HY | DDB | 960 |
| c   7-year property | | 23,000 | 7 yr | HY | DDB | 3,288 |
| d   10-year property | | | | | | |
| e   15-year property | | | | | | |
| f   20-year property | | | | | | |
| g   25-year property | | | 25 yrs. | | S/L | |
| h   Residential rental property | | | 27.5 yrs. | MM | S/L | |
| | | | 27.5 yrs. | MM | S/L | |
| i   Nonresidential real property | 7/21 | 120,000 | 39 yrs. | MM | S/L | 1,412 |
| | | | | MM | S/L | |

**Section C—Assets Placed in Service During 2021 Tax Year Using the Alternative Depreciation System**

| | | | | | | |
|---|---|---|---|---|---|---|
| 20a  Class life | | | | | S/L | |
| b   12-year | | | 12 yrs. | | S/L | |
| c   30-year | | | 30 yrs. | MM | S/L | |
| d   40-year | | | 40 yrs. | MM | S/L | |

### Part IV    Summary (See instructions.)

| | | | |
|---|---|---|---|
| 21 | Listed property. Enter amount from line 28 | **21** | 3,960 |
| 22 | **Total.** Add amounts from line 12, lines 14 through 17, lines 19 and 20 in column (g), and line 21. Enter here and on the appropriate lines of your return. Partnerships and S corporations—see instructions | **22** | 9,620 |
| 23 | For assets shown above and placed in service during the current year, enter the portion of the basis attributable to section 263A costs . . . . . . . . . **23** | | |

For Paperwork Reduction Act Notice, see separate instructions.          Cat. No. 12906N          Form **4562** (2021)

Source: U.S. Department of the Treasury, Internal Revenue Service, Form 4562. Washington, DC: 2021.

**EXHIBIT 6-9** *(concluded)*

Form 4562 (2021)      Page **2**

## Part V   Listed Property   (Include automobiles, certain other vehicles, certain aircraft, and property used for entertainment, recreation, or amusement.)

**Note:** For any vehicle for which you are using the standard mileage rate or deducting lease expense, complete **only** 24a, 24b, columns (a) through (c) of Section A, all of Section B, and Section C if applicable.

### Section A—Depreciation and Other Information (Caution: See the instructions for limits for passenger automobiles.)

**24a** Do you have evidence to support the business/investment use claimed? ☑ **Yes** ☐ **No**    **24b** If "Yes," is the evidence written? ☑ **Yes** ☐ **No**

| (a) Type of property (list vehicles first) | (b) Date placed in service | (c) Business/ investment use percentage | (d) Cost or other basis | (e) Basis for depreciation (business/investment use only) | (f) Recovery period | (g) Method/ Convention | (h) Depreciation deduction | (i) Elected section 179 cost |
|---|---|---|---|---|---|---|---|---|
| **25** Special depreciation allowance for qualified listed property placed in service during the tax year and used more than 50% in a qualified business use. See instructions . | | | | | **25** | | | |
| **26** Property used more than 50% in a qualified business use: | | | | | | | | |
| Auto | 7/15/21 | 90 % | 22,000 | 19,800 | 5 yr | DDB | 3,960 | |
| | | % | | | | | | |
| | | % | | | | | | |
| **27** Property used 50% or less in a qualified business use: | | | | | | | | |
| | | % | | | | S/L – | | |
| | | % | | | | S/L – | | |
| | | % | | | | S/L – | | |
| **28** Add amounts in column (h), lines 25 through 27. Enter here and on line 21, page 1 | | | | | **28** | | 3,960 | |
| **29** Add amounts in column (i), line 26. Enter here and on line 7, page 1 . . . . . . . . . | | | | | | | **29** | |

### Section B—Information on Use of Vehicles

Complete this section for vehicles used by a sole proprietor, partner, or other "more than 5% owner," or related person. If you provided vehicles to your employees, first answer the questions in Section C to see if you meet an exception to completing this section for those vehicles.

| | | (a) Vehicle 1 | | (b) Vehicle 2 | | (c) Vehicle 3 | | (d) Vehicle 4 | | (e) Vehicle 5 | | (f) Vehicle 6 | |
|---|---|---|---|---|---|---|---|---|---|---|---|---|---|
| **30** | Total business/investment miles driven during the year (**don't** include commuting miles) . | | | | | | | | | | | | |
| **31** | Total commuting miles driven during the year | | | | | | | | | | | | |
| **32** | Total other personal (noncommuting) miles driven . . . . . . . . . | | | | | | | | | | | | |
| **33** | Total miles driven during the year. Add lines 30 through 32 . . . . . . | | | | | | | | | | | | |
| **34** | Was the vehicle available for personal use during off-duty hours? | Yes | No | Yes | No | Yes | No | Yes | No | Yes | No | Yes | No |
| **35** | Was the vehicle used primarily by a more than 5% owner or related person? . . | | | | | | | | | | | | |
| **36** | Is another vehicle available for personal use? | | | | | | | | | | | | |

### Section C—Questions for Employers Who Provide Vehicles for Use by Their Employees

Answer these questions to determine if you meet an exception to completing Section B for vehicles used by employees who **aren't** more than 5% owners or related persons. See instructions.

| | | Yes | No |
|---|---|---|---|
| **37** | Do you maintain a written policy statement that prohibits all personal use of vehicles, including commuting, by your employees? . . . | | |
| **38** | Do you maintain a written policy statement that prohibits personal use of vehicles, except commuting, by your employees? See the instructions for vehicles used by corporate officers, directors, or 1% or more owners . . | | |
| **39** | Do you treat all use of vehicles by employees as personal use? . . . . . . | | |
| **40** | Do you provide more than five vehicles to your employees, obtain information from your employees about the use of the vehicles, and retain the information received? . . . . . . . . | | |
| **41** | Do you meet the requirements concerning qualified automobile demonstration use? See instructions. . . . . | | |

**Note:** If your answer to 37, 38, 39, 40, or 41 is "Yes," don't complete Section B for the covered vehicles.

## Part VI   Amortization

| (a) Description of costs | (b) Date amortization begins | (c) Amortizable amount | (d) Code section | (e) Amortization period or percentage | (f) Amortization for this year |
|---|---|---|---|---|---|
| **42** Amortization of costs that begins during your 2021 tax year (see instructions): | | | | | |
| | | | | | |
| | | | | | |
| **43** Amortization of costs that began before your 2021 tax year . . . . . . . . . . . . . . . . **43** | | | | | |
| **44** **Total.** Add amounts in column (f). See the instructions for where to report . . . . . . . . **44** | | | | | |

Form **4562** (2021)

**EXHIBIT 6-10**

| SCHEDULE SE (Form 1040) | Self-Employment Tax | OMB No. 1545-0074 |
|---|---|---|
| Department of the Treasury Internal Revenue Service (99) | ▶ Go to *www.irs.gov/ScheduleSE* for instructions and the latest information.<br>▶ Attach to Form 1040, 1040-SR, or 1040-NR. | 2021<br>Attachment Sequence No. 17 |

Name of person with self-employment income (as shown on Form 1040, 1040-SR, or 1040-NR)
**Alan Masters**

Social security number of person with **self-employment** income ▶  412-34-5670

### Part I    Self-Employment Tax

**Note:** If your only income subject to self-employment tax is **church employee income,** see instructions for how to report your income and the definition of church employee income.

**A**  If you are a minister, member of a religious order, or Christian Science practitioner **and** you filed Form 4361, but you had $400 or more of **other** net earnings from self-employment, check here and continue with Part I . . . . . . . . ▶ ☐

Skip lines 1a and 1b if you use the farm optional method in Part II. See instructions.

| | | | |
|---|---|---|---|
| 1a | Net farm profit or (loss) from Schedule F, line 34, and farm partnerships, Schedule K-1 (Form 1065), box 14, code A | 1a | |
| b | If you received social security retirement or disability benefits, enter the amount of Conservation Reserve Program payments included on Schedule F, line 4b, or listed on Schedule K-1 (Form 1065), box 20, code AH | 1b | ( ) |

Skip line 2 if you use the nonfarm optional method in Part II. See instructions.

| | | | |
|---|---|---|---|
| 2 | Net profit or (loss) from Schedule C, line 31; and Schedule K-1 (Form 1065), box 14, code A (other than farming). See instructions for other income to report or if you are a minister or member of a religious order | 2 | 33,005 |
| 3 | Combine lines 1a, 1b, and 2 | 3 | 33,005 |
| 4a | If line 3 is more than zero, multiply line 3 by 92.35% (0.9235). Otherwise, enter amount from line 3 | 4a | 30,480 |
| | **Note:** If line 4a is less than $400 due to Conservation Reserve Program payments on line 1b, see instructions. | | |
| b | If you elect one or both of the optional methods, enter the total of lines 15 and 17 here | 4b | |
| c | Combine lines 4a and 4b. If less than $400, **stop;** you don't owe self-employment tax. **Exception:** If less than $400 and you had **church employee income,** enter -0- and continue ▶ | 4c | 30,480 |
| 5a | Enter your **church employee income** from Form W-2. See instructions for definition of church employee income | 5a | |
| b | Multiply line 5a by 92.35% (0.9235). If less than $100, enter -0- | 5b | |
| 6 | Add lines 4c and 5b | 6 | 30,480 |
| 7 | Maximum amount of combined wages and self-employment earnings subject to social security tax or the 6.2% portion of the 7.65% railroad retirement (tier 1) tax for 2021 | 7 | 142,800 |
| 8a | Total social security wages and tips (total of boxes 3 and 7 on Form(s) W-2) and railroad retirement (tier 1) compensation. If $142,800 or more, skip lines 8b through 10, and go to line 11 · · · 8a | 112,505 | |
| b | Unreported tips subject to social security tax from Form 4137, line 10 · · · 8b | | |
| c | Wages subject to social security tax from Form 8919, line 10 · · · 8c | | |
| d | Add lines 8a, 8b, and 8c | 8d | 112,505 |
| 9 | Subtract line 8d from line 7. If zero or less, enter -0- here and on line 10 and go to line 11 ▶ | 9 | 30,295 |
| 10 | Multiply the **smaller** of line 6 or line 9 by 12.4% (0.124) | 10 | 3,757 |
| 11 | Multiply line 6 by 2.9% (0.029) | 11 | 884 |
| 12 | **Self-employment tax.** Add lines 10 and 11. Enter here and on **Schedule 2 (Form 1040), line 4** | 12 | 4,641 |
| 13 | **Deduction for one-half of self-employment tax.**<br>Multiply line 12 by 50% (0.50). Enter here and on **Schedule 1 (Form 1040), line 15** · · · 13 | 2,321 | |

### Part II    Optional Methods To Figure Net Earnings (see instructions)

**Farm Optional Method.** You may use this method **only** if **(a)** your gross farm income[1] wasn't more than $8,820, **or (b)** your net farm profits[2] were less than $6,367.

| | | | |
|---|---|---|---|
| 14 | Maximum income for optional methods | 14 | 5,880 |
| 15 | Enter the **smaller** of: two-thirds (2/3) of gross farm income[1] (not less than zero) **or** $5,880. Also, include this amount on line 4b above | 15 | |

**Nonfarm Optional Method.** You may use this method **only** if **(a)** your net nonfarm profits[3] were less than $6,367 and also less than 72.189% of your gross nonfarm income,[4] **and (b)** you had net earnings from self-employment of at least $400 in 2 of the prior 3 years. **Caution:** You may use this method no more than five times.

| | | | |
|---|---|---|---|
| 16 | Subtract line 15 from line 14 | 16 | |
| 17 | Enter the **smaller** of: two-thirds (2/3) of gross nonfarm income[4] (not less than zero) **or** the amount on line 16. Also, include this amount on line 4b above | 17 | |

[1] From Sch. F, line 9; and Sch. K-1 (Form 1065), box 14, code B.
[2] From Sch. F, line 34; and Sch. K-1 (Form 1065), box 14, code A—minus the amount you would have entered on line 1b had you not used the optional method.
[3] From Sch. C, line 31; and Sch. K-1 (Form 1065), box 14, code A.
[4] From Sch. C, line 7; and Sch. K-1 (Form 1065), box 14, code C.

**For Paperwork Reduction Act Notice, see your tax return instructions.**    Cat. No. 11358Z    **Schedule SE (Form 1040) 2021**

Source: U.S. Department of the Treasury, Internal Revenue Service, Schedule SE (Form 1040). Washington, DC: 2021.

## Qualified Business Income Deduction

One of the most drastic changes by the Tax Cuts and Jobs Act of 2017 is the IRC § 199A deduction for qualified business income. Taxpayers are allowed a deduction up to 20% of the qualified business income (QBI). QBI includes business income from sole proprietorships (Schedule C) and flow-through entities such as partnerships, limited liability companies, S corporations, trusts, and estates. The purpose of the 20% deduction is to make the taxation of these entities (Schedule Cs and flow-throughs) essentially similar to C corporations, where the tax rate was reduced from 35% to 21% by the 2017 Tax Act.

The 20% deduction is from AGI, so this deduction does not affect any of the AGI limitations. The deduction is shown on line 10 of Form 1040 and is calculated by multiplying line 31 of Schedule C less the deductible part of self-employment tax (50%) and deductible health insurance by 20% (for the Schedule C income in Exhibit 6-8).[66] The deduction is the lesser of 20% of QBI or 20% of taxable income (less net capital gains).

The QBI deduction is not without some limitations. If the business income is from a "specified business" that includes service fields (health, law, accounting, consulting, athletics, brokerage services, or where the business income is generated from the reputation or skill of one or more employees), the deduction is limited when "taxable" income (the whole return) exceeds $329,800 for married filing jointly (phased out at $429,800) and $164,900 for all other individuals (phased out at $214,900). The deduction phases out ratably over the range ($100,000 for married filing jointly or $50,000 for all other taxpayers). For example, married taxpayers with taxable income of $361,600 would lose 32% of the QBI deduction ($31,800 excess over $329,800 divided by the $100,000 phase-out range).

If taxpayers are above the threshold income limit ($329,800 married, $164,900 all others), and not in the service fields mentioned above, the taxpayer is subject to an additional W-2 wage limitation. In this case, the QBI deduction is the lesser of

1. 20% of the QBI, or
2. The greater of 50% of the W-2 wages with respect to the qualified business or the sum of 25% of W-2 wages plus 2.5% of the basis of qualified property in the business.

Examples 6-36, 6-37, 6-38, and 6-39 illustrate the basic calculations:

**EXAMPLE 6-36**  Allison (married) makes $200,000 in QBI from her Schedule C net of her deductible self-employment tax. Allison's taxable income on her Form 1040 (less any capital gains) is $260,000. The IRC § 199A deduction would be $40,000 (the lesser of 20% of QBI or 20% of taxable income less capital gains).

---

[66] The Schedule C income for QBI purposes is also reduced by deductible self-employed retirement contributions.

**EXAMPLE 6-37**     Allison (married) makes $200,000 in QBI from her Schedule C net of her deductible self-employment tax. Allison's taxable income on her Form 1040 (less any capital gains) is $180,000. Taxable income could definitely be less due to *for* AGI deductions for self-employment tax, self-employed health insurance, and itemized deductions. The IRC § 199A deduction would be $36,000 (the lesser of 20% of QBI or 20% of taxable income less capital gains).

**EXAMPLE 6-38**     Allison (married) makes $500,000 in QBI from her Schedule C net of her deductible self-employment tax—a law practice. Allison's taxable income on her Form 1040 (less any capital gains) is $620,000. The IRC § 199A would be $0 because her law practice is a "specified business" and her income exceeds the married income threshold of $429,800.

**EXAMPLE 6-39**     Allison (married) makes $600,000 in QBI from her solely owned S Corporation—a manufacturing business with $1,000,000 in depreciable assets and $150,000 of W-2 wages. She is above the $429,800 threshold amount so the W-2 limitation must be used. The IRC § 199A deduction would be $75,000. The QBI deduction is the lesser of

1. 20% × $600,000 = $120,000 or
2. The greater of 50% of $150,000 = $75,000 or (2.5% × 1,000,000) + (25% × 150,000 wages) = $62,500.

## Summary

**LO 6-1:** Describe how income and expenses for a self-employed individual are recognized and reported.
- Reported on Schedule C.
- Usually reported on 1099-NEC.
- Usually reported on the cash basis except for inventory, which is reported on the accrual basis.

**LO 6-2:** Explain the concept of ordinary and necessary business expenses.
- Expenses must be ordinary, necessary, and reasonable.
  - Ordinary—customary or usual.
  - Necessary—appropriate and helpful.
  - Reasonable—amount and relation to business.
- Illegal payments, lobbying, or payments for fines and penalties not allowed.

**LO 6-3:** Explain the calculation of depreciation for trade or business assets.
- Basis—typically the cost of the asset.
- Periods—3, 5, or 7 years for personal property; 27.5 and 39 years for real property.
- Conventions—half-year, mid-quarter, and mid-month conventions.
- Methods—200% declining balance (DB), 150% DB, and straight-line.
- § 179 expense up to $1,050,000 in 2021.
- Luxury autos limited to $18,200 in 2021.

**LO 6-4:** Describe travel and entertainment expenses and discuss their deductibility.

- Transportation deductible unless for commuting.
- Standard mileage rate is 56 cents per mile for 2021.
- Travel—overnight stay for business purposes, meals included.

**LO 6-5:** Apply the rules for deducting the business portion of a residence and business bad debts.

- Portion of the home must be used exclusively and regularly in the trade or business.
- Direct expenses 100% deductible.
- Indirect expenses deductible in relation to business ratio.
- Deductions limited to the gross income from the business.
- Business bad debts create an ordinary deduction.

**LO 6-6:** Explain the hobby loss rules and the limits on education expense deductibility.

- Hobby—primarily for personal pleasure.
- Not a hobby if a profit is shown for 3 of the last 5 years.
- No deduction in 2021 due to Miscellaneous Deductions being eliminated
- Education expenses deductible if the education maintains or improves skills.

**LO 6-7:** Describe the calculation of self-employment taxes.

- Reported on Schedule SE.
- Social security 12.40%.
- Medicare 2.9%.
- Social security limit $142,800 in 2021.

# Appendix

## General Depreciation System

**TABLE 6A-1**
**General Depreciation System: 200% or 150% Declining Balance Switching to Straight-Line***

| | Half-Year Convention | | | | | |
|---|---|---|---|---|---|---|
| **Recovery Year** | **3-Year** | **5-Year** | **7-Year** | **10-Year** | **15-Year** | **20-Year** |
| 1 | 33.33 | 20.00 | 14.29 | 10.00 | 5.00 | 3.750 |
| 2 | 44.45 | 32.00 | 24.49 | 18.00 | 9.50 | 7.219 |
| 3 | 14.81 | 19.20 | 17.49 | 14.40 | 8.55 | 6.677 |
| 4 | 7.41 | 11.52 | 12.49 | 11.52 | 7.70 | 6.177 |
| 5 | | 11.52 | 8.93 | 9.22 | 6.93 | 5.713 |
| 6 | | 5.76 | 8.92 | 7.37 | 6.23 | 5.285 |
| 7 | | | 8.93 | 6.55 | 5.90 | 4.888 |
| 8 | | | 4.46 | 6.55 | 5.90 | 4.522 |
| 9 | | | | 6.56 | 5.91 | 4.462 |
| 10 | | | | 6.55 | 5.90 | 4.461 |
| 11 | | | | 3.28 | 5.91 | 4.462 |
| 12 | | | | | 5.90 | 4.461 |
| 13 | | | | | 5.91 | 4.462 |
| 14 | | | | | 5.90 | 4.461 |
| 15 | | | | | 5.91 | 4.462 |
| 16 | | | | | 2.95 | 4.461 |
| 17 | | | | | | 4.462 |
| 18 | | | | | | 4.461 |
| 19 | | | | | | 4.462 |
| 20 | | | | | | 4.461 |
| 21 | | | | | | 2.231 |

\* May not be used for farm business property generally placed in service after 1988. See Table 14, Rev. Proc. 87-57, 1987-2 CB 687.

**TABLE 6A-2**

**General Depreciation System: 200% or 150% Declining Balance Switching to Straight-Line***

| | Mid-Quarter Convention (Property Placed in Service in 1st Quarter) | | | | | |
|---|---|---|---|---|---|---|
| Recovery Year | 3-Year | 5-Year | 7-Year | 10-Year | 15-Year | 20-Year |
| 1 | 58.33 | 35.00 | 25.00 | 19.50 | 8.75 | 6.563 |
| 2 | 27.78 | 26.00 | 21.43 | 16.50 | 9.13 | 7.000 |
| 3 | 12.35 | 15.60 | 15.31 | 13.20 | 8.21 | 6.482 |
| 4 | 1.54 | 11.01 | 10.93 | 10.56 | 7.39 | 5.996 |
| 5 | | 11.01 | 8.75 | 8.45 | 6.65 | 5.546 |
| 6 | | 1.38 | 8.74 | 6.76 | 5.99 | 5.130 |
| 7 | | | 8.75 | 6.55 | 5.90 | 4.746 |
| 8 | | | 1.09 | 6.55 | 5.91 | 4.459 |
| 9 | | | | 6.56 | 5.90 | 4.459 |
| 10 | | | | 6.55 | 5.91 | 4.459 |
| 11 | | | | 0.82 | 5.90 | 4.459 |
| 12 | | | | | 5.91 | 4.460 |
| 13 | | | | | 5.90 | 4.459 |
| 14 | | | | | 5.91 | 4.460 |
| 15 | | | | | 5.90 | 4.459 |
| 16 | | | | | 0.74 | 4.460 |
| 17 | | | | | | 4.459 |
| 18 | | | | | | 4.460 |
| 19 | | | | | | 4.459 |
| 20 | | | | | | 4.460 |
| 21 | | | | | | 0.557 |

* May not be used for farm business property generally placed in service after 1988. See Table 15, Rev. Proc. 87-57, 1987-2 CB 687.

**TABLE 6A-3**

**General Depreciation System: 200% or 150% Declining Balance Switching to Straight-Line***

| | Mid-Quarter Convention (Property Placed in Service in 2nd Quarter) | | | | | |
|---|---|---|---|---|---|---|
| Recovery Year | 3-Year | 5-Year | 7-Year | 10-Year | 15-Year | 20-Year |
| 1 | 41.67 | 25.00 | 17.85 | 12.50 | 6.25 | 4.688 |
| 2 | 38.89 | 30.00 | 23.47 | 17.50 | 9.38 | 7.148 |
| 3 | 14.14 | 18.00 | 16.76 | 14.00 | 8.44 | 6.612 |
| 4 | 5.30 | 11.37 | 11.97 | 11.20 | 7.59 | 6.116 |
| 5 | | 11.37 | 8.87 | 8.96 | 6.83 | 5.658 |
| 6 | | 4.26 | 8.87 | 7.17 | 6.15 | 5.233 |
| 7 | | | 8.87 | 6.55 | 5.91 | 4.841 |
| 8 | | | 3.33 | 6.55 | 5.90 | 4.478 |
| 9 | | | | 6.56 | 5.91 | 4.463 |
| 10 | | | | 6.55 | 5.90 | 4.463 |
| 11 | | | | 2.46 | 5.91 | 4.463 |
| 12 | | | | | 5.90 | 4.463 |
| 13 | | | | | 5.91 | 4.463 |
| 14 | | | | | 5.90 | 4.463 |
| 15 | | | | | 5.91 | 4.462 |
| 16 | | | | | 2.21 | 4.463 |
| 17 | | | | | | 4.462 |
| 18 | | | | | | 4.463 |
| 19 | | | | | | 4.462 |
| 20 | | | | | | 4.463 |
| 21 | | | | | | 1.673 |

* May not be used for farm business property generally placed in service after 1988. See Table 16, Rev. Proc. 87-57, 1987-2 CB 687.

**TABLE 6A-4**

General Depreciation System: 200% or 150% Declining Balance Switching to Straight-Line*

| | Mid-Quarter Convention (Property Placed in Service in 3rd Quarter) | | | | | |
|---|---|---|---|---|---|---|
| Recovery Year | 3-Year | 5-Year | 7-Year | 10-Year | 15-Year | 20-Year |
| 1 | 25.00 | 15.00 | 10.71 | 7.50 | 3.75 | 2.813 |
| 2 | 50.00 | 34.00 | 25.51 | 18.50 | 9.63 | 7.289 |
| 3 | 16.67 | 20.40 | 18.22 | 14.80 | 8.66 | 6.742 |
| 4 | 16.67 | 12.24 | 13.02 | 11.84 | 7.80 | 6.237 |
| 5 | 8.33 | 11.30 | 9.30 | 9.47 | 7.02 | 5.769 |
| 6 | | 7.06 | 8.85 | 7.58 | 6.31 | 5.336 |
| 7 | | | 8.86 | 6.55 | 5.90 | 4.936 |
| 8 | | | 5.53 | 6.55 | 5.90 | 4.566 |
| 9 | | | | 6.56 | 5.91 | 4.460 |
| 10 | | | | 6.55 | 5.90 | 4.460 |
| 11 | | | | 4.10 | 5.91 | 4.460 |
| 12 | | | | | 5.90 | 4.460 |
| 13 | | | | | 5.91 | 4.461 |
| 14 | | | | | 5.90 | 4.460 |
| 15 | | | | | 5.91 | 4.461 |
| 16 | | | | | 3.69 | 4.460 |
| 17 | | | | | | 4.461 |
| 18 | | | | | | 4.460 |
| 19 | | | | | | 4.461 |
| 20 | | | | | | 4.460 |
| 21 | | | | | | 2.788 |

* May not be used for farm business property generally placed in service after 1988. See Table 17, Rev. Proc. 87–57, 1987-2 CB 687.

**TABLE 6A-5**

General Depreciation System: 200% or 150% Declining Balance Switching to Straight-Line*

| | Mid-Quarter Convention (Property Placed in Service in 4th Quarter) | | | | | |
|---|---|---|---|---|---|---|
| Recovery Year | 3-Year | 5-Year | 7-Year | 10-Year | 15-Year | 20-Year |
| 1 | 8.33 | 5.00 | 3.57 | 2.50 | 1.25 | 0.938 |
| 2 | 61.11 | 38.00 | 27.55 | 19.50 | 9.88 | 7.430 |
| 3 | 20.37 | 22.80 | 19.68 | 15.60 | 8.89 | 6.872 |
| 4 | 10.19 | 13.68 | 14.06 | 12.48 | 8.00 | 6.357 |
| 5 | | 10.94 | 10.04 | 9.98 | 7.20 | 5.880 |
| 6 | | 9.58 | 8.73 | 7.99 | 6.48 | 5.439 |
| 7 | | | 8.73 | 6.55 | 5.90 | 5.031 |
| 8 | | | 7.64 | 6.55 | 5.90 | 4.654 |
| 9 | | | | 6.56 | 5.90 | 4.458 |
| 10 | | | | 6.55 | 5.91 | 4.458 |
| 11 | | | | 5.74 | 5.90 | 4.458 |
| 12 | | | | | 5.91 | 4.458 |
| 13 | | | | | 5.90 | 4.458 |
| 14 | | | | | 5.91 | 4.458 |
| 15 | | | | | 5.90 | 4.458 |
| 16 | | | | | 5.17 | 4.458 |
| 17 | | | | | | 4.458 |
| 18 | | | | | | 4.459 |
| 19 | | | | | | 4.458 |
| 20 | | | | | | 4.459 |
| 21 | | | | | | 3.901 |

* May not be used for farm business property generally placed in service after 1988. See Table 18, Rev. Proc. 87–57, 1987-2 CB 687.

**TABLE 6A-6** General Depreciation System: Straight-Line; Applicable Recovery Period: 27.5 Years; Mid-Month Convention

| | Month in the First Recovery Year the Property Is Placed in Service | | | | | | | | | | | |
|---|---|---|---|---|---|---|---|---|---|---|---|---|
| Recovery Year | 1 | 2 | 3 | 4 | 5 | 6 | 7 | 8 | 9 | 10 | 11 | 12 |
| 1 | 3.485 | 3.182 | 2.879 | 2.576 | 2.273 | 1.970 | 1.667 | 1.364 | 1.061 | 0.758 | 0.455 | 0.152 |
| 2 | 3.636 | 3.636 | 3.636 | 3.636 | 3.636 | 3.636 | 3.636 | 3.636 | 3.636 | 3.636 | 3.636 | 3.636 |
| 3 | 3.636 | 3.636 | 3.636 | 3.636 | 3.636 | 3.636 | 3.636 | 3.636 | 3.636 | 3.636 | 3.636 | 3.636 |
| 4 | 3.636 | 3.636 | 3.636 | 3.636 | 3.636 | 3.636 | 3.636 | 3.636 | 3.636 | 3.636 | 3.636 | 3.636 |
| 5 | 3.636 | 3.636 | 3.636 | 3.636 | 3.636 | 3.636 | 3.636 | 3.636 | 3.636 | 3.636 | 3.636 | 3.636 |
| 6 | 3.636 | 3.636 | 3.636 | 3.636 | 3.636 | 3.636 | 3.636 | 3.636 | 3.636 | 3.636 | 3.636 | 3.636 |
| 7 | 3.636 | 3.636 | 3.636 | 3.636 | 3.636 | 3.636 | 3.636 | 3.636 | 3.636 | 3.636 | 3.636 | 3.636 |
| 8 | 3.636 | 3.636 | 3.636 | 3.636 | 3.636 | 3.636 | 3.636 | 3.636 | 3.636 | 3.636 | 3.636 | 3.636 |
| 9 | 3.636 | 3.636 | 3.636 | 3.636 | 3.636 | 3.636 | 3.636 | 3.636 | 3.636 | 3.636 | 3.636 | 3.636 |
| 10 | 3.637 | 3.637 | 3.637 | 3.637 | 3.637 | 3.637 | 3.636 | 3.636 | 3.636 | 3.636 | 3.636 | 3.636 |
| 11 | 3.636 | 3.636 | 3.636 | 3.636 | 3.636 | 3.636 | 3.637 | 3.637 | 3.637 | 3.637 | 3.637 | 3.637 |
| 12 | 3.637 | 3.637 | 3.637 | 3.637 | 3.637 | 3.637 | 3.636 | 3.636 | 3.636 | 3.636 | 3.636 | 3.636 |
| 13 | 3.636 | 3.636 | 3.636 | 3.636 | 3.636 | 3.636 | 3.637 | 3.637 | 3.637 | 3.637 | 3.637 | 3.637 |
| 14 | 3.637 | 3.637 | 3.637 | 3.637 | 3.637 | 3.637 | 3.636 | 3.636 | 3.636 | 3.636 | 3.636 | 3.636 |
| 15 | 3.636 | 3.636 | 3.636 | 3.636 | 3.636 | 3.636 | 3.637 | 3.637 | 3.637 | 3.637 | 3.637 | 3.637 |
| 16 | 3.637 | 3.637 | 3.637 | 3.637 | 3.637 | 3.637 | 3.636 | 3.636 | 3.636 | 3.636 | 3.636 | 3.636 |
| 17 | 3.636 | 3.636 | 3.636 | 3.636 | 3.636 | 3.636 | 3.637 | 3.637 | 3.637 | 3.637 | 3.637 | 3.637 |
| 18 | 3.637 | 3.637 | 3.637 | 3.637 | 3.637 | 3.637 | 3.636 | 3.636 | 3.636 | 3.636 | 3.636 | 3.636 |
| 19 | 3.636 | 3.636 | 3.636 | 3.636 | 3.636 | 3.636 | 3.637 | 3.637 | 3.637 | 3.637 | 3.637 | 3.637 |
| 20 | 3.637 | 3.637 | 3.637 | 3.637 | 3.637 | 3.637 | 3.636 | 3.636 | 3.636 | 3.636 | 3.636 | 3.636 |
| 21 | 3.636 | 3.636 | 3.636 | 3.636 | 3.636 | 3.636 | 3.637 | 3.637 | 3.637 | 3.637 | 3.637 | 3.637 |
| 22 | 3.637 | 3.637 | 3.637 | 3.637 | 3.637 | 3.637 | 3.636 | 3.636 | 3.636 | 3.636 | 3.636 | 3.636 |
| 23 | 3.636 | 3.636 | 3.636 | 3.636 | 3.636 | 3.636 | 3.637 | 3.637 | 3.637 | 3.637 | 3.637 | 3.637 |
| 24 | 3.637 | 3.637 | 3.637 | 3.637 | 3.637 | 3.637 | 3.636 | 3.636 | 3.636 | 3.636 | 3.636 | 3.636 |
| 25 | 3.636 | 3.636 | 3.636 | 3.636 | 3.636 | 3.636 | 3.637 | 3.637 | 3.637 | 3.637 | 3.637 | 3.637 |
| 26 | 3.637 | 3.637 | 3.637 | 3.637 | 3.637 | 3.637 | 3.636 | 3.636 | 3.636 | 3.636 | 3.636 | 3.636 |
| 27 | 3.636 | 3.636 | 3.636 | 3.636 | 3.636 | 3.636 | 3.637 | 3.637 | 3.637 | 3.637 | 3.637 | 3.637 |
| 28 | 1.970 | 2.273 | 2.576 | 2.879 | 3.182 | 3.485 | 3.636 | 3.636 | 3.636 | 3.636 | 3.636 | 3.636 |
| 29 | 0.000 | 0.000 | 0.000 | 0.000 | 0.000 | 0.000 | 0.152 | 0.455 | 0.758 | 1.061 | 1.364 | 1.667 |

**TABLE 6A-7**    General Depreciation System: Straight-Line; Applicable Recovery Period: 31.5 Years; Mid-Month Convention

| | Month in the First Recovery Year the Property Is Placed in Service | | | | | | | | | | | |
|---|---|---|---|---|---|---|---|---|---|---|---|---|
| Recovery Year | 1 | 2 | 3 | 4 | 5 | 6 | 7 | 8 | 9 | 10 | 11 | 12 |
| 1 | 3.042 | 2.778 | 2.513 | 2.249 | 1.984 | 1.720 | 1.455 | 1.190 | 0.926 | 0.661 | 0.390 | 0.132 |
| 2 | 3.175 | 3.175 | 3.175 | 3.175 | 3.175 | 3.175 | 3.175 | 3.175 | 3.175 | 3.175 | 3.170 | 3.175 |
| 3 | 3.175 | 3.175 | 3.175 | 3.175 | 3.175 | 3.175 | 3.175 | 3.175 | 3.175 | 3.175 | 3.170 | 3.175 |
| 4 | 3.175 | 3.175 | 3.175 | 3.175 | 3.175 | 3.175 | 3.175 | 3.175 | 3.175 | 3.175 | 3.170 | 3.175 |
| 5 | 3.175 | 3.175 | 3.175 | 3.175 | 3.175 | 3.175 | 3.175 | 3.175 | 3.175 | 3.175 | 3.170 | 3.175 |
| 6 | 3.175 | 3.175 | 3.175 | 3.175 | 3.175 | 3.175 | 3.175 | 3.175 | 3.175 | 3.175 | 3.170 | 3.175 |
| 7 | 3.175 | 3.175 | 3.175 | 3.175 | 3.175 | 3.175 | 3.175 | 3.175 | 3.175 | 3.175 | 3.170 | 3.175 |
| 8 | 3.175 | 3.174 | 3.175 | 3.174 | 3.175 | 3.174 | 3.175 | 3.175 | 3.175 | 3.175 | 3.170 | 3.175 |
| 9 | 3.174 | 3.175 | 3.174 | 3.175 | 3.174 | 3.175 | 3.174 | 3.175 | 3.174 | 3.175 | 3.170 | 3.175 |
| 10 | 3.175 | 3.174 | 3.175 | 3.174 | 3.175 | 3.174 | 3.175 | 3.174 | 3.175 | 3.174 | 3.170 | 3.174 |
| 11 | 3.174 | 3.175 | 3.174 | 3.175 | 3.174 | 3.175 | 3.174 | 3.175 | 3.174 | 3.175 | 3.170 | 3.175 |
| 12 | 3.175 | 3.174 | 3.175 | 3.174 | 3.175 | 3.174 | 3.175 | 3.174 | 3.175 | 3.174 | 3.170 | 3.174 |
| 13 | 3.174 | 3.175 | 3.174 | 3.175 | 3.174 | 3.175 | 3.174 | 3.175 | 3.174 | 3.175 | 3.170 | 3.175 |
| 14 | 3.175 | 3.174 | 3.175 | 3.174 | 3.175 | 3.174 | 3.175 | 3.174 | 3.175 | 3.174 | 3.170 | 3.174 |
| 15 | 3.174 | 3.175 | 3.174 | 3.175 | 3.174 | 3.175 | 3.174 | 3.175 | 3.174 | 3.175 | 3.170 | 3.175 |
| 16 | 3.175 | 3.174 | 3.175 | 3.174 | 3.175 | 3.174 | 3.175 | 3.174 | 3.175 | 3.174 | 3.170 | 3.174 |
| 17 | 3.174 | 3.175 | 3.174 | 3.175 | 3.174 | 3.175 | 3.174 | 3.175 | 3.174 | 3.175 | 3.170 | 3.175 |
| 18 | 3.175 | 3.174 | 3.175 | 3.174 | 3.175 | 3.174 | 3.175 | 3.174 | 3.175 | 3.174 | 3.170 | 3.174 |
| 19 | 3.174 | 3.175 | 3.174 | 3.175 | 3.174 | 3.175 | 3.174 | 3.175 | 3.174 | 3.175 | 3.170 | 3.175 |
| 20 | 3.175 | 3.174 | 3.175 | 3.174 | 3.175 | 3.174 | 3.175 | 3.174 | 3.175 | 3.174 | 3.170 | 3.174 |
| 21 | 3.174 | 3.175 | 3.174 | 3.175 | 3.174 | 3.175 | 3.174 | 3.175 | 3.174 | 3.175 | 3.170 | 3.175 |
| 22 | 3.175 | 3.174 | 3.175 | 3.174 | 3.175 | 3.174 | 3.175 | 3.174 | 3.175 | 3.174 | 3.170 | 3.174 |
| 23 | 3.174 | 3.175 | 3.174 | 3.175 | 3.174 | 3.175 | 3.174 | 3.175 | 3.174 | 3.175 | 3.170 | 3.175 |
| 24 | 3.175 | 3.174 | 3.175 | 3.174 | 3.175 | 3.174 | 3.175 | 3.174 | 3.175 | 3.174 | 3.170 | 3.174 |
| 25 | 3.174 | 3.175 | 3.174 | 3.175 | 3.174 | 3.175 | 3.174 | 3.175 | 3.174 | 3.175 | 3.170 | 3.175 |
| 26 | 3.175 | 3.174 | 3.175 | 3.174 | 3.175 | 3.174 | 3.175 | 3.174 | 3.175 | 3.174 | 3.170 | 3.174 |
| 27 | 3.174 | 3.175 | 3.174 | 3.175 | 3.174 | 3.175 | 3.174 | 3.175 | 3.174 | 3.175 | 3.170 | 3.175 |
| 28 | 3.175 | 3.174 | 3.175 | 3.174 | 3.175 | 3.174 | 3.175 | 3.174 | 3.175 | 3.174 | 3.170 | 3.174 |
| 29 | 3.174 | 3.175 | 3.174 | 3.175 | 3.174 | 3.175 | 3.174 | 3.175 | 3.174 | 3.175 | 3.170 | 3.175 |
| 30 | 3.175 | 3.174 | 3.175 | 3.174 | 3.175 | 3.174 | 3.175 | 3.174 | 3.175 | 3.174 | 3.170 | 3.174 |
| 31 | 3.174 | 3.175 | 3.174 | 3.175 | 3.174 | 3.175 | 3.174 | 3.175 | 3.174 | 3.175 | 3.170 | 3.175 |
| 32 | 1.720 | 1.984 | 2.249 | 2.513 | 2.778 | 3.042 | 3.175 | 3.174 | 3.175 | 3.174 | 3.170 | 3.174 |
| 33 | 0.000 | 0.000 | 0.000 | 0.000 | 0.000 | 0.000 | 0.132 | 0.397 | 0.661 | 0.926 | 1.190 | 1.455 |

**TABLE 6A-8**    General Depreciation System: Straight-Line; Applicable Recovery Period: 39 Years; Mid-Month Convention

| | Month in the First Recovery Year the Property Is Placed in Service | | | | | | | | | | | |
|---|---|---|---|---|---|---|---|---|---|---|---|---|
| Recovery Year | 1 | 2 | 3 | 4 | 5 | 6 | 7 | 8 | 9 | 10 | 11 | 12 |
| 1 | 2.461 | 2.247 | 2.033 | 1.819 | 1.605 | 1.391 | 1.177 | .963 | .749 | .535 | .32 | .107 |
| 2–39 | 2.564 | 2.564 | 2.564 | 2.564 | 2.564 | 2.564 | 2.564 | 2.564 | 2.564 | 2.564 | 2.564 | 2.564 |
| 40 | 0.107 | 0.321 | 0.535 | 0.749 | 0.963 | 1.177 | 1.391 | 1.605 | 1.819 | 2.033 | 2.24 | 2.461 |

## EA Fast Fact

ADMITTED TO PRACTICE BEFORE THE IRS

**ENROLLED AGENT**

The Special Enrollment Exam, or EA Exam, is administered by the Department of the Treasury in conjunction with Prometric, a national provider of certification exams. The three-part exam tests knowledge of taxation in the areas of individuals (part 1), businesses (part 2) and representation, practice & procedures (part 3). When candidates believe they are ready to begin the exam process, they must register with Prometric and complete an application. Additional information on the testing process can be had by going to https://www.prometric.com/test-takers/search/irs.

### IMPORTANT

You are eligible to receive absolutely free, the Surgent Enrolled Agent review program for Part I of the EA exam as a result of purchasing this text. To activate your free access, go to https://Surgent.com/McGrawHill/EA.

## Discussion Questions   Mc Graw Hill connect

All applicable Discussion Questions are available with **Connect**©

**EA**  **LO 6-1**   1. Discuss the definition of *trade or business*. Why does it matter whether a taxpayer is classified as an employee or as self-employed?

**EA**  **LO 6-2**   2. Discuss the concepts of *ordinary, necessary,* and *reasonable* in relation to trade or business expenses.

**EA**  **LO 6-3**   3. On what form is depreciation reported, and how does it relate to other forms such as Schedules C, E, and F?

**EA**  **LO 6-3**   4. On what type of property is depreciation allowed?

**EA**  **LO 6-3**   5. Discuss the word *basis* in relation to the financial accounting term *book value*. What is meant by the term *adjusted basis?*

**EA**  **LO 6-3**   6. Discuss the difference between personal property and real property. Give examples of each.

**EA** LO 6-3    7. What is a *depreciation convention?* What conventions are available under MACRS?

_____

_____

_____

**EA** LO 6-3    8. When calculating depreciation for personal property (assuming the half-year convention) using the IRS depreciation tables, does the taxpayer need to multiply the first-year table depreciation percentage by one-half? What about in the year of disposal, assuming the property is disposed of prior to the end of its recovery period?

_____

_____

_____

**EA** LO 6-3    9. Discuss the concept of electing § 179 expense. Does the election allow a larger expense deduction in the year of asset acquisition?

_____

_____

_____

**EA** LO 6-3    10. Discuss the concept of *listed property.*

_____

_____

_____

**EA** LO 6-4    11. Distinguish between travel and transportation expenses.

_____

_____

_____

**EA** LO 6-4    12. When can a taxpayer use the standard mileage rate? Is the standard mileage rate better than the actual auto costs?

_____

_____

_____

**EA** LO 6-4    13. Discuss the limits on meals.

_____

_____

_____

**EA** LO 6-5    14. Discuss the limits on home office expense deductibility.

_____

_____

_____

**EA** LO 6-6    15. Why were the hobby loss rules established? What factors determine whether an activity is a trade or business or a hobby? Is any one factor controlling?

_____

_____

_____

**EA** LO 6-7    16. What are the two components of the self-employment tax? Is either component limited?

_____

_____

_____

## Multiple-Choice Questions

All applicable multiple-choice questions are available with **Connect**©

**EA** **LO 6-1** 17. Trade or business expenses are treated as

    *a.* A deduction *for* AGI.

    *b.* An itemized deduction if not reimbursed.

    *c.* A deduction *from* AGI.

    *d.* A deduction *from* AGI limited to the amount in excess of 2% of AGI.

**EA** **LO 6-1** 18. Which of the following is *not* a "trade or business" expense?

    *a.* Interest on investment indebtedness.

    *b.* Property taxes on business equipment.

    *c.* Depreciation on business property.

    *d.* Cost of goods sold.

**EA** **LO 6-1** 19. Atlas, a financial consultant, had the following income and expenses in his business:

| | |
|---|---:|
| Fee income | $235,000 |
| Expenses: | |
| Rent expense | 18,000 |
| Penalties assessed by the SEC | 2,500 |
| Office expenses | 6,000 |
| Supplies | 6,000 |
| Interest paid on note used to acquire office equipment | 2,700 |
| Speeding tickets going to see clients | 650 |

How much net income must Atlas report from this business?

    *a.* $199,150.

    *b.* $202,300.

    *c.* $202,950.

    *d.* $205,450.

**EA** **LO 6-2** 20. Mandy, a CPA, flew from Raleigh to Seattle to attend an accounting conference that lasted four days. Then she took three days of vacation to go sightseeing. Mandy's expenses for the trip are as follows:

| | |
|---|---:|
| Airfare | $ 625 |
| Lodging (7 days × $145) | 1,015 |
| Meals (7 days × $75) | 525 |
| Taxi from airport to hotel and back | 70 |

Mandy's travel expense deduction is

    *a.* $1,425.

    *b.* $1,575.

    *c.* $1,973.

    *d.* $2,235.

**EA** **LO 6-3** 21. On May 5, 2016, Jillian purchased equipment for $40,000 to be used in her business. She did not elect to expense the equipment under § 179 or bonus depreciation. On January 1, 2021, she sells the equipment to a scrap metal dealer. What is the cost recovery deduction for 2021?

    *a.* $892.

    *b.* $1,784.

    *c.* $3,568.

    *d.* No deduction allowed.

**EA**  LO 6-3   22. On April 15, 2019, Andy purchased some furniture and fixtures (seven-year property) for $10,000 to be used in his business. He did not elect to expense the equipment under § 179 or bonus depreciation. On June 30, 2021, he sells the equipment. What is the cost recovery deduction for 2021?

    *a.* $0.
    *b.* $875.
    *c.* $1,429.
    *d.* $1,749.

**EA**  LO 6-3   23. Lawrence purchased an apartment building on February 10, 2021, for $330,000, $30,000 of which was for the land. What is the cost recovery deduction for 2021?

    *a.* $0.
    *b.* $6,741.
    *c.* $9,546.
    *d.* $10,660.

**EA**  LO 6-3   24. Cosmo purchased an office building on March 30, 2018, for $250,000, $25,000 of which was for the land. On July 30, 2021, he sold the office building. What is the cost recovery deduction for 2021?

    *a.* $0.
    *b.* $3,125.
    *c.* $5,769.
    *d.* $6,410.

**EA**  LO 6-3   25. On June 30, 2021, Dion purchased an apartment building for $500,000. Determine the cost recovery deduction for 2021.

    *a.* $4,925.
    *b.* $5,335.
    *c.* $6,955.
    *d.* $9,850.

**EA**  LO 6-3   26. During the year, Cory purchased a log skidder (seven-year property) for $55,000 for his business. Assume that he has income from his business of $30,000, and he and his wife have combined salaries and wages income of $40,000. What is the maximum deduction he can take for his business in relation to the log skidder purchase?

    *a.* $7,860.
    *b.* $30,000.
    *c.* $31,429.
    *d.* $55,000.

**EA**  LO 6-3   27. Section 179 expense is available for all of the following business assets *except*

    *a.* Office building.
    *b.* Office furniture.
    *c.* Computer.
    *d.* Delivery truck.

**EA**  LO 6-4   28. Jordan has two jobs. She works as a night auditor at the Moonlight Motel. When her shift at the motel is over, she works as a short-order cook at the Greasy Spoon Restaurant. On a typical day, she drives the following number of miles:

| | |
|---|---|
| Home to Moonlight Motel | 4 |
| Moonlight Motel to Greasy Spoon Restaurant | 7 |
| Greasy Spoon Restaurant to home | 12 |

How many miles would qualify as transportation expenses for tax purposes?

*a.* 4.

*b.* 7.

*c.* 11.

*d.* 12.

**EA** **LO 6-4** 29. Jasmine purchased a $70,000 BMW in 2021 and used it 80% for business. What is her maximum cost recovery on the BMW in 2021.

*a.* $11,200.

*b.* $14,560.

*c.* $56,000.

*d.* $70,000.

**EA** **LO 6-4** 30. Frankie purchased a vehicle for business and personal use. In 2021, he used the vehicle 70% for business (11,000 business miles incurred equally throughout the year) and calculated his vehicle expenses using the standard mileage rate. Frank also paid $1,800 in interest and $480 in county property tax on the car. What is the total business deduction related to business use of the car?

*a.* $6,160.

*b.* $6,640.

*c.* $7,756.

*d.* $8,440.

**EA** **LO 6-1, 6-4** 31. Florian took a business trip from Dallas to Brazil. He was there for a total of seven days, of which two were weekend days. Over the weekend, he spent his time sightseeing and relaxing. His expenses were as follows:

| | |
|---|---|
| Airfare | $1,400 |
| Lodging (7 days × $300) | 2,100 |
| Meals (7 days) | 595 |
| Taxi fares ($600 to and from business meetings) | 800 |

How much is Florian allowed to deduct?

*a.* $3,500.

*b.* $4,300.

*c.* $4,895.

*d.* $4,598.

**EA** **LO 6-5** 32. Jake runs a business out of his home. He uses 600 square feet of his home exclusively for the business. His home is 2,400 square feet in total. Jake had $27,000 of business revenue and $22,000 of business expenses from his home-based business. The following expenses relate to his home:

| | |
|---|---|
| Mortgage interest | $10,800 |
| Real estate taxes | 1,600 |
| Utilities | 2,400 |
| Insurance | 600 |
| Repairs | 2,400 |
| Depreciation (on business-use portion of home) | 1,200 |

What is Jake's net income from his business? What amount of expenses is carried over to the following year, if any?

a. ($14,000) and $0 carryover.

b. ($650) and $0 carryover.

c. $0 and $650 carryover.

d. $550 and $0 carryover.

**EA**   **LO 6-6**   33. Which of the following is *not* a relevant factor to be considered in deciding whether an activity is profit seeking or a hobby?

a. Manner in which the taxpayer carries on the activity.

b. Expertise of the taxpayer or his or her advisers.

c. Time and effort expended by the taxpayer in carrying on the activity.

d. All of the above are relevant factors.

**EA**   **LO 6-6**   34. Which of the following individuals can deduct education expenses?

a. A real estate broker who attends college to get an accounting degree.

b. A CPA who attends a review course to obtain a contractor's license.

c. A corporate executive attending an executive MBA program.

d. An accounting bookkeeper taking a CPA review course to pass the CPA exam and become a CPA.

**EA**   **LO 6-7**   35. Annie is self-employed and has $58,000 in income from her business. She also has investments that generated dividends of $3,000 and interest of $2,500. What is Annie's self-employment tax for the year?

a. $8,195.

b. $8,619.

c. $8,874.

d. $8,972.

**EA**   **LO 6-7**   36. The maximum tax bases and percentages for 2021 for the two portions of the self-employment tax are which of the following?

| Social Security | Medicare |
| --- | --- |
| a. $142,800; 12.4% | Unlimited; 2.9%. |
| b. $142,800; 12.4% | Unlimited; 15.3%. |
| c. $137,700; 12.4% | Unlimited; 2.9%. |
| d. $137,700; 15.3% | Unlimited; 15.3%. |

## Problems  Mc Graw Hill  connect

All applicable problems are available with *Connect*

**EA**   **LO 6-1**   37. Kelly is a self-employed tax attorney whose practice primarily involves tax planning. During the year, she attended a three-day seminar regarding new changes to the tax law. She incurred the following expenses:

| | |
| --- | --- |
| Lodging | $400 |
| Meals | 95 |
| Course registration | 350 |
| Transportation | 150 |

a. How much can Kelly deduct? _____

b. Kelly believes that obtaining a CPA license would improve her skills as a tax attorney. She enrolls as a part-time student at a local college to take CPA review courses. During the current year, she spends $1,500 for tuition and $300 for books. How much of these expenses can Kelly deduct? Why?

_____

_____

_____

**LO 6-1, 6-2, 6-4**

**EA**

38. Jackie owns a temporary employment agency that hires personnel to perform accounting services for clients. During the year, her expenses for her clients include the following:

| | |
|---|---:|
| Cab fare to and from restaurants | $ 350 |
| Gratuity at restaurants | 300 |
| Meals | 4,000 |
| Cover charges | 250 |

All expenses are reasonable.

*a.* Can Jackie deduct any of these expenses? If so, how much? _____

*b.* How is the deduction classified? _____

**EA** **LO 6-5**

39. David is a college professor who does some consulting work on the side. He uses 25% of his home exclusively for the consulting practice. He is single and 63 years old. His AGI (without consideration of consulting income) is $45,000. Other information follows:

| | |
|---|---:|
| Income from consulting business | $4,000 |
| Consulting expenses other than home office | 1,500 |
| Total costs relating to home: | |
| Interest and taxes | 6,500 |
| Utilities | 1,500 |
| Maintenance and repairs | 450 |
| Depreciation (business part only) | 1,500 |

Calculate David's AGI. _____

**EA** **LO 6-5**

40. In 2019, Gerald loaned Main Street Bakery $55,000 with whom he had a business relationship. In 2020, he learned that he would probably receive only $6,400 of the loan. In 2021, Gerald received $3,000 in final settlement of the loan. Calculate Gerald's possible deductions with respect to the loan for 2019, 2020, and 2021.

2019: _____

2020: _____

2021: _____

**EA** **LO 6-1, 6-2**

41. Charles, a self-employed real estate agent, attended a conference on the impact of some new building codes on real estate investments. His unreimbursed expenses were as follows:

| | |
|---|---:|
| Airfare | $480 |
| Lodging | 290 |
| Meals | 100 |
| Tuition and fees | 650 |

How much can Charles deduct on his return? _____

**EA**   **LO 6-3**   42. Lars acquired a new network system on June 5, 2021 (five-year class property), for $75,000. She expects taxable income from the business will always be about $175,000 without regard to the § 179 election. Lars will elect § 179 expensing. She also acquired seven-year property in July 2021 for $350,000. Determine Lars's maximum cost recovery deduction with respect to her purchases in 2021: _____

**EA**   **LO 6-3**   43. Janet purchased her personal residence in 2011 for $250,000. In January 2021, she converted it to rental property. The fair market value at the time of conversion was $210,000.

   *a.* Determine the amount of cost recovery that can be taken in 2021: _____

   *b.* Determine the amount of cost recovery that could be taken in 2021 if the fair market value of the property were $350,000: _____

**EA**   **LO 6-3**   44. On February 4, 2021, Jackie purchased and placed in service a car she purchased for $21,500. The car was used exclusively for her business. Compute Jackie's cost recovery deduction in 2021 assuming no § 179 expense but the bonus was taken: _____

**EA**   **LO 6-3**   45. Rueben acquires a warehouse on September 1, 2021, for $3 million. On March 1, 2025, he sells the warehouse. Determine Rueben's cost recovery for 2021–2025:

   _____

**EA**   **LO 6-3**   46. Michael is the sole proprietor of a small business. In June 2021, his business income is $12,000 before consideration of any §179 deduction. He spends $245,000 on furniture and equipment in 2021. If Michael elects to take the §179 deduction and no bonus on a conference table that cost $25,000 (included in the $245,000 total), determine the maximum cost recovery for 2021 with respect to the conference table: _____

**EA**   **LO 6-3**   47. On June 10, 2021, Huron purchased equipment (seven-year class property) for $75,000. Determine Huron's cost recovery deduction for computing 2021 taxable income. Assume that Huron does not make the § 179 and bonus elections. _____

**EA**   **LO 6-3**   48. Brittany purchased a building for $500,000 on January 1, 2013. The purchase price does not include land. Calculate the cost recovery for 2013 and 2021 if the real property is

   *a.* Residential real property: _____

   *b.* A warehouse: _____

**EA**   **LO 6-3**   49. Walt purchased electronic equipment (five-year property) for $5,000. He could use the electronic equipment exclusively for his business, or he could allow his family to use the electronic equipment 60% of the time and 40% would be for business use. Determine the tax deduction for the year of acquisition under both alternatives. What is the overall tax savings between the two alternatives? Assume that Walt would not elect § 179 expensing or bonus and that he is in the 24% tax bracket.

   _____

**EA**   **LO 6-3, 6-4**   50. In 2019, Jessica bought a new heavy truck for $45,000 to use 80% for her sole proprietorship. Total miles driven include 12,000 in 2019, 14,500 in 2020, and 13,000 in 2021.

   *a.* If Jessica uses the standard mileage method, how much may she deduct on her 2021 tax return (miles were incurred ratably throughout the year)? _____

   *b.* What is the deduction for 2021 assuming the actual method was used from the beginning? Calculate depreciation only; the truck is not limited by the luxury auto rules. Also assume § 179 was not elected in the year of purchase. _____

**EA** **LO 6-3, 6-4** 51. Jose purchased a vehicle for business and personal use. In 2021, he used the vehicle 18,000 miles (80% of total) for business and calculated his vehicle expenses using the standard mileage rate (mileage was incurred ratably throughout the year). He paid $1,400 in interest and $150 in property taxes on the car. Calculate the total business deduction related to the car:

_____

**EA** **LO 6-4** 52. Jordan took a business trip from New York to Denver. She spent two days in travel, conducted business for nine days, and visited friends for five days. She incurred the following expenses:

| | |
|---|---|
| Airfare | $ 550 |
| Lodging | 3,000 |
| Meals | 900 |
| Entertainment of clients | 750 |

How much of these expenses can Jordan deduct?

_____

**EA** **LO 6-5** 53. Derrick owns a farm in eastern North Carolina. A hurricane hit the area (a national disaster area was declared) and destroyed a farm building and some farm equipment and damaged a barn.

| Item | Adjusted Basis | FMV before Damage | FMV after Damage | Insurance Proceeds |
|---|---|---|---|---|
| Building | $85,000 | $115,000 | $ –0– | $55,000 |
| Equipment | 68,000 | 49,000 | –0– | 15,000 |
| Barn | 95,000 | 145,000 | 95,000 | 35,000 |

Due to the extensive damage throughout the area, the president of the United States declared all areas affected by the hurricane as a disaster area. Derrick, who files a joint return with his wife, had $45,000 of taxable income last year. Their taxable income for the current year is $150,000, excluding the loss from the hurricane. Calculate the amount of the loss deductible by Derrick and his wife and the years in which they should deduct the loss. (*Hint:* Chapter 5 provides information concerning nationally declared disaster areas.)

_____

_____

_____

**EA** **LO 6-6** 54. Rebecca is a doctor with an AGI of $125,000 before consideration of income or loss from her dog breeding business. Her home is on 15 acres, 10 of which she uses to house the animals and provide them with ample space to play and exercise. Her records show the following related income and expenses for the current year:

| | |
|---|---|
| Income from fees and sales | $2,500 |
| Expenses: | |
| Dog food | $4,000 |
| Veterinary bills | 3,500 |
| Supplies | 1,200 |
| Publications and dues | 350 |

*a.* How must Rebecca treat the income and expenses of the operation if the dog breeding business is held to be a hobby? _____

_____

*b.* How would your answer differ if the operation were held to be a business?

_____

**LO 6-6**    55. Eric, who is single, has income from his Schedule C of $150,000 net of deductible self-employment taxes. His taxable income is $120,000 after his other deductions. What is Eric's QBI deduction for 2021?

**EA**    **LO 6-7**    56. In 2021, Landon has self-employment earnings of $195,000. Compute Landon's self-employment tax liability and the allowable income tax deduction of the self-employment tax paid. SE tax: _____ SE deduction: _____

**EA**    **LO 6-3**    57. (Comprehensive) Casper used the following assets in his Schedule C trade or business in the tax year 2021.

| Asset | Date Purchased | Date Sold | Business Use (percentage) | Cost |
|---|---|---|---|---|
| Computer 1 | 03/12/18 | | 100% | $  3,000 |
| Computer 2 | 05/05/18 | 05/15/21 | 100 | 2,500 |
| Printer | 08/25/21 | | 100 | 2,200 |
| Computer 3 | 05/25/21 | | 100 | 2,800 |
| Equipment | 03/20/19 | | 100 | 2,700 |
| Auto | 05/01/21 | | 90 | 20,000 |
| Furniture 1 | 02/12/19 | 08/25/21 | 100 | 22,000 |
| Furniture 2 | 08/15/19 | | 100 | 3,600 |
| Office building | 04/01/21 | | 100 | 330,000 |

Casper is a new client and unfortunately does not have a copy of his prior year's tax return. He recalls that all of the assets purchased in prior years used MACRS depreciation (no § 179 expense or bonus). Casper does not wish to take a § 179. Calculate the current-year depreciation allowance for Casper's business. Correctly report the amounts on Form 4562.

**Tax Return Problems**    Mc Graw Hill **connect**

All applicable tax return problems are available with **Connect**©

Use your tax software to complete the following problems. If you are manually preparing the tax returns, the problems indicate the forms or schedules you will need.

For the following tax return problems, assume the taxpayer does NOT wish to contribute to the Presidential Election Fund, unless otherwise stated in the problem. In addition, the taxpayers did not receive, sell, send, exchange, or otherwise acquire any financial interest in any virtual currency during the year. For any Tax Return Problems for which the taxpayers are entitled to a child tax credit, assume that the taxpayers did NOT receive any advance child tax credit payments during 2021. Thus, the entire child tax credit (if permitted) will be claimed on the 2021 tax return.

**Tax Return Problem 1**    Cassi (SSN 412-34-5670) has a home cleaning business she runs as a sole proprietorship. The following are the results from business operations for the tax year 2021:

| | |
|---|---|
| Gross receipts | $203,000 |
| Business mileage: 27,000 (miles incurred ratably throughout the year) | |
| 35,000 miles total during the year 2021 | |
| Van (over 6,000 lb) placed in service 1/01/2021, cost 27,000 | |
| Postage | (500) |
| Wages | (26,000) |
| Payroll taxes | (1,950) |
| Supplies | (12,500) |

| | |
|---|---:|
| Phone | (1,250) |
| Internet service | (600) |
| Rent | (2,400) |
| Insurance | (2,800) |
| Van expenses | (4,500) |

| Business assets | Date Purchased | Cost |
|---|---|---:|
| Computer 1 | 5/18/21 | $2,200 |
| Computer 2 | 6/01/21 | 2,700 |
| Printer | 3/01/20 | 900 |
| Copier | 3/02/20 | 2,100 |
| Furniture | 3/01/20 | 6,000 |

Determine Cassi's self-employment income and QBI deduction. Cassi does not elect to defer her self-employment tax under the Cares Act. Prepare Schedule C and Schedule SE. Section 179 expense is elected on all eligible assets (§ 179 was not taken on assets purchased last year). Cassi had qualifying health care coverage at all times during the tax year.

**Tax Return Problem 2**   During 2021, Cassandra Albright, who is single, worked part-time at a doctor's office and received a W-2. She also had a consulting practice that had the following income and expenses:

| | |
|---|---:|
| Revenue | $53,000 |
| Laptop computer purchased 4/23/21 (§ 179 elected) | 3,300 |
| Travel: 2,500 miles for business, 13,000 personal | |
| Supplies | 500 |
| Cell phone charge | 960 |

Cassandra (SSN 412-34-5670) resides at 1400 Medical Street, Apt. 3A, Lowland, CA 92273. Her W-2 shows the following:

| | |
|---|---:|
| Wages | $49,000 |
| Federal withholding | 5,200 |
| Social security wages | 49,000 |
| Social security withholding | 3,038 |
| Medicare withholding | 711 |
| State withholding | 2,265 |
| Other income: | |
| 1099-INT Old Bank | 2,200 |
| 1099-DIV Bake Co., Inc.—Ordinary dividends | 3,500 |
| Qualified dividends | 3,500 |

Cassandra had the following itemized deductions:

| | |
|---|---:|
| State income tax withholding | $ 2,265 |
| State income tax paid with the 2020 return | 350 |
| Real estate tax | 3,450 |
| Mortgage interest | 12,300 |

Cassandra made two federal estimated payments of $6,500 each on April 15 and June 15. Prepare Form 1040 for Cassandra for 2021. You will need Form 1040, Schedule A, Schedule B, Schedule C, Form 4562, and Schedule SE. Cassandra does not elect to defer her self-employment tax under the Cares Act. Cassandra had qualifying health care coverage at all times during the tax year.

**Tax Return Problem 3**

During 2021, Jason and Vicki Hurting, who are married with two children, had the following tax information. Jason owns a landscaping business, and Vicki works as a sales executive for a manufacturing business.

Jason (SSN 412-34-5670) and Vicki (SSN 412-34-5671) reside at 123 Bate Street, Bright, AL 36116. Both children are under the age of 17:

Jason Jr. (412-34-5672), date of birth 7/20/13
Catlin (412-34-5673), date of birth 1/08/17
Vicki's W-2 information is as follows:

| | |
|---|---|
| Wages | $94,000 |
| Federal withholding | 22,000 |
| Social security wages | 94,000 |
| Social security withholding | 5,828 |
| Medicare withholding | 1,363 |
| State withholding | 4,700 |

Other income:

| | |
|---|---|
| 1099-G Alabama state tax refund is taxable because $4,900 was deducted on last year's return | $423 |
| 1099-INT First Bank of Alabama | 225 |
| 1099-DIV IBM, Inc.—Ordinary dividends | 125 |
| Qualified dividends | 125 |

The following information is for Jason's landscaping business:

| | |
|---|---|
| Revenue | $153,000 |
| Wages | 41,600 |
| Payroll tax | 3,182 |
| Cell phone charge | 425 |
| Assets (§ 179 elected) | |

| Item | Date Purchased | Business Use Amount | Percentage |
|---|---|---|---|
| Truck (100% business) | 2/05/2021 | $28,000 | 100% |
| Mower 1 | 3/08/2021 | 12,000 | 100 |
| Mower 2 | 3/08/2021 | 3,400 | 100 |
| Equipment | 6/25/2021 | 1,595 | 100 |

The truck was over 6,000 lb. The Hurtings had the following itemized deductions:

| | |
|---|---|
| State income tax withholding (from above) | $4,700 |
| Real estate tax | 2,100 |
| Personal property tax | 425 |
| Mortgage interest | 8,300 |
| Charitable contributions | 2,400 |

The Hurtings made four federal estimated payments of $2,500 each on their due dates. Prepare Form 1040 plus appropriate schedules for the Hurtings for 2021. The Hurtings do not elect to defer their self-employment tax under the Cares Act. The Hurtings had qualifying health care coverage at all times during the tax year.

We have provided selected filled-in source documents that are available in the *Connect Library*.

# Chapter **Seven**

# Capital Gains and Other Sales of Property (Schedule D and Form 4797)

Gains and losses from the sale of assets are included in taxable income. The gain or loss can appear on a tax return in different locations, depending on the type of asset sold. Before determining the tax implications of asset sales, the property must be classified as a personal-use asset, a trade or business asset, or an investment asset. Also, the length of time the taxpayer owned the property and whether the asset is subject to depreciation must be determined. Each of these items affects the taxability of asset sales. This chapter focuses on the tax treatment of asset sales with particular attention on the determination of capital gain versus ordinary gain treatment. At present, gains from the sale of capital assets receive preferential tax treatment (lower rate of tax). Thus, the chapter emphasizes the proper classification and reporting of capital gain properties. IRS Publication 544 (Sales and Other Dispositions of Assets), Publication 550 (Investment Income and Expenses), and Publication 551 (Basis of Assets) can be helpful as you study this chapter.

## Learning Objectives

When you have completed this chapter, you should understand the following learning objectives (LO):

LO 7-1  Define the terms and identify the tax forms used in sales of property transactions.

LO 7-2  Classify assets sold as ordinary assets, § 1221 capital assets, or § 1231 business assets.

LO 7-3  Explain and apply the tax rules for recognizing gains or losses on the sale of ordinary assets.

LO 7-4  Explain and apply the tax rules for recognizing short-term and long-term gains or losses on the sale of capital assets (§ 1221).

LO 7-5  Calculate the recognized gain or loss on the sale of § 1231 business assets, including gain recapture provisions of § 1245 and § 1250 property.

LO 7-6  Describe the tax rules for special types of sales, including block stock sales, capital gain distributions, sales of mutual funds, worthless securities, and sales of property received as a gift or through inheritance.

# INTRODUCTION

*Gross income* includes gains derived from dealings in property.[1] The tax code also allows the deductibility of losses on the sale of property in certain situations.[2] The purpose of this chapter is to discuss the taxability and reporting of gains and losses from the sale of various asset types. Depending on the classification of the assets sold, gains on the sale are subject to different tax rates; however, losses on the sales of assets may be limited, may be deducted in full, or may not be deductible. Form 4797 and Schedule D are the forms used to record all gains and losses from sales of property. Form 8949—Sales and Other Dispositions of Capital Assets is completed first and the subtotals are then recorded on Schedule D, Part I and Part II.

# TERMS AND TAX FORMS
## LO 7-1

Before any gain or loss on the sale or transfer of property can be calculated, the asset's basis first must be determined. In general, the *basis* of property purchased is the cost of the asset, including cash, debt obligations, and other property or services involved in acquiring the asset. For example, if you buy stocks, the basis is the purchase price plus commission and transfer fees. If you buy a copier, additional costs could include sales tax, freight, and installation. The cost basis is adjusted for certain items such as improvements to the property, which increase basis, and depreciation deductions, which decrease basis. The result of these adjustments to the property is termed the *adjusted basis.* Using the copier as an example, assume it was purchased for use in a business at an initial cost of $10,000. Freight and installation costs added $500. The adjusted basis of the copier is $10,500. Assume depreciation allowed was $4,200; the adjusted basis of the copier is now $6,300 ($10,000 + $500 − $4,200). The concept of adjusted basis is important because this basis will be used to determine the amount of the gain or loss on the sale or disposition of the property. The lower the adjusted basis, the greater the potential gain will be when the property is sold. How these gains are taxed is explained in detail later in the chapter. Sometimes basis is other than the cost of the asset. For example, if the taxpayer receives investment property in exchange for services rendered, the basis is the fair market value (FMV) of the property. If the value of the services was known beforehand, then the asset's basis would be based on the price of the services.

The basis of assets transferred by inheritance is generally valued at the FMV of the property at the date of the individual's death or the FMV on the alternate valuation date if the personal representative for the estate chooses and qualifies to use this date. If no federal estate tax return is filed, the appraised value on the date of death for state inheritance taxes is used.[3] The basis of property transferred to a taxpayer from a spouse or former spouse incident to a divorce settlement is the same as the spouse's or former spouse's adjusted basis before the transfer.[4] The transfer must occur within one year after the date on which the marriage ends if the transfer is related to the ending of the marriage.

The rules for assets transferred by gift depend on whether the FMV is less than, equal to, or more than the donor's adjusted basis. If the FMV of the property at the time of the gift is less than the donor's adjusted basis before the gift, the donee's basis for a gain on the sale or other disposition is the donor's adjusted basis. The basis for a loss is the FMV of the property at the time the gift was given. If the FMV is equal to or greater than the donor's adjusted basis just before the gift, the donee's basis for calculating a gain or loss is the donor's adjusted basis. (Refer to the special sales section at the end of the chapter for an example.) Table 7-1 outlines some specific definitions of basis used in this chapter.[5]

---

[1] IRC § 61(a)(3).

[2] IRC § 165.

[3] Additional rules for valuation of assets transferred by inheritance are beyond the scope of this discussion. For specific rules, refer to Publication 559, *Survivors, Executors, and Administrators.*

[4] Refer to Publication 504, *Divorced or Separated Individuals.*

[5] Publication 551, *Basis of Assets.*

**TABLE 7-1** Definitions

| | |
|---|---|
| **Basis** | The amount of investment in property for tax purposes. *Basis* is the starting point in determining gain or loss on the sale or disposition of investment property. |
| **Cost Basis** | The cost of the property bought in cash, debt obligations, other property, or services. |
| **Other Cost Basis** | Property acquired other than through a purchase:<br>• Gift<br>• Inheritance<br>• Divorce<br>• Exchanges |
| **Adjusted Basis** | Increases and/or decreases to the original cost basis of an asset.<br><br>• Examples of increases: a room addition to a home, replacing an entire roof, the cost of defending and perfecting a title to property or a patent, commission fees for purchasing stock, and stock dividends received through dividend reinvestment plans.<br>• Examples of decreases: § 179 deductions, deductions previously allowed such as depreciation or amortization, nontaxable stock dividends or stock splits, or postponed gain from the sale of a home (discussed in Chapter 12). |
| **Fair Market Value** | The price at which the property would change hands between a buyer and a seller, neither being forced to buy or sell and both having reasonable knowledge of all the relevant facts. Sales of similar property, around the same date, are typically used in figuring fair market value. |

Also important terms to know are *amount realized* and *amount recognized*. The *amount realized* from a sale or trade of property is everything the taxpayer receives in the transaction. This is also termed the *proceeds from the sale*. This includes cash received plus the FMV of any property or services received plus the amount of any debt assumed by the purchaser. If a taxpayer trades property and cash for other property, the amount realized is the FMV of the asset that the taxpayer is receiving. The difference between the amount realized and the adjusted basis determines whether there is a gain or loss on the sale. The following chart summarizes this process:

| | |
|---|---|
| Amount realized < Adjusted basis | Loss |
| Amount realized > Adjusted basis | Gain |

The last term to discuss is the amount of gain or loss that will be recognized for tax purposes. The *amount recognized* from a sale or trade of property is the amount that will be recorded on the tax return as a gain or loss. Gains and losses can be realized and recognized, or they can be realized and not recognized, such as in a nontaxable exchange, or a loss on the disposition of property that is held for personal use, or a gain that is excluded as with the sale of a residence (see Chapter 12).

For example, if the adjusted basis of the property sold is $8,000 and the amount realized is $10,000, there is a gain of $2,000. This $2,000 gain is recognized for tax purposes because it is not from a nontaxable exchange. If the adjusted basis of the property sold is $8,000 and the amount realized is $7,000, there is a loss of $1,000. If the loss is from the disposition of personal-use property, the $1,000 is not recognized for tax purposes. If the loss is *not* from the disposition of personal-use property, it is recognized as a loss for tax purposes.

It is possible that, when a sale occurs, the sales proceeds (amount the seller realizes) include not only cash but also the FMV of other property received as well as any assumption of liabilities by the buyer, as illustrated in Examples 7-1 and 7-2.[6]

**EXAMPLE 7-1**

Indra sold a parcel of land for $55,000 cash. The buyer also assumed a $15,000 note attached to the land. Indra originally purchased the land for $34,000, so Indra reports a gain on the land of $36,000 ($55,000 cash + $15,000 release of liability less the $34,000 basis).

---

[6] Reg. § 1.1001-2(a)(1).

**EXAMPLE 7-2**

Larry needed cash and sold a parcel of land for $55,000. The buyer also assumed a $15,000 note attached to the land. Larry originally purchased the land for $72,000, so Larry reports a loss on the land of $2,000 ($55,000 cash + $15,000 release of liability less the $72,000 basis).

The nature of the tax reporting for gains and losses on the sale of property depends primarily on the use of the asset rather than on its form. After the appropriate asset use has been determined, the taxpayer will possibly record the taxable event on different tax forms. Examples 7-1 and 7-2 involved the sale of land. If the land were used in a trade or business, the gain or loss would be reported on Form 4797. If the land were an investment held in a trade or business, the gain or loss would be reported on Schedule D. Exhibit 7-1 is a sample of Form 4797 and Exhibit 7-2 is a sample of Schedule D including Form 8949. These exhibits can be found on pages 7-8 and 7-14.

**CONCEPT CHECK 7-1— LO 7-1**

1. A gain or loss on a sale is the difference between the cash received and the original cost of the asset. True or false?
2. The gain or loss on the sale of an asset used for investment or in a trade or business appears on Form 4797. True or false?
3. When the buyer assumes the seller's liability, the seller includes this amount in computing the amount realized from the sale. True or false?

# CLASSIFICATION OF ASSETS
## LO 7-2

All assets can be classified into one of three categories. The classification of the asset determines how gains and losses on the sale are reported for tax purposes. The three asset categories follow:

1. Ordinary income property.
2. § 1221 property (capital assets).
3. § 1231 trade or business property.

The following sections discuss the rules associated with classifying assets into each of the categories. (Refer to Table 7-2 for a summary of asset classifications.)

### Ordinary Income Property

The tax code does not directly define *ordinary income property* except to state that it is any asset that is "not a capital asset." The two most common ordinary assets are

**TABLE 7-2**
**Asset Classification Summary**

| Ordinary Income Asset | § 1221—Capital Asset | § 1231—Trade or Business |
|---|---|---|
| Short-term asset used in a trade or business | Any asset held for investment | Long-term depreciable trade or business property |
| Inventory | Personal-use property | Long-term land used in the trade or business |
| Accounts receivable | Not inventory | Not short-term trade or business property |
| Notes receivable | Not depreciable trade or business property | Not inventory |
|  | Not a copyright* | Not a copyright |
|  | Not accounts receivable |  |
|  | Not notes receivable |  |

* Refer to new election provision for musical compositions and copyrights in musical works.

inventory and accounts or notes receivable, defined in Chapter 2 of IRS Publication 544 as follows:

- Inventory: property held mainly for sale to customers or property that will physically become part of merchandise for sale to customers.
- Receivables: accounts or notes receivable acquired in the ordinary course of business or from the sale of any inventory properties.

Typically, the sale of inventory appears on the income statement of a business as a cost of goods sold. Gross profit (sales − cost of goods sold) is ordinary income subject to tax and is entered on Schedule C for a sole proprietorship.[7] The collection of an account or note receivable is ordinary income to a cash basis taxpayer when the cash is collected. Neither selling inventory nor collecting accounts or notes receivable requires reporting on Form 4797 or Schedule D. Other assets such as copyrights and literary, musical, and artistic compositions are also ordinary assets in the hands of the creator or artist.

### § 1221 Capital Property (Capital Assets)

In general, a *capital asset* is any asset used for personal purposes or investment.[8] A common example of a capital asset is an investment in stocks or bonds. Other capital assets include

- A home owned and occupied by the taxpayer and the taxpayer's family.
- Timber grown on home property or investment property, even if the taxpayer makes only casual sales of the timber.
- Household furnishings.
- A car used for pleasure or commuting.
- Coin or stamp collections, gems, and jewelry.
- Gold, silver, and other metals.[9]

The Internal Revenue Code (IRC) actually defines a capital asset not by what it *is* but by what it is *not*. Capital assets include all assets held by the taxpayer *except*[10]

1. Those held mainly for sale to customers, including stock in trade, inventory, and other property held mainly for sale to customers in a trade or business.
2. Property used in a trade or business subject to depreciation.
3. A copyright; a literary, musical, or artistic composition; a letter or memorandum; or similar property held by a taxpayer whose personal efforts created the property or, in the case of a letter or memo, for which the letter was prepared.
4. Accounts or notes receivable acquired in the ordinary course of business.
5. Real property used in the taxpayer's trade or business.
6. Any commodities derivative financial instrument held by a dealer.
7. Certain hedging transactions entered in the normal course of a trade or business.
8. Supplies used or consumed by the taxpayer in the ordinary course of a trade or business of the taxpayer.

**TAX YOUR BRAIN**

Is land a capital asset?

**ANSWER**

The answer is the typical tax answer—it depends. Land held for investment is a capital asset. However, land used in a trade or business is not a capital asset but a § 1231 asset (discussed in the next section). Additionally, land held for resale by a real estate developer is inventory (an ordinary asset).

---

[7] The sale, related cost of goods sold, and gross profit are reported directly on Schedule C.

[8] IRS Publication 544, *Sales and Other Dispositions of Assets,* Chapter 2.

[9] IRS Publication 544, p. 20.

[10] IRC § 1221.

Musical compositions and copyrights in musical works are generally not capital assets. However, there is an election available to treat these types of property as capital assets if they are sold or exchanged in the years beginning after May 17, 2006, and

- The taxpayer's personal efforts created the property or
- The taxpayer under certain circumstances (such as by gift) is entitled to the basis of the person who created the property or for whom it was prepared or produced.

By definition, artistic works are specifically not capital assets of the taxpayer who created the property (the artist), but any artistic work purchased is a capital asset in the hands of the purchaser. In all instances of artistic works, copyrights, letters, or publications of the U.S. government, if the taxpayer's basis is determined by reference to the basis of the property in the hands of the creator of the property (such as by gift from the creator), then the property is not a capital asset.[11]

| | |
|---|---|
| **EXAMPLE 7-3** | Jacque, a world-renowned artist, painted a lovely new work. Jacque then gave the painting to a close friend as a gift. Because the property is a gift, the friend's basis is the same as the basis to Jacque. Consequently, the painting is not a capital asset to the friend and would be treated as ordinary income property. |

## Trade or Business Property (§ 1231 Asset)

*IRC § 1231 property* is depreciable or nondepreciable property (such as land) used in a trade or business and held for more than one year.[12] Land purchased and held for investment (even if purchased through the business) is a capital asset under § 1221.

Timber, coal, domestic iron ore, and certain livestock held for breeding, dairy, or sporting purposes are also considered § 1231 property.[13] The most typical examples of § 1231 assets are machinery and equipment used in a business, business buildings, and business land. If a business asset is disposed of within one year of acquisition, it is treated as a short-term asset, and the amount received for it is considered ordinary income. Furthermore, § 1231 assets do not include property that is considered inventory or artistic works.

| | |
|---|---|
| **EXAMPLE 7-4** | Vlad, a sole proprietor, purchased a three-acre lot for $55,000. Vlad constructed a building for the business on a portion of the land and used the rest of the land for customer parking. The land, building, and pavement for the parking lot are considered § 1231 property. |

| | |
|---|---|
| **CONCEPT CHECK 7-2—** <br> **LO 7-2** <br>  | 1. Inventory sold by a company is an ordinary income asset that appears on Form 4797—Sale of Business Assets. True or false? <br> 2. A capital asset includes all of the following *except* <br>    *a.* A taxpayer's vacation home. <br>    *b.* Inherited property. <br>    *c.* Property used in a trade or business. <br>    *d.* A stock portfolio. <br> 3. An ordinary income asset is any short-term or long-term asset used in a business. True or false? <br> 4. A § 1221 asset is any asset held for investment. True or false? <br> 5. A § 1231 asset is any depreciable or nondepreciable property used in a trade or business and not considered an ordinary income asset. True or false? |

[11] IRC § 1221(a)(3)(A), (5)(B). When property is received by gift, the new basis is determined by the basis (old basis) to the person giving the gift (donor).
[12] IRC § 1231(b)(1).
[13] IRC § 1231(b)(3).

# From Shoebox to Software

To report ordinary income or loss from the sale of an ordinary asset, use Form 4797, Part II. The description of the property sold, the date acquired, the date sold, the gross sales price, the depreciation allowed, the cost basis, and the gain or loss are shown on Form 4797. Exhibit 7-1 illustrates the reporting of Examples 7-5 and 7-6. Note that the gains are combined (netted if a loss had occurred) on line 18. If any ordinary gains or losses had resulted from the sale of § 1231 property (discussed later), they would also be included in the final figure on line 18. For an individual taxpayer, the $15,140 ordinary income is reported on line 4 of Schedule 1.

**TAX PREPARATION SOFTWARE**

The sale of a receivable is a unique transaction (it does not happen often in practice). To enter this type of sale in tax preparation software, enter the information directly on Part II of Form 4797. For an asset that has already been entered on Form 4562, Asset Depreciation worksheet (see Chapter 6), simply go to the Asset Depreciation worksheet and enter the date sold. Then click the Asset Disposed Of link and enter the sales price. The depreciation should recalculate, and the gain or loss will appear in the appropriate section of Form 4797.[14]

# SALES OF ORDINARY ASSETS

## LO 7-3

When an asset is sold (or otherwise disposed of), the gain or loss produced is considered either "ordinary" or "capital." For example, when an ordinary asset is sold, the gain or loss is termed "an ordinary gain or loss." When a capital asset (§ 1221 asset) is sold, the gain or loss is a "capital gain or loss." When a § 1231 asset is sold, the gain can be either ordinary or capital.

Why is the distinction between ordinary and capital so important? The primary reason is that capital gains are taxed at lower capital gains tax rates, compared to ordinary gains that are taxed at ordinary rates. Capital losses are also limited in their deductibility.[15] The specifics of ordinary gains and losses, capital gains and losses, and § 1231 gains and losses are described in detail in the following sections.

### Recognized Gain or Loss from Ordinary Assets

Recall that the primary ordinary income assets are inventory and accounts receivable. Inventory sold in the normal course of a trade or business generates sales revenue. The cost of the inventory is a deduction (cost of goods sold). The type of transaction discussed in this chapter is the sale of an ordinary asset outside the normal course of business. Typically, ordinary gains or losses produced outside (not part of) the normal course of business relate to the sale of business property held less than one year or the sale of accounts receivable.[16]

---

**EXAMPLE 7-5**

Sheetal, a sole proprietor who needs cash, decides to sell some outstanding accounts receivable. They have a $10,000 FMV and a zero basis. Sheetal, is able to sell the receivables on July 1, 2021, for $8,500. Sheetal, recognizes an $8,500 ordinary gain ($8,500 received less $0 basis).

---

**EXAMPLE 7-6**

Sheetal sold some equipment for $22,000 on March 7, 2021, that was originally purchased for $24,000 on April 8, 2020. The equipment was subject to depreciation of $8,640 for 2020 and 2021. The adjusted basis is $15,360 ($24,000 cost − $8,640 depreciation). Sheetal recognizes a $6,640 ordinary gain ($22,000 amount realized − $15,360 adjusted basis).

---

[14] Remember from Chapter 6 that only a half year of depreciation is allowed in the year of disposal for half year convention assets. Depreciation for mid-quarter and mid-month convention assets also changes in the year of disposal.

[15] Capital gains and losses are treated differently for corporate taxpayers. The discussion in this chapter pertains exclusively to noncorporate taxpayers.

[16] The sale of § 1231 property where the gain is a result of depreciation taken also produces an ordinary gain. These gains are discussed later in the chapter.

**EXHIBIT 7-1** Form 4797 for Examples 7-5 and 7-6

| Form **4797** | **Sales of Business Property** | OMB No. 1545-0184 |
|---|---|---|
| | (Also Involuntary Conversions and Recapture Amounts Under Sections 179 and 280F(b)(2)) | **2021** |
| Department of the Treasury Internal Revenue Service | ► Attach to your tax return. ► Go to *www.irs.gov/Form4797* for instructions and the latest information. | Attachment Sequence No. **27** |

| Name(s) shown on return | Identifying number |
|---|---|
| Sheetal Taxpayer | 412-34-5670 |

| | | |
|---|---|---|
| **1a** | Enter the gross proceeds from sales or exchanges reported to you for 2021 on Form(s) 1099-B or 1099-S (or substitute statement) that you are including on line 2, 10, or 20. See instructions | **1a** |
| **b** | Enter the total amount of gain that you are including on lines 2, 10, and 24 due to the partial dispositions of MACRS assets | **1b** |
| **c** | Enter the total amount of loss that you are including on lines 2 and 10 due to the partial dispositions of MACRS assets | **1c** |

**Part I**   **Sales or Exchanges of Property Used in a Trade or Business and Involuntary Conversions From Other Than Casualty or Theft—Most Property Held More Than 1 Year** (see instructions)

| 2 | (a) Description of property | (b) Date acquired (mo., day, yr.) | (c) Date sold (mo., day, yr.) | (d) Gross sales price | (e) Depreciation allowed or allowable since acquisition | (f) Cost or other basis, plus improvements and expense of sale | (g) Gain or (loss) Subtract (f) from the sum of (d) and (e) |
|---|---|---|---|---|---|---|---|
| | | | | | | | |
| | | | | | | | |
| | | | | | | | |
| | | | | | | | |

| | | | |
|---|---|---|---|
| **3** | Gain, if any, from Form 4684, line 39 | **3** | |
| **4** | Section 1231 gain from installment sales from Form 6252, line 26 or 37 | **4** | |
| **5** | Section 1231 gain or (loss) from like-kind exchanges from Form 8824 | **5** | |
| **6** | Gain, if any, from line 32, from other than casualty or theft | **6** | |
| **7** | Combine lines 2 through 6. Enter the gain or (loss) here and on the appropriate line as follows | **7** | |

    **Partnerships and S corporations.** Report the gain or (loss) following the instructions for Form 1065, Schedule K, line 10, or Form 1120-S, Schedule K, line 9. Skip lines 8, 9, 11, and 12 below.

    **Individuals, partners, S corporation shareholders, and all others.** If line 7 is zero or a loss, enter the amount from line 7 on line 11 below and skip lines 8 and 9. If line 7 is a gain and you didn't have any prior year section 1231 losses, or they were recaptured in an earlier year, enter the gain from line 7 as a long-term capital gain on the Schedule D filed with your return and skip lines 8, 9, 11, and 12 below.

| | | | |
|---|---|---|---|
| **8** | Nonrecaptured net section 1231 losses from prior years. See instructions | **8** | |
| **9** | Subtract line 8 from line 7. If zero or less, enter -0-. If line 9 is zero, enter the gain from line 7 on line 12 below. If line 9 is more than zero, enter the amount from line 8 on line 12 below and enter the gain from line 9 as a long-term capital gain on the Schedule D filed with your return. See instructions. | **9** | |

**Part II**   **Ordinary Gains and Losses** (see instructions)

**10**   Ordinary gains and losses not included on lines 11 through 16 (include property held 1 year or less):

| | | | | | | |
|---|---|---|---|---|---|---|
| Accounts Receivable | various | various | 8,500 | 0 | 0 | 8,500 |
| Equipment | 04/08/20 | 03/07/21 | 22,000 | 8,640 | 24,000 | 6,640 |
| | | | | | | |

| | | | |
|---|---|---|---|
| **11** | Loss, if any, from line 7 | **11** ( ) | |
| **12** | Gain, if any, from line 7 or amount from line 8, if applicable | **12** | |
| **13** | Gain, if any, from line 31 | **13** | |
| **14** | Net gain or (loss) from Form 4684, lines 31 and 38a | **14** | |
| **15** | Ordinary gain from installment sales from Form 6252, line 25 or 36 | **15** | |
| **16** | Ordinary gain or (loss) from like-kind exchanges from Form 8824 | **16** | |
| **17** | Combine lines 10 through 16 | **17** | 15,140 |
| **18** | For all except individual returns, enter the amount from line 17 on the appropriate line of your return and skip lines a and b below. For individual returns, complete lines a and b below. | | |
| **a** | If the loss on line 11 includes a loss from Form 4684, line 35, column (b)(ii), enter that part of the loss here. Enter the loss from income-producing property on Schedule A (Form 1040), line 16. (Do not include any loss on property used as an employee.) Identify as from "Form 4797, line 18a." See instructions | **18a** | |
| **b** | Redetermine the gain or (loss) on line 17 excluding the loss, if any, on line 18a. Enter here and on Schedule 1 (Form 1040), Part I, line 4 | **18b** | 15,140 |

For Paperwork Reduction Act Notice, see separate instructions.     Cat. No. 13086I     Form **4797** (2021)

Source: U.S. Department of the Treasury, Internal Revenue Service, Form 4797. Washington, DC: 2021.

---

**CONCEPT CHECK 7-3—**

**LO 7-3**

1. When an ordinary asset is sold, the gain or loss is subject to capital gain or loss tax treatment. True or false?

2. Why is the distinction between "ordinary" and "capital" so important?

3. Ordinary gains or losses produced outside the normal course of business relate to the sale of business property held for less than one year or the sale of receivables. True or false?

**TABLE 7-3**
**Summary of the Different Holding Periods for Capital Assets**

Source: IRS Publication 544.

| Type of Acquisition | When the Holding Period Starts |
|---|---|
| Stock or bond purchased on a securities market | The day after the trading day the taxpayer purchased the security. |
| Nontaxable exchanges | The day after the taxpayer acquired the old property. |
| Gift | If the taxpayer's basis is the donor's basis, the holding period includes the donor's holding period. If the taxpayer's basis is the FMV, the holding period starts the day after the date of the gift. |
| Inherited property | The property is considered to be held longer than one year regardless of how long the property was actually held. |
| Real property purchase | The day after the date the taxpayer received title to the property. |
| Real property repossessed | The date the taxpayer originally received title to the property, but not including the time between the original sale and the date of repossession. |

# SALES OF CAPITAL ASSETS
## LO 7-4

Recall that a capital asset is any personal-use asset or any asset held for investment that is not one of the exclusions listed earlier. The tax treatment of a capital gain or loss varies depending on several factors:

- The period of time the capital asset is held.
- Whether the sale of the asset produced a gain or loss.
- The type of capital asset sold (for example, collectibles are treated differently).
- The taxpayer's tax bracket.
- The combination (or netting) of all capital gains and losses to derive a net capital gain or a net capital loss.
- Whether a capital asset sold is stock of a qualified small business.

### Holding Period of a Capital Asset

Only long-term capital gains receive preferential tax treatment. A *long-term capital asset* is any capital asset held for more than one year.[17] A *short-term capital asset* is any capital asset held for one year or less, and any gain or loss on its sale is taxed using ordinary tax rates. Typically, the holding period starts the day after the taxpayer acquired the property and includes the day the property is sold. Table 7-3 summarizes the determination of holding periods for capital assets.

**EXAMPLE 7-7**   Jackie purchased 100 shares of IBM stock on January 6, 2020. The stock is a long-term asset on January 7, 2021. If the stock is sold prior to January 7, 2021, the gain or loss is short-term and no preferential treatment is applicable on any gain.

Capital assets are typically acquired through a purchase. However, what if an asset is received by gift, nontaxable exchange, or inheritance?[18] Generally, if the property received has the same basis as the basis in the hands of the transferor (the person giving the property), the holding period includes the transferor's holding period. The exception to this rule is for property received by inheritance. Inherited property is *always* long-term property regardless of how long the asset belonged to the decedent or beneficiary.[19]

[17] IRC § 1222(3).
[18] Often when one asset is traded for another asset, no gain or loss is recognized. These are nontaxable exchanges covered in Chapter 12.
[19] IRC § 1223(9).

**TABLE 7-4**
**2021 Capital Gains Tax Rate Income Thresholds**

| Source of Net Capital Gain | |
|---|---|
| Collectibles gain | 28% |
| § 1202 gain | 28% |
| Unrecaptured § 1250 gain | 25% |
| Other capital gains based on taxable income:<br>  Single: Over $445,850<br>  MFS: Over $250,800<br>  MFJ: Over $501,600<br>  HoH: Over $473,750 | 20% |
| Other capital gains based on taxable income:<br>  Single: $40,401 to $445,850<br>  MFS: $40,401 to $250,800<br>  MFJ: $80,801 to $501,600<br>  HoH: $54,101 to $473,750 | 15% |
| Other capital gains based on taxable income:<br>  Single: Up to $40,400<br>  MFS: Up to $40,400<br>  MFJ: Up to $80,800<br>  HoH: Up to $54,100 | 0% |

**EXAMPLE 7-8**

Matias gave a gift of 500 shares of GM stock to Sienna, a sibling on November 12, 2020, when the stock was worth $50 per share. Matias had purchased the stock for $30 per share in 1991. Because the basis to Sienna would be the same as in the hands of Matias, the holding period for Sienna includes Matias's holding period. Thus, Sienna's holding period is more than one year, and the stock is considered a long-term capital asset. When Sienna sells the stock, any gain will be taxed using capital gain rates.

## Capital Gain Rates

The taxes on net long-term capital gains are calculated using 15%, 20%, 25%, and 28% rates. Under the Tax Cuts and Jobs Act, the three capital gain rates are applied to maximum taxable income levels rather than tax brackets as before. It should be noted that these thresholds do not match up perfectly with the income tax brackets for ordinary income as they did in prior years. For example, the rate for a single person with taxable income of $40,401 would be 15% for long-term capital gains. However, ordinary gains at $40,401 for a single taxpayer would be taxed at the 12% bracket. If the single taxpayer's taxable income was $100,000, the long-term capital gain rate would be 15%, while the ordinary income tax rate would be 24%. The lower rates of 0%, 15%, and 20% are called *maximum capital gain rates*. Table 7-4 summarizes the capital gain tax rates in effect for 2021.

**EXAMPLE 7-9**

Basha is a married taxpayer who files a joint return. In tax year 2021, their taxable income is $115,000. Basha sold stock in April 2021 that was held for four years. The gain on the sale was $30,000. Basha is in the 22% tax bracket, so the $30,000 capital gain is taxed using a 15% tax rate.

The 25% bracket is a special rate that relates to capital gains generated from depreciable real property (buildings) used in a trade or business. The Internal Revenue Code has special tax rules for depreciable real property (buildings) used in a trade or business, called *§ 1250 property*. In general, when depreciable real property is sold for a gain, the taxpayer has to bring back (recapture) as income that part of the gain due to the difference between MACRS depreciation and straight-line depreciation. As of 1987, all § 1250 property is depreciated using the straight-line method; therefore, there is no recapture of depreciation. However, the IRS implemented a special provision for this nonrecaptured depreciation of real property; it is called *unrecaptured § 1250 gain*. Instead of the entire gain from § 1250 real property being taxed at preferential capital gain rates, the gain attributable to any depreciation allowable is taxed at a special 25% rate, and any gain in excess of this amount is given preferential capital gains tax treatment. To avoid the possibility that a taxpayer might get around this special tax provision by not claiming depreciation, the IRS included depreciation recapture in the tax law so the taxpayer must include depreciation deductions whether or not the taxpayer actually took depreciation deductions on the real property. IRS § 1250 property is covered in more detail under LO 7-5 (Sales of Business Property) later in this chapter.

**EXAMPLE 7-10**

Mustafa purchased a business building in November 2007 for $200,000 and assumes that $69,655 of depreciation was taken on the building. The adjusted basis is $130,345 ($200,000 cost − $69,655 depreciation). If Mustafa sold the building for $190,000 in June 2021, the $59,655 gain ($190,000 amount realized − $130,345 adjusted basis) would be a long-term capital gain subject to the 25% rate because the gain is attributable to the depreciation recapture requirement.

**EXAMPLE 7-11**

If Mustafa sold the building for $220,000, the total gain would be $89,655 ($220,000 amount realized − $130,345 adjusted basis). Of that gain, $69,655 would be subject to the 25% rate (the unrecaptured depreciation) and $20,000 would be a § 1231 gain subject to a potential 0%, 15%, or 20% rate.

The 28% capital gain rate applies to collectibles gains. A *collectibles gain or loss* is a gain or loss from the sale or exchange of a work of art, rug, antique, metal, gem, stamp, coin, or alcoholic beverage held longer than one year.[20]

The 28% rate also applies to § 1202 gains. IRC § 1202 has a provision to limit the taxation on a gain from the sale of *qualified small business (QSB) stock,* which is stock from any domestic corporation whose aggregate gross assets at all times after August 10, 1993, up to the date of issue have been less than $50,000,000.[21] In the case of a taxpayer other than a corporation who purchased the stock after August 10, 1993, and prior to February 17, 2009, gross income excludes 50% of any gain from the sale or exchange of qualified small business stock held for more than five years.[22] Any remaining gain is taxed at a 28% rate.

**EXAMPLE 7-12**

Aiya invested in a midsize local corporation with gross assets of $15,000,000. Aiya purchased 500 shares for $25,000 in 1999. On April 6, 2021, Aiya sold the stock for $45,000, realizing a gain of $20,000. One-half of the $20,000 gain is excluded from gross income under § 1202. The remaining $10,000 gain is recognized and taxed at a rate of 28%.

There is a 3.8% Medicare surtax (IRC § 1411) on certain net investment income (NII) on individuals who have modified AGI above a threshold amount. In general, NII includes some of the more common types of investments such as interest, dividends, rental, and royalty income. It also includes, but is not limited to, gains from the sale of stocks, bonds, and mutual funds; capital gain distributions from mutual funds; gains from the sale of investment real estate (a second home that is not a primary residence); and sales of interests in passive investments from a partnership or S corporation.

The 3.8% surtax is imposed on the lesser of

- Net investment income (NII) for the year or
- Modified Adjusted Gross Income (modified AGI) over $250,000 for married filing jointly and qualifying widow(er) with dependent child; $200,000 for single and head of household (with qualified person); and $125,000 for married filing separately.

For example, a single taxpayer who has NII of $40,000 and modified AGI of $180,000 will not be subject to this surtax because the modified AGI did not exceed the threshold amount of $200,000. Remember that the $40,000 is included in the modified AGI calculation. What if the

[20] IRC § 408(m)(2).

[21] IRC § 1202(d)(1).

[22] IRC § 1202(a). *Note:* For stock acquired after February 17, 2009, and before September 27, 2010, this exclusion is 75%. For stock acquired after September 27, 2010, and before January 1, 2012, this exclusion is 100%. Remember that these exclusion rates are not applicable until the stock has been held for more than five years. This exclusion has been extended for stock acquired before January 1, 2014, and held for more than five years.

# From Shoebox to Software

When capital gains or losses occur, the taxpayer must file Schedule D to report the gain or loss. The following examples illustrate the preparation of Schedule D.

Taxpayers receive Form 1099-B from corporations and brokerage firms. These forms report information concerning the sale of stock by the taxpayer (see Exhibit 7-7). Often brokerage firms send a "substitute" 1099-B form to report multiple sales transactions occurring throughout the year.

Exhibit 7-2 illustrates the reporting of the gains from Example 7-14 on Form 8949 and Schedule D. A taxpayer who has 28% capital gains also uses the 28% Rate Gain worksheet shown. The taxpayer uses the rates from the tax rate schedules to calculate the tax on the ordinary income and calculates the tax on qualified dividends.

## TAX PREPARATION SOFTWARE

Open the tax return for the Masters and go to the forms. Open Schedule D and double-click on the first sales price cell. This will open the Form 1099-B box. The taxpayer receives a sales confirmation after a sale throughout the year and a 1099-B (Brokerage Sales) at year-end from the brokerage company.

Open a new copy for each 1099-B received. Enter the name of the stock, the sales price, the dates purchased, and the dates sold. For the collectibles, make sure you check the box on the bottom of the input form that indicates that the asset sold is a collectible. Tax preparation software will classify the gains as short- or long-term and enter them on the correct section of Schedule D.

same single taxpayer had NII of $40,000 and modified AGI of $210,000? The surtax would apply because modified AGI is more than the threshold of $200,000. The tax would be applied to the $10,000 amount because it is less than the NII income of $40,000. If the taxpayer had NII of $80,000 and modified AGI of $300,000, the amount of surtax would be calculated on the full NII of $80,000 because the modified AGI exceeds the threshold by $100,000. The surtax applies to the lower amount, which in this case is $80,000; the additional tax would be $3,040 ($80,000 × 3.8%). The surtax is calculated on Form 1040.

## Netting Capital Gains and Capital Losses

After all long- and short-term capital gains and losses have been calculated, they need to be combined in a certain manner before applying special tax rate provisions. First, combine all short-term capital gains and short-term capital losses to obtain a *net* short-term gain or loss. Next, combine all long-term capital gains and losses to obtain a *net* long-term capital gain or loss. Finally, combine the net short-term gain or loss with the net long-term gain or loss. If netting results in a net short-term capital gain and a net long-term capital gain or a net short-term capital loss and a net long-term capital loss, the netting process ends. In this final phase, taxpayers must take care to separate the gains that are taxed at 28% (collectibles and § 1202 gains). If an overall net loss results, IRC § 1211 permits the taxpayer to deduct up to a maximum of $3,000 against other income.[23] IRC § 1212 allows any net loss exceeding $3,000 to be carried over to future years (indefinitely) to offset other capital gains.[24]

The netting process can result in the following outcomes:

- **Net short-term gain and net long-term gain:** Short-term gains are taxed at regular tax rates, and net long-term gains are taxed at the appropriate capital gain rate of 0%, 15%, 20%, 25%, or 28%.
- **Net short-term gain and net long-term loss:** A long-term loss is offset against a short-term gain. If a net short-term gain results, the short-term gain is taxed using regular tax rates. If a long-term loss results, the loss, up to $3,000, reduces other income, and any excess carries forward indefinitely.
- **Net short-term loss and net long-term gain:** In this case, separate the long-term gains into 28%, 25%, 20%, and 15% or 0% groups. Any net short-term loss is first offset against the 28% group, then the 25% group, and if any loss remains, the 20%, 15%, or 0% group.[25]
- **Net short-term loss and net long-term loss:** In this case, only $3,000 of the loss is deductible against other income in any one year. First, the short-term losses are deducted against

[23] IRC § 1211(b)—only a $1,500 loss is allowed for married taxpayers filing a separate return.
[24] IRC § 1212(b).
[25] IRS Notice 97-59, 1997-2 CB 309.

other income, and if any of the $3,000 maximum remains, deduct the long-term loss up to the maximum $3,000 annual loss limit.

Excess losses are carried forward to the next year and retain their original character. A short-term loss carries over as a short-term loss, and a long-term loss carries over as a long-term loss.

---

**EXAMPLE 7-13**

Adrian and Pat Reynolds sold property in 2021. The sale resulted in a long-term loss of $8,000. They had no other capital transactions and filed a joint return for 2021. They had 2021 taxable income of $50,000. They deduct $3,000 of the loss in 2021. The unused $5,000 of the loss ($8,000 − $3,000) carries over to 2022 as a long-term loss. If their loss had been less than $3,000, there would be no carryover to 2022.

---

**EXAMPLE 7-14**

Alan Masters, the taxpayer from previous chapters, had the following capital transactions:

|  | Purchased | Sold | Sale Price | Basis | Gain/Loss |
|---|---|---|---|---|---|
| Stock 1 (held 9 months) | 12/01/2020 | 09/01/2021 | $15,000 | $ 9,000 | $ 6,000 |
| Stock 2 (held 4 months) | 12/01/2020 | 04/01/2021 | 17,000 | 25,000 | (8,000) |
| Stock 3 (held 30 months) | 06/05/2019 | 12/05/2021 | 38,000 | 20,000 | 18,000 |
| Collectibles | 07/01/2020 | 08/01/2021 | 20,000 | 14,000 | 6,000 |

The results follow:

| | |
|---|---|
| Net short-term capital loss ($8,000 − $6,000) | $ (2,000) |
| Net long-term capital gain | 18,000 |
| 28% collectibles capital gain | 6,000 |

The net short-term loss of $2,000 first offsets the 28% gain on the collectibles. The result is a long-term capital gain of $18,000 and a $4,000, 28% gain. The appropriate rates are applied:

$18,000 × 15%  = $2,700
$ 4,000 × 28%  =  1,120
  $3,820 increase in tax due to capital gains

Form 8949, Schedule D, and the 28% gains worksheet are illustrated in Exhibit 7-2.

---

**EXAMPLE 7-15**

Assume similar facts from Example 7-14, except that stock 3 was sold for $20,000 with a basis of $38,000, producing a loss of $18,000.

|  | Purchased | Sold | Sale Price | Basis | Gain/Loss |
|---|---|---|---|---|---|
| Stock 1 (9 months) | 12/01/2020 | 09/01/2021 | $ 15,000 | $ 9,000 | $ 6,000 |
| Stock 2 (4 months) | 12/01/2020 | 04/01/2021 | 17,000 | 25,000 | (8,000) |
| Stock 3 (30 months) | 06/05/2019 | 12/05/2021 | 20,000 | 38,000 | (18,000) |
| Collectibles | 07/01/2020 | 08/01/2021 | 20,000 | 14,000 | 6,000 |

The results follow:

| | |
|---|---|
| Net short-term capital loss ($8,000 − $6,000) | $ (2,000) |
| Net long-term loss against collectibles gain ($18,000 − $6,000) | (12,000) |

Only $3,000 of the $14,000 loss can be taken this year. The net short-term loss of $2,000 is allowed plus $1,000 of the long-term loss. The $11,000 remaining loss is carried forward indefinitely.

Form 8949 and Schedule D, created from Example 7-15, are shown in Exhibit 7-3.

**EXHIBIT 7-2** Form 8949 and Schedule D for Example 7-14

| Form **8949** | **Sales and Other Dispositions of Capital Assets** | OMB No. 1545-0074 |
|---|---|---|
| Department of the Treasury Internal Revenue Service | ▶ Go to *www.irs.gov/Form8949* for instructions and the latest information. ▶ File with your Schedule D to list your transactions for lines 1b, 2, 3, 8b, 9, and 10 of Schedule D. | **2021** Attachment Sequence No. **12A** |

| Name(s) shown on return | Social security number or taxpayer identification number |
|---|---|
| Alan and Cherie Masters          For Example 7-14 | 412-34-5670 |

*Before you check Box A, B, or C below, see whether you received any Form(s) 1099-B or substitute statement(s) from your broker. A substitute statement will have the same information as Form 1099-B. Either will show whether your basis (usually your cost) was reported to the IRS by your broker and may even tell you which box to check.*

**Part I**   **Short-Term.** Transactions involving capital assets you held 1 year or less are generally short-term (see instructions). For long-term transactions, see page 2.

**Note:** You may aggregate all short-term transactions reported on Form(s) 1099-B showing basis was reported to the IRS and for which no adjustments or codes are required. Enter the totals directly on Schedule D, line 1a; you aren't required to report these transactions on Form 8949 (see instructions).

**You *must* check Box A, B, *or* C below. Check only one box.** If more than one box applies for your short-term transactions, complete a separate Form 8949, page 1, for each applicable box. If you have more short-term transactions than will fit on this page for one or more of the boxes, complete as many forms with the same box checked as you need.

- ☑ **(A)** Short-term transactions reported on Form(s) 1099-B showing basis was reported to the IRS (see **Note** above)
- ☐ **(B)** Short-term transactions reported on Form(s) 1099-B showing basis **wasn't** reported to the IRS
- ☐ **(C)** Short-term transactions not reported to you on Form 1099-B

| 1 (a) Description of property (Example: 100 sh. XYZ Co.) | (b) Date acquired (Mo., day, yr.) | (c) Date sold or disposed of (Mo., day, yr.) | (d) Proceeds (sales price) (see instructions) | (e) Cost or other basis. See the **Note** below and see *Column (e)* in the separate instructions | (f) Code(s) from instructions | (g) Amount of adjustment | (h) Gain or (loss). Subtract column (e) from column (d) and combine the result with column (g) |
|---|---|---|---|---|---|---|---|
| Stock #1 | 12/01/20 | 09/01/21 | 15,000 | 9,000 | | | 6,000 |
| Stock #2 | 12/01/20 | 04/01/21 | 17,000 | 25,000 | | | (8,000) |
| Totals to Schedule D | | | 32,000 | 34,000 | | | (2,000) |

**You *must* check Box D, E, *or* F below. Check only one box.** If more than one box applies for your long-term transactions, complete a separate Form 8949, page 2, for each applicable box. If you have more long-term transactions than will fit on this page for one or more of the boxes, complete as many forms with the same box checked as you need.

- ☑ **(D)** Long-term transactions reported on Form(s) 1099-B showing basis was reported to the IRS (see **Note** above)
- ☐ **(E)** Long-term transactions reported on Form(s) 1099-B showing basis **wasn't** reported to the IRS
- ☐ **(F)** Long-term transactions not reported to you on Form 1099-B

| 1 (a) Description of property (Example: 100 sh. XYZ Co.) | (b) Date acquired (Mo., day, yr.) | (c) Date sold or disposed of (Mo., day, yr.) | (d) Proceeds (sales price) (see instructions) | (e) Cost or other basis. See the **Note** below and see *Column (e)* in the separate instructions | (f) Code(s) from instructions | (g) Amount of adjustment | (h) Gain or (loss). Subtract column (e) from column (d) and combine the result with column (g) |
|---|---|---|---|---|---|---|---|
| Stock #3 | 06/05/19 | 12/05/21 | 38,000 | 20,000 | | | 18,000 |

**You *must* check Box D, E, *or* F below. Check only one box.** If more than one box applies for your long-term transactions, complete a separate Form 8949, page 2, for each applicable box. If you have more long-term transactions than will fit on this page for one or more of the boxes, complete as many forms with the same box checked as you need.

- ☐ **(D)** Long-term transactions reported on Form(s) 1099-B showing basis was reported to the IRS (see **Note** above)
- ☐ **(E)** Long-term transactions reported on Form(s) 1099-B showing basis **wasn't** reported to the IRS
- ☑ **(F)** Long-term transactions not reported to you on Form 1099-B

| 1 (a) Description of property (Example: 100 sh. XYZ Co.) | (b) Date acquired (Mo., day, yr.) | (c) Date sold or disposed of (Mo., day, yr.) | (d) Proceeds (sales price) (see instructions) | (e) Cost or other basis. See the **Note** below and see *Column (e)* in the separate instructions | (f) Code(s) from instructions | (g) Amount of adjustment | (h) Gain or (loss). Subtract column (e) from column (d) and combine the result with column (g) |
|---|---|---|---|---|---|---|---|
| Collectibles | 07/01/20 | 08/01/21 | 20,000 | 14,000 | | | 6,000 |

Source: U.S. Department of the Treasury, Internal Revenue Service, Form 8949 and Schedule D (Form 1040). Washington, DC: 2021.

**EXHIBIT 7-2**   *(continued)*

| SCHEDULE D<br>(Form 1040)<br><br>Department of the Treasury<br>Internal Revenue Service (99) | **Capital Gains and Losses**<br><br>► Attach to Form 1040, 1040-SR, or 1040-NR.<br>► Go to *www.irs.gov/ScheduleD* for instructions and the latest information.<br>► Use Form 8949 to list your transactions for lines 1b, 2, 3, 8b, 9, and 10. | OMB No. 1545-0074<br><br>2021<br><br>Attachment<br>Sequence No. 12 |
|---|---|---|

| Name(s) shown on return<br>Alan and Cherie Masters        For Example 7-14 | Your social security number<br>412-34-5670 |
|---|---|

Did you dispose of any investment(s) in a qualified opportunity fund during the tax year? ☐ Yes   ☑ No
If "Yes," attach Form 8949 and see its instructions for additional requirements for reporting your gain or loss.

**Part I**   **Short-Term Capital Gains and Losses—Generally Assets Held One Year or Less** (see instructions)

| See instructions for how to figure the amounts to enter on the lines below.<br><br>This form may be easier to complete if you round off cents to whole dollars. | (d)<br>Proceeds<br>(sales price) | (e)<br>Cost<br>(or other basis) | (g)<br>Adjustments<br>to gain or loss from<br>Form(s) 8949, Part I,<br>line 2, column (g) | (h) Gain or (loss)<br>Subtract column (e)<br>from column (d) and<br>combine the result<br>with column (g) |
|---|---|---|---|---|
| **1a** Totals for all short-term transactions reported on Form 1099-B for which basis was reported to the IRS and for which you have no adjustments (see instructions). However, if you choose to report all these transactions on Form 8949, leave this line blank and go to line 1b . | | | | |
| **1b** Totals for all transactions reported on Form(s) 8949 with **Box A** checked . | 32,000 | 34,000 | | (2,000) |
| **2** Totals for all transactions reported on Form(s) 8949 with **Box B** checked   . . . . . . . . . | | | | |
| **3** Totals for all transactions reported on Form(s) 8949 with **Box C** checked   . . . . . . . . . | | | | |

| **4** Short-term gain from Form 6252 and short-term gain or (loss) from Forms 4684, 6781, and 8824   . . | **4** | |
|---|---|---|
| **5** Net short-term gain or (loss) from partnerships, S corporations, estates, and trusts from Schedule(s) K-1 . . . . . . . . . . . . . . . . . . . . . . . . . | **5** | |
| **6** Short-term capital loss carryover. Enter the amount, if any, from line 8 of your **Capital Loss Carryover Worksheet** in the instructions   . . . . . . . . . . . . . . . . . . | **6** (              ) |
| **7** **Net short-term capital gain or (loss).** Combine lines 1a through 6 in column (h). If you have any long-term capital gains or losses, go to Part II below. Otherwise, go to Part III on the back   . . . . . . | **7** | (2,000) |

**Part II**   **Long-Term Capital Gains and Losses—Generally Assets Held More Than One Year** (see instructions)

| See instructions for how to figure the amounts to enter on the lines below.<br><br>This form may be easier to complete if you round off cents to whole dollars. | (d)<br>Proceeds<br>(sales price) | (e)<br>Cost<br>(or other basis) | (g)<br>Adjustments<br>to gain or loss from<br>Form(s) 8949, Part II,<br>line 2, column (g) | (h) Gain or (loss)<br>Subtract column (e)<br>from column (d) and<br>combine the result<br>with column (g) |
|---|---|---|---|---|
| **8a** Totals for all long-term transactions reported on Form 1099-B for which basis was reported to the IRS and for which you have no adjustments (see instructions). However, if you choose to report all these transactions on Form 8949, leave this line blank and go to line 8b . | | | | |
| **8b** Totals for all transactions reported on Form(s) 8949 with **Box D** checked   . . . . . . . . . | 38,000 | 20,000 | | 18,000 |
| **9** Totals for all transactions reported on Form(s) 8949 with **Box E** checked   . . . . . . . . . | | | | |
| **10** Totals for all transactions reported on Form(s) 8949 with **Box F** checked.  . . . . . . . . . | 20,000 | 14,000 | | 6,000 |

| **11** Gain from Form 4797, Part I; long-term gain from Forms 2439 and 6252; and long-term gain or (loss) from Forms 4684, 6781, and 8824   . . . . . . . . . . . . . . . . . . . | **11** | |
|---|---|---|
| **12** Net long-term gain or (loss) from partnerships, S corporations, estates, and trusts from Schedule(s) K-1 | **12** | |
| **13** Capital gain distributions. See the instructions   . . . . . . . . . . . . . . | **13** | |
| **14** Long-term capital loss carryover. Enter the amount, if any, from line 13 of your **Capital Loss Carryover Worksheet** in the instructions   . . . . . . . . . . . . . . . . . | **14** (              ) |
| **15** **Net long-term capital gain or (loss).** Combine lines 8a through 14 in column (h). Then, go to Part III on the back   . . . . . . . . . . . . . . . . . . . . . . . . . | **15** | 24,000 |

For Paperwork Reduction Act Notice, see your tax return instructions.          Cat. No. 11338H          Schedule D (Form 1040) 2021

*(continued)*

**EXHIBIT 7-2** *(concluded)*

Schedule D (Form 1040) 2021      Page **2**

**Part III**    **Summary**

| | | | |
|---|---|---|---|
| **16** | Combine lines 7 and 15 and enter the result . . . . . . . . . . . . . . | **16** | 22,000 |

- If line 16 is a **gain,** enter the amount from line 16 on Form 1040, 1040-SR, or 1040-NR, line 7. Then, go to line 17 below.
- If line 16 is a **loss,** skip lines 17 through 20 below. Then, go to line 21. Also be sure to complete line 22.
- If line 16 is **zero,** skip lines 17 through 21 below and enter -0- on Form 1040, 1040-SR, or 1040-NR, line 7. Then, go to line 22.

**17**   Are lines 15 and 16 **both** gains?
     ☑ **Yes.** Go to line 18.
     ☐ **No.** Skip lines 18 through 21, and go to line 22.

| | | | |
|---|---|---|---|
| **18** | If you are required to complete the **28% Rate Gain Worksheet** (see instructions), enter the amount, if any, from line 7 of that worksheet . . . . . . . . . . . ▶ | **18** | 4,000 |
| **19** | If you are required to complete the **Unrecaptured Section 1250 Gain Worksheet** (see instructions), enter the amount, if any, from line 18 of that worksheet . . . . . . ▶ | **19** | |

**20**   Are lines 18 and 19 both zero or blank and are you not filing Form 4952?
     ☐ **Yes.** Complete the **Qualified Dividends and Capital Gain Tax Worksheet** in the instructions for Forms 1040 and 1040-SR, line 16. **Don't** complete lines 21 and 22 below.

     ☑ **No.** Complete the **Schedule D Tax Worksheet** in the instructions. **Don't** complete lines 21 and 22 below.

**21**   If line 16 is a loss, enter here and on Form 1040, 1040-SR, or 1040-NR, line 7, the **smaller** of:

- The loss on line 16; or
- ($3,000), or if married filing separately, ($1,500)

. . . . . . . . . . . .    **21** (        )

**Note:** When figuring which amount is smaller, treat both amounts as positive numbers.

**22**   Do you have qualified dividends on Form 1040, 1040-SR, or 1040-NR, line 3a?

     ☐ **Yes.** Complete the **Qualified Dividends and Capital Gain Tax Worksheet** in the instructions for Forms 1040 and 1040-SR, line 16.

     ☐ **No.** Complete the rest of Form 1040, 1040-SR, or 1040-NR.

Schedule D (Form 1040) 2021

---

**28% Rate Gain Worksheet—Line 18**        *Keep for Your Records*

| | | | |
|---|---|---|---|
| **1.** | Enter the total of all collectibles gain or (loss) from items you reported on Form 8949, Part II . . . . . . . . . . . . | **1.** | 6,000 |
| **2.** | Enter as a positive number the total of: <br>• Any section 1202 exclusion you reported in column (g) of Form 8949, Part II, with code "Q" in column (f), that is 50% of the gain; <br>• ⅔ of any section 1202 exclusion you reported in column (g) of Form 8949, Part II, with code "Q" in column (f), that is 60% of the gain; and <br>• ⅓ of any section 1202 exclusion you reported in column (g) of Form 8949, Part II, with code "Q" in column (f), that is 75% of the gain. <br>Don't make an entry for any section 1202 exclusion that is 100% of the gain. | **2.** | 0 |
| **3.** | Enter the total of all collectibles gain or (loss) from Form 4684, line 4 (but only if Form 4684, line 15, is more than zero); Form 6252; Form 6781, Part II; and Form 8824 . . . . . . . . . . | **3.** | 0 |
| **4.** | Enter the total of any collectibles gain reported to you on: <br>• Form 1099-DIV, box 2d; <br>• Form 2439, box 1d; and <br>• Schedule K-1 from a partnership, S corporation, estate, or trust. | **4.** | 0 |
| **5.** | Enter your long-term capital loss carryovers from Schedule D, line 14, and Schedule K-1 (Form 1041), box 11, code C . . . . . . . . . . . . . . . | **5.** | (   0 ) |
| **6.** | If Schedule D, line 7, is a (loss), enter that (loss) here. Otherwise, enter -0- . . . . . . . . . . | **6.** | ( 2,000 ) |
| **7.** | Combine lines 1 through 6. If zero or less, enter -0-. If more than zero, also enter this amount on Schedule D, line 18 . . . . . . . . . . . . . . . | **7.** | 4,000 |

**EXHIBIT 7-3** **Schedule D and Capital Loss Carryover Worksheet for Example 7-15**

| Form **8949** | **Sales and Other Dispositions of Capital Assets** | OMB No. 1545-0074 |
|---|---|---|
| Department of the Treasury Internal Revenue Service | ▶ Go to *www.irs.gov/Form8949* for instructions and the latest information.<br>▶ File with your Schedule D to list your transactions for lines 1b, 2, 3, 8b, 9, and 10 of Schedule D. | 20**21**<br>Attachment Sequence No. **12A** |

| Name(s) shown on return | Social security number or taxpayer identification number |
|---|---|
| Alan and Cherie Masters    For Example 7-15 | 412-34-5670 |

Before you check Box A, B, or C below, see whether you received any Form(s) 1099-B or substitute statement(s) from your broker. A substitute statement will have the same information as Form 1099-B. Either will show whether your basis (usually your cost) was reported to the IRS by your broker and may even tell you which box to check.

**Part I** **Short-Term.** Transactions involving capital assets you held 1 year or less are generally short-term (see instructions). For long-term transactions, see page 2.

**Note:** You may aggregate all short-term transactions reported on Form(s) 1099-B showing basis was reported to the IRS and for which no adjustments or codes are required. Enter the totals directly on Schedule D, line 1a; you aren't required to report these transactions on Form 8949 (see instructions).

**You *must* check Box A, B, *or* C below. Check only one box.** If more than one box applies for your short-term transactions, complete a separate Form 8949, page 1, for each applicable box. If you have more short-term transactions than will fit on this page for one or more of the boxes, complete as many forms with the same box checked as you need.

- [✓] **(A)** Short-term transactions reported on Form(s) 1099-B showing basis was reported to the IRS (see **Note** above)
- [ ] **(B)** Short-term transactions reported on Form(s) 1099-B showing basis **wasn't** reported to the IRS
- [ ] **(C)** Short-term transactions not reported to you on Form 1099-B

| 1<br>(a)<br>Description of property<br>(Example: 100 sh. XYZ Co.) | (b)<br>Date acquired<br>(Mo., day, yr.) | (c)<br>Date sold or disposed of<br>(Mo., day, yr.) | (d)<br>Proceeds<br>(sales price)<br>(see instructions) | (e)<br>Cost or other basis.<br>See the **Note** below and see *Column (e)* in the separate instructions | Adjustment, if any, to gain or loss. If you enter an amount in column (g), enter a code in column (f). See the separate instructions.<br>(f)<br>Code(s) from instructions | (g)<br>Amount of adjustment | (h)<br>Gain or (loss).<br>Subtract column (e) from column (d) and combine the result with column (g) |
|---|---|---|---|---|---|---|---|
| Stock #1 | 12/01/20 | 09/01/21 | 15,000 | 9,000 | | | 6,000 |
| Stock #2 | 12/01/20 | 04/01/21 | 17,000 | 25,000 | | | (8,000) |
| Totals to Schedule D | | | 32,000 | 34,000 | | | (2,000) |

---

**You *must* check Box D, E, *or* F below. Check only one box.** If more than one box applies for your long-term transactions, complete a separate Form 8949, page 2, for each applicable box. If you have more long-term transactions than will fit on this page for one or more of the boxes, complete as many forms with the same box checked as you need.

- [✓] **(D)** Long-term transactions reported on Form(s) 1099-B showing basis was reported to the IRS (see **Note** above)
- [ ] **(E)** Long-term transactions reported on Form(s) 1099-B showing basis **wasn't** reported to the IRS
- [ ] **(F)** Long-term transactions not reported to you on Form 1099-B

| 1<br>(a)<br>Description of property<br>(Example: 100 sh. XYZ Co.) | (b)<br>Date acquired<br>(Mo., day, yr.) | (c)<br>Date sold or disposed of<br>(Mo., day, yr.) | (d)<br>Proceeds<br>(sales price)<br>(see instructions) | (e)<br>Cost or other basis.<br>See the **Note** below and see *Column (e)* in the separate instructions | Adjustment, if any, to gain or loss. If you enter an amount in column (g), enter a code in column (f). See the separate instructions.<br>(f)<br>Code(s) from instructions | (g)<br>Amount of adjustment | (h)<br>Gain or (loss).<br>Subtract column (e) from column (d) and combine the result with column (g) |
|---|---|---|---|---|---|---|---|
| Stock #3 | 06/05/19 | 12/05/21 | 20,000 | 38,000 | | | (18,000) |

---

**You *must* check Box D, E, *or* F below. Check only one box.** If more than one box applies for your long-term transactions, complete a separate Form 8949, page 2, for each applicable box. If you have more long-term transactions than will fit on this page for one or more of the boxes, complete as many forms with the same box checked as you need.

- [ ] **(D)** Long-term transactions reported on Form(s) 1099-B showing basis was reported to the IRS (see **Note** above)
- [ ] **(E)** Long-term transactions reported on Form(s) 1099-B showing basis **wasn't** reported to the IRS
- [✓] **(F)** Long-term transactions not reported to you on Form 1099-B

| 1<br>(a)<br>Description of property<br>(Example: 100 sh. XYZ Co.) | (b)<br>Date acquired<br>(Mo., day, yr.) | (c)<br>Date sold or disposed of<br>(Mo., day, yr.) | (d)<br>Proceeds<br>(sales price)<br>(see instructions) | (e)<br>Cost or other basis.<br>See the **Note** below and see *Column (e)* in the separate instructions | Adjustment, if any, to gain or loss. If you enter an amount in column (g), enter a code in column (f). See the separate instructions.<br>(f)<br>Code(s) from instructions | (g)<br>Amount of adjustment | (h)<br>Gain or (loss).<br>Subtract column (e) from column (d) and combine the result with column (g) |
|---|---|---|---|---|---|---|---|
| Collectibles | 07/01/20 | 08/01/21 | 20,000 | 14,000 | | | 6,000 |

Source: U.S. Department of the Treasury, Internal Revenue Service, Form 8949 and Schedule D (Form 1040). Washington, DC: 2021.

*(continued)*

**EXHIBIT 7-3** *(continued)*

| SCHEDULE D<br>(Form 1040)<br><br>Department of the Treasury<br>Internal Revenue Service (99) | **Capital Gains and Losses**<br><br>▶ Attach to Form 1040, 1040-SR, or 1040-NR.<br>▶ Go to *www.irs.gov/ScheduleD* for instructions and the latest information.<br>▶ Use Form 8949 to list your transactions for lines 1b, 2, 3, 8b, 9, and 10. | OMB No. 1545-0074<br><br>**2021**<br><br>Attachment<br>Sequence No. **12** |
|---|---|---|

| Name(s) shown on return<br>**Alan and Cherie Masters**        For Example 7-15 | Your social security number<br>**412-34-5670** |
|---|---|

Did you dispose of any investment(s) in a qualified opportunity fund during the tax year?  ☐ Yes  ☑ No
If "Yes," attach Form 8949 and see its instructions for additional requirements for reporting your gain or loss.

**Part I    Short-Term Capital Gains and Losses—Generally Assets Held One Year or Less** (see instructions)

| See instructions for how to figure the amounts to enter on the lines below.<br><br>This form may be easier to complete if you round off cents to whole dollars. | (d)<br>Proceeds<br>(sales price) | (e)<br>Cost<br>(or other basis) | (g)<br>Adjustments<br>to gain or loss from<br>Form(s) 8949, Part I,<br>line 2, column (g) | (h) Gain or (loss)<br>Subtract column (e)<br>from column (d) and<br>combine the result<br>with column (g) |
|---|---|---|---|---|
| **1a** Totals for all short-term transactions reported on Form 1099-B for which basis was reported to the IRS and for which you have no adjustments (see instructions). However, if you choose to report all these transactions on Form 8949, leave this line blank and go to line 1b | | | | |
| **1b** Totals for all transactions reported on Form(s) 8949 with **Box A** checked | 32,000 | 34,000 | | (2,000) |
| **2** Totals for all transactions reported on Form(s) 8949 with **Box B** checked | | | | |
| **3** Totals for all transactions reported on Form(s) 8949 with **Box C** checked | | | | |

| **4** Short-term gain from Form 6252 and short-term gain or (loss) from Forms 4684, 6781, and 8824 | **4** | |
|---|---|---|
| **5** Net short-term gain or (loss) from partnerships, S corporations, estates, and trusts from Schedule(s) K-1 | **5** | |
| **6** Short-term capital loss carryover. Enter the amount, if any, from line 8 of your **Capital Loss Carryover Worksheet** in the instructions | **6** ( | ) |
| **7** **Net short-term capital gain or (loss).** Combine lines 1a through 6 in column (h). If you have any long-term capital gains or losses, go to Part II below. Otherwise, go to Part III on the back | **7** | (2,000) |

**Part II    Long-Term Capital Gains and Losses—Generally Assets Held More Than One Year** (see instructions)

| See instructions for how to figure the amounts to enter on the lines below.<br><br>This form may be easier to complete if you round off cents to whole dollars. | (d)<br>Proceeds<br>(sales price) | (e)<br>Cost<br>(or other basis) | (g)<br>Adjustments<br>to gain or loss from<br>Form(s) 8949, Part II,<br>line 2, column (g) | (h) Gain or (loss)<br>Subtract column (e)<br>from column (d) and<br>combine the result<br>with column (g) |
|---|---|---|---|---|
| **8a** Totals for all long-term transactions reported on Form 1099-B for which basis was reported to the IRS and for which you have no adjustments (see instructions). However, if you choose to report all these transactions on Form 8949, leave this line blank and go to line 8b | | | | |
| **8b** Totals for all transactions reported on Form(s) 8949 with **Box D** checked | 20,000 | 38,000 | | (18,000) |
| **9** Totals for all transactions reported on Form(s) 8949 with **Box E** checked | | | | |
| **10** Totals for all transactions reported on Form(s) 8949 with **Box F** checked | 20,000 | 14,000 | | 6,000 |

| **11** Gain from Form 4797, Part I; long-term gain from Forms 2439 and 6252; and long-term gain or (loss) from Forms 4684, 6781, and 8824 | **11** | |
|---|---|---|
| **12** Net long-term gain or (loss) from partnerships, S corporations, estates, and trusts from Schedule(s) K-1 | **12** | |
| **13** Capital gain distributions. See the instructions | **13** | |
| **14** Long-term capital loss carryover. Enter the amount, if any, from line 13 of your **Capital Loss Carryover Worksheet** in the instructions | **14** ( | ) |
| **15** **Net long-term capital gain or (loss).** Combine lines 8a through 14 in column (h). Then, go to Part III on the back | **15** | (12,000) |

For Paperwork Reduction Act Notice, see your tax return instructions.        Cat. No. 11338H        Schedule D (Form 1040) 2021

**EXHIBIT 7-3**  *(concluded)*

Schedule D (Form 1040) 2021                                                                 Page **2**

**Part III**   **Summary**

**16**   Combine lines 7 and 15 and enter the result . . . . . . . . . . . . . .   **16**   (14,000)

- If line 16 is a **gain,** enter the amount from line 16 on Form 1040, 1040-SR, or 1040-NR, line 7. Then, go to line 17 below.
- If line 16 is a **loss,** skip lines 17 through 20 below. Then, go to line 21. Also be sure to complete line 22.
- If line 16 is **zero,** skip lines 17 through 21 below and enter -0- on Form 1040, 1040-SR, or 1040-NR, line 7. Then, go to line 22.

**17**   Are lines 15 and 16 **both** gains?
☐ **Yes.** Go to line 18.
☑ **No.** Skip lines 18 through 21, and go to line 22.

**18**   If you are required to complete the **28% Rate Gain Worksheet** (see instructions), enter the amount, if any, from line 7 of that worksheet . . . . . . . . . . . . . . . . ▶  **18**

**19**   If you are required to complete the **Unrecaptured Section 1250 Gain Worksheet** (see instructions), enter the amount, if any, from line 18 of that worksheet . . . . . . . . . ▶  **19**

**20**   Are lines 18 and 19 both zero or blank and are you not filing Form 4952?
☐ **Yes.** Complete the **Qualified Dividends and Capital Gain Tax Worksheet** in the instructions for Forms 1040 and 1040-SR, line 16. **Don't** complete lines 21 and 22 below.

☐ **No.** Complete the **Schedule D Tax Worksheet** in the instructions. **Don't** complete lines 21 and 22 below.

**21**   If line 16 is a loss, enter here and on Form 1040, 1040-SR, or 1040-NR, line 7, the **smaller** of:

- The loss on line 16; or
- ($3,000), or if married filing separately, ($1,500)   } . . . . . . . . . . . . . . . . .   **21** (    3,000 )

**Note:** When figuring which amount is smaller, treat both amounts as positive numbers.

**22**   Do you have qualified dividends on Form 1040, 1040-SR, or 1040-NR, line 3a?

☐ **Yes.** Complete the **Qualified Dividends and Capital Gain Tax Worksheet** in the instructions for Forms 1040 and 1040-SR, line 16.

☐ **No.** Complete the rest of Form 1040, 1040-SR, or 1040-NR.

Schedule D (Form 1040) 2021

**CONCEPT CHECK 7-4— LO 7-4**

1. The tax treatment of a capital gain or loss varies, depending on all of the following *except*
   a. The holding period.
   b. The basis of the asset sold.
   c. The taxpayer's regular taxable income.
   d. The netting of all gains and losses.

2. If property received has the same basis as the basis in the hands of the transferor, the holding period includes the holding period of the transferor. True or false?

3. The holding period of inherited property can be either short-term or long-term to the beneficiary. True or false?

4. The 3.8% surtax is charged on long-term capital gains only if a taxpayer is in the top tax bracket. True or false?

5. For sales after 2017, what are the maximum capital gain rates on the following?
   a. Collectibles gains.
   b. § 1202 gains.
   c. Unrecaptured § 1250 gains.
   d. Single taxpayer's regular taxable income of $40,350.
   e. Married taxpayers filing jointly with regular taxable income of $490,000.
   f. Married taxpayers filing separately with regular taxable income of $260,000.

# SALES OF BUSINESS PROPERTY
## LO 7-5

IRC § 1231 assets are assets used in a trade or business that are held longer than one year. The sales treatment of a § 1231 asset varies depending on three factors:

1. Whether the asset was sold at a gain or loss.
2. If a gain, whether the asset had been depreciated.
3. Whether the asset was depreciable real property (such as a building) or depreciable personal property (such as equipment).

As with capital assets, gains and losses from the sale of § 1231 assets must be netted. If a net § 1231 gain results, the net gain is taxed as a long-term capital gain subject to the depreciation recapture provisions discussed in the next section.[26] Thus, net § 1231 gains receive preferential tax rate treatment. If a net § 1231 loss results, the loss is treated as an ordinary loss. Ordinary loss treatment allows an unlimited loss deduction rather than the $3,000 limit placed on capital losses. The sale of § 1231 assets (both gains and losses) is initially reported on Form 4797.

---

**EXAMPLE 7-16**

Yenh sold land used in a trade or business for $15,000 in 2021. Yenh had purchased the land in 1991 for $7,000. The $8,000 gain is a § 1231 gain and goes on Form 4797, Part I. The $8,000 gain would be netted with other § 1231 transactions, and if a net § 1231 gain results, the gain is transferred to Schedule D as a long-term capital gain. If the netted transactions result in a net § 1231 loss, the loss from Form 4797 is transferred to line 4 of Schedule 1, as an ordinary loss.

---

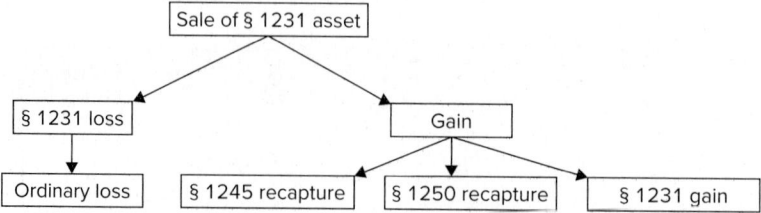

---

[26] IRC § 1231(a)(1).

# From Shoebox to Software

Tax preparation software makes most of the calculations for you. When a § 1245 asset is sold, simply go to the asset's Form 4562—Asset Depreciation worksheet and double-click on the Asset Disposed of icon. Enter the date sold and the proceeds from the sale. The gain and recapture amounts will automatically be calculated and placed in the appropriate section of Form 4797. This transaction cannot be done for existing clients Alan and Cherie Masters because none of Alan's business assets have been held longer than one year. Thus, do not enter this transaction on the Masters's tax return file.

## Recapture Provisions

The term *depreciation recapture* can be a difficult concept to understand. Recall from Chapter 6 that depreciation is an income tax deduction that permits the taxpayer to recover the cost or other basis of an asset used in a trade or business. The longer the taxpayer owns and uses the property, the more cost is "recovered"; therefore, the adjusted basis is reduced. The lower the adjusted basis, the greater the gain to be included in the taxpayer's taxable income. When the taxpayer sells § 1231 property for a gain, this gain can qualify for capital gain tax preference. The position of the IRS is that if a taxpayer was allowed to reduce taxable income by taking a depreciation deduction and paid less in taxes, when the property is sold, some of that gain attributable to depreciation deductions should be taxed at regular rates; this is depreciation recapture. The theory is to transform (recapture), as ordinary income, the portion of a gain that was created by taking a deduction for depreciation. For personal property (§ 1245 property) used in a business, this gain attributable to depreciation is taxed as ordinary income, whereas the gain attributable to depreciation for real property (§ 1250 property) is taxed at a special rate of 25%. Note that when a § 1231 asset is sold at a loss, the loss is always treated as an ordinary loss provided there are no § 1231 gains to offset the loss. The chart above illustrates the treatment of gains or losses on depreciable § 1231 assets. Recall that the only § 1231 asset that is not depreciated is land.

### § 1245 Recapture

IRC § 1245 property is personal trade or business property subject to depreciation. This definition encompasses most assets used in a trade or business with the exception of real property. Land, buildings, and building structural components (with the exception to be noted) are *not* included as § 1245 property. Although the most common example of § 1245 property is machinery and equipment used in a business, the § 1245 definition also includes such assets as autos, livestock, and certain buildings placed in service between 1981 and 1986.[27] The general rule concerning § 1245 recapture is that any gain recognized on the sale of § 1245 property is "ordinary" to the extent of depreciation taken.

For example, in May 2019, a taxpayer purchased a truck to be used 100% in a trade or business (5-year property) for $10,000. Using MACRS and the half-year convention, $6,160 of depreciation was taken. In May 2021, the truck was sold for $7,000. Here is how the gain on the sale is calculated and taxed:

| | |
|---|---|
| Truck cost basis | $10,000 |
| Less depreciation | 6,160 |
| Adjusted basis | $ 3,840 |
| | |
| Selling price | $ 7,000 |
| Less adjusted basis | 3,840 |
| Realized gain | $ 3,160 |

The gain treated as ordinary income is the lesser of the depreciation taken ($6,160) or the realized gain ($3,160); in this example, that would be $3,160. In practice, however, a § 1231 gain (in excess of depreciation) on § 1245 property is unusual because equipment rarely appreciates, and any gain is usually caused by the depreciation taken.

[27] IRC § 1245(a)(3). The only buildings considered § 1245 property are buildings placed in service from 1981 through 1986 and depreciated under the 15-, 18-, or 19-year ACRS rules.

**EXAMPLE 7-17**

On May 1, 2019, Noor purchased equipment costing $12,000 for business use. Depreciation deducted on the equipment from 2019 to 2021 was $7,392; the adjusted basis of the equipment is $4,608. Using the following independent situations, calculate the amount of any gain or loss assuming the equipment was sold on July 8, 2021, for the following amounts:

| Situation | Amount Realized | Adjusted Basis ($12,000 – $7,392) (Cost – Depreciation) | Gain (Loss) | § 1245 Recapture* | § 1231 Gain/Loss |
|---|---|---|---|---|---|
| 1 | $13,000 | $4,608 | $8,392 | $7,392 | $1,000 |
| 2 | 9,000 | 4,608 | 4,392 | 4,392 | –0– |
| 3 | 4,000 | 4,608 | (608) | –0– | (608) Ordinary loss/ no recapture |

* Amount up to depreciation taken or allowed.

Exhibit 7-4 shows the reporting of the first sale situation in Example 7-17 on Form 4797. The sale and total gain appear on Part III, lines 19–24. Lines 25a and 25b separate the recapture amount. The ordinary income of $7,392 is transferred to Part II on page 1 of Form 4797, and the § 1231 gain of $1,000 is transferred to Part I on page 1 of Form 4797. Business property sales that occur during the year are netted, and these netted gains and losses are reported on page 1 of Form 4797.

On January 18, 2019 the Treasury and Internal Revenue Service issued final IRC 199A regulations; [Section 1.199A-3(b)(2)} – Gains and Losses as QBI (1231, 1245, 1250). The final regulations removed the specific reference to Section 1231 assets and provided that any short term or long-term gain or loss are not taken into account for calculating QBI. However, if the item is not treated as capital, such as Section 1245 recapture, it is included in the QBI calculation. Section 1245 recapture provision is due to depreciation taken in previous years, and as depreciation deductions are made which reduce business income, the adjusted basis of the property is also adjusted. When the Section 1245 property is sold for a gain, to the extent any gain is from depreciation recapture, this amount is ordinary income and is included in the calculation for QBI. Any excess gain over depreciation taken is considered to be a capital gain.

For purposes of illustration of the effect of Section 1245 gain and depreciation recapture, this is a simplified example. There are many other items that could affect a taxpayer's completion of Form 1040 and all related schedules. The focus for Chapter 7 is how the Section 1245 ordinary gain affects the QBI calculation per Section 199A.

For example, on July 28, 2021, LMN Company sold office equipment for $6,500 that was purchased in May 10, 2019 at a cost basis of 8,000. This a section 1245 asset and was depreciated over 7-year MACRS using the half-year convention. Accumulated depreciation for the period 2019–2021 is $3,802. The adjusted basis is $8,000 – $3,802 = $4,198. The gain on the sale (from Form 4797) is $6,500 – $4,198 = $2,302. The gain is considered ordinary income to the extent of depreciation taken. In this example, the entire gain $2,302 is considered ordinary income and would be added to income to calculate QBI. Assume taxable income from Schedule C is $45,000 and ½ of self-employment tax is $3,179; then the total income for QBI on Form 8995 – Qualified Business Income Deduction Simplified Computation line 1 is calculated as follows:

| | |
|---|---|
| Income from Schedule C = $45,000 | |
| ½ SE tax | – 3,179 |
| Section 1245 recapture | + 2,302 |
| Total | $44,123 |

If there are no other entities to include on line 1 of Form 8995, the QBI deduction of 20% of $44,123 = $8,825 goes on line 5. After completing Form 8995, the amount on line 15 is then transferred to line 13 on Form 1040. The amount of income on line 8 on the Form 1040 is from Schedule 1 – line 3 – Schedule C income of $45,000 and line 4 – Gain from Form 4797 of $2,302.

### § 1250 Recapture

The phrase "§ 1250 recapture" refers to the portion of the capital gain from § 1250 property representing the tax benefit of a depreciation deduction previously taken. IRC § 1250 property includes depreciable real property used in a trade or business that has never been considered § 1245 property. Thus, § 1250 property includes all buildings, residential and nonresidential, used in a business or for the production of income.[28] The general rule for § 1250 recapture is that any gain on § 1250 property is considered ordinary to the extent the depreciation taken exceeds straight-line depreciation. Any other gain is considered § 1231 gain.

**EXHIBIT 7-4**  **Example of § 1245 Recapture on Form 4797 from Example 7-17, Situation 1**

| Form **4797** | **Sales of Business Property** | OMB No. 1545-0184 |
|---|---|---|
| | (Also Involuntary Conversions and Recapture Amounts Under Sections 179 and 280F(b)(2)) | 20**21** |
| Department of the Treasury Internal Revenue Service | ▶ Attach to your tax return. ▶ Go to *www.irs.gov/Form4797* for instructions and the latest information. | Attachment Sequence No. **27** |

Name(s) shown on return: **Noor Taxpayer**   Identifying number: **412-34-5670**

| | | |
|---|---|---|
| 1a | Enter the gross proceeds from sales or exchanges reported to you for 2021 on Form(s) 1099-B or 1099-S (or substitute statement) that you are including on line 2, 10, or 20. See instructions | 1a |
| b | Enter the total amount of gain that you are including on lines 2, 10, and 24 due to the partial dispositions of MACRS assets | 1b |
| c | Enter the total amount of loss that you are including on lines 2 and 10 due to the partial dispositions of MACRS assets | 1c |

**Part I**  Sales or Exchanges of Property Used in a Trade or Business and Involuntary Conversions From Other Than Casualty or Theft—Most Property Held More Than 1 Year (see instructions)

| 2 | (a) Description of property | (b) Date acquired (mo., day, yr.) | (c) Date sold (mo., day, yr.) | (d) Gross sales price | (e) Depreciation allowed or allowable since acquisition | (f) Cost or other basis, plus improvements and expense of sale | (g) Gain or (loss) Subtract (f) from the sum of (d) and (e) |
|---|---|---|---|---|---|---|---|
| | | | | | | | |
| | | | | | | | |
| | | | | | | | |

| | | |
|---|---|---|
| 3 | Gain, if any, from Form 4684, line 39 | 3 |
| 4 | Section 1231 gain from installment sales from Form 6252, line 26 or 37 | 4 |
| 5 | Section 1231 gain or (loss) from like-kind exchanges from Form 8824 | 5 |
| 6 | Gain, if any, from line 32, from other than casualty or theft | 6  1,000 |
| 7 | Combine lines 2 through 6. Enter the gain or (loss) here and on the appropriate line as follows | 7  1,000 |

**Partnerships and S corporations.** Report the gain or (loss) following the instructions for Form 1065, Schedule K, line 10, or Form 1120-S, Schedule K, line 9. Skip lines 8, 9, 11, and 12 below.

**Individuals, partners, S corporation shareholders, and all others.** If line 7 is zero or a loss, enter the amount from line 7 on line 11 below and skip lines 8 and 9. If line 7 is a gain and you don't have any prior year section 1231 losses, or they were recaptured in an earlier year, enter the gain from line 7 as a long-term capital gain on the Schedule D filed with your return and skip lines 8, 9, 11, and 12 below.

| | | |
|---|---|---|
| 8 | Nonrecaptured net section 1231 losses from prior years. See instructions | 8 |
| 9 | Subtract line 8 from line 7. If zero or less, enter -0-. If line 9 is zero, enter the gain from line 7 on line 12 below. If line 9 is more than zero, enter the amount from line 8 on line 12 below and enter the gain from line 9 as a long-term capital gain on the Schedule D filed with your return. See instructions | 9 |

**Part II**  Ordinary Gains and Losses (see instructions)

| 10 | Ordinary gains and losses not included on lines 11 through 16 (include property held 1 year or less): | | | | | | |
|---|---|---|---|---|---|---|---|
| | | | | | | | |
| | | | | | | | |
| | | | | | | | |

| | | |
|---|---|---|
| 11 | Loss, if any, from line 7 | 11 ( ) |
| 12 | Gain, if any, from line 7 or amount from line 8, if applicable | 12 |
| 13 | Gain, if any, from line 31 | 13  7,392 |
| 14 | Net gain or (loss) from Form 4684, lines 31 and 38a | 14 |
| 15 | Ordinary gain from installment sales from Form 6252, line 25 or 36 | 15 |
| 16 | Ordinary gain or (loss) from like-kind exchanges from Form 8824 | 16 |
| 17 | Combine lines 10 through 16 | 17  7,392 |

| | | |
|---|---|---|
| 18 | For all except individual returns, enter the amount from line 17 on the appropriate line of your return and skip lines a and b below. For individual returns, complete lines a and b below. | |
| a | If the loss on line 11 includes a loss from Form 4684, line 35, column (b)(ii), enter that part of the loss here. Enter the loss from income-producing property on Schedule A (Form 1040), line 16. (Do not include any loss on property used as an employee.) Identify as from "Form 4797, line 18a." See instructions | 18a |
| b | Redetermine the gain or (loss) on line 17 excluding the loss, if any, on line 18a. Enter here and on Schedule 1 (Form 1040), Part I, line 4 | 18b  7,392 |

For Paperwork Reduction Act Notice, see separate instructions.   Cat. No. 13086I   Form **4797** (2021)

Source: U.S. Department of the Treasury, Internal Revenue Service, Form 4797. Washington, DC: 2021.   *(continued)*

---

[28] One exception is for buildings placed in service from 1981 through 1986, as noted in footnote 27.

**EXHIBIT 7-4** *(concluded)*

Form 4797 (2021)                                                                                     Page **2**

### Part III — Gain From Disposition of Property Under Sections 1245, 1250, 1252, 1254, and 1255 (see instructions)

| 19 | (a) Description of section 1245, 1250, 1252, 1254, or 1255 property: | (b) Date acquired (mo., day, yr.) | (c) Date sold (mo., day, yr.) |
|---|---|---|---|
| A | Equipment | 05/01/19 | 07/08/21 |
| B | | | |
| C | | | |
| D | | | |

| | These columns relate to the properties on lines 19A through 19D. ▶ | | Property A | Property B | Property C | Property D |
|---|---|---|---|---|---|---|
| 20 | Gross sales price (**Note:** *See line 1a before completing.*) | 20 | 13,000 | | | |
| 21 | Cost or other basis plus expense of sale | 21 | 13,000 | | | |
| 22 | Depreciation (or depletion) allowed or allowable | 22 | 7,392 | | | |
| 23 | Adjusted basis. Subtract line 22 from line 21 | 23 | 4,608 | | | |
| 24 | Total gain. Subtract line 23 from line 20 | 24 | 8,392 | | | |
| 25 | **If section 1245 property:** | | | | | |
| a | Depreciation allowed or allowable from line 22 | 25a | 7,392 | | | |
| b | Enter the **smaller** of line 24 or 25a | 25b | 7,392 | | | |
| 26 | **If section 1250 property:** If straight line depreciation was used, enter -0- on line 26g, except for a corporation subject to section 291. | | | | | |
| a | Additional depreciation after 1975. See instructions | 26a | | | | |
| b | Applicable percentage multiplied by the **smaller** of line 24 or line 26a. See instructions. | 26b | | | | |
| c | Subtract line 26a from line 24. If residential rental property **or** line 24 isn't more than line 26a, skip lines 26d and 26e | 26c | | | | |
| d | Additional depreciation after 1969 and before 1976. | 26d | | | | |
| e | Enter the **smaller** of line 26c or 26d | 26e | | | | |
| f | Section 291 amount (corporations only) | 26f | | | | |
| g | Add lines 26b, 26e, and 26f | 26g | | | | |
| 27 | **If section 1252 property:** Skip this section if you didn't dispose of farmland or if this form is being completed for a partnership. | | | | | |
| a | Soil, water, and land clearing expenses | 27a | | | | |
| b | Line 27a multiplied by applicable percentage. See instructions | 27b | | | | |
| c | Enter the **smaller** of line 24 or 27b | 27c | | | | |
| 28 | **If section 1254 property:** | | | | | |
| a | Intangible drilling and development costs, expenditures for development of mines and other natural deposits, mining exploration costs, and depletion. See instructions | 28a | | | | |
| b | Enter the **smaller** of line 24 or 28a. | 28b | | | | |
| 29 | **If section 1255 property:** | | | | | |
| a | Applicable percentage of payments excluded from income under section 126. See instructions | 29a | | | | |
| b | Enter the **smaller** of line 24 or 29a. See instructions | 29b | | | | |

**Summary of Part III Gains.** Complete property columns A through D through line 29b before going to line 30.

| 30 | Total gains for all properties. Add property columns A through D, line 24 | 30 | 8,392 |
|---|---|---|---|
| 31 | Add property columns A through D, lines 25b, 26g, 27c, 28b, and 29b. Enter here and on line 13 | 31 | 7,392 |
| 32 | Subtract line 31 from line 30. Enter the portion from casualty or theft on Form 4684, line 33. Enter the portion from other than casualty or theft on Form 4797, line 6 | 32 | 1,000 |

### Part IV — Recapture Amounts Under Sections 179 and 280F(b)(2) When Business Use Drops to 50% or Less (see instructions)

| | | | (a) Section 179 | (b) Section 280F(b)(2) |
|---|---|---|---|---|
| 33 | Section 179 expense deduction or depreciation allowable in prior years. | 33 | | |
| 34 | Recomputed depreciation. See instructions | 34 | | |
| 35 | Recapture amount. Subtract line 34 from line 33. See the instructions for where to report | 35 | | |

Form **4797** (2021)

**TAX YOUR BRAIN**

Why are fewer building sales resulting in ordinary gains for taxpayers?

**ANSWER**

The main reason is that any depreciable real property purchased after 1986 must be depreciated using the straight-line method.[29] If the required depreciation is straight-line, there cannot be any depreciation in *excess* of straight-line.

In recent years, few § 1250 sales have been subject to the § 1250 recapture provisions. Most real property placed in service from 1981 through 1986 used accelerated depreciation methods over periods of 15, 18, or 19 years. Although it is likely that the same taxpayers still own many of these buildings, recall that these properties are considered § 1245 property. Most other buildings placed in service prior to 1981 are likely to be fully depreciated under either straight-line or some other method.[30] Thus, the depreciation taken would be the same under all methods.

The more important aspect of § 1250 property in recent years is the capital gain rate applied to the gain. The term *unrecaptured* refers to the amount of capital gain attributable to depreciation previously taken and is taxed at a 25% capital gain rate rather than the 0%, 15%, or 20% rate. For example, in February 2012, a taxpayer purchased for $200,000 a building to be used 100% in a trade or business (39-year property) and took $48,296 in total depreciation deductions. In July 2021, the taxpayer sold the building for $275,000. Assume the taxpayer is in the 35% tax bracket, is not subject to the surtax, and will not increase to the next tax bracket with the gain on the sale of the building. Here is how the gain on the sale is calculated and taxed:

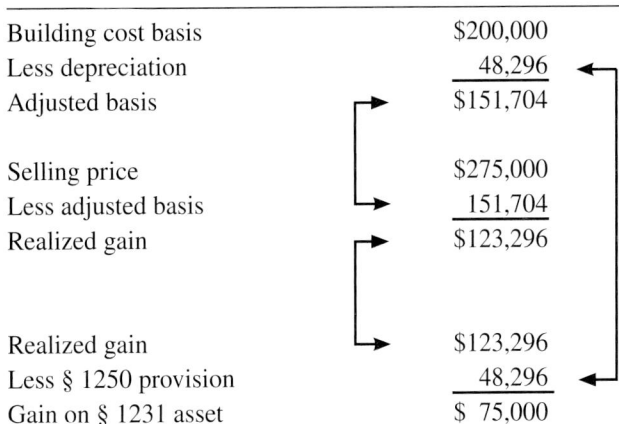

| | |
|---|---|
| Building cost basis | $200,000 |
| Less depreciation | 48,296 |
| Adjusted basis | $151,704 |
| | |
| Selling price | $275,000 |
| Less adjusted basis | 151,704 |
| Realized gain | $123,296 |
| | |
| Realized gain | $123,296 |
| Less § 1250 provision | 48,296 |
| Gain on § 1231 asset | $ 75,000 |

The gain treated as income subject to the 25% tax is the lesser of the depreciation taken ($48,296) or the realized gain ($123,296); in this example, that would be $48,296, taxed at a rate of 25%, resulting in $12,074 tax. If this was the only sale of a § 1231 asset, the remaining $75,000 gain due to the appreciation in value (selling price $275,000 − cost basis $200,000) would qualify for the 15% rate, resulting in $11,250 additional tax. Given this example, the total tax liability on the sale of the building would be $23,324. If there were no recapture provisions, the entire $123,296 gain would have been taxed at the 15% rate, generating only $18,494 in tax liability.

The portion of the gain that is attributable to depreciation is taxed at 25%; any gain in excess of the depreciation taken is considered a normal § 1231 gain and is potentially taxed at the preferential rate.

[29] Recall from Chapter 6 that the required MACRS depreciation for nonresidential real property is 39-year straight-line for property acquired after May 13, 1993, and the required method for residential real property is 27.5-year straight-line.

[30] If the § 1250 property purchased before 1981 is not fully depreciated, it will be late in its depreciation life. Because most accelerated methods for tax purposes switch to straight-line late in the asset's life or the depreciation allowed goes below straight-line, any possible recapture would be limited.

**EXAMPLE 7-18**

Abhay used a building in a trade or business that was purchased in June 2017 for $165,000. Abhay sold the building in June 2021. Assume straight-line depreciation was taken in the amount of $16,927. The adjusted basis is $148,073 ($165,000 − $16,927). Using the following independent situations, calculate the amount of any gain or loss, assuming the building sells in 2021 for the following amounts. Assume the maximum gain rate of 15%.

| Situation | Amount Realized | Adjusted Basis | Gain/(Loss) | § 1250 Amount | § 1231 Gain/Loss |
|---|---|---|---|---|---|
| 1 | $172,000 | $148,073 | $23,927 | $16,927 × 25% 4,232 | $7,000 × 15% 1,050 |
| 2 | 160,000 | 148,073 | 11,927 | 11,927 × 25% 2,982 | –0– |
| 3 | 140,000 | 148,073 | (8,073) | –0– | (8,073) ordinary loss |

# From Shoebox to Software

Any sale of § 1250 property is originally reported on page 2 of Form 4797, and the gain is transferred to Schedule D. Exhibit 7-5 illustrates the reporting on Form 4797 for situation 1 in Example 7-18. Note that the entire gain appears on page 1 of Form 4797. Because the gain is all capital, the gain transfers to Schedule D. On page 2 of Schedule D, separate the 25% gain and the 15% gain, and then calculate the tax. The tax preparation software will calculate the § 1250 gain. The unrecaptured § 1250 Gain worksheet shows the tax effect of this transaction.

**CONCEPT CHECK 7-5—**

**LO 7-5**

1. Under § 1231, gains receive preferential tax rate treatment, but losses are limited to $3,000 per year. True or false?
2. The only pure § 1231 asset is land used in a trade or business. True or false?
3. What is meant by the term *depreciation recapture?*
4. What is the difference between a § 1245 asset and a § 1250 asset?
5. What is the difference between recaptured and unrecaptured gain provisions?

# TAX ISSUES FOR SPECIAL TYPES OF SALES
## LO 7-6

### Sales of Block Stock, Mutual Fund Capital Gain Distributions, and Sales of Shares from Mutual Funds

When shares of stock are purchased on different dates or for different prices, the shares are termed purchases of *blocks* of stock. Each block of stock may differ in basis and holding period (short-term or long-term). The taxpayer can specify which block is being sold (specific identification), or if the blocks are not specified, they are treated as coming from the earliest purchases (first-in, first-out).

A *mutual fund* is an investment vehicle that pools the resources of numerous taxpayers and purchases shares of stock in a portfolio. Tax treatment of a mutual fund investment can be difficult. For example, a mutual fund buys and sells individual stocks throughout the year, generating capital gains and losses from these sales. At year-end, the individual

**EXHIBIT 7-5**   Sale of § 1250 Property on Form 4797 and Schedule D from Example 7-18, Situation 1

| | |
|---|---|
| Form **4797** | **Sales of Business Property** (Also Involuntary Conversions and Recapture Amounts Under Sections 179 and 280F(b)(2)) |

OMB No. 1545-0184

2021

Department of the Treasury
Internal Revenue Service

▶ Attach to your tax return.
▶ Go to *www.irs.gov/Form4797* for instructions and the latest information.

Attachment Sequence No. **27**

Name(s) shown on return: **Abhay Taxpayer** — Information from Example 7-18, Situation 1

Identifying number: **412-34-5670**

**1a** Enter the gross proceeds from sales or exchanges reported to you for 2021 on Form(s) 1099-B or 1099-S (or substitute statement) that you are including on line 2, 10, or 20. See instructions . . . . **1a**

**b** Enter the total amount of gain that you are including on lines 2, 10, and 24 due to the partial dispositions of MACRS assets . . . . **1b**

**c** Enter the total amount of loss that you are including on lines 2 and 10 due to the partial dispositions of MACRS assets . . . . **1c**

**Part I   Sales or Exchanges of Property Used in a Trade or Business and Involuntary Conversions From Other Than Casualty or Theft—Most Property Held More Than 1 Year** (see instructions)

| 2 (a) Description of property | (b) Date acquired (mo., day, yr.) | (c) Date sold (mo., day, yr.) | (d) Gross sales price | (e) Depreciation allowed or allowable since acquisition | (f) Cost or other basis, plus improvements and expense of sale | (g) Gain or (loss) Subtract (f) from the sum of (d) and (e) |
|---|---|---|---|---|---|---|
| | | | | | | |

| | | |
|---|---|---|
| **3** Gain, if any, from Form 4684, line 39 | **3** | |
| **4** Section 1231 gain from installment sales from Form 6252, line 26 or 37 | **4** | |
| **5** Section 1231 gain or (loss) from like-kind exchanges from Form 8824 | **5** | |
| **6** Gain, if any, from line 32, from other than casualty or theft | **6** | 23,927 |
| **7** Combine lines 2 through 6. Enter the gain or (loss) here and on the appropriate line as follows | **7** | 23,927 |

**Partnerships and S corporations.** Report the gain or (loss) following the instructions for Form 1065, Schedule K, line 10, or Form 1120-S, Schedule K, line 9. Skip lines 8, 9, 11, and 12 below.

**Individuals, partners, S corporation shareholders, and all others.** If line 7 is zero or a loss, enter the amount from line 7 on line 11 below and skip lines 8 and 9. If line 7 is a gain and you didn't have any prior year section 1231 losses, or they were recaptured in an earlier year, enter the gain from line 7 as a long-term capital gain on the Schedule D filed with your return and skip lines 8, 9, 11, and 12 below.

**8** Nonrecaptured net section 1231 losses from prior years. See instructions . . . **8**

**9** Subtract line 8 from line 7. If zero or less, enter -0-. If line 9 is zero, enter the gain from line 7 on line 12 below. If line 9 is more than zero, enter the amount from line 8 on line 12 below and enter the gain from line 9 as a long-term capital gain on the Schedule D filed with your return. See instructions. . . . **9**

**Part II   Ordinary Gains and Losses** (see instructions)

**10** Ordinary gains and losses not included on lines 11 through 16 (include property held 1 year or less):

| | | |
|---|---|---|
| **11** Loss, if any, from line 7 | **11** ( ) | |
| **12** Gain, if any, from line 7 or amount from line 8, if applicable | **12** | |
| **13** Gain, if any, from line 31 | **13** | |
| **14** Net gain or (loss) from Form 4684, lines 31 and 38a | **14** | |
| **15** Ordinary gain from installment sales from Form 6252, line 25 or 36 | **15** | |
| **16** Ordinary gain or (loss) from like-kind exchanges from Form 8824 | **16** | |
| **17** Combine lines 10 through 16 | **17** | |

**18** For all except individual returns, enter the amount from line 17 on the appropriate line of your return and skip lines a and b below. For individual returns, complete lines a and b below.

**a** If the loss on line 11 includes a loss from Form 4684, line 35, column (b)(ii), enter that part of the loss here. Enter the loss from income-producing property on Schedule A (Form 1040), line 16. (Do not include any loss on property used as an employee.) Identify as from "Form 4797, line 18a." See instructions . . . **18a**

**b** Redetermine the gain or (loss) on line 17 excluding the loss, if any, on line 18a. Enter here and on Schedule 1 (Form 1040), Part I, line 4 . . . **18b**

For Paperwork Reduction Act Notice, see separate instructions.   Cat. No. 13086I   Form **4797** (2021)

Source: U.S. Department of the Treasury, Internal Revenue Service, Form 4797 and Schedule D (Form 1040). Washington, DC: 2021.

*(continued)*

**EXHIBIT 7-5** *(continued)*

Form 4797 (2021)                                                                                                                 Page **2**

### Part III    Gain From Disposition of Property Under Sections 1245, 1250, 1252, 1254, and 1255 (see instructions)

| 19 | (a) Description of section 1245, 1250, 1252, 1254, or 1255 property: | | (b) Date acquired (mo., day, yr.) | (c) Date sold (mo., day, yr.) |
|---|---|---|---|---|
| A | Building | | 06/01/17 | 06/01/21 |
| B | | | | |
| C | | | | |
| D | | | | |

| | These columns relate to the properties on lines 19A through 19D. ▶ | | Property A | Property B | Property C | Property D |
|---|---|---|---|---|---|---|
| 20 | Gross sales price (**Note:** *See line 1a before completing.*) | 20 | 172,000 | | | |
| 21 | Cost or other basis plus expense of sale | 21 | 165,000 | | | |
| 22 | Depreciation (or depletion) allowed or allowable | 22 | 16,927 | | | |
| 23 | Adjusted basis. Subtract line 22 from line 21 | 23 | 148,073 | | | |
| 24 | Total gain. Subtract line 23 from line 20 | 24 | 23,927 | | | |
| 25 | **If section 1245 property:** | | | | | |
| a | Depreciation allowed or allowable from line 22 | 25a | | | | |
| b | Enter the **smaller** of line 24 or 25a. | 25b | | | | |
| 26 | **If section 1250 property:** If straight line depreciation was used, enter -0- on line 26g, except for a corporation subject to section 291. | | | | | |
| a | Additional depreciation after 1975. See instructions | 26a | | | | |
| b | Applicable percentage multiplied by the **smaller** of line 24 or line 26a. See instructions. | 26b | | | | |
| c | Subtract line 26a from line 24. If residential rental property **or** line 24 isn't more than line 26a, skip lines 26d and 26e | 26c | | | | |
| d | Additional depreciation after 1969 and before 1976. | 26d | | | | |
| e | Enter the **smaller** of line 26c or 26d | 26e | | | | |
| f | Section 291 amount (corporations only) | 26f | | | | |
| g | Add lines 26b, 26e, and 26f | 26g | | | | |
| 27 | **If section 1252 property:** Skip this section if you didn't dispose of farmland or if this form is being completed for a partnership. | | | | | |
| a | Soil, water, and land clearing expenses | 27a | | | | |
| b | Line 27a multiplied by applicable percentage. See instructions | 27b | | | | |
| c | Enter the **smaller** of line 24 or 27b | 27c | | | | |
| 28 | **If section 1254 property:** | | | | | |
| a | Intangible drilling and development costs, expenditures for development of mines and other natural deposits, mining exploration costs, and depletion. See instructions | 28a | | | | |
| b | Enter the **smaller** of line 24 or 28a. | 28b | | | | |
| 29 | **If section 1255 property:** | | | | | |
| a | Applicable percentage of payments excluded from income under section 126. See instructions | 29a | | | | |
| b | Enter the **smaller** of line 24 or 29a. See instructions | 29b | | | | |

**Summary of Part III Gains.** Complete property columns A through D through line 29b before going to line 30.

| 30 | Total gains for all properties. Add property columns A through D, line 24 | 30 | 23,927 |
|---|---|---|---|
| 31 | Add property columns A through D, lines 25b, 26g, 27c, 28b, and 29b. Enter here and on line 13 | 31 | 0 |
| 32 | Subtract line 31 from line 30. Enter the portion from casualty or theft on Form 4684, line 33. Enter the portion from other than casualty or theft on Form 4797, line 6 | 32 | 23,927 |

### Part IV    Recapture Amounts Under Sections 179 and 280F(b)(2) When Business Use Drops to 50% or Less (see instructions)

| | | | (a) Section 179 | (b) Section 280F(b)(2) |
|---|---|---|---|---|
| 33 | Section 179 expense deduction or depreciation allowable in prior years. | 33 | | |
| 34 | Recomputed depreciation. See instructions | 34 | | |
| 35 | Recapture amount. Subtract line 34 from line 33. See the instructions for where to report | 35 | | |

Form **4797** (2021)

**EXHIBIT 7-5**  *(continued)*

| SCHEDULE D<br>(Form 1040)<br>Department of the Treasury<br>Internal Revenue Service (99) | **Capital Gains and Losses**<br>▶ Attach to Form 1040, 1040-SR, or 1040-NR.<br>▶ Go to *www.irs.gov/ScheduleD* for instructions and the latest information.<br>▶ Use Form 8949 to list your transactions for lines 1b, 2, 3, 8b, 9, and 10. | OMB No. 1545-0074<br>2021<br>Attachment<br>Sequence No. **12** |
|---|---|---|

| Name(s) shown on return | | Your social security number |
|---|---|---|
| Abhay Taxpayer | Information from Example 7-18, Situation 1 | 412-34-5670 |

Did you dispose of any investment(s) in a qualified opportunity fund during the tax year? ☐ **Yes** ☐ **No**
If "Yes," attach Form 8949 and see its instructions for additional requirements for reporting your gain or loss.

**Part I  Short-Term Capital Gains and Losses—Generally Assets Held One Year or Less** (see instructions)

| | (d)<br>Proceeds<br>(sales price) | (e)<br>Cost<br>(or other basis) | (g)<br>Adjustments<br>to gain or loss from<br>Form(s) 8949, Part I,<br>line 2, column (g) | (h) Gain or (loss)<br>Subtract column (e)<br>from column (d) and<br>combine the result<br>with column (g) |
|---|---|---|---|---|
| **1a** Totals for all short-term transactions reported on Form 1099-B for which basis was reported to the IRS and for which you have no adjustments (see instructions). However, if you choose to report all these transactions on Form 8949, leave this line blank and go to line 1b . | | | | |
| **1b** Totals for all transactions reported on Form(s) 8949 with **Box A** checked | | | | |
| **2** Totals for all transactions reported on Form(s) 8949 with **Box B** checked | | | | |
| **3** Totals for all transactions reported on Form(s) 8949 with **Box C** checked | | | | |

| | | |
|---|---|---|
| **4** Short-term gain from Form 6252 and short-term gain or (loss) from Forms 4684, 6781, and 8824 | **4** | |
| **5** Net short-term gain or (loss) from partnerships, S corporations, estates, and trusts from Schedule(s) K-1 | **5** | |
| **6** Short-term capital loss carryover. Enter the amount, if any, from line 8 of your **Capital Loss Carryover Worksheet** in the instructions | **6** | ( ) |
| **7** **Net short-term capital gain or (loss).** Combine lines 1a through 6 in column (h). If you have any long-term capital gains or losses, go to Part II below. Otherwise, go to Part III on the back | **7** | |

**Part II  Long-Term Capital Gains and Losses—Generally Assets Held More Than One Year** (see instructions)

| | (d)<br>Proceeds<br>(sales price) | (e)<br>Cost<br>(or other basis) | (g)<br>Adjustments<br>to gain or loss from<br>Form(s) 8949, Part II,<br>line 2, column (g) | (h) Gain or (loss)<br>Subtract column (e)<br>from column (d) and<br>combine the result<br>with column (g) |
|---|---|---|---|---|
| **8a** Totals for all long-term transactions reported on Form 1099-B for which basis was reported to the IRS and for which you have no adjustments (see instructions). However, if you choose to report all these transactions on Form 8949, leave this line blank and go to line 8b . | | | | |
| **8b** Totals for all transactions reported on Form(s) 8949 with **Box D** checked | | | | |
| **9** Totals for all transactions reported on Form(s) 8949 with **Box E** checked | | | | |
| **10** Totals for all transactions reported on Form(s) 8949 with **Box F** checked. | | | | |

| | | |
|---|---|---|
| **11** Gain from Form 4797, Part I; long-term gain from Forms 2439 and 6252; and long-term gain or (loss) from Forms 4684, 6781, and 8824 | **11** | 23,927 |
| **12** Net long-term gain or (loss) from partnerships, S corporations, estates, and trusts from Schedule(s) K-1 | **12** | |
| **13** Capital gain distributions. See the instructions | **13** | |
| **14** Long-term capital loss carryover. Enter the amount, if any, from line 13 of your **Capital Loss Carryover Worksheet** in the instructions | **14** | ( ) |
| **15** **Net long-term capital gain or (loss).** Combine lines 8a through 14 in column (h). Then, go to Part III on the back | **15** | 23,927 |

For Paperwork Reduction Act Notice, see your tax return instructions.　　Cat. No. 11338H　　Schedule D (Form 1040) 2021

*(continued)*

**EXHIBIT 7-5**
*(concluded)*

Schedule D (Form 1040) 2021

Page **2**

**Part III** Summary

| | | | |
|---|---|---|---|
| 16 | Combine lines 7 and 15 and enter the result | 16 | 23,927 |

• If line 16 is a **gain,** enter the amount from line 16 on Form 1040, 1040-SR, or 1040-NR, line 7. Then, go to line 17 below.

• If line 16 is a **loss,** skip lines 17 through 20 below. Then, go to line 21. Also be sure to complete line 22.

• If line 16 is **zero,** skip lines 17 through 21 below and enter -0- on Form 1040, 1040-SR, or 1040-NR, line 7. Then, go to line 22.

17  Are lines 15 and 16 **both** gains?
☑ **Yes.** Go to line 18.
☐ **No.** Skip lines 18 through 21, and go to line 22.

18  If you are required to complete the **28% Rate Gain Worksheet** (see instructions), enter the amount, if any, from line 7 of that worksheet ▶ | **18** |

19  If you are required to complete the **Unrecaptured Section 1250 Gain Worksheet** (see instructions), enter the amount, if any, from line 18 of that worksheet ▶ | **19** | 16,927

20  Are lines 18 and 19 both zero or blank and are you not filing Form 4952?
☐ **Yes.** Complete the **Qualified Dividends and Capital Gain Tax Worksheet** in the instructions for Forms 1040 and 1040-SR, line 16. **Don't** complete lines 21 and 22 below.

☐ **No.** Complete the **Schedule D Tax Worksheet** in the instructions. **Don't** complete lines 21 and 22 below.

21  If line 16 is a loss, enter here and on Form 1040, 1040-SR, or 1040-NR, line 7, the **smaller** of:

• The loss on line 16; or
• ($3,000), or if married filing separately, ($1,500) | **21** | ( | ) |

**Note:** When figuring which amount is smaller, treat both amounts as positive numbers.

22  Do you have qualified dividends on Form 1040, 1040-SR, or 1040-NR, line 3a?

☐ **Yes.** Complete the **Qualified Dividends and Capital Gain Tax Worksheet** in the instructions for Forms 1040 and 1040-SR, line 16.

☐ **No.** Complete the rest of Form 1040, 1040-SR, or 1040-NR.

Schedule D (Form 1040) 2021

---

**Unrecaptured Section 1250 Gain Worksheet—Line 19**

*Keep for Your Records*

**If you are not reporting a gain on Form 4797, line 7, skip lines 1 through 9 and go to line 10.**

1. If you have a section 1250 property in Part III of Form 4797 for which you made an entry in Part I of Form 4797 (but not on Form 6252), enter the **smaller** of line 22 or line 24 of Form 4797 for that property. If you did not have any such property, go to line 4. If you had more than one such property, see instructions .......... | **1.** | 16,927
2. Enter the amount from Form 4797, line 26g, for the property for which you made an entry on line 1 ........ | **2.** | 0
3. Subtract line 2 from line 1 ..................... | **3.** | 16,927
4. Enter the total unrecaptured section 1250 gain included on line 26 or line 37 of Form(s) 6252 from installment sales of trade or business property held more than 1 year (see instructions) ..................... | **4.** | 0
5. Enter the total of any amounts reported to you on a Schedule K-1 from a partnership or an S corporation as "unrecaptured section 1250 gain" ..................... | **5.** | 0
6. Add lines 3 through 5 ..................... | **6.** | 16,927
7. Enter the **smaller** of line 6 or the gain from Form 4797, line 7 ................. | **7.** | 16,927 |
8. Enter the amount, if any, from Form 4797, line 8 .................. | **8.** | 0 |
9. Subtract line 8 from line 7. If zero or less, enter -0- ..................... | **9.** | 16,927
10. Enter the amount of any gain from the sale or exchange of an interest in a partnership attributable to unrecaptured section 1250 gain (see instructions) ..................... | **10.** | 0
11. Enter the total of any amounts reported to you as "unrecaptured section 1250 gain" on a Schedule K-1, Form 1099-DIV, or Form 2439 from an estate, trust, real estate investment trust, or mutual fund (or other regulated investment company) or in connection with a Form 1099-R ..................... | **11.** | 0
12. Enter the total of any unrecaptured section 1250 gain from sales (including installment sales) or other dispositions of section 1250 property held more than 1 year for which you did not make an entry in Part I of Form 4797 for the year of sale (see instructions) ..................... | **12.** | 0
13. Add lines 9 through 12 ..................... | **13.** | 16,927
14. If you had any section 1202 gain or collectibles gain or (loss), enter the total of lines 1 through 4 of the **28% Rate Gain Worksheet.** Otherwise, enter -0- ......... | **14.** | 0
15. Enter the (loss), if any, from Schedule D, line 7. If Schedule D, line 7, is zero or a gain, enter -0- ..................... | **15.** | ( 0)
16. Enter your long-term capital loss carryovers from Schedule D, line 14, and Schedule K-1 (Form 1041), box 11, code C* ..................... | **16.** | ( 0)
17. Combine lines 14 through 16. If the result is a (loss), enter it as a positive amount. If the result is zero or a gain, enter -0- ..................... | **17.** | 0
18. **Unrecaptured section 1250 gain.** Subtract line 17 from line 13. If zero or less, enter -0-. If more than zero, enter the result here and on Schedule D, line 19 ..................... | **18.** | 16,927

**EXAMPLE 7-19**

Mashun purchased the following blocks of stock:

| Date | Shares | Price |
|------|--------|-------|
| February 5, 2019 | 100 | $10 |
| August 15, 2019 | 50 | 9 |
| December 9, 2020 | 150 | 8 |

Mashun sold 200 shares of stock on July 26, 2021, for $8.50 per share, for a total of $1,700.

*Using the specific identification method:*

The shares sold were identified as being 100 shares from the February 5, 2019, and 100 shares from the December 9, 2020, purchases. The basis for each block is calculated as follows:

| | | |
|---|---|---|
| February 5, 2019, purchase | 100 shares × $10 | = $1,000 |
| July 26, 2021, sale | 100 shares × $8.50 | = 850 |
| Loss on sale | | $ (150) long-term |

| | | |
|---|---|---|
| December 9, 2020, purchase | 100 shares × $8 | = $800 |
| July 26, 2021, sale | 100 shares × $8.50 | = 850 |
| Gain on sale | | $ 50 short-term |

*Using the first-in, first-out method:*

| | | |
|---|---|---|
| February 5, 2019, purchase | 100 shares × $10 | = $1,000 |
| August 15, 2019, purchase | 50 shares × $9 | = 450 |
| Basis | | 1,450 |
| July 26, 2021, sale | 150 shares × $8.50 | = 1,275 |
| Loss on the sale | | $ (175) long-term |

| | | |
|---|---|---|
| December 9, 2020, purchase | 50 shares × $8 | = $400 |
| July 26, 2021, sale | 50 shares × $8.50 | = 425 |
| Gain on sale | | $ 25 short-term |

investors are responsible for paying taxes on their share of these gains and losses, which are considered to be long-term regardless of how long they are held by shareholders. These capital gains, known as *capital gain distributions,* are reported to the taxpayer (investor) on Form 1099-DIV.[31] The taxpayer reports the capital gain distribution on line 13 of Schedule D (any gains subject to a rate of 28% appear on the annual mutual fund statement and are reported by the taxpayer on Schedule D). If there are no other capital gains or losses, the amounts on Form 1099-DIV, line 2a, can go directly on Form 1040, line 7 (see Exhibit 7-6).

Remember that ordinary dividends are a distribution from the earnings and profits of the corporation, are ordinary income, and include short-term capital gains.[32] Ordinary dividends are reported to taxpayers on Form 1099-DIV, and sales of stock are reported on Form 1099-B. Many mutual funds and stock brokerages use a substitute Form 1099-DIV or 1099-B to record multiple events under the taxpayer's account.

Many brokerage firms provide the taxpayer with an annual statement on which all activity for the year is reported. Many firms, but not all, automatically calculate the average cost of the shares for the taxpayer's convenience. Form 1099-B—Proceeds from Broker and Barter

[31] The mutual fund may also pass through dividends to the investors.

[32] Publication 550, *Investment Income and Expenses,* Chapter 1—"Dividends and Other Corporate Distributions".

**EXHIBIT 7-6**

| Standard Deduction for— • Single or Married filing | 6a | Social security benefits . . | 6a | | **b** Taxable amount . . . . . . | 6b | |
|---|---|---|---|---|---|---|---|
| | 7 | Capital gain or (loss). Attach Schedule D if required. If not required, check here . . . . . ▶ ☐ | | | | 7 | |
| | 8 | Other income from Schedule 1, line 10   . . . . . . . . . . . . . . . . . . . . . | | | | 8 | |

| 12 | Net long-term gain or (loss) from partnerships, S corporations, estates, and trusts from Schedule(s) K-1 | 12 | |
|---|---|---|---|
| 13 | Capital gain distributions. See the instructions . . . . . . . . . . . . . . . . . . | 13 | |
| 14 | Long-term capital loss carryover. Enter the amount, if any, from line 13 of your **Capital Loss Carryover Worksheet** in the instructions   . . . . . . . . . . . . . . . . . . . . | 14 | ( ) |
| 15 | **Net long-term capital gain or (loss).** Combine lines 8a through 14 in column (h). Then, go to Part III on the back . . . . . . . . . . . . . . . . . . . . . . . . . . . . . | 15 | |

Source: U.S. Department of the Treasury, Internal Revenue Service, Form 1040. Washington, DC: 2021.

Exchange Transactions—has been redesigned to accommodate changes to Form 8949. One of the important changes to Form 1099-B is to box 3—if checked, basis reported to IRS. Refer to Exhibit 7-7 for a completed Form 1099-B.

A tax challenge occurs in determining the basis of units or shares of the mutual funds sold. Often mutual fund stock purchases can occur at different times with regular purchases, dividend reinvestment programs, or automatic monthly investments. The simplest case is the sale of *all* shares. The gain or loss is the difference between the sales price and the total cost basis of the shares. However, if a taxpayer who has invested in a mutual fund for 10 years at $200 per month with all of the capital gains and dividends reinvested sells *some* (not all) of those shares, the taxpayer will have a challenge in establishing a cost basis from which to calculate gain or loss. For example, suppose the taxpayer has 1,000 mutual fund shares acquired at many different times over decades. This taxpayer then sells 56.125 units of the mutual fund for $5,000. The challenge is in establishing a cost of these shares that had different purchase prices to calculate the gain or loss on the sale. To simplify this challenge, the taxpayer can use one of three methods in determining the basis of the units in the mutual fund:[33]

- **First-in, first-out:** The first shares purchased are assumed to be the first shares sold. This usually results in the largest gain when the value of the mutual fund units appreciates.
- **Specific identification:** The taxpayer specifies exactly which units are sold from the fund.
- **Average basis:** The taxpayer takes the total cost basis and divides by the total number of units to get an average cost per unit (single-category method).

After the basis has been determined, with an entry in box 3 of Form 1099-B or by separate calculations, any gain or loss is reported on Form 8949 and the totals transferred to Schedule D. Using the information in Example 7-20, the gain on the sale of the stock held in this mutual fund will be $3,500 using the first-in, first-out method; $1,500 using the specific identification method; and $2,000 using the single-category average basis method. Using the information from Example 7-20, Exhibits 7-7 and 7-8 illustrate the recording of mutual fund dividends and sales on Form 8949, Schedule D, and the Qualified Dividends and Capital Gain Tax worksheet.

[33] Reg. § 1.1012-1(e).

**EXAMPLE 7-20**

Jane purchased the following shares in the Get Rich Quick Mutual Fund:

| Date | Shares | Price per Share | Total Cost |
|------|--------|-----------------|------------|
| 2018 | 1,000 | $5 | $ 5,000 |
| 2019 | 1,500 | 7 | 10,500 |
| 2020 | 500 | 9 | 4,500 |

The basis of the block stock purchases can be calculated as follows:

**First-In, First-Out**

| Shares | Price per Share | Total Cost | Sale Price | Gain/Loss |
|--------|-----------------|------------|------------|-----------|
| 1,000 | $5 | $5,000 | | |
| 500 | 7 | 3,500 | | |
| | | **$8,500** | **$12,000** | **$3,500** |

**Specific Identification**

| Shares | Price per Share | Total Cost | Sale Price | Gain/Loss |
|--------|-----------------|------------|------------|-----------|
| 2018: 500 | $5 | $ 2,500 | | |
| 2019: 500 | 7 | 3,500 | | |
| 2020: 500 | 9 | 4,500 | | |
| | | **$10,500** | **$12,000** | **$1,500** |

**Average Basis—Single Category**

| Shares | Price per Share | Total Cost | Sale Price | Gain/Loss |
|--------|-----------------|------------|------------|-----------|
| 1,000 | $5 | $ 5,000 | | |
| 1,500 | 7 | 10,500 | | |
| 500 | 9 | 4,500 | | |
| | | $20,000/3,000 shares = $6.667/share: 1,500 × $6.667 = | | |
| | | **$10,000** | **$12,000** | **$2,000** |

Assume that on May 15, 2021, Jane sold 1,500 shares at a unit price of $8 for a total sale of $12,000. Jane also received Form 1099-DIV (see Exhibit 7-7) from Get Rich Quick Mutual Fund showing $500 in ordinary dividends, $300 in qualified dividends, and $1,000 in capital gain distributions. Assume she has gross wages of $50,000, is filing as a single taxpayer, takes the standard deduction, and has taxable income (Form 1040, line 11b) of $41,100. She is using the single-category average cost method to value her shares. See Exhibit 7-8 for a completed Schedule D and Qualified Dividends and Capital Gains worksheet.

## Worthless Securities

A taxpayer cannot deduct a loss on a security until the security is sold or it becomes worthless. At issue is the definition of *worthless*. Treasury Reg. § 1.165-5 states that the act of abandonment establishes worthlessness. Therefore, worthless securities follow the capital loss limitation rules for deductibility. If a security becomes worthless during the year, the taxpayer reports a loss from a sale or exchange of a capital asset on the last day of the taxable year.[34]

---

[34] IRC § 165(g).

**EXHIBIT 7-7** **Form 1099-B and 1099-DIV from Example 7-20**

☐ CORRECTED (if checked)

PAYER'S name, street address, city or town, state or province, country, ZIP or foreign postal code, and telephone no.

**Get Rich Quick Mutual Fund**

| Applicable checkbox on Form 8949 | OMB No. 1545-0715 | **Proceeds From Broker and Barter Exchange Transactions** |
|---|---|---|

**2021** Form **1099-B**

**1a** Description of property (Example: 100 sh. XYZ Co.)
**1,500 shares of mutual fund**

| 1b Date acquired | 1c Date sold or disposed |
|---|---|
| **various** | **05/15/2021** |

| 1d Proceeds | 1e Cost or other basis |
|---|---|
| $ 12,000.00 | $ |

| 1f Accrued market discount | 1g Wash sale loss disallowed |
|---|---|
| $ | $ |

PAYER'S TIN: 36-8156713   RECIPIENT'S TIN: 412-34-5670

**Copy B** **For Recipient**

RECIPIENT'S name

**Jane Taxpayer**

Street address (including apt. no.)

**123 Main Street**

City or town, state or province, country, and ZIP or foreign postal code

**Anywhere, USA 54321**

Account number (see instructions)

2 Short-term gain or loss ☐  Long-term gain or loss ☑  Ordinary ☐
3 If checked, proceeds from: Collectibles ☐  QOF ☐
4 Federal income tax withheld $
5 If checked, noncovered security ☐
6 Reported to IRS: Gross proceeds ☐  Net proceeds ☐
7 If checked, loss is not allowed based on amount in 1d ☐
8 Profit or (loss) realized in 2021 on closed contracts $
9 Unrealized profit or (loss) on open contracts—12/31/2020 $
10 Unrealized profit or (loss) on open contracts—12/31/2021 $
11 Aggregate profit or (loss) on contracts $
12 If checked, basis reported to IRS ☐
13 Bartering $

CUSIP number   FATCA filing requirement ☐
14 State name  15 State identification no.  16 State tax withheld $ $

This is important tax information and is being furnished to the IRS. If you are required to file a return, a negligence penalty or other sanction may be imposed on you if this income is taxable and the IRS determines that it has not been reported.

Form **1099-B**   (Keep for your records)   www.irs.gov/Form1099B   Department of the Treasury - Internal Revenue Service

---

☐ CORRECTED (if checked)

PAYER'S name, street address, city or town, state or province, country, ZIP or foreign postal code, and telephone no.

**Get Rich Quick Mutual Fund**

| 1a Total ordinary dividends | OMB No. 1545-0110 | **Dividends and Distributions** |
|---|---|---|

1a Total ordinary dividends $ 500.00
1b Qualified dividends $ 300.00
**2021** Form **1099-DIV**
2a Total capital gain distr. $ 1,000.00  2b Unrecap. Sec. 1250 gain $

**Copy B** **For Recipient**

2c Section 1202 gain $   2d Collectibles (28%) gain $
2e Section 897 ordinary dividends $   2f Section 897 capital gain $

PAYER'S TIN: 36-8156713   RECIPIENT'S TIN: 412-34-5670

RECIPIENT'S name

**Jane Taxpayer**

3 Nondividend distributions $   4 Federal income tax withheld $

Street address (including apt. no.)

5 Section 199A dividends $   6 Investment expenses $

**123 Main Street**

7 Foreign tax paid $   8 Foreign country or U.S. possession

City or town, state or province, country, and ZIP or foreign postal code

9 Cash liquidation distributions $   10 Noncash liquidation distributions $

**Anywhere, USA 54321**

FATCA filing requirement ☐
11 Exempt-interest dividends $   12 Specified private activity bond interest dividends $

Account number (see instructions)

13 State  14 State identification no.  15 State tax withheld $ $

This is important tax information and is being furnished to the IRS. If you are required to file a return, a negligence penalty or other sanction may be imposed on you if this income is taxable and the IRS determines that it has not been reported.

Form **1099-DIV**   (keep for your records)   www.irs.gov/Form1099DIV   Department of the Treasury - Internal Revenue Service

Source: U.S. Department of the Treasury, Internal Revenue Service, Form 1099-B and 1099-DIV. Washington, DC: 2021.

**EXHIBIT 7-8** Form 8949 and Schedule D from Example 7-20

## SCHEDULE D
### (Form 1040)

Department of the Treasury
Internal Revenue Service (99)

# Capital Gains and Losses

► Attach to Form 1040, 1040-SR, or 1040-NR.
► Go to *www.irs.gov/ScheduleD* for instructions and the latest information.
► Use Form 8949 to list your transactions for lines 1b, 2, 3, 8b, 9, and 10.

OMB No. 1545-0074

**2021**

Attachment
Sequence No. **12**

Name(s) shown on return
Jane Taxpayer

Information from Example 7-20

Your social security number
412-34-5670

Did you dispose of any investment(s) in a qualified opportunity fund during the tax year? ☐ Yes ☑ No
If "Yes," attach Form 8949 and see its instructions for additional requirements for reporting your gain or loss.

*DRAFT AS OF August 18, 2021 DO NOT FILE*

### Part I    Short-Term Capital Gains and Losses—Generally Assets Held One Year or Less (see instructions)

| See instructions for how to figure the amounts to enter on the lines below.<br><br>This form may be easier to complete if you round off cents to whole dollars. | (d)<br>Proceeds<br>(sales price) | (e)<br>Cost<br>(or other basis) | (g)<br>Adjustments<br>to gain or loss from<br>Form(s) 8949, Part I,<br>line 2, column (g) | (h) Gain or (loss)<br>Subtract column (e)<br>from column (d) and<br>combine the result<br>with column (g) |
|---|---|---|---|---|
| **1a** Totals for all short-term transactions reported on Form 1099-B for which basis was reported to the IRS and for which you have no adjustments (see instructions). However, if you choose to report all these transactions on Form 8949, leave this line blank and go to line 1b | | | | |
| **1b** Totals for all transactions reported on Form(s) 8949 with **Box A** checked . . . . . . . . . . | | | | |
| **2** Totals for all transactions reported on Form(s) 8949 with **Box B** checked . . . . . . . . . . | | | | |
| **3** Totals for all transactions reported on Form(s) 8949 with **Box C** checked . . . . . . . . . . | | | | |

| | | |
|---|---|---|
| **4** Short-term gain from Form 6252 and short-term gain or (loss) from Forms 4684, 6781, and 8824 . . | **4** | |
| **5** Net short-term gain or (loss) from partnerships, S corporations, estates, and trusts from Schedule(s) K-1 . . . . . . . . . . . . . . . . . . . . . | **5** | |
| **6** Short-term capital loss carryover. Enter the amount, if any, from line 8 of your **Capital Loss Carryover Worksheet** in the instructions . . . . . . . . . . . . . | **6** | ( ) |
| **7** **Net short-term capital gain or (loss).** Combine lines 1a through 6 in column (h). If you have any long-term capital gains or losses, go to Part II below. Otherwise, go to Part III on the back . . . . . . . | **7** | |

### Part II    Long-Term Capital Gains and Losses—Generally Assets Held More Than One Year (see instructions)

| See instructions for how to figure the amounts to enter on the lines below.<br><br>This form may be easier to complete if you round off cents to whole dollars. | (d)<br>Proceeds<br>(sales price) | (e)<br>Cost<br>(or other basis) | (g)<br>Adjustments<br>to gain or loss from<br>Form(s) 8949, Part II,<br>line 2, column (g) | (h) Gain or (loss)<br>Subtract column (e)<br>from column (d) and<br>combine the result<br>with column (g) |
|---|---|---|---|---|
| **8a** Totals for all long-term transactions reported on Form 1099-B for which basis was reported to the IRS and for which you have no adjustments (see instructions). However, if you choose to report all these transactions on Form 8949, leave this line blank and go to line 8b . | | | | |
| **8b** Totals for all transactions reported on Form(s) 8949 with **Box D** checked . . . . . . . . . . | | | | |
| **9** Totals for all transactions reported on Form(s) 8949 with **Box E** checked . . . . . . . . . . | 12,000 | 10,000 | | 2,000 |
| **10** Totals for all transactions reported on Form(s) 8949 with **Box F** checked. . . . . . . . . . | | | | |

| | | |
|---|---|---|
| **11** Gain from Form 4797, Part I; long-term gain from Forms 2439 and 6252; and long-term gain or (loss) from Forms 4684, 6781, and 8824 . . . . . . . . . . . . . . . | **11** | |
| **12** Net long-term gain or (loss) from partnerships, S corporations, estates, and trusts from Schedule(s) K-1 | **12** | |
| **13** Capital gain distributions. See the instructions . . . . . . . . . . . . . . . | **13** | 1,000 |
| **14** Long-term capital loss carryover. Enter the amount, if any, from line 13 of your **Capital Loss Carryover Worksheet** in the instructions . . . . . . . . . . . . . | **14** | ( ) |
| **15** **Net long-term capital gain or (loss).** Combine lines 8a through 14 in column (h). Then, go to Part III on the back . . . . . . . . . . . . . . . . . . . . | **15** | 3,000 |

For Paperwork Reduction Act Notice, see your tax return instructions.          Cat. No. 11338H          Schedule D (Form 1040) 2021

Source: U.S. Department of the Treasury, Internal Revenue Service, Form 8949 and Schedule D (Form 1040). Washington, DC: 2021.

*(continued)*

**EXHIBIT 7-8** *(continued)*

Schedule D (Form 1040) 2021                                                                                             Page **2**

**Part III** Summary

| | | | |
|---|---|---|---|
| 16 | Combine lines 7 and 15 and enter the result . . . . . . . . . . . . . . | **16** | 3,000 |

- If line 16 is a **gain**, enter the amount from line 16 on Form 1040, 1040-SR, or 1040-NR, line 7. Then, go to line 17 below.
- If line 16 is a **loss**, skip lines 17 through 20 below. Then, go to line 21. Also be sure to complete line 22.
- If line 16 is **zero**, skip lines 17 through 21 below and enter -0- on Form 1040, 1040-SR, or 1040-NR, line 7. Then, go to line 22.

17 Are lines 15 and 16 **both** gains?
  ☑ **Yes.** Go to line 18.
  ☐ **No.** Skip lines 18 through 21, and go to line 22.

18 If you are required to complete the **28% Rate Gain Worksheet** (see instructions), enter the amount, if any, from line 7 of that worksheet . . . . . . . . . . ▶ | **18** |

19 If you are required to complete the **Unrecaptured Section 1250 Gain Worksheet** (see instructions), enter the amount, if any, from line 18 of that worksheet . . . . . . . ▶ | **19** |

20 Are lines 18 and 19 both zero or blank and are you not filing Form 4952?
  ☑ **Yes.** Complete the **Qualified Dividends and Capital Gain Tax Worksheet** in the instructions for Forms 1040 and 1040-SR, line 16. **Don't** complete lines 21 and 22 below.

  ☐ **No.** Complete the **Schedule D Tax Worksheet** in the instructions. **Don't** complete lines 21 and 22 below.

21 If line 16 is a loss, enter here and on Form 1040, 1040-SR, or 1040-NR, line 7, the **smaller** of:

- The loss on line 16; or
- ($3,000), or if married filing separately, ($1,500)  } . . . . . . . . . | **21** | ( ) |

**Note:** When figuring which amount is smaller, treat both amounts as positive numbers.

22 Do you have qualified dividends on Form 1040, 1040-SR, or 1040-NR, line 3a?

  ☐ **Yes.** Complete the **Qualified Dividends and Capital Gain Tax Worksheet** in the instructions for Forms 1040 and 1040-SR, line 16.

  ☐ **No.** Complete the rest of Form 1040, 1040-SR, or 1040-NR.

Schedule D (Form 1040) 2021

---

Form 8949 (2021)                                                            Attachment Sequence No. **12A**    Page **2**

| Name(s) shown on return. Name and SSN or taxpayer identification no. not required if shown on other side | Social security number or taxpayer identification number |
|---|---|
| Jane Taxpayer | 412-34-5670 |

*Before you check Box D, E, or F below, see whether you received any Form(s) 1099-B or substitute statement(s) from your broker. A substitute statement will have the same information as Form 1099-B. Either will show whether your basis (usually your cost) was reported to the IRS by your broker and may even tell you which box to check.*

**Part II** **Long-Term.** Transactions involving capital assets you held more than 1 year are generally long-term (see instructions). For short-term transactions, see page 1.

**Note:** You may aggregate all long-term transactions reported on Form(s) 1099-B showing basis was reported to the IRS and for which no adjustments or codes are required. Enter the totals directly on Schedule D, line 8a; you aren't required to report these transactions on Form 8949 (see instructions).

**You** *must* **check Box D, E, *or* F below. Check only one box.** If more than one box applies for your long-term transactions, complete a separate Form 8949, page 2, for each applicable box. If you have more long-term transactions than will fit on this page for one or more of the boxes, complete as many forms with the same box checked as you need.

☐ **(D)** Long-term transactions reported on Form(s) 1099-B showing basis was reported to the IRS (see **Note** above)
☑ **(E)** Long-term transactions reported on Form(s) 1099-B showing basis **wasn't** reported to the IRS
☐ **(F)** Long-term transactions not reported to you on Form 1099-B

| 1 (a) Description of property (Example: 100 sh. XYZ Co.) | (b) Date acquired (Mo., day, yr.) | (c) Date sold or disposed of (Mo., day, yr.) | (d) Proceeds (sales price) (see instructions) | (e) Cost or other basis. See the **Note** below and see *Column (e)* in the separate instructions | (f) Code(s) from instructions | (g) Amount of adjustment | (h) Gain or (loss). Subtract column (e) from column (d) and combine the result with column (g) |
|---|---|---|---|---|---|---|---|
| 1,500 shares GRQ Mutual Fund | various | 05/15/21 | 12,000 | 10,000 | | | 2,000 |

EXHIBIT 7-8 *(concluded)*

## Qualified Dividends and Capital Gain Tax Worksheet—Line 16 — *Keep for Your Records*

**Before you begin:**
✓ See the earlier instructions for line 16 to see if you can use this worksheet to figure your tax.
✓ Before completing this worksheet, complete Form 1040 or 1040-SR through line 15.
✓ If you don't have to file Schedule D and you received capital gain distributions, be sure you checked the box on Form 1040 or 1040-SR, line 7.

| | | | |
|---|---|---|---|
| 1. | Enter the amount from Form 1040 or 1040-SR, line 15. However, if you are filing Form 2555 (relating to foreign earned income), enter the amount from line 3 of the Foreign Earned Income Tax Worksheet | **1.** | 41,300 |
| 2. | Enter the amount from Form 1040 or 1040-SR, line 3a* | **2.** | 300 |
| 3. | Are you filing Schedule D?* <br> ☒ **Yes.** Enter the **smaller** of line 15 or 16 of Schedule D. If either line 15 or 16 is blank or a loss, enter -0-. <br> ☐ **No.** Enter the amount from Form 1040 or 1040-SR, line 7. | **3.** | 3,000 |
| 4. | Add lines 2 and 3 | **4.** | 3,300 |
| 5. | Subtract line 4 from line 1. If zero or less, enter -0- | **5.** | 38,000 |
| 6. | Enter: <br> $40,000 if single or married filing separately, <br> $80,000 if married filing jointly or qualifying widow(er), <br> $53,600 if head of household. | **6.** | 40,000 |
| 7. | Enter the smaller of line 1 or line 6 | **7.** | 40,000 |
| 8. | Enter the smaller of line 5 or line 7 | **8.** | 38,000 |
| 9. | Subtract line 8 from line 7. This amount is taxed at 0% | **9.** | 2,000 |
| 10. | Enter the smaller of line 1 or line 4 | **10.** | 3,300 |
| 11. | Enter the amount from line 9 | **11.** | 2,000 |
| 12. | Subtract line 11 from line 10 | **12.** | 1,300 |
| 13. | Enter: <br> $441,450 if single, <br> $248,300 if married filing separately, <br> $496,600 if married filing jointly or qualifying widow(er), <br> $469,050 if head of household. | **13.** | 441,450 |
| 14. | Enter the smaller of line 1 or line 13 | **14.** | 41,300 |
| 15. | Add lines 5 and 9 | **15.** | 40,000 |
| 16. | Subtract line 15 from line 14. If zero or less, enter -0- | **16.** | 1,300 |
| 17. | Enter the smaller of line 12 or line 16 | **17.** | 1,300 |
| 18. | Multiply line 17 by 15% (0.15) | **18.** | 195 |
| 19. | Add lines 9 and 17 | **19.** | 3,300 |
| 20. | Subtract line 19 from line 10 | **20.** | 0 |
| 21. | Multiply line 20 by 20% (0.20) | **21.** | 0 |
| 22. | Figure the tax on the amount on line 5. If the amount on line 5 is less than $100,000, use the Tax Table to figure the tax. If the amount on line 5 is $100,000 or more, use the Tax Computation Worksheet | **22.** | 4,364 |
| 23. | Add lines 18, 21, and 22 | **23.** | 4,559 |
| 24. | Figure the tax on the amount on line 1. If the amount on line 1 is less than $100,000, use the Tax Table to figure the tax. If the amount on line 1 is $100,000 or more, use the Tax Computation Worksheet | **24.** | 4,840 |
| 25. | **Tax on all taxable income.** Enter the **smaller** of line 23 or 24. Also include this amount on the entry space on Form 1040 or 1040-SR, line 16. If you are filing Form 2555, don't enter this amount on the entry space on Form 1040 or 1040-SR, line 16. Instead, enter it on line 4 of the Foreign Earned Income Tax Worksheet | **25.** | 4,559 |

*\* If you are filing Form 2555, see the footnote in the Foreign Earned Income Tax Worksheet before completing this line.*

As of the date this text went to print, the 2021 qualified dividends and capital gain tax worksheet had not been released by the IRS. The worksheet above was created using the 2020 form. The tax calculations on lines 22 to 25 were computed using the 2021 Tax Tables so they accurately reflect 2021 taxes. The only difference of substance between 2020 and 2021 is that the income thresholds noted on line 13 will slightly increase, but the revised numbers will not affect the tax calculations at the end of the form above. When the 2021 form is released, an updated Exhibit will be posted to Connect.

The mere fact that a company declares bankruptcy is not sufficient to indicate worthlessness. It is often difficult to pinpoint exactly when a security became worthless and hence determine a sale date for long-term versus short-term treatment. Thus, for these purposes, a loss on a worthless security is assumed to occur on the last day of the taxable year.[35]

[35] IRC § 165(g).

**EXAMPLE 7-21**

Eleonora purchased 500 shares in Bad News, Inc., for $10,000 on December 12, 2020. The company promptly went bankrupt in February 2021 with no hope of recovery for the shareholders. Accordingly, the date the stock is deemed to be worthless occurs on December 31, 2021; Eleonora would have a long-term capital loss of $10,000 in tax year 2021.

## Sales of Inherited Property

Remember that in this situation the basis to the beneficiaries is the FMV at the date of death or alternate valuation date (if the estate qualifies for and elects to use the alternate date) and that the holding period is always considered long-term. If no federal estate tax return is filed, use the FMV at the date of death. For example, Taylor inherits property from a relative with an FMV of $5,000 on June 13, 2021. On November 21, 2021, Taylor sells the property for $7,000, for a $2,000 gain. Even though Taylor held the property for less than one year, the gain is taxed as a long-term capital gain.

## Sales of Property Received as a Gift

To figure the gain or loss from the sale of property received as a gift, the person who received the gift must know the adjusted basis of the property to the donor and the FMV when the gift was given. If the FMV is less than the donor's adjusted basis at the time of the gift, the basis for figuring the gain is the donor's basis and the FMV is the basis for figuring a loss. If the FMV is equal to or more than the donor's adjusted basis, the basis for any gain or loss on a sale is the donor's adjusted basis.[36]

**EXAMPLE 7-22**

Juan receives property as a gift. At the time of the gift, the property had an FMV of $7,000. The donor's basis was $9,000. Using the following situations, calculate Juan's gain or loss on the sale of the gifted property:

| Situation | Sale Price | Donor Basis | FMV at Date of Gift | Gain/Loss |
|---|---|---|---|---|
| 1 | $11,000 | $9,000 | $7,000 | $2,000 gain (use donor basis) |
| 2 | 6,000 | 9,000 | 7,000 | $(1,000) loss (use FMV at date of gift) |
| 3 | 8,000 | 9,000 | 7,000 | No gain or loss; sale price in between basis and FMV |

*Note:* If the FMV of the gift was $10,000 at the date of the gift, the donor's basis of $9,000 would be used to calculate any gains or losses on a subsequent sale.

**CONCEPT CHECK 7-6— LO 7-6**

1. Explain the three types of methods used to determine the basis of the units in a mutual fund.
2. It is often difficult to pinpoint exactly when a security becomes worthless, so the loss on a worthless security is treated as occurring on the last day of the taxable year. True or false?
3. The basis for property given as a gift is always the FMV of the property at the time of the gift. True or false?
4. The tax treatment of a gain on the sale of inherited property depends on the holding period of the deceased taxpayer. True or false?

Table 7-5 is a summary table for the sale of all assets. These assets include ordinary assets, § 1221 capital assets, § 1231 assets, § 1245 assets, and § 1250 assets.

---

[36] See Chapter 4 in Publication 550 for more detailed information about sales of property received as a gift subject to gift tax.

**TABLE 7-5   Summary of Asset Sales**

| | Asset Type | | | | |
|---|---|---|---|---|---|
| | **Ordinary Asset** | **§ 1221 Capital Asset** | **§ 1231 Asset** | **§ 1245 Asset** | **§ 1250 Asset** |
| | 1. Short-term business assets<br>2. Short-term gains or losses<br>3. Inventory<br>4. Accounts receivable or notes receivable | 1. Not inventory<br>2. Not depreciable business assets<br>3. Not copyrights*<br>4. Not accounts receivable or notes receivable | 1. Depreciable or nondepreciable business assets held ≥ 1 year<br>2. Long-term depreciable or nondepreciable real property<br>3. Not inventory<br>4. Not copyrights<br>5. Not short-term business assets | 1. Subset of § 1231<br>2. Depreciable personal property | 1. Subset of § 1231<br>2. Depreciable real property |
| | | | **Gain (Loss)** | | |
| Gain (loss) treatment | Ordinary income/loss | **Gains**<br>Net short-term capital gains held ≤ 1 year<br>Net long-term capital gains held > 1 year 0%, 15%, or 20% rate†<br>Collectibles 28%<br>§ 1202 investments<br>**Losses**<br>Net short-term capital losses held ≤ 1 year<br>Net long-term capital losses held > 1 year | **Gains**<br>Net long-term taxed at long-term capital gains preferential rates<br>**Losses**<br>Net capital losses deducted as an ordinary loss | **Gains**<br>Ordinary to the extent of depreciation taken; excess is true § 1231 capital gain<br>**Losses**<br>§ 1231 loss—ordinary loss | **Gains**<br>Ordinary to the extent that depreciation taken exceeds straight-line; subject to 25% rate to the extent of depreciation taken; excess is true § 1231 capital gain<br>**Losses**<br>§ 1231 loss—ordinary loss |
| | | | **Form Reported** | | |
| | Form 4797, Part II | Schedule D | Form 4797, Part I | Form 4797, Part III | Form 4797, Part III |
| | | | **Asset Example** | | |
| | Inventory or account receivable | Stocks and securities | Business land | Business equipment | Business building |

* Refer to new election provisions for musical works.
† Sales after 2012.

# Summary

**LO 7-1:** Define the terms and identify the tax forms used in sales of property transactions.

- The amount realized (or sales proceeds) and the adjusted basis of the asset must be determined before a gain or loss on the sale of the asset can be determined.
- *A gain or loss on the sale of property* is the difference between the amount realized from the sale and the asset's adjusted basis.
- The nature of tax reporting for gains and losses on the sale of property depends primarily on the use of the asset.
- Form 8949, Schedule D, and Form 4797 are used to record sales of property.

**LO 7-2:** Classify assets sold as ordinary assets, § 1221 capital assets, or § 1231 business assets.

- Ordinary income property is any asset that is "not a capital asset."
- In general, any asset used for personal purposes or investment is a *capital asset,* but there are eight basic exceptions to this definition.
- IRC § 1231 property is property used in a trade or business that is depreciable or real and held for more than one year.
- Any business asset that is disposed of within one year of acquisition is an ordinary income asset.

**LO 7-3:** Explain and apply the tax rules for recognizing gains or losses on the sale of ordinary assets.

- Inventory and accounts receivable are not ordinary income assets unless they are outside (not part of) the normal course of business.
- Inventory sold is a part of the cost of goods sold, whereas accounts receivable are generated from sales of the inventory.
- Gains are taxed at the taxpayer's regular tax rate; there is no preferential tax treatment.

**LO 7-4:** Explain and apply the tax rules for recognizing short-term and long-term gains or losses on the sale of capital assets (§ 1221).

- Tax treatment for a capital gain or loss depends on the holding period of the asset. Assets must be held for more than one year for preferential treatment.
- Generally, the property received through a gift or nontaxable exchange has the same basis as the basis in the hands of the transferor.
- The exception to this rule is property received through inheritance, in which case the asset is always long-term property.
- Tax rates differ, depending on the holding period; short-term assets are taxed at regular taxpayer rates, whereas long-term assets are taxed at preferential rates.
- The 0%, 15%, and 20% rates are for long-term gains on capital assets.
- The 25% rate is applied to that portion of the gain attributable to the depreciation on real property used in a trade or business.
- The 28% rate applies to "collectibles" gains and gains on § 1202 property (qualified small business stock).
- There is a 3.8% surtax applied to the lesser of net investment income (NII) or when modified AGI exceeds $250,000 for MFJ, $200,000 for single taxpayers, and $125,000 for MFS.
- All short-term gains and losses are netted, as are all long-term gains and losses. The resultant gain or loss determines the deductibility of a loss and the tax rate used for gains.

**LO 7-5:** Calculate the recognized gain or loss on the sale of § 1231 business assets, including gain recapture provisions of § 1245 and § 1250 property.

- Gains and losses from the sale of § 1231 assets must be netted before tax rates are applied.
- A net § 1231 gain is taxed as a long-term capital gain subject to recapture provisions.
- Net § 1231 gains receive preferential tax rate treatment.
- Net § 1231 losses are treated as ordinary losses and are fully deductible.
- Losses disallowed in the current year can be carried over to future years.
- Depreciation recapture rules are designed to transform some or all of a § 1231 gain into an ordinary gain.
- IRC § 1245 (personal trade or business property) and § 1250 (buildings, residential and nonresidential) are subsets of § 1231 property and apply only when there is a gain on the sale of a property that has been depreciated.
- The tax rate for unrecaptured depreciation on § 1250 property is 25%.

**LO 7-6:** Describe the tax rules for special types of sales, including block stock sales, capital gain distributions, sales of mutual funds, worthless securities, and sales of property received as a gift or through inheritance.

- Block stock sales are shares that are sold at one time but were purchased at different times or prices. Use either specific identification or the first-in, first-out method to calculate share basis.
- A mutual fund pools resources from various sources and purchases shares of stock in a portfolio.
- Capital gain distributions from mutual funds can be reported either on Schedule D or directly on Form 1040 if Schedule D is not being prepared.
- Determining the basis of mutual fund shares can be challenging. Three methods are available for calculating the basis of the shares: first-in, first-out; specific identification; and single-category average basis. Form 1099-B has been redesigned to show cost basis if known.
- Worthless securities are treated as losses from a sale or exchange of a capital asset on the last day of the taxable year.
- Property received through an inheritance is always considered to be long-term property regardless of the holding period by the beneficiary. The basis to the beneficiary is valued at the FMV at the date of death or alternate valuation date chosen by the personal representative if qualified under estate tax rules.
- The FMV and adjusted basis of the property at the date given by the donor must be known for the donee to properly calculate a gain or loss on the sale of gifted property in the future.

## EA Fast Fact

ADMITTED TO PRACTICE BEFORE THE IRS  **ENROLLED AGENT**

The Enrolled Agent exam is an online examination that is given at one of Prometric's 300 test sites throughout the US and internationally. The exam is offered year-round except for the months of March and April, which allows the IRS time to update the next exam cycle for any new tax law, as well as changes to existing tax code. Candidates may schedule each part of the exam at their convenience, and in any order. Additionally, candidates may choose to take just one part of the exam at a time. You can find more information on taking the exam at https://www.prometric.com/test-takers/search/irs

### IMPORTANT

You are eligible to receive absolutely free, the Surgent Enrolled Agent review program for Part I of the EA exam as a result of purchasing this text. To activate your free access, go to https://Surgent.com/McGrawHill/EA.

## Discussion Questions

All applicable discussion questions are available with **Connect**

EA  LO 7-1  1. How are the terms *basis, adjusted basis,* and *fair market value* defined as they apply to the calculation of gains and losses?

_____

_____

_____

EA  LO 7-1  2. What is meant by the terms *realized gain (loss)* and *recognized gain (loss)* as they apply to the sale of assets by a taxpayer?

_____

_____

_____

EA LO 7-2   3. How can the gain from the sale of property be characterized? Why is it important to correctly characterize the gain on the sale of property?

_____

_____

_____

EA LO 7-2   4. What is a *capital asset?* What factors affect the determination of whether an asset is classified as a capital asset?

_____

_____

_____

EA LO 7-2   5. What determines whether land is a capital asset? How else can land be classified?

_____

_____

_____

EA LO 7-2   6. What is a § 1231 asset? How are gains and losses from the sale of § 1231 assets treated? On what tax form are gains and losses from the sale of § 1231 assets reported?

_____

_____

_____

EA LO 7-2   7. When we determine whether an asset is a § 1231 asset, does the length of time the asset is held affect the classification? Explain.

_____

_____

_____

EA LO 7-2, 7-4   8. What are the different classifications of capital assets? List each classification and the rate at which the gains are taxed.

_____

_____

_____

EA LO 7-3   9. Discuss the concept of ordinary income property and give some examples.

_____

_____

_____

EA LO 7-4   10. What factors affect the taxability of capital gains and losses?

_____

_____

_____

**EA**   LO 7-4   11. Does the length of time a capital asset is held affect the gain or loss on the sale of the asset? Explain.

_____

_____

_____

**EA**   LO 7-4   12. How is a net capital loss treated? Include in your answer a discussion of how a net capital loss is treated in relation to other income.

_____

_____

_____

**EA**   LO 7-4   13. In what ways can a capital asset be acquired, and how is the holding period determined for each method of acquisition?

_____

_____

_____

**EA**   LO 7-4   14. Capital gains can be taxed at several different rates. What determines the rate?

_____

_____

_____

**EA**   LO 7-4   15. What is a § 1202 gain, and how is it taxed?

_____

_____

_____

**EA**   LO 7-4   16. Discuss the netting process of capital gains and losses. What are the possible outcomes of the netting process, and how would each situation be taxed?

_____

_____

_____

**EA**   LO 7-5   17. What is a § 1245 asset? How is it related to a § 1231 asset?

_____

_____

_____

**EA**   LO 7-5   18. What is a § 1250 asset? How is it related to a § 1231 asset?

_____

_____

_____

**EA** LO 7-5 19. Explain the terms *recapture* and *unrecaptured provisions* as they apply to § 1250 assets.

_____

_____

_____

**EA** LO 7-6 20. What is a capital gain distribution, and how is it taxed?

_____

_____

_____

**EA** LO 7-6 21. How can a taxpayer determine the basis of units from a mutual fund?

_____

_____

_____

**EA** LO 7-6 22. How are gains (losses) from the sale of property acquired from a decedent taxed?

_____

_____

_____

**EA** LO 7-6 23. Explain how gains (losses) from the sale of property acquired as a gift are taxed.

_____

_____

_____

## Multiple-Choice Questions

All applicable multiple-choice questions are available with **Connect**©

**EA** LO 7-1 24. Yakov sells a parcel of land for $75,000 cash, and the buyer assumes Yakov's liability of $10,000 on the land. Yakov's basis is $64,000. What is the gain or loss on the sale?

  a. $1,000 loss.
  b. $1,000 gain.
  c. $11,000 gain.
  d. $21,000 gain.

**EA** LO 7-1 25. All of the following statements regarding the definition of basis other than cost are true *except*

  a. The basis for assets received as a gift depends on whether the FMV is greater than, equal to, or less than the donor's basis at the time of the gift.
  b. The basis of property transferred to a taxpayer from a former spouse pursuant to a divorce decree is valued at the FMV at the date of the decree.
  c. The basis of inherited property is the FMV at the date of death or alternate valuation date that the personal representative is allowed by law to choose.
  d. The basis for property received in exchange for services rendered is the FMV of the property if the FMV of the services is not known beforehand.

**EA** LO 7-1 26. All of the following increase the basis of stock held for investment *except*

  a. Commission fees on the purchase of the stock.
  b. Stock splits.

  *c.* Stock dividends from a dividend reinvestment plan.

  *d.* All of the above increase the basis of stock held for investment.

**EA** **LO 7-2** 27. In 2018 Grant purchased land for $103,000 for use in a business. Grant sold it in 2021 for $114,000. What are the amount and type of gain on this sale before netting any other gains and/or losses?

  *a.* $11,000 § 1231 gain.

  *b.* $11,000 ordinary gain.

  *c.* $11,000 short-term capital gain

  *d.* $11,000 long-term capital gain.

**EA** **LO 7-3** 28. On May 20, 2020, Jessica purchased land for $105,647 to use in a business. Jessica sold it on May 21, 2021, for $102,595. What are the amount and type of loss on this sale if Jessica does not have any other sales from a trade or business?

  *a.* $3,052 deferred loss.

  *b.* $3,052 long-term capital loss.

  *c.* $3,052 ordinary loss.

  *d.* $3,052 § 1231 loss.

**EA** **LO 7-4** 29. Medhat and Neveen, married filing jointly, have $420,000 in modified AGI and $101,000 of NII. They will pay a surtax of

  *a.* $0.

  *b.* $3,268.

  *c.* $3,458.

  *d.* $3,838.

**EA** **LO 7-4** 30. In 2007, Duncan purchased 2,000 shares of stock for $50,000 in a midsize local company with gross assets of $15,000,000. In 2021, Duncan sold the stock for $68,000. How is the gain treated for tax purposes?

  *a.* $18,000 capital gain and taxed at preferential rates.

  *b.* $9,000 excluded from gross income under § 1202 and $9,000 taxed at regular rates.

  *c.* $9,000 excluded from gross income under § 1202 and $9,000 taxed at 28%.

  *d.* $13,500 excluded from gross income under § 1202 and $4,500 taxed at preferential rates.

**EA** **LO 7-4** 31. Mishka sold the following stocks in 2021: 200 shares of Dearborn Investments, purchased May 15, 2020, for $3,050 and sold January 9, 2021, for $4,135; and 40 shares of State Street Investments, purchased November 7, 2018, for $11,875 and sold March 29, 2021, for $8,675. What are the pre-net amount and nature of the gain (loss) on the sale of these transactions on Mishka's 1040 return for 2021?

  *a.* $1,085 short-term gain and $3,000 long-term loss.

  *b.* $1,085 short-term gain and $3,200 long-term loss.

  *c.* $1,915 net long-term loss.

  *d.* $2,115 net long-term loss.

**EA** **LO 7-4** 32. Which statement is true regarding short-term capital gains?

  *a.* If there are a net short-term gain and a net long-term gain, both gains are taxed at regular rates.

  *b.* A long-term loss offsets a short-term gain, and if a gain results, the gain is taxed at regular rates.

  *c.* A long-term loss offsets a short-term gain, and if a gain results, the gain is taxed at preferential rates.

  *d.* If there are a net short-term gain and a net long-term gain, both gains are taxed at preferential rates.

**EA**  **LO 7-4**  33. Which is true regarding long-term capital gains?

    *a.* A net long-term gain can be taxed at 28%, 25%, 20%, 15%, or 0%, depending on the type of gain generated.

    *b.* A net long-term loss can be offset against a long-term gain, and if there is a resulting long-term gain, it is taxed at regular rates.

    *c.* A long-term loss can offset a long-term gain only if the netting result produces a loss of more than $3,000.

    *d.* A net long-term gain can offset a short-term gain but not a short-term loss.

**EA**  **LO 7-4**  34. When there are a net short-term loss and a net long-term loss, which of the following is true?

    *a.* The entire short-term loss is used to reduce other income before the long-term loss can be used to offset other income.

    *b.* A long-term loss is used to reduce other income before the short-term loss.

    *c.* Regardless of the amount of a short-term or long-term loss, the maximum amount of loss that can be taken in any one year is $3,000. Any remaining loss amounts can be carried forward for three years for individual taxpayers.

    *d.* Regardless of the amount of a short-term or long-term loss, the maximum amount of loss that can be taken in any one year is $3,000. Any remaining loss amounts can be carried forward indefinitely for individual taxpayers.

**EA**  **LO 7-4**  35. Alton received a Form 1099-B that shows a net sales price of $3,750 on the sale of 600 shares of FNP Company. The stock was bought on October 21, 2020, and sold on October 22, 2021. The basis in the stock is $2,225, of which $30 is a commission fee. What are the amount and nature of Alton's gain?

    *a.* $1,525 short-term gain.

    *b.* $1,525 long-term gain.

    *c.* $1,555 short-term gain.

    *d.* $1,555 long-term gain.

**EA**  **LO 7-4, 7-6**  36. Amal received a Form 1099-DIV with a capital gain distribution of $210 and also a Form 1099-B from the sale of 240 shares of AMS stock purchased for $2,900 plus a $28 commission fee on February 22, 2020. The net proceeds of the stock sale were $2,700 (the commission fee was $14) and the trade date was February 22, 2021. What are the amount and nature of Amal's gain (loss) on these transactions?

    *a.* $214 short-term loss and $210 long-term gain.

    *b.* $214 long-term loss and $210 short-term gain.

    *c.* $228 long-term loss and $210 short-term gain.

    *d.* $228 short-term loss and $210 long-term gain.

**EA**  **LO 7-5**  37. Rayna bought an apartment building in July 2015 for $360,000 and sold it for $480,000 in 2021. There was $77,994 of accumulated depreciation allowed on the apartment building. If Rayna is in the 35% tax bracket, how much of the gain is taxed at 25%?

    *a.* $0.

    *b.* $42,006.

    *c.* $77,994.

    *d.* $120,000.

**LO 7-5**  38. Francisco, a single taxpayer, is self-employed and files Schedule C. Francisco has taxable income of $68,000 from a business which qualifies as Qualified Business Income (QBI). Francisco has no other income to be considered for income limitation calculation for the year. In 2021, some office furniture used in this business was sold for $3,000. The furniture was purchased in 2018 for a cost of $4,500 and $2,813 in allowable deprecation has been taken. What is QBI for 2021?

    *a.* $59,307.

    *b.* $64,111.

    *c.* $64,509.

    *d.* $66,009.

**EA**   **LO 7-4**   39. Renaldo, a single taxpayer, has a W-2 showing income of $95,360. Renaldo also has a short-term capital loss of $6,309, a short-term capital gain of $2,400, and a long-term capital gain of $3,656. What is Renaldo's AGI for 2021?

    *a.* $92,719.

    *b.* $95,107.

    *c.* $95,360.

    *d.* $95,613.

**EA**   **LO 7-6**   40. In 2021 Ann received 1,000 shares of stock as a gift from Tim, who had purchased them in 2012. At the time of the gift, the FMV of the stock was $29,300 and Tim's basis was $31,000. If Ann sells the stock for $32,834 in 2021, what are the nature and amount of the gain from the sale?

    *a.* $1,834 long-term gain.

    *b.* $3,534 long-term gain.

    *c.* $1,834 short-term gain and $1,700 long-term gain.

    *d.* $1,834 long-term gain and $1,700 short-term gain.

**EA**   **LO 7-3, 7-6**   41. In 2021 Ann received 1,000 shares of stock as a gift from Tim, who had purchased them in 2012. At the time of the gift, the FMV of the stock was $29,300 and Tim's basis was $31,000. If Ann sells the stock for $26,834 in 2021, what are the nature and amount of the loss from the sale?

    *a.* $2,466 short-term loss.

    *b.* $1,700 long-term loss.

    *c.* $4,166 long-term loss.

    *d.* $2,466 short-term loss and $1,700 long-term loss.

## Problems   Mc Graw Hill  **connect**

All applicable problems are available with **Connect**©

**EA**   **LO 7-3**   42. Umair sold some equipment he used in his business on August 29, 2021, that was originally purchased for $65,000 on November 21, 2019. The equipment was depreciated using the 7-year MACRS method for a total of $17,249. Assume there is no additional netting of gains and losses for this taxpayer.

    *a.* Assume Umair sold the equipment for $45,000:

      (1) What is the amount of realized gain or loss on the sale of the equipment?

      (2) Is the nature of the gain or loss considered ordinary or long-term?

      ———————————————————————————————

      ———————————————————————————————

      ———————————————————————————————

    *b.* Assume Umair sold the equipment for $49,000:

      (1) What is the amount of realized gain or loss on the sale of the equipment?

      (2) Is the nature of the gain or loss considered ordinary or long-term?

      ———————————————————————————————

      ———————————————————————————————

      ———————————————————————————————

**LO 7-1, 7-2, 7-4**   43. Amna owns undeveloped land with an adjusted basis of $375,000. Amna sells the property to George for $435,000.

**EA**

    *a.* What is Amna's realized and recognized gain?

    ———————————————————————————————

    ———————————————————————————————

b. To what IRC section does the gain on the property apply?

_____

_____

c. If the land is used in a trade or business, to what IRC section does the gain on the property apply?

_____

_____

**EA**　**LO 7-4**　44. Haneen has taxable income of $124,000 without consideration of capital gain or loss transactions. Haneen has a short-term capital gain of $19,000, a long-term capital loss of $11,000, and a short-term capital gain of $5,000. Assume none of the gains or losses are from collectibles or unrecaptured § 1250 property and Haneen is in the 24% tax bracket.

a. What is the total short-term gain or loss?

_____

_____

b. What is the total long-term gain or loss?

_____

_____

c. What is the carryover amount?

_____

_____

d. Is the gain or loss after netting taxed at the ordinary or capital rate?

_____

_____

**EA**　**LO 7-4**　45. Respond to the following independent situations:

a. Jacob is a single taxpayer who has net investment income consisting of $10,000 interest on a certificate of deposit, $5,000 from dividends from a mutual fund, $5,000 from capital gain distributions from mutual funds, and $40,000 in long-term capital gains from selling some stocks, and a modified AGI of $190,000.

(1) How much in surtax will Jacob be assessed on his Form 1040 for 2021?

_____

_____

b. Jacob is a single taxpayer who has net investment income consisting of $10,000 interest on a certificate of deposit, $5,000 from dividends from a mutual fund, $5,000 from capital gain distributions from mutual funds, and $40,000 in long-term capital gains from selling some stocks, and a modified AGI of $250,000.

(1) How much in surtax will Jacob be assessed on Form 1040 for 2021?

_____

_____

c. Jacob is a single taxpayer who has net investment income consisting of $30,000 interest on a certificate of deposit, $15,000 from dividends from a mutual fund, $15,000 from capital gain distributions from mutual funds, and $40,000 in long-term capital gains from selling some stocks, and a modified AGI of $300,000.

(1) How much in surtax will Jacob be assessed on Form 1040 for 2021?

_____

_____

**EA  LO 7-4  46.** Respond to the following independent situations:

    *a.* Chris and Casey, married filing jointly, earn $300,000 in salaries and do not have any net investment income.

        (1) How much in surtax will Chris and Casey be assessed on their Form 1040 for 2021? _____

    *b.* Chris and Casey, married filing jointly, earn $214,500 in salaries and $50,000 in capital gains, $50,000 in dividends, and $25,000 in savings interest for a total modified AGI of $339,500.

        (1) How much in surtax will Chris and Casey be assessed on their Form 1040 for 2021? _____

    *c.* Chris and Casey, married filing jointly, earn $336,000 in salaries and $56,000 in capital gains for a total modified AGI of $392,000.

        (1) How much in surtax will Chris and Casey be assessed on their Form 1040 for 2021? _____

**EA  LO 7-5  47.** Joaquin purchased a $235,000 crane for a construction business. The crane was sold for $175,000 after taking $115,000 of depreciation. Assume Joaquin is in the 35% tax rate bracket.

    *a.* On what form would the gain or loss originally be reported?

    _____

    _____

    *b.* What is the amount of gain or loss on the sale?

    _____

    _____

    *c.* What amount of the gain or loss is subject to ordinary tax rates?

    _____

    _____

**EA  LO 7-5  48.** Zofia is self-employed, files a Schedule C, and owns a qualified business for calculation of QBI. Zofia had 86,000 in taxable business income on Schedule C. On 10/30/2021, Zofia sold some office equipment was sold for $6,000 which was purchased on 04/01/2018 for a cost of $7,500. The office equipment is being depreciated over 7-year MACRS half-year convention. Zofia has no other qualified businesses. Zofia's taxable income for the income limitation is $102,000. (Hint: it will be useful to use information from Chapter 6, Form 8995, Schedule 1, and Form 1040 as a guide.)

    *a.* What is the Section 1245 depreciation recapture (if any) on the sale of the office equipment?

    *b.* What is the self-employment deduction on the income from Zofia's business?

    *c.* What is Zofia's Qualified Business Income (QBI) for Form 8995?

    *d.* What is Zofia's Qualified Business Income Deduction (QBID) for Form 8995?

    *e.* Assuming there are no other items for Form 8995, what amount(s) will be entered on line 13 of Form 1040?

    *f.* Assuming there are no other items for Schedule 1, what amount(s) will be entered on line 8 of Form 1040?

    *g.* Assuming there are other items for Schedule 1, what amount (s) will be entered on line 10a of Form 1040?

**EA  LO 7-4  49.** Maddie owns an automobile for personal use. The adjusted basis is $19,500, and the FMV is $16,000. Assume Maddie has owned the automobile for two years.

    *a.* Respond to the following if Maddie sells the vehicle for $16,000.

        (1) What is the amount of realized gain or loss on the sale? _____

        (2) What is the amount Maddie will recognize on her Form 1040? _____

b. Respond to the following if Maddie sells the vehicle for $20,000.

   (1) What is the amount of realized gain or loss on the sale? _____

   (2) What is the amount Maddie will recognize on her Form 1040? _____

**EA**  **LO 7-4**  50. Saleh sold the following stock in 2021. ABC, Inc., is a § 1202 qualified small business (QSB).

| Asset | Cost | Acquired | Sale Price | Sale Date |
|---|---|---|---|---|
| ABC, Inc., 200 shares | $153,000 | 01/10/2020 | $200,000 | 04/30/2021 |
| DEF, Inc., 100 shares | 24,600 | 11/15/2017 | 14,000 | 02/28/2021 |
| GHI, Inc., 50 shares | 19,350 | 03/31/2020 | 17,000 | 08/30/2021 |

a. Complete this chart.

| Asset | Amount of Realized Gain (Loss) | Amount of Recognized Gain (Loss) | IRC Section |
|---|---|---|---|
| ABC | _____ | _____ | _____ |
| DEF | _____ | _____ | _____ |
| GHI | _____ | _____ | _____ |

b. After netting, what is the total gain or loss?

_____

_____

_____

c. If Saleh is in the 37% tax rate bracket, at what rate is the net gain or loss taxed?

_____

_____

_____

**EA**  **LO 7-5**  51. Kwan acquired a warehouse for business purposes on August 30, 2002. The building cost $420,000. Kwan took $227,600 of depreciation on the building and then sold it for $500,000 on July 1, 2021. What are the amount and nature of Kwan's gain or loss on the sale of the warehouse?

a. What is the adjusted basis for the warehouse?

_____

_____

_____

b. What amount of the gain or loss is realized on the sale of the warehouse?

_____

_____

_____

c. What amount of the gain or loss is unrecaptured?

_____

_____

_____

d. At what rate is the unrecaptured gain or loss taxed?

_____

_____

_____

e. What amount of gain or loss qualifies as a § 1231 gain or loss ?

_____

_____

_____

**LO 7-1, 7-2, 7-3, 7-4, 7-5**

**EA**

52. Patel Industries, a sole proprietorship, sold the following assets in 2021:

| Asset | Cost | Acquired | Depreciation | Sale Price | Sale Date |
|---|---|---|---|---|---|
| Warehouse | $150,000 | 10/10/2014 | $25,801 | $175,000 | 03/15/2021 |
| Truck | 18,000 | 01/15/2020 | 6,480 | 16,000 | 01/14/2021 |
| Computer | 25,000 | 07/31/2020 | 6,634 | 17,000 | 08/31/2021 |

a. The following questions relate to the sale of the warehouse:

(1) What is the adjusted basis of the warehouse?

_____

(2) What is the realized gain on the warehouse?

_____

(3) What amount of the gain is taxed according to § 1250 rules?

_____

(4) What amount is considered a § 1231 gain before netting?

_____

b. The following questions relate to the sale of the truck:

(1) What is the adjusted basis of the truck?

_____

(2) What is the realized gain on the truck?

_____

(3) What amount of the gain is taxed according to § 1245 rules?

_____

(4) What amount of the gain is taxed as ordinary income?

_____

c. The following questions relate to the sale of the computer:

(1) What is the adjusted basis of the computer?

_____

(2) What is the realized gain or loss on the sale?

_____

(3) Which IRC section code applies to this asset?

_____

_____

**LO 7-3, 7-4, 7-5**

**EA**

53. In 2021 Rosalva sold stock considered short-term for a gain of $1,631 and stock considered long-term for a loss of $2,537. Rosalva also had a $3,000 short-term loss carryover from 2020 and a $1,350 long-term loss carryover from 2020.

*a.* What amount will be shown as a short-term gain (loss) for 2021? _____

*b.* What amount will be shown as a long-term gain (loss) for 2021? _____

*c.* How much of the loss is deductible in 2021? _____

*d.* What is the amount of long-term carryover to 2022? _____

**EA** **LO 7-6**

54. Dale purchased the following blocks of Westgate stock:

| Date | Shares | Price |
|---|---|---|
| June 12, 2018 | 1,000 | $4.225 |
| October 21, 2018 | 2,000 | 4.775 |
| December 18, 2020 | 1,500 | 5.500 |

Dale sold 1,600 shares of the stock on November 20, 2021, for $5.00 per share for a total of $8,000. Using the first-in, first-out method, determine the gain or loss on the sale of the Westgate stock.

_____

_____

What if 750 of the shares sold were identified as being from the October 21, 2018 purchase and the remaining 850 shares from the December 18, 2020 purchase? Using the specific identification method, determine the gain or loss on the sale of the Westgate stock.

_____

_____

**EA** **LO 7-6**

55. During 2021 Roberto sold 830 shares of Casual Investor Mutual Fund for $8.875 per share. The shares were purchased on the following dates:

| Date | Shares | Price |
|---|---|---|
| May 31, 2017 | 400 | $ 9.375 |
| September 18, 2018 | 225 | 8.500 |
| October 21, 2018 | 425 | 10.000 |
| January 12, 2020 | 276 | 7.125 |

Calculate the gain (loss) on the sale under the following assumptions (carry your calculations to three places):

*a.* Basis is calculated using the first-in, first-out method.

_____

*b.* Basis is calculated using the average cost method (assume all shares are long-term).

_____

**LO 7-3, 7-4, 7-5, 7-6**
**EA**

56. Suzette inherited property from her father on April 19, 2021. The FMV at the date of death was $45,000. The property was worth $43,000 six months later and had a basis to Suzette father of $25,000.
   a. What is the basis of the inherited property to Suzette
      (1) If the alternate valuation date was not elected? _____
      (2) If this property qualifies for using the alternate valuation date? _____
   b. If Suzette sold the property on November 1, 2021, for $48,750, what are the amount and nature of the gain
      (1) If the alternate valuation date was not elected? _____
      (2) If this property qualifies for using the alternate valuation date? _____

**EA** **LO 7-6**

57. Using the following independent situations, answer the following questions:

**Situation 1**

Kerry received property from an aunt with a FMV of $40,000 on the date of the gift. The aunt had purchased the property five years ago for $35,000. Kerry sold the property for $43,000.
   a. What is the basis to Kerry? _____
   b. What is Kerry's gain on the sale? _____
   c. If Kerry is in the 37% tax bracket, what is the tax on the gain (assuming there are no other gains/losses to be netted)? _____
   d. If Kerry is in the 24% tax bracket, what is the tax on the gain (assuming there are no other gains/losses to be netted)? _____

**Situation 2**

Kerry received property from an aunt with a FMV of $30,000 on the date of the gift. The aunt had purchased the property five years ago for $35,000.
   a. If Kerry sold the property for $43,000, what is the gain or loss on the sale?

   _____

   b. If Kerry sold the property for $33,000, what is the gain or loss on the sale?

   _____

   c. If Kerry sold the property for $28,000, what is the gain or loss on the sale?

   _____

**EA** **LO 7-6**

58. Ramon received a gift of stock from an uncle. The basis of the stock to the uncle was $25,000, and it had an FMV of $18,000 at the date of the gift. The donor held the property for more than one year. Complete the following chart under the independent situations shown:

| | Situation 1 | Situation 2 | Situation 3 |
|---|---|---|---|
| Donor's basis | $25,000 | $25,000 | $25,000 |
| FMV at gift date | 18,000 | 18,000 | 18,000 |
| Ramon's selling price | 30,000 | 15,000 | 20,000 |
| Basis to Ramon | ––––– | ––––– | ––––– |
| Taxable gain (if any) | ––––– | ––––– | ––––– |
| Deductible loss (if any) | ––––– | ––––– | ––––– |

## Tax Return Problems  Mc Graw Hill Connect

All applicable tax return problems are available with **Connect**©

Use your tax software to complete the following problems. If you are manually preparing the tax returns, you will need Form 1040, Schedule A, Schedule B, Schedule D, Schedule D worksheets, and Form 4797, Form 8949, or other forms, depending on the problems.

For the following tax return problems, assume the taxpayer does NOT wish to contribute to the Presidential Election Fund, unless otherwise stated in the problem. In addition, the taxpayers did *not* receive, sell, send, exchange, or otherwise acquire any financial interest in any virtual currency during the year.

**Tax Return Problem 1**

Maribel Gomez is a single taxpayer, SSN 412-34-5670, living at 5037 Circle Court, Crestview, IL 60543. Maribel is a supervisor whose 2021 W-2 shows gross wages of $94,850 with $5,881 of social security and $1,375 of Medicare taxes withheld. Maribel has $14,500 of federal withholding and $2,595 in state withholding, does not itemize, and had the following stock transactions for the year:

| Stock Shares | Date Purchased | Date Sold | Sale Price | Cost Basis |
|---|---|---|---|---|
| 5,500 | 7/8/2020 | 9/12/2021 | $15,000 | $18,000 |
| 800 | 3/12/2021 | 10/21/2021 | 43,000 | 47,000 |
| 2,800 | 2/13/2014 | 10/21/2021 | 30,000 | 22,000 |

Maribel also has interest from a savings account with Local Neighborhood Bank of $250 and a dividend from a Form 1099-DIV of $1,600 in ordinary dividends, of which $1,350 are considered qualified dividends.

Prepare a 2021 Form 1040 for Maribel and all related schedules and forms. Assume that each box 3 of the 1099-Bs was not checked for all sales transactions. Maribel had qualifying health care coverage at all times during the tax year.

**Tax Return Problem 2**

Kai Sato is single and lives at 5411 Melbourne Avenue, Chicago, IL 60455. Kai is a manager whose SSN is 412-34-5670. Using the following information, complete Kai's tax return for 2021:

Kimber Company W-2:

| | |
|---|---|
| Gross | $90,000 |
| Social security tax | 5,580 |
| Medicare tax | 1,305 |
| Federal withholding tax | 16,300 |
| State withholding tax | 2,700 |

Lee Company W-2:

| | |
|---|---|
| Gross | $22,500 |
| Social security tax | 1,395 |
| Medicare tax | 326 |
| Federal withholding tax | 2,300 |
| State withholding tax | 600 |

Kai has the following itemized deductions:

| | |
|---|---|
| Real estate tax | $7,633 |
| Mortgage interest | 8,445 |
| Charitable contributions | 3,000 |

Kai has the following investments:

| | |
|---|---|
| 1099-INT | $2,510 |
| 1099-DIV | |

| Ordinary dividends | 2,389 |
|---|---|
| Qualified dividends | 1,963 |
| Capital gain distribution | 4,711 |
| 2020 short-term loss carryover | (1,000) |

Kai received a gift of 2,000 shares of FNP Inc. stock from Aunt Jane on January 19, 2021. The basis of the shares to Aunt Jane was $4,300, and they had an FMV of $4,600 on the date of the gift. Aunt Jane purchased the stock on December 30, 2019. On June 30, 2021, Kai sold all the shares for $6,000.

Kai is an avid stamp collector and purchased a rare stamp on March 20, 2011, for $4,000. Kai sold the stamp for $6,000 on April 8, 2021.

Prepare Form 1040 and all related schedules, forms, and worksheets for 2021. Kai does not donate to the presidential election campaign. Kai is a manager at Kimber Company and had qualifying health care coverage at all times during the tax year.

**Tax Return Problem 3**

Pat and Jordan Beber are married and file a joint return in 2021. They live at 12345 Hemenway Avenue, Marlborough, MA 01752. Pat is a self-employed tax prepare whose SSN is 412-34-5670. Jordan is a software programmer whose SSN is 412-34-5671. Jordan had the following income and expenses for the year:

| Jordan's W-2: | |
|---|---|
| Gross wages | $100,776 |
| Social security tax | 6,248 |
| Medicare tax | 1,461 |
| Federal withholding tax | 18,735 |
| State withholding tax | 4,800 |

Pat was the sole proprietor of NAMA Tax Service. The business is located at 123 Main Street, Marlborough, MA 01752, and the business code is 541213. Pat had the following revenue and expenses:

| Revenue | $80,000 |
|---|---|
| Expenses: | |
| Advertising | 1,200 |
| Insurance | 3,200 |
| Telephone | 2,400 |
| Office rent | 18,000 |
| Utilities | 4,800 |
| Office supplies | 5,000 |
| Depreciation | 6,041 (must be allocated to the § 1231 assets listed next) |

Pat had the following business assets:

- Office furniture: Purchased for $4,950 on May 20, 2019. The equipment is being depreciated over seven-year MACRS 200% declining balance. Norman sold it on May 15, 2021, for $4,000.

- Office equipment: Purchased a copier for $13,800 on January 10, 2021. The copier is being depreciated over five-year MACRS 200% declining balance. Pat makes no elections for § 179 or bonus depreciation.
- Computer and equipment: Purchased a computer system for $8,900 on January 2, 2020. The computer is being depreciated over five-year MACRS 200% declining balance. Pat makes no elections for § 179 or bonus depreciation.

Pat and Jordan had the following other sources of income and deductions:

- Interest from a CD in the amount of $1,410.
- Long-term loss carryover from 2019 of $5,000.
- Real estate taxes of $8,459.
- Home mortgage interest of $16,600.
- Charitable contributions in cash over the year of $2,500; all receipts and acknowledgments were received from the charitable organizations.

Pat has made four (4) quarterly installments of $250 each as estimated taxes for 2021. All estimated tax payments were paid by the due date using the 1040-ES coupons.

Prepare Form 1040 and all related schedules, forms, and worksheets for Pat and Jordan Beber for 2021. The Bebers do not donate to the presidential election campaign. Pat and Jordan had qualifying health care coverage at all times during the tax year.

We have provided selected filled-in source documents that are available in the *Connect Library*.

BUS
LANE
TOW &
FINE

# Chapter **Eight**

# Rental Property, Royalties, and Income from Flow-Through Entities (Line 5, Schedule 1, and Schedule E)

The Internal Revenue Code often uses the term *for the production of income*. This term relates to activities that are not trades or businesses but are activities with a profit motive. Rental property is the most common example. Because these activities have a profit motive, taxpayers can deduct most ordinary and necessary expenses to offset income. In this chapter, we discuss the most common types of activities for the production of income. Rental properties, royalty-producing property or investments, and flow-through entities such as partnerships, S corporations, LLCs, trusts, and estates are covered.

### Learning Objectives

When you have completed this chapter, you should understand the following learning objectives (LO):

LO 8-1 Explain how income and expenses are recognized and reported for rental property.

LO 8-2 Understand how to report personal use of a rental property (vacation home).

LO 8-3 Know how to report royalty income on Schedule E.

LO 8-4 Discuss the different types of flow-through entities reported on Schedule E, such as partnerships, S corporations, LLCs, trusts, and estates.

## INTRODUCTION

This chapter focuses on property described as *for the production of income*. These activities produce income and expenses that are *for* AGI, similar to a trade or business. Income and expenses associated with rental, royalty, and flow-through entities[1] are for the production of

---

[1] Common flow-through entities are partnerships, S corporations, LLCs, trusts, and estates. They are referred to in this way because, in most instances, they do not pay income taxes. Instead the net share of income or loss from the entity flows through to the tax returns of its individual partners/shareholders/owners. The partners and others then pay tax on their share of the flow-through income.

income property. Generally, taxpayers report these items on Schedule E of Form 1040. The income and expense items are netted on Schedule E and are accumulated on line 5 of Form 1040, Schedule 1. Examples of Schedule E can be found throughout this chapter.

On Schedule E, income and expenses from rental properties and royalties are reported on Part I, page 1 (Exhibit 8-1), and certain items from flow-through entities such as partnerships, S corporations, LLCs, trusts, and estates are reported on Part II and Part III, page 2 (Exhibit 8-7).

# RENTAL PROPERTY
## LO 8-1

Taxable income includes rental income.[2] This includes any rental income received or accrued for the occupancy of real estate or for the use of personal property.[3] The taxpayer must differentiate between rental property and a trade or business involving rental property. Generally, if the taxpayer is a real estate professional and materially participates in a real property trade or business, then the business side of the rental activity should be reported on Schedule C. The business side, such as real property development, construction, acquisition, conversion, rental operation, management, leasing, or brokerage, all should be reported on Schedule C. Items related to the real estate rental activity such as rental income and related expenses should be reported on Schedule E. Rental income is not subject to self-employment tax.[4] Rentals are allowed the 20% QBI deduction discussed in Chapter 6 if the taxpayer is a rental professional or works in the rental more than 250 hours (See Rev. Proc. 2019-38).

**EXAMPLE 8-1**

Jack is a real estate professional who owns and operates a bed and breakfast in the North Carolina mountains. Jack provides significant services to the renters and has no other trade or business. As such, the activity is treated as a trade or business, not as rental property. Consequently, Jack reports the rental (lodging) income and expenses of this property on Schedule C.

## Farm Rental Income

Any rental income from farming activities is reported on Form 4835 rather than on Schedule E. However, the provisions concerning the reporting of farm rental income are similar to the rules for reporting regular rental income. Net farm rental income or loss from Form 4835 is transferred to line 40 of Schedule E.

## Rental Income

The rental activities reported on Schedule E are proceeds from the rental of real estate such as office buildings, rental houses, condominiums or town houses, and vacation homes. Taxpayers report gross rents on line 3 of Schedule E. Ordinary and necessary expenses are deducted on lines 5 through 20 to arrive at net rental income or loss on line 26. The net amount from line 26 of Schedule E is reported on line 5 of Schedule 1 of Form 1040.

*Gross rent* is the total rent collected from each individual property. Gross rental income includes advance rentals in the year of receipt regardless of the rental period covered or the method of accounting employed.[5] Advance rental does *not* include security deposits. Generally, if the payment is subject to an obligation to repay, it is not included in taxable income.[6]

---

[2] IRC § 61(a)(5).

[3] Reg. § 1.61-8(a).

[4] Additional information concerning rental activities treated as trades or businesses, and *who* qualifies as a real estate professional, is given in Chapter 13 under passive activity losses. As discussed later in this chapter, rental activities are, by definition, considered passive activities.

[5] Reg. § 1.61-8(b).

[6] The Supreme Court in *Commissioner v. Indianapolis Power & Light Co.* [493 U.S. 203 (1990)] ruled that if the taxpayer had no guarantee to keep the advance payment (contingent on events outside the taxpayer's control), the payment was not includable in taxable income.

**EXAMPLE 8-2**

On December 12, 2021, Della receives $7,000 from Philip to cover six months of rent from December 15, 2021, to June 15, 2022. The payment includes a $1,000 security deposit. Della must include $6,000 as rental income in the tax year 2021. The $1,000 security deposit is not reported as income.

Expenses paid by the tenant or services provided by the tenant in lieu of rent payments are also components of rental income. If the tenant pays an expense normally paid by the taxpayer, the taxpayer must include that payment in rental income. Likewise, if the tenant performs services in exchange for free rent or reduced rent, the fair market value of those services is included in rental income.[7]

**EXAMPLE 8-3**

Bill is the owner of a house that rents for $900 per month. During the winter while Bill was on vacation, the furnace failed. The tenants of the house had the furnace repaired and paid $300 in repair costs. On the first of the following month, the tenants reduced the rent payment by $300, paying just $600. Bill is required to include $900 as rental income: the net rental payment plus the repair cost paid by the tenants. Bill can then deduct a repair expense of $300.

**EXAMPLE 8-4**

Bill owns a second rental house in need of repairs. He allows a new tenant (a carpenter) to live rent-free for three months ($1,800 value); in exchange, the tenant will complete the necessary repairs. Bill must include $1,800 in rental income. He can then take a corresponding deduction for the repairs, assuming that they are not capital improvements.

## Rental Expenses

Recall that an ordinary expense is customary or usual for the taxpayer's business or activity (in this case, rental property). The "necessary" criterion refers to an expense that is appropriate and helpful rather than one that is essential to the taxpayer's activity. Table 8-1 summarizes expenses that are common to most rental activities.

The information in Table 8-1 is not comprehensive because any expense that meets the ordinary and necessary criteria is deductible. We discussed the rules concerning the deductibility of many of these expenses in Chapter 6. For example, we distinguished between travel and transportation. The same rules apply to rental property. Consequently, travel costs from the taxpayer's home to a rental property are deductible if the travel is for business purposes (such as to conduct repairs or attend a condominium association meeting). Likewise, if a taxpayer stays overnight, meals are also deductible. Use caution when deducting meals, however, especially if elements of personal vacation are involved.[8] Typically the standard mileage rate is used to calculate any travel expenses concerning

**TABLE 8-1**
**Common Rental Activity Expenses**

| Expense | Purpose |
|---|---|
| Advertising | Payments to advertise property for rent. |
| Travel | Travel to and from property for rental business such as repairs or maintenance. |
| Repair and maintenance costs | Normal repair and maintenance costs that are not capital improvements. |
| Insurance | Policy to guard the property against casualty and liability. |
| Management fees | Fees paid to have someone manage the property and provide services such as security, rental agency, repairs, and maintenance. |
| Interest | Payments on mortgage to purchase or improve rental property. |
| Taxes | Payments for property taxes (e.g., county property taxes). |
| Depreciation | Residential: 27.5-year MACRS straight-line. Nonresidential: 39-year MACRS straight-line. |

[7] IRS Publication 527, *Residential Rental Property*, p. 3.

[8] The rules concerning the deduction of expenses on vacation homes that are also rented are presented in the next section.

**TABLE 8-2**
**Examples of Capital Improvements**

Source: IRS Publication 527.

| Additions | Heating and air conditioning | Lawn and grounds landscaping | Plumbing |
|---|---|---|---|
| Bedroom | Heating system | Driveway | Septic system |
| Bathroom | Central air | Walkway | Water heater |
| Deck | conditioning | Fence | Soft water system |
| Garage | Furnace | Retaining wall | Filtration system |
| Porch | Ductwork | Sprinkler system | **Miscellaneous** |
| Patio | Central humidifier | Swimming pool | Storm windows, |
| **Interior improvements** | Filtration system | | doors |
| Built-in appliances | | **Insulation** | New roof |
| Kitchen modernization | | Attic | Central vacuum |
| Flooring | | Walls, floor | Wiring upgrades |
| Wall-to-wall carpeting | | Pipes, ductwork | Satellite dish |
| | | | Security system |

rental property because the rental activity (on Schedule E) is not the taxpayer's trade or business, and thus the taxpayer likely does not drive enough to merit using actual auto costs.

**EXAMPLE 8-5**

Bryan lives in Birmingham, Alabama, and owns a rental condominium on the beach in Destin, Florida. Twice a year (in March and June) he drives to Destin to perform general maintenance on the condominium. The round-trip mileage from Birmingham to Destin is 602 miles. In tax year 2021, Bryan could deduct $674 in travel costs (602 miles × 2 trips × 56 cents per mile).

General repairs and maintenance are also deductible from gross rental income. However, the taxpayer cannot deduct amounts that are "capital improvements"; allowable repairs are expenditures that neither materially add to the value of the property nor appreciably prolong the property's life.[9] Any repairs as part of an extensive remodeling or restoration of the property are considered *capital improvements* and are, consequently, capitalized and depreciated over the appropriate depreciable life.[10] The distinction is important because a taxpayer receives an immediate expense deduction for repairs, whereas capital improvements require depreciation over 27.5 years (residential) or 39 years (nonresidential). Table 8-2 shows examples of expenditures that are considered capital improvements.[11] Starting in 2014, certain small rentals can elect to deduct certain improvements as expenses up to a maximum of

1. 2% of the building's unadjusted basis, or
2. $10,000.

Taxpayers with average rental receipts over $10 million and properties with basis greater than $1 million are not eligible.[12]

Rental property is also depreciated. We provided a complete review of depreciation in Chapter 6. However, some aspects specifically relating to rental property merit additional discussion. For the rental structure, the depreciable life is 27.5 years for residential structures and 39 years for nonresidential structures. The applicable depreciation method is straight-line. The IRC § 179 deduction is not allowed for rental property. However, the 100% bonus would be allowed for property with a less-than-20-year life.

When a furnished rental property is purchased for a lump sum, depreciation may be calculated over 27.5 (or 39) years on the total purchase price of the rental property. However, to accelerate the tax deduction, the taxpayer should allocate the purchase price to the structure separately from the furniture, appliances, carpet, and even shrubbery or fences (because depreciating over 5 or 7 years allows a much faster deduction than over 27.5 or 39 years). A 5-year life is allowed for furniture (normally 7 years) for rental properties. The depreciable lives and methods for these asset types are as follows:

[9] Reg. § 1.162–4.
[10] Reg. § 1.162–4.
[11] IRS Publication 527, p. 5.
[12] Reg. § 1.263(a)-3(h).

| Asset | MACRS Life | MACRS Method |
|---|---|---|
| Furniture used in rental* | 5 years | 200% declining balance |
| Appliances | 5 years | 200% declining balance |
| Carpets | 5 years | 200% declining balance |
| Office furniture | 7 years | 200% declining balance |
| Shrubbery | 15 years | 150% declining balance |
| Fences | 15 years | 150% declining balance |

\* In Chapter 6, we depreciated furniture and fixtures for a trade or business over a seven-year period. Furniture used in a rental activity has a five-year depreciation period. IRS Publication 527 makes a distinction between furniture used in a rental (five years) and office furniture and equipment (seven years).

**EXAMPLE 8-6**

Alan and Cherie Masters purchased a furnished beach house in San Clemente, California, for $1,364,000 on June 1, 2021. The land was valued at $700,000; furniture, $15,000; appliances, $3,000; carpet, $4,000; and landscaping, $8,000. The Masters rent the house full time (no personal use). If the Masters depreciate the house as a single lump sum (as 27.5-year property), their first-year depreciation would be as follows (see Table 6A-6 in Chapter 6):

$$\$664,000 \times 1.970\% = \$13,081$$

On the other hand, if the Masters divided the assets into depreciable components, their first-year depreciation would be as calculated here:

| | | |
|---|---|---|
| House | $634,000 (27.5 years, straight-line) × 1.970% = | $12,490 |
| Furniture | $15,000 (5 years, 200% declining balance [DB]) × 20.00% = | 3,000 |
| Appliances | $3,000 (5 years, 200% DB) × 20.00% = | 600 |
| Carpet | $4,000 (5 years, 200% DB) × 20.00% = | 800 |
| Landscaping | $8,000 (15 years, 150% DB) × 5.00% = | 400 |
| Total depreciation | | $17,290 |

By allocating the purchase price to the structure and to the other assets, the Masters would benefit from an additional depreciation deduction of $4,209 ($17,290 − $13,081) in the first year. This example assumes we did not elect the 100% allowed bonus, which would make the difference even larger.

# From Shoebox to Software

In this section, we present a comprehensive example of rental income and expenses. The Masters, from Example 8-6, have the following income and expenses in addition to the depreciation deduction calculated earlier. During the tax year, neither the Masters nor their family used the house at any time for personal reasons.

| | |
|---|---|
| Rental income (12 wks @ $3,500 per week) | $42,000 |
| Rental management company (10% of gross) | 4,200 |
| Travel (1 round-trip [in April] for maintenance at 893 miles: 893 miles × 56.0 cents per mile) | 500 |
| Repairs (leaking roof & plumbing repairs) | 2,500 |
| Mortgage interest | 1,300 |
| Property taxes | 3,800 |
| Insurance | 1,800 |
| Utilities | 2,000 |
| Depreciation (see Example 8-6) | 17,290 |

Open the Masters' tax return file. Then open Schedule E and enter the type and location of the property (123 Beach Rd., San Clemente, CA 92672). Next, enter the income and the expenses. Enter the auto (2019 Yukon, placed in service on June 1, 2021), and enter the Business Use worksheet to fill in the mileage. Then check the box to use the standard mileage rate and answer the questions in step 3 (all "yes" in this case).

Click on line 18 on Schedule E and add each individual asset on the asset entry worksheet (as in Chapter 6 and Schedule C). Some tax software programs do not provide an "asset type" for rental furniture, appliances, or carpet.[13] If this is the case, use the Other asset type and enter the five-year life and MACRS method on the life and method input lines. Exhibit 8-1 shows the presentation of the preceding information on Schedule E, and Exhibit 8-2 shows the depreciation reported on Form 4562.

---

[13] If you choose "office furniture and fixtures" on some programs, seven-year MACRS is used for the depreciation life when a five-year life is allowed.

**EXHIBIT 8-1**

| SCHEDULE E<br>(Form 1040)<br><br>Department of the Treasury<br>Internal Revenue Service (99) | **Supplemental Income and Loss**<br>(From rental real estate, royalties, partnerships, S corporations, estates, trusts, REMICs, etc.)<br>▶ Attach to Form 1040, 1040-SR, 1040-NR, or 1041.<br>▶ Go to *www.irs.gov/ScheduleE* for instructions and the latest information. | OMB No. 1545-0074<br>**2021**<br>Attachment<br>Sequence No. **13** |
|---|---|---|

| Name(s) shown on return<br>**Alan and Cherie Masters** | Your social security number<br>**412-34-5670** |
|---|---|

**Part I**   Income or Loss From Rental Real Estate and Royalties   **Note:** If you are in the business of renting personal property, use **Schedule C.** See instructions. If you are an individual, report farm rental income or loss from **Form 4835** on page 2, line 40.

**A** Did you make any payments in 2021 that would require you to file Form(s) 1099? See instructions . . . ☐ Yes ☑ No
**B** If "Yes," did you or will you file required Form(s) 1099? . . . . . . . . . . . ☐ Yes ☐ No

**1a**   Physical address of each property (street, city, state, ZIP code)
**A**   123 Beach Road, San Clemente, CA 92672
**B**
**C**

| 1b | Type of Property<br>(from list below) | 2 | For each rental real estate property listed above, report the number of fair rental and personal use days. Check the **QJV** box only if you meet the requirements to file as a qualified joint venture. See instructions. | | Fair Rental Days | Personal Use Days | QJV |
|---|---|---|---|---|---|---|---|
| A | 1 | | | A | 365 | 0 | ☐ |
| B | | | | B | | | ☐ |
| C | | | | C | | | ☐ |

**Type of Property:**
1 Single Family Residence    3 Vacation/Short-Term Rental   5 Land      7 Self-Rental
2 Multi-Family Residence     4 Commercial               6 Royalties    8 Other (describe)

| Income: | Properties: | | A | B | C |
|---|---|---|---|---|---|
| **3** Rents received . . . . . . . . . . . | | 3 | 42,000 | | |
| **4** Royalties received . . . . . . . . . | | 4 | | | |
| **Expenses:** | | | | | |
| **5** Advertising . . . . . . . . . | | 5 | | | |
| **6** Auto and travel (see instructions) . . . . . . | | 6 | 500 | | |
| **7** Cleaning and maintenance . . . . . . . . | | 7 | | | |
| **8** Commissions. . . . . . . . . . | | 8 | | | |
| **9** Insurance . . . . . . . . . . | | 9 | 1,800 | | |
| **10** Legal and other professional fees . . . . . . | | 10 | | | |
| **11** Management fees . . . . . . . . . | | 11 | 4,200 | | |
| **12** Mortgage interest paid to banks, etc. (see instructions) | | 12 | 1,300 | | |
| **13** Other interest. . . . . . . . . . | | 13 | | | |
| **14** Repairs. . . . . . . . . . . | | 14 | 2,500 | | |
| **15** Supplies . . . . . . . . . . | | 15 | | | |
| **16** Taxes . . . . . . . . . . . | | 16 | 3,800 | | |
| **17** Utilities . . . . . . . . . . . | | 17 | 2,000 | | |
| **18** Depreciation expense or depletion . . . . . . | | 18 | 17,290 | | |
| **19** Other (list) ▶ _____ | | 19 | | | |
| **20** Total expenses. Add lines 5 through 19 . . . . . | | 20 | 33,390 | | |
| **21** Subtract line 20 from line 3 (rents) and/or 4 (royalties). If result is a (loss), see instructions to find out if you must file **Form 6198** . . . . . . . | | 21 | 8,610 | | |
| **22** Deductible rental real estate loss after limitation, if any, on **Form 8582** (see instructions) . . . . . . . | | 22 | (       ) | (       ) | (       ) |

| **23a** Total of all amounts reported on line 3 for all rental properties . . . . | **23a** | 42,000 |
|---|---|---|
|    **b** Total of all amounts reported on line 4 for all royalty properties . . . . | **23b** | 0 |
|    **c** Total of all amounts reported on line 12 for all properties . . . . . | **23c** | 1,300 |
|    **d** Total of all amounts reported on line 18 for all properties . . . . . | **23d** | 17,290 |
|    **e** Total of all amounts reported on line 20 for all properties . . . . . | **23e** | 33,390 |

| **24** | **Income.** Add positive amounts shown on line 21. **Do not** include any losses . . . . . . . . | **24** | 8,610 |
|---|---|---|---|
| **25** | **Losses.** Add royalty losses from line 21 and rental real estate losses from line 22. Enter total losses here . | **25** | (          ) |
| **26** | **Total rental real estate and royalty income or (loss).** Combine lines 24 and 25. Enter the result here. If Parts II, III, IV, and line 40 on page 2 do not apply to you, also enter this amount on Schedule 1 (Form 1040), line 5. Otherwise, include this amount in the total on line 41 on page 2 . | **26** | 8,610 |

For Paperwork Reduction Act Notice, see the separate instructions.      Cat. No. 11344L      Schedule E (Form 1040) 2021

**EXHIBIT 8-2**

| Form **4562** | **Depreciation and Amortization** (Including Information on Listed Property) ▶ Attach to your tax return. ▶ Go to *www.irs.gov/Form4562* for instructions and the latest information. | OMB No. 1545-0172 **2021** Attachment Sequence No. **179** |
|---|---|---|
| Department of the Treasury Internal Revenue Service (99) | | |

| Name(s) shown on return | Business or activity to which this form relates | Identifying number |
|---|---|---|
| Alan and Cherie Masters | Rental | 412-34-5670 |

### Part I  Election To Expense Certain Property Under Section 179
**Note:** If you have any listed property, complete Part V before you complete Part I.

| | | |
|---|---|---|
| 1 | Maximum amount (see instructions) . . . . . . . . . . . . . . . . . | **1** |
| 2 | Total cost of section 179 property placed in service (see instructions) . . . . . . . | **2** |
| 3 | Threshold cost of section 179 property before reduction in limitation (see instructions) . . | **3** |
| 4 | Reduction in limitation. Subtract line 3 from line 2. If zero or less, enter -0- . . . . . | **4** |
| 5 | Dollar limitation for tax year. Subtract line 4 from line 1. If zero or less, enter -0-. If married filing separately, see instructions . . . . . . . . . . . . . . . . . | **5** |

| 6 | **(a)** Description of property | **(b)** Cost (business use only) | **(c)** Elected cost |
|---|---|---|---|
| | | | |
| | | | |

| | | |
|---|---|---|
| 7 | Listed property. Enter the amount from line 29 . . . . . . . . . . | **7** |
| 8 | Total elected cost of section 179 property. Add amounts in column (c), lines 6 and 7 . . . . | **8** |
| 9 | Tentative deduction. Enter the **smaller** of line 5 or line 8 . . . . . . . . . . . | **9** |
| 10 | Carryover of disallowed deduction from line 13 of your 2020 Form 4562 . . . . . . | **10** |
| 11 | Business income limitation. Enter the smaller of business income (not less than zero) or line 5. See instructions | **11** |
| 12 | Section 179 expense deduction. Add lines 9 and 10, but don't enter more than line 11 . . . . . | **12** |
| 13 | Carryover of disallowed deduction to 2022. Add lines 9 and 10, less line 12 ▶ | **13** |

**Note:** Don't use Part II or Part III below for listed property. Instead, use Part V.

### Part II  Special Depreciation Allowance and Other Depreciation (Don't include listed property. See instructions.)

| | | |
|---|---|---|
| 14 | Special depreciation allowance for qualified property (other than listed property) placed in service during the tax year. See instructions . . . . . . . . . . . . . . . . . | **14** |
| 15 | Property subject to section 168(f)(1) election . . . . . . . . . . . . . . | **15** |
| 16 | Other depreciation (including ACRS) . . . . . . . . . . . . . . . . | **16** |

### Part III  MACRS Depreciation (Don't include listed property. See instructions.)

**Section A**

| | | |
|---|---|---|
| 17 | MACRS deductions for assets placed in service in tax years beginning before 2021 . . . . . . . | **17** |
| 18 | If you are electing to group any assets placed in service during the tax year into one or more general asset accounts, check here . . . . . . . . . . . . . . . . . . ▶ ☐ | |

**Section B—Assets Placed in Service During 2021 Tax Year Using the General Depreciation System**

| (a) Classification of property | (b) Month and year placed in service | (c) Basis for depreciation (business/investment use only—see instructions) | (d) Recovery period | (e) Convention | (f) Method | (g) Depreciation deduction |
|---|---|---|---|---|---|---|
| 19a 3-year property | | | | | | |
| b 5-year property | | 22,000 | 5 yr | HY | 200 DB | 4,400 |
| c 7-year property | | | | | | |
| d 10-year property | | | | | | |
| e 15-year property | | 8,000 | 15 yr | HY | 150 DB | 400 |
| f 20-year property | | | | | | |
| g 25-year property | | | 25 yrs. | | S/L | |
| h Residential rental property | 06/01/21 | 634,000 | 27.5 yrs. | MM | S/L | 12,490 |
| | | | 27.5 yrs. | MM | S/L | |
| i Nonresidential real property | | | 39 yrs. | MM | S/L | |
| | | | | MM | S/L | |

**Section C—Assets Placed in Service During 2021 Tax Year Using the Alternative Depreciation System**

| 20a Class life | | | | | S/L | |
|---|---|---|---|---|---|---|
| b 12-year | | | 12 yrs. | | S/L | |
| c 30-year | | | 30 yrs. | MM | S/L | |
| d 40-year | | | 40 yrs. | MM | S/L | |

### Part IV  Summary (See instructions.)

| | | |
|---|---|---|
| 21 | Listed property. Enter amount from line 28 . . . . . . . . . . . . . | **21** |
| 22 | **Total.** Add amounts from line 12, lines 14 through 17, lines 19 and 20 in column (g), and line 21. Enter here and on the appropriate lines of your return. Partnerships and S corporations—see instructions . | **22** 17,920 |
| 23 | For assets shown above and placed in service during the current year, enter the portion of the basis attributable to section 263A costs . . . . . . . . . | **23** |

| For Paperwork Reduction Act Notice, see separate instructions. | Cat. No. 12906N | Form **4562** (2021) |
|---|---|---|

*(continued)*

**EXHIBIT 8-2**  *(concluded)*

Form 4562 (2021)                                                                                                    Page **2**

### Part V  Listed Property  (Include automobiles, certain other vehicles, certain aircraft, and property used for entertainment, recreation, or amusement.)

**Note:** For any vehicle for which you are using the standard mileage rate or deducting lease expense, complete **only** 24a, 24b, columns (a) through (c) of Section A, all of Section B, and Section C if applicable.

#### Section A—Depreciation and Other Information (Caution: See the instructions for limits for passenger automobiles.)

**24a** Do you have evidence to support the business/investment use claimed?  ☑ Yes ☐ No  **24b** If "Yes," is the evidence written? ☑ Yes ☐ No

| (a) Type of property (list vehicles first) | (b) Date placed in service | (c) Business/ investment use percentage | (d) Cost or other basis | (e) Basis for depreciation (business/investment use only) | (f) Recovery period | (g) Method/ Convention | (h) Depreciation deduction | (i) Elected section 179 cost |
|---|---|---|---|---|---|---|---|---|
| **25** Special depreciation allowance for qualified listed property placed in service during the tax year and used more than 50% in a qualified business use. See instructions . | | | | | **25** | | | |
| **26** Property used more than 50% in a qualified business use: | | | | | | | | |
| | | % | | | | | | |
| | | % | | | | | | |
| | | % | | | | | | |
| **27** Property used 50% or less in a qualified business use: | | | | | | | | |
| 2019 Yukon | 06/01/21 | % | | | | S/L – | | |
| | | % | | | | S/L – | | |
| | | % | | | | S/L – | | |

**28** Add amounts in column (h), lines 25 through 27. Enter here and on line 21, page 1 . | **28** |
**29** Add amounts in column (i), line 26. Enter here and on line 7, page 1 . . . . . . . . . . . . . . | **29** |

#### Section B—Information on Use of Vehicles

Complete this section for vehicles used by a sole proprietor, partner, or other "more than 5% owner," or related person. If you provided vehicles to your employees, first answer the questions in Section C to see if you meet an exception to completing this section for those vehicles.

| | (a) Vehicle 1 | | (b) Vehicle 2 | | (c) Vehicle 3 | | (d) Vehicle 4 | | (e) Vehicle 5 | | (f) Vehicle 6 | |
|---|---|---|---|---|---|---|---|---|---|---|---|---|
| **30** Total business/investment miles driven during the year (**don't** include commuting miles) | | | | | | | | | | | | |
| **31** Total commuting miles driven during the year | | | | | | | | | | | | |
| **32** Total other personal (noncommuting) miles driven . . . . . . . . | | | | | | | | | | | | |
| **33** Total miles driven during the year. Add lines 30 through 32 . . . . . . | | | | | | | | | | | | |
| **34** Was the vehicle available for personal use during off-duty hours? . . . . | Yes | No | Yes | No | Yes | No | Yes | No | Yes | No | Yes | No |
| **35** Was the vehicle used primarily by a more than 5% owner or related person? . . . | | | | | | | | | | | | |
| **36** Is another vehicle available for personal use? | | | | | | | | | | | | |

#### Section C—Questions for Employers Who Provide Vehicles for Use by Their Employees

Answer these questions to determine if you meet an exception to completing Section B for vehicles used by employees who **aren't** more than 5% owners or related persons. See instructions.

| | | Yes | No |
|---|---|---|---|
| **37** | Do you maintain a written policy statement that prohibits all personal use of vehicles, including commuting, by your employees? . . . . . . . . . | | |
| **38** | Do you maintain a written policy statement that prohibits personal use of vehicles, except commuting, by your employees? See the instructions for vehicles used by corporate officers, directors, or 1% or more owners . . | | |
| **39** | Do you treat all use of vehicles by employees as personal use? . . . . . . . . | | |
| **40** | Do you provide more than five vehicles to your employees, obtain information from your employees about the use of the vehicles, and retain the information received? . . . . . . . . . | | |
| **41** | Do you meet the requirements concerning qualified automobile demonstration use? See instructions. . . . . | | |

**Note:** If your answer to 37, 38, 39, 40, or 41 is "Yes," don't complete Section B for the covered vehicles.

### Part VI  Amortization

| (a) Description of costs | (b) Date amortization begins | (c) Amortizable amount | (d) Code section | (e) Amortization period or percentage | (f) Amortization for this year |
|---|---|---|---|---|---|
| **42** Amortization of costs that begins during your 2021 tax year (see instructions): | | | | | |
| | | | | | |
| | | | | | |

**43** Amortization of costs that began before your 2021 tax year . . . . . . . . | **43** | |
**44 Total.** Add amounts in column (f). See the instructions for where to report . . . . . . . | **44** | |

Form **4562** (2021)

One important exception to trade or business depreciation rules is that the IRC § 179 deduction *cannot* be claimed for property held to produce rental income. Any 100% bonus is allowed, however.

If a rental property incurs a loss, there are potential limitations on the deductibility of the losses. By definition, rental property is a *passive activity*. The rules concerning passive activity losses are complex and are discussed briefly at the end of this chapter and more fully in Chapter 13.[14]

**CONCEPT CHECK 8-1— LO 8-1**

1. Rental income is generally reported on Schedule E. True or false?
2. All expenses related to rental property are deductible in the current year, including capital improvements. True or false?
3. Rental property structures must be depreciated using the straight-line method. True or false?
4. If a taxpayer's rental property is considered a trade or business, the taxpayer reports the income on Schedule E. True or false?
5. If a tenant provides a service in lieu of rent, the taxpayer is not required to report the value of that amount as rental income. True or false?

# RENTAL OF VACATION HOMES
## LO 8-2

When a taxpayer uses a property both for personal use (vacation home) and as rental property, tax complexities arise. Vacation home rental property falls into one of the following three possible categories: (1) primarily rental use, (2) primarily personal use, and (3) personal/rental use.

The appropriate category is determined by comparing the number of rental use days to the number of personal use days. The category determines how much of the rental income and expenses for the property may be reported. If the property

1. Is not used for more than 14 days (or 10% of the total rental days, if more) for personal use, and it is rented for 15 days or more, it is categorized as primarily rental.
2. Is rented for less than 15 days, it is categorized as primarily personal.
3. Is rented for 15 days or more and the personal use of the property is more than the greater of[15]

   a. 14 days or

   b. 10% of the total rental days at the fair rental value,

   it is categorized as personal/rental property.

**EXAMPLE 8-7**

Jose owns a cabin in the mountains. If he rents the cabin for the ski season (four months) and uses the property for personal use for 13 days, the cabin would be categorized as primarily rental property. If John used the property for personal use for 21 days, the property would be categorized as personal/rental. If John rented the cabin for less than 15 days, the cabin would be categorized as primarily personal.

Personal use of a dwelling is any use by

1. The taxpayer, any member of the taxpayer's family, or any other person with an interest in the unit.
2. Any individual who uses the unit under an arrangement that enables the taxpayer to use some other dwelling unit (reciprocal-use arrangement).
3. Any individual unless for such day the dwelling unit is rented for its fair rental value.[16]

---

[14] For a detailed discussion of the passive activity loss rules, and the loss rules of rental property in particular, see Chapter 13.

[15] IRC § 280A(d)(1).

[16] IRC § 280A(d)(2).

If a taxpayer lets anyone, family or nonfamily, use the rental property free of a rental charge, those days are considered personal-use days by the taxpayer. If any family member uses the rental property (even if the family member pays the full rental value), the days are considered personal-use days.[17] *Family* is defined as the taxpayer's brothers and sisters (whether whole or half blood), spouse, ancestors, and lineal descendants.[18] Any day spent working substantially full time repairing and maintaining the property does not count as a personal-use day. This is true even if other family members use the property for recreational purposes on the same day.[19]

| | |
|---|---|
| **EXAMPLE 8-8** | Javier owns a rental beach house. He and his two daughters spend two days at the beach house, where Nick repairs the deck and the screened porch while his daughters relax on the beach. The two days are not considered personal-use days. |

## Primarily Rental Use

If rental property is not used for more than 14 days for personal purposes (or 10% of the total rental days if more) and is rented for 15 days or more, it is primarily rental property. As such, the taxpayer must report all of the income and ordinary and necessary expenses (rental portion). The portion of expenses that are allocated to the personal use are not deductible unless they are normally allowed as itemized deductions (such as mortgage interest and property taxes). If a net loss results, it is deductible to the extent allowed by the passive activity loss rules (see the end of this chapter and Chapter 13).

## Primarily Personal Use

A property rented for less than 15 days but otherwise used as a personal residence is considered primarily personal property. When property is rented for less than 15 days, *none* of the rental income derived from the short rental period is included in gross income. Likewise, no deduction is allowed for rental expenses (other than those normally allowed as itemized deductions).

| | |
|---|---|
| **EXAMPLE 8-9** | Kirk and his family live in Augusta, Georgia. Each year during the Masters golf tournament, they rent their house to a major corporation for $10,000 for the entire week. Because Kirk rents his house for only seven days, the property is considered primarily personal, and Kirk reports none of the rental income or expenses. |

## Personal/Rental Property

When a rental property is used for personal use for more than 14 days, or 10% of the total rental days, and is rented for 15 days or more, the property is considered personal/rental property. In the case of personal/rental property, a taxpayer can deduct expenses only to the extent that there is rental income (that is, no net loss is allowed). A summary of vacation home rental rules is presented in Table 8-3.

| | |
|---|---|
| **EXAMPLE 8-10** | **Case 1: Primarily Rental Property:** Frank owns a condominium at the beach that he rents for 90 days during the summer and uses the property for personal use for 13 days.<br>**Case 2: Personal/Rental Property:** Frank rents the condominium for 90 days and uses it for personal use for 16 days.<br>**Case 3: Primarily Personal Property:** Frank rents the property for 10 days, and he uses the condominium for the remainder of the year for personal use. |

---

[17] Prop. Reg. § 1.280A-1(e)(7), ex. (1).

[18] IRC § 267(c)(4).

[19] IRS Publication 527, p. 20.

**TABLE 8-3   Summary of Vacation Home Rental Rules**

|  | Primarily Personal | Primarily Rental | Personal/Rental |
|---|---|---|---|
| Rental days | Rented less than 15 days. |  | Rented 15 days or more. |
| Personal days | No limit. | Personal use no more than the greater of (a) 14 days or (b) 10% of the total rental days. | More than the greater of (a) 14 days or (b) 10% of the total rental days. |
| Income and expense reporting | The income does not have to be reported. (It is not taxable!) Mortgage interest and property taxes are allowed as itemized deductions, as with any personal residence. | All rental income must be reported on Schedule E. The expenses must be allocated between personal and rental days and reported on Schedule E. | All rental income must be reported on Schedule E. The expenses must be allocated between personal and rental days and reported on Schedule E. |
| Net loss treatment | Not allowed; none of the net income or net loss is reported. | Losses are allowed (limited by passive activity loss rules). Usually limited to losses up to $25,000 by passive loss rules discussed in Chapter 13. | Not allowed; expenses deducted only to the extent there is rental income (i.e., breakeven). |

**EXAMPLE 8-11**

Tan owns a beach house in Seal Beach, California. Each year she uses her beach house for four months and rents it for three months in the summer. The property is considered personal/rental, and the expenses related to the beach house must be allocated between personal and rental use. Remember that if the rental portion of her expenses is higher than her rental income, the resulting net loss is not allowed.

**CONCEPT CHECK 8-2—**
**LO 8-2**

Indicate the correct letter that identifies whether the rental property in the following situations would be categorized as (a) primarily rental, (b) primarily personal, or (c) personal/rental:

1. Jamie rented her lake home for $2,000 for 12 days, and she and her family used it for the rest of the year, usually on weekends and holidays.
2. Julie rented her home in Solano Beach for 180 days for $12,000; she used it for 17 days.
3. Darren rented his beach house for 45 days for $9,000 and stayed there on weekends with his family for a total of 16 days. During his stay, he spent 7 of the days rebuilding the deck while his family enjoyed the beach.
4. Alex rented her mountain cabin for 90 days for $13,500, and she and her family used it for 50 days.

## Allocation of Rental Expenses

For both primarily rental and personal/rental properties, the expenses related to those properties must be allocated between personal and rental uses. The following are the two methods used to allocate expenses between the personal and rental uses of a rental property:

1. **The IRS method:** The expenses should be allocated between personal and rental days based on the ratio of the number of rental days to the total number of days used.
2. **The Tax Court method:** The interest and taxes on the rental property should be allocated based on the ratio of the number of rental days to the total number of days in the year (365),[20] and the remaining rental expenses should be allocated using the IRS method.[21] The court's

---

[20] The denominator in the allocation is the number of days owned during the year if the property was purchased or sold during the year.

[21] Dorance Bolton, 77 T.C. 104 (1981), *aff'd sub nom Bolton v. Comm'r*, 694 F.2d 556 (9th Cir. 1982); *McKinney v. Comm'r*, 732 F.2d 414 (10th Cir. 1983).

rationale is that interest and taxes occur ratably over the entire year whereas other expenses occur only when the property is used.

Regardless of the allocation method used, certain expenses are not allocated but are deducted in full, subject to sufficient rental income. These are expenses that have no personal element to them such as travel costs and management fees. The Tax Court method nearly always results in a larger deduction for the taxpayer.

In addition, expenses must be deducted in a certain order. First, mortgage interest and property taxes and those expenses that are directly related to the rental activity (such as management fees) are deducted. Next to be deducted are indirect expenses such as utilities, insurance, and repairs. Lastly, depreciation expense is deducted and for personal/rental properties, deducted only to the extent that there is income still remaining.

**EXAMPLE 8-12**

Assume the same rental property example as illustrated in the "From Shoebox to Software" box for the Masters (following Example 8-6) except that rental income was $21,600 and the taxpayer used the property for 22 days for personal use and rented it for 84 days (therefore, the property would be categorized as personal/rental property). Also assume that the property was held the entire year when using the Tax Court method.

| | |
|---|---|
| Rent income (12 weeks at $1,800 per week) | $21,600 |
| Mortgage interest | 1,300 |
| Property taxes | 3,800 |
| Management fees (10% of gross rent) | 2,160 |
| Travel (1 round-trip [in April] for maintenance at 893 miles: 893 miles × 56 cents per mile) | 500 |
| Repairs (leaking roof and plumbing repairs) | 2,500 |
| Insurance | 1,800 |
| Utilities | 2,000 |
| Depreciation | 17,290 |

## IRS Method

The rental expenses are allocated based on the ratio of the number of rental days (84) to the total days used (106). The remaining expenses are allocated to personal use.

| Expense | Total | Rental Ratio | Allocated to Personal | Deductible on Schedule E |
|---|---|---|---|---|
| Mortgage interest | $ 1,300 | 84/106 | $270* | $1,030 |
| Property taxes | 3,800 | 84/106 | 789* | 3,011 |
| Management fees | 2,160 | 100% | –0– | 2,160 |
| Travel | 500 | 100% | –0– | 500 |
| Repairs | 2,500 | 84/106 | 519 | 1,981 |
| Insurance | 1,800 | 84/106 | 374 | 1,426 |
| Utilities | 2,000 | 84/106 | 415 | 1,585 |
| Depreciation | 17,290 | 84/106 | –0– | 9,907[†] |

\* These amounts are deducted on Schedule A.
[†] The depreciation is $17,920. However, the deduction is limited to the remaining rental income of $9,907.
*Note:* Remember that the taxpayer cannot have a net loss on a personal/rental property.

## Tax Court Method

Using the Tax Court allocation method, taxpayers allocate mortgage interest and property taxes by the ratio of rental days (84) to the entire year (365).[22] This yields a smaller percentage

---

[22] If the property was held for less than the entire year (i.e., purchased or sold during the year), the number of days owned during the year is substituted for 365 days.

of the interest and taxes being allocated to rental income on Schedule E and more allocated to personal use as itemized deductions on Schedule A. The remaining expenses are allocated using the IRS method (84/106).

| Expense | Total | Rental Ratio | Allocated to Personal | Deductible on Schedule E |
|---|---|---|---|---|
| Mortgage interest | $ 1,300 | 84/365 | $1,001* | $   299 |
| Property taxes | 3,800 | 84/365 | 2,925* | 875 |
| Management fees | 2,160 | 100% | –0– | 2,160 |
| Travel | 500 | 100% | –0– | 500 |
| Repairs | 2,500 | 84/106 | 519 | 1,981 |
| Insurance | 1,800 | 84/106 | 374 | 1,426 |
| Utilities | 2,000 | 84/106 | 415 | 1,585 |
| Depreciation | 17,290 | 84/106 | –0– | 12,774† |

\* These amounts are deducted on Schedule A.
† The depreciation is $17,290. However, the deduction is limited to the remaining rental income of $12,774.
*Note:* Remember that the taxpayer cannot have a net loss on a personal/rental property.

### Multifamily Residential Homes

If a taxpayer owns a multifamily home (such as a duplex or a triplex) and lives in one of the units and rents the other unit(s), the units are treated as independent units and the expenses are allocated accordingly. The expenses are allocated based on the proportion of the property that is used for rental purposes versus the portion that is used for personal purposes and deducted from the rental income.

**EXAMPLE 8-13**    Guadalupe owns and lives in a fourplex of identical two-bedroom units in Anaheim, California. During the year, the entire fourplex had $100,000 in expenses: She would allocate three-fourths of the expenses and deduct $75,000 in rental expenses against rental income for the year. The remaining $25,000 would be considered personal and deducted to the extent that Guadalupe can if she itemizes.

# From Shoebox to Software

Tax software allocates rental expenses for you. Check whether your software calculates the expense allocation using the IRS method or the Tax Court method. Usually, if you enter the number of personal days on Schedule E (line 2), a note appears stating that the "vacation home limits will be applied." If you double-click on this note, the Vacation Home worksheet appears showing the allocation. If you wish to use a method different from the one your software normally does, you must make the calculations yourself and enter the expense items directly on Schedule E. Some software programs just have a selection of Tax Court method or IRS method and will do both calculations for you. Exhibits 8-3 and 8-4 illustrate the IRS method and the Tax Court method, respectively, on Schedule E, for the Masters using Example 8-12.

Note that the Tax Court method allocates more interest and taxes to personal use and deducts them on Schedule A as itemized deductions.[23] By allocating a higher percentage of interest and taxes to Schedule A, the taxpayer is able to deduct an additional $2,867 of depreciation expense ($12,774 versus $9,907) and increase the overall deductible expenses. Also note that the travel costs and management fees are 100% deductible. As discussed earlier, these expenses are 100% deductible because if this property was not rented, these expenses would not have occurred.

[23] Mortgage interest is deductible on Schedule A for interest on a personal residence and one vacation home; but if the taxpayer has more than one vacation home, the interest may not be deductible on Schedule A (for details on mortgage interest, see Chapter 5). Also, with the cap of $10,000 on taxes on Schedule A, the IRS method may be more attractive.

**EXHIBIT 8-3   Schedule E Using the IRS Method**

| SCHEDULE E<br>(Form 1040)<br>Department of the Treasury<br>Internal Revenue Service (99) | **Supplemental Income and Loss**<br>(From rental real estate, royalties, partnerships, S corporations, estates, trusts, REMICs, etc.)<br>▶ Attach to Form 1040, 1040-SR, 1040-NR, or 1041.<br>▶ Go to *www.irs.gov/ScheduleE* for instructions and the latest information. | OMB No. 1545-0074<br>2021<br>Attachment<br>Sequence No. **13** |
|---|---|---|

| Name(s) shown on return<br>**Alan and Cherie Masters**             IRS METHOD | Your social security number<br>412-34-5670 |
|---|---|

**Part I**   Income or Loss From Rental Real Estate and Royalties   Note: If you are in the business of renting personal property, use Schedule C. See instructions. If you are an individual, report farm rental income or loss from **Form 4835** on page 2, line 40.

A  Did you make any payments in 2021 that would require you to file Form(s) 1099? See instructions . . . . .   ☐ Yes  ☑ No

B  If "Yes," did you or will you file required Form(s) 1099? . . . . . . . . . . . . . . . . . .   ☐ Yes  ☐ No

1a  Physical address of each property (street, city, state, ZIP code)

| | |
|---|---|
| A | 123 Beach Road, San Clemente, CA  92672 |
| B | |
| C | |

| 1b | Type of Property<br>(from list below) | 2  For each rental real estate property listed above, report the number of fair rental and personal use days. Check the **QJV** box only if you meet the requirements to file as a qualified joint venture. See instructions. | | Fair Rental Days | Personal Use Days | QJV |
|---|---|---|---|---|---|---|
| A | 1 | | A | 84 | 22 | ☐ |
| B | | | B | | | ☐ |
| C | | | C | | | ☐ |

**Type of Property:**
1 Single Family Residence   3 Vacation/Short-Term Rental   5 Land   7 Self-Rental
2 Multi-Family Residence   4 Commercial   6 Royalties   8 Other (describe)

| Income: | Properties: | | A | B | C |
|---|---|---|---|---|---|
| 3 | Rents received . . . . . . . . . . . . . . . | 3 | 21,600 | | |
| 4 | Royalties received . . . . . . . . . . . . | 4 | | | |
| **Expenses:** | | | | | |
| 5 | Advertising . . . . . . . . . . . . . | 5 | | | |
| 6 | Auto and travel (see instructions) . . . . . | 6 | 500 | | |
| 7 | Cleaning and maintenance . . . . . . . | 7 | | | |
| 8 | Commissions. . . . . . . . . . . . | 8 | | | |
| 9 | Insurance . . . . . . . . . . . . . | 9 | 1,426 | | |
| 10 | Legal and other professional fees . . . . . | 10 | | | |
| 11 | Management fees . . . . . . . . . . | 11 | 2,160 | | |
| 12 | Mortgage interest paid to banks, etc. (see instructions) | 12 | 1,030 | | |
| 13 | Other interest. . . . . . . . . . . . | 13 | | | |
| 14 | Repairs. . . . . . . . . . . . . . | 14 | 1,981 | | |
| 15 | Supplies . . . . . . . . . . . . . | 15 | | | |
| 16 | Taxes . . . . . . . . . . . . . . | 16 | 3,011 | | |
| 17 | Utilities . . . . . . . . . . . . . . | 17 | 1,585 | | |
| 18 | Depreciation expense or depletion . . . . . | 18 | 9,907 | | |
| 19 | Other (list) ▶ _____ | 19 | | | |
| 20 | Total expenses. Add lines 5 through 19 . . . . . | 20 | 21,600 | | |
| 21 | Subtract line 20 from line 3 (rents) and/or 4 (royalties). If result is a (loss), see instructions to find out if you must file **Form 6198** . . . . . . . . . . . . . . | 21 | 0 | | |
| 22 | Deductible rental real estate loss after limitation, if any, on **Form 8582** (see instructions) . . . . . . . | 22 | ( ) | ( ) | ( ) |

| 23a | Total of all amounts reported on line 3 for all rental properties . . . . | 23a | 21,600 | |
|---|---|---|---|---|
| b | Total of all amounts reported on line 4 for all royalty properties . . . . | 23b | 0 | |
| c | Total of all amounts reported on line 12 for all properties . . . . . | 23c | 1,060 | |
| d | Total of all amounts reported on line 18 for all properties . . . . . | 23d | 9,907 | |
| e | Total of all amounts reported on line 20 for all properties . . . . . | 23e | 21,600 | |
| 24 | **Income.** Add positive amounts shown on line 21. **Do not** include any losses . . . . . . . | 24 | 0 |
| 25 | **Losses.** Add royalty losses from line 21 and rental real estate losses from line 22. Enter total losses here . | 25 | ( 0 ) |
| 26 | **Total rental real estate and royalty income or (loss).** Combine lines 24 and 25. Enter the result here. If Parts II, III, IV, and line 40 on page 2 do not apply to you, also enter this amount on Schedule 1 (Form 1040), line 5. Otherwise, include this amount in the total on line 41 on page 2 . | 26 | 0 |

For Paperwork Reduction Act Notice, see the separate instructions.        Cat. No. 11344L        Schedule E (Form 1040) 2021

Source: U.S. Department of the Treasury, Internal Revenue Service, Schedule E (Form 1040). Washington, DC: 2021.

**EXHIBIT 8-4** **Schedule E Using the Tax Court Method**

| SCHEDULE E (Form 1040) | Supplemental Income and Loss | OMB No. 1545-0074 |
|---|---|---|
| Department of the Treasury Internal Revenue Service (99) | (From rental real estate, royalties, partnerships, S corporations, estates, trusts, REMICs, etc.) ▶ Attach to Form 1040, 1040-SR, 1040-NR, or 1041. ▶ Go to *www.irs.gov/ScheduleE* for instructions and the latest information. | 2021 Attachment Sequence No. **13** |

| Name(s) shown on return | Your social security number |
|---|---|
| **Alan and Cherie Masters**     TAX COURT METHOD | **412-34-5670** |

**Part I** **Income or Loss From Rental Real Estate and Royalties** **Note:** If you are in the business of renting personal property, use **Schedule C**. See instructions. If you are an individual, report farm rental income or loss from **Form 4835** on page 2, line 40.

A Did you make any payments in 2021 that would require you to file Form(s) 1099? See instructions . . . . ☐ Yes ☑ No
B If "Yes," did you or will you file required Form(s) 1099? . . . . . . . . . . . . . . . . . . . ☐ Yes ☐ No

| 1a | Physical address of each property (street, city, state, ZIP code) |
|---|---|
| A | 123 Beach Road, San Clemente, CA 92672 |
| B | |
| C | |

| 1b | Type of Property (from list below) | 2 For each rental real estate property listed above, report the number of fair rental and personal use days. Check the **QJV** box only if you meet the requirements to file as a qualified joint venture. See instructions. | | Fair Rental Days | Personal Use Days | QJV |
|---|---|---|---|---|---|---|
| A | 1 | | A | 84 | 22 | ☐ |
| B | | | B | | | ☐ |
| C | | | C | | | ☐ |

**Type of Property:**
1  Single Family Residence    3  Vacation/Short-Term Rental   5  Land     7  Self-Rental
2  Multi-Family Residence     4  Commercial     6  Royalties      8  Other (describe)

| Income: | Properties: | | A | B | C |
|---|---|---|---|---|---|
| 3 | Rents received . . . . . . . . . . | 3 | 21,600 | | |
| 4 | Royalties received . . . . . . . . . . | 4 | | | |
| **Expenses:** | | | | | |
| 5 | Advertising . . . . . . . . . . | 5 | | | |
| 6 | Auto and travel (see instructions) . . . . . | 6 | 500 | | |
| 7 | Cleaning and maintenance . . . . . . . | 7 | | | |
| 8 | Commissions. . . . . . . . . . | 8 | | | |
| 9 | Insurance . . . . . . . . . . | 9 | 1,426 | | |
| 10 | Legal and other professional fees . . . . . | 10 | | | |
| 11 | Management fees . . . . . . . . . | 11 | 2,160 | | |
| 12 | Mortgage interest paid to banks, etc. (see instructions) | 12 | 299 | | |
| 13 | Other interest. . . . . . . . . . | 13 | | | |
| 14 | Repairs. . . . . . . . . . | 14 | 1,981 | | |
| 15 | Supplies . . . . . . . . . . | 15 | | | |
| 16 | Taxes . . . . . . . . . . | 16 | 875 | | |
| 17 | Utilities . . . . . . . . . . | 17 | 1,585 | | |
| 18 | Depreciation expense or depletion . . . . . | 18 | 12,774 | | |
| 19 | Other (list) ▶ _____ | 19 | | | |
| 20 | Total expenses. Add lines 5 through 19 . . . . . | 20 | 21,600 | | |
| 21 | Subtract line 20 from line 3 (rents) and/or 4 (royalties). If result is a (loss), see instructions to find out if you must file **Form 6198** . . . . . . . . . . | 21 | 0 | | |
| 22 | Deductible rental real estate loss after limitation, if any, on **Form 8582** (see instructions) . . . . . . . | 22 | ( ) | ( ) | ( ) |

| 23a | Total of all amounts reported on line 3 for all rental properties . . . . | 23a | 21,600 | |
| b | Total of all amounts reported on line 4 for all royalty properties . . . . | 23b | 0 | |
| c | Total of all amounts reported on line 12 for all properties . . . . . . | 23c | 299 | |
| d | Total of all amounts reported on line 18 for all properties . . . . . . | 23d | 12,774 | |
| e | Total of all amounts reported on line 20 for all properties . . . . . . | 23e | 21,600 | |
| 24 | **Income.** Add positive amounts shown on line 21. **Do not** include any losses . . . . . . . . | 24 | 0 |
| 25 | **Losses.** Add royalty losses from line 21 and rental real estate losses from line 22. Enter total losses here . | 25 | ( 0 ) |
| 26 | **Total rental real estate and royalty income or (loss).** Combine lines 24 and 25. Enter the result here. If Parts II, III, IV, and line 40 on page 2 do not apply to you, also enter this amount on Schedule 1 (Form 1040), line 5. Otherwise, include this amount in the total on line 41 on page 2 . | 26 | 0 |

| For Paperwork Reduction Act Notice, see the separate instructions. | Cat. No. 11344L | Schedule E (Form 1040) 2021 |
|---|---|---|

Source: U.S. Department of the Treasury, Internal Revenue Service, Schedule E (Form 1040). Washington, DC: 2021.

**CONCEPT CHECK 8-3— LO 8-2**

Lynn and Dave Wood own a vacation home in Park City, Utah. During the year, the Woods rented the home for 75 days and used it for personal use for 30 days. The following are income and expenses related to the property for the year:

| | |
|---|---:|
| Rental income | $15,000 |
| Mortgage interest | 6,000 |
| Property taxes | 1,000 |
| Insurance | 1,400 |
| Repairs and maintenance | 800 |
| Depreciation | 2,000 |

1. Which of the three categories of rental property would apply to this property and why?
2. If using the IRS method, how much of the expenses can be allocated to the rental property?
3. If using the Tax Court method, how much of the expenses can be allocated to the rental property?
4. If using the IRS method, determine the net income or loss that should be reported for this rental property.

# ROYALTY INCOME
## LO 8-3

A *royalty* is a payment for the right to use intangible property. Royalties are paid for the use of books, stories, plays, copyrights, trademarks, formulas, and patents and from the exploitation of natural resources such as coal, gas, or timber.[24] When royalties are paid, the payer sends the recipient a 1099-MISC noting the amount paid in box 2. The recipient (taxpayer) reports that amount on line 4 of Schedule E. A sample 1099-MISC is shown in Exhibit 8-5.

**EXHIBIT 8-5**

| | | | |
|---|---|---|---|
| ☐ **CORRECTED (if checked)** | | | |

| PAYER'S name, street address, city or town, state or province, country, ZIP or foreign postal code, and telephone no. | **1 Rents**<br>$ | OMB No. 1545-0115<br><br>20**21**<br><br>Form **1099-MISC** | **Miscellaneous Information** |
|---|---|---|---|
| | **2 Royalties**<br>$ | | |
| | **3 Other income**<br>$ | **4 Federal income tax withheld**<br>$ | **Copy B**<br>**For Recipient** |
| PAYER'S TIN        RECIPIENT'S TIN | **5 Fishing boat proceeds**<br><br>$ | **6 Medical and health care payments**<br><br>$ | |
| RECIPIENT'S name | **7 Payer made direct sales totaling $5,000 or more of consumer products to recipient for resale** ☐ | **8 Substitute payments in lieu of dividends or interest**<br>$ | This is important tax information and is being furnished to the IRS. If you are required to file a return, a negligence penalty or other sanction may be imposed on you if this income is taxable and the IRS determines that it has not been reported. |
| Street address (including apt. no.) | **9 Crop insurance proceeds**<br><br>$ | **10 Gross proceeds paid to an attorney**<br>$ | |
| City or town, state or province, country, and ZIP or foreign postal code | **11 Fish purchased for resale**<br><br>$ | **12 Section 409A deferrals**<br><br>$ | |
| Account number (see instructions)        FATCA filing requirement ☐ | **13 Excess golden parachute payments**<br>$ | **14 Nonqualified deferred compensation**<br>$ | |
| | **15 State tax withheld**<br>$<br>$ | **16 State/Payer's state no.** | **17 State income**<br>$<br>$ |

Form **1099-MISC**        (keep for your records)        www.irs.gov/Form1099MISC        Department of the Treasury - Internal Revenue Service

Source: U.S. Department of the Treasury, Internal Revenue Service, Form 1099-MISC. Washington, DC: 2021.

[24] Reg. § 1.61-8.

Royalty payments do not include payments for services even when the services performed relate to a royalty-producing asset. Likewise, payments received for the transfer or sale of a copyright or patent are not royalties but proceeds from the sale of a capital asset.[25] Should royalty income be reported on Schedule E or Schedule C? If the royalty is a result of a trade or business, the taxpayer should report the royalty on Schedule C. If the royalty is from a nontrade or business activity, such as an investment, then the royalty income should be reported on line 4 of Schedule E.

| | |
|---|---|
| **EXAMPLE 8-14** | Shea is the author of a best-selling book of poetry for which he receives royalties. He also presents seminars and readings of his book of poetry throughout the country. Shea's payments for the readings and seminars are not royalties. He reports his income from the readings and seminars on Schedule C and the royalties on Schedule E. |

**TAX YOUR BRAIN**

Would the taxpayer prefer royalty income to be reported on Schedule E or on Schedule C? The royalty must be included in income from both forms, so why does it matter?

**ANSWER**

It is true that the royalty will be included in income on either form. However, if the royalty is reported on Schedule C, the net income is subject to self-employment tax, whereas on Schedule E, it is not.

| | |
|---|---|
| **EXAMPLE 8-15** | Nihal is a full-time author of mystery novels. He has an office in his home and has no other source of income. The royalties Nihal receives from his novels are trade or business income and are reported on Schedule C. |

| | |
|---|---|
| **EXAMPLE 8-16** | Lilly is a business executive with a large import/export company. She also owns some land in south Texas. Recently a small oil reserve was discovered on her land, and she began receiving royalties for the oil produced. Lilly reports these royalties on Schedule E because owning the land is not a trade or a business but an investment. |

Whether royalties are reported on Schedule C or Schedule E, any ordinary and necessary expenses are allowed as deductions.

**CONCEPT CHECK 8-4— LO 8-3**

Indicate whether the following items would be reported on Schedule E (E) or Schedule C (C).

1. Royalty income received by Debra, a full-time author, for her mystery novel.
2. Royalty income received by Mark, a professional baseball player, for coal mined on his land in Wyoming.
3. Nathan recently wrote a book about proverbs. He received income for his readings at various bookstores throughout the country.
4. Royalty income that Jane, a full-time philosophy professor at the University of San Diego, received for a textbook she wrote.

# FLOW-THROUGH ENTITIES
## LO 8-4

Every partnership, limited liability company (LLC), S corporation, and certain types of trusts and estates must file a tax return indicating the amount of income or loss that flows through to the taxpayer (partner, shareholder, or owner). These entities are known as *flow-through entities* because they are not taxed directly. Instead, the income or loss items of these entities

---

[25] Reg. § 1.61-8.

"flow through" to the partners, shareholders, or owners, who then report the income or loss on their individual Forms 1040.[26]

The flow-through entity must supply each partner (shareholder or owner) with a Schedule K-1 indicating the partner's distributive share of income, expenses, or losses. The partners (shareholders or owners) report the income and loss from the K-1s in Part II and Part III on Schedule E. Although trusts and estates are technically considered separate taxable entities, any income or property distributed to a beneficiary must also be reported on a Schedule K-1 as a flow-through entity. Exhibit 8-6 is a sample Schedule K-1 from a partnership Form 1065.

The K-1s from LLCs, S corporations, trusts, and estates are similar in appearance to the partnership K-1 presented in Exhibit 8-6.

## Reporting of Flow-Through Items

Flow-through entities file "informational returns" because the returns do just that: provide tax information to the taxpayer and the IRS regarding the income or loss from the entity. The K-1 provides not only specific income or loss data but also the type of entity (a partnership in this case) and the partner relationship. Typically, a partnership is either an active trade or business or a passive activity.[27] A passive activity usually involves an investor relationship, whereas, in general, a partner materially participates in an active trade or business.

| EXAMPLE 8-17 | Dave is a partner in a local CPA firm (partnership) and works there full time. He is also an investor as a limited partner in several real estate partnerships. The CPA firm partnership is an active trade or business partnership, and the real estate partnerships are passive investments.[28] |
|---|---|

In this section, the focus is on a trade or business partnership in which the partner materially participates in the business (an active trade or business). The K-1 in Exhibit 8-6 reports the partner's share of ordinary income (line 1, Schedule K-1) from the partnership and other separately stated items (all other lines). The amounts of separately stated items (such as interest income or capital gains and losses) are not included in the income or expenses of the partnership but are allocated separately to each of the partners. All of the ordinary income from flow-through entities is eligible for the Qualified Business Income deduction (20%) subject to the limits discussed in Chapter 6.

**TAX YOUR BRAIN**

Why are the different types of income and expenses that flow through from a partnership (ordinary income, interest, dividends, royalties, capital gains, charitable contributions, § 179 expense deductions, etc.) separately stated? Why not just lump them all together and have one income or loss number from the partnership?

**ANSWER**

Any item that could be treated differently by different partners (individuals, corporations, etc.) is separately stated. For example, one individual partner might have capital gains from other sources to offset capital losses from the partnership, whereas another individual partner might not have any capital gains and be limited in the amount of capital losses allowed. Another example concerns a corporate partner[29] who receives a dividends-received deduction and no deduction for net capital losses. An individual partner in the same partnership would have to include the dividends in income but could deduct up to $3,000 of net capital losses. Additionally, for an individual taxpayer, most charitable deductions are limited to 60% of AGI in 2021. The limit occurs at the individual level and could result in a different outcome, depending on the individual partner's particular tax situation.

---

[26] Of course, partners, shareholders, and owners can be entities as well. For example, a corporation can be a partner in a partnership. If this is the case, the corporate partner is taxed on the flow-through income. The focus in this text is the individual partner, shareholder, or owner.

[27] All of the various partnership forms file a Form 1065 and issue related Schedule K-1s to partners. A partnership form can be a limited liability company, a limited liability partnership, a limited partnership, or a general partnership.

[28] Chapter 13 focuses, in part, on passive activities.

[29] Corporate partners are taxed differently than individual partners with respect to many items. Thus, various items must be separately stated because the tax treatment by the partners may differ.

# From Shoebox to Software

If Jose Ramirez were to receive the K-1 from W&S Woodworking, shown in Exhibit 8-6, how would he report those amounts on Form 1040? The amounts reported will flow through to numerous forms and schedules.

To enter the amounts from the K-1 in the tax software, you should first open the saved file of Jose and Maria Ramirez used in earlier chapters. Open the forms and go to the Documents Received section. Open the Federal Partnership Schedule K-1. Note that it is a duplicate of Schedule K-1. Simply enter the information from the K-1 received (Exhibit 8-6) in

the K-1 pro forma. The tax software will transfer the amounts to the appropriate forms. Jose materially participates in the business, so the activity is not a passive activity. Table 8-4 indicates where Jose reports the items from Schedule K-1.

Exhibit 8-7 illustrates the correct reporting of Schedule E, page 2, assuming that the taxpayer did not have any other activities with § 179 expenses. Thus, all of the partnership's § 179 expense is allowed. Column (j) has an amount of $2,130—the ordinary income. Make sure you save the Ramirezes' file for future use.

**TABLE 8-4**

**Form 1040 Reporting of K-1 Items from W&S Woodworking**

| K-1 Items | Location Reported on Form 1040 | Amount Reported | Chapter Where Item Was Covered |
|---|---|---|---|
| Line 1—Ordinary income | Form 1040, Schedule E, p. 2, col. (j) | $2,130 | Chapter 8 |
| Dividends | Form 1040, Schedule B | 201 | Chapter 3 |
| Net short-term capital gain/loss | Form 1040, Schedule D | 133 | Chapter 7 |
| Net long-term capital gain/loss | Form 1040, Schedule D | (400) | Chapter 7 |
| Charitable contributions | Schedule A | 2,000 | Chapter 5 |
| § 179 expense | Form 4562 to Schedule E, p. 2, col. (i)* | 7,600 | Chapter 6 |
| Earnings from self-employment | Schedule SE, p. 2, line 2 | –0–† | Chapter 6 |

\* The § 179 expense must first go to Form 4562 to determine how much is allowed if the taxpayer has other activities where § 179 expense was taken or allowed. The allowable amount is then transferred to Schedule E.
† The amount on line 14 of the K-1 is $0. However, recall from earlier discussion that the § 179 expense allowed from this entity reduces self-employment income below zero.

*Separately stated items* are items that the partnership does not deduct or include in income, but each partner's share is reported directly to the partner. When dealing with an individual partner, items from the K-1s are placed in various locations on the tax return. For example, the income or loss from the partnership (line 1, 2, or 3 of Schedule K-1) is reported on Schedule E, interest and dividends are reported on Schedule B, royalties on Schedule E, and capital gains and losses on Schedule D. Charitable contributions from a partnership are reported on Schedule A, and § 179 expense deductions are reported on Schedule E, page 2.

Two other pieces of essential information are reported on Schedule K-1: line 4— guaranteed payments and line 14—self-employment earnings (loss). A partner is not an employee of the partnership and thus cannot have a deductible salary (to the partnership). A partner can receive a guaranteed payment, however, for services rendered to the partnership.[30] The guaranteed payment reduces the ordinary income of the partnership. Because

**EXHIBIT 8-6**

| | |
|---|---|
| 651121 | |

☐ Final K-1   ☐ Amended K-1   OMB No. 1545-0123

**Schedule K-1**
**(Form 1065)**
Department of the Treasury
Internal Revenue Service

**2021**

For calendar year 2021, or tax year

beginning  /  / 2021  ending  /  /

**Partner's Share of Income, Deductions, Credits, etc.** ▶ See back of form and separate instructions.

### Part I  Information About the Partnership

**A** Partnership's employer identification number
22-7234567

**B** Partnership's name, address, city, state, and ZIP code

W&S Woodworking
2144 Playground Ave.
Ellenwood, GA 30294

**C** IRS center where partnership filed return ▶ Kansas City, MO

**D** ☐ Check if this is a publicly traded partnership (PTP)

### Part II  Information About the Partner

**E** Partner's SSN or TIN (Do not use TIN of a disregarded entity. See instructions.)
412-34-5670

**F** Name, address, city, state, and ZIP code for partner entered in E. See instructions.

Jose Ramirez
1234 West Street
Ellenwood, GA 30294

**G** ☒ General partner or LLC member-manager ☐ Limited partner or other LLC member

**H1** ☒ Domestic partner ☐ Foreign partner

**H2** ☐ If the partner is a disregarded entity (DE), enter the partner's:
TIN _____  Name _____

**I1** What type of entity is this partner? Individual

**I2** If this partner is a retirement plan (IRA/SEP/Keogh/etc.), check here ▶ ☐

**J** Partner's share of profit, loss, and capital (see instructions):

| | Beginning | Ending |
|---|---|---|
| Profit | % | 40 % |
| Loss | % | 40 % |
| Capital | % | 40 % |

Check if decrease is due to sale or exchange of partnership interest . ▶ ☐

**K** Partner's share of liabilities:

| | Beginning | Ending |
|---|---|---|
| Nonrecourse . . $ | $ | |
| Qualified nonrecourse financing . . $ | $ | 23,000 |
| Recourse . . $ | $ | 40,000 |

Check this box if Item K includes liability amounts from lower tier partnerships ▶ ☐

**L** **Partner's Capital Account Analysis**

Beginning capital account . . . $ _____
Capital contributed during the year . . $ _____
Current year net income (loss) . . . $ _____
Other increase (decrease) (attach explanation) $ _____
Withdrawals and distributions . . . $ ( _____ )
Ending capital account . . . . $ _____

**M** Did the partner contribute property with a built-in gain (loss)?
☐ Yes ☒ No If "Yes," attach statement. See instructions.

**N** Partner's Share of Net Unrecognized Section 704(c) Gain or (Loss)
Beginning . . . . . . . . $ _____
Ending . . . . . . . . . $ _____

### Part III  Partner's Share of Current Year Income, Deductions, Credits, and Other Items

| | | | |
|---|---|---|---|
| 1 | Ordinary business income (loss)   2,130 | 14 | Self-employment earnings (loss)   0 |
| 2 | Net rental real estate income (loss) | | |
| 3 | Other net rental income (loss) | 15 | Credits |
| 4a | Guaranteed payments for services | | |
| 4b | Guaranteed payments for capital | 16 | Schedule K-3 is attached if checked . . . . . ▶ ☐ |
| 4c | Total guaranteed payments | 17 | Alternative minimum tax (AMT) items |
| 5 | Interest income | | |
| 6a | Ordinary dividends   201 | | |
| 6b | Qualified dividends   201 | 18 | Tax-exempt income and nondeductible expenses |
| 6c | Dividend equivalents | | |
| 7 | Royalties | | |
| 8 | Net short-term capital gain (loss)   133 | 19 | Distributions |
| 9a | Net long-term capital gain (loss)   (400) | | |
| 9b | Collectibles (28%) gain (loss) | | |
| 9c | Unrecaptured section 1250 gain | 20 | Other information |
| 10 | Net section 1231 gain (loss) | | |
| 11 | Other income (loss) | | |
| 12 | Section 179 deduction   7,600 | 21 | Foreign taxes paid or accrued |
| 13 | Other deductions   G   2,000 | | |
| 22 | ☐ More than one activity for at-risk purposes* | | |
| 23 | ☐ More than one activity for passive activity purposes* | | |

*See attached statement for additional information.

For IRS Use Only

For Paperwork Reduction Act Notice, see the Instructions for Form 1065.   www.irs.gov/Form1065   Cat. No. 11394R   Schedule K-1 (Form 1065) 2021

Source: U.S. Department of the Treasury, Internal Revenue Service, Schedule-K (Form 1065). Washington, DC: 2021.

**EXHIBIT 8-7**

| Schedule E (Form 1040) 2021 | | Attachment Sequence No. **13** | | Page **2** |
|---|---|---|---|---|

Name(s) shown on return. Do not enter name and social security number if shown on other side.
**Jose and Maria Ramirez**

Your social security number
**412-34-5670**

**Caution:** The IRS compares amounts reported on your tax return with amounts shown on Schedule(s) K-1.

**Part II   Income or Loss From Partnerships and S Corporations** — **Note:** If you report a loss, receive a distribution, dispose of stock, or receive a loan repayment from an S corporation, you **must** check the box in column **(e)** on line 28 and attach the required basis computation. If you report a loss from an at-risk activity for which **any** amount is **not** at risk, you **must** check the box in column **(f)** on line 28 and attach **Form 6198**. See instructions.

27  Are you reporting any loss not allowed in a prior year due to the at-risk or basis limitations, a prior year unallowed loss from a passive activity (if that loss was not reported on Form 8582), or unreimbursed partnership expenses? If you answered "Yes," see instructions before completing this section . . . . . . . . . . . . . . . . .   ☐ Yes   ☐ No

| 28 | (a) Name | (b) Enter **P** for partnership; **S** for S corporation | (c) Check if foreign partnership | (d) Employer identification number | (e) Check if basis computation is required | (f) Check if any amount is not at risk |
|---|---|---|---|---|---|---|
| A | W&S Woodworking | P | ☐ | 22-7234567 | ☐ | ☐ |
| B | | | ☐ | | ☐ | ☐ |
| C | | | ☐ | | ☐ | ☐ |
| D | | | ☐ | | ☐ | ☐ |

| | Passive Income and Loss | | Nonpassive Income and Loss | | |
|---|---|---|---|---|---|
| | (g) Passive loss allowed (attach **Form 8582** if required) | (h) Passive income from **Schedule K-1** | (i) Nonpassive loss allowed (see **Schedule K-1**) | (j) Section 179 expense deduction from **Form 4562** | (k) Nonpassive income from **Schedule K-1** |
| A | | | | (7,600) | 2,130 |
| B | | | | | |
| C | | | | | |
| D | | | | | |
| 29a Totals | | | | | 2,130 |
| b Totals | | | | (7,600) | |

| 30 | Add columns (h) and (k) of line 29a. . . . . . . . . . . . . ▶ | 30 | 2,130 |
|---|---|---|---|
| 31 | Add columns (g), (i), and (j) of line 29b. . . . . . . . . . . ▶ | 31 | ( 7,600 ) |
| 32 | **Total partnership and S corporation income or (loss).** Combine lines 30 and 31 . . . . . | 32 | (5,470) |

**Part III   Income or Loss From Estates and Trusts**

| 33 | (a) Name | (b) Employer identification number |
|---|---|---|
| A | | |
| B | | |

| | Passive Income and Loss | | Nonpassive Income and Loss | |
|---|---|---|---|---|
| | (c) Passive deduction or loss allowed (attach **Form 8582** if required) | (d) Passive income from **Schedule K-1** | (e) Deduction or loss from **Schedule K-1** | (f) Other income from **Schedule K-1** |
| A | | | | |
| B | | | | |
| 34a Totals | | | | |
| b Totals | | | | |

| 35 | Add columns (d) and (f) of line 34a . . . . . . . . . . . . | 35 | |
|---|---|---|---|
| 36 | Add columns (c) and (e) of line 34b . . . . . . . . . . . . | 36 | ( ) |
| 37 | **Total estate and trust income or (loss).** Combine lines 35 and 36 . . . . . . . . . | 37 | |

**Part IV   Income or Loss From Real Estate Mortgage Investment Conduits (REMICs)—Residual Holder**

| 38 | (a) Name | (b) Employer identification number | (c) Excess inclusion from **Schedules Q**, line 2c (see instructions) | (d) Taxable income (net loss) from **Schedules Q**, line 1b | (e) Income from **Schedules Q**, line 3b |
|---|---|---|---|---|---|
| | | | | | |

| 39 | Combine columns (d) and (e) only. Enter the result here and include in the total on line 41 below | 39 | |
|---|---|---|---|

**Part V   Summary**

| 40 | Net farm rental income or (loss) from **Form 4835**. Also, complete line 42 below . . . . . . | 40 | |
|---|---|---|---|
| 41 | **Total income or (loss).** Combine lines 26, 32, 37, 39, and 40. Enter the result here and on Schedule 1 (Form 1040), line 5 ▶ | 41 | (5,470) |

| 42 | **Reconciliation of farming and fishing income.** Enter your **gross** farming and fishing income reported on Form 4835, line 7; Schedule K-1 (Form 1065), box 14, code B; Schedule K-1 (Form 1120-S), box 17, code AD; and Schedule K-1 (Form 1041), box 14, code F. See instructions . . | 42 | |
|---|---|---|---|
| 43 | **Reconciliation for real estate professionals.** If you were a real estate professional (see instructions), enter the net income or (loss) you reported anywhere on Form 1040, Form 1040-SR, or Form 1040-NR from all rental real estate activities in which you materially participated under the passive activity loss rules . . . . . . | 43 | |

Schedule E (Form 1040) 2021

Source: U.S. Department of the Treasury, Internal Revenue Service, Schedule E (Form 1040). Washington, DC: 2021.

the guaranteed payment is not salary, the partnership does not pay social security tax on the payment. However, the partner must consider the guaranteed payment as self-employment income. From the partner's point of view, the details of the self-employment calculation are unimportant because the number on line 14 (less § 179 expense) is the amount of self-employment earnings that must be reported on Schedule SE.

The income from all other flow-through entities is not considered self-employment income (as it is in a partnership). For example, an employee/shareholder in an S corporation receives a salary like any other employee, and the S corporation and employee each pays its share of social security tax. Ordinary income from an S corporation is not self-employment income.

### Partnership Income or Loss—Passive Activities

We discuss passive activities in detail in Chapter 13. However, some explanation is needed at this point. A *passive activity* is an activity in which the taxpayer does not materially participate in the operations. An investment often is a passive activity, whereas an actual trade or business is considered active. After all, a trade or business such as a bakery or a retail store does not operate by itself; some person(s) must actively run the business. Rental activity and limited partnership interests are, by definition, passive activities (even if the taxpayer actively participated in that activity).[31]

Thus, if the limited partner box on a K-1 (Part II) is checked or income from rental activities is shown on line 2 or 3, the activity is likely a passive activity. The passive rules require that the taxpayer categorize income and losses into three types: active, passive, and portfolio. In general, taxpayers can deduct passive losses to the extent that there is passive income (that is, no loss is allowed). Any excess losses cannot be used to offset active or portfolio income but are carried forward instead to offset passive income in future years. In cases of rental activity, however, a taxpayer is allowed up to $25,000 of rental losses against other nonpassive income, subject to phaseout above certain AGI amounts (see Chapter 13 for details and limitations). Income or losses from passive activities are reported on line 28, column (g) or (h), of page 2, Schedule E. Form 8582 may also be required.

---

**CONCEPT CHECK 8-5— LO 8-4**

1. Flow-through entities allocate an appropriate share of the entity's income, expenses, or loss to their partners, shareholders, or owners on Schedule K-1. True or false?
2. Ordinary income from all flow-through entities is considered self-employment income. True or false?
3. The partners (shareholders and owners) must report the income and loss from the K-1s they received on Schedule E of their individual tax returns. True or false?
4. By definition, rental properties are passive activities. However, in certain cases, a taxpayer may deduct rental losses, subject to limitations and phaseouts. True or false?

---

## Summary

**LO 8-1:** Explain how income and expenses are recognized and reported for rental property.

- Income and expenses from rental property are generally reported on Schedule E.
- Gross rent is total rent collected regardless of the period covered and includes expenses paid by the tenant or services provided by the tenant in lieu of rent payments.
- All ordinary and necessary expenses related to a rental property are deductible.

---

[31] IRC § 469.

- Rental property is depreciated using straight-line depreciation over 27.5 or 39 years.
- If a taxpayer's rental property is considered a trade or business, the related income and expenses are reported on Schedule C.

**LO 8-2:** Understand how to report personal use of a rental property (vacation home).

- A property that is used for both personal and rental activities falls into one of three categories for tax purposes: (a) primarily rental, (b) primarily personal, and (c) personal/rental.
- The three categories are determined by comparing the number of rental-use days versus the number of personal-use days.
- If a rental property is primarily personal, no income is taxable and no expenses are deductible other than deductions usually allowed as itemized deductions.
- If a rental property is primarily rental or personal/rental, the expenses must be allocated between personal and rental uses.
- Two methods available to allocate expenses between personal and rental uses are the IRS and the Tax Court methods.
- No net loss is allowed if a rental property is considered personal/rental (i.e., expenses are deducted only to the extent that there is rental income).
- In the case of multifamily homes when the taxpayer owns the home, lives in one of the units, and rents the remaining units, the units are treated as independent units and expenses allocated accordingly.

**LO 8-3:** Know how to report royalty income on Schedule E.

- A *royalty* is a payment for the right to use intangible property.
- Royalty income is generally reported on Schedule E.
- If a payment is received while performing a service related to the royalty-producing asset or the royalty is a result of a trade or business, the royalty income is reported on Schedule C.

**LO 8-4:** Discuss the different types of flow-through entities reported on Schedule E, such as partnerships, S corporations, LLCs, trusts, and estates.

- Partnerships, LLCs, S corporations, trusts, and estates are known as *flow-through entities*.
- Flow-through entities file "informational returns" and provide their partners (shareholders or owners) with Schedule K-1s.
- The income and expenses from K-1s are reported on the individual partner's (shareholder or owner) Schedule E.
- Certain limited partnerships and rental activity are considered passive activities; as such, the amounts of net loss that are deductible against nonpassive income are limited by the passive activity rules (discussed in detail in Chapter 13).
- Ordinary income from flow-through entities is eligible for the 20% qualified business income deduction, subject to the limitations discussed in Chapter 6.

## EA Fast Fact

The Enrolled Agent exam is a three-part exam that covers all aspects of tax practice. Part 1 covers Individual taxation, which is the primary focus of this textbook. Applicants are allowed to take each part of the exam separately, and once a single part has been passed, they generally have two years to complete the remaining two parts. The Enrolled Agent Designation is awarded by the US Treasury Department once the candidate has passed all three parts and has completed a tax background check.

**IMPORTANT**

You are eligible to receive absolutely free, the Surgent Enrolled Agent review program for Part I of the EA exam as a result of purchasing this text. To activate your tree access, go to https://Surgent.com/McGrawHill/EA

## Discussion Questions   Mc Graw Hill connect

All applicable discussion questions are available with **Connect**©

LO 8-1   1. Can an owner of a rental property be treated as conducting a trade or business with respect to the rental property? If so, what must the owner do for it to be considered a trade or business?

EA   LO 8-1   2. For rental expenses to be deductible, what criteria must be met? For this question, assume no personal use of the rental property.

EA   LO 8-1   3. What is the difference between a deductible repair expense and capital improvement of rental property?

EA   LO 8-1   4. When depreciation is deducted on a rental property, why is it beneficial for the taxpayer to allocate the cost of the property to other assets (furniture, appliances, etc.) connected with the property rather than allocating the entire lump sum to the building itself?

EA   LO 8-1   5. Can travel expenses to and from rental property be deducted? If so, what are the rules concerning the deductibility of travel, and how is the deduction calculated? (*Hint:* You may need to review Chapter 6 to help with this answer.)

EA   LO 8-2   6. Les's personal residence is in uptown New Orleans. Every year during Mardi Gras, Les rents his house for 10 days to a large corporation that uses it to entertain clients. How does Les treat the rental income? Explain.

EA   LO 8-2   7. Two methods are used to allocate expenses between personal and rental uses of property. Explain the Tax Court method and the IRS method. Which method is more beneficial to the taxpayer?

LO 8-2   8. Discuss the three categories of vacation home rentals. Include in your discussion how personal use of the property affects the reporting of income and losses of vacation homes.

LO 8-2    9. What is considered personal use of a vacation rental property?

_____

_____

_____

LO 8-2    10. Jake has a vacation rental house at the beach. During the tax year, he and his immediate family used the house for 12 days for personal vacation. Jake and his son spent two more weekends (4 days) repairing the steps from the property to the beach. The beach house was rented for 100 days. How is the beach house categorized this year? Explain your answer.

_____

_____

_____

LO 8-2    11. Would your answer to Question 10 change if Jake also rented his house (at fair value) to his brother and his family for 7 days?

_____

_____

_____

EA  LO 8-3    12. What is royalty income, and which forms are used to report it? What factors determine which forms should be used?

_____

_____

_____

LO 8-1, 8-2, 8-3, 8-4    13. Briefly describe the types of income that are reported on Schedule E.
EA

_____

_____

_____

LO 8-4    14. What is meant by the term *flow-through entity?* Give some examples.

_____

_____

_____

EA  LO 8-4    15. How are the income and losses from a flow-through entity reported to the taxpayer (partner, shareholder, or owner)? Are all of the items from the flow-through entity reported on the same form? Explain.

_____

_____

_____

LO 8-4    16. Why are the income and losses (or expenses) separately stated to the partner, shareholder, or owner, and on what form are they reported?

_____

_____

_____

LO 8-4    17. Why are charitable contributions stated separately on the K-1 but not deducted on a partnership return?

_____

_____

_____

## Multiple-Choice Questions  Mc Graw Hill  connect

All applicable multiple-choice questions are available with **Connect**©

**EA**  LO 8-1  18. On August 1 of the current year, Jennifer and Tyler purchased a cabin for $950,000. Of that amount, $500,000 was for the land. How much depreciation deduction can Jennifer and Tyler take in the current year assuming that the cabin was rented starting on the purchase date? (You may need to refer to the depreciation tables in Chapter 6.)

    *a.* 0.

    *b.* $6,138.

    *c.* $8,865.

    *d.* $16,364.

**EA**  LO 8-1  19. Jermaine owns a rental home in Lake Tahoe and traveled there from his home in San Francisco for maintenance and repairs three times this year. The round trip from San Francisco to Lake Tahoe is approximately 167 miles. How much travel cost can Jermaine deduct for the current year related to the rental home in Lake Tahoe?

    *a.* 0.

    *b.* $96.

    *c.* $167.

    *d.* $281.

**EA**  LO 8-1  20. Dennis receives $11,100 during the current tax year from Blanca for some office space in Anaheim, California. The rent covers eight months, from August 1 of the current year to March 31 of the following year. The amount also includes a security deposit of $1,500. How much should Dennis report as rental income in the current tax year?

    *a.* $1,200.

    *b.* $6,000.

    *c.* $9,600.

    *d.* $11,100.

**EA**  LO 8-1  21. Ginny owns a house in northern Wisconsin that she rents for $1,600 per month. Ginny does not use the property personally. While she was in Europe for Christmas, the water heater on the property failed, and her tenants repaired it for $1,200. For the following month's rent (January), her tenants paid her $400 for rent ($1,600 − $1,200). What amounts should Ginny include for rental income and repair expense, respectively, for January?

    *a.* $400; $0.

    *b.* $1,200; $400.

    *c.* $1,600; $400.

    *d.* $1,600; $1,200.

**EA**  LO 8-2  22. James owns a home in Lake Tahoe, Nevada, that he rented for $1,600 for two weeks during the summer. He lived there for a total of 120 days, and the rest of the year the house was vacant. The expenses for the home included $6,000 in mortgage interest, $900 in property taxes, $1,300 in maintenance and utilities, and $2,500 in depreciation.

How much rental income from the Lake Tahoe home would James report for the current year?

a. $0.

b. $567.

c. $1,600.

d. $9,100.

**EA** LO 8-2 23. Assume the same facts as Question 22 except that James rented the Lake Tahoe home for 40 days for $4,600. What is his net income or loss from the rental of his home (without considering the passive loss limitation)? Use the IRS method for allocation of expenses.

a. $0.

b. $1,925 net income.

c. $4,600 net income.

d. $6,100 net loss.

**EA** LO 8-2 24. Which of the following items is *not* deductible as rental expense?

a. Advertising.

b. Repairs and maintenance.

c. New bathroom addition.

d. Insurance.

**EA** LO 8-2 25. Darren and Nikki own a cabin in Mammoth, California. During the year, they rented it for 45 days for $9,000 and used it for 12 days for personal use. The house remained vacant for the remainder of the year. The expenses for the house included $8,000 in mortgage interest, $2,000 in property taxes, $1,200 in utilities, $750 in maintenance, and $4,000 in depreciation. What is their net income or loss from their cabin rental (without considering the passive loss limitation)? Use the IRS method for allocation of expenses.

a. $0.

b. $3,592 net loss.

c. $6,950 net loss.

d. $9,000 net income.

**EA** LO 8-2 26. Aron and Nino own a home in Boulder City, Nevada, near Lake Mead. During the year, they rented the house for 40 days for $3,000 and used it for personal use for 18 days. The house remained vacant for the remainder of the year. The expenses for the house included $14,000 in mortgage interest, $3,500 in property taxes, $1,100 in utilities, $1,300 in maintenance, and $10,900 in depreciation. What is the deductible net loss for the rental of their home (without considering the passive loss limitation)? Use the Tax Court method for allocation of expenses.

a. $0.

b. $388.

c. $8,090.

d. $27,800.

EA    LO 8-2    27. Nicolette and Brady own a cabin in Lake Arrowhead, California, that they rent out during the winter and use the rest of the year. The rental property is categorized as personal/rental property, and their personal use is determined to be 68% (based on the IRS method). They had the following income and expenses for the year (after allocation):

| | |
|---|---|
| Gross rental income | $9,500 |
| Interest and taxes | 6,000 |
| Utilities and maintenance | 2,500 |
| Depreciation | 4,300 |

How much can Nicolette and Brady deduct for depreciation expense related to this property for the year on their tax return?

a. $0.

b. $1,000.

c. $4,300.

d. The answer cannot be determined.

EA    LO 8-3    28. Colin is a high school chemistry teacher who owns some land in Oklahoma that produces oil from its small oil reserve. On what schedule should Colin report the royalty income he receives?

a. Schedule A.

b. Schedule C.

c. Schedule E.

d. Schedule SE.

EA    LO 8-3    29. Sally is a full-time author and recently published her third mystery novel. The royalty income she receives from the publisher this year should be reported on what schedule?

a. Schedule E.

b. Schedule D.

c. Schedule A.

d. Schedule C.

LO 8-4    30. What is the maximum amount of passive losses from a rental activity that a taxpayer can deduct against active and portfolio income per year (assuming no passive loss limitation due to AGI or personal use of the property)?

a. $0.

b. $15,000.

c. $25,000.

d. $50,000.

LO 8-4    31. Which of the following entity(ies) is (are) considered flow-through?

a. Partnership.

b. S corporation.

c. LLC.

d. All are considered flow-through entities.

LO 8-4    32. From which of the following flow-through entities is ordinary income (K-1) considered self-employment income?

a. Partnership.

b. S corporation.

c. Trusts.

d. Estates.

## Problems   Mc Graw Hill **connect**

All applicable problems are available with ***Connect***©

**LO 8-1**   33. Ramone is a tax attorney, and he owns an office building that he rents for $8,500/month. He is responsible for paying all taxes and expenses relating to the building's operation and maintenance. Is Ramone engaged in the trade or business of renting real estate?

_____

_____

_____

_____

_____

**EA**   **LO 8-1, 8-2**   34. Kelvin owns and lives in a duplex. He rents the other unit for $750 per month. He incurs the following expenses during the current year for the entire property:

| | |
|---|---|
| Mortgage interest | $7,500 |
| Property taxes | 2,000 |
| Utilities | 1,500 |
| Fixed light fixture in rental unit | 100 |
| Fixed dishwasher in personal unit | 250 |
| Painted entire exterior | 1,300 |
| Insurance | 1,800 |
| Depreciation (entire structure) | 7,000 |

How are these income and expenses reported on Kelvin's tax return? On what tax form(s) are these amounts reported?

_____

_____

_____

_____

_____

**EA**   **LO 8-2**   35. In the current year, Sandra rented her vacation home for 75 days, used it for personal use for 22 days, and left it vacant for the remainder of the year. Her income and expenses before allocation are as follows:

| | |
|---|---|
| Rental income | $15,000 |
| Real estate taxes | 2,000 |
| Utilities | 1,500 |
| Mortgage interest | 3,800 |
| Depreciation | 7,200 |
| Repairs and maintenance | 1,300 |

What is Sandra's net income or loss from the rental of her vacation home? Use the Tax Court method.

_____

_____

_____

_____

_____

**EA** **LO 8-2** 36. Alice rented her personal residence for 13 days to summer vacationers for $4,500. She has AGI of $105,000 before the rental income. Related expenses for the year include the following:

| | |
|---|---|
| Real property taxes | $ 4,500 |
| Utilities | 5,000 |
| Insurance | 900 |
| Mortgage interest | 7,000 |
| Repairs | 800 |
| Depreciation | 15,000 |

Calculate the effect of the rental on Alice's AGI. Explain your rationale, citing tax authority.

_____

_____

_____

_____

_____

_____

**EA** **LO 8-2** 37. Alicia and Marie own a vacation home at the beach. During the year, they rented the house for 42 days (6 weeks) at $890 per week and used it for personal use for 58 days. The total costs of maintaining the home are as follows:

| | |
|---|---|
| Mortgage interest | $4,200 |
| Property taxes | 700 |
| Insurance | 1,200 |
| Utilities | 3,200 |
| Repairs | 1,900 |
| Depreciation | 5,500 |

*a.* What is the proper tax treatment of this information on their tax return using the Tax Court method?

*b.* Are there options available for how to allocate the expenses between personal and rental use? Explain.

*c.* What is the proper tax treatment of the rental income and expenses if Alicia and Marie rented the house for only 14 days?

_____

_____

_____

_____

_____

_____

**EA** **LO 8-2** 38. Janet owns a home at the lake. She incurs the following expenses:

| | |
|---|---|
| Mortgage interest | $1,300 |
| Property taxes | 800 |
| Insurance | 1,500 |
| Utilities | 1,800 |
| Repairs | 300 |
| Depreciation | 4,000 |

What is the proper treatment of the rental income and expenses in each of the following cases? Use the Tax Court allocation method, if applicable.

| Case | Rental Income | Days Rented | Personal-Use Days |
|------|--------------|-------------|-------------------|
| A | $ 9,000 | 45 | 10 |
| B | 12,000 | 55 | 25 |
| C | 6,000 | 10 | 30 |
| D | 22,000 | 365 | –0– |

_____

_____

_____

_____

_____

_____

**EA**   **LO 8-2**   39. Randolph and Tammy own a second home. They spent 45 days there and rented it for 88 days at $150 per day during the year. The total costs relating to the home include the following:

| | |
|---|---|
| Mortgage interest | $4,500 |
| Property taxes | 1,200 |
| Insurance | 1,800 |
| Utilities | 2,300 |
| Repairs | 1,500 |
| Depreciation | 6,500 |

What is the proper treatment of these items relating to the second home? Would you use the Tax Court allocation or the IRS allocation? Explain.

_____

_____

_____

_____

_____

_____

**EA**   **LO 8-4**   40. Mabel, Loretta, and Margaret are equal partners in a local restaurant. The restaurant reports the following items for the current year:

| | |
|---|---|
| Revenue | $ 600,000 |
| Business expenses | 310,000 |
| Investment expenses | 150,000 |
| Short-term capital gains | 157,000 |
| Short-term capital losses | (213,000) |

Each partner receives a Schedule K-1 with one-third of the preceding items reported to her. How must each individual report these results on her Form 1040?

_____

_____

_____

_____

_____

_____

EA  LO 8-4   41. Nicole and Mohammad (married taxpayers filing jointly) are equal owners in an S corporation. The company reported sales revenue of $450,000 and expenses of $310,000. The corporation also earned $20,000 in taxable interest and dividend income and had $15,000 investment interest expense. How are these amounts treated for tax purposes?

_____

_____

_____

_____

_____

_____

EA  LO 8-4   42. Dominique and Terrell are joint owners of a bookstore. The business operates as an S corporation. Dominique owns 65%, and Terrell owns 35%. The business has the following results in the current year:

| | |
|---|---:|
| Revenue | $1,500,000 |
| Business expenses | 750,000 |
| Charitable contributions | 50,000 |
| Short-term capital losses | 4,500 |
| Long-term capital gains | 6,000 |

How do Dominique and Terrell report these items for tax purposes?

_____

_____

_____

_____

_____

_____

EA  LO 8-4   43. Shirelle and Newman are each 50% partners of a business that operates as a partnership. The business reports the following results:

| | |
|---|---:|
| Revenue | $95,000 |
| Business expenses | 48,000 |
| Investment expenses | 8,000 |
| Short-term capital gains | 15,000 |
| Short-term capital losses | (22,000) |

How do Shirelle and Newman report these items for tax purposes?

_____

_____

_____

_____

_____

_____

## Tax Return Problems

All applicable tax return problems are available with ***Connect***<sup></sup>

Use your tax software to complete the following problems. If you are manually preparing the tax returns, see each problem for the forms you may need.

For the following tax return problems, assume the taxpayer does NOT wish to contribute to the Presidential Election Fund, unless otherwise stated in the problem. In addition, the taxpayers did *not* receive, sell, send, exchange, or otherwise acquire any financial interest in any virtual currency during the year. For any Tax Return Problems for which the taxpayers are entitled to a child tax credit, assume that the taxpayers did NOT receive any advance child tax credit payments during 2021. Thus, the entire child tax credit (if permitted) will be claimed on the 2021 tax return.

**Tax Return Problem 1**

Derrick and Ani Jones are married taxpayers, filing jointly, and have a son named Jackson. They live at 474 Rustic Drive, Spokane, WA 99201. Ani works as the director of information systems at Washington Community College District (WCCD). Derrick is a stay-at-home dad. Their SSNs are Derrick, 412-34-5670; Ani, 412-34-5671; and Jackson, 412-34-5672. Their birth dates are as follows: Derrick, June 7, 1981; Ani, March 20, 1982; and Jackson, October 10, 2014. The Joneses own their home and paid $15,000 in mortgage interest during the year to Chase Bank and property taxes of $3,200. Assume they have no other deductible expenses.

The Form W-2 Ani received from WCCD contained the following information:

Wages (box 1) = $79,002.50
Federal W/H (box 2) = $ 7,000.14
Social security wages (box 3) = $79,002.50
Social security W/H (box 4) = $ 4,898.16
Medicare wages (box 5) = $79,002.50
Medicare W/H (box 6) = $ 1,145.54

In addition, the Joneses own a small, four-unit rental at 12345 Rainbow Way, Sultan, WA 98294. The rental was purchased and placed in service on July 1, 2008, and was rented for the entire year. The following income and expense information relates to the rental activity. For the purpose of this return problem, do not consider passive activity rules or limitations.

| | |
|---|---:|
| Rental income | $24,000 |
| Real estate taxes | 2,000 |
| State sales taxes | 1,349 |
| Utilities | 1,500 |
| Mortgage interest | 3,800 |
| Depreciation | 7,200 |
| Repairs and maintenance | 1,300 |

Prepare the Joneses' federal tax return for 2021. Use Form 1040, Schedule A, Schedule E, and any other appropriate schedules. Assume they do not qualify for any credits other than the child care credit. If using tax software, the software will calculate Child Tax Credit automatically. The taxpayers had qualifying health care coverage at all times during the tax year. For any missing information, make reasonable assumptions.

We have provided selected filled-in source documents available in the *Connect Library.*

**Tax Return Problem 2**

Warren and Young Kim are married taxpayers, filing jointly. They live at 777 Kingston Place, Anaheim, CA 92805. They are both retired. Their SSNs are Warren, 412-34-5670; and Young, 412-34-5671. Their birth dates are as follows: Warren, January 8, 1951; and Young, August 21, 1951.

They own their home, which they paid off in 2012, and another home that they paid for in cash as an investment (Warren considers it his pension). Their investment home was rented for the entire year and is located just one block over at 9021 Jasmine Way. The following income and expense information relates to the rental activity. For the purpose of this return problem, do not consider passive activity rules or limitations.

| | |
|---|---|
| Rental income | $27,600 |
| Real estate taxes | 7,952 |
| Utilities | 1,603 |
| Mortgage interest | –0– |
| Repairs and maintenance | 3,616 |
| Depreciation | See following information |

They placed the rental home into service on March 1, 2015, and of the $515,000 purchase price, $426,000 was allocated to the land.

In addition to the rental, they received interest of $1,086 from American Credit Union and $2,200 from Bank of California. Social security benefits were $13,910 for Warren and $8,822 for Young, respectively.

Prepare the Kims' federal tax return for 2021. Use Form 1040, Schedule B, Schedule E, and Form 4562. Assume they do not qualify for any credits (although they may). The taxpayers had qualifying health care coverage at all times during the tax year. For any missing information, make reasonable assumptions.

We have provided selected filled-in source documents available in the *Connect Library*.

**Tax Return Problem 3**

Lou and Joann Girardi are married and file a joint return. They recently bought a new home at 21680 Skyline Drive, Henderson, NV, 89077. Their son, Stuart, attends the University of Pennsylvania full time on a full scholarship. Stuart is claimed as a dependent on the Girardis' tax return. Their SSNs are Lou, 412-34-5670; Joann, 412-34-5671; and Stuart, 412-34-5672. Their birth dates are as follows: Lou, May 18, 1968; Joann, December 24, 1968; and Stuart, May 9, 2021. Their relevant tax information follows:

Joann is an attorney and owns her law firm, which is operating as an S corporation. Her W-2 information and Schedule K-1 from her law firm are as follows:

Wages (box 1) = $114,800.50

Federal W/H (box 2) = $ 13,000.14

Social security wages (box 3) = $114,800.50

Social security W/H (box 4) = $ 7,117.63

Medicare wages (box 5) = $114,800.50

Medicare W/H (box 6) = $ 1,664.61

Schedule K-1 from the law offices of Joann Girardi: Girardi—Attorney at Law

ID # 12-3456789

100% Owner

Material participation – yes

Line 1 = $22,582.00 (ordinary business income)
Line 11 = $22,582.00 (§ 179 deduction)

Lou is a full-time lecturer at Arizona State University. His W-2 information from ASU is as follows:

Wages (box 1) = $65,000.00

Federal W/H (box 2) = $ 8,950.25

Social security wages (box 3) = $65,000.00

Social security W/H (box 4) = $ 4,030.00

Medicare wages (box 5) = $65,000.00

Medicare W/H (box 6) = $ 942.50

The following are other income and expenses they received and incurred during the year:

| | |
|---|---:|
| Income | |
|    Dividends (all qualified) | $    666 |
|    Interest | 765 |
| Expenses | |
|    Real estate taxes | 7,836 |
|    State sales tax | 1,629 |
|    Mortgage interest | 32,562 |
|    Charitable contribution | 2,598 |

Prepare the Girardis' federal tax return for 2021. Use Form 1040, Schedules A, B, and E, and a Qualified Dividends worksheet. Assume that the Girardis do not qualify for any credits (although they may). For any missing information, make reasonable assumptions. The taxpayers had qualifying health care coverage at all times during the tax year. (Assume no AMT although it may apply; Form 6251 or the AMT calculation is not required.)

We have provided selected filled-in source documents that are available in the *Connect Library.*

# Chapter **Nine**

# Tax Credits (Form 1040, Lines 19, 20, 27 through 29, and 31, Schedule 3, Lines 1 through 14)

Congress has provided a variety of tax credits designed to reduce the tax liability of specific groups of taxpayers. The intended purpose of these tax credits is to accomplish certain social or economic goals or to encourage participation in certain activities deemed desirable by policymakers. Tax credits are different from tax deductions. A tax credit is subtracted directly from the total amount of tax liability, thus reducing or even eliminating the taxpayer's tax obligation. Tax deductions decrease the taxable income used to calculate tax liability. Thus, tax credits provide equal relief to all taxpayers regardless of their marginal tax rate and are more beneficial to the taxpayer than a deduction.

### Learning Objectives

When you have completed this chapter, you should understand the following learning objectives (LO):

LO 9-1  Apply the tax rules and calculate the credit for child and dependent care expenses.

LO 9-2  Apply the tax rules and calculate the credit for the elderly or the disabled.

LO 9-3  Apply the tax rules and calculate the education credits.

LO 9-4  Apply the tax rules and calculate the foreign tax credit (FTC).

LO 9-5  Apply the tax rules and calculate the child tax credit.

LO 9-6  Apply the tax rules and calculate the retirement savings contributions credit.

LO 9-7  Apply the tax rules and calculate the adoption credit.

LO 9-8  Apply the tax rules and calculate the Earned Income Credit (EIC).

LO 9-9  Apply the tax rules for the premium tax credit under the Affordable Care Act.

## INTRODUCTION

We discussed many kinds of deductions in Chapter 5. Deductions reduce taxable income, which then reduces tax liability in an amount equal to the deduction multiplied by the marginal tax rate. So, a taxpayer who has a $100 deduction in the 24% marginal bracket will save $24 in tax. Credits are covered in this chapter. Credits are more valuable than deductions because credits reduce tax liability dollar-for-dollar. Thus, subject to possible limitation, a $100 credit will reduce tax liability by $100.

Congress has elected to offer a number of tax credits, generally enacted to encourage certain outcomes or to accomplish specified societal goals. Some of these goals include assisting families with children, ensuring additional tax relief for low-income taxpayers, encouraging taxpayers to enhance their education, encouraging adoptions, and providing incentives for taxpayers to work.

Most individual income tax credits are *nonrefundable.* This means that taxpayers whose credits exceed their tax liability will reduce tax owed to zero but will *not* receive a refund for the excess amount. There are some tax credits that are *refundable,* such as the Earned Income Credit (EIC) and others. In these cases, a taxpayer with credits in excess of the tax liability will receive the excess amount as a refund.

Most tax credits are reported on Form 1040, lines 19, 20, 27 through 29, and 31, Schedule 3, lines 1 through 14, and some may require additional forms or schedules. This chapter also discusses the premium tax credit, which can create additional tax on Schedule 2, line 2, or an additional credit on Schedule 3, line 9. The more commonly used tax credits are discussed under the appropriate learning objectives of this chapter.

# CREDIT FOR CHILD AND DEPENDENT CARE EXPENSES (SCHEDULE 3, LINE 2 [FORM 2441])
## LO 9-1

 **NEW LAW**

Many taxpayers with dependents incur expenses to care for those dependents while they work. The credit for child and dependent care expenses provides some relief for working taxpayers by providing a credit for a portion of the expenses incurred to care for a qualified dependent.[1] To qualify for the credit, the taxpayer must incur employment-related expenses to care for one or more qualifying individuals. For 2021, the credit is fully refundable for taxpayers who have a principal place of abode in the United States for more than one-half of the year.

### Qualifying Expenses

All necessary expenses, including those paid for household services and expenses for the care of qualified individuals so that the taxpayer can be gainfully employed,[2] are eligible. Appropriate expenses include those incurred in the home for a babysitter, housekeeper, cook, or nanny. Expenses paid to a family member (such as a grandparent) are eligible as long as the relative is not a child of the taxpayer under the age of 19 and cannot be claimed as a dependent by the taxpayer.[3]

If the expenses are incurred outside the home at a dependent care facility (such as a day care center) that provides care for a fee for six or more individuals, the expenses qualify only if the facility complies with all of the applicable state and local laws related to licensing.[4] In addition, out-of-the-home expenses incurred while caring for an older dependent or spouse (who is incapacitated) qualify. However, the qualifying individual(s) must live in the household of the taxpayer for at least eight hours a day. These rules allow credit for expenses incurred for an incapacitated dependent who otherwise would be institutionalized.

### Qualifying Individual

A qualifying individual includes (1) a person under age 13 who is a dependent of the taxpayer or (2) a dependent or spouse of the taxpayer who is incapable of caring for themselves and who lived with the taxpayer for at least half of the year.[5] A child under age 13 meeting the special dependency test of divorced parents is deemed to be a qualifying individual for the custodial parent even if that parent cannot claim the child as a dependent.[6]

Generally, married taxpayers must file a joint return to claim the credit (legally separated taxpayers are not considered to be married). Married taxpayers filing a separate return are entitled to claim the credit only if they meet *all* the following conditions:

---

[1] IRC § 21.
[2] IRC § 21(b)(2)(A).
[3] *Family member* is defined in IRC § 152(c)(2).
[4] IRC § 21(b)(2)(C), (D).
[5] IRC § 21(b)(1).
[6] IRC § 21(e)(5), § 152(e).

- Lived apart from their spouse.
- Furnished more than half of the cost of maintaining a household that a qualified individual lived in for more than half the year.
- Have a spouse who was not a member of the household for the last six months of the year.[7]

### Credit Calculation

**NEW LAW**

The credit is calculated as a percentage of employment-related expenses paid during the year. For tax year 2021 only, the percentage varies between 20% and 50%, depending on the taxpayer's AGI. The maximum amount of qualifying expenses for 2021 is limited to $8,000 if there is one qualifying individual and to $16,000 for two or more qualifying individuals.[8] These amounts are further limited to the amount of earned income of the taxpayer (or the earned income of the taxpayer's spouse, if smaller).[9] Earned income includes wages, salaries, tips, other taxable employee compensation, and net earnings from self-employment. Generally, only taxable compensation is included. Therefore, earned income does not include noncompensation income such as interest and dividends, unemployment compensation, or child support payments, among others. If a taxpayer receives dependent care assistance from an employer that is excluded from gross income, the expense limit is reduced by the amount excluded from income.[10] The amount of the credit is limited to the taxpayer's tax liability.

If the taxpayer's spouse is unable to care for themselves or is a full-time student, the spouse is deemed to have earned income for the purpose of the credit calculation. That amount of earned income is $250 per month if the taxpayer cares for one qualifying person and $500 per month if caring for two or more persons. In case of a full-time student, the amount is further limited by the number of months the taxpayer (or the spouse) attended school.

**EXAMPLE 9-1**

Bill and Suzie each earned $120,000 and they paid $21,400 in qualified employment-related expenses for their three children. Suzie received $2,500 of dependent care assistance that her employer properly excluded from Suzie's gross income. The amount of employment-related expenses Bill and Suzie can use to determine their credit is $13,500 (the maximum amount allowed of $16,000 reduced by $2,500 of excluded dependent care assistance). Note that the taxpayer must apply the dependent care assistance exclusion against the $16,000 maximum for two or more qualifying individuals, not against the total amount paid (unless the amount paid is less than the limitation amount).

**EXAMPLE 9-2**

Sofia and Elijah paid $3,800 in qualified employment-related expenses for their dependent daughter. Their AGI was $42,000, which included $40,500 from Sofia's job and $1,500 of net self-employment income from Elijah's business (as reported on Schedule C). Qualified employment-related expenses would be limited to $1,500.

**EXAMPLE 9-3**

Ethan and Riley paid $4,200 in qualified employment-related expenses for their dependent son. Ethan's AGI was $42,000; Riley was a full-time student for nine months of the year. Ethan and Riley's qualified employment-related expenses would be limited to $2,250 ($250 × 9 months).

The percentage used to determine the credit, which ranges from 50% to 0% in 2021, depends on the taxpayer's AGI. The percentage is 50% for taxpayers with AGI of $125,000 or less. Above $125,000, the credit is reduced by 1% for each additional $2,000 of AGI (or fraction thereof), until AGI of $183,000 when the percentage reaches 20%. It stays at 20% until AGI of $400,000 when it is again reduced by 1% for each $2,000 of AGI (or fraction thereof). At AGI over $438,000, the credit is zero. The following chart provides applicable percentages:

[7] IRC § 21(e)(4).

[8] IRC § 21(c).

[9] IRC § 21(d).

[10] IRC § 21(c). The income exclusion would be made in accordance with IRC § 129.

| Adjusted Gross Income | Applicable Percentage | Adjusted Gross Income | Applicable Percentage | Adjusted Gross Income | Applicable Percentage |
|---|---|---|---|---|---|
| $125,000 or less | 50% | $157,001–159,000 | 33% | $406,001–408,000 | 16% |
| $125,001–127,000 | 49% | $159,001–161,000 | 32% | $408,001–410,000 | 15% |
| $127,001–129,000 | 48% | $161,001–163,000 | 31% | $410,001–412,000 | 14% |
| $129,001–131,000 | 47% | $163,001–165,000 | 30% | $412,001–414,000 | 13% |
| $131,001–133,000 | 46% | $165,001–167,000 | 29% | $414,001–416,000 | 12% |
| $133,001–135,000 | 45% | $167,001–169,000 | 28% | $416,001–418,000 | 11% |
| $135,001–137,000 | 44% | $169,001–171,000 | 27% | $418,001–420,000 | 10% |
| $137,001–139,000 | 43% | $171,001–173,000 | 26% | $420,001–422,000 | 9% |
| $139,001–141,000 | 42% | $173,001–175,000 | 25% | $422,001–424,000 | 8% |
| $141,001–143,000 | 41% | $175,001–177,000 | 24% | $424,001–426,000 | 7% |
| $143,001–145,000 | 40% | $177,001–179,000 | 23% | $426,001–428,000 | 6% |
| $145,001–147,000 | 39% | $179,001–181,000 | 22% | $428,001–430,000 | 5% |
| $147,001–149,000 | 38% | $181,001–183,000 | 21% | $430,001–432,000 | 4% |
| $149,001–151,000 | 37% | $183,001–400,000 | 20% | $432,001–434,000 | 3% |
| $151,001–153,000 | 36% | $400,001–402,000 | 19% | $434,001–436,000 | 2% |
| $153,001–155,000 | 35% | $402,001–404,000 | 18% | $436,001–438,000 | 1% |
| $155,001–157,000 | 34% | $404,001–406,000 | 17% | $438,001 or more | 0% |

# From Shoebox to Software

Taxpayers use Form 2441 to calculate and report the child and dependent care credit (Exhibit 9-1).

Complete identification of the qualifying child is required. Taxpayers must also provide information for the person or entity that provided the care, including taxpayer ID numbers. Most established day care programs provide taxpayers with end-of-year statements listing the amounts paid for day care and the taxpayer ID of the day care establishment.

Within the tax software, you enter most required information directly on Form 2441. Part I is used to report information about the child care provider, including the amount paid. Part II shows data on the qualifying individual(s) and the expenses paid for each one. The tax software automatically determines lines 3 through 11. If taxpayers received any nontaxable dependent care benefits from their employer, the software will then complete Part III (not shown). The amount of tax-free benefit is in box 10 of Form W-2.

If the taxpayer has checked box B on Form 2441, the tax software reports the final refundable credit amount (Form 2441, line 10) on line 13g of on Schedule 3.

---

**EXAMPLE 9-4**    Cheng has AGI of $88,744 from his employment, and he spent $1,240 on qualified expenses for his child during the year. He is entitled to a tax credit of $620 ($1,240 × 50%). If Cheng's AGI were $133,744, his credit would be $558 ($1,240 × 45%). If his AGI were $450,000, his credit would be zero.

---

**EXAMPLE 9-5**    Rachel, a single mother, maintains a household for her four-year-old son, Eric. Rachel had AGI of $148,217 and incurred $10,800 in child care expenses for Eric during the year. Her child and dependent care tax credit will be $3,040 ($8,000 × 38%). Rachel is entitled to 38% of qualifying expenses, which are limited to $8,000 for one child.

---

**TAX YOUR BRAIN**    Why would Congress want to provide a credit for child and dependent care expenses?

**ANSWER**

Remember that the credit pertains to qualifying expenses paid to enable the taxpayer to be gainfully employed. It is reasonable to expect that the credit will allow more individuals to be employed (or be employed more hours), resulting in higher payroll and other taxes to offset at least some of the cost of providing the credit. In addition, overall employment levels should increase, which is beneficial to the economy in general.

**EXHIBIT 9-1**

| Form **2441** | **Child and Dependent Care Expenses** | | OMB No. 1545-0074 |
|---|---|---|---|

**Form 2441**

**Child and Dependent Care Expenses**

▶ Attach to Form 1040, 1040-SR, or 1040-NR.

▶ Go to *www.irs.gov/Form2441* for instructions and the latest information.

OMB No. 1545-0074

2021

Attachment Sequence No. **21**

Department of the Treasury
Internal Revenue Service (99)

Name(s) shown on return

Your social security number

**A** You can't claim a credit for child and dependent care expenses if your filing status is married filing separately unless you meet the requirements listed in the instructions under "Married Persons Filing Separately." If you meet these requirements, check this box . ☐

**B** For 2021, your credit for child and dependent care expenses is refundable if you, or your spouse if married filing jointly, had a principal place of abode in the United States for more than half of 2021. If you meet these requirements, check this box . . . ☐

**Part I**   **Persons or Organizations Who Provided the Care—**You **must** complete this part.

If you have more than three care providers, see the instructions and check this box . . . . . . . ☐

| 1 | (a) Care provider's name | (b) Address (number, street, apt. no., city, state, and ZIP code) | (c) Identifying number (SSN or EIN) | (d) Amount paid (see instructions) |
|---|---|---|---|---|
| | | | | |
| | | | | |
| | | | | |

**Did you receive dependent care benefits?** — No ⟶ Complete only Part II below.

— Yes ⟶ Complete Part III on page 2 next.

**Caution:** If the care was provided in your home, you may owe employment taxes. For details, see the instructions for Schedule 2 (Form 1040), line 9. If you incurred care expenses in 2021 but didn't pay them until 2022, or if you prepaid in 2021 for care to be provided in 2022, don't include these expenses in column (c) of line 2 for 2021. See the instructions.

**Part II**   **Credit for Child and Dependent Care Expenses**

**2** Information about your **qualifying person(s).** If you have more than three qualifying persons, see the instructions and check this box . . . . . . . . . . . . . . . . . . . . . . ☐

| (a) Qualifying person's name | | (b) Qualifying person's social security number | (c) Qualified expenses you incurred and paid in 2021 for the person listed in column (a) |
|---|---|---|---|
| First | Last | | |
| | | | |
| | | | |
| | | | |

**3** Add the amounts in column (c) of line 2. **Don't** enter more than $8,000 if you had one qualifying person or $16,000 if you had two or more persons. If you completed Part III, enter the amount from line 31 . . . . . . . . . . . . . . . . . . . . . . . . | **3** | |

**4** Enter your **earned income.** See instructions | **4** | |

**5** If married filing jointly, enter your spouse's earned income (if you or your spouse was a student or was disabled, see the instructions); **all others,** enter the amount from line 4 . . . . . . | **5** | |

**6** Enter the **smallest** of line 3, 4, or 5 . | **6** | |

**7** Enter the amount from Form 1040, 1040-SR, or 1040-NR, line 11 | **7** | |

**8** Enter on line 8 the decimal amount shown below that applies to the amount on line 7.

- If line 7 is $125,000 or less, enter .50 on line 8.
- If line 7 is over $125,000 and no more than $438,000, see the instructions for line 8 for the amount to enter.
- If line 7 is over $438,000, don't complete line 8. Enter zero on line 9a. You may be able to claim a credit on line 9b. | **8** | X . |

**9a** Multiply line 6 by the decimal amount on line 8 . . . . . . . . . . . . | **9a** | |

**b** If you paid 2020 expenses in 2021, complete Worksheet A in the instructions. Enter the amount from line 13 of the worksheet here. Otherwise, go to line 10 . . . . . . . . . | **9b** | |

**10** Add lines 9a and 9b and enter the result. If you checked the box on line B above, this is your **refundable credit for child and dependent care expenses;** enter the amount from this line on Schedule 3 (Form 1040), line 13g, and don't complete line 11. If you didn't check the box on line B above, go to line 11 . . . . . . . . . . . . . . . . . . . . . . . . . . . | **10** | |

**11** **Nonrefundable credit for child and dependent care expenses.** If you didn't check the box on line B above, your credit is nonrefundable and limited by the amount of your tax; see the instructions to figure the portion of line 10 that you can claim and enter that amount here and on Schedule 3 (Form 1040), line 2 . . . . . . . . . . . . . . . . . . . . . . . . . | **11** | |

For Paperwork Reduction Act Notice, see your tax return instructions.    Cat. No. 11862M    Form **2441** (2021)

Source: U.S. Department of the Treasury, Internal Revenue Service, Form 2441. Washington, DC: 2021.

**CONCEPT CHECK 9-1—**
**LO 9-1**

1. Rohini is a single mother with one dependent child, Vanya, age 7. She has AGI of $176,000, and she paid $4,500 to a qualified day care center for after-school care for Vanya. Calculate Rohini's child and dependent care credit.

2. Tom and Katie are married, file a joint return, and have two dependent children: Jack, age 11, and Jordan, age 5. Tom has earned income of $41,000; Katie was a full-time student (for nine months) with no income. They paid a qualified day care/after-school care center $6,000. What is the maximum amount of qualified employment-related expenses that would be allowed for the child and dependent care credit calculation for Tom and Katie?

3. Antonio is a widower and cares for his son Elio, age 4. Antonio has AGI of $24,000 and paid qualified child care expenses for Elio of $2,900. In addition, Antonio received $1,000 of dependent care assistance that his employer properly excluded from Antonio's gross income. Calculate Antonio's child and dependent care credit.

# CREDIT FOR THE ELDERLY OR THE DISABLED (SCHEDULE 3, LINE 6d [SCHEDULE R])
## LO 9-2

The credit for the elderly or the disabled was originally enacted to provide some tax relief to low-income elderly or disabled individuals.[11] To be eligible, the taxpayer must be age 65 or older or have retired on permanent and total disability and be receiving taxable disability income. In addition, certain AGI and nontaxable social security income limits apply.

### Credit Calculation

The maximum allowable credit is equal to 15% of the taxpayer's base amount (depending on the filing status) as follows:

- $5,000 for single individuals or joint returns when only one spouse qualifies.
- $7,500 for joint returns when both spouses qualify.
- $3,750 for a married person filing a separate return.[12]

This base amount must first be reduced by (1) the amount of nontaxable social security (or similar) payments received and (2) one-half of the amount of AGI that exceeds $7,500 for single returns, $10,000 for joint returns, or $5,000 for married filing separately.[13]

**EXAMPLE 9-6**

Lou and Greta file a joint return. Lou is age 66, and Greta is 63. Note that only Lou is eligible for this credit. They have AGI of $11,500 and received $1,000 of nontaxable social security benefits. They would be entitled to a credit for the elderly or the disabled of $488, calculated as follows:

| | |
|---|---:|
| Base amount | $5,000 |
| Less: Nontaxable social security | (1,000) |
| One-half of AGI over $10,000 | (750) |
| Allowable base amount | $3,250 |
| Applicable percentage | × 15% |
| Tax credit allowed | $ 488* |

\* Lou and Greta would have had a maximum credit for the elderly or disabled of $750 ($5,000 × 15%). However, the base amount must be reduced by social security and one-half of the amount of AGI over $10,000 ($750).

In practice, few elderly or disabled taxpayers are eligible for the credit because they generally receive nontaxable social security benefits in excess of the income limitations. In fact, if some social security benefits are taxable, the taxpayer will have exceeded the AGI limits. Furthermore, because the credit is not a refundable credit, the allowed credit is often zero because low-income elderly taxpayers often have no tax liability.

[11] IRC § 22.

[12] IRC § 22(c)(2).

[13] IRC § 22(c)(3), (d).

# From Shoebox to Software

Taxpayers use Schedule R to report the credit for the elderly or disabled. (For page 2 of Schedule R, see Exhibit 9-2.)

With the exception of checking an appropriate box in Part I denoting the taxpayer's age and filing status, the tax software automatically determines the credit for the person who is elderly or disabled. The amount on line 22 of Schedule R is included on Schedule 3, line 6d (other credits).

---

**TAX YOUR BRAIN**

What is the maximum AGI amount a single taxpayer receiving no social security benefits would have to earn to become ineligible for the elderly or disabled credit?

**ANSWER**

The base amount for a single taxpayer is $5,000, reduced by one-half of the amount in excess of AGI of $7,500. Once excess AGI is more than $10,000, the base amount is reduced to zero. Thus, if total AGI exceeds $17,500 ($7,500 + $10,000), a single taxpayer would not be eligible for the credit.

---

**CONCEPT CHECK 9-2—**
**LO 9-2**

1. Vincent and Maria are ages 70 and 67, respectively, and file a joint return. They have AGI of $21,000 and received $1,000 in nontaxable social security benefits. Calculate Vincent and Maria's credit for the elderly or the disabled.

---

# EDUCATION CREDITS (FORM 1040, LINE 29 AND SCHEDULE 3, LINE 3 [FORM 8863])
## LO 9-3

There are two education credits available: the American opportunity tax credit (AOTC), also known as the Hope scholarship credit, and the lifetime learning credit. Both credits are available to taxpayers for qualified higher education expenses paid for themselves, their spouses, or a dependent.[14] Qualifying expenses are amounts paid for tuition, fees, and other related expenses paid to an eligible educational institution while taxpayers (or their spouses and dependents) are pursuing undergraduate, graduate, or vocational degrees.[15] Qualified tuition and related expenses include amounts paid for course materials such as books and supplies. The qualifying expenses do not include room and board or student activity fees. The expenses must be for an academic period that begins in the same tax year as the year of the payment or that begins in the first three months of the following year. See Table 9-1 for a comparison of the two education credits.

An eligible educational institution is a postsecondary educational institution (college, university, vocational school, or the like) that is eligible to participate in a student aid program administered by the U.S. Department of Education. Almost all postsecondary institutions qualify.

---

**EXAMPLE 9-7**

In December 2021, Fred pays his son's college tuition for spring semester 2022. The semester starts in February 2022. Fred can deduct the expenses in tax year 2021.

---

Payments made using borrowed funds (such as student loans) are qualifying expenses. If a student receives a scholarship or other income that is excludable from gross income (such as Pell grants or employer-provided educational assistance), the excludable income reduces

[14] IRC § 25A.
[15] IRC § 25A(f)(1).

**EXHIBIT 9-2**

Schedule R (Form 1040) 2021      Page **2**

**Part III**   **Figure Your Credit**

**10** If you checked (in Part I):     Enter:
Box 1, 2, 4, or 7 . . . . . . . . . . . . . $5,000
Box 3, 5, or 6 . . . . . . . . . . . . . . $7,500        . . . . . . . . . . . . **10**
Box 8 or 9 . . . . . . . . . . . . . . . . $3,750

Did you check box 2, 4, 5, 6, or 9 in Part I? —— **Yes** ➤ You **must** complete line 11.
—— **No** ➤ Enter the amount from line 10 on line 12 and go to line 13.

**11** If you checked (in Part I):
• Box 6, add $5,000 to the taxable disability income of the spouse who was under age 65. Enter the total.
• Box 2, 4, or 9, enter your taxable disability income.    **11**
• Box 5, add your taxable disability income to your spouse's taxable disability income. Enter the total.

**TIP** *For more details on what to include on line 11, see* Figure Your Credit *in the instructions.*

**12** If you completed line 11, enter the **smaller** of line 10 or line 11. **All others,** enter the amount from line 10 . . . . . . . . . . . . . . . . . . . . . . . . . **12**

**13** Enter the following pensions, annuities, or disability income that you (and your spouse if filing jointly) received in 2021.
**a** Nontaxable part of social security benefits and nontaxable part of railroad retirement benefits treated as social security (see instructions)   **13a**
**b** Nontaxable veterans' pensions and any other pension, annuity, or disability benefit that is excluded from income under any other provision of law (see instructions) . . . . . . . . . . . . . . **13b**
**c** Add lines 13a and 13b. (Even though these income items aren't taxable, they **must** be included here to figure your credit.) If you didn't receive any of the types of nontaxable income listed on line 13a or 13b, enter -0- on line 13c . . . . . . . . . . . . . **13c**
**14** Enter the amount from Form 1040 or 1040-SR, line 11. . . . . . . . . . . . . . **14**
**15** If you checked (in Part I):   Enter:
Box 1 or 2 . . . . . . . . $7,500
Box 3, 4, 5, 6, or 7 . . . . . . $10,000   **15**
Box 8 or 9 . . . . . . . . $5,000
**16** Subtract line 15 from line 14. If zero or less, enter -0- . . . . . . . . . . . . . **16**
**17** Enter one-half of line 16 . . . . . . . . . . . . **17**
**18** Add lines 13c and 17 . . . . . . . . . . . . . . . . . . . . . . . . . **18**
**19** Subtract line 18 from line 12. If zero or less, **stop; you can't** take the credit. Otherwise, go to line 20. . . . . . **19**
**20** Multiply line 19 by 15% (0.15) . . . . . . . . . . . . . . . . **20**
**21** Tax liability limit. Enter the amount from the Credit Limit Worksheet in the instructions . . **21**
**22** **Credit for the elderly or the disabled.** Enter the **smaller** of line 20 or line 21. Also enter this amount on Schedule 3 (Form 1040), line 6d . . . . . . . . . . . . . . . . . **22**

Schedule R (Form 1040) 2021

Source: U.S. Department of the Treasury, Internal Revenue Service, Schedule R (Form 1040). Washington, DC: 2021.

qualifying expenses.[16] If a dependent pays for qualified expenses, the expenses are deemed paid by the taxpayer. Similarly, if someone other than the taxpayer, spouse, or dependent pays the expenses directly to the educational institution on behalf of the student, the expenses are deemed paid by the student.

[16] IRC § 25A(g)(2). Gifts, bequests, or inheritances are not excluded.

| **TABLE 9-1**<br>Comparison of American Opportunity Tax and Lifetime Learning Credits<br><br>Source: IRS Publication 17, chapter 35. | **American Opportunity Tax (or Hope) Credit** | **Lifetime Learning Credit** |
|---|---|---|
| | Up to $2,500 credit per **eligible student.** | Up to $2,000 credit per **taxpayer.** |
| | Available for the first four years of postsecondary education. | Available for all years of postsecondary education and for courses to acquire or improve job skills. |
| | Up to 40% of credit may be refundable. | Credit is nonrefundable. |
| | Student must be pursuing an undergraduate degree or other recognized education credential. | Student does not need to be pursuing a degree or other recognized education credential. |
| | Student must be enrolled at least half-time for at least one academic period beginning during the year. | Available for one or more courses. |
| | Qualified tuition and related expenses include books and supplies whether or not the materials are bought at the educational institution as a condition of enrollment or attendance. | Qualified tuition and related expenses include course-related books and supplies if the amount was required to be paid to the institution as part of the enrollment and attendance. |
| | No felony drug conviction on student's record. | Felony drug conviction rule does not apply. |

**EXAMPLE 9-8**    Aunt Juanita pays the college tuition for her nephew, Finell. For purposes of the education credits, the expenses are deemed paid by Finell. If Finell is a dependent of his parents, his parents can take the credit.

## American Opportunity Tax Credit

Also known as the *Hope credit,* the American opportunity tax credit (AOTC) is equal to 100% of the first $2,000 and 25% of the next $2,000 paid for qualified tuition and related expenses,[17] for a maximum of $2,500 per student per year.

To be eligible, a student must be carrying at least *half* of the normal full-time course load applicable to their course of study for at least one academic period (semester or quarter) during the year.[18] The student must be enrolled in a program leading to a degree or other educational credential. The AOTC is available for a student's first four years of postsecondary education, measured as of the beginning of the year.

Generally, up to 40% of the AOTC (that is, $1,000) may be a refundable credit. This means that taxpayers may receive a refund even if they owe no taxes. However, none of the credit is refundable if the taxpayer claiming the credit (a) is a child under age 18 (or a student who is at least 18 and under 24) whose earned income is less than one-half of his or her own support, (b) has at least one living parent, and (c) does not file a joint return.

**EXAMPLE 9-9**    Lauren and Ed paid $3,600 of qualified tuition and related expenses for their daughter, who is in her fourth year of college. These expenses included $450 for books and supplies. Without regard to AGI limitations or other credits, they can take an American opportunity tax credit of $2,400 ([$2,000 × 100%] + [$1,600 × 25%]).

## Lifetime Learning Credit

The lifetime learning credit is equal to 20% of up to $10,000 of qualified tuition and related expenses paid during the year.[19] The credit is determined per taxpayer, not per student. Thus, the maximum credit allowed for a taxpayer is $2,000 per year.

[17] These amounts are indexed for inflation.

[18] IRC § 25A(b)(2), (3).

[19] IRC § 25A(c).

**EXAMPLE 9-10**

During the year, Emmit and Francine paid qualified higher education expenses of $3,000 for their daughter and $4,000 for their son. Without regard to AGI limitations or other credits, they can claim a lifetime learning credit of $1,400 ($7,000 × 20%).

A student can qualify for the lifetime learning credit regardless of whether they enroll in a degree program or the number of courses taken in a semester. Qualified expenses for courses taken to acquire or improve job skills are eligible as well as expenses for any postsecondary education, including graduate school.

## Phaseout of the Education Credits

The AOTC and the lifetime learning credit are intended to defray the cost of higher education for low- to middle-income taxpayers. As such, the credit is phased out when modified AGI (MAGI) exceeds certain limits. MAGI is equal to AGI plus income earned abroad or in certain U.S. territories or possessions.[20]

 **NEW LAW**

Prior to 2021, the AOTC and the lifetime learning credit had different phaseout rules. With passage of the ARPA, both credits begin to phase out at $80,000 of MAGI for single taxpayers and $160,000 for joint filers.[21] You cannot claim the AOTC if your MAGI is $90,000 or more ($180,000 or more if you are filing jointly).

When MAGI is within the phaseout range, the amount of the credit is reduced by multiplying the amount by a fraction, calculated as follows:

| American Opportunity Tax Credit and Lifetime Learning Credit | |
| --- | --- |
| **For Married Taxpayers** | **For Single Taxpayers** |
| $180,000 − MAGI | $90,000 − MAGI |
| $20,000 | $10,000 |

**EXAMPLE 9-11**

Quinn and Andy are married filing jointly and have modified AGI of $164,000 and a pre-limitation lifetime learning credit of $1,200. Because of their MAGI, their lifetime learning credit is limited to $960 ([$180,000 − $164,000]/$20,000 × $1,200). If they had MAGI of $160,000 or less, they would have received the entire $1,200 as credit. If they had MAGI of $180,000 or more, they would be entitled to no credit.

## Coordination with Other Education-Related Benefits

Taxpayers can use qualifying expenses for the American opportunity tax credit or lifetime learning credit, but not both. A taxpayer who is an eligible student, or has dependents that are eligible students, should take the credit or deduction (or a combination thereof) that yields the greater tax savings for his or her individual tax situation.

[20] IRC § 25A(d).
[21] These income limitation amounts are indexed for inflation.

# From Shoebox to Software

Taxpayers report education credits on Form 8863 (Exhibit 9-3). AOTC are in Part I, lifetime learning credits in Part II, and limitations are determined in Part III. With the tax software, you initially enter information concerning qualified expenses on a Federal Information for Higher Education worksheet located in the worksheet section. The software will automatically take the credit or deduction that is most advantageous. Alternatively, you can force the software to take the deduction or credit of your choice by placing an x in the appropriate box on the worksheet.

The data for the worksheet generally come from Form 1098-T (Exhibit 9-4). Schools and universities provide this form to report the amount of qualifying tuition and related expenses paid. You must reduce the amount in box 1 by any amount shown in box 4 prior to entering the information on the tax worksheet.

The information on the worksheet carries forward to Form 8863, and the credit is automatically calculated. Note that on line 18 of Form 8863, allowed credits may be limited to tax liability minus various other credits.

---

**EXAMPLE 9-12**

Art and Arlene paid $3,200 of qualified expenses for their dependent son, Albert, who is a freshman at State University. Their MAGI is $73,000, and they are married filing jointly. The couple could choose to take either an AOTC of $2,300 ($2,000 plus 25% of the next $1,200) or a lifetime learning credit of $640 ($3,200 × 20%), but not both.

---

**TAX YOUR BRAIN**

Using the information from Example 9-12, assume that Art and Arlene also have a dependent daughter, Chris, who is a sophomore at the same university, and they paid $6,000 of qualified expenses for her. What are the credit options for Art and Arlene? Which option should they choose?

**ANSWER**

Art and Arlene could take (1) two AOTCs of $2,300 and $2,500 (for a total of $4,800) or (2) an AOTC of $2,300 for Albert and a lifetime learning credit of $1,200 for Chris or (3) a lifetime learning credit of $640 for Albert and an AOTC of $2,500 for Chris or (4) a single lifetime learning credit of $1,840. In this case, they should obviously choose option 1.

Taxpayers can claim an AOTC or a lifetime learning credit in the same year they take a tax-free distribution from a Coverdell Education Savings Account, as long as they do not use the same expenses for both benefits.

---

**CONCEPT CHECK 9-3—**

**LO 9-3**

1. Jewels is a single taxpayer and paid $2,900 in qualifying expenses for her dependent daughter, who attended the University of Arizona full time as a freshman. How much is Jewels's lifetime learning credit without regard to modified AGI limitations or other credits?
2. Assume the same facts as in Question 1. Jewels has modified AGI of $85,000 and wants to claim the AOTC. What is her allowable credit after the credit phaseout based on AGI is taken into account?
3. Assume the same facts as in Question 1. Jewels has modified AGI of $98,000 and wants to claim the AOTC. What is her allowable credit after the credit phaseout based on AGI is taken into account?
4. Vern and Whitney paid $1,600 and $2,100 in qualifying expenses for their children Jayla and Caden, respectively, to attend the nursing program at the community college. Without regard to modified AGI limitations or other credits, how much is their lifetime learning credit?

**EXHIBIT 9-3**

| Form **8863** | **Education Credits** | OMB No. 1545-0074 |
|---|---|---|
| Department of the Treasury Internal Revenue Service (99) | **(American Opportunity and Lifetime Learning Credits)** ▶ Attach to Form 1040 or 1040-SR. ▶ Go to *www.irs.gov/Form8863* for instructions and the latest information. | **2021** Attachment Sequence No. **50** |

Name(s) shown on return | Your social security number

⚠ **CAUTION**  *Complete a separate Part III on page 2 for each student for whom you're claiming either credit before you complete Parts I and II.*

**Part I — Refundable American Opportunity Credit**

| 1 | After completing Part III for each student, enter the total of all amounts from all Parts III, line 30 . . . | 1 | |
| 2 | Enter: $180,000 if married filing jointly; $90,000 if single, head of household, or qualifying widow(er) . . . . . . . . . . . . . . . . . 2 | | |
| 3 | Enter the amount from Form 1040 or 1040-SR, line 11. If you're filing Form 2555 or 4563, or you're excluding income from Puerto Rico, see Pub. 970 for the amount to enter . . . . . . . . . . . . . . . . . 3 | | |
| 4 | Subtract line 3 from line 2. If zero or less, **stop**; you can't take any education credit . . . . . . . . . . . . . . . . . . . . . . 4 | | |
| 5 | Enter: $20,000 if married filing jointly; $10,000 if single, head of household, or qualifying widow(er) . . . . . . . . . . . . . . 5 | | |
| 6 | If line 4 is: • Equal to or more than line 5, enter 1.000 on line 6 . . . . . . . . . • Less than line 5, divide line 4 by line 5. Enter the result as a decimal (rounded to at least three places) . . . . . . . . . . . . . . . . | 6 | . |
| 7 | Multiply line 1 by line 6. **Caution:** If you were under age 24 at the end of the year **and** meet the conditions described in the instructions, you **can't** take the refundable American opportunity credit; skip line 8, enter the amount from line 7 on line 9, and check this box . . . . . . . . ▶ ☐ | 7 | |
| 8 | **Refundable American opportunity credit.** Multiply line 7 by 40% (0.40). Enter the amount here and on Form 1040 or 1040-SR, line 29. Then go to line 9 below. . . . . . . . . . . . | 8 | |

**Part II — Nonrefundable Education Credits**

| 9 | Subtract line 8 from line 7. Enter here and on line 2 of the Credit Limit Worksheet (see instructions) . | 9 | |
| 10 | After completing Part III for each student, enter the total of all amounts from all Parts III, line 31. If zero, skip lines 11 through 17, enter -0- on line 18, and go to line 19 . . . . . . . . . . . | 10 | |
| 11 | Enter the smaller of line 10 or $10,000 . . . . . . . . . . . . . . | 11 | |
| 12 | Multiply line 11 by 20% (0.20) . . . . . . . . . . . . . . . . | 12 | |
| 13 | Enter: $180,000 if married filing jointly; $90,000 if single, head of household, or qualifying widow(er) . . . . . . . . . . 13 | | |
| 14 | Enter the amount from Form 1040 or 1040-SR, line 11. If you're filing Form 2555 or 4563, or you're excluding income from Puerto Rico, see Pub. 970 for the amount to enter . . . . . . . . . . . . . . . . . 14 | | |
| 15 | Subtract line 14 from line 13. If zero or less, skip lines 16 and 17, enter -0- on line 18, and go to line 19 . . . . . . . . . . . . 15 | | |
| 16 | Enter: $20,000 if married filing jointly; $10,000 if single, head of household, or qualifying widow(er) . . . . . . . . . . . 16 | | |
| 17 | If line 15 is: • Equal to or more than line 16, enter 1.000 on line 17 and go to line 18 • Less than line 16, divide line 15 by line 16. Enter the result as a decimal (rounded to at least three places) . . . . . . . . . . . . . . . . | 17 | . |
| 18 | Multiply line 12 by line 17. Enter here and on line 1 of the Credit Limit Worksheet (see instructions) ▶ | 18 | |
| 19 | **Nonrefundable education credits.** Enter the amount from line 7 of the Credit Limit Worksheet (see instructions) here and on Schedule 3 (Form 1040), line 3 . . . . . . . . . . . | 19 | |

For Paperwork Reduction Act Notice, see your tax return instructions. | Cat. No. 25379M | Form **8863** (2021)

Source: U.S. Department of the Treasury, Internal Revenue Service, Form 8863. Washington, DC: 2021.

**EXHIBIT 9-4**

| | | | |
|---|---|---|---|
| ☐ CORRECTED | | | |

| FILER'S name, street address, city or town, state or province, country, ZIP or foreign postal code, and telephone number | **1** Payments received for qualified tuition and related expenses<br><br>$ | OMB No. 1545-1574<br><br>20**21**<br><br>Form **1098-T** | **Tuition Statement** |
| | **2** | | |
| FILER'S employer identification no. | STUDENT'S TIN | **3** | **Copy B**<br>**For Student** |
| STUDENT'S name | | **4** Adjustments made for a prior year<br><br>$ | **5** Scholarships or grants<br><br>$ | This is important tax information and is being furnished to the IRS. This form must be used to complete Form 8863 to claim education credits. Give it to the tax preparer or use it to prepare the tax return. |
| Street address (including apt. no.) | | **6** Adjustments to scholarships or grants for a prior year<br><br>$ | **7** Checked if the amount in box 1 includes amounts for an academic period beginning January–March 2022  ☐ | |
| City or town, state or province, country, and ZIP or foreign postal code | | | | |
| Service Provider/Acct. No. (see instr.) | **8** Checked if at least half-time student ☐ | **9** Checked if a graduate student ☐ | **10** Ins. contract reimb./refund<br>$ | |

Form **1098-T**          (keep for your records)          www.irs.gov/Form1098T          Department of the Treasury - Internal Revenue Service

Source: U.S. Department of the Treasury, Internal Revenue Service, Form 1098-T. Washington, DC: 2021.

# FOREIGN TAX CREDIT (FTC) (SCHEDULE 3, LINE 1 [FORM 1116])

## LO 9-4

U.S. citizens and residents are subject to taxation on income earned worldwide. Although most U.S. taxpayers earn income solely from U.S. sources, taxpayers with income from foreign sources may be subject to double taxation (the same income is taxed both in the United States and in the foreign country). Most often this foreign-source income is investment income such as interest or dividends, although other types are possible.[22] To mitigate double taxation, the Internal Revenue Code (IRC) provides a foreign tax credit for income taxes paid or accrued to a foreign country or U.S. possession.[23]

The foreign tax credit is available for taxes levied on income such as wages, interest, dividends, and royalties. The amount of the credit is equal to the foreign tax paid or accrued. However, the credit cannot exceed that portion of U.S. income tax attributable to the foreign income.[24] The limitation is determined as follows:[25]

$$\frac{\text{Foreign-source taxable income}}{\text{Worldwide taxable income}} \times \begin{array}{c}\text{U.S. income}\\\text{tax liability}\\\text{before FTC}\end{array} = \begin{array}{c}\text{Foreign tax}\\\text{credit}\\\text{limitation}\end{array}$$

**EXAMPLE 9-13**

Kim reported worldwide taxable income of $84,010 that included $1,000 of foreign-source interest income. Her U.S. tax liability was $18,273. She paid foreign taxes of $250 on the foreign income. Kim is entitled to a foreign tax credit of $218. Although she paid $250 in foreign tax, her credit is limited to $218, calculated as follows: ($1,000/$84,010) × $18,273 = $218. If Kim's foreign tax paid were $218 or less, the limitation would not apply and her credit would be equal to the amount of foreign tax paid.

---

[22] This section does not discuss foreign-source income earned by U.S. citizens living abroad. Law concerning the taxation and credits associated with such income is found in IRC § 911. Taxation of foreign-source wages is complex and is not discussed in this text.

[23] IRC § 901.

[24] IRC § 904(a).

[25] In practice, the limitation is calculated separately for certain categories of income as indicated in IRC § 904(d) and as shown on the top of Form 1116. This text focuses only on the passive income category because the other categories seldom apply to individual taxpayers.

## From Shoebox to Software

The majority of taxpayers who earn foreign-source income do so through mutual funds that invest in foreign stocks or bonds. These taxpayers will receive a Form 1099-INT or 1099-DIV from their mutual fund company. The statements report the amount of income and the corresponding foreign tax paid. Some taxpayers may own foreign stocks or bonds directly. If the investment is through a brokerage firm, the taxpayer will receive an appropriate Form 1099. If the taxpayer owns foreign investments outside of a brokerage account, the taxpayer often needs to gather the income and tax information separately.

Taxpayers report the foreign tax credit on Form 1116 (Exhibit 9-5). A taxpayer may elect to claim the credit without filing Form 1116 if they meet *all* of the following:[26]

- All of the foreign-source income is passive income.
- All of the income and foreign taxes paid are reported to the taxpayer on the appropriate Form 1099.
- Total foreign taxes paid were less than $300 ($600 if married filing a joint return).

- The taxpayer is not subject to the foreign tax limitation rules.

A taxpayer who meets all of these rules reports the foreign tax credit directly on Schedule 3, line 1. No Form 1116 is required.

You enter the appropriate information directly onto Form 1116 when using the tax software. Most taxpayers enter information concerning the gross income that was taxed by the foreign country on line 1, columns (a) through (c), and enter the appropriate amount of foreign taxes paid in Part II, columns (m) through (s). In most situations, the tax software completes the remainder of the form and shows the total credit on line 35.

A taxpayer who earns passive income through investment in a mutual fund often provides the foreign country name in Parts I and II as "various" because there is seldom one country from which the income is earned. If the passive income were from a direct investment in one country, the taxpayer would enter that country's name.

Cash basis taxpayers take the foreign tax credit in the year paid. However, cash basis taxpayers can make a binding election to take the credit for all foreign taxes in the year they accrue.[27]

Taxpayers may also choose to deduct foreign taxes as an itemized deduction rather than as a credit. From a practical standpoint, it is seldom advantageous to use a deduction instead of a credit. However, there are at least two instances for which a deduction is preferred. One is when a taxpayer has income from one country (on which tax was paid) and an equal loss from another country. The net foreign taxable income would be zero, and the taxpayer would receive no credit. In such a case, the benefit for the taxes paid in the positive-income country would be lost unless the taxpayer took the foreign taxes as an itemized deduction. Another instance relates to foreign taxes not based on income (e.g., property taxes). Taxpayers can take these foreign taxes as a deduction because the foreign tax credit is available only for foreign taxes paid based on income.[28]

**CONCEPT CHECK 9-4— LO 9-4**

1. Joy has $63,000 worldwide taxable income, which includes $8,000 of taxable income from New Zealand. She paid $2,500 in foreign income taxes, and her U.S. tax liability is $17,640. Calculate Joy's foreign tax credit.

---

[26] U.S. Department of the Treasury, Internal Revenue Service, IRS instructions for Form 1116. Washington, DC: 2019.

[27] IRC § 905(a).

[28] Reg. § 1.901-2(a)(1).

**EXHIBIT 9-5**

Form **1116**

Department of the Treasury
Internal Revenue Service    (99)

# Foreign Tax Credit
## (Individual, Estate, or Trust)
▶ Attach to Form 1040, 1040-SR, 1040-NR, 1041, or 990-T.
▶ Go to *www.irs.gov/Form1116* for instructions and the latest information.

OMB No. 1545-0121

**2021**

Attachment
Sequence No. **19**

Name

**Identifying number** as shown on page 1 of your tax return

Use a separate Form 1116 for each category of income listed below. See *Categories of Income* in the instructions. Check only one box on each Form 1116. Report all amounts in U.S. dollars except where specified in Part II below.

a ☐ Section 951A category income
b ☐ Foreign branch category income
c ☐ Passive category income
d ☐ General category income
e ☐ Section 901(j) income
f ☐ Certain income re-sourced by treaty
g ☐ Lump-sum distributions

**h** Resident of (name of country) ▶

**Note:** If you paid taxes to only one foreign country or U.S. possession, use column A in Part I and line A in Part II. If you paid taxes to **more than one** foreign country or U.S. possession, use a separate column and line for each country or possession.

### Part I  Taxable Income or Loss From Sources Outside the United States (for category checked above)

| | | Foreign Country or U.S. Possession | | | Total (Add cols. A, B, and C.) |
|---|---|---|---|---|---|
| | | A | B | C | |
| i | Enter the name of the foreign country or U.S. possession . . . . . . . . ▶ | | | | |
| 1a | Gross income from sources within country shown above and of the type checked above (see instructions): | | | | 1a |
| b | Check if line 1a is compensation for personal services as an employee, your total compensation from all sources is $250,000 or more, and you used an alternative basis to determine its source. See instructions . . ▶ ☐ | | | | |
| | **Deductions and losses (Caution: See instructions.):** | | | | |
| 2 | Expenses **definitely related** to the income on line 1a (attach statement) . . . . . . | | | | |
| 3 | Pro rata share of other deductions **not definitely related:** | | | | |
| a | Certain itemized deductions or standard deduction (see instructions) . . . . . . . | | | | |
| b | Other deductions (attach statement) . . . . . | | | | |
| c | Add lines 3a and 3b . . . . . . . . | | | | |
| d | Gross foreign source income (see instructions) . | | | | |
| e | Gross income from all sources (see instructions) . | | | | |
| f | Divide line 3d by line 3e (see instructions) . . . | | | | |
| g | Multiply line 3c by line 3f . . . . . . | | | | |
| 4 | Pro rata share of interest expense (see instructions): | | | | |
| a | Home mortgage interest (use the Worksheet for Home Mortgage Interest in the instructions) . . | | | | |
| b | Other interest expense . . . . . . . | | | | |
| 5 | Losses from foreign sources . . . . . . | | | | |
| 6 | Add lines 2, 3g, 4a, 4b, and 5 . . . . . . | | | | 6 |
| 7 | Subtract line 6 from line 1a. Enter the result here and on line 15, page 2 . . . . . . . . . ▶ | | | 7 | |

### Part II  Foreign Taxes Paid or Accrued (see instructions)

| Country | Credit is claimed for taxes (you must check one) | | Foreign taxes paid or accrued | | | | | | | |
|---|---|---|---|---|---|---|---|---|---|---|
| | | | In foreign currency | | | | In U.S. dollars | | | |
| | (j) ☐ Paid | | Taxes withheld at source on: | | | (p) Other foreign taxes paid or accrued | Taxes withheld at source on: | | | (t) Other foreign taxes paid or accrued |
| | (k) ☐ Accrued | | | | | | | | | (u) Total foreign taxes paid or accrued (add cols. (q) through (t)) |
| | (l) Date paid or accrued | (m) Dividends | (n) Rents and royalties | (o) Interest | | (q) Dividends | (r) Rents and royalties | (s) Interest | | |
| A | | | | | | | | | | |
| B | | | | | | | | | | |
| C | | | | | | | | | | |
| 8 | Add lines A through C, column (u). Enter the total here and on line 9, page 2 . . . . . . . . . ▶ | | | | | | | | 8 | |

For Paperwork Reduction Act Notice, see instructions.

Cat. No. 11440U

Form **1116** (2021)

**EXHIBIT 9-5** *(concluded)*

Form 1116 (2021)                                                                                              Page **2**

**Part III   Figuring the Credit**

| | | | |
|---|---|---|---|
| 9 | Enter the amount from line 8. These are your total foreign taxes paid or accrued for the category of income checked above Part I . . | 9 | |
| 10 | Enter the sum of any carryover of foreign taxes (from Schedule B, line 3, column (xiv)) plus any carrybacks to the current tax year . . . . | 10 | |
| | (If your income was section 951A category income (box a above Part I), leave line 10 blank.) | | |
| 11 | Add lines 9 and 10 . . . . . . . . . . . . . . . . . . | 11 | |
| 12 | Reduction in foreign taxes (see instructions) . . . . . . . . | 12 ( ) | |
| 13 | Taxes reclassified under high tax kickout (see instructions) . . . | 13 | |
| 14 | Combine lines 11, 12, and 13. This is the total amount of foreign taxes available for credit . . . | | 14 |
| 15 | Enter the amount from line 7. This is your taxable income or (loss) from sources outside the United States (before adjustments) for the category of income checked above Part I. See instructions . . . . . | 15 | |
| 16 | Adjustments to line 15 (see instructions) . . . . . . . . . | 16 | |
| 17 | Combine the amounts on lines 15 and 16. This is your net foreign source taxable income. (If the result is zero or less, you have no foreign tax credit for the category of income you checked above Part I. Skip lines 18 through 24. However, if you are filing more than one Form 1116, you must complete line 20.) . . . . . . . | 17 | |
| 18 | **Individuals:** Enter the amount from line 15 of your Form 1040, 1040-SR, or 1040-NR. **Estates and trusts:** Enter your taxable income without the deduction for your exemption . . . . . | 18 | |
| | **Caution:** If you figured your tax using the lower rates on qualified dividends or capital gains, see instructions. | | |
| 19 | Divide line 17 by line 18. If line 17 is more than line 18, enter "1" . . . . . . . . . | | 19 |
| 20 | **Individuals:** Enter the total of Form 1040, 1040-SR, or 1040-NR, line 16, and Schedule 2 (Form 1040), line 2. **Estates and trusts:** Enter the amount from Form 1041, Schedule G, line 1a; or the total of Form 990-T, Part II, lines 2, 3, 4, and 6. Foreign estates and trusts should enter the amount from Form 1040-NR, line 16 . . . . . | | 20 |
| | **Caution:** If you are completing line 20 for separate category **g** (lump-sum distributions), or, if you file Form 8978, Partner's Additional Reporting Year Tax, see instructions. | | |
| 21 | Multiply line 20 by line 19 (maximum amount of credit) . . . . . . . . . . . | | 21 |
| 22 | Increase in limitation (section 960(c)) . . . . . . . . . . . . . . | | 22 |
| 23 | Add lines 21 and 22 . . . . . . . . . . . . . . . . . . . . | | 23 |
| 24 | Enter the **smaller** of line 14 or line 23. If this is the only Form 1116 you are filing, skip lines 25 through 32 and enter this amount on line 33. Otherwise, complete the appropriate line in Part IV. See instructions . . . . . . . . . . . . . . . . . . . . . . . ▶ | | 24 |

**Part IV   Summary of Credits From Separate Parts III** (see instructions)

| | | | |
|---|---|---|---|
| 25 | Credit for taxes on section 951A category income . . . . . | 25 | |
| 26 | Credit for taxes on foreign branch category income . . . . . | 26 | |
| 27 | Credit for taxes on passive category income . . . . . . . | 27 | |
| 28 | Credit for taxes on general category income . . . . . . . | 28 | |
| 29 | Credit for taxes on section 901(j) income . . . . . . . . | 29 | |
| 30 | Credit for taxes on certain income re-sourced by treaty . . . . | 30 | |
| 31 | Credit for taxes on lump-sum distributions . . . . . . . . | 31 | |
| 32 | Add lines 25 through 31 . . . . . . . . . . . . . . . . | | 32 |
| 33 | Enter the **smaller** of line 20 or line 32 . . . . . . . . . . . . . . . | | 33 |
| 34 | Reduction of credit for international boycott operations. See instructions for line 12 . . . . . | | 34 |
| 35 | Subtract line 34 from line 33. This is your **foreign tax credit.** Enter here and on Schedule 3 (Form 1040), line 1; Form 1041, Schedule G, line 2a; or Form 990-T, Part III, line 1a . . . . . . . . . ▶ | | 35 |

Form **1116** (2021)

# CHILD TAX CREDIT (FORM 1040, LINE 19 AND 28)

## LO 9-5

 **NEW LAW**

We first introduced the Child Tax Credit in Chapter 2. Recall that taxpayers are allowed a $3,000 refundable tax credit for each qualifying child who is 6 to 17 years of age and $3,600 for children under age 6.[29] The definition of a qualifying child is the same as a qualifying child for dependent purposes (see Chapter 2, beginning on page 2-13). The qualifying child must also be under age 18 as of the end of the tax year, be a U.S. citizen or resident,[30] be younger than the person claiming the credit for the child, and be unmarried.

[29] IRC § 24(a).

[30] IRC § 24(c).

**EXAMPLE 9-14**

Xavier and Paula have a son Marco, age 14, who qualifies as a dependent. The family are all U.S. citizens. Because Marco meets the requirements to be claimed as a dependent, is under age 18, and is a U.S. citizen, Xavier and Paula are eligible to claim a $3,000 child tax credit.

A $500 nonrefundable credit is also provided for qualifying dependents who are not qualifying children. A qualifying dependent is one who meets the definition of a qualifying relative as discussed in Chapter 2, beginning on page 2-16. In addition, the qualifying relative must also be a U.S. citizen or resident, not be filing a joint return with their spouse, and not claimed for the child tax credit. This credit may be taken for certain dependents who are not a qualifying child, such as adult dependents or a dependent child age 18 or a dependent child age 19 to 24 who is a fulltime student in college.

**EXAMPLE 9-15**

Use the information in Example 9-14 except that Marco is age 20, lives at home, does not work, and attends university full time. Marco is a dependent, but he is not under the age of 17. Thus, he is not eligible for the child tax credit. However, Marco meets the tests to be a qualifying relative, so Xavier and Paula can claim the $500 credit for qualifying dependents for Marco.

The child tax credit is subject to two different phaseout calculations. In prior years, the child tax credit was $2,000 per child. As noted above, for 2021 the credit is either $3,000 or $3,600 depending on the age of the qualifying child.

The first phaseout reduces the credit from $3,000 or $3,600 per child to $2,000 per child. Thus, the maximum reduction for the first phaseout calculation is either $1,000 (for a qualifying child age 6 to 17) or $1,600 (for a child under age 6). The phaseout threshold is modified AGI of $75,000 for single filers, $112,500 for head of household filers, and $150,000 for married joint filers. The credit reduction is 5% of the amount of income in excess of the threshold amount. Modified AGI is AGI plus income earned abroad or in certain U.S. territories or possessions.

**EXAMPLE 9-16**

Here are three examples that illustrate the rules related to the first phaseout.

Taxpayer A is single and has two qualifying children, ages 8 and 10. With income of $65,000, the taxpayer will be entitled to a fully refundable credit of $3,000 per child, or $6,000. If the taxpayer's income is $80,000, the credit is reduced. The income in excess of the threshold amount is $5,000 ($80,000 − $75,000). The reduction is $5,000 × 5%, or $250, and the allowed credit would then be $5,750.

Now assume Taxpayer A has income of $165,000. This income is $90,000 greater than the threshold amount. This suggests that the reduction would be $90,000 × 5%, or $4,500. However, recall that the first phaseout calculation is designed to reduce the original credit amount down to $2,000 per qualifying child. So, the amount of reduction is $2,000 in total (reducing the credit for each child from $3,000 to $2,000), leaving a remaining credit of $2,000 per child, or $4,000 in total.

Taxpayer B is married with one qualifying child, age 4. With income of less than $150,000, the taxpayer will be entitled to a fully refundable credit of $3,600. If the taxpayer's income is $160,000, the income in excess of the threshold would be $10,000 and the credit reduction would be $500 ($10,000 × 5%). If, instead, income was $185,000, the excess income would be $35,000. The preliminary credit reduction would be $35,000 × 5% = $1,750. However, remember that the first phaseout calculation is designed to reduce the credit to $2,000 per child. In this case, the maximum reduction is $1,600 ($3,600 original credit minus the desired ending credit of $2,000). Thus, with an income of $185,000 the child tax credit would be $2,000.

Once the credits have been reduced to $2,000 per child, the credits are then reduced by $50 for each $1,000, or fraction thereof, for modified AGI in excess of $400,000 for taxpayers who are married filing jointly or $200,000 for all other taxpayers.[31]

**EXAMPLE 9-17**

Taylor and Drew have two qualifying children and file jointly. Their modified AGI was $416,322. Their child tax credit will be $3,150, calculated as $416,322 − $400,000)/$1,000 = 16.3 rounded up to 17. The credit reduction is 17 × $50 = $850. The permitted credit is $4,000 − $850 = $3,150.

[31] IRC § 24(b).

## From Shoebox to Software

Taxpayers calculate the child tax credit using a worksheet found in the instructions to Form 1040. In the tax software, this document is in the worksheet section. When you examine the worksheet, you will see that the software automatically creates virtually all of it.

When we entered the tax information for Jose and Maria Ramirez in Chapter 3, we noted that they had a $9,000 child

tax credit shown on Form 1040, line 28. This amount is $3,000 for each child. If you open the Ramirezes' tax return, click on line 28, and then click on the yellow folder, you will see the Child Tax Credit worksheet. You will note that the amount of the preliminary credit on line 1 is not limited. The same is true for the tax return of Alan and Cherie Masters.

The credit is reported on Form 1040, line 28.

Normally, the child tax credit is reported on the tax return filed for tax year 2021 in April 2022. In order to disburse the 2021 credits more quickly, the ARPA legislation that increased the child tax credit to $3,000 or $3,600, also contained a provision that the IRS must issue half the credit in periodic advanced payments beginning after July 1, 2021. The remaining half will be claimed on the 2021 tax return.

The IRS will estimate the credit amounts based on 2020 tax return data or, if unavailable, 2019 data.

If a taxpayer receives more in advanced payments than they are eligible for, the taxpayer will need to repay the excess. The excess payments could be the result of a change in the amount of modified AGI, or filing status, or number of eligible children.

However, low- and moderate-income taxpayers may not be required to repay some or all excess payments if the excess is due to changes in the number of qualifying children. If AGI is below $40,000 (single), $50,000 (head of household), or $60,000 (MFJ), the taxpayer does not need to repay up to $2,000 per qualifying child (this is referred to as the "safe harbor amount"). If income is between $40,000 and $80,000 (single), $50,000 and $100,000 (head of household), or $60,000 and $120,000 (MFJ), the $2,000 safe harbor amount is reduced ratably to zero as income rises to the upper limit. For AGI over those limits, any excess advance payments must be returned.

**CONCEPT CHECK 9-5—**

**LO 9-5**

1. Pat and Lisa have two qualifying children, ages 11 and 8, and file jointly. Their AGI is $112,000. What amount of child tax credit can they claim after their AGI limitation is considered?

2. A child tax credit cannot be taken for a dependent child age 18. True or false?

3. Glen is an unemployed widower, is a U.S. citizen, is unrelated to Fred and Marlene, and has lived the entire year in their residence. Glen is between jobs and Fred and Marlene are paying all his living expenses until he finds employment. Can Fred and Marlene claim a $500 credit for other dependents for Glen? Why or why not?

## RETIREMENT SAVINGS CONTRIBUTIONS CREDIT (SAVER'S CREDIT) (SCHEDULE 3, LINE 4 [FORM 8880])
**LO 9-6**

Eligible individuals can take a tax credit based on contributions toward a retirement savings account, multiplied by an applicable percentage ranging from 0% to 50%.[32] The percentage is based on the taxpayer's modified AGI and filing status. Subject to the maximum, the credit is determined using Table 9-2.

Contributions can be made to Individual Retirement Accounts (traditional or Roth); 401(k), 403(b), or 457 plans; a SIMPLE or SEP plan; or other qualified retirement plans.[33] Distributions from the noted retirement accounts will reduce the allowed contribution. Modified AGI is equal to AGI plus income earned abroad or in certain U.S. territories or possessions. The maximum contribution amount for the credit is $2,000 per person, and on a joint return, $2,000 for each spouse.

[32] IRC § 25B(a)

[33] These plans are discussed in more detail in Chapter 11.

# From Shoebox to Software

Taxpayers claim the retirement savings contributions credit on Form 8880 (Exhibit 9-6).

The information shown on line 1 comes from an IRA Contribution Summary in the worksheet section. You must enter any retirement account distributions on line 4. The software will calculate the remainder of the form and will report the appropriate credit on Schedule 3, line 4. Distributions are generally reported to taxpayers on Form 1099-R.

**TABLE 9-2**
**Rates for Retirement Savings Contributions Credit**

| | Modified Adjusted Gross Income | | | | | | Applicable Percentage |
| | Joint Return | | Head of Household | | All Other Filing Status | | |
| | Over | Not Over | Over | Not Over | Over | Not Over | |
|---|---|---|---|---|---|---|---|
| | $ 0 | $39,500 | $ 0 | $29,625 | $ 0 | $19,750 | 50% |
| | 39,500 | 43,000 | 29,625 | 32,250 | 19,750 | 21,500 | 20% |
| | 43,000 | 66,000 | 32,250 | 49,500 | 21,500 | 33,000 | 10% |
| | 66,000 | | 49,500 | | 33,000 | | 0% |

**EXAMPLE 9-18**

Hector is a single filer with modified AGI of $25,000. He makes a $1,000 contribution to an IRA. His retirement savings contributions credit is $100 ($1,000 × 10%). If Hector's modified AGI was $19,750 or less, his credit would be $500 ($1,000 × 50%).

**EXAMPLE 9-19**

Bo and Rachelle are married filing jointly with modified AGI of $39,700. Bo makes a $2,000 contribution to a qualified retirement plan. Their credit is $400 ($2,000 × 20%).

**CONCEPT CHECK 9-6—**
**LO 9-6**

1. Enrique and Lupe have AGI of $52,000, are married filing jointly, and contributed $1,500 during the year to a qualified retirement plan for Enrique. How much is their retirement savings contributions credit?
2. Roger is a head of household taxpayer with AGI of $26,000. He made a $2,200 contribution to a qualified retirement plan. How much is his retirement savings contributions credit?

# ADOPTION CREDIT (SCHEDULE 3, LINE 6c [FORM 8839])
**LO 9-7**

Taxpayers can claim an adoption credit of 100% of qualified adoption expenses paid, up to a maximum of $14,440 per eligible child adopted.[34] Married taxpayers generally must file jointly to take the credit.

Qualified adoption expenses include reasonable and necessary expenses such as adoption fees, court costs, attorney fees, and similar expenses directly related to the legal adoption of an eligible child.[35] Qualified expenses do not include reimbursements under an employer program. An eligible child is one who is under age 18 or is incapable of caring for themself but does not include a child of an individual's spouse.

Adoption proceedings are often protracted. Taxpayers often pay expenses in a tax year other than the year in which the adoption becomes final. In the case of expenses paid in the years before the adoption becomes final, taxpayers take the credit in the year immediately after it is paid. For expenses paid in the year the adoption is finalized or after, taxpayers take the credit in the year paid.[36] The total amount of qualified adoption expenses over all years cannot exceed $14,440 per child.

[34] IRC § 23(a), (b).
[35] IRC § 23(d)(1).
[36] IRC § 23(a)(2).

EXHIBIT 9-6

| Form **8880** | **Credit for Qualified Retirement Savings Contributions** | OMB No. 1545-0074 |
|---|---|---|
| Department of the Treasury Internal Revenue Service | ▶ Attach to Form 1040, 1040-SR, or 1040-NR. ▶ Go to *www.irs.gov/Form8880* for the latest information. | **2021** Attachment Sequence No. **54** |

Name(s) shown on return | | Your social security number

**You cannot take this credit if either of the following applies.**

- *The amount on Form 1040, 1040-SR, or 1040-NR, line 11, is more than $33,000 ($49,500 if head of household; $66,000 if married filing jointly).*
- *The person(s) who made the qualified contribution or elective deferral (a) was born after January 1, 2004; (b) is claimed as a dependent on someone else's 2021 tax return; or (c) was a student (see instructions).*

|  |  | (a) You | (b) Your spouse |
|---|---|---|---|
| **1** | Traditional and Roth IRA contributions, and ABLE account contributions by the designated beneficiary for 2021. **Do not** include rollover contributions . . . . **1** |  |  |
| **2** | Elective deferrals to a 401(k) or other qualified employer plan, voluntary employee contributions, and 501(c)(18)(D) plan contributions for 2021 (see instructions) **2** |  |  |
| **3** | Add lines 1 and 2 . . . . . . . . . . . . . . . . **3** |  |  |
| **4** | Certain distributions received **after** 2018 and **before** the due date (including extensions) of your 2021 tax return (see instructions). If married filing jointly, include **both** spouses' amounts in **both** columns. See instructions for an exception . . . . **4** |  |  |
| **5** | Subtract line 4 from line 3. If zero or less, enter -0- . . . . . . . . **5** |  |  |
| **6** | In each column, enter the **smaller** of line 5 or $2,000 . . . . . . . **6** |  |  |
| **7** | Add the amounts on line 6. If zero, **stop;** you can't take this credit . . . . . . . . **7** |  |
| **8** | Enter the amount from Form 1040, 1040-SR, or 1040-NR, line 11* . . . . **8** |  |
| **9** | Enter the applicable decimal amount from the table below. |  |

| If line 8 is— | | And your filing status is— | | |
|---|---|---|---|---|
| Over— | But not over— | Married filing jointly | Head of household | Single, Married filing separately, or Qualifying widow(er) |
| | | Enter on line 9— | | |
| --- | $19,750 | 0.5 | 0.5 | 0.5 |
| $19,750 | $21,500 | 0.5 | 0.5 | 0.2 |
| $21,500 | $29,625 | 0.5 | 0.5 | 0.1 |
| $29,625 | $32,250 | 0.5 | 0.2 | 0.1 |
| $32,250 | $33,000 | 0.5 | 0.1 | 0.1 |
| $33,000 | $39,500 | 0.5 | 0.1 | 0.0 |
| $39,500 | $43,000 | 0.2 | 0.1 | 0.0 |
| $43,000 | $49,500 | 0.1 | 0.1 | 0.0 |
| $49,500 | $66,000 | 0.1 | 0.0 | 0.0 |
| $66,000 | --- | 0.0 | 0.0 | 0.0 |

**9** x 0 .

**Note:** If line 9 is zero, **stop;** you can't take this credit.

| **10** | Multiply line 7 by line 9 . . . . . . . . . . . . . . . . . . **10** |  |
|---|---|---|
| **11** | Limitation based on tax liability. Enter the amount from the Credit Limit Worksheet in the instructions **11** |  |
| **12** | **Credit for qualified retirement savings contributions.** Enter the **smaller** of line 10 or line 11 here and on Schedule 3 (Form 1040), line 4 . . . . . . . . . . . . . . . . **12** |  |

* See Pub. 590-A for the amount to enter if you claim any exclusion or deduction for foreign earned income, foreign housing, or income from Puerto Rico or for bona fide residents of American Samoa.

**For Paperwork Reduction Act Notice, see your tax return instructions.** | Cat. No. 33394D | Form **8880** (2021)

Source: U.S. Department of the Treasury, Internal Revenue Service, Form 8880. Washington, DC: 2021.

**EXAMPLE 9-20**

Mila and Layla legally adopted a child in 2021. They incurred and paid qualified adoption expenses of $6,000 in 2020, $4,000 in 2021, and $5,000 in 2022 ($15,000 in total). Without any AGI limitations, they would be entitled to an adoption credit of $10,000 ($6,000 + $4,000) in 2021 and an additional $4,440 credit in 2022. Expenses over $14,440 are disallowed.

If a taxpayer adopts a child who is not a citizen or resident of the United States (a foreign adoption), the credit is allowed only in the year in which the adoption becomes final or in a later year if the expenses were paid or incurred in a later year.

Additional rules apply to a special-needs child. This is a child who has a special factor or condition that a state agency determines prevents the child from being placed with adoptive

# From Shoebox to Software

Taxpayers report the adoption credit on Form 8839 (see Exhibit 9-7).

You enter most of the required information directly onto Form 8839. In Part I, you provide information concerning the adopted child. On line 3, you enter the amount of any adoption credit taken in a prior year for the child. The tax software completes the remainder of the form. It also transfers the total

adoption credit shown on line 12 onto Schedule 3, line 6c.

Part III of Form 8839 (not shown) is used to report and account for employer-provided adoption benefits. Employers report any such benefits on Form W-2, box 12, with a code of T. The tax software will automatically record the box 12 amount on the proper lines on Part III of Form 8839.

parents without providing adoption assistance. Such a child must also be a U.S. citizen or resident.[37] In the case of adoption of a special-needs child, taxpayers can take a $14,440 credit regardless of whether the taxpayer incurred any qualifying expenses.[38] Taxpayers take the credit in the year the adoption becomes final.

## Phaseout of Adoption Credit

The adoption credit is subject to phaseout when modified AGI exceeds certain limits. Modified AGI is equal to AGI plus income earned abroad or in certain U.S. territories or possessions. The phaseout begins when modified AGI exceeds $216,660 and the credit is completely phased out when modified AGI reaches $256,660.

For taxpayers with modified AGI that is within the phaseout range (between $216,660 and $256,660), the allowable credit is equal to the tentative credit multiplied by the following fraction:

$$\frac{\$256,660 - \text{Modified AGI}}{\$40,000}$$

---

**EXAMPLE 9-21**

Nicholas and Elaine spent $18,000 in qualified adoption expenses. Their modified AGI is $220,000. Their adoption credit would be $13,234: [($256,660 − $220,000)/$40,000] × $14,440. Note that the fraction is multiplied by the $14,440 maximum amount allowed, not the total spent of $18,000.

---

If a taxpayer receives employer-provided adoption benefits, the amount of qualified adoption expenses for purposes of the adoption credit is limited to the amount paid or incurred in excess of the employer-provided assistance, if any. If the assistance exceeds the expenses, the excess is taxable income. In order to claim the credit, Form 8839 must be filed along with documents supporting the adoption such as final adoption decree, court documents, and so on.

---

**CONCEPT CHECK 9-7—**

**LO 9-7**

1. Levi and Isaiah incurred the following expenses in the adoption of their infant daughter, which was finalized in 2021:

   2020   $10,800
   2021    3,950

   If their 2021 modified AGI is $120,000, how much can they claim in 2020? How about in 2021?

2. Zhang and Umiko spent $16,000 in qualified adoption expenses in the adoption of their son. The adoption was finalized and all of the expenses were incurred in the current year. Zhang and Umiko's modified AGI for the current year is $236,000. How much is their adoption credit?

# EARNED INCOME CREDIT (EIC) (FORM 1040, LINE 27a)

**LO 9-8**

The Earned Income Credit (EIC) is designed to help working taxpayers who are economically disadvantaged and to alleviate the burden of certain additional taxes such as gasoline and social security taxes.[39] Unlike most of the other personal credits, the EIC is a refundable tax credit. As discussed earlier, this means that the EIC amount is treated like payments made and may result

---

[37] IRC § 23(d)(3).
[38] IRC § 23(a)(3).
[39] IRC § 32.

**EXHIBIT 9-7**

| Form **8839** | **Qualified Adoption Expenses** | OMB No. 1545-0074 |
|---|---|---|
| Department of the Treasury Internal Revenue Service (99) | ▶ Attach to Form 1040, 1040-SR, or 1040-NR. ▶ Go to *www.irs.gov/Form8839* for instructions and the latest information. | **2021** Attachment Sequence No. **38** |

Name(s) shown on return | Your social security number

**Part I**  **Information About Your Eligible Child or Children**—You **must** complete this part.
See instructions for details, including what to do if you need more space.

*(DRAFT AS OF August 18, 2021 DO NOT FILE)*

**1**

| | (a) Child's name | | (b) Child's year of birth | Check if child was— | | | (f) Child's identifying number | (g) Check if adoption became final in 2021 or earlier |
|---|---|---|---|---|---|---|---|---|
| | First | Last | | (c) born **before 2004** and disabled | (d) a child with special needs | (e) a foreign child | | |
| Child 1 | | | | ☐ | ☐ | ☐ | | ☐ |
| Child 2 | | | | ☐ | ☐ | ☐ | | ☐ |
| Child 3 | | | | ☐ | ☐ | ☐ | | ☐ |

**Caution:** If the child was a foreign child, see **Special rules** in the instructions for line 1, column (e), before you complete Part II or Part III. If you received **employer-provided adoption benefits**, complete Part III on the back next.

**Part II**  **Adoption Credit**

| | | | Child 1 | Child 2 | Child 3 |
|---|---|---|---|---|---|
| **2** | Maximum adoption credit per child. Enter $14,440 (see instructions) . . . . . . . . . | **2** | | | |
| **3** | Did you file Form 8839 for a prior year for the same child? ☐ **No.** Enter -0-. ☐ **Yes.** See instructions for the amount to enter. | **3** | | | |
| **4** | Subtract line 3 from line 2 . . . . . . . . | **4** | | | |
| **5** | **Qualified adoption expenses** (see instructions) . . | **5** | | | |
| | **Caution:** Your qualified adoption expenses may not be equal to the adoption expenses you paid in 2021. | | | | |
| **6** | Enter the **smaller** of line 4 or line 5 . . . . . . | **6** | | | |
| **7** | Enter modified adjusted gross income (see instructions) . . . . . . | **7** | | | |
| **8** | Is line 7 more than $216,660? ☐ **No.** Skip lines 8 and 9, and enter -0- on line 10. ☐ **Yes.** Subtract $216,660 from line 7 . . . . . . . . . . | **8** | | | |
| **9** | Divide line 8 by $40,000. Enter the result as a decimal (rounded to at least three places). Do not enter more than 1.000 . . . . . . . . . . . . . . . . . . . . | **9** | × . | | |
| **10** | Multiply each amount on line 6 by line 9 . . . . . | **10** | | | |
| **11** | Subtract line 10 from line 6 . . . . . . . . . | **11** | | | |
| **12** | Add the amounts on line 11 . . . . . . . . . . . . . . . . . . . | **12** | | | |
| **13** | Credit carryforward, if any, from prior years. See your Adoption Credit Carryforward Worksheet in the 2020 Form 8839 instructions . . . . . . . . . . . . . . . . . . | **13** | | | |
| **14** | Add lines 12 and 13 . . . . . . . . . . . . . . . . . . . | **14** | | | |
| **15** | Enter the amount from line 5 of the Credit Limit Worksheet in the instructions . . . . . . . . . | **15** | | | |
| **16** | **Adoption Credit.** Enter the smaller of line 14 or line 15 here and on Schedule 3 (Form 1040), line 6c. If line 15 is smaller than line 14, you may have a credit carryforward (see instructions) . . . . . . . | **16** | | | |

For Paperwork Reduction Act Notice, see your tax return instructions. | Cat. No. 22843L | Form **8839** (2021)

Source: U.S. Department of the Treasury, Internal Revenue Service, Form 8839. Washington, DC: 2021.

in a tax refund even if a taxpayer has no tax liability. To claim the credit, the taxpayer must meet certain requirements and file a tax return. Taxpayers may claim the EIC with or without a qualifying child, but the amount of the credit will vary, depending on their earned income and whether the taxpayer has no qualifying children, or one, two, or three or more qualifying children.

### Earned Income

The EIC is determined by multiplying the taxpayer's earned income (up to a certain maximum amount) by the appropriate EIC percentage. *Earned income* includes wages, salaries, tips, and earnings from self-employment (minus one-half of the self-employment taxes).[40] A taxpayer who has a net loss from self-employment must reduce earned income by the amount of the loss.[41]

### Qualifying Child

To be eligible for the credit, a taxpayer must either have a qualifying child or meet certain criteria. A qualifying child is one of the following:

- The taxpayer's son or daughter, grandchild, or descendant.
- A stepson or stepdaughter, or descendant of either.
- An eligible foster child, defined as someone the taxpayer cares for as their own child and who is (1) a brother, sister, stepbrother, or stepsister, or (2) a descendant of a person in (1), or (3) a child placed with the taxpayer by an authorized placement agency.
- An adopted child.[42]

In addition, the child must

- Live with the taxpayer in the United States for more than half the year and be under the age of 19 (or be a full-time student under the age of 24).
- Be younger than the person claiming the child.
- Not have filed a joint return other than to claim a refund.
- Have a valid social security number.

### No Qualifying Child

If a taxpayer has no qualifying child, to be eligible for the credit, *all* of the following criteria must be met:

- Have a principal place of abode in the United States for more than half the tax year.

**NEW LAW**

- Be older than 24 but younger than 65 before the end of the tax year. In the case of married individuals, at least one spouse must satisfy this requirement. For 2021 ONLY, the minimum age is reduced to 19 and there is no maximum age.
- Not be claimed as a dependent of another taxpayer.
- Not be a nonresident alien for any part of the tax year.

### Calculating the Earned Income Credit

To calculate the EIC, multiply earned income up to a certain amount by a percentage; when earned income exceeds certain levels, the credit begins to phase out. The percentages for the credit and phaseout amounts vary depending on filing status and the number of qualifying children claimed by the taxpayer. The appropriate percentages and earned income amounts are shown in Table 9-3.[43] For 2021, taxpayers can use their earned income from 2019 to determine their EIC. This provision means taxpayers can determine their EIC using 2021 earned income or 2019 earned income and choose the larger EIC.

At first glance, the table may appear intimidating, but its application is straightforward. For example, married taxpayers with two eligible children use the column "Two" (the second column from the right). For earned income up to $14,950, the taxpayer is entitled to a credit of 40% of earned income. For tax year 2021, $5,980 ($14,950 × 40%) is the maximum EIC for a joint filer with two qualifying children.

[40] IRC § 32(c)(2).

[41] Reg. § 1.32-2(c)(2).

[42] IRC § 32(c)(3).

[43] Derived from IRC § 32(b).

**TABLE 9-3\***
**Earned Income Credit**
**Tax Year 2021**

| | None | One | Two | Three or More |
|---|---|---|---|---|
| | \multicolumn{4}{c}{**Number of Eligible Children**} | | | |
| EIC percentage | 15.30% | 34.0% | 40.0% | 45.0% |
| For earned income up to | $9,820 | $10,640 | $14,950 | $14,950 |
| Maximum EIC | $1,502 | $3,618 | $5,980 | $6,728 |
| Phaseout percentage | 15.30% | 15.98% | 21.06% | 21.06% |
| For joint filers: | | | | |
|   Phaseout starts at earned income of | $17,560 | $25,470 | $25,470 | $25,470 |
|   Phaseout ends at earned income of | $27,380 | $48,108 | $53,865 | $57,414 |
| For all other filers: | | | | |
|   Phaseout starts at earned income of | $11,610 | $19,520 | $19,520 | $19,520 |
|   Phaseout ends at earned income of | $21,430 | $42,158 | $47,915 | $51,464 |

\* The dollar amounts in the table are subject to annual adjustments for inflation.

Married joint return filers (with two qualifying children) with earned income between $14,950 and the phaseout starting point of $25,470 are also entitled to the maximum credit. However, once earned income rises above $25,470, the EIC is reduced by 21.06% of the excess (that is, amounts over $25,470) until earned income reaches $53,865. Once earned income reaches $53,865, the EIC is eliminated.

 **NEW LAW**

For 2021, the maximum EIC for qualified taxpayers with no children has been almost tripled from prior law. This change is incorporated into Table 9-3.

In practice, the EIC is determined by referencing the EIC table provided by the IRS and completing a Schedule EIC (if there is a qualifying child) shown in Exhibit 9-8. A copy of the EIC table can be found at the end of this chapter in Appendix A.

---

**EXAMPLE 9-22**

Danny and Wanda have two eligible children and file a joint return. They have earned income of $38,025. Their EIC is $3,223, calculated as follows:

| | |
|---|---|
| Maximum credit ............................................. | $5,980 |
| Less: ($38,025 − $25,470) × 21.06% ...... | 2,644 |
| Earned Income Credit ......................... | $3,336 |

---

**EXAMPLE 9-23**

Using the same information as in Example 9-22, look up the amount of EIC for Danny and Wanda using the EIC table in the Appendix at the end of this chapter. They have earned income of $38,025, which falls between $38,000 and $38,050. Be sure to use the column for married filing jointly and "two children." The EIC amount should be $3,336, same as the amount calculated in Example 9-22.

---

**EXAMPLE 9-24**

Saul and Tammy have a 4-year-old daughter, Brenda, who is a dependent. Their combined earned income was $26,500. The couple had no other income. In this case, the couple qualifies for the EIC with one qualifying child. Their EIC is $3,379, calculated as follows:

| | |
|---|---|
| Maximum credit ............................................. | $3,618 |
| Less: ($26,500 − $25,470) × 15.98% ...... | 165 |
| Earned Income Credit ......................... | $3,453 |

# From Shoebox to Software

Taxpayers use Schedule EIC and Worksheet A to claim the EIC credit (Exhibits 9-8 and 9-9). The tax software will automatically calculate the amount of the credit based on the information provided elsewhere in the tax return. Taxpayers claim the credit directly on Form 1040, line 27a.

To obtain the credit, the taxpayer must provide ID numbers of the taxpayer, the taxpayer's spouse (if applicable), and the name, age, and taxpayer ID of any qualifying child (if applicable).

 **NEW LAW**

A taxpayer is ineligible to take the EIC if they have disqualified income in excess of $10,000.[44] *Disqualified income* includes dividends, interest (taxable and nontaxable), net rental income, net royalty income, net capital gains, and net passive income.[45]

If certain required forms are filed, a taxpayer with a qualifying child may receive advance payments of the EIC through their employer, not to exceed 60% of the total available credit.

**CONCEPT CHECK 9-8— LO 9-8**

1. Josh and Danielle both work and have one qualifying child. They had earned income of $20,000. Using the EIC table at the end of the chapter, look up the amount of their EIC.

2. Assume the same facts as above for Josh and Danielle except their earned income is $32,000. Calculate their EIC using the formula as shown in Example 9-24 of this chapter.

3. Tiffany is a head of household taxpayer with two qualifying children. She had earned income of $16,000. (*a*) If she qualifies for the EIC, how much is her credit (either the EIC table or the EIC formula may be used)? (*b*) If her tax liability is $800 for the tax year (before the EIC), what is the amount of her tax refund or tax owed after the EIC is taken into account?

# From Shoebox to Software   Comprehensive Example

Using the tax software, open the tax return for Mr. and Mrs. Ramirez.

The Ramirezes already have a $9,000 child tax credit—$3,000 for each of their three children. We will now add some education credits.

Maria Ramirez attended State University, where she is working on an undergraduate degree in accounting. She is taking three classes a semester (a full load is four classes). During the current year (while Maria was a sophomore), she paid the university $9,000 for tuition and fees, the local bookstore $700 for books, and $235 for food at the student union between classes.

Jose is taking a few graduate classes at State University to help him with certain aspects of his job. He paid the university $1,300 for tuition. He was not enrolled in a degree program.

Go to Form 1040 for the Ramirezes. Click on Schedule 3, line 3, education credits. Click on the yellow file folder, and then click on the information sheet. Alternatively, you could go to the Documents Received section and click on the Federal Information for Higher Education sheet.

Jose and Maria's allowable expenses are tuition, fees, and books. The expenses for food are not qualified expenses for purposes of the credits. Enter the $9,700 of expenses for Maria and the $1,300 for Jose. Then click the Qualifies for the American opportunity tax credit box beside Maria's name because she is in her first four years of higher education.

Now open the Ramirezes' Form 8863. Part I should show a $2,500 credit for Maria, and Part II should show a $260 credit for Jose. If the Ramirezes have modified AGI in excess of $180,000, their credit of $2,760 will be limited in Part III. Line 19 of Form 8863 and line 3 of Schedule 3 should both reflect this limited credit.

Save the Ramirezes' return for future chapters.

---

[44] This amount is adjusted annually for inflation.

[45] IRC § 32(i).

**EXHIBIT 9-8**

---

| SCHEDULE EIC<br>(Form 1040)<br><br>Department of the Treasury<br>Internal Revenue Service (99) | **Earned Income Credit**<br>Qualifying Child Information<br><br>▶ **Complete and attach to Form 1040 or 1040-SR only if you have a qualifying child.**<br>▶ **Go to** *www.irs.gov/ScheduleEIC* **for the latest information.** | 1040<br>1040-SR<br>EIC | OMB No. 1545-0074<br><br>2021<br><br>Attachment<br>Sequence No. **43** |
|---|---|---|---|

| Name(s) shown on return | Your social security number |
|---|---|

If you are separated from your spouse, filing a separate return and meet the requirements to claim the EIC (see instructions), check here ☐

**Before you begin:**
- See the instructions for Form 1040, lines 27a, 27b, and 27c, to make sure that **(a)** you can take the EIC, and **(b)** you have a qualifying child.
- Be sure the child's name on line 1 and social security number (SSN) on line 2 agree with the child's social security card. Otherwise, at the time we process your return, we may reduce your EIC. If the name or SSN on the child's social security card is not correct, call the Social Security Administration at 1-800-772-1213.

⚠ **CAUTION**
- You can't claim the EIC for a child who didn't live with you for more than half of the year.
- If you take the EIC even though you are not eligible, you may not be allowed to take the credit for up to 10 years. See the instructions for details.
- It will take us longer to process your return and issue your refund if you do not fill in all lines that apply for each qualifying child.

| Qualifying Child Information | Child 1 | Child 2 | Child 3 |
|---|---|---|---|
| **1 Child's name**<br>If you have more than three qualifying children, you have to list only three to get the maximum credit. | First name __ Last name | First name __ Last name | First name __ Last name |
| **2 Child's SSN**<br>The child must have an SSN as defined in the instructions for Form 1040, lines 27a, 27b, and 27c, unless the child was born and died in 2021. If your child was born and died in 2021 and did not have an SSN, enter "Died" on this line and attach a copy of the child's birth certificate, death certificate, or hospital medical records showing a live birth. | | | |
| **3 Child's year of birth** | Year ____ ____ ____ ____<br>*If born after 2002 **and** the child is younger than you (or your spouse, if filing jointly), skip lines 4a and 4b; go to line 5.* | Year ____ ____ ____ ____<br>*If born after 2002 **and** the child is younger than you (or your spouse, if filing jointly), skip lines 4a and 4b; go to line 5.* | Year ____ ____ ____ ____<br>*If born after 2002 **and** the child is younger than you (or your spouse, if filing jointly), skip lines 4a and 4b; go to line 5.* |
| **4 a** Was the child under age 24 at the end of 2021, a student, and younger than you (or your spouse, if filing jointly)? | ☐ **Yes.** *Go to line 5.*  ☐ **No.** *Go to line 4b.* | ☐ **Yes.** *Go to line 5.*  ☐ **No.** *Go to line 4b.* | ☐ **Yes.** *Go to line 5.*  ☐ **No.** *Go to line 4b.* |
| **b** Was the child permanently and totally disabled during any part of 2021? | ☐ **Yes.** *Go to line 5.*  ☐ **No.** The child is not a qualifying child. | ☐ **Yes.** *Go to line 5.*  ☐ **No.** The child is not a qualifying child. | ☐ **Yes.** *Go to line 5.*  ☐ **No.** The child is not a qualifying child. |
| **5 Child's relationship to you**<br>(for example, son, daughter, grandchild, niece, nephew, eligible foster child, etc.) | | | |
| **6 Number of months child lived with you in the United States during 2021**<br>• If the child lived with you for more than half of 2021 but less than 7 months, enter "7."<br>• If the child was born or died in 2021 and your home was the child's home for more than half the time he or she was alive during 2021, enter "12." | _____ months<br>*Do not enter more than 12 months.* | _____ months<br>*Do not enter more than 12 months.* | _____ months<br>*Do not enter more than 12 months.* |

| For Paperwork Reduction Act Notice, see your tax return instructions. | Cat. No. 13339M | Schedule EIC (Form 1040) 2021 |
|---|---|---|

*DRAFT AS OF JULY 16, 2021 DO NOT FILE*

Source: U.S. Department of the Treasury, Internal Revenue Service, Schedule EIC (Form 1040). Washington, DC: 2021.

# PREMIUM TAX CREDIT (SCHEDULE 2, LINE 2, OR SCHEDULE 3, LINE 9)

## LO 9-9

The Affordable Care Act (ACA) requires all individuals to either have health care coverage or qualify for a health coverage exemption or make a shared responsibility payment with their tax return. As we noted in Chapter 1, the shared responsibility payment is zero beginning in 2019. A tax credit is available for some taxpayers.

Taxpayers can obtain health insurance from an employer or from Medicare, or they can purchase an individual plan.

Individuals without insurance can obtain health insurance through a Health Insurance Marketplace ("Marketplace" or "Exchange"). Millions of Americans have purchased their health insurance in this manner.

Taxpayers who purchased qualified health insurance through the Marketplace may be eligible for a premium tax credit. This credit can be claimed in full on the taxpayer's Form 1040. Most often, the credit is used during the year to reduce the out-of-pocket cost of the insurance premiums—in effect, the taxpayer will pay for part of the premium and the credit will pay for the remainder.

 **NEW LAW**

In general, to receive the credit, eligible taxpayers must have household income between 100% and 400% of the federal poverty level for the taxpayer's family size. For 2021 and 2022, the 400% upper limit has been eliminated. The taxpayer must also be ineligible for coverage through an employer or government plan. In general, taxpayers with income less than 100% of the federal poverty level are eligible for health coverage from other federal or state programs.

Taxpayers eligible for the credit can choose to apply the credit toward their insurance premium or to receive the entire credit when they file their tax return. This determination is made at the time a taxpayer obtains insurance through the Marketplace.

At the end of the year, taxpayers who receive the credit must file a tax return and complete Form 8962. This form claims the premium tax credit and reconciles any advanced tax credits received with the tax credit for which the taxpayer is eligible. The credit is a refundable credit. Taxpayers receiving a credit will receive a Form 1095-A from the Marketplace, and the information on this form is used to complete Form 8962.

The amount of the credit is the lesser of

- The premium for the insurance obtained from the Marketplace.
- The premium for the applicable second lowest cost silver plan (SLCSP) minus the taxpayer's contribution amount.

To calculate the monthly contribution amount, the taxpayer uses an "applicable figure" determined with reference to Table 2 in the instructions to Form 8962. The table is shown in Appendix B of this chapter.

The applicable figure is based on the taxpayer's household income as a percentage of the federal poverty level for the applicable family size. The applicable poverty guidelines are those from the preceding calendar year. So, the 2020 guidelines are used to determine the 2021 premium tax credit. The 2020 federal poverty levels are as follows:

| 2020 Poverty Guidelines for the 48 Contiguous States and the District of Columbia | |
|---|---|
| Persons in Family/Household | Poverty Guideline |
| 1 | $12,760 |
| 2 | 17,240 |
| 3 | 21,720 |
| 4 | 26,200 |
| 5 | 30,680 |
| 6 | 35,160 |
| 7 | 39,640 |
| 8 | 44,120 |

**EXAMPLE 9-25**

Shantae is married with one dependent and a household size of three. Her household income is $59,370. This household income is 273% of the federal poverty level for a household size of three ($59,370/$21,720 = 273%). The applicable figure from Table 2 is 0.0492.

The contribution amount is equal to the household income multiplied by the applicable figure from Table 2. This calculated contribution amount is subtracted from the taxpayer's SLCSP cost.

Let's put it all together with the following example.

**EXAMPLE 9-26**

Gordon is single with no dependents. He enrolled in a qualified health care plan with an annual premium of $5,000 through the Marketplace. His SLCSP premium (shown on his Form 1095-A) is $5,200. His household income was $29,900, which is 234% of the federal poverty level for a family size of one ($29,900/$12,760 = 234%). His applicable figure using Table 2 in the instructions to Form 8962 or in Appendix B in this chapter is 0.0336. His contribution amount is equal to $1,005 (household income of $29,900 multiplied by the Table 2 factor of 0.0336).

Gordon's premium tax credit is the lesser of

- His health plan premium of $5,000 or
- His SLCSP cost of $5,200 minus his contribution amount of $1,005, which is $4,195.

Thus, his premium tax credit is $4,195.

In practice, the premium credit is calculated based on expected household income and expected family size. To the extent that actual household income varies from expected, the taxpayer may receive an additional credit (on Schedule 3, line 9) or may have additional tax (Schedule 2, line 2). In general, if actual income is greater than expected income, the taxpayer will owe additional tax because the credit decreases as income increases. If actual income is less than expected, the taxpayer will receive an additional credit. Similarly, if actual family size is larger than expected, the taxpayer will receive an additional credit, and if actual size is smaller, the taxpayer will owe additional tax.

The rules associated with the credit can be complex. In fact, the IRS suggests taxpayers use tax software to file a return. Refer to IRS Publications 974, 5187, and 5201 for additional information.

**CONCEPT CHECK 9-9— LO 9-9**

1. Taxpayers with income greater than 400% of the federal poverty guidelines are ineligible for the premium tax credit. True or false?

## Other Personal Credits

The IRC provides for various other credits that are not discussed in detail here. As with the credit for the elderly or the disabled, some of these credits are reported on line 6 a through z of Schedule 3 (most require additional forms to be attached). Recall that tax credits are often used by Congress to encourage certain societal and economic outcomes and in some cases are available for only a short term.

# Summary

**LO 9-1:** Apply the tax rules and calculate the credit for child and dependent care expenses.

- The credit is available to working taxpayers with dependent care expenses (of qualifying individuals).
- The credit is calculated as a percentage of the qualified expenses incurred to care for dependents.
- The maximum amount of qualifying expenses is limited to $8,000 for one and $16,000 for two or more qualifying individuals.
- For qualifying expenses and qualifying individuals, certain criteria must be met.
- The percentage (50% to 0%) used in the calculation is dependent on AGI.
- Certain expense limitations exist.

**LO 9-2:** Apply the tax rules and calculate the credit for the elderly or the disabled.

- The credit is available to taxpayers over 65 years of age or permanently and totally disabled.
- The credit is equal to 15% of allowable base amounts.
- The base amount is reduced by certain amounts of social security benefits and excess AGI.
- The base amounts vary depending on the filing status and age of the taxpayer.

**LO 9-3:** Apply the tax rules and calculate the education credits.

- Two credits available are the American opportunity tax credit (AOTC) and the lifetime learning credit.
- Both allow credit for higher education expenses for the taxpayer, spouse, or dependent.
- The AOTC has a maximum of $2,500 per student.
- The lifetime learning credit has a maximum of $2,000 per taxpayer.
- Both credits are phased out at certain amounts of AGI.
- For married filing jointly and single filers credits phase out completely at MAGI amounts of $180,000 and $90,000, respectively.

**LO 9-4:** Apply the tax rules and calculate the foreign tax credit (FTC).

- The credit is available to taxpayers who paid foreign income taxes.
- The credit is equal to the amount of foreign taxes paid.
- The FTC, however, is limited to the portion of the U.S. income tax liability that is attributable to foreign income.

**LO 9-5:** Apply the tax rules and calculate the child tax credit.

- The credit is provided to taxpayers with dependent children under age 18.
- The credit is $3,000 for each child 6 to 17 years of age and $3,600 for a child under age 6.
- The credit is reduced to $2,000 per child starting at MAGI of $75,000 (single), $112,500 (HoH), and $150,000 (MFJ).
- The credit is further reduced to zero beginning at AGI of $400,000 for married filing jointly and $200,000 for all others.
- The entire credit is refundable.
- A $500 nonrefundable credit is provided for qualifying dependents other than qualifying children.

**LO 9-6:** Apply the tax rules and calculate the retirement savings contributions credit.

- The credit is available to taxpayers who made contributions to certain qualified retirement accounts.
- The credit is based on a percentage of the contributions made.
- The maximum amount of contributions for credit purposes is $2,000 per individual (or per spouse if filed jointly).
- The percentage used depends on filing status and AGI.
- Over certain amounts of AGI, no credit is available.

**LO 9-7:** Apply the tax rules and calculate the adoption credit.

- The credit is available up to $14,440 per child adopted.
- The credit is phased out for AGI above $216,660.
- No credit is available for AGI above $256,660.
- If married, the credit is generally allowed only for taxpayers filing jointly.
- To claim the credit, Form 8839 must be filed.

**LO 9-8:** Apply the tax rules and calculate the Earned Income Credit (EIC).

- The credit is allowed for working taxpayers who are economically disadvantaged.
- It is a refundable tax credit.
- The credit is based on filing status, number of qualifying children (including none), and AGI.
- The credit can completely phase out at certain AGI levels.
- Certain types of income (mostly unearned) in excess of $10,000 make taxpayers ineligible for the credit.

**LO 9-9:** Apply the tax rules for the premium tax credit under the Affordable Care Act.

- Taxpayers with health insurance purchased through the Marketplace may be eligible.
- Household income must be between 100% and 400% of the federal poverty level for the family size. For 2021 and 2022, the upper limit is eliminated.
- The credit can be used to pay a portion of the insurance premium.
- To claim the credit or to reconcile advanced payments, taxpayers must file Form 8962.

# Appendix A

## 2021 Earned Income Credit (EIC) Table
## Caution. This is **not** a tax table.

**1.** To find your credit, read down the "At least - But less than" columns and find the line that includes the amount you were told to look up from your EIC Worksheet.

**2.** Then, go to the column that includes your filing status and the number of qualifying children you have. Enter the credit from that column on your EIC Worksheet.

**Example.** If your filing status is single, you have one qualifying child, and the amount you are looking up from your EIC Worksheet is $2,455, you would enter $842.

| If the amount you are looking up from the worksheet is— | | And your filing status is— | | | |
|---|---|---|---|---|---|
| | | Single, head of household, or qualifying widow(er) and the number of children you have is— | | | |
| At least | But less than | 0 | 1 | 2 | 3 |
| | | Your credit is— | | | |
| 2,400 | 2,450 | 371 | 825 | 970 | 1,091 |
| 2,450 | 2,500 | 379 | 842 | 990 | 1,114 |

| If the amount you are looking up from the worksheet is— | | Single, head of household, or qualifying widow(er)★ and you have— | | | | Married filing jointly and you have— | | | |
|---|---|---|---|---|---|---|---|---|---|
| | | 0 | 1 | 2 | 3 | 0 | 1 | 2 | 3 |
| At least | But less than | Your credit is— | | | | Your credit is— | | | |
| $1 | $50 | $4 | $9 | $10 | $11 | $4 | $9 | $10 | $11 |
| 50 | 100 | 11 | 26 | 30 | 34 | 11 | 26 | 30 | 34 |
| 100 | 150 | 19 | 43 | 50 | 56 | 19 | 43 | 50 | 56 |
| 150 | 200 | 27 | 60 | 70 | 79 | 27 | 60 | 70 | 79 |
| 200 | 250 | 34 | 77 | 90 | 101 | 34 | 77 | 90 | 101 |
| 250 | 300 | 42 | 94 | 110 | 124 | 42 | 94 | 110 | 124 |
| 300 | 350 | 50 | 111 | 130 | 146 | 50 | 111 | 130 | 146 |
| 350 | 400 | 57 | 128 | 150 | 169 | 57 | 128 | 150 | 169 |
| 400 | 450 | 65 | 145 | 170 | 191 | 65 | 145 | 170 | 191 |
| 450 | 500 | 73 | 162 | 190 | 214 | 73 | 162 | 190 | 214 |
| 500 | 550 | 80 | 179 | 210 | 236 | 80 | 179 | 210 | 236 |
| 550 | 600 | 88 | 196 | 230 | 259 | 88 | 196 | 230 | 259 |
| 600 | 650 | 96 | 213 | 250 | 281 | 96 | 213 | 250 | 281 |
| 650 | 700 | 103 | 230 | 270 | 304 | 103 | 230 | 270 | 304 |
| 700 | 750 | 111 | 247 | 290 | 326 | 111 | 247 | 290 | 326 |
| 750 | 800 | 119 | 264 | 310 | 349 | 119 | 264 | 310 | 349 |
| 800 | 850 | 126 | 281 | 330 | 371 | 126 | 281 | 330 | 371 |
| 850 | 900 | 134 | 298 | 350 | 394 | 134 | 298 | 350 | 394 |
| 900 | 950 | 142 | 315 | 370 | 416 | 142 | 315 | 370 | 416 |
| 950 | 1,000 | 149 | 332 | 390 | 439 | 149 | 332 | 390 | 439 |
| 1,000 | 1,050 | 157 | 349 | 410 | 461 | 157 | 349 | 410 | 461 |
| 1,050 | 1,100 | 164 | 366 | 430 | 484 | 164 | 366 | 430 | 484 |
| 1,100 | 1,150 | 172 | 383 | 450 | 506 | 172 | 383 | 450 | 506 |
| 1,150 | 1,200 | 180 | 400 | 470 | 529 | 180 | 400 | 470 | 529 |
| 1,200 | 1,250 | 187 | 417 | 490 | 551 | 187 | 417 | 490 | 551 |
| 1,250 | 1,300 | 195 | 434 | 510 | 574 | 195 | 434 | 510 | 574 |
| 1,300 | 1,350 | 203 | 451 | 530 | 596 | 203 | 451 | 530 | 596 |
| 1,350 | 1,400 | 210 | 468 | 550 | 619 | 210 | 468 | 550 | 619 |
| 1,400 | 1,450 | 218 | 485 | 570 | 641 | 218 | 485 | 570 | 641 |
| 1,450 | 1,500 | 226 | 502 | 590 | 664 | 226 | 502 | 590 | 664 |
| 1,500 | 1,550 | 233 | 519 | 610 | 686 | 233 | 519 | 610 | 686 |
| 1,550 | 1,600 | 241 | 536 | 630 | 709 | 241 | 536 | 630 | 709 |
| 1,600 | 1,650 | 249 | 553 | 650 | 731 | 249 | 553 | 650 | 731 |
| 1,650 | 1,700 | 256 | 570 | 670 | 754 | 256 | 570 | 670 | 754 |
| 1,700 | 1,750 | 264 | 587 | 690 | 776 | 264 | 587 | 690 | 776 |
| 1,750 | 1,800 | 272 | 604 | 710 | 799 | 272 | 604 | 710 | 799 |
| 1,800 | 1,850 | 279 | 621 | 730 | 821 | 279 | 621 | 730 | 821 |
| 1,850 | 1,900 | 287 | 638 | 750 | 844 | 287 | 638 | 750 | 844 |
| 1,900 | 1,950 | 295 | 655 | 770 | 866 | 295 | 655 | 770 | 866 |
| 1,950 | 2,000 | 302 | 672 | 790 | 889 | 302 | 672 | 790 | 889 |
| 2,000 | 2,050 | 310 | 689 | 810 | 911 | 310 | 689 | 810 | 911 |
| 2,050 | 2,100 | 317 | 706 | 830 | 934 | 317 | 706 | 830 | 934 |
| 2,100 | 2,150 | 325 | 723 | 850 | 956 | 325 | 723 | 850 | 956 |
| 2,150 | 2,200 | 333 | 740 | 870 | 979 | 333 | 740 | 870 | 979 |
| 2,200 | 2,250 | 340 | 757 | 890 | 1,001 | 340 | 757 | 890 | 1,001 |
| 2,250 | 2,300 | 348 | 774 | 910 | 1,024 | 348 | 774 | 910 | 1,024 |
| 2,300 | 2,350 | 356 | 791 | 930 | 1,046 | 356 | 791 | 930 | 1,046 |
| 2,350 | 2,400 | 363 | 808 | 950 | 1,069 | 363 | 808 | 950 | 1,069 |
| 2,400 | 2,450 | 371 | 825 | 970 | 1,091 | 371 | 825 | 970 | 1,091 |
| 2,450 | 2,500 | 379 | 842 | 990 | 1,114 | 379 | 842 | 990 | 1,114 |
| 2,500 | 2,550 | 386 | 859 | 1,010 | 1,136 | 386 | 859 | 1,010 | 1,136 |
| 2,550 | 2,600 | 394 | 876 | 1,030 | 1,159 | 394 | 876 | 1,030 | 1,159 |
| 2,600 | 2,650 | 402 | 893 | 1,050 | 1,181 | 402 | 893 | 1,050 | 1,181 |
| 2,650 | 2,700 | 409 | 910 | 1,070 | 1,204 | 409 | 910 | 1,070 | 1,204 |
| 2,700 | 2,750 | 417 | 927 | 1,090 | 1,226 | 417 | 927 | 1,090 | 1,226 |
| 2,750 | 2,800 | 425 | 944 | 1,110 | 1,249 | 425 | 944 | 1,110 | 1,249 |

| If the amount you are looking up from the worksheet is— | | Single, head of household, or qualifying widow(er)★ and you have— | | | | Married filing jointly and you have— | | | |
|---|---|---|---|---|---|---|---|---|---|
| | | 0 | 1 | 2 | 3 | 0 | 1 | 2 | 3 |
| At least | But less than | Your credit is— | | | | Your credit is— | | | |
| 2,800 | 2,850 | 432 | 961 | 1,130 | 1,271 | 432 | 961 | 1,130 | 1,271 |
| 2,850 | 2,900 | 440 | 978 | 1,150 | 1,294 | 440 | 978 | 1,150 | 1,294 |
| 2,900 | 2,950 | 448 | 995 | 1,170 | 1,316 | 448 | 995 | 1,170 | 1,316 |
| 2,950 | 3,000 | 455 | 1,012 | 1,190 | 1,339 | 455 | 1,012 | 1,190 | 1,339 |
| 3,000 | 3,050 | 463 | 1,029 | 1,210 | 1,361 | 463 | 1,029 | 1,210 | 1,361 |
| 3,050 | 3,100 | 470 | 1,046 | 1,230 | 1,384 | 470 | 1,046 | 1,230 | 1,384 |
| 3,100 | 3,150 | 478 | 1,063 | 1,250 | 1,406 | 478 | 1,063 | 1,250 | 1,406 |
| 3,150 | 3,200 | 486 | 1,080 | 1,270 | 1,429 | 486 | 1,080 | 1,270 | 1,429 |
| 3,200 | 3,250 | 493 | 1,097 | 1,290 | 1,451 | 493 | 1,097 | 1,290 | 1,451 |
| 3,250 | 3,300 | 501 | 1,114 | 1,310 | 1,474 | 501 | 1,114 | 1,310 | 1,474 |
| 3,300 | 3,350 | 509 | 1,131 | 1,330 | 1,496 | 509 | 1,131 | 1,330 | 1,496 |
| 3,350 | 3,400 | 516 | 1,148 | 1,350 | 1,519 | 516 | 1,148 | 1,350 | 1,519 |
| 3,400 | 3,450 | 524 | 1,165 | 1,370 | 1,541 | 524 | 1,165 | 1,370 | 1,541 |
| 3,450 | 3,500 | 532 | 1,182 | 1,390 | 1,564 | 532 | 1,182 | 1,390 | 1,564 |
| 3,500 | 3,550 | 539 | 1,199 | 1,410 | 1,586 | 539 | 1,199 | 1,410 | 1,586 |
| 3,550 | 3,600 | 547 | 1,216 | 1,430 | 1,609 | 547 | 1,216 | 1,430 | 1,609 |
| 3,600 | 3,650 | 555 | 1,233 | 1,450 | 1,631 | 555 | 1,233 | 1,450 | 1,631 |
| 3,650 | 3,700 | 562 | 1,250 | 1,470 | 1,654 | 562 | 1,250 | 1,470 | 1,654 |
| 3,700 | 3,750 | 570 | 1,267 | 1,490 | 1,676 | 570 | 1,267 | 1,490 | 1,676 |
| 3,750 | 3,800 | 578 | 1,284 | 1,510 | 1,699 | 578 | 1,284 | 1,510 | 1,699 |
| 3,800 | 3,850 | 585 | 1,301 | 1,530 | 1,721 | 585 | 1,301 | 1,530 | 1,721 |
| 3,850 | 3,900 | 593 | 1,318 | 1,550 | 1,744 | 593 | 1,318 | 1,550 | 1,744 |
| 3,900 | 3,950 | 601 | 1,335 | 1,570 | 1,766 | 601 | 1,335 | 1,570 | 1,766 |
| 3,950 | 4,000 | 608 | 1,352 | 1,590 | 1,789 | 608 | 1,352 | 1,590 | 1,789 |
| 4,000 | 4,050 | 616 | 1,369 | 1,610 | 1,811 | 616 | 1,369 | 1,610 | 1,811 |
| 4,050 | 4,100 | 623 | 1,386 | 1,630 | 1,834 | 623 | 1,386 | 1,630 | 1,834 |
| 4,100 | 4,150 | 631 | 1,403 | 1,650 | 1,856 | 631 | 1,403 | 1,650 | 1,856 |
| 4,150 | 4,200 | 639 | 1,420 | 1,670 | 1,879 | 639 | 1,420 | 1,670 | 1,879 |
| 4,200 | 4,250 | 646 | 1,437 | 1,690 | 1,901 | 646 | 1,437 | 1,690 | 1,901 |
| 4,250 | 4,300 | 654 | 1,454 | 1,710 | 1,924 | 654 | 1,454 | 1,710 | 1,924 |
| 4,300 | 4,350 | 662 | 1,471 | 1,730 | 1,946 | 662 | 1,471 | 1,730 | 1,946 |
| 4,350 | 4,400 | 669 | 1,488 | 1,750 | 1,969 | 669 | 1,488 | 1,750 | 1,969 |
| 4,400 | 4,450 | 677 | 1,505 | 1,770 | 1,991 | 677 | 1,505 | 1,770 | 1,991 |
| 4,450 | 4,500 | 685 | 1,522 | 1,790 | 2,014 | 685 | 1,522 | 1,790 | 2,014 |
| 4,500 | 4,550 | 692 | 1,539 | 1,810 | 2,036 | 692 | 1,539 | 1,810 | 2,036 |
| 4,550 | 4,600 | 700 | 1,556 | 1,830 | 2,059 | 700 | 1,556 | 1,830 | 2,059 |
| 4,600 | 4,650 | 708 | 1,573 | 1,850 | 2,081 | 708 | 1,573 | 1,850 | 2,081 |
| 4,650 | 4,700 | 715 | 1,590 | 1,870 | 2,104 | 715 | 1,590 | 1,870 | 2,104 |
| 4,700 | 4,750 | 723 | 1,607 | 1,890 | 2,126 | 723 | 1,607 | 1,890 | 2,126 |
| 4,750 | 4,800 | 731 | 1,624 | 1,910 | 2,149 | 731 | 1,624 | 1,910 | 2,149 |
| 4,800 | 4,850 | 738 | 1,641 | 1,930 | 2,171 | 738 | 1,641 | 1,930 | 2,171 |
| 4,850 | 4,900 | 746 | 1,658 | 1,950 | 2,194 | 746 | 1,658 | 1,950 | 2,194 |
| 4,900 | 4,950 | 754 | 1,675 | 1,970 | 2,216 | 754 | 1,675 | 1,970 | 2,216 |
| 4,950 | 5,000 | 761 | 1,692 | 1,990 | 2,239 | 761 | 1,692 | 1,990 | 2,239 |
| 5,000 | 5,050 | 769 | 1,709 | 2,010 | 2,261 | 769 | 1,709 | 2,010 | 2,261 |
| 5,050 | 5,100 | 776 | 1,726 | 2,030 | 2,284 | 776 | 1,726 | 2,030 | 2,284 |
| 5,100 | 5,150 | 784 | 1,743 | 2,050 | 2,306 | 784 | 1,743 | 2,050 | 2,306 |
| 5,150 | 5,200 | 792 | 1,760 | 2,070 | 2,329 | 792 | 1,760 | 2,070 | 2,329 |
| 5,200 | 5,250 | 799 | 1,777 | 2,090 | 2,351 | 799 | 1,777 | 2,090 | 2,351 |
| 5,250 | 5,300 | 807 | 1,794 | 2,110 | 2,374 | 807 | 1,794 | 2,110 | 2,374 |
| 5,300 | 5,350 | 815 | 1,811 | 2,130 | 2,396 | 815 | 1,811 | 2,130 | 2,396 |
| 5,350 | 5,400 | 822 | 1,828 | 2,150 | 2,419 | 822 | 1,828 | 2,150 | 2,419 |
| 5,400 | 5,450 | 830 | 1,845 | 2,170 | 2,441 | 830 | 1,845 | 2,170 | 2,441 |
| 5,450 | 5,500 | 838 | 1,862 | 2,190 | 2,464 | 838 | 1,862 | 2,190 | 2,464 |
| 5,500 | 5,550 | 845 | 1,879 | 2,210 | 2,486 | 845 | 1,879 | 2,210 | 2,486 |
| 5,550 | 5,600 | 853 | 1,896 | 2,230 | 2,509 | 853 | 1,896 | 2,230 | 2,509 |

★ Use this column if your filing status is married filing separately and you qualify to claim the EIC. See the instructions for line 27a.

*(Continued)*

- 16 -

Source: U.S. Department of the Treasury, Internal Revenue Service, 2019 Earned Income Credit (EIC) Table. Washington, DC: 2021.

**Earned Income Credit (EIC) Table** - *Continued*  (**Caution.** This is **not** a tax table.)

| If the amount you are looking up from the worksheet is— | | Single, head of household, or qualifying widow(er)★ and you have— | | | | Married filing jointly and you have— | | | |
|---|---|---|---|---|---|---|---|---|---|
| At least | But less than | 0 | 1 | 2 | 3 | 0 | 1 | 2 | 3 |
| | | Your credit is— | | | | Your credit is— | | | |
| 5,600 | 5,650 | 861 | 1,913 | 2,250 | 2,531 | 861 | 1,913 | 2,250 | 2,531 |
| 5,650 | 5,700 | 868 | 1,930 | 2,270 | 2,554 | 868 | 1,930 | 2,270 | 2,554 |
| 5,700 | 5,750 | 876 | 1,947 | 2,290 | 2,576 | 876 | 1,947 | 2,290 | 2,576 |
| 5,750 | 5,800 | 884 | 1,964 | 2,310 | 2,599 | 884 | 1,964 | 2,310 | 2,599 |
| 5,800 | 5,850 | 891 | 1,981 | 2,330 | 2,621 | 891 | 1,981 | 2,330 | 2,621 |
| 5,850 | 5,900 | 899 | 1,998 | 2,350 | 2,644 | 899 | 1,998 | 2,350 | 2,644 |
| 5,900 | 5,950 | 907 | 2,015 | 2,370 | 2,666 | 907 | 2,015 | 2,370 | 2,666 |
| 5,950 | 6,000 | 914 | 2,032 | 2,390 | 2,689 | 914 | 2,032 | 2,390 | 2,689 |
| 6,000 | 6,050 | 922 | 2,049 | 2,410 | 2,711 | 922 | 2,049 | 2,410 | 2,711 |
| 6,050 | 6,100 | 929 | 2,066 | 2,430 | 2,734 | 929 | 2,066 | 2,430 | 2,734 |
| 6,100 | 6,150 | 937 | 2,083 | 2,450 | 2,756 | 937 | 2,083 | 2,450 | 2,756 |
| 6,150 | 6,200 | 945 | 2,100 | 2,470 | 2,779 | 945 | 2,100 | 2,470 | 2,779 |
| 6,200 | 6,250 | 952 | 2,117 | 2,490 | 2,801 | 952 | 2,117 | 2,490 | 2,801 |
| 6,250 | 6,300 | 960 | 2,134 | 2,510 | 2,824 | 960 | 2,134 | 2,510 | 2,824 |
| 6,300 | 6,350 | 968 | 2,151 | 2,530 | 2,846 | 968 | 2,151 | 2,530 | 2,846 |
| 6,350 | 6,400 | 975 | 2,168 | 2,550 | 2,869 | 975 | 2,168 | 2,550 | 2,869 |
| 6,400 | 6,450 | 983 | 2,185 | 2,570 | 2,891 | 983 | 2,185 | 2,570 | 2,891 |
| 6,450 | 6,500 | 991 | 2,202 | 2,590 | 2,914 | 991 | 2,202 | 2,590 | 2,914 |
| 6,500 | 6,550 | 998 | 2,219 | 2,610 | 2,936 | 998 | 2,219 | 2,610 | 2,936 |
| 6,550 | 6,600 | 1,006 | 2,236 | 2,630 | 2,959 | 1,006 | 2,236 | 2,630 | 2,959 |
| 6,600 | 6,650 | 1,014 | 2,253 | 2,650 | 2,981 | 1,014 | 2,253 | 2,650 | 2,981 |
| 6,650 | 6,700 | 1,021 | 2,270 | 2,670 | 3,004 | 1,021 | 2,270 | 2,670 | 3,004 |
| 6,700 | 6,750 | 1,029 | 2,287 | 2,690 | 3,026 | 1,029 | 2,287 | 2,690 | 3,026 |
| 6,750 | 6,800 | 1,037 | 2,304 | 2,710 | 3,049 | 1,037 | 2,304 | 2,710 | 3,049 |
| 6,800 | 6,850 | 1,044 | 2,321 | 2,730 | 3,071 | 1,044 | 2,321 | 2,730 | 3,071 |
| 6,850 | 6,900 | 1,052 | 2,338 | 2,750 | 3,094 | 1,052 | 2,338 | 2,750 | 3,094 |
| 6,900 | 6,950 | 1,060 | 2,355 | 2,770 | 3,116 | 1,060 | 2,355 | 2,770 | 3,116 |
| 6,950 | 7,000 | 1,067 | 2,372 | 2,790 | 3,139 | 1,067 | 2,372 | 2,790 | 3,139 |
| 7,000 | 7,050 | 1,075 | 2,389 | 2,810 | 3,161 | 1,075 | 2,389 | 2,810 | 3,161 |
| 7,050 | 7,100 | 1,082 | 2,406 | 2,830 | 3,184 | 1,082 | 2,406 | 2,830 | 3,184 |
| 7,100 | 7,150 | 1,090 | 2,423 | 2,850 | 3,206 | 1,090 | 2,423 | 2,850 | 3,206 |
| 7,150 | 7,200 | 1,098 | 2,440 | 2,870 | 3,229 | 1,098 | 2,440 | 2,870 | 3,229 |
| 7,200 | 7,250 | 1,105 | 2,457 | 2,890 | 3,251 | 1,105 | 2,457 | 2,890 | 3,251 |
| 7,250 | 7,300 | 1,113 | 2,474 | 2,910 | 3,274 | 1,113 | 2,474 | 2,910 | 3,274 |
| 7,300 | 7,350 | 1,121 | 2,491 | 2,930 | 3,296 | 1,121 | 2,491 | 2,930 | 3,296 |
| 7,350 | 7,400 | 1,128 | 2,508 | 2,950 | 3,319 | 1,128 | 2,508 | 2,950 | 3,319 |
| 7,400 | 7,450 | 1,136 | 2,525 | 2,970 | 3,341 | 1,136 | 2,525 | 2,970 | 3,341 |
| 7,450 | 7,500 | 1,144 | 2,542 | 2,990 | 3,364 | 1,144 | 2,542 | 2,990 | 3,364 |
| 7,500 | 7,550 | 1,151 | 2,559 | 3,010 | 3,386 | 1,151 | 2,559 | 3,010 | 3,386 |
| 7,550 | 7,600 | 1,159 | 2,576 | 3,030 | 3,409 | 1,159 | 2,576 | 3,030 | 3,409 |
| 7,600 | 7,650 | 1,167 | 2,593 | 3,050 | 3,431 | 1,167 | 2,593 | 3,050 | 3,431 |
| 7,650 | 7,700 | 1,174 | 2,610 | 3,070 | 3,454 | 1,174 | 2,610 | 3,070 | 3,454 |
| 7,700 | 7,750 | 1,182 | 2,627 | 3,090 | 3,476 | 1,182 | 2,627 | 3,090 | 3,476 |
| 7,750 | 7,800 | 1,190 | 2,644 | 3,110 | 3,499 | 1,190 | 2,644 | 3,110 | 3,499 |
| 7,800 | 7,850 | 1,197 | 2,661 | 3,130 | 3,521 | 1,197 | 2,661 | 3,130 | 3,521 |
| 7,850 | 7,900 | 1,205 | 2,678 | 3,150 | 3,544 | 1,205 | 2,678 | 3,150 | 3,544 |
| 7,900 | 7,950 | 1,213 | 2,695 | 3,170 | 3,566 | 1,213 | 2,695 | 3,170 | 3,566 |
| 7,950 | 8,000 | 1,220 | 2,712 | 3,190 | 3,589 | 1,220 | 2,712 | 3,190 | 3,589 |
| 8,000 | 8,050 | 1,228 | 2,729 | 3,210 | 3,611 | 1,228 | 2,729 | 3,210 | 3,611 |
| 8,050 | 8,100 | 1,235 | 2,746 | 3,230 | 3,634 | 1,235 | 2,746 | 3,230 | 3,634 |
| 8,100 | 8,150 | 1,243 | 2,763 | 3,250 | 3,656 | 1,243 | 2,763 | 3,250 | 3,656 |
| 8,150 | 8,200 | 1,251 | 2,780 | 3,270 | 3,679 | 1,251 | 2,780 | 3,270 | 3,679 |
| 8,200 | 8,250 | 1,258 | 2,797 | 3,290 | 3,701 | 1,258 | 2,797 | 3,290 | 3,701 |
| 8,250 | 8,300 | 1,266 | 2,814 | 3,310 | 3,724 | 1,266 | 2,814 | 3,310 | 3,724 |
| 8,300 | 8,350 | 1,274 | 2,831 | 3,330 | 3,746 | 1,274 | 2,831 | 3,330 | 3,746 |
| 8,350 | 8,400 | 1,281 | 2,848 | 3,350 | 3,769 | 1,281 | 2,848 | 3,350 | 3,769 |
| 8,400 | 8,450 | 1,289 | 2,865 | 3,370 | 3,791 | 1,289 | 2,865 | 3,370 | 3,791 |
| 8,450 | 8,500 | 1,297 | 2,882 | 3,390 | 3,814 | 1,297 | 2,882 | 3,390 | 3,814 |
| 8,500 | 8,550 | 1,304 | 2,899 | 3,410 | 3,836 | 1,304 | 2,899 | 3,410 | 3,836 |
| 8,550 | 8,600 | 1,312 | 2,916 | 3,430 | 3,859 | 1,312 | 2,916 | 3,430 | 3,859 |
| 8,600 | 8,650 | 1,320 | 2,933 | 3,450 | 3,881 | 1,320 | 2,933 | 3,450 | 3,881 |
| 8,650 | 8,700 | 1,327 | 2,950 | 3,470 | 3,904 | 1,327 | 2,950 | 3,470 | 3,904 |
| 8,700 | 8,750 | 1,335 | 2,967 | 3,490 | 3,926 | 1,335 | 2,967 | 3,490 | 3,926 |
| 8,750 | 8,800 | 1,343 | 2,984 | 3,510 | 3,949 | 1,343 | 2,984 | 3,510 | 3,949 |

| If the amount you are looking up from the worksheet is— | | Single, head of household, or qualifying widow(er)★ and you have— | | | | Married filing jointly and you have— | | | |
|---|---|---|---|---|---|---|---|---|---|
| At least | But less than | 0 | 1 | 2 | 3 | 0 | 1 | 2 | 3 |
| | | Your credit is— | | | | Your credit is— | | | |
| 8,800 | 8,850 | 1,350 | 3,001 | 3,530 | 3,971 | 1,350 | 3,001 | 3,530 | 3,971 |
| 8,850 | 8,900 | 1,358 | 3,018 | 3,550 | 3,994 | 1,358 | 3,018 | 3,550 | 3,994 |
| 8,900 | 8,950 | 1,366 | 3,035 | 3,570 | 4,016 | 1,366 | 3,035 | 3,570 | 4,016 |
| 8,950 | 9,000 | 1,373 | 3,052 | 3,590 | 4,039 | 1,373 | 3,052 | 3,590 | 4,039 |
| 9,000 | 9,050 | 1,381 | 3,069 | 3,610 | 4,061 | 1,381 | 3,069 | 3,610 | 4,061 |
| 9,050 | 9,100 | 1,388 | 3,086 | 3,630 | 4,084 | 1,388 | 3,086 | 3,630 | 4,084 |
| 9,100 | 9,150 | 1,396 | 3,103 | 3,650 | 4,106 | 1,396 | 3,103 | 3,650 | 4,106 |
| 9,150 | 9,200 | 1,404 | 3,120 | 3,670 | 4,129 | 1,404 | 3,120 | 3,670 | 4,129 |
| 9,200 | 9,250 | 1,411 | 3,137 | 3,690 | 4,151 | 1,411 | 3,137 | 3,690 | 4,151 |
| 9,250 | 9,300 | 1,419 | 3,154 | 3,710 | 4,174 | 1,419 | 3,154 | 3,710 | 4,174 |
| 9,300 | 9,350 | 1,427 | 3,171 | 3,730 | 4,196 | 1,427 | 3,171 | 3,730 | 4,196 |
| 9,350 | 9,400 | 1,434 | 3,188 | 3,750 | 4,219 | 1,434 | 3,188 | 3,750 | 4,219 |
| 9,400 | 9,450 | 1,442 | 3,205 | 3,770 | 4,241 | 1,442 | 3,205 | 3,770 | 4,241 |
| 9,450 | 9,500 | 1,450 | 3,222 | 3,790 | 4,264 | 1,450 | 3,222 | 3,790 | 4,264 |
| 9,500 | 9,550 | 1,457 | 3,239 | 3,810 | 4,286 | 1,457 | 3,239 | 3,810 | 4,286 |
| 9,550 | 9,600 | 1,465 | 3,256 | 3,830 | 4,309 | 1,465 | 3,256 | 3,830 | 4,309 |
| 9,600 | 9,650 | 1,473 | 3,273 | 3,850 | 4,331 | 1,473 | 3,273 | 3,850 | 4,331 |
| 9,650 | 9,700 | 1,480 | 3,290 | 3,870 | 4,354 | 1,480 | 3,290 | 3,870 | 4,354 |
| 9,700 | 9,750 | 1,488 | 3,307 | 3,890 | 4,376 | 1,488 | 3,307 | 3,890 | 4,376 |
| 9,750 | 9,800 | 1,496 | 3,324 | 3,910 | 4,399 | 1,496 | 3,324 | 3,910 | 4,399 |
| 9,800 | 9,850 | 1,502 | 3,341 | 3,930 | 4,421 | 1,502 | 3,341 | 3,930 | 4,421 |
| 9,850 | 9,900 | 1,502 | 3,358 | 3,950 | 4,444 | 1,502 | 3,358 | 3,950 | 4,444 |
| 9,900 | 9,950 | 1,502 | 3,375 | 3,970 | 4,466 | 1,502 | 3,375 | 3,970 | 4,466 |
| 9,950 | 10,000 | 1,502 | 3,392 | 3,990 | 4,489 | 1,502 | 3,392 | 3,990 | 4,489 |
| 10,000 | 10,050 | 1,502 | 3,409 | 4,010 | 4,511 | 1,502 | 3,409 | 4,010 | 4,511 |
| 10,050 | 10,100 | 1,502 | 3,426 | 4,030 | 4,534 | 1,502 | 3,426 | 4,030 | 4,534 |
| 10,100 | 10,150 | 1,502 | 3,443 | 4,050 | 4,556 | 1,502 | 3,443 | 4,050 | 4,556 |
| 10,150 | 10,200 | 1,502 | 3,460 | 4,070 | 4,579 | 1,502 | 3,460 | 4,070 | 4,579 |
| 10,200 | 10,250 | 1,502 | 3,477 | 4,090 | 4,601 | 1,502 | 3,477 | 4,090 | 4,601 |
| 10,250 | 10,300 | 1,502 | 3,494 | 4,110 | 4,624 | 1,502 | 3,494 | 4,110 | 4,624 |
| 10,300 | 10,350 | 1,502 | 3,511 | 4,130 | 4,646 | 1,502 | 3,511 | 4,130 | 4,646 |
| 10,350 | 10,400 | 1,502 | 3,528 | 4,150 | 4,669 | 1,502 | 3,528 | 4,150 | 4,669 |
| 10,400 | 10,450 | 1,502 | 3,545 | 4,170 | 4,691 | 1,502 | 3,545 | 4,170 | 4,691 |
| 10,450 | 10,500 | 1,502 | 3,562 | 4,190 | 4,714 | 1,502 | 3,562 | 4,190 | 4,714 |
| 10,500 | 10,550 | 1,502 | 3,579 | 4,210 | 4,736 | 1,502 | 3,579 | 4,210 | 4,736 |
| 10,550 | 10,600 | 1,502 | 3,596 | 4,230 | 4,759 | 1,502 | 3,596 | 4,230 | 4,759 |
| 10,600 | 10,650 | 1,502 | 3,618 | 4,250 | 4,781 | 1,502 | 3,618 | 4,250 | 4,781 |
| 10,650 | 10,700 | 1,502 | 3,618 | 4,270 | 4,804 | 1,502 | 3,618 | 4,270 | 4,804 |
| 10,700 | 10,750 | 1,502 | 3,618 | 4,290 | 4,826 | 1,502 | 3,618 | 4,290 | 4,826 |
| 10,750 | 10,800 | 1,502 | 3,618 | 4,310 | 4,849 | 1,502 | 3,618 | 4,310 | 4,849 |
| 10,800 | 10,850 | 1,502 | 3,618 | 4,330 | 4,871 | 1,502 | 3,618 | 4,330 | 4,871 |
| 10,850 | 10,900 | 1,502 | 3,618 | 4,350 | 4,894 | 1,502 | 3,618 | 4,350 | 4,894 |
| 10,900 | 10,950 | 1,502 | 3,618 | 4,370 | 4,916 | 1,502 | 3,618 | 4,370 | 4,916 |
| 10,950 | 11,000 | 1,502 | 3,618 | 4,390 | 4,939 | 1,502 | 3,618 | 4,390 | 4,939 |
| 11,000 | 11,050 | 1,502 | 3,618 | 4,410 | 4,961 | 1,502 | 3,618 | 4,410 | 4,961 |
| 11,050 | 11,100 | 1,502 | 3,618 | 4,430 | 4,984 | 1,502 | 3,618 | 4,430 | 4,984 |
| 11,100 | 11,150 | 1,502 | 3,618 | 4,450 | 5,006 | 1,502 | 3,618 | 4,450 | 5,006 |
| 11,150 | 11,200 | 1,502 | 3,618 | 4,470 | 5,029 | 1,502 | 3,618 | 4,470 | 5,029 |
| 11,200 | 11,250 | 1,502 | 3,618 | 4,490 | 5,051 | 1,502 | 3,618 | 4,490 | 5,051 |
| 11,250 | 11,300 | 1,502 | 3,618 | 4,510 | 5,074 | 1,502 | 3,618 | 4,510 | 5,074 |
| 11,300 | 11,350 | 1,502 | 3,618 | 4,530 | 5,096 | 1,502 | 3,618 | 4,530 | 5,096 |
| 11,350 | 11,400 | 1,502 | 3,618 | 4,550 | 5,119 | 1,502 | 3,618 | 4,550 | 5,119 |
| 11,400 | 11,450 | 1,502 | 3,618 | 4,570 | 5,141 | 1,502 | 3,618 | 4,570 | 5,141 |
| 11,450 | 11,500 | 1,502 | 3,618 | 4,590 | 5,164 | 1,502 | 3,618 | 4,590 | 5,164 |
| 11,500 | 11,550 | 1,502 | 3,618 | 4,610 | 5,186 | 1,502 | 3,618 | 4,610 | 5,186 |
| 11,550 | 11,600 | 1,502 | 3,618 | 4,630 | 5,209 | 1,502 | 3,618 | 4,630 | 5,209 |
| 11,600 | 11,650 | 1,502 | 3,618 | 4,650 | 5,231 | 1,502 | 3,618 | 4,650 | 5,231 |
| 11,650 | 11,700 | 1,493 | 3,618 | 4,670 | 5,254 | 1,502 | 3,618 | 4,670 | 5,254 |
| 11,700 | 11,750 | 1,485 | 3,618 | 4,690 | 5,276 | 1,502 | 3,618 | 4,690 | 5,276 |
| 11,750 | 11,800 | 1,477 | 3,618 | 4,710 | 5,299 | 1,502 | 3,618 | 4,710 | 5,299 |
| 11,800 | 11,850 | 1,470 | 3,618 | 4,730 | 5,321 | 1,502 | 3,618 | 4,730 | 5,321 |
| 11,850 | 11,900 | 1,462 | 3,618 | 4,750 | 5,344 | 1,502 | 3,618 | 4,750 | 5,344 |
| 11,900 | 11,950 | 1,454 | 3,618 | 4,770 | 5,366 | 1,502 | 3,618 | 4,770 | 5,366 |
| 11,950 | 12,000 | 1,447 | 3,618 | 4,790 | 5,389 | 1,502 | 3,618 | 4,790 | 5,389 |

★ Use this column if your filing status is married filing separately and you qualify to claim the EIC. See the instructions for line 27a.

*(Continued)*

**Earned Income Credit (EIC) Table** - *Continued*      (**Caution.** This is **not** a tax table.)

| If the amount you are looking up from the worksheet is— | | Single, head of household, or qualifying widow(er)★ and you have— | | | | Married filing jointly and you have— | | | |
|---|---|---|---|---|---|---|---|---|---|
| At least | But less than | 0 | 1 | 2 | 3 | 0 | 1 | 2 | 3 |
| | | Your credit is— | | | | Your credit is— | | | |
| 12,000 | 12,050 | 1,439 | 3,618 | 4,810 | 5,411 | 1,502 | 3,618 | 4,810 | 5,411 |
| 12,050 | 12,100 | 1,431 | 3,618 | 4,830 | 5,434 | 1,502 | 3,618 | 4,830 | 5,434 |
| 12,100 | 12,150 | 1,424 | 3,618 | 4,850 | 5,456 | 1,502 | 3,618 | 4,850 | 5,456 |
| 12,150 | 12,200 | 1,416 | 3,618 | 4,870 | 5,479 | 1,502 | 3,618 | 4,870 | 5,479 |
| 12,200 | 12,250 | 1,408 | 3,618 | 4,890 | 5,501 | 1,502 | 3,618 | 4,890 | 5,501 |
| 12,250 | 12,300 | 1,401 | 3,618 | 4,910 | 5,524 | 1,502 | 3,618 | 4,910 | 5,524 |
| 12,300 | 12,350 | 1,393 | 3,618 | 4,930 | 5,546 | 1,502 | 3,618 | 4,930 | 5,546 |
| 12,350 | 12,400 | 1,385 | 3,618 | 4,950 | 5,569 | 1,502 | 3,618 | 4,950 | 5,569 |
| 12,400 | 12,450 | 1,378 | 3,618 | 4,970 | 5,591 | 1,502 | 3,618 | 4,970 | 5,591 |
| 12,450 | 12,500 | 1,370 | 3,618 | 4,990 | 5,614 | 1,502 | 3,618 | 4,990 | 5,614 |
| 12,500 | 12,550 | 1,362 | 3,618 | 5,010 | 5,636 | 1,502 | 3,618 | 5,010 | 5,636 |
| 12,550 | 12,600 | 1,355 | 3,618 | 5,030 | 5,659 | 1,502 | 3,618 | 5,030 | 5,659 |
| 12,600 | 12,650 | 1,347 | 3,618 | 5,050 | 5,681 | 1,502 | 3,618 | 5,050 | 5,681 |
| 12,650 | 12,700 | 1,340 | 3,618 | 5,070 | 5,704 | 1,502 | 3,618 | 5,070 | 5,704 |
| 12,700 | 12,750 | 1,332 | 3,618 | 5,090 | 5,726 | 1,502 | 3,618 | 5,090 | 5,726 |
| 12,750 | 12,800 | 1,324 | 3,618 | 5,110 | 5,749 | 1,502 | 3,618 | 5,110 | 5,749 |
| 12,800 | 12,850 | 1,317 | 3,618 | 5,130 | 5,771 | 1,502 | 3,618 | 5,130 | 5,771 |
| 12,850 | 12,900 | 1,309 | 3,618 | 5,150 | 5,794 | 1,502 | 3,618 | 5,150 | 5,794 |
| 12,900 | 12,950 | 1,301 | 3,618 | 5,170 | 5,816 | 1,502 | 3,618 | 5,170 | 5,816 |
| 12,950 | 13,000 | 1,294 | 3,618 | 5,190 | 5,839 | 1,502 | 3,618 | 5,190 | 5,839 |
| 13,000 | 13,050 | 1,286 | 3,618 | 5,210 | 5,861 | 1,502 | 3,618 | 5,210 | 5,861 |
| 13,050 | 13,100 | 1,278 | 3,618 | 5,230 | 5,884 | 1,502 | 3,618 | 5,230 | 5,884 |
| 13,100 | 13,150 | 1,271 | 3,618 | 5,250 | 5,906 | 1,502 | 3,618 | 5,250 | 5,906 |
| 13,150 | 13,200 | 1,263 | 3,618 | 5,270 | 5,929 | 1,502 | 3,618 | 5,270 | 5,929 |
| 13,200 | 13,250 | 1,255 | 3,618 | 5,290 | 5,951 | 1,502 | 3,618 | 5,290 | 5,951 |
| 13,250 | 13,300 | 1,248 | 3,618 | 5,310 | 5,974 | 1,502 | 3,618 | 5,310 | 5,974 |
| 13,300 | 13,350 | 1,240 | 3,618 | 5,330 | 5,996 | 1,502 | 3,618 | 5,330 | 5,996 |
| 13,350 | 13,400 | 1,232 | 3,618 | 5,350 | 6,019 | 1,502 | 3,618 | 5,350 | 6,019 |
| 13,400 | 13,450 | 1,225 | 3,618 | 5,370 | 6,041 | 1,502 | 3,618 | 5,370 | 6,041 |
| 13,450 | 13,500 | 1,217 | 3,618 | 5,390 | 6,064 | 1,502 | 3,618 | 5,390 | 6,064 |
| 13,500 | 13,550 | 1,209 | 3,618 | 5,410 | 6,086 | 1,502 | 3,618 | 5,410 | 6,086 |
| 13,550 | 13,600 | 1,202 | 3,618 | 5,430 | 6,109 | 1,502 | 3,618 | 5,430 | 6,109 |
| 13,600 | 13,650 | 1,194 | 3,618 | 5,450 | 6,131 | 1,502 | 3,618 | 5,450 | 6,131 |
| 13,650 | 13,700 | 1,187 | 3,618 | 5,470 | 6,154 | 1,502 | 3,618 | 5,470 | 6,154 |
| 13,700 | 13,750 | 1,179 | 3,618 | 5,490 | 6,176 | 1,502 | 3,618 | 5,490 | 6,176 |
| 13,750 | 13,800 | 1,171 | 3,618 | 5,510 | 6,199 | 1,502 | 3,618 | 5,510 | 6,199 |
| 13,800 | 13,850 | 1,164 | 3,618 | 5,530 | 6,221 | 1,502 | 3,618 | 5,530 | 6,221 |
| 13,850 | 13,900 | 1,156 | 3,618 | 5,550 | 6,244 | 1,502 | 3,618 | 5,550 | 6,244 |
| 13,900 | 13,950 | 1,148 | 3,618 | 5,570 | 6,266 | 1,502 | 3,618 | 5,570 | 6,266 |
| 13,950 | 14,000 | 1,141 | 3,618 | 5,590 | 6,289 | 1,502 | 3,618 | 5,590 | 6,289 |
| 14,000 | 14,050 | 1,133 | 3,618 | 5,610 | 6,311 | 1,502 | 3,618 | 5,610 | 6,311 |
| 14,050 | 14,100 | 1,125 | 3,618 | 5,630 | 6,334 | 1,502 | 3,618 | 5,630 | 6,334 |
| 14,100 | 14,150 | 1,118 | 3,618 | 5,650 | 6,356 | 1,502 | 3,618 | 5,650 | 6,356 |
| 14,150 | 14,200 | 1,110 | 3,618 | 5,670 | 6,379 | 1,502 | 3,618 | 5,670 | 6,379 |
| 14,200 | 14,250 | 1,102 | 3,618 | 5,690 | 6,401 | 1,502 | 3,618 | 5,690 | 6,401 |
| 14,250 | 14,300 | 1,095 | 3,618 | 5,710 | 6,424 | 1,502 | 3,618 | 5,710 | 6,424 |
| 14,300 | 14,350 | 1,087 | 3,618 | 5,730 | 6,446 | 1,502 | 3,618 | 5,730 | 6,446 |
| 14,350 | 14,400 | 1,079 | 3,618 | 5,750 | 6,469 | 1,502 | 3,618 | 5,750 | 6,469 |
| 14,400 | 14,450 | 1,072 | 3,618 | 5,770 | 6,491 | 1,502 | 3,618 | 5,770 | 6,491 |
| 14,450 | 14,500 | 1,064 | 3,618 | 5,790 | 6,514 | 1,502 | 3,618 | 5,790 | 6,514 |
| 14,500 | 14,550 | 1,056 | 3,618 | 5,810 | 6,536 | 1,502 | 3,618 | 5,810 | 6,536 |
| 14,550 | 14,600 | 1,049 | 3,618 | 5,830 | 6,559 | 1,502 | 3,618 | 5,830 | 6,559 |
| 14,600 | 14,650 | 1,041 | 3,618 | 5,850 | 6,581 | 1,502 | 3,618 | 5,850 | 6,581 |
| 14,650 | 14,700 | 1,034 | 3,618 | 5,870 | 6,604 | 1,502 | 3,618 | 5,870 | 6,604 |
| 14,700 | 14,750 | 1,026 | 3,618 | 5,890 | 6,626 | 1,502 | 3,618 | 5,890 | 6,626 |
| 14,750 | 14,800 | 1,018 | 3,618 | 5,910 | 6,649 | 1,502 | 3,618 | 5,910 | 6,649 |
| 14,800 | 14,850 | 1,011 | 3,618 | 5,930 | 6,671 | 1,502 | 3,618 | 5,930 | 6,671 |
| 14,850 | 14,900 | 1,003 | 3,618 | 5,950 | 6,694 | 1,502 | 3,618 | 5,950 | 6,694 |
| 14,900 | 14,950 | 995 | 3,618 | 5,970 | 6,716 | 1,502 | 3,618 | 5,970 | 6,716 |
| 14,950 | 15,000 | 988 | 3,618 | 5,980 | 6,728 | 1,502 | 3,618 | 5,980 | 6,728 |
| 15,000 | 15,050 | 980 | 3,618 | 5,980 | 6,728 | 1,502 | 3,618 | 5,980 | 6,728 |
| 15,050 | 15,100 | 972 | 3,618 | 5,980 | 6,728 | 1,502 | 3,618 | 5,980 | 6,728 |
| 15,100 | 15,150 | 965 | 3,618 | 5,980 | 6,728 | 1,502 | 3,618 | 5,980 | 6,728 |
| 15,150 | 15,200 | 957 | 3,618 | 5,980 | 6,728 | 1,502 | 3,618 | 5,980 | 6,728 |
| 15,200 | 15,250 | 949 | 3,618 | 5,980 | 6,728 | 1,502 | 3,618 | 5,980 | 6,728 |
| 15,250 | 15,300 | 942 | 3,618 | 5,980 | 6,728 | 1,502 | 3,618 | 5,980 | 6,728 |
| 15,300 | 15,350 | 934 | 3,618 | 5,980 | 6,728 | 1,502 | 3,618 | 5,980 | 6,728 |
| 15,350 | 15,400 | 926 | 3,618 | 5,980 | 6,728 | 1,502 | 3,618 | 5,980 | 6,728 |
| 15,400 | 15,450 | 919 | 3,618 | 5,980 | 6,728 | 1,502 | 3,618 | 5,980 | 6,728 |
| 15,450 | 15,500 | 911 | 3,618 | 5,980 | 6,728 | 1,502 | 3,618 | 5,980 | 6,728 |
| 15,500 | 15,550 | 903 | 3,618 | 5,980 | 6,728 | 1,502 | 3,618 | 5,980 | 6,728 |
| 15,550 | 15,600 | 896 | 3,618 | 5,980 | 6,728 | 1,502 | 3,618 | 5,980 | 6,728 |
| 15,600 | 15,650 | 888 | 3,618 | 5,980 | 6,728 | 1,502 | 3,618 | 5,980 | 6,728 |
| 15,650 | 15,700 | 881 | 3,618 | 5,980 | 6,728 | 1,502 | 3,618 | 5,980 | 6,728 |
| 15,700 | 15,750 | 873 | 3,618 | 5,980 | 6,728 | 1,502 | 3,618 | 5,980 | 6,728 |
| 15,750 | 15,800 | 865 | 3,618 | 5,980 | 6,728 | 1,502 | 3,618 | 5,980 | 6,728 |
| 15,800 | 15,850 | 858 | 3,618 | 5,980 | 6,728 | 1,502 | 3,618 | 5,980 | 6,728 |
| 15,850 | 15,900 | 850 | 3,618 | 5,980 | 6,728 | 1,502 | 3,618 | 5,980 | 6,728 |
| 15,900 | 15,950 | 842 | 3,618 | 5,980 | 6,728 | 1,502 | 3,618 | 5,980 | 6,728 |
| 15,950 | 16,000 | 835 | 3,618 | 5,980 | 6,728 | 1,502 | 3,618 | 5,980 | 6,728 |
| 16,000 | 16,050 | 827 | 3,618 | 5,980 | 6,728 | 1,502 | 3,618 | 5,980 | 6,728 |
| 16,050 | 16,100 | 819 | 3,618 | 5,980 | 6,728 | 1,502 | 3,618 | 5,980 | 6,728 |
| 16,100 | 16,150 | 812 | 3,618 | 5,980 | 6,728 | 1,502 | 3,618 | 5,980 | 6,728 |
| 16,150 | 16,200 | 804 | 3,618 | 5,980 | 6,728 | 1,502 | 3,618 | 5,980 | 6,728 |
| 16,200 | 16,250 | 796 | 3,618 | 5,980 | 6,728 | 1,502 | 3,618 | 5,980 | 6,728 |
| 16,250 | 16,300 | 789 | 3,618 | 5,980 | 6,728 | 1,502 | 3,618 | 5,980 | 6,728 |
| 16,300 | 16,350 | 781 | 3,618 | 5,980 | 6,728 | 1,502 | 3,618 | 5,980 | 6,728 |
| 16,350 | 16,400 | 773 | 3,618 | 5,980 | 6,728 | 1,502 | 3,618 | 5,980 | 6,728 |
| 16,400 | 16,450 | 766 | 3,618 | 5,980 | 6,728 | 1,502 | 3,618 | 5,980 | 6,728 |
| 16,450 | 16,500 | 758 | 3,618 | 5,980 | 6,728 | 1,502 | 3,618 | 5,980 | 6,728 |
| 16,500 | 16,550 | 750 | 3,618 | 5,980 | 6,728 | 1,502 | 3,618 | 5,980 | 6,728 |
| 16,550 | 16,600 | 743 | 3,618 | 5,980 | 6,728 | 1,502 | 3,618 | 5,980 | 6,728 |
| 16,600 | 16,650 | 735 | 3,618 | 5,980 | 6,728 | 1,502 | 3,618 | 5,980 | 6,728 |
| 16,650 | 16,700 | 728 | 3,618 | 5,980 | 6,728 | 1,502 | 3,618 | 5,980 | 6,728 |
| 16,700 | 16,750 | 720 | 3,618 | 5,980 | 6,728 | 1,502 | 3,618 | 5,980 | 6,728 |
| 16,750 | 16,800 | 712 | 3,618 | 5,980 | 6,728 | 1,502 | 3,618 | 5,980 | 6,728 |
| 16,800 | 16,850 | 705 | 3,618 | 5,980 | 6,728 | 1,502 | 3,618 | 5,980 | 6,728 |
| 16,850 | 16,900 | 697 | 3,618 | 5,980 | 6,728 | 1,502 | 3,618 | 5,980 | 6,728 |
| 16,900 | 16,950 | 689 | 3,618 | 5,980 | 6,728 | 1,502 | 3,618 | 5,980 | 6,728 |
| 16,950 | 17,000 | 682 | 3,618 | 5,980 | 6,728 | 1,502 | 3,618 | 5,980 | 6,728 |
| 17,000 | 17,050 | 674 | 3,618 | 5,980 | 6,728 | 1,502 | 3,618 | 5,980 | 6,728 |
| 17,050 | 17,100 | 666 | 3,618 | 5,980 | 6,728 | 1,502 | 3,618 | 5,980 | 6,728 |
| 17,100 | 17,150 | 659 | 3,618 | 5,980 | 6,728 | 1,502 | 3,618 | 5,980 | 6,728 |
| 17,150 | 17,200 | 651 | 3,618 | 5,980 | 6,728 | 1,502 | 3,618 | 5,980 | 6,728 |
| 17,200 | 17,250 | 643 | 3,618 | 5,980 | 6,728 | 1,502 | 3,618 | 5,980 | 6,728 |
| 17,250 | 17,300 | 636 | 3,618 | 5,980 | 6,728 | 1,502 | 3,618 | 5,980 | 6,728 |
| 17,300 | 17,350 | 628 | 3,618 | 5,980 | 6,728 | 1,502 | 3,618 | 5,980 | 6,728 |
| 17,350 | 17,400 | 620 | 3,618 | 5,980 | 6,728 | 1,502 | 3,618 | 5,980 | 6,728 |
| 17,400 | 17,450 | 613 | 3,618 | 5,980 | 6,728 | 1,502 | 3,618 | 5,980 | 6,728 |
| 17,450 | 17,500 | 605 | 3,618 | 5,980 | 6,728 | 1,502 | 3,618 | 5,980 | 6,728 |
| 17,500 | 17,550 | 597 | 3,618 | 5,980 | 6,728 | 1,502 | 3,618 | 5,980 | 6,728 |
| 17,550 | 17,600 | 590 | 3,618 | 5,980 | 6,728 | 1,502 | 3,618 | 5,980 | 6,728 |
| 17,600 | 17,650 | 582 | 3,618 | 5,980 | 6,728 | 1,493 | 3,618 | 5,980 | 6,728 |
| 17,650 | 17,700 | 575 | 3,618 | 5,980 | 6,728 | 1,485 | 3,618 | 5,980 | 6,728 |
| 17,700 | 17,750 | 567 | 3,618 | 5,980 | 6,728 | 1,477 | 3,618 | 5,980 | 6,728 |
| 17,750 | 17,800 | 559 | 3,618 | 5,980 | 6,728 | 1,470 | 3,618 | 5,980 | 6,728 |
| 17,800 | 17,850 | 552 | 3,618 | 5,980 | 6,728 | 1,462 | 3,618 | 5,980 | 6,728 |
| 17,850 | 17,900 | 544 | 3,618 | 5,980 | 6,728 | 1,454 | 3,618 | 5,980 | 6,728 |
| 17,900 | 17,950 | 536 | 3,618 | 5,980 | 6,728 | 1,447 | 3,618 | 5,980 | 6,728 |
| 17,950 | 18,000 | 529 | 3,618 | 5,980 | 6,728 | 1,439 | 3,618 | 5,980 | 6,728 |
| 18,000 | 18,050 | 521 | 3,618 | 5,980 | 6,728 | 1,431 | 3,618 | 5,980 | 6,728 |
| 18,050 | 18,100 | 513 | 3,618 | 5,980 | 6,728 | 1,424 | 3,618 | 5,980 | 6,728 |
| 18,100 | 18,150 | 506 | 3,618 | 5,980 | 6,728 | 1,416 | 3,618 | 5,980 | 6,728 |
| 18,150 | 18,200 | 498 | 3,618 | 5,980 | 6,728 | 1,408 | 3,618 | 5,980 | 6,728 |
| 18,200 | 18,250 | 490 | 3,618 | 5,980 | 6,728 | 1,401 | 3,618 | 5,980 | 6,728 |
| 18,250 | 18,300 | 483 | 3,618 | 5,980 | 6,728 | 1,393 | 3,618 | 5,980 | 6,728 |
| 18,300 | 18,350 | 475 | 3,618 | 5,980 | 6,728 | 1,385 | 3,618 | 5,980 | 6,728 |
| 18,350 | 18,400 | 467 | 3,618 | 5,980 | 6,728 | 1,378 | 3,618 | 5,980 | 6,728 |

★  Use this column if your filing status is married filing separately and you qualify to claim the EIC. See the instructions for line 27a.

*(Continued)*

**Earned Income Credit (EIC) Table** - *Continued*     (**Caution.** This is **not** a tax table.)

| If the amount you are looking up from the worksheet is— | | Single, head of household, or qualifying widow(er)★ and you have— | | | | Married filing jointly and you have— | | | | If the amount you are looking up from the worksheet is— | | Single, head of household, or qualifying widow(er)★ and you have— | | | | Married filing jointly and you have— | | | |
|---|---|---|---|---|---|---|---|---|---|---|---|---|---|---|---|---|---|---|---|
| At least | But less than | 0 | 1 | 2 | 3 | 0 | 1 | 2 | 3 | At least | But less than | 0 | 1 | 2 | 3 | 0 | 1 | 2 | 3 |
| | | Your credit is— | | | | Your credit is— | | | | | | Your credit is— | | | | Your credit is— | | | |
| 18,400 | 18,450 | 460 | 3,618 | 5,980 | 6,728 | 1,370 | 3,618 | 5,980 | 6,728 | 21,600 | 21,650 | 0 | 3,281 | 5,537 | 6,284 | 881 | 3,618 | 5,980 | 6,728 |
| 18,450 | 18,500 | 452 | 3,618 | 5,980 | 6,728 | 1,362 | 3,618 | 5,980 | 6,728 | 21,650 | 21,700 | 0 | 3,273 | 5,526 | 6,274 | 873 | 3,618 | 5,980 | 6,728 |
| 18,500 | 18,550 | 444 | 3,618 | 5,980 | 6,728 | 1,355 | 3,618 | 5,980 | 6,728 | 21,700 | 21,750 | 0 | 3,265 | 5,516 | 6,263 | 865 | 3,618 | 5,980 | 6,728 |
| 18,550 | 18,600 | 437 | 3,618 | 5,980 | 6,728 | 1,347 | 3,618 | 5,980 | 6,728 | 21,750 | 21,800 | 0 | 3,257 | 5,505 | 6,253 | 858 | 3,618 | 5,980 | 6,728 |
| 18,600 | 18,650 | 429 | 3,618 | 5,980 | 6,728 | 1,340 | 3,618 | 5,980 | 6,728 | 21,800 | 21,850 | 0 | 3,249 | 5,495 | 6,242 | 850 | 3,618 | 5,980 | 6,728 |
| 18,650 | 18,700 | 422 | 3,618 | 5,980 | 6,728 | 1,332 | 3,618 | 5,980 | 6,728 | 21,850 | 21,900 | 0 | 3,241 | 5,484 | 6,232 | 842 | 3,618 | 5,980 | 6,728 |
| 18,700 | 18,750 | 414 | 3,618 | 5,980 | 6,728 | 1,324 | 3,618 | 5,980 | 6,728 | 21,900 | 21,950 | 0 | 3,233 | 5,474 | 6,221 | 835 | 3,618 | 5,980 | 6,728 |
| 18,750 | 18,800 | 406 | 3,618 | 5,980 | 6,728 | 1,317 | 3,618 | 5,980 | 6,728 | 21,950 | 22,000 | 0 | 3,225 | 5,463 | 6,210 | 827 | 3,618 | 5,980 | 6,728 |
| 18,800 | 18,850 | 399 | 3,618 | 5,980 | 6,728 | 1,309 | 3,618 | 5,980 | 6,728 | 22,000 | 22,050 | 0 | 3,217 | 5,452 | 6,200 | 819 | 3,618 | 5,980 | 6,728 |
| 18,850 | 18,900 | 391 | 3,618 | 5,980 | 6,728 | 1,301 | 3,618 | 5,980 | 6,728 | 22,050 | 22,100 | 0 | 3,209 | 5,442 | 6,189 | 812 | 3,618 | 5,980 | 6,728 |
| 18,900 | 18,950 | 383 | 3,618 | 5,980 | 6,728 | 1,294 | 3,618 | 5,980 | 6,728 | 22,100 | 22,150 | 0 | 3,201 | 5,431 | 6,179 | 804 | 3,618 | 5,980 | 6,728 |
| 18,950 | 19,000 | 376 | 3,618 | 5,980 | 6,728 | 1,286 | 3,618 | 5,980 | 6,728 | 22,150 | 22,200 | 0 | 3,193 | 5,421 | 6,168 | 796 | 3,618 | 5,980 | 6,728 |
| 19,000 | 19,050 | 368 | 3,618 | 5,980 | 6,728 | 1,278 | 3,618 | 5,980 | 6,728 | 22,200 | 22,250 | 0 | 3,185 | 5,410 | 6,158 | 789 | 3,618 | 5,980 | 6,728 |
| 19,050 | 19,100 | 360 | 3,618 | 5,980 | 6,728 | 1,271 | 3,618 | 5,980 | 6,728 | 22,250 | 22,300 | 0 | 3,177 | 5,400 | 6,147 | 781 | 3,618 | 5,980 | 6,728 |
| 19,100 | 19,150 | 353 | 3,618 | 5,980 | 6,728 | 1,263 | 3,618 | 5,980 | 6,728 | 22,300 | 22,350 | 0 | 3,169 | 5,389 | 6,137 | 773 | 3,618 | 5,980 | 6,728 |
| 19,150 | 19,200 | 345 | 3,618 | 5,980 | 6,728 | 1,255 | 3,618 | 5,980 | 6,728 | 22,350 | 22,400 | 0 | 3,161 | 5,379 | 6,126 | 766 | 3,618 | 5,980 | 6,728 |
| 19,200 | 19,250 | 337 | 3,618 | 5,980 | 6,728 | 1,248 | 3,618 | 5,980 | 6,728 | 22,400 | 22,450 | 0 | 3,153 | 5,368 | 6,116 | 758 | 3,618 | 5,980 | 6,728 |
| 19,250 | 19,300 | 330 | 3,618 | 5,980 | 6,728 | 1,240 | 3,618 | 5,980 | 6,728 | 22,450 | 22,500 | 0 | 3,145 | 5,358 | 6,105 | 750 | 3,618 | 5,980 | 6,728 |
| 19,300 | 19,350 | 322 | 3,618 | 5,980 | 6,728 | 1,232 | 3,618 | 5,980 | 6,728 | 22,500 | 22,550 | 0 | 3,137 | 5,347 | 6,095 | 743 | 3,618 | 5,980 | 6,728 |
| 19,350 | 19,400 | 314 | 3,618 | 5,980 | 6,728 | 1,225 | 3,618 | 5,980 | 6,728 | 22,550 | 22,600 | 0 | 3,129 | 5,337 | 6,084 | 735 | 3,618 | 5,980 | 6,728 |
| 19,400 | 19,450 | 307 | 3,618 | 5,980 | 6,728 | 1,217 | 3,618 | 5,980 | 6,728 | 22,600 | 22,650 | 0 | 3,121 | 5,326 | 6,074 | 728 | 3,618 | 5,980 | 6,728 |
| 19,450 | 19,500 | 299 | 3,618 | 5,980 | 6,728 | 1,209 | 3,618 | 5,980 | 6,728 | 22,650 | 22,700 | 0 | 3,113 | 5,316 | 6,063 | 720 | 3,618 | 5,980 | 6,728 |
| 19,500 | 19,550 | 291 | 3,618 | 5,980 | 6,728 | 1,202 | 3,618 | 5,980 | 6,728 | 22,700 | 22,750 | 0 | 3,105 | 5,305 | 6,053 | 712 | 3,618 | 5,980 | 6,728 |
| 19,550 | 19,600 | 284 | 3,609 | 5,968 | 6,716 | 1,194 | 3,618 | 5,980 | 6,728 | 22,750 | 22,800 | 0 | 3,097 | 5,294 | 6,042 | 705 | 3,618 | 5,980 | 6,728 |
| 19,600 | 19,650 | 276 | 3,601 | 5,958 | 6,705 | 1,187 | 3,618 | 5,980 | 6,728 | 22,800 | 22,850 | 0 | 3,089 | 5,284 | 6,031 | 697 | 3,618 | 5,980 | 6,728 |
| 19,650 | 19,700 | 269 | 3,593 | 5,947 | 6,695 | 1,179 | 3,618 | 5,980 | 6,728 | 22,850 | 22,900 | 0 | 3,081 | 5,273 | 6,021 | 689 | 3,618 | 5,980 | 6,728 |
| 19,700 | 19,750 | 261 | 3,585 | 5,937 | 6,684 | 1,171 | 3,618 | 5,980 | 6,728 | 22,900 | 22,950 | 0 | 3,073 | 5,263 | 6,010 | 682 | 3,618 | 5,980 | 6,728 |
| 19,750 | 19,800 | 253 | 3,577 | 5,926 | 6,674 | 1,164 | 3,618 | 5,980 | 6,728 | 22,950 | 23,000 | 0 | 3,065 | 5,252 | 6,000 | 674 | 3,618 | 5,980 | 6,728 |
| 19,800 | 19,850 | 246 | 3,569 | 5,916 | 6,663 | 1,156 | 3,618 | 5,980 | 6,728 | 23,000 | 23,050 | 0 | 3,058 | 5,242 | 5,989 | 666 | 3,618 | 5,980 | 6,728 |
| 19,850 | 19,900 | 238 | 3,561 | 5,905 | 6,653 | 1,148 | 3,618 | 5,980 | 6,728 | 23,050 | 23,100 | 0 | 3,050 | 5,231 | 5,979 | 659 | 3,618 | 5,980 | 6,728 |
| 19,900 | 19,950 | 230 | 3,553 | 5,895 | 6,642 | 1,141 | 3,618 | 5,980 | 6,728 | 23,100 | 23,150 | 0 | 3,042 | 5,221 | 5,968 | 651 | 3,618 | 5,980 | 6,728 |
| 19,950 | 20,000 | 223 | 3,545 | 5,884 | 6,632 | 1,133 | 3,618 | 5,980 | 6,728 | 23,150 | 23,200 | 0 | 3,034 | 5,210 | 5,958 | 643 | 3,618 | 5,980 | 6,728 |
| 20,000 | 20,050 | 215 | 3,537 | 5,874 | 6,621 | 1,125 | 3,618 | 5,980 | 6,728 | 23,200 | 23,250 | 0 | 3,026 | 5,200 | 5,947 | 636 | 3,618 | 5,980 | 6,728 |
| 20,050 | 20,100 | 207 | 3,529 | 5,863 | 6,611 | 1,118 | 3,618 | 5,980 | 6,728 | 23,250 | 23,300 | 0 | 3,018 | 5,189 | 5,937 | 628 | 3,618 | 5,980 | 6,728 |
| 20,100 | 20,150 | 200 | 3,521 | 5,853 | 6,600 | 1,110 | 3,618 | 5,980 | 6,728 | 23,300 | 23,350 | 0 | 3,010 | 5,179 | 5,926 | 620 | 3,618 | 5,980 | 6,728 |
| 20,150 | 20,200 | 192 | 3,513 | 5,842 | 6,590 | 1,102 | 3,618 | 5,980 | 6,728 | 23,350 | 23,400 | 0 | 3,002 | 5,168 | 5,916 | 613 | 3,618 | 5,980 | 6,728 |
| 20,200 | 20,250 | 184 | 3,505 | 5,832 | 6,579 | 1,095 | 3,618 | 5,980 | 6,728 | 23,400 | 23,450 | 0 | 2,994 | 5,158 | 5,905 | 605 | 3,618 | 5,980 | 6,728 |
| 20,250 | 20,300 | 177 | 3,497 | 5,821 | 6,568 | 1,087 | 3,618 | 5,980 | 6,728 | 23,450 | 23,500 | 0 | 2,986 | 5,147 | 5,895 | 597 | 3,618 | 5,980 | 6,728 |
| 20,300 | 20,350 | 169 | 3,489 | 5,810 | 6,558 | 1,079 | 3,618 | 5,980 | 6,728 | 23,500 | 23,550 | 0 | 2,978 | 5,137 | 5,884 | 590 | 3,618 | 5,980 | 6,728 |
| 20,350 | 20,400 | 161 | 3,481 | 5,800 | 6,547 | 1,072 | 3,618 | 5,980 | 6,728 | 23,550 | 23,600 | 0 | 2,970 | 5,126 | 5,874 | 582 | 3,618 | 5,980 | 6,728 |
| 20,400 | 20,450 | 154 | 3,473 | 5,789 | 6,537 | 1,064 | 3,618 | 5,980 | 6,728 | 23,600 | 23,650 | 0 | 2,962 | 5,115 | 5,863 | 575 | 3,618 | 5,980 | 6,728 |
| 20,450 | 20,500 | 146 | 3,465 | 5,779 | 6,526 | 1,056 | 3,618 | 5,980 | 6,728 | 23,650 | 23,700 | 0 | 2,954 | 5,105 | 5,852 | 567 | 3,618 | 5,980 | 6,728 |
| 20,500 | 20,550 | 138 | 3,457 | 5,768 | 6,516 | 1,049 | 3,618 | 5,980 | 6,728 | 23,700 | 23,750 | 0 | 2,946 | 5,094 | 5,842 | 559 | 3,618 | 5,980 | 6,728 |
| 20,550 | 20,600 | 131 | 3,449 | 5,758 | 6,505 | 1,041 | 3,618 | 5,980 | 6,728 | 23,750 | 23,800 | 0 | 2,938 | 5,084 | 5,831 | 552 | 3,618 | 5,980 | 6,728 |
| 20,600 | 20,650 | 123 | 3,441 | 5,747 | 6,495 | 1,034 | 3,618 | 5,980 | 6,728 | 23,800 | 23,850 | 0 | 2,930 | 5,073 | 5,821 | 544 | 3,618 | 5,980 | 6,728 |
| 20,650 | 20,700 | 116 | 3,433 | 5,737 | 6,484 | 1,026 | 3,618 | 5,980 | 6,728 | 23,850 | 23,900 | 0 | 2,922 | 5,063 | 5,810 | 536 | 3,618 | 5,980 | 6,728 |
| 20,700 | 20,750 | 108 | 3,425 | 5,726 | 6,474 | 1,018 | 3,618 | 5,980 | 6,728 | 23,900 | 23,950 | 0 | 2,914 | 5,052 | 5,800 | 529 | 3,618 | 5,980 | 6,728 |
| 20,750 | 20,800 | 100 | 3,417 | 5,716 | 6,463 | 1,011 | 3,618 | 5,980 | 6,728 | 23,950 | 24,000 | 0 | 2,906 | 5,042 | 5,789 | 521 | 3,618 | 5,980 | 6,728 |
| 20,800 | 20,850 | 93 | 3,409 | 5,705 | 6,453 | 1,003 | 3,618 | 5,980 | 6,728 | 24,000 | 24,050 | 0 | 2,898 | 5,031 | 5,779 | 513 | 3,618 | 5,980 | 6,728 |
| 20,850 | 20,900 | 85 | 3,401 | 5,695 | 6,442 | 995 | 3,618 | 5,980 | 6,728 | 24,050 | 24,100 | 0 | 2,890 | 5,021 | 5,768 | 506 | 3,618 | 5,980 | 6,728 |
| 20,900 | 20,950 | 77 | 3,393 | 5,684 | 6,432 | 988 | 3,618 | 5,980 | 6,728 | 24,100 | 24,150 | 0 | 2,882 | 5,010 | 5,758 | 498 | 3,618 | 5,980 | 6,728 |
| 20,950 | 21,000 | 70 | 3,385 | 5,674 | 6,421 | 980 | 3,618 | 5,980 | 6,728 | 24,150 | 24,200 | 0 | 2,874 | 5,000 | 5,747 | 490 | 3,618 | 5,980 | 6,728 |
| 21,000 | 21,050 | 62 | 3,377 | 5,663 | 6,411 | 972 | 3,618 | 5,980 | 6,728 | 24,200 | 24,250 | 0 | 2,866 | 4,989 | 5,737 | 483 | 3,618 | 5,980 | 6,728 |
| 21,050 | 21,100 | 54 | 3,369 | 5,653 | 6,400 | 965 | 3,618 | 5,980 | 6,728 | 24,250 | 24,300 | 0 | 2,858 | 4,979 | 5,726 | 475 | 3,618 | 5,980 | 6,728 |
| 21,100 | 21,150 | 47 | 3,361 | 5,642 | 6,389 | 957 | 3,618 | 5,980 | 6,728 | 24,300 | 24,350 | 0 | 2,850 | 4,968 | 5,716 | 467 | 3,618 | 5,980 | 6,728 |
| 21,150 | 21,200 | 39 | 3,353 | 5,631 | 6,379 | 949 | 3,618 | 5,980 | 6,728 | 24,350 | 24,400 | 0 | 2,842 | 4,958 | 5,705 | 460 | 3,618 | 5,980 | 6,728 |
| 21,200 | 21,250 | 31 | 3,345 | 5,621 | 6,368 | 942 | 3,618 | 5,980 | 6,728 | 24,400 | 24,450 | 0 | 2,834 | 4,947 | 5,695 | 452 | 3,618 | 5,980 | 6,728 |
| 21,250 | 21,300 | 24 | 3,337 | 5,610 | 6,358 | 934 | 3,618 | 5,980 | 6,728 | 24,450 | 24,500 | 0 | 2,826 | 4,936 | 5,684 | 444 | 3,618 | 5,980 | 6,728 |
| 21,300 | 21,350 | 16 | 3,329 | 5,600 | 6,347 | 926 | 3,618 | 5,980 | 6,728 | 24,500 | 24,550 | 0 | 2,818 | 4,926 | 5,673 | 437 | 3,618 | 5,980 | 6,728 |
| 21,350 | 21,400 | 8 | 3,321 | 5,589 | 6,337 | 919 | 3,618 | 5,980 | 6,728 | 24,550 | 24,600 | 0 | 2,810 | 4,915 | 5,663 | 429 | 3,618 | 5,980 | 6,728 |
| 21,400 | 21,450 | * | 3,313 | 5,579 | 6,326 | 911 | 3,618 | 5,980 | 6,728 | 24,600 | 24,650 | 0 | 2,802 | 4,905 | 5,652 | 422 | 3,618 | 5,980 | 6,728 |
| 21,450 | 21,500 | 0 | 3,305 | 5,568 | 6,316 | 903 | 3,618 | 5,980 | 6,728 | 24,650 | 24,700 | 0 | 2,794 | 4,894 | 5,642 | 414 | 3,618 | 5,980 | 6,728 |
| 21,500 | 21,550 | 0 | 3,297 | 5,558 | 6,305 | 896 | 3,618 | 5,980 | 6,728 | 24,700 | 24,750 | 0 | 2,786 | 4,884 | 5,631 | 406 | 3,618 | 5,980 | 6,728 |
| 21,550 | 21,600 | 0 | 3,289 | 5,547 | 6,295 | 888 | 3,618 | 5,980 | 6,728 | 24,750 | 24,800 | 0 | 2,778 | 4,873 | 5,621 | 399 | 3,618 | 5,980 | 6,728 |

★ Use this column if your filing status is married filing separately and you qualify to claim the EIC. See the instructions for line 27a.

* If the amount you are looking up from the worksheet is at least $21,400 but less than $21,430, and you have no qualifying children, your credit is $2.

If the amount you are looking up from the worksheet is $21,430 or more, and you have no qualifying children, you can't take the credit.

*(Continued)*

## Earned Income Credit (EIC) Table - Continued

(**Caution.** This is **not** a tax table.)

| If the amount you are looking up from the worksheet is– | | Single, head of household, or qualifying widow(er)★ and you have– | | | | Married filing jointly and you have– | | | |
|---|---|---|---|---|---|---|---|---|---|
| At least | But less than | 0 | 1 | 2 | 3 | 0 | 1 | 2 | 3 |
| | | Your credit is– | | | | Your credit is– | | | |
| 24,800 | 24,850 | 0 | 2,770 | 4,863 | 5,610 | 391 | 3,618 | 5,980 | 6,728 |
| 24,850 | 24,900 | 0 | 2,762 | 4,852 | 5,600 | 383 | 3,618 | 5,980 | 6,728 |
| 24,900 | 24,950 | 0 | 2,754 | 4,842 | 5,589 | 376 | 3,618 | 5,980 | 6,728 |
| 24,950 | 25,000 | 0 | 2,746 | 4,831 | 5,579 | 368 | 3,618 | 5,980 | 6,728 |
| 25,000 | 25,050 | 0 | 2,738 | 4,821 | 5,568 | 360 | 3,618 | 5,980 | 6,728 |
| 25,050 | 25,100 | 0 | 2,730 | 4,810 | 5,558 | 353 | 3,618 | 5,980 | 6,728 |
| 25,100 | 25,150 | 0 | 2,722 | 4,800 | 5,547 | 345 | 3,618 | 5,980 | 6,728 |
| 25,150 | 25,200 | 0 | 2,714 | 4,789 | 5,537 | 337 | 3,618 | 5,980 | 6,728 |
| 25,200 | 25,250 | 0 | 2,706 | 4,779 | 5,526 | 330 | 3,618 | 5,980 | 6,728 |
| 25,250 | 25,300 | 0 | 2,698 | 4,768 | 5,515 | 322 | 3,618 | 5,980 | 6,728 |
| 25,300 | 25,350 | 0 | 2,690 | 4,757 | 5,505 | 314 | 3,618 | 5,980 | 6,728 |
| 25,350 | 25,400 | 0 | 2,682 | 4,747 | 5,494 | 307 | 3,618 | 5,980 | 6,728 |
| 25,400 | 25,450 | 0 | 2,674 | 4,736 | 5,484 | 299 | 3,618 | 5,980 | 6,728 |
| 25,450 | 25,500 | 0 | 2,666 | 4,726 | 5,473 | 291 | 3,618 | 5,980 | 6,728 |
| 25,500 | 25,550 | 0 | 2,658 | 4,715 | 5,463 | 284 | 3,609 | 5,968 | 6,716 |
| 25,550 | 25,600 | 0 | 2,650 | 4,705 | 5,452 | 276 | 3,601 | 5,958 | 6,705 |
| 25,600 | 25,650 | 0 | 2,642 | 4,694 | 5,442 | 269 | 3,593 | 5,947 | 6,695 |
| 25,650 | 25,700 | 0 | 2,634 | 4,684 | 5,431 | 261 | 3,585 | 5,937 | 6,684 |
| 25,700 | 25,750 | 0 | 2,626 | 4,673 | 5,421 | 253 | 3,577 | 5,926 | 6,674 |
| 25,750 | 25,800 | 0 | 2,618 | 4,663 | 5,410 | 246 | 3,569 | 5,916 | 6,663 |
| 25,800 | 25,850 | 0 | 2,610 | 4,652 | 5,400 | 238 | 3,561 | 5,905 | 6,653 |
| 25,850 | 25,900 | 0 | 2,602 | 4,642 | 5,389 | 230 | 3,553 | 5,895 | 6,642 |
| 25,900 | 25,950 | 0 | 2,594 | 4,631 | 5,379 | 223 | 3,545 | 5,884 | 6,632 |
| 25,950 | 26,000 | 0 | 2,586 | 4,621 | 5,368 | 215 | 3,537 | 5,874 | 6,621 |
| 26,000 | 26,050 | 0 | 2,578 | 4,610 | 5,358 | 207 | 3,529 | 5,863 | 6,611 |
| 26,050 | 26,100 | 0 | 2,570 | 4,600 | 5,347 | 200 | 3,521 | 5,853 | 6,600 |
| 26,100 | 26,150 | 0 | 2,562 | 4,589 | 5,336 | 192 | 3,513 | 5,842 | 6,590 |
| 26,150 | 26,200 | 0 | 2,554 | 4,578 | 5,326 | 184 | 3,505 | 5,832 | 6,579 |
| 26,200 | 26,250 | 0 | 2,546 | 4,568 | 5,315 | 177 | 3,497 | 5,821 | 6,568 |
| 26,250 | 26,300 | 0 | 2,538 | 4,557 | 5,305 | 169 | 3,489 | 5,810 | 6,558 |
| 26,300 | 26,350 | 0 | 2,530 | 4,547 | 5,294 | 161 | 3,481 | 5,800 | 6,547 |
| 26,350 | 26,400 | 0 | 2,522 | 4,536 | 5,284 | 154 | 3,473 | 5,789 | 6,537 |
| 26,400 | 26,450 | 0 | 2,514 | 4,526 | 5,273 | 146 | 3,465 | 5,779 | 6,526 |
| 26,450 | 26,500 | 0 | 2,506 | 4,515 | 5,263 | 138 | 3,457 | 5,768 | 6,516 |
| 26,500 | 26,550 | 0 | 2,498 | 4,505 | 5,252 | 131 | 3,449 | 5,758 | 6,505 |
| 26,550 | 26,600 | 0 | 2,490 | 4,494 | 5,242 | 123 | 3,441 | 5,747 | 6,495 |
| 26,600 | 26,650 | 0 | 2,482 | 4,484 | 5,231 | 116 | 3,433 | 5,737 | 6,484 |
| 26,650 | 26,700 | 0 | 2,474 | 4,473 | 5,221 | 108 | 3,425 | 5,726 | 6,474 |
| 26,700 | 26,750 | 0 | 2,466 | 4,463 | 5,210 | 100 | 3,417 | 5,716 | 6,463 |
| 26,750 | 26,800 | 0 | 2,458 | 4,452 | 5,200 | 93 | 3,409 | 5,705 | 6,453 |
| 26,800 | 26,850 | 0 | 2,450 | 4,442 | 5,189 | 85 | 3,401 | 5,695 | 6,442 |
| 26,850 | 26,900 | 0 | 2,442 | 4,431 | 5,179 | 77 | 3,393 | 5,684 | 6,432 |
| 26,900 | 26,950 | 0 | 2,434 | 4,421 | 5,168 | 70 | 3,385 | 5,674 | 6,421 |
| 26,950 | 27,000 | 0 | 2,426 | 4,410 | 5,157 | 62 | 3,377 | 5,663 | 6,411 |
| 27,000 | 27,050 | 0 | 2,418 | 4,399 | 5,147 | 54 | 3,369 | 5,653 | 6,400 |
| 27,050 | 27,100 | 0 | 2,410 | 4,389 | 5,136 | 47 | 3,361 | 5,642 | 6,389 |
| 27,100 | 27,150 | 0 | 2,402 | 4,378 | 5,126 | 39 | 3,353 | 5,631 | 6,379 |
| 27,150 | 27,200 | 0 | 2,394 | 4,368 | 5,115 | 31 | 3,345 | 5,621 | 6,368 |
| 27,200 | 27,250 | 0 | 2,386 | 4,357 | 5,105 | 24 | 3,337 | 5,610 | 6,358 |
| 27,250 | 27,300 | 0 | 2,378 | 4,347 | 5,094 | 16 | 3,329 | 5,600 | 6,347 |
| 27,300 | 27,350 | 0 | 2,370 | 4,336 | 5,084 | 8 | 3,321 | 5,589 | 6,337 |
| 27,350 | 27,400 | 0 | 2,362 | 4,326 | 5,073 | * | 3,313 | 5,579 | 6,326 |
| 27,400 | 27,450 | 0 | 2,354 | 4,315 | 5,063 | 0 | 3,305 | 5,568 | 6,316 |
| 27,450 | 27,500 | 0 | 2,346 | 4,305 | 5,052 | 0 | 3,297 | 5,558 | 6,305 |
| 27,500 | 27,550 | 0 | 2,338 | 4,294 | 5,042 | 0 | 3,289 | 5,547 | 6,295 |
| 27,550 | 27,600 | 0 | 2,330 | 4,284 | 5,031 | 0 | 3,281 | 5,537 | 6,284 |
| 27,600 | 27,650 | 0 | 2,322 | 4,273 | 5,021 | 0 | 3,273 | 5,526 | 6,274 |
| 27,650 | 27,700 | 0 | 2,314 | 4,263 | 5,010 | 0 | 3,265 | 5,516 | 6,263 |
| 27,700 | 27,750 | 0 | 2,306 | 4,252 | 5,000 | 0 | 3,257 | 5,505 | 6,253 |
| 27,750 | 27,800 | 0 | 2,298 | 4,241 | 4,989 | 0 | 3,249 | 5,495 | 6,242 |
| 27,800 | 27,850 | 0 | 2,290 | 4,231 | 4,978 | 0 | 3,241 | 5,484 | 6,232 |
| 27,850 | 27,900 | 0 | 2,282 | 4,220 | 4,968 | 0 | 3,233 | 5,474 | 6,221 |
| 27,900 | 27,950 | 0 | 2,274 | 4,210 | 4,957 | 0 | 3,225 | 5,463 | 6,210 |
| 27,950 | 28,000 | 0 | 2,266 | 4,199 | 4,947 | 0 | 3,217 | 5,452 | 6,200 |

| If the amount you are looking up from the worksheet is– | | Single, head of household, or qualifying widow(er)★ and you have– | | | | Married filing jointly and you have– | | | |
|---|---|---|---|---|---|---|---|---|---|
| At least | But less than | 0 | 1 | 2 | 3 | 0 | 1 | 2 | 3 |
| | | Your credit is– | | | | Your credit is– | | | |
| 28,000 | 28,050 | 0 | 2,259 | 4,189 | 4,936 | 0 | 3,209 | 5,442 | 6,189 |
| 28,050 | 28,100 | 0 | 2,251 | 4,178 | 4,926 | 0 | 3,201 | 5,431 | 6,179 |
| 28,100 | 28,150 | 0 | 2,243 | 4,168 | 4,915 | 0 | 3,193 | 5,421 | 6,168 |
| 28,150 | 28,200 | 0 | 2,235 | 4,157 | 4,905 | 0 | 3,185 | 5,410 | 6,158 |
| 28,200 | 28,250 | 0 | 2,227 | 4,147 | 4,894 | 0 | 3,177 | 5,400 | 6,147 |
| 28,250 | 28,300 | 0 | 2,219 | 4,136 | 4,884 | 0 | 3,169 | 5,389 | 6,137 |
| 28,300 | 28,350 | 0 | 2,211 | 4,126 | 4,873 | 0 | 3,161 | 5,379 | 6,126 |
| 28,350 | 28,400 | 0 | 2,203 | 4,115 | 4,863 | 0 | 3,153 | 5,368 | 6,116 |
| 28,400 | 28,450 | 0 | 2,195 | 4,105 | 4,852 | 0 | 3,145 | 5,358 | 6,105 |
| 28,450 | 28,500 | 0 | 2,187 | 4,094 | 4,842 | 0 | 3,137 | 5,347 | 6,095 |
| 28,500 | 28,550 | 0 | 2,179 | 4,084 | 4,831 | 0 | 3,129 | 5,337 | 6,084 |
| 28,550 | 28,600 | 0 | 2,171 | 4,073 | 4,821 | 0 | 3,121 | 5,326 | 6,074 |
| 28,600 | 28,650 | 0 | 2,163 | 4,062 | 4,810 | 0 | 3,113 | 5,316 | 6,063 |
| 28,650 | 28,700 | 0 | 2,155 | 4,052 | 4,799 | 0 | 3,105 | 5,305 | 6,053 |
| 28,700 | 28,750 | 0 | 2,147 | 4,041 | 4,789 | 0 | 3,097 | 5,294 | 6,042 |
| 28,750 | 28,800 | 0 | 2,139 | 4,031 | 4,778 | 0 | 3,089 | 5,284 | 6,031 |
| 28,800 | 28,850 | 0 | 2,131 | 4,020 | 4,768 | 0 | 3,081 | 5,273 | 6,021 |
| 28,850 | 28,900 | 0 | 2,123 | 4,010 | 4,757 | 0 | 3,073 | 5,263 | 6,010 |
| 28,900 | 28,950 | 0 | 2,115 | 3,999 | 4,747 | 0 | 3,065 | 5,252 | 6,000 |
| 28,950 | 29,000 | 0 | 2,107 | 3,989 | 4,736 | 0 | 3,058 | 5,242 | 5,989 |
| 29,000 | 29,050 | 0 | 2,099 | 3,978 | 4,726 | 0 | 3,050 | 5,231 | 5,979 |
| 29,050 | 29,100 | 0 | 2,091 | 3,968 | 4,715 | 0 | 3,042 | 5,221 | 5,968 |
| 29,100 | 29,150 | 0 | 2,083 | 3,957 | 4,705 | 0 | 3,034 | 5,210 | 5,958 |
| 29,150 | 29,200 | 0 | 2,075 | 3,947 | 4,694 | 0 | 3,026 | 5,200 | 5,947 |
| 29,200 | 29,250 | 0 | 2,067 | 3,936 | 4,684 | 0 | 3,018 | 5,189 | 5,937 |
| 29,250 | 29,300 | 0 | 2,059 | 3,926 | 4,673 | 0 | 3,010 | 5,179 | 5,926 |
| 29,300 | 29,350 | 0 | 2,051 | 3,915 | 4,663 | 0 | 3,002 | 5,168 | 5,916 |
| 29,350 | 29,400 | 0 | 2,043 | 3,905 | 4,652 | 0 | 2,994 | 5,158 | 5,905 |
| 29,400 | 29,450 | 0 | 2,035 | 3,894 | 4,642 | 0 | 2,986 | 5,147 | 5,895 |
| 29,450 | 29,500 | 0 | 2,027 | 3,883 | 4,631 | 0 | 2,978 | 5,137 | 5,884 |
| 29,500 | 29,550 | 0 | 2,019 | 3,873 | 4,620 | 0 | 2,970 | 5,126 | 5,874 |
| 29,550 | 29,600 | 0 | 2,011 | 3,862 | 4,610 | 0 | 2,962 | 5,115 | 5,863 |
| 29,600 | 29,650 | 0 | 2,003 | 3,852 | 4,599 | 0 | 2,954 | 5,105 | 5,852 |
| 29,650 | 29,700 | 0 | 1,995 | 3,841 | 4,589 | 0 | 2,946 | 5,094 | 5,842 |
| 29,700 | 29,750 | 0 | 1,987 | 3,831 | 4,578 | 0 | 2,938 | 5,084 | 5,831 |
| 29,750 | 29,800 | 0 | 1,979 | 3,820 | 4,568 | 0 | 2,930 | 5,073 | 5,821 |
| 29,800 | 29,850 | 0 | 1,971 | 3,810 | 4,557 | 0 | 2,922 | 5,063 | 5,810 |
| 29,850 | 29,900 | 0 | 1,963 | 3,799 | 4,547 | 0 | 2,914 | 5,052 | 5,800 |
| 29,900 | 29,950 | 0 | 1,955 | 3,789 | 4,536 | 0 | 2,906 | 5,042 | 5,789 |
| 29,950 | 30,000 | 0 | 1,947 | 3,778 | 4,526 | 0 | 2,898 | 5,031 | 5,779 |
| 30,000 | 30,050 | 0 | 1,939 | 3,768 | 4,515 | 0 | 2,890 | 5,021 | 5,768 |
| 30,050 | 30,100 | 0 | 1,931 | 3,757 | 4,505 | 0 | 2,882 | 5,010 | 5,758 |
| 30,100 | 30,150 | 0 | 1,923 | 3,747 | 4,494 | 0 | 2,874 | 5,000 | 5,747 |
| 30,150 | 30,200 | 0 | 1,915 | 3,736 | 4,484 | 0 | 2,866 | 4,989 | 5,737 |
| 30,200 | 30,250 | 0 | 1,907 | 3,726 | 4,473 | 0 | 2,858 | 4,979 | 5,726 |
| 30,250 | 30,300 | 0 | 1,899 | 3,715 | 4,462 | 0 | 2,850 | 4,968 | 5,716 |
| 30,300 | 30,350 | 0 | 1,891 | 3,704 | 4,452 | 0 | 2,842 | 4,958 | 5,705 |
| 30,350 | 30,400 | 0 | 1,883 | 3,694 | 4,441 | 0 | 2,834 | 4,947 | 5,695 |
| 30,400 | 30,450 | 0 | 1,875 | 3,683 | 4,431 | 0 | 2,826 | 4,936 | 5,684 |
| 30,450 | 30,500 | 0 | 1,867 | 3,673 | 4,420 | 0 | 2,818 | 4,926 | 5,673 |
| 30,500 | 30,550 | 0 | 1,859 | 3,662 | 4,410 | 0 | 2,810 | 4,915 | 5,663 |
| 30,550 | 30,600 | 0 | 1,851 | 3,652 | 4,399 | 0 | 2,802 | 4,905 | 5,652 |
| 30,600 | 30,650 | 0 | 1,843 | 3,641 | 4,389 | 0 | 2,794 | 4,894 | 5,642 |
| 30,650 | 30,700 | 0 | 1,835 | 3,631 | 4,378 | 0 | 2,786 | 4,884 | 5,631 |
| 30,700 | 30,750 | 0 | 1,827 | 3,620 | 4,368 | 0 | 2,778 | 4,873 | 5,621 |
| 30,750 | 30,800 | 0 | 1,819 | 3,610 | 4,357 | 0 | 2,770 | 4,863 | 5,610 |
| 30,800 | 30,850 | 0 | 1,811 | 3,599 | 4,347 | 0 | 2,762 | 4,852 | 5,600 |
| 30,850 | 30,900 | 0 | 1,803 | 3,589 | 4,336 | 0 | 2,754 | 4,842 | 5,589 |
| 30,900 | 30,950 | 0 | 1,795 | 3,578 | 4,326 | 0 | 2,746 | 4,831 | 5,579 |
| 30,950 | 31,000 | 0 | 1,787 | 3,568 | 4,315 | 0 | 2,738 | 4,821 | 5,568 |
| 31,000 | 31,050 | 0 | 1,779 | 3,557 | 4,305 | 0 | 2,730 | 4,810 | 5,558 |
| 31,050 | 31,100 | 0 | 1,771 | 3,547 | 4,294 | 0 | 2,722 | 4,800 | 5,547 |
| 31,100 | 31,150 | 0 | 1,763 | 3,536 | 4,283 | 0 | 2,714 | 4,789 | 5,537 |
| 31,150 | 31,200 | 0 | 1,755 | 3,525 | 4,273 | 0 | 2,706 | 4,779 | 5,526 |

★  Use this column if your filing status is married filing separately and you qualify to claim the EIC. See the instructions for line 27a.

*  If the amount you are looking up from the worksheet is at least $27,350 but less than $27,380, and you have no qualifying children, your credit is $2.

If the amount you are looking up from the worksheet is $27,380 or more, and you have no qualifying children, you can't take the credit.

*(Continued)*

**Earned Income Credit (EIC) Table** - *Continued*      (**Caution.** This is **not** a tax table.)

| At least | But less than | Single, head of household, or qualifying widow(er)★ and you have— 0 | 1 | 2 | 3 | Married filing jointly and you have— 0 | 1 | 2 | 3 |
|---|---|---|---|---|---|---|---|---|---|
| 31,200 | 31,250 | 0 | 1,747 | 3,515 | 4,262 | 0 | 2,698 | 4,768 | 5,515 |
| 31,250 | 31,300 | 0 | 1,739 | 3,504 | 4,252 | 0 | 2,690 | 4,757 | 5,505 |
| 31,300 | 31,350 | 0 | 1,731 | 3,494 | 4,241 | 0 | 2,682 | 4,747 | 5,494 |
| 31,350 | 31,400 | 0 | 1,723 | 3,483 | 4,231 | 0 | 2,674 | 4,736 | 5,484 |
| 31,400 | 31,450 | 0 | 1,715 | 3,473 | 4,220 | 0 | 2,666 | 4,726 | 5,473 |
| 31,450 | 31,500 | 0 | 1,707 | 3,462 | 4,210 | 0 | 2,658 | 4,715 | 5,463 |
| 31,500 | 31,550 | 0 | 1,699 | 3,452 | 4,199 | 0 | 2,650 | 4,705 | 5,452 |
| 31,550 | 31,600 | 0 | 1,691 | 3,441 | 4,189 | 0 | 2,642 | 4,694 | 5,442 |
| 31,600 | 31,650 | 0 | 1,683 | 3,431 | 4,178 | 0 | 2,634 | 4,684 | 5,431 |
| 31,650 | 31,700 | 0 | 1,675 | 3,420 | 4,168 | 0 | 2,626 | 4,673 | 5,421 |
| 31,700 | 31,750 | 0 | 1,667 | 3,410 | 4,157 | 0 | 2,618 | 4,663 | 5,410 |
| 31,750 | 31,800 | 0 | 1,659 | 3,399 | 4,147 | 0 | 2,610 | 4,652 | 5,400 |
| 31,800 | 31,850 | 0 | 1,651 | 3,389 | 4,136 | 0 | 2,602 | 4,642 | 5,389 |
| 31,850 | 31,900 | 0 | 1,643 | 3,378 | 4,126 | 0 | 2,594 | 4,631 | 5,379 |
| 31,900 | 31,950 | 0 | 1,635 | 3,368 | 4,115 | 0 | 2,586 | 4,621 | 5,368 |
| 31,950 | 32,000 | 0 | 1,627 | 3,357 | 4,104 | 0 | 2,578 | 4,610 | 5,358 |
| 32,000 | 32,050 | 0 | 1,619 | 3,346 | 4,094 | 0 | 2,570 | 4,600 | 5,347 |
| 32,050 | 32,100 | 0 | 1,611 | 3,336 | 4,083 | 0 | 2,562 | 4,589 | 5,336 |
| 32,100 | 32,150 | 0 | 1,603 | 3,325 | 4,073 | 0 | 2,554 | 4,578 | 5,326 |
| 32,150 | 32,200 | 0 | 1,595 | 3,315 | 4,062 | 0 | 2,546 | 4,568 | 5,315 |
| 32,200 | 32,250 | 0 | 1,587 | 3,304 | 4,052 | 0 | 2,538 | 4,557 | 5,305 |
| 32,250 | 32,300 | 0 | 1,579 | 3,294 | 4,041 | 0 | 2,530 | 4,547 | 5,294 |
| 32,300 | 32,350 | 0 | 1,571 | 3,283 | 4,031 | 0 | 2,522 | 4,536 | 5,284 |
| 32,350 | 32,400 | 0 | 1,563 | 3,273 | 4,020 | 0 | 2,514 | 4,526 | 5,273 |
| 32,400 | 32,450 | 0 | 1,555 | 3,262 | 4,010 | 0 | 2,506 | 4,515 | 5,263 |
| 32,450 | 32,500 | 0 | 1,547 | 3,252 | 3,999 | 0 | 2,498 | 4,505 | 5,252 |
| 32,500 | 32,550 | 0 | 1,539 | 3,241 | 3,989 | 0 | 2,490 | 4,494 | 5,242 |
| 32,550 | 32,600 | 0 | 1,531 | 3,231 | 3,978 | 0 | 2,482 | 4,484 | 5,231 |
| 32,600 | 32,650 | 0 | 1,523 | 3,220 | 3,968 | 0 | 2,474 | 4,473 | 5,221 |
| 32,650 | 32,700 | 0 | 1,515 | 3,210 | 3,957 | 0 | 2,466 | 4,463 | 5,210 |
| 32,700 | 32,750 | 0 | 1,507 | 3,199 | 3,947 | 0 | 2,458 | 4,452 | 5,200 |
| 32,750 | 32,800 | 0 | 1,499 | 3,188 | 3,936 | 0 | 2,450 | 4,442 | 5,189 |
| 32,800 | 32,850 | 0 | 1,491 | 3,178 | 3,925 | 0 | 2,442 | 4,431 | 5,179 |
| 32,850 | 32,900 | 0 | 1,483 | 3,167 | 3,915 | 0 | 2,434 | 4,421 | 5,168 |
| 32,900 | 32,950 | 0 | 1,475 | 3,157 | 3,904 | 0 | 2,426 | 4,410 | 5,157 |
| 32,950 | 33,000 | 0 | 1,467 | 3,146 | 3,894 | 0 | 2,418 | 4,399 | 5,147 |
| 33,000 | 33,050 | 0 | 1,460 | 3,136 | 3,883 | 0 | 2,410 | 4,389 | 5,136 |
| 33,050 | 33,100 | 0 | 1,452 | 3,125 | 3,873 | 0 | 2,402 | 4,378 | 5,126 |
| 33,100 | 33,150 | 0 | 1,444 | 3,115 | 3,862 | 0 | 2,394 | 4,368 | 5,115 |
| 33,150 | 33,200 | 0 | 1,436 | 3,104 | 3,852 | 0 | 2,386 | 4,357 | 5,105 |
| 33,200 | 33,250 | 0 | 1,428 | 3,094 | 3,841 | 0 | 2,378 | 4,347 | 5,094 |
| 33,250 | 33,300 | 0 | 1,420 | 3,083 | 3,831 | 0 | 2,370 | 4,336 | 5,084 |
| 33,300 | 33,350 | 0 | 1,412 | 3,073 | 3,820 | 0 | 2,362 | 4,326 | 5,073 |
| 33,350 | 33,400 | 0 | 1,404 | 3,062 | 3,810 | 0 | 2,354 | 4,315 | 5,063 |
| 33,400 | 33,450 | 0 | 1,396 | 3,052 | 3,799 | 0 | 2,346 | 4,305 | 5,052 |
| 33,450 | 33,500 | 0 | 1,388 | 3,041 | 3,789 | 0 | 2,338 | 4,294 | 5,042 |
| 33,500 | 33,550 | 0 | 1,380 | 3,031 | 3,778 | 0 | 2,330 | 4,284 | 5,031 |
| 33,550 | 33,600 | 0 | 1,372 | 3,020 | 3,768 | 0 | 2,322 | 4,273 | 5,021 |
| 33,600 | 33,650 | 0 | 1,364 | 3,009 | 3,757 | 0 | 2,314 | 4,263 | 5,010 |
| 33,650 | 33,700 | 0 | 1,356 | 2,999 | 3,746 | 0 | 2,306 | 4,252 | 5,000 |
| 33,700 | 33,750 | 0 | 1,348 | 2,988 | 3,736 | 0 | 2,298 | 4,241 | 4,989 |
| 33,750 | 33,800 | 0 | 1,340 | 2,978 | 3,725 | 0 | 2,290 | 4,231 | 4,978 |
| 33,800 | 33,850 | 0 | 1,332 | 2,967 | 3,715 | 0 | 2,282 | 4,220 | 4,968 |
| 33,850 | 33,900 | 0 | 1,324 | 2,957 | 3,704 | 0 | 2,274 | 4,210 | 4,957 |
| 33,900 | 33,950 | 0 | 1,316 | 2,946 | 3,694 | 0 | 2,266 | 4,199 | 4,947 |
| 33,950 | 34,000 | 0 | 1,308 | 2,936 | 3,683 | 0 | 2,258 | 4,189 | 4,936 |
| 34,000 | 34,050 | 0 | 1,300 | 2,925 | 3,673 | 0 | 2,251 | 4,178 | 4,926 |
| 34,050 | 34,100 | 0 | 1,292 | 2,915 | 3,662 | 0 | 2,243 | 4,168 | 4,915 |
| 34,100 | 34,150 | 0 | 1,284 | 2,904 | 3,652 | 0 | 2,235 | 4,157 | 4,905 |
| 34,150 | 34,200 | 0 | 1,276 | 2,894 | 3,641 | 0 | 2,227 | 4,147 | 4,894 |
| 34,200 | 34,250 | 0 | 1,268 | 2,883 | 3,631 | 0 | 2,219 | 4,136 | 4,884 |
| 34,250 | 34,300 | 0 | 1,260 | 2,873 | 3,620 | 0 | 2,211 | 4,126 | 4,873 |
| 34,300 | 34,350 | 0 | 1,252 | 2,862 | 3,610 | 0 | 2,203 | 4,115 | 4,863 |
| 34,350 | 34,400 | 0 | 1,244 | 2,852 | 3,599 | 0 | 2,195 | 4,105 | 4,852 |
| 34,400 | 34,450 | 0 | 1,236 | 2,841 | 3,589 | 0 | 2,187 | 4,094 | 4,842 |
| 34,450 | 34,500 | 0 | 1,228 | 2,830 | 3,578 | 0 | 2,179 | 4,084 | 4,831 |
| 34,500 | 34,550 | 0 | 1,220 | 2,820 | 3,567 | 0 | 2,171 | 4,073 | 4,821 |
| 34,550 | 34,600 | 0 | 1,212 | 2,809 | 3,557 | 0 | 2,163 | 4,062 | 4,810 |
| 34,600 | 34,650 | 0 | 1,204 | 2,799 | 3,546 | 0 | 2,155 | 4,052 | 4,799 |
| 34,650 | 34,700 | 0 | 1,196 | 2,788 | 3,536 | 0 | 2,147 | 4,041 | 4,789 |
| 34,700 | 34,750 | 0 | 1,188 | 2,778 | 3,525 | 0 | 2,139 | 4,031 | 4,778 |
| 34,750 | 34,800 | 0 | 1,180 | 2,767 | 3,515 | 0 | 2,131 | 4,020 | 4,768 |
| 34,800 | 34,850 | 0 | 1,172 | 2,757 | 3,504 | 0 | 2,123 | 4,010 | 4,757 |
| 34,850 | 34,900 | 0 | 1,164 | 2,746 | 3,494 | 0 | 2,115 | 3,999 | 4,747 |
| 34,900 | 34,950 | 0 | 1,156 | 2,736 | 3,483 | 0 | 2,107 | 3,989 | 4,736 |
| 34,950 | 35,000 | 0 | 1,148 | 2,725 | 3,473 | 0 | 2,099 | 3,978 | 4,726 |
| 35,000 | 35,050 | 0 | 1,140 | 2,715 | 3,462 | 0 | 2,091 | 3,968 | 4,715 |
| 35,050 | 35,100 | 0 | 1,132 | 2,704 | 3,452 | 0 | 2,083 | 3,957 | 4,705 |
| 35,100 | 35,150 | 0 | 1,124 | 2,694 | 3,441 | 0 | 2,075 | 3,947 | 4,694 |
| 35,150 | 35,200 | 0 | 1,116 | 2,683 | 3,431 | 0 | 2,067 | 3,936 | 4,684 |
| 35,200 | 35,250 | 0 | 1,108 | 2,673 | 3,420 | 0 | 2,059 | 3,926 | 4,673 |
| 35,250 | 35,300 | 0 | 1,100 | 2,662 | 3,409 | 0 | 2,051 | 3,915 | 4,663 |
| 35,300 | 35,350 | 0 | 1,092 | 2,651 | 3,399 | 0 | 2,043 | 3,905 | 4,652 |
| 35,350 | 35,400 | 0 | 1,084 | 2,641 | 3,388 | 0 | 2,035 | 3,894 | 4,642 |
| 35,400 | 35,450 | 0 | 1,076 | 2,630 | 3,378 | 0 | 2,027 | 3,883 | 4,631 |
| 35,450 | 35,500 | 0 | 1,068 | 2,620 | 3,367 | 0 | 2,019 | 3,873 | 4,620 |
| 35,500 | 35,550 | 0 | 1,060 | 2,609 | 3,357 | 0 | 2,011 | 3,862 | 4,610 |
| 35,550 | 35,600 | 0 | 1,052 | 2,599 | 3,346 | 0 | 2,003 | 3,852 | 4,599 |
| 35,600 | 35,650 | 0 | 1,044 | 2,588 | 3,336 | 0 | 1,995 | 3,841 | 4,589 |
| 35,650 | 35,700 | 0 | 1,036 | 2,578 | 3,325 | 0 | 1,987 | 3,831 | 4,578 |
| 35,700 | 35,750 | 0 | 1,028 | 2,567 | 3,315 | 0 | 1,979 | 3,820 | 4,568 |
| 35,750 | 35,800 | 0 | 1,020 | 2,557 | 3,304 | 0 | 1,971 | 3,810 | 4,557 |
| 35,800 | 35,850 | 0 | 1,012 | 2,546 | 3,294 | 0 | 1,963 | 3,799 | 4,547 |
| 35,850 | 35,900 | 0 | 1,004 | 2,536 | 3,283 | 0 | 1,955 | 3,789 | 4,536 |
| 35,900 | 35,950 | 0 | 996 | 2,525 | 3,273 | 0 | 1,947 | 3,778 | 4,526 |
| 35,950 | 36,000 | 0 | 988 | 2,515 | 3,262 | 0 | 1,939 | 3,768 | 4,515 |
| 36,000 | 36,050 | 0 | 980 | 2,504 | 3,252 | 0 | 1,931 | 3,757 | 4,505 |
| 36,050 | 36,100 | 0 | 972 | 2,494 | 3,241 | 0 | 1,923 | 3,747 | 4,494 |
| 36,100 | 36,150 | 0 | 964 | 2,483 | 3,230 | 0 | 1,915 | 3,736 | 4,484 |
| 36,150 | 36,200 | 0 | 956 | 2,472 | 3,220 | 0 | 1,907 | 3,726 | 4,473 |
| 36,200 | 36,250 | 0 | 948 | 2,462 | 3,209 | 0 | 1,899 | 3,715 | 4,462 |
| 36,250 | 36,300 | 0 | 940 | 2,451 | 3,199 | 0 | 1,891 | 3,704 | 4,452 |
| 36,300 | 36,350 | 0 | 932 | 2,441 | 3,188 | 0 | 1,883 | 3,694 | 4,441 |
| 36,350 | 36,400 | 0 | 924 | 2,430 | 3,178 | 0 | 1,875 | 3,683 | 4,431 |
| 36,400 | 36,450 | 0 | 916 | 2,420 | 3,167 | 0 | 1,867 | 3,673 | 4,420 |
| 36,450 | 36,500 | 0 | 908 | 2,409 | 3,157 | 0 | 1,859 | 3,662 | 4,410 |
| 36,500 | 36,550 | 0 | 900 | 2,399 | 3,146 | 0 | 1,851 | 3,652 | 4,399 |
| 36,550 | 36,600 | 0 | 892 | 2,388 | 3,136 | 0 | 1,843 | 3,641 | 4,389 |
| 36,600 | 36,650 | 0 | 884 | 2,378 | 3,125 | 0 | 1,835 | 3,631 | 4,378 |
| 36,650 | 36,700 | 0 | 876 | 2,367 | 3,115 | 0 | 1,827 | 3,620 | 4,368 |
| 36,700 | 36,750 | 0 | 868 | 2,357 | 3,104 | 0 | 1,819 | 3,610 | 4,357 |
| 36,750 | 36,800 | 0 | 860 | 2,346 | 3,094 | 0 | 1,811 | 3,599 | 4,347 |
| 36,800 | 36,850 | 0 | 852 | 2,336 | 3,083 | 0 | 1,803 | 3,589 | 4,336 |
| 36,850 | 36,900 | 0 | 844 | 2,325 | 3,073 | 0 | 1,795 | 3,578 | 4,326 |
| 36,900 | 36,950 | 0 | 836 | 2,315 | 3,062 | 0 | 1,787 | 3,568 | 4,315 |
| 36,950 | 37,000 | 0 | 828 | 2,304 | 3,051 | 0 | 1,779 | 3,557 | 4,305 |
| 37,000 | 37,050 | 0 | 820 | 2,293 | 3,041 | 0 | 1,771 | 3,547 | 4,294 |
| 37,050 | 37,100 | 0 | 812 | 2,283 | 3,030 | 0 | 1,763 | 3,536 | 4,283 |
| 37,100 | 37,150 | 0 | 804 | 2,272 | 3,020 | 0 | 1,755 | 3,525 | 4,273 |
| 37,150 | 37,200 | 0 | 796 | 2,262 | 3,009 | 0 | 1,747 | 3,515 | 4,262 |
| 37,200 | 37,250 | 0 | 788 | 2,251 | 2,999 | 0 | 1,739 | 3,504 | 4,252 |
| 37,250 | 37,300 | 0 | 780 | 2,241 | 2,988 | 0 | 1,731 | 3,494 | 4,241 |
| 37,300 | 37,350 | 0 | 772 | 2,230 | 2,978 | 0 | 1,723 | 3,483 | 4,231 |
| 37,350 | 37,400 | 0 | 764 | 2,220 | 2,967 | 0 | 1,715 | 3,473 | 4,220 |
| 37,400 | 37,450 | 0 | 756 | 2,209 | 2,957 | 0 | 1,707 | 3,462 | 4,210 |
| 37,450 | 37,500 | 0 | 748 | 2,199 | 2,946 | 0 | 1,699 | 3,452 | 4,199 |
| 37,500 | 37,550 | 0 | 740 | 2,188 | 2,936 | 0 | 1,691 | 3,441 | 4,189 |
| 37,550 | 37,600 | 0 | 732 | 2,178 | 2,925 | 0 | 1,683 | 3,431 | 4,178 |

★ Use this column if your filing status is married filing separately and you qualify to claim the EIC. See the instructions for line 27a.

*(Continued)*

**Earned Income Credit (EIC) Table** - *Continued*     (**Caution.** This is **not** a tax table.)

| At least | But less than | Single, head of household, or qualifying widow(er)★ and you have– 0 | 1 | 2 | 3 | Married filing jointly and you have– 0 | 1 | 2 | 3 | At least | But less than | Single, head of household, or qualifying widow(er)★ and you have– 0 | 1 | 2 | 3 | Married filing jointly and you have– 0 | 1 | 2 | 3 |
|---|---|---|---|---|---|---|---|---|---|---|---|---|---|---|---|---|---|---|---|
| 37,600 | 37,650 | 0 | 724 | 2,167 | 2,915 | 0 | 1,675 | 3,420 | 4,168 | 40,800 | 40,850 | 0 | 213 | 1,493 | 2,241 | 0 | 1,164 | 2,746 | 3,494 |
| 37,650 | 37,700 | 0 | 716 | 2,157 | 2,904 | 0 | 1,667 | 3,410 | 4,157 | 40,850 | 40,900 | 0 | 205 | 1,483 | 2,230 | 0 | 1,156 | 2,736 | 3,483 |
| 37,700 | 37,750 | 0 | 708 | 2,146 | 2,894 | 0 | 1,659 | 3,399 | 4,147 | 40,900 | 40,950 | 0 | 197 | 1,472 | 2,220 | 0 | 1,148 | 2,725 | 3,473 |
| 37,750 | 37,800 | 0 | 700 | 2,135 | 2,883 | 0 | 1,651 | 3,389 | 4,136 | 40,950 | 41,000 | 0 | 189 | 1,462 | 2,209 | 0 | 1,140 | 2,715 | 3,462 |
| 37,800 | 37,850 | 0 | 692 | 2,125 | 2,872 | 0 | 1,643 | 3,378 | 4,126 | 41,000 | 41,050 | 0 | 181 | 1,451 | 2,199 | 0 | 1,132 | 2,704 | 3,452 |
| 37,850 | 37,900 | 0 | 684 | 2,114 | 2,862 | 0 | 1,635 | 3,368 | 4,115 | 41,050 | 41,100 | 0 | 173 | 1,441 | 2,188 | 0 | 1,124 | 2,694 | 3,441 |
| 37,900 | 37,950 | 0 | 676 | 2,104 | 2,851 | 0 | 1,627 | 3,357 | 4,104 | 41,100 | 41,150 | 0 | 165 | 1,430 | 2,177 | 0 | 1,116 | 2,683 | 3,431 |
| 37,950 | 38,000 | 0 | 668 | 2,093 | 2,841 | 0 | 1,619 | 3,346 | 4,094 | 41,150 | 41,200 | 0 | 157 | 1,419 | 2,167 | 0 | 1,108 | 2,673 | 3,420 |
| 38,000 | 38,050 | 0 | 661 | 2,083 | 2,830 | 0 | 1,611 | 3,336 | 4,083 | 41,200 | 41,250 | 0 | 149 | 1,409 | 2,156 | 0 | 1,100 | 2,662 | 3,409 |
| 38,050 | 38,100 | 0 | 653 | 2,072 | 2,820 | 0 | 1,603 | 3,325 | 4,073 | 41,250 | 41,300 | 0 | 141 | 1,398 | 2,146 | 0 | 1,092 | 2,651 | 3,399 |
| 38,100 | 38,150 | 0 | 645 | 2,062 | 2,809 | 0 | 1,595 | 3,315 | 4,062 | 41,300 | 41,350 | 0 | 133 | 1,388 | 2,135 | 0 | 1,084 | 2,641 | 3,388 |
| 38,150 | 38,200 | 0 | 637 | 2,051 | 2,799 | 0 | 1,587 | 3,304 | 4,052 | 41,350 | 41,400 | 0 | 125 | 1,377 | 2,125 | 0 | 1,076 | 2,630 | 3,378 |
| 38,200 | 38,250 | 0 | 629 | 2,041 | 2,788 | 0 | 1,579 | 3,294 | 4,041 | 41,400 | 41,450 | 0 | 117 | 1,367 | 2,114 | 0 | 1,068 | 2,620 | 3,367 |
| 38,250 | 38,300 | 0 | 621 | 2,030 | 2,778 | 0 | 1,571 | 3,283 | 4,031 | 41,450 | 41,500 | 0 | 109 | 1,356 | 2,104 | 0 | 1,060 | 2,609 | 3,357 |
| 38,300 | 38,350 | 0 | 613 | 2,020 | 2,767 | 0 | 1,563 | 3,273 | 4,020 | 41,500 | 41,550 | 0 | 101 | 1,346 | 2,093 | 0 | 1,052 | 2,599 | 3,346 |
| 38,350 | 38,400 | 0 | 605 | 2,009 | 2,757 | 0 | 1,555 | 3,262 | 4,010 | 41,550 | 41,600 | 0 | 93 | 1,335 | 2,083 | 0 | 1,044 | 2,588 | 3,336 |
| 38,400 | 38,450 | 0 | 597 | 1,999 | 2,746 | 0 | 1,547 | 3,252 | 3,999 | 41,600 | 41,650 | 0 | 85 | 1,325 | 2,072 | 0 | 1,036 | 2,578 | 3,325 |
| 38,450 | 38,500 | 0 | 589 | 1,988 | 2,736 | 0 | 1,539 | 3,241 | 3,989 | 41,650 | 41,700 | 0 | 77 | 1,314 | 2,062 | 0 | 1,028 | 2,567 | 3,315 |
| 38,500 | 38,550 | 0 | 581 | 1,978 | 2,725 | 0 | 1,531 | 3,231 | 3,978 | 41,700 | 41,750 | 0 | 69 | 1,304 | 2,051 | 0 | 1,020 | 2,557 | 3,304 |
| 38,550 | 38,600 | 0 | 573 | 1,967 | 2,715 | 0 | 1,523 | 3,220 | 3,968 | 41,750 | 41,800 | 0 | 61 | 1,293 | 2,041 | 0 | 1,012 | 2,546 | 3,294 |
| 38,600 | 38,650 | 0 | 565 | 1,956 | 2,704 | 0 | 1,515 | 3,210 | 3,957 | 41,800 | 41,850 | 0 | 53 | 1,283 | 2,030 | 0 | 1,004 | 2,536 | 3,283 |
| 38,650 | 38,700 | 0 | 557 | 1,946 | 2,693 | 0 | 1,507 | 3,199 | 3,947 | 41,850 | 41,900 | 0 | 45 | 1,272 | 2,020 | 0 | 996 | 2,525 | 3,273 |
| 38,700 | 38,750 | 0 | 549 | 1,935 | 2,683 | 0 | 1,499 | 3,188 | 3,936 | 41,900 | 41,950 | 0 | 37 | 1,262 | 2,009 | 0 | 988 | 2,515 | 3,262 |
| 38,750 | 38,800 | 0 | 541 | 1,925 | 2,672 | 0 | 1,491 | 3,178 | 3,925 | 41,950 | 42,000 | 0 | 29 | 1,251 | 1,998 | 0 | 980 | 2,504 | 3,252 |
| 38,800 | 38,850 | 0 | 533 | 1,914 | 2,662 | 0 | 1,483 | 3,167 | 3,915 | 42,000 | 42,050 | 0 | 21 | 1,240 | 1,988 | 0 | 972 | 2,494 | 3,241 |
| 38,850 | 38,900 | 0 | 525 | 1,904 | 2,651 | 0 | 1,475 | 3,157 | 3,904 | 42,050 | 42,100 | 0 | 13 | 1,230 | 1,977 | 0 | 964 | 2,483 | 3,230 |
| 38,900 | 38,950 | 0 | 517 | 1,893 | 2,641 | 0 | 1,467 | 3,146 | 3,894 | 42,100 | 42,150 | 0 | 5 | 1,219 | 1,967 | 0 | 956 | 2,472 | 3,220 |
| 38,950 | 39,000 | 0 | 509 | 1,883 | 2,630 | 0 | 1,460 | 3,136 | 3,883 | 42,150 | 42,200 | 0 | * | 1,209 | 1,956 | 0 | 948 | 2,462 | 3,209 |
| 39,000 | 39,050 | 0 | 501 | 1,872 | 2,620 | 0 | 1,452 | 3,125 | 3,873 | 42,200 | 42,250 | 0 | 0 | 1,198 | 1,946 | 0 | 940 | 2,451 | 3,199 |
| 39,050 | 39,100 | 0 | 493 | 1,862 | 2,609 | 0 | 1,444 | 3,115 | 3,862 | 42,250 | 42,300 | 0 | 0 | 1,188 | 1,935 | 0 | 932 | 2,441 | 3,188 |
| 39,100 | 39,150 | 0 | 485 | 1,851 | 2,599 | 0 | 1,436 | 3,104 | 3,852 | 42,300 | 42,350 | 0 | 0 | 1,177 | 1,925 | 0 | 924 | 2,430 | 3,178 |
| 39,150 | 39,200 | 0 | 477 | 1,841 | 2,588 | 0 | 1,428 | 3,094 | 3,841 | 42,350 | 42,400 | 0 | 0 | 1,167 | 1,914 | 0 | 916 | 2,420 | 3,167 |
| 39,200 | 39,250 | 0 | 469 | 1,830 | 2,578 | 0 | 1,420 | 3,083 | 3,831 | 42,400 | 42,450 | 0 | 0 | 1,156 | 1,904 | 0 | 908 | 2,409 | 3,157 |
| 39,250 | 39,300 | 0 | 461 | 1,820 | 2,567 | 0 | 1,412 | 3,073 | 3,820 | 42,450 | 42,500 | 0 | 0 | 1,146 | 1,893 | 0 | 900 | 2,399 | 3,146 |
| 39,300 | 39,350 | 0 | 453 | 1,809 | 2,557 | 0 | 1,404 | 3,062 | 3,810 | 42,500 | 42,550 | 0 | 0 | 1,135 | 1,883 | 0 | 892 | 2,388 | 3,136 |
| 39,350 | 39,400 | 0 | 445 | 1,799 | 2,546 | 0 | 1,396 | 3,052 | 3,799 | 42,550 | 42,600 | 0 | 0 | 1,125 | 1,872 | 0 | 884 | 2,378 | 3,125 |
| 39,400 | 39,450 | 0 | 437 | 1,788 | 2,536 | 0 | 1,388 | 3,041 | 3,789 | 42,600 | 42,650 | 0 | 0 | 1,114 | 1,862 | 0 | 876 | 2,367 | 3,115 |
| 39,450 | 39,500 | 0 | 429 | 1,777 | 2,525 | 0 | 1,380 | 3,031 | 3,778 | 42,650 | 42,700 | 0 | 0 | 1,104 | 1,851 | 0 | 868 | 2,357 | 3,104 |
| 39,500 | 39,550 | 0 | 421 | 1,767 | 2,514 | 0 | 1,372 | 3,020 | 3,768 | 42,700 | 42,750 | 0 | 0 | 1,093 | 1,841 | 0 | 860 | 2,346 | 3,094 |
| 39,550 | 39,600 | 0 | 413 | 1,756 | 2,504 | 0 | 1,364 | 3,009 | 3,757 | 42,750 | 42,800 | 0 | 0 | 1,082 | 1,830 | 0 | 852 | 2,336 | 3,083 |
| 39,600 | 39,650 | 0 | 405 | 1,746 | 2,493 | 0 | 1,356 | 2,999 | 3,746 | 42,800 | 42,850 | 0 | 0 | 1,072 | 1,819 | 0 | 844 | 2,325 | 3,073 |
| 39,650 | 39,700 | 0 | 397 | 1,735 | 2,483 | 0 | 1,348 | 2,988 | 3,736 | 42,850 | 42,900 | 0 | 0 | 1,061 | 1,809 | 0 | 836 | 2,315 | 3,062 |
| 39,700 | 39,750 | 0 | 389 | 1,725 | 2,472 | 0 | 1,340 | 2,978 | 3,725 | 42,900 | 42,950 | 0 | 0 | 1,051 | 1,798 | 0 | 828 | 2,304 | 3,051 |
| 39,750 | 39,800 | 0 | 381 | 1,714 | 2,462 | 0 | 1,332 | 2,967 | 3,715 | 42,950 | 43,000 | 0 | 0 | 1,040 | 1,788 | 0 | 820 | 2,293 | 3,041 |
| 39,800 | 39,850 | 0 | 373 | 1,704 | 2,451 | 0 | 1,324 | 2,957 | 3,704 | 43,000 | 43,050 | 0 | 0 | 1,030 | 1,777 | 0 | 812 | 2,283 | 3,030 |
| 39,850 | 39,900 | 0 | 365 | 1,693 | 2,441 | 0 | 1,316 | 2,946 | 3,694 | 43,050 | 43,100 | 0 | 0 | 1,019 | 1,767 | 0 | 804 | 2,272 | 3,020 |
| 39,900 | 39,950 | 0 | 357 | 1,683 | 2,430 | 0 | 1,308 | 2,936 | 3,683 | 43,100 | 43,150 | 0 | 0 | 1,009 | 1,756 | 0 | 796 | 2,262 | 3,009 |
| 39,950 | 40,000 | 0 | 349 | 1,672 | 2,420 | 0 | 1,300 | 2,925 | 3,673 | 43,150 | 43,200 | 0 | 0 | 998 | 1,746 | 0 | 788 | 2,251 | 2,999 |
| 40,000 | 40,050 | 0 | 341 | 1,662 | 2,409 | 0 | 1,292 | 2,915 | 3,662 | 43,200 | 43,250 | 0 | 0 | 988 | 1,735 | 0 | 780 | 2,241 | 2,988 |
| 40,050 | 40,100 | 0 | 333 | 1,651 | 2,399 | 0 | 1,284 | 2,904 | 3,652 | 43,250 | 43,300 | 0 | 0 | 977 | 1,725 | 0 | 772 | 2,230 | 2,978 |
| 40,100 | 40,150 | 0 | 325 | 1,641 | 2,388 | 0 | 1,276 | 2,894 | 3,641 | 43,300 | 43,350 | 0 | 0 | 967 | 1,714 | 0 | 764 | 2,220 | 2,967 |
| 40,150 | 40,200 | 0 | 317 | 1,630 | 2,378 | 0 | 1,268 | 2,883 | 3,631 | 43,350 | 43,400 | 0 | 0 | 956 | 1,704 | 0 | 756 | 2,209 | 2,957 |
| 40,200 | 40,250 | 0 | 309 | 1,620 | 2,367 | 0 | 1,260 | 2,873 | 3,620 | 43,400 | 43,450 | 0 | 0 | 946 | 1,693 | 0 | 748 | 2,199 | 2,946 |
| 40,250 | 40,300 | 0 | 301 | 1,609 | 2,356 | 0 | 1,252 | 2,862 | 3,610 | 43,450 | 43,500 | 0 | 0 | 935 | 1,683 | 0 | 740 | 2,188 | 2,936 |
| 40,300 | 40,350 | 0 | 293 | 1,598 | 2,346 | 0 | 1,244 | 2,852 | 3,599 | 43,500 | 43,550 | 0 | 0 | 925 | 1,672 | 0 | 732 | 2,178 | 2,925 |
| 40,350 | 40,400 | 0 | 285 | 1,588 | 2,335 | 0 | 1,236 | 2,841 | 3,589 | 43,550 | 43,600 | 0 | 0 | 914 | 1,662 | 0 | 724 | 2,167 | 2,915 |
| 40,400 | 40,450 | 0 | 277 | 1,577 | 2,325 | 0 | 1,228 | 2,830 | 3,578 | 43,600 | 43,650 | 0 | 0 | 903 | 1,651 | 0 | 716 | 2,157 | 2,904 |
| 40,450 | 40,500 | 0 | 269 | 1,567 | 2,314 | 0 | 1,220 | 2,820 | 3,567 | 43,650 | 43,700 | 0 | 0 | 893 | 1,640 | 0 | 708 | 2,146 | 2,894 |
| 40,500 | 40,550 | 0 | 261 | 1,556 | 2,304 | 0 | 1,212 | 2,809 | 3,557 | 43,700 | 43,750 | 0 | 0 | 882 | 1,630 | 0 | 700 | 2,135 | 2,883 |
| 40,550 | 40,600 | 0 | 253 | 1,546 | 2,293 | 0 | 1,204 | 2,799 | 3,546 | 43,750 | 43,800 | 0 | 0 | 872 | 1,619 | 0 | 692 | 2,125 | 2,872 |
| 40,600 | 40,650 | 0 | 245 | 1,535 | 2,283 | 0 | 1,196 | 2,788 | 3,536 | 43,800 | 43,850 | 0 | 0 | 861 | 1,609 | 0 | 684 | 2,114 | 2,862 |
| 40,650 | 40,700 | 0 | 237 | 1,525 | 2,272 | 0 | 1,188 | 2,778 | 3,525 | 43,850 | 43,900 | 0 | 0 | 851 | 1,598 | 0 | 676 | 2,104 | 2,851 |
| 40,700 | 40,750 | 0 | 229 | 1,514 | 2,262 | 0 | 1,180 | 2,767 | 3,515 | 43,900 | 43,950 | 0 | 0 | 840 | 1,588 | 0 | 668 | 2,093 | 2,841 |
| 40,750 | 40,800 | 0 | 221 | 1,504 | 2,251 | 0 | 1,172 | 2,757 | 3,504 | 43,950 | 44,000 | 0 | 0 | 830 | 1,577 | 0 | 661 | 2,083 | 2,830 |

★   Use this column if your filing status is married filing separately and you qualify to claim the EIC. See the instructions for line 27a.

·   If the amount you are looking up from the worksheet is at least $42,150 but less than $42,158, and you have one qualifying child, your credit is $1.

If the amount you are looking up from the worksheet is $42,158 or more, and you have one qualifying child, you can't take the credit.

*(Continued)*

## Earned Income Credit (EIC) Table - *Continued*

(**Caution.** This is **not** a tax table.)

| If the amount you are looking up from the worksheet is– | | And your filing status is– | | | | | | | |
|---|---|---|---|---|---|---|---|---|---|
| | | Single, head of household, or qualifying widow(er)★ and you have– | | | | Married filing jointly and you have– | | | |
| At least | But less than | 0 | 1 | 2 | 3 | 0 | 1 | 2 | 3 |
| | | Your credit is– | | | | Your credit is– | | | |
| 44,000 | 44,050 | 0 | 0 | 819 | 1,567 | 0 | 653 | 2,072 | 2,820 |
| 44,050 | 44,100 | 0 | 0 | 809 | 1,556 | 0 | 645 | 2,062 | 2,809 |
| 44,100 | 44,150 | 0 | 0 | 798 | 1,546 | 0 | 637 | 2,051 | 2,799 |
| 44,150 | 44,200 | 0 | 0 | 788 | 1,535 | 0 | 629 | 2,041 | 2,788 |
| 44,200 | 44,250 | 0 | 0 | 777 | 1,525 | 0 | 621 | 2,030 | 2,778 |
| 44,250 | 44,300 | 0 | 0 | 767 | 1,514 | 0 | 613 | 2,020 | 2,767 |
| 44,300 | 44,350 | 0 | 0 | 756 | 1,504 | 0 | 605 | 2,009 | 2,757 |
| 44,350 | 44,400 | 0 | 0 | 746 | 1,493 | 0 | 597 | 1,999 | 2,746 |
| 44,400 | 44,450 | 0 | 0 | 735 | 1,483 | 0 | 589 | 1,988 | 2,736 |
| 44,450 | 44,500 | 0 | 0 | 724 | 1,472 | 0 | 581 | 1,978 | 2,725 |
| 44,500 | 44,550 | 0 | 0 | 714 | 1,461 | 0 | 573 | 1,967 | 2,715 |
| 44,550 | 44,600 | 0 | 0 | 703 | 1,451 | 0 | 565 | 1,956 | 2,704 |
| 44,600 | 44,650 | 0 | 0 | 693 | 1,440 | 0 | 557 | 1,946 | 2,693 |
| 44,650 | 44,700 | 0 | 0 | 682 | 1,430 | 0 | 549 | 1,935 | 2,683 |
| 44,700 | 44,750 | 0 | 0 | 672 | 1,419 | 0 | 541 | 1,925 | 2,672 |
| 44,750 | 44,800 | 0 | 0 | 661 | 1,409 | 0 | 533 | 1,914 | 2,662 |
| 44,800 | 44,850 | 0 | 0 | 651 | 1,398 | 0 | 525 | 1,904 | 2,651 |
| 44,850 | 44,900 | 0 | 0 | 640 | 1,388 | 0 | 517 | 1,893 | 2,641 |
| 44,900 | 44,950 | 0 | 0 | 630 | 1,377 | 0 | 509 | 1,883 | 2,630 |
| 44,950 | 45,000 | 0 | 0 | 619 | 1,367 | 0 | 501 | 1,872 | 2,620 |
| 45,000 | 45,050 | 0 | 0 | 609 | 1,356 | 0 | 493 | 1,862 | 2,609 |
| 45,050 | 45,100 | 0 | 0 | 598 | 1,346 | 0 | 485 | 1,851 | 2,599 |
| 45,100 | 45,150 | 0 | 0 | 588 | 1,335 | 0 | 477 | 1,841 | 2,588 |
| 45,150 | 45,200 | 0 | 0 | 577 | 1,325 | 0 | 469 | 1,830 | 2,578 |
| 45,200 | 45,250 | 0 | 0 | 567 | 1,314 | 0 | 461 | 1,820 | 2,567 |
| 45,250 | 45,300 | 0 | 0 | 556 | 1,303 | 0 | 453 | 1,809 | 2,557 |
| 45,300 | 45,350 | 0 | 0 | 545 | 1,293 | 0 | 445 | 1,799 | 2,546 |
| 45,350 | 45,400 | 0 | 0 | 535 | 1,282 | 0 | 437 | 1,788 | 2,536 |
| 45,400 | 45,450 | 0 | 0 | 524 | 1,272 | 0 | 429 | 1,777 | 2,525 |
| 45,450 | 45,500 | 0 | 0 | 514 | 1,261 | 0 | 421 | 1,767 | 2,514 |
| 45,500 | 45,550 | 0 | 0 | 503 | 1,251 | 0 | 413 | 1,756 | 2,504 |
| 45,550 | 45,600 | 0 | 0 | 493 | 1,240 | 0 | 405 | 1,746 | 2,493 |
| 45,600 | 45,650 | 0 | 0 | 482 | 1,230 | 0 | 397 | 1,735 | 2,483 |
| 45,650 | 45,700 | 0 | 0 | 472 | 1,219 | 0 | 389 | 1,725 | 2,472 |
| 45,700 | 45,750 | 0 | 0 | 461 | 1,209 | 0 | 381 | 1,714 | 2,462 |
| 45,750 | 45,800 | 0 | 0 | 451 | 1,198 | 0 | 373 | 1,704 | 2,451 |
| 45,800 | 45,850 | 0 | 0 | 440 | 1,188 | 0 | 365 | 1,693 | 2,441 |
| 45,850 | 45,900 | 0 | 0 | 430 | 1,177 | 0 | 357 | 1,683 | 2,430 |
| 45,900 | 45,950 | 0 | 0 | 419 | 1,167 | 0 | 349 | 1,672 | 2,420 |
| 45,950 | 46,000 | 0 | 0 | 409 | 1,156 | 0 | 341 | 1,662 | 2,409 |
| 46,000 | 46,050 | 0 | 0 | 398 | 1,146 | 0 | 333 | 1,651 | 2,399 |
| 46,050 | 46,100 | 0 | 0 | 388 | 1,135 | 0 | 325 | 1,641 | 2,388 |
| 46,100 | 46,150 | 0 | 0 | 377 | 1,124 | 0 | 317 | 1,630 | 2,378 |
| 46,150 | 46,200 | 0 | 0 | 366 | 1,114 | 0 | 309 | 1,620 | 2,367 |
| 46,200 | 46,250 | 0 | 0 | 356 | 1,103 | 0 | 301 | 1,609 | 2,356 |
| 46,250 | 46,300 | 0 | 0 | 345 | 1,093 | 0 | 293 | 1,598 | 2,346 |
| 46,300 | 46,350 | 0 | 0 | 335 | 1,082 | 0 | 285 | 1,588 | 2,335 |
| 46,350 | 46,400 | 0 | 0 | 324 | 1,072 | 0 | 277 | 1,577 | 2,325 |
| 46,400 | 46,450 | 0 | 0 | 314 | 1,061 | 0 | 269 | 1,567 | 2,314 |
| 46,450 | 46,500 | 0 | 0 | 303 | 1,051 | 0 | 261 | 1,556 | 2,304 |
| 46,500 | 46,550 | 0 | 0 | 293 | 1,040 | 0 | 253 | 1,546 | 2,293 |
| 46,550 | 46,600 | 0 | 0 | 282 | 1,030 | 0 | 245 | 1,535 | 2,283 |
| 46,600 | 46,650 | 0 | 0 | 272 | 1,019 | 0 | 237 | 1,525 | 2,272 |
| 46,650 | 46,700 | 0 | 0 | 261 | 1,009 | 0 | 229 | 1,514 | 2,262 |
| 46,700 | 46,750 | 0 | 0 | 251 | 998 | 0 | 221 | 1,504 | 2,251 |
| 46,750 | 46,800 | 0 | 0 | 240 | 988 | 0 | 213 | 1,493 | 2,241 |
| 46,800 | 46,850 | 0 | 0 | 230 | 977 | 0 | 205 | 1,483 | 2,230 |
| 46,850 | 46,900 | 0 | 0 | 219 | 967 | 0 | 197 | 1,472 | 2,220 |
| 46,900 | 46,950 | 0 | 0 | 209 | 956 | 0 | 189 | 1,462 | 2,209 |
| 46,950 | 47,000 | 0 | 0 | 198 | 945 | 0 | 181 | 1,451 | 2,199 |
| 47,000 | 47,050 | 0 | 0 | 187 | 935 | 0 | 173 | 1,441 | 2,188 |
| 47,050 | 47,100 | 0 | 0 | 177 | 924 | 0 | 165 | 1,430 | 2,177 |
| 47,100 | 47,150 | 0 | 0 | 166 | 914 | 0 | 157 | 1,419 | 2,167 |
| 47,150 | 47,200 | 0 | 0 | 156 | 903 | 0 | 149 | 1,409 | 2,156 |

| If the amount you are looking up from the worksheet is– | | And your filing status is– | | | | | | | |
|---|---|---|---|---|---|---|---|---|---|
| | | Single, head of household, or qualifying widow(er)★ and you have– | | | | Married filing jointly and you have– | | | |
| At least | But less than | 0 | 1 | 2 | 3 | 0 | 1 | 2 | 3 |
| | | Your credit is– | | | | Your credit is– | | | |
| 47,200 | 47,250 | 0 | 0 | 145 | 893 | 0 | 141 | 1,398 | 2,146 |
| 47,250 | 47,300 | 0 | 0 | 135 | 882 | 0 | 133 | 1,388 | 2,135 |
| 47,300 | 47,350 | 0 | 0 | 124 | 872 | 0 | 125 | 1,377 | 2,125 |
| 47,350 | 47,400 | 0 | 0 | 114 | 861 | 0 | 117 | 1,367 | 2,114 |
| 47,400 | 47,450 | 0 | 0 | 103 | 851 | 0 | 109 | 1,356 | 2,104 |
| 47,450 | 47,500 | 0 | 0 | 93 | 840 | 0 | 101 | 1,346 | 2,093 |
| 47,500 | 47,550 | 0 | 0 | 82 | 830 | 0 | 93 | 1,335 | 2,083 |
| 47,550 | 47,600 | 0 | 0 | 72 | 819 | 0 | 85 | 1,325 | 2,072 |
| 47,600 | 47,650 | 0 | 0 | 61 | 809 | 0 | 77 | 1,314 | 2,062 |
| 47,650 | 47,700 | 0 | 0 | 51 | 798 | 0 | 69 | 1,304 | 2,051 |
| 47,700 | 47,750 | 0 | 0 | 40 | 788 | 0 | 61 | 1,293 | 2,041 |
| 47,750 | 47,800 | 0 | 0 | 29 | 777 | 0 | 53 | 1,283 | 2,030 |
| 47,800 | 47,850 | 0 | 0 | 19 | 766 | 0 | 45 | 1,272 | 2,020 |
| 47,850 | 47,900 | 0 | 0 | 8 | 756 | 0 | 37 | 1,262 | 2,009 |
| 47,900 | 47,950 | 0 | 0 | * | 745 | 0 | 29 | 1,251 | 1,998 |
| 47,950 | 48,000 | 0 | 0 | 0 | 735 | 0 | 21 | 1,240 | 1,988 |
| 48,000 | 48,050 | 0 | 0 | 0 | 724 | 0 | 13 | 1,230 | 1,977 |
| 48,050 | 48,100 | 0 | 0 | 0 | 714 | 0 | 5 | 1,219 | 1,967 |
| 48,100 | 48,150 | 0 | 0 | 0 | 703 | 0 | ** | 1,209 | 1,956 |
| 48,150 | 48,200 | 0 | 0 | 0 | 693 | 0 | 0 | 1,198 | 1,946 |
| 48,200 | 48,250 | 0 | 0 | 0 | 682 | 0 | 0 | 1,188 | 1,935 |
| 48,250 | 48,300 | 0 | 0 | 0 | 672 | 0 | 0 | 1,177 | 1,925 |
| 48,300 | 48,350 | 0 | 0 | 0 | 661 | 0 | 0 | 1,167 | 1,914 |
| 48,350 | 48,400 | 0 | 0 | 0 | 651 | 0 | 0 | 1,156 | 1,904 |
| 48,400 | 48,450 | 0 | 0 | 0 | 640 | 0 | 0 | 1,146 | 1,893 |
| 48,450 | 48,500 | 0 | 0 | 0 | 630 | 0 | 0 | 1,135 | 1,883 |
| 48,500 | 48,550 | 0 | 0 | 0 | 619 | 0 | 0 | 1,125 | 1,872 |
| 48,550 | 48,600 | 0 | 0 | 0 | 609 | 0 | 0 | 1,114 | 1,862 |
| 48,600 | 48,650 | 0 | 0 | 0 | 598 | 0 | 0 | 1,104 | 1,851 |
| 48,650 | 48,700 | 0 | 0 | 0 | 587 | 0 | 0 | 1,093 | 1,841 |
| 48,700 | 48,750 | 0 | 0 | 0 | 577 | 0 | 0 | 1,082 | 1,830 |
| 48,750 | 48,800 | 0 | 0 | 0 | 566 | 0 | 0 | 1,072 | 1,819 |
| 48,800 | 48,850 | 0 | 0 | 0 | 556 | 0 | 0 | 1,061 | 1,809 |
| 48,850 | 48,900 | 0 | 0 | 0 | 545 | 0 | 0 | 1,051 | 1,798 |
| 48,900 | 48,950 | 0 | 0 | 0 | 535 | 0 | 0 | 1,040 | 1,788 |
| 48,950 | 49,000 | 0 | 0 | 0 | 524 | 0 | 0 | 1,030 | 1,777 |
| 49,000 | 49,050 | 0 | 0 | 0 | 514 | 0 | 0 | 1,019 | 1,767 |
| 49,050 | 49,100 | 0 | 0 | 0 | 503 | 0 | 0 | 1,009 | 1,756 |
| 49,100 | 49,150 | 0 | 0 | 0 | 493 | 0 | 0 | 998 | 1,746 |
| 49,150 | 49,200 | 0 | 0 | 0 | 482 | 0 | 0 | 988 | 1,735 |
| 49,200 | 49,250 | 0 | 0 | 0 | 472 | 0 | 0 | 977 | 1,725 |
| 49,250 | 49,300 | 0 | 0 | 0 | 461 | 0 | 0 | 967 | 1,714 |
| 49,300 | 49,350 | 0 | 0 | 0 | 451 | 0 | 0 | 956 | 1,704 |
| 49,350 | 49,400 | 0 | 0 | 0 | 440 | 0 | 0 | 946 | 1,693 |
| 49,400 | 49,450 | 0 | 0 | 0 | 430 | 0 | 0 | 935 | 1,683 |
| 49,450 | 49,500 | 0 | 0 | 0 | 419 | 0 | 0 | 925 | 1,672 |
| 49,500 | 49,550 | 0 | 0 | 0 | 408 | 0 | 0 | 914 | 1,662 |
| 49,550 | 49,600 | 0 | 0 | 0 | 398 | 0 | 0 | 903 | 1,651 |
| 49,600 | 49,650 | 0 | 0 | 0 | 387 | 0 | 0 | 893 | 1,640 |
| 49,650 | 49,700 | 0 | 0 | 0 | 377 | 0 | 0 | 882 | 1,630 |
| 49,700 | 49,750 | 0 | 0 | 0 | 366 | 0 | 0 | 872 | 1,619 |
| 49,750 | 49,800 | 0 | 0 | 0 | 356 | 0 | 0 | 861 | 1,609 |
| 49,800 | 49,850 | 0 | 0 | 0 | 345 | 0 | 0 | 851 | 1,598 |
| 49,850 | 49,900 | 0 | 0 | 0 | 335 | 0 | 0 | 840 | 1,588 |
| 49,900 | 49,950 | 0 | 0 | 0 | 324 | 0 | 0 | 830 | 1,577 |
| 49,950 | 50,000 | 0 | 0 | 0 | 314 | 0 | 0 | 819 | 1,567 |
| 50,000 | 50,050 | 0 | 0 | 0 | 303 | 0 | 0 | 809 | 1,556 |
| 50,050 | 50,100 | 0 | 0 | 0 | 293 | 0 | 0 | 798 | 1,546 |
| 50,100 | 50,150 | 0 | 0 | 0 | 282 | 0 | 0 | 788 | 1,535 |
| 50,150 | 50,200 | 0 | 0 | 0 | 272 | 0 | 0 | 777 | 1,525 |
| 50,200 | 50,250 | 0 | 0 | 0 | 261 | 0 | 0 | 767 | 1,514 |
| 50,250 | 50,300 | 0 | 0 | 0 | 250 | 0 | 0 | 756 | 1,504 |
| 50,300 | 50,350 | 0 | 0 | 0 | 240 | 0 | 0 | 746 | 1,493 |
| 50,350 | 50,400 | 0 | 0 | 0 | 229 | 0 | 0 | 735 | 1,483 |

★   Use this column if your filing status is married filing separately and you qualify to claim the EIC. See the instructions for line 27a.

*   If the amount you are looking up from the worksheet is at least $47,900 but less than $47,915, and you have two qualifying children, your credit is $2.
   If the amount you are looking up from the worksheet is $47,915 or more, and you have two qualifying children, you can't take the credit.

**   If the amount you are looking up from the worksheet is at least $48,100 but less than $48,108, and you have one qualifying child, your credit is $1.
   If the amount you are looking up from the worksheet is $48,108 or more, and you have one qualifying child, you can't take the credit.

*(Continued)*

**Earned Income Credit (EIC) Table** - *Continued*                    (**Caution.** This is **not** a tax table.)

| If the amount you are looking up from the worksheet is– | | Single, head of household, or qualifying widow(er)★ and you have– | | | | Married filing jointly and you have– | | | |
|---|---|---|---|---|---|---|---|---|---|
| At least | But less than | 0 | 1 | 2 | 3 | 0 | 1 | 2 | 3 |
| | | Your credit is– | | | | Your credit is– | | | |
| 50,400 | 50,450 | 0 | 0 | 0 | 219 | 0 | 0 | 724 | 1,472 |
| 50,450 | 50,500 | 0 | 0 | 0 | 208 | 0 | 0 | 714 | 1,461 |
| 50,500 | 50,550 | 0 | 0 | 0 | 198 | 0 | 0 | 703 | 1,451 |
| 50,550 | 50,600 | 0 | 0 | 0 | 187 | 0 | 0 | 693 | 1,440 |
| 50,600 | 50,650 | 0 | 0 | 0 | 177 | 0 | 0 | 682 | 1,430 |
| 50,650 | 50,700 | 0 | 0 | 0 | 166 | 0 | 0 | 672 | 1,419 |
| 50,700 | 50,750 | 0 | 0 | 0 | 156 | 0 | 0 | 661 | 1,409 |
| 50,750 | 50,800 | 0 | 0 | 0 | 145 | 0 | 0 | 651 | 1,398 |
| 50,800 | 50,850 | 0 | 0 | 0 | 135 | 0 | 0 | 640 | 1,388 |
| 50,850 | 50,900 | 0 | 0 | 0 | 124 | 0 | 0 | 630 | 1,377 |
| 50,900 | 50,950 | 0 | 0 | 0 | 114 | 0 | 0 | 619 | 1,367 |
| 50,950 | 51,000 | 0 | 0 | 0 | 103 | 0 | 0 | 609 | 1,356 |
| 51,000 | 51,050 | 0 | 0 | 0 | 93 | 0 | 0 | 598 | 1,346 |
| 51,050 | 51,100 | 0 | 0 | 0 | 82 | 0 | 0 | 588 | 1,335 |
| 51,100 | 51,150 | 0 | 0 | 0 | 71 | 0 | 0 | 577 | 1,325 |
| 51,150 | 51,200 | 0 | 0 | 0 | 61 | 0 | 0 | 567 | 1,314 |
| 51,200 | 51,250 | 0 | 0 | 0 | 50 | 0 | 0 | 556 | 1,303 |
| 51,250 | 51,300 | 0 | 0 | 0 | 40 | 0 | 0 | 545 | 1,293 |
| 51,300 | 51,350 | 0 | 0 | 0 | 29 | 0 | 0 | 535 | 1,282 |
| 51,350 | 51,400 | 0 | 0 | 0 | 19 | 0 | 0 | 524 | 1,272 |
| 51,400 | 51,450 | 0 | 0 | 0 | 8 | 0 | 0 | 514 | 1,261 |
| 51,450 | 51,500 | 0 | 0 | 0 | * | 0 | 0 | 503 | 1,251 |
| 51,500 | 51,550 | 0 | 0 | 0 | 0 | 0 | 0 | 493 | 1,240 |
| 51,550 | 51,600 | 0 | 0 | 0 | 0 | 0 | 0 | 482 | 1,230 |
| 51,600 | 51,650 | 0 | 0 | 0 | 0 | 0 | 0 | 472 | 1,219 |
| 51,650 | 51,700 | 0 | 0 | 0 | 0 | 0 | 0 | 461 | 1,209 |
| 51,700 | 51,750 | 0 | 0 | 0 | 0 | 0 | 0 | 451 | 1,198 |
| 51,750 | 51,800 | 0 | 0 | 0 | 0 | 0 | 0 | 440 | 1,188 |
| 51,800 | 51,850 | 0 | 0 | 0 | 0 | 0 | 0 | 430 | 1,177 |
| 51,850 | 51,900 | 0 | 0 | 0 | 0 | 0 | 0 | 419 | 1,167 |
| 51,900 | 51,950 | 0 | 0 | 0 | 0 | 0 | 0 | 409 | 1,156 |
| 51,950 | 52,000 | 0 | 0 | 0 | 0 | 0 | 0 | 398 | 1,146 |
| 52,000 | 52,050 | 0 | 0 | 0 | 0 | 0 | 0 | 388 | 1,135 |
| 52,050 | 52,100 | 0 | 0 | 0 | 0 | 0 | 0 | 377 | 1,124 |
| 52,100 | 52,150 | 0 | 0 | 0 | 0 | 0 | 0 | 366 | 1,114 |
| 52,150 | 52,200 | 0 | 0 | 0 | 0 | 0 | 0 | 356 | 1,103 |
| 52,200 | 52,250 | 0 | 0 | 0 | 0 | 0 | 0 | 345 | 1,093 |
| 52,250 | 52,300 | 0 | 0 | 0 | 0 | 0 | 0 | 335 | 1,082 |
| 52,300 | 52,350 | 0 | 0 | 0 | 0 | 0 | 0 | 324 | 1,072 |
| 52,350 | 52,400 | 0 | 0 | 0 | 0 | 0 | 0 | 314 | 1,061 |
| 52,400 | 52,450 | 0 | 0 | 0 | 0 | 0 | 0 | 303 | 1,051 |
| 52,450 | 52,500 | 0 | 0 | 0 | 0 | 0 | 0 | 293 | 1,040 |
| 52,500 | 52,550 | 0 | 0 | 0 | 0 | 0 | 0 | 282 | 1,030 |
| 52,550 | 52,600 | 0 | 0 | 0 | 0 | 0 | 0 | 272 | 1,019 |
| 52,600 | 52,650 | 0 | 0 | 0 | 0 | 0 | 0 | 261 | 1,009 |
| 52,650 | 52,700 | 0 | 0 | 0 | 0 | 0 | 0 | 251 | 998 |
| 52,700 | 52,750 | 0 | 0 | 0 | 0 | 0 | 0 | 240 | 988 |
| 52,750 | 52,800 | 0 | 0 | 0 | 0 | 0 | 0 | 230 | 977 |
| 52,800 | 52,850 | 0 | 0 | 0 | 0 | 0 | 0 | 219 | 967 |
| 52,850 | 52,900 | 0 | 0 | 0 | 0 | 0 | 0 | 209 | 956 |
| 52,900 | 52,950 | 0 | 0 | 0 | 0 | 0 | 0 | 198 | 945 |
| 52,950 | 53,000 | 0 | 0 | 0 | 0 | 0 | 0 | 187 | 935 |
| 53,000 | 53,050 | 0 | 0 | 0 | 0 | 0 | 0 | 177 | 924 |
| 53,050 | 53,100 | 0 | 0 | 0 | 0 | 0 | 0 | 166 | 914 |
| 53,100 | 53,150 | 0 | 0 | 0 | 0 | 0 | 0 | 156 | 903 |
| 53,150 | 53,200 | 0 | 0 | 0 | 0 | 0 | 0 | 145 | 893 |
| 53,200 | 53,250 | 0 | 0 | 0 | 0 | 0 | 0 | 135 | 882 |
| 53,250 | 53,300 | 0 | 0 | 0 | 0 | 0 | 0 | 124 | 872 |
| 53,300 | 53,350 | 0 | 0 | 0 | 0 | 0 | 0 | 114 | 861 |
| 53,350 | 53,400 | 0 | 0 | 0 | 0 | 0 | 0 | 103 | 851 |
| 53,400 | 53,450 | 0 | 0 | 0 | 0 | 0 | 0 | 93 | 840 |
| 53,450 | 53,500 | 0 | 0 | 0 | 0 | 0 | 0 | 82 | 830 |
| 53,500 | 53,550 | 0 | 0 | 0 | 0 | 0 | 0 | 72 | 819 |
| 53,550 | 53,600 | 0 | 0 | 0 | 0 | 0 | 0 | 61 | 809 |

| If the amount you are looking up from the worksheet is– | | Single, head of household, or qualifying widow(er)★ and you have– | | | | Married filing jointly and you have– | | | |
|---|---|---|---|---|---|---|---|---|---|
| At least | But less than | 0 | 1 | 2 | 3 | 0 | 1 | 2 | 3 |
| | | Your credit is– | | | | Your credit is– | | | |
| 53,600 | 53,650 | 0 | 0 | 0 | 0 | 0 | 0 | 51 | 798 |
| 53,650 | 53,700 | 0 | 0 | 0 | 0 | 0 | 0 | 40 | 788 |
| 53,700 | 53,750 | 0 | 0 | 0 | 0 | 0 | 0 | 29 | 777 |
| 53,750 | 53,800 | 0 | 0 | 0 | 0 | 0 | 0 | 19 | 766 |
| 53,800 | 53,850 | 0 | 0 | 0 | 0 | 0 | 0 | 8 | 756 |
| 53,850 | 53,900 | 0 | 0 | 0 | 0 | 0 | 0 | ** | 745 |
| 53,900 | 53,950 | 0 | 0 | 0 | 0 | 0 | 0 | 0 | 735 |
| 53,950 | 54,000 | 0 | 0 | 0 | 0 | 0 | 0 | 0 | 724 |
| 54,000 | 54,050 | 0 | 0 | 0 | 0 | 0 | 0 | 0 | 714 |
| 54,050 | 54,100 | 0 | 0 | 0 | 0 | 0 | 0 | 0 | 703 |
| 54,100 | 54,150 | 0 | 0 | 0 | 0 | 0 | 0 | 0 | 693 |
| 54,150 | 54,200 | 0 | 0 | 0 | 0 | 0 | 0 | 0 | 682 |
| 54,200 | 54,250 | 0 | 0 | 0 | 0 | 0 | 0 | 0 | 672 |
| 54,250 | 54,300 | 0 | 0 | 0 | 0 | 0 | 0 | 0 | 661 |
| 54,300 | 54,350 | 0 | 0 | 0 | 0 | 0 | 0 | 0 | 651 |
| 54,350 | 54,400 | 0 | 0 | 0 | 0 | 0 | 0 | 0 | 640 |
| 54,400 | 54,450 | 0 | 0 | 0 | 0 | 0 | 0 | 0 | 630 |
| 54,450 | 54,500 | 0 | 0 | 0 | 0 | 0 | 0 | 0 | 619 |
| 54,500 | 54,550 | 0 | 0 | 0 | 0 | 0 | 0 | 0 | 609 |
| 54,550 | 54,600 | 0 | 0 | 0 | 0 | 0 | 0 | 0 | 598 |
| 54,600 | 54,650 | 0 | 0 | 0 | 0 | 0 | 0 | 0 | 587 |
| 54,650 | 54,700 | 0 | 0 | 0 | 0 | 0 | 0 | 0 | 577 |
| 54,700 | 54,750 | 0 | 0 | 0 | 0 | 0 | 0 | 0 | 566 |
| 54,750 | 54,800 | 0 | 0 | 0 | 0 | 0 | 0 | 0 | 556 |
| 54,800 | 54,850 | 0 | 0 | 0 | 0 | 0 | 0 | 0 | 545 |
| 54,850 | 54,900 | 0 | 0 | 0 | 0 | 0 | 0 | 0 | 535 |
| 54,900 | 54,950 | 0 | 0 | 0 | 0 | 0 | 0 | 0 | 524 |
| 54,950 | 55,000 | 0 | 0 | 0 | 0 | 0 | 0 | 0 | 514 |
| 55,000 | 55,050 | 0 | 0 | 0 | 0 | 0 | 0 | 0 | 503 |
| 55,050 | 55,100 | 0 | 0 | 0 | 0 | 0 | 0 | 0 | 493 |
| 55,100 | 55,150 | 0 | 0 | 0 | 0 | 0 | 0 | 0 | 482 |
| 55,150 | 55,200 | 0 | 0 | 0 | 0 | 0 | 0 | 0 | 472 |
| 55,200 | 55,250 | 0 | 0 | 0 | 0 | 0 | 0 | 0 | 461 |
| 55,250 | 55,300 | 0 | 0 | 0 | 0 | 0 | 0 | 0 | 451 |
| 55,300 | 55,350 | 0 | 0 | 0 | 0 | 0 | 0 | 0 | 440 |
| 55,350 | 55,400 | 0 | 0 | 0 | 0 | 0 | 0 | 0 | 430 |
| 55,400 | 55,450 | 0 | 0 | 0 | 0 | 0 | 0 | 0 | 419 |
| 55,450 | 55,500 | 0 | 0 | 0 | 0 | 0 | 0 | 0 | 408 |
| 55,500 | 55,550 | 0 | 0 | 0 | 0 | 0 | 0 | 0 | 398 |
| 55,550 | 55,600 | 0 | 0 | 0 | 0 | 0 | 0 | 0 | 387 |
| 55,600 | 55,650 | 0 | 0 | 0 | 0 | 0 | 0 | 0 | 377 |
| 55,650 | 55,700 | 0 | 0 | 0 | 0 | 0 | 0 | 0 | 366 |
| 55,700 | 55,750 | 0 | 0 | 0 | 0 | 0 | 0 | 0 | 356 |
| 55,750 | 55,800 | 0 | 0 | 0 | 0 | 0 | 0 | 0 | 345 |
| 55,800 | 55,850 | 0 | 0 | 0 | 0 | 0 | 0 | 0 | 335 |
| 55,850 | 55,900 | 0 | 0 | 0 | 0 | 0 | 0 | 0 | 324 |
| 55,900 | 55,950 | 0 | 0 | 0 | 0 | 0 | 0 | 0 | 314 |
| 55,950 | 56,000 | 0 | 0 | 0 | 0 | 0 | 0 | 0 | 303 |
| 56,000 | 56,050 | 0 | 0 | 0 | 0 | 0 | 0 | 0 | 293 |
| 56,050 | 56,100 | 0 | 0 | 0 | 0 | 0 | 0 | 0 | 282 |
| 56,100 | 56,150 | 0 | 0 | 0 | 0 | 0 | 0 | 0 | 272 |
| 56,150 | 56,200 | 0 | 0 | 0 | 0 | 0 | 0 | 0 | 261 |
| 56,200 | 56,250 | 0 | 0 | 0 | 0 | 0 | 0 | 0 | 250 |
| 56,250 | 56,300 | 0 | 0 | 0 | 0 | 0 | 0 | 0 | 240 |
| 56,300 | 56,350 | 0 | 0 | 0 | 0 | 0 | 0 | 0 | 229 |
| 56,350 | 56,400 | 0 | 0 | 0 | 0 | 0 | 0 | 0 | 219 |
| 56,400 | 56,450 | 0 | 0 | 0 | 0 | 0 | 0 | 0 | 208 |
| 56,450 | 56,500 | 0 | 0 | 0 | 0 | 0 | 0 | 0 | 198 |
| 56,500 | 56,550 | 0 | 0 | 0 | 0 | 0 | 0 | 0 | 187 |
| 56,550 | 56,600 | 0 | 0 | 0 | 0 | 0 | 0 | 0 | 177 |
| 56,600 | 56,650 | 0 | 0 | 0 | 0 | 0 | 0 | 0 | 166 |
| 56,650 | 56,700 | 0 | 0 | 0 | 0 | 0 | 0 | 0 | 156 |
| 56,700 | 56,750 | 0 | 0 | 0 | 0 | 0 | 0 | 0 | 145 |
| 56,750 | 56,800 | 0 | 0 | 0 | 0 | 0 | 0 | 0 | 135 |

★ Use this column if your filing status is married filing separately and you qualify to claim the EIC. See the instructions for line 27a.

* If the amount you are looking up from the worksheet is at least $51,450 but less than $51,464, and you have three qualifying children, your credit is $2.

If the amount you are looking up from the worksheet is $51,464 or more, and you have three qualifying children, you can't take the credit.

** If the amount you are looking up from the worksheet is at least $53,850 but less than $53,865, and you have two qualifying children, your credit is $2.

If the amount you are looking up from the worksheet is $53,865 or more, and you have two qualifying children, you can't take the credit.

*(Continued)*

**Earned Income Credit (EIC) Table** - *Continued*

**(Caution. This is not a tax table.)**

| If the amount you are looking up from the worksheet is– | | And your filing status is– | | | | | | | | If the amount you are looking up from the worksheet is– | | And your filing status is– | | | | | | | |
|---|---|---|---|---|---|---|---|---|---|---|---|---|---|---|---|---|---|---|---|
| | | Single, head of household, or qualifying widow(er)★ and you have– | | | | Married filing jointly and you have– | | | | | | Single, head of household, or qualifying widow(er)★ and you have– | | | | Married filing jointly and you have– | | | |
| At least | But less than | 0 | 1 | 2 | 3 | 0 | 1 | 2 | 3 | At least | But less than | 0 | 1 | 2 | 3 | 0 | 1 | 2 | 3 |
| | | Your credit is– | | | | Your credit is– | | | | | | Your credit is– | | | | Your credit is– | | | |
| 56,800 | 56,850 | 0 | 0 | 0 | 0 | 0 | 0 | 0 | 124 | 57,200 | 57,250 | 0 | 0 | 0 | 0 | 0 | 0 | 0 | 40 |
| 56,850 | 56,900 | 0 | 0 | 0 | 0 | 0 | 0 | 0 | 114 | 57,250 | 57,300 | 0 | 0 | 0 | 0 | 0 | 0 | 0 | 29 |
| 56,900 | 56,950 | 0 | 0 | 0 | 0 | 0 | 0 | 0 | 103 | 57,300 | 57,350 | 0 | 0 | 0 | 0 | 0 | 0 | 0 | 19 |
| 56,950 | 57,000 | 0 | 0 | 0 | 0 | 0 | 0 | 0 | 93 | 57,350 | 57,400 | 0 | 0 | 0 | 0 | 0 | 0 | 0 | 8 |
| 57,000 | 57,050 | 0 | 0 | 0 | 0 | 0 | 0 | 0 | 82 | 57,400 | 57,414 | 0 | 0 | 0 | 0 | 0 | 0 | 0 | * |
| 57,050 | 57,100 | 0 | 0 | 0 | 0 | 0 | 0 | 0 | 71 | | | | | | | | | | |
| 57,100 | 57,150 | 0 | 0 | 0 | 0 | 0 | 0 | 0 | 61 | | | | | | | | | | |
| 57,150 | 57,200 | 0 | 0 | 0 | 0 | 0 | 0 | 0 | 50 | | | | | | | | | | |

★ Use this column if your filing status is married filing separately and you qualify to claim the EIC. See the instructions for line 27a.

* If the amount you are looking up from the worksheet is at least $57,400 but less than $57,414, and you have three qualifying children, your credit is $2.

If the amount you are looking up from the worksheet is $57,414 or more, and you have three qualifying children, you can't take the credit.

# Appendix B

*TIP: If the amount on line 5 is 150 or less, your applicable figure is 0.0000. If the amount on line 5 is 400 or more, your applicable figure is 0.0850.*

| IF Form 8962, line 5, is... | ENTER on Form 8962, line 7... | IF Form 8962, line 5, is... | ENTER on Form 8962, line 7... | IF Form 8962, line 5, is... | ENTER on Form 8962, line 7... | IF Form 8962, line 5, is... | ENTER on Form 8962, line 7... | IF Form 8962, line 5, is... | ENTER on Form 8962, line 7... |
|---|---|---|---|---|---|---|---|---|---|
| less than 150 | 0.0000 | 200 | 0.0200 | 251 | 0.0404 | 302 | 0.0605 | 353 | 0.0733 |
| 150 | 0.0000 | 201 | 0.0204 | 252 | 0.0408 | 303 | 0.0608 | 354 | 0.0735 |
| 151 | 0.0004 | 202 | 0.0208 | 253 | 0.0412 | 304 | 0.0610 | 355 | 0.0738 |
| 152 | 0.0008 | 203 | 0.0212 | 254 | 0.0416 | 305 | 0.0613 | 356 | 0.0740 |
| 153 | 0.0012 | 204 | 0.0216 | 255 | 0.0420 | 306 | 0.0615 | 357 | 0.0743 |
| 154 | 0.0016 | 205 | 0.0220 | 256 | 0.0424 | 307 | 0.0618 | 358 | 0.0745 |
| 155 | 0.0020 | 206 | 0.0224 | 257 | 0.0428 | 308 | 0.0620 | 359 | 0.0748 |
| 156 | 0.0024 | 207 | 0.0228 | 258 | 0.0432 | 309 | 0.0623 | 360 | 0.0750 |
| 157 | 0.0028 | 208 | 0.0232 | 259 | 0.0436 | 310 | 0.0625 | 361 | 0.0753 |
| 158 | 0.0032 | 209 | 0.0236 | 260 | 0.0440 | 311 | 0.0628 | 362 | 0.0755 |
| 159 | 0.0036 | 210 | 0.0240 | 261 | 0.0444 | 312 | 0.0630 | 363 | 0.0758 |
| 160 | 0.0040 | 211 | 0.0244 | 262 | 0.0448 | 313 | 0.0633 | 364 | 0.0760 |
| 161 | 0.0044 | 212 | 0.0248 | 263 | 0.0452 | 314 | 0.0635 | 365 | 0.0763 |
| 162 | 0.0048 | 213 | 0.0252 | 264 | 0.0456 | 315 | 0.0638 | 366 | 0.0765 |
| 163 | 0.0052 | 214 | 0.0256 | 265 | 0.0460 | 316 | 0.0640 | 367 | 0.0768 |
| 164 | 0.0056 | 215 | 0.0260 | 266 | 0.0464 | 317 | 0.0643 | 368 | 0.0770 |
| 165 | 0.0060 | 216 | 0.0264 | 267 | 0.0468 | 318 | 0.0645 | 369 | 0.0773 |
| 166 | 0.0064 | 217 | 0.0268 | 268 | 0.0472 | 319 | 0.0648 | 370 | 0.0775 |
| 167 | 0.0068 | 218 | 0.0272 | 269 | 0.0476 | 320 | 0.0650 | 371 | 0.0778 |
| 168 | 0.0072 | 219 | 0.0276 | 270 | 0.0480 | 321 | 0.0653 | 372 | 0.0780 |
| 169 | 0.0076 | 220 | 0.0280 | 271 | 0.0484 | 322 | 0.0655 | 373 | 0.0783 |
| 170 | 0.0080 | 221 | 0.0284 | 272 | 0.0488 | 323 | 0.0658 | 374 | 0.0785 |
| 171 | 0.0084 | 222 | 0.0288 | 273 | 0.0492 | 324 | 0.0660 | 375 | 0.0788 |
| 172 | 0.0088 | 223 | 0.0292 | 274 | 0.0496 | 325 | 0.0663 | 376 | 0.0790 |
| 173 | 0.0092 | 224 | 0.0296 | 275 | 0.0500 | 326 | 0.0665 | 377 | 0.0793 |
| 174 | 0.0096 | 225 | 0.0300 | 276 | 0.0504 | 327 | 0.0668 | 378 | 0.0795 |
| 175 | 0.0100 | 226 | 0.0304 | 277 | 0.0508 | 328 | 0.0670 | 379 | 0.0798 |
| 176 | 0.0104 | 227 | 0.0308 | 278 | 0.0512 | 329 | 0.0673 | 380 | 0.0800 |
| 177 | 0.0108 | 228 | 0.0312 | 279 | 0.0516 | 330 | 0.0675 | 381 | 0.0803 |
| 178 | 0.0112 | 229 | 0.0316 | 280 | 0.0520 | 331 | 0.0678 | 382 | 0.0805 |
| 179 | 0.0116 | 230 | 0.0320 | 281 | 0.0524 | 332 | 0.0680 | 383 | 0.0808 |
| 180 | 0.0120 | 231 | 0.0324 | 282 | 0.0528 | 333 | 0.0683 | 384 | 0.0810 |
| 181 | 0.0124 | 232 | 0.0328 | 283 | 0.0532 | 334 | 0.0685 | 385 | 0.0813 |
| 182 | 0.0128 | 233 | 0.0332 | 284 | 0.0536 | 335 | 0.0688 | 386 | 0.0815 |
| 183 | 0.0132 | 234 | 0.0336 | 285 | 0.0540 | 336 | 0.0690 | 387 | 0.0818 |
| 184 | 0.0136 | 235 | 0.0340 | 286 | 0.0544 | 337 | 0.0693 | 388 | 0.0820 |
| 185 | 0.0140 | 236 | 0.0344 | 287 | 0.0548 | 338 | 0.0695 | 389 | 0.0823 |
| 186 | 0.0144 | 237 | 0.0348 | 288 | 0.0552 | 339 | 0.0698 | 390 | 0.0825 |
| 187 | 0.0148 | 238 | 0.0352 | 289 | 0.0556 | 340 | 0.0700 | 391 | 0.0828 |
| 188 | 0.0152 | 239 | 0.0356 | 290 | 0.0560 | 341 | 0.0703 | 392 | 0.0830 |
| 189 | 0.0156 | 240 | 0.0360 | 291 | 0.0564 | 342 | 0.0705 | 393 | 0.0833 |
| 190 | 0.0160 | 241 | 0.0364 | 292 | 0.0568 | 343 | 0.0708 | 394 | 0.0835 |
| 191 | 0.0164 | 242 | 0.0368 | 293 | 0.0572 | 344 | 0.0710 | 395 | 0.0838 |
| 192 | 0.0168 | 243 | 0.0372 | 294 | 0.0576 | 345 | 0.0713 | 396 | 0.0840 |
| 193 | 0.0172 | 244 | 0.0376 | 295 | 0.0580 | 346 | 0.0715 | 397 | 0.0843 |
| 194 | 0.0176 | 245 | 0.0380 | 296 | 0.0584 | 347 | 0.0718 | 398 | 0.0845 |
| 195 | 0.0180 | 246 | 0.0384 | 297 | 0.0588 | 348 | 0.0720 | 399 | 0.0848 |
| 196 | 0.0184 | 247 | 0.0388 | 298 | 0.0592 | 349 | 0.0723 | 400 or more | 0.0850 |
| 197 | 0.0188 | 248 | 0.0392 | 299 | 0.0596 | 350 | 0.0725 | | |
| 198 | 0.0192 | 249 | 0.0396 | 300 | 0.0600 | 351 | 0.0728 | | |
| 199 | 0.0196 | 250 | 0.0400 | 301 | 0.0603 | 352 | 0.0730 | | |

Source: U.S. Department of the Treasury, Internal Revenue Service Table 2 for Form 8962. Washington, DC: 2021.

## EA Fast Fact

The Enrolled Agent exam is a multiple-choice test, and each question has four potential answers. The question styles may include direct questions, incomplete statements or "all of the following except" questions. Each part of the exam is approximately 100 questions. An applicant needs a minimum passing score of 70% for each part. Test results are available immediately following the exam. If failed, each part may be taken up to four times in any testing year, but the goal here is to put the preparation time in so that, for each part, you are one and done.

**IMPORTANT**

You are eligible to receive absolutely free, the Surgent Enrolled Agent review program for Part I of the EA exam as a result of purchasing this text. To activate your free access, go to https://Surgent.com/McGrawHill/EA.

## Discussion Questions

All applicable discussion questions are available with **Connect©**

**EA** **LO 9-1**
1. A taxpayer has $4,000 of qualified employment-related expenses paid on behalf of one qualifying child. Determine the maximum and minimum amounts of the child and dependent care tax credit available to the taxpayer, and explain the circumstances in which the maximum and minimum credits would be permitted.

_____

_____

_____

**EA** **LO 9-1**
2. Briefly explain the requirements that must be met to receive a tax credit for child and dependent care expenses.

_____

_____

_____

**EA** **LO 9-1**
3. For purposes of the tax credit for child and dependent care expenses, explain the limitations concerning the amount of qualified expenses that can be used to calculate the credit.

_____

_____

_____

**EA** **LO 9-1**
4. A taxpayer maintains a household and is entitled to claim an incapacitated adult child as a dependent. The child lives during the week at an adult day care center and on the weekends at home with the taxpayer. The taxpayer pays a fee to the center so the taxpayer can be gainfully employed. Does the fee qualify for treatment as a qualifying expense for purposes of the child and dependent care tax credit? Why or why not?

_____

_____

_____

**LO 9-2**
5. To determine the amount of the credit for the elderly or the disabled, the appropriate base amount must be adjusted by the effect of two items. What are those two items, and in what way is the base amount adjusted?

_____

_____

_____

EA   LO 9-3   6. Two kinds of educational tax credits are available. Name them and briefly discuss the criteria necessary to claim each of the credits.

_____
_____
_____

EA   LO 9-3   7. Explain what qualifies as educational expenses for the purposes of educational tax credits.

_____
_____
_____

EA   LO 9-3   8. Jerome is single and cannot be claimed by anyone as a dependent. He is a student at a local university enrolled full time in an MBA program. His tuition bill was $5,000. He paid the bill by withdrawing $2,000 from his savings account and borrowing the remainder from a local bank. For purposes of the educational tax credits, what is the amount of Jerome's qualifying expenses?

_____
_____
_____

EA   LO 9-3   9. Briefly explain when and how each of the two education credits is phased out.

_____
_____
_____

LO 9-4   10. Explain the two instances in which taxpayers may choose to deduct foreign taxes as an itemized deduction rather than as a credit.

_____
_____
_____

LO 9-4   11. Explain how the foreign tax credit limitation works.

_____
_____
_____

EA   LO 9-5   12. Taxpayers can claim a child tax credit for a qualifying child. Define *qualifying child*.

_____
_____
_____

EA   LO 9-5   13. Paul and Olivia filed a joint tax return and reported modified AGI of $142,000. They have two qualifying children, ages 7 and 9, for the purposes of the child tax credit. What is the amount of their child tax credit? What is the amount of their credit if their modified AGI is $167,000? What is the amount of their credit if their modified AGI is $432,000?

_____
_____
_____

EA   LO 9-6   14. Explain the limitations pertaining to the retirement savings contributions credit.

_____
_____

**EA** LO 9-6 15. Leonardo's filing status is head of household. He has modified AGI of $34,000, and he made a $3,000 contribution to his IRA. What is the amount of his retirement savings contributions credit? What would the credit be if he had a filing status of single?

_____

_____

_____

LO 9-7 16. What limitations are associated with the adoption credit in terms of both dollar amounts and eligibility?

_____

_____

_____

LO 9-7 17. In the case of the adoption credit, what special rules apply when adopting a child who is a *child with special needs?*

_____

_____

_____

LO 9-7 18. In the case of the adoption credit, what special rules apply when adopting a child who is a citizen of another country?

_____

_____

_____

**EA** LO 9-8 19. What is the definition of *qualifying child* for purposes of the Earned Income Credit?

_____

_____

_____

**EA** LO 9-8 20. Briefly explain the difference between a refundable and a nonrefundable tax credit and give three examples of tax credits that may be refundable (or partly refundable) discussed in this chapter.

_____

_____

_____

**EA** LO 9-9 21. Briefly explain the purpose of the premium tax credit.

_____

_____

_____

**EA** LO 9-9 22. The amount of the premium tax credit is the lesser of what two factors?

_____

_____

_____

## Multiple-Choice Questions ![Mc Graw Hill] connect

All applicable multiple-choice questions are available with **Connect**©

**EA** **LO 9-1** 23. Jamison is a single dad with two dependent children: Zoey, age 7, and Conner, age 3. He has an AGI of $63,000 and paid $3,600 to a qualified day care center for the two children. What amount can Jamison receive for the child and dependent care credit?

a. $720.

b. $1,800.

c. $3,600.

d. $31,500.

**EA** **LO 9-1** 24. Allie and Buddy are married, file a joint return, and have one son, Zack, age 5. Buddy has earned income of $48,000, and Allie was a full-time student for nine months (with no income). They paid a qualified child care center $3,450. How much is Allie and Buddy's child and dependent care credit for the year?

a. $0.

b. $1,125.

c. $1,725.

d. $3,450.

**LO 9-2** 25. Avril and John are ages 70 and 72, respectively, and file a joint return. They have an AGI of $17,000 and received $1,000 in nontaxable social security benefits. How much can Avril and John take as a credit for the elderly or the disabled?

a. $2,550.

b. $975.

c. $450.

d. $375.

**LO 9-2** 26. Dennis and Vera are ages 69 and 59, respectively, and file a joint return. They have an AGI of $28,000 and received $2,000 in nontaxable social security benefits. How much can Dennis and Vera take as a credit for the elderly or the disabled?

a. $0.

b. $1,125.

c. $2,000.

d. $7,500.

**EA** **LO 9-3** 27. Nathan paid $2,750 in qualifying expenses for his daughter, who attended a community college. How much is Nathan's lifetime learning credit *without* regard to AGI limitations or other credits?

a. $250.

b. $550.

c. $825.

d. $1,375.

**EA** **LO 9-3** 28. DJ and Gwen paid $3,200 in qualifying expenses for their son, Nikko, who is a freshman attending the University of Colorado. DJ and Gwen have AGI of $170,000 and file a joint return. What is their allowable American opportunity tax credit?

a. $0.

b. $1,150.

c. $2,300.

d. $3,200.

EA  LO 9-3  29. Darren paid the following expenses during November 2021 for his son Sean's college expenses for the spring 2022 semester, which begins in January 2022:

| Tuition | $12,000 |
|---------|---------|
| Housing | 8,000 |
| Books | 1,500 |

In addition, Sean's uncle paid $500 in fees on behalf of Sean directly to the college. Sean is claimed as Darren's dependent on his tax return. How much of the expenses qualify for the purpose of the AOTC deduction for Darren in 2021?

a. $12,000.

b. $13,500.

c. $14,000.

d. $22,000.

EA  LO 9-3  30. Which of the following expenses are qualifying expenses for the purposes of the education credits?

a. Books (purchased at the institution as a condition of enrollment).

b. Tuition.

c. Room and board.

d. Both *(a)* and *(b)*.

LO 9-4  31. Which of the following conditions must be met for a taxpayer to be able to claim the foreign tax credit (FTC) *without* filing Form 1116?

a. All of the foreign-source income is passive income.

b. All of the foreign-source income was reported on Form 1099.

c. Total foreign taxes paid were less than $300 (or $600 if married filing jointly).

d. All of the above must be met to claim the FTC without Form 1116.

LO 9-4  32. Joyce has $82,000 worldwide taxable income, which includes $10,000 of taxable income from China. She paid $2,800 in foreign income taxes to China, and her U.S. tax liability is $21,610. Joyce's foreign tax credit is

a. $0.

b. $2,635.

c. $2,800.

d. $10,000.

LO 9-4  33. Michael paid $3,350 in foreign income taxes to Argentina. His total worldwide taxable income was $75,000, which included $9,800 of income from Argentina. His U.S. tax liability is $18,750. How much can Michael claim as foreign tax credit?

a. $2,450.

b. $2,800.

c. $3,350.

d. $15,400.

LO 9-4  34. Under which of the following situations would a taxpayer most likely take the foreign taxes paid as an itemized deduction rather than as a foreign tax credit?

a. The foreign tax paid was less than 15%.

b. The foreign tax was paid to a European country.

c. The foreign tax paid was a property tax.

d. The foreign tax paid was a tax on dividend income.

**EA** **LO 9-5** 35. Justin and Janet, whose modified AGI is $456,000, have one daughter, age 5. How much child tax credit can they take?

    *a.* $0.

    *b.* $2,000.

    *c.* $3,000.

    *d.* $3,600.

**EA** **LO 9-5** 36. Julian is a single father with a son, Alex, who is 8 years old. If Julian's modified AGI is $135,000, what is his child tax credit for Alex?

    *a.* $0.

    *b.* $1,000.

    *c.* $2,000.

    *d.* $3,000.

**EA** **LO 9-6** 37. Alexis and Ashton are married filing jointly with AGI of $45,000. They made a $1,500 contribution to a qualified retirement plan. How much is their retirement savings contributions credit?

    *a.* $0.

    *b.* $150.

    *c.* $300.

    *d.* $750.

**EA** **LO 9-6** 38. Camila is a single filer and has AGI of $26,000. During the year, she contributed $800 to a Roth IRA. What amount of retirement savings contributions credit can Camila take?

    *a.* $0.

    *b.* $80.

    *c.* $160.

    *d.* $400.

**LO 9-7** 39. After two and one-half years of working with the orphanage and the government, Jake and Nikki adopted a two-year-old girl from Korea. The adoption process, which became final in January 2021, incurred the following qualified adoption expenses. For how much and in which year can Jake and Nikki take the adoption credit? (Assume no limitation of the credit due to AGI.)

| | |
|---|---|
| Year 2020 | $6,000 |
| Year 2021 | 1,000 |

    *a.* $6,000 in 2020.

    *b.* $1,000 in 2021.

    *c.* $7,000 in 2020.

    *d.* $7,000 in 2021.

**LO 9-7** 40. Abel and Loni adopted a boy (a U.S. citizen) during the current tax year and incurred a total of $15,675 in qualified adoption expenses. Abel and Loni have modified AGI of $225,000. What is the amount of adoption credit they can take?

    *a.* $11,429.

    *b.* $12,407.

    *c.* $14,440.

    *d.* $15,675.

**EA** | **LO 9-8** 41. Juan and Lydia both work, file a joint return, and have one qualifying child. They have earned income of $23,000. What is their EIC?

    *a.* $1,502.

    *b.* $3,618.

    *c.* $3,675.

    *d.* $7,820.

**EA** | **LO 9-8** 42. Thomas and Stephani are married with four qualifying children. Their earned income is $29,500. Calculate their EIC using the EIC formula.

    *a.* $4,626.

    *b.* $5,879.

    *c.* $6,213.

    *d.* $6,728.

**LO 9-8** 43. Which of the following credits is *never* a refundable credit?

    *a.* Earned Income Credit.

    *b.* Foreign tax credit.

    *c.* Child tax credit.

    *d.* American opportunity tax credit.

**EA** | **LO 9-9** 44. Which of the following statements is *incorrect?*

    *a.* Taxpayers who purchased qualified health insurance through the Marketplace may be eligible for a premium tax credit.

    *b.* Taxpayers must apply the premium tax credit toward their health insurance premium.

    *c.* The premium tax credit is designed to help eligible taxpayers pay some of their health insurance premium.

    *d.* Taxpayers who receive a credit must file a federal tax return and attach Form 8962.

**EA** | **LO 9-9** 45. Dwayne is single with two dependents. He enrolled in a qualified health care plan through the Marketplace at a cost of $4,200 per year. His household income was $43,730. The SLCSP premium is $4,950. What is Dwayne's premium tax credit?

    *a.* $0.

    *b.* $892.

    *c.* $4,058.

    *d.* $4,200.

## Problems Mc Graw Hill connect

All applicable problems are available with *Connect©*

**EA** | **LO 9-1** 46. Tim and Martha paid $17,900 in qualified employment-related expenses for their three young children who live with them in their household. Martha received $1,800 of dependent care assistance from her employer, which was properly excluded from gross income. The couple had $156,500 of AGI earned equally. What amount of child and dependent care credit can they claim on their Form 1040? How would your answer differ (if at all) if the couple had AGI of $136,500 that was earned entirely by Martha?

**EA**  **LO 9-1**  47. Adrienne is a single mother with a six-year-old daughter who lived with her during the entire year. Adrienne paid $3,900 in child care expenses so that she would be able to work. Of this amount, $500 was paid to Adrienne's mother, whom Adrienne cannot claim as a dependent. Adrienne had net earnings of $1,900 from her jewelry business. In addition, she received child support payments of $21,000 from her ex-husband. What amount, if any, of child and dependent care credit can Adrienne claim?

_____

_____

_____

_____

_____

**LO 9-2**  48. What is the AGI limit above which each of the following taxpayers would *not* be eligible to receive a credit for the elderly or the disabled?

a. A single taxpayer eligible for the credit who receives $1,000 of nontaxable social security benefits.

b. Taxpayers filing a joint return for which one taxpayer is eligible for the credit and the taxpayers have received no social security benefits.

c. Taxpayers filing a joint return, and both are eligible for the credit and received $3,000 of nontaxable social security benefits.

_____

_____

_____

_____

_____

_____

**LO 9-2**  49. Assuming that an AGI limitation does not apply, what amounts of credit for the elderly or the disabled would be permitted in each of the instances in Problem 48?

_____

_____

_____

_____

_____

_____

**EA**  **LO 9-3**  50. In each of the following cases, certain qualifying education expenses were paid during the tax year for individuals who were the taxpayer, spouse, or dependent. The taxpayer has a tax liability and no other credits. Determine the amount of the American opportunity tax credit (AOTC) and/or the lifetime learning credit that should be taken in each instance:

a. A single individual with modified AGI of $32,900 and expenses of $3,400 for a child who is a full-time college freshman.

b. A single individual with modified AGI of $44,500 and expenses of $3,800 for a child who is a full-time college junior.

c. A couple, married filing jointly, with modified AGI of $79,300 and expenses of $8,000 for a child who is a full-time graduate student.

_____

_____

_____

_____

**EA** **LO 9-3** 51. Ariana and John, who file a joint return, have two dependent children, Kai and Angel. Kai is a freshman at State University, and Angel is working on her graduate degree. The couple paid qualified expenses of $3,900 for Kai (who is a half-time student) and $7,800 for Angel. What are the amount and type of education tax credits that Ariana and John can take, assuming they have no modified AGI limitation?

**EA** **LO 9-3** 52. Use the information in Problem 51. What education tax credits are available if Ariana and John report modified AGI of $173,700? Does your answer change if Angel is taking one class a semester (is less than a half-time student) and not taking classes in a degree program? Why or why not?

**EA** **LO 9-3** 53. In 2021, Jeremy and Celeste, who file a joint return, paid the following amounts for their daughter, Alyssa, to attend the University of Colorado during academic year 2021–2022. Alyssa was in her first year of college and attended full-time.

| | |
|---|---|
| Tuition and fees (for fall semester 2021) | $1,950 |
| Tuition and fees (for spring semester 2022) | 1,000 |
| Required books | 600 |
| Room and board | 1,200 |

The spring semester at the University of Colorado begins in January. In addition to the above, Alyssa's Uncle Devin sent $800 for her tuition directly to the university. Jeremy and Celeste have modified AGI of $168,000. What is the amount of qualifying expenses for the purposes of the American opportunity tax credit (AOTC) in tax year 2021? What is the amount of qualifying expenses and the amount of AOTC that Jeremy and Celeste can claim based on their AGI?

**LO 9-4** 54. Jenna paid foreign income tax of $1,326 on foreign income of $8,112. Her worldwide taxable income was $91,400, and her U.S. tax liability was $23,000. What is the amount of the foreign tax credit (FTC) allowed? What would be the allowed FTC if Jenna had paid foreign income tax of $2,400 instead?

_____
_____
_____
_____
_____
_____

**EA**   LO 9-5   55. Determine the amount of the child tax credit in each of the following cases:

   *a.* A single parent with modified AGI of $213,400 and one child age 4.

   *b.* A single parent with modified AGI of $78,000 and three children ages 7, 9, and 12.

   *c.* A married couple, filing jointly, with modified AGI of $407,933 and two children age 14 and 16.

   *d.* A married couple, filing jointly, with modified AGI of $132,055 and one child, age 13.

_____
_____
_____
_____

**EA**   LO 9-6   56. Determine the retirement savings contributions credit in each of the following independent cases:

   *a.* A married couple filing jointly with modified AGI of $37,500 and an IRA contribution of $1,600.

   *b.* A married couple filing jointly with modified AGI of $58,000 and an IRA contribution of $1,500.

   *c.* A head of household taxpayer with modified AGI of $33,000 and Roth IRA contribution of $2,000.

   *d.* A single taxpayer with modified AGI of $12,000 and an IRA contribution of $2,300.

_____
_____
_____
_____
_____
_____

   LO 9-7   57. Niles and Marsha adopted an infant boy (a U.S. citizen). They paid $15,500 in 2020 for adoption-related expenses. The adoption was finalized in early 2021. Marsha received $4,000 of employer-provided adoption benefits. For part *(a)*, assume that any adoption credit is not limited by modified AGI or by the amount of tax liability.

   *a.* What amount of adoption credit, if any, can Niles and Marsha take in 2021?

   *b.* Using the information in part *(a)*, assume that their modified AGI was $223,000 in 2021. What amount of adoption credit is allowed in 2021?

_____
_____
_____
_____

_____

_____

**EA**   **LO 9-8**   58. Determine the amount of the Earned Income Credit in each of the following cases. Assume that the person or persons are eligible to take the credit. Calculate the credit using the formulas.

    *a.* A single person with earned income of $7,554 and no qualifying children.

    *b.* A single person with earned income of $27,500 and two qualifying children.

    *c.* A married couple filing jointly with earned income of $34,190 and one qualifying child.

_____

_____

_____

_____

_____

_____

## Tax Return Problems  

All applicable tax return problems are available with **Connect©**

Use your tax software to complete the following problems. If you are manually preparing the tax returns, see each problem for the forms you may need.

For the following tax return problems, assume the taxpayers do not wish to contribute to the Presidential Election Fund, unless otherwise stated in the problem. In addition, the taxpayers did not receive, sell, send, exchange, or otherwise acquire any financial interest in any virtual currency during the year.

For any Tax Return Problems for which the taxpayers are entitled to a child tax credit, assume that the taxpayers did NOT receive any advance child tax credit payments during 2021. Thus, the entire child tax credit (if permitted) will be claimed on the 2021 tax return.

**Tax Return Problem 1**   Juliette White is a head of household taxpayer with a daughter named Sabrina. They live at 1009 Olinda Terrace, Apt. 5B, Reno, NV 78887. Juliette works at a local law firm, Law Offices of Dane Gray, and attends school in the evenings at Reno Community College (RCC). She is taking some general classes and is not sure what degree she wants to pursue yet. She is taking three units this semester. Full-time status at RCC is nine units. Juliette's mother watches Sabrina after school and in the evenings (no charge) so that Juliette can work and take classes at RCC. Social security numbers are 412-34-5670 for Juliette and 412-34-5672 for Sabrina. Their birth dates are as follows: Juliette, 10/31/1989; and Sabrina, 3/1/2014.

    The Form W-2 Juliette received from the Law Offices of Dane Gray contained the following information:

$$
\begin{aligned}
\text{Wages (box 1)} &= \$29,502.30 \\
\text{Federal W/H (box 2)} &= \$ \quad 997.14 \\
\text{Social security wages (box 3)} &= \$29,502.30 \\
\text{Social security W/H (box 4)} &= \$ \ 1,829.14 \\
\text{Medicare wages (box 5)} &= \$29,502.30 \\
\text{Medicare W/H (box 6)} &= \$ \quad 427.78
\end{aligned}
$$

Juliette also had the following expenses:

| Education expenses: | |
| --- | --- |
| Tuition for Reno Community College | $775 |

Juliette had qualifying health care coverage at all times during the tax year.

Prepare Juliette's federal tax return. Use Form 1040 and any additional appropriate schedules or forms she may need for credits. For any missing information, make reasonable assumptions.

**Tax Return Problem 2**

Married taxpayers David and Lillian Perdue file jointly and have a daughter, Erin. They live at 9510 Bluebird Canyon Drive, Seattle, WA 99201. The Perdues own their home, which was paid off last year. David works as a salesman for the Canyon Honda car dealer and Lillian works at the same dealer as the manager of the service department. The social security number for David is 412-34-5670; for Lillian, 412-34-5671; and for Erin, 412-34-5672. Their birth dates are as follows: David, 1/18/1971; Lillian, 3/14/1971; and Erin, 11/21/2011.

Erin attends school during the day and in the afternoon attends Seattle Day Care (1 Day Street, Seattle WA 99201, EIN 92-6789012). The Perdues paid $2,800 during the year to the school for the after-school care.

The Forms W-2 from Canyon Honda contained the following information:

Lillian Perdue:

| | |
| --- | --- |
| Wages (box 1) = | $72,000.00 |
| Federal W/H (box 2) = | $ 7,165.00 |
| Social security wages (box 3) = | $72,000.00 |
| Social security W/H (box 4) = | $ 4,464.00 |
| Medicare wages (box 5) = | $72,000.00 |
| Medicare W/H (box 6) = | $ 1,044.00 |

David Perdue:

| | |
| --- | --- |
| Wages (box 1) = | $62,434.91 |
| Federal W/H (box 2) = | $ 6,492.14 |
| Social security wages (box 3) = | $62,434.91 |
| Social security W/H (box 4) = | $ 3,870.96 |
| Medicare wages (box 5) = | $62,434.91 |
| Medicare W/H (box 6) = | $   905.30 |

David and Lillian had qualifying health care coverage at all times during the tax year.

Prepare the Perdues' federal tax return. Use Form 1040 and any additional appropriate schedules or forms they may need for credits. For any missing information, make reasonable assumptions.

**Tax Return Problem 3**

Brian and Corrine Lee are married taxpayers filing jointly. They live in the home they own, located at 3301 Pacific Coast Hwy., Laguna Beach, CA 92651. Brian is an optometrist who owns his business; Corrine is a social worker for Orange County. They have two sons, Brady and Hank. During their trip to China last year, they fell in love with a beautiful one-year-old girl from an orphanage near Shanghai and are in the process of adopting her. The social security numbers of the four current members of their household are 412-34-5670 for Brian, 412-34-5671 for Corrine, 412-34-5672 for Brady, and 412-34-5673 for Hank. Their birth dates are as follows: Brian, 5/20/1976; Corrine, 7/23/1976; Brady, 9/1/2009; and Hank, 10/12/2011. The following are Brian's income and expense information from his business and Corrine's W-2 from Orange County.

Brian's optometrist office income and expenses for the current year:

| | |
|---|---:|
| Gross income | $260,000 |
| Cost of goods sold | |
| (beginning inventory $45,000; purchases $63,000; ending inventory $20,000) | 88,000 |
| Advertising | 5,000 |
| Wages | 32,000 |
| Office rent | 9,600 |
| Other | 2,100 |

The Lees also made $25,000 in federal estimated tax payments during the year on the applicable due dates ($6,250 per quarter).

The Form W-2 Corrine received from Orange County contained this information:

| | |
|---:|---|
| Wages (box 1) = | $76,925.04 |
| Federal W/H (box 2) = | $ 9,956.70 |
| Social security wages (box 3) = | $76,925.04 |
| Social security W/H (box 4) = | $ 4,769.35 |
| Medicare wages (box 5) = | $76,925.04 |
| Medicare W/H (box 6) = | $ 1,115.41 |
| State income taxes (box 17) = | $ 2,944.89 |

In addition, the Lees had the following income and expenses during the year:

| | |
|---|---:|
| **Income** | |
| Interest from CDs at Pacific Coast Bank | $3,500 |
| **Expenses** | |
| Mortgage interest paid to PC Bank for their home | $29,500 |
| Property taxes paid on their residence | 7,000 |
| Adoption expenses (fees, court costs, and attorney's fees) | 8,850 |
| Child care costs at LB Parks and Recreations (550 Main St, Laguna Beach, CA 92651, EIN 94-3344556) after-school program for Hank | 3,500 |

Brian and Corrine had qualifying health care coverage at all times during the tax year. Prepare the Lees' federal tax return. Use Form 1040, Schedule A, Schedule B, Schedule C, and any additional appropriate schedules or forms they may need for credits. Do *not* complete Form 4562 (with Schedule C). (Assume no AMT although it may apply; Form 6251 or the AMT calculation is not required.) For any missing information, make reasonable assumptions.

**Tax Return Problem 4**    Jermaine Watson is a single father with a son, Jamal, who qualifies as a dependent. They live at 5678 SE Stark St., Portland, OR 97233. Jermaine works at First Bank of Oregon. Jamal attends school and at the end of the school day he goes to a dependent care facility next door to his school, where Jermaine picks him up after work. Jermaine pays $800 per month to the care facility (Portland Day Care, 4567 SE Stark St., Portland, OR 97233. EIN 90-6543210).

Jermaine's W-2 from First Bank of Oregon is as follows:

$$\text{Wages (box 1)} = \$71,510.00$$
$$\text{Federal W/H (box 2)} = \$\ 3,197.00$$
$$\text{Social security wages (box 3)} = \$71,510.00$$
$$\text{Social security W/H (box 4)} = \$\ 4,433.62$$
$$\text{Medicare wages (box 5)} = \$71,510.00$$
$$\text{Medicare W/H (box 6)} = \$\ 1,036.90$$
$$\text{State income taxes (box 17)} = \$\ 1,134.90$$

Jermaine takes one class a semester at Portland State University toward an MBA degree. In 2019, he paid $1,300 in tuition, $300 for books, and $200 for a meal card.

Jermaine has some investments in a New Zealand public company. He received foreign-source dividends (nonqualified) of $750 during the year. He paid $225 of foreign tax on the foreign income. He also received $350 of interest income from First Bank of Oregon.

Jermaine's birthdate is 9/14/1987 and Jamal's is 4/22/2011. Their social security numbers are 412-34-5670 and 412-34-5672, respectively.

They had qualifying health care coverage at all times during the tax year.

Prepare Jermaine's federal tax return. Use Form 1040 and any additional appropriate schedules or forms he may need for credits. For any missing information, make reasonable assumptions.

We have provided selected filled-in source documents that are available in the *Connect Library*.

# Chapter Ten

# Payroll Taxes

The majority of taxpayers receive wages or other compensation from an employer. This employer–employee relationship has tax implications and responsibilities for both parties. In this chapter, we focus on the withholding tax collection and payment responsibilities of employers. We also discuss employment tax issues associated with household employees, such as nannies and similar individuals. IRS Publication 15, *(Circular E), Employer's Tax Guide,* and Publication 15-A, *Employer's Supplemental Tax Guide,* are sources of additional information for taxpayers. State withholding and reporting requirements often differ. Thus the discussion in this chapter focuses mainly on federal payroll tax requirements.

### Learning Objectives

When you have completed this chapter, you should understand the following learning objectives (LO):

**LO 10-1** Explain the tax issues associated with payroll and Form 1040.

**LO 10-2** Calculate federal income tax withholding, social security, and Medicare taxes on wages and tips.

**LO 10-3** Describe the rules for reporting and paying payroll taxes, including deposit penalties and Form 941.

**LO 10-4** Calculate self-employment taxes, unemployment taxes, Form 940, taxes for household employees, and Schedule H.

**LO 10-5** Determine employer payroll reporting requirements, including Forms W-2 and W-3.

**LO 10-6** Explain supplemental wage payments, backup withholding, Form W-9, estimated tax payments, and Form 1040-ES.

# TAX ISSUES ASSOCIATED WITH PAYROLL AND FORM 1040
## LO 10-1

Everyone who is an employee of a business receives a paycheck. Employees typically receive checks on a weekly, biweekly, semimonthly, or monthly basis. Some employees may receive daily or miscellaneous wages. Many employees look only at their net check amount with little understanding of how that net amount was determined. Often, employees are not sure how their paychecks relate to the Form 1040 they file on or before April 15 of the next year.

Briefly, the federal government (as well as state and local governments) expects taxpayers to help fund programs and keep the government operational. Even though income tax returns are filed once a year, the government operates 365 days of the year and requires a steady flow of money to operate. To provide part of that flow of money, a payroll tax withholding system was established, sometimes referred to as a *pay-as-you-go* system. Employees pay into the system as they earn their wages rather than waiting until the end of the year.

At the end of the year, the employer is required to summarize all of an employee's earnings and taxes withheld on a Form W-2, which is the starting point for completing Form 1040. Federal withholding taxes are the payments made by the employer on behalf of the employee. Form 1040 compares tax liability with tax payments to determine whether a taxpayer will receive a refund or will owe more money.

The payroll system also covers special tax situations for a person who is a tipped employee, a self-employed person, or a domestic worker within a home. The remaining sections of this chapter discuss general federal payroll, withholding, and reporting requirements as well as these special situations.

---

**CONCEPT CHECK 10-1— LO 10-1**

1. The payroll tax withholding system was established to produce a stream of revenue for governmental operations. True or false?
2. Forms W-2 and 1040 are used to match tax liability with tax payments. True or false?

# FEDERAL INCOME TAX WITHHOLDING, SOCIAL SECURITY, AND MEDICARE TAXES ON WAGES AND TIPS
## LO 10-2

### Income Tax Withholding from Wages

Wages and other compensation earned by employees are taxable. Rather than have taxpayers pay their entire tax liability when they file their tax returns, the IRC has established a payroll tax withholding system.[1] These rules require employers to retain (withhold) a portion of each paycheck based on the gross wages paid to the employee. This withholding represents an approximation of the proportionate share of total tax liability the employee will owe to the federal government. The IRS encourages taxpayers to check their withholding amounts to avoid potential tax issues as a result of these changes. The withholding tax calculator can be found at www.irs.gov/individuals/irs-withholding-calculator. Employers must then remit (deposit) those withholdings to the U.S. Treasury on behalf of their employees. This system of withholding taxes has some advantages. First, employees pay their tax liability in small amounts throughout the year rather than in a large sum on April 15. Second, the federal government receives the tax revenue throughout the year, thus reducing the need to borrow money to fund operations.

Wages subject to withholding and other employment taxes include all pay given to employees for services performed. The payment may be in cash or other forms of compensation and includes, for example, salaries, vacation allowances, bonuses, commissions, and taxable fringe benefits. Employers withhold federal taxes on this compensation using withholding tax tables based on the number of withholding allowances selected by employees.[2]

Employees provide their employers a Form W-4 indicating their filing status and number of withholding allowances (see Exhibit 10-1). There is also a withholding calculator on the IRS website at www.irs.gov/w4app for help in determining the appropriate amount of withholding taxes to be withheld. The employee gives the Form W-4 to the employer. Employees are strongly encouraged to submit the revised Form W-4 to their employers.

Employees complete Form W4—Employee's Withholding Certificate so the employer can withhold the correct federal income tax from their pay. Starting in 2020, the W-4 form has

---

[1] IRC § 3402.
[2] IRC § 3402(f).

**EXHIBIT 10-1**

| Form **W-4**<br>(Rev. December 2020)<br>Department of the Treasury<br>Internal Revenue Service | **Employee's Withholding Certificate**<br>▶ Complete Form W-4 so that your employer can withhold the correct federal income tax from your pay.<br>▶ Give Form W-4 to your employer.<br>▶ Your withholding is subject to review by the IRS. | OMB No. 1545-0074<br>**2021** |

**Step 1:**
**Enter Personal Information**

| (a) First name and middle initial | Last name | (b) Social security number |
|---|---|---|
| Mauro Valdez | | 412-34-5670 |

Address

▶ **Does your name match the name on your social security card?** If not, to ensure you get credit for your earnings, contact SSA at 800-772-1213 or go to *www.ssa.gov.*

City or town, state, and ZIP code

(c) ☐ Single or **Married filing separately**

☑ **Married filing jointly** or **Qualifying widow(er)**

☐ **Head of household** (Check only if you're unmarried and pay more than half the costs of keeping up a home for yourself and a qualifying individual.)

**Complete Steps 2–4 ONLY if they apply to you; otherwise, skip to Step 5.** See page 2 for more information on each step, who can claim exemption from withholding, when to use the estimator at *www.irs.gov/W4App*, and privacy.

**Step 2:**
**Multiple Jobs or Spouse Works**

Complete this step if you (1) hold more than one job at a time, or (2) are married filing jointly and your spouse also works. The correct amount of withholding depends on income earned from all of these jobs.

Do **only one** of the following.

(a) Use the estimator at *www.irs.gov/W4App* for most accurate withholding for this step (and Steps 3–4); **or**

(b) Use the Multiple Jobs Worksheet on page 3 and enter the result in Step 4(c) below for roughly accurate withholding; **or**

(c) If there are only two jobs total, you may check this box. Do the same on Form W-4 for the other job. This option is accurate for jobs with similar pay; otherwise, more tax than necessary may be withheld . . . . . . ▶ ☐

**TIP:** To be accurate, submit a 2021 Form W-4 for all other jobs. If you (or your spouse) have self-employment income, including as an independent contractor, use the estimator.

**Complete Steps 3–4(b) on Form W-4 for only ONE of these jobs.** Leave those steps blank for the other jobs. (Your withholding will be most accurate if you complete Steps 3–4(b) on the Form W-4 for the highest paying job.)

**Step 3:**
**Claim Dependents**

If your total income will be $200,000 or less ($400,000 or less if married filing jointly):

Multiply the number of qualifying children under age 17 by $2,000 ▶ $ _____ 4,000

Multiply the number of other dependents by $500 . . . . ▶ $ _____

Add the amounts above and enter the total here . . . . . . . . . . . . . . . . **3** | $ _____ 4,000

**Step 4 (optional):**
**Other Adjustments**

(a) **Other income (not from jobs).** If you want tax withheld for other income you expect this year that won't have withholding, enter the amount of other income here. This may include interest, dividends, and retirement income . . . . . . . . . . . . . **4(a)** | $ _____

(b) **Deductions.** If you expect to claim deductions other than the standard deduction and want to reduce your withholding, use the Deductions Worksheet on page 3 and enter the result here . . . . . . . . . . . . . . . . **4(b)** | $ _____

(c) **Extra withholding.** Enter any additional tax you want withheld each **pay period** . **4(c)** | $ _____ 50

**Step 5:**
**Sign Here**

Under penalties of perjury, I declare that this certificate, to the best of my knowledge and belief, is true, correct, and complete.

▶ _____  ▶ _____
**Employee's signature** (This form is not valid unless you sign it.)   **Date**

**Employers Only**

| Employer's name and address | First date of employment | Employer identification number (EIN) |
|---|---|---|

**For Privacy Act and Paperwork Reduction Act Notice, see page 3.**   Cat. No. 10220Q   Form **W-4** (2021)

Source: U.S. Department of the Treasury, Internal Revenue Service, Form W-4. Washington, DC: 2021.

*(continued)*

**EXHIBIT 10-1** *(concluded)*

Form W-4 (2021)                                                                                                    Page **3**

### Step 2(b) — Multiple Jobs Worksheet *(Keep for your records.)*

If you choose the option in Step 2(b) on Form W-4, complete this worksheet (which calculates the total extra tax for all jobs) on **only ONE** Form W-4. Withholding will be most accurate if you complete the worksheet and enter the result on the Form W-4 for the highest paying job.

**Note:** If more than one job has annual wages of more than $120,000 or there are more than three jobs, see Pub. 505 for additional tables; or, you can use the online withholding estimator at *www.irs.gov/W4App*.

1   **Two jobs.** If you have two jobs or you're married filing jointly and you and your spouse each have one job, find the amount from the appropriate table on page 4. Using the "Higher Paying Job" row and the "Lower Paying Job" column, find the value at the intersection of the two household salaries and enter that value on line 1. Then, **skip** to line 3 . . . . . . . . . . . . . . . . . . . . . . **1** $ _____

2   **Three jobs.** If you and/or your spouse have three jobs at the same time, complete lines 2a, 2b, and 2c below. Otherwise, skip to line 3.

     **a**  Find the amount from the appropriate table on page 4 using the annual wages from the highest paying job in the "Higher Paying Job" row and the annual wages for your next highest paying job in the "Lower Paying Job" column. Find the value at the intersection of the two household salaries and enter that value on line 2a . . . . . . . . . . . . . . . **2a** $ _____

     **b**  Add the annual wages of the two highest paying jobs from line 2a together and use the total as the wages in the "Higher Paying Job" row and use the annual wages for your third job in the "Lower Paying Job" column to find the amount from the appropriate table on page 4 and enter this amount on line 2b . . . . . . . . . . . . . . . . . . . . **2b** $ _____

     **c**  Add the amounts from lines 2a and 2b and enter the result on line 2c . . . . . . . **2c** $ _____

3   Enter the number of pay periods per year for the highest paying job. For example, if that job pays weekly, enter 52; if it pays every other week, enter 26; if it pays monthly, enter 12, etc. . . . . . **3** _____

4   **Divide** the annual amount on line 1 or line 2c by the number of pay periods on line 3. Enter this amount here and in **Step 4(c)** of Form W-4 for the highest paying job (along with any other additional amount you want withheld) . . . . . . . . . . . . . . . . . . . . . . . **4** $ _____

### Step 4(b) — Deductions Worksheet *(Keep for your records.)*

1   Enter an estimate of your 2021 itemized deductions (from Schedule A (Form 1040)). Such deductions may include qualifying home mortgage interest, charitable contributions, state and local taxes (up to $10,000), and medical expenses in excess of 7.5% of your income . . . . . . . . . **1** $ _____

2   Enter:  { • $25,100 if you're married filing jointly or qualifying widow(er)<br>          • $18,800 if you're head of household                  } . . . . . . . . **2** $ _____<br>          • $12,550 if you're single or married filing separately

3   If line 1 is greater than line 2, subtract line 2 from line 1 and enter the result here. If line 2 is greater than line 1, enter "-0-" . . . . . . . . . . . . . . . . . . . . . **3** $ _____

4   Enter an estimate of your student loan interest, deductible IRA contributions, and certain other adjustments (from Part II of Schedule 1 (Form 1040)). See Pub. 505 for more information . . . . **4** $ _____

5   **Add** lines 3 and 4. Enter the result here and in **Step 4(b)** of Form W-4 . . . . . . . . . . **5** $ _____

been completely redesigned (see Exhibit 10-1 for the Form W-4 for 2021). The new Form W-4 was developed to more accurately correlate the amount of income tax withholding for taxpayer with multiple jobs and/or a working spouse, with and without dependents.

There are four steps to complete the form. Step 1 is for taxpayer personal information, step 2 is for multiple jobs or if your spouse works, step 3 is where you claim dependents, and step 4 is other adjustments (optional). Step 2 is completed if the taxpayer holds more than one job or is married filing jointly and the spouse is working. The correct amount of withholding depends on the income earned from these jobs. Within step 2 is the option to use the IRS estimator (www.irs.gov/W4App), or the multiple jobs worksheet (page 3 of the form), or if there are only two jobs you can check a box. Step 3 is where the taxpayer claims dependents. Step 4 is where the taxpayer can have additional taxes withheld for other income, can claim deductions other than the standard deduction, or claim an extra withholding amount. The employer will need the information on the Form W-4 to calculate the federal income tax withholding amounts per pay period.

There is also a new Publication 15-T, "Federal Income Tax Withholding Methods." This publication supplements Publication 15, "Employer's Tax Guide." There are seven new tables that can used to calculate federal income tax withholding:

1. Percentage Method Tables for Automated Payroll Systems.
2. Wage Bracket Method Tables for Manual Payroll Systems with Forms W-4 from 2020 or Later.
3. Wage Bracket Method Tables for Manual Payroll Systems with Forms W-4 from 2019 or Earlier.
4. Percentage Method Tables for Manual Payroll Systems with Forms W-4 from 2020 or Later.
5. Percentage Method Tables for Manual Payroll Systems with Forms W-4 from 2019 or Earlier.
6. Alternative Methods of Figuring Withholding.
7. Tables for Withholding on Distributions of Indian Gaming Profits to Tribal Members.

Examples of worksheets and selected tables for 1, 2, and 4 above are found in the Appendix at the end of the chapter. For most situations throughout this chapter, Table 1 will be assumed to be the method most often used. Examples using Tables 2 and 4 will be presented when appropriate. Using Table 1 and Worksheet 1, "Employer's Withholding Worksheet for Percentage Method Tables for Automated Payroll Systems" (Exhibit 10-2), the employer will complete the four steps for each employee. In order to determine the amount of tax to withhold using either a percentage or wage bracket method, the employer must have an accurate W-4 form on file. Because most payroll systems are computerized, Table 1 (Exhibit 10-2) will be most commonly used; see Example 10-1. However, for purposes of illustration, Table 4 (Exhibit 10-3) will also be illustrated in Example 10-2.

| **EXAMPLE 10-1** | Audrey is single and earns $1,000 per week for a total of $52,000 annually. Audrey has only one job, no dependents, and did not complete steps 2, 3, or 4 of the Form W-4, which was provided to the employer. Audrey's employer uses Table 1, Percentage Method Table for Automated Payroll Systems, to calculate employee payroll. The amount of federal income tax withholding from Audrey's paycheck is $87.21. |
| --- | --- |

**EXHIBIT 10-2**

# 1. Percentage Method Tables for Automated Payroll Systems

to figure federal income tax withholding. This method works for Forms W-4 for all prior, current, and future years. This method also works for any amount of wages. If the Form W-4 is from 2019 or earlier, this method works for any number of withholding allowances claimed.

If you have an automated payroll system, use the worksheet below and the Percentage Method tables that follow

## Worksheet 1. Employer's Withholding Worksheet for Percentage Method Tables for Automated Payroll Systems

*Keep for Your Records*

| Table 3 | Semiannually | Quarterly | Monthly | Semimonthly | Biweekly | Weekly | Daily |
|---|---|---|---|---|---|---|---|
| | 2 | 4 | 12 | 24 | 26 | 52 | 260 |

**Step 1.** **Adjust the empoyee's payment amount**

1a Enter the employee's total taxable wages this payroll period . . . . . . . . . . . . . . . . . . . . . . . . . . . . . 1a $ 1,000

1b Enter the number of pay periods you have per year (see Table 3) . . . . . . . . . . . . . . . . . . . . . . . . 1b 52

1c Multiply the amount on line 1a by the number on line 1b . . . . . . . . . . . . . . . . . . . . . . . . . . . 1c $ 52,000

If the employee **HAS** submitted a Form W-4 for 2020 or later, figure the Adjusted Annual Wage Amount as follows:

1d Enter the amount from Step 4(a) of the employee's Form W-4 . . . . . . . . . . . . . . . . . . . . . . . . . 1d $ 0

1e Add lines 1c and 1d . . . . . . . . . . . . . . . . . . . . . . . . . . . . . . . . . . . . . . . . . . . . . . . . . 1e $ 52,000

1f Enter the amount from Step 4(b) of the employee's Form W-4 . . . . . . . . . . . . . . . . . . . . . . . . . 1f $ 0

1g If the box in Step 2 of Form W-4 is checked, enter -0-. If the box is not checked, enter $12,900 if the taxpayor ic married filing jointly or $8,600 otherwise . . . . . . . . . . . . . . . . . . . . . . . . . . . . . 1g $ 8,600

1h Add lines 1f and 1g . . . . . . . . . . . . . . . . . . . . . . . . . . . . . . . . . . . . . . . . . . . . . . . . . 1h $ 8,600

1i Subtract line 1h from line 1e. If zero or less, enter -0-. This is the **Adjusted Annual Wage Amount** . . . . . . . . . . . . . . . . . . . . . . . . . . . . . . . . . . . . . . . . . . . . . . . . . . . . . 1i $ 43,400

If the employee **HAS NOT** submitted a Form W-4 for 2020 or later, figure the Adjusted Annual Wage Amount as follows:

1j Enter the number of allowances claimed on the employee's most recent Form W-4 . . . . . . . . . . . . . . 1j

1k Multiply line 1j by $4,300 . . . . . . . . . . . . . . . . . . . . . . . . . . . . . . . . . . . . . . . . . . . . . 1k $

1l Subtract line 1k from line 1c. If zero or less, enter -0-. This is the **Adjusted Annual Wage Amount** . . . . . . . . . . . . . . . . . . . . . . . . . . . . . . . . . . . . . . . . . . . . . . . . . . . . . . . 1l $

**Step 2.** **Figure the Tentative Withholding Amount**
based on the employee's Adjusted Annual Wage Amount; filing status (Step 1(c) of the 2020 or later Form W-4) or marital status (line 3 of Form W-4 from 2019 or earlier); and whether the box in Step 2 of 2020 or later Form W-4 is checked.
**Note.** Don't use the Head of Household table if the Form W-4 is from 2019 or earlier.

2a Enter the employee's **Adjusted Annual Wage Amount** from line 1i or 1l above . . . . . . . . . . . . . . . . 2a $ 43,400

2b Find the row in the appropriate **Annual** Percentage Method table in which the amount on line 2a is at least the amount in column A but less than the amount in column B, then enter here the amount from column A of that row . . . . . . . . . . . . . . . . . . . . . . . . . . . . . . . . . . . . . . . . . . . . . . 2b $ 13,900

2c Enter the amount from column C of that row . . . . . . . . . . . . . . . . . . . . . . . . . . . . . . . . . . . 2c $ 995

2d Enter the percentage from column D of that row . . . . . . . . . . . . . . . . . . . . . . . . . . . . . . . . . 2d 12 %

2e Subtract line 2b from line 2a . . . . . . . . . . . . . . . . . . . . . . . . . . . . . . . . . . . . . . . . . . . 2e $ 29,500

2f Multiply the amount on line 2e by the percentage on line 2d . . . . . . . . . . . . . . . . . . . . . . . . . . 2f $ 3,540

2g Add lines 2c and 2f . . . . . . . . . . . . . . . . . . . . . . . . . . . . . . . . . . . . . . . . . . . . . . . . 2g $ 4,535

2h Divide the amount on line 2g by the number of pay periods on line 1b. This is the **Tentative Withholding Amount** . . . . . . . . . . . . . . . . . . . . . . . . . . . . . . . . . . . . . . . . . . . . . . . . . 2h $ 87.21

**Step 3.** **Account for tax credits**

3a If the employee's Form W-4 is from 2020 or later, enter the amount from Step 3 of that form; otherwise enter -0- . . . . . . . . . . . . . . . . . . . . . . . . . . . . . . . . . . . . . . . . . . . . . . . . . . . . . . 3a $

3b Divide the amount on line 3a by the number of pay periods on line 1b . . . . . . . . . . . . . . . . . . . . . 3b $

3c Subtract line 3b from line 2h. If zero or less, enter -0- . . . . . . . . . . . . . . . . . . . . . . . . . . . . . 3c $ 87.21

**Step 4.** **Figure the final amount to withhold**

4a Enter the additional amount to withhold from the employee's Form W-4 (Step 4(c) of the 2020 or later form or line 6 on earlier forms) . . . . . . . . . . . . . . . . . . . . . . . . . . . . . . . . . . . . . . . . . 4a $

4b Add lines 3c and 4a. **This is the amount to withhold from the employee's wages this pay period** . . . . . . . . . . . . . . . . . . . . . . . . . . . . . . . . . . . . . . . . . . . . . . . . . . . . . 4b $ 87.21

**EXHIBIT 10-2** *(concluded)*

## 2021 Percentage Method Tables for Automated Payroll Systems

| STANDARD Withholding Rate Schedules | | | | |
|---|---|---|---|---|
| (Use these if the Form W-4 is from 2019 or earlier, or if the Form W-4 is from 2020 or later and the box in Step 2 of Form W-4 is **NOT** checked) | | | | |

| If the Adjusted Annual Wage Amount (line 2a) is: | | The tentative amount to withhold is: | Plus this percentage— | of the amount that the Adjusted Annual Wage exceeds— |
|---|---|---|---|---|
| At least— | But less than— | | | |
| A | B | C | D | E |
| **Married Filing Jointly** | | | | |
| $0 | $12,200 | $0.00 | 0% | $0 |
| $12,200 | $32,100 | $0.00 | 10% | $12,200 |
| $32,100 | $93,250 | $1,990.00 | 12% | $32,100 |
| $93,250 | $184,950 | $9,328.00 | 22% | $93,250 |
| $184,950 | $342,050 | $29,502.00 | 24% | $184,950 |
| $342,050 | $431,050 | $67,206.00 | 32% | $342,050 |
| $431,050 | $640,500 | $95,686.00 | 35% | $431,050 |
| $640,500 | | $168,993.50 | 37% | $640,500 |
| **Single or Married Filing Separately** | | | | |
| $0 | $3,950 | $0.00 | 0% | $0 |
| $3,950 | $13,900 | $0.00 | 10% | $3,950 |
| $13,900 | $44,475 | $995.00 | 12% | $13,900 |
| $44,475 | $90,325 | $4,664.00 | 22% | $44,475 |
| $90,325 | $168,875 | $14,751.00 | 24% | $90,325 |
| $168,875 | $213,375 | $33,603.00 | 32% | $168,875 |
| $213,375 | $527,550 | $47,843.00 | 35% | $213,375 |
| $527,550 | | $157,804.25 | 37% | $527,550 |
| **Head of Household** | | | | |
| $0 | $10,200 | $0.00 | 0% | $0 |
| $10,200 | $24,400 | $0.00 | 10% | $10,200 |
| $24,400 | $64,400 | $1,420.00 | 12% | $24,400 |
| $64,400 | $96,550 | $6,220.00 | 22% | $64,400 |
| $96,550 | $175,100 | $13,293.00 | 24% | $96,550 |
| $175,100 | $219,600 | $32,145.00 | 32% | $175,100 |
| $219,600 | $533,800 | $46,385.00 | 35% | $219,600 |
| $533,800 | | $156,355.00 | 37% | $533,800 |

| Form W-4, Step 2, Checkbox, Withholding Rate Schedules | | | | |
|---|---|---|---|---|
| (Use these if the Form W-4 is from 2020 or later and the box in Step 2 of Form W-4 **IS** checked) | | | | |

| If the Adjusted Annual Wage Amount (line 2a) is: | | The tentative amount to withhold is: | Plus this percentage— | of the amount that the Adjusted Annual Wage exceeds— |
|---|---|---|---|---|
| At least— | But less than— | | | |
| A | B | C | D | E |
| **Married Filing Jointly** | | | | |
| $0 | $12,550 | $0.00 | 0% | $0 |
| $12,550 | $22,500 | $0.00 | 10% | $12,550 |
| $22,500 | $53,075 | $995.00 | 12% | $22,500 |
| $53,075 | $98,925 | $4,664.00 | 22% | $53,075 |
| $98,925 | $177,475 | $14,751.00 | 24% | $98,925 |
| $177,475 | $221,975 | $33,603.00 | 32% | $177,475 |
| $221,975 | $326,700 | $47,843.00 | 35% | $221,975 |
| $326,700 | | $84,496.75 | 37% | $326,700 |
| **Single or Married Filing Separately** | | | | |
| $0 | $6,275 | $0.00 | 0% | $0 |
| $6,275 | $11,250 | $0.00 | 10% | $6,275 |
| $11,250 | $26,538 | $497.50 | 12% | $11,250 |
| $26,538 | $49,463 | $2,332.00 | 22% | $26,538 |
| $49,463 | $88,738 | $7,375.50 | 24% | $49,463 |
| $88,738 | $110,988 | $16,801.50 | 32% | $88,738 |
| $110,988 | $268,075 | $23,921.50 | 35% | $110,988 |
| $268,075 | | $78,902.13 | 37% | $268,075 |
| **Head of Household** | | | | |
| $0 | $9,400 | $0.00 | 0% | $0 |
| $9,400 | $16,500 | $0.00 | 10% | $9,400 |
| $16,500 | $36,500 | $710.00 | 12% | $16,500 |
| $36,500 | $52,575 | $3,110.00 | 22% | $36,500 |
| $52,575 | $91,850 | $6,646.50 | 24% | $52,575 |
| $91,850 | $114,100 | $16,072.50 | 32% | $91,850 |
| $114,100 | $271,200 | $23,192.50 | 35% | $114,100 |
| $271,200 | | $78,177.50 | 37% | $271,200 |

**Publication 15-T (2021)**

**EXHIBIT 10-3**

# 4. Percentage Method Tables for Manual Payroll Systems With Forms W-4 From 2020 or Later

If you compute payroll manually, your employee has submitted a Form W-4 for 2020 or later, and you prefer to use the Percentage Method or you can't use the Wage Bracket Method tables because the employee's annual wages exceed $100,000, use the worksheet below and the Percentage Method tables that follow to figure federal income tax withholding. This method works for any amount of wages.

**Worksheet 4. Employer's Withholding Worksheet for Percentage Method Tables for Manual Payroll Systems With Forms W-4 From 2020 or Later**

*Keep for Your Records*

| Table 5 | Monthly | Semimonthly | Biweekly | Weekly | Daily |
|---|---|---|---|---|---|
| | 12 | 24 | 26 | 52 | 260 |

**Step 1.** **Adjust the employee's wage amount**

| | | | | |
|---|---|---|---|---|
| 1a | Enter the employee's total taxable wages this payroll period .......................... | 1a | $ | 5,000.00 |
| 1b | Enter the number of pay periods you have per year (see Table 5) ....................... | 1b | | 24 |
| 1c | Enter the amount from Step 4(a) of the employee's Form W-4 .......................... | 1c | $ | |
| 1d | Divide line 1c by the number on line 1b ........................ | 1d | $ | |
| 1e | Add lines 1a and 1d .................... | 1e | $ | 5,000.00 |
| 1f | Enter the amount from Step 4(b) of the employee's Form W-4 ....................... | 1f | $ | |
| 1g | Divide line 1f by the number on line 1b ....................... | 1g | $ | |
| 1h | Subtract line 1g from line 1e. If zero or less, enter -0-. This is the **Adjusted Wage Amount** ...... | 1h | $ | 5,000.00 |

**Step 2.** **Figure the Tentative Withholding Amount**

based on your pay frequency, the employee's Adjusted Wage Amount, filing status (Step 1(c) of Form W-4), and whether the box in Step 2 of Form W-4 is checked.

| | | | | |
|---|---|---|---|---|
| 2a | Find the row in the *STANDARD Withholding Rate Schedules* (if the box in Step 2 of Form W-4 is NOT checked) or the *Form W-4, Step 2, Checkbox, Withholding Rate Schedules* (if it HAS been checked) of the Percentage Method tables in this section in which the amount on line 1h is at least the amount in column A but less than the amount in column B, then enter here the amount from column A of that row ......... | 2a | $ | 4,423.00 |
| 2b | Enter the amount from column C of that row ................................. | 2b | $ | 388.66 |
| 2c | Enter the percentage from column D of that row ................................. | 2c | | 22 % |
| 2d | Subtract line 2a from line 1h ................................. | 2d | $ | 577.00 |
| 2e | Multiply the amount on line 2d by the percentage on line 2c ........................... | 2e | $ | 126.94 |
| 2f | Add lines 2b and 2e. This is the **Tentative Withholding Amount** ........................ | 2f | $ | 515.60 |

**Step 3.** **Account for tax credits**

| | | | | |
|---|---|---|---|---|
| 3a | Enter the amount from Step 3 of the employee's Form W-4 ........................... | 3a | $ | 4,000.00 |
| 3b | Divide the amount on line 3a by the number of pay periods on line 1b ..................... | 3b | $ | 166.67 |
| 3c | Subtract line 3b from line 2f. If zero or less, enter -0- ............................. | 3c | $ | 348.93 |

**Step 4.** **Figure the final amount to withhold**

| | | | | |
|---|---|---|---|---|
| 4a | Enter the additional amount to withhold from Step 4(c) of the employee's Form W-4 ........... | 4a | $ | 50.00 |
| 4b | Add lines 3c and 4a. **This is the amount to withhold from the employee's wages this pay period** .................................................................... | 4b | $ | 398.93 |

**EXHIBIT 10-3** *(concluded)*

## 2021 Percentage Method Tables for Manual Payroll Systems With Forms W-4 from 2020 or Later
### SEMIMONTHLY Payroll Period

| STANDARD Withholding Rate Schedules (Use these if the box in Step 2 of Form W-4 is **NOT** checked) | | | | | Form W-4, Step 2, Checkbox, Withholding Rate Schedules (Use these if the box in Step 2 of Form W-4 **IS** checked) | | | | |
|---|---|---|---|---|---|---|---|---|---|
| If the Adjusted Wage Amount (line 1h) is: | | The tentative amount to withhold is: | Plus this percentage— | of the amount that the Adjusted Wage exceeds— | If the Adjusted Wage Amount (line 1h) is: | | The tentative amount to withhold is: | Plus this percentage— | of the amount that the Adjusted Wage exceeds— |
| At least— | But less than— | | | | At least— | But less than— | | | |
| A | B | C | D | E | A | B | C | D | E |
| **Married Filing Jointly** | | | | | **Married Filing Jointly** | | | | |
| $0 | $1,046 | $0.00 | 0% | $0 | $0 | $523 | $0.00 | 0% | $0 |
| $1,046 | $1,875 | $0.00 | 10% | $1,046 | $523 | $938 | $0.00 | 10% | $523 |
| $1,875 | $4,423 | $82.90 | 12% | $1,875 | $938 | $2,211 | $41.50 | 12% | $938 |
| $4,423 | $8,244 | $388.66 | 22% | $4,423 | $2,211 | $4,122 | $194.26 | 22% | $2,211 |
| $8,244 | $14,790 | $1,229.28 | 24% | $8,244 | $4,122 | $7,395 | $614.68 | 24% | $4,122 |
| $14,790 | $18,498 | $2,800.32 | 32% | $14,790 | $7,395 | $9,249 | $1,400.20 | 32% | $7,395 |
| $18,498 | $27,225 | $3,986.88 | 35% | $18,498 | $9,249 | $13,613 | $1,993.48 | 35% | $9,249 |
| $27,225 | | $7,041.33 | 37% | $27,225 | $13,613 | | $3,520.88 | 37% | $13,613 |
| **Single or Married Filing Separately** | | | | | **Single or Married Filing Separately** | | | | |
| $0 | $523 | $0.00 | 0% | $0 | $0 | $261 | $0.00 | 0% | $0 |
| $523 | $938 | $0.00 | 10% | $523 | $261 | $469 | $0.00 | 10% | $261 |
| $938 | $2,211 | $41.50 | 12% | $938 | $469 | $1,106 | $20.80 | 12% | $469 |
| $2,211 | $4,122 | $194.26 | 22% | $2,211 | $1,106 | $2,061 | $97.24 | 22% | $1,106 |
| $4,122 | $7,395 | $614.68 | 24% | $4,122 | $2,061 | $3,697 | $307.34 | 24% | $2,061 |
| $7,395 | $9,249 | $1,400.20 | 32% | $7,395 | $3,697 | $4,624 | $699.98 | 32% | $3,697 |
| $9,249 | $22,340 | $1,993.48 | 35% | $9,249 | $4,624 | $11,170 | $996.62 | 35% | $4,624 |
| $22,340 | | $6,575.33 | 37% | $22,340 | $11,170 | | $3,287.72 | 37% | $11,170 |
| **Head of Household** | | | | | **Head of Household** | | | | |
| $0 | $783 | $0.00 | 0% | $0 | $0 | $392 | $0.00 | 0% | $0 |
| $783 | $1,375 | $0.00 | 10% | $783 | $392 | $688 | $0.00 | 10% | $392 |
| $1,375 | $3,042 | $59.20 | 12% | $1,375 | $688 | $1,521 | $29.60 | 12% | $688 |
| $3,042 | $4,381 | $259.24 | 22% | $3,042 | $1,521 | $2,191 | $129.56 | 22% | $1,521 |
| $4,381 | $7,654 | $553.82 | 24% | $4,381 | $2,191 | $3,827 | $276.96 | 24% | $2,191 |
| $7,654 | $9,508 | $1,339.34 | 32% | $7,654 | $3,827 | $4,754 | $669.60 | 32% | $3,827 |
| $9,508 | $22,600 | $1,932.62 | 35% | $9,508 | $4,754 | $11,300 | $966.24 | 35% | $4,754 |
| $22,600 | | $6,514.82 | 37% | $22,600 | $11,300 | | $3,257.34 | 37% | $11,300 |

**Publication 15-T (2021)**

**EXAMPLE 10-2**     Mauro Valdez is married filing jointly with a spouse who does not work, and who claims two dependents. Mauro is paid twice a month (semimonthly) and has gross wages of $5,000 each pay period. The proper amount of federal income tax withholding from Mauro's paycheck is $398.93. Use the Form W-4 from Exhibit 10-1 for his current information.

Note that the withholding tables are structured so that employees withhold approximately the same amount for a given annual income regardless of how often the employee is paid.

**EXAMPLE 10-3**     Using the information from Example 10-1, assume Audrey is paid biweekly; $52,000/26 = $2,000 per pay period. Using Table 1 and Worksheet 1 from Example 10-1, the amount of federal income tax withholding from Audrey's paycheck is $174.42. Over the period of a year, the withholdings total is $4,535.00. If Audrey is paid on a weekly basis, over the period of a year, the withholdings total $4,534.92. The difference is due to rounding.

Use Table 2, Wage Bracket Method Tables for Manual Payroll Systems with Form W-4 from 2020 or Later, if the payroll is manual and the employer prefers to use the wage bracket method. Note, these tables cover only up to approximately $100,000 in annual wages; if annual wages are in excess of $100,000, use the percentage method tables (typically Table 4). See Example 10-4 and Exhibit 10-4 for an illustration of a wage bracket table. Notice that the amount of federal withholding is a whole amount based on a range of wages. This "averaging" accounts for differences in withholding using the percent method.

**EXAMPLE 10-4**     Using the information from Example 10-1, assume Audrey's employer prefers to use Table 2, Wage Bracket Method Tables for Manual Payroll Systems with Forms W-4 from 2020 or Later.

1.   Using the Worksheet for Table 2, complete the form to 1h.
2.   Find the wage bracket table for a "Weekly Payroll Period."
3.   Go down the left side of the table and find the range for the adjusted wage amount from line 1h which is $995–$1,005.
4.   Go across to find the heading "Single or Married Filing Separately."
5.   Choose Standard Withholding.
6.   The intersection is $87.

Note that when the percentage method is used, the amount of federal withholding is $87.21, and when the wage bracket method is used, the amount of federal withholding is $87. This is due to averaging within the range of gross wages ($995–$1,005).

Generally, the largest amount of federal income tax withholding occurs when an employee is single and claims no exemption allowances. The more exemptions claimed, the less tax is withheld and the higher the net paycheck. In such cases, that may not provide for sufficient withholding during the year if, for example, an individual works multiple jobs. The withholding tables are constructed under the assumption that an individual works only one job. Remember that the U.S. tax system is a *progressive tax system* in which individuals with higher levels of income are taxed at higher rates. If a single employee works one job and

**EXHIBIT 10-4**

# 2. Wage Bracket Method Tables for Manual Payroll Systems With Forms W-4 From 2020 or Later

If you compute payroll manually, your employee has submitted a Form W-4 for 2020 or later, and you prefer to use the Wage Bracket method, use the worksheet below and the Wage Bracket Method tables that follow to figure federal income tax withholding.

The Wage Bracket Method tables cover only up to approximately $100,000 in annual wages. If you can't use the Wage Bracket Method tables because taxable wages exceed the amount from the last bracket of the table (based on filing status and pay period), use the Percentage Method tables in section 4.

**Worksheet 2. Employer's Withholding Worksheet for Wage Bracket Method Tables for Manual Payroll Systems With Forms W-4 From 2020 or Later**

*Keep for Your Records*

| Table 4 | Monthly | Semimonthly | Biweekly | Weekly | Daily |
|---|---|---|---|---|---|
| | 12 | 24 | 26 | 52 | 260 |

**Step 1.** **Adjust the employee's wage amount**

1a Enter the employee's total taxable wages this payroll period . . . . . . . . . . . . . . . . . . . . . . . . . . . . 1a $ 1,000

1b Enter the number of pay periods you have per year (see Table 4) . . . . . . . . . . . . . . . . . . . . . . . 1b 52

1c Enter the amount from Step 4(a) of the employee's Form W-4 . . . . . . . . . . . . . . . . . . . . . . . . . 1c $

1d Divide the amount on line 1c by the number of pay periods on line 1b . . . . . . . . . . . . . . . . . . 1d $

1e Add lines 1a and 1d . . . . . . . . . . . . . . . . . . . . . . . . . . . . . . . . . . . . . . . . . 1e $ 1,000

1f Enter the amount from Step 4(b) of the employee's Form W-4 . . . . . . . . . . . . . . . . . . . . . . . . . 1f $

1g Divide the amount on line 1f by the number of pay periods on line 1b . . . . . . . . . . . . . . . . . . 1g $

1h Subtract line 1g from line 1e. If zero or less, enter -0-. This is the **Adjusted Wage Amount** . . . . . . 1h $ 1,000

**Step 2.** **Figure the Tentative Withholding Amount**

2a Use the amount on line 1h to look up the tentative amount to withhold in the appropriate Wage Bracket Table in this section for your pay frequency, given the employee's filing status and whether the employee has checked the box in Step 2 of Form W-4. This is the **Tentative Withholding Amount** . . . . . . . . . . . . . . . . . . . . . . . . . . . . . . . . . . . . . . . . . 2a $ 87

**Step 3.** **Account for tax credits**

3a Enter the amount from Step 3 of the employee's Form W-4 . . . . . . . . . . . . . . . . . . . . . . . . . 3a $

3b Divide the amount on line 3a by the number of pay periods on line 1b . . . . . . . . . . . . . . . . . . 3b $

3c Subtract line 3b from line 2a. If zero or less, enter -0- . . . . . . . . . . . . . . . . . . . . . . . . . . . . . . 3c $ 87

**Step 4.** **Figure the final amount to withhold**

4a Enter the additional amount to withhold from Step 4(c) of the employee's Form W-4 . . . . . . . . . . . 4a $

4b Add lines 3c and 4a. **This is the amount to withhold from the employee's wages this pay period** . . . . . . . . . . . . . . . . . . . . . . . . . . . . . . . . . . . . . . . . . . . . . . . . . . 4b $ 87

**EXHIBIT 10-4** *(concluded)*

## 2021 Wage Bracket Method Tables for Manual Payroll Systems with Forms W-4 From 2020 or Later
### WEEKLY Payroll Period

| If the Adjusted Wage Amount (line 1h) is | | Married Filing Jointly | | Head of Household | | Single or Married Filing Separately | |
|---|---|---|---|---|---|---|---|
| | | Standard withholding | Form W-4, Step 2, Checkbox withholding | Standard withholding | Form W-4, Step 2, Checkbox withholding | Standard withholding | Form W-4, Step 2, Checkbox withholding |
| At least | But less than | The Tentative Withholding Amount is: | | | | | |
| $765 | $775 | $29 | $60 | $44 | $75 | $60 | $102 |
| $775 | $785 | $30 | $61 | $45 | $77 | $61 | $104 |
| $785 | $795 | $31 | $62 | $46 | $79 | $62 | $106 |
| $795 | $805 | $32 | $63 | $47 | $81 | $63 | $109 |
| $805 | $815 | $33 | $64 | $48 | $84 | $64 | $111 |
| $815 | $825 | $34 | $66 | $50 | $86 | $66 | $113 |
| $825 | $835 | $35 | $67 | $51 | $88 | $67 | $115 |
| $835 | $845 | $36 | $68 | $52 | $90 | $68 | $117 |
| $845 | $855 | $37 | $69 | $53 | $92 | $69 | $120 |
| $855 | $865 | $38 | $70 | $54 | $95 | $70 | $122 |
| $865 | $875 | $39 | $72 | $56 | $97 | $72 | $124 |
| $875 | $885 | $40 | $73 | $57 | $99 | $73 | $126 |
| $885 | $895 | $41 | $74 | $58 | $101 | $74 | $128 |
| $895 | $905 | $42 | $75 | $59 | $103 | $75 | $131 |
| $905 | $915 | $44 | $76 | $60 | $106 | $76 | $133 |
| $915 | $925 | $45 | $78 | $62 | $108 | $78 | $135 |
| $925 | $935 | $46 | $79 | $63 | $110 | $79 | $137 |
| $935 | $945 | $47 | $80 | $64 | $112 | $80 | $139 |
| $945 | $955 | $48 | $81 | $65 | $114 | $81 | $142 |
| $955 | $965 | $50 | $82 | $66 | $117 | $82 | $144 |
| $965 | $975 | $51 | $84 | $68 | $119 | $84 | $146 |
| $975 | $985 | $52 | $85 | $69 | $121 | $85 | $149 |
| $985 | $995 | $53 | $86 | $70 | $123 | $86 | $151 |
| $995 | $1,005 | $54 | $87 | $71 | $125 | $87 | $154 |
| $1,005 | $1,015 | $56 | $88 | $72 | $128 | $88 | $156 |
| $1,015 | $1,025 | $57 | $90 | $74 | $130 | $90 | $158 |
| $1,025 | $1,035 | $58 | $92 | $75 | $132 | $92 | $161 |
| $1,035 | $1,045 | $59 | $94 | $76 | $135 | $94 | $163 |
| $1,045 | $1,055 | $60 | $96 | $77 | $137 | $96 | $166 |
| $1,055 | $1,065 | $62 | $98 | $78 | $140 | $98 | $168 |
| $1,065 | $1,075 | $63 | $101 | $80 | $142 | $101 | $170 |
| $1,075 | $1,085 | $64 | $103 | $81 | $144 | $103 | $173 |
| $1,085 | $1,095 | $65 | $105 | $82 | $147 | $105 | $175 |
| $1,095 | $1,105 | $66 | $107 | $83 | $149 | $107 | $178 |
| $1,105 | $1,115 | $68 | $109 | $84 | $152 | $109 | $180 |
| $1,115 | $1,125 | $69 | $112 | $86 | $154 | $112 | $182 |
| $1,125 | $1,135 | $70 | $114 | $87 | $156 | $114 | $185 |
| $1,135 | $1,145 | $71 | $116 | $88 | $159 | $116 | $187 |
| $1,145 | $1,155 | $72 | $118 | $89 | $161 | $118 | $190 |
| $1,155 | $1,165 | $74 | $120 | $90 | $164 | $120 | $192 |
| $1,165 | $1,175 | $75 | $123 | $92 | $166 | $123 | $194 |
| $1,175 | $1,185 | $76 | $125 | $93 | $168 | $125 | $197 |
| $1,185 | $1,195 | $77 | $127 | $94 | $171 | $127 | $199 |
| $1,195 | $1,205 | $78 | $129 | $95 | $173 | $129 | $202 |
| $1,205 | $1,215 | $80 | $131 | $96 | $176 | $131 | $204 |
| $1,215 | $1,225 | $81 | $134 | $98 | $178 | $134 | $206 |
| $1,225 | $1,235 | $82 | $136 | $99 | $180 | $136 | $209 |
| $1,235 | $1,245 | $83 | $138 | $100 | $183 | $138 | $211 |
| $1,245 | $1,255 | $84 | $140 | $101 | $185 | $140 | $214 |
| $1,255 | $1,265 | $86 | $142 | $102 | $188 | $142 | $216 |
| $1,265 | $1,275 | $87 | $145 | $104 | $190 | $145 | $218 |
| $1,275 | $1,285 | $88 | $147 | $105 | $192 | $147 | $221 |
| $1,285 | $1,295 | $89 | $149 | $106 | $195 | $149 | $223 |
| $1,295 | $1,305 | $90 | $151 | $107 | $197 | $151 | $226 |
| $1,305 | $1,315 | $92 | $153 | $108 | $200 | $153 | $228 |
| $1,315 | $1,325 | $93 | $156 | $110 | $202 | $156 | $230 |
| $1,325 | $1,335 | $94 | $158 | $111 | $204 | $158 | $233 |
| $1,335 | $1,345 | $95 | $160 | $112 | $207 | $160 | $235 |
| $1,345 | $1,355 | $96 | $162 | $113 | $209 | $162 | $238 |
| $1,355 | $1,365 | $98 | $164 | $114 | $212 | $164 | $240 |
| $1,365 | $1,375 | $99 | $167 | $116 | $214 | $167 | $242 |
| $1,375 | $1,385 | $100 | $169 | $117 | $216 | $169 | $245 |
| $1,385 | $1,395 | $101 | $171 | $118 | $219 | $171 | $247 |
| $1,395 | $1,405 | $102 | $173 | $119 | $221 | $173 | $250 |
| $1,405 | $1,415 | $104 | $175 | $121 | $224 | $175 | $252 |

earns $25,000 per year, the marginal withholding rate is 12%. If that same person works two jobs paying $25,000 each, the second job is added to the first job for purposes of taxation. The second job causes the marginal withholding rate to be 22% (when both jobs are added together), yet each employer will withhold at a marginal 12% rate as though the individual works only one job.

Unless the employee requests one or both employers to withhold an amount in excess of the statutory requirement, the employee will likely be underwithheld and will be required to pay additional taxes when filing their return and could incur an underpayment penalty. Step 4c on the Form W-4 informs the employer to take out "extra withholding" for each pay period to cover for a potential shortfall in federal withholding taxes.

## FICA Taxes—Social Security Tax and Medicare Tax Withholding

Employers must also withhold Federal Insurance Contributions Act (FICA) taxes from the paychecks of employees. There are two parts to FICA taxes. One is the old age, survivors, and disability insurance (OASDI), commonly referred to as *social security*.[3] The other is hospital insurance for the elderly and other specified individuals, called *Medicare*.[4]

Unlike income tax withholding, which is deducted entirely from the paycheck of the employee, social security and Medicare taxes are collected equally from the employee and the employer. The employer withholds the appropriate amount from the employee (as with income tax withholding), and that amount is added to the amount from the pocket of the employer. Thus, the employer pays a portion of the total FICA liability and the employee pays their portion.

If a taxpayer works two jobs, both employers are required to withhold FICA and match the amounts withheld. A taxpayer who has overpaid the social security portion of the tax because their combined taxable income from both jobs exceeds the annual wage base is entitled to receive the excess amount back when they file Form 1040. The excess social security tax withheld is recorded on the second page of Form 1040 under the Payments section.

In 2021 the social security tax rate is 6.2% of taxable wages for the employee and 6.2% of taxable wages for the employer, up to an annual wage base of $142,800.[5] For Medicare taxes, the rate is 1.45% for each party on an unlimited wage base. Thus, the total amount collected by the federal government is 15.3%, 12.4% on the social security wages of an individual up to $142,800 and 2.9% on individual wages above that threshold. A 0.9% Additional Medicare Tax applies to combined Medicare wages and self-employment income over the threshold amount based on the taxpayer's filing status. The threshold is $250,000 for married filing jointly; $200,000 for single, head of household, and qualifying widow(er); and $125,000 for married filing separately. Self-employment losses are not considered for purposes of these threshold amounts. It also requires the employer to withhold the 0.9% on Medicare wages that it pays to the employee in excess of $200,000 in 2021. The employer is not required to match this additional Medicare tax; it is an employee-only tax.

**EXAMPLE 10-5**    Lamar earned $72,000 during 2021. Without regard to federal income taxes, the employer will withhold $4,464.00 ($72,000 × 0.062) from the paycheck for social security taxes and $1,044.00 ($72,000 × 0.0145) for Medicare taxes, for a total of $5,508.00. Lamar's employer pays its share and will deposit a total of $11,016.00 with the federal government during the year.

[3] IRC § 3101(a).
[4] IRC § 3101(b).
[5] This annual wage base is subject to annual inflation adjustment.

**EXAMPLE 10-6**

Haito earned $145,000 during 2021. Haito's employer will withhold social security taxes of $8,853.60 (maximum wage base of $142,800 × 0.062) and Medicare taxes of $2,102.50 ($145,000 × 0.0145) for a total of $10,956.10. The employer pays its share and sends the federal government $21,912.20 during the year for social security and Medicare taxes.

## Tips

Employees at restaurants or other establishments may receive tips from customers for services performed. Employees are required to report cash tips to their employer by the 10th of the month after the month in which the employee receives the tips. Employees can use Form 4070 to report tips. The report must include the employee's name, address, and social security number; the period the report covers; and the total amount of tips received during the period. The report includes tips known to the employer (from credit card charges, for example) and cash tips, and the employee must sign the report. If the tips in any one month from any one job are less than $20, no reporting is required. Employers must withhold income tax, social security, and Medicare taxes on the amount of employee tips.[6]

Large food and beverage establishments may be required to "allocate" tips to employees. A large establishment is one with more than 10 employees on a typical business day during the preceding year that provides food or beverages for consumption on the premises and where tipping is customary.[7] In effect, if employees do not report tips in an amount of at least 8% of gross receipts, the employer must allocate the difference to the employees. Employers are required to report allocated tips to the IRS on Form 8027.

**CONCEPT CHECK 10-2—**
**LO 10-2**

1. Withholding and other employment taxes are levied only on cash wages and salaries paid to the employee. True or false?
2. The employer fills out Form W-4 to determine how many withholding allowances the employee is entitled to take. True or false?
3. Reza is single and earns $1,200 per week. Using the percentage method for a manual system (Table 4 in the Appendix). What amount of federal withholding tax will be deducted from this gross compensation?
4. Luis earns $146,500 in 2021. How much social security tax will be withheld from this compensation? How much Medicare tax will be withheld from this compensation?
5. Form 4070 is completed by tipped employees for any and all tips earned for the period. True or false?

Employers must use one of the following methods to allocate tips:

1. Gross receipts per employee.
2. Hours worked per employee.
3. Good-faith agreement between the employee and employer.

Employers are *not* required to withhold income, social security, or Medicare taxes on allocated tips. Allocated tips appear in box 8 on Form W-2.

[6] IRC § 3121(q), § 3402(k).
[7] IRC § 6053(c).

# REPORTING AND PAYING PAYROLL TAXES

## LO 10-3

### Payment of Payroll Taxes

Employers are required to pay withheld taxes (income tax, social security, Medicare) to the federal government on a timely basis.[8] These payments are called *payroll tax deposits.* The frequency of the deposits depends, in large part, on the dollar amounts withheld or otherwise owed to the government. The employer must use the electronic funds transfer to make all federal tax deposits;[9] the Electronic Federal Tax Payment System (EFTPS) is a free service provided by the Department of Treasury. This service is available for all employers. When the employer identification number (EIN) is requested from the IRS, the employer is pre-enrolled with instructions on how to activate the EFTPS account. For more information, go to www.eftps.gov.

Employers typically deposit taxes either monthly or semiweekly. New employers are deemed monthly schedule depositors except in unusual circumstances. The deposit schedule is based on the total tax liability that the employer reported on Form 941 during a four-quarter lookback period. For 2021, the lookback period runs from the quarters starting July 1, 2019, through June 30, 2020. If the employer reported total payroll taxes of $50,000 or less during the lookback period, the employer is a monthly schedule depositor. If total taxes exceed $50,000, the employer is a semiweekly schedule depositor.[10]

---

**EXAMPLE 10-7**

Wong Company is determining how often it needs to deposit payroll taxes for calendar year 2021. The company made quarterly payroll tax deposits during the lookback period as follows:

| | |
|---|---:|
| Quarter July 1–September 30, 2019 | $ 8,000 |
| Quarter October 1–December 31, 2019 | 9,000 |
| Quarter January 1–March 31, 2020 | 10,000 |
| Quarter April 1–June 30, 2020 | 10,000 |
| Total payroll taxes paid in lookback period | $37,000 |

Because the total payroll taxes deposited in the lookback period were less than $50,000, Wong Company will be a monthly payroll tax depositor during 2021.

---

Monthly depositors are required to deposit payroll taxes through EFTPS on or before the 15th day of the following month. The taxes that must be deposited are the sum of (a) withheld income taxes, (b) social security and Medicare taxes withheld from the employee, and (c) the employer's share for social security and Medicare taxes.

---

**EXAMPLE 10-8**

XYZ Company is a monthly depositor. For payroll paid during the month of April, the company withheld $4,000 in income taxes, $2,500 in social security, and $863 in Medicare taxes. The company is required to pay [$4,000 + ($2,500 + $863) + ($2,500 + $863)] and to deposit $10,726 through EFTPS no later than May 15.

---

[8] IRC § 6302(a); Reg. § 31.6302-1(a).

[9] Refer to Publication 15 under "How to Deposit."

[10] Reg. §31.6302-1(b).

Semiweekly schedule depositors must remit payroll taxes more often. Payroll taxes associated with payrolls paid on a Wednesday, Thursday, or Friday must be deposited by the following Wednesday. For payrolls paid on Saturday, Sunday, Monday, or Tuesday, the semiweekly schedule depositor must deposit the taxes no later than the following Friday.

---

**EXAMPLE 10-9**     LMNO Company, which pays its employees every Friday, is a semiweekly schedule depositor. When the company paid its employees on Friday, it incurred a payroll tax liability of $19,000 on that date. LMNO must deposit applicable payroll taxes no later than Wednesday of the next week.

---

It is important to note that the applicable payroll date is the date the payroll is *paid,* not the end of the payroll period.

---

**EXAMPLE 10-10**     Nichols Company is a monthly schedule depositor that pays its employees on the first day of the month for the payroll period ending on the last day of the prior month. Payroll taxes withheld on June 1 are due no later than July 15 even though the payroll is for work performed by employees through May 31.

---

If the day on which taxes are due is a weekend or holiday, taxes are payable on the next banking day. Semiweekly schedule depositors have at least three banking days to make a deposit. Thus, if a banking holiday means that an employer does not get three banking days, the payment date is extended.

---

**EXAMPLE 10-11**     LMNO Company (from Example 10-9) pays employees on Friday. The following Monday is a banking holiday. Because LMNO is a semiweekly schedule depositor, it must normally deposit applicable payroll taxes on the following Wednesday. Because Monday is a banking holiday, the company does not have at least three banking days to make its deposit. Thus, the company has until Thursday to make its deposit.

---

Employers with a payroll tax liability of less than $2,500 at the end of any quarter can pay the payroll tax liability using Form 941-V when they file their quarterly payroll tax reports rather than with the EFTPS.

If an employer accumulates $100,000 or more in taxes on any day during a deposit period, it must deposit the tax by the next banking day, whether it is a monthly or semiweekly schedule depositor. This rule applies to a single day, and the taxes do not accumulate during the period. For example, if $100,000 of taxes are accumulated on a Monday, they must be deposited by Tuesday. If on that Tuesday, additional accumulated taxes are $90,000, the taxes are deposited by Friday. An employer who is a monthly schedule depositor and accumulates a $100,000 tax liability on any day becomes a semiweekly schedule depositor on the next day and remains so for at least the rest of the calendar year and for the following year.

---

**EXAMPLE 10-12**     Patel Company started its business on July 26, 2021. On August 2 it paid wages for the first time and accumulated a tax liability of $30,000. On Friday, August 13, Patel Company paid wages and incurred a tax liability of $70,000, which brings the accumulated tax liability to $100,000. Because this is the first year of its business, the tax liability for its lookback period is zero, so the company would be a monthly schedule depositor. However, because Patel Company accumulated a $100,000 tax liability, it became a semiweekly schedule depositor. It will be a semiweekly schedule depositor for the remainder of 2021 and 2022. In this example, Patel Company is required to deposit the $100,000 by Monday, August 16, the next banking day.

## Deposit Penalties

If payroll taxes are not paid on a timely basis, the employer is subject to penalty. The penalty is based on the amount not properly or timely deposited. The penalties are as follows:

- 2% for deposits made 1 to 5 days late.
- 5% for deposits made 6 to 15 days late.
- 10% for deposits made 16 or more days late, but before 10 days from the due date of the first notice the IRS sent asking for the tax due.
- 10% if electronic deposit is required but not used.
- 10% if deposits are paid directly to the IRS, paid with the return, or paid to an unauthorized financial institution.
- 15% for amounts unpaid more than 10 days after the date of the first notice the IRS sent asking for the tax due.

Employers who withhold taxes from employee paychecks are holding the withheld taxes in trust for the employee. As such, employers have a high level of responsibility. Individuals may be personally responsible for unpaid payroll taxes. If the IRS determines that an individual is responsible for collecting, accounting for, and paying payroll taxes and that the person acted willfully in not paying the taxes, the IRS can assess a penalty on the individual equal to the amount of tax due. Refer to Publication 15 under "Deposit Penalties" for additional rules.

## Reporting Payroll Taxes and Form 941

Each quarter, if a company pays wages subject to income tax withholding or social security and Medicare taxes, a Form 941 must be completed. Refer to Exhibit 10-5 and Example 10-13 for a filled-in Form 941 and Schedule B. There is a requirement that any return prepared by a paid preparer be signed by the preparer. Note: All references to the 2021 Form 941 assume regular payroll data excluding specific provisions for legislation due to COVID-19. Additional information related to this legislation is covered at the end of the chapter.

---

**EXAMPLE 10-13**

Kahn Company (EIN: 36-1234567), located at 123 Main Street, Seattle, WA 98107, had the following payroll data for the first quarter, ended March 31, 2021:

| | |
|---|---|
| Number of employees | 6 |
| Gross wages | $300,000 |
| Total income tax withheld from wages | $ 24,000* |
| Social security wages | $300,000 |
| Medicare wages | $300,000 |

\* Assume $4,000 per pay period.

Assume that Kahn Company pays wages on a semimonthly basis ($50,000 per pay period). Deposits for the quarter were $69,800. Exhibit 10-5 is the filled-in Form 941 (including Schedule B) for Kahn Company for the second quarter of 2021. Exhibit 10-6 is a filled-in voucher coupon for the amount of additional tax due for the quarter. Anmal Kumar is the paid preparer of Form 941.

The payroll tax liability per pay period is calculated as follows:

| | | |
|---|---|---|
| Social security tax | $50,000 × 12.4% = | $ 6,200 |
| Medicare tax | $50,000 × 2.9% = | 1,450 |
| Federal income tax | | 4,000 |
| Total tax liability per period | | $11,650 |
| Total tax liability for the quarter | | $69,900 |
| Deposits made for the quarter | | 69,800 |
| Deposit due with 941 return | | $ 100 |

**EXHIBIT 10-5**

Form **941 for 2021:** **Employer's QUARTERLY Federal Tax Return**
(Rev. March 2021)    Department of the Treasury — Internal Revenue Service

950121

OMB No. 1545-0029

Employer identification number (EIN)  3 6 – 1 2 3 4 5 6 7

Name *(not your trade name)* Khan Company

Trade name *(if any)*

Address  123 Main Street
Number     Street                              Suite or room number

Seattle                          WA          98107
City                            State        ZIP code

Foreign country name        Foreign province/county        Foreign postal code

**Report for this Quarter of 2021**
(Check one.)

[X] **1:** January, February, March

[ ] **2:** April, May, June

[ ] **3:** July, August, September

[ ] **4:** October, November, December

Go to *www.irs.gov/Form941* for
instructions and the latest information.

Read the separate instructions before you complete Form 941. Type or print within the boxes.

**Part 1:**    **Answer these questions for this quarter.**

| | | |
|---|---|---|
| 1 | Number of employees who received wages, tips, or other compensation for the pay period including: *Mar. 12* (Quarter 1), *June 12* (Quarter 2), *Sept. 12* (Quarter 3), or *Dec. 12* (Quarter 4) | 1 | 6 |
| 2 | Wages, tips, and other compensation . . . . . . . . . . | 2 | 300,000 . |
| 3 | Federal income tax withheld from wages, tips, and other compensation . . . . . . | 3 | 24,000 . |
| 4 | If no wages, tips, and other compensation are subject to social security or Medicare tax | [ ] Check and go to line 6. |

|  |  | Column 1 | | Column 2 |
|---|---|---|---|---|
| 5a | Taxable social security wages . . | 300,000 . | × 0.124 = | 37,200 . |
| 5a | (i) Qualified sick leave wages . . | . | × 0.062 = | . |
| 5a | (ii) Qualified family leave wages . | . | × 0.062 = | . |
| 5b | Taxable social security tips . . . | . | × 0.124 = | . |
| 5c | Taxable Medicare wages & tips . . | 300,000 . | × 0.029 = | 8,700 . |
| 5d | Taxable wages & tips subject to Additional Medicare Tax withholding | . | × 0.009 = | . |

| | | |
|---|---|---|
| 5e | Total social security and Medicare taxes. Add Column 2 from lines 5a, 5a(i), 5a(ii), 5b, 5c, and 5d | 5e | 45,900 . |
| 5f | Section 3121(q) Notice and Demand—Tax due on unreported tips (see instructions) . . | 5f | . |
| 6 | Total taxes before adjustments. Add lines 3, 5e, and 5f . . . . . . . . . | 6 | 69,900 . |
| 7 | Current quarter's adjustment for fractions of cents . . . . . . . . . . | 7 | |
| 8 | Current quarter's adjustment for sick pay . . . . . . . . . . . . | 8 | . |
| 9 | Current quarter's adjustments for tips and group-term life insurance . . . . . . | 9 | . |
| 10 | Total taxes after adjustments. Combine lines 6 through 9 . . . . . . . | 10 | 69,900 . |
| 11a | Qualified small business payroll tax credit for increasing research activities. Attach Form 8974 | 11a | . |
| 11b | Nonrefundable portion of credit for qualified sick and family leave wages from Worksheet 1 | 11b | . |
| 11c | Nonrefundable portion of employee retention credit from Worksheet 1 . . . . . . | 11c | . |

▶ **You MUST complete all three pages of Form 941 and SIGN it.**

Next ▶

For Privacy Act and Paperwork Reduction Act Notice, see the back of the Payment Voucher.     Cat. No. 17001Z     Form **941** (Rev. 3-2021)

Source: U.S. Department of the Treasury, Internal Revenue Service, Form 941. Washington, DC: 2021.

*(continued)*

**EXHIBIT 10-5**   *(continued)*

950221

| Name *(not your trade name)* | Employer identification number (EIN) |
|---|---|
| Khan Company | 36-1234567 |

| Part 1: | Answer these questions for this quarter. *(continued)* |
|---|---|

**11d** Total nonrefundable credits. Add lines 11a, 11b, and 11c . . . . . . . . . .   **11d** [ . ]

**12** Total taxes after adjustments and nonrefundable credits. Subtract line 11d from line 10 .   **12** [ 69,900 . ]

**13a** Total deposits for this quarter, including overpayment applied from a prior quarter and overpayments applied from Form 941-X, 941-X (PR), 944-X, or 944-X (SP) filed in the current quarter   **13a** [ 69,800 . ]

**13b** Reserved for future use . . . . . . . . . . . . . . . . .   **13b** [ . ]

**13c** Refundable portion of credit for qualified sick and family leave wages from Worksheet 1   **13c** [ . ]

**13d** Refundable portion of employee retention credit from Worksheet 1 . . . . . . . .   **13d** [ . ]

**13e** Total deposits and refundable credits. Add lines 13a, 13c, and 13d . . . . . . .   **13e** [ 69,800 . ]

**13f** Total advances received from filing Form(s) 7200 for the quarter . . . . . . . .   **13f** [ . ]

**13g** Total deposits and refundable credits less advances. Subtract line 13f from line 13e . . . .   **13g** [ 69,800 . ]

**14** Balance due. If line 12 is more than line 13g, enter the difference and see instructions . . .   **14** [ 100 . ]

**15** Overpayment. If line 13g is more than line 12, enter the difference [ . ]   Check one: ☐ Apply to next return.   ☐ Send a refund.

| Part 2: | Tell us about your deposit schedule and tax liability for this quarter. |
|---|---|

If you're unsure about whether you're a monthly schedule depositor or a semiweekly schedule depositor, see section 11 of Pub. 15.

**16   Check one:** ☐   **Line 12 on this return is less than $2,500 or line 12 on the return for the prior quarter was less than $2,500, and you didn't incur a $100,000 next-day deposit obligation during the current quarter.** If line 12 for the prior quarter was less than $2,500 but line 12 on this return is $100,000 or more, you must provide a record of your federal tax liability. If you're a monthly schedule depositor, complete the deposit schedule below; if you're a semiweekly schedule depositor, attach Schedule B (Form 941). Go to Part 3.

☐   **You were a monthly schedule depositor for the entire quarter.** Enter your tax liability for each month and total liability for the quarter, then go to Part 3.

Tax liability:   Month 1   [ . ]

Month 2   [ . ]

Month 3   [ . ]

Total liability for quarter   [ . ]   Total must equal line 12.

☒   **You were a semiweekly schedule depositor for any part of this quarter.** Complete Schedule B (Form 941), Report of Tax Liability for Semiweekly Schedule Depositors, and attach it to Form 941. Go to Part 3.

▶ **You MUST complete all three pages of Form 941 and SIGN it.**   Next ▶

Page **2**   Form **941** (Rev. 3-2021)

**EXHIBIT 10-5** *(concluded)*

| Name (not your trade name) | Employer identification number (EIN) |
|---|---|
| Khan Company | 36-1234567 |

950921

**Part 3:** Tell us about your business. If a question does NOT apply to your business, leave it blank.

17 If your business has closed or you stopped paying wages . . . . . . . . . . . . . . □ Check here, and

enter the final date you paid wages [ / / ] ; also attach a statement to your return. See instructions.

18 If you're a seasonal employer and you don't have to file a return for every quarter of the year . . . □ Check here.

19 Qualified health plan expenses allocable to qualified sick leave wages . . . . . . . 19 [ . ]

20 Qualified health plan expenses allocable to qualified family leave wages . . . . . . 20 [ . ]

21 Qualified wages for the employee retention credit . . . . . . . . . 21 [ . ]

22 Qualified health plan expenses allocable to wages reported on line 21 . . . . . . . . 22 [ . ]

23 Credit from Form 5884-C, line 11, for this quarter . . . . . . . . 23 [ . ]

24 Reserved for future use . . . . . . . . . . . . 24 [ . ]

25 Reserved for future use . . . . . . . . . . . 25 [ . ]

**Part 4:** May we speak with your third-party designee?

Do you want to allow an employee, a paid tax preparer, or another person to discuss this return with the IRS? See the instructions for details.

□ **Yes.** Designee's name and phone number [                    ] [                    ]

Select a 5-digit personal identification number (PIN) to use when talking to the IRS. [ ] [ ] [ ] [ ] [ ]

□ **No.**

**Part 5:** Sign here. You MUST complete all three pages of Form 941 and SIGN it.

Under penalties of perjury, I declare that I have examined this return, including accompanying schedules and statements, and to the best of my knowledge and belief, it is true, correct, and complete. Declaration of preparer (other than taxpayer) is based on all information of which preparer has any knowledge.

✗ **Sign your name here** [                    ]   Print your name here [                    ]

Print your title here [                    ]

Date [ / / ]   Best daytime phone [                    ]

**Paid Preparer Use Only**   Check if you're self-employed . . . □

| Preparer's name | [                    ] | PTIN | [                    ] |
|---|---|---|---|
| Preparer's signature | [                    ] | Date | [ / / ] |
| Firm's name (or yours if self-employed) | [                    ] | EIN | [                    ] |
| Address | [                    ] | Phone | [                    ] |
| City | [                    ] State [ ] | ZIP code | [                    ] |

Form **941** (Rev. 3-2021)

**EXHIBIT 10-5**   *(continued)*

# Schedule B (Form 941):

960311

## Report of Tax Liability for Semiweekly Schedule Depositors

(Rev. January 2017)                    Department of the Treasury — Internal Revenue Service

OMB No. 1545-0029

**Employer identification number (EIN)**    3  6 – 1  2  3  4  5  6  7

**Name** *(not your trade name)*   Khan Company

**Calendar year**   2  0  2  1   *(Also check quarter)*

**Report for this Quarter...**
**(Check one.)**

- [X] **1:** January, February, March
- [ ] **2:** April, May, June
- [ ] **3:** July, August, September
- [ ] **4:** October, November, December

Use this schedule to show your TAX LIABILITY for the quarter; don't use it to show your deposits. When you file this form with Form 941 or Form 941-SS, don't change your tax liability by adjustments reported on any Forms 941-X or 944-X. You must fill out this form and attach it to Form 941 or Form 941-SS if you're a semiweekly schedule depositor or became one because your accumulated tax liability on any day was $100,000 or more. Write your daily tax liability on the numbered space that corresponds to the date wages were paid. See Section 11 in Pub. 15 for details.

**Month 1**

| # | | # | | # | | # | | Tax liability for Month 1 |
|---|---|---|---|---|---|---|---|---|
| 1 | . | 9 | . | 17 | . | 25 | . | |
| 2 | . | 10 | . | 18 | . | 26 | . | |
| 3 | . | 11 | . | 19 | . | 27 | . | **23,300** . |
| 4 | . | 12 | . | 20 | . | 28 | . | |
| 5 | . | 13 | . | 21 | . | 29 | . | |
| 6 | . | 14 | . | 22 | . | 30 | . | |
| 7 | . | 15 | 11,650 . | 23 | . | 31 | 11,650 . | |
| 8 | . | 16 | . | 24 | | | | |

**Month 2**

| # | | # | | # | | # | | Tax liability for Month 2 |
|---|---|---|---|---|---|---|---|---|
| 1 | . | 9 | . | 17 | . | 25 | . | |
| 2 | . | 10 | . | 18 | . | 26 | . | |
| 3 | . | 11 | . | 19 | . | 27 | . | **23,300** . |
| 4 | . | 12 | . | 20 | . | 28 | 11,650 . | |
| 5 | . | 13 | . | 21 | . | 29 | . | |
| 6 | . | 14 | . | 22 | . | 30 | . | |
| 7 | . | 15 | 11,650 . | 23 | . | 31 | . | |
| 8 | . | 16 | . | 24 | . | | | |

**Month 3**

| # | | # | | # | | # | | Tax liability for Month 3 |
|---|---|---|---|---|---|---|---|---|
| 1 | . | 9 | . | 17 | . | 25 | . | |
| 2 | . | 10 | . | 18 | . | 26 | . | |
| 3 | . | 11 | . | 19 | . | 27 | . | **23,300** . |
| 4 | . | 12 | . | 20 | . | 28 | . | |
| 5 | . | 13 | . | 21 | . | 29 | . | |
| 6 | . | 14 | . | 22 | . | 30 | . | |
| 7 | . | 15 | 11,650 . | 23 | . | 31 | 11,650 . | |
| 8 | . | 16 | . | 24 | . | | | |

Fill in your total liability for the quarter (Month 1 + Month 2 + Month 3) ▶
**Total must equal line 12 on Form 941 or Form 941-SS.**

**Total liability for the quarter**

**69,900** .

**For Paperwork Reduction Act Notice, see separate instructions.**    IRS.gov/form941    Cat. No. 11967Q    **Schedule B (Form 941)** (Rev. 1-2017)

Source: U.S. Department of the Treasury, Internal Revenue Service, Form 941. Washington, DC: 2021.

**EXHIBIT 10-6**

| Form **941-V** | **Payment Voucher** | OMB No. 1545-0029 |
|---|---|---|
| Department of the Treasury Internal Revenue Service | ▶ Don't staple this voucher or your payment to Form 941. | 20**21** |

| 1 Enter your employer identification number (EIN). | 2 **Enter the amount of your payment.** ▶ | | Dollars | Cents |
|---|---|---|---|---|
| 36-1234567 | Make your check or money order payable to "**United States Treasury**" | | 100 | 00 |

| 3 Tax Period | | 4 Enter your business name (individual name if sole proprietor). |
|---|---|---|
| ◉ 1st Quarter | ○ 3rd Quarter | Khan Company |
| | | Enter your address. |
| ○ 2nd Quarter | ○ 4th Quarter | 123 Main Street |
| | | Enter your city, state, and ZIP code; or your city, foreign country name, foreign province/county, and foreign postal code. |
| | | Seattle, WA 98107 |

Source: U.S. Department of the Treasury, Internal Revenue Service, Form 941-V. Washington, DC: 2021.

Schedule B is used to report an employer's payroll tax liability for each period, not for the amount of payroll tax deposits. Therefore, the amounts entered on Schedule B relate to the payroll tax liability for each month in the quarter. Using the previous example, the amount of payroll tax liability is $69,900; this amount will be allocated according to the employer payroll periods on the schedule.

There may be situations in which the total liability from Schedule B will not agree with the calculated amounts on line 6 of Form 941 by "fractions of cents" due to rounding. The difference is recorded on line 7 and is included in the totals on Line 10. Lines 11a-11c (special items) are totaled on line 11d. Line 12 is the total after subtracting line 11d from line 10. Schedule B totals will then be equal to line 12 on Form 941.

Small business employers may have the option of filing these taxes on an annual basis. Form 944—Employer's Annual Federal Tax Return is for employers who have received written notification from the IRS that they qualify for the Form 944 program. Refer to Publication 15, "Chapter 12. Filing Form 941 or Form 944," for a detailed explanation of qualification requirements. Employers who are required to file Form 944 can notify the IRS if they want to file quarterly Form 941 instead of the annual form.

**CONCEPT CHECK 10-3— LO 10-3**

1. All new employers must use the semiweekly deposit system. True or false?
2. The deposit schedule for an employer is based on the total tax liability that the employer reported on Form 941 during the prior four quarters starting on July 1 and ending on March 31 of the next year. The lookback period runs from the quarters starting July 1 of the current year through June 30 of the next year. True or false?
3. Semiweekly schedule depositors remit taxes on the following Wednesday if the payroll is paid on a Wednesday, Thursday, or Friday. True or false?
4. The penalty for not paying the appropriate federal taxes on time is based on the total amount of the tax liability whether or not a partial payment was made on time. True or false?
5. Form 941 is prepared by the employer to record all federal taxes withheld, including federal withholding, social security, and Medicare taxes and amounts paid for these taxes. True or false?

# SELF-EMPLOYMENT TAXES, UNEMPLOYMENT TAXES, FORM 940, TAXES FOR HOUSEHOLD EMPLOYEES, AND SCHEDULE H
## LO 10-4

### Self-Employment Tax

To this point, this chapter has covered the rules associated with payroll taxes derived from an employee–employer relationship. Self-employed individuals (those filing Schedule C or Schedule F) pay similar taxes, called *self-employment taxes.*

Self-employment taxes are based on net earnings (profit) generated by the business. Because the self-employed taxpayer acts, in effect, as an employee and an employer, the self-employed taxpayer pays both parts of social security and Medicare taxes. For 2021, these individuals pay 12.4% social security tax on net earnings from self-employment of up to $142,800 and a 2.9% Medicare tax on all net earnings without limit.[11] If net earnings from self-employment are less than $400, no self-employment tax is payable.[12] Self-employment tax is reported on Schedule SE.

Remember that self-employed taxpayers are allowed a deduction for self-employment tax in determining AGI (Schedule 1, line 15). This deduction gives the sole proprietor a share of the employer tax expense that would be allowed for corporate businesses. The amount of net self-employment earnings subject to FICA taxes is first reduced by 7.65% before calculating the taxes. Remember from Chapter 6 that sole proprietors are not considered employees; therefore, there is no employer match of FICA taxes and no business expense allowed in reducing taxable income. To compensate self-employed individuals for this inability to take the employer share as a business deduction, they are permitted to reduce net self-employment earnings by 7.65% so that only 92.35% (100% − 7.65%) of net self-employment earnings are subject to FICA taxes.

In some situations, a taxpayer is an employee of a company as well as a sole proprietor. For example, a taxpayer can work as a teacher and sell real estate as a part-time business. The school district withholds the teacher's FICA taxes while the teacher must pay FICA taxes on the net earnings generated by the real estate business. If the earnings from the teacher's Form W-2 and the net earnings from the real estate business are less than the ceiling for social security ($142,800 in 2021), there is no problem. What if both activities combined generate more than $142,800 in earnings? In this type of situation, wages subject to social security are deducted from the ceiling amount of $142,800. The balance is then compared with the earnings from self-employment. If the taxpayer in this situation earned $100,000 as a teacher and $47,500 from the real estate business, the calculation for FICA tax is as follows:

| | | |
|---|---|---|
| Earnings (profit) from business (Schedule C) | | $47,500 |
| Net earnings from self-employment ($47,500 × 92.35%) | | $43,866 |
| Social security ceiling | $ 142,800 | |
| − W2 wages | 100,000 | |
| Base for social security self-employment tax | $ 42,800 | |
| Self-employment rate | Social security | Medicare |
| | $ 42,800.00 | $43,866.00 |
| | × 12.4 % | × 2.9 % |
| Self-employment tax | $5,307.20 | $1,272.11 |
| | (rounded to $5,307) | (rounded to $1,272) |

The total self-employment tax is $6,579 ($5,307 + $1,272). The taxpayer's 2021 return will show net earnings from the business of $47,500 (on Schedule C), a deduction for Adjusted Gross Income of $3,290 (calculated from Schedule SE and transferred to line 15 of Schedule 1), and self-employment tax of $6,579 (on Schedule SE, shown in Exhibit 10-7, and Schedule 2, line 4). Note that amounts are rounded on the appropriate forms.

## Unemployment Taxes

The Social Security Act of 1935 required every state to institute an unemployment compensation program to provide payments to people during temporary periods of unemployment.

[11] IRC § 1401(a), (b).
[12] IRC § 1402(b).

**EXHIBIT 10-7**

| SCHEDULE SE<br>(Form 1040)<br><br>Department of the Treasury<br>Internal Revenue Service (99) | **Self-Employment Tax**<br><br>▶ Go to *www.irs.gov/ScheduleSE* for instructions and the latest information.<br>▶ Attach to Form 1040, 1040-SR, or 1040-NR. | OMB No. 1545-0074<br><br>**2021**<br>Attachment<br>Sequence No. **17** |
|---|---|---|

| Name of person with self-employment income (as shown on Form 1040, 1040-SR, or 1040-NR) | Social security number of person<br>with **self-employment** income ▶ |
|---|---|

**Part I**   **Self-Employment Tax**

**Note:** If your only income subject to self-employment tax is **church employee income,** see instructions for how to report your income and the definition of church employee income.

**A**   If you are a minister, member of a religious order, or Christian Science practitioner **and** you filed Form 4361, but you had $400 or more of **other** net earnings from self-employment, check here and continue with Part I . . . . . . . . ▶ ☐

Skip lines 1a and 1b if you use the farm optional method in Part II. See instructions.

| | | | |
|---|---|---|---:|
| **1a** | Net farm profit or (loss) from Schedule F, line 34, and farm partnerships, Schedule K-1 (Form 1065), box 14, code A . . . . . . . . . . . . . | **1a** | |
| **b** | If you received social security retirement or disability benefits, enter the amount of Conservation Reserve Program payments included on Schedule F, line 4b, or listed on Schedule K-1 (Form 1065), box 20, code AH | **1b** | (        ) |

Skip line 2 if you use the nonfarm optional method in Part II. See instructions.

| | | | |
|---|---|---|---:|
| **2** | Net profit or (loss) from Schedule C, line 31; and Schedule K-1 (Form 1065), box 14, code A (other than farming). See instructions for other income to report or if you are a minister or member of a religious order | **2** | 47,500 |
| **3** | Combine lines 1a, 1b, and 2 . . . . . . . . . . . . . . . . . . . | **3** | 47,500 |
| **4a** | If line 3 is more than zero, multiply line 3 by 92.35% (0.9235). Otherwise, enter amount from line 3 | **4a** | 43,866 |
| | **Note:** If line 4a is less than $400 due to Conservation Reserve Program payments on line 1b, see instructions. | | |
| **b** | If you elect one or both of the optional methods, enter the total of lines 15 and 17 here . . . . . | **4b** | |
| **c** | Combine lines 4a and 4b. If less than $400, **stop;** you don't owe self-employment tax. **Exception:** If less than $400 and you had **church employee income,** enter -0- and continue . . . . . . . ▶ | **4c** | 43,866 |
| **5a** | Enter your **church employee income** from Form W-2. See instructions for definition of church employee income . . . . . .    **5a** | | |
| **b** | Multiply line 5a by 92.35% (0.9235). If less than $100, enter -0- . . . . . . . . | **5b** | |
| **6** | Add lines 4c and 5b . . . . . . . . . . . . . . . . . . . . | **6** | 43,866 |
| **7** | Maximum amount of combined wages and self-employment earnings subject to social security tax or the 6.2% portion of the 7.65% railroad retirement (tier 1) tax for 2021 . . . . . . . . . | **7** | 142,800 |
| **8a** | Total social security wages and tips (total of boxes 3 and 7 on Form(s) W-2) and railroad retirement (tier 1) compensation. If $142,800 or more, skip lines 8b through 10, and go to line 11 . . . . . . . .    **8a**   100,000 | | |
| **b** | Unreported tips subject to social security tax from Form 4137, line 10 . . .    **8b** | | |
| **c** | Wages subject to social security tax from Form 8919, line 10 . . . . . .    **8c** | | |
| **d** | Add lines 8a, 8b, and 8c . . . . . . . . . . . . . . . . . . | **8d** | 100,000 |
| **9** | Subtract line 8d from line 7. If zero or less, enter -0- here and on line 10 and go to line 11 . . . ▶ | **9** | 42,800 |
| **10** | Multiply the **smaller** of line 6 or line 9 by 12.4% (0.124) . . . . . . . . . . | **10** | 5,307 |
| **11** | Multiply line 6 by 2.9% (0.029) . . . . . . . . . . . . . . . . . | **11** | 1,272 |
| **12** | **Self-employment tax.** Add lines 10 and 11. Enter here and on **Schedule 2 (Form 1040), line 4** . . | **12** | 6,579 |
| **13** | **Deduction for one-half of self-employment tax.**<br>Multiply line 12 by 50% (0.50). Enter here and on **Schedule 1 (Form 1040), line 15** . . . . . . . . . . . . . . . .    **13**   3,290 | | |

**Part II**   **Optional Methods To Figure Net Earnings** (see instructions)

**Farm Optional Method.** You may use this method **only** if (a) your gross farm income[1] wasn't more than $8,820, **or** (b) your net farm profits[2] were less than $6,367.

| | | | |
|---|---|---|---:|
| **14** | Maximum income for optional methods . . . . . . . . . . . . . . . | **14** | 5,880 |
| **15** | Enter the **smaller** of: two-thirds (2/3) of gross farm income[1] (not less than zero) or $5,880. Also, include this amount on line 4b above . . . . . . . . . . . . . . . . . | **15** | |

**Nonfarm Optional Method.** You may use this method **only** if (a) your net nonfarm profits[3] were less than $6,367 and also less than 72.189% of your gross nonfarm income,[4] **and** (b) you had net earnings from self-employment of at least $400 in 2 of the prior 3 years. **Caution:** You may use this method no more than five times.

| | | | |
|---|---|---|---:|
| **16** | Subtract line 15 from line 14 . . . . . . . . . . . . . . . . . | **16** | |
| **17** | Enter the **smaller** of: two-thirds (2/3) of gross nonfarm income[4] (not less than zero) **or** the amount on line 16. Also, include this amount on line 4b above . . . . . . . . . . . . . | **17** | |

[1] From Sch. F, line 9; and Sch. K-1 (Form 1065), box 14, code B.
[2] From Sch. F, line 34; and Sch. K-1 (Form 1065), box 14, code A—minus the amount you would have entered on line 1b had you not used the optional method.
[3] From Sch. C, line 31; and Sch. K-1 (Form 1065), box 14, code A.
[4] From Sch. C, line 7; and Sch. K-1 (Form 1065), box 14, code C.

| For Paperwork Reduction Act Notice, see your tax return instructions. | Cat. No. 11358Z | Schedule SE (Form 1040) 2021 |
|---|---|---|

Source: U.S. Department of the Treasury, Internal Revenue Service, Schedule SE (Form 1040). Washington, DC: 2021.

The Federal Unemployment Tax Act (FUTA) and the State Unemployment Tax Act (SUTA) provide for payments of unemployment compensation to workers who have lost their jobs. The federal and state governments fund these unemployment compensation payments in part through an unemployment tax assessed on employers.[13]

The actual benefits paid to taxpayers are from the taxpayer's SUTA program. The federal government has the responsibility of administering the state programs to ensure that each state pays into its state trust fund. Employers who pay employees who are not farmworkers or household workers are subject to the FUTA tax if *either* of these criteria applies to them:

1. Paid wages of $1,500 or more in any calendar quarter in the current or preceding calendar year.
2. Had one or more employees for at least some part of a day in any 20 or more different weeks in 2020 or 20 or more different weeks in 2021.

The tax rate is 6.0% of employee wages up to $7,000.[14] Employers get a credit for state unemployment taxes paid up to 5.4%. Thus, the effective federal tax rate is 0.6% if employers pay the maximum amount of state tax on time. To receive the maximum credit, the employer's state agency must make the state's contributions on or before the due date for filing the annual return (Form 940) for FUTA. If the employer is late in depositing its funds, the credit is limited to 10% of the amount of deposit that would have been allowed as a credit.

---

**EXAMPLE 10-14**

Boersma Company, located at 567 Main St., Columbus OH 43215, has three employees who were paid the following amounts during 2021. Boersma pays state unemployment taxes and is entitled to the maximum credit of 5.4%, and thus subject to a federal unemployment tax rate of 0.6%.

|  | **Wages** | **FUTA Tax** |
|---|---|---|
| Theodore | $3,000 × 0.006 | = $18 |
| Ursula | $28,000, limited to $7,000 × 0.006 = | $42 |
| Vanessa | $51,000, limited to $7,000 × 0.006 = | $42 |

Boersma will owe FUTA tax of $102.

---

**EXAMPLE 10-15**

Everhart Company had state wages of $100,000 subject to SUTA but did not make timely deposits for SUTA. Therefore, the credit for FUTA is limited to 90% of $5,400, or $4,860. If its payroll subject to FUTA tax is $100,000, the following amount is due on Form 940:

| | | |
|---|---|---|
| $100,000 × 0.060 | = | $6,000 |
| Less 90% credit | = | 4,860 |
| Amount of net FUTA = | | $1,140 |

If Everhart had made timely deposits to its state fund, the amount of FUTA tax would have been $100,000 × 0.6% = $600.

---

Those who employ household workers (see the next section) are subject to FUTA tax *only* if they pay cash wages of $1,000 or more in any calendar quarter in 2020 or 2021. Employers

[13] IRC § 3301.
[14] IRC § 3301.

must also pay FUTA tax for farmworkers if they paid cash wages of $20,000 or more to farmworkers during any calendar quarter in 2020 or 2021 or if the employer employed 10 or more farmworkers during at least some part of a day during any 20 or more different weeks in 2020 or 2021.

FUTA taxes are deposited quarterly with an authorized depository if the taxes for a quarter (plus undeposited taxes from prior quarters) exceed $500. The tax is deposited using EFTPS. The employer must record that the tax paid is for FUTA tax and indicate the quarter to which the payment applies. The deposit is due no later than the last day of the month following the end of the quarter. If the employer does not specify to which tax the payment is to be applied, the default is for the Form 941 tax payment (withholding and FICA taxes).

To report FUTA taxes, employers must file Form 940 on an annual basis. (See Exhibit 10-8 for a filled-in Form 940 using data from Example 10-14.) Form 940 is due no later than January 31 of the following year or the next business day if January 31 falls on a holiday or weekend. Deposits must be accompanied by a Form 940-V payment voucher.

## Household Employees

A household worker is an employee who performs household work in a private home, local college club, or local fraternity or sorority chapter. These individuals may be nannies, gardeners, maintenance workers, cooks, maids, or the like. These workers are generally classified as employees, and the employer must pay payroll taxes.[15]

Individuals employing household workers are subject to tax rules if any of the following are true:

- They paid any one household employee wages of $2,300 or more in 2021; pay social security and Medicare tax.
- Federal income taxes were withheld from employee wages.
- Household wages of at least $1,000 were paid to all household workers combined in any calendar quarter in 2020 or 2021; pay FUTA tax.

Household workers do not include the taxpayer's spouse, father or mother, children under age 21, or anyone under age 18 unless providing household services is their primary occupation. An example of someone falling into the last category is a high school student who occasionally babysits for neighbors.

Household workers may be classified as employees or as independent contractors. This section deals with workers who are employees. These individuals generally work for one person and are under the direction of the employer. Independent contractors are likely to work for many individuals. For example, you may have someone clean your house every two weeks. That person may clean houses for 40 other people. It is likely that your household worker is an independent contractor, not an employee. Thus, you would not need to withhold taxes from the individual.

Instead of filing Form 941 and Form 940, individuals who employ household workers report employment taxes on Schedule H (see Exhibit 10-9 for a filled-in illustration of Example 10-16). The form is not filed separately but is attached to Form 1040. If line 27 is answered "yes," the amount of tax due on line 26 of Schedule H is carried forward to line 9 of Schedule 2. Thus, the employment taxes due for household employees are paid when Form 1040 is filed or extended.

A taxpayer who has nonhousehold workers (that is, a taxpayer with a business) and household workers can elect to account for and report the latter according to the rules pertaining to their regular employees.

[15] IRC § 3510.

**EXHIBIT 10-8**

Form **940 for 2021:** **Employer's Annual Federal Unemployment (FUTA) Tax Return**

850113

Department of the Treasury — Internal Revenue Service

OMB No. 1545-0028

| Employer identification number (EIN) | 3 6 – 5 6 7 8 9 0 1 |
|---|---|

**Name** *(not your trade name)*   Boersma Company

**Trade name** *(if any)*

**Address**   567 Main Street

Number   Street   Suite or room number

Columbus   OH   43215

City   State   ZIP code

Foreign country name   Foreign province/county   Foreign postal code

**Type of Return**
(Check all that apply.)

☐ **a.** Amended

☐ **b.** Successor employer

☐ **c.** No payments to employees in 2021

☐ **d.** Final: Business closed or stopped paying wages

Go to *www.irs.gov/Form940* for instructions and the latest information.

Read the separate instructions before you complete this form. Please type or print within the boxes.

**Part 1:**   **Tell us about your return. If any line does NOT apply, leave it blank. See instructions before completing Part 1.**

**1a**  If you had to pay state unemployment tax in one state only, enter the state abbreviation   **1a**  [ O  H ]

**1b**  If you had to pay state unemployment tax in more than one state, you are a multi-state employer   **1b** ☐ Check here. Complete Schedule A (Form 940).

**2**  If you paid wages in a state that is subject to **CREDIT REDUCTION**   **2** ☐ Check here. Complete Schedule A (Form 940).

**Part 2:**   **Determine your FUTA tax before adjustments. If any line does NOT apply, leave it blank.**

**3**  Total payments to all employees   **3**  82,000 .

**4**  Payments exempt from FUTA tax   **4**

Check all that apply:  **4a** ☐ Fringe benefits   **4c** ☐ Retirement/Pension   **4e** ☐ Other

**4b** ☐ Group-term life insurance   **4d** ☐ Dependent care

**5**  Total of payments made to each employee in excess of $7,000   **5**  65,000 .

**6**  Subtotal (line 4 + line 5 = line 6)   **6**  65,000 .

**7**  Total taxable FUTA wages (line 3 – line 6 = line 7). See instructions   **7**  17,000 .

**8**  FUTA tax before adjustments (line 7 x 0.006 = line 8)   **8**  102 .

**Part 3:**   **Determine your adjustments. If any line does NOT apply, leave it blank.**

**9**  If ALL of the taxable FUTA wages you paid were excluded from state unemployment tax, multiply line 7 by 0.054 (line 7 × 0.054 = line 9). Go to line 12   **9**  .

**10**  If SOME of the taxable FUTA wages you paid were excluded from state unemployment tax, OR you paid ANY state unemployment tax late (after the due date for filing Form 940), complete the worksheet in the instructions. Enter the amount from line 7 of the worksheet   **10**  .

**11**  If credit reduction applies, enter the total from Schedule A (Form 940)   **11**  .

**Part 4:**   **Determine your FUTA tax and balance due or overpayment. If any line does NOT apply, leave it blank.**

**12**  Total FUTA tax after adjustments (lines 8 + 9 + 10 + 11 = line 12)   **12**  102 .

**13**  FUTA tax deposited for the year, including any overpayment applied from a prior year   **13**  0 .

**14**  Balance due. If line 12 is more than line 13, enter the excess on line 14.
- If line 14 is more than $500, you must deposit your tax.
- If line 14 is $500 or less, you may pay with this return. See instructions   **14**  102 .

**15**  Overpayment. If line 13 is more than line 12, enter the excess on line 15 and check a box below   **15**  .

▶ You **MUST** complete both pages of this form and **SIGN** it.   Check one: ☐ Apply to next return.   ☐ Send a refund.

Next ➡

**For Privacy Act and Paperwork Reduction Act Notice, see the back of the Payment Voucher.**   Cat. No. 11234O   Form **940** (2021)

Source: U.S. Department of the Treasury, Internal Revenue Service, Form 940. Washington, DC: 2021.

*(continued)*

**EXHIBIT 10-8** *(concluded)*

850212

| Name *(not your trade name)* | Employer identification number (EIN) |
|---|---|
| Boersma Company | 36-5678901 |

**Part 5:** Report your FUTA tax liability by quarter only if line 12 is more than $500. If not, go to Part 6.

16 Report the amount of your FUTA tax liability for each quarter; do NOT enter the amount you deposited. If you had no liability for a quarter, leave the line blank.

16a 1st quarter (January 1 – March 31) . . . . . . . . . 16a ▢ .

16b 2nd quarter (April 1 – June 30) . . . . . . . . . 16b ▢ .

16c 3rd quarter (July 1 – September 30) . . . . . . . 16c ▢ .

16d 4th quarter (October 1 – December 31) . . . . . 16d ▢ .

17 Total tax liability for the year (lines 16a + 16b + 16c + 16d = line 17) **17** ▢ . **Total must equal line 12.**

**Part 6:** May we speak with your third-party designee?

Do you want to allow an employee, a paid tax preparer, or another person to discuss this return with the IRS? See the instructions for details.

☐ **Yes.** Designee's name and phone number

Select a 5-digit personal identification number (PIN) to use when talking to the IRS. ▢ ▢ ▢ ▢ ▢

☒ **No.**

**Part 7:** Sign here. You MUST complete both pages of this form and SIGN it.

Under penalties of perjury, I declare that I have examined this return, including accompanying schedules and statements, and to the best of my knowledge and belief, it is true, correct, and complete, and that no part of any payment made to a state unemployment fund claimed as a credit was, or is to be, deducted from the payments made to employees. Declaration of preparer (other than taxpayer) is based on all information of which preparer has any knowledge.

✗ **Sign your name here**

Print your name here

Print your title here

Date / /

Best daytime phone

**Paid Preparer Use Only**

Check if you are self-employed ☐

| Preparer's name | | PTIN | |
| Preparer's signature | | Date | / / |
| Firm's name (or yours if self-employed) | | EIN | |
| Address | | Phone | |
| City | | State | ZIP code |

Form **940** (2021)

**EXHIBIT 10-9**

| SCHEDULE H<br>(Form 1040)<br><br>Department of the Treasury<br>Internal Revenue Service (99) | **Household Employment Taxes**<br>(For Social Security, Medicare, Withheld Income, and Federal Unemployment (FUTA) Taxes)<br>▶ **Attach to Form 1040, 1040-SR, 1040-NR, 1040-SS, or 1041.**<br>▶ **Go to** *www.irs.gov/ScheduleH* **for instructions and the latest information.** | OMB No. 1545-0074<br>**2021**<br>Attachment<br>Sequence No. **44** |
|---|---|---|

| Name of employer<br><br>**Dale and Kerry Cohen** | Social security number<br>**412-34-5670** |
|---|---|
| | Employer identification number |

Calendar year taxpayers having no household employees in 2021 don't have to complete this form for 2021.

**A**   Did you pay **any one** household employee cash wages of $2,300 or more in 2021? (If any household employee was your spouse, your child under age 21, your parent, or anyone under age 18, see the line A instructions before you answer this question.)
     ☑ **Yes.** Skip lines B and C and go to line 1a.
     ☐ **No.** Go to line B.

**B**   Did you withhold federal income tax during 2021 for any household employee?
     ☐ **Yes.** Skip line C and go to line 7.
     ☐ **No.** Go to line C.

**C**   Did you pay **total** cash wages of $1,000 or more in **any** calendar **quarter** of 2020 or 2021 to **all** household employees? (**Don't** count cash wages paid in 2020 or 2021 to your spouse, your child under age 21, or your parent.)
     ☐ **No. Stop.** Don't file this schedule.
     ☐ **Yes.** Skip lines 1a–9 and go to line 10.

**Part I**   **Social Security, Medicare, and Federal Income Taxes**

| | | | | |
|---|---|---:|---|---:|
| **1a** | Total cash wages subject to social security tax | **1a** 4,800 | | |
| **b** | Qualified sick and family wages for leave taken before April 1, 2021, included on line 1a | **1b** 0 | | |
| **2a** | Social security tax. Multiply line 1a by 12.4% (0.124) | | **2a** | 595 |
| **b** | Employer share of social security tax on qualified sick and family leave wages for leave taken before April 1, 2021. Multiply line 1b by 6.2% (0.062) | | **2b** | 0 |
| **c** | Total social security tax. Subtract line 2b from line 2a | | **2c** | 595 |
| **3** | Total cash wages subject to Medicare tax | **3** 4,800 | | |
| **4** | Medicare tax. Multiply line 3 by 2.9% (0.029) | | **4** | 139 |
| **5** | Total cash wages subject to Additional Medicare Tax withholding | **5** 0 | | |
| **6** | Additional Medicare Tax withholding. Multiply line 5 by 0.9% (0.009) | | **6** | 0 |
| **7** | Federal income tax withheld, if any | | **7** | 0 |
| **8a** | Total social security, Medicare, and federal income taxes. Add lines 2c, 4, 6, and 7. | | **8a** | 734 |
| **b** | Nonrefundable portion of credit for qualified sick and family leave wages for leave taken before April 1, 2021 | | **8b** | |
| **c** | Nonrefundable portion of credit for qualified sick and family leave wages for leave taken after March 31, 2021 | | **8c** | |
| **d** | Total social security, Medicare, and federal income taxes after nonrefundable credits. Add lines 8b and 8c and then subtract that total from line 8a | | **8d** | 734 |
| **e** | Refundable portion of credit for qualified sick and family leave wages for leave taken before April 1, 2021 | | **8e** | |
| **f** | Refundable portion of credit for qualified sick and family leave wages for leave taken after March 31, 2021 | | **8f** | |
| **g** | Qualified sick leave wages for leave taken before April 1, 2021 | | **8g** | |
| **h** | Qualified health plan expenses allocable to qualified sick leave wages reported on line 8g | | **8h** | |
| **i** | Qualified family leave wages for leave taken before April 1, 2021 | | **8i** | |
| **j** | Qualified health plan expenses allocable to qualified family leave wages reported on line 8i | | **8j** | |
| **k** | Qualified sick wages for leave taken after March 31, 2021 | | **8k** | |
| **l** | Qualified health plan expenses allocable to qualified sick leave wages reported on line 8k | | **8l** | |
| **m** | Qualified family leave wages for leave taken after March 31, 2021 | | **8m** | |
| **n** | Qualified health plan expenses allocable to qualified family leave wages reported on line 8m | | **8n** | |

**9**   Did you pay **total** cash wages of $1,000 or more in **any** calendar **quarter** of 2020 or 2021 to **all** household employees? (**Don't** count cash wages paid in 2020 or 2021 to your spouse, your child under age 21, or your parent.)
     ☐ **No. Stop.** Include the amount from line 8d above on Schedule 2 (Form 1040), line 9. Include the amounts, if any, from line 8e on Schedule 3 (Form 1040), line 13b, and line 8f on Schedule 3 (Form 1040), line 13h. If you're not required to file Form 1040, see the line 9 instructions.
     ☑ **Yes.** Go to line 10.

| For Privacy Act and Paperwork Reduction Act Notice, see the instructions. | Cat. No. 12187K | Schedule H (Form 1040) 2021 |
|---|---|---|

Source: U.S. Department of the Treasury, Internal Revenue Service, Schedule H (Form 1040). Washington, DC: 2021.

*(continued)*

**EXHIBIT 10-9** *(concluded)*

Schedule H (Form 1040) 2021 | Page **2**

## Part II  Federal Unemployment (FUTA) Tax

|  |  | Yes | No |
|---|---|---|---|
| 10 | Did you pay unemployment contributions to only one state? If you paid contributions to a credit reduction state, see instructions and check **"No"** . . . . . . . . . . . . . . . . **10** | ✓ |  |
| 11 | Did you pay all state unemployment contributions for 2021 by April 18, 2022? Fiscal year filers, see instructions **11** | ✓ |  |
| 12 | Were all wages that are taxable for FUTA tax also taxable for your state's unemployment tax? . . . . . **12** | ✓ |  |

**Next:** If you checked the **"Yes"** box on **all** the lines above, complete Section A.
If you checked the **"No"** box on **any** of the lines above, skip Section A and complete Section B.

### Section A

| 13 | Name of the state where you paid unemployment contributions ► New Mexico |  |  |
|---|---|---|---|
| 14 | Contributions paid to your state unemployment fund . . . . . . . . **14** | 480 |  |
| 15 | Total cash wages subject to FUTA tax . . . . . . . . . . . | **15** | 4,800 |
| 16 | **FUTA tax.** Multiply line 15 by 0.6% (0.006). Enter the result here, skip Section B, and go to line 25 . | **16** | 29 |

### Section B

17  Complete all columns below that apply (if you need more space, see instructions):

| (a) Name of state | (b) Taxable wages (as defined in state act) | (c) State experience rate period | | (d) State experience rate | (e) Multiply col. (b) by 0.054 | (f) Multiply col. (b) by col. (d) | (g) Subtract col. (f) from col. (e). If zero or less, enter -0-. | (h) Contributions paid to state unemployment fund |
|---|---|---|---|---|---|---|---|---|
|  |  | From | To |  |  |  |  |  |
|  |  |  |  |  |  |  |  |  |
|  |  |  |  |  |  |  |  |  |

| 18 | Totals . . . . . . . . . . . **18** |  |  |
|---|---|---|---|
| 19 | Add columns (g) and (h) of line 18 . . . . . . **19** |  |  |
| 20 | Total cash wages subject to FUTA tax (see the line 15 instructions) . . . . . . . . | **20** |  |
| 21 | Multiply line 20 by 6.0% (0.06) . . . . . . . . . . . . . | **21** |  |
| 22 | Multiply line 20 by 5.4% (0.054) . . . . . . . **22** |  |  |
| 23 | Enter the **smaller** of line 19 or line 22. (If you paid state unemployment contributions late or you're in a credit reduction state, see instructions and check here) . . ☐ | **23** |  |
| 24 | **FUTA tax.** Subtract line 23 from line 21. Enter the result here and go to line 25 . . . . . . . . | **24** |  |

## Part III  Total Household Employment Taxes

| 25 | Enter the amount from line 8d. If you checked the **"Yes"** box on line C of page 1, enter -0- . . . . | **25** | 734 |
|---|---|---|---|
| 26 | Add line 16 (or line 24) and line 25 . . . . . . . . . . | **26** | 763 |
| 27 | Are you required to file Form 1040? | | |

☑ **Yes. Stop.** Include the amount from line 26 above on Schedule 2 (Form 1040), line 9. Include the amounts, if any, from line 8e, on Schedule 3 (Form 1040), line 13b, and line 8f on Schedule 3 (Form 1040), line 13h. **Don't** complete Part IV below.

☐ **No.** You may have to complete Part IV. See instructions for details.

## Part IV  Address and Signature — Complete this part **only** if required. See the line 27 instructions.

| Address (number and street) or P.O. box if mail isn't delivered to street address | Apt., room, or suite no. |
|---|---|
| City, town or post office, state, and ZIP code | |

Under penalties of perjury, I declare that I have examined this schedule, including accompanying statements, and to the best of my knowledge and belief, it is true, correct, and complete. No part of any payment made to a state unemployment fund claimed as a credit was, or is to be, deducted from the payments to employees. Declaration of preparer (other than taxpayer) is based on all information of which preparer has any knowledge.

| ► Employer's signature | ► Date | | |
|---|---|---|---|

| **Paid Preparer Use Only** | Print/Type preparer's name | Preparer's signature | Date | Check ☐ if self-employed | PTIN |
|---|---|---|---|---|---|
| | Firm's name ► | | | Firm's EIN ► | |
| | Firm's address ► | | | Phone no. | |

Schedule H (Form 1040) 2021

**EXAMPLE 10-16**

Dale and Kerry Cohen employed a household worker for the entire year. They paid the household worker $400 per month, for a total of $4,800 for the year. For purposes of this example, assume they live in New Mexico, have a state reporting number of J1234, and have paid $480 of state unemployment taxes for this worker.

They paid cash wages of $4,800 for the year and answered yes to Question A on Schedule H.

**Part I Calculations**

| | | |
|---|---|---|
| Social security tax $4,800 × 12.4% = | | $595 |
| Medicare tax | $4,800 × 2.9%  = | 139 |
| Total taxes | | $734 |

**Part II Calculations**

Answer yes to Questions 9, 10, 11, and 12 and enter NM on line 13. On line 14, enter $480. All wages were subject to FUTA tax, so line 15 is $4,800. Calculate the amount for line 16.

**Part III Calculations**

Add the FUTA tax and the FICA taxes for a total amount due and reportable on Form 1040, Schedule 2, line 9.

---

**CONCEPT CHECK 10-4—**
**LO 10-4**

1. A self-employed taxpayer is treated both as an employee and an employer and thus pays a combined total of 15.3% for FICA taxes. True or false?
2. What is the effective tax rate for FUTA, provided that employers pay into their state SUTA programs on a timely basis?
   a.  0.6%.
   b.  6.2%.
   c.  5.4%.
   d.  10%.
3. Who can use Schedule H? _____
4. Taxpayers who employ household workers are subject to payroll taxes under what conditions?
   _____
   _____

# EMPLOYER PAYROLL REPORTING REQUIREMENTS INCLUDING FORMS W-2 AND W-3
**LO 10-5**

### Employer Payroll Reporting to Employees

Employers must annually report payroll-related information to employees and to the IRS.[16] The information is reported to both parties on Form W-2, Wage and Tax Statement.

The W-2 is a multipart form labeled Copies A, B, C, D, 1, and 2. Each labeled part is used for a different purpose. The employer sends the employee Copies 1 and 2 (filed with the employee's state and local tax returns), Copy B (filed with the employee's federal tax return—see Exhibit 10-10), and Copy C (retained by the employee). The employer retains Copy D. The employee uses the information from the W-2 to prepare their federal and state income tax returns. The employer must mail each employee their W-2 copies no later than January 31.

Both paper and electronically filed Forms W-2 and W-3 must be filed with the Social Security Administration (SSA) no later than January 31, 2022. Also, both paper and electronically filed Forms 1099-MISC must be filed with the IRS no later than January 31, 2022. The SSA uses Copy A to track wages for social security purposes. The SSA also transmits the W-2 information to the IRS. Employers with 250 or more employees are required to file their W-2s electronically. The employer completes Form 4419—Application for Filing Information Returns Electronically (not shown here) and files it with the IRS.

[16] IRC § 6051.

**EXHIBIT 10-10**

| a Employee's social security number 412-34-5670 | OMB No. 1545-0008 | Safe, accurate, FAST! Use | IRS e-file | Visit the IRS website at www.irs.gov/efile |
|---|---|---|---|---|

| | 1 Wages, tips, other compensation 144,664.00 | 2 Federal income tax withheld 24,703.50 |
|---|---|---|
| **b** Employer identification number (EIN) 36-3456789 | | |
| **c** Employer's name, address, and ZIP code | 3 Social security wages 142,800.00 | 4 Social security tax withheld 8,853.60 |
| Jakub Company 1250 Chicago Avenue Chicago, IL 60622 | 5 Medicare wages and tips 144,664.00 | 6 Medicare tax withheld 2,097.63 |
| | 7 Social security tips | 8 Allocated tips |
| **d** Control number | 9 | 10 Dependent care benefits |
| **e** Employee's first name and initial    Last name    Suff. | 11 Nonqualified plans | 12a See instructions for box 12 |
| Basha Nowak 2390 Northwestern Ave. Chicago, IL 60618 | 13 Statutory employee / Retirement plan / Third-party sick pay | 12b |
| | 14 Other | 12c |
| | | 12d |
| **f** Employee's address and ZIP code | | |

| 15 State  Employer's state ID number | 16 State wages, tips, etc. | 17 State income tax | 18 Local wages, tips, etc. | 19 Local income tax | 20 Locality name |
|---|---|---|---|---|---|
| | | | | | |

Form **W-2** Wage and Tax Statement    **2021**    Department of the Treasury—Internal Revenue Service

Copy B—To Be Filed With Employee's FEDERAL Tax Return.
This information is being furnished to the Internal Revenue Service.

Source: U.S. Department of the Treasury, Internal Revenue Service, Form W-2 Wages and Tax Statement. Washington, DC: 2021.

Form W-3 (Transmittal of Wage and Tax Statements) accompanies the W-2s sent by the employer (see Exhibit 10-11). The W-3 summarizes the information contained on the attached W-2s. The totals on the W-3 must equal the accumulated amounts on the W-2s. Recording payroll and preparing the governmental forms is time-consuming, so many employers use accountants or payroll services to provide these services and to prepare year-end W-2 and W-3 information in a timely manner.

**EXAMPLE 10-17**

Jakub Company had four employees. Selected 2021 information for the company is as follows:

| | |
|---|---|
| Total wages, tips, and other compensation | = $480,000.00 |
| Total social security wages | = 427,200.00 |
| Total Medicare wages | = 480,000.00 |
| Total federal income tax withheld | = 102,631.80 |
| Total social security tax withheld | = 26,486.40 |
| Total Medicare tax withheld | = 6,960.00 |

One of the employees is Basha Nowak who has the following payroll information for 2021:

| | |
|---|---|
| Wages, tips, and other compensation | = $144,664.00 |
| Federal income tax withheld | = 24,703.50 |
| Social security tax withheld | = 8,853.60 |
| Medicare tax withheld | = 2,097.63 |

Exhibit 10-10 is the completed 2021 Form W-2 for Basha Nowak, and Exhibit 10-11 is the completed 2021 Form W-3 for Jakub Company.

**EXHIBIT 10-11**

| | | | | | | | | |
|---|---|---|---|---|---|---|---|---|
| **33333** | **a** Control number | | **For Official Use Only ▶** OMB No. 1545-0008 | | | | | |

| **b** **Kind of Payer** (Check one) | 941 ☒    Military ☐    943 ☐    944 ☐ <br> CT-1 ☐   Hshld. emp. ☐   Medicare govt. emp. ☐ | **Kind of Employer** (Check one) | None apply ☐   501c non-govt. ☐ <br> State/local non-501c ☒   State/local 501c ☐   Federal govt. ☐ | Third-party sick pay (Check if applicable) ☐ |
|---|---|---|---|---|

| **c** Total number of Forms W-2 <br> 4 | **d** Establishment number | **1** Wages, tips, other compensation <br> 480,000.00 | **2** Federal income tax withheld <br> 102,631.80 |
|---|---|---|---|
| **e** Employer identification number (EIN) <br> 36-3456789 | | **3** Social security wages <br> 427,200.00 | **4** Social security tax withheld <br> 26,486.40 |
| **f** Employer's name <br> Jakub Company | | **5** Medicare wages and tips <br> 480,000.00 | **6** Medicare tax withheld <br> 6,960.00 |
| 1250 Chicago Avenue <br> Chicago, IL 60622 | | **7** Social security tips | **8** Allocated tips |
| | | **9** | **10** Dependent care benefits |
| | | **11** Nonqualified plans | **12a** Deferred compensation |
| **g** Employer's address and ZIP code | | | |
| **h** Other EIN used this year | | **13** For third-party sick pay use only | **12b** |
| **15** State    Employer's state ID number | | **14** Income tax withheld by payer of third-party sick pay | |
| **16** State wages, tips, etc. | **17** State income tax | **18** Local wages, tips, etc. | **19** Local income tax |
| Employer's contact person | | Employer's telephone number | For Official Use Only |
| Employer's fax number | | Employer's email address | |

Under penalties of perjury, I declare that I have examined this return and accompanying documents, and, to the best of my knowledge and belief, they are true, correct, and complete.

Signature ▶      Title ▶      Date ▶

Form **W-3** **Transmittal of Wage and Tax Statements**     **2021**     Department of the Treasury Internal Revenue Service

Source: U.S. Department of the Treasury, Internal Revenue Service, Form W-3 Transmittal of Wage and Tax Statements. Washington, DC: 2021.

An employer prepares a Form W-2C (Statement of Corrected Income and Tax Amounts) to correct a W-2 and provides appropriate copies to the employee. The employer files Copy A with the Social Security Administration, and a Form W-3C (Transmittal of Corrected Income and Tax Statements) accompanies Copy A to the Social Security Administration. These forms can be accessed through the IRS website.

The following penalties are imposed on employers for incorrect or late filing of W-2s:

- A W-2 filed within 30 days of the due date: $50 per return ($571,000 maximum penalty/$199,500 for small businesses).

- A W-2 filed between 30 days late and August 1: $110 per return ($1,713,000 maximum penalty/$571,000 for small businesses).

- A W-2 filed after August 1: $280 per return ($3,426,000 maximum penalty/$1,142,000 for small businesses).

- Penalty of $570 per return for intentional disregard of filing requirements, providing payees with incorrect statements, or reporting incorrect information (no maximum penalty).

**CONCEPT CHECK 10-5— LO 10-5**

1. The employee uses the information from a W-2 to prepare their federal, state, and local (if applicable) tax returns. True or false?
2. Where and when must the employer send Copy A of the W-2 form?
3. Explain the process by which an employer corrects an employee's W-2.
4. What are the maximum penalty amounts per return imposed on a company that prepares incorrect W-2s?

# SUPPLEMENTAL WAGE PAYMENTS, BACKUP WITHHOLDING, FORM W-9, ESTIMATED TAX PAYMENTS, AND FORM 1040-ES
## LO 10-6

### Supplemental Wage Payments

Supplemental wages are compensation paid in addition to an employee's regular wages and include vacation pay, commissions, bonuses, accumulated sick pay, severance pay, taxable fringe benefits, and expense allowances paid under a nonaccountable plan. The amount withheld from these supplemental payments depends on whether the employer accounts for the payment separately from regular wages.

Supplemental wages can be combined with regular wages, and the total amount will be taxed as if it were a single payment for a regular payroll period. If the supplemental payments are identified separately from regular wages, the federal income tax withholding method depends on whether the employer withholds income tax from the employee's regular wages.

1. Method 1: If taxes are withheld from the employee's wages:

    *a.* Withhold a flat 22% (no other percentage is allowed) or

    *b.* Add the supplemental and regular wages for the period and figure the income tax withholding as if the total were a single payment. Subtract the tax already withheld from regular wages. Withhold the remaining tax from the supplemental wages.

2. Method 2: If taxes are not withheld from the employee's wages:

    *a.* Add the supplemental and regular wages and calculate the withholding tax as in part *b* of method 1.

Regardless of the method used to withhold income tax on supplemental wages, the wages are subject to social security, Medicare, and FUTA taxes as well as state withholding (if applicable) and SUTA.

---

**EXAMPLE 10-18**

Zofia has a base salary of $2,000, is paid on the first of the month, is single, and claims no dependents. On June 1, 2021, she is paid $2,000, and $97.90 (using Table 4) is withheld from her earnings. In July 2021, she receives a commission of $1,000, which is included in the regular wages. The amount of withholding is based on a total of $3,000. The amount withheld from these wages is $217.90 (using Table 4).

---

**EXAMPLE 10-19**

Farid is paid a base salary of $2,000 on the first of each month, is single and claims no dependents. For the pay period of August 1, 2021, the amount of tax withheld (using Table 4) is $97.90. On August 19, 2021, Farid receives a bonus of $1,000. Using method 1*b,* the amount subject to withholding is $3,000. The amount of withholding on the combined $3,000 is $217.90. Subtract the amount already withheld for the month. The difference of $120.00 is the amount to be withheld from the bonus payment.

---

**EXAMPLE 10-20**

Using the information from Example 10-19, the employer elects to use a flat rate of 22% of withholding on the bonus. In this situation, the amount of withholding on the bonus is $1,000 × 22% = $220.00.

## Backup Withholding

Generally an employer must withhold 24% of certain taxable payments if the payee fails to furnish the employer with a correct taxpayer identification number (TIN). Payments subject to backup withholding include interest, dividends, rents, royalties, commissions, nonemployee compensation, and certain other payments made in the course of a trade or business. In addition, certain payments made by brokers and barter exchanges and certain payments made by fishing boat operators are subject to backup withholding.[17]

Payments a taxpayer receives are subject to backup withholding under these circumstances:

- The taxpayer does not furnish a TIN to the requester.
- The IRS tells the requester that a taxpayer has furnished an incorrect TIN.
- The IRS informs the payee that they are subject to backup withholding due to nonreporting of any interest and dividends on a tax return.
- The payee did not certify to the requester that they were not subject to backup withholding.

Backup withholding does not apply to wages, pensions, annuities, IRAs, Section 404(k) distributions from an employee stock ownership plan (ESOP), health savings accounts, long-term care benefits, and real estate transactions. The IRS lists specific payees exempt from backup withholding as well as specific types of payments that are exempt from backup withholding. To avoid this backup withholding, payees must furnish a correct TIN to the payer via Form W-9.

## Form W-9

Anyone who is required to file an information return with the IRS must supply the payer a correct TIN to report transactions such as income paid to the taxpayer, a real estate transaction, any mortgage interest the taxpayer paid, and contributions to an IRA. The form used to report this information to the payer is a Form W-9.

A U.S. person (or resident alien) uses Form W-9 to

- Certify that the TIN the taxpayer is giving is correct.
- Certify that the taxpayer is not subject to backup withholding.
- Claim exemption from backup withholding if the taxpayer is a U.S. exempt payee.

For federal purposes, a U.S. person includes but is not limited to

- An individual who is a citizen or resident of the United States.
- A partnership, corporation, company, or association created or organized in the United States or under the laws of the United States.
- Any estate (other than a foreign estate) or trust.

Special rules apply to partnerships, corporations, associations, and estates. There are 15 provisions for exemption from backup withholding; refer to the W-9 instructions located at the IRS Web site (www.irs.gov) for a complete list. Failure to furnish a correct TIN to a requester can result in a penalty of $50 for each failure unless the failure is due to reasonable cause, not willful neglect. If a taxpayer makes a false statement with no reasonable basis that results in no backup withholding, the taxpayer is subject to a $500 penalty. Willfully falsifying certifications may subject the taxpayer to criminal penalties including fines and imprisonment.[18] For example, Joe Zonca has a landscaping and snow removal service. One of his clients, Village Apartments, requires that all vendors complete Form W-9. Joe is a sole proprietor, social security number 412-34-5670, and he resides at 632 Main Street, Savoy, IL 61874. See Exhibit 10-12 for a completed Form W-9.

---

[17] Publication 15, page 7.

[18] IRS instructions for Requester of Form W-9 and Form W-9.

**EXHIBIT 10-12**

| Form **W-9**<br>(Rev. October 2018)<br>Department of the Treasury<br>Internal Revenue Service | **Request for Taxpayer<br>Identification Number and Certification**<br><br>▶ Go to *www.irs.gov/FormW9* for instructions and the latest information. | **Give Form to the<br>requester. Do not<br>send to the IRS.** |
|---|---|---|

**1** Name (as shown on your income tax return). Name is required on this line; do not leave this line blank.

**Joe Zonca**

**2** Business name/disregarded entity name, if different from above

**3** Check appropriate box for federal tax classification of the person whose name is entered on line 1. Check only **one** of the following seven boxes.

[✓] Individual/sole proprietor or single-member LLC  [ ] C Corporation  [ ] S Corporation  [ ] Partnership  [ ] Trust/estate

[ ] Limited liability company. Enter the tax classification (C=C corporation, S=S corporation, P=Partnership) ▶ _____

**Note:** Check the appropriate box in the line above for the tax classification of the single-member owner. Do not check LLC if the LLC is classified as a single-member LLC that is disregarded from the owner unless the owner of the LLC is another LLC that is **not** disregarded from the owner for U.S. federal tax purposes. Otherwise, a single-member LLC that is disregarded from the owner should check the appropriate box for the tax classification of its owner.

[ ] Other (see instructions) ▶

**4** Exemptions (codes apply only to certain entities, not individuals; see instructions on page 3):

Exempt payee code (if any) _____

Exemption from FATCA reporting code (if any) _____

*(Applies to accounts maintained outside the U.S.)*

**5** Address (number, street, and apt. or suite no.) See instructions.

**632 Main Street**

**6** City, state, and ZIP code

**Savoy, IL 61874**

Requester's name and address (optional)

**7** List account number(s) here (optional)

**Part I  Taxpayer Identification Number (TIN)**

Enter your TIN in the appropriate box. The TIN provided must match the name given on line 1 to avoid backup withholding. For individuals, this is generally your social security number (SSN). However, for a resident alien, sole proprietor, or disregarded entity, see the instructions for Part I, later. For other entities, it is your employer identification number (EIN). If you do not have a number, see *How to get a TIN*, later.

**Note:** If the account is in more than one name, see the instructions for line 1. Also see *What Name and Number To Give the Requester* for guidelines on whose number to enter.

Social security number: **4 1 2 – 3 4 – 5 6 7 0**

or

Employer identification number

**Part II  Certification**

Under penalties of perjury, I certify that:

1. The number shown on this form is my correct taxpayer identification number (or I am waiting for a number to be issued to me); and
2. I am not subject to backup withholding because: (a) I am exempt from backup withholding, or (b) I have not been notified by the Internal Revenue Service (IRS) that I am subject to backup withholding as a result of a failure to report all interest or dividends, or (c) the IRS has notified me that I am no longer subject to backup withholding; and
3. I am a U.S. citizen or other U.S. person (defined below); and
4. The FATCA code(s) entered on this form (if any) indicating that I am exempt from FATCA reporting is correct.

**Certification instructions.** You must cross out item 2 above if you have been notified by the IRS that you are currently subject to backup withholding because you have failed to report all interest and dividends on your tax return. For real estate transactions, item 2 does not apply. For mortgage interest paid, acquisition or abandonment of secured property, cancellation of debt, contributions to an individual retirement arrangement (IRA), and generally, payments other than interest and dividends, you are not required to sign the certification, but you must provide your correct TIN. See the instructions for Part II, later.

**Sign Here**  Signature of U.S. person ▶  Date ▶

## General Instructions

Section references are to the Internal Revenue Code unless otherwise noted.

**Future developments.** For the latest information about developments related to Form W-9 and its instructions, such as legislation enacted after they were published, go to *www.irs.gov/FormW9*.

## Purpose of Form

An individual or entity (Form W-9 requester) who is required to file an information return with the IRS must obtain your correct taxpayer identification number (TIN) which may be your social security number (SSN), individual taxpayer identification number (ITIN), adoption taxpayer identification number (ATIN), or employer identification number (EIN), to report on an information return the amount paid to you, or other amount reportable on an information return. Examples of information returns include, but are not limited to, the following.

• Form 1099-INT (interest earned or paid)

• Form 1099-DIV (dividends, including those from stocks or mutual funds)

• Form 1099-MISC (various types of income, prizes, awards, or gross proceeds)

• Form 1099-B (stock or mutual fund sales and certain other transactions by brokers)

• Form 1099-S (proceeds from real estate transactions)

• Form 1099-K (merchant card and third party network transactions)

• Form 1098 (home mortgage interest), 1098-E (student loan interest), 1098-T (tuition)

• Form 1099-C (canceled debt)

• Form 1099-A (acquisition or abandonment of secured property)

Use Form W-9 only if you are a U.S. person (including a resident alien), to provide your correct TIN.

*If you do not return Form W-9 to the requester with a TIN, you might be subject to backup withholding. See* What is backup withholding, *later.*

Cat. No. 10231X  Form **W-9** (Rev. 10-2018)

**EXHIBIT 10-13**

| Form 1040-ES Department of the Treasury Internal Revenue Service | 2021 Estimated Tax | Payment Voucher 1 OMB No. 1545-0074 |
|---|---|---|

File only if you are making a payment of estimated tax by check or money order. Mail this voucher with your check or money order payable to **"United States Treasury."** Write your social security number and "2021 Form 1040-ES" on your check or money order. Do not send cash. Enclose, but do not staple or attach, your payment with this voucher.

**Calendar year—Due April 15, 2021**

Amount of estimated tax you are paying by check or money order.

| | Dollars | Cents |
|---|---|---|
| | 441 | 25 |

Pay online at www.irs.gov/etpay

Simple. Fast. Secure.

Print or type

| Your first name and middle initial Luis | Your last name Diaz | Your social security number 412-34-5670 |
|---|---|---|
| If joint payment, complete for spouse | | |
| Spouse's first name and middle initial | Spouse's last name | Spouse's social security number |
| Address (number, street, and apt. no.) 1234 Main Street | | |
| City, town, or post office. If you have a foreign address, also complete spaces below. Savoy | State IL | ZIP code 61874 |
| Foreign country name | Foreign province/county | Foreign postal code |

For Privacy Act and Paperwork Reduction Act Notice, see instructions.

Form 1040-ES (2021)

Source: U.S. Department of the Treasury, Internal Revenue Service, Form 1040-ES. Washington, DC: 2021.

## Estimated Tax Payments and Form 1040-ES

Estimated tax is the method individuals use to pay tax on income that is taxable but not subject to payroll withholding such as earnings from self-employment, interest, dividends, rents, and alimony. In most cases, a taxpayer must make estimated tax payments if they expect to owe at least $1,000 in tax and the taxpayer expects their withholding and credits to be less than the smaller of

- 90% of the tax shown on the taxpayer's current return.
- 100% of the tax shown on the taxpayer's prior year tax return if the AGI shown on that return is less than or equal to $150,000 or, if married filing separately, is less than or equal to $75,000.
- 110% of the tax shown on the taxpayer's prior-year tax return if the AGI shown on that return is more than $150,000 or, if married filing separately, is more than $75,000.

If a taxpayer meets one of the percentage criteria just noted, it is said that they have met the "safe harbor" rule. *Safe harbor* is a term used to describe a provision of the IRC that protects a taxpayer from penalty.

The estimated tax payments can be paid in total by April 15 (provided this date is a business day—otherwise, the next business day) or in four equal amounts by the following dates:

- 1st payment—April 15, 2021.
- 2nd payment—June 15, 2021.
- 3rd payment—September 15, 2021.
- 4th payment—January 18, 2022.

Taxpayers make estimated payments using Form 1040-ES (see Exhibit 10-13). The taxpayer submits the coupon for the appropriate period. It is important to remember to include the correct taxpayer identification number (social security number) and remit the payment to the address given in the instructions. This form is also accessible on the IRS Web site. Using information from Example 10-21, Form 1040-ES is completed in Exhibit 10-13. It shows the first-quarter estimated payment due from Ramon. The total amount of all the estimated payments appears on 2021 Form 1040 line 26.

| | |
|---|---|
| **EXAMPLE 10-21** | Luis Diaz works as a professor at a local college and also sells real estate as a part-time business. During 2021 Luis earned $87,500 from the college and also earned $15,000 in commissions for selling real estate. Luis operates the real estate business as a sole proprietorship and estimates $1,765 more in taxes will be owed for 2021. A payment will be made for this amount using Form 1040-ES. Assuming self-employment earnings are consistent throughout the year, estimated tax payments would be made based on the commissions earned each period. In this case, if $3,750 in commissions was earned each period, $441.25 ($1,765/4) could be remitted to the IRS on each of the due dates. |

| | |
|---|---|
| **CONCEPT CHECK 10-6— LO 10-6**  | 1. Describe the two methods that are available to calculate the withholding from supplemental payments.<br>2. Payments subject to backup withholding are withheld at a flat tax rate of 24% if the payee fails to furnish the payer with a correct TIN. True or false?<br>3. What is a Form W-9?<br>4. What is the penalty for failing to furnish a correct TIN to a requester?<br>5. Taxpayers use Form 1040-ES to remit additional amounts to the IRS so that they receive a refund when they file Form 1040. True or false? |

# ADDITIONAL INFORMATION REGARDING LEGISLATION AND PAYROLL

Within the Families First Coronavirus Response Act (Families First Act, March 18, 2020) and the Coronavirus Aid, Relief, and Economic Security Act (CARES Act, March 27, 2020), employers have relief from depositing employment taxes and receiving a refundable tax credit. Notice 2020-22, "Relief from Penalty for Failure to Deposit Employment Taxes," provides the details for employers.

Under the CARES Act, the bill is intended to help those financially struggling due to the coronavirus. This bill has four areas for small business owners; the two areas covered here are the Employee Retention Credit and the Payroll Tax Postponement. The Families First Act generally requires employers of fewer than 500 employees to provide paid sick leave (EPSL) and expanded family medical leave (FMLA), up to certain limits. This covers employees unable to work or telework due to certain circumstances related to COVID-19.

The act provides a refundable tax credit against an employer's share of the social security portion of FICA and the employer's share of social security and Medicare portions of RRTA (collectively called Creditable Employment Taxes) for each quarter in an amount equal to 100% of qualified leave wages paid by the employer plus qualified health plan expenses with respect to that calendar quarter. Also, for employers subject to FICA tax, this can be increased by the employer's share of Medicare tax imposed on qualified leave wages. This refundable tax credit typically is reported on Form 941. However, the employer may claim an advance payment of the refundable tax credits by filing Form 7200—Advance Payment of Employer Credits Due to COVID-19 (see Instructor's Resources).

Employers paying qualified sick leave wages and qualified family leave wages required by the Families First Act (qualified leave wages), in addition to qualified health plan expenses allocable to qualified leave wages (qualified health plan expenses), are eligible for refundable tax credits under Families First Act. Also, certain employers who experienced partial or full suspension due to orders from a governmental authority due to COVID-19 are allowed a refundable tax credit under the CARES Act up to 50% of the qualified wages, including qualified health expenses and limited to $10,000 per employee over all calendar quarters combined (qualified retention wages).

Under both acts, an employer paying qualified leaves wages or qualified retention wages may take refundable tax credits against a specified portion of the employer's share of certain employment taxes (social security portion of FICA as well as for social security portion for RRTA).

Additionally, the notice applies to deposits of employment taxes reduced of credits with respect to qualified leave wages paid beginning April 1, 2020, and ending December 31, 2020. Also, in anticipation of credits to qualified retention wages paid beginning March 13, 2020, and ending December 31, 2020. There are three main areas that are covered in the notice.

## Employee Retention Tax Credit

The Taxpayer Certainty and Disaster Tax Relief Act of 2020 (Relief Act), enacted December 27, 2020 (see IR-2021-21, January 26, 2021) made changes to the employee retention tax credit for 2021. Eligible employers can now claim a refundable tax credit against the employer share of Social Security tax equal to 70% of qualified wages paid to employees starting after December 31, 2020, through June 30, 2021. Qualified wages are limited to $10,000 per employee per calendar quarter in 2021. The maximum ERC amount available is $7,000 per employee for the first 2 quarters totally $14,000.

This credit can be claimed on Form 7200 (prior to paying employees) or on Form 941 to recover any payroll taxes already paid in the quarter.

To qualify for the credit effective January 1, 2021, one of the two following events had to occur:

1. The employer had to fully or partially suspend operations of their trade or business during this period because of governmental orders limiting commerce, travel, or group meeting due to COVID-19.

2. A decline in gross receipts in a calendar quarter in 2021 where the gross receipts of that calendar quarter are less than 80% of gross receipts in the same calendar quarter in 2019. (To be eligible based on a decline in gross receipts in 2020, the gross receipts were required to less than 50%.) For employers that did not exist in 2019, there are special provisions to qualify.

In all situations, the employer must maintain documentation to support the determination of the decline in gross receipts, including the calendar quarter an eligible employer elects to use in measuring the decline.

In addition, effective January 1, 2021, the definition of qualified wages was changed to provide:

- For an employer that averaged more than 500 full-time employees in 2019, qualified wages are generally those wages paid to employees that are not providing services because operations were fully or partially suspended or due to the decline in gross receipts.

- For an employer that averaged 500 or fewer full-time employees in 2019, qualified wages are generally those wages paid to all employees during a period that operations were fully or partially suspended or during the quarter that the employer had a decline in gross receipts regardless of whether the employees are providing services.

On March 11, 2021, Notice 2021-23 extended the employee retention credit for wages paid after June 30, 2021, and before January 1, 2022, as part of the American Rescue Plan Act of 2021 (ARP Act). The extended retention credit for these quarters is addressed in IRS revised Form 941 (June 2021 and instructions).

## Payroll Tax Postponement

This provision (deferred amount of the employer share of social security tax) applied only to line 13 b on Form 941 for 2020. However, in 2021, the first deposit (50%) is not due before December 21, 2021, and the second deposit (50%) is not due before December 31,2022. Under this provision, the employer will be considered to make timely deposits of taxes due.

## Relief from Failure to Make a Deposit of Taxes

Also, included in Notice 2020-22 is a special section that outlines the relief from penalty pursuant to the Families First Act and the CARES Act.

1. *Employment taxes related to qualified leave wages.* An employer will not be subject to a penalty for failing to deposit employment taxes relating to qualified leave wages in a calendar quarter if

    *a.* The employer paid qualified leave wages to its employees in the calendar quarter prior to the time of the required deposit.

*b.* The amount of employment taxes that the employer does not timely deposit is less than or equal to the amount of the employer's anticipated credits under sections 7001 and 7003 of the Families First Act for the calendar quarter as of the time of the required deposit.

*c.* The employer did not seek payment of an advance credit by filing Form 7200—Advance Payment of Employer Credits Due to COVID-19, with respect to the anticipated credits it relied upon to reduce its deposits.

2. *Employment taxes related to qualified retention wages.* An eligible employer will not be subject to a penalty (under section 6656) for failing to deposit employment taxes relating to qualified retention wages in a calendar quarter if

*a.* The employer paid qualified retention wages to its employees in the calendar quarter prior to the time of the required deposit.

*b.* The amount of employment taxes that the employer does not timely deposit reduce by the amount of employment taxes not deposited in anticipation of the credits claimed for qualified leave wages, qualified health plan expenses, and the employer's share of Medicare tax on the qualified leave wages is less than or equal to the amount of the employer's anticipated credits under the CARES Act for the calendar quarter as of the time of the required deposit.

*c.* The employer did not seek payment of an advance credit by filing Form 7200—Advance Payment of Employers Credits Due to Covid-19, with respect to the anticipated credits it relied upon to reduce its deposits.

The employer can reduce the amount of a deposit if the employer does not also seek an advance credit regarding such amount. After a reduction, if any, of a deposit of employment taxes by the amount of credits anticipated for qualified leave wages, an employer may further reduce, without a penalty, the amount of the deposit of employment taxes by the amount of qualified retention wages paid by the employer in the calendar quarter prior to the required deposit, as long as the employer does not also seek an advance credit with regard to the same amount.

## Revised Form 941

Form 941 was revised again for 2021. See Exhibit 10-5 for the 2021 Form 941. In general, the form has been expanded to cover the following items:

- Qualified sick wages. (line 5a(i))
- Qualified family leave wages. (line 5a(ii))
- Nonrefundable portion of credit for qualified sick and family leave wages from Worksheet 1. (line 11b)
- Nonrefundable portion of employee retention credit from Worksheet 1. (line 11c)
- Refundable portion of credit for qualified sick and family leave wages from Worksheet 1. (line 13c)
- Refundable portion of employee retention credit from Worksheet 1. (line 13d)
- Total advances received from filing Form(s) 7200 for the quarter. (line 13f)
- Qualified health plan expenses allocable to qualified sick leave. (line 19)
- Qualified health plan expenses allocable to qualified family leave wages. (line 20)
- Qualified wages for the employee retention credit. (line 21)
- Qualified health plan expenses allocable to wages reported on line 21. (line 22)
- Credit from Form 5884-C, line 11, for this quarter. (line 23)

The Internal Revenue Service has provided more details on its Web site: https://www.irs.gov/coronavirus/coronavirus-tax-relief-for-businesses-and-tax-exempt-entities. There are also FAQs under the more information section at https://www.irs.gov/coronavirus/coronavirus-and-economic-impact-payments-resources-and-guidance.

Because the impact of these changes is both complex and temporary, this coverage is for informational purposes and does not include any end-of-chapter activities or test questions.

## EA Fast Fact

There are numerous practice opportunities available to Enrolled Agents. While some Enrolled Agents work only during tax season or by appointment only, others have year-round practices that provide additional opportunities to grow their business and increase their income stream. In addition to tax preparation and representation, many EAs offer other related services such as Bookkeeping, Financial Planning, and Payroll Services to name but a few. Whether it be a part-time or a full-time vocation, the Enrolled Agent certification can provide the opportunity for a fulfilling career.

**IMPORTANT**

You are eligible to receive absolutely free, the Surgent Enrolled Agent review program for Part I of the EA exam as a result of purchasing this text. To activate your free access, go to https://Surgent.com/McGrawHill/EA.

## Summary

**LO 10-1:** Explain the tax issues associated with payroll and Form 1040.

- Withholding taxes are imposed on taxpayers to help fund government operations using a *pay-as-you-go* system.
- Form W-2 is the starting point for Form 1040.

**LO 10-2:** Calculate federal income tax withholding, social security, and Medicare taxes on wages and tips.

- Withholding of taxes is an approximation of the proportionate share of total tax liability the employee will owe to the federal government.
- Form W-4 is completed by the employee to list filing status and claim withholding allowances. This information is used by the employer to calculate withholding.
- Two withholding methods are allowed: the wage bracket method and the percentage method.
- FICA taxes encompass social security taxes and Medicare taxes.
- Social security tax withholding is 6.2% of each employee's wages up to a maximum of $142,800 of wages for 2021. Medicare withholding is 1.45% of all wages.
- The employer must pay an additional amount equal to the amount withheld from employees.
- The employer must withhold a 0.9% additional Medicare tax on wages paid in excess of $200,000. This is an employee-only tax.
- The 0.9% additional Medicare tax is assessed on combined wage and self-employment income in excess of the threshold amounts. A loss on self-employment is excluded from this calculation.

**LO 10-3:** Describe the rules for reporting and paying payroll taxes, including deposit penalties and Form 941.

- Employers must make payroll tax deposits of amounts withheld from employees' wages.
- Employers typically deposit taxes monthly or semiweekly. A lookback period generally determines the frequency of required deposits.
- Employers must make timely deposits through the Electronic Federal Tax Payment System (EFTPS).
- Payroll taxes not paid on a timely basis are subject to deposit penalties that range from 2% to 15%.
- Form 941 is used to report amounts withheld for income, social security, and Medicare taxes for the quarter. It is due by the end of the month following the end of a quarter.
- With IRS permission, Form 944 can be filed for small business employers, or there can be an election to file quarterly Forms 941.

**LO 10-4:** Calculate self-employment taxes, unemployment taxes, Form 940, taxes for household employees, and Schedule H.

- Self-employment taxes are based on net earnings of $400 or more generated by a sole proprietor taxpayer. The rate paid is based on both the employee and employer portions.
- 50% of self-employment taxes is a permitted *for* AGI deduction on Form 1040.
- The federal unemployment tax (FUTA) is 6.0% of wages up to $7,000. The maximum credit for state unemployment taxes (SUTA) is 5.4%, reducing the amount due to the IRS to 0.6%.
- Form 940 is filed annually by the employer to report and reconcile FUTA liabilities and payments.
- Household workers are considered employees subject to federal income, social security, Medicare, and FUTA taxes.
- Schedule H reports tax information for household workers. It is filed with Form 1040.

**LO 10-5:** Determine employer payroll reporting requirements, including Forms W-2 and W-3.

- Employers report wages earned and taxes withheld to employees on Form W-2.
- A Form W-2 must be given to each employee no later than January 31, with a copy to the Social Security Administration by January 31 as well.
- Form W-3 is a transmittal form that summarizes all employee W-2s prepared by a company and is due no later than January 31.

**LO 10-6:** Explain supplemental wage payments, backup withholding, Form W-9, estimated tax payments, and Form 1040-ES.

- Supplemental wages are compensation paid in addition to an employee's regular wages.
- Withholding on supplemental wages can be calculated using one of two methods: using a flat tax rate of 22% or combining the supplemental wages with regular wages.
- Anyone required to file an information return with the IRS must supply the payer a correct taxpayer ID number (TIN) using Form W-9.
- Failure of a taxpayer to furnish a TIN to a requester can result in a $50 penalty. A taxpayer making a false statement that results in no backup withholding is subject to a civil penalty of $500.
- Failure to provide a correct TIN can result in 24% withholding on certain taxable payments.
- Form 1040-ES is used when a taxpayer must make tax payments for estimated taxes due.
- Estimated payments are required if unpaid tax liability ≥$1,000 and withholding and credits do not meet certain "safe harbor" thresholds.
- Estimated taxes are due April 15, June 15, September 15, and January 18, or on the next business day if any of these dates falls on a weekend or holiday.

## Discussion Questions

All applicable discussion questions are available with **Connect**©

LO 10-2

1. What type of compensation is subject to employer withholding?

   _____

   _____

   _____

LO 10-2

2. Who completes Form W-4, and what is its purpose? What information does it provide to employers?

   _____

   _____

   _____

LO 10-2

3. If a taxpayer makes $30,000 per year, will the annual withholding differ, depending on whether the taxpayer is paid weekly, semimonthly, or monthly? Explain.

   _____

   _____

   _____

LO 10-2

4. If a taxpayer works more than one job, will the withholding from the various jobs necessarily cover their tax liability? Explain.

   _____

   _____

   _____

LO 10-2    5. In addition to federal tax withholding, what other taxes are employers required to withhold from an employee's paycheck? How are the calculations made?

_____

_____

_____

LO 10-2    6. Who pays FICA? What are the percentages and limits on the payments?

_____

_____

_____

LO 10-2    7. When are employees required to report tips to their employer? Are tips subject to the same withholding requirements as regular salary?

_____

_____

_____

LO 10-2    8. What are the tip reporting requirements for large food and beverage establishments?

_____

_____

_____

LO 10-3    9. When must employers make payroll tax deposits?

_____

_____

_____

LO 10-3    10. What is a *lookback* period?

_____

_____

_____

LO 10-3    11. When must monthly and semiweekly schedule depositors make their deposits? What taxes must be deposited?

_____

_____

_____

LO 10-3    12. What are the penalties for not making timely payroll deposits?

_____

_____

_____

LO 10-3    13. If a business fails to make payroll deposits, who is held responsible?

_____

_____

_____

**LO 10-3**    14. How often must employers report payroll taxes to the IRS? What form must the employer file?

_____

_____

_____

**LO 10-3**    15. Why are self-employed taxpayers allowed a deduction for self-employment tax in determining Adjusted Gross Income (AGI)?

_____

_____

_____

**LO 10-4**    16. What is the FUTA tax, and at what percentage is it assessed?

_____

_____

_____

**LO 10-4**    17. What individuals are subject to the payroll taxes on household employees?

_____

_____

_____

**LO 10-4**    18. How are household payroll taxes reported? When are they due?

_____

_____

_____

**LO 10-5**    19. How does an employer report wages to the employee, the federal government, and the Social Security Administration? When is this notification due?

_____

_____

_____

**LO 10-5**    20. What are the penalties imposed on employers for filing incorrect W-2s?

_____

_____

_____

**LO 10-6**    21. What are supplemental wage payments?

_____

_____

_____

**LO 10-6**    22. Explain the two methods for income tax withholding on supplemental wage payments.

_____

_____

_____

**LO 10-6**  23. Explain the provisions of backup withholding and the conditions under which an employer must comply with these provisions.

_____

_____

_____

**LO 10-6**  24. What is a Form W-9? Why must this form be filed?

_____

_____

_____

**LO 10-6**  25. Explain the purpose of Form 1040-ES. Under what conditions are taxpayers required to file Form 1040-ES? When is Form 1040-ES filed?

_____

_____

_____

## Multiple-Choice Questions   Mc Graw Hill **connect**

All applicable multiple-choice questions are available with **Connect**©

**LO 10-2**  26. Juanita is single and receives gross wages of $1,468.50 per week. The employer uses the Percentage Method Tables for Automated Payroll Systems (see appendix). Calculate all employee federal income tax withholding. Juanita has no dependents and does not have additional withholding taken out on the 2021 Form W-4. What is the amount of income tax withheld on Juanita's gross wages for the week?

  a. $186.00.
  b. $188.21.
  c. $189.65.
  d. $196.58.

**LO 10-2**  27. Ely is single, claims one dependent, and receives gross wages of $3,450.85 paid semi-monthly. A 2021 Form W-4 is filed with the employer who uses the Percentage Method Tables for Manual Payroll Systems with Forms W-4 from 2020 or Later (see appendix). What is the amount of income tax withheld on Ely's gross wages for each pay period?

  a. $383.70.
  b. $386.77.
  c. $397.51.
  d. $462.50.

**LO 10-2**  28. Jade is single and receives gross wages of $635 per week. On the 2021 Form W-4, Jade also wants an additional $10 withheld from each pay period. The employer uses the Wage Bracket Method Tables for Manual Payroll Systems with Forms W-4 From 2020 or Later (see appendix). What is the amount of income tax withheld on Jade gross wages for each pay period?

  a. $44.
  b. $45.
  c. $54.
  d. $55.

**LO 10-2**  29. Ernesto earned $144,895 during 2021. How much will the employer withhold from Ernesto, in total, for FICA taxes?

  a. $10,550.00.
  b. $10,638.38.

      *c.* $10,954.58.

      *d.* $11,084.47.

LO 10-2   30. Adenike has two jobs and earned $123,984.20 from the first job and $20,612.40 from the second job. How much total FICA taxes will Adenike have withheld from working two jobs?

      *a.* $10,327.50.

      *b.* $11,061.64.

      *c.* $11,138.14.

      *d.* $11,600.93.

LO 10-2   31. Carmine earned a total of $236,824.75 for 2021. How much in FICA tax will the employer be required to withhold in Carmine name?

      *a.* $12,283.40.

      *b.* $12,287.56.

      *c.* $12,569.38.

      *d.* $12,618.98.

LO 10-2   32. Dewoun has two jobs, and both employers withheld FICA tax. From the first job, $111,670.45 was earned, and from the second job, $32,186.90 was earned. How much can Dewoun claim as an additional payment on the Form 1040 as excess social security paid in 2021?

      *a.* $0.

      *b.* $58.44.

      *c.* $65.56.

      *d.* $142.60.

LO 10-2   33. Kim earned $75 in tips in September. When must the employer be informed of the tips on Form 4070 for federal income tax and FICA withholding purposes?

      *a.* By September 30.

      *b.* By October 10.

      *c.* By October 31.

      *d.* Kim is not subject to payroll taxes on tips of less than $80 in any one month.

LO 10-2   34. In a large food or beverage establishment, any tip shortfall from a directly tipped employee is recorded on the employee's W-2 as

      *a.* W-2 box 8—Allocated tips.

      *b.* W-2 box 14—Other.

      *c.* W-2 box 1—Wages, tips, other compensation.

      *d.* W-2 box 7—Social security tips.

LO 10-3   35. An employer will prepare Schedule B of Form 941 under which circumstances?

      *a.* Line 12 on Form 941 is less than $2,500.

      *b.* The employer is a semimonthly depositor.

      *c.* The employer is a monthly depositor.

      *d.* The employer is a semiweekly depositor.

LO 10-3   36. Amour Company started its business on July 23, 2021. On August 6 it paid wages for the first time and accumulated a tax liability of $48,000. On Friday, August 13, it incurred a tax liability of $52,000. How is Amour Company treated as a depositor?

      *a.* Monthly because new companies do not have a lookback period.

      *b.* Semiweekly because its accumulated tax liability is $100,000.

   *c.* Monthly because its accumulated tax liability is not more than $100,000 on any one day.

   *d.* Semiweekly for this pay period only and then monthly for the remainder of the year.

**LO 10-3**   37. What is the penalty for sending a required tax payment (unless specifically allowed) directly to the IRS?

   *a.* 2%.

   *b.* 5%.

   *c.* 10%.

   *d.* 15%.

**LO 10-3**   38. A semiweekly schedule depositor's payroll period ends and is paid on Friday, June 21. The depositor (employer) must deposit the federal taxes for this pay period on or before

   *a.* The following Wednesday.

   *b.* The following Friday.

   *c.* June 24.

   *d.* June 27.

**LO 10-3**   39. To what amount of employer tax accumulation does the one-day deposit rule apply?

   *a.* $75,000.

   *b.* $100,000.

   *c.* More than $100,000.

   *d.* An amount between $75,000 and $99,999.

**LO 10-4**   40. Employers are required to deposit FUTA taxes when their liability exceeds

   *a.* $100.

   *b.* $500.

   *c.* $1,000.

   *d.* $1,500.

**LO 10-4**   41. Household employees are subject to FICA withholding if they are paid at least what amount during 2021?

   *a.* $2,000.

   *b.* $2,100.

   *c.* $2,200.

   *d.* $2,300.

**LO 10-4**   42. Employers pay a maximum federal unemployment tax of 6.0% on how much of an employee's taxable wages for 2021?

   *a.* $1,800.

   *b.* $3,800.

   *c.* $5,800.

   *d.* $7,000.

**LO 10-2, 10-4**   43. Jordan has two jobs, as an attorney (not a partner) in a law firm and as the owner of a small legal practice (sole proprietorship) providing real estate legal services. How does compute the federal income tax for the year?

   *a.* Jordan's wages from the law firm are taxed as an employee, as are the wages from the private practice.

b. Jordan's wages from the law firm are considered self-employment, as are the earnings from the private practice.

c. Jordan's wages from the law firm are taxed as an employee, and the earnings from the private practice are taxed as a self-employed proprietor.

d. Jordan's wages from the law firm are taxed as an employee, and the earnings from self-employment are taxed up to the maximum for social security only.

LO 10-4   44. Lucia is a self-employed attorney with net earnings (profit) from the practice of $106,800. Lucia self-employment taxes for the year are

a. $13,117.76.

b. $13,338.85.

c. $14,204.40.

d. $15,090.36.

LO 10-4   45. Akio works for ABC Company and earned $63,000 for the entire year 2021. How much in FUTA tax is the employer required to withhold in Akio's name? Assume that the employer receives the maximum credit for state unemployment taxes.

a. $0.

b. $42.00.

c. $43.40.

d. $420.00.

LO 10-4   46. On January 4, 2021, Irina employed a part-time household worker. The household worker was paid $375 per month for doing various work around the house. What amount of FICA tax is Irina required to record on Schedule H?

a. $344.25.

b. $558.60.

c. $642.60.

d. $688.50.

LO 10-6   47. A taxpayer with 2021 AGI of $160,000 has no income tax withholding and is required to pay estimated taxes. The taxpayer can avoid an underpayment penalty by paying

a. At least 90% of the 2021 tax liability ratably over four quarterly payments.

b. At least 110% of the 2021 tax liability ratably over four quarterly payments.

c. At least 90% of the 2020 tax liability ratably over four quarterly payments.

d. 100% of the 2021 tax liability ratably over four quarterly payments.

LO 10-6   48. Nico received a bonus of $6,000 from an employer. Which one of the following federal income withholding tax amounts is *not* in accordance with IRS rules regarding supplemental wage payments? Nico earns biweekly wages of $5,000, and is single with no dependents. Assume the employer uses the Percentage Method Tables for Manual Payroll Systems with Forms W-4 from 2020 or Later (see appendix).

a. $1,847.90 on the bonus if taxes had already been withheld from regular pay.

b. $1,948.38 if the bonus and wages are paid on different dates within the pay period.

c. $2,174.19 if the bonus is taxed at the supplemental wage percentage and added to regular wages paid in the same period.

d. $2,701.99 if the bonus and wages are paid at the same time during the pay period.

## Problems ![McGraw Hill] **connect**

All applicable problems are available with *Connect*©

**LO 10-2** 49. Morgan is paid $2,616.35 per week. What is the amount of federal income tax withheld from Morgan paycheck under the following conditions? Assume that Morgan has only one job or that step 2 of Form W-4 is not checked. Use the Percentage Method Tables for Automated Payroll Systems (see appendix).

    *a.* Morgan is single and no dependents.

_____

    *b.* Morgan is married (spouse does not work) and claims two dependents who are under the age of 17.

_____

    *c.* Morgan is single, claims no dependents, but wants $50 in additional withholding.

_____

**LO 10-2** 50. Saleh is married (spouse does not work), claims two dependents who are under the age of 17. What is the amount of federal income tax withholding under the following conditions? Assume Saleh has only one job or that step 2 of Form W-4 is not checked. Use the Percentage Method Tables for Manual Payroll Systems with Forms W-4 from 2020 or Later (see appendix).

    *a.* Saleh is paid semimonthly, and the gross pay is $3,622.58 per paycheck.

_____

    *b.* Saleh is paid monthly, and the gross pay is $6,712.97 per paycheck.

_____

    *c.* Saleh is paid weekly, and the gross pay is $4,605.25 per paycheck.

_____

**LO 10-2** 51. Valentina is single and claims no dependents. Assume that Valentina has only one job or that step 2 of Form W-4 is not checked. Use the Wage Bracket Method Tables for Manual Payroll Systems with Forms W-4 from 2020 or Later available online in Publication 15, Publication 15-T, "Federal Income Tax Withholding Methods."

    *a.* If Valentina is paid weekly and her annual wages are $78,325.00, what is the amount of withholding per paycheck?

_____

    *b.* If Valentina is paid monthly with annual wages of $60,841.80, what is the amount of withholding per paycheck?

_____

    *c.* If Valentina is paid biweekly with annual wages of $61,825.92, what is the amount of withholding per paycheck?

_____

    *d.* If Valentina is paid semimonthly with annual wages of $75,000, what is the amount of withholding per paycheck?

_____

**LO 10-2** 52. Kendall, who earned $120,000 during 2021, is paid on a monthly basis, is married, (spouse does not work) and claims two dependents who are under the age of 17. Use the Percentage Method Tables for Automated Payroll Systems (see appendix).

    *a.* What is Kendall federal tax withholding for each pay period?

_____

    *b.* What is Kendall FICA withholding for each pay period?

_____

LO 10-2    53. Roberto's salary is $147,860.40 in 2021. Roberto is paid on a semimonthly basis, is single, and claims one dependent who is under the age of 17. Use the Percentage Method Tables for Manual Payroll Systems with Forms W-4 from 2020 or Later (see appendix).

  *a.* What is Roberto's federal tax withholding per pay period?

  _____

  *b.* What is Roberto's FICA withholding per pay period before the social security limit is reached?

  _____

  *c.* For the last pay period in 2021, what is Roberto's FICA withholding?

  _____

LO 10-3    54. Chang Company is trying to determine how often it needs to deposit payroll taxes for calendar year 2021. The company made the following quarterly payroll tax deposits during the last two years:

| | |
|---|---|
| Quarter beginning January 1, 2019 | $10,000 |
| Quarter beginning April 1, 2019 | 10,000 |
| Quarter beginning July 1, 2019 | 11,000 |
| Quarter beginning October 1, 2019 | 12,000 |
| Quarter beginning January 1, 2020 | 12,000 |
| Quarter beginning April 1, 2020 | 12,000 |
| Quarter beginning July 1, 2020 | 11,000 |
| Quarter beginning October 1, 2020 | 12,000 |

  *a.* What is the amount from the lookback period?

  _____

  *b.* In 2021, how often must Chang Company make payroll deposits?

  _____

LO 10-4    55. CFG Company has the following employees:

| | Wages Paid |
|---|---|
| Edwardo | $12,000 |
| Melanie | 6,000 |
| Navaeh | 22,000 |

  CFG receives the maximum credit for state unemployment taxes. What is the FUTA tax that CFG Company would owe for the year?

LO 10-4    56. Angel hired Chris as a housekeeper starting on January 2 at $750 monthly. Angel does not withhold any federal taxes. Assume that Chris is not a housekeeper for anyone else. Assume that Angel paid $2,250 in wages for the fourth quarter of 2021.

  *a.* How much in social security tax should Angel pay? _____

  _____

  *b.* How much Medicare tax should Angel pay?

  _____

  *c.* How much FUTA tax should Angel pay?

  _____

LO 10-2, 10-4   57.  Lauprechta Inc. has the following employees on payroll:

| | Semimonthly Payroll | Number of Dependents from Form W-4 | Marital Status |
|---|---|---|---|
| Naila | $6,000 | 3 | Married |
| Wilfred | $5,300 | 2 | Married |
| Byron | $3,900 | 0 | Single |
| Annie | $4,500 | 1 | Single |

Complete the table for taxes to be withheld for each pay period using the Percentage Method Tables for Manual Payroll Systems with Forms W-4 from 2020 or Later (see appendix).

| Employee | Federal Withholding Tax | Social Security Tax | Medicare Tax | Total Taxes Withheld |
|---|---|---|---|---|
| Naila | _____ | _____ | _____ | _____ |
| Wilfred | _____ | _____ | _____ | _____ |
| Byron | _____ | _____ | _____ | _____ |
| Annie | _____ | _____ | _____ | _____ |

## Tax Return Problems

All applicable tax return problems are available with **Connect** ©

These problems are intended to be completed manually. Go to the IRS Web site at www.irs.gov to obtain 2021 forms.

**Tax Return Problem 1**   Use the information from Problem 57. Prepare Form 941 including Schedule B for the first quarter of 2021. Assume that the payroll is consistent every pay period beginning in January through March 31 and that all tax deposits were made on a timely basis as required. Lauprechta Inc.'s Employer Identification Number (EIN) is 36-1238975, and its address is 1825 Elkhart Way, Columbus, GA 31904.

**Tax Return Problem 2**   Use the information from Problem 57. Prepare Form 940 for 2021. Assume that Lauprechta Inc. has timely paid all amounts due to the state unemployment fund (assume a total amount of $3,471) and that the payroll was consistent throughout the entire year. No FUTA deposits were made during the year.

**Tax Return Problem 3**   Use the information from Problem 57. Prepare a Form W-2 for Naila Neffa. Her SSN is 412-34-5670, and her address is 988 Main Street, Midland, GA 31820. The EIN for Lauprechta Inc. is 36-1238975, and its address is 1825 Elkhart Way, Columbus, GA 31904.

We have provided selected filled-in source documents that are available in the *Connect Library.*

# Appendix

# PARTIAL WAGE BRACKET METHOD WITHHOLDING

## 1. Percentage Method Tables for Automated Payroll Systems

If you have an automated payroll system, use the worksheet below and the Percentage Method tables that follow

to figure federal income tax withholding. This method works for Forms W-4 for all prior, current, and future years. This method also works for any amount of wages. If the Form W-4 is from 2019 or earlier, this method works for any number of withholding allowances claimed.

### Worksheet 1. Employer's Withholding Worksheet for Percentage Method Tables for Automated Payroll Systems

*Keep for Your Records*

| Table 3 | Semiannually | Quarterly | Monthly | Semimonthly | Biweekly | Weekly | Daily |
|---|---|---|---|---|---|---|---|
| | 2 | 4 | 12 | 24 | 26 | 52 | 260 |

**Step 1.** **Adjust the employee's payment amount**

1a  Enter the employee's total taxable wages this payroll period . . . . . . . . . . . . . . . . . . . . . . . . . . 1a  $ _____

1b  Enter the number of pay periods you have per year (see Table 3) . . . . . . . . . . . . . . . . . . . . . . 1b  _____

1c  Multiply the amount on line 1a by the number on line 1b . . . . . . . . . . . . . . . . . . . . . . . . . 1c  $ _____

If the employee **HAS** submitted a Form W-4 for 2020 or later, figure the Adjusted Annual Wage Amount as follows:

1d  Enter the amount from Step 4(a) of the employee's Form W-4 . . . . . . . . . . . . . . . . . . . 1d  $ _____

1e  Add lines 1c and 1d . . . . . . . . . . . . . . . . . . . . . . . . . . . . . . . . . . . . . . . . . . 1e  $ _____

1f  Enter the amount from Step 4(b) of the employee's Form W-4 . . . . . . . . . . . . . . . . . . . 1f  $ _____

1g  If the box in Step 2 of Form W-4 is checked, enter -0-. If the box is not checked, enter $12,900 if the taxpayer is married filing jointly or $8,600 otherwise . . . . . . . . . . . . . . . . . . . . . . . . 1g  $ _____

1h  Add lines 1f and 1g . . . . . . . . . . . . . . . . . . . . . . . . . . . . . . . . . . . . . . . . . . 1h  $ _____

1i  Subtract line 1h from line 1e. If zero or less, enter -0-. This is the **Adjusted Annual Wage Amount** . . . . . . . . . . . . . . . . . . . . . . . . . . . . . . . . . . . . . . . . . . . . . . 1i  $ _____

If the employee **HAS NOT** submitted a Form W-4 for 2020 or later, figure the Adjusted Annual Wage Amount as follows:

1j  Enter the number of allowances claimed on the employee's most recent Form W-4 . . . . . . . . . . . . . 1j  _____

1k  Multiply line 1j by $4,300 . . . . . . . . . . . . . . . . . . . . . . . . . . . . . . . . . . . . . . . 1k  $ _____

1l  Subtract line 1k from line 1c. If zero or less, enter -0-. This is the **Adjusted Annual Wage Amount** . . . . . . . . . . . . . . . . . . . . . . . . . . . . . . . . . . . . . . . . . . . . . . 1l  $ _____

**Step 2.** **Figure the Tentative Withholding Amount**

based on the employee's Adjusted Annual Wage Amount; filing status (Step 1(c) of the 2020 or later Form W-4) or marital status (line 3 of Form W-4 from 2019 or earlier); and whether the box in Step 2 of 2020 or later Form W-4 is checked.
**Note.** Don't use the Head of Household table if the Form W-4 is from 2019 or earlier.

2a  Enter the employee's **Adjusted Annual Wage Amount** from line 1i or 1l above . . . . . . . . . . . . . . . 2a  $ _____

2b  Find the row in the appropriate **Annual** Percentage Method table in which the amount on line 2a is at least the amount in column A but less than the amount in column B, then enter here the amount from column A of that row . . . . . . . . . . . . . . . . . . . . . . . . . . . . . . . . . . . . . . . . . . 2b  $ _____

2c  Enter the amount from column C of that row . . . . . . . . . . . . . . . . . . . . . . . . . . . . . . 2c  $ _____

2d  Enter the percentage from column D of that row . . . . . . . . . . . . . . . . . . . . . . . . . . . . 2d  _____ %

2e  Subtract line 2b from line 2a . . . . . . . . . . . . . . . . . . . . . . . . . . . . . . . . . . . . . 2e  $ _____

2f  Multiply the amount on line 2e by the percentage on line 2d . . . . . . . . . . . . . . . . . . . . . . 2f  $ _____

2g  Add lines 2c and 2f . . . . . . . . . . . . . . . . . . . . . . . . . . . . . . . . . . . . . . . . . . 2g  $ _____

2h  Divide the amount on line 2g by the number of pay periods on line 1b. This is the **Tentative Withholding Amount** . . . . . . . . . . . . . . . . . . . . . . . . . . . . . . . . . . . . . . . . 2h  $ _____

**Step 3.** **Account for tax credits**

3a  If the employee's Form W-4 is from 2020 or later, enter the amount from Step 3 of that form; otherwise enter -0- . . . . . . . . . . . . . . . . . . . . . . . . . . . . . . . . . . . . . . . . . . . . . . . . 3a  $ _____

3b  Divide the amount on line 3a by the number of pay periods on line 1b . . . . . . . . . . . . . . . . . . 3b  $ _____

3c  Subtract line 3b from line 2h. If zero or less, enter -0- . . . . . . . . . . . . . . . . . . . . . . . . . 3c  $ _____

**Step 4.** **Figure the final amount to withhold**

4a  Enter the additional amount to withhold from the employee's Form W-4 (Step 4(c) of the 2020 or later form or line 6 on earlier forms) . . . . . . . . . . . . . . . . . . . . . . . . . . . . . . . . . . . . 4a  $ _____

4b  Add lines 3c and 4a. **This is the amount to withhold from the employee's wages this pay period** . . . . . . . . . . . . . . . . . . . . . . . . . . . . . . . . . . . . . . . . . . . . . . 4b  $ _____

Source: U.S. Department of the Treasury, Internal Revenue Service, Publication 15. Washington, DC: 2021.

# TABLES

## 2021 Percentage Method Tables for Automated Payroll Systems

| STANDARD Withholding Rate Schedules (Use these if the Form W-4 is from 2019 or earlier, or if the Form W-4 is from 2020 or later and the box in Step 2 of Form W-4 is **NOT** checked) | | | | | Form W-4, Step 2, Checkbox, Withholding Rate Schedules (Use these if the Form W-4 is from 2020 or later and the box in Step 2 of Form W-4 **IS** checked) | | | | |
|---|---|---|---|---|---|---|---|---|---|
| If the Adjusted Annual Wage Amount (line 2a) is: | | The tentative amount to withhold is: | Plus this percentage— | of the amount that the Adjusted Annual Wage exceeds— | If the Adjusted Annual Wage Amount (line 2a) is: | | The tentative amount to withhold is: | Plus this percentage— | of the amount that the Adjusted Annual Wage exceeds— |
| At least— | But less than— | | | | At least— | But less than— | | | |
| A | B | C | D | E | A | B | C | D | E |
| **Married Filing Jointly** | | | | | **Married Filing Jointly** | | | | |
| $0 | $12,200 | $0.00 | 0% | $0 | $0 | $12,550 | $0.00 | 0% | $0 |
| $12,200 | $32,100 | $0.00 | 10% | $12,200 | $12,550 | $22,500 | $0.00 | 10% | $12,550 |
| $32,100 | $93,250 | $1,990.00 | 12% | $32,100 | $22,500 | $53,075 | $995.00 | 12% | $22,500 |
| $93,250 | $184,950 | $9,328.00 | 22% | $93,250 | $53,075 | $98,925 | $4,664.00 | 22% | $53,075 |
| $184,950 | $342,050 | $29,502.00 | 24% | $184,950 | $98,925 | $177,475 | $14,751.00 | 24% | $98,925 |
| $342,050 | $431,050 | $67,206.00 | 32% | $342,050 | $177,475 | $221,975 | $33,603.00 | 32% | $177,475 |
| $431,050 | $640,500 | $95,686.00 | 35% | $431,050 | $221,975 | $326,700 | $47,843.00 | 35% | $221,975 |
| $640,500 | | $168,993.50 | 37% | $640,500 | $326,700 | | $84,496.75 | 37% | $326,700 |
| **Single or Married Filing Separately** | | | | | **Single or Married Filing Separately** | | | | |
| $0 | $3,950 | $0.00 | 0% | $0 | $0 | $6,275 | $0.00 | 0% | $0 |
| $3,950 | $13,900 | $0.00 | 10% | $3,950 | $6,275 | $11,250 | $0.00 | 10% | $6,275 |
| $13,900 | $44,475 | $995.00 | 12% | $13,900 | $11,250 | $26,538 | $497.50 | 12% | $11,250 |
| $44,475 | $90,325 | $4,664.00 | 22% | $44,475 | $26,538 | $49,463 | $2,332.00 | 22% | $26,538 |
| $90,325 | $168,875 | $14,751.00 | 24% | $90,325 | $49,463 | $88,738 | $7,375.50 | 24% | $49,463 |
| $168,875 | $213,375 | $33,603.00 | 32% | $168,875 | $88,738 | $110,988 | $16,801.50 | 32% | $88,738 |
| $213,375 | $527,550 | $47,843.00 | 35% | $213,375 | $110,988 | $268,075 | $23,921.50 | 35% | $110,988 |
| $527,550 | | $157,804.25 | 37% | $527,550 | $268,075 | | $78,902.13 | 37% | $268,075 |
| **Head of Household** | | | | | **Head of Household** | | | | |
| $0 | $10,200 | $0.00 | 0% | $0 | $0 | $9,400 | $0.00 | 0% | $0 |
| $10,200 | $24,400 | $0.00 | 10% | $10,200 | $9,400 | $16,500 | $0.00 | 10% | $9,400 |
| $24,400 | $64,400 | $1,420.00 | 12% | $24,400 | $16,500 | $36,500 | $710.00 | 12% | $16,500 |
| $64,400 | $96,550 | $6,220.00 | 22% | $64,400 | $36,500 | $52,575 | $3,110.00 | 22% | $36,500 |
| $96,550 | $175,100 | $13,293.00 | 24% | $96,550 | $52,575 | $91,850 | $6,646.50 | 24% | $52,575 |
| $175,100 | $219,600 | $32,145.00 | 32% | $175,100 | $91,850 | $114,100 | $16,072.50 | 32% | $91,850 |
| $219,600 | $533,800 | $46,385.00 | 35% | $219,600 | $114,100 | $271,200 | $23,192.50 | 35% | $114,100 |
| $533,800 | | $156,355.00 | 37% | $533,800 | $271,200 | | $78,177.50 | 37% | $271,200 |

**Publication 15-T (2021)**

# 2. Wage Bracket Method Tables for Manual Payroll Systems With Forms W-4 From 2020 or Later

If you compute payroll manually, your employee has submitted a Form W-4 for 2020 or later, and you prefer to use the Wage Bracket method, use the worksheet below and the Wage Bracket Method tables that follow to figure federal income tax withholding.

The Wage Bracket Method tables cover only up to approximately $100,000 in annual wages. If you can't use the Wage Bracket Method tables because taxable wages exceed the amount from the last bracket of the table (based on filing status and pay period), use the Percentage Method tables in section 4.

## Worksheet 2. Employer's Withholding Worksheet for Wage Bracket Method Tables for Manual Payroll Systems With Forms W-4 From 2020 or Later

*Keep for Your Records*

| Table 4 | Monthly | Semimonthly | Biweekly | Weekly | Daily |
|---|---|---|---|---|---|
| | 12 | 24 | 26 | 52 | 260 |

**Step 1.** **Adjust the employee's wage amount**

1a Enter the employee's total taxable wages this payroll period . . . . . . . . . . . . . . . . . . . . . . . . . . . .   1a $ _____

1b Enter the number of pay periods you have per year (see Table 4) . . . . . . . . . . . . . . . . . . . . . . .   1b _____

1c Enter the amount from Step 4(a) of the employee's Form W-4 . . . . . . . . . . . . . . . . . . . . . . . . .   1c $ _____

1d Divide the amount on line 1c by the number of pay periods on line 1b . . . . . . . . . . . . . . . . . . . .   1d $ _____

1e Add lines 1a and 1d . . . . . . . . . . . . . . . . . . . . . . . . . . . . . . . . . . . . . . . . . . . . . . . . . . . . . . .   1e $ _____

1f Enter the amount from Step 4(b) of the employee's Form W-4 . . . . . . . . . . . . . . . . . . . . . . . . .   1f $ _____

1g Divide the amount on line 1f by the number of pay periods on line 1b . . . . . . . . . . . . . . . . . . . .   1g $ _____

1h Subtract line 1g from line 1e. If zero or less, enter -0-. This is the **Adjusted Wage Amount** . . . . . .   1h $ _____

**Step 2.** **Figure the Tentative Withholding Amount**

2a Use the amount on line 1h to look up the tentative amount to withhold in the appropriate Wage Bracket Table in this section for your pay frequency, given the employee's filing status and whether the employee has checked the box in Step 2 of Form W-4. This is the **Tentative Withholding Amount** . . . . . . . . . . . . . . . . . . . . . . . . . . . . . . . . . . . . . . . . . . . . . . . . . . . . . . . . .   2a $ _____

**Step 3.** **Account for tax credits**

3a Enter the amount from Step 3 of the employee's Form W-4 . . . . . . . . . . . . . . . . . . . . . . . . . . . .   3a $ _____

3b Divide the amount on line 3a by the number of pay periods on line 1b . . . . . . . . . . . . . . . . . . . .   3b $ _____

3c Subtract line 3b from line 2a. If zero or less, enter -0- . . . . . . . . . . . . . . . . . . . . . . . . . . . . . . .   3c $ _____

**Step 4.** **Figure the final amount to withhold**

4a Enter the additional amount to withhold from Step 4(c) of the employee's Form W-4 . . . . . . . . . .   4a $ _____

4b Add lines 3c and 4a. **This is the amount to withhold from the employee's wages this pay period** . . . . . . . . . . . . . . . . . . . . . . . . . . . . . . . . . . . . . . . . . . . . . . . . . . . . . . . . . . . . . . . .   4b $ _____

## 2021 Wage Bracket Method Tables for Manual Payroll Systems with Forms W-4 From 2020 or Later
### WEEKLY Payroll Period

| If the Adjusted Wage Amount (line 1h) is | | Married Filing Jointly | | Head of Household | | Single or Married Filing Separately | |
|---|---|---|---|---|---|---|---|
| At least | But less than | Standard withholding | Form W-4, Step 2, Checkbox withholding | Standard withholding | Form W-4, Step 2, Checkbox withholding | Standard withholding | Form W-4, Step 2, Checkbox withholding |
| | | The Tentative Withholding Amount is: | | | | | |
| $0 | $125 | $0 | $0 | $0 | $0 | $0 | $0 |
| $125 | $135 | $0 | $0 | $0 | $0 | $0 | $1 |
| $135 | $145 | $0 | $0 | $0 | $0 | $0 | $2 |
| $145 | $155 | $0 | $0 | $0 | $0 | $0 | $3 |
| $155 | $165 | $0 | $0 | $0 | $0 | $0 | $4 |
| $165 | $175 | $0 | $0 | $0 | $0 | $0 | $5 |
| $175 | $185 | $0 | $0 | $0 | $0 | $0 | $6 |
| $185 | $195 | $0 | $0 | $0 | $1 | $0 | $7 |
| $195 | $205 | $0 | $0 | $0 | $2 | $0 | $8 |
| $205 | $215 | $0 | $0 | $0 | $3 | $0 | $9 |
| $215 | $225 | $0 | $0 | $0 | $4 | $0 | $10 |
| $225 | $235 | $0 | $0 | $0 | $5 | $0 | $11 |
| $235 | $245 | $0 | $0 | $0 | $6 | $0 | $12 |
| $245 | $255 | $0 | $1 | $0 | $7 | $1 | $14 |
| $255 | $265 | $0 | $2 | $0 | $8 | $2 | $15 |
| $265 | $275 | $0 | $3 | $0 | $9 | $3 | $16 |
| $275 | $285 | $0 | $4 | $0 | $10 | $4 | $17 |
| $285 | $295 | $0 | $5 | $0 | $11 | $5 | $18 |
| $295 | $305 | $0 | $6 | $0 | $12 | $6 | $20 |
| $305 | $315 | $0 | $7 | $0 | $13 | $7 | $21 |
| $315 | $325 | $0 | $8 | $0 | $14 | $8 | $22 |
| $325 | $335 | $0 | $9 | $0 | $15 | $9 | $23 |
| $335 | $345 | $0 | $10 | $0 | $16 | $10 | $24 |
| $345 | $355 | $0 | $11 | $0 | $18 | $11 | $26 |
| $355 | $365 | $0 | $12 | $0 | $19 | $12 | $27 |
| $365 | $375 | $0 | $13 | $1 | $20 | $13 | $28 |
| $375 | $385 | $0 | $14 | $2 | $21 | $14 | $29 |
| $385 | $395 | $0 | $15 | $3 | $22 | $15 | $30 |
| $395 | $405 | $0 | $16 | $4 | $24 | $16 | $32 |
| $405 | $415 | $0 | $17 | $5 | $25 | $17 | $33 |
| $415 | $425 | $0 | $18 | $6 | $26 | $18 | $34 |
| $425 | $435 | $0 | $19 | $7 | $27 | $19 | $35 |
| $435 | $445 | $0 | $20 | $8 | $28 | $20 | $36 |
| $445 | $455 | $0 | $21 | $9 | $30 | $21 | $38 |
| $455 | $465 | $0 | $22 | $10 | $31 | $22 | $39 |
| $465 | $475 | $0 | $24 | $11 | $32 | $24 | $40 |
| $475 | $485 | $0 | $25 | $12 | $33 | $25 | $41 |
| $485 | $495 | $1 | $26 | $13 | $34 | $26 | $42 |
| $495 | $505 | $2 | $27 | $14 | $36 | $27 | $44 |
| $505 | $515 | $3 | $28 | $15 | $37 | $28 | $45 |
| $515 | $525 | $4 | $30 | $16 | $38 | $30 | $47 |
| $525 | $535 | $5 | $31 | $17 | $39 | $31 | $49 |
| $535 | $545 | $6 | $32 | $18 | $40 | $32 | $51 |
| $545 | $555 | $7 | $33 | $19 | $42 | $33 | $54 |
| $555 | $565 | $8 | $34 | $20 | $43 | $34 | $56 |
| $565 | $575 | $9 | $36 | $21 | $44 | $36 | $58 |
| $575 | $585 | $10 | $37 | $22 | $45 | $37 | $60 |
| $585 | $595 | $11 | $38 | $23 | $46 | $38 | $62 |
| $595 | $605 | $12 | $39 | $24 | $48 | $39 | $65 |
| $605 | $615 | $13 | $40 | $25 | $49 | $40 | $67 |
| $615 | $625 | $14 | $42 | $26 | $50 | $42 | $69 |
| $625 | $635 | $15 | $43 | $27 | $51 | $43 | $71 |
| $635 | $645 | $16 | $44 | $28 | $52 | $44 | $73 |
| $645 | $655 | $17 | $45 | $29 | $54 | $45 | $76 |
| $655 | $665 | $18 | $46 | $30 | $55 | $46 | $78 |
| $665 | $675 | $19 | $48 | $32 | $56 | $48 | $80 |
| $675 | $685 | $20 | $49 | $33 | $57 | $49 | $82 |
| $685 | $695 | $21 | $50 | $34 | $58 | $50 | $84 |
| $695 | $705 | $22 | $51 | $35 | $60 | $51 | $87 |
| $705 | $715 | $23 | $52 | $36 | $62 | $52 | $89 |
| $715 | $725 | $24 | $54 | $38 | $64 | $54 | $91 |
| $725 | $735 | $25 | $55 | $39 | $66 | $55 | $93 |
| $735 | $745 | $26 | $56 | $40 | $68 | $56 | $95 |
| $745 | $755 | $27 | $57 | $41 | $70 | $57 | $98 |
| $755 | $765 | $28 | $58 | $42 | $73 | $58 | $100 |

**Publication 15-T (2021)**

# 4. Percentage Method Tables for Manual Payroll Systems With Forms W-4 From 2020 or Later

the Percentage Method or you can't use the Wage Bracket Method tables because the employee's annual wages exceed $100,000, use the worksheet below and the Percentage Method tables that follow to figure federal income tax withholding. This method works for any amount of wages.

If you compute payroll manually, your employee has submitted a Form W-4 for 2020 or later, and you prefer to use

## Worksheet 4. Employer's Withholding Worksheet for Percentage Method Tables for Manual Payroll Systems With Forms W-4 From 2020 or Later

*Keep for Your Records*

| Table 5 | Monthly | Semimonthly | Biweekly | Weekly | Daily |
|---|---|---|---|---|---|
| | 12 | 24 | 26 | 52 | 260 |

**Step 1.** **Adjust the employee's wage amount**

1a  Enter the employee's total taxable wages this payroll period .......................... 1a $ _____

1b  Enter the number of pay periods you have per year (see Table 5) ..................... 1b _____

1c  Enter the amount from Step 4(a) of the employee's Form W-4 ......................... 1c $ _____

1d  Divide line 1c by the number on line 1b ............................................. 1d $ _____

1e  Add lines 1a and 1d ................................................................ 1e $ _____

1f  Enter the amount from Step 4(b) of the employee's Form W-4 ......................... 1f $ _____

1g  Divide line 1f by the number on line 1b ............................................. 1g $ _____

1h  Subtract line 1g from line 1e. If zero or less, enter -0-. This is the **Adjusted Wage Amount** ...... 1h $ _____

**Step 2.** **Figure the Tentative Withholding Amount**

based on your pay frequency, the employee's Adjusted Wage Amount, filing status (Step 1(c) of Form W-4), and whether the box in Step 2 of Form W-4 is checked.

2a  Find the row in the *STANDARD Withholding Rate Schedules* (if the box in Step 2 of Form W-4 is NOT checked) or the *Form W-4, Step 2, Checkbox, Withholding Rate Schedules* (if it HAS been checked) of the Percentage Method tables in this section in which the amount on line 1h is at least the amount in column A but less than the amount in column B, then enter here the amount from column A of that row ................................................................ 2a $ _____

2b  Enter the amount from column C of that row .......................................... 2b $ _____

2c  Enter the percentage from column D of that row ...................................... 2c _____ %

2d  Subtract line 2a from line 1h ....................................................... 2d $ _____

2e  Multiply the amount on line 2d by the percentage on line 2c ......................... 2e $ _____

2f  Add lines 2b and 2e. This is the **Tentative Withholding Amount** ................... 2f $ _____

**Step 3.** **Account for tax credits**

3a  Enter the amount from Step 3 of the employee's Form W-4 ............................. 3a $ _____

3b  Divide the amount on line 3a by the number of pay periods on line 1b ............... 3b $ _____

3c  Subtract line 3b from line 2f. If zero or less, enter -0- ........................... 3c $ _____

**Step 4.** **Figure the final amount to withhold**

4a  Enter the additional amount to withhold from Step 4(c) of the employee's Form W-4 ........... 4a $ _____

4b  Add lines 3c and 4a. **This is the amount to withhold from the employee's wages this pay period** ......................................................................... 4b $ _____

# 2021 Percentage Method Tables for Manual Payroll Systems With Forms W-4 from 2020 or Later

WEEKLY Payroll Period

| STANDARD Withholding Rate Schedules (Use these if the box in Step 2 of Form W-4 is **NOT** checked) | | | | | Form W-4, Step 2, Checkbox, Withholding Rate Schedules (Use these if the box in Step 2 of Form W-4 **IS** checked) | | | | |
|---|---|---|---|---|---|---|---|---|---|
| **If the Adjusted Wage Amount (line 1h) is:** | | **The tentative amount to withhold is:** | **Plus this percentage—** | **of the amount that the Adjusted Wage exceeds—** | **If the Adjusted Wage Amount (line 1h) is:** | | **The tentative amount to withhold is:** | **Plus this percentage—** | **of the amount that the Adjusted Wage exceeds—** |
| At least— | But less than— | | | | At least— | But less than— | | | |
| A | B | C | D | E | A | B | C | D | E |
| **Married Filing Jointly** | | | | | **Married Filing Jointly** | | | | |
| $0 | $483 | $0.00 | 0% | $0 | $0 | $241 | $0.00 | 0% | $0 |
| $483 | $865 | $0.00 | 10% | $483 | $241 | $433 | $0.00 | 10% | $241 |
| $865 | $2,041 | $38.20 | 12% | $865 | $433 | $1,021 | $19.20 | 12% | $433 |
| $2,041 | $3,805 | $179.32 | 22% | $2,041 | $1,021 | $1,902 | $89.76 | 22% | $1,021 |
| $3,805 | $6,826 | $567.40 | 24% | $3,805 | $1,902 | $3,413 | $283.58 | 24% | $1,902 |
| $6,826 | $8,538 | $1,292.44 | 32% | $6,826 | $3,413 | $4,269 | $646.22 | 32% | $3,413 |
| $8,538 | $12,565 | $1,840.28 | 35% | $8,538 | $4,269 | $6,283 | $920.14 | 35% | $4,269 |
| $12,565 | | $3,249.73 | 37% | $12,565 | $6,283 | | $1,625.04 | 37% | $6,283 |
| **Single or Married Filing Separately** | | | | | **Single or Married Filing Separately** | | | | |
| $0 | $241 | $0.00 | 0% | $0 | $0 | $121 | $0.00 | 0% | $0 |
| $241 | $433 | $0.00 | 10% | $241 | $121 | $216 | $0.00 | 10% | $121 |
| $433 | $1,021 | $19.20 | 12% | $433 | $216 | $510 | $9.50 | 12% | $216 |
| $1,021 | $1,902 | $89.76 | 22% | $1,021 | $510 | $951 | $44.78 | 22% | $510 |
| $1,902 | $3,413 | $283.58 | 24% | $1,902 | $951 | $1,706 | $141.80 | 24% | $951 |
| $3,413 | $4,269 | $646.22 | 32% | $3,413 | $1,706 | $2,134 | $323.00 | 32% | $1,706 |
| $4,269 | $10,311 | $920.14 | 35% | $4,269 | $2,134 | $5,155 | $459.96 | 35% | $2,134 |
| $10,311 | | $3,034.84 | 37% | $10,311 | $5,155 | | $1,517.31 | 37% | $5,155 |
| **Head of Household** | | | | | **Head of Household** | | | | |
| $0 | $362 | $0.00 | 0% | $0 | $0 | $181 | $0.00 | 0% | $0 |
| $362 | $635 | $0.00 | 10% | $362 | $181 | $317 | $0.00 | 10% | $181 |
| $635 | $1,404 | $27.30 | 12% | $635 | $317 | $702 | $13.60 | 12% | $317 |
| $1,404 | $2,022 | $119.58 | 22% | $1,404 | $702 | $1,011 | $59.80 | 22% | $702 |
| $2,022 | $3,533 | $255.54 | 24% | $2,022 | $1,011 | $1,766 | $127.78 | 24% | $1,011 |
| $3,533 | $4,388 | $618.18 | 32% | $3,533 | $1,766 | $2,194 | $308.98 | 32% | $1,766 |
| $4,388 | $10,431 | $891.78 | 35% | $4,388 | $2,194 | $5,215 | $445.94 | 35% | $2,194 |
| $10,431 | | $3,006.83 | 37% | $10,431 | $5,215 | | $1,503.29 | 37% | $5,215 |

**Publication 15-T (2021)**

## 2021 Percentage Method Tables for Manual Payroll Systems With Forms W-4 from 2020 or Later
### BIWEEKLY Payroll Period

| STANDARD Withholding Rate Schedules (Use these if the box in Step 2 of Form W-4 is **NOT** checked) | | | | | Form W-4, Step 2, Checkbox, Withholding Rate Schedules (Use these if the box in Step 2 of Form W-4 **IS** checked) | | | | |
|---|---|---|---|---|---|---|---|---|---|
| If the Adjusted Wage Amount (line 1h) is: | | The tentative amount to withhold is: | Plus this percentage— | of the amount that the Adjusted Wage exceeds— | If the Adjusted Wage Amount (line 1h) is: | | The tentative amount to withhold is: | Plus this percentage— | of the amount that the Adjusted Wage exceeds— |
| At least— | But less than— | | | | At least— | But less than— | | | |
| A | B | C | D | E | A | B | C | D | E |
| Married Filing Jointly | | | | | Married Filing Jointly | | | | |
| $0 | $965 | $0.00 | 0% | $0 | $0 | $483 | $0.00 | 0% | $0 |
| $965 | $1,731 | $0.00 | 10% | $965 | $483 | $865 | $0.00 | 10% | $483 |
| $1,731 | $4,083 | $76.60 | 12% | $1,731 | $865 | $2,041 | $38.20 | 12% | $865 |
| $4,083 | $7,610 | $358.84 | 22% | $4,083 | $2,041 | $3,805 | $179.32 | 22% | $2,041 |
| $7,610 | $13,652 | $1,134.78 | 24% | $7,610 | $3,805 | $6,826 | $567.40 | 24% | $3,805 |
| $13,652 | $17,075 | $2,584.86 | 32% | $13,652 | $6,826 | $8,538 | $1,292.44 | 32% | $6,826 |
| $17,075 | $25,131 | $3,680.22 | 35% | $17,075 | $8,538 | $12,565 | $1,840.28 | 35% | $8,538 |
| $25,131 | | $6,499.82 | 37% | $25,131 | $12,565 | | $3,249.73 | 37% | $12,565 |
| Single or Married Filing Separately | | | | | Single or Married Filing Separately | | | | |
| $0 | $483 | $0.00 | 0% | $0 | $0 | $241 | $0.00 | 0% | $0 |
| $483 | $865 | $0.00 | 10% | $483 | $241 | $433 | $0.00 | 10% | $241 |
| $865 | $2,041 | $38.20 | 12% | $865 | $433 | $1,021 | $19.20 | 12% | $433 |
| $2,041 | $3,805 | $179.32 | 22% | $2,041 | $1,021 | $1,902 | $89.76 | 22% | $1,021 |
| $3,805 | $6,826 | $567.40 | 24% | $3,805 | $1,902 | $3,413 | $283.58 | 24% | $1,902 |
| $6,826 | $8,538 | $1,292.44 | 32% | $6,826 | $3,413 | $4,269 | $646.22 | 32% | $3,413 |
| $8,538 | $20,621 | $1,840.28 | 35% | $8,538 | $4,269 | $10,311 | $920.14 | 35% | $4,269 |
| $20,621 | | $6,069.33 | 37% | $20,621 | $10,311 | | $3,034.84 | 37% | $10,311 |
| Head of Household | | | | | Head of Household | | | | |
| $0 | $723 | $0.00 | 0% | $0 | $0 | $362 | $0.00 | 0% | $0 |
| $723 | $1,269 | $0.00 | 10% | $723 | $362 | $635 | $0.00 | 10% | $362 |
| $1,269 | $2,808 | $54.60 | 12% | $1,269 | $635 | $1,404 | $27.30 | 12% | $635 |
| $2,808 | $4,044 | $239.28 | 22% | $2,808 | $1,404 | $2,022 | $119.58 | 22% | $1,404 |
| $4,044 | $7,065 | $511.20 | 24% | $4,044 | $2,022 | $3,533 | $255.54 | 24% | $2,022 |
| $7,065 | $8,777 | $1,236.24 | 32% | $7,065 | $3,533 | $4,388 | $618.18 | 32% | $3,533 |
| $8,777 | $20,862 | $1,784.08 | 35% | $8,777 | $4,388 | $10,431 | $891.78 | 35% | $4,388 |
| $20,862 | | $6,013.83 | 37% | $20,862 | $10,431 | | $3,006.83 | 37% | $10,431 |

## 2021 Percentage Method Tables for Manual Payroll Systems With Forms W-4 from 2020 or Later

SEMIMONTHLY Payroll Period

| STANDARD Withholding Rate Schedules (Use these if the box in Step 2 of Form W-4 is **NOT** checked) | | | | | Form W-4, Step 2, Checkbox, Withholding Rate Schedules (Use these if the box in Step 2 of Form W-4 **IS** checked) | | | | |
|---|---|---|---|---|---|---|---|---|---|
| If the Adjusted Wage Amount (line 1h) is: | | The tentative amount to withhold is: | Plus this percentage— | of the amount that the Adjusted Wage exceeds— | If the Adjusted Wage Amount (line 1h) is: | | The tentative amount to withhold is: | Plus this percentage— | of the amount that the Adjusted Wage exceeds— |
| At least— | But less than— | | | | At least— | But less than— | | | |
| A | B | C | D | E | A | B | C | D | E |
| Married Filing Jointly | | | | | Married Filing Jointly | | | | |
| $0 | $1,046 | $0.00 | 0% | $0 | $0 | $523 | $0.00 | 0% | $0 |
| $1,046 | $1,875 | $0.00 | 10% | $1,046 | $523 | $938 | $0.00 | 10% | $523 |
| $1,875 | $4,423 | $82.90 | 12% | $1,875 | $938 | $2,211 | $41.50 | 12% | $938 |
| $4,423 | $8,244 | $388.66 | 22% | $4,423 | $2,211 | $4,122 | $194.26 | 22% | $2,211 |
| $8,244 | $14,790 | $1,229.28 | 24% | $8,244 | $4,122 | $7,395 | $614.68 | 24% | $4,122 |
| $14,790 | $18,498 | $2,800.32 | 32% | $14,790 | $7,395 | $9,249 | $1,400.20 | 32% | $7,395 |
| $18,498 | $27,225 | $3,986.88 | 35% | $18,498 | $9,249 | $13,613 | $1,993.48 | 35% | $9,249 |
| $27,225 | | $7,041.33 | 37% | $27,225 | $13,613 | | $3,520.88 | 37% | $13,613 |
| Single or Married Filing Separately | | | | | Single or Married Filing Separately | | | | |
| $0 | $523 | $0.00 | 0% | $0 | $0 | $261 | $0.00 | 0% | $0 |
| $523 | $938 | $0.00 | 10% | $523 | $261 | $469 | $0.00 | 10% | $261 |
| $938 | $2,211 | $41.50 | 12% | $938 | $469 | $1,106 | $20.80 | 12% | $469 |
| $2,211 | $4,122 | $194.26 | 22% | $2,211 | $1,106 | $2,061 | $97.24 | 22% | $1,106 |
| $4,122 | $7,395 | $614.68 | 24% | $4,122 | $2,061 | $3,697 | $307.34 | 24% | $2,061 |
| $7,395 | $9,249 | $1,400.20 | 32% | $7,395 | $3,697 | $4,624 | $699.98 | 32% | $3,697 |
| $9,249 | $22,340 | $1,993.48 | 35% | $9,249 | $4,624 | $11,170 | $996.62 | 35% | $4,624 |
| $22,340 | | $6,575.33 | 37% | $22,340 | $11,170 | | $3,287.72 | 37% | $11,170 |
| Head of Household | | | | | Head of Household | | | | |
| $0 | $783 | $0.00 | 0% | $0 | $0 | $392 | $0.00 | 0% | $0 |
| $783 | $1,375 | $0.00 | 10% | $783 | $392 | $688 | $0.00 | 10% | $392 |
| $1,375 | $3,042 | $59.20 | 12% | $1,375 | $688 | $1,521 | $29.60 | 12% | $688 |
| $3,042 | $4,381 | $259.24 | 22% | $3,042 | $1,521 | $2,191 | $129.56 | 22% | $1,521 |
| $4,381 | $7,654 | $553.82 | 24% | $4,381 | $2,191 | $3,827 | $276.96 | 24% | $2,191 |
| $7,654 | $9,508 | $1,339.34 | 32% | $7,654 | $3,827 | $4,754 | $669.60 | 32% | $3,827 |
| $9,508 | $22,600 | $1,932.62 | 35% | $9,508 | $4,754 | $11,300 | $966.24 | 35% | $4,754 |
| $22,600 | | $6,514.82 | 37% | $22,600 | $11,300 | | $3,257.34 | 37% | $11,300 |

**Publication 15-T (2021)**

## 2021 Percentage Method Tables for Manual Payroll Systems With Forms W-4 from 2020 or Later

### MONTHLY Payroll Period

| STANDARD Withholding Rate Schedules (Use these if the box in Step 2 of Form W-4 is **NOT** checked) | | | | | Form W-4, Step 2, Checkbox, Withholding Rate Schedules (Use these if the box in Step 2 of Form W-4 **IS** checked) | | | | |
|---|---|---|---|---|---|---|---|---|---|
| If the Adjusted Wage Amount (line 1h) is: | | The tentative amount to withhold is: | Plus this percentage— | of the amount that the Adjusted Wage exceeds— | If the Adjusted Wage Amount (line 1h) is: | | The tentative amount to withhold is: | Plus this percentage— | of the amount that the Adjusted Wage exceeds— |
| At least— | But less than— | | | | At least— | But less than— | | | |
| A | B | C | D | E | A | B | C | D | E |
| **Married Filing Jointly** | | | | | **Married Filing Jointly** | | | | |
| $0 | $2,092 | $0.00 | 0% | $0 | $0 | $1,046 | $0.00 | 0% | $0 |
| $2,092 | $3,750 | $0.00 | 10% | $2,092 | $1,046 | $1,875 | $0.00 | 10% | $1,046 |
| $3,750 | $8,846 | $165.80 | 12% | $3,750 | $1,875 | $4,423 | $82.90 | 12% | $1,875 |
| $8,846 | $16,488 | $777.32 | 22% | $8,846 | $4,423 | $8,244 | $388.66 | 22% | $4,423 |
| $16,488 | $29,579 | $2,458.56 | 24% | $16,488 | $8,244 | $14,790 | $1,229.28 | 24% | $8,244 |
| $29,579 | $36,996 | $5,600.40 | 32% | $29,579 | $14,790 | $18,498 | $2,800.32 | 32% | $14,790 |
| $36,996 | $54,450 | $7,973.84 | 35% | $36,996 | $18,498 | $27,225 | $3,986.88 | 35% | $18,498 |
| $54,450 | | $14,082.74 | 37% | $54,450 | $27,225 | | $7,041.33 | 37% | $27,225 |
| **Single or Married Filing Separately** | | | | | **Single or Married Filing Separately** | | | | |
| $0 | $1,046 | $0.00 | 0% | $0 | $0 | $523 | $0.00 | 0% | $0 |
| $1,046 | $1,875 | $0.00 | 10% | $1,046 | $523 | $938 | $0.00 | 10% | $523 |
| $1,875 | $4,423 | $82.90 | 12% | $1,875 | $938 | $2,211 | $41.50 | 12% | $938 |
| $4,423 | $8,244 | $388.66 | 22% | $4,423 | $2,211 | $4,122 | $194.26 | 22% | $2,211 |
| $8,244 | $14,790 | $1,229.28 | 24% | $8,244 | $4,122 | $7,395 | $614.68 | 24% | $4,122 |
| $14,790 | $18,498 | $2,800.32 | 32% | $14,790 | $7,395 | $9,249 | $1,400.20 | 32% | $7,395 |
| $18,498 | $44,679 | $3,986.88 | 35% | $18,498 | $9,249 | $22,340 | $1,993.48 | 35% | $9,249 |
| $44,679 | | $13,150.23 | 37% | $44,679 | $22,340 | | $6,575.33 | 37% | $22,340 |
| **Head of Household** | | | | | **Head of Household** | | | | |
| $0 | $1,567 | $0.00 | 0% | $0 | $0 | $783 | $0.00 | 0% | $0 |
| $1,567 | $2,750 | $0.00 | 10% | $1,567 | $783 | $1,375 | $0.00 | 10% | $783 |
| $2,750 | $6,083 | $118.30 | 12% | $2,750 | $1,375 | $3,042 | $59.20 | 12% | $1,375 |
| $6,083 | $8,763 | $518.26 | 22% | $6,083 | $3,042 | $4,381 | $259.24 | 22% | $3,042 |
| $8,763 | $15,308 | $1,107.86 | 24% | $8,763 | $4,381 | $7,654 | $553.82 | 24% | $4,381 |
| $15,308 | $19,017 | $2,678.66 | 32% | $15,308 | $7,654 | $9,508 | $1,339.34 | 32% | $7,654 |
| $19,017 | $45,200 | $3,865.54 | 35% | $19,017 | $9,508 | $22,600 | $1,932.62 | 35% | $9,508 |
| $45,200 | | $13,029.59 | 37% | $45,200 | $22,600 | | $6,514.82 | 37% | $22,600 |

# Chapter **Eleven**

# Retirement and Other Tax-Deferred Plans and Annuities

The rules concerning contributions to and distributions from qualified retirement and other tax-deferred plans and annuities are voluminous and often complex. Entire books are devoted to portions of the subject matter we discuss in this chapter. We begin with an explanation of what a tax-deferred plan is and what it is intended to accomplish. We discuss the rules pertaining to contributions to each type of plan and then close with a presentation of plan distribution rules and annuities.

### Learning Objectives

When you have completed this chapter, you should understand the following learning objectives (LO):

**LO 11-1** Discuss the basic tax and operational structure of tax-deferred plans and annuities.

**LO 11-2** Explain details about and contributions to employer-sponsored retirement plans.

**LO 11-3** Describe the tax rules related to contributions to individual-sponsored retirement plans.

**LO 11-4** Explain details about and contributions to tax-deferred nonretirement plans.

**LO 11-5** Apply the tax rules for distributions from tax-deferred plans and the tax treatment of those distributions.

**LO 11-6** Determine the tax treatment of annuity contracts.

## TAX-DEFERRED PLANS AND ANNUITIES: THE BASICS

**LO 11-1**

Assume that you have decided to save $100,000 for retirement. You go to the bank, open a savings account, and start to make monthly deposits. At the end of the year, the bank sends you a Form 1099-INT, and you must pay taxes on the interest you earned on your savings account. To pay the taxes, you withdraw some money from your savings account. Because you now do not have as much money in your savings account, you are not as close to your goal of saving $100,000 for retirement. Saving money for retirement is an important goal. You would think that the government would give you some incentives to help you save. It has.

As mentioned in other chapters, tax law is not designed solely to raise tax revenue. Sometimes Congress uses the tax law to encourage or discourage certain activities. For example, the deductibility of mortgage interest encourages home ownership, tax credits, or deductions for higher education expenses help individuals attend college, and tax penalties discourage illegal tax avoidance by taxpayers.

Congress believes that it is important for individuals to save for retirement, so it has enacted laws to encourage such activity. These laws allow taxpayers to establish various types of tax-deferred plans.[1] They permit a taxpayer to set aside money in a special account, invest that money, and defer paying taxes on the interest, dividends, or capital gains earned by the investments until the taxpayer withdraws money after retirement.

It is important to note that Congress has not said that taxpayers will *never* need to pay tax on the investment earnings—only that the day of reckoning (the day to pay the tax) can be put off until later. That is why these accounts are called *tax-deferred* accounts, not *tax-free* accounts.

Now that you have a better understanding of why tax-deferred accounts exist, let's take a brief look at how they work. Operationally, an eligible individual who wants to start a tax-deferred account opens an account with a trustee (such as a bank or brokerage firm). The trustee exists to ensure the tax rules are followed; after all, Congress is going to give taxpayers a tax break to support a specific purpose, so it wants to make sure the funds are used for that purpose.

All tax-deferred plans have an accumulation period and a distribution period. In the *accumulation period,* a donor contributes assets (usually cash) to the plan. Making a contribution to a tax-deferred plan is similar in concept to making a deposit in a savings account. Contributions are often made monthly or annually over as many as 30 or 40 years. The plan trustee invests the contributed assets. Investments may be CDs, stocks, bonds, or similar assets. Investment decisions may be made solely by the trustee, solely by the donor, or jointly. During the accumulation period, no taxes are due on the earnings from the plan's investments.

During the *distribution period,* the trustee distributes (pays) accumulated assets to the plan beneficiary (or for their benefit) to be used for the purpose for which the plan was established. A distribution from a retirement plan is conceptually similar to a withdrawal from a savings account. If the plan is a retirement plan, the assets are distributed to the beneficiaries during their retirement. If the plan is an education plan, the assets are distributed to pay education-related bills of the beneficiaries while they are in school. Distributions may be in a lump sum or may be spread out in payments over many years.

Plan contributions and distributions are subject to numerous tax rules. For example, contributions are generally limited in amount and timing. Distributions must be for specific purposes and are subject to rules pertaining to when they can be made and how they are taxed.

In this chapter, we cover the tax rules associated with contributions to and distributions from retirement plans, other tax-deferred or tax-advantaged plans, and annuities.

*Retirement plans* can be categorized into employer-sponsored plans (including plans for the self-employed) and individual-sponsored plans. *Employer-sponsored plans* encompass qualified pension and profit-sharing plans, 401(k) or 403(b) plans, Keogh plans, SEPs, and SIMPLE plans. An employer creates and administers these plans. In some cases, only the employer contributes to the plan; in other cases, both the employer and the employee make contributions. *Individual-sponsored retirement plans* are individual retirement accounts (IRAs), which include traditional IRAs and Roth IRAs. These plans are created and funded by the individual.

*Tax-deferred nonretirement plans* are also available for health-related or education expenses. The most common health plans are health savings accounts, discussed in Chapter 4. We cover Coverdell Education Savings Accounts (CESAs) and qualified tuition plans (also known as 529 plans) in this chapter.

Sometimes the taxability of distributions or the deductibility of contributions can be a source of confusion. A good rule of thumb to keep in mind when learning about retirement

---

[1] As you will see, most of these accounts are tax-deferred accounts in which taxability of benefits is postponed to a later date. However, some of these accounts receive different types of tax benefits and are sometimes called *tax-advantaged accounts.* For ease of exposition, we generically refer to all of these accounts as *tax-deferred accounts.*

# Buzzwords

*Annuity:* Series of payments made pursuant to a contract usually between an individual and an insurance company, brokerage firm, or bank. Payments are normally uniformly spaced (monthly, quarterly, or annually).

*Beneficiary:* Person(s) entitled to receive the benefits from a plan.

*Contributions:* Amounts deposited into the tax-deferred plan by the donor. Contributions may or may not be tax-deductible, depending on the plan. When making a contribution to the plan, the donor is said to have "funded" the plan.

*Distributions:* Amounts withdrawn from the tax-deferred plan. Distributions are made to, or for the benefit of, the beneficiary and must be made in accordance with applicable tax rules. Distributions may or may not be taxable, depending on the plan.

*Donor:* Person(s) or entity(ies) responsible for making contributions to a plan. The donor and the beneficiary can be, and often are, the same individual.

*Taxability of plan earnings:* Except in unusual circumstances, earnings derived from the investment of plan assets are not taxed in the year earned.

*Tax-deferred retirement plan:* Account held by a trustee to accumulate and invest assets to be distributed to a beneficiary during retirement.

*Tax-deferred plans for other purposes:* Account held by a trustee to accumulate and invest assets to pay for a specific purpose such as health care or education.

*Trustee:* Entity—often a bank, brokerage firm, or insurance company—legally responsible to ensure that a plan's contributions and distributions follow legal and tax rules.

and tax-deferred plans is that if the plan is funded with dollars that have *not* been taxed, the distributions will be fully taxed; if the plan is funded with already-taxed dollars, some or all of the distributions will not be taxed. This rule of thumb is not always true, but it is a good place to start.

In this chapter, we also discuss the tax rules pertaining to distributions from an *annuity,* which is a series of payments made pursuant to a contract. The contract is usually between an individual and an insurance company, a financial services company, or an employer. Annuities often arise in conjunction with the payout phase of a retirement plan. The primary tax issue associated with an annuity payment is how much of each payment is taxable.

Payments to a tax-advantaged retirement plan are often tax-deductible and are shown as a *for* AGI deduction on Form 1040, Schedule 1, line 20 (for an IRA) or line 16 (for Keogh, SEP, or SIMPLE plans). Deductible payments made by employers (with respect to pension plans and 401(k) plans) are reported on the employer's tax return. Distributions from retirement plans and annuities are usually taxable, at least in part, and are found on Form 1040, lines 4a/4b and 5a/5b.

**CONCEPT
CHECK 11-1—
LO 11-1**

1. Tax-deferred retirement accounts are essentially tax-free accounts. True or false?
2. The period in which accumulated assets are paid to plan beneficiaries is known as the _____ period.
3. A Keogh plan is an example of an individual-based retirement plan. True or false?
4. Two examples of employer-based retirement plans are _____ and _____.
5. Distributions from pension plans are taxable if the contributions were made using dollars that were not previously taxed. True or false?

# EMPLOYER-SPONSORED RETIREMENT PLANS
## LO 11-2

### Qualified Pension Plans

A *qualified pension plan* provides systematic and definite payments to employees and their beneficiaries after retirement. Individuals receive payments over a period of years, often for life. Most often, the payments are made monthly. The *retirement benefit* amount is determined using factors such as years of employee service and compensation received.[2] The amount of payment must be "definitely determinable" using actuarial assumptions in a manner not subject to employer discretion.[3]

A qualified pension plan must meet strict requirements including (1) not discriminating in favor of highly compensated employees, (2) forming and operating for the exclusive benefit of employees or their beneficiaries, (3) having certain vesting and funding requirements, and (4) having certain minimum participation standards.[4]

A qualified pension plan provides significant tax benefits to both employers and employees. The primary benefits follow:

- The employer gets an immediate deduction for contributions.[5]
- Employer contributions are not compensation to the employee.
- Earnings from investments held by the plan are not taxable when earned.[6]
- Plan assets or earnings are not taxable to employees until the amounts are distributed.[7]

Qualified pension plans may be noncontributory or contributory. In a noncontributory plan, only the employer (not the employee) contributes. In a contributory plan, the employee can choose to contribute beyond employer contributions. The employer can require employee contributions as long as the plan is nondiscriminatory toward highly paid individuals.

A pension plan can also be a qualified profit-sharing plan. Contributions are not required on an annual basis, and it does not matter whether the employer has positive income in a contribution year.[8] Profit-sharing plans must have a definite, predetermined formula for allocating plan contributions to participants and for establishing benefit payments. Note that the required formula applies to the allocation of those contributions once made, not to the amount of the contributions.

Qualified plans may be either a defined contribution plan or a defined benefit plan. *Defined contribution plans* establish the contribution but do not establish the amount of retirement benefits. These plans provide an individual account for each participant and pay benefits based on those accounts.[9] Thus, the amount of eventual retirement benefits is unknown. *Defined benefit plans* are those plans that are not defined contribution plans.[10] These defined benefit plans provide a stream of definitely determinable retirement benefits. Defined benefit plans are often deemed to be "less risky" to beneficiaries because, by design, they provide greater certainty as to the amount and timing of future benefits.

---

**TAX YOUR BRAIN**

Are qualified pension plans likely to be defined contribution or defined benefit plans? Which are qualified profit-sharing plans likely to be?

**ANSWER**

Pension plans are more likely to be defined benefit plans, and profit-sharing plans are more likely to be defined contribution plans. By their very nature, defined benefit plans require a more precisely defined stream of inputs (contributions) to enable them to provide a precisely defined stream of outputs (benefits). Contributions to profit-sharing plans are more variable, which makes it less likely there will be a "stream of definitely determinable benefits."

---

[2] An example is a pension plan that pays each retired employee an annual pension (payable on a monthly basis) equal to 2% of the employee's final salary for each year of service to the company. Thus, an employee who worked 30 years for the company would receive an annual pension equal to 60% of their final annual salary.

[3] IRC § 401(a)(25).

[4] IRC § 401(a).

[5] IRC § 404.

[6] IRC § 501(a).

[7] IRC § 402.

[8] IRC § 401(a)(27).

[9] IRC § 414(i).

[10] IRC § 414(j).

Normally a bank, insurance company, or financial services company administers a trust that receives the contributions made to pension or profit-sharing plans. One reason for the trust arrangement is that, in the event that the business has financial difficulties or declares bankruptcy, creditors cannot attach the assets set aside for the benefit of the employees. From a practical matter, few companies are in the business of running a pension plan.

To obtain and retain qualified status, a pension or profit-sharing plan must meet complex rules, including the following:

- Be for the exclusive benefit of the employees and their beneficiaries.[11]
- Not discriminate in favor of highly compensated employees—employees who either (a) own more than 5% of the corporation's stock in the current or prior year or (b) received more than $130,000 compensation in the previous year and were in the top 20% of employees based on compensation.[12]
- Have adequate coverage for rank-and-file employees. In general, the plan must benefit at least 70% of those employees who are not highly compensated.[13] A defined benefit plan must also meet certain minimum participation requirements.[14]
- Meet certain minimum vesting standards.[15] *Vesting* occurs when an employee obtains a nonforfeitable right to their benefits. Employee contributions must vest immediately. Employer contributions must fully vest after five years of service or must vest 20% in the third year of service and increase 20% per year thereafter until fully vested after seven years of service.

**TAX YOUR BRAIN**

Why would Congress require vesting rules for employer contributions?

**ANSWER**

It did so for at least two reasons. First, by design, pension plans provide benefits to participants during retirement. By requiring vesting, Congress ensured that participants will receive payments because the payments cannot go to others or back to the company. Second, qualified plans give employers an immediate tax deduction for contributions. With vesting, Congress has reasonable assurance that the employer deductions are valid in the long run.

Qualified plans must also meet certain limitations on contributions and benefits. Annual per employee additions to a defined contribution plan cannot exceed the lower of $58,000 or 100% of the employee's compensation.[16] Annual additions include employer contributions, employee contributions, and forfeitures (for employees leaving the company before full vesting).

Defined benefit plans have no restrictions on contributions. However, these plans are restricted to annual benefits to a participant equal to the lower of $230,000 or 100% of average compensation of the participant for the highest three years.[17]

For profit-sharing plans, employers can take a maximum annual deduction of 25% of compensation paid.[18]

---

[11] IRC § 401(a).

[12] IRC § 414(q). The 20% criterion is effective only if the taxpayer elects. The $130,000 amount is subject to annual inflation adjustment.

[13] IRC § 410(b).

[14] IRC § 401(a)(26).

[15] IRC § 411(a).

[16] IRC § 415(c)(1). The contribution limit is subject to annual inflation adjustment.

[17] IRC § 415(b)(1). The contribution limit is subject to annual inflation adjustment.

[18] IRC § 404(a)(3)(A).

## 401(k) Plans

An employer can provide a 401(k) plan (named after the IRC section from which it comes) in addition to, or in the place of, a qualified pension or profit-sharing plan. A 401(k) plan is a qualified profit-sharing plan under which an employee can choose to receive a specified portion of their wages directly in cash or can elect to have the employer pay the amount on the employee's behalf into a qualified trust for the benefit of the employee on retirement.[19] Trust payments are made with pretax dollars. A 403(b) plan (again named after the IRC section that created it) is equivalent to a 401(k) plan but is for employees of educational and certain tax-exempt organizations.

An employee may elect to defer up to $19,500 under a 401(k) plan.[20] Employees age 50 or over can defer an additional $6,500. Any excess contributions must either be returned to the employee by April 15 of the following year or be included in the employee's gross income.

---

**EXAMPLE 11-1**

Fouad earns $80,000 in taxable wages. His employer establishes a 401(k) plan in which he participates. Fouad elects to have 3% of his wages paid into the 401(k) plan. For the year, his employer withholds $2,400 ($80,000 × 3%) from his paychecks on a pretax basis and deposits the amount in trust on Fouad's behalf. As a result, Fouad's taxable wages for the year are $77,600 ($80,000 − $2,400).

---

A 401(k) plan must meet all of the qualification rules established for pension and profit-sharing plans. In addition, amounts held in the trust cannot be distributed except in the case of termination of the plan or the employee's (a) separation from service, death, or disability; (b) attainment of the age of 59½; or (c) hardship.[21] Hardship distributions are permitted if the employee has an "immediate heavy financial need" that can be met with the distribution and that cannot be relieved by alternative sources such as loans or insurance.[22] Additional nondiscrimination rules apply to 401(k) plans as enumerated in IRC § 401(k)(3).

## Keogh Plans

Self-employed individuals are not employees, so they cannot participate in a qualified pension or profit-sharing plan established by an employer. However, they can establish an individual Keogh plan, which is subject to the same contribution and benefit limitations as pension or profit-sharing plans. For defined contribution Keogh plans, self-employed individuals can contribute the lower of $58,000 or 25% of earned income from self-employment.[23] For purposes of the calculation, earned income cannot exceed $290,000.[24] Earned income from self-employment is determined after the deduction for one-half of the self-employment taxes paid and after the amount of the Keogh contribution.

---

**EXAMPLE 11-2**

Ahmed is a self-employed architect. In 2021 his earnings, before the Keogh deduction but after deduction for one-half the self-employment tax, are $60,000. His Keogh deduction for purposes of the 25% calculation is

$$\$60,000 - 0.25X = X$$

$$\text{Thus, } X = \$48,000$$

where $X$ is the amount of self-employment income after the Keogh deduction.

Ahmed is entitled to contribute the lower of $58,000 or $12,000 (25% of $48,000). Thus, his maximum Keogh contribution is $12,000.

---

[19] IRC § 401(k)(2).

[20] IRC § 402(g)(1). The contribution limit is subject to annual inflation adjustment.

[21] IRC Section 401(k)(2)(B)(i).

[22] Reg. Section 1.401(k)-1(d)(2).

[23] IRC § 415(c). The contribution limit is subject to annual inflation adjustment.

[24] IRC § 404(l). The earned income limit is subject to annual inflation adjustment.

Defined benefit Keogh plans are subject to the $230,000/100% benefit limitations given previously for qualified defined benefit plans. Keogh plans must be established by the end of the tax year (once established, the plan continues from year to year). Contributions are required no later than the due date of the return, including extensions.[25]

If a self-employed individual has employees, the Keogh plan must also cover full-time employees under the same nondiscrimination, vesting, and other rules established for qualified plans. Contributions for these employees are deductible by the self-employed individual on Schedule C.

## Simplified Employee Pensions

Qualified pension and profit-sharing plans are complex and can be difficult to establish and administer. Small businesses can establish a *simplified employee pension* (SEP).[26] With a SEP, an employer contributes to IRA accounts of its employees, up to a specified maximum contribution. SEPs must conform to the following rules:

- All employees who have reached the age of 21, who have worked for the employer for at least three of the preceding five years, and who received at least $650 in compensation must be covered.[27]
- Contributions cannot discriminate in favor of highly compensated employees.
- Annual deductible contributions cannot exceed the lower of 25% of the employee's compensation (with a maximum of $290,000) or the $58,000 limitation for defined contribution plans.[28]
- The employer cannot restrict the employee's withdrawals.[29]

Initial SEP adoption must be effective no later than the due date of the employer's return, including extensions. Most small employers adopt a SEP by using Form 5305-SEP. Contributions to the SEP are required no later than the due date of the return of the employer, including extensions.

Self-employed individuals can create and contribute to a SEP. Contribution limits are determined in the same manner as for Keogh plans.

## SIMPLE Plans

Employers with 100 or fewer employees who do not have a qualified pension or profit-sharing plan can establish a *SIMPLE retirement plan* for their employees.[30] Under a SIMPLE plan, the employer creates an IRA or a 401(k) account for each employee. Eligible employees are those who earned at least $5,000 during any two preceding years and who are reasonably expected to earn at least $5,000 in the current year. Employees are not required to contribute. SIMPLE plans are not subject to the nondiscrimination rules that apply to other qualified plans. Thus, there is no requirement that a certain number or percentage of employees must participate in the SIMPLE plan.

Employees can elect to contribute an employer-specified percentage (or dollar amount if the employer agrees) of their pretax wages with a maximum annual contribution of $13,500.[31] Employees age 50 or older can elect to make additional contributions of up to $3,000 (for a maximum of $16,500 per year).

---

[25] IRC § 404(a)(6).

[26] IRC § 408(k).

[27] IRC § 408(k)(2). The $650 compensation amount is subject to annual inflation adjustment.

[28] Both dollar amounts are subject to annual inflation adjustment.

[29] IRC § 408(k)(4)(B).

[30] IRC § 408(p).

[31] IRC § 408(p)(2)(A)(ii). The maximum contribution is subject to annual inflation adjustment.

# From Shoebox to Software

Contributions to qualified plans, Keogh plans, SEPs, and SIMPLE plans are deductible as a *for* AGI deduction to the extent contributed by the individual. The portion contributed by the employer is not deductible (remember that the employer contribution is not taxable to the employee in the first place).

In tax software, employee contributions to these plans are generally reported on a worksheet. You enter the amount of the deductible contribution in the appropriate box, and that amount carries forward to Form 1040, Schedule 1, line 16.

The plan's trustee will report for an individual covered by a SEP or SIMPLE plan the amount of employee contribution in box 8 or 9 of Form 5498 (see Exhibit 11-1).

The trustees of qualified pension plans report employee contributions to employees on a similar form.

Employers either must make a matching contribution of up to 3% (in most instances) of the employee's compensation or must make a nonelective contribution of 2% of compensation for each employee eligible to participate (whether or not the employee actually participates). Contributions to a SIMPLE plan fully and immediately vest to the employee.

| EXAMPLE 11-3 | Acme Corporation established a SIMPLE plan for its 10 eligible employees, each of whom earned more than $5,000 in the current and prior years. Seven employees elect to contribute 5% of their pretax wages, while the other three decline to participate. Acme can choose to make either matching contributions of 3% of wages for the seven employees who elected to participate or a contribution of 2% of wages for all 10 employees. |
|---|---|

## EXHIBIT 11-1

☐ **CORRECTED (if checked)**

| TRUSTEE'S or ISSUER'S name, street address, city or town, state or province, country, and ZIP or foreign postal code | **1** IRA contributions (other than amounts in boxes 2–4, 8–10, 13a, and 14a) $ | OMB No. 1545-0747 2021 Form **5498** | **IRA Contribution Information** |
|---|---|---|---|
| | **2** Rollover contributions $ | | |
| | **3** Roth IRA conversion amount $ | **4** Recharacterized contributions $ | **Copy B** |
| TRUSTEE'S or ISSUER'S TIN \| PARTICIPANT'S TIN | **5** FMV of account $ | **6** Life insurance cost included in box 1 $ | **For Participant** |
| PARTICIPANT'S name | **7** IRA ☐  SEP ☐  SIMPLE ☐  Roth IRA ☐ | | This information is being furnished to the IRS. |
| | **8** SEP contributions $ | **9** SIMPLE contributions $ | |
| Street address (including apt. no.) | **10** Roth IRA contributions $ | **11** If checked, required minimum distribution for 2022 ☐ | |
| | **12a** RMD date | **12b** RMD amount $ | |
| City or town, state or province, country, and ZIP or foreign postal code | **13a** Postponed/late contrib. $ | **13b** Year \| **13c** Code | |
| | **14a** Repayments $ | **14b** Code | |
| Account number (see instructions) | **15a** FMV of certain specified assets $ | **15b** Code(s) | |

Form **5498**          (keep for your records)          www.irs.gov/Form5498          Department of the Treasury - Internal Revenue Service

Source: U.S. Department of the Treasury, Internal Revenue Service, Form 5498. Washington, DC: 2021.

Employers establish a SIMPLE plan using Form 5305-S or 5305-SA. The employer retains the form and does not file it with the IRS. Employers must initially adopt the plan between January 1 and October 1. The employer must make contributions no later than the due date of the employer's return, including extensions.

---

**CONCEPT CHECK 11-2— LO 11-2**

1. Qualified pension plans are either defined _____ plans or defined _____ plans.
2. Employees must make contributions to qualified pension plans. True or false?
3. The maximum contribution to a 401(k) plan is _____ for individuals under age 50.
4. A Keogh plan can be used by self-employed individuals. True or false?
5. A SIMPLE plan can be used by employers with 100 or fewer employees who also meet other requirements. True or false?

# INDIVIDUAL-SPONSORED RETIREMENT PLANS
## LO 11-3

Individual-sponsored retirement plans are individual retirement accounts (IRAs). There are two types: a traditional IRA and a Roth IRA. Although the accounts sound similar, they have significant differences.

### Traditional IRA

A traditional IRA is a tax-deferred retirement account for individuals with earned income (employees and self-employed individuals). Qualified individuals can make IRA contributions and take a *for* AGI deduction equal to the lower of $6,000 or the amount of compensation for the year.[32] Individuals who are age 50 or older as of the end of the tax year can contribute the lower of $7,000 or the amount of annual compensation. Earnings on invested contributions grow tax-deferred until distribution.

A qualified individual is someone who is not an active participant and whose spouse is not an active participant in an employer-sponsored retirement plan (qualified pension or profit-sharing plan, Keogh, 401(k), SEP, SIMPLE). Even if an individual (or spouse) is an active participant, they can make a deductible IRA contribution if their AGI is below certain limits. The allowed IRA deduction begins to be phased out for active participants when AGI exceeds certain amounts, depending on the filing status of the taxpayer.[33] For joint filers, the amount is $105,000, for single or head of household filers the amount is $66,000, and for married filing separately the amount is zero.[34]

Once AGI reaches the indicated amounts, the taxpayer can use the following formula to determine the disallowed portion of the IRA deduction:

$$\frac{\text{AGI} - \text{Applicable limit}}{\$10,000 \text{ or } \$20,000} \times \$6,000 = \text{Disallowed deduction}$$

The denominator of the fraction is $10,000 for taxpayers filing as single or head of household and $20,000 for married filing jointly. For taxpayers over 50 years old, the $6,000 figure is $7,000.

[32] IRC § 219(b)(1).

[33] IRC § 219(g)(3)(B).

[34] These amounts increase each year in accordance with an IRC schedule.

**EXAMPLE 11-4**

Teresa, age 31, is single and reported AGI of $68,400 in tax year 2021. She is an active participant in her employer's pension plan. Her disallowed deduction is $1,440 ([$68,400 − $66,000]/$10,000 × $6,000). Thus, she would be entitled to make a deductible IRA contribution of $4,560 ($6,000 − $1,440). If Teresa's AGI exceeded $75,000, her deductible contribution would be zero. If her employer did not have a pension plan, her deductible contribution would be $6,000.

Special rules apply to married taxpayers. If both spouses are employed and neither is covered by an employer plan, each spouse can make a deductible contribution to separate IRA accounts, subject to the lower of $6,000 or earned income limits.

**EXAMPLE 11-5**

Earl and Amanda are both under age 50 and file a joint return. Neither is covered under an employer plan. Each of them contributed equally to their AGI of $125,000. Both Earl and Amanda are entitled to make a deductible $6,000 contribution to an IRA (total of $12,000). Note that the AGI limitations do not apply because neither spouse was covered under an employer plan.

If only one spouse is employed, and that spouse is not covered under an employer plan (or their AGI is less than the phaseout limitation), the working spouse and the nonworking spouse may *each* make a deductible $6,000 contribution toward an IRA. This result is also true if the "nonworking" spouse earned less than $6,000 as long as the couple's *combined* earned income is at least $12,000. This is an exception to the general rule that contributions are permitted only when the taxpayer has earned income.

If one spouse is covered under an employer-sponsored plan but the other spouse is not covered, the noncovered spouse may contribute up to $6,000 toward a deductible IRA.[35] The deduction is phased out for joint AGI between $198,000 and $208,000.

Taxpayers who are not eligible to make a deductible contribution to an IRA because they are an active participant in an employer plan and earn too much can make a designated *nondeductible IRA* contribution.[36] The contribution is limited to the lower of $6,000 or 100% of compensation ($7,000 for those age 50 or over) but must be reduced by the amount of any deductible contribution allowed.[37] Even though the contribution may be nondeductible, the earnings of the IRA will grow tax-deferred until withdrawn.

**EXAMPLE 11-6**

Aalyiah is 45 years old and an active participant in an employer plan. Because of AGI limitations, her deductible IRA contribution is limited to $1,200. She can also make a nondeductible IRA contribution of up to $4,800. If Aalyiah's AGI were high enough that she was ineligible to make any *deductible* contribution, she would be permitted a $6,000 *nondeductible* contribution.

The IRA trust account must be established and contributions, both deductible and nondeductible, must be made no later than the due date of the taxpayer's income tax return, not including extensions (April 15 for most taxpayers). Contributions made after January 1 and before April 15 may be treated as a deduction in the prior year. No form or statement is filed with the tax return for the year the traditional IRA is established.

Beginning January 1, 2020, contributions are permitted to an IRA (deductible or nondeductible) at any age as long as the taxpayer has sufficient earned income. Prior to 2020, deductible contributions were *not* permitted once a taxpayer reached age 70½. Taxpayers can make deductible and nondeductible contributions to the same IRA, although determining the taxability of distributions becomes problematic.

Contributions in excess of the amount allowable are subject to a 6% excise tax,[38] which is reported on Form 5329.

[35] IRC § 219(g)(7).

[36] IRC § 408(o).

[37] Thus, for those under age 50, a maximum contribution of $6,000 can be made, whether deductible or not deductible.

[38] Section 4973(a).

## Roth IRA

With a traditional IRA, contributions are deductible (assuming eligibility requirements are met), the account grows tax-deferred, and distributions are fully taxable. With a Roth IRA, contributions are not deductible, the account grows tax-free, and distributions are not taxable. In effect, when choosing between traditional and Roth IRAs, taxpayers are trading the nondeductibility of contributions for the nontaxability of distributions.

A *Roth IRA* is an IRA designated as a Roth when it is established.[39] Taxpayers can make nondeductible contributions to a Roth IRA in an amount equal to the lower of $6,000 or 100% of compensation, reduced by the amount of contributions for the year to other IRAs (not including SEP or SIMPLE plans).[40] Taxpayers who are age 50 or over at the end of the year are permitted a contribution of $7,000 or 100% of compensation. Permitted contributions are phased out ratably starting when AGI reaches $198,000 for joint returns, $125,000 for those filing single or head of household, and $0 for married filing separately.[41] The phaseout range is $15,000 for single and head of household and $10,000 for joint filers. The formulas to determine the disallowed contribution in the phaseout range follow.

Use this formula for joint returns:

$$\frac{\text{AGI} - \text{Applicable limit}}{\$10,000} \times \$6,000 = \text{Disallowed contribution}$$

Use this formula for single or head of household returns:

$$\frac{\text{AGI} - \text{Applicable limit}}{\$15,000} \times \$6,000 = \text{Disallowed contribution}$$

For taxpayers age 50 or older, the $6,000 figure is $7,000.

AGI limits do not include any income resulting from the conversion of a traditional IRA to a Roth IRA.

Roth IRAs, like traditional ones, are established with a trustee and must be established and funded no later than the due date of the return for the contribution year, not including extensions.[42] Taxpayers use Form 5305-R (or -RA or -RB) to set up the account. This form is not filed with the taxpayer's return. Contributions to a Roth IRA are permitted at any age subject to normal funding rules.

Excess contributions to a Roth IRA are subject to a 6% excise tax under the rules applicable to a traditional IRA.

Roth 401(k) plans are permitted. A Roth 401(k) has the funding characteristics of a 401(k) (can defer up to $19,500 or $26,000 if age 50 or over) and the tax characteristics of a Roth IRA (contributions are not deductible and distributions are not taxable).

---

**CONCEPT CHECK 11-3—**
**LO 11-3**

1. Two types of individual-sponsored retirement plans are _____ and _____.
2. A single individual, age 58, with wages of $30,000 can make a tax-deductible contribution of up to $_____ to a traditional IRA.
3. A married couple with earned income of $200,000 is ineligible to make a deductible contribution to a traditional IRA. True or false?
4. Distributions from a Roth IRA generally are not taxable. True or false?

---

[39] IRC § 408A(b).
[40] IRC § 408A(c)(2)(B), (f)(2).
[41] IRC § 408A(c)(3).
[42] IRC § 408A(c)(7), § 219(f)(3).

## From Shoebox to Software

Qualified individuals can make deductible contributions to a traditional IRA. Trustees report contributions on Form 5498 (see Exhibit 11-1).

In your software, you generally enter information concerning IRA contributions on a worksheet or directly on Form 5498. If the requirements to make a deductible contribution are met, the amount in box 1 of Form 5498 is entered as a contribution at the top of the form. It is important to realize that the amount in box 1 is only the amount *contributed*—the trustee makes no determination as to whether the amount is deductible. It is the responsibility of the taxpayer or preparer to report the proper deduction.

Information from the worksheet is carried forward to Form 1040, Schedule 1, line 20.

If you open the tax return file for Jose and Maria Ramirez and then open the IRA summary sheet, you will see that the maximum allowable IRA contribution for Jose is zero. This is so because he was covered by a retirement plan at work and he earned in excess of the income limitation.

Contributions to a Roth IRA are in box 10 of Form 5498. You record this amount in the appropriate place on the IRA worksheet or the form.

# TAX-DEFERRED NONRETIREMENT PLANS
## LO 11-4

The two major types of tax-deferred nonretirement plans are health-related plans and education-related plans. In Chapter 4 we discussed health savings accounts. Here we describe the Coverdell Education Savings Account and the qualified tuition plan (also known as a 529 plan).

### Coverdell Education Savings Account

Taxpayers who meet AGI limitations can contribute to a Coverdell Education Savings Account (CESA) exclusively to pay the qualified elementary, secondary, or higher education expenses of the beneficiary.[43] CESAs are similar to Roth IRAs in that contributions are not deductible, earnings accumulate tax-free, and distributions are not taxable (if used for their intended purpose).

Contributions are limited to $2,000 per year per beneficiary, must be in cash, and must be made before the beneficiary turns 18.[44]

Subject to limitations as to the amount, any person can contribute to a CESA for any person (themselves included). The contributor is not required to report a certain amount of earned income, nor must the contributor be related to the beneficiary. A contributor (or contributors) can establish multiple CESAs for multiple beneficiaries, and an individual can be the beneficiary of multiple CESAs. However, for any given tax year, the aggregate contributions to all CESAs for a specific individual beneficiary cannot exceed $2,000.

**EXAMPLE 11-7**

Roger and Shelly have one child, Caroline. They established a CESA for Caroline. Shelly's parents can establish a separate CESA for Caroline or can contribute to the CESA already established. The total permitted contributions to all CESAs for which Caroline is the beneficiary cannot exceed $2,000. Thus, if Caroline's parents contribute $1,500 to her CESA, the grandparents can contribute a maximum of $500.

Permitted contributions begin to phase out ratably when the contributor's AGI reaches $190,000 for joint returns or $95,000 for single and head of household returns.[45] When AGI exceeds $220,000 for married taxpayers or $110,000 for single or head of household taxpayers,

---

[43] IRC § 530(b)(1).

[44] IRC § 530(b)(1)(A).

[45] AGI is increased by foreign income excluded from AGI under IRC §§ 911, 931, and 933.

no CESA contribution is allowed. The formulas to determine the disallowed contribution in the phaseout range are as follows.

Use this formula for joint returns:

$$\frac{\text{AGI} - \text{Applicable limit}}{\$30,000} \times \$2,000 = \text{Disallowed contribution}$$

Use this formula for single or head of household returns:

$$\frac{\text{AGI} - \text{Applicable limit}}{\$15,000} \times \$2,000 = \text{Disallowed contribution}$$

---

**EXAMPLE 11-8**

Vance and Martha file a joint return showing AGI of $196,300. Their disallowed CESA contribution is $420 ([$196,300 − $190,000]/[$30,000 × $2,000]), so their permitted contribution is $1,580 ($2,000 − $420). If their AGI was more than $220,000, Vance and Martha would not be permitted to make a CESA contribution.

---

Taxpayers establish the trust using a Form 5305-E or 5305-EA. As with the Roth IRA, the form is not filed with the taxpayer's return but is retained in the tax files. The trustee must be a bank or other entity or person who will administer the account properly.[46]

You can find additional information about CESAs in Chapter 7 of IRS Publication 970, "Tax Benefits for Education."

## Qualified Tuition Plans

A qualified tuition plan (QTP) is a state-based savings plan designed to encourage saving for future education costs. A QTP is also known as a 529 plan, named from the IRS Code Section that governs these plans.[47] A QTP is, in effect, a tax-free savings account if the proceeds are used exclusively for qualified education expenses.[48]

A QTP can be established by anyone for a designated beneficiary, such as a child, grandchild, spouse, or even the taxpayer. There is no limit on the number of QTP plans an individual can set up or the number of individuals who can contribute to a QTP. The plan belongs to the person who establishes the account, and this individual is known as the plan holder.

Taxpayers contribute to a QTP offered by a state. While a taxpayer can contribute to a state QTP in any state, there may be state-based deductions or credits that may make it beneficial for taxpayers to contribute to the state in which they live. No federal deduction is permitted for QTP contributions. Depending on the state, a deduction may be permitted on a state tax return. Contributions cannot exceed the amount necessary to provide for the qualified education expenses of the beneficiary.

Contributions are invested in various permitted investments, which will vary from state to state. Earnings grow tax-free.

Withdrawals are not taxable if the proceeds are used for qualified educational expenses of the beneficiary at a qualified educational institution. Qualified expenses include tuition and mandatory fees; required books, supplies, and equipment; computers and software; and room and board (if the student is attending at least half-time).[49] The cost for room and board cannot exceed the greater of (a) the actual amount charged the student for school-owned or operated housing or (b) the allowance for room and board in the "cost of attendance" figures provided by the school.

[46] IRC § 530(b)(1)(B).
[47] IRC § 529(b)(1)(A)(ii).
[48] IRC § 529(c)(1).
[49] IRC § 529(e)(3).

Some expenses do not qualify. These include student health insurance, transportation costs, elective activities such as sports and clubs, entertainment costs, and student loan repayments.

A qualified educational institution is a post-secondary institution eligible to participate in a student aid program administered by the U.S. Department of Education.[50] This includes virtually all post-secondary institutions in the United States. A beneficiary can be taking classes as an undergraduate or graduate student and can be attending full or part time (note that room and board is a qualified expense only if the beneficiary is at least a half-time student).

The 2017 Tax Act expanded QTP rules to allow a tax-free distribution of up to $10,000 per year, per beneficiary, to pay tuition expenses (only) at K–12 public, private, or religious schools.[51]

Distributions from the QTP can be made directly to the account holder, the beneficiary, or the school. Distributions are reported on Form 1099-Q (see Exhibit 11-2).

If the distribution in box 1 has been used for qualified educational expenses at a qualified educational institution or used to pay up to $10,000 of tuition at a K–12 school, none of the distribution is taxable and it does not need to be reported.[52]

If withdrawals are used for nonqualified purposes, the earnings will be subject to taxes and penalties. Nonqualified withdrawals are subject to tax on the earnings plus a penalty of 10% of the nonqualified withdrawal.[53] The penalty is waived if the beneficiary receives a tax-free scholarship or attends a U.S. military academy, or dies, or becomes disabled. If some or all of the distribution was used for a nonqualified expense, see IRS Publication 970 for details on how to report income in such case.

A QTP can be rolled over into the QTP of another family member.[54] A family member is defined broadly and includes son, daughter, brother, sister, grandparent, niece, nephew, aunt, uncle, in-law, and others noted in IRS Publication 970.

---

**EXAMPLE 11-9**    Mario and Ellen Kelly have two children, Enya and Ian. Each child is the beneficiary of a QTP with a balance of $20,000 each. Total withdrawals from Ian's QTP were $15,000. The remaining $5,000 can be rolled into the QTP of Enya or into a new or existing QTP for any other family member.

---

**EXHIBIT 11-2**

Source: U.S. Department of the Treasury, Internal Revenue Service, Form 1099-Q. Washington, DC: 2021.

[50] IRC § 529(e)(5).
[51] IRC § 529(c)(7).
[52] IRC § 529(c)(1).
[53] IRC § 529(c)(6), § 530(d)(4).
[54] IRC § 529(c)(3)(C)(i).

Qualified education expenses must be reduced by the amount of any tax-free tuition scholarship.

---

**EXAMPLE 11-10**    Basha is a full-time student at State University. Her tuition and fees were $7,000 and room and board was $6,000. She also received a $2,000 tax-free scholarship. Her qualified education expenses were $11,000 ($7,000 + $6,000 − $2,000).

---

Individuals can contribute to both a QTP and a Coverdell Education Savings Account in the same year for the same beneficiary.[55] The same is true for expenses used to claim an American Opportunity Credit or a Lifetime Learning Credit.[56] So, a taxpayer could take a QTP distribution to pay for room and board, use non-QTP funds to pay tuition, and take a tuition and fees deduction for the tuition expense or one of the two credits.

Some colleges and universities offer a prepaid tuition plan, which is a different type of QTP. These plans allow plan holders to prepay for one or more semesters at a specific college or university at current tuition prices or to purchase tuition credits.[57] These plans are less flexible, and less popular, than QTP savings plans.

You can find additional information about Qualified Tuition Plans in Chapter 8 of IRS Publication 970.

---

**CONCEPT CHECK 11-4— LO 11-4**

1. Contributions to Coverdell Education Savings Accounts (CESAs) are not deductible. True or false?
2. The maximum annual contribution to a CESA is $_____.
3. Contributions to CESA accounts begin to be phased out when AGI reaches $_____ for a single taxpayer.
4. Distributions from a Qualified Tuition Plan can be used for a computer used by the beneficiary student. True or False?

# DISTRIBUTIONS FROM TAX-DEFERRED PENSION PLANS
## LO 11-5

### General

All pension plans have an accumulation period when contributions are received and invested and a distribution period when assets are paid to owners or beneficiaries. Individuals with pension plan assets normally withdraw those assets during their retirement. The payments received during retirement are *distributions* or *withdrawals.*

Recall that a defined benefit plan provides a retiree certain specified distributions over a specified period or for life. Normally retirees receive fixed distributions (often with inflation adjustments) on a regular basis (such as monthly or quarterly). Many large corporations and unions have defined benefit plans. Retirees do not have an ownership interest in any portion of the plan assets; they are simply entitled to a stream of payments (called an *annuity*).

The second category of pension plans is a defined contribution plan. These plans accumulate assets from contributions and earnings that belong to a specific individual but that are not predetermined as to the value upon retirement. An IRA is an example of a defined contribution plan. While the retiree worked, they contributed to the IRA and invested those contributions. The IRA assets belong to the retiree, but there is no guarantee as to either their value at retirement or the date the assets will be exhausted once withdrawals commence. Because assets in defined contribution plans belong to the retiree, they usually can specify the amount and timing of plan withdrawals.

[55] IRC § 529(c)(3)(B)(vi).
[56] IRC § 529(c)(3)(B)(v).
[57] IRC §529(b)(1)(A)(i).

To reduce the chance of living beyond the point that their pension plan assets are exhausted, beneficiaries of defined contribution plans sometimes choose to buy an annuity contract using some or all of the plan assets. In doing so, the beneficiary is trading a lump sum for a stream of payments. Effectively, the beneficiary becomes a participant in a defined benefit plan to the extent of the annuity.

You can find additional information pertaining to distributions from tax-deferred pension plans in IRS Publication 575, *Pension and Annuity Income*.

## Distributions from Qualified Pension Plans

A distribution from a qualified pension plan (pension and profit-sharing plan, Keogh, 401(k), 403(b), IRA, SEP, SIMPLE) may be fully taxable, nontaxable, or a combination of both. Generally proceeds are tax-free if they are attributable to contributions made with taxed dollars (a nondeductible contribution), and proceeds are taxable if they are attributable to contributions made with untaxed dollars (a deduction was allowed or income was excluded) or if they are attributable to tax-deferred earnings. The annuity provisions govern taxability of distributions from qualified employer retirement plans.[58]

To apply the simplified method of taxing payments from a qualified plan, the taxpayer must first determine the amount that they contributed to the plan with previously taxed dollars. The previously taxed investment is divided by the number of anticipated future payments (see the following table). The resulting fraction represents the proportion of each payment that will be tax-free. The remainder of the annuity payment is taxable as ordinary income. If the employee contributed nothing to the plan, or if employee contributions were made entirely with untaxed dollars, the entire payment is taxable.

If the annuity is payable over the life of a single individual, the number of anticipated payments is determined as of the starting date of the payments as follows:

| Age of the Individual | Number of Anticipated Monthly Payments |
|---|---|
| 55 or under | 360 |
| 56–60 | 310 |
| 61–65 | 260 |
| 66–70 | 210 |
| 71 or over | 160[59] |

If the annuity is payable over the life of more than one individual (the lives of a retiree and their spouse), the number of anticipated payments is determined as of the starting date of the payments as follows:

| Combined Ages of the Individuals | Number of Anticipated Monthly Payments |
|---|---|
| 110 or under | 410 |
| 111–120 | 360 |
| 121–130 | 310 |
| 131–140 | 260 |
| 141 or over | 210[60] |

**EXAMPLE 11-11**

Jungwoo is entitled to monthly payments of $2,000 over his life from his employer's qualified pension plan. He contributed $97,500 to the plan with previously taxed dollars prior to his retirement at age 64. Jungwoo would be able to exclude $375 ($97,500/260) from each payment as a nontaxable return of his contributions. The remaining $1,625 would be taxable at ordinary income rates.

---

[58] Specifically, the simplified rules under IRC § 72(d).

[59] IRC § 72(d)(1)(B)(iii).

[60] IRC § 72(d)(1)(B)(iv).

**EXAMPLE 11-12**     Instead of taking $2,000 a month over his life, Jungwoo chose to receive monthly payments of $1,800 a month over his life and that of his 62-year-old wife, Seo-yeon. The combined ages of Jungwoo and Seo-yeon are 126. Thus, Jungwoo would be permitted to exclude $314.52 ($97,500/310) from each payment, with the remaining $1,485.48 being taxable.

    The anticipated payment tables assume monthly payments. If payments are received other than monthly, appropriate adjustments are made. For example, the number of anticipated monthly payments for an individual age 55 or under is 360. If the actual payments are made quarterly, the number of anticipated quarterly payments will be 120 (360/12 = 30 years × 4 quarters per year). This would be the number used in the denominator to determine the exclusion amount.

    Retirement plans (other than Roth IRAs) must make required distributions.[61] For many plans (especially qualified pension and profit-sharing plans), the plan administrator determines the required distribution rules. Such determination is not a concern to the recipient. However, especially in the case of a traditional IRA, the taxpayer may be required to make the appropriate required minimum distribution calculations.

    Generally, distributions from a retirement plan can be taken without penalty once the owner (the person who made the contributions) reaches age 59½. However, it is usually good tax planning to defer withdrawals for as long as practical so that the account balance can continue to grow tax-deferred. Tax deferral cannot continue indefinitely—the tax code mandates certain minimum withdrawals. A minimum withdrawal is called a required minimum distribution (RMD).

    If the plan owner reaches age 70½ before January 1, 2020, then the first RMD must occur no later than April 1 of the following year. Thus, for example, someone reaching age 70½ on November 8, 2019, must make their first RMD no later than April 1, 2020.

    However, if the plan owner has not reached age 70½ before January 1, 2020, then the applicable age is 72. In this case, the first RMD must be made no later than April 1 of the year after the plan owner reaches age 72. Subsequent RMDs must occur no later than December 31 of each year.

    As a result of the passage of the CARES Act, all RMDs are waived for calendar year 2020 for IRAs and certain defined contribution plans. Taxpayers are permitted to take a distribution, but for 2020 only, they are not required to do so.

    The RMD for a year is equal to the account balance at the end of the prior year divided by the minimum distribution period. The minimum distribution period is determined in accordance with life expectancy tables provided by the IRS in Publication 590. Some of these tables are provided in the Appendix to this chapter. Table III is the one used by owners of the retirement plan who either are unmarried or whose spouse is not more than 10 years younger. Table I is used by the beneficiary of a retirement plan after the original owner has died. Table II (not provided but available in Publication 590) is used by owners whose spouse is more than 10 years younger. When referring to the tables, the age used is the age of the taxpayer as of the end of the year for which the distribution is calculated.

**EXAMPLE 11-13**     Arlene is age 77 and must determine her required minimum distribution for tax year 2021. She would use the balance in her retirement account as of the end of 2020 and would refer to the proper life expectancy table using her age as of the end of 2021.

**EXAMPLE 11-14**     Mort is unmarried and has been receiving distributions from his retirement plan. He must determine his required minimum distribution for 2021. He is age 76 at the end of 2021. At the end of 2020, his plan had a balance of $110,000. Using Table III, his life expectancy is 22.0 years. Mort must receive at least $5,000 ($110,000/22.0) from his retirement plan in 2021. If Mort were married and the age difference between Mort and his spouse was 10 years or less, the answer to this question would be the same. If the age difference were more than 10 years, Mort would need to use Table II in IRS Publication 590 to determine the appropriate life expectancy.

---

[61] IRC § 401(a)(9).

If a plan owner reaches age 70½ or 72, as appropriate, and they have have not received any distributions from the plan, there are special rules associated with determining and distributing the very first payment.

Plans can distribute each employee's interest either (1) in a lump sum on the required *beginning date* or (2) in payments starting on the required beginning date, over the life expectancy of the employee or of the employee and a designated beneficiary. The required beginning date is April 1 of the calendar year following the year in which the taxpayer reaches age 70½ or 72.[62]

Note that the first distribution is calculated for the tax year in which the taxpayer reaches age 70½ or 72. However, that first distribution does not need to be made until April 1 of the tax year after the taxpayer reaches age 70½ or 72.

---

**EXAMPLE 11-15**

Taxpayer A's 70th birthday was February 1, 2019, so the taxpayer reaches age 70½ on August 1, 2019. The distribution calculated for 2019 must be distributed to the taxpayer no later than April 1, 2020. Taxpayer B's 70th birthday was November 1, 2019, so the taxpayer has not reached age 70 1/2 by January 1, 2020. Thus, taxpayer B falls under the rules pertaining to age 72. Taxpayer B will reach age 72 on November 1, 2021. The first distribution must occur no later than April 1, 2022.

---

**EXAMPLE 11-16**

Mort is unmarried. His 70th birthday was March 1, 2019. Thus, he reached age 70½ on September 1, 2019, and his required beginning date is April 1, 2020. At the end of 2018, the balance in his retirement plan was $300,000. He needs to calculate his tax year 2019 required minimum distribution (2019 is the year he turned 70½). At the end of 2019 he will be 70 years old. Using Table III, the life expectancy to use in the calculations is 27.4 years. Thus, he must receive at least $10,949 ($300,000/27.4) from his retirement plan no later than April 1, 2020.

---

**EXAMPLE 11-17**

Jamal's 72nd birthday was August 10, 2021. Thus, his first distribution must occur no later than April 1, 2022. The first distribution pertains to calendar year 2021 (the year he turned age 72) and it can be made anytime in the August 10, 2021 to April 1, 2022, period. To calculate the minimum RMD, he will use his account balance at the end of 2020 which is the account balance at the end of the prior year. His December 31, 2020, account balance was $612,608. Using Table III, the life expectancy of someone age 72 is 25.6 years. Thus, he must receive a distribution of at least $23,930 ($612,608/25.6) from his retirement plan no later than April 1, 2022.

---

When the owner of a retirement plan dies, special rules apply. These rules depend on whether the beneficiary of the plan (the person who inherits the plan assets) is the spouse or someone else. If the sole beneficiary is the spouse, they can elect to be treated as the owner. If so, the beneficiary would account for the retirement plan using the rules just indicated. If the beneficiary is not the spouse (or if the spouse does not make the election to be treated as the owner), the beneficiary generally determines the required minimum distribution for the year of death using their age with reference to Table I. For each subsequent year, that factor is reduced by 1. There are special rules for beneficiaries that are not individuals.

---

**EXAMPLE 11-18**

Fernando died in 2020 at age 80. His nephew Jose was the sole beneficiary and was age 67. Using Table I, Jose would use 19.4 as the appropriate factor in 2020, 18.4 in 2021, and so forth.

---

*Caution:* The distribution rules for beneficiaries can be complex. Refer to the Internal Revenue Code and to IRS Publication 590 for additional information.

If required minimum distributions are not made properly, the taxpayer is subject to a nondeductible excise tax equal to 50% of the shortfall.[63] The penalty is reported on Form 5329.

---

[62] In the case of non-IRA accounts, it is the later of 70½ (72 in 2020 or later) or the year in which the employee retires.

[63] IRC § 4974(a).

**TAX YOUR BRAIN**

Why are minimum withdrawal provisions required?

**ANSWER**

Recall that, for the most part, funds in a pension plan have never been taxed. If there were no minimum distribution standards, the assets could remain in the account and continue to accumulate tax-free indefinitely. In an effort to ensure eventual taxation of contributions and earnings, Congress enacted the minimum withdrawal provisions.

Retirement plan distributions that are includable in income are subject to a 10% additional tax unless the distributions meet *one* of the following exceptions:

- Distributed to an employee or retiree at or after age 59½ (age 55 for certain employees in the building and construction industry).
- Made to a beneficiary or estate on or after the death of the employee.
- Paid attributable to a total and permanent disability.
- Made to an employee over the age of 55 after separation from service (in the case of qualified pension and profit-sharing plans).
- Paid for deductible medical expenses (above the 10% threshold) whether or not the employee itemizes.
- Paid from an IRA, SEP, or SIMPLE to unemployed individuals for health insurance premiums (NOT for qualified plans).
- Paid from a CESA, IRA, SEP, or SIMPLE for higher education expenses.
- Paid from an IRA for "first home" purchases with a $10,000 lifetime maximum.
- Paid from a qualified plan to an alternative payee under provisions of a qualified domestic relations order.
- Distributed to pay an IRS tax levy on the plan.
- Made for certain distributions to qualified military reservists called to active duty.
- Paid as part of a series of substantially equal periodic payments over the life expectancy of the employee (an annuity). In the case of qualified pension and profit-sharing plans, these payments can start only after separation from service.[64]

In the case of SIMPLE plans, distributions not meeting one or more of the preceding exceptions made during the first two years of participation are subject to a 25% additional tax rather than 10%.

The purpose of the additional tax is to discourage withdrawals from retirement plans until the beneficiary retires unless the distribution is for one of the special purposes.

Taxpayers can choose to have the plan administrator withhold taxes on distributions. These withholdings are reported on Form 1099-R, box 4 (see Exhibit 11-4 later in this chapter).

**CONCEPT CHECK 11-5—**

**LO 11-5**

1. A participant in a defined benefit plan is entitled to only a stream of payments. True or false?
2. Distributions from qualified pension plans may be taxable, nontaxable, or both. True or false?
3. The number of anticipated payments from a pension plan for a single individual, age 68, is _____.
4. The number of anticipated payments from a pension plan for a married couple aged 59 and 63 is _____.
5. Distributions are required from a traditional IRA. True or false?

---

[64] IRC § 72(t)(1)–(8).

## Taxation of Traditional IRA Distributions

Distributions from traditional IRAs are fully taxable if the IRA was entirely funded with deductible contributions. If an IRA was funded partially with deductible contributions and partially with nondeductible contributions, a portion of each distribution is nontaxable. If such is the case, the taxpayer must first determine their tax basis in the IRA. The tax basis is equal to the sum of all nondeductible contributions made to the IRA minus the sum of all nontaxable distributions received as of the beginning of the year. Calculation of the tax-free portion is determined as follows:

$$\frac{\text{Tax basis in the IRA (i.e., after-tax contributions)}}{\text{End-of-year asset value} + \text{Distribution for the year}} \times \text{Distribution for the year} = \text{Nontaxable distribution}$$

**EXAMPLE 11-19**

Michael, age 65, retired in 2021. During the year, he received distributions of $7,000 from his IRA. He made nondeductible contributions of $10,000 to the IRA in prior years and has never received a nontaxable distribution. As of December 31, 2021, the value of his IRA was $100,000. The nontaxable portion of Michael's distribution is $654, calculated as follows:

$$[\$10,000/(\$100,000 + \$7,000)] \times \$7,000 = \$654$$

Michael's taxable distribution is $6,346 ($7,000 − $654), and his tax basis carried forward to tax year 2022 is $9,346 ($10,000 − $654). This $9,346 figure will be used as the numerator of the fraction in 2022.

Distributions from IRAs with nondeductible contributions are reported on Form 8606, Part I (see Exhibit 11-3). The exclusion percentage is on line 10, and the nontaxable distribution is on line 13. The distribution and the taxable amount are carried forward to Form 1040, lines 4a and 4b, respectively.

## Taxation of Roth IRA Distributions

Unlike traditional IRAs, no minimum withdrawal from a Roth IRA is required. Roth IRA withdrawals are not taxable when distributed unless they fail to meet a five-year holding period requirement.[65] Specifically, the distribution must be made after the five-tax-year period beginning with the first tax year in which a Roth contribution was made.[66] Roth withdrawals are deemed to come first from contributions and then from earnings. Thus, withdrawals within the five-year window are not taxable to the extent that they do not exceed contributions.

**EXAMPLE 11-20**

Parker and Reese established and funded their Roth IRA in tax year 2017 and have made an annual $2,000 contribution in every year since (even though the 2021 contribution maximum is $6,000, the maximum was smaller in some prior years so we will assume equal $2,000 contributions). If other distribution requirements are met, Parker and Reese can make tax-free withdrawals from their Roth beginning in 2022. If they were to make a withdrawal earlier in 2021, they could withdraw up to $10,000 tax-free ($2,000 contribution per year for 2017 through 2021).

The 10% additional tax for retirement plan withdrawals does not apply to Roth distributions because the distributions are not included in income. However, before the five-year holding period, Roth distributions are taxable (and subject to a 10% penalty) to the extent they come from earnings unless they are made (1) on or after the taxpayer's reaching age 59½, (2) as a result of death, (3) on account of disability, or (4) for a first-time home purchase with a maximum cap of $10,000.[67]

## Distributions from a Coverdell Education Savings Account

Distributions from a CESA are tax-free to the beneficiary if used for their qualified education expenses. Qualified expenses include required tuition, fees, books, supplies, tutoring,

[65] IRC § 408A(d)(1).
[66] IRC § 408A(d)(2)(B).
[67] IRC § 408A(d)(2)(A).

**EXHIBIT 11-3**

| Form **8606** | **Nondeductible IRAs** | OMB No. 1545-0074 |
|---|---|---|
| Department of the Treasury<br>Internal Revenue Service (99) | ▶ Go to *www.irs.gov/Form8606* for instructions and the latest information.<br>▶ **Attach to 2021 Form 1040, 1040-SR, or 1040-NR.** | 20**21**<br>Attachment<br>Sequence No. **48** |

Name. If married, file a separate form for each spouse required to file 2021 Form 8606. See instructions. | Your social security number

**Fill in Your Address Only if You Are Filing This Form by Itself and Not With Your Tax Return** ▶

Home address (number and street, or P.O. box if mail is not delivered to your home) | Apt. no.

City, town or post office, state, and ZIP code. If you have a foreign address, also complete the spaces below (see instructions).

Foreign country name | Foreign province/state/county | Foreign postal code

**Part I** | **Nondeductible Contributions to Traditional IRAs and Distributions From Traditional, SEP, and SIMPLE IRAs**

Complete this part only if one or more of the following apply.

- You made nondeductible contributions to a traditional IRA for 2021.
- You took distributions from a traditional, SEP, or SIMPLE IRA in 2021 **and** you made nondeductible contributions to a traditional IRA in 2021 or an earlier year. For this purpose, a distribution does not include a rollover (other than a repayment of a qualified disaster distribution (see 2021 Forms 8915-D and 8915-F)), qualified charitable distribution, one-time distribution to fund an HSA, conversion, recharacterization, or return of certain contributions.
- You converted part, but not all, of your traditional, SEP, and SIMPLE IRAs to Roth IRAs in 2021 **and** you made nondeductible contributions to a traditional IRA in 2021 or an earlier year.

| | | |
|---|---|---|
| **1** | Enter your nondeductible contributions to traditional IRAs for 2021, including those made for 2021 from January 1, 2022, through April 18, 2022. See instructions . . . . . . . . . . . . | **1** |
| **2** | Enter your total basis in traditional IRAs. See instructions . . . . . . . . . . . . . | **2** |
| **3** | Add lines 1 and 2 | **3** |

In 2021, did you take a distribution from traditional, SEP, or SIMPLE IRAs, or make a Roth IRA conversion? → **No** → Enter the amount from line 3 on line 14. Do not complete the rest of Part I.

→ **Yes** → Go to line 4.

| | | |
|---|---|---|
| **4** | Enter those contributions included on line 1 that were made from January 1, 2022, through April 18, 2022 | **4** |
| **5** | Subtract line 4 from line 3 . . . . . . . . . . . . . . . . . . . . | **5** |
| **6** | Enter the value of **all** your traditional, SEP, and SIMPLE IRAs as of December 31, 2021, plus any outstanding rollovers. Subtract any repayments of qualified disaster distributions (see 2021 Forms 8915-D and 8915-F) . . . . . | **6** |
| **7** | Enter your distributions from traditional, SEP, and SIMPLE IRAs in 2021. **Do not** include rollovers (other than repayments of qualified disaster distributions (see 2021 Forms 8915-D and 8915-F)), qualified charitable distributions, a one-time distribution to fund an HSA, conversions to a Roth IRA, certain returned contributions, or recharacterizations of traditional IRA contributions (see instructions) . . . . . . . . . . . . . . . . . | **7** |
| **8** | Enter the net amount you converted from traditional, SEP, and SIMPLE IRAs to Roth IRAs in 2021. Also, enter this amount on line 16 . . . . . . . . . | **8** |
| **9** | Add lines 6, 7, and 8 . . . . . . . . | **9** |
| **10** | Divide line 5 by line 9. Enter the result as a decimal rounded to at least 3 places. If the result is 1.000 or more, enter "1.000" . . . . . . . . | **10** × . |
| **11** | Multiply line 8 by line 10. This is the nontaxable portion of the amount you converted to Roth IRAs. Also, enter this amount on line 17 . . . . . . . | **11** |
| **12** | Multiply line 7 by line 10. This is the nontaxable portion of your distributions that you did not convert to a Roth IRA . . . . . . . . . . . . . . | **12** |
| **13** | Add lines 11 and 12. This is the nontaxable portion of all your distributions . . . . . . . | **13** |
| **14** | Subtract line 13 from line 3. This is **your total basis in traditional IRAs for 2021 and earlier years** . | **14** |
| **15a** | Subtract line 12 from line 7 . . . . . . . . . . . . . . . . . . | **15a** |
| **b** | Enter the amount on line 15a attributable to qualified disaster distributions from 2021 Forms 8915-D and 8915-F (see instructions). Also, enter this amount on 2021 Form 8915-D, line 23; **or** 2021 Form 8915-F, line 18, as applicable . . . . . . . . . . . . . . . . . . | **15b** |
| **c** | **Taxable amount.** Subtract line 15b from line 15a. If more than zero, also include this amount on 2021 Form 1040, 1040-SR, **or** 1040-NR, line 4b . . . . . . . . . . . . | **15c** |

**Note:** You may be subject to an additional 10% tax on the amount on line 15c if you were under age 59½ at the time of the distribution. See instructions.

**For Privacy Act and Paperwork Reduction Act Notice, see separate instructions.** | Cat. No. 63966F | Form **8606** (2021)

Source: U.S. Department of the Treasury, Internal Revenue Service, Form 8606. Washington, DC: 2021.

equipment, and similar expenses incurred in conjunction with the enrollment or attendance of the beneficiary at an elementary or secondary school or at an accredited post-secondary educational institution.[68] Qualified expenses must be reduced by scholarships or other tax-free income. Expenses for room and board are qualified expenses if either (1) the student is enrolled at least half-time at a qualified post-secondary school or (2) the expense is required in the case of eligible elementary or secondary schools.

If distributions exceed qualified expenses, the excess attributable to contributions is tax-free and the amount attributable to earnings is taxable as ordinary income. The taxable excess is generally subject to a 10% penalty tax. Taxable CESA distributions are reported on Schedule 1, line 8z, other income.

Expenses used to determine American opportunity/Hope or lifetime learning credits or the tuition and fees deduction cannot be used again as qualified expenses for CESA distributions. In other words, you cannot double-count the expenses.

Funds remaining in a CESA when the beneficiary reaches age 30 must be distributed to the beneficiary within 30 days. If the distribution is not used for qualified education expenses, the amount will be taxable to the extent that it represents earnings. The distribution will also be subject to an additional 10% tax.[69] However, if the CESA is transferred (rolled over) within 60 days to a CESA for a member of the beneficiary's family under age 30, the transfer is tax-free.[70]

## Rollovers

Taxpayers can transfer plan assets from one retirement plan to another retirement plan tax- and penalty-free if they follow certain rules.[71] Taxpayers may choose to do so to consolidate numerous pension accounts into one account or to change plan administrators.

Normally, transfers are from trustee to trustee. In this case, the taxpayer notifies the current plan trustee to transfer some or all of their plan assets to the trustee of another plan. The transfer is made directly from the first trustee to the second trustee, and the taxpayer never has any control over the funds. Such transfers are not subject to tax or withholding.[72]

Alternatively, the taxpayer may choose (subject to plan restrictions) to have some or all of the plan assets distributed to them and, within a 60-day period, transfer those assets into another eligible retirement plan. The amount distributed is subject to a 20% mandatory withholding.[73] If the taxpayer fails to properly transfer the funds within the 60-day period, the entire amount distributed (including the amount withheld) is taxable as ordinary income.

Permissible types of tax-free rollovers follow:

- From one IRA to the same or another type except that (a) a transfer to a Roth IRA is taxable and (b) a transfer from a SIMPLE during the first two years of an employee's participation can be made only to another SIMPLE.

- From a qualified plan to an IRA.

- From a qualified plan to another qualified plan.

- From a tax-sheltered annuity to another tax-sheltered annuity or to an IRA.

Taxpayers are permitted to roll over a traditional IRA to a Roth IRA without being subject to the 10% penalty tax. This rollover is also called a *Roth conversion.* If the IRA was funded with tax-deductible contributions, the entire amount must be included in taxable income. If the IRA was funded with tax-deductible and non-tax-deductible contributions, then a pro rata allocation is made.

[68] IRC § 529(e)(3)(A), (5)(A).
[69] IRC § 530(d)(4)(A).
[70] IRC § 530(d)(5).
[71] Any such transfers must meet the administrative requirements set by the plan administrators.
[72] IRC § 401(a)(31)(A).
[73] IRC § 3405(c)(1)(B).

**TAX YOUR BRAIN**

Amounts transferred from a traditional IRA to a Roth IRA are moving from one IRA to another. Why must the amount transferred be included in income?

**ANSWER**

Even though both accounts are IRAs, they have different deductibility and taxability rules. Recall that the traditional account is funded with untaxed dollars, whereas the Roth is funded with dollars that have already been taxed. In addition, distributions from the traditional IRA will normally be fully taxed, whereas Roth distributions will be tax-free. Thus, the funds are moving from an account that has never been taxed (traditional) to an account that will not be taxed upon withdrawal (Roth). If the government does not tax the transfer when it occurs, it will never collect tax on the funds.

**CONCEPT CHECK 11-6—**

**LO 11-5**

1. IRA distributions are taxable if funded with deductible contributions. True or false?
2. Distributions are never required from a Roth IRA. True or false?
3. For an individual age 65, Roth IRA distributions are not taxable if they have been held for at least five years. True or false?
4. Distributions from Coverdell Education Savings Accounts can be used for any purpose once the beneficiary reaches age 30. True or false?

# TAX TREATMENT OF ANNUITY CONTRACTS

**LO 11-6**

Taxpayers may choose to invest in an annuity (either taxable or tax-deferred). An *annuity* is defined as a series of payments made under a contract. The payments can be in a variable or fixed amount and can be for a specified period or for the life of the contract holder. The contract can be with an insurance company, a financial services company, a bank, or an employer. Annuities often arise in conjunction with the payout phase of a retirement plan (the taxability of these plans has previously been discussed).

An annuity contract generally requires the taxpayer to pay a lump sum for the right to receive periodic payments (usually monthly, quarterly, or annually). The portion of these payments attributable to the amount invested is tax-free; the remainder is taxable. The taxable nontaxable split is calculated based on the proportion that the cost of the contract bears to the expected return from the contract.

The expected return on an annuity that will last for a specified amount of time is easy to determine. If a contract will provide payments of $1,000 per month for five years, the expected return is $60,000 ($1,000 × 12 × 5). The expected return on a contract that will provide payments for the life of the contract owner is determined based on the life expectancy tables provided in IRS Publication 939. We have provided Table V, for single life annuities, in the Appendix to this chapter. For dual life annuities, refer to Publication 939. The expected return is equal to the annual payout from the contract multiplied by the appropriate factor.

**EXAMPLE 11-21**

Bart is 57 years old and purchased a single life annuity contract that will pay him $5,000 per year for life. Bart paid $90,000 for the contract. The expected return on Bart's contract is $134,000 ($5,000 × 26.8).

The exclusion ratio is 0.672 ($90,000/$134,000). Thus each $5,000 annual payment will have a tax-free component of $3,360 (5,000 × 0.672) and a taxable component of $1,640 ($5,000 − $3,360).

## From Shoebox to Software   Reporting Contributions and Distributions

Contributions to employer-provided qualified pension and profit-sharing plans are not reported on Form 1040 or attachments. Employees will receive certain notification from the plan administrator in accordance with the rules of the plan. Generally, the employee contribution information is reported in box 9b of Form 1099-R (see Exhibit 11-4) in the year distributions commence.

Contributions to traditional IRAs, Keogh plans, SEPs, and SIMPLE plans are calculated in accordance with the rules outlined in this chapter and, if deductible, are reported as a *for* AGI deduction on line 20 (for an IRA) or line 16 (for the other plans) of Form 1040, Schedule 1.

Nondeductible contributions to a traditional IRA are reported on Form 8606, Part I, line 1 (see Exhibit 11-3). These contributions create a tax basis that determines the taxability of future distributions. It is important for a taxpayer to have good recordkeeping practices because, when calculating the nontaxable portion of IRA distributions, the taxpayer will need to use information that may be up to 30 or 40 years old.

In tax software, IRA contributions and contributions to self-employed pension plans are generally reported on a worksheet.

Distributions from pension plans, IRAs, and similar plans are reported to taxpayers on Form 1099-R. If a taxpayer receives distributions from multiple plans, they will receive multiple Forms 1099-R, and the amounts therein must be added together. A Form 1099-R is shown in Exhibit 11-4.

The information in the various boxes of Form 1099-R is important when preparing a tax return. The following is an explanation of the information most commonly provided:

- Box 1 represents the total distribution from the pension plan during the year, including any taxes withheld.

- Box 2a is the taxable amount of the distribution. In box 2b, if the "total distribution" box is checked, the entire distribution is taxable. If the "taxable amount not determined" box is checked, the plan administrator does not have sufficient information to determine the amount of the payment that is taxable. In such case, the taxpayer must calculate the appropriate amount.

- Box 4 is the amount of tax withheld by the plan administrator. It is added to other withholdings and reported on Form 1040, line 25b. Generally, taxpayers must elect to have amounts withheld from pension payments. In the case of a rollover amount distributed directly to the taxpayer, box 4 will reflect the 20% mandatory withholding.

- Box 7 contains the number or letter code that corresponds to the type of distribution being made. The most common code is 7 for a normal distribution. Other codes are 1 for an early distribution; 3 or 4 as a result of the death or disability, respectively, of the employee; G or H for most rollovers; J for a Roth distribution; and M for a Coverdell Education Savings Account distribution.

- Boxes 14 and 17 provide any state or local tax withholdings. These are used as part of any itemized deductions and in preparation of state and local tax returns.

In tax software, information from Form 1099-R is generally entered directly on the Form 1099-R.

The software transfers the information you enter on the worksheets and the Form 1099-R input form onto the appropriate tax return form. Contributions are not normally reported but are used to determine tax basis. An exception is a nondeductible contribution to a traditional IRA.

Distributions from a pension plan will be reported on Form 1040, lines 5a and 5b. Traditional IRA distributions are initially reported on Form 8606, Part 1 (see Exhibit 11-3), and will be transferred to Form 1040, on lines 4a and 4b.

Taxpayers also use Form 8606 to report distributions from a Roth IRA and a nondeductible IRA. Distributions from IRAs with nondeductible contributions are also on Form 8606, Part I. The exclusion percentage is on line 10, and the nontaxable distribution is on line 13. The tax software carries the distribution and the taxable amount to Form 1040, lines 4a and 4b, respectively.

Distributions from a Coverdell Education Savings Account are to be used for qualified education expenses. If distributions exceed expenses, report the excess on Form 1040, Schedule 1, line 8z, Other income.

**EXAMPLE 11-22**

Beverly is 60 years old and has purchased a single life annuity for $35,000. The annuity contract will provide Beverly payments of $300 per month for the rest of her life. Beverly's life expectancy from Table V in the Appendix is 24.2 years. The expected return from the contract is $87,120 ($300 × 12 × 24.2). The exclusion ratio is 0.4017 ($35,000/$87,120). Thus, each $300 payment will have a tax-free component of $120.51 ($300 × 0.4017) and a taxable component of $179.49 ($300.00 − $120.51).

**EXHIBIT 11-4**

| | | |
|---|---|---|
| ☐ CORRECTED (if checked) | | |

| PAYER'S name, street address, city or town, state or province, country, ZIP or foreign postal code, and telephone no. | **1** Gross distribution<br><br>$ | OMB No. 1545-0119<br><br>**2021**<br><br>Form **1099-R** | **Distributions From Pensions, Annuities, Retirement or Profit-Sharing Plans, IRAs, Insurance Contracts, etc.** |
| | **2a** Taxable amount<br><br>$ | | |
| | **2b** Taxable amount not determined ☐   Total distribution ☐ | | **Copy B** |
| PAYER'S TIN          RECIPIENT'S TIN | **3** Capital gain (included in box 2a)<br><br>$ | **4** Federal income tax withheld<br><br>$ | **Report this income on your federal tax return. If this form shows federal income tax withheld in box 4, attach this copy to your return.** |
| RECIPIENT'S name | **5** Employee contributions/ Designated Roth contributions or insurance premiums<br><br>$ | **6** Net unrealized appreciation in employer's securities<br><br>$ | |
| Street address (including apt. no.) | **7** Distribution code(s)   IRA/ SEP/ SIMPLE ☐ | **8** Other<br><br>$                    % | **This information is being furnished to the IRS.** |
| City or town, state or province, country, and ZIP or foreign postal code | **9a** Your percentage of total distribution          % | **9b** Total employee contributions<br>$ | |
| **10** Amount allocable to IRR within 5 years<br><br>$ | **11** 1st year of desig. Roth contrib. | **12** FATCA filing requirement ☐ | **14** State tax withheld<br>$<br>$ | **15** State/Payer's state no. | **16** State distribution<br>$<br>$ |
| Account number (see instructions) | **13** Date of payment | | **17** Local tax withheld<br>$<br>$ | **18** Name of locality | **19** Local distribution<br>$<br>$ |

Form **1099-R**          www.irs.gov/Form1099R          Department of the Treasury - Internal Revenue Service

Source: U.S. Department of the Treasury, Internal Revenue Service, Form 1099-R. Washington, DC: 2021.

After the entire cost of the annuity has been recovered, all additional payments are fully taxable. If an individual dies before recovering the entire cost, the unrecovered cost can be used as an itemized deduction on the individual's final return.

---

**TAX YOUR BRAIN**

Under what circumstances will the entire cost of an annuity be recovered?

**ANSWER**

In the case of an annuity that is payable for a fixed period, the entire cost will be recovered when the last payment is received. For annuities payable over the life of the recipient, the entire cost will be recovered if the annuitant lives exactly as long as the life expectancy used to determine the exclusion ratio. Mathematically, once the recipient reaches the life expectancy originally anticipated, the entire cost will have been recovered.

---

**CONCEPT CHECK 11-7—**

**LO 11-6**

1. An annuity is a _____ of payments under a _____.
2. Annuity payments are always the same amount each period. True or false?
3. Annuity payments often have a taxable component and a nontaxable component. True or false?

## Summary

**LO 11-1:** Discuss the basic tax and operational structure of tax-deferred plans and annuities.

- Specified retirement plans are encouraged and receive tax advantages.
- Important related terminology includes *donor, beneficiary, contributions, distributions, annuity,* and *trustee.*
- Tax-deferred does not mean tax-free.
- Generally, untaxed contributions are taxed on distribution, but taxed contributions are not.
- Contributions to retirement plans can provide a tax deduction.

**LO 11-2:** Explain details about and contributions to employer-sponsored retirement plans.

- Employer-sponsored plans include qualified pension and profit-sharing, 401(k), 403(b), Keogh, SEP, and SIMPLE plans.
- Plans provide significant benefits to both employers and employees.
- Qualified plans are either defined contribution or defined benefit plans.
- All employer-sponsored plans have contribution limits that vary by plan.

**LO 11-3:** Describe the tax rules related to contributions to individual-sponsored retirement plans.

- Individual-sponsored IRAs include both traditional and Roth.
- Contributions are limited to the lower of $6,000 or 100% of compensation. Individuals over 50 can contribute up to $7,000.
- Special rules apply to compensation for married taxpayers and for individuals covered by employer-related plans.
- Contribution restrictions are based on AGI.
- Deductibility of contributions and taxability of distributions for traditional and Roth IRAs differ.

**LO 11-4:** Explain details about and contributions to tax-deferred nonretirement plans.

- A Coverdell Education Savings Account is a tax-deferred plan used for qualified elementary, secondary, or higher education expenses.
- The maximum annual contribution is $2,000, subject to AGI limitations.
- A qualified tuition plan (also known as a 529 plan) is a tax-deferred plan used to pay for qualified expenses at K–12 and post-secondary schools.
- Contributions cannot exceed the amount necessary to provide for qualified expenses of the beneficiary.
- QTPs can be used in the same year as a Coverdell Education Savings Account, tuition and fees deduction, American opportunity credit, or lifetime learning credit as long as the same expenses are not counted twice.

**LO 11-5:** Apply the tax rules for distributions from tax-deferred plans and the tax treatment of those distributions.

- Generally, distributions are taxable if contributions were deductible.
- The simplified method is used to determine taxability of qualified plan distributions.
- Other retirement plans have required minimum distributions that must begin by April 1 of the year after the taxpayer reaches age 70½ (pre-2020) or 72 (2020 or later).
- Distributions are determined using life expectancy tables.
- Premature distributions are subject to 10% penalty; some exceptions apply.
- Rollovers are generally tax-free, but rollovers to a Roth IRA are subject to tax.

**LO 11-6:** Determine the tax treatment of annuity contracts.

- Normally, annuity payments are partially taxable and partially tax-free.
- The tax-free component is based on the cost of the annuity contract.
- The expected return must be determined. The expected return is the amount the annuity recipient expects to receive from the contract. Life expectancy tables may be needed to determine the amount.

# Appendix

## LIFE EXPECTANCY TABLES

### Table I
### (Single Life Expectancy)
### (For Use by Beneficiaries)

| Age | Life Expectancy | Age | Life Expectancy |
|---|---|---|---|
| 56 | 28.7 | 84 | 8.1 |
| 57 | 27.9 | 85 | 7.6 |
| 58 | 27.0 | 86 | 7.1 |
| 59 | 26.1 | 87 | 6.7 |
| 60 | 25.2 | 88 | 6.3 |
| 61 | 24.4 | 89 | 5.9 |
| 62 | 23.5 | 90 | 5.5 |
| 63 | 22.7 | 91 | 5.2 |
| 64 | 21.8 | 92 | 4.9 |
| 65 | 21.0 | 93 | 4.6 |
| 66 | 20.2 | 94 | 4.3 |
| 67 | 19.4 | 95 | 4.1 |
| 68 | 18.6 | 96 | 3.8 |
| 69 | 17.8 | 97 | 3.6 |
| 70 | 17.0 | 98 | 3.4 |
| 71 | 16.3 | 99 | 3.1 |
| 72 | 15.5 | 100 | 2.9 |
| 73 | 14.8 | 101 | 2.7 |
| 74 | 14.1 | 102 | 2.5 |
| 75 | 13.4 | 103 | 2.3 |
| 76 | 12.7 | 104 | 2.1 |
| 77 | 12.1 | 105 | 1.9 |
| 78 | 11.4 | 106 | 1.7 |
| 79 | 10.8 | 107 | 1.5 |
| 80 | 10.2 | 108 | 1.4 |
| 81 | 9.7 | 109 | 1.2 |
| 82 | 9.1 | 110 | 1.1 |
| 83 | 8.6 | 111 and over | 1.0 |

Generally this table is to be used for IRAs by beneficiaries as a result of the death of the original IRA owner.

Source: Life Expectancy Tables, IRA.

## Table III
## (Uniform Lifetime)

**(For Use by:**
- **Unmarried Owners,**
- **Married Owners Whose Spouses Are Not More Than 10 Years Younger, and**
- **Married Owners Whose Spouses Are Not the Sole Beneficiaries of Their IRAs)**

| Age | Distribution Period | Age | Distribution Period |
|---|---|---|---|
| 70 | 27.4 | 93 | 9.6 |
| 71 | 26.5 | 94 | 9.1 |
| 72 | 25.6 | 95 | 8.6 |
| 73 | 24.7 | 96 | 8.1 |
| 74 | 23.8 | 97 | 7.6 |
| 75 | 22.9 | 98 | 7.1 |
| 76 | 22.0 | 99 | 6.7 |
| 77 | 21.2 | 100 | 6.3 |
| 78 | 20.3 | 101 | 5.9 |
| 79 | 19.5 | 102 | 5.5 |
| 80 | 18.7 | 103 | 5.2 |
| 81 | 17.9 | 104 | 4.9 |
| 82 | 17.1 | 105 | 4.5 |
| 83 | 16.3 | 106 | 4.2 |
| 84 | 15.5 | 107 | 3.9 |
| 85 | 14.8 | 108 | 3.7 |
| 86 | 14.1 | 109 | 3.4 |
| 87 | 13.4 | 110 | 3.1 |
| 88 | 12.7 | 111 | 2.9 |
| 89 | 12.0 | 112 | 2.6 |
| 90 | 11.4 | 113 | 2.4 |
| 91 | 10.8 | 114 | 2.1 |
| 92 | 10.2 | 115 and over | 1.9 |

Generally this table is to be used by the original owner of an IRA.

## TABLE V—ORDINARY LIFE ANNUITIES
## ONE LIFE—EXPECTED RETURN MULTIPLES

| AGE | MULTIPLE | AGE | MULTIPLE | AGE | MULTIPLE |
|---|---|---|---|---|---|
| 5 | 76.6 | 42 | 40.6 | 79 | 10.0 |
| 6 | 75.6 | 43 | 39.6 | 80 | 9.5 |
| 7 | 74.7 | 44 | 38.7 | 81 | 8.9 |
| 8 | 73.7 | 45 | 37.7 | 82 | 8.4 |
| 9 | 72.7 | 46 | 36.8 | 83 | 7.9 |
| 10 | 71.7 | 47 | 35.9 | 84 | 7.4 |
| 11 | 70.7 | 48 | 34.9 | 85 | 6.9 |
| 12 | 69.7 | 49 | 34.0 | 86 | 6.5 |
| 13 | 68.8 | 50 | 33.1 | 87 | 6.1 |
| 14 | 67.8 | 51 | 32.2 | 88 | 5.7 |
| 15 | 66.8 | 52 | 31.3 | 89 | 5.3 |
| 16 | 65.8 | 53 | 30.4 | 90 | 5.0 |
| 17 | 64.8 | 54 | 29.5 | 91 | 4.7 |
| 18 | 63.9 | 55 | 28.6 | 92 | 4.4 |
| 19 | 62.9 | 56 | 27.7 | 93 | 4.1 |
| 20 | 61.9 | 57 | 26.8 | 94 | 3.9 |
| 21 | 60.9 | 58 | 25.9 | 95 | 3.7 |
| 22 | 59.9 | 59 | 25.0 | 96 | 3.4 |
| 23 | 59.0 | 60 | 24.2 | 97 | 3.2 |
| 24 | 58.0 | 61 | 23.3 | 98 | 3.0 |
| 25 | 57.0 | 62 | 22.5 | 99 | 2.8 |
| 26 | 56.0 | 63 | 21.6 | 100 | 2.7 |
| 27 | 55.1 | 64 | 20.8 | 101 | 2.5 |
| 28 | 54.1 | 65 | 20.0 | 102 | 2.3 |
| 29 | 53.1 | 66 | 19.2 | 103 | 2.1 |
| 30 | 52.2 | 67 | 18.4 | 104 | 1.9 |
| 31 | 51.2 | 68 | 17.6 | 105 | 1.8 |
| 32 | 50.2 | 69 | 16.8 | 106 | 1.6 |
| 33 | 49.3 | 70 | 16.0 | 107 | 1.4 |
| 34 | 48.3 | 71 | 15.3 | 108 | 1.3 |
| 35 | 47.3 | 72 | 14.6 | 109 | 1.1 |
| 36 | 46.4 | 73 | 13.9 | 110 | 1.0 |
| 37 | 45.4 | 74 | 13.2 | 111 | .9 |
| 38 | 44.4 | 75 | 12.5 | 112 | .8 |
| 39 | 43.5 | 76 | 11.9 | 113 | .7 |
| 40 | 42.5 | 77 | 11.2 | 114 | .6 |
| 41 | 41.5 | 78 | 10.6 | 115 | .5 |

This table is to be used by taxpayers with payments from an annuity not associated with a qualified pension or profit-sharing plan.

## *EA Fast Fact*

Primary Topics on Part I of the EA exam, Individuals, include:

☐ *Part I – Individuals – 3.5 hrs.*

- Filing Requirements for Tax Returns and Extensions
- Gross Income
- Business Deductions
- Taxability of Wages, Salaries, and Other Earnings
- Interest Income
- Rental Income and Expenses
- Scholarships and Fellowships
- Moving Expenses
- Other Income
- Basis of Property

**IMPORTANT**

You are eligible to receive absolutely free, the Surgent Enrolled Agent review program for Part I of the EA exam as a result of purchasing this text. To activate your free access, go to https://Surgent.com/McGrawHill/EA.

## Discussion Questions   McGraw Hill **connect**

All applicable discussion questions are available with *Connect*©

LO 11-1
1. What is the purpose of a retirement plan? Why does the government provide tax benefits to retirement plans?

EA   LO 11-1
2. What is the rule of thumb noted in the text pertaining to the taxability of retirement plan distributions?

LO 11-1
3. Pension plans have an *accumulation period* and a *distribution period*. Explain what those terms mean.

LO 11-1
4. What are the two broad categories of retirement plans? Give some examples of each.

LO 11-2
5. What are the differences between a defined benefit pension plan and a defined contribution pension plan?

LO 11-2    6. What are the differences between a contributory and a noncontributory pension plan?

_____

_____

_____

LO 11-2    7. What are the similarities and differences between a pension plan and a profit-sharing plan?

_____

_____

_____

LO 11-2    8. Pension plans are subject to certain vesting requirements. What does the word *vesting* mean? Describe the vesting rules for pension plans.

_____

_____

_____

LO 11-2    9. Briefly discuss the conditions necessary for a taxpayer to be permitted to make tax-deductible contributions to a Keogh plan.

_____

_____

_____

LO 11-2   10. What is the maximum annual contribution that can be made to a Keogh plan, and how is the maximum calculated?

_____

_____

_____

LO 11-2   11. Briefly discuss the conditions necessary for a taxpayer to be permitted to make tax-deductible contributions to a SIMPLE plan.

_____

_____

_____

LO 11-2   12. What is the maximum annual contribution that can be made to a SIMPLE plan, and how is the maximum calculated?

_____

_____

_____

LO 11-2   13. Briefly discuss the conditions necessary for a taxpayer to be permitted to make tax-deductible contributions to a simplified employee pension (SEP).

_____

_____

_____

LO 11-2   14. What is the maximum annual contribution that can be made to a SEP, and how is the maximum calculated?

_____

_____

_____

**EA** **LO 11-3** 15. Briefly discuss the conditions necessary for a taxpayer to be permitted to make tax-deductible contributions to a traditional IRA.

_____

_____

_____

**EA** **LO 11-3** 16. What is the maximum annual contribution that can be made to a traditional IRA, and how is the maximum calculated?

_____

_____

_____

**EA** **LO 11-3** 17. What is the deadline by which contributions must be made to a traditional IRA to obtain a tax deduction in the current year?

_____

_____

_____

**EA** **LO 11-3** 18. What is the maximum annual contribution that can be made to a Roth IRA, and how is the maximum calculated?

_____

_____

_____

**LO 11-3** 19. Anne, a single taxpayer under age 50, has wage income of $74,000 and is not covered under a retirement plan by her employer. She would like to start a retirement plan if possible. What options are available to her?

_____

_____

_____

**LO 11-4** 20. What is the maximum annual contribution that can be made to a Coverdell Education Savings Account? Can an eligible beneficiary have more than one CESA?

_____

_____

_____

**LO 11-4** 21. Tax-free distributions from a Coverdell Education Savings Account can be used for what purpose? Be specific.

_____

_____

_____

**LO 11-4** 22. What is a qualified tuition plan? What can nontaxable distributions from such a plan be used for?

_____

_____

_____

**LO 11-5** 23. Hao has $20,000 in a traditional IRA at a bank. He decided to change trustees from a bank to a financial services firm. He requests, and receives, a check from the bank that he intends to take to the financial services firm to open a new account. He puts the check in his drawer and forgets it. Three months later, he remembers the check and takes it to the financial services firm and opens an IRA account. What are the tax implications of Hao's actions?

_____

_____

_____

LO 11-6    24. What is meant by an *expected return* on an annuity contract? How do you calculate the expected return for a single person?

_____

_____

_____

## Multiple-Choice Questions    Mc Graw Hill **connect**

All applicable multiple-choice questions are available with *Connect*©

LO 11-1    25. Which of the following is an individual-sponsored pension plan?
  *a.* Defined benefit plan.
  *b.* Keogh plan.
  *c.* Roth IRA.
  *d.* SIMPLE plan.

LO 11-1    26. Which of the following statements is true?
  *a.* Only employers can establish tax-deferred retirement plans.
  *b.* Generally, plan distributions are taxable if the contributions were made with untaxed dollars.
  *c.* The donor and the beneficiary of a retirement plan are almost never the same.
  *d.* Retirement plan distributions can be made for any purpose and at any time.

LO 11-2    27. A participant in a Keogh plan over the age of 50 may contribute up to what amount in 2021?
  *a.* $7,000.
  *b.* $26,000.
  *c.* The lower of $58,000 or 25% of earned income from self-employment.
  *d.* The greater of $58,000 or 25% of earned income from self-employment.

LO 11-2    28. A qualified pension plan provides significant tax benefits to both employers and employees, including
  *a.* Employer contributions are not treated as compensation to the employee.
  *b.* Earnings from the investments held in the plan are tax-deferred.
  *c.* No tax on plan assets until the amounts are distributed.
  *d.* All of the above.

LO 11-2    29. To obtain and retain qualified status, a pension or profit-sharing plan must not discriminate in favor of highly compensated employees, who include
  *a.* Employees who own more than 5% of the corporation's stock.
  *b.* Employees who received more than $100,000 compensation in the previous year.
  *c.* Employees who were in the top 25% of employees based on compensation.
  *d.* All of the above.

**LO 11-2** 30. A participant in a 401(k) plan under the age of 50 may contribute up to what amount in 2021?

    *a.* $6,000.

    *b.* $13,500.

    *c.* $19,500.

    *d.* $58,000.

**LO 11-2** 31. Thomas is a self-employed plumber under the age of 50. His earnings from self-employment, before the Keogh deduction but after deducting half of the self-employment tax, are $80,000. What is his deductible Keogh contribution for 2021?

    *a.* $64,000.

    *b.* $58,000.

    *c.* $20,000.

    *d.* $16,000.

**LO 11-2** 32. Which of the following is true regarding SEPs?

    *a.* The plan cannot discriminate in favor of highly compensated employees.

    *b.* Deductible contributions cannot exceed the lower of 15% of the employee's compensation or $58,000.

    *c.* Self-employed individuals cannot create and contribute to a SEP.

    *d.* The plan must cover all employees who have reached the age of 18, who have worked for the employer for at least two of the preceding five years, and who received at least $650 in compensation.

**LO 11-2** 33. Generous Corporation provides a SIMPLE plan for its employees. Under the plan, employees can contribute up to 6% of their salary, and Generous Corporation will match each employee's contribution up to 3% of the employee's salary. Erika is an employee of Generous Corporation and elects to contribute 6% of her $60,000 salary to the SIMPLE plan. What is the total contribution made to her SIMPLE account?

    *a.* $12,500.

    *b.* $5,400.

    *c.* $3,600.

    *d.* $1,800.

**EA** **LO 11-3** 34. Terri is single and age 32. She reported AGI of $70,000 in tax year 2021. She is an active participant in her employer's pension plan. What is the maximum deductible IRA contribution she can make for 2021?

    *a.* $6,000.

    *b.* $3,600.

    *c.* $2,400.

    *d.* $0.

**EA** **LO 11-3** 35. Eli and Adriana, both under age 50, file a joint return. Neither is covered under an employer pension plan. Adriana earned compensation of $53,000 in 2020. Eli worked part time and earned $1,200. What is the maximum deductible IRA contribution they can make for 2021?

    *a.* $0.

    *b.* $6,000.

    *c.* $7,200.

    *d.* $12,000.

**EA** **LO 11-3**  36. Jack is single and age 53. He reported AGI of $69,000 in 2021. He is an active participant in his employer's pension plan. What is the maximum deductible IRA contribution he can make for 2021?

a. $2,100.

b. $4,900.

c. $6,000.

d. $7,000.

**EA** **LO 11-3**  37. Patrice is single and age 26. She reported AGI of $70,000 in tax year 2021. She is an active participant in her employer's pension plan. What is the maximum deductible Roth IRA contribution she can make for 2021?

a. $6,000.

b. $3,600.

c. $2,400.

d. $0.

**EA** **LO 11-3**  38. Vickie is single and age 43. She reported AGI of $136,000 in tax year 2021. She is an active participant in her employer's pension plan. What is the maximum Roth IRA contribution she can make for 2021?

a. $0.

b. $1,600.

c. $4,400.

d. $6,000.

**LO 11-4**  39. Without regard to AGI limitations, what is the maximum contribution permitted to a Coverdell Education Savings Account?

a. $500.

b. $2,000.

c. $6,000.

d. The lower of $6,000 or 100% of earned income.

**LO 11-4**  40. Vanessa and Martin file a joint return for 2021. They have one child, age 12. They have combined AGI of $208,000. What is their maximum permitted contribution to a Coverdell Education Savings Account for 2021?

a. $0.

b. $800.

c. $1,200.

d. $2,000.

**LO 11-4**  41. Which of the following statements is true for a qualified tuition plan (QTP)?

a. Undergraduate or graduate students must be attending full time.

b. Tax-free distributions are permitted of up to $10,000 per year for tuition and room and board at K–12 schools.

c. Amounts in a QTP can be rolled over to a QTP of another family member.

d. In a year that a tax-free distribution is taken from a qualified tuition plan, the taxpayer cannot also claim a lifetime learning credit.

**LO 11-4**  42. Ellen is attending college less than half time. In the current year, she had education-related expenses of $8,000 for tuition and fees, $4,000 for room and board, $500 in transportation to and from her parent's house, and $1,000 for required books. What is the amount of her qualified expenses for purposes of a qualified tuition plan?

a. $0.

b. $9,000.

c. $13,000.

d. $13,500.

**EA  LO 11-5**  43. Juan is single and retired on January 1, 2021, at age 62. He is entitled to receive monthly payments of $1,500 over his life from his employer's qualified pension plan. The payments began January 1, 2021. He contributed $71,500 to the plan prior to his retirement. Using the simplified method, how much of the payments will be included in his income for 2021?

a. $1,225.

b. $3,300.

c. $14,700.

d. $18,000.

**EA  LO 11-5**  44. If a qualified pension plan is being distributed using joint life expectancy,

a. The taxpayers cannot choose to refigure their life expectancy.

b. If the beneficiary dies, no adjustment of the denominator used to calculate minimum distributions is required.

c. If the beneficiary dies, the life expectancy of a different beneficiary is substituted for the original beneficiary.

d. None of the above.

**EA  LO 11-5**  45. Mark, who is single, must start making distributions from his pension plan beginning April 1, 2022. At the end of 2020, when Mark was 71 years old, the plan had a balance of $220,000. He will use a single life expectancy. What amount must Mark take as a distribution from the pension plan no later than April 1, 2022?

a. $8,302.

b. $8,594.

c. $8,907.

d. $14,193.

**EA  LO 11-5**  46. Juanita, age 62, retired in 2021. During the year, she received distributions of $9,000 from her IRA. She made nondeductible contributions of $20,000 to the IRA in prior years and has never received a nontaxable distribution. As of December 31, 2021, the value of her IRA was $150,000. Calculate the nontaxable portion of Juanita's distribution.

a. $1,132.

b. $1,200.

c. $7,868.

d. $9,000.

**EA  LO 11-5**  47. Withdrawals from a Roth IRA are

a. Subject to the required minimum distribution rules.

b. Taxable if made after the five-tax-year period beginning with the first tax year in which a Roth contribution was made.

c. Deemed to come first from contributions and then from earnings.

d. Not taxable to the extent they exceed contributions if the five-year holding period requirement is not met.

**LO 11-5**  48. Regarding a Coverdell Education Savings Account,

a. Distributions are tax-free to the beneficiary if they are used for their qualified education expenses.

b. Qualified education expenses include required tuition, fees, books, supplies, and equipment at an eligible educational institution.

c. Qualified expenses must be reduced by scholarships or other tax-free income.

d. All of the above apply.

**EA**  **LO 11-6**  49. Julio is 62 and single. He purchased a single life annuity contract that will pay him $1,000 a month for life with a minimum payout of 10 years. His expected return on the contract

a. Is $120,000.

b. Is $270,000.

c. Is $282,000.

d. Cannot be determined with the information given.

**EA**  **LO 11-6**  50. June, age 76, and Augustus, age 78, are married. They purchased a single life annuity contract that will pay $1,500 per month for June's lifetime. The expected return on the contract

a. Is $190,800.

b. Is $214,200.

c. Is $405,000.

d. Cannot be determined with the information given.

**EA**  **LO 11-6**  51. Sanjay purchased a single life annuity contract for $200,000. The contract will pay $15,000 per year beginning in 2021 for the remainder of his life and has an expected return of $330,000. What amount of taxable income must Sanjay report in 2021?

a. $5,909.

b. $9,091.

c. $15,000.

d. $130,000.

## Problems  **Mc Graw Hill** **connect**

All applicable problems are available with **Connect**©

**LO 11-2, 11-3**  52. Will, who is single and age 50, is employed as a full-time tax accountant at a local manufacturing company where he earns $83,000 per year. He participates in a pension plan through his employer. Will also operates a small tax practice in his spare time during tax season and has net Schedule C income of $8,000. He is interested in establishing and contributing to other retirement plans. What options are available to Will?

_____

_____

_____

_____

_____

**LO 11-2**  53. Teak Company is considering the establishment of a pension plan. The proposed plan has the following features:

- Contributions for employees earning less than $100,000 will be based on 3% of salary, while contributions for those earning over $100,000 will be based on 4% of salary.
- To reduce employee turnover, company contributions will vest in 10 years.
- Employees with more than five years of service will be required to contribute 2% to the pension plan.
- Employee contributions will completely vest in one year.

Will the proposed pension plan be deemed a qualified pension plan? Why or why not?

_____

_____

_____

_____

_____

LO 11-2    54. Determine the maximum contribution that can be made to a Keogh plan in each of the following cases. In all instances, the individual is self-employed, and the self-employment tax reduction has already been taken.

    *a.* Self-employment income of $58,000.

    *b.* Self-employment income of $58,000 and wage income of $30,000.

    *c.* Self-employment income of $125,000.

    *d.* Self-employment income of $295,000.

_____

_____

_____

_____

_____

LO 11-2    55. Ken is a self-employed architect in a small firm with four employees: himself, his office assistant, and two drafters, all of whom have worked for Ken full time for the last four years. The office assistant earns $30,000 per year and each drafter earns $40,000. Ken's net earnings from self-employment (after deducting all expenses and one-half of self-employment taxes) are $310,000. Ken is considering whether to establish a SEP plan and has a few questions:

    *a.* Is he eligible to establish a SEP plan?

    *b.* Is he required to cover his employees under the plan? Why or why not?

    *c.* If his employees must be covered, what is the maximum amount that can be contributed on their behalf?

    *d.* If the employees are not covered, what is the maximum amount Ken can contribute for himself?

    *e.* If Ken is required to contribute for his employees and chooses to contribute the maximum amount, what is the maximum amount Ken can contribute for himself? (*Hint:* Calculate the employee amounts first.) Ignore any changes in Ken's self-employment tax.

_____

_____

_____

_____

_____

LO 11-2    56. Use the same information as in Problem 55. Answer the questions there, assuming that Ken is considering a SIMPLE plan.

_____

_____

_____

_____

_____

**EA** LO 11-3   57. Under what circumstances is it advantageous for a taxpayer to make a nondeductible contribution to a traditional IRA rather than a contribution to a Roth IRA?

LO 11-3   58. April, who is under age 50, is considering investing in tax-free state government bonds or making a permitted tax-deductible contribution to a traditional IRA. Assume that the amounts are the same for either alternative and that she can reinvest the interest income from the government bonds indefinitely. What tax and nontax factors should she consider?

LO 11-3   59. Lance is single and has a traditional IRA into which he has made deductible contributions for several years. This year he changed employers and is now an active participant in his employer's pension plan. His AGI is $95,000. He wants to make a nondeductible contribution to his IRA in the current year. What advice would you give Lance?

**EA** LO 11-3, 11-5   60. What are the differences between a traditional IRA and a Roth IRA regarding the deductibility of contributions, taxability of IRA earnings, and taxability of distributions?

**EA** LO 11-5   61. Using the simplified method, determine the tax-free amount of the following distributions from a qualified pension plan. Individual contributions, if any, are made with previously taxed dollars.

a. Person A, age 59, made no contributions to the pension plan and will receive a $500 monthly check for life.

b. Person B, age 66, made contributions of $23,000 to the pension plan and will receive a monthly check of $1,300 for life.

c. Person C, age 64, made contributions of $19,000 to the pension plan and will receive monthly payments of $1,200 over her life and the life of her 67-year-old husband.

d. Person D, age 55, made contributions of $62,000 to the pension plan. He will receive quarterly payments of $5,000 over his life and the life of his 58-year-old wife.

**EA** **LO 11-5** 62. Pablo and his wife Bernita are both age 45. Their combined AGI is $90,000. Neither is a participant in an employer-sponsored retirement plan. They have been contributing to a traditional IRA for many years and have built up an IRA balance of $120,000. They are considering rolling the traditional IRA into a Roth IRA.

    *a.* Is the couple eligible to make the conversion? Why or why not?

    *b.* Assume that the couple does not make the conversion but, instead, establishes a separate Roth IRA in the current year and properly contributes $2,000 per year for four years, at which point the balance in the Roth is $21,000 (contributions plus investment earnings). At the end of four years, they withdraw $12,000 to pay for an addition to their house. What is the tax effect, if anything, of the withdrawal?

    *c.* Does your answer to part (*b*) change if they instead withdraw only $6,000? Why or why not?

    *d.* What if the $12,000 withdrawal is used to pay qualified education expenses for their daughter who is attending college?

**EA** **LO 11-6** 63. Determine the tax-free amount of the monthly payment in each of the following instances. Use the life expectancy tables.

    *a.* Person A is age 57 and purchased an annuity for $82,000. The annuity pays $600 per month for life.

    *b.* Person B is 73 and purchased an annuity for $80,000. The annuity pays $950 per month for life.

    *c.* Person C is 68 and purchased an annuity for $40,000 that pays a monthly payment of $550 for 10 years.

## Complex Problems

**LO 11-5** 64. Terrance is age 71 and retired. Beginning in 2021, he must start taking minimum distributions from his IRA account that had a balance of $150,000 as of December 31, 2020. Make these three assumptions: His IRA will earn 8% per year, he will withdraw the minimum distribution on the last day of each calendar year, and only one distribution will be taken in 2021. Calculate the amount of his distribution for years 2021 through 2025 and the ending balance in his IRA account on December 31, 2025.

LO 11-5    65. Jennifer is age 50 and is seeking your advice. She has a traditional IRA with a balance of $100,000 and is considering whether to convert it (roll it over) to a Roth IRA. She has sufficient money in CDs to pay any required tax resulting from the rollover. Her current AGI is $70,000. She expects her income will be slightly higher upon retirement at age 65. What advice would you give Jennifer?

_____

_____

_____

_____

_____

_____

_____

_____

_____

_____

_____

LO 11-5    66. Use the information from Problem 65. Would your advice change if the fact(s) changed in each of the following independent instances? Why or why not?

   *a.* Jennifer cannot cash the CDs and would need to pay any additional tax liability from the IRA funds.

   *b.* She expects her income on retirement to decrease slightly.

   *c.* Jennifer is age 30.

_____

_____

_____

_____

_____

_____

_____

_____

_____

_____

_____

_____

_____

# Chapter **Twelve**

# Special Property Transactions

In Chapter 7, we discussed the sale of capital assets and the associated preferential tax treatment as well as the sale of business property and ordinary income property. The Internal Revenue Code (IRC) has other provisions that allow special tax treatment for certain transactions. In this chapter, we cover many special provisions that permit taxpayers to exclude or defer gains in certain situations, including like-kind exchanges, involuntary conversions, installment sales, and the sale of a personal residence. Not all of the provisions discussed in this chapter are favorable to the taxpayer. For example, losses are not allowed on transactions between related parties.

### Learning Objectives

When you have completed this chapter, you should understand the following learning objectives (LO):

**LO 12-1** Explain how to defer gains using the like-kind exchange rules.

**LO 12-2** Describe how to account for and report involuntary conversions.

**LO 12-3** Apply the tax rules to report an installment sale.

**LO 12-4** Explain how to exclude a gain on the sale of a personal residence.

**LO 12-5** Apply the rules affecting related parties and wash sales.

## INTRODUCTION

Numerous provisions in the IRC allow the taxpayer either to defer a gain to future years or to exclude the gain entirely from taxable income. A general rule of tax practice is that if a taxpayer must recognize a gain, it is best to defer the gain for as long as legally possible. Other provisions in the IRC disallow losses in certain circumstances. We discuss many of these provisions in this chapter. The topics discussed in this chapter include:

- Exchange of real property held for productive use or investment (like-kind exchanges).
- Involuntary conversions.
- Installment sales.
- Exclusion of gain from the sale of a principal residence.
- Losses with respect to transactions between related parties.
- Wash sales of stock or securities.

# LIKE-KIND EXCHANGES
## LO 12-1

Consider the following.

---

**EXAMPLE 12-1**

Bert and Alice purchased a house for rental in Emerald Isle, North Carolina, in 1965 for $15,000 (now fully depreciated). The same house and land are now worth $500,000. The house produces $25,000 of rental income a year. However, Bert and Alice's children and grandchildren live in Louisiana, so a beach house in Gulf Shores, Alabama, would be better because it could be used by the children when it is not rented. If Bert and Alice sell the property in North Carolina, a taxable § 1231 gain of $500,000 would result. If a 15% capital gains tax rate were assumed, Bert and Alice would pay tax of $75,000 on that gain, thereby reducing the proceeds available to purchase a new house in Alabama.[1] This is a perfect scenario for a like-kind exchange. Instead of selling their North Carolina house and buying another one in Alabama, if Bert and Alice exchange one house for the other, no tax will be owed.

---

Taxpayers often balk at the idea of a like-kind exchange because of the perceived difficulty in locating a desirable property for which the seller is willing to participate in an exchange. As discussed here, a properly executed like-kind exchange can take place even though the seller has no desire to exchange properties. A properly executed like-kind exchange in Example 12-1 would save $75,000 in taxes and allow the purchase of a nicer property or properties.

## Requirements of Nontaxable Exchanges

Three criteria must be met to qualify for a like-kind exchange:

1. An exchange must occur.
2. The real property transferred and the real property received must be held for productive use in a trade or business or for investment.
3. The property exchanged must be like-kind.[2]

One important aspect of a like-kind exchange is that it is *not* an elective provision. In other words, when an exchange occurs that meets the above criteria, the taxpayer must defer the gain or loss.

Generally, an *exchange* is loosely defined as receiving property of a like (similar) use in trade for similar property. The sale of old property and the purchase of new property are *not* an exchange. Additionally, the property must be held for productive use or investment to qualify. Prior to the Tax Cuts and Jobs Act of 2017 (2017 Act), any business asset was eligible for like-kind treatment.[3] After the 2017 Act, only real property (e.g., land and buildings) used in a business or held for investment can receive like-kind treatment.[4]

---

[1] As discussed in Chapter 7, the sale of real property results in a § 1250 gain. Thus, any of this gain attributable to depreciation is taxed at a 25% rate (unrecaptured § 1250 gain). In this case, only $15,000 is an unrecaptured § 1250 gain. The excess is taxed as a § 1231 gain that could result in a 15% rate, assuming that Bert and Alice are in a regular tax bracket higher than 15%.

[2] Only business assets such as inventory, stocks and bonds, and partnership interest were not eligible for like-kind treatment prior to the 2017 Act.

[3] IRC § 1031(a).

[4] IRC § 1031(a)(2).

Land or buildings held primarily for sale (e.g., inventory) is still excluded from the like-kind provision.[5]

Note that because inventory does not qualify for like-kind treatment, a dealer cannot participate in a like-kind exchange on a trade-in.

---

**EXAMPLE 12-2**

Marius, a dealer in real estate, allows a trade of one piece of land toward the purchase of a piece of land. He cannot use the like-kind rules to defer any taxable gain. However, the customer could use the like-kind rules to defer gain, assuming the customer is not also a dealer in land.

---

## What Is a "Like-Kind" Asset?

The requirement that the property be like-kind does not require the asset received be an exact duplicate of the property exchanged. To qualify as "like-kind," the property must be of the same nature or character. The grade or quality of the exchanged assets does not matter.[6]

---

**EXAMPLE 12-3**

Johnny exchanges a parcel of farm real property for city real property. Because both properties are real properties held for productive use, the exchange would qualify as a like-kind exchange.[7]

---

Real property located in the United States traded for real property outside the United States is not considered like-kind.[8]

## Boot Property

When two taxpayers wish to exchange properties, the fair market values (FMVs) of the properties rarely are equal. Thus, to make an exchange a viable option, one participant gives extra consideration (usually cash or a note payable) to make the exchange values equitable. This extra consideration is called *boot,* defined as property given or received in a like-kind exchange that is *not* like-kind property. The receipt of boot property often triggers the recognition of gain. The following is the general rule concerning the receipt of boot: When boot is received, the recognized gain is the *lesser* of

1. The FMV of the boot received or
2. The realized gain on the exchange.[9]

Gain or loss is determined by comparing the FMV received with the basis of the assets given. The receipt of boot causes the recognition of gain but not loss.[10] Giving boot does not trigger gain recognition.

[5] IRC § 1031(a)(2).
[6] Reg. §1.1031(a)-1(b).
[7] Reg. §1.1031(a)-1(b).
[8] IRC § 1031(h).
[9] IRC § 1031(b).
[10] IRC § 1031(c).

**EXAMPLE 12-4**

Sonja exchanges a lot used in business with Kelly for another lot. The basis of Sonja's old lot is $25,000, its FMV is $33,000, and she gives cash of $7,000. Kelly's basis in her lot is $35,000, and its FMV is $40,000.

| | Sonja | | Kelly |
|---|---|---|---|
| New lot—FMV | $40,000 | Amount received | $40,000* |
| Basis of old | (25,000) | Basis of old | (35,000) |
| Cash given | (7,000) | Gain—recognized | $ 5,000 |
| Gain—not recognized | $ 8,000 | | |

\* The amount received was the $33,000 FMV of Sonja's lot plus the $7,000 cash (boot).

Kelly recognizes the gain because she received boot in the transaction. The gain recognized is $5,000 because it is the lower of the boot received ($7,000 cash) or the gain realized ($5,000). Sonja defers her gain of $8,000.

## Tax Basis of New Property Received

An important calculation in a nontaxable exchange is the basis calculation. The basis calculation is the method by which the taxpayer defers gain. Generally, the basis of the new property is calculated as follows:

**Basis Calculation of New Property Received[11]**

| | Adjusted basis of the property given up |
|---|---|
| + | Adjusted basis of the boot given |
| + | Gain recognized |
| − | FMV of boot received |
| − | Loss recognized |
| = | Adjusted basis of new asset |

Alternatively, the taxpayer can calculate the adjusted basis by taking the FMV of the property received (like-kind asset) less the gain postponed (or plus the loss postponed).

**TAX YOUR BRAIN**

Why is the term *deferred* used instead of *excluded* when referring to the realized gain in a nontaxable exchange?

**ANSWER**

The gain is deferred because the unrecognized gain reduces the basis in the new asset received. Thus, the gain is deferred until the new asset is sold or disposed of. The reduced basis also causes less depreciation allowed on the new asset.

[11] IRC § 1031(d).

**EXAMPLE 12-5**

Assuming the same facts as in Example 12-4, what is the basis in the new properties for Sonja and Kelly?

|  | Sonja | Kelly |
|---|---|---|
| Adjusted basis of property given | $25,000 | $35,000 |
| + Adjusted basis of boot given | 7,000 | –0– |
| + Gain recognized | –0– | 5,000 |
| – FMV of boot received | –0– | 7,000 |
| – Loss recognized | –0– | –0– |
| Basis of new property | $32,000 | $33,000 |

| Or | FMV of Property Received | – | Gain Postponed | + | Loss Postponed | = | Basis |
|---|---|---|---|---|---|---|---|
| Sonja | $40,000 | – | $8,000 | + | $–0– | = | $32,000 |
| Kelly | 33,000 | – | –0– | + | –0– | = | 33,000 |

The holding period used to determine any short-term or long-term treatment on the sale of the new asset includes the holding period of the old asset exchanged. Thus, if a taxpayer exchanges a property held for 20 years for a new property, the new property has a holding period of 20 years plus the holding period of the new property.

## Time Period for Finding Exchange Property

The taxpayer does not have an unlimited amount of time to find exchange property. After relinquishing the property, the taxpayer has 45 days to identify replacement property. In addition, the taxpayer must receive the replacement property within the earlier of 180 days after the property was given up or the due date for filing a return (including extensions) for the year of the transfer.

**EXAMPLE 12-6**

Dang transfers property to Joey, and Joey places cash with an escrow agent on December 10, 2021. Dang has until January 24, 2022 (45 days), to identify a replacement property and must receive the replacement property by April 15, 2022. If the tax return were extended, Dan would have 180 days from December 10 to receive the property.

## Liabilities Assumed on the Exchange

The assumption or release of a liability adds complexity to a nontaxable exchange. When a taxpayer is released from a liability in an exchange, its release is considered boot received.[12] In other words, the taxpayer who assumes the debt is treated as having paid cash, and the taxpayer released from the debt is treated as having received cash. Because liabilities released are boot, the presence of a liability can trigger gain to the lesser of boot received or gain realized.

---

[12] IRC § 1031(d).

**EXAMPLE 12-7**

Jack exchanges land used in his business (FMV $200,000) for Dave's land (FMV $150,000). Jack's basis in the land is $75,000 and is subject to a liability of $50,000, which Dave assumes.

| | |
|---|---|
| Proceeds | $200,000* |
| Basis | (75,000) |
| Realized gain | $125,000† |

\* The FMV of the land received of $150,000 plus the release of a liability of $50,000.
† The realized gain is $125,000, of which $50,000 is recognized (the lesser of boot received or gain realized). The released liability is boot. The basis in the new land is $75,000 (FMV of land received of $150,000 less the deferred gain of $75,000).

## Exchanges between Related Parties

Exchanges between related parties are not like-kind exchanges if either party disposes of the property within two years of the exchange. Any gain realized on the exchange is recognized in the year of the subsequent sale.[13] A *related party* includes the taxpayer's spouse, child, grandchild, parent, brother, or sister; or a related corporation, S corporation, partnership, or trust. Death or involuntary conversions within the two-year period do not trigger the gain.[14]

**TAX YOUR BRAIN**

Why does the tax law disallow a nontaxable exchange between related parties if the property is sold within two years?

**ANSWER**

Suppose one brother was in the 35% tax bracket and the other brother was in the 15% tax bracket. The brothers could exchange gain property held by the high-bracket brother at no gain, and the low-bracket brother could sell the property and pay tax at a lower tax rate. Corporations and shareholders owning more than 50% of the stock are also related parties. Without the disallowance, the same type of transaction could occur between the corporation and a related shareholder.

## Deferred Exchanges

One problem with a like-kind exchange is finding someone willing to exchange properties. However, with a properly executed like-kind exchange, the exchange can be nontaxable even if a seller of a property is unwilling to exchange properties. As noted, a like-kind exchange does not need to be simultaneous to be tax-free. The Ninth Circuit Court of Appeals held that the contractual right to receive like-kind property is the same as the ownership rights themselves.[15] The court did not specify a time period, so Congress imposed the 45- and 180-day time requirements discussed earlier.

The most common arrangement for a deferred exchange occurs when the title to the property to be exchanged is placed in an escrow account with a custodian (usually an attorney or CPA). The custodian sells the property and places the cash in an escrow account. The taxpayer then has 45 days to identify like-kind property. When the property has been identified, the custodian purchases the new asset and distributes the title to the taxpayer. The main restriction is

---

[13] IRC § 1031(f).
[14] IRC § 1031(f)(2).
[15] *Starker v. United States*, 602 F.2d 1341, 79-2 USTC (CCH) ¶ 9541 (9th Cir. 1979).

## From Shoebox to Software

The reporting requirements for like-kind exchanges are not complex for single asset exchanges. The taxpayer is required to file Form 8824. On Form 8824, the taxpayer reports the FMV of property given up, the basis of the property given, and the gain or loss realized. The taxpayer compares the boot property to the realized gain to determine how much gain, if any, must be recognized.

Exhibit 12-1 illustrates the reporting for the exchange in Example 12-7. Recall that Jack traded land with an FMV of $200,000 and a liability of $50,000 for land with an FMV of $150,000.[16] Because the gain of $50,000 is recognized on the like-kind exchange and the land was used in a business, the land is considered § 1231 property. Thus, the gain transfers to page 1 of Form 4797.

that the taxpayer cannot, at any time, have actual or constructive receipt of the proceeds from the sale of old property. In other words, the taxpayer cannot touch or be able to use the cash proceeds; otherwise, the nontaxable exchange will be disqualified.[17]

| **EXAMPLE 12-8** | On May 1, 2021, Riko offers to purchase real property from Zack for $100,000. However, Riko is unwilling to participate in a like-kind exchange. Thus, Zack enters into an exchange agreement with Carri (an attorney) to facilitate an exchange with respect to the real property. The exchange agreement between Zack and Carri provides that Zack will deliver a deed conveying real property to Carri, who, in turn, will deliver a deed conveying the real property to Riko in exchange for $100,000. The exchange agreement expressly limits Zack's rights to receive, pledge, borrow, or otherwise obtain benefits of the money or other property held by Carri. On May 17, 2021, Zack delivers to Carri a deed conveying the real property to Carri. On the same date, Carri delivers to Riko a deed conveying real property to him, and Riko deposits $100,000 in escrow. The escrow agreement provides that the money in escrow be used to purchase replacement property. On June 3, 2021 (within 45 days), Zack identifies replacement real property. On August 9, 2021, Carri uses $80,000 from the escrow to purchase the new real property. On the same date (within 180 days), Carri delivers to Zack a deed conveying new real property to him, and the escrow holder pays Zack $20,000, the balance of the escrow account (considered boot). Zack recognizes gain of the lesser of the realized gain or the boot received ($20,000). |
|---|---|

| **CONCEPT CHECK 12-1—** **LO 12-1**  | 1. With a correctly executed like-kind exchange, gain is never recognized unless the taxpayer receives boot. True or false? <br> 2. For a transaction to qualify for a like-kind exchange, an exchange of assets must occur and the assets must be held for trade or business use or for investment and be like-kind assets. True or false? <br> 3. A taxpayer has 180 days after relinquishing their property to identify a replacement property. True or false? <br> 4. The basis in the replacement property is typically the FMV of the property received less the gain postponed. True or false? |
|---|---|

# INVOLUNTARY CONVERSIONS
## LO 12-2

An *involuntary conversion* occurs when property is destroyed, stolen, condemned, or disposed of under the threat of condemnation and the taxpayer receives other property or payment such as an insurance or condemnation award. If the taxpayer receives other property for the converted property of similar or related use, the taxpayer recognizes no gain.[18]

---

[16] The dates included on the tax form were not given in the example.

[17] Reg. § 1.1031(k)-1(g). This regulation section gives safe harbor rules to protect against the actual or constructive receipt of the money.

[18] IRC § 1033(a)(1).

**EXHIBIT 12-1**

| Form **8824** | **Like-Kind Exchanges** | OMB No. 1545-1190 |
|---|---|---|
| Department of the Treasury Internal Revenue Service | **(and section 1043 conflict-of-interest sales)** ▶ **Attach to your tax return.** ▶ **Go to** *www.irs.gov/Form8824* **for instructions and the latest information.** | **2021** Attachment Sequence No. **109** |

| Name(s) shown on tax return | Identifying number |
|---|---|
| Jack A. Trade | 412-34-5670 |

**Part I**    Information on the Like-Kind Exchange

**Note:** Generally, only real property should be described on lines 1 and 2. However, you may describe personal property transferred prior to January 1, 2018, as part of an exchange subject to the like-kind exchange transition rule described in the instructions, and/or real property on lines 1 and 2, if you are filing this form to report the disposition of property exchanged in a previously reported related party like-kind exchange. If the property described on line 1 or line 2 is real or personal property located outside the United States, indicate the country.

1    Description of like-kind property given up:
     Land located at 519 Exchange Avenue, Anywhere, USA

2    Description of like-kind property received:
     Land located at 321 Exchange Avenue, Anywhere, USA

| | | | |
|---|---|---|---|
| 3 | Date like-kind property given up was originally acquired (month, day, year) . . . . . . . | **3** | 10/15/2018 |
| 4 | Date you actually transferred your property to the other party (month, day, year) . . . . . . | **4** | 05/01/2021 |
| 5 | Date like-kind property you received was identified by written notice to another party (month, day, year). See instructions for 45-day written identification requirement . . . . . . . . . . | **5** | 05/01/2021 |
| 6 | Date you actually received the like-kind property from other party (month, day, year). See instructions | **6** | 05/01/2021 |

7    Was the exchange of the property given up or received made with a related party, either directly or indirectly (such as through an intermediary)? See instructions. If "Yes," complete Part II. If "No," go to Part III . . .    ☐ **Yes**    ☑ **No**

**Note:** Do not file this form if a related party sold property into the exchange, directly or indirectly (such as through an intermediary); that property became your replacement property; and none of the exceptions on line 11 applies to the exchange. Instead, report the disposition of the property as if the exchange had been a sale. If one of the exceptions on line 11 applies to the exchange, complete Part II.

**Part II**    Related Party Exchange Information

| 8 | Name of related party | Relationship to you | Related party's identifying number |
|---|---|---|---|
| | | | |

Address (no., street, and apt., room, or suite no.; city or town; state; and ZIP code)

9    During this tax year (and before the date that is 2 years after the last transfer of property that was part of the exchange), did the related party sell or dispose of any part of the like-kind property received from you (or an intermediary) in the exchange? . . . . . . . . . . . . . . .    ☐ **Yes**    ☐ **No**

10    During this tax year (and before the date that is 2 years after the last transfer of property that was part of the exchange), did you sell or dispose of any part of the like-kind property you received? . . . . . .    ☐ **Yes**    ☐ **No**

     *If both lines 9 and 10 are "No" and this is the year of the exchange, go to Part III. If both lines 9 and 10 are "No" and this is* **not** *the year of the exchange, stop here. If either line 9 or line 10 is "Yes," complete Part III and report on this year's tax return the deferred gain or (loss) from line 24* **unless** *one of the exceptions on line 11 applies.*

11    If one of the exceptions below applies to the disposition, check the applicable box.

   a    ☐ The disposition was after the death of either of the related parties.

   b    ☐ The disposition was an involuntary conversion, and the threat of conversion occurred after the exchange.

   c    ☐ You can establish to the satisfaction of the IRS that neither the exchange nor the disposition had tax avoidance as one of its principal purposes. If this box is checked, attach an explanation. See instructions.

| For Paperwork Reduction Act Notice, see the instructions. | Cat. No. 12311A | Form **8824** (2021) |
|---|---|---|

Source: U.S. Department of the Treasury, Internal Revenue Service, Form 8824. Washington, DC: 2021.

**EXHIBIT 12-1**   *(concluded)*

Form 8824 (2021)                                                                                         Page **2**

Name(s) shown on tax return. Do not enter name and social security number if shown on other side.   | Your social security number

**Part III   Realized Gain or (Loss), Recognized Gain, and Basis of Like-Kind Property Received**

**Caution:** If you transferred **and** received **(a)** more than one group of like-kind properties, or **(b)** cash or other (not like-kind) property, see *Reporting of multi-asset exchanges* in the instructions.

**Note:** Complete lines 12 through 14 **only** if you gave up property that was not like-kind. Otherwise, go to line 15.

| | | |
|---|---|---:|
| 12 | Fair market value (FMV) of other property given up. See instructions **12** | |
| 13 | Adjusted basis of other property given up **13** | |
| 14 | Gain or (loss) recognized on other property given up. Subtract line 13 from line 12. Report the gain or (loss) in the same manner as if the exchange had been a sale **14** | |

**Caution:** If the property given up was used previously or partly as a home, see ***Property used as home*** in the instructions.

| | | |
|---|---|---:|
| 15 | Cash received, FMV of other property received, plus net liabilities assumed by other party, reduced (but not below zero) by any exchange expenses you incurred. See instructions **15** | 50,000 |
| 16 | FMV of like-kind property you received **16** | 150,000 |
| 17 | Add lines 15 and 16 **17** | 200,000 |
| 18 | Adjusted basis of like-kind property you gave up, net amounts paid to other party, plus any exchange expenses **not** used on line 15. See instructions **18** | 75,000 |
| 19 | **Realized gain or (loss).** Subtract line 18 from line 17 **19** | 125,000 |
| 20 | Enter the smaller of line 15 or line 19, but not less than zero **20** | 50,000 |
| 21 | Ordinary income under recapture rules. Enter here and on Form 4797, line 16. See instructions **21** | |
| 22 | Subtract line 21 from line 20. If zero or less, enter -0-. If more than zero, enter here and on Schedule D or Form 4797, unless the installment method applies. See instructions **22** | 50,000 |
| 23 | **Recognized gain.** Add lines 21 and 22 **23** | 50,000 |
| 24 | Deferred gain or (loss). Subtract line 23 from line 19. If a related party exchange, see instructions **24** | 75,000 |
| 25 | **Basis of like-kind property received.** Subtract line 15 from the sum of lines 18 and 23. See instructions **25** | 75,000 |

**Part IV   Deferral of Gain From Section 1043 Conflict-of-Interest Sales**

**Note:** This part is to be used **only** by officers or employees of the executive branch of the federal government or judicial officers of the federal government (including certain spouses, minor or dependent children, and trustees as described in section 1043) for reporting nonrecognition of gain under section 1043 on the sale of property to comply with the conflict-of-interest requirements. This part can be used **only** if the cost of the replacement property is more than the basis of the divested property.

| | | |
|---|---|---|
| 26 | Enter the number from the upper right corner of your certificate of divestiture. (**Do not** attach a copy of your certificate. Keep the certificate with your records.) ▶ | – |
| 27 | Description of divested property ▶ | |
| 28 | Description of replacement property ▶ | |
| 29 | Date divested property was sold (month, day, year) **29** | MM/DD/YYYY |
| 30 | Sales price of divested property. See instructions **30** | |
| 31 | Basis of divested property **31** | |
| 32 | **Realized gain.** Subtract line 31 from line 30 **32** | |
| 33 | Cost of replacement property purchased within 60 days after date of sale **33** | |
| 34 | Subtract line 33 from line 30. If zero or less, enter -0- **34** | |
| 35 | Ordinary income under recapture rules. Enter here and on Form 4797, line 10. See instructions **35** | |
| 36 | Subtract line 35 from line 34. If zero or less, enter -0-. If more than zero, enter here and on Schedule D or Form 4797. See instructions **36** | |
| 37 | **Deferred gain.** Subtract the sum of lines 35 and 36 from line 32 **37** | |
| 38 | **Basis of replacement property.** Subtract line 37 from line 33 **38** | |

Form **8824** (2021)

**EXAMPLE 12-9**

The state of Alabama condemned 300 acres of Art's land. In payment to Art, the state awarded him 300 acres of similar land. In this case, Art recognizes no gain or loss, and the basis of his new land is the same as his old land.

A far more likely scenario is that the taxpayer receives cash either from the condemning authority or from an insurance policy (in the case of a casualty). In this case, the taxpayer must recognize any gain unless they elect the nonrecognition provisions.[19] This election provides that, in general, no gain will be recognized on an involuntary conversion if the taxpayer replaces the converted property with similar property of equal or greater value within a certain time.

**EXAMPLE 12-10**

A tornado destroyed Kelly's building used in a trade or business. Kelly purchased the building in 1987 for $100,000, and it is now fully depreciated (zero adjusted basis). She received $250,000 in insurance proceeds for the replacement cost. Unless Kelly elects to replace the property with similar-use property costing $250,000 or more, she must recognize the $250,000 gain.

To defer the entire gain, the replacement property must be purchased for an amount equal to or greater than the proceeds from the conversion. The gain is recognized at the lower of the gain realized or the proceeds *not* used for replacement. If, in this example, the replacement building costs only $240,000, Kelly would recognize $10,000 of the $250,000 realized gain.

The involuntary conversion provisions do not apply to losses. Losses are deducted without reference to the involuntary conversion rules and are allowed to the extent allowed by the casualty loss rules for either personal property (see Chapter 5) or business property (see Chapter 6).

## Replacement Property

To postpone any gain, the taxpayer must purchase qualifying replacement property with the specific purpose of replacing the converted property. However, qualifying property depends on the type of property held prior to the involuntary conversion. If the property lost is anything other than real property, the replacement property must be "similar or related in service or use."[20] This test is more restrictive than the like-kind test.

**EXAMPLE 12-11**

A delivery van used in Chris's business was destroyed in an auto accident. The van was fully depreciated. Chris received $8,000 in insurance proceeds. To qualify as replacement property, Chris must replace the van with a vehicle of similar or related use.[21]

If the property destroyed or condemned is real property, the similar use restrictions are lowered. The replacement property for real property must be only like-kind.[22]

---

[19] IRC § 1033(a)(2)(A).

[20] IRC § 1033(a)(2)(A).

[21] If the property was lost in a presidentially declared disaster zone, any tangible property held for productive use in the business qualifies. In this case, any tangible business property qualifies as replacement property.

[22] IRC § 1033(g)(1).

**EXAMPLE 12-12**

The city condemned an office building owned by Alice. Her basis in the building was $120,000, and she received $200,000 in condemnation proceeds. If Alice invests $200,000 or more in a residential building instead of an office building, she meets the like-kind test even though the similar use test is not met.

The IRC also allows the taxpayer to purchase stock in a corporation that holds property similar to the converted property. However, the taxpayer must have control of the corporation with similar-use property for the acquisition to qualify as replacement property.[23]

### Replacement Period

The time to purchase replacement property is limited. The replacement period ends two years after the close of the first taxable year in which any part of the gain is realized.[24]

The two years to replace involuntarily converted property is the norm for most property. However, for real property held for use in a trade or business or investment that is condemned, the replacement period is three years.[25]

**EXAMPLE 12-13**

The state condemned Connie's land with a $200,000 basis on October 23, 2021. Connie received proceeds of $310,000 on December 12, 2021. Because the $110,000 gain was realized in 2021, she has until December 31, 2024, to replace the property and defer the gain. If the proceeds were received on January 5, 2022, Connie would have until December 31, 2025, to replace the property (three years from the end of the tax year in which the gain was realized because the property was real property).

### Basis and Holding Period of Replacement Property

The basis calculation for the replacement property is similar to like-kind exchanges. The basis is calculated as follows when property is converted directly to similar property:[26]

|   | Adjusted basis of converted property |
|---|---|
| + | Increased by money reinvested in excess of proceeds received |
| − | Decreased by money received not used to replace the property |
| + | Amount of gain recognized by the taxpayer on the conversion |
| − | Amount of loss recognized by the taxpayer on the conversion |
| = | Adjusted basis of replacement property |

When the conversion results in money received (which is usually the case through either insurance proceeds or a condemnation award) and replacement property is purchased within the two-year period, the basis of the new property is its cost less the deferred gain.[27]

**EXAMPLE 12-14**

Assume the same facts as in Example 12-13. However, in June 2021, Connie finds suitable replacement land and acquires it for $325,000. She recognizes none of the $110,000 gain because the property is replaced within the three-year period and the acquisition price is more than $310,000. The basis of the new land is $215,000 ($325,000 purchase price less $110,000 deferred gain).

[23] IRC § 1033(a)(2)(A).
[24] IRC § 1033(a)(2)(B)(i).
[25] IRC § 1033(g)(4).
[26] IRC § 1033(b)(1).
[27] IRC § 1033(b)(2).

## From Shoebox to Software

As mentioned previously, there is no form to elect deferral of gain on an involuntary conversion. The taxpayer simply attaches a schedule or statement to the end of the tax return noting the election. If the replacement property is purchased in a subsequent tax year, another statement is attached to the subsequent return detailing the replacement property. Exhibit 12-2 is an example of a sample statement attached to a tax return regarding involuntary conversions.

**EXHIBIT 12-2**
**(for year of involuntary conversion)**
**Connie Erwin**
**SSN 123-45-6789**
**Tax Year 2021**

The land parcel at 104 Asphalt Drive, Cary, AZ, was taken by eminent domain by the state of Arizona on October 23, 2021. The proceeds from the state amounted to $310,000. I elect the deferral of gain under IRC § 1033.

| | |
|---|---|
| Proceeds | $310,000 |
| Adjusted basis | (200,000) |
| Deferred gain | $110,000 |

**(for the tax year when replacement property is acquired)**
**Connie Erwin**
**SSN 123-45-6789**
**Tax Year 2022**

A land parcel at 112 Fix Drive, Cary, AZ, was purchased for $325,000 as replacement property for land conveyed to the state of Arizona on October 23, 2021. The gain is deferred under IRC § 1033.

| | |
|---|---|
| State proceeds | $310,000 |
| Adjusted basis | (200,000) |
| Deferred gain | $110,000 |
| | |
| Cost of new land | $325,000 |
| Deferred gain | (110,000) |
| Basis of new land | $215,000 |

---

**EXAMPLE 12-15**   Assume the same facts as in Example 12-14 ($310,000 in condemnation proceeds). Suppose the purchase price of the new land was only $260,000. In this case, $50,000 of the gain is recognized because $50,000 of the proceeds is not used to replace the converted property. The basis of the new property would be $200,000 ($260,000 purchase price less $60,000 deferred gain).

---

The holding period for the replacement property includes the holding period of the converted property.[28]

In two instances concerning involuntary conversions, taxpayers must file an amended tax return (Form 1040X):

1. The taxpayer does not buy replacement property within the replacement period. In this case, the gain on the sale of the asset and any tax due must be reported in the year of the conversion.

2. The replacement property purchased by the taxpayer costs less than the amount realized for the converted property.[29]

The taxpayer reports the gain either on Form 4797 for business property or on Schedule D for personal investment property.

---

[28] IRC § 1223(1)(A).
[29] IRS Publication 544, *Sales and Other Disposition of Assets,* pp. 7–10.

**CONCEPT CHECK 12-2— LO 12-2**

Assume these facts to answer the following questions: A fire destroyed Andrew's building used in his woodworking business. He had purchased the building several years ago for $75,000, and it now has a $50,000 adjusted basis. Andrew received $105,000 in insurance proceeds for the replacement cost.

1. If Andrew does not replace the building, what is his taxable gain?
2. How many years does Andrew have to replace the building to defer any recognized gain?
3. How much gain would Andrew be required to recognize if he replaced the building (within the replacement period) with another building costing $95,000?
4. How much gain would Andrew be required to recognize if he replaced the building with another building costing $115,000?
5. Assuming the same facts as in Question (4), how much would Andrew's basis be in the new building?

# INSTALLMENT SALES

## LO 12-3

When an asset is sold, any gain or loss is usually recognized in the year of sale. The IRC allows the taxpayer a method to defer some of the gain to future years.[30] An *installment sale* is a disposition of property for which at least one payment is to be received after the year of the sale.[31]

Typically, payments on installment sales consist of three components:

1. Interest income.
2. Return of adjusted basis in the property sold.
3. Gain on the sale.

Taxpayers report the interest income separately (on Form 1040, Schedule B) from the gain on the sale. The return of basis and the gain portion of each payment are determined based on the gross profit percentage of the asset sold. The gross profit percentage is calculated as follows:

| | | |
|---|---|---|
| Selling price | | $100,000 |
| Installment sale basis | | |
|   Adjusted basis of the property | $25,000 | |
|   Selling expenses | 3,000 | |
|   Depreciation recapture | –0– | (28,000) |
| Gross profit | | $ 72,000 |
| Contract price | | $100,000 |
| Gross profit percentage | | |
| (gross profit/contract price) | 72% | |

Most installment payments have an interest component. However, the interest charges do not affect the gross profit calculation. If the taxpayer in the preceding example were to receive

[30] IRC § 453.

[31] IRC § 453(b)(1).

a $20,000 cash down payment and $20,000 for the next four years, income would be recognized as follows:

| | Cash Received* | Income | Return of Basis |
|---|---|---|---|
| Year of sale | $ 20,000 × 72% | $14,400 | $ 5,600 |
| 1st payment | 20,000 × 72% | 14,400 | 5,600 |
| 2nd payment | 20,000 × 72% | 14,400 | 5,600 |
| 3rd payment | 20,000 × 72% | 14,400 | 5,600 |
| 4th payment | 20,000 × 72% | 14,400 | 5,600 |
| | $100,000 | $72,000 | $28,000 |

\* In this example, the interest component is ignored for simplicity. If a 10% interest rate were assumed, the first installment payment would also have $8,000 of interest ($6,000 for payment 2, $4,000 for payment 3, and $2,000 for payment 4). Thus, the first-year cash received is actually $28,000 ($20,000 installment plus $8,000 in interest).

The contract price is the selling price or the selling price reduced by any debt assumed by the buyer. In the preceding example, the contract price and the selling price are the same.[32]

---

**EXAMPLE 12-16**

Assume the same facts as just given except that the buyer agrees to pay $80,000 in cash over four years and assume a $20,000 liability attached to the asset.

| | | |
|---|---|---|
| Selling price | | $100,000 |
| Installment sale basis | | |
|     Adjusted basis of the property | $25,000 | |
|     Selling expenses | 3,000 | |
|     Depreciation recapture | –0– | (28,000) |
| Gross profit | | $ 72,000 |
| Contract price ($100,000 − $20,000) | | $ 80,000 |
| Gross profit percentage | | |
| (gross profit/contract price) | 90% | |

---

If the taxpayer in the same example were to receive a $20,000 cash down payment and $15,000 for the next four years, income would be recognized as follows:

| | Cash Received* | Income | Return of Basis |
|---|---|---|---|
| Year of sale | $20,000 × 90% | $18,000 | $2,000 |
| 1st payment | 15,000 × 90% | 13,500 | 1,500 |
| 2nd payment | 15,000 × 90% | 13,500 | 1,500 |
| 3rd payment | 15,000 × 90% | 13,500 | 1,500 |
| 4th payment | 15,000 × 90% | 13,500 | 1,500 |
| | $80,000 | $72,000 | $8,000 |

\* Again, the interest component would be separate from the gross profit calculations, but the additional cash for interest would be received.

---

[32] Reg. § 15a.453-1(b)(5), Ex. 2.

## Dealers, Inventory, and Depreciation Recapture

An installment sale does not include any dispositions by a taxpayer who is a dealer in the item sold (for example, a car dealership cannot use the installment method to account for the sale of a car).[33] Likewise, a taxpayer cannot use the installment method to report a gain from the sale of stock or securities traded on an established securities market.

Note in the preceding examples that depreciation recapture is added to the basis in the gross profit calculation. We discussed depreciation recapture in Chapter 7. Any depreciation deducted on personal assets used in a trade or business (§1245 assets) must be recaptured as ordinary income when the asset is disposed of. If that asset is sold on the installment method, the depreciation recapture is recognized in the year of sale and cannot be deferred.

Other limitations apply to installment sales between related parties. If the related party resells the property before *all* installment payments have been made or within two years of the sale, any payment received by the related party on the second sale is treated as an amount received by the original seller.[34]

## Electing Out of the Installment Method

Taxpayers must use the installment method for deferred payments unless they elect not to use the installment method.

**TAX YOUR BRAIN**

Why might a taxpayer wish to elect out of the installment method and not defer any gain?

**ANSWER**

A taxpayer may want to report the entire gain in the year of sale if the gain were a capital gain and the taxpayer had a large capital loss that would go unused in the current year.

To elect out of the installment method, the taxpayer simply reports the sale in its entirety on Form 4797 or Schedule D, whichever applies.

**CONCEPT CHECK 12-3— LO 12-3**

1. Tamaria sold a tract of land for $30,000. The land has a basis of $18,000, and she incurred $2,000 of selling expenses. Tamaria received $5,000 down and will receive five additional annual payments of $5,000 each. What is Tamaria's gross profit percentage on the sale?
   a. 33.3%.
   b. 60.0%.
   c. 66.7%.
   d. 100.0%.

2. Assume the same facts. How much income will Tamaria recognize in year 2 when she receives the first additional payment of $5,000?
   a. $0.
   b. $1,667.
   c. $3,335.
   d. $5,000.

[33] IRC § 453(b)(2).
[34] IRC § 453(e).

# From Shoebox to Software

A taxpayer initially reports installment sales on Form 6252 and transfers any recognized gain to Schedule D or Form 4797, as appropriate. Exhibit 12-3 illustrates the tax reporting for Example 12-16. In this example, the taxpayer received $80,000 cash ($20,000 down and the remainder over four years). The buyer also assumed a $20,000 liability.

To record an installment sale in most software programs, open Form 6252 on the Forms menu. Fill in the proceeds, basis, commissions, and the amount of cash received during the tax year. The software calculates the gross profit percentage and the recognized gain. The software then transfers the gain to Schedule D or Form 4797.

# SALE OF A PERSONAL RESIDENCE
## LO 12-4

The Taxpayer Relief Act of 1997 changed the treatment of the sale of personal residences in favor of taxpayers. Under certain conditions (explained later), a taxpayer can exclude up to $500,000 ($250,000 for a single taxpayer) of gain on the sale of his or her primary residence.[35] Note that this provision is an exclusion, not a deferral of gain.

Even though a taxpayer is allowed tax deductions for more than one home for various other provisions in the IRC,[36] the residence exclusion applies only to the taxpayer's principal residence. To qualify for the exclusion, the taxpayer must meet the ownership test and the use test. During the five-year period ending on the date of the sale, the taxpayer must have satisfied

- The ownership test: owned the home for at least two years.
- The use test: lived in the home as the main home for at least two years.[37]

The ownership and use tests do not have to be continuous. The taxpayer need only show that they lived in the main home for either 24 full months or 730 days during the five-year period.

**EXAMPLE 12-17**

David purchased a house on May 1, 2019. He lived in the house from May 1, 2019, until April 15, 2020. He then lived in Germany from April 15, 2020, to April 1, 2021. David moved back into the house from April 1, 2021, until June 5, 2022, when he sold the house. Because David has lived in the house for 24 full months in the five years prior to the sale of the home, he is eligible for the exclusion (11 months the first time and 14 months after he returned from Germany).

## Reduced Maximum Exclusion

The exclusion applies to only one sale every two years. The taxpayer is ineligible for the exclusion if, during the two-year period ending on the date of sale of the present home, the taxpayer sold another home at a gain and excluded all or part of that gain.[38] If the second sale is caused by a change in the place of employment, health reasons, or other unforeseen circumstances, the taxpayer is still eligible for some reduced exclusion. In this situation, a portion of the gain can be excluded by dividing the number of days used by 730 days and multiplying by the full exclusion amount.[39]

---

[35] IRC § 121(a), (b).

[36] For example, a taxpayer can deduct the mortgage interest on a primary residence and a second vacation home as an itemized deduction.

[37] IRC § 121(a).

[38] IRC § 121(b)(3).

[39] IRC § 121(c)(2)(B).

**EXHIBIT 12-3**

| Form **6252** | **Installment Sale Income** | OMB No. 1545-0228 |
|---|---|---|
| Department of the Treasury Internal Revenue Service | ▶ Attach to your tax return.<br>▶ Use a separate form for each sale or other disposition of property on the installment method.<br>▶ Go to *www.irs.gov/Form6252* for the latest information. | 2021<br>Attachment Sequence No. **67** |

| Name(s) shown on return | Identifying number |
|---|---|
| Juan Taxpayer | 412-34-5670 |

| | | |
|---|---|---|
| **1** | Description of property ▶ Land, 303 Anywhere Road | |
| **2a** | Date acquired (mm/dd/yyyy) ▶   02/05/2001      **b** Date sold (mm/dd/yyyy) ▶   10/23/2021 | |
| **3** | Was the property sold to a related party (see instructions) after May 14, 1980? If "No," skip line 4 . . . | ☐ Yes  ☑ No |
| **4** | Was the property you sold to a related party a marketable security? If "Yes," complete Part III. If "No," complete Part III for the year of sale and the 2 years after the year of sale . . . . . . . . . . . . | ☐ Yes  ☐ No |

| **Part I** | **Gross Profit and Contract Price.** Complete this part for all years of the installment agreement. | | |
|---|---|---|---|
| **5** | Selling price including mortgages and other debts. **Don't** include interest, whether stated or unstated | **5** | 100,000 |
| **6** | Mortgages, debts, and other liabilities the buyer assumed or took the property subject to (see instructions) . . . . . . . . . . . . . . . **6** | 20,000 | |
| **7** | Subtract line 6 from line 5 . . . . . . . . . . . . . . . . **7** | 80,000 | |
| **8** | Cost or other basis of property sold . . . . . . . . . . . **8** | 25,000 | |
| **9** | Depreciation allowed or allowable . . . . . . . . . . . . **9** | 0 | |
| **10** | Adjusted basis. Subtract line 9 from line 8 . . . . . . . . **10** | 25,000 | |
| **11** | Commissions and other expenses of sale . . . . . . . . **11** | 3,000 | |
| **12** | Income recapture from Form 4797, Part III (see instructions) . **12** | | |
| **13** | Add lines 10, 11, and 12 . . . . . . . . . . . . . . . . | **13** | 28,000 |
| **14** | Subtract line 13 from line 5. If zero or less, **don't** complete the rest of this form. See instructions . . | **14** | 72,000 |
| **15** | If the property described on line 1 above was your main home, enter the amount of your excluded gain. See instructions. Otherwise, enter -0- . . . . . . . . . . . . . . . . | **15** | 0 |
| **16** | **Gross profit.** Subtract line 15 from line 14 . . . . . . . . . . . . . . . . | **16** | 72,000 |
| **17** | Subtract line 13 from line 6. If zero or less, enter -0- . . . . . . . . . . . . . . | **17** | 0 |
| **18** | **Contract price.** Add line 7 and line 17 . . . . . . . . . . . . . . . . . . | **18** | 80,000 |

| **Part II** | **Installment Sale Income.** Complete this part for all years of the installment agreement. | | |
|---|---|---|---|
| **19** | Gross profit percentage (expressed as a decimal amount). Divide line 16 by line 18. (For years after the year of sale, see instructions.) . . . . . . . . . . . . . . . . | **19** | 0.90 |
| **20** | If this is the year of sale, enter the amount from line 17. Otherwise, enter -0- . . . . . . . | **20** | 0 |
| **21** | Payments received during year (see instructions). **Don't** include interest, whether stated or unstated . | **21** | 20,000 |
| **22** | Add lines 20 and 21 . . . . . . . . . . . . . . . . . . . . . . | **22** | 20,000 |
| **23** | Payments received in prior years (see instructions). **Don't** include interest, whether stated or unstated . . . . . . . . . . . . . . . . . **23** | 0 | |
| **24** | **Installment sale income.** Multiply line 22 by line 19 . . . . . . . . . . . . . | **24** | 18,000 |
| **25** | Enter the part of line 24 that is ordinary income under the recapture rules. See instructions . . . . | **25** | 0 |
| **26** | Subtract line 25 from line 24. Enter here and on Schedule D or Form 4797. See instructions . . . | **26** | 18,000 |

| **Part III** | **Related Party Installment Sale Income. Don't** complete if you received the final payment this tax year. | | |
|---|---|---|---|
| **27** | Name, address, and taxpayer identifying number of related party ▶ | | |
| **28** | Did the related party resell or dispose of the property ("second disposition") during this tax year? . . . . . | ☐ Yes  ☐ No | |
| **29** | **If the answer to question 28 is "Yes," complete lines 30 through 37 below unless one of the following conditions is met. Check the box that applies.** | | |
| **a** | ☐ The second disposition was more than 2 years after the first disposition (other than dispositions of marketable securities). If this box is checked, enter the date of disposition (mm/dd/yyyy) . . . . . . . . . . . ▶ | | |
| **b** | ☐ The first disposition was a sale or exchange of stock to the issuing corporation. | | |
| **c** | ☐ The second disposition was an involuntary conversion and the threat of conversion occurred after the first disposition. | | |
| **d** | ☐ The second disposition occurred after the death of the original seller or buyer. | | |
| **e** | ☐ It can be established to the satisfaction of the IRS that tax avoidance wasn't a principal purpose for either of the dispositions. If this box is checked, attach an explanation. See instructions. | | |
| **30** | Selling price of property sold by related party (see instructions) . . . . . . . . . . **30** | | |
| **31** | Enter contract price from line 18 for year of first sale . . . . . . . . . . **31** | | |
| **32** | Enter the **smaller** of line 30 or line 31 . . . . . . . . . . **32** | | |
| **33** | Total payments received by the end of your 2021 tax year (see instructions) . . . . . . **33** | | |
| **34** | Subtract line 33 from line 32. If zero or less, enter -0- . . . . . . . . . **34** | | |
| **35** | Multiply line 34 by the gross profit percentage on line 19 for year of first sale . . . . . **35** | | |
| **36** | Enter the part of line 35 that is ordinary income under the recapture rules. See instructions . . . . **36** | | |
| **37** | Subtract line 36 from line 35. Enter here and on Schedule D or Form 4797. See instructions . . . **37** | | |

| For Paperwork Reduction Act Notice, see page 4. | Cat. No. 13601R | Form **6252** (2021) |
|---|---|---|

Source: U.S. Department of the Treasury, Internal Revenue Service, Form 6252. Washington, DC: 2021.

**EXHIBIT 12-4** **Worksheet for the Reduced Maximum Exclusion**

| Worksheet 3. **Reduced Maximum Exclusion** | | *Keep for Your Records* | |
|---|---|---|---|
| **Caution:** *Complete this worksheet only if you qualify for a reduced maximum exclusion (see* Reduced Maximum Exclusion*). Complete column (a).* | | **(a)** You | **(b)** Your Spouse |
| **1.** | Maximum amount ................................................. **1.** | $250,000 | $250,000 |
| **2a.** | Enter the number of days (or months) that you used the property as a main home during the 5-year period* ending on the date of sale ................................... **2a.** | | |
| **b.** | Enter the number of days (or months) that you owned the property during the 5-year period* ending on the date of sale. If you used days on line 2a, you also must use days on this line and on lines 3 and 5. If you used months on line 2a, you also must use months on this line and on lines 3 and 5. (If married filing jointly and one spouse owned the property longer than the other spouse, both spouses are treated as owning the property for the longer period.) .......... **b.** | | |
| **c.** | Enter the smaller of line 2a or 2b ...................................... **c.** | | |
| **3.** | Have you (or your spouse, if filing jointly) excluded gain from the sale of another home during the 2-year period ending on the date of this sale? | | |
| | ☐ **No.** Skip line 3 and enter the number of days (or months) from line 2c on line 4. ☐ **Yes.** Enter the number of days (or months) between the date of the most recent sale of another home on which you excluded gain and the date of sale of this home ...................................................... **3.** | | |
| **4.** | Enter the smaller of line 2c or 3 ....................................... **4.** | | |
| **5.** | Divide the amount on line 4 by 730 days (or 24 months). Enter the result as a decimal (rounded to at least 3 places). But do not enter an amount greater than 1.000 ......................................................... **5.** | | |
| **6.** | Multiply the amount on line 1 by the decimal amount on line 5 ................... **6.** | | |
| **7.** | **Reduced maximum exclusion.** Add the amounts in columns (a) and (b) of line 6. Enter it here and on Worksheet 2, line 13 ........................... **7.** | | |

*\*If you were a member of the uniformed services or Foreign Service, an employee of the intelligence community, or an employee or volunteer of the Peace Corps during the time you owned the home, see* Members of the uniformed services or Foreign Service, employees of the intelligence community, or employees or volunteers of the Peace Corps *to determine your 5-year period.*

Source: IRS Publication 523, *Selling Your Home.*

**EXAMPLE 12-18**    Rob (single) sold his house in Charlotte, North Carolina, at a gain of $130,000 on May 5, 2021. He properly excluded the gain. He left Charlotte to take a job in Richmond, Virginia, where he purchased a new home for $325,000 on June 10, 2021. On October 1, 2021, Rob's employer offered him a transfer to Orlando to manage the firm's Orlando office. Rob took the job and sold his Richmond home for $350,000 (a $25,000 gain) on October 10, 2021. Because the move was employment-related, Rob can exclude his gain up to $41,781. He lived in the home for 122 days from June 10, 2021, to October 10, 2021. Rob calculates his exclusion as follows:

$$122 \text{ days}/730 \text{ days} \times \$250{,}000 \text{ exclusion}[40]$$

$$= \$41{,}781 \text{ allowed exclusion}$$

Exhibit 12-4 provides a worksheet to help determine the reduced maximum exclusion.

Another exception to the two-year rule involves an individual who has a disability. The use test is modified if during the five-year period before the sale of the home, a taxpayer

- Became physically or mentally unable to care for themselves.

- Owned and lived in the home as the main residence for a total of at least one year.

In this case, the taxpayer is deemed to live in the home during any time he or she lived in a care facility licensed by a state or political subdivision.

[40] The exclusion is $250,000 if the taxpayer is single and $500,000 if the taxpayer is married and files a joint return.

# From Shoebox to Software

Because most post-1997 sales of residences produce gains of less than $250,000 for single taxpayers and $500,000 for married taxpayers, the reporting requirements involving the sale of a residence are minimal. If no gain is recognized on the sale of a residence, the taxpayer is not required to report the sale on any form or statement. If, however, the gain is larger than the allowed exclusion, the taxpayer is required to report the gain as a sale of a capital asset on Schedule D. When the gain is partially excluded, the taxpayer should write the amount excluded on Schedule D. Exhibit 12-5 illustrates the presentation on Schedule D of a gain recognized on the sale of a residence when some of the gain is excluded.

Tax software usually performs the exclusion calculation for you. With most software programs, you go to the Schedule D Home Sale worksheet and fill in the house sale information.

## Special Problems with Married Individuals

Married individuals can exclude up to $500,000 from the gain on a personal residence. However, what happens when one spouse is eligible for the exclusion and the other is not? In this case, each individual is treated separately.

| **EXAMPLE 12-19** | Diya sold her personal residence on July 10, 2020, at a $190,000 gain. She excluded the gain. On August 15, 2021, she married Gus. He sold his house on December 12, 2021, at a gain of $480,000. Because Diya is not eligible for the exclusion (she sold a residence within two years of the sale), only $250,000 of the $480,000 gain is excluded from income. |
|---|---|

Other special provisions for married individuals are summarized in Table 12-1.

**TABLE 12-1**
**Provisions for Married Individuals**

Source: IRS Publication 523, *Selling Your Home,* p. 13.

| | |
|---|---|
| One spouse sells a home | The other spouse is still allowed an exclusion of gain up to $250,000. |
| Death of spouse before sale | The surviving spouse is deemed to have owned and lived in the property for any period when the decedent spouse owned and lived in the home. Starting in 2008, a surviving spouse can qualify for up to $500,000 if the sale of the residence occurs not later than two years after one spouse's death. |
| Home transferred from spouse | The transferee spouse is considered to have owned the residence for any period of time when the transferor spouse owned the residence. |
| Use of home after divorce | The taxpayer is considered to have used the house during any period when (1) the taxpayer owned it and (2) the spouse or former spouse is allowed to live in it under a divorce or separation agreement. |

**CONCEPT CHECK 12-4—**
**LO 12-4**

1. If married taxpayers live in their personal residence for more than two years, the couple can exclude the gain on the sale of their residence up to $500,000. True or false?
2. Taxpayers cannot exclude any gain on the sale of a residence if they have lived there less than two years. True or false?
3. Sharon and Johnny were recently married, and Sharon moved into Johnny's house. She then sold her home and took the exclusion. Because Sharon took the exclusion, Johnny must forfeit his exclusion if he were to sell his home within the next two years. True or false?

**EXHIBIT 12-5**

Form 8949 (2021)     Attachment Sequence No. **12A**   Page **2**

Name(s) shown on return. Name and SSN or taxpayer identification no. not required if shown on other side
**Rob Johnson**

Social security number or taxpayer identification number
**412-34-5670**

*Before you check Box D, E, or F below, see whether you received any Form(s) 1099-B or substitute statement(s) from your broker. A substitute statement will have the same information as Form 1099-B. Either will show whether your basis (usually your cost) was reported to the IRS by your broker and may even tell you which box to check.*

**Part II**   **Long-Term.** Transactions involving capital assets you held more than 1 year are generally long-term (see instructions). For short-term transactions, see page 1.

**Note:** You may aggregate all long-term transactions reported on Form(s) 1099-B showing basis was reported to the IRS and for which no adjustments or codes are required. Enter the totals directly on Schedule D, line 8a; you aren't required to report these transactions on Form 8949 (see instructions).

You *must* check Box D, E, *or* F below. Check only one box. If more than one box applies for your long-term transactions, complete a separate Form 8949, page 2, for each applicable box. If you have more long-term transactions than will fit on this page for one or more of the boxes, complete as many forms with the same box checked as you need.

- ☐ **(D)** Long-term transactions reported on Form(s) 1099-B showing basis was reported to the IRS (see **Note** above)
- ☐ **(E)** Long-term transactions reported on Form(s) 1099-B showing basis **wasn't** reported to the IRS
- ☑ **(F)** Long-term transactions not reported to you on Form 1099-B

| 1 (a) Description of property (Example: 100 sh. XYZ Co.) | (b) Date acquired (Mo., day, yr.) | (c) Date sold or disposed of (Mo., day, yr.) | (d) Proceeds (sales price) (see instructions) | (e) Cost or other basis. | (f) Code(s) from instructions | (g) Amount of adjustment | (h) Gain or (loss). |
|---|---|---|---|---|---|---|---|
| Sale of Personal Residence | 04/05/07 | 05/05/21 | 470,000 | 325,000 | H | (135,000) | 10,000 |
| Adj. above is Sec 121 exclusion | | | | | | | |

**Part II**   **Long-Term Capital Gains and Losses—Generally Assets Held More Than One Year** (see instructions)

| | (d) Proceeds (sales price) | (e) Cost (or other basis) | (g) Adjustments to gain or loss from Form(s) 8949, Part II, line 2, column (g) | (h) Gain or (loss) Subtract column (e) from column (d) and combine the result with column (g) |
|---|---|---|---|---|
| **8a** Totals for all long-term transactions reported on Form 1099-B for which basis was reported to the IRS and for which you have no adjustments (see instructions). However, if you choose to report all these transactions on Form 8949, leave this line blank and go to line 8b . | | | | |
| **8b** Totals for all transactions reported on Form(s) 8949 with **Box D** checked . . . . . . . . . . | | | | |
| **9** Totals for all transactions reported on Form(s) 8949 with **Box E** checked . . . . . . . . . . | | | | |
| **10** Totals for all transactions reported on Form(s) 8949 with **Box F** checked. . . . . . . . . . | 470,000 | 325,000 | (135,000) | 10,000 |

| | | |
|---|---|---|
| **11** Gain from Form 4797, Part I; long-term gain from Forms 2439 and 6252; and long-term gain or (loss) from Forms 4684, 6781, and 8824 . . . . . . . . . . . . . . . . . | **11** | |
| **12** Net long-term gain or (loss) from partnerships, S corporations, estates, and trusts from Schedule(s) K-1 | **12** | |
| **13** Capital gain distributions. See the instructions . . . . . . . . . . . . . . . | **13** | |
| **14** Long-term capital loss carryover. Enter the amount, if any, from line 13 of your **Capital Loss Carryover Worksheet** in the instructions . . . . . . . . . . . . . . . | **14** ( ) | |
| **15** **Net long-term capital gain or (loss).** Combine lines 8a through 14 in column (h). Then, go to Part III on the back . . . . . . . . . . . . . . . . . . . . . | **15** | 10,000 |

Source: U.S. Department of the Treasury, Internal Revenue Service, Form 8949 and Form 1040, Schedule D. Washington, DC: 2021.

# RELATED-PARTY LOSSES AND WASH SALES
## LO 12-5

The related-party rules and wash sale rules limit losses (but not gains) when the taxpayer still has control over the property that caused the loss. In other words, these rules apply when the taxpayer creates a tax loss but does not substantially change the ownership of the property.

### Related-Party Losses

A taxpayer cannot deduct any loss from the sale or exchange of property, directly or indirectly, between related parties.[41] The following relationships are considered related parties:

- Members of a family including spouse, ancestors, lineal descendants, and brothers and sisters (whether whole or half blood).[42]
- An individual and a corporation when more than 50% in value of the outstanding stock is owned, directly or indirectly, by or for the individual.
- Two corporations that are members of the same controlled group.
- A grantor and a fiduciary of any trust.
- A fiduciary of a trust and a beneficiary of such trust.
- Any corporation or partnership where there is more than 50% ownership.

*Constructive ownership* rules also apply.[43] With constructive ownership, a taxpayer is deemed to also own the stock of anyone or any entity they control. A taxpayer constructively owns stock in the following instances:

- Stock owned by a corporation, partnership, estate, or trust shall be considered as being owned proportionately by its shareholders, partners, or beneficiaries.
- An individual is considered to own any stock owned by their family.
- An individual owning any stock in a corporation is considered to own the stock owned by or for their partner in a partnership.

---

**EXAMPLE 12-20**

Following are several examples concerning the constructive ownership rules:

Al owns 75% of Mama Corp.
Alice (Al's wife) owns 25% of Mama Corp.
Dad (Alice's dad) owns 0% of Mama Corp.
Pizza Corp. is owned 80% by Mama Corp.
Pizza Corp. is owned 20% by unrelated parties.

Tables 12-2 and 12-3 illustrate the ownership of the two corporations.

**TABLE 12-2**
**Stock Ownership of Mama Corp.**

| Person | Actual (percentage) | Constructive (percentage) | Total under Section 267 (percentage) |
|--------|--------------------|--------------------------|-------------------------------------|
| Al | 75% | From Alice 25% | 100% |
| Alice | 25 | From Al    75 | 100 |
| Dad | –0– | From Alice 25 | 25 |

*(continued)*

---

[41] IRC § 267(a)(1).
[42] IRC § 267(c)(4).
[43] Reg. § 1.267(c)-1(b).

**TABLE 12-3**
**Stock Ownership of Pizza Corp.**

| Person | Actual (percentage) | Constructive (percentage) | Total under Section 267 (percentage) |
|---|---|---|---|
| Al | –0–% | 60% & 20%* | 80% |
| Alice | –0– | 20 & 60† | 80 |
| Dad | –0– | 20‡ | 20 |
| Mama Corp. | 80 | –0– | 80 |

\* Deemed ownership through Mama Corp. 80% × 75% = 60% and through Alice 80% × 25% = 20%.
† Deemed ownership through Mama Corp. 80% × 25% = 20% and through Al 80% × 75% = 60%.
‡ Through Alice 80% × 25% = 20%.

Because Al and Alice control Mama Corp. and Mama Corp. controls Pizza Corp., Al and Alice are deemed to own Pizza Corp. Al and Alice are considered related parties to both Mama and Pizza.

**EXAMPLE 12-21**

Building Supply Inc. is owned 50% by Jake and 50% by his partner, Mia. Both Jake and Mia are related parties to Building Supply because each partner is considered as owning the stock of the other partner. Thus, both are considered to own more than 50% of the stock of Building Supply Inc.[44]

Once a relationship is considered a related party, any losses on the sale of property between related parties are disallowed. This rule can be especially harsh because the disallowance of the loss does not affect the basis of the property to the buyer. The basis is the cost of the property. IRC § 267(d) does provide some relief in that if the related buyer subsequently sells the property at a gain, the taxpayer reduces the recognized gain by the previously disallowed related-party loss.[45]

**EXAMPLE 12-22**

Jake sells land (basis $15,000) to related party Building Supply Inc. for $8,000. The $7,000 loss is disallowed to Jake, and the basis to Building Supply is $8,000. If Building Supply Inc. subsequently sells the land to an unrelated party for $10,000, the $2,000 gain is reduced to $0. The $5,000 leftover loss remains unused and is lost.

## Wash Sales of Stock

The purpose of the wash sale rules is to disallow a tax loss when the ownership of a company is not reduced. A *wash sale* occurs when a taxpayer sells stock or securities at a loss, and within a period of 30 days before or 30 days after the sale, the taxpayer acquires substantially identical stock or securities.[46]

**EXAMPLE 12-23**

On December 15, 2021, Kathy sold 300 shares of Electronics Inc. (a publicly traded company) at a loss of $2,500. On January 5, 2022, Kathy repurchased 300 shares of Electronics. The $2,500 loss is disallowed.

The wash sale rule does not apply to dealers in securities.

[44] Reg. § 1.267(c)–1(b) ex. 2.
[45] IRC § 267(d)(2).
[46] IRC § 1091(a).

**EXAMPLE 12-24**

Jackie made the following acquisitions of ABC Inc.:

> January 15, 2021, 300 shares @ $50/share = $15,000
> February 1, 2021, 200 shares @ $30/share = $6,000

To offset other capital gains, Jackie sells all 500 shares of ABC Inc. for $25 per share on December 15, 2021. Because she believes ABC is a good investment, she buys 600 shares of ABC on January 5, 2022, for $28 per share. Because she repurchased identical stock, Jackie cannot deduct the losses on the blocks of stock.

**EXAMPLE 12-25**

Assume the same facts as Example 12-24, but Jackie repurchased only 300 shares of ABC stock. In this case, a proportionate share of the loss is allowed. Because 300 of the 500 shares were repurchased, Jackie can deduct 40% of the losses.

A disallowed loss under the wash sale rule is not lost forever but only deferred. The taxpayer adds any disallowed loss to the basis of the newly acquired stock. Thus, the future disposal of the stock results in a reduced gain or greater loss.[47]

**EXAMPLE 12-26**

Serena purchased 100 shares of XYZ Corp. for $10 per share in 2009. She sold the 100 shares on December 1, 2020, for $6 per share. Within 30 days, she subsequently purchased 100 shares for $8 per share. No loss is recognized. The basis of the new 100 shares is $12 per share. This basis is the $8 per share cost plus the deferred loss of $4 per share.

**CONCEPT CHECK 12-5—**
**LO 12-5**

1. Leslie sold 500 shares of Bluff Co. stock to her brother for $5,000. Leslie purchased the stock three years ago for $7,000. How much of the loss can Leslie deduct on her tax return in the current year?
2. Would the answer to Question 1 change if Leslie had sold the stock to Leslie Co. instead of to her brother? Explain assuming the following facts:
   a. Leslie owns 25% of the outstanding stock in Leslie Co.
   b. Leslie owns 75% of the outstanding stock in Leslie Co.
3. What is the purpose of the wash sale rules?

# Summary

**LO 12-1:** Explain how to defer gains using the like-kind exchange rules.
- There must be an exchange.
- The property exchanged must be real property held for business use or for investment.
- The property exchanged must be like-kind.
- Boot property received can cause the recognition of gain.

**LO 12-2:** Describe how to account for and report involuntary conversions.
- If the taxpayer receives other property for the converted property of similar or related use, the taxpayer recognizes no gain.
- If the taxpayer receives cash for the converted property, the taxpayer must use the proceeds to replace the converted property with similar property of equal or greater value within two years (generally) to defer all of the gain.
- The basis of the property is typically its cost less any deferred gain.

**LO 12-3:** Apply the tax rules to report an installment sale.
- The taxpayer calculates a gross profit percentage based on the basis of the property sold divided by the selling price.
- As the taxpayer receives cash in installments, the gain is recognized based on the gross profit percentage.
- The interest income on any note receivable is a separate calculation.

[47] Reg. § 1.1091-2(a).

**LO 12-4:** Explain how to exclude a gain on the sale of a personal residence.

- A taxpayer can exclude up to $500,000 ($250,000 if single) of gain on the sale of a personal residence.
- The residence exclusion applies only to the taxpayer's principal residence.
- The taxpayer must have lived there two of the last five years.
- Reduced exclusions are available if a move is the result of employment transfers or health issues.

**LO 12-5:** Apply the rules affecting related parties and wash sales.

- A taxpayer cannot deduct any loss from the sale or exchange of property between related parties.
- Related parties include family members and controlled entities.
- The wash sale rules disallow a tax loss when the ownership of a company is not reduced.
- A wash sale occurs when a taxpayer sells stock and within a period of 30 days (before or after the sale) the taxpayer acquires substantially the same stock.

## EA Fast Fact

ADMITTED TO PRACTICE BEFORE THE IRS **ENROLLED AGENT**

Primary Topics on Part II of the EA exam, Business, include:

☐ *Part II—Businesses—3.5 hrs.*
- Definition of a Corporation
- Filing Requirements and Due Dates
- Forming a Corporation
- Special Provisions Applicable to Corporations
- Corporate Tax and Estimated Payment Requirements
- Reconciling Books to Return
- Distributions and Recognition Requirements
- Liquidations and Stock Redemptions
- Subchapter S Corporations
- Trusts

**IMPORTANT**

You are eligible to receive absolutely free, the Surgent Enrolled Agent review program for Part I of the EA exam as a result of purchasing this text. To activate your free access, go to https://Surgent.com/McGrawHill/EA.

## Discussion Questions  Mc Graw Hill connect

All applicable discussion questions are available with *Connect*©

LO 12-1   1. Can the exchange of personal-use property qualify as a like-kind exchange? Why or why not?

_____
_____
_____

LO 12-1   2. What types of properties do *not* qualify for like-kind exchange treatment?

_____
_____
_____

LO 12-1   3. Discuss the characteristics of a like-kind asset. Must the asset received in a like-kind exchange be an exact duplicate of the asset given? Explain.

_____
_____
_____

LO 12-1    4. What is *boot?* How does the receipt of boot affect a like-kind exchange?

LO 12-1    5. What is the difference between a *deferred gain* and an *excluded gain?*

LO 12-1    6. How is the basis calculated in a like-kind exchange? How does the receipt of boot affect the basis of the asset received? How does the giving of boot affect the basis of the asset received?

LO 12-1    7. Often, when assets are exchanged, liabilities are assumed in the exchange. How does the assumption of liabilities in a like-kind exchange affect the gain or loss recognized? How does it affect the basis of an asset received in a like-kind exchange?

LO 12-1    8. What are the special provisions for like-kind exchanges between related parties? Why are these special provisions included in the IRC?

LO 12-1    9. Must both parties in a potential like-kind exchange agree to the exchange? If not, how can the transaction be structured to defer any gain?

LO 12-2    10. What is an *involuntary conversion?*

LO 12-2    11. When an involuntary conversion occurs and the taxpayer receives insurance proceeds, what must the taxpayer do to guarantee that no gain is recognized?

LO 12-2    12. When faced with an involuntary conversion, does the taxpayer have an unlimited amount of time to replace the converted property? Explain.

_____

_____

_____

LO 12-2    13. How are the basis and holding period of the replacement property in an involuntary conversion determined? Explain.

_____

_____

_____

LO 12-2    14. What information must be reported to the IRS concerning an involuntary conversion?

_____

_____

_____

LO 12-3    15. How is income reported from an installment sale? What are the components of the payments received in an installment sale, and how is the gross profit percentage calculated?

_____

_____

_____

EA    LO 12-4    16. Discuss the rules concerning the sale of a personal residence. Include in your discussion the specifics regarding the *ownership test* and the *use test*.

_____

_____

_____

EA    LO 12-4    17. Is a taxpayer allowed to take the § 121 exclusion for a vacation home that was never rented? Explain.

_____

_____

_____

EA    LO 12-4    18. If a taxpayer moves within two years after moving into a new home and uses the exclusion on their former home, is any gain taxable on the sale of the new home? Under what conditions can some of the exclusion be used?

_____

_____

_____

EA    LO 12-4    19. What happens in the following circumstances if a wife, prior to marriage, uses the exclusion on the sale of a residence and subsequently (after marriage) sells a second residence within two years?

*a.* The new husband sells a residence.

_____
_____
_____

*b.* The new husband dies within two years and the wife sells the residence.

_____
_____
_____

**EA** LO 12-5 20. What is a *related-party loss,* and why is it disallowed?

_____
_____
_____

**EA** LO 12-5 21. Explain the constructive ownership rules and how they relate to related-party transactions.

_____
_____
_____

**EA** LO 12-5 22. What is a *wash sale,* and why are losses from wash sales disallowed?

_____
_____
_____

## Multiple-Choice Questions

All applicable multiple-choice questions are available with **Connect**©

LO 12-1 23. For an exchange to qualify as a nontaxable exchange, what criteria must be present?
   *a.* There must be an exchange.
   *b.* The property transferred and received must be real property held for use in a trade or business or for investment.
   *c.* The property exchanged must be like-kind.
   *d.* All of these must be present.

LO 12-1 24. For the asset received in a like-kind exchange, how is the holding period of the new asset determined?
   *a.* According to the date the new asset is received.
   *b.* According to the date the old asset is given away.
   *c.* According to the holding period of the old asset.
   *d.* None of the above apply.

LO 12-1 25. Which of the following exchanges qualifies as like-kind property?
   *a.* Partnership interest for partnership interest.
   *b.* Inventory for equipment.
   *c.* Investment land for land used as a business parking lot.
   *d.* Business-use delivery truck for a business-use van.

LO 12-1    26. Eric exchanged land used in his business with Geoff for another lot of land. Eric exchanged the land with a $75,000 FMV and $45,000 basis along with $15,000 cash. Geoff's basis in his land is $60,000, and the FMV is $90,000. Which of the following statements is correct?

*a.* Geoff must recognize a gain of $15,000 on the exchange.

*b.* Geoff must recognize a gain of $5,000 on the exchange.

*c.* Neither Eric nor Geoff must recognize a gain.

*d.* Eric must recognize a gain of $15,000 on the exchange.

LO 12-1    27. Ava exchanges a land used in her business with Gail for another parcel of land. The basis of Ava's old land is $50,000, the FMV is $66,000, and she gives Gail cash of $14,000. Gail's basis in her land is $70,000, and the FMV is $80,000. What is Ava's adjusted basis in the new land she receives?

*a.* $50,000.

*b.* $64,000.

*c.* $66,000.

*d.* $80,000.

LO 12-1    28. Janel exchanges a building she uses in her rental business for a building owned by Russel that she will use in her rental business. The adjusted basis of Janel's building is $160,000, and the FMV is $250,000. The adjusted basis of Russel's building is $80,000, and the FMV is $250,000. Which of the following statements is correct?

*a.* Janel's recognized gain is $0, and her basis for the building received is $160,000.

*b.* Janel's recognized gain is $90,000, and her basis for the building received is $160,000.

*c.* Janel's recognized gain is $0, and her basis for the building received is $250,000.

*d.* Janel's recognized gain is $90,000, and her basis for the building received is $250,000.

LO 12-1    29. Jason exchanged land for another lot of land. The old land had an adjusted basis of $14,000, and the new land had an FMV of $22,000. Jason also paid $5,000 cash in the exchange. What are the recognized gain or loss and the basis of the land?

*a.* $0 and $14,000.

*b.* $0 and $19,000.

*c.* $6,000 and $14,000.

*d.* ($8,000) and $9,000.

LO 12-1    30. Gretel exchanges a warehouse with an adjusted basis of $150,000 and an FMV of $160,000 for a mini-storage building with an FMV of $100,000 and $60,000 cash. What are the recognized gain or loss and the basis of the mini-storage building?

*a.* $0 gain and $150,000 basis.

*b.* $10,000 gain and $100,000 basis.

*c.* $10,000 gain and $150,000 basis.

*d.* $(10,000) loss and $160,000 basis.

LO 12-2    31. What tax form is completed to elect deferral of gain on an involuntary conversion?

*a.* No form is required.

*b.* Form 4797.

*c.* Form 4562.

*d.* Form 1040, Schedule D.

**LO 12-2**  32. In order to build a new road, the city of Oxford annexed 20 acres of Michael's farmland with an FMV of $30,000 and basis of $18,000. In return, Michael received 50 acres of similar land, which was appraised at $45,000. In this involuntary conversion, what gain or loss should Michael recognize, and what is his basis in the new land?

 a. $0 gain and $18,000 basis.

 b. $0 gain and $27,000 basis.

 c. $12,000 gain and $30,000 basis.

 d. $27,000 gain and $45,000 basis.

**LO 12-2**  33. A warehouse with an adjusted basis of $125,000 was destroyed by a tornado on April 15, 2021. On June 15, 2021, the insurance company paid the owner $195,000. The owner reinvested $170,000 in another warehouse. What is the basis of the new warehouse if nonrecognition of gain from an involuntary conversion is elected?

 a. $100,000.

 b. $125,000.

 c. $170,000.

 d. $195,000.

**LO 12-2**  34. A warehouse with an adjusted basis of $250,000 was destroyed by a tornado on April 15, 2021. On June 15, 2021, the insurance company paid the owner $395,000. The owner reinvested $470,000 in a new warehouse. What is the basis of the new warehouse if nonrecognition of gain from an involuntary conversion is elected?

 a. $105,000.

 b. $250,000.

 c. $325,000.

 d. $395,000.

**LO 12-2**  35. Kyla owns a convenience store with an adjusted basis of $215,000 that was destroyed by a flood on August 15, 2021. Kyla received a check for $275,000 from her insurance company on January 10, 2022, compensating her for the damage to her store. What is the latest date on which Kyla can buy replacement property to avoid recognition of any realized gain?

 a. August 15, 2023.

 b. December 31, 2023.

 c. January 10, 2024.

 d. December 31, 2025.

**LO 12-3**  36. On June 15, 2021, Allen sold land held for investment to Stan for $50,000 and an installment note of $250,000 payable in five equal annual installments beginning on June 15, 2022, plus interest at 10%. Allen's basis in the land is $150,000. What amount of gain is recognized in 2021 under the installment method?

 a. $0.

 b. $25,000.

 c. $50,000.

 d. $150,000.

**LO 12-3**  37. On July 1, 2021, Andrea sold land held for investment to Taylor. Andrea's land had a $300,000 basis and was subject to a $150,000 mortgage. Under the contractual agreement, Taylor will pay Andrea $85,000 on the date of the sale, will assume the mortgage, and will give Andrea a note for $375,000 (plus interest at the federal rate) due the following year. What is the contract price in the year of sale?

a. $460,000.

b. $525,000.

c. $610,000.

d. $760,000.

**LO 12-3** 38. Which of the following statements is correct with regard to installment sales?

a. The contract price is generally the amount of cash the seller will receive.

b. Sales by a taxpayer who is a dealer in the item sold are not eligible for installment sale treatment.

c. The installment method cannot be used to report gain from the sale of stock or securities that are traded on an established securities market.

d. All of the above are correct.

**LO 12-3** 39. A taxpayer who sells their personal residence in 2021 may exclude some or all of the gain on the sale if the residence was owned and lived in for

a. At least four years before the sale date.

b. Any two years of a five-year period before the sale.

c. Any of the last four years of an eight-year period before the sale.

d. At least one year prior to the sale date.

**EA** **LO 12-4** 40. Marcus purchased Vinnie and Marie's personal residence for $225,000 cash and the assumption of their $100,000 mortgage. Vinnie and Marie bought the house six years ago for $275,000 and have used it as a primary residence. What amount of gain should Vinnie and Marie recognize on the sale of their personal residence?

a. $0.

b. $50,000.

c. $100,000.

d. $225,000.

**EA** **LO 12-4** 41. Daniel, who is single, purchased a house on May 15, 1998, for $115,000. During the years he owned the house, he installed a swimming pool at a cost of $24,000 and replaced the driveway at a cost of $12,000. On April 28, 2021, Daniel sold the house for $470,000. He paid a Realtor commission of $28,000 and legal fees of $1,000 connected with the sale of the house. What is Daniel's recognized gain on the sale of the house?

a. $0.

b. $40,000.

c. $290,000.

d. $319,000.

**EA** **LO 12-5** 42. All of the following relationships are considered related parties *except*

a. A corporation and a taxpayer whose spouse owns 80% of the corporation's stock.

b. A trust and a taxpayer who is the grantor of the trust.

c. A corporation and a taxpayer who owns 20% of the corporation's stock.

d. A partnership and a taxpayer who is a two-thirds partner.

**EA** **LO 12-5** 43. On June 1, 2021, Nigel sells land (basis $55,000) to his daughter Ana for $40,000, the land's FMV on the date of the sale. On September 21, 2021, Ana sells the land to an unrelated party. Which of the following statements is correct?

    *a.* If Ana sells the land for $35,000, he has a $20,000 recognized loss on the sale.

    *b.* If Ana sells the land for $65,000, he has a $25,000 recognized gain on the sale.

    *c.* If Ana sells the land for $45,000, he has a $5,000 recognized gain on the sale.

    *d.* If Ana sells the land for $57,000, he has a $2,000 recognized gain on the sale.

**EA**   **LO 12-5**  44. Bryce owns 200 shares of Basic Company stock that he purchased for $8,000 three years ago. On December 28, 2021, Bryce sold 100 shares of the stock for $2,500. On January 3, 2022, Bryce repurchased 50 shares for $1,100. How much of the loss can Bryce deduct in 2021?

    *a.* $0.

    *b.* $750.

    *c.* $4,400.

    *d.* $5,500.

## Problems   Mc Graw Hill **connect**

All applicable problems are available with **Connect**©

**LO 12-1**  45. Carlton holds undeveloped land for investment. His adjusted basis in the land is $200,000, and the FMV is $325,000. On November 1, 2021, he exchanges this land for land owned by his son, who is 31 years old. The appraised value of his son's land is $320,000 with a basis of $310,000.

    *a.* Calculate Carlton's realized and recognized gain or loss from the exchange with his son and on Carlton's subsequent sale of the land to a real estate agent on July 19, 2022, for $375,000.

    *b.* Calculate Carlton's realized and recognized gain or loss from the exchange with his son if Carlton does not sell the land received from his son, but his son sells the land received from Carlton on July 19, 2022. Calculate Carlton's basis for the land on November 1, 2021, and July 19, 2022.

    *c.* What could Carlton do to avoid any recognition of gain associated with the first exchange prior to his sale of the land?

**LO 12-1**  46. Elana exchanges a lot of land that is used exclusively for business purposes for another lot that also is to be used exclusively for business. The adjusted basis for the old lot is $18,000, and its FMV is $14,500.

    *a.* Calculate Elana's recognized gain or loss on the exchange.

    *b.* Calculate Elana's basis for the lot she receives.

_____

_____

_____

**LO 12-1**  47. What is the basis of the new property in each of the following situations? Is any gain recognized in the following transactions?

    *a.* Rental house with an adjusted basis of $100,000 exchanged for a personal-use river cottage with an FMV of $130,000.

_____

_____

_____

    *b.* General Motors common stock with an adjusted basis of $19,000 exchanged for Quaker Oats common stock with an FMV of $14,000.

_____

_____

_____

    *c.* Land and building with an adjusted basis of $25,000 used as a furniture repair shop exchanged for land and a building with an FMV of $52,000 used as a car dealership.

_____

_____

_____

    *d.* An office building with an adjusted basis of $22,000 exchanged for a heavy-duty truck with an FMV of $28,000. Both properties are held for 100% business purposes.

_____

_____

_____

    *e.* A residential rental property held for investment with an adjusted basis of $230,000 exchanged for a warehouse to be held for investment with an FMV of $180,000.

_____

_____

_____

**LO 12-1**  48. Viktor exchanges stock (adjusted basis $18,000, FMV $25,000) and real estate (adjusted basis $18,000, FMV $44,000) held for investment for other real estate to be held for investment. The real estate acquired in the exchange has a suggested FMV of $67,000.

    *a.* What are Viktor's realized and recognized gain or loss?

_____

_____

_____

    *b.* What is the basis of the acquired real estate?

_____

_____

_____

**LO 12-1**  49. LaRhonda owns an office building that has an adjusted basis of $45,000. The building is subject to a mortgage of $20,000. She transfers the building to Miguel in exchange for

$15,000 cash and a warehouse with an FMV of $50,000. Miguel assumes the mortgage on the building.

*a.* What are LaRhonda's realized and recognized gain or loss?

_____

_____

_____

*b.* What is her basis in the newly acquired warehouse?

_____

_____

_____

LO 12-1   50. Kim owns equipment that is used exclusively in her business. The building has an adjusted basis of $8,500 (FMV $5,000). Kim transfers the building and $2,000 cash to David for another building (also used for business purposes) that has an FMV of $7,000.

*a.* What is Kim's recognized gain or loss on the exchange?

_____

_____

_____

*b.* What is Kim's adjusted basis in the storage building?

_____

_____

_____

LO 12-1   51. Joshua owns undeveloped land that has an adjusted basis of $45,000. He exchanges it for other undeveloped land with an FMV of $70,000.

*a.* What are his realized and recognized gain or loss on the exchange?

_____

_____

_____

*b.* What is his basis in the acquired land?

_____

_____

_____

LO 12-2   52. Patti's garage (used to store business property) is destroyed by a fire. She decides not to replace it and uses the insurance proceeds to invest in her business. The garage had an adjusted basis of $50,000.

*a.* If the insurance proceeds total $20,000, what is Patti's recognized gain or loss?

_____

_____

_____

*b.* If the insurance proceeds total $60,000, what is Patti's recognized gain or loss?

_____

_____

_____

LO 12-2    53. Indicate whether the property acquired qualifies as replacement property for each of the following involuntary conversions:

    *a.* The Harts' personal residence is destroyed by a hurricane. They decide not to acquire a replacement residence but to invest the insurance proceeds in a house that they rent to tenants.

    _____

    _____

    _____

    *b.* Faiqa's personal residence is condemned. She uses the proceeds to invest in another personal residence.

    _____

    _____

    _____

    *c.* Tonya owns a storage warehouse used for business purposes. A flood destroys the building, and she decides to use the insurance proceeds to rebuild the warehouse in another state.

    _____

    _____

    _____

    *d.* Ramona owns an apartment building that is destroyed by a flood. She uses the insurance proceeds to build an apartment building nearby that is out of the flood zone.

    _____

    _____

    _____

LO 12-2    54. Jessica's office building is destroyed by fire on November 15, 2021. The adjusted basis of the building is $410,000. She receives insurance proceeds of $550,000 on December 12, 2021.

    *a.* Calculate her realized and recognized gain or loss for the replacement property if she acquires an office building in December 2021 for $550,000.

    _____

    _____

    _____

    *b.* Calculate her realized and recognized gain or loss for the replacement property if she acquires an office building in December 2021 for $495,000.

    _____

    _____

    _____

    *c.* What is her basis for the replacement property in parts (*a*) and (*b*)?

    _____

    _____

    _____

    *d.* Calculate Jessica's realized and recognized gain or loss if she does not invest in replacement property.

    _____

    _____

    _____

LO 12-2   55. Reid's personal residence is condemned on September 12, 2021, as part of a plan to add two lanes to the existing highway. His adjusted basis is $300,000. He receives condemnation proceeds of $340,000 on September 30, 2021. He purchases another personal residence for $325,000 on October 15, 2021. What are Reid's realized and recognized gain or loss?

_____

_____

_____

_____

LO 12-3   56. Pedro sells investment land on September 1, 2021. Information pertaining to the sale follows:

| | |
|---|---:|
| Adjusted basis | $25,000 |
| Selling price | 90,000 |
| Selling expenses | 1,500 |
| Down payment | 12,000 |
| Four installment payments | 15,000 |
| Mortgage assumed by the buyer | 18,000 |

Each installment payment is due on September 1 of 2022, 2023, 2024, and 2025 (ignore interest). Determine the tax consequences in 2021, 2022, 2023, 2024, and 2025.

_____

_____

_____

_____

EA   LO 12-4   57. Aisha is an accountant for a global CPA firm. She is being temporarily transferred from the Raleigh, North Carolina, office to Tokyo. She will leave Raleigh on October 7, 2021, and will be out of the country for four years. She sells her personal residence on September 30, 2021, for $250,000 (her adjusted basis is $190,000). Upon her return to the United States in 2025, she purchases a new residence in Los Angeles for $220,000, where she will continue working for the same firm.

*a.* What are Aisha's realized and recognized gain or loss?

_____

_____

_____

*b.* What is Aisha's basis in the new residence?

_____

_____

_____

EA   LO 12-4   58. On February 1, 2021, Mariah buys a new residence for $150,000. Three months later, she sells her old residence for $310,000 (adjusted basis of $120,000). Selling expenses totaled $21,000. She lived in the old house for 15 years.

*a.* What are Mariah's realized and recognized gain or loss?

_____

_____

_____

b. What is her basis in the new residence?

_____

_____

_____

**EA** LO 12-4   59. Dominique is a manager for a regional bank. He is being relocated several states away to act as a temporary manager while a new branch is interviewing for a permanent manager. He will leave on May 1, 2021, and will be at the new location for less than one year. He sells his personal residence on April 15, 2021, for $123,000 (adjusted basis $95,000). Upon completion of the assignment, he purchases a new residence for $200,000.

a. What are Dominique's realized and recognized gain or loss?

_____

_____

_____

b. What is Dominique's basis in the new residence?

_____

_____

_____

c. Assume that Dominique is transferred out of state and sells his new residence for $230,000 two months later (he is single). What are the realized and recognized gains?

_____

_____

_____

**EA** LO 12-5   60. Crystal owns 150 shares of Carson Inc. stock that has an adjusted basis of $100,000. On December 18, 2021, she sells the 150 shares for FMV ($88,000). On January 7, 2022, she purchases 200 shares of Carson stock for $127,500.

a. What are Crystal's realized and recognized gain or loss on the sale of the 150 shares sold on December 18, 2021?

_____

_____

_____

b. What is Crystal's adjusted basis for the shares purchased on January 7, 2022?

_____

_____

_____

c. How would your answers in parts (*a*) and (*b*) change if she purchased only 100 shares for $98,000 in January?

_____

_____

_____

**EA** LO 12-5   61. On January 1, 2021, Antonio sells stock that has a $50,000 FMV on the date of the sale (basis $75,000) to his daughter Tiana. On October 21, 2021, Tiana sells the stock to an unrelated party. In each of the following, determine the tax consequences of these transactions to Antonio and Tiana:

 *a.* Tiana sells the stock for $40,000.

_____

_____

_____

 *b.* Tiana sells the stock for $80,000.

_____

_____

_____

 *c.* Tiana sells the stock for $65,000.

_____

_____

_____

**EA**   **LO 12-5**   62. Harold owns 130 shares of stock in Becker Corporation. His adjusted basis for the stock is $210,000. On December 15, 2021, he sells the stock for $180,000. He purchases 200 shares of Becker Corporation stock on January 12, 2022, for $195,000.

 *a.* What are Harold's realized and recognized gain or loss on the sale?

_____

_____

_____

 *b.* What is Harold's adjusted basis for the 200 shares purchased on January 12, 2022?

_____

_____

_____

 *c.* How would your answers in parts (*a*) and (*b*) change if he purchased only 100 shares for $95,000 in January?

_____

_____

_____

**EA**   **LO 12-5**   63. Lewis owns 200 shares of stock in Modlin Corporation. His adjusted basis for the stock is $180,000. On December 15, 2021, he sells the stock for $170,000. He purchases 200 shares of Modlin Corporation stock on January 8, 2021 for $170,000.

 *a.* What are Lewis's realized and recognized gain or loss on the sale?

_____

_____

_____

 *b.* What is Lewis's adjusted basis for the 200 shares purchased on January 8, 2022?

_____

_____

_____

 *c.* How would your answers in parts (*a*) and (*b*) change if he purchased only 100 shares for $105,000 in January?

_____

_____

_____

d. What tax treatment is Lewis trying to achieve?

_____

_____

_____

## Tax Return Problems  Mc Graw Hill **connect**

All applicable tax return problems are available with **Connect**©

Use your tax software to complete the following problems. If you are manually preparing the tax returns, the problem indicates the forms or schedules you will need.

**Tax Return Problem 1**

Wendy O'Neil (SSN 412-34-5670), who is single, worked full time as the director at a local charity. She resides at 1501 Front Street, Highland, AZ 85711. For the year, she had the following reported on her W-2:

| | |
|---|---|
| Wages | $46,200 |
| Federal withholding | 7,930 |
| Social security wages | 46,200 |
| Social security withholding | 2,864 |
| Medicare withholding | 670 |
| State withholding | 2,310 |

Other information follows:

| | |
|---|---|
| 1099-INT New Bank | $300 |
| 1099-DIV Freeze, Inc. Ordinary dividends | 400 |
| Qualified dividends | 400 |

Wendy had the following itemized deductions:

| | |
|---|---|
| State income tax withholding | $2,310 |
| State income tax paid with the 2019 return | 100 |
| Real estate tax | 2,600 |
| Mortgage interest | 8,060 |

Wendy inherited a beach house in North Carolina (rental only) on January 2, 2021, from her father. The FMV at the father's death was $850,000. He had purchased the house 20 years earlier for $100,000.

| | |
|---|---|
| Summer rental income | $45,000 |
| Repairs | 2,500 |
| Real estate taxes | 6,500 |
| Utilities | 2,400 |
| Depreciation | (Calculate) |

On December 29, 2021, Wendy properly conducted a like-kind exchange for rental real estate located at 128 Lake Blvd., Hot Town, AZ. She received rental property with an FMV of $950,000 and $20,000 cash in exchange for the North Carolina beach house. The Arizona property did not produce any income until 2021.

Prepare Form 1040 for Wendy for 2021. The taxpayer had qualifying health care coverage at all times during the tax year. You will also need Schedule A, Schedule D, Schedule E, Form 4562, and Form 8824.

**Tax Return Problem 2**   Dave (SSN 412-34-5670) and Alicia (SSN 412-34-5671) Stanley are married and retired at age 51. The couple's income consists of rental property, stock investments, and royalties from an invention. They sold their large house that they had purchased six years ago for $580,000 on October 18, 2021, for $1 million. They now live in a condo at 101 Magnolia Lane, Suite 15, Highland Park, FL 33853.

The rental property is an apartment complex (building cost $1.5 million and was purchased January 5, 2020) with 30 units that rent for $27,000 per month and are at 90% occupancy.

| | |
|---|---|
| Rental income | $291,600 |
| Salaries | 115,000 |
| Payroll taxes | 8,798 |
| Real estate taxes | 18,750 |
| Interest | 45,000 |
| Repairs and maintenance | 29,000 |
| Depreciation | (Calculate) |

The following information is also for the year:

| | | | |
|---|---|---|---|
| 1099-INT | Old Bank | | $ 22,000 |
| 1099-DIV | Dell, Inc. | Ordinary dividends | 15,250 |
| | | Qualified dividends | 15,250 |
| 1099-DIV | IBM, Inc. | Ordinary dividends | 8,650 |
| | | Qualified dividends | 8,650 |
| 1099-DIV | Pepsi, Inc. | Ordinary dividends | 18,785 |
| | | Qualified dividends | 18,785 |
| 1099-MISC | Box 2 royalties | | 152,300 |

| | Purchased | Sold | Sale Price | Basis | Gain/Loss |
|---|---|---|---|---|---|
| Dell (held 9 mo.) | 12/01/20 | 09/01/21 | $15,000 | $ 9,000 | $ 6,000 |
| Pepsi (held 4 mo.) | 09/01/21 | 12/29/21 | 17,000 | 25,000 | (8,000) |
| IBM (held 30 mo.) | 06/05/19 | 12/05/21 | 38,000 | 20,000 | 18,000 |

On January 3, 2022, Dave repurchased the exact number of shares he sold on December 29, 2021. The Stanleys paid $12,000 each quarter (four payments) in federal estimated income taxes.

Prepare Form 1040 for the Stanleys. Taxpayers had qualifying health care coverage at all times during the tax year. You will also need Schedule B, Schedule D, Schedule E, Form 4562, and Form 8960.

We have provided selected filled-in source documents that are available in *Connect.*

# Chapter **Thirteen**

# At-Risk/Passive Activity Loss Rules and the Individual Alternative Minimum Tax

In this chapter, we provide a detailed examination of the at-risk rules and the passive activity loss rules. At-risk rules and passive activity loss rules work together to limit the deductibility of losses from activities in which the taxpayer does not materially participate in the business or in which an economic loss does not occur. We also discuss the Alternative Minimum Tax (AMT) for individual taxpayers. Congress enacted the AMT to ensure that taxpayers with substantial economic income cannot avoid significant tax liability using exclusions, deductions, and credits permitted in the Internal Revenue Code (IRC).

### Learning Objectives

When you have completed this chapter, you should understand the following learning objectives (LO):

**LO 13-1**  Explain the process of applying the at-risk rules.

**LO 13-2**  Describe the rules and applications related to passive activities.

**LO 13-3**  Explain how the passive activity loss rules and at-risk rules work together to limit the deductibility of losses.

**LO 13-4**  Explain the alternative minimum tax and how it is calculated.

## INTRODUCTION

A pervasive problem for the government prior to 1976 was taxpayer use of tax shelters to reduce taxable income. Tax shelters were (and still are) investment schemes that produce substantial tax losses but, at the same time, produce either a neutral or a positive cash flow. In 1976 Congress established the *at-risk rules* to combat such tax shelters. When it was apparent that the at-risk rules alone were not sufficient to quell abusive tax shelters, Congress enacted the *passive activity loss* (PAL) rules in 1986.

To understand the rules developed to combat tax shelters, you need to understand the government's problem in the first place. Example 13-1 is an example of a typical tax shelter.

**EXAMPLE 13-1**

Abbott, Bart, and Calvin had some extra cash to invest. They also wanted to reduce their taxable income. The three individuals each invested $33,333 into a partnership. The partnership borrowed $900,000 on a 10% interest-only nonrecourse note and purchased an equipment-intensive oil and gas venture for $1,000,000.[1] The venture produced $150,000 per year in royalty income.

| | Total | Abbott | Bart | Calvin |
|---|---|---|---|---|
| Income | $150,000 | $ 50,000 | $ 50,000 | $ 50,000 |
| Interest ($900,000 × 10%) | (90,000) | (30,000) | (30,000) | (30,000) |
| Cash flow | 60,000 | 20,000 | 20,000 | 20,000 |
| Depreciation* ($1 million × 15%) | (150,000) | (50,000) | (50,000) | (50,000) |
| Tax loss | $ (90,000) | $(30,000) | $(30,000) | $(30,000) |

\* The depreciation rate would vary depending on the type of asset being depreciated. For simplicity, a conservative 15% rate was used.

Assuming no at-risk rules or PAL rules, Abbott, Bart, and Calvin each would have a $30,000 tax loss from this activity, yet the venture has positive cash flow of $20,000 to each taxpayer plus tax savings related to the $30,000 loss. By the end of the tax year, the partners would have received more cash and tax savings than the amount they invested in the first place. Furthermore, if the losses remained the same for year 2, each partner would have deducted a total of $60,000 in tax losses from a venture in which each initially had only $33,333 to lose (the "at-risk" amount).

Congress established the at-risk rules to limit the deductible losses that the taxpayer could economically lose. In Example 13-1, this amount is only $33,333. Thus, if losses in the second year were also $30,000 per partner, the deductible loss of each partner would be limited to $3,333 (the initial $33,333 at-risk amount minus the $30,000 loss in year 1).

# AT-RISK RULES
## LO 13-1

The following types of activities are subject to the at-risk rules:

1. Holding, producing, or distributing motion picture films or videotapes.
2. Farming.
3. Leasing any § 1245 property.
4. Exploring for, or exploiting, oil and gas resources as a trade or business or for the production of income.
5. Exploring for, or exploiting, geothermal deposits.[2]

In addition to the activities specifically listed, the IRC also includes a catch-all provision that causes *any* activity "engaged in by the taxpayer in carrying on a trade or business or for the production of income" to be subject to the at-risk rules. The film, farming, leasing, and oil and gas exploration ventures are specifically listed because they were the most common tax-sheltering activities at the time. The at-risk rules often affect investments that have some form of limited liability to the investors (such as limited partnerships).

---

[1] A *nonrecourse debt* is one for which no one is personally liable. The notions of recourse, nonrecourse, and qualified nonrecourse are discussed in greater detail later in the chapter. Financial institutions rarely lend money for which no security is pledged or no individual is personally liable. The availability of nonrecourse financing is the primary reason that the at-risk rules were ineffective in limiting abusive tax shelters, thus leading to the passage of the PAL rules.

[2] IRC § 465(c).

**TAX YOUR BRAIN**

Assume that Jack invests $20,000 cash in a plant nursery for a 20% share in the business. The 80% owner is Jill, who contributes $20,000 and personally borrows $60,000 to put in the business. Jack does no work in the business and is not liable for any of the debt. Is either Jack or Jill subject to at-risk limitations?

**ANSWER**

Both Jack and Jill are subject to the at-risk rules. Jack's initial at-risk amount is $20,000 because that is all he can lose. Jill, on the other hand, would have an initial at-risk amount of $80,000 (her $20,000 cash contribution plus the $60,000 she personally borrowed).

## What Is At-Risk?

Generally, the initial *at-risk* amount is the money plus the adjusted basis of property contributed to the activity. The at-risk amount also includes certain amounts borrowed in connection with the activity.[3] The taxpayer's at-risk amount increases each tax year by income/gain items and any additional contributions of money or property. Likewise, the at-risk amount decreases each tax year by loss items and distributions of money or property. Table 13-1 summarizes the increases and decreases in the at-risk amount.

Factors that either increase or decrease the at-risk amount are considered prior to determining the amount of allowed loss items.[4]

**EXAMPLE 13-2**

In 2021, Zeke contributed land with an adjusted basis of $15,000 and a fair market value (FMV) of $30,000 to Land Developers Limited Partnership (LDLP) in return for a 5% limited partnership interest. LDLP issued Zeke the K-1 shown in Exhibit 13-1. What are Zeke's allowed losses and ending at-risk amount? Assume, perhaps unrealistically, that LDLP has no liabilities.

| | |
|---|---:|
| Zeke's initial at-risk amount | $15,000 |
| Interest income | 123 |
| Dividend income | 600 |
| Capital gain | 700 |
| At-risk amount prior to loss | $16,423 |
| Loss allowed under at-risk rules | (7,000)* |
| Ending at-risk amount | $ 9,423 |

\* The $7,000 loss is allowed under the at-risk rules. However, as noted earlier, the loss may still be disallowed under the passive activity loss rules. We discuss these rules in a few pages.

**TABLE 13-1**
**At-Risk Calculation**

| | |
|---|---|
| + | Cash contributions |
| + | Property contributions |
| + | Share of liabilities |
| + | Income items (net income, interest, dividends, etc.) |
| + | Gain items (gain on asset sales, capital gains) |
| (−) | Cash distributions |
| (−) | Property distributions |
| (−) | Release of liabilities |
| = | Amount at risk |
| (−) | Loss items (i.e., net losses allowed to the extent at risk) |
| = | Ending at-risk amount |

[3] IRC § 465(b)(1)(A), (B).

[4] Proposed Reg. § 1.465-39(a). Proposed Regulations are weak authority until they become permanent. However, in this case, the inclusion of increase/decrease items is common and has been treated similarly in practice for numerous years.

**EXHIBIT 13-1**

| | |
|---|---|
| | 651121 |

☐ Final K-1    ☐ Amended K-1    OMB No. 1545-0123

**Schedule K-1**
**(Form 1065)**
Department of the Treasury
Internal Revenue Service

**2021**

For calendar year 2021, or tax year

beginning    /    / 2021    ending    /    /

**Partner's Share of Income, Deductions, Credits, etc.**    ▶ See back of form and separate instructions.

*DRAFT AS OF August 6, 2021 DO NOT FILE*

**Part I    Information About the Partnership**

**A**    Partnership's employer identification number
52-1234567

**B**    Partnership's name, address, city, state, and ZIP code

Land Developers, LP
P.O. Box 999
Wayne, MS  38765

**C**    IRS center where partnership filed return ▶ Ogden, UT

**D**    ☐ Check if this is a publicly traded partnership (PTP)

**Part II    Information About the Partner**

**E**    Partner's SSN or TIN (Do not use TIN of a disregarded entity. See instructions.)
412-34-5670

**F**    Name, address, city, state, and ZIP code for partner entered in E. See instructions.

Zeke Johnson
123 Ash Street
Wayne, MS  38765

**G**    ☐ General partner or LLC member-manager    ☐ Limited partner or other LLC member

**H1**    ☒ Domestic partner    ☐ Foreign partner

**H2**    ☐ If the partner is a disregarded entity (DE), enter the partner's:
TIN _____ Name _____

**I1**    What type of entity is this partner?  Individual

**I2**    If this partner is a retirement plan (IRA/SEP/Keogh/etc.), check here ▶ ☐

**J**    Partner's share of profit, loss, and capital (see instructions):

| | Beginning | Ending |
|---|---|---|
| Profit | % | 5 % |
| Loss | % | 5 % |
| Capital | % | 5 % |

Check if decrease is due to sale or exchange of partnership interest  ▶ ☐

**K**    Partner's share of liabilities:

| | Beginning | Ending |
|---|---|---|
| Nonrecourse | $ | $ |
| Qualified nonrecourse financing | $ | $ |
| Recourse | $ | $ |

Check this box if Item K includes liability amounts from lower tier partnerships ▶ ☐

**L**    **Partner's Capital Account Analysis**

Beginning capital account    .    .    .  $ _____
Capital contributed during the year  .    .  $ _____
Current year net income (loss)  .    .  $ _____
Other increase (decrease) (attach explanation)  $ _____
Withdrawals and distributions  .    .  $ ( _____ )
Ending capital account    .    .    .  $ _____

**M**    Did the partner contribute property with a built-in gain (loss)?
☒ Yes    ☐ No    If "Yes," attach statement. See instructions.

**N**    **Partner's Share of Net Unrecognized Section 704(c) Gain or (Loss)**
Beginning  .    .    .    .    .    .    .  $ _____
Ending  .    .    .    .    .    .    .  $ _____

**Part III    Partner's Share of Current Year Income, Deductions, Credits, and Other Items**

| | | | | |
|---|---|---|---|---|
| 1 | Ordinary business income (loss) (7,000) | 14 | Self-employment earnings (loss) | |
| 2 | Net rental real estate income (loss) | | | |
| 3 | Other net rental income (loss) | 15 | Credits | |
| 4a | Guaranteed payments for services | | | |
| 4b | Guaranteed payments for capital | 16 | Schedule K-3 is attached if checked . . . . . ▶ ☐ | |
| 4c | Total guaranteed payments | 17 | Alternative minimum tax (AMT) items | |
| 5 | Interest income 123 | | | |
| 6a | Ordinary dividends 600 | | | |
| 6b | Qualified dividends 600 | 18 | Tax-exempt income and nondeductible expenses | |
| 6c | Dividend equivalents | | | |
| 7 | Royalties | | | |
| 8 | Net short-term capital gain (loss) | | | |
| 9a | Net long-term capital gain (loss) 700 | 19 | Distributions | |
| 9b | Collectibles (28%) gain (loss) | | | |
| 9c | Unrecaptured section 1250 gain | 20 | Other information | |
| 10 | Net section 1231 gain (loss) | | | |
| 11 | Other income (loss) | | | |
| 12 | Section 179 deduction | 21 | Foreign taxes paid or accrued | |
| 13 | Other deductions | | | |

**22** ☐ More than one activity for at-risk purposes*
**23** ☐ More than one activity for passive activity purposes*
*See attached statement for additional information.

*For IRS Use Only*

For Paperwork Reduction Act Notice, see the Instructions for Form 1065.    www.irs.gov/Form1065    Cat. No. 11394R    **Schedule K-1 (Form 1065) 2021**

**EXAMPLE 13-3**

Assume that in 2022, Zeke's K-1 from LDLP had only one item: an $11,500 ordinary loss on line 1.

| | |
|---|---:|
| Beginning at-risk amount (Example 13-2) | $9,423 |
| Increase or decrease items | –0– |
| At-risk amount prior to loss | 9,423 |
| Loss allowed under at-risk rules | (9,423) |
| Ending at-risk amount | $   –0– |

In this case, a $2,077 loss is disallowed under the at-risk rules ($11,500 K-1 loss minus the permitted $9,423 loss).[5] Zeke cannot deduct the disallowed loss until he has additional amounts at-risk. Zeke will increase his at-risk amount by contributing additional capital, by incurring additional liabilities, or by waiting for LDLP to generate income or gain items.

A taxpayer uses Form 6198 to report an activity that is subject to at-risk limitations. The taxpayer is not required to file Form 6198 if the activity has net income or is not subject to the at-risk limitation. Thus, in Example 13-2 (for tax year 2021), Zeke would not file Form 6198 because he was not subject to any at-risk limitations. However, because Zeke's loss was limited in Example 13-3, he would file Form 6198 in 2022 (see Exhibit 13-2).

Other income or gain items from Zeke's LDLP investment, if any, are reported on Form 6198, line 2 or 3. Any losses are allowable to the extent of income and gains from the current year. For example, if LDLP reported an additional $200 of interest income in 2022, $200 of the $11,500 loss would have automatically been deductible regardless of the at-risk amount (current year first). Thus, a total of $9,623 could have been deducted, although line 10b on Form 6198 would still show only $9,423.

## Liabilities for At-Risk Purposes

Liabilities fall into three categories:

1. Recourse
2. Nonrecourse
3. Qualified nonrecourse[6]

A *recourse liability* is one in which the taxpayer is personally liable for the debt. A taxpayer's at-risk amount increases by their share of recourse debt.

**EXAMPLE 13-4**

Lee invested $10,000 cash in S&W Properties General Partnership and received a 25% interest in the partnership. The partnership borrowed $100,000 in full recourse debt. Assuming that Lee is personally liable for $25,000 (25% × $100,000 debt) if the partnership defaults on the loan, Lee's at-risk amount would be $35,000 ($10,000 cash + $25,000 debt).

Recourse debt is not included in the at-risk amount if the amounts are borrowed from any person (or entity) that has an interest in the activity or someone who is related to any person who has an interest in the activity.[7] In this case, the related-party lender would receive the at-risk increase.

---

[5] Some tax practitioners prefer to say that the at-risk amount is a negative $2,077. However, tax basis can never go below zero. It is true that tax basis and the at-risk amount may or may not be the same. When liabilities are ignored in the at-risk calculation (which often occurs in practice unless they are needed to deduct a loss), the at-risk amount and the tax basis are identical. In this text, we refer to the situation in Example 13-3 as zero at-risk with a disallowed loss.

[6] IRC § 465(b)(2).

[7] IRC § 465(b)(3)(A), (B), (C).

**EXHIBIT 13-2**

| Form **6198** | **At-Risk Limitations** | OMB No. 1545-0712 |
|---|---|---|
| (Rev. December 2020)<br>Department of the Treasury<br>Internal Revenue Service | ▶ **Attach to your tax return.**<br>▶ Go to *www.irs.gov/Form6198* for instructions and the latest information. | Attachment<br>Sequence No. **31** |

| Name(s) shown on return | Identifying number |
|---|---|
| Zeke Johnson | 412-34-5670 |

Description of activity (see instructions)

Land Developers, L.P.

### Part I — Current Year Profit (Loss) From the Activity, Including Prior Year Nondeductible Amounts. See instructions.

| | | | |
|---|---|---|---:|
| 1 | Ordinary income (loss) from the activity (see instructions) . . . . . . . . . . . . . | **1** | (11,500) |
| 2 | Gain (loss) from the sale or other disposition of assets used in the activity (or of your interest in the activity) that you are reporting on: | | |
| a | Schedule D . . . . . . . . . . . . . . . . | **2a** | |
| b | Form 4797 . . . . . . . . . . . . . . . | **2b** | |
| c | Other form or schedule . . . . . . . . . . | **2c** | |
| 3 | Other income and gains from the activity, from Schedule K-1 (Form 1065) or Schedule K-1 (Form 1120-S), that were not included on lines 1 through 2c . . . . . . . . . . . | **3** | |
| 4 | Other deductions and losses from the activity, including investment interest expense allowed from Form 4952, that were not included on lines 1 through 2c . . . . . . . . . . | **4** | ( ) |
| 5 | Current year profit (loss) from the activity. Combine lines 1 through 4. See the instructions before completing the rest of this form . . . . . . . . . . . . . . . . . . | **5** | (11,500) |

### Part II — Simplified Computation of Amount at Risk. See the instructions before completing this part.

| | | | |
|---|---|---|---:|
| 6 | Adjusted basis (as defined in section 1011) in the activity (or in your interest in the activity) on the first day of the tax year. **Do not** enter less than zero . . . . . . . . | **6** | 9,423 |
| 7 | Increases for the tax year (see instructions) . . . . . . . . . . . . . | **7** | 0 |
| 8 | Add lines 6 and 7 . . . . . . . . . . . . . . . . . | **8** | 9,423 |
| 9 | Decreases for the tax year (see instructions) . . . . . . . . . . . | **9** | 0 |
| 10a | Subtract line 9 from line 8 . . . . . . . . . . ▶ \|10a\| 9,423 | | |
| b | If line 10a is **more** than zero, enter that amount here and go to line 20 (or complete Part III). Otherwise, enter -0- and see **Pub. 925** for information on the recapture rules . . . . . . . . | **10b** | 9,423 |

### Part III — Detailed Computation of Amount at Risk. If you completed Part III of Form 6198 for the prior year, see the instructions.

| | | | |
|---|---|---|---:|
| 11 | Investment in the activity (or in your interest in the activity) at the effective date. **Do not** enter less than zero . . . . . . . . . . . . . . . . . . . | **11** | |
| 12 | Increases at effective date . . . . . . . . . . . . | **12** | |
| 13 | Add lines 11 and 12 . . . . . . . . . . . . | **13** | |
| 14 | Decreases at effective date . . . . . . . . . . | **14** | |
| 15 | Amount at risk (check box that applies): | | |
| a | ☐ At effective date. Subtract line 14 from line 13. **Do not** enter less than zero. | | |
| b | ☐ From your prior year Form 6198, line 19b. **Do not** enter the amount from line 10b of your prior year form. | **15** | |
| 16 | Increases since (check box that applies): | | |
| a | ☐ Effective date    b ☐ The end of your prior year . . . . . . . . | **16** | |
| 17 | Add lines 15 and 16 . . . . . . . . . . | **17** | |
| 18 | Decreases since (check box that applies): | | |
| a | ☐ Effective date    b ☐ The end of your prior year . . . . . . . . | **18** | |
| 19a | Subtract line 18 from line 17 . . . . . . . . . ▶ \|19a\| | | |
| b | If line 19a is **more** than zero, enter that amount here and go to line 20. Otherwise, enter -0- and see **Pub. 925** for information on the recapture rules . . . . . . . . . . . . . | **19b** | |

### Part IV — Deductible Loss

| | | | |
|---|---|---|---:|
| 20 | **Amount at risk.** Enter the **larger** of line 10b or line 19b . . . . . . . . | **20** | 9,423 |
| 21 | **Deductible loss.** Enter the **smaller** of the line 5 loss (treated as a positive number) or line 20. See the instructions to find out how to report any deductible loss and any carryover . . . . . . . . | **21** | ( 9,423) |

**Note:** If the loss is from a passive activity, see the Instructions for Form 8582, Passive Activity Loss Limitations, or the Instructions for Form 8810, Corporate Passive Activity Loss and Credit Limitations, to find out if the loss is allowed under the passive activity rules. If only part of the loss is subject to the passive activity loss rules, report only that part on Form 8582 or Form 8810, whichever applies.

**For Paperwork Reduction Act Notice, see the Instructions for Form 6198.**    Cat. No. 50012Y    Form **6198** (Rev. 12-2020)

Source: U.S. Department of the Treasury, Internal Revenue Service, Form 6198. Washington, DC: 2021.

| **EXAMPLE 13-5** | Assume the same facts as in Example 13-4. However, the partnership borrowed $100,000 from Stan, who is a 50% partner in S&W Properties. In this case, the debt would not count as an at-risk amount for Lee. The result would be the same had the $100,000 been borrowed from Stan Corporation, a corporation 100% owned by Stan. |
| --- | --- |

*Nonrecourse debts* are loans in which no individual is personally liable for the debt. Because no one is personally liable, a taxpayer's share of nonrecourse liabilities does not increase at-risk amounts.

The final category of debt is *qualified nonrecourse financing,* which applies to the activity of holding real property (real estate). Taxpayers are deemed to be at risk for their share of such amounts.[8] Qualified nonrecourse financing is any debt that meets all of the following criteria:[9]

1. The taxpayer borrowed it with respect to the activity of holding real property.[10]
2. The taxpayer borrowed it from a qualified person or government.[11]
3. No person is personally liable for repayment.
4. The debt is not convertible debt.

This provision limited the effectiveness of the general at-risk rules in reducing tax shelter abuses for real estate investments. Most financial institutions are unwilling to finance business activities without security. In practice, borrowings for real estate ventures often meet the requirements of qualified nonrecourse financing because the financial institution requires the real estate to secure the loan but may not require the individuals to be personally liable.

| **EXAMPLE 13-6** | Jane, Danielle, and Dora each invested $20,000 in a real estate venture. The partnership borrowed $300,000 from a local bank and purchased an apartment building for $360,000. The bank required that the apartment building secure the loan, but none of the partners was personally liable for repayment of the debt. Assuming that each partner is a one-third partner, each has a beginning at-risk amount of $120,000 (1/3 of $300,000 debt + $20,000 cash investment). |
| --- | --- |

## Carryover of Disallowed Losses

Losses disallowed under the at-risk rules are carried over indefinitely. The taxpayer can deduct the suspended losses in later years when the taxpayer's at-risk amount increases by income from the activity, cash or property contributions, or an increased share of recourse debt.

---

[8] IRC § 465(b)(6).

[9] IRC § 465(b)(6)(B).

[10] IRC § 465(b)(6)(E)(ii) specifically excludes holding of mineral property from the definition of holding real property.

[11] A *qualified person* is any person who is actively and regularly engaged in the business of lending money and who is not a related party to the taxpayer or the person from whom the taxpayer acquired the property. Any financial institution qualifies as a qualified person assuming there is no owner relationship with the taxpayer.

**EXAMPLE 13-7**

Kim invested $100,000 in an activity years ago. In 2017, Kim's at-risk amount was $25,000 at the beginning of the year. Kim's shares of losses from the activity were as follows (ignore passive loss rules):

| Year | Gain (Loss) |
|------|-------------|
| 2017 | $(30,000) |
| 2018 | (20,000) |
| 2019 | (10,000) |
| 2020 | 20,000 |
| 2021 | 20,000 |

For each year, Kim can deduct the following amounts under the at-risk rules:

| | At-Risk Amount | Loss Carryover |
|---|---|---|
| Beginning at-risk amount | $ 25,000 | |
| 2017 loss allowed | (25,000) | $ 5,000 disallowed |
| Ending at-risk amount | $ –0– | |
| 2018 loss allowed | –0– | 20,000 disallowed |
| Ending at-risk amount | –0– | $25,000 carryover |
| 2019 loss allowed | –0– | 10,000 disallowed |
| Ending at-risk amount | –0– | $35,000 carryover |
| 2020 increase in at-risk amount | 20,000 | |
| 2020 loss allowed | (20,000) | 20,000 allowed |
| Ending at-risk amount | $ –0– | $15,000 carryover |
| 2021 increase in at-risk amount | 20,000 | |
| 2021 loss allowed | (15,000) | 15,000 allowed |
| Ending at-risk amount | $ 5,000 | $ –0– carryover |

On her 2021 tax return, Kim reports $5,000 of net income ($20,000 income minus the $15,000 loss allowed). The amount would be reported on Schedule E (if this were a partnership or S corporation) or Schedule C (if this activity were a sole proprietorship). All of the carryover losses are gone, and the 2022 tax year starts with an at-risk amount of $5,000.

**CONCEPT CHECK 13-1—LO 13-1**

1. Which of the following items will increase a taxpayer's at-risk amount?
   a. A cash contribution made by the taxpayer into the activity.
   b. The taxpayer's share of income from the activity.
   c. The taxpayer's share of the activity's liabilities for which the taxpayer is personally liable.
   d. All of the above.

2. Which of the following types of liability do *not* increase the taxpayer's at-risk amount in an activity?
   a. Nonrecourse debt.
   b. Recourse debt.
   c. Qualified nonrecourse debt.
   d. All of the above increase at-risk amount.

3. When a loss is disallowed by the at-risk rules, which of the following is true?
   a. The loss is lost forever.
   b. The loss can be used only upon the activity's disposal.
   c. The loss is indefinitely carried forward.
   d. The loss can be used only if the taxpayer makes a contribution to the activity.

# PASSIVE ACTIVITY LOSSES
## LO 13-2

The goal of the passive activity loss (PAL) rules is to restrict deductibility of tax losses created from activities that are not the taxpayer's primary source of income. The PAL rules supplement the at-risk rules. The loss must first be allowed under the at-risk rules and then must pass through PAL rule filters to ultimately be deductible and reduce taxable income.

### Definition of Passive Activity

A *passive activity* is one in which the taxpayer does not materially participate. The IRC defines material participation by the taxpayer as participating in the activity on a regular, continuous, and substantial basis.[12]

Most rental activities and limited partnership interests are, by definition, passive activities. An additional potential passive activity is a trade or business in which the taxpayer does not materially participate. Table 13-2 summarizes passive activities.

**TABLE 13-2**
**Passive Activities**

Most rental properties
Any ownership interests as a limited partner
Any trade or business in which the taxpayer does not materially participate

---

**TAX YOUR BRAIN**

What constitutes regular, continuous, and substantial participation in an activity?

**ANSWER**
The IRS issued regulations that list seven tests to determine material participation. It is clear, however, that investor-only participation is not sufficient to be classified as a material participant in an activity.

---

The regulations provide seven tests to help determine whether a taxpayer materially participates in an activity.[13] Material participation exists if the taxpayer meets any of the following seven tests.

### Test 1: The 500-Hour Test

The individual participates in the activity for more than 500 hours. This test is the general test for most activities. The main premise is that if a taxpayer participates more than 500 hours in an activity, that taxpayer is more than a mere investor. Any work normally completed in the activity counts toward the 500-hour requirement.

### Test 2: Sole Participant

The individual's participation in the activity for the taxable year constitutes all of the participation in such activity of all individuals (including individuals who are not owners of interest in the activity) for such year. If no one else works in the activity, the taxpayer must be a material participant. This rule is pertinent to many small sole proprietorships that operate cyclical or seasonal businesses.

---

**EXAMPLE 13-8**

Nidar is the sole owner and operator of a small coffee and hot chocolate shop in the mountains. The shop is open only in the winter during high-traffic times such as weekends and holidays. Even though Nidar works fewer than 500 hours in the activity, the work is not a passive activity because he is the only one who participates in the business.

---

[12] IRC § 469(h).
[13] IRS Reg. 1.469-5T.

### Test 3: More Than 100 Participation Hours

The individual participates in the activity for more than 100 hours during the tax year, and the individual's participation is not less than that of any other individual for the year.

---

**EXAMPLE 13-9**   Assume the same facts as in Example 13-8, but Nidar hires several part-time employees to help run the coffee and hot chocolate shop. If he works more than 100 hours and none of the other employees works more hours, the activity is not a passive activity.

---

### Test 4: Aggregate Significant Participation

The activity is a significant participation activity (participation more than 100 hours) for the tax year, and the individual's aggregate participation in all significant participation activities during such year exceeds 500 hours. Test 4 is important to taxpayers who own and operate several businesses during the year but participate fewer than 500 hours in any one of them.

---

**EXAMPLE 13-10**   Let's assume that Nidar operates his coffee and hot chocolate shop in the mountains for 130 hours in the winter, operates a daiquiri shop at the beach for 200 hours in the summer, and works in a landscaping business of which he is a part owner for 250 hours during the year. All of these businesses are significant participation activities because Nidar worked more than 100 hours in each. Furthermore, in aggregate, his participation in all significant participation activities is more than 500 hours. Thus, he is a material participant in all three activities.

---

### Test 5: History of Material Participation

The individual materially participated in the activity for any 5 taxable years during the 10 taxable years immediately preceding the current taxable year.

### Test 6: Personal Service Activity

The activity is a personal service activity, and the individual materially participated in it for any three taxable years (whether or not consecutive) preceding the taxable year.

Tests 5 and 6 are extremely important to individuals who cease to work in the activity (because of retirement, disability, or otherwise) but retain an ownership interest.

---

**EXAMPLE 13-11**   Tom is part owner in a furniture store with his son but retired from working in the business last year. Assuming that Tom worked more than 500 hours for 5 of the last 10 years, the current profit or loss from the activity is not passive. If Tom and his son operated a personal service activity such as a CPA firm, Tom needs to have been a material participant for only any three taxable years preceding the current year.

---

### Test 7: Facts and Circumstances

Based on all of the facts and circumstances, the individual participates in the activity on a regular, continuous, and substantial basis during the tax year.

Test 7 is a catchall for taxpayers who do not meet one of the first six tests. However, the temporary regulations are silent about the conditions required to meet Test 7. Based on the lack of guidance in the regulations regarding Test 7, it would be prudent to rely on Tests 1 through 6 in determining material participation.

## Passive Activity Losses: General Rule

Taxpayers subject to PAL rules include any individual, estate, trust, closely held C corporation, or personal service corporation.[14] The general rule for passive activities generating a loss

[14] IRC § 469(a)(2). In this text, the focus is exclusively on the individual taxpayer. However, these same PAL rules also apply to the other entity types.

is that a taxpayer can deduct the passive loss to the extent of passive income. The PAL rules are applied on an individual-by-individual basis.

| **TAX YOUR BRAIN**  | Can two partners in a passive activity with identical passive losses from the activity be treated differently concerning the deductibility of the losses? |
|---|---|

**ANSWER**

Yes, one of the partners who has passive income from another source can deduct the passive loss while the partner with no other passive activity cannot. Remember that PAL rules are applied on an individual basis, and any losses are allowed only to the extent of passive income.

**EXAMPLE 13-12**

Suppose Edna has an ownership interest in three passive activities. In the current tax year, the activities had the following income and losses:

| | |
|---|---|
| Partnership A | $10,000 |
| Partnership B | (8,000) |
| Partnership C | (6,000) |

Edna can deduct passive losses only to the extent of passive income. Here she can deduct $10,000 of the $14,000 in passive losses. This assumes that Edna is at risk for each of the loss activities. The excess $4,000 loss would be suspended and carried forward to future tax years until Edna has additional passive income (or until the activity is sold).

The IRC separates all income/loss items into three categories:[15]

1. **Active income/loss:** includes wages and profit or loss from a trade or business with material participation.
2. **Portfolio income:** includes interest, dividends, royalties, and capital gains.
3. **Passive income/loss:** includes any income or loss from a trade or business in which the taxpayer did not materially participate. It also includes income or loss from most rental activities whether or not there was material participation.[16]

Net passive losses cannot offset portfolio income or active income. In other words, all passive activities are first appropriately combined. If the result is net passive income, the income is reported. If the result is a net passive loss, the loss is suspended until additional passive income is generated.

## Rental Activities

A *rental activity* is any activity in which a taxpayer receives payments principally for the use of tangible property. In general, rental activities are passive activities. One exception concerns real estate professionals. A rental business can qualify for active treatment if more than one-half of the personal services performed in a business during the year are performed in a real property trade or business and the taxpayer performs more than 750 hours of services in the activity.[17]

**EXAMPLE 13-13**

Richard owns and operates several rental houses and apartment complexes in a college town. This is his only business activity, and he works full time in the venture. In this case, Richard meets the exception as a real estate professional, and the rental income and losses are not passive activities.

---

[15] IRC § 469(e).

[16] The sale of an asset (such as a piece of equipment) used in the passive activity would be considered passive. This does not include gains on investment property (that is, capital gains or losses).

[17] IRC § 469(c)(7)(B).

# From Shoebox to Software

**EXAMPLE 13-14**    Assume that Jose Ramirez (from the earlier chapters) received a K-1 (shown in Exhibit 13-3) from College Repairs Limited Partnership.

Upon reviewing the K-1, you must apply one of the seven material participation tests to determine whether the activity is passive. The interest and dividends ($500 and $200, respectively) are portfolio income, which you report on Schedule B. The $1,200 capital gain transfers to Schedule D. However, the $3,523 loss is a passive loss and is deductible on Schedule E only if Jose had passive income from another passive activity.

In Chapter 8 you entered information from a K-1 on Jose Ramirez's return. However, Jose materially participated in that partnership. In the College Repairs partnership, Jose is a limited partner, and thus the activity is passive.

In your tax software, open the Ramirez file and open a new K-1. Enter the information from the College Repairs LP from Exhibit 13-3. Assume that Jose is at risk for this activity. After you complete the K-1 information, the tax software transfers the information to Schedule B, Schedule D, and Form 8582. Note that the allowed loss on Form 8582 is zero because Jose had no other passive income. Also note that Schedule E, page 2, shows the College Repairs LP, but zero loss is allowed. Form 8582 is shown in Exhibit 13-4.

In addition to the real estate professional exception to the PAL rules, rental activities are not passive activities in six other cases.[18]

### Case 1: Average Rental Period Fewer Than Seven Days

The average period for customer use is fewer than seven days. Businesses that rent or lease tangible property for short periods are active (nonpassive) activities. For example, businesses that rent automobiles, tools, or DVDs are not passive activities.

### Case 2: Average Rental Period 30 or Fewer Days with Significant Personal Services

The average period of customer use is 30 or fewer days, and the owner provides significant personal services. An example meeting this exception for nonpassive classification would be the rental of a large crane for a construction site. If the average use were more than 7 days but fewer than 30 days and the rental company provided the crane operator, the rental would qualify as an active activity.

### Case 3: Extraordinary Personal Services

The owner provides extraordinary personal services in connection with the rental of tangible property. The most common rental property meeting this exception includes hospitals and university dormitories. Dorm rooms and hospital rooms are essentially rented, but the extraordinary services provided (the education or medical care) qualify the business for active treatment.

### Case 4: Incidental Rental Activity

The rental activity is incidental to a nonrental activity. This occurs if the property was predominantly used in a trade or business for at least two of the last five tax years. The gross rental income must be less than 2% of the lower of the basis of the property or its FMV. For example, suppose that a farmer leases a portion of his rice farm for duck hunting over the winter. If the rent received is less than 2% of the lower of the basis or FMV, the rent is incidental to the farming activity.

---

[18] Reg. § 1.469-1(e)(3).

**EXHIBIT 13-3**

| | |
|---|---|
| ☐ Final K-1    ☐ Amended K-1 | OMB No. 1545-0123 |

651121

**Schedule K-1**
**(Form 1065)**
Department of the Treasury
Internal Revenue Service

20**21**

For calendar year 2021, or tax year

beginning  /  / 2021  ending  /  /

**Partner's Share of Income, Deductions, Credits, etc.**

▶ See back of form and separate instructions.

| **Part I** | **Information About the Partnership** |
|---|---|
| A | Partnership's employer identification number |
| | 58-1234567 |
| B | Partnership's name, address, city, state, and ZIP code |

College Repairs, LP
123 University Drive
State University, NC  28765

| C | IRS center where partnership filed return ▶ Kansas City, MO |
|---|---|
| D | ☐ Check if this is a publicly traded partnership (PTP) |

| **Part II** | **Information About the Partner** |
|---|---|
| E | Partner's SSN or TIN (Do not use TIN of a disregarded entity. See instructions.) |
| | 412-34-5670 |
| F | Name, address, city, state, and ZIP code for partner entered in E. See instructions. |

Jose Ramirez
1234 West Street
Ellenwood, GA  30294

| G | ☐ General partner or LLC member-manager | ☐ Limited partner or other LLC member |
|---|---|---|
| H1 | ☒ Domestic partner | ☐ Foreign partner |
| H2 | ☐ If the partner is a disregarded entity (DE), enter the partner's: | |
| | TIN _____  Name _____ | |
| I1 | What type of entity is this partner? Individual | |
| I2 | If this partner is a retirement plan (IRA/SEP/Keogh/etc.), check here ▶ ☐ | |
| J | Partner's share of profit, loss, and capital (see instructions): | |

| | Beginning | Ending |
|---|---|---|
| Profit | % | 5 % |
| Loss | % | 5 % |
| Capital | % | 5 % |

Check if decrease is due to sale or exchange of partnership interest  ▶ ☐

| K | Partner's share of liabilities: | | |
|---|---|---|---|
| | | Beginning | Ending |
| Nonrecourse | $ | $ | |
| Qualified nonrecourse financing | $ | $ | |
| Recourse | $ | $ | |

Check this box if Item K includes liability amounts from lower tier partnerships ▶ ☐

| L | **Partner's Capital Account Analysis** |
|---|---|
| **Beginning capital account** | $ _____ |
| Capital contributed during the year | $ _____ |
| Current year net income (loss) | $ _____ |
| Other increase (decrease) (attach explanation) | $ _____ |
| Withdrawals and distributions | $ (_____ ) |
| **Ending capital account** | $ _____ |

| M | Did the partner contribute property with a built-in gain (loss)? |
|---|---|
| | ☐ Yes  ☒ No  If "Yes," attach statement. See instructions. |
| N | **Partner's Share of Net Unrecognized Section 704(c) Gain or (Loss)** |
| | Beginning .  .  .  .  .  .  . $ _____ |
| | Ending .  .  .  .  .  .  .  . $ _____ |

| **Part III** | **Partner's Share of Current Year Income, Deductions, Credits, and Other Items** | |
|---|---|---|
| 1 | Ordinary business income (loss)  (3,523) | 14  Self-employment earnings (loss) |
| 2 | Net rental real estate income (loss) | |
| 3 | Other net rental income (loss) | 15  Credits |
| 4a | Guaranteed payments for services | |
| 4b | Guaranteed payments for capital | 16  Schedule K-3 is attached if checked . . . . . ▶ ☐ |
| 4c | Total guaranteed payments | 17  Alternative minimum tax (AMT) items |
| 5 | Interest income  500 | |
| 6a | Ordinary dividends  200 | |
| 6b | Qualified dividends  200 | 18  Tax-exempt income and nondeductible expenses |
| 6c | Dividend equivalents | |
| 7 | Royalties | |
| 8 | Net short-term capital gain (loss) | |
| | | 19  Distributions |
| 9a | Net long-term capital gain (loss)  1,200 | |
| 9b | Collectibles (28%) gain (loss) | |
| | | 20  Other information |
| 9c | Unrecaptured section 1250 gain | |
| 10 | Net section 1231 gain (loss) | |
| 11 | Other income (loss) | |
| 12 | Section 179 deduction | 21  Foreign taxes paid or accrued |
| 13 | Other deductions | |
| 22 | ☐ More than one activity for at-risk purposes* | |
| 23 | ☐ More than one activity for passive activity purposes* | |

*See attached statement for additional information.

For IRS Use Only

**For Paperwork Reduction Act Notice, see the Instructions for Form 1065.**   www.irs.gov/Form1065   Cat. No. 11394R   **Schedule K-1 (Form 1065) 2021**

Source: U.S. Department of the Treasury, Internal Revenue Service, Schedule K-1 (Form 1065). Washington, DC: 2021.

**EXHIBIT 13-4**

| Form **8582** | **Passive Activity Loss Limitations** | OMB No. 1545-1008 |
|---|---|---|
| Department of the Treasury<br>Internal Revenue Service (99) | ▶ See separate instructions.<br>▶ Attach to Form 1040, 1040-SR, or 1041.<br>▶ Go to *www.irs.gov/Form8582* for instructions and the latest information. | **2021**<br>Attachment<br>Sequence No. **858** |

| Name(s) shown on return | Identifying number |
|---|---|
| Jose and Maria Ramirez | 412-34-5670 |

**Part I**    **2021 Passive Activity Loss**

**Caution:** Complete Parts IV and V before completing Part I.

**Rental Real Estate Activities With Active Participation** (For the definition of active participation, see *Special Allowance for Rental Real Estate Activities* in the instructions.)

| | | | |
|---|---|---|---|
| 1a | Activities with net income (enter the amount from Part IV, column (a)) | **1a** | |
| b | Activities with net loss (enter the amount from Part IV, column (b)) | **1b** ( ) | |
| c | Prior years' unallowed losses (enter the amount from Part IV, column (c)) | **1c** ( ) | |
| d | Combine lines 1a, 1b, and 1c | | **1d** |

**All Other Passive Activities**

| | | | |
|---|---|---|---|
| 2a | Activities with net income (enter the amount from Part V, column (a)) | **2a** | |
| b | Activities with net loss (enter the amount from Part V, column (b)) | **2b** ( 3,523 ) | |
| c | Prior years' unallowed losses (enter the amount from Part V, column (c)) | **2c** ( ) | |
| d | Combine lines 2a, 2b, and 2c | | **2d** (3,523) |
| 3 | Combine lines 1d and 2d. If this line is zero or more, stop here and include this form with your return; all losses are allowed, including any prior year unallowed losses entered on line 1c or 2c. Report the losses on the forms and schedules normally used | | **3** (3,523) |

If line 3 is a loss and:    • Line 1d is a loss, go to Part II.

                       • Line 2d is a loss (and line 1d is zero or more), skip Part II and go to line 10.

**Caution:** If your filing status is married filing separately and you lived with your spouse at any time during the year, **do not** complete Part II. Instead, go to line 10.

**Part II**    **Special Allowance for Rental Real Estate Activities With Active Participation**

**Note:** Enter all numbers in Part II as positive amounts. See instructions for an example.

| | | | |
|---|---|---|---|
| 4 | Enter the **smaller** of the loss on line 1d or the loss on line 3 | | **4** |
| 5 | Enter $150,000. If married filing separately, see instructions | **5** | |
| 6 | Enter modified adjusted gross income, but not less than zero. See instructions | **6** | |
| | **Note:** If line 6 is greater than or equal to line 5, skip lines 7 and 8 and enter -0- on line 9. Otherwise, go to line 7. | | |
| 7 | Subtract line 6 from line 5 | **7** | |
| 8 | Multiply line 7 by 50% (0.50). **Do not** enter more than $25,000. If married filing separately, see instructions | | **8** |
| 9 | Enter the **smaller** of line 4 or line 8 | | **9** |

**Part III**    **Total Losses Allowed**

| | | | |
|---|---|---|---|
| 10 | Add the income, if any, on lines 1a and 2a and enter the total | | **10** 0 |
| 11 | **Total losses allowed from all passive activities for 2021.** Add lines 9 and 10. See instructions to find out how to report the losses on your tax return | | **11** 0 |

**Part IV**    **Complete This Part Before Part I, Lines 1a, 1b, and 1c.** See instructions.

| Name of activity | Current year | | Prior years | Overall gain or loss | |
|---|---|---|---|---|---|
| | **(a)** Net income (line 1a) | **(b)** Net loss (line 1b) | **(c)** Unallowed loss (line 1c) | **(d)** Gain | **(e)** Loss |
| | | | | | |
| | | | | | |
| | | | | | |
| | | | | | |
| **Total.** Enter on Part I, lines 1a, 1b, and 1c ▶ | | | | | |

| For Paperwork Reduction Act Notice, see instructions. | Cat. No. 63704F | Form **8582** (2021) |
|---|---|---|

Source: U.S. Department of the Treasury, Internal Revenue Service, Form 8582. Washington, DC: 2021.

### Case 5: Nonexclusive Use by Customers

The taxpayer customarily makes the property available during defined business hours for non-exclusive use by customers. The regulations provide the example of the rental of golf carts on a golf course. The carts are customarily available during business hours for nonexclusive use by customers. This example could also qualify for the exception of average rental for fewer than seven days or the rental being incidental to the trade or business activity.

### Case 6: Use in a Partnership, S Corporation, or Joint Venture

The property is provided for use in an activity conducted by a partnership, S corporation, or joint venture in which the taxpayer owns an interest. If a taxpayer owns an interest in one of these (other than a rental activity) and rents property to that entity for use in the trade or business, the rental of that property is not considered a passive activity.

## $25,000 Offset for Rental Activities with Active Participation

Thus far in our discussion, passive losses are deducted only to the extent of passive income. One exception to this rule is the "$25,000 loss offset" for real estate rental activities for certain lower-income taxpayers.[19] A taxpayer who qualifies for this exception can offset up to $25,000 in passive losses from a rental activity against active and/or portfolio income. To qualify for the $25,000 offset, a taxpayer must actively participate in the rental activity.

To actively participate, an individual must have at least a 10% ownership interest in a rental activity. A taxpayer who participates in making management decisions or arranges for others to provide services (such as repairs) is treated as actively participating in a rental activity. Approving new tenants, deciding on rental terms, and approving expenditures also count in determining active participation.

Do not confuse *active participation* with *material participation*. Material participation is the test to determine whether an activity is passive. Active participation concerns rental property (which is already considered passive) and is a far less stringent requirement than material participation.

The $25,000 loss offset starts to phase out once a taxpayer's Adjusted Gross Income (AGI) reaches $100,000 (before rental loss). The $25,000 amount is reduced by 50% of the taxpayer's AGI in excess of $100,000 and is eliminated when a taxpayer's AGI reaches $150,000.

---

**EXAMPLE 13-15**   Alexandra has AGI (before any rental loss) of $85,000. She also owns a rental condo in Florida in which she actively participates. The condo produced a $12,000 loss in the current year. Alexandra has no passive income but can deduct the entire $12,000 rental loss against other active and portfolio income because her AGI is less than $100,000.

---

**EXAMPLE 13-16**   Assume the same facts as in Example 13-15, but in this case, Alexandra's pre-rental AGI is $140,000. With $140,000 in AGI, her deductible rental loss would be only $5,000. The available offset is reduced by $20,000 ([$140,000 AGI − $100,000 threshold] × 50%). If Alexandra's AGI were at or above $150,000, none of the rental loss could offset active or portfolio income. The nondeductible rental loss is a passive loss and would be suspended until passive income is generated or the activity is disposed of.

---

[19] The $25,000 amount becomes $12,500 for married taxpayers who file separate returns and do not live together at any time during the tax year.

### Disposition of a Passive Activity

When a taxpayer disposes of a passive activity in a taxable transaction (taxable gain or loss is recognized), suspended passive losses from past years are allowed, and any excess passive losses can be used to offset nonpassive income.[20]

| EXAMPLE 13-17 | Jamal sells his entire interest in a rental property in which he actively participated at a gain of $15,525. The activity has a current year loss of $2,800 and $12,650 in prior-year suspended losses. The $15,525 would most likely be reported on Form 4797, Part I, as a § 1231 gain. Jamal deducts the total $15,450 in current and suspended losses ($2,800 + $12,650) on Schedule E. If this were Jamal's only passive activity, Form 8582 would not be required. If Jamal had other passive activities, Form 8582 would be required because the sale resulted in a net gain of $75 ($15,525 gain from sale less $15,450 in total losses). The excess $75 is passive income and offsets other passive losses. |
| --- | --- |

If less than the entire interest in a passive activity is sold, the gains and losses from disposition are treated as part of the net income or loss from that activity. In other words, the gain or loss from a partial disposition of a passive activity is passive. The disposition of less than all of a passive interest does not trigger the allowance of prior-year suspended losses.

Additionally, a gift of a passive interest does not trigger the use of suspended PALs because a gift is not a taxable transaction. In the gift situation, the suspended PALs are added to the basis assumed by the donee.[21] A similar rule applies when a passive property transfers at death. Typically, the beneficiary receives the property with a basis equal to the FMV at the date of death. To the extent any suspended PALs exceed the increase in basis to the beneficiary, the suspended PALs are deducted on the decedent's final tax return.[22]

| CONCEPT CHECK 13-2— LO 13-2  | 1. Rental properties are almost always considered passive activities. True or false?<br>2. The general rule concerning the deductibility of passive losses is that they can be deducted only to the extent of passive income. True or false?<br>3. For low-income taxpayers, passive rental losses can be deducted against other income up to a maximum of $50,000. True or false?<br>4. Generally, suspended passive losses can be deducted against other income when the activity is sold or disposed of. True or false? |
| --- | --- |

## AT-RISK AND PAL RULES IN CONJUNCTION
### LO 13-3

In this section, we illustrate how the at-risk rules and the PAL rules work together to limit tax shelter abuses. When an investment in an activity is at risk, a Form 6198 is filed for each at-risk activity. Form 8582 (see Exhibit 13-4) is used to report PALs. A taxpayer files only one Form 8582 regardless of the number of passive activities with losses. The instructions relating to Form 8582 provide worksheets to determine the correct allocations between allowed and disallowed losses.

| TAX YOUR BRAIN | Do the PAL rules come into play for an activity that has a loss but has no amount at risk? |
| --- | --- |
| | **ANSWER** |
| | No, the loss must first be allowed under the at-risk rules, and then the PAL rules are applied. The PAL cannot be deducted unless the taxpayer had some passive income or was eligible for the $25,000 loss offset for rental real estate. |

[20] IRC § 469(g).

[21] IRC § 469(j)(6)(A).

[22] IRC § 469(g)(2)(A).

**EXAMPLE 13-18**

At the beginning of 2019, Marcella's at-risk amount in an activity was $60,000. The income/losses from the activity for 2019, 2020, and 2021 are as follows:

| Year | Gain/Loss |
|------|-----------|
| 2019 | $(80,000) |
| 2020 | (60,000) |
| 2021 | 100,000 |

How are the income and losses treated for each year? Apply both the at-risk rules and PAL rules assuming that this is Marcella's only passive activity:

| 2019 | | |
|------|------|------|
| Beginning at-risk amount | $60,000 | |
| Loss | (60,000) | $20,000 disallowed at-risk |
| Ending at-risk amount | $ –0– | |

Therefore, $60,000 of the loss passes through the at-risk rules. The PAL rules are now applied to the $60,000. Because Marcella has no other passive income and did not dispose of the activity, the $60,000 PAL is suspended and carried forward to 2020:

| Carryforwards to 2020 | $20,000 disallowed at-risk |
|-----------------------|----------------------------|
| | $60,000 suspended PAL* |

* These carryforward items should be noted in a prominent place (usually on the first page) in the 2019 working papers. When the 2020 tax return is prepared, a quick review of the prior-year working papers will bring the suspended losses to the attention of the preparer.

| 2020 | | |
|------|------|------|
| Beginning at-risk amount | $–0– | |
| Loss | –0– | $60,000 disallowed at-risk |
| Ending at-risk amount | $–0– | |

Because the $60,000 loss did not make it through the at-risk rules, the PAL rules are not applied. The $60,000 disallowed at-risk loss adds to the carryforward:

| Carryforwards to 2021 | $20,000 disallowed at-risk from 2019 |
|-----------------------|--------------------------------------|
| | $60,000 disallowed at-risk from 2020 |
| | $60,000 suspended PAL from 2019 |
| | $–0– suspended PAL from 2020 |

| 2021 | | |
|------|------|------|
| Beginning at-risk amount | $ –0– | |
| Income | 100,000 | |
| Prior-year disallowed losses | (80,000) | |
| Ending at-risk amount | $ 20,000 | |

Because the activity had $100,000 of income, the entire amount of prior-year disallowed losses is allowed under the at-risk rules. Now that the entire amount of losses ($140,000) has made it through the at-risk rules, the PAL rules are applied. Because the activity now has passive income of $100,000, Marcella can deduct $100,000 of the suspended PAL from 2019 and 2020. See Exhibit 13-5 (Form 8582) and Exhibit 13-6 (page 2 of Schedule E assumes the activity was a partnership) for the tax form presentation for 2021:

| Carryforwards to 2021 | $–0– disallowed at-risk from 2019 |
|-----------------------|-----------------------------------|
| | $–0– disallowed at-risk from 2020 |
| | $40,000 suspended PALs |

**EXHIBIT 13-5**

| Form **8582** | **Passive Activity Loss Limitations** | OMB No. 1545-1008 |
|---|---|---|
| Department of the Treasury Internal Revenue Service (99) | ▶ See separate instructions.<br>▶ Attach to Form 1040, 1040-SR, or 1041.<br>▶ Go to *www.irs.gov/Form8582* for instructions and the latest information. | 20**21**<br>Attachment Sequence No. **858** |

| Name(s) shown on return | Identifying number |
|---|---|
| Marcella Doe | 412-34-5670 |

**Part I    2021 Passive Activity Loss**

**Caution:** Complete Parts IV and V before completing Part I.

**Rental Real Estate Activities With Active Participation** (For the definition of active participation, see *Special Allowance for Rental Real Estate Activities* in the instructions.)

| | | | |
|---|---|---|---|
| 1a | Activities with net income (enter the amount from Part IV, column (a)) . . . | **1a** | |
| b | Activities with net loss (enter the amount from Part IV, column (b)) . . . . | **1b** ( ) | |
| c | Prior years' unallowed losses (enter the amount from Part IV, column (c)) . . | **1c** ( ) | |
| d | Combine lines 1a, 1b, and 1c . . . . . . . . . . . . . . . . . . . . | | **1d** |

**All Other Passive Activities**

| | | | |
|---|---|---|---|
| 2a | Activities with net income (enter the amount from Part V, column (a)) . . . | **2a** 100,000 | |
| b | Activities with net loss (enter the amount from Part V, column (b)) . . . . | **2b** ( ) | |
| c | Prior years' unallowed losses (enter the amount from Part V, column (c)) . . | **2c** ( 140,000 ) | |
| d | Combine lines 2a, 2b, and 2c . . . . . . . . . . . . . . . . . . . . | | **2d** (40,000) |
| 3 | Combine lines 1d and 2d. If this line is zero or more, stop here and include this form with your return; all losses are allowed, including any prior year unallowed losses entered on line 1c or 2c. Report the losses on the forms and schedules normally used . . . . . . . . . . . . . . . . . . . | | **3** (40,000) |

If line 3 is a loss and: • Line 1d is a loss, go to Part II.
                                    • Line 2d is a loss (and line 1d is zero or more), skip Part II and go to line 10.

**Caution:** If your filing status is married filing separately and you lived with your spouse at any time during the year, **do not** complete Part II. Instead, go to line 10.

**Part II    Special Allowance for Rental Real Estate Activities With Active Participation**

**Note:** Enter all numbers in Part II as positive amounts. See instructions for an example.

| | | | |
|---|---|---|---|
| 4 | Enter the **smaller** of the loss on line 1d or the loss on line 3 . . . . . . . | | **4** |
| 5 | Enter $150,000. If married filing separately, see instructions . . . . . . | **5** | |
| 6 | Enter modified adjusted gross income, but not less than zero. See instructions | **6** | |
| | **Note:** If line 6 is greater than or equal to line 5, skip lines 7 and 8 and enter -0- on line 9. Otherwise, go to line 7. | | |
| 7 | Subtract line 6 from line 5 . . . . . . . . . . . . . . . . . . . . | **7** | |
| 8 | Multiply line 7 by 50% (0.50). **Do not** enter more than $25,000. If married filing separately, see instructions | | **8** |
| 9 | Enter the **smaller** of line 4 or line 8 . . . . . . . . . . . . . . . . | | **9** |

**Part III    Total Losses Allowed**

| | | | |
|---|---|---|---|
| 10 | Add the income, if any, on lines 1a and 2a and enter the total . . . . . . . . | **10** | 100,000 |
| 11 | **Total losses allowed from all passive activities for 2021.** Add lines 9 and 10. See instructions to find out how to report the losses on your tax return . . . . . . . . . . . . . . . . . . . | **11** | 100,000 |

**Part IV    Complete This Part Before Part I, Lines 1a, 1b, and 1c.** See instructions.

| Name of activity | Current year | | Prior years | Overall gain or loss | |
|---|---|---|---|---|---|
| | **(a)** Net income (line 1a) | **(b)** Net loss (line 1b) | **(c)** Unallowed loss (line 1c) | **(d)** Gain | **(e)** Loss |
| | | | | | |
| | | | | | |
| | | | | | |
| | | | | | |
| **Total.** Enter on Part I, lines 1a, 1b, and 1c ▶ | | | | | |

For Paperwork Reduction Act Notice, see instructions.     Cat. No. 63704F     Form **8582** (2021)

Source: U.S. Department of the Treasury, Internal Revenue Service, Form 8582. Washington, DC: 2021.

**EXHIBIT 13-6**

| Schedule E (Form 1040) 2021 | Attachment Sequence No. **13** | Page **2** |
|---|---|---|

| Name(s) shown on return. Do not enter name and social security number if shown on other side.<br><br>Marcella Doe | Your social security number<br><br>412-34-5670 |
|---|---|

**Caution:** The IRS compares amounts reported on your tax return with amounts shown on Schedule(s) K-1.

**Part II** **Income or Loss From Partnerships and S Corporations** — **Note:** If you report a loss, receive a distribution, dispose of stock, or receive a loan repayment from an S corporation, you **must** check the box in column **(e)** on line 28 and attach the required basis computation. If you report a loss from an at-risk activity for which **any** amount is **not** at risk, you **must** check the box in column **(f)** on line 28 and attach **Form 6198.** See instructions.

27   Are you reporting any loss not allowed in a prior year due to the at-risk or basis limitations, a prior year unallowed loss from a passive activity (if that loss was not reported on Form 8582), or unreimbursed partnership expenses? If you answered "Yes," see instructions before completing this section . . . . . . . . . . . . . . . . .   ☐ **Yes**   ☐ **No**

| 28 | (a) Name | (b) Enter **P** for partnership; **S** for S corporation | (c) Check if foreign partnership | (d) Employer identification number | (e) Check if basis computation is required | (f) Check if any amount is not at risk |
|---|---|---|---|---|---|---|
| **A** | Marcella's Partnership | P | ☐ | 56-1234567 | ☐ | ☐ |
| **B** | | | ☐ | | ☐ | ☐ |
| **C** | | | ☐ | | ☐ | ☐ |
| **D** | | | ☐ | | ☐ | ☐ |

| | Passive Income and Loss | | Nonpassive Income and Loss | | |
|---|---|---|---|---|---|
| | (g) Passive loss allowed (attach **Form 8582** if required) | (h) Passive income from **Schedule K-1** | (i) Nonpassive loss allowed (see **Schedule K-1**) | (j) Section 179 expense deduction from **Form 4562** | (k) Nonpassive income from **Schedule K-1** |
| **A** | 100,000 | 100,000 | | | |
| **B** | | | | | |
| **C** | | | | | |
| **D** | | | | | |
| **29a** Totals | | 100,000 | | | |
| **b** Totals | 100,000 | | | | |

| 30 | Add columns (h) and (k) of line 29a. . . . . . . . . . . . . . . | 30 | 100,000 |
|---|---|---|---|
| 31 | Add columns (g), (i), and (j) of line 29b. . . . . . . . . . . . . . | 31 | ( 100,000 ) |
| 32 | **Total partnership and S corporation income or (loss).** Combine lines 30 and 31 . . . . | 32 | 0 |

**Part III** **Income or Loss From Estates and Trusts**

| 33 | (a) Name | (b) Employer identification number |
|---|---|---|
| **A** | | |
| **B** | | |

| | Passive Income and Loss | | Nonpassive Income and Loss | |
|---|---|---|---|---|
| | (c) Passive deduction or loss allowed (attach **Form 8582** if required) | (d) Passive income from **Schedule K-1** | (e) Deduction or loss from **Schedule K-1** | (f) Other income from **Schedule K-1** |
| **A** | | | | |
| **B** | | | | |
| **34a** Totals | | | | |
| **b** Totals | | | | |

| 35 | Add columns (d) and (f) of line 34a . . . . . . . . . . . . | 35 | |
|---|---|---|---|
| 36 | Add columns (c) and (e) of line 34b . . . . . . . . . . . | 36 | ( ) |
| 37 | **Total estate and trust income or (loss).** Combine lines 35 and 36 . . . . . . . . . . | 37 | |

**Part IV** **Income or Loss From Real Estate Mortgage Investment Conduits (REMICs)—Residual Holder**

| 38 | (a) Name | (b) Employer identification number | (c) Excess inclusion from **Schedules Q**, line 2c (see instructions) | (d) Taxable income (net loss) from **Schedules Q**, line 1b | (e) Income from **Schedules Q**, line 3b |
|---|---|---|---|---|---|
| | | | | | |

| 39 | Combine columns (d) and (e) only. Enter the result here and include in the total on line 41 below | 39 | |
|---|---|---|---|

**Part V** **Summary**

| 40 | Net farm rental income or (loss) from **Form 4835.** Also, complete line 42 below . . . . . . | 40 | |
|---|---|---|---|
| 41 | **Total income or (loss).** Combine lines 26, 32, 37, 39, and 40. Enter the result here and on Schedule 1 (Form 1040), line 5 ▶ | 41 | 0 |

| 42 | **Reconciliation of farming and fishing income.** Enter your **gross** farming and fishing income reported on Form 4835, line 7; Schedule K-1 (Form 1065), box 14, code B; Schedule K-1 (Form 1120-S), box 17, code AD; and Schedule K-1 (Form 1041), box 14, code F. See instructions . . | 42 | |
|---|---|---|---|
| 43 | **Reconciliation for real estate professionals.** If you were a real estate professional (see instructions), enter the net income or (loss) you reported anywhere on Form 1040, Form 1040-SR, or Form 1040-NR from all rental real estate activities in which you materially participated under the passive activity loss rules . . . . . . | 43 | |

Schedule E (Form 1040) 2021

Source: U.S. Department of the Treasury, Internal Revenue Service, Schedule E (Form 1040). Washington, DC: 2021.

**EXAMPLE 13-19**

Over the years, Lori purchased interests in four passive partnerships. Partnerships A, B, and C conduct a trade or business, and Partnership D is a rental real estate company. Lori's AGI prior to the partnership gains/losses is $80,003. The four partnerships had the following gains and losses in the current year. Lori is sufficiently at risk in each partnership.

| Partnership | Income/Loss | Type |
|---|---|---|
| A | $60,000 | Trade or business |
| B | (60,000) | Trade or business |
| C | (30,000) | Trade or business |
| D | (10,000) | Rental real estate |

In this case, Lori can deduct $70,000 of the $100,000 in losses under the PAL rules: $60,000 is allowed to the extent of passive income (allocated to B and C), and the $10,000 loss from the rental real estate is allowed under the $25,000 offset rule. Lori allocates the suspended PALs to the loss properties as follows:

$30,000 in suspended PAL
70,000 in PAL allowed

Suspended
| Partnership B | $60,000/$90,000 × $30,000 suspended | = | $20,000 suspended to B |
| Partnership C | 30,000/90,000 × 30,000 suspended | = | 10,000 suspended to C |

PAL allowed
| Partnership B | 60,000/90,000 × 60,000 allowed PAL | = | 40,000 allowed to B |
| Partnership C | 30,000/90,000 × 60,000 allowed PAL | = | 20,000 allowed to C |
| Partnership D | | = | 10,000 allowed to D |

Partnership A shows $60,000 of income on Schedule E, and Partnerships B, C, and D show losses of $40,000, $20,000, and $10,000, respectively. See Exhibits 13-7 and 13-8 for the correct presentation on Form 8582 and Schedule E, page 2, respectively.

---

**TAX YOUR BRAIN**

Why is it important that suspended losses be properly allocated to the various loss properties?

**ANSWER**
The primary reason is that when a passive activity is disposed of, the suspended losses are allowed. The suspended losses should be deducted in proportion to the activities that created the losses.

---

**CONCEPT CHECK 13-3— LO 13-3**

1. Which rules are applied *first* to a passive activity: the at-risk rules or the passive activity loss rules? Explain.
2. Why must suspended passive losses from several passive activities be allocated among the activities?
3. If a taxpayer has AGI of $105,000 before considering a $23,000 loss from a rental activity, how much can the taxpayer deduct from the rental activity, if any?

---

# ALTERNATIVE MINIMUM TAX (AMT)
## LO 13-4

The *alternative minimum tax* (AMT) is a separate tax system that attempts to levy tax on individuals who might otherwise escape taxation by using advanced tax incentives and programs provided in the IRC. The following is an excerpt from the Senate Finance Committee report providing the reasoning for the change in AMT rules:

**EXHIBIT 13-7**

| Form **8582** | **Passive Activity Loss Limitations** | OMB No. 1545-1008 |
|---|---|---|
| Department of the Treasury Internal Revenue Service (99) | ▶ See separate instructions.<br>▶ Attach to Form 1040, 1040-SR, or 1041.<br>▶ Go to *www.irs.gov/Form8582* for instructions and the latest information. | 20**21**<br>Attachment Sequence No. **858** |

| Name(s) shown on return | Identifying number |
|---|---|
| Lori Doe | 412-34-5670 |

**Part I**  **2021 Passive Activity Loss**

**Caution:** Complete Parts IV and V before completing Part I.

**Rental Real Estate Activities With Active Participation** (For the definition of active participation, see *Special Allowance for Rental Real Estate Activities* in the instructions.)

| | | | |
|---|---|---|---|
| 1a | Activities with net income (enter the amount from Part IV, column (a)) . . . | **1a** | |
| b | Activities with net loss (enter the amount from Part IV, column (b)) . . . . | **1b** ( 10,000 ) | |
| c | Prior years' unallowed losses (enter the amount from Part IV, column (c)) . . | **1c** ( ) | |
| d | Combine lines 1a, 1b, and 1c . . . . . . . . . . . . . . . . . . . | **1d** (10,000) |

**All Other Passive Activities**

| | | | |
|---|---|---|---|
| 2a | Activities with net income (enter the amount from Part V, column (a)) . . . | **2a** 60,000 | |
| b | Activities with net loss (enter the amount from Part V, column (b)) . . . . | **2b** ( 90,000 ) | |
| c | Prior years' unallowed losses (enter the amount from Part V, column (c)) . . | **2c** ( ) | |
| d | Combine lines 2a, 2b, and 2c . . . . . . . . . . . . . . . . . . . | **2d** (30,000) |

**3**  Combine lines 1d and 2d. If this line is zero or more, stop here and include this form with your return; all losses are allowed, including any prior year unallowed losses entered on line 1c or 2c. Report the losses on the forms and schedules normally used  .  .  .  .  .  .  .  .  .  .  .  .  .  .  .  | **3** (40,000)

If line 3 is a loss and:  • Line 1d is a loss, go to Part II.
• Line 2d is a loss (and line 1d is zero or more), skip Part II and go to line 10.

**Caution:** If your filing status is married filing separately and you lived with your spouse at any time during the year, **do not** complete Part II. Instead, go to line 10.

**Part II**  **Special Allowance for Rental Real Estate Activities With Active Participation**

**Note:** Enter all numbers in Part II as positive amounts. See instructions for an example.

| | | | |
|---|---|---|---|
| **4** | Enter the **smaller** of the loss on line 1d or the loss on line 3 . . . . . . . . . . . . . . . | **4** | 10,000 |
| **5** | Enter $150,000. If married filing separately, see instructions | **5** 150,000 | |
| **6** | Enter modified adjusted gross income, but not less than zero. See instructions | **6** 80,003 | |
| | **Note:** If line 6 is greater than or equal to line 5, skip lines 7 and 8 and enter -0- on line 9. Otherwise, go to line 7. | | |
| **7** | Subtract line 6 from line 5 . . . . . . . . . . . . . . . . . . . | **7** 69,997 | |
| **8** | Multiply line 7 by 50% (0.50). **Do not** enter more than $25,000. If married filing separately, see instructions | **8** | 25,000 |
| **9** | Enter the **smaller** of line 4 or line 8  .  .  .  .  .  .  .  .  .  .  .  .  .  .  .  .  .  .  .  | **9** | 10,000 |

**Part III**  **Total Losses Allowed**

| | | | |
|---|---|---|---|
| **10** | Add the income, if any, on lines 1a and 2a and enter the total .  .  .  .  .  .  .  .  .  .  . | **10** | 60,000 |
| **11** | **Total losses allowed from all passive activities for 2021.** Add lines 9 and 10. See instructions to find out how to report the losses on your tax return  .  .  .  .  .  .  .  .  .  .  .  .  .  .  . | **11** | 70,000 |

**Part IV**  **Complete This Part Before Part I, Lines 1a, 1b, and 1c.** See instructions.

| Name of activity | Current year | | Prior years | Overall gain or loss | |
|---|---|---|---|---|---|
| | **(a)** Net income (line 1a) | **(b)** Net loss (line 1b) | **(c)** Unallowed loss (line 1c) | **(d)** Gain | **(e)** Loss |
| Partnership D | 0 | (10,000) | 0 | | (10,000) |
| | | | | | |
| | | | | | |
| | | | | | |
| | | | | | |
| **Total.** Enter on Part I, lines 1a, 1b, and 1c ▶ | 0 | (10,000) | 0 | | |

| For Paperwork Reduction Act Notice, see instructions. | Cat. No. 63704F | Form **8582** (2021) |
|---|---|---|

Source: U.S. Department of the Treasury, Internal Revenue Service, Form 8582. Washington, DC: 2021.

**EXHIBIT 13-8**

Schedule E (Form 1040) 2021　　　　　　　　　　　　Attachment Sequence No. **13**　　　Page **2**

| Name(s) shown on return. Do not enter name and social security number if shown on other side. | Your social security number |
|---|---|
| Lori Doe | 412-34-5670 |

**Caution:** The IRS compares amounts reported on your tax return with amounts shown on Schedule(s) K-1.

**Part II　Income or Loss From Partnerships and S Corporations — Note:** If you report a loss, receive a distribution, dispose of stock, or receive a loan repayment from an S corporation, you **must** check the box in column **(e)** on line 28 and attach the required basis computation. If you report a loss from an at-risk activity for which **any** amount is **not** at risk, you **must** check the box in column **(f)** on line 28 and attach **Form 6198.** See instructions.

**27** Are you reporting any loss not allowed in a prior year due to the at-risk or basis limitations, a prior year unallowed loss from a passive activity (if that loss was not reported on Form 8582), or unreimbursed partnership expenses? If you answered "Yes," see instructions before completing this section . . . . . . . . . . . . . . . . ☐ **Yes** ☐ **No**

| 28 | (a) Name | (b) Enter **P** for partnership; **S** for S corporation | (c) Check if foreign partnership | (d) Employer identification number | (e) Check if basis computation is required | (f) Check if any amount is not at risk |
|---|---|---|---|---|---|---|
| A | Partnership A | P | ☐ | 56-1234567 | ☐ | ☐ |
| B | Partnership B | P | ☐ | 56-1234568 | ☐ | ☐ |
| C | Partnership C | P | ☐ | 56-1234569 | ☐ | ☐ |
| D | Partnership D | P | ☐ | 56-1234560 | ☐ | ☐ |

| | Passive Income and Loss | | Nonpassive Income and Loss | | |
|---|---|---|---|---|---|
| | (g) Passive loss allowed (attach **Form 8582** if required) | (h) Passive income from **Schedule K-1** | (i) Nonpassive loss allowed (see **Schedule K-1**) | (j) Section 179 expense deduction from **Form 4562** | (k) Nonpassive income from **Schedule K-1** |
| A | | 60,000 | | | |
| B | 40,000 | | | | |
| C | 20,000 | | | | |
| D | 10,000 | | | | |
| 29a Totals | | 60,000 | | | |
| b Totals | 70,000 | | | | |

| 30 | Add columns (h) and (k) of line 29a. . . . . . . . . . | 30 | 60,000 |
|---|---|---|---|
| 31 | Add columns (g), (i), and (j) of line 29b. . . . . . . . | 31 | ( 70,000 ) |
| 32 | **Total partnership and S corporation income or (loss).** Combine lines 30 and 31 . . . . . | 32 | (10,000) |

**Part III　Income or Loss From Estates and Trusts**

| 33 | (a) Name | (b) Employer identification number |
|---|---|---|
| A | | |
| B | | |

| | Passive Income and Loss | | Nonpassive Income and Loss | |
|---|---|---|---|---|
| | (c) Passive deduction or loss allowed (attach **Form 8582** if required) | (d) Passive income from **Schedule K-1** | (e) Deduction or loss from **Schedule K-1** | (f) Other income from **Schedule K-1** |
| A | | | | |
| B | | | | |
| 34a Totals | | | | |
| b Totals | | | | |

| 35 | Add columns (d) and (f) of line 34a . . . . . . . . . . | 35 | |
|---|---|---|---|
| 36 | Add columns (c) and (e) of line 34b . . . . . . . . . . | 36 | ( ) |
| 37 | **Total estate and trust income or (loss).** Combine lines 35 and 36 . . . . . . . . | 37 | |

**Part IV　Income or Loss From Real Estate Mortgage Investment Conduits (REMICs)—Residual Holder**

| 38 | (a) Name | (b) Employer identification number | (c) Excess inclusion from **Schedules Q,** line 2c (see instructions) | (d) Taxable income (net loss) from **Schedules Q,** line 1b | (e) Income from **Schedules Q,** line 3b |
|---|---|---|---|---|---|
| | | | | | |

| 39 | Combine columns (d) and (e) only. Enter the result here and include in the total on line 41 below | 39 | |
|---|---|---|---|

**Part V　Summary**

| 40 | Net farm rental income or (loss) from **Form 4835.** Also, complete line 42 below . . . . . . | 40 | |
|---|---|---|---|
| 41 | **Total income or (loss).** Combine lines 26, 32, 37, 39, and 40. Enter the result here and on Schedule 1 (Form 1040), line 5 ▶ | 41 | (10,000) |

| 42 | **Reconciliation of farming and fishing income.** Enter your **gross** farming and fishing income reported on Form 4835, line 7; Schedule K-1 (Form 1065), box 14, code B; Schedule K-1 (Form 1120-S), box 17, code AD; and Schedule K-1 (Form 1041), box 14, code F. See instructions . . | 42 | |
|---|---|---|---|
| 43 | **Reconciliation for real estate professionals.** If you were a real estate professional (see instructions), enter the net income or (loss) you reported anywhere on Form 1040, Form 1040-SR, or Form 1040-NR from all rental real estate activities in which you materially participated under the passive activity loss rules . . . . . . | 43 | |

Schedule E (Form 1040) 2021

Source: U.S. Department of the Treasury, Internal Revenue Service, Schedule E (Form 1040). Washington, DC: 2021.

**Reason for Change:** The committee believes that the minimum tax should serve one overriding objective: to ensure that no taxpayer with substantial economic income can avoid significant tax liability by using exclusions, deductions, and credits. Although these provisions may provide incentives for worthy goals, they become counterproductive when taxpayers are allowed to use them to avoid virtually all tax liability. The ability of high-income individuals and highly profitable corporations to pay little or no tax undermines respect for the entire tax system and, thus, for the incentive provisions themselves. In addition, even aside from public perceptions, the committee believes that it is inherently unfair for high-income individuals and highly profitable corporations to pay little or no tax due to their ability to utilize various tax preferences.[23]

The AMT rules are based on the notion of alternative minimum taxable income (AMTI). To determine AMTI, the taxpayer starts with regular taxable income calculated in accordance with the laws discussed throughout this text. The taxpayer then makes adjustments to regular taxable income to arrive at AMTI, which is used to calculate the minimum tax liability. The AMT tax rate is 26% on the first $199,900 and then moves to 28%. The AMT for an individual taxpayer is reported on Form 6251. The 2017 Tax Act virtually eliminated the AMT for nearly all individual taxpayers. Recall that the top regular tax rate is 37% and the top AMT rate is 28%, so most high-income taxpayers will pay more under the regular tax system. Only taxpayers with significant special adjustments (e.g., incentive stock options or long-term construction contracts–discussed later) will be subject to AMT.

## AMT Formula

The base formula for calculating AMT is this:[24]

| | | |
|---|---|---|
| Regular taxable income | | |
| | + | Standard deduction if the taxpayer does not itemize[a] |
| | +/− | Adjustment items[b] |
| | + | Tax preference items[c] |
| | = | Alternative minimum taxable income (AMTI) |
| | − | AMT exemption amount[d] |
| | = | Alternative minimum tax base |
| | × | Tax rate of either 26% (or 28% less $3,998[e]) |
| | = | Tentative minimum tax |
| | − | Regular tax |
| | = | Alternative minimum tax |

[a] IRC § 56(b)(1)(E).
[b] IRC § 56.
[c] IRC § 57.
[d] IRC § 55(d)(1).
[e] IRC § 55(b)(1)(A).

It is important to note that a taxpayer does not owe any AMT unless the AMT calculation results in an amount higher tax than the regular tax. Also note that the AMT tax rate is either 26% or 28%. If the taxpayer's AMTI is $199,900 or less, the AMT rate is 26%. If the AMTI amount is more than $199,900, the AMT rate is 28%. When the rate is 28%, $3,998 is then subtracted from the resulting AMT tax calculation. For taxpayers with net capital gains or qualified dividend income, the tax rates for these items are the same for both AMT and regular tax purposes.

## AMT Adjustment Items

Adjustments to regular income to arrive at AMTI can be either positive or negative.[25] The adjustments could reduce AMTI to the point that a taxpayer will not be subject to AMT. However, most adjustments increase AMTI. Table 13-3 lists the primary AMT adjustments.[26]

---

[23] Senate Report No. 99-313 (Pub. L. No. 99-514), 1986-3 CB (Part 3), p. 518. The Senate Report accompanied the Tax Reform Act of 1986.

[24] The format on Form 6251 is somewhat different, but the calculation is the same.

[25] A positive adjustrent increases AMTI, and a negative adjustment decreases AMTI. Thus, a negative adjustment is good for the taxpayer.

[26] IRC § 56.

**TABLE 13-3**
**Adjustments to AMT**

Standard deduction not allowed.

Depreciation for assets placed in service after 1986 and before 1999.

Depreciation exceeding 150% declining balance for some assets placed in service after 1998.

Adjustments to gains and losses on the sale of assets (different gains are caused by different depreciation methods).

Treatment of incentive stock options.

Passive activities (differences in regular tax passive loss and AMT passive loss allowed).

Beneficiaries of estates and trusts (differences in regular income or loss and amount of AMT income or loss).

Treatment of long-term contracts.

Others.

Only those adjustments affecting numerous taxpayers are covered in detail in this section. For more obscure adjustments, see the instructions for Form 6251 and IRC § 56.

### Standard Deduction and Itemized Deduction Limits

If the taxpayer does not itemize and takes the standard deduction for regular tax purposes, the standard deduction is added back as a positive adjustment to AMTI.[27]

---

**EXAMPLE 13-20**

Roland is married, files a joint return, and has two children. Because he rents his home (pays no mortgage interest) and lives in Florida (has no state income tax), he does not itemize his deductions but takes the standard deduction. Roland would have a positive adjustment for his standard deduction of $25,100.*

* Prior to 2018, personal exemptions were a positive adjustment. Exemptions were eliminated in the 2017 Tax Act.

---

### Itemized Deductions

The 2017 Tax Act simplified the treatment for itemized deductions. Medical, mortgage interest, charity, and miscellaneous deductions are now all treated the same for regular tax purposes as for AMT. Prior to 2018 all could create positive AMT adjustments. The 3% overall limitation of itemized deductions was also eliminated by the 2017 Tax Act so that AMT adjustment is also no longer necessary. State and local taxes are limited to $10,000 for regular tax so the adjustment for AMT is a maximum of $10,000.[28]

### Depreciation Adjustment for AMT

Nearly every taxpayer who calculates depreciation on their tax return will have a depreciation adjustment for AMT purposes. For most assets, depreciation must be recalculated using methods allowable for AMT. The method and life used vary depending on when the asset was placed in service and the type of property (real property or personal property).

### Real Property Placed in Service after 1986 and before 1999

Depreciation (for regular tax purposes) on all depreciable real property placed in service after 1986 and before 1999 is calculated using the straight-line method. The only

---

[27] IRC § 56(b)(1)(E).
[28] IRC § 56(b)(1)(A).

difference is the depreciation life of 27.5 years for residential real property and 39 years for nonresidential real property.[29] For AMT purposes, the depreciation life is 40 years for *all* real property (straight-line and mid-month conventions stay the same). Table 13 in Revenue Procedure 87-57 is the appropriate table to use for the depreciation calculation for real property under the AMT rules. Table 13 is reproduced in the Appendix to this chapter (Table 13A-1).

**EXAMPLE 13-21**

For tax years 2018 through 2025 there should be no adjustments for itemized deductions with the exception of $10,000 for taxes. Suppose that Jergen had the Schedule A shown in Exhibit 13-9 for his regular tax return. The mortgage interest is all qualified mortgage interest to purchase his personal residence.

For AMT purposes, Jergen has the following adjustments:

| Itemized Deduction | Regular Tax | Permitted AMT Deduction | AMT Adjustment |
|---|---|---|---|
| Medical | $65,450 | $65,450 | $  –0– |
| Taxes | 10,000 | –0– | 10,000 |
| Mortgage interest | 15,400 | 15,400 | –0– |
| Charitable contributions | 12,800 | 12,800 | –0– |
| | Total AMT adjustment for itemized deductions | | $10,000[30] |

**EXAMPLE 13-22**

Alex purchased a warehouse for $310,000 in August 1998. The regular depreciation and AMT depreciation for 2021 are calculated as follows:

| Regular Tax Depreciation (Table 6A-8—Chapter 6) | AMT Depreciation (Appendix Table 13A-1) | Adjustment |
|---|---|---|
| $310,000 × 2.564% = $7,948 | $310,000 × 2.5% = $7,750 | $198 |

The depreciation adjustment is only $198 for this asset. This is a small adjustment because the depreciation lives are virtually the same: 39 years for regular taxes compared to 40 years for AMT purposes.

[29] For assets placed in service prior to 1986, the difference in depreciation is called *a tax preference item* rather than an *adjustment* and thus is discussed in the preference section. Also, nonresidential real property purchased between December 31, 1986, and May 13, 1993, has a depreciable life of 31.5 years.

[30] Recall that tax refunds are included in income only if the taxpayer deducted the taxes in a prior year.

**EXHIBIT 13-9**

| SCHEDULE A (Form 1040)<br>Department of the Treasury<br>Internal Revenue Service (99) | **Itemized Deductions**<br>▶ Go to *www.irs.gov/ScheduleA* for instructions and the latest information.<br>▶ Attach to Form 1040 or 1040-SR.<br>**Caution:** If you are claiming a net qualified disaster loss on Form 4684, see the instructions for line 16. | OMB No. 1545-0074<br>**2021**<br>Attachment<br>Sequence No. **07** |
|---|---|---|

Name(s) shown on Form 1040 or 1040-SR

Jergen Taxpayer

Your social security number

412-34-5670

| Medical and Dental Expenses | | **Caution:** Do not include expenses reimbursed or paid by others. | | |
|---|---|---|---|---|
| | 1 | Medical and dental expenses (see instructions) | **1** | 83,900 |
| | 2 | Enter amount from Form 1040 or 1040-SR, line 11 | **2** | 246,000 |
| | 3 | Multiply line 2 by 7.5% (0.075) | **3** | 18,450 |
| | 4 | Subtract line 3 from line 1. If line 3 is more than line 1, enter -0- | **4** | 65,450 |
| Taxes You Paid | 5 | State and local taxes. | | |
| | a | State and local income taxes or general sales taxes. You may include either income taxes or general sales taxes on line 5a, but not both. If you elect to include general sales taxes instead of income taxes, check this box ▶ ☐ | **5a** | 10,000 |
| | b | State and local real estate taxes (see instructions) | **5b** | |
| | c | State and local personal property taxes | **5c** | |
| | d | Add lines 5a through 5c | **5d** | 10,000 |
| | e | Enter the smaller of line 5d or $10,000 ($5,000 if married filing separately) | **5e** | 10,000 |
| | 6 | Other taxes. List type and amount ▶ | **6** | |
| | 7 | Add lines 5e and 6 | **7** | 10,000 |
| Interest You Paid<br>**Caution:** Your mortgage interest deduction may be limited (see instructions). | 8 | Home mortgage interest and points. If you didn't use all of your home mortgage loan(s) to buy, build, or improve your home, see instructions and check this box ▶ ☐ | | |
| | a | Home mortgage interest and points reported to you on Form 1098. See instructions if limited | **8a** | 15,400 |
| | b | Home mortgage interest not reported to you on Form 1098. See instructions if limited. If paid to the person from whom you bought the home, see instructions and show that person's name, identifying no., and address ▶ | **8b** | |
| | c | Points not reported to you on Form 1098. See instructions for special rules | **8c** | |
| | d | Mortgage insurance premiums (see instructions) | **8d** | |
| | e | Add lines 8a through 8d | **8e** | 15,400 |
| | 9 | Investment interest. Attach Form 4952 if required. See instructions | **9** | |
| | 10 | Add lines 8e and 9 | **10** | 15,400 |
| Gifts to Charity<br>**Caution:** If you made a gift and got a benefit for it, see instructions. | 11 | Gifts by cash or check. If you made any gift of $250 or more, see instructions | **11** | 12,800 |
| | 12 | Other than by cash or check. If you made any gift of $250 or more, see instructions. You **must** attach Form 8283 if over $500. | **12** | |
| | 13 | Carryover from prior year | **13** | |
| | 14 | Add lines 11 through 13 | **14** | 12,800 |
| Casualty and Theft Losses | 15 | Casualty and theft loss(es) from a federally declared disaster (other than net qualified disaster losses). Attach Form 4684 and enter the amount from line 18 of that form. See instructions | **15** | |
| Other Itemized Deductions | 16 | Other—from list in instructions. List type and amount ▶ | **16** | |
| Total Itemized Deductions | 17 | Add the amounts in the far right column for lines 4 through 16. Also, enter this amount on Form 1040 or 1040-SR, line 12a | **17** | 103,650 |
| | 18 | If you elect to itemize deductions even though they are less than your standard deduction, check this box ▶ ☐ | | |

For Paperwork Reduction Act Notice, see the Instructions for Forms 1040 and 1040-SR.   Cat. No. 17145C   **Schedule A (Form 1040) 2021**

Source: U.S. Department of the Treasury, Internal Revenue Service, Schedule A (Form 1040). Washington, DC: 2021.

**EXAMPLE 13-23**     Assume the same facts as in Example 13-22, but the property is an apartment building instead of a warehouse.

| Regular Tax Depreciation (Table 6A-6—Chapter 6) | AMT Depreciation (Appendix Table 13A-1) | Adjustment |
|---|---|---|
| $310,000 × 3.636% = $11,272 | $310,000 × 2.5% = $7,750 | $3,522 |

In Example 13-23, the adjustment of $3,522 is higher because the depreciable lives are 27.5 years for regular tax purposes and 40 years for AMT purposes.

### Real Property Placed in Service after 1998

Congress changed the law for real property placed in service after 1998. Because the depreciation difference affected only the depreciation life and the difference was only one year in the case of nonresidential real property, Congress eliminated this adjustment. For real property placed in service after 1998, there is no adjustment for depreciation.

### Personal Property Placed in Service after 1986 and before 1999

For personal property, both the depreciation method and the class life are different under AMT rules. Regular MACRS depreciation for personal property is 200% declining balance (DB), and the life is determined under the general depreciation system (GDS). However, only 150% declining balance is allowed for AMT, and the life is determined under the alternative depreciation system (ADS). Both Revenue Procedure 87-56 and IRS Publication 946 present the different depreciation systems and corresponding lives.

The AMT lives are almost always longer (*never* shorter) than the regular tax lives. Longer lives and a less-aggressive depreciation method (150% DB versus 200% DB) ensure that a positive AMTI adjustment results for personal property. This adjustment is becoming less important because most of these assets were fully depreciated for regular tax purposes during the 2006 tax year and fully depreciated for AMT in the 2009 tax year.

**TAX YOUR BRAIN**

Will the AMT depreciation adjustment for these assets be larger or smaller as the years progress?

**ANSWER**

It will be smaller. Because a higher amount of depreciation is taken in the early years with accelerated methods, the 200% declining balance depreciation will decline more rapidly than the 150% declining balance as the assets get older. Thus, the difference between the two numbers will narrow. The adjustment will actually become negative in the last years of depreciation.

### Personal Property Placed in Service after 1998

In an attempt to simplify AMT calculations, Congress again changed the treatment of AMT depreciation for personal property. For any personal assets placed in service after 1998, the depreciation lives for AMT purposes are the same as for regular taxes (both will use the GDS life). The method still differs (150% DB for AMT and 200% DB for MACRS) for assets placed in service before then. Bonus depreciation and Section 179 expense are allowed for AMT so there is no adjustment if these provisions are used for regular tax purposes.

**EXAMPLE 13-24**

Andrew has two depreciable business assets. AMT depreciation is calculated using 150% DB; the MACRS method is 200% DB. Depreciation for tax year 2021 (the eighth year of depreciation) yields the following AMT adjustment.[31] The AMT depreciation percentages are found in Table 14 of Revenue Procedure 87-57. This table is partially reproduced in Table 13A-2 in the Appendix to this chapter.[32]

| Asset | Date Purchased | Cost | MACRS Life/ AMT Life | MACRS Depreciation | AMT Depreciation | Adjustment |
|-------|----------------|------|----------------------|--------------------|-------------------|------------|
| Furniture 1 | 02/12/2014 | $ 7,000 | 7-year | $312 | $429 | $(117) |
| Furniture 2 | 11/15/2014 | 12,000 | 7-year | 535 | 736 | (201) |
| | | | | | AMT adjustment | $(318) |

## Basis Calculation: Different Gains and Losses for AMT Purposes

Because of the different depreciation methods for AMT and for regular tax, accumulated depreciation and the adjusted basis of the assets are different. The different basis causes different gains and losses when assets are disposed.

**EXAMPLE 13-25**

Suppose we purchased furniture on February 10, 2019, for $6,000. On March 2, 2021, we sold the furniture for $4,300. The depreciation expense and gain for regular tax purposes are calculated as follows (seven-year, 200% DB):

| Year | Adjusted Basis | Depreciation Expense | Accumulated Depreciation |
|------|----------------|----------------------|--------------------------|
| 2019 | $6,000 | $ 857 | $ 857 |
| 2020 | 5,143* | 1,469 | 2,326 |
| 2021 | 3,674 | 525† | 2,851 |
| | | | $3,149 |
| Regular tax gain | | $4,300 − $3,149 = $1,151 | |

* The depreciation tables are structured such that depreciation is always calculated by multiplying the original cost basis by the appropriate percentage.
† One-half year of depreciation is allowed in the year of disposal.

The AMT depreciation, AMT adjusted basis, and AMT gain are calculated as follows (seven-year, 150% DB):

| Year | Adjusted Basis | Depreciation Expense | Accumulated Depreciation |
|------|----------------|----------------------|--------------------------|
| 2019 | $6,000 | $ 643 | $ 643 |
| 2020 | 5,357 | 1,148 | 1,791 |
| 2021 | 4,209 | 451 | 2,242 |
| | | | $3,758 |
| AMT gain | | $4,300 − $3,758 = $542 | |

The sale of this asset would result in a negative AMT adjustment of $609 ($1,151 regular tax gain less the $542 AMT gain).

---

[31] Recall that because the half-year convention is used for most assets, the depreciation calculation goes into the eighth year for seven-year assets.

[32] The regular depreciation percentages are found in the Appendix of Chapter 6, Table 6A-1. For MACRS depreciation of personal property, the percentages are also found in Table 1 of Rev. Proc. 87-57.

| TAX YOUR BRAIN | Why does the difference in gains result in a negative AMT adjustment that reduces AMT income? |
|---|---|

**ANSWER**

The regular tax gain of $1,151 is already included in taxable income (the starting point for AMT calculations). The AMT gain is $609 less than the regular tax gain. Therefore, AMT income should be reduced to reflect the lower gain.

### *Incentive Stock Options Adjustment*

For regular tax purposes, no income is recognized when an incentive stock option is exercised. This is not the case with AMT. For AMT purposes, the positive adjustment is equal to the FMV of the stock less the amount the taxpayer paid for it (including any amount paid for the option).[33]

---

**EXAMPLE 13-26**

Bob works for a large publicly traded company and regularly receives incentive stock options as bonuses. Bob exercises options to purchase 10,000 shares at $13 per share when the market value is $18. Bob's AMT adjustment is calculated as follows:

| | | | |
|---|---|---|---|
| Market value | 10,000 shares × $18 per share | = | $180,000 |
| Cost of stock | 10,000 shares × $13 per share | = | 130,000 |
| AMT adjustment | | | $ 50,000 |

---

The AMT basis in the stock is increased by the amount of the adjustment. Thus, when the stock is sold, the gain or loss will be different for AMT purposes than for regular tax purposes. In Example 13-26, the stock basis is $130,000 for regular tax purposes and $180,000 for AMT.

### *Passive Activity Adjustment and K-1 Adjustments*

AMTI is also adjusted for differences in passive losses and other adjustments originating from flow-through entities such as partnerships, estates, and trusts. The rule that passive activity losses are allowed only to the extent of passive income pertains to both regular tax and AMT calculations. However, the amount of passive loss and passive income will be different for AMT because all of the adjustments and preferences discussed in this chapter also apply to the passive activities (e.g., depreciation must be calculated differently using the AMT rules). These adjustments are reported to the taxpayer via the K-1 received from the flow-through entity.

### *Treatment of Long-Term Contracts*

For AMT purposes, a taxpayer must use the percentage of completion method rather than the completed contract method to report the income from long-term contracts. The adjustment is the difference between the income under the percentage of completion method and income determined for regular tax. In the year in question, if AMT income is smaller, the adjustment is negative. A negative adjustment is likely to occur in the year the contract is completed. This adjustment rarely, if ever, affects individual taxpayers unless the adjustment flows through from a partnership or LLC via a K-1.

### Tax Preference Items

Unlike adjustments, tax items result only in additions to AMTI. Tax preference items are typically more specific and affect taxpayers only in certain industries. This is true for individual taxpayers because individuals are unlikely to conduct business in certain industries other than a corporation or other entity form. Tax preference items are more likely to flow through from a K-1 than be directly calculated by the taxpayer. Some preference items can, however, affect

---

[33] IRC § 56(b)(3).

individual taxpayers. The following is a summary of the pertinent tax preference items that could affect an individual taxpayer. Form 6251 gives a complete list of tax preferences.

### Depreciation on Pre-1987 Assets

For all real property placed in service prior to 1987 and depreciated under an accelerated method, depreciation must be recalculated for AMT using the straight-line method over a 19-year life. The excess of regular tax depreciation over the straight-line depreciation is a *tax preference item*. Only a positive amount is reported. If the 19-year straight-line method results in more depreciation, no preference item is included. In tax year 2008, straight-line depreciation should be higher because the newest asset in this category was purchased in 1986. This preference item is considerably less important as time passes and pre-1986 assets approach the end of their depreciable lives.

### IRC § 1202 Exclusion

One preference item that can cause a substantial increase in AMTI for an individual taxpayer is the preference for the § 1202 exclusion (discussed in Chapter 7), which allows 50% (and possibly as much as 75%) of any gain from the sale of "qualified small business stock" to be excluded from regular tax. However, for AMT purposes, 7% of the amount excluded must be added as a tax preference item for post–May 5, 2003, sales.[34] The 2012 Taxpayer Relief Act made the 7% AMT preference item permanent. This preference will not apply to qualified small business stock purchased between September 1, 2010, and January 1, 2014. Additional dates of purchase apply to this provision; see IRC § 57(a)(7) for more information.

---

**EXAMPLE 13-27**

Ahkar invested in a local corporation with gross assets of $15,000,000. He purchased 500 shares for $25,000 in 2005. On June 6, 2021, Richard sold the stock for $45,000. One-half of the $20,000 gain is excluded from gross income for regular tax purposes under § 1202. For AMT, a tax preference item of $700 ($10,000 exclusion × 7%) is added to AMTI.

---

### Other Preference Items

The following is a list of other preference items that an individual taxpayer may be subject to in certain limited situations. A detailed discussion of these items is beyond the scope of this text. Preference items include:

- Percentage depletion taken in excess of the basis of the property.
- Excess intangible drilling and development costs.
- Tax-exempt interest on private activity bonds.
- Amortization of pollution control facilities placed in service before 1987.[35]

### Exemption Amount

After all of the tax preference items and AMT adjustments have been included, the taxpayer reduces AMTI by an exemption amount. The exemption amount varies depending on the filing status of the taxpayer and level of AMTI. The exemption amounts follow:

| Filing Status | AMTI Not More Than | 2021 Exemption Amount |
|---|---|---|
| Single/head of household | $ 523,600 | $ 73,600 |
| Married filing jointly/qualifying widow(er) | 1,047,200 | 114,600 |
| Married filing separately | 523,600 | 57,300 |

---

[34] IRC § 57(a)(7).
[35] IRC § 57(a)(6).

The exemption amount is reduced by 25% of AMTI in excess of the income limit in the "AMTI Not More Than" column.

**EXAMPLE 13-28**

After computing all tax preferences and AMT adjustments, Alex and Angel have AMTI of $1,100,000. Because Alex and Angel file a joint tax return, their initial exemption is $114,600. However, because their AMTI is more than $1,047,200, the exemption is reduced to $101,400: [$114,600 − 0.25($1,100,000 − $1,047,200)].

**COMPREHENSIVE AMT EXAMPLE**

This comprehensive AMT example uses components of many of the examples throughout this chapter.

Jergen Trade is married with two children. His Form 1040 shows regular taxable income of $142,350 (AGI $246,000 − Itemized deductions of $103,650). His regular tax liability is $22,814. He also has the following AMT adjustments and preferences:

1. Taxes are not allowed for AMT so there is only a $10,000 adjustment for the itemized deductions on Schedule A.

2. Depreciation of an apartment purchased in August 1998 for $310,000 (Example 13-23):

| Regular Tax Depreciation | AMT Depreciation | Adjustment |
|---|---|---|
| 2019  $310,000 × 3.636% = $11,272 | $310,000 × 2.5% = $7,750 | $3,522 |

3. Depreciation on personal property (Example 13-24):

| Asset | Date Purchased | Cost | MACRS Life/AMT Life | MACRS Depreciation | AMT Depreciation | Adjustment |
|---|---|---|---|---|---|---|
| Furniture 1 | 02/12/2013 | $ 7,000 | 7-year | $312 | $429 | $(117) |
| Furniture 2 | 11/15/2013 | 12,000 | 7-year | 535 | 736 | (201) |
| | | | | | AMT adjustment | $(318) |

4. Different basis (gain or loss) on the sale of an asset (see Example 13-25 for the calculations):

| Regular tax gain | $4,300 − $3,149 = $1,151 |
|---|---|
| AMT gain | $4,300 − $3,758 =   542 |

The sale of this asset would result in a $609 negative AMT adjustment ($1,151 tax gain − $542 AMT gain).

5. Incentive stock option adjustment (Example 13-26): Jergen exercises options to purchase 10,000 shares at $13 per share when the market value is $18. His AMT adjustment is calculated as follows:

| Market value | 10,000 shares × $18 per share | = | $180,000 |
|---|---|---|---|
| Cost of stock | 10,000 shares × $13 per share | = | 130,000 |
| AMT adjustment | | | $ 50,000 |

Exhibit 13-10 illustrates a completed Form 6251 and the calculated AMT of $676.

**EXHIBIT 13-10**

| Form **6251** | **Alternative Minimum Tax—Individuals** | OMB No. 1545-0074 |
|---|---|---|
| Department of the Treasury Internal Revenue Service (99) | ▶ Go to *www.irs.gov/Form6251* for instructions and the latest information.  ▶ Attach to Form 1040, 1040-SR, or 1040-NR. | **20**21  Attachment Sequence No. **32** |

Name(s) shown on Form 1040, 1040-SR, or 1040-NR

Jergan Trade

Your social security number

### Part I   Alternative Minimum Taxable Income (See instructions for how to complete each line.)

| | | | |
|---|---|---|---|
| 1 | Enter the amount from Form 1040 or 1040-SR, line 15, if more than zero. If Form 1040 or 1040-SR, line 15, is zero, subtract line 14 of Form 1040 or 1040-SR from line 11 of Form 1040 or 1040-SR and enter the result here. (If less than zero, enter as a negative amount.) . . . . . . . . . | **1** | 142,350 |
| 2a | If filing Schedule A (Form 1040), enter the taxes from Schedule A, line 7; otherwise, enter the amount from Form 1040 or 1040-SR, line 12a . . . . . . . | **2a** | 10,000 |
| b | Tax refund from Schedule 1 (Form 1040), line 1 or line 8z | **2b** | ( ) |
| c | Investment interest expense (difference between regular tax and AMT) . | **2c** | |
| d | Depletion (difference between regular tax and AMT) . . . . . . | **2d** | |
| e | Net operating loss deduction from Schedule 1 (Form 1040), line 8a. Enter as a positive amount | **2e** | |
| f | Alternative tax net operating loss deduction . . . . . . . . | **2f** | |
| g | Interest from specified private activity bonds exempt from the regular tax . . . . . . . | **2g** | |
| h | Qualified small business stock, see instructions . . . . . . . | **2h** | |
| i | Exercise of incentive stock options (excess of AMT income over regular tax income) . . . | **2i** | 50,000 |
| j | Estates and trusts (amount from Schedule K-1 (Form 1041), box 12, code A) . . . | **2j** | |
| k | Disposition of property (difference between AMT and regular tax gain or loss) . . . . | **2k** | (609) |
| l | Depreciation on assets placed in service after 1986 (difference between regular tax and AMT) . . . | **2l** | 3,204 |
| m | Passive activities (difference between AMT and regular tax income or loss) . . . | **2m** | |
| n | Loss limitations (difference between AMT and regular tax income or loss) . . . | **2n** | |
| o | Circulation costs (difference between regular tax and AMT). . . . . . . | **2o** | |
| p | Long-term contracts (difference between AMT and regular tax income) . . . | **2p** | |
| q | Mining costs (difference between regular tax and AMT) . . . . . . | **2q** | |
| r | Research and experimental costs (difference between regular tax and AMT) . . . | **2r** | |
| s | Income from certain installment sales before January 1, 1987 . . . . . | **2s** | ( ) |
| t | Intangible drilling costs preference . . . . . . . . . . | **2t** | |
| 3 | Other adjustments, including income-based related adjustments . . . . . | **3** | |
| 4 | **Alternative minimum taxable income.** Combine lines 1 through 3. (If married filing separately and line 4 is more than $752,800, see instructions.) . . . . . . . . . . . | **4** | 204,945 |

### Part II   Alternative Minimum Tax (AMT)

| | | |
|---|---|---|
| 5 | Exemption. | |

| **IF your filing status is . . .** | **AND line 4 is not over . . .** | **THEN enter on line 5 . . .** | | |
|---|---|---|---|---|
| Single or head of household . . . . | $    523,600 . . . . . | $ 73,600 | | |
| Married filing jointly or qualifying widow(er) | 1,047,200 . . . . . | 114,600 | | |
| Married filing separately . . . . . | 523,600 . . . . . | 57,300 | **5** | 114,600 |
| If line 4 is **over** the amount shown above for your filing status, see instructions. | | | | |

| | | | |
|---|---|---|---|
| 6 | Subtract line 5 from line 4. If more than zero, go to line 7. If zero or less, enter -0- here and on lines 7, 9, and 11, and go to line 10. . . . . . . . . . . . . . . . | **6** | 90,345 |
| 7 | • If you are filing Form 2555, see instructions for the amount to enter.  • If you reported capital gain distributions directly on Form 1040 or 1040-SR, line 7; you reported qualified dividends on Form 1040 or 1040-SR, line 3a; **or** you had a gain on both lines 15 and 16 of Schedule D (Form 1040) (as refigured for the AMT, if necessary), complete Part III on the back and enter the amount from line 40 here.  • **All others:** If line 6 is $199,900 or less ($99,950 or less if married filing separately), multiply line 6 by 26% (0.26). Otherwise, multiply line 6 by 28% (0.28) and subtract $3,998 ($1,999 if married filing separately) from the result. | **7** | 23,490 |
| 8 | Alternative minimum tax foreign tax credit (see instructions) . . . . . . . | **8** | 0 |
| 9 | Tentative minimum tax. Subtract line 8 from line 7 . . . . . . . . . | **9** | 23,490 |
| 10 | Add Form 1040 or 1040-SR, line 16 (minus any tax from Form 4972), and Schedule 2 (Form 1040), line 2. Subtract from the result any foreign tax credit from Schedule 3 (Form 1040), line 1. If you used Schedule J to figure your tax on Form 1040 or 1040-SR, line 16, refigure that tax without using Schedule J before completing this line (see instructions) . . . . . . . . . . . . . . . | **10** | 22,814 |
| 11 | **AMT.** Subtract line 10 from line 9. If zero or less, enter -0-. Enter here and on Schedule 2 (Form 1040), line 1 | **11** | 676 |

| | | |
|---|---|---|
| For Paperwork Reduction Act Notice, see your tax return instructions. | Cat. No. 13600G | Form **6251** (2021) |

Source: U.S. Department of the Treasury, Internal Revenue Service, Form 6251. Washington, DC: 2021.

# From Shoebox to Software

Tax software performs most of the AMT calculation automatically. All of the itemized deduction adjustments and the AMT depreciation calculations transfer to Form 6251. For some of the unique adjustments, the taxpayer must enter the adjustments and preferences directly on Form 6251.

Some explanation is necessary concerning certain items on Form 6251 in Exhibit 13-10:

Line 1: This is taxable income ($142,350), which is the total income less itemized deductions.

Line 2l: The depreciation adjustment of $3,204 is a combination of the real property depreciation adjustment

of $3,522 and the personal property depreciation adjustment of $(318).

Line 7: Because AMTI after the exemption is less than $199,900, the AMT rate is 26%. The resulting tentative tax is $23,490 (90,345 × 26%).

Line 11: The regular tax is $22,814. The difference between the tax calculated under the AMT rules and the regular tax is equal to the AMT of $676. If the taxpayer had capital gains and the regular tax was calculated on page 2 of Schedule D, the AMT would be calculated on page 2 of Form 6251 (not shown). The preferential capital gain rates are allowed for AMT purposes.

---

**CONCEPT CHECK 13-4—**
**LO 13-4**

1. Medical expenses are allowed in full (same as the regular tax) for AMT purposes. True or false?
2. No taxes are allowed as a deduction for AMT purposes. True or false?
3. If a taxpayer is married and has eight children, no exemption would be allowed for AMT purposes. True or false?
4. If a taxpayer's AMTI is $199,900 or less, the AMT tax rate would be 26%. True or false?

---

# Summary

**LO 13-1:** Explain the process of applying the at-risk rules.

- The initial at-risk amount is the money plus the adjusted basis of property contributed.
- The at-risk amount is increased by income/gain items, additional contributions, and the taxpayer's share of recourse liabilities.
- Loss deductions and distributions are limited to the amount that the taxpayer has at risk.

**LO 13-2:** Describe the rules and applications related to passive activities.

- A passive activity is one in which the taxpayer does not materially participate.
- A passive loss is generally deductible only to the extent of passive income.
- Low-income taxpayers could be able to offset up to $25,000 of passive rental loss against other income.
- When a passive activity is sold, suspended passive losses from past years are allowed to offset nonpassive income.

**LO 13-3:** Explain how the passive activity loss rules and at-risk rules work together to limit the deductibility of losses.

- For a loss to be deductible, it must first be allowed under the at-risk rules before the PAL rules can be applied.
- Suspended PALs must be allocated to individual properties.

**LO 13-4:** Explain the alternative minimum tax and how it is calculated.

- The AMT is a separate tax system to limit taxpayers with substantial income from avoiding paying tax by using exclusions, deductions, and credits.
- Itemized deductions for taxes are disallowed for AMT.
- The AMT rate is 26% for AMTI of $199,900 or less, and 28% for AMTI over $199,900.

## Appendix

Tables 13A-1 and 13A-2 are reproductions of Tables 13 and 14 in Revenue Procedure 87-57.

**DEPRECIATION TABLE 13A-1**  Alternative Depreciation System Straight-Line Applicable Recovery Period: 40 Years

| | **Mid-Month Convention** | | | | | | | | | | | |
| | **Month in the First Recovery Year the Property Is Placed in Service** | | | | | | | | | | | |
| Recovery Year | **1** | **2** | **3** | **4** | **5** | **6** | **7** | **8** | **9** | **10** | **11** | **12** |
|---|---|---|---|---|---|---|---|---|---|---|---|---|
| 1 | 2.396 | 2.188 | 1.979 | 1.771 | 1.563 | 1.354 | 1.146 | .938 | .729 | .521 | .313 | .104 |
| 2–40 | 2.500 | 2.500 | 2.500 | 2.500 | 2.500 | 2.500 | 2.500 | 2.500 | 2.500 | 2.500 | 2.500 | 2.500 |
| 41 | .104 | .312 | .521 | .729 | .937 | 1.146 | 1.354 | 1.562 | 1.771 | 1.979 | 2.187 | 2.396 |

**DEPRECIATION TABLE 13A-2**
**Alternative Minimum Tax 150% Declining Balance Switching to Straight-Line Recovery Period: 2.5–50 Years**

| | **Half-Year Convention** | | | | | |
| | **Partial Table of Table 14 in Revenue Procedure 87-57** | | | | | |
| Recovery Year | **4.0** | **5.0** | **6.0** | **7.0** | **10.0** | **12.0** |
|---|---|---|---|---|---|---|
| 1 | 18.75 | 15.00 | 12.50 | 10.71 | 7.50 | 6.25 |
| 2 | 30.47 | 25.50 | 21.88 | 19.13 | 13.88 | 11.72 |
| 3 | 20.31 | 17.85 | 16.41 | 15.03 | 11.79 | 10.25 |
| 4 | 20.31 | 16.66 | 14.06 | 12.25 | 10.02 | 8.97 |
| 5 | 10.16 | 16.66 | 14.06 | 12.25 | 8.74 | 7.85 |
| 6 | | 8.33 | 14.06 | 12.25 | 8.74 | 7.33 |
| 7 | | | 7.03 | 12.25 | 8.74 | 7.33 |
| 8 | | | | 6.13 | 8.74 | 7.33 |
| 9 | | | | | 8.74 | 7.33 |
| 10 | | | | | 8.74 | 7.33 |
| 11 | | | | | 4.37 | 7.32 |
| 12 | | | | | | 7.33 |
| 13 | | | | | | 3.66 |

## *EA Fast Fact*

**ADMITTED TO PRACTICE BEFORE THE IRS**

**ENROLLED AGENT**

Primary Topics on Part III of the EA exam, Representation, Practice, and Procedures, include:

☐ ***Part III–Representation, Practices, and Procedures–3.5 hrs.***
- Recordkeeping Requirements
- Rules for Tax Returns Preparers
- Electronic Filing
- Powers of Attorney and Disclosure
- Tax Returns Examinations and Appeals
- Tax Law and Authority
- Provisions in Circular 230
- Record Maintenance
- Exempt Organizations
- Accountant privilege and disclosure

**IMPORTANT**

You are eligible to receive absolutely free, the Surgent Enrolled Agent review program for Part I of the EA exam as a result of purchasing this text. To activate your free access, go to https://Surgent.com/McGrawHill/EA.

## Discussion Questions   <sub>Mc Graw Hill</sub> **connect**

All applicable discussion questions are available with **Connect**

LO 13-1   1. Discuss the *at-risk* concept and how it applies to the deductibility of investment losses.

LO 13-1   2. What amounts are considered at risk when making the determination of a deductible loss?

LO 13-1   3. What are the differences between recourse, nonrecourse, and qualified nonrecourse liabilities? Which liabilities are considered at risk?

LO 13-2   4. What is a *passive activity?* What types of activities are automatically considered passive?

LO 13-2   5. Discuss the concept of *material participation.* To be considered a material participant, what tests must the taxpayer satisfy?

LO 13-2   6. When a loss is disallowed under the passive activity loss rules, what happens to that loss in future years?

LO 13-2   7. Discuss the rules concerning the $25,000 loss offset for rental activities. Why are losses of $25,000 allowed for some taxpayers?

LO 13-2    8. What are the differences between material participation, active participation, and significant participation?

_____

_____

_____

_____

LO 13-2    9. When a passive activity is sold or otherwise disposed of, what happens to any suspended losses from that activity?

_____

_____

_____

_____

LO 13-3    10. When must Form 6198 and Form 8582 be filed? Does the taxpayer file more than one Form 6198 or Form 8582?

_____

_____

_____

_____

LO 13-3    11. How do the passive loss rules and the at-risk rules work in conjunction to limit losses?

_____

_____

_____

_____

**EA**   LO 13-4    12. Discuss the AMT formula and how it relates to the regular income tax. Include in your discussion factors that cause AMT to be assessed.

_____

_____

_____

_____

**EA**   LO 13-4    13. What AMT adjustment items are likely to affect all taxpayers who itemize their deductions? Give examples.

_____

_____

_____

_____

**EA**   LO 13-4    14. Are medical expenses treated differently for AMT purposes than for regular tax purposes? If so, explain.

_____

_____

_____

_____

**EA** **LO 13-4** 15. Are the depreciation lives the same for AMT purposes as for regular tax purposes? If not, how are the lives determined for AMT?

_____

_____

_____

_____

**EA** **LO 13-4** 16. Discuss the tax basis calculation adjustment. Why is the gain or loss on the sale of depreciable assets different for AMT purposes than for regular tax purposes?

_____

_____

_____

_____

## Multiple-Choice Questions

All applicable multiple-choice questions are available with **Connect**

**LO 13-1** 17. Which of the following increases a taxpayer's at-risk amount?
 *a.* Cash and the adjusted basis of property contributed to the activity.
 *b.* Borrowed amounts used in the activity for which the taxpayer is personally liable.
 *c.* Income from the activity.
 *d.* All of the above.

**LO 13-1** 18. Which of the following increases a taxpayer's at-risk amount?
 *a.* Cash distributions.
 *b.* Property distributions.
 *c.* Increased share of liabilities.
 *d.* Loss items.

**LO 13-1** 19. In 2021, Kirsten invested $20,000 for a 10% partnership interest (not a passive activity). The partnership has losses of $150,000 in 2021 and $250,000 in 2022. Kirsten's share of the partnership's losses is $15,000 in 2021 and $25,000 in 2022. How much of the losses from the partnership can Kirsten deduct?
 *a.* $0 in 2021 and $0 in 2022.
 *b.* $15,000 in 2021 and $5,000 in 2022.
 *c.* $15,000 in 2021 and $25,000 in 2022.
 *d.* $20,000 in 2021 and $0 in 2022.

**LO 13-1** 20. Leonardo invests $10,000 cash in an equipment-leasing activity for a 15% share in the business. The 85% owner is Rebecca, who contributes $10,000 and borrows $75,000 to put in the business. Only Rebecca is liable for repayment of the loan. The partnership incurs a loss of $125,000 during the year. What amounts of the loss are deductible currently by Leonardo and Rebecca (ignore passive loss rules)?
 *a.* $0 by Leonard and $0 by Rebecca.
 *b.* $10,000 by Leonardo and $85,000 by Rebecca.
 *c.* $18,750 by Leonardo and $106,250 by Rebecca.
 *d.* $21,250 by Leonardo and $73,750 by Rebecca.

**LO 13-1**    21. Myer owns a 20% interest in a partnership (not involved in real estate) in which his at-risk amount was $50,000 at the beginning of the year. During the year, he receives a $40,000 distribution from the partnership. The partnership produces a $160,000 loss during the year. What is Myer's deductible loss for the year (ignore passive loss rules)?

  *a.* $0.

  *b.* $10,000.

  *c.* $32,000.

  *d.* $50,000.

**LO 13-1**    22. Alcott invested $20,000 for a 25% interest in a partnership (not a passive activity) on January 1, 2021. The partnership borrowed $100,000 (with full recourse to the partners) on January 15, 2021, to cover short-term cash flow requirements. During the year, the partnership generated a $60,000 loss. By December 31, 2021, the partnership had paid off $20,000 of the loan. What is Alcott's at-risk amount on January 1, 2022?

  *a.* $20,000.

  *b.* $25,000.

  *c.* $40,000.

  *d.* $45,000.

**LO 13-1**    23. Agnes and Aunt Sue each invested $140,000 cash in the A&S Partnership, and each received a 50% interest in the partnership. To finance her investment in the partnership, Agnes borrowed $60,000 on a full recourse basis from her partner, Aunt Sue. Which of the following is correct?

  *a.* Agnes's at-risk amount in her partnership interest is $80,000.

  *b.* Aunt Sue's at-risk amount in her partnership interest is $140,000.

  *c.* Agnes's at-risk amount in her partnership interest is $140,000.

  *d.* Aunt Sue's at-risk amount in her partnership interest is $80,000.

**LO 13-2**    24. Which of the following would be considered a passive activity?

  *a.* A limited partnership interest.

  *b.* Most rental real estate activities.

  *c.* A trade or business in which the taxpayer does not materially participate.

  *d.* All of the above.

**LO 13-2**    25. Sylvester, an accountant, owns a mail-order business in which he participates. He has one employee who works part time in the business. Which of the following statements is *not* correct?

  *a.* If Sylvester participates for 600 hours and the employee participates for 1,000 hours during the year, Sylvester qualifies as a material participant.

  *b.* If Sylvester participates for 120 hours and the employee participates for 125 hours during the year, Sylvester does not qualify as a material participant.

  *c.* If Sylvester participates for 495 hours and the employee participates for 520 hours during the year, Sylvester qualifies as a material participant.

  *d.* If Sylvester participates for 105 hours and the employee participates for 5 hours during the year, Sylvester probably qualifies as a material participant.

**LO 13-2**    26. Janel owns five small businesses, each of which has its own manager and employees. Janel spends the following number of hours this year working in the various businesses: Business A, 130 hours; Business B, 160 hours; Business C, 110 hours; Business D, 120 hours; Business E, 100 hours. Which of the following statements is correct?

  *a.* Businesses A, B, C, D, and E are all significant participation activities.

  *b.* Businesses A, B, C, and D are all significant participation activities.

c. Janel is considered a material participant in Businesses A, B, C, and D.

d. Both *b* and *c* are correct.

**LO 13-2**   27. Santiago is a CPA and earns $150,000 from his practice in the current year. He also has an ownership interest in three passive activities. Assume he is sufficiently at risk in each of the three partnerships. In the current tax year, the activities had the following income and losses:

| | |
|---|---|
| Partnership A | $40,000 |
| Partnership B | (32,000) |
| Partnership C | (24,000) |

What is Santiago AGI for the current year?

a. $134,000.

b. $144,000.

c. $150,000.

d. $190,000.

**LO 13-2**   28. Nathaniel has AGI (before any rental loss) of $65,000. He also owns several rental properties in which he actively participates. The rental properties produced a $30,000 loss in the current year. Nathaniel also has $5,000 of income from a limited partnership interest. How much, if any, of the rental loss can he deduct in the current year?

a. $0.

b. $5,000.

c. $25,000.

d. $30,000.

**LO 13-2**   29. Basil has $130,000 AGI (before any rental loss). He also owns several rental properties in which he actively participates. The rental properties produced a $30,000 loss in the current year. How much, if any, of the rental loss can Basil deduct in the current year?

a. $0.

b. $10,000.

c. $15,000.

d. $25,000.

**LO 13-2**   30. Raymond sells his entire interest in a rental property in which he actively participated at a gain of $18,000. The activity has a current year loss of $5,500 and $18,500 in prior-year suspended losses. During the year, Raymond has $55,000 in salary. What is Raymond's AGI for the year?

a. $49,000.

b. $55,000.

c. $67,500.

d. $73,000.

**EA**   **LO 13-4**   31. Jacob is single with no dependents. During 2021 he has $48,000 of taxable income. He also has $28,000 of positive AMT adjustments and $12,000 of tax preferences. Jacob does not itemize his deductions but takes the standard deduction. Calculate his AMTI.

a. $60,000.

b. $76,000.

c. $88,000.

d. $100,550.

EA LO 13-4 32. Which of the following itemized deductions is *not* allowed for AMT?

    *a.* Medical expenses.

    *b.* Taxes.

    *c.* Charitable contributions.

    *d.* Interest on loan to purchase principal residence.

EA LO 13-4 33. Which of the following statements is correct with regard to the medical expense deduction?

    *a.* Medical expenses are not deductible for AMT.

    *b.* The medical expense deduction is decreased for AMT.

    *c.* The medical expense deduction is increased for AMT.

    *d.* The same amount of medical expenses that is deductible for regular tax purposes is deductible for AMT.

EA LO 13-4 34. Paul reported the following itemized deductions on his 2021 tax return. His AGI for 2021 was $65,000. The mortgage interest is all qualified mortgage interest to purchase his personal residence. For AMT, compute his total adjustment for itemized deductions.

| | |
|---|---:|
| Medical expenses (after the 7.5% of AGI floor) | $ 6,000 |
| State income taxes | 3,600 |
| Home mortgage interest | 11,500 |
| Charitable contributions | 3,200 |

    *a.* $0.

    *b.* $3,600.

    *c.* $9,600.

    *d.* $24,300.

EA LO 13-4 35. After computing all tax preferences and AMT adjustments, Phillip and his wife Carmin have AMTI of $1,210,000. If Phillip and Carmin file a joint tax return, what exemption amount can they claim for AMT for 2021?

    *a.* $0.

    *b.* $73,900.

    *c.* $73,600.

    *d.* $114,600.

## Problems McGraw Hill connect

All applicable problems are available with **Connect**

LO 13-1 36. In 2021, Andrew contributed equipment with an adjusted basis of $20,000 and an FMV of $18,000 to Construction Limited Partnership (CLP) in return for a 3% limited partnership interest. Andrew's share of CLP income and losses for the year was as follows:

| | |
|---|---:|
| Interest | $ 500 |
| Dividends | 300 |
| Capital gains | 900 |
| Ordinary loss | (4,325) |

CLP had no liabilities. What are Andrew's initial basis, allowed losses, and ending at-risk amount?

_____

_____

_____

_____

**LO 13-1**  37. Cindy, Casey, and Kara each invested $30,000 in a real estate venture. The partnership borrowed $200,000 and purchased a warehouse for $290,000. The note was secured by the building; there was no personal recourse against the partners. What is each partner's beginning at-risk amount in the venture?

_____

_____

_____

_____

**LO 13-2**  38. During the current year, Joshua worked 1,300 hours as a tax consultant and 450 hours as a real estate agent. His one other employee (his spouse) worked 300 hours in the real estate business. Joshua earned $50,000 as a tax consultant, and together the couple lost $20,000 in the real estate business. How should Joshua treat the loss on his federal income tax return?

_____

_____

_____

_____

**LO 13-2**  39. Donald has two investments in activities that are considered nonrental passive activities. He acquired Activity A six years ago, and it was profitable until the current year. He acquired Activity B in the current year. His share of the loss from Activity A in the current year is $15,000, and his share of the loss from Activity B is $4,000. What is the total of Donald's suspended losses from these activities as of the end of the current year?

_____

_____

_____

_____

**LO 13-2**  40. Darrell acquired an activity eight years ago. The loss from it in the current year was $65,000. The activity involves residential rental real estate in which he is an active participant. Calculate Darrell's AGI after considering that Darrell's AGI was $100,000 before including any potential loss.

_____

_____

_____

_____

LO 13-2    41. Evelyn has rental income of $48,000 and passive income of $18,000. She also has $148,000 of losses from a real estate rental activity in which she actively participates. Evelyn's AGI is $95,000 before considering this activity. How much rental loss can she deduct against other income sources without regard to the at-risk rules?

_____

_____

_____

_____

LO 13-2    42. Christine died owning an interest in a passive activity property. The property had an adjusted basis of $210,000, a fair market value of $224,000, and suspended losses of $21,000. What can be deducted on her final income tax return?

_____

_____

_____

_____

LO 13-2    43. Judy acquired passive Activity A in January 2015 and Activity B in July 2016. Until 2020 Activity A was profitable. Activity A produced a loss of $50,000 in 2020 and a loss of $75,000 in 2021. She has $45,000 passive income from Activity B in 2020 and $35,000 in 2021. After offsetting passive income, how much of the net losses may she deduct?

_____

_____

_____

_____

LO 13-2    44. This year Robert had the following income and losses from four passive activities:

| | |
|---|---:|
| Activity 1 | $(20,000) |
| Activity 2 | (10,000) |
| Activity 3 | (5,000) |
| Activity 4 | 33,000 |

Activity 4 had $10,000 of passive losses that are carried over from a prior year. Robert also had wages of $110,000.

*a.* How much income or loss does Robert have from the four activities?

*b.* How are the suspended PALs allocated?

*c.* If Activity 1 were sold at an $18,000 gain, what would be the total income or loss from the four activities?

_____

_____

_____

_____

_____

_____

LO 13-2    45. Lucy has AGI of $120,000 before considering losses from some rental real estate she owns (she actively participates). She had the following losses from her rental property:

| | |
|---|---|
| Rental property 1 | $(22,000) |
| Rental property 2 | (5,000) |

*a.* How much of the losses can Lucy deduct?

*b.* If Lucy's AGI before the losses was $90,000, how much of the losses can she deduct?

_____

_____

_____

_____

_____

_____

**LO 13-2**   46. Julia acquired passive Activity A in January 2017 and passive Activity B in July 2019. Until 2020 Activity A was profitable. Activity A produced a loss of $150,000 in 2020 and a loss of $150,000 in 2021. She had passive income from Activity B of $50,000 in 2020 and $35,000 in 2021. How much of the net passive losses may she deduct in 2020 and 2021, respectively? (Ignore at-risk rules.)

_____

_____

_____

_____

_____

**LO 13-3**   47. Jackson invested $190,000 in a passive activity five years ago. On January 1, 2019, his at-risk amount in the activity was $45,000. His share of the income and losses in the activity were $52,000 loss in 2019, $20,000 loss in 2020, and $80,000 gain in 2021. How much can Jackson deduct in 2019 and 2020? What is his taxable income from the activity in 2021? Keep in mind the at-risk rules as well as the passive loss rules.

_____

_____

_____

_____

_____

**LO 13-3**   48. Hunter has a $38,000 loss from an investment in a partnership in which he does not participate. His basis in the interest is $35,000.

*a.* How much of the loss is disallowed by the at-risk rules?

*b.* How much of the loss is disallowed by the passive loss rules?

_____

_____

_____

_____

_____

_____

LO 13-3    49. Reva gave her daughter a passive activity last year that had an adjusted basis of $75,000. The activity had suspended losses of $35,000 and a fair market value of $120,000. In the current year, her daughter realized income of $18,000 from the passive activity. What is the tax effect on Reva and her daughter last year and in the current year?

_____

_____

_____

_____

_____

_____

LO 13-4    50. In 2019, Jerry acquired an interest in a partnership in which he is not a material participant. The partnership was profitable until 2020. Jerry's basis in the partnership interest at the beginning of 2020 was $55,000. In 2020, his share of the partnership loss was $40,000. In 2021, his share of the partnership income was $18,000. How much can Jerry deduct in 2020 and 2021?

_____

_____

_____

_____

_____

_____

**EA**  LO 13-4    51. Benny sells an apartment building. His adjusted basis for regular income tax purposes is $450,000, and it is $475,000 for AMT purposes. He receives $700,000 from the sale.

   *a.* Calculate Benny's gain for regular income tax purposes.

   *b.* Calculate Benny's gain for AMT purposes.

   *c.* Calculate any applicable AMT adjustment.

_____

_____

_____

_____

_____

_____

**EA**  LO 13-4    52. Carson had the following itemized deductions in 2021:

| | |
|---|---:|
| State income taxes | $ 1,500 |
| Charitable contributions | 9,900 |
| Mortgage interest (personal residence) | 12,000 |
| Medical expenses ($9,875 − [7.5% × $75,000]) | 4,250 |

   *a.* What are Carson's itemized deductions for AMT purposes?

   *b.* What is the amount of the AMT adjustment?

_____

_____

_____

**EA   LO 13-4**   53. William is not married, nor does he have any dependents. He does not itemize deductions. His taxable income for 2021 was $87,000 and his regular tax was $14,907. His AMT adjustments totaled $125,000. What is William's AMT for 2021?

**EA   LO 13-4**   54. Herbie is the owner of two apartment buildings. Following is information related to the two buildings:

|  | Date Acquired | Total Cost | Cost Allocated to Land |
|---|---|---|---|
| Building A | 3/15/98 | $300,000 | $40,000 |
| Building B | 8/31/07 | 600,000 | 95,000 |

Herbie elected the maximum depreciation available for each asset. What is the effect of depreciation on AMTI for 2021?

**EA   LO 13-4**   55. Clay Company uses the completed contract method on a contract that requires 14 months to complete. The contract is for $750,000 and has estimated costs of $425,000. At the end of 2021, $210,000 of the costs had been incurred. The contract is completed on schedule; however, total costs equal $435,000. What is the amount of AMT adjustments for 2021 and 2022?

**EA   LO 13-4**   56. Arnold exercised an incentive stock option in 2018, acquiring 1,500 shares of stock at an option price of $80 per share. The FMV of the stock at the date of exercise was $110 per share. In 2020, the rights became freely transferable and were not subject to a substantial risk of forfeiture. Arnold sells the shares in 2021 for $165 per share. How do these transactions affect his AMTI in 2018, 2020, and 2021?

**EA** **LO 13-4** 57. Barbara is single and owns a home in the city, which is her primary residence. She also owns a cottage at the beach, which she treats as a vacation home. In April 2021, she borrowed $50,000 on a home equity loan and used the proceeds to pay off credit card obligations and other debt. She paid the following in 2021:

| | |
|---|---:|
| Mortgage interest (personal residence) | $15,000 |
| Mortgage interest (cottage) | 8,000 |
| Interest on the home equity loan | 5,000 |
| Interest on credit card | 2,500 |

Calculate any AMT adjustment concerning interest in 2021.

# Tax Return Problems

All applicable tax return problems are available with **Connect**©

Use your tax software to complete the following problems. If you are manually preparing the tax returns, the problem indicates the forms or schedules you will need.

**Tax Return Problem 1**

Kia Lopez (SSN 412-34-5670) resides at 101 Poker Street, Apt. 12A, Hickory, FL 34714. Her W-2 shows the following:

| | |
|---|---:|
| Wages | $56,500 |
| Federal withholding | 5,100 |
| Social security wages | 56,500 |
| Social security withholding | 3,503 |
| Medicare withholding | 819 |
| State withholding | –0– |

In 2021, Kia contributed cash of $7,000 to Apartment Rentals Limited Partnership (ARLP) in return for a 13% limited partnership interest. She is an active participant. Kia's shares of ARLP income and losses for the year per her K-1 were as follows:

| | |
|---|---:|
| Interest | $ 35 |
| Dividends (qualified) | 290 |
| Capital gains (long-term) | 700 |
| Rental loss | (8,300) |

ARLP had no liabilities. Kia does not itemize and has no other investments or passive activities.

Prepare Form 1040 for Kia Lopez for 2021. The taxpayer had qualifying health care coverage at all times during the tax year. You will need Form 1040, Schedule E (page 2), Form 6198, and Form 8582.

**Tax Return Problem 2**

Kurt and Ashley Tallo (SSNs 412-34-5670 and 412-34-5671) reside at 1901 Princess Ave., Park City, UT 84060. Kurt does not work outside the home. Ashley's W-2 shows the following:

| | |
|---|---:|
| Wages | $340,000 |
| Federal withholding | 65,000 |
| Social security wages | 137,700 |
| Social security withholding | 8,537 |
| Medicare withholding | 6,190 |
| State withholding | 23,800 |

The Tallos also have the following:

| | |
|---|---|
| Mortgage interest | $12,600 |
| Charitable contributions | 10,000 |

Kurt and Ashley have four passive activities. They received K-1s from four partnerships with the following income or loss on line 1. They are at risk in each activity, so the passive loss rules are the only obstacle.

| | |
|---|---|
| Activity 1 | $(40,000) |
| Activity 2 | (20,000) |
| Activity 3 | (10,000) |
| Activity 4 | 63,000 |

Prepare Form 1040 for the Tallos for 2021. The taxpayers had qualifying health care coverage at all times during the tax year. You will need Form 1040, Schedule A, Schedule E (page 2), Form 6251, and Form 8582. Do not compute the underpayment penalty, if any.

**Tax Return Problem 3**   Nathan is married with two children and has AGI of $405,000. He also has the following AMT adjustments and preferences:

    *a.* Itemized deductions:

| Itemized Deduction | Regular Tax | AMT Deduction | AMT Adjustment |
|---|---|---|---|
| Medical after floor | $ 5,375 | | |
| Taxes | 34,354 | | |
| Mortgage interest | 14,900 | | |
| Charitable contributions | 18,000 | | |

    *b.* Depreciation of a rental property purchased in August 2010 for $210,000.

    *c.* Depreciation on personal property:

| Asset | Date Purchased | Cost | MACRS Life/ AMT | MACRS Depreciation | AMT Depreciation | Adjustment |
|---|---|---|---|---|---|---|
| Computer 1 | 02/12/17 | $ 2,900 | | | | |
| Furniture 1 | 02/12/17 | 12,000 | | | | |

    *d.* Incentive stock option: Nathan exercises options to purchase 3,000 shares at $19 per share when the market value is $26.

Prepare Form 6251 for the calculation of AMT. The regular tax is $76,183.[36]

We have provided selected filled-in source documents that are available in *Connect.*

[36] This regular tax number may vary slightly if software is used to complete this problem. This number was calculated using the tax rate schedules published prior to software and tax table publication dates.

John Fedele/Blend Images LLC

# Chapter Fourteen

# Partnership Taxation

In this chapter, we discuss taxation of partnerships. As noted earlier in this text, the partnership itself does not pay income tax. However, a partnership must annually report each partner's share of its income or loss and other items on a Schedule K-1. This chapter presents the tax consequences of the partnership entity from formation to liquidation. We also examine Form 1065, the annual information tax return filed by partnerships.

### Learning Objectives

When you have completed this chapter, you should understand the following learning objectives (LO):

**LO 14-1**  Explain the rules dealing with the formation of a partnership.

**LO 14-2**  Be able to report partnership ordinary income or loss.

**LO 14-3**  Determine separately stated items.

**LO 14-4**  Calculate partner basis.

**LO 14-5**  Apply the rules for partnership distributions.

**LO 14-6**  Correctly report partnership liquidations and dispositions.

## INTRODUCTION

Taxpayers are increasingly using the partnership organizational form for tax purposes. The partnership form allows substantial flexibility in terms of contributions and distributions. A partnership is subject to tax only at the partner level. In contrast to a corporation that pays a corporate tax, and then the individual shareholder is subject to tax on the dividends (double taxation), a partnership's income flows through to its partners, and the partnership pays no income tax at the entity level.

A historic disadvantage of a general partnership has been a lack of limited liability; all general partners were individually liable for partnership actions and liabilities. With the increasing availability of limited liability companies (LLCs), limited liability partnerships (LLPs), and limited partnerships (LPs), all of which are taxed as partnerships for federal purposes and which also limit the liability of at least some partners, this disadvantage has been eliminated. The discussions in this chapter encompass each of these organizational forms under the generic term *partnerships*.

## FORMATION OF A PARTNERSHIP
## LO 14-1

Generally a partner recognizes no gain or loss on the formation of a partnership.[1] The most common way to form a partnership is for two or more partners (individuals or entities) to contribute cash, property, or services in exchange for a partnership interest.

[1] IRC § 721.

**EXAMPLE 14-1**

Jason and Spence form a partnership to perform lawn care and landscaping. Each contributes $25,000 and receives a 50% interest in J&S Landscaping. No gain or loss is recognized in this transaction.

## Beginning Partner Basis

The concept of *basis* is extremely important when dealing with partnerships. A partnership has two types of tax basis. One is the *outside basis,* which is the basis of the partnership interest in the hands of the partner. The second type is *inside basis,* the partner's share of the basis of the individual assets in the partnership.

When a partner contributes property to a partnership, the basis of the property carries over to the partnership (inside basis), and the partner's basis increases by the basis of the property contributed (outside basis).[2] This concept is known as *basis-in, basis-out.*

**EXAMPLE 14-2**

Bart and Alan form an LLC to construct personal residences. Each is a 50% partner in sharing income and loss items. Bart contributes the following assets to the partnership:

|  | Basis | FMV |
|---|---|---|
| Undeveloped land | $55,000 | $100,000 |
| Equipment | 35,000 | 50,000 |
| Total | $90,000 | $150,000 |

Alan contributes the following assets to the partnership:

|  | Basis | FMV |
|---|---|---|
| Cash | $ 90,000 | $ 90,000 |
| Office equipment | 30,000 | 40,000 |
| Truck | 5,000 | 20,000 |
| Total | $125,000 | $150,000 |

Bart's outside basis in his partnership interest is $90,000, the sum of the contributed assets' basis. Alan's outside basis in his partnership interest is $125,000, the sum of his contributed assets' basis.

In Example 14-2, Bart's partnership basis is only $90,000 while Alan's basis is $125,000, yet both own a 50% interest in the partnership. This happens because Bart's contributed assets had higher unrecognized gains. If Bart were to sell his partnership interest for its fair market value of $150,000, he would recognize a $60,000 gain—the same gain he deferred upon contributing the assets to the partnership.

In summary, a partner's basis in his or her partnership interest (outside basis) is the sum of any money contributed plus the adjusted basis of property contributed.

**TAX YOUR BRAIN**

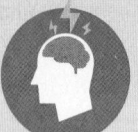

Dave and Alisa form a law partnership. Dave gave $100,000 cash to the partnership, and Alisa gave $100,000 of unrealized accounts receivable from her cash basis sole proprietorship. What is the basis of the partnership interest for each partner?

**ANSWER**

Dave has a partnership basis of $100,000. Alisa, on the other hand, has a zero basis in her partnership interest. Even though she gave something of value for a 50% interest in the partnership, her basis is zero because the accounts receivable have a zero basis due to the fact that her sole proprietorship uses the cash basis of accounting. As these receivables are collected, Alisa's partnership basis will increase.

---

[2] IRC § 722.

## Partnership Basis

The term *basis-in, basis-out* also applies to the partnership. The assets contributed to the partnership must have a tax basis for various purposes (such as depreciation or gain/loss determination). The partnership "steps into the shoes" of the partner. In other words, the basis in the hands of the partnership is the same as the basis in the hands of the partner (that is, the partner's basis carries over to the partnership).[3]

In the following example, we introduce a *tax basis balance sheet*. Thus far, in your accounting education, you probably have never been exposed to any method of accounting other than that following generally accepted accounting principles (GAAP). In practice, many small partnerships and other entities keep their books on the tax basis to eliminate the need and cost of keeping two sets of books, one for taxes and one for GAAP.

**EXAMPLE 14-3**

Assume the same facts as in Example 14-2. The basis of the contributed assets from Bart and Alan carries over to the partnership. Following is the tax basis balance sheet for the partnership:

| | | | |
|---|---|---|---|
| Cash | $ 90,000 | | |
| Equipment | 35,000 | | |
| Office equipment | 30,000 | | |
| Truck | 5,000 | Capital, Bart | $ 90,000 |
| Undeveloped land | 55,000 | Capital, Alan | 125,000 |
| Total assets | $215,000 | Total capital | $215,000 |

For depreciable assets, the partnership assumes the depreciation schedule of the partner at the point of contribution. For example, if a partner is in the third year of depreciation for an asset and contributes that asset to the partnership, the partnership starts depreciating it in the third year. If a personal-use asset is contributed to a partnership for business use, the partnership's basis in the asset is the lower of the partner's cost or the FMV of the asset on the date contributed.

**EXAMPLE 14-4**

Jose contributed a piece of equipment to JWS Partnership on March 1, 2021. The cost of the equipment was $20,000, and year 2021 was the third year of depreciation under seven-year MACRS. The depreciation for the equipment for 2021 would be calculated as follows:

| **Jose's Schedule C** | | **Depreciation Expense** |
|---|---|---|
| 2019 | | $2,858 |
| 2020 | | 4,898 |
| 2021 | $(20,000 \times 0.1749 \times 2/12)$ | 583 |

| **JWS Partnership** | | **Depreciation Expense** |
|---|---|---|
| 2021 | $(20,000 \times 0.1749 \times 10/12)$ | $2,915 |

Jose deducts two months of depreciation ($583) in 2021 on his Schedule C, and JWS Partnership deducts the other 10 months of 2021 depreciation ($2,915) on its Form 1065.

**EXAMPLE 14-5**

Jose also contributed a truck to JWS Partnership that he had used personally for four years. The truck cost $28,000 four years ago; its current fair market value is $8,300. The basis to the partnership is $8,300, and depreciation would start for a five-year MACRS asset.

---

[3] IRC § 723.

## Holding Periods

Chapter 7 discussed the importance of holding periods for § 1231 assets and capital assets. A partnership interest is a capital asset to the partner. Likewise, partners are likely to contribute capital assets, § 1231 assets, and ordinary assets (such as inventory) when forming partnerships. As a general rule, the holding period of the partnership interest includes the partner's holding period for the § 1231 assets and capital assets contributed.[4] If ordinary assets are contributed (such as inventory or accounts receivable), the holding period of the partnership interest begins on the date of the transfer.[5]

The same holding period concept holds true for the partnership. The partnership holding period for the individual assets includes the contributing partner's holding period for § 1231 and capital assets.

---

**EXAMPLE 14-6**

Casey contributed the following business assets to CWS Partnership on June 5, 2021:

|  | Basis | FMV | Date Purchased by Casey |
|---|---|---|---|
| Building | $175,000 | $300,000 | 07/01/12 |
| Inventory | 50,000 | 100,000 | 05/08/16 |

The building is a § 1231 asset and has a $175,000 basis to CWS. The building has a long-term holding period to the partnership. Because the inventory is an ordinary asset, its basis is $50,000 with a short-term holding period.[6]

---

## Contribution of Services

Nonrecognition of gain does not apply when a partner receives a partnership interest in exchange for services. When forming a partnership, one or more partners frequently invest capital and other partners perform services in exchange for a partnership interest. A partner providing services recognizes income to the extent of the fair market value of their partnership interest.[7]

---

**EXAMPLE 14-7**

Russell, Kevin, and David form a partnership. Russell and Kevin are wealthy investors; David is an expert construction contractor. Russell contributes a 20-acre parcel of land, and Kevin contributes cash. David agrees to perform all of the work to develop the land into a high-end subdivision.

|  | Basis | FMV | Partnership Percentage |
|---|---|---|---|
| Russell's land | $200,000 | $300,000 | 30% |
| Kevin's cash | 300,000 | 300,000 | 30 |
| David's services | –0– | –0– | 40 |

David must recognize $240,000 of income in the tax year of formation ($600,000 FMV of assets × 40% partnership interest). In essence, Russell and Kevin are paying David for his future services.

---

[4] IRC § 1223.

[5] If a mixture of capital assets and ordinary assets is contributed to a partnership, the holding period of the partnership interest should be fragmented into interests with different holding periods. This is an issue only when the partnership interest is disposed of within a year of contribution. See *Aliber v. Commissioner* for more information [52 TCM 1316 (1987)].

[6] The inventory maintains its inventory characteristic (ordinary income property) for five years even if the partnership does not hold it out for sale to customers; see IRC § 724(b).

[7] Reg. § 1.721-1(b).

Example 14-7 is a drastic example that shows how an unknowing service partner may be burdened with a high unexpected tax liability without cash available to pay the bill.

## Contributed Property with Liabilities

Complexities arise when a partnership assumes a partner's liability. A partner who is released from a liability is treated as receiving money from the partnership, which reduces their partnership basis. If other partners assume a portion of the liability, they are treated as making a money contribution that increases their partnership basis.[8]

**EXAMPLE 14-8**

Angie contributes an office building to a newly formed partnership for a 25% interest. The building has a $300,000 FMV and a $160,000 basis and is subject to a $100,000 mortgage. The partnership assumes the mortgage. Each of the other three partners contributes $200,000 cash. The partners calculate their basis as follows:

|  | Angie | Maria | Bess | Kiley |
|---|---|---|---|---|
| Beginning basis | $160,000 | $200,000 | $200,000 | $200,000 |
| Plus: Share of liability ($100,000 × 25%) | 25,000 | 25,000 | 25,000 | 25,000 |
| Less: Release of liability | (100,000) | –0– | –0– | –0– |
| Partner basis | $ 85,000 | $225,000 | $225,000 | $225,000 |

An important point to note is that a partner's basis can *never* go below zero. If the release of liability causes the basis to become negative, the contributing partner must recognize a gain.[9]

**EXAMPLE 14-9**

Assume the same facts as in Example 14-8 except that the basis of the office building is $45,000. Angie's basis would change as follows:

| | |
|---|---|
| Beginning basis | $ 45,000 |
| Plus: Share of liability | 25,000 |
| Less: Liability release | (100,000) |
| Liability in excess of basis | (30,000) |
| Gain recognized by Angie | 30,000 |
| Partnership basis | $  –0– |

The gain recognized causes the negative basis to return to zero.

In summary, the only time a partner recognizes a gain on partnership formation is upon contributing services or when the partnership assumes a partner's liability in excess of basis.

**CONCEPT CHECK 14-1— LO 14-1**

1. Generally, a partner does not recognize a gain on the formation of a partnership. True or false?
2. Typically, the basis of the assets contributed to a partnership is the same in the hands of the partnership as it was in the hands of the contributing partner. True or false?
3. If two taxpayers form a partnership and each has a 50% interest in it, each partner's outside basis must be equal. True or false?
4. A partner does not have to recognize a gain on the receipt of a partnership interest in exchange for services. True or false?
5. A partner who assumes an increased portion of the partnership debt is treated as making a cash contribution, and their basis in the partnership increases. True or false?

[8] IRC § 752. The term *money contribution* is used in place of *cash contribution* because the partner is not actually contributing cash but is assuming a liability. However, the effect on basis is the same.

[9] IRC § 731.

# PARTNERSHIP ORDINARY INCOME OR LOSS
## LO 14-2

Partnership income consists of two components: ordinary income or loss and separately stated items. Both flow through to the individual partners. *Ordinary income or loss* consists of all ordinary income and expense items; *separately stated items* are those that could affect individual partners differently at the partner level.

### Ordinary Income or Loss

See Exhibit 14-1 for the five main pages of Form 1065, the annual informational tax return that every partnership must file. Each partnership calculates ordinary income or loss and reports the amount on page 1 of Form 1065. The tax rules used to calculate ordinary income are generally similar to those used by a Schedule C business. All ordinary income items are accumulated and reduced by ordinary and necessary expenses to derive net ordinary income or loss, shown on line 22 of Form 1065. Several partnership expense items require some additional discussion: guaranteed payments to partners, depreciation, and health insurance premiums.

### *Guaranteed Payments*

Partners of a partnership are not employees of the partnership; thus, they cannot receive a salary. Partners are owners of the partnership and are considered self-employed individuals (or entities) that have merged together to run a business. *Guaranteed payments* are payments made to partners for services rendered. To qualify as a guaranteed payment, the payment must be calculated without regard to partnership income.[10]

---

**EXAMPLE 14-10**

Junius is a 20% partner in the DJ Real Estate partnership. He does substantial work for the partnership and receives $1,000 per month for his services. The $1,000 a month is a guaranteed payment and, as such, the partnership deducts it from ordinary income on line 10. He would include the $12,000 guaranteed payment on page 2 of his Form 1040, Schedule E.

---

**EXAMPLE 14-11**

Donna is an 80% partner in the DJ Real Estate partnership. She also works for the partnership and receives a monthly payment of 50% of the net income for the month. Because Donna's payment is calculated *with regard to partnership income,* it is *not* considered a guaranteed payment, and the partnership cannot take a deduction for the payment.

---

Guaranteed payments are the only items that are reported both as a deduction for ordinary income and as a separately stated item (discussed in the next section).

---

**TAX YOUR BRAIN**

Refer to Examples 14-10 and 14-11. How can Junius and Donna, partners in the same partnership, be treated differently? Donna is an 80% partner in the business but receives only 50% of the net income.

**ANSWER**

This is one of the benefits of the partnership form. Due to the flexibility of a partnership agreement, the partners can receive the returns of the business in any way they agree upon. In Examples 14-10 and 14-11, Junius may get a flat fee because he works a fixed number of hours in the office, whereas Donna is the sales agent and makes her money based on the sales she makes. How Donna and Junius share the net income at the end of the year is based on their agreement, but in this example it is likely to be 80% to Donna and 20% to Junius. He, however, is guaranteed $12,000 per year no matter the partnership income or loss.

---

[10] IRC § 707(c).

**EXHIBIT 14-1**

# Form 1065

## U.S. Return of Partnership Income

OMB No. 1545-0123

Department of the Treasury
Internal Revenue Service

For calendar year 2021, or tax year beginning _____ , 2021, ending _____ , 20 ____

▶ Go to *www.irs.gov/Form1065* for instructions and the latest information.

**2021**

| | |
|---|---|
| A Principal business activity | Name of partnership |
| B Principal product or service | Number, street, and room or suite no. If a P.O. box, see instructions. |
| C Business code number | City or town, state or province, country, and ZIP or foreign postal code |

Type or Print

D Employer identification number

E Date business started

F Total assets (see instructions) $

G Check applicable boxes: **(1)** ☐ Initial return **(2)** ☐ Final return **(3)** ☐ Name change **(4)** ☐ Address change **(5)** ☐ Amended return

H Check accounting method: **(1)** ☐ Cash **(2)** ☐ Accrual **(3)** ☐ Other (specify) ▶ _____

I Number of Schedules K-1. Attach one for each person who was a partner at any time during the tax year ▶

J Check if Schedules C and M-3 are attached . . . . . . . . . . . . . . . . ▶ ☐

K Check if partnership: **(1)** ☐ Aggregated activities for section 465 at-risk purposes **(2)** ☐ Grouped activities for section 469 passive activity purposes

**Caution:** Include **only** trade or business income and expenses on lines 1a through 22 below. See instructions for more information.

**Income**

| | | | |
|---|---|---|---|
| 1a | Gross receipts or sales | 1a | |
| b | Returns and allowances | 1b | |
| c | Balance. Subtract line 1b from line 1a | | 1c |
| 2 | Cost of goods sold (attach Form 1125-A) | | 2 |
| 3 | Gross profit. Subtract line 2 from line 1c | | 3 |
| 4 | Ordinary income (loss) from other partnerships, estates, and trusts (attach statement) | | 4 |
| 5 | Net farm profit (loss) (attach Schedule F (Form 1040)) | | 5 |
| 6 | Net gain (loss) from Form 4797, Part II, line 17 (attach Form 4797) | | 6 |
| 7 | Other income (loss) (attach statement) | | 7 |
| 8 | **Total income (loss).** Combine lines 3 through 7 | | 8 |

**Deductions** (see instructions for limitations)

| | | | |
|---|---|---|---|
| 9 | Salaries and wages (other than to partners) (less employment credits) | | 9 |
| 10 | Guaranteed payments to partners | | 10 |
| 11 | Repairs and maintenance | | 11 |
| 12 | Bad debts | | 12 |
| 13 | Rent | | 13 |
| 14 | Taxes and licenses | | 14 |
| 15 | Interest (see instructions) | | 15 |
| 16a | Depreciation (if required, attach Form 4562) | 16a | |
| b | Less depreciation reported on Form 1125-A and elsewhere on return | 16b | 16c |
| 17 | Depletion **(Do not deduct oil and gas depletion.)** | | 17 |
| 18 | Retirement plans, etc. | | 18 |
| 19 | Employee benefit programs | | 19 |
| 20 | Other deductions (attach statement) | | 20 |
| 21 | **Total deductions.** Add the amounts shown in the far right column for lines 9 through 20 | | 21 |
| 22 | **Ordinary business income (loss).** Subtract line 21 from line 8 | | 22 |

**Tax and Payment**

| | | |
|---|---|---|
| 23 | Interest due under the look-back method—completed long-term contracts (attach Form 8697) | 23 |
| 24 | Interest due under the look-back method—income forecast method (attach Form 8866) | 24 |
| 25 | BBA AAR imputed underpayment (see instructions) | 25 |
| 26 | Other taxes (see instructions) | 26 |
| 27 | **Total balance due.** Add lines 23 through 26 | 27 |
| 28 | Payment (see instructions) | 28 |
| 29 | **Amount owed.** If line 28 is smaller than line 27, enter amount owed | 29 |
| 30 | **Overpayment.** If line 28 is larger than line 27, enter overpayment | 30 |

**Sign Here**

Under penalties of perjury, I declare that I have examined this return, including accompanying schedules and statements, and to the best of my knowledge and belief, it is true, correct, and complete. Declaration of preparer (other than partner or limited liability company member) is based on all information of which preparer has any knowledge.

▶ _____ Signature of partner or limited liability company member   ▶ Date _____

May the IRS discuss this return with the preparer shown below? See instructions. ☐ Yes ☐ No

**Paid Preparer Use Only**

| Print/Type preparer's name | Preparer's signature | Date | Check ☐ if self-employed | PTIN |
|---|---|---|---|---|

Firm's name ▶

Firm's address ▶

Firm's EIN ▶

Phone no.

For Paperwork Reduction Act Notice, see separate instructions.   Cat. No. 11390Z   Form **1065** (2021)

*(continued)*

**EXHIBIT 14-1**　*(continued)*

Form 1065 (2021)　　　　　　　　　　　　　　　　　　　　　　　　　Page **2**

| Schedule B | Other Information |

| | | Yes | No |
|---|---|---|---|

**1** What type of entity is filing this return? Check the applicable box:

**a** ☐ Domestic general partnership　　**b** ☐ Domestic limited partnership

**c** ☐ Domestic limited liability company　**d** ☐ Domestic limited liability partnership

**e** ☐ Foreign partnership　　　　　　**f** ☐ Other ▶

**2** At the end of the tax year:

**a** Did any foreign or domestic corporation, partnership (including any entity treated as a partnership), trust, or tax-exempt organization, or any foreign government own, directly or indirectly, an interest of 50% or more in the profit, loss, or capital of the partnership? For rules of constructive ownership, see instructions. If "Yes," attach Schedule B-1, Information on Partners Owning 50% or More of the Partnership

**b** Did any individual or estate own, directly or indirectly, an interest of 50% or more in the profit, loss, or capital of the partnership? For rules of constructive ownership, see instructions. If "Yes," attach Schedule B-1, Information on Partners Owning 50% or More of the Partnership

**3** At the end of the tax year, did the partnership:

**a** Own directly 20% or more, or own, directly or indirectly, 50% or more of the total voting power of all classes of stock entitled to vote of any foreign or domestic corporation? For rules of constructive ownership, see instructions. If "Yes," complete (i) through (iv) below

| (i) Name of Corporation | (ii) Employer Identification Number (if any) | (iii) Country of Incorporation | (iv) Percentage Owned in Voting Stock |
|---|---|---|---|
| | | | |
| | | | |
| | | | |

**b** Own directly an interest of 20% or more, or own, directly or indirectly, an interest of 50% or more in the profit, loss, or capital in any foreign or domestic partnership (including an entity treated as a partnership) or in the beneficial interest of a trust? For rules of constructive ownership, see instructions. If "Yes," complete (i) through (v) below

| (i) Name of Entity | (ii) Employer Identification Number (if any) | (iii) Type of Entity | (iv) Country of Organization | (v) Maximum Percentage Owned in Profit, Loss, or Capital |
|---|---|---|---|---|
| | | | | |
| | | | | |
| | | | | |
| | | | | |

**4** Does the partnership satisfy **all four** of the following conditions?

**a** The partnership's total receipts for the tax year were less than $250,000.

**b** The partnership's total assets at the end of the tax year were less than $1 million.

**c** Schedules K-1 are filed with the return and furnished to the partners on or before the due date (including extensions) for the partnership return.

**d** The partnership is not filing and is not required to file Schedule M-3

If "Yes," the partnership is not required to complete Schedules L, M-1, and M-2; item F on page 1 of Form 1065; or item L on Schedule K-1.

**5** Is this partnership a publicly traded partnership, as defined in section 469(k)(2)?

**6** During the tax year, did the partnership have any debt that was canceled, was forgiven, or had the terms modified so as to reduce the principal amount of the debt?

**7** Has this partnership filed, or is it required to file, Form 8918, Material Advisor Disclosure Statement, to provide information on any reportable transaction?

**8** At any time during calendar year 2021, did the partnership have an interest in or a signature or other authority over a financial account in a foreign country (such as a bank account, securities account, or other financial account)? See instructions for exceptions and filing requirements for FinCEN Form 114, Report of Foreign Bank and Financial Accounts (FBAR). If "Yes," enter the name of the foreign country ▶

**9** At any time during the tax year, did the partnership receive a distribution from, or was it the grantor of, or transferor to, a foreign trust? If "Yes," the partnership may have to file Form 3520, Annual Return To Report Transactions With Foreign Trusts and Receipt of Certain Foreign Gifts. See instructions

**10a** Is the partnership making, or had it previously made (and not revoked), a section 754 election?
See instructions for details regarding a section 754 election.

**b** Did the partnership make for this tax year an optional basis adjustment under section 743(b) or 734(b)? If "Yes," attach a statement showing the computation and allocation of the basis adjustment. See instructions

Form **1065** (2021)

**EXHIBIT 14-1** *(continued)*

Form 1065 (2021) Page **3**

**Schedule B** Other Information *(continued)*

| | | Yes | No |
|---|---|---|---|
| c | Is the partnership required to adjust the basis of partnership assets under section 743(b) or 734(b) because of a substantial built-in loss (as defined under section 743(d)) or substantial basis reduction (as defined under section 734(d))? If "Yes," attach a statement showing the computation and allocation of the basis adjustment. See instructions | | |
| 11 | Check this box if, during the current or prior tax year, the partnership distributed any property received in a like-kind exchange or contributed such property to another entity (other than disregarded entities wholly owned by the partnership throughout the tax year) ▶ ☐ | | |
| 12 | At any time during the tax year, did the partnership distribute to any partner a tenancy-in-common or other undivided interest in partnership property? | | |
| 13 | If the partnership is required to file Form 8858, Information Return of U.S. Persons With Respect To Foreign Disregarded Entities (FDEs) and Foreign Branches (FBs), enter the number of Forms 8858 attached. See instructions ▶ | | |
| 14 | Does the partnership have any foreign partners? If "Yes," enter the number of Forms 8805, Foreign Partner's Information Statement of Section 1446 Withholding Tax, filed for this partnership ▶ | | |
| 15 | Enter the number of Forms 8865, Return of U.S. Persons With Respect to Certain Foreign Partnerships, attached to this return ▶ | | |
| 16a | Did you make any payments in 2021 that would require you to file Form(s) 1099? See instructions | | |
| b | If "Yes," did you or will you file required Form(s) 1099? | | |
| 17 | Enter the number of Forms 5471, Information Return of U.S. Persons With Respect To Certain Foreign Corporations, attached to this return ▶ | | |
| 18 | Enter the number of partners that are foreign governments under section 892 ▶ | | |
| 19 | During the partnership's tax year, did the partnership make any payments that would require it to file Forms 1042 and 1042-S under chapter 3 (sections 1441 through 1464) or chapter 4 (sections 1471 through 1474)? | | |
| 20 | Was the partnership a specified domestic entity required to file Form 8938 for the tax year? See the Instructions for Form 8938 | | |
| 21 | Is the partnership a section 721(c) partnership, as defined in Regulations section 1.721(c)-1(b)(14)? | | |
| 22 | During the tax year, did the partnership pay or accrue any interest or royalty for which one or more partners are not allowed a deduction under section 267A? See instructions | | |
| | If "Yes," enter the total amount of the disallowed deductions ▶ $ | | |
| 23 | Did the partnership have an election under section 163(j) for any real property trade or business or any farming business in effect during the tax year? See instructions | | |
| 24 | Does the partnership satisfy one or more of the following? See instructions | | |
| a | The partnership owns a pass-through entity with current, or prior year carryover, excess business interest expense. | | |
| b | The partnership's aggregate average annual gross receipts (determined under section 448(c)) for the 3 tax years preceding the current tax year are more than $26 million and the partnership has business interest. | | |
| c | The partnership is a tax shelter (see instructions) and the partnership has business interest expense. If "Yes" to any, complete and attach Form 8990. | | |
| 25 | Is the partnership attaching Form 8996 to certify as a Qualified Opportunity Fund? If "Yes," enter the amount from Form 8996, line 15 ▶ $ | | |
| 26 | Enter the number of foreign partners subject to section 864(c)(8) as a result of transferring all or a portion of an interest in the partnership or of receiving a distribution from the partnership ▶ Complete Schedule K-3 (Form 1065), Part XIII, for each foreign partner subject to section 864(c)(8) on a transfer or distribution. | | |
| 27 | At any time during the tax year, were there any transfers between the partnership and its partners subject to the disclosure requirements of Regulations section 1.707-8? | | |
| 28 | Since December 22, 2017, did a foreign corporation directly or indirectly acquire substantially all of the properties constituting a trade or business of your partnership, and was the ownership percentage (by vote or value) for purposes of section 7874 greater than 50% (for example, the partners held more than 50% of the stock of the foreign corporation)? If "Yes," list the ownership percentage by vote and by value. See instructions. Percentage: By Vote By Value | | |
| 29 | Is the partnership electing out of the centralized partnership audit regime under section 6221(b)? See instructions. If "Yes," the partnership must complete Schedule B-2 (Form 1065). Enter the total from Schedule B-2, Part III, line 3 ▶ If "No," complete Designation of Partnership Representative below. | | |

**Designation of Partnership Representative** (see instructions)
Enter below the information for the partnership representative (PR) for the tax year covered by this return.

Name of PR ▶

| U.S. address of PR | U.S. phone number of PR |
|---|---|

If the PR is an entity, name of the designated individual for the PR ▶

| U.S. address of designated individual | U.S. phone number of designated individual |
|---|---|

Form **1065** (2021)

*(continued)*

**EXHIBIT 14-1** *(continued)*

| Form 1065 (2021) | | | | Page **4** |
|---|---|---|---|---|

| Schedule K | | Partners' Distributive Share Items | | Total amount |
|---|---|---|---|---|
| **Income (Loss)** | 1 | Ordinary business income (loss) (page 1, line 22) . . . . . . . . . . . . . | **1** | |
| | 2 | Net rental real estate income (loss) (attach Form 8825) . . . . . . . . . . | **2** | |
| | 3a | Other gross rental income (loss) . . . . . . . . . . . . | **3a** | |
| | b | Expenses from other rental activities (attach statement) . . . . . | **3b** | |
| | c | Other net rental income (loss). Subtract line 3b from line 3a . . . . | **3c** | |
| | 4 | Guaranteed payments: **a** Services **4a**    **b** Capital **4b** | | |
| | | **c** Total. Add lines 4a and 4b . . . . . . . . . . . . . . . . . . | **4c** | |
| | 5 | Interest income . . . . . . . . . . . . . . . . . . . . . . . | **5** | |
| | 6 | Dividends and dividend equivalents: **a** Ordinary dividends | **6a** | |
| | | **b** Qualified dividends **6b**    **c** Dividend equivalents **6c** | | |
| | 7 | Royalties . . . . . . . . . . . . . . . . . . . . . . . . . | **7** | |
| | 8 | Net short-term capital gain (loss) (attach Schedule D (Form 1065)) . . . . | **8** | |
| | 9a | Net long-term capital gain (loss) (attach Schedule D (Form 1065)) . . . . | **9a** | |
| | b | Collectibles (28%) gain (loss) **9b** | | |
| | c | Unrecaptured section 1250 gain (attach statement) **9c** | | |
| | 10 | Net section 1231 gain (loss) (attach Form 4797) . . . . . . . . . . . | **10** | |
| | 11 | Other income (loss) (see instructions)    Type ▶ | **11** | |
| **Deductions** | 12 | Section 179 deduction (attach Form 4562) . . . . . . . . . . . . | **12** | |
| | 13a | Contributions . . . . . . . . . . . . . . . . . . . . . . | **13a** | |
| | b | Investment interest expense . . . . . . . . . . . . . . . . | **13b** | |
| | c | Section 59(e)(2) expenditures: **(1)** Type ▶ _____ **(2)** Amount ▶ | **13c(2)** | |
| | d | Other deductions (see instructions)    Type ▶ | **13d** | |
| **Self-Employ-ment** | 14a | Net earnings (loss) from self-employment . . . . . . . . . . . | **14a** | |
| | b | Gross farming or fishing income . . . . . . . . . . . . . . | **14b** | |
| | c | Gross nonfarm income . . . . . . . . . . . . . . . . . . | **14c** | |
| **Credits** | 15a | Low-income housing credit (section 42(j)(5)) . . . . . . . . . . | **15a** | |
| | b | Low-income housing credit (other) . . . . . . . . . . . . . | **15b** | |
| | c | Qualified rehabilitation expenditures (rental real estate) (attach Form 3468, if applicable) . . | **15c** | |
| | d | Other rental real estate credits (see instructions)    Type ▶ _____ | **15d** | |
| | e | Other rental credits (see instructions)    Type ▶ _____ | **15e** | |
| | f | Other credits (see instructions)    Type ▶ | **15f** | |
| **International Transactions** | 16 | Attach Schedule K-2 (Form 1065), Partners' Distributive Share Items-International, and check this box to indicate that you are reporting items of international tax relevance . . . . . ▶ ☐ | | |
| **Alternative Minimum Tax (AMT) Items** | 17a | Post-1986 depreciation adjustment . . . . . . . . . . . . . | **17a** | |
| | b | Adjusted gain or loss . . . . . . . . . . . . . . . . . . | **17b** | |
| | c | Depletion (other than oil and gas) . . . . . . . . . . . . . | **17c** | |
| | d | Oil, gas, and geothermal properties—gross income . . . . . . . | **17d** | |
| | e | Oil, gas, and geothermal properties—deductions . . . . . . . | **17e** | |
| | f | Other AMT items (attach statement) . . . . . . . . . . . . | **17f** | |
| **Other Information** | 18a | Tax-exempt interest income . . . . . . . . . . . . . . . . | **18a** | |
| | b | Other tax-exempt income . . . . . . . . . . . . . . . . | **18b** | |
| | c | Nondeductible expenses . . . . . . . . . . . . . . . . . | **18c** | |
| | 19a | Distributions of cash and marketable securities . . . . . . . . | **19a** | |
| | b | Distributions of other property . . . . . . . . . . . . . . | **19b** | |
| | 20a | Investment income . . . . . . . . . . . . . . . . . . . | **20a** | |
| | b | Investment expenses . . . . . . . . . . . . . . . . . . | **20b** | |
| | c | Other items and amounts (attach statement) | | |
| | 21 | Total foreign taxes paid or accrued . . . . . . . . . . . . . | **21** | |

Form **1065** (2021)

**EXHIBIT 14-1**  *(concluded)*

Form 1065 (2021)                                                                                                           Page **5**

## Analysis of Net Income (Loss)

| 1 | Net income (loss). Combine Schedule K, lines 1 through 11. From the result, subtract the sum of Schedule K, lines 12 through 13d, and 21 . . . . . . . . . . . . . . . . . . . . | | **1** | |

| 2 | Analysis by partner type: | (i) Corporate | (ii) Individual (active) | (iii) Individual (passive) | (iv) Partnership | (v) Exempt Organization | (vi) Nominee/Other |
|---|---|---|---|---|---|---|---|
| a | General partners | | | | | | |
| b | Limited partners | | | | | | |

## Schedule L  Balance Sheets per Books

| | | Beginning of tax year | | End of tax year | |
|---|---|---|---|---|---|
| | **Assets** | (a) | (b) | (c) | (d) |
| 1 | Cash . . . . . . . . . . . | | | | |
| 2a | Trade notes and accounts receivable . . . . . | | | | |
| b | Less allowance for bad debts . . . . . . . | | | | |
| 3 | Inventories . . . . . . . . . . . | | | | |
| 4 | U.S. government obligations . . . . . . . | | | | |
| 5 | Tax-exempt securities . . . . . . . . | | | | |
| 6 | Other current assets (attach statement) . . . . | | | | |
| 7a | Loans to partners (or persons related to partners) | | | | |
| b | Mortgage and real estate loans . . . . . . | | | | |
| 8 | Other investments (attach statement) . . . . | | | | |
| 9a | Buildings and other depreciable assets . . . . | | | | |
| b | Less accumulated depreciation . . . . . . | | | | |
| 10a | Depletable assets . . . . . . . . . | | | | |
| b | Less accumulated depletion . . . . . . . | | | | |
| 11 | Land (net of any amortization) . . . . . . . | | | | |
| 12a | Intangible assets (amortizable only) . . . . . | | | | |
| b | Less accumulated amortization . . . . . . | | | | |
| 13 | Other assets (attach statement) . . . . . . | | | | |
| 14 | Total assets . . . . . . . . . . | | | | |
| | **Liabilities and Capital** | | | | |
| 15 | Accounts payable . . . . . . . . . | | | | |
| 16 | Mortgages, notes, bonds payable in less than 1 year | | | | |
| 17 | Other current liabilities (attach statement) . . . . | | | | |
| 18 | All nonrecourse loans . . . . . . . . | | | | |
| 19a | Loans from partners (or persons related to partners) . | | | | |
| b | Mortgages, notes, bonds payable in 1 year or more . | | | | |
| 20 | Other liabilities (attach statement) . . . . . . | | | | |
| 21 | Partners' capital accounts . . . . . . . | | | | |
| 22 | Total liabilities and capital . . . . . . . | | | | |

## Schedule M-1  Reconciliation of Income (Loss) per Books With Income (Loss) per Return
**Note:** The partnership may be required to file Schedule M-3. See instructions.

| 1 | Net income (loss) per books . . . . | | 6 | Income recorded on books this year not included on Schedule K, lines 1 through 11 (itemize): | |
|---|---|---|---|---|---|
| 2 | Income included on Schedule K, lines 1, 2, 3c, 5, 6a, 7, 8, 9a, 10, and 11, not recorded on books this year (itemize): _____ | | a | Tax-exempt interest $ _____ | |
| 3 | Guaranteed payments (other than health insurance) . . . . . . . . . | | 7 | Deductions included on Schedule K, lines 1 through 13d, and 21, not charged against book income this year (itemize): | |
| 4 | Expenses recorded on books this year not included on Schedule K, lines 1 through 13d, and 21 (itemize): | | a | Depreciation $ _____ | |
| a | Depreciation $ _____ | | 8 | Add lines 6 and 7 . . . . . . . . | |
| b | Travel and entertainment $ _____ | | 9 | Income (loss) (Analysis of Net Income (Loss), line 1). Subtract line 8 from line 5 | |
| 5 | Add lines 1 through 4 . . . . . . | | | | |

## Schedule M-2  Analysis of Partners' Capital Accounts

| 1 | Balance at beginning of year . . . | | 6 | Distributions: a Cash . . . . . . | |
|---|---|---|---|---|---|
| 2 | Capital contributed: a Cash . . . . | | | b Property . . . . . | |
| | b Property . . | | 7 | Other decreases (itemize): _____ | |
| 3 | Net income (loss) (see instructions) . | | | | |
| 4 | Other increases (itemize): _____ | | 8 | Add lines 6 and 7 . . . . . . . . | |
| 5 | Add lines 1 through 4 . . . . . . | | 9 | Balance at end of year. Subtract line 8 from line 5 | |

Form **1065** (2021)

### Depreciation

A partnership calculates depreciation following the same rules as a sole proprietorship using Schedule C. Form 4562 must be completed and attached. One major exception concerns the § 179 expense deduction. A partnership can use the § 179 expense deduction, but the deduction cannot reduce the partnership ordinary income; § 179 expense must be reported separately to each partner.

---

**TAX YOUR BRAIN**

Why must § 179 expense be reported separately to each partner?

**ANSWER**

If you recall from Chapter 6, each individual is allowed to deduct a maximum of $1,050,000 of § 179 expense in tax year 2021. If the partnership deducts the § 179 expense and does not separately state it to partners, an individual could set up numerous partnerships for their businesses and, effectively, have an unlimited § 179 expense (up to $1,050,000 for each partnership).

---

### Partner Health Premiums

Most employees can exclude from income the cost of employer-provided health and accident insurance. For employees of a partnership, this is certainly the case. However, because partners are not employees, partners cannot exclude from income the cost of their health insurance premiums paid by the partnership. The partnership treats the premiums as guaranteed payments to the partner, and the partner can deduct the premiums as a *for* AGI deduction on Form 1040.

### Business Interest Expense Limitation

The 2017 Tax Act added a limitation for business interest expense. For businesses with average annual gross receipts (in the prior three years) over $26 million, business interest expense is only allowed to the extent it does not exceed 50% of Adjusted Taxable Income (ATI). In general, ATI is taxable income before interest, depreciation, amortization, and depletion. The applicability to partnerships is limited (due to size), so for more information see IRC § 163(j). We discuss this limitation in more detail in Chapter 15.

---

**CONCEPT CHECK 14-2—**

**LO 14-2**

1. A partnership can deduct which of the following in determining partnership ordinary income or loss?
   a. All ordinary and necessary expenses.
   b. Guaranteed payments.
   c. Depreciation.
   d. All of the above.

2. What tax form is a partnership required to file each year?
   a. Form 1120.
   b. Form 1040.
   c. Form 1065.
   d. Form 1120S.

3. A payment made to a partner that is calculated without regard to partnership income is a
   a. Partner salary.
   b. Partner withdrawal.
   c. Loan to a partner.
   d. Guaranteed payment.

**TABLE 14-1**
**Common Partnership Ordinary and Separately Stated Items**

| Ordinary Items (page 1, Form 1065) | Separately Stated Items (Schedule K, page 4, Form 1065) |
|---|---|
| Gross profit | Net income from rental real estate |
| Ordinary income from Form 4797 | Net income from other rentals |
| Salary and wages (nonpartners) | Interest income |
| Guaranteed payments (partners) | Guaranteed payments (partners) |
| Repairs and maintenance | Dividends |
| Bad debts | Royalty income |
| Rent | Capital gains and losses |
| Taxes and licenses | § 1231 gains and losses |
| Interest | Charitable contributions |
| Depreciation | § 179 expense |
| Retirement plans | Tax credits |
| Employee benefits | AMT adjustments and preferences |
| Other ordinary and necessary expenses | |

# SEPARATELY STATED ITEMS

**LO 14-3**

As noted earlier, a partnership must allocate income and expense items between ordinary items and separately stated items. The general rule regarding income and expense items of a partnership and their classification follows:

> All income and expense items of a partnership that may be treated differently at the partner level must be separately stated.

Table 14-1 lists the most common ordinary items and separately stated items.

Form 1065, Schedule K (page 4), lists the partners' shares of income, credits, and deductions. Schedule K is the total for all partners, whereas Schedule K-1 (discussed later) provides the individual partner's share of each item.

**TAX YOUR BRAIN**

Why are items such as rental loss or capital gains separately stated?

**ANSWER**

Rental losses are passive activities. One partner may have rental income or other passive income to offset the losses, whereas another partner may not. Thus, the rental loss from the partnership could be treated differently from partner to partner. Likewise, an individual partner receives preferential tax treatment for capital gains. A corporate partner, in the same partnership, receives no preferential treatment and can deduct capital losses only to the extent of capital gains. Again, the different tax treatment at the partner level mandates that these items be separately reported to the partners.

## Allocations to Partners (Schedule K-1)

Every year, each partner in a partnership must receive a Schedule K-1 (shown in Exhibit 14-2), which reports the partner's share of ordinary income or loss and each separately stated item. Section J of the K-1 shows the partner's percentage share of profit, loss, and ownership. Notice that the line items on the K-1 correspond directly to the line items on Schedule K of Form 1065. The summation (line 1, for example) of all the K-1s, whether for 2 or 5,000 partners, should equal the total on Schedule K. In the majority of cases, the allocation to the partner is the year-end percentage multiplied by the total amount for each item on Schedule K (page 4 of Form 1065).[11] This calculation differs if changes in ownership occurred during the year or special allocations are made between the partners.

[11] This is not always the case. One of the benefits of the partnership form is flexibility in the allocations. Allocations are based on the partnership agreement, and as long as the agreement has substantial economic effect, the allocations can vary. *Substantial economic effect* basically means that tax minimization is not the only reason for the allocation. Complete coverage of substantial economic effect is beyond the scope of this text.

**EXHIBIT 14-2**

| | |
|---|---|
| **651121** | |

<table>
<tr><td colspan="2">☐ Final K-1        ☐ Amended K-1</td><td>OMB No. 1545-0123</td></tr>
</table>

**Schedule K-1**
**(Form 1065)**
20**21**

Department of the Treasury
Internal Revenue Service

For calendar year 2021, or tax year

beginning  /  / 2021  ending  /  /

**Partner's Share of Income, Deductions, Credits, etc.**  ▶ See back of form and separate instructions.

**Part I    Information About the Partnership**

A    Partnership's employer identification number
22-7892345

B    Partnership's name, address, city, state, and ZIP code

W&J Woodworking
2155 Playground Ave.
Kinston, NC  23849

C    IRS center where partnership filed return ▶ Kansas City, MO

D    ☐ Check if this is a publicly traded partnership (PTP)

**Part II    Information About the Partner**

E    Partner's SSN or TIN (Do not use TIN of a disregarded entity. See instructions.)
412-34-5670

F    Name, address, city, state, and ZIP code for partner entered in E. See instructions.

Luleng Wu
118 Nail Road
Kinston, NC  23849

G    ☐ General partner or LLC member-manager    ☐ Limited partner or other LLC member

H1    ☒ Domestic partner    ☐ Foreign partner

H2    ☐ If the partner is a disregarded entity (DE), enter the partner's:

TIN _____    Name _____

I1    What type of entity is this partner?  Individual

I2    If this partner is a retirement plan (IRA/SEP/Keogh/etc.), check here ▶ ☐

J    Partner's share of profit, loss, and capital (see instructions):

| | Beginning | Ending |
|---|---|---|
| Profit | % | 40 % |
| Loss | % | 40 % |
| Capital | % | 40 % |

Check if decrease is due to sale or exchange of partnership interest  . ▶ ☐

K    Partner's share of liabilities:

| | Beginning | Ending |
|---|---|---|
| Nonrecourse     . . $ | $ | |
| Qualified nonrecourse financing . . . $ | $ | 26,300 |
| Recourse . . . $ | $ | 43,000 |

Check this box if Item K includes liability amounts from lower tier partnerships ▶ ☐

L    **Partner's Capital Account Analysis**

| | |
|---|---|
| **Beginning capital account** . . . $ | 116,900 |
| Capital contributed during the year . . $ | |
| Current year net income (loss) . . . $ | 64,755 |
| Other increase (decrease) (attach explanation) $ | |
| Withdrawals and distributions . . . $ ( | 26,000 ) |
| **Ending capital account** . . . . $ | 145,655 |

M    Did the partner contribute property with a built-in gain (loss)?
☐ Yes    ☒ No    If "Yes," attach statement. See instructions.

N    **Partner's Share of Net Unrecognized Section 704(c) Gain or (Loss)**
Beginning . . . . . . . . $ _____
Ending . . . . . . . . $ _____

**Part III    Partner's Share of Current Year Income, Deductions, Credits, and Other Items**

| | | | | |
|---|---|---|---|---|
| 1 | Ordinary business income (loss) | 60,540 | 14 | Self-employment earnings (loss) |
| | | | A | 91,940 |
| 2 | Net rental real estate income (loss) | | | |
| 3 | Other net rental income (loss) | | 15 | Credits |
| 4a | Guaranteed payments for services | 42,000 | | |
| 4b | Guaranteed payments for capital | | 16 | Schedule K-3 is attached if checked . . . . . ▶ ☐ |
| 4c | Total guaranteed payments | 42,000 | 17 | Alternative minimum tax (AMT) items |
| 5 | Interest income | | | |
| 6a | Ordinary dividends | 1,100 | | |
| 6b | Qualified dividends | 1,100 | 18 | Tax-exempt income and nondeductible expenses |
| 6c | Dividend equivalents | | | |
| 7 | Royalties | | | |
| 8 | Net short-term capital gain (loss) | 400 | 19 | Distributions |
| 9a | Net long-term capital gain (loss) | 600 | A | 26,000 |
| 9b | Collectibles (28%) gain (loss) | | | |
| 9c | Unrecaptured section 1250 gain | | 20 | Other information |
| 10 | Net section 1231 gain (loss) | 115 | | |
| 11 | Other income (loss) | | | |
| A | | 2,600 | | |
| 12 | Section 179 deduction | | 21 | Foreign taxes paid or accrued |
| 13 | Other deductions | | | |
| 22 | ☐ More than one activity for at-risk purposes* | | | |
| 23 | ☐ More than one activity for passive activity purposes* | | | |

*See attached statement for additional information.

For IRS Use Only

For Paperwork Reduction Act Notice, see the Instructions for Form 1065.    www.irs.gov/Form1065    Cat. No. 11394R    **Schedule K-1 (Form 1065) 2021**

**EXAMPLE 14-12**

Knox is a partner in Knox, Smith, & Wood partnership. He owned 33.3% from January 1, 2021, to March 31, 2021, when he bought Smith's 33.3% interest. He owned 66.6% for the rest of the year. The partnership had $76,000 of ordinary income and $8,000 in long-term capital gains. Barring any special allocations in a partnership agreement, Knox's share of the income items follows:

| | | |
|---|---|---:|
| Ordinary income | $76,000 × 33.3% × 3/12 = | $ 6,333* |
| | $76,000 × 66.6% × 9/12 = | 38,000 |
| Ordinary income allocated to Knox | | $44,333 |
| Capital gain | $8,000 × 33.3% × 3/12 = | $ 667 |
| | $8,000 × 66.6% × 9/12 = | 4,000 |
| Capital gain allocated to Knox | | $ 4,667 |

\* Use of expanded decimal places reduces rounding errors.

## Self-Employment Income

Another important item affecting a partner is self-employment income. As we have mentioned, a partner is not an employee of a partnership and, thus, must consider income from the partnership to be self-employment income. In Chapter 6, we noted that a self-employed individual must pay 15.3% of self-employment tax on the first $142,800 of self-employment income (wages in excess of $142,800 will be subject only to the Medicare rate of 2.9%). Normally, only ordinary income and guaranteed payments are included as self-employment income from the partnership.[12] Table 14-2 illustrates the basic computation of self-employment income using the information on the Schedule K-1 in Exhibit 14-2.

The partnership reports self-employment income to the partner on line 14 of Schedule K-1. The sum of all the partners' self-employment income should equal the total self-employment income on Form 1065, Schedule K, line 14a.

**TABLE 14-2**
**Calculation of Self-Employment Income from a Partnership**

| | |
|---|---:|
| 1. Ordinary income from Schedule K-1, line 1 | $60,540 |
| 2. Plus: Any guaranteed payments from Schedule K-1, line 4c | 42,000 |
| 3. Less: Any § 1231 gain included in ordinary income | –0– |
| 4. Less: Any § 179 expense from Schedule K-1, line 12 | (10,600) |
| Self-employment income, Schedule K-1, line 14 | $91,940 |

## Qualified Business Income Deduction

Taxpayers are allowed a deduction of 20% of income from a partnership, S corporation, or sole proprietorship. The QBI deduction is allowed on the partner return (Form 1040 for an individual partner) and is typically 20% of line 1 of the K-1—the ordinary income from the partnership. Full coverage of the QBI deduction is shown at the end of Chapter 6.

**TAX YOUR BRAIN**

Why are items such as dividends, capital gains, and royalty income not included in self-employment income? Likewise, why do charitable contributions not reduce self-employment income?

**ANSWER**

Only income and expenses from the operations of the partnership are included. Dividends, capital gains, and royalty income are not included as self-employment income because they are investment income. The partnership is just a conduit for the partners' charitable contributions.

**CONCEPT CHECK 14-3—**

**LO 14-3**

1. Why are items such as rental income/loss, capital gains/losses, and charitable contributions that flow through a partnership treated as separately stated?
2. Why is income from a partnership treated as self-employment income?

[12] Rental of real estate may be included in self-employment income if the property is held for sale to customers in the course of a trade or business as a real estate dealer or if the rental income is for rentals for which service is rendered to the occupants (such as a bed and breakfast).

# BASIS OF THE PARTNERSHIP INTEREST
## LO 14-4

A partner's basis in their partnership interest changes over time. It is extremely important to continue to recalculate basis for various reasons. For example, a partner must use the basis to determine any gain or loss on the sale or disposal of the interest, to determine the basis of property distributed from the partnership, and to determine whether losses from the partnership are deductible (see the at-risk rules in Chapter 13). Table 14-3 summarizes the process to calculate a partner's basis.[13]

Although it is advisable to keep a running total of a partner's basis each year, the basis calculation is mandatory at the following times:

1. In a year the partnership had a loss.
2. At the liquidation or disposition of a partner's interest.
3. In a year a partner receives nonliquidating distributions.

### Increases and Decreases in Partnership Basis

Table 14-3 notes that the partner's share of separately stated items increases or decreases their basis. Do separately stated income items such as tax-exempt income increase basis? Do separately stated nondeductible loss or deduction items (such as life insurance premiums) decrease basis? The answers are yes. All income/gain or expense/loss items increase or decrease outside basis.

---

**TAX YOUR BRAIN**

Why do tax-exempt and nondeductible items increase or decrease basis?

**ANSWER**

If these items do not increase or decrease a partner's basis (outside basis), they will have a tax effect when the partnership interest is sold or disposed of. For example, if a partner's share of tax-exempt interest is $500, that $500 should never be taxed. If the partner's basis does not increase by $500, the partnership basis will be $500 lower. When the interest is sold, $500 in additional gain will be recognized. Thus, the tax-exempt interest income will effectively be taxed. The same concept applies to nondeductible items but in the opposite direction.

---

There is a specific sequence to the basis adjustments. The order of adjustment follows:

1. Basis is first increased and decreased by all adjustments except for losses.
2. The adjustment is reduced by money distributed (including release of liabilities).
3. The adjustment is reduced by the basis of any property distributed.

**TABLE 14-3**
**Basis of the Partnership Interest**

Starting basis = Basis of property contributed + FMV of services rendered (or cost if partnership interest was purchased)*
Plus: Basis of property contributions after formation (cash or property)
Plus: Partner's share of partnership ordinary income
Plus: Partner's share of separately stated income or gain items
Plus: Partner's share in partnership liabilities
Less: Basis of property distributed (cash or property—but not below zero)
Less: Partner's share of partnership ordinary loss (but not below zero)
Less: Partner's share of separately stated loss/expense items
Less: Partner's release of partnership liabilities

* A partnership interest could be inherited or received by gift as well. If the interest is inherited, the beginning partnership basis is the FMV at the date of death of the decedent. The gift basis is typically the donor's basis plus any gift tax paid on the appreciation.

[13] IRC § 705(a).

The basis that remains is used for the determination of any deductible losses from the partnership.

**EXAMPLE 14-13**

Partner Allison has a basis of $5,000 in a partnership at the beginning of the year. She receives $3,000 in cash distributions, her distributive share of income is $2,500, and she receives a land distribution with a basis of $4,000 (FMV $10,000).

| | |
|---|---:|
| Beginning basis | $5,000 |
| Share of income | 2,500 |
| Cash distribution | (3,000) |
| Land distribution | (4,000) |
| Year-end basis | $ 500 |

**EXAMPLE 14-14**

Use the information on the Schedule K-1 shown in Exhibit 14-2. If Luleng Wu's partnership basis at the beginning of 2021 was $22,000, calculate his basis at the end of 2021.

| | |
|---|---:|
| Beginning basis | $22,000 |
| Share of ordinary income | 60,540 |
| Share of dividends | 1,110 |
| Share of short-term capital gains | 440 |
| Share of long-term capital gains | 600 |
| Share of net § 1231 gain | 105 |
| Charitable contributions | (2,600) |
| Section 179 expense | (10,600) |
| Wu's ending basis | $71,595 |

Notice in Example 14-14 and Table 14-3 that guaranteed payments are *not* used in the basis calculation. Typically, guaranteed payments do not have an impact on basis. The partner recognizes income from the guaranteed payment but receives a payment for the exact amount. Thus, the increase (income recognized) and the decrease (cash distribution) exactly cancel out.[14]

## Liabilities

In Example 14-14, you may have noticed that we did not include any liabilities in the basis even though the partner's Schedule K-1 clearly shows the partner's share of liabilities in Section K. In practice, most tax preparers calculate basis but ignore the liability implications. In most cases, liabilities are considered only if the increase in basis is necessary to deduct a loss from the partnership. The primary reason for this common practice is that the liability level of the partnership is consistently changing, and most of the time the calculation is simply not necessary.

**EXAMPLE 14-15**

Using the same facts as in Example 14-14, we calculate the ending basis including liabilities as follows:

| | |
|---|---:|
| Ending basis | $ 71,595 |
| Qualified nonrecourse | 26,300 |
| Other debt | 43,000 |
| Total basis including liabilities | $140,895 |

---

[14] One instance in which this is not the case occurs when a partner receives a capital interest for services to the partnership. Income is recognized as a guaranteed payment, but no cash payment is made. The partner's basis is increased in this instance.

**CONCEPT CHECK 14-4— LO 14-4**

1. A partner must use basis to determine the gain or loss on a sale of the partnership interest and to determine whether losses are deductible. True or false?
2. A partner's basis is not increased by their share of tax-exempt income items. True or false?
3. In the calculation of basis, the order of the basis adjustments is not important. True or false?
4. A partner's basis is never increased by their share of recourse liabilities. True or false?

# PARTNERSHIP DISTRIBUTIONS
## LO 14-5

One of the convenient features of a partnership is flexibility concerning distributions. As a general rule, a partner recognizes no gain or loss on a nonliquidating distribution.[15]

**EXAMPLE 14-16**

Davis, a 50% partner in ABCD partnership, has a basis of $85,000 in his partnership interest. He receives a cash distribution of $84,000 at year-end. Davis recognizes no gain or loss on the distribution but reduces his basis to $1,000.

**TAX YOUR BRAIN**

Why does the IRS allow the tax-free distribution in Example 14-16?

**ANSWER**

For Davis to have a predistribution basis of $85,000, he would have made past contributions or have been taxed on income to increase his basis. Therefore, he is receiving either a distribution of previously taxed income or a distribution of his own capital, neither of which is taxed. This is a significant advantage of the partnership form over the corporate form. A distribution from a corporation is usually considered a taxable dividend.

### Gain on Current Distributions

The two exceptions to the general rule of no gain or loss on current distributions follow:

1. When money or marketable securities are distributed in excess of the partner's basis, a gain is recognized to the extent of the excess.[16]
2. The current distribution triggers a precontribution gain.[17]

Basis can never go below zero. Thus, if money or marketable securities (cashlike assets) exceed the partner's basis, the partner recognizes the excess as a capital gain.[18]

**EXAMPLE 14-17**

Assume the same facts as in Example 14-16. If Davis received a cash distribution of $86,000, he must recognize a $1,000 capital gain. After the distribution and recognized gain, he would have a zero basis in the partnership at year-end.

A precontribution gain occurs when a partner contributes appreciated property to a partnership and, within seven years, the partnership distributes the same property to another partner. In essence, the contributing partner is selling the property to the distributing partner and attempting to eliminate the gain by passing it through the partnership. If the contributed property is distributed to another partner within the seven-year time frame, the contributing partner recognizes the deferred gain.

[15] IRC § 731.
[16] Remember that *money* in this case refers to cash distributions and the release of liabilities.
[17] IRC § 737.
[18] IRC § 741.

**EXAMPLE 14-18**

Bailey contributes land to a partnership with a basis of $8,000 and an FMV of $12,000 in 2020. In 2021, when the FMV of the land is $14,000, the partnership distributes the land to Jessica, another partner. The distribution triggers a precontribution gain of $4,000 to Bailey. Jessica has no gain or loss on the distribution and would have a basis of $12,000 in the land ($8,000 carryover basis plus the $4,000 gain recognized by Bailey).

## Basis of Distributed Property

When property is distributed to a partner from a partnership, neither the partner nor the partnership recognizes any gain. The basis and the holding period of the distributed property carry over to the partner.[19] Hence, the partner steps into the shoes of the partnership. The only exception to the carryover basis rule occurs when the basis in the distributed property exceeds the basis in the partnership interest. The basis of the distributed property is limited to the basis of the partnership interest. Recall that the partner recognizes a gain only if the distribution exceeds basis and the distribution consists only of money and marketable securities.[20]

**EXAMPLE 14-19**

Fonda has a partnership basis of $6,000. She receives, from the partnership, a distribution of equipment with a basis to the partnership of $8,000 and an FMV of $5,000. The basis in the equipment to Fonda after the distribution is limited to her basis in the partnership of $6,000. Fonda recognizes no gain or loss and has a zero basis in her partnership interest after the distribution.

**EXAMPLE 14-20**

Assume the same facts as in Example 14-19 except that Fonda receives a $2,000 cash distribution and the equipment. In this case, she would first reduce her partnership basis by the $2,000 cash distribution. Fonda still does not recognize any gain but now has a basis of $4,000 in the equipment.

**CONCEPT CHECK 14-5—LO 14-5**

1. Which of the following is true concerning the recognition of gain on a distribution from a partnership?
   a. Gain is recognized if the partner receives property with a basis higher than their partnership interest basis.
   b. Gain is recognized if the partner receives cash in excess of their basis.
   c. The partner never recognizes a gain on a partnership distribution.
   d. The partner always recognizes a gain on a partnership distribution.

2. Nelson has a partnership basis of $12,000. He receives, from the partnership, a distribution of furniture with a basis to the partnership of $16,000 and an FMV of $10,000. Nelson's basis in the furniture after the distribution from the partnership is
   a. $10,000.
   b. $12,000.
   c. $16,000.
   d. None of the above.

3. Assume the same facts as in Question 2. However, Nelson receives a cash distribution of $4,000 with the furniture. The basis in the furniture after the distributions is
   a. $8,000.
   b. $10,000.
   c. $12,000.
   d. $16,000.

[19] See IRC § 732(a) for the basis and IRC § 735(b) for the holding period.
[20] This is assuming there is no triggered precontribution gain.

# DISPOSAL OR LIQUIDATION OF A PARTNERSHIP INTEREST
## LO 14-6

The most common way to dispose of a partnership interest is either through partnership liquidation or by selling the interest.[21]

### Liquidation of a Partnership Interest

*Liquidation* occurs when a partner's entire interest is redeemed by the partnership. Most of the rules concerning nonliquidating distributions (discussed previously) also apply to liquidating distributions. Thus, a distribution of money in excess of basis causes a capital gain. If property is received in the liquidating distribution, no gain is recognized, and the basis of the property is adjusted as shown in Example 14-19.

One substantial difference in the liquidation rules and regular distribution rules is that a loss can be recognized on liquidating distributions. A loss occurs when the amounts received in liquidation are less than the partner's outside basis. One major caveat is that the loss can be recognized only after the final payment is received from the partnership and when only money, receivables, and/or inventory is/are distributed.

---

**EXAMPLE 14-21**

Cassandra has a $20,000 basis in her partnership interest when she receives liquidating distributions from the partnership. She receives cash of $12,000 and equipment with a basis to the partnership of $6,000. Cassandra recognizes no gain or loss on the liquidating distribution. The equipment will have a basis to her of $8,000 ($20,000 partnership basis minus cash received of $12,000).

---

**EXAMPLE 14-22**

Assume the same facts as in Example 14-21 except that Cassandra receives cash of $12,000 and inventory with a basis to the partnership of $6,000. Cassandra recognizes a loss of $2,000 on the liquidation (cash and inventory basis of $18,000 minus the $20,000 partnership basis); the inventory will have a basis to her of $6,000.

---

If several assets are distributed in liquidation and the partner does not have outside basis to cover the basis in the partnership assets distributed, the outside basis is allocated among the distributed assets as follows:

1. The partnership basis is first reduced by money distributions.
2. Any remaining basis covers the basis in receivables and inventory distributed.
3. Any remaining basis is allocated to the other assets distributed in proportion to each asset's basis.[22]

---

**EXAMPLE 14-23**

Kelsey has a basis in her partnership interest of $10,000. She receives the following assets in complete liquidation of the partnership interest:

| | |
|---|---|
| Cash | $3,000 |
| Inventory (basis) | 2,000 |
| Equipment (basis) | 2,000 |
| Land (basis) | 4,000 |

---

[21] Of course, a partnership interest could be disposed of through inheritance or by gift, but these disposals have limited income tax effects to the partner. There may be estate tax issues or gift tax considerations, but these are beyond the scope of this text.

[22] Reg. § 1.732-1(c).

Kelsey has no recognized gain or loss, and her $10,000 outside basis is allocated to the assets as follows:

| | |
|---|---:|
| Cash | $3,000 |
| Inventory | 2,000 |
| Equipment ($5,000 × $2,000/$6,000) | 1,667 |
| Land ($5,000 × $4,000/$6,000) | 3,333 |

## Sale of a Partnership Interest

The sale of a partnership interest is similar to the sale of any capital asset. The partner determines the amount realized from the sale and subtracts the basis of the partnership interest at the date of sale. The gain or loss is a capital item and, assuming that the partner is an individual, he or she is reported on Schedule D of Form 1040.

**EXAMPLE 14-24**

Jana purchased a 30% partnership interest for $23,000 in February 2019. Her share of partnership income in subsequent years was $12,000 in 2019, $15,000 in 2020, and $8,000 in 2021. She made no additional contributions to, or withdrawals from, the partnership. On December 18, 2021, Jana sold her partnership interest for $74,000. Her long-term capital gain is $16,000.

| | | |
|---|---:|---:|
| Amount realized | | $ 74,000 |
| Basis: Beginning | $ 23,000 | |
| 2019 income | +12,000 | |
| 2020 income | +15,000 | |
| 2021 income | + 8,000 | (58,000) |
| Long-term capital gain | | $ 16,000 |

The partner may be subject to ordinary income from the sale if the partnership has substantially appreciated inventory or accounts receivable.[23] If the partnership sold or collected these items, ordinary income would result, and the partner would share in that ordinary income. A partner who is allowed capital gain treatment on the sale of the partnership interest would effectively convert the ordinary income to capital gain income and benefit from the preferential capital gain rates. IRC § 751 prevents this conversion.

**EXAMPLE 14-25**

Assume the same facts as in Example 14-24. However, the partnership has uncollected accounts receivable with an FMV of $20,000 and a basis of $0.[24] Because Jana's share in the receivables is $6,000 (30% interest × $20,000), $6,000 of the $16,000 gain is ordinary, and the remaining $10,000 is capital gain.

**CONCEPT CHECK 14-6— LO 14-6**

1. Shelly has a basis in her partnership interest of $30,000. She receives the following assets in complete liquidation of the partnership interest:

| | |
|---|---:|
| Cash | $ 9,000 |
| Inventory (basis) | 6,000 |
| Equipment (basis) | 8,000 |
| Land (basis) | 12,000 |

   *a.* What is Shelly's recognized gain?

   *b.* What is Shelly's basis in each of the assets distributed?    *(continued)*

[23] IRC § 751.

[24] Typically, a cash basis partnership will have a zero basis in accounts receivable because income is not recognized until the partnership collects the cash.

2. Callie purchased a 60% partnership interest for $55,000 in March 2020. She had income of $18,000 from the partnership in 2020 and $26,000 in 2021. She made no additional contributions to, or withdrawals from, the partnership. On December 30, 2021, Callie sold her partnership interest for $107,000.

   a. What is Callie's basis before the sale?

   b. What is Callie's gain or loss?

   c. Is the gain or loss (if any) capital or ordinary?

## Comprehensive Example

Shafer and Jones Consulting LLC is a partnership formed on January 1, 2018, to perform business consulting services. The business is located at 1482 Jones Business Complex, Anywhere, NC 27858. Its Employer ID is 92-1234567; it uses the tax/cash basis of accounting, is not subject to partnership audit procedures, has no foreign interests, and is not a tax shelter.

The home address for David A. Shafer (SSN 412-34-5670) is 103 Flower Road, Anywhere, NC 27858. He is a 60% partner. Robert B. Jones (SSN 412-34-5671) lives at 534 Bates Road, Anywhere, NC 27858. He is a 40% partner.

In 2021, David received a distribution of $60,000 and Robert received a $40,000 distribution. Both of these distributions are in addition to the guaranteed payments.

**SHAFER AND JONES CONSULTING, LLC**
**Comparative Balance Sheet**
**As of December 31, 2020, and December 31, 2021**

|  | 12/31/20 | 12/31/21 |
|---|---|---|
| Assets |  |  |
| Cash | $ 29,452 | $ 35,452 |
| Investments | 153,345 | 105,480 |
| Office equipment | 123,000 | 143,800 |
| Accumulated depreciation (equipment) | (68,880) | (71,852) |
| Building | 245,600 | 245,600 |
| Accumulated depreciation (building) | (18,616) | (24,913) |
| Total assets | $463,901 | $433,567 |
| Liabilities and equity |  |  |
| Notes payable | $233,800 | $228,333 |
| Capital accounts |  |  |
| Capital, Shafer | 138,061 | 123,140 |
| Capital, Jones | 92,040 | 82,094 |
| Total liabilities and equity | $463,901 | $433,567 |

**SHAFER AND JONES CONSULTING, LLC**
**Income Statement**
**For the Year Ending December 31, 2021**

| Revenue |  |
|---|---|
| Consulting income | $554,897 |
| Interest income | 1,231 |
| Dividend income (qualified) | 3,234 |
| Long-term capital losses | (12,435) |
| Total revenue | $546,927 |

| Expenses | |
|---|---|
| Salaries and wages (nonpartners) | $153,000 |
| Guaranteed payments | |
| Shafer | 100,000 |
| Jones | 96,000 |
| Depreciation (MACRS—includes $5,000 § 179 expense) | 31,448 |
| Interest expense | 15,983 |
| Taxes and licenses | 15,548 |
| Utilities | 12,132 |
| Travel | 11,458 |
| Meals (100%) | 11,345 |
| Auto | 9,880 |
| Insurance (nonpartner health) | 5,000 |
| Accounting and legal | 4,800 |
| Repairs | 3,200 |
| Charitable contributions | 1,500 |
| Payroll penalties | 500 |
| Total expenses | $471,794 |
| Net income | $ 75,133 |

See Table 14-4 for a spreadsheet of partnership ordinary income and separately stated items. Exhibits 14-3 and 14-4 show the presentation of Form 1065 and Schedule K-1s for Shafer and Jones Consulting. Form 4562 (depreciation), Schedule D (capital gains and losses), and a statement listing other deductions (line 20 of Form 1065) are omitted from the example.

**TABLE 14-4**

**SHAFER AND JONES CONSULTING, LLC**

**Income Statement**

**For the Year Ending December 31, 2021**

| | Adjustments | Ordinary | Separately Stated |
|---|---|---|---|
| Consulting income | $ | $554,897 | $ |
| Interest income | | | 1,231 |
| Dividend income (qualified) | | | 3,234 |
| Long-term capital losses | | | (12,435) |
| | | | |
| Expenses | | | |
| Salaries and wages (nonpartners) | | 153,000 | |
| Guaranteed payments | | | |
| Shafer | | 100,000 | 100,000 |
| Jones | | 96,000 | 96,000 |
| Depreciation (MACRS—includes $5,000 § 179 expense) | | 26,448 | 5,000 |
| Interest expense | | 15,983 | |
| Taxes and licenses | | 15,548 | |
| Utilities | | 12,132 | |
| Travel | | 11,458 | |
| Meals (100%) | (5,673)* | 5,672* | |
| Auto | | 9,880 | |
| Insurance (nonpartner health) | | 5,000 | |
| Accounting and legal | | 4,800 | |
| Repairs | | 3,200 | |
| Charitable contributions | | | 1,500 |
| Payroll penalties | (500)† | | |
| Net income | | $ 95,776 | |

* Only 50% of meals are allowed.
† Penalties are not deductible.

**EXHIBIT 14-3**

| Form **1065** | U.S. Return of Partnership Income | OMB No. 1545-0123 |
|---|---|---|

Department of the Treasury
Internal Revenue Service

For calendar year 2021, or tax year beginning _____, 2021, ending _____, 20___.
▶ Go to *www.irs.gov/Form1065* for instructions and the latest information.

**2021**

| A Principal business activity | | Name of partnership | D Employer identification number |
|---|---|---|---|
| Consulting | | Shafer and Jones Consulting, LLC | 92-1234567 |
| B Principal product or service | Type or Print | Number, street, and room or suite no. If a P.O. box, see instructions. | E Date business started |
| Consulting | | 1482 Jones Business Center | 01/01/18 |
| C Business code number | | City or town, state or province, country, and ZIP or foreign postal code | F Total assets (see instructions) |
| 541600 | | Anywhere, NC 27858 | $ 433,567 |

G Check applicable boxes: (1) ☐ Initial return (2) ☐ Final return (3) ☐ Name change (4) ☐ Address change (5) ☐ Amended return
H Check accounting method: (1) ☑ Cash (2) ☐ Accrual (3) ☐ Other (specify) ▶
I Number of Schedules K-1. Attach one for each person who was a partner at any time during the tax year ▶ **Two**
J Check if Schedules C and M-3 are attached ▶ ☐
K Check if partnership: (1) ☐ Aggregated activities for section 465 at-risk purposes (2) ☐ Grouped activities for section 469 passive activity purposes

**Caution:** Include **only** trade or business income and expenses on lines 1a through 22 below. See instructions for more information.

**Income**

| | | | | |
|---|---|---|---|---|
| 1a | Gross receipts or sales | 1a | 554,897 | |
| b | Returns and allowances | 1b | | |
| c | Balance. Subtract line 1b from line 1a | | 1c | 554,897 |
| 2 | Cost of goods sold (attach Form 1125-A) | | 2 | |
| 3 | Gross profit. Subtract line 2 from line 1c | | 3 | 554,897 |
| 4 | Ordinary income (loss) from other partnerships, estates, and trusts (attach statement) | | 4 | |
| 5 | Net farm profit (loss) (attach Schedule F (Form 1040)) | | 5 | |
| 6 | Net gain (loss) from Form 4797, Part II, line 17 (attach Form 4797) | | 6 | |
| 7 | Other income (loss) (attach statement) | | 7 | |
| 8 | **Total income (loss).** Combine lines 3 through 7 | | 8 | 554,897 |

**Deductions** (see instructions for limitations)

| | | | | |
|---|---|---|---|---|
| 9 | Salaries and wages (other than to partners) (less employment credits) | | 9 | 153,000 |
| 10 | Guaranteed payments to partners | | 10 | 196,000 |
| 11 | Repairs and maintenance | | 11 | 3,200 |
| 12 | Bad debts | | 12 | |
| 13 | Rent | | 13 | |
| 14 | Taxes and licenses | | 14 | 15,548 |
| 15 | Interest (see instructions) | | 15 | 15,983 |
| 16a | Depreciation (if required, attach Form 4562) | 16a | 26,448 | |
| b | Less depreciation reported on Form 1125-A and elsewhere on return | 16b | | |
| | | | 16c | 26,448 |
| 17 | Depletion (**Do not deduct oil and gas depletion.**) | | 17 | |
| 18 | Retirement plans, etc. | | 18 | |
| 19 | Employee benefit programs | | 19 | |
| 20 | Other deductions (attach statement) | | 20 | 48,942 |
| 21 | **Total deductions.** Add the amounts shown in the far right column for lines 9 through 20 | | 21 | 459,121 |
| 22 | **Ordinary business income (loss).** Subtract line 21 from line 8 | | 22 | 95,776 |

**Tax and Payment**

| | | | |
|---|---|---|---|
| 23 | Interest due under the look-back method—completed long-term contracts (attach Form 8697) | 23 | |
| 24 | Interest due under the look-back method—income forecast method (attach Form 8866) | 24 | |
| 25 | BBA AAR imputed underpayment (see instructions) | 25 | |
| 26 | Other taxes (see instructions) | 26 | |
| 27 | **Total balance due.** Add lines 23 through 26 | 27 | 0 |
| 28 | Payment (see instructions) | 28 | |
| 29 | **Amount owed.** If line 28 is smaller than line 27, enter amount owed | 29 | |
| 30 | **Overpayment.** If line 28 is larger than line 27, enter overpayment | 30 | |

**Sign Here**

Under penalties of perjury, I declare that I have examined this return, including accompanying schedules and statements, and to the best of my knowledge and belief, it is true, correct, and complete. Declaration of preparer (other than partner or limited liability company member) is based on all information of which preparer has any knowledge.

▶ Signature of partner or limited liability company member   Date

May the IRS discuss this return with the preparer shown below? See instructions. ☐ Yes ☐ No

**Paid Preparer Use Only**

| Print/Type preparer's name | Preparer's signature | Date | Check ☐ if self-employed | PTIN |
|---|---|---|---|---|
| Firm's name ▶ | | | Firm's EIN ▶ | |
| Firm's address ▶ | | | Phone no. | |

For Paperwork Reduction Act Notice, see separate instructions.  Cat. No. 11390Z  Form **1065** (2021)

**EXHIBIT 14-3**  *(continued)*

Form 1065 (2021)

## Schedule B     Other Information

| | | | | Yes | No |
|---|---|---|---|---|---|
| **1** | What type of entity is filing this return? Check the applicable box: | | | | |
| **a** | ☐ Domestic general partnership | **b** | ☐ Domestic limited partnership | | |
| **c** | ☑ Domestic limited liability company | **d** | ☐ Domestic limited liability partnership | | |
| **e** | ☐ Foreign partnership | **f** | ☐ Other ▶ | | |
| **2** | At the end of the tax year: | | | | |
| **a** | Did any foreign or domestic corporation, partnership (including any entity treated as a partnership), trust, or tax-exempt organization, or any foreign government own, directly or indirectly, an interest of 50% or more in the profit, loss, or capital of the partnership? For rules of constructive ownership, see instructions. If "Yes," attach Schedule B-1, Information on Partners Owning 50% or More of the Partnership . . . . . . . . . . . . . . | | | | | ✓ |
| **b** | Did any individual or estate own, directly or indirectly, an interest of 50% or more in the profit, loss, or capital of the partnership? For rules of constructive ownership, see instructions. If "Yes," attach Schedule B-1, Information on Partners Owning 50% or More of the Partnership . . . . . . . . . . . | | | | ✓ | |
| **3** | At the end of the tax year, did the partnership: | | | | | |
| **a** | Own directly 20% or more, or own, directly or indirectly, 50% or more of the total voting power of all classes of stock entitled to vote of any foreign or domestic corporation? For rules of constructive ownership, see instructions. If "Yes," complete (i) through (iv) below . . . . . . . . . . . . . . . . . . | | | | | ✓ |

| **(i)** Name of Corporation | **(ii)** Employer Identification Number (if any) | **(iii)** Country of Incorporation | **(iv)** Percentage Owned in Voting Stock |
|---|---|---|---|
| | | | |
| | | | |
| | | | |
| | | | |
| | | | |

| | | Yes | No |
|---|---|---|---|
| **b** | Own directly an interest of 20% or more, or own, directly or indirectly, an interest of 50% or more in the profit, loss, or capital in any foreign or domestic partnership (including an entity treated as a partnership) or in the beneficial interest of a trust? For rules of constructive ownership, see instructions. If "Yes," complete (i) through (v) below . . | | | ✓ |

| **(i)** Name of Entity | **(ii)** Employer Identification Number (if any) | **(iii)** Type of Entity | **(iv)** Country of Organization | **(v)** Maximum Percentage Owned in Profit, Loss, or Capital |
|---|---|---|---|---|
| | | | | |
| | | | | |
| | | | | |
| | | | | |
| | | | | |

| | | | Yes | No |
|---|---|---|---|---|
| **4** | Does the partnership satisfy **all four** of the following conditions? | | | |
| **a** | The partnership's total receipts for the tax year were less than $250,000. | | | |
| **b** | The partnership's total assets at the end of the tax year were less than $1 million. | | | |
| **c** | Schedules K-1 are filed with the return and furnished to the partners on or before the due date (including extensions) for the partnership return. | | | |
| **d** | The partnership is not filing and is not required to file Schedule M-3 . . . . . . . . . . | | | ✓ |
| | If "Yes," the partnership is not required to complete Schedules L, M-1, and M-2; item F on page 1 of Form 1065; or item L on Schedule K-1. | | | |
| **5** | Is this partnership a publicly traded partnership, as defined in section 469(k)(2)? . . . . . . . . . . | | | ✓ |
| **6** | During the tax year, did the partnership have any debt that was canceled, was forgiven, or had the terms modified so as to reduce the principal amount of the debt? . . . . . . . . . . . . . . . . . | | | ✓ |
| **7** | Has this partnership filed, or is it required to file, Form 8918, Material Advisor Disclosure Statement, to provide information on any reportable transaction? . . . . . . . . . . . . . . . . . . . . . | | | ✓ |
| **8** | At any time during calendar year 2021, did the partnership have an interest in or a signature or other authority over a financial account in a foreign country (such as a bank account, securities account, or other financial account)? See instructions for exceptions and filing requirements for FinCEN Form 114, Report of Foreign Bank and Financial Accounts (FBAR). If "Yes," enter the name of the foreign country ▶ | | | ✓ |
| **9** | At any time during the tax year, did the partnership receive a distribution from, or was it the grantor of, or transferor to, a foreign trust? If "Yes," the partnership may have to file Form 3520, Annual Return To Report Transactions With Foreign Trusts and Receipt of Certain Foreign Gifts. See instructions . . . . . . . . . | | | ✓ |
| **10a** | Is the partnership making, or had it previously made (and not revoked), a section 754 election? . . . . . . See instructions for details regarding a section 754 election. | | | ✓ |
| **b** | Did the partnership make for this tax year an optional basis adjustment under section 743(b) or 734(b)? If "Yes," attach a statement showing the computation and allocation of the basis adjustment. See instructions . . . . | | | ✓ |

Form **1065** (2021)

*(continued)*

**EXHIBIT 14-3** *(continued)*

Form 1065 (2021)                                                                 Page **3**

**Schedule B**    **Other Information** *(continued)*

| | | Yes | No |
|---|---|---|---|
| c | Is the partnership required to adjust the basis of partnership assets under section 743(b) or 734(b) because of a substantial built-in loss (as defined under section 743(d)) or substantial basis reduction (as defined under section 734(d))? If "Yes," attach a statement showing the computation and allocation of the basis adjustment. See instructions | | ✓ |
| 11 | Check this box if, during the current or prior tax year, the partnership distributed any property received in a like-kind exchange or contributed such property to another entity (other than disregarded entities wholly owned by the partnership throughout the tax year) . . . . . . . . . . . . . . . . . . . . ▶ ☐ | | |
| 12 | At any time during the tax year, did the partnership distribute to any partner a tenancy-in-common or other undivided interest in partnership property? . . . . . . . . . . . . . . . | | ✓ |
| 13 | If the partnership is required to file Form 8858, Information Return of U.S. Persons With Respect To Foreign Disregarded Entities (FDEs) and Foreign Branches (FBs), enter the number of Forms 8858 attached. See instructions . . . . . . . . . . . . . . . . . . . ▶ | | |
| 14 | Does the partnership have any foreign partners? If "Yes," enter the number of Forms 8805, Foreign Partner's Information Statement of Section 1446 Withholding Tax, filed for this partnership . . . ▶ | | ✓ |
| 15 | Enter the number of Forms 8865, Return of U.S. Persons With Respect to Certain Foreign Partnerships, attached to this return . . . . . . . . . . . . . . . . . . . . . . ▶ | | |
| 16a | Did you make any payments in 2021 that would require you to file Form(s) 1099? See instructions . . . . . | ✓ | |
| b | If "Yes," did you or will you file required Form(s) 1099? . . . . . . . . . . . . . . . | ✓ | |
| 17 | Enter the number of Forms 5471, Information Return of U.S. Persons With Respect To Certain Foreign Corporations, attached to this return . . . . . . . . . . . . . . . . . ▶ | | |
| 18 | Enter the number of partners that are foreign governments under section 892 . . . . . . ▶ | | |
| 19 | During the partnership's tax year, did the partnership make any payments that would require it to file Forms 1042 and 1042-S under chapter 3 (sections 1441 through 1464) or chapter 4 (sections 1471 through 1474)? . . . . | | ✓ |
| 20 | Was the partnership a specified domestic entity required to file Form 8938 for the tax year? See the Instructions for Form 8938 | | ✓ |
| 21 | Is the partnership a section 721(c) partnership, as defined in Regulations section 1.721(c)-1(b)(14)? . . . . . | | ✓ |
| 22 | During the tax year, did the partnership pay or accrue any interest or royalty for which one or more partners are not allowed a deduction under section 267A? See instructions | | ✓ |
| | If "Yes," enter the total amount of the disallowed deductions . . . . . . . . . . ▶ $ | | |
| 23 | Did the partnership have an election under section 163(j) for any real property trade or business or any farming business in effect during the tax year? See instructions . . . . . . . . . . . . . . . . . | | ✓ |
| 24 | Does the partnership satisfy one or more of the following? See instructions . . . . . . . . . . | | ✓ |
| a | The partnership owns a pass-through entity with current, or prior year carryover, excess business interest expense. | | |
| b | The partnership's aggregate average annual gross receipts (determined under section 448(c)) for the 3 tax years preceding the current tax year are more than $26 million and the partnership has business interest. | | |
| c | The partnership is a tax shelter (see instructions) and the partnership has business interest expense. | | |
| | If "Yes" to any, complete and attach Form 8990. | | |
| 25 | Is the partnership attaching Form 8996 to certify as a Qualified Opportunity Fund? . . . . . . . | | ✓ |
| | If "Yes," enter the amount from Form 8996, line 15 . . . . . . . . . . . . ▶ $ | | |
| 26 | Enter the number of foreign partners subject to section 864(c)(8) as a result of transferring all or a portion of an interest in the partnership or of receiving a distribution from the partnership . . . . . ▶ _____ | | |
| | Complete Schedule K-3 (Form 1065), Part XIII, for each foreign partner subject to section 864(c)(8) on a transfer or distribution. | | |
| 27 | At any time during the tax year, were there any transfers between the partnership and its partners subject to the disclosure requirements of Regulations section 1.707-8? . . . . . . . . . . . . . . . . . | | ✓ |
| 28 | Since December 22, 2017, did a foreign corporation directly or indirectly acquire substantially all of the properties constituting a trade or business of your partnership, and was the ownership percentage (by vote or value) for purposes of section 7874 greater than 50% (for example, the partners held more than 50% of the stock of the foreign corporation)? If "Yes," list the ownership percentage by vote and by value. See instructions. Percentage:      By Vote           By Value | | ✓ |
| 29 | Is the partnership electing out of the centralized partnership audit regime under section 6221(b)? See instructions. | | ✓ |
| | If "Yes," the partnership must complete Schedule B-2 (Form 1065). Enter the total from Schedule B-2, Part III, line 3 ▶ | | |
| | If "No," complete Designation of Partnership Representative below. | | |

**Designation of Partnership Representative** (see instructions)

Enter below the information for the partnership representative (PR) for the tax year covered by this return.

Name of PR ▶

| U.S. address of PR ▶ | U.S. phone number of PR ▶ |
|---|---|

If the PR is an entity, name of the designated individual for the PR ▶

| U.S. address of designated individual ▶ | U.S. phone number of designated individual ▶ |
|---|---|

Form **1065** (2021)

**EXHIBIT 14-3**  *(continued)*

Form 1065 (2021)

Page **4**

| **Schedule K** | **Partners' Distributive Share Items** | | **Total amount** |
|---|---|---|---|
| | **Income (Loss)** | | |
| 1 | Ordinary business income (loss) (page 1, line 22) . . . . . . . . . . | 1 | 95,776 |
| 2 | Net rental real estate income (loss) (attach Form 8825) . . . . . . . . | 2 | |
| 3a | Other gross rental income (loss) . . . . . . . . . . 3a | | |
| b | Expenses from other rental activities (attach statement) . . . . . 3b | | |
| c | Other net rental income (loss). Subtract line 3b from line 3a . . . . . . | 3c | |
| 4 | Guaranteed payments: **a** Services 4a 196,000 **b** Capital 4b | | |
| | **c** Total. Add lines 4a and 4b . . . . . . . . . . . . . . . | 4c | 196,000 |
| 5 | Interest income . . . . . . . . . . . . . . . . . | 5 | 1,231 |
| 6 | Dividends and dividend equivalents: **a** Ordinary dividends . . . . | 6a | 3,234 |
| | **b** Qualified dividends 6b 3,234 **c** Dividend equivalents 6c | | |
| 7 | Royalties . . . . . . . . . . . . . . . . . . | 7 | |
| 8 | Net short-term capital gain (loss) (attach Schedule D (Form 1065)) . . . . | 8 | |
| 9a | Net long-term capital gain (loss) (attach Schedule D (Form 1065)) . . . . | 9a | (12,435) |
| b | Collectibles (28%) gain (loss) . . . . . . . . . . 9b | | |
| c | Unrecaptured section 1250 gain (attach statement) . . . . . 9c | | |
| 10 | Net section 1231 gain (loss) (attach Form 4797) . . . . . . . . . | 10 | |
| 11 | Other income (loss) (see instructions)  Type ▶ | 11 | |
| | **Deductions** | | |
| 12 | Section 179 deduction (attach Form 4562) . . . . . . . . . . | 12 | 5,000 |
| 13a | Contributions . . . . . . . . . . . . . . . . . | 13a | 1,500 |
| b | Investment interest expense . . . . . . . . . . . . . | 13b | |
| c | Section 59(e)(2) expenditures: **(1)** Type ▶ _____ **(2)** Amount ▶ | 13c(2) | |
| d | Other deductions (see instructions)  Type ▶ | 13d | |
| | **Self-Employ-ment** | | |
| 14a | Net earnings (loss) from self-employment . . . . . . . . . . | 14a | 286,776 |
| b | Gross farming or fishing income . . . . . . . . . . . . | 14b | |
| c | Gross nonfarm income . . . . . . . . . . . . . . | 14c | |
| | **Credits** | | |
| 15a | Low-income housing credit (section 42(j)(5)) | 15a | |
| b | Low-income housing credit (other) . . . . . . . . . . . | 15b | |
| c | Qualified rehabilitation expenditures (rental real estate) (attach Form 3468, if applicable) . . | 15c | |
| d | Other rental real estate credits (see instructions)  Type ▶ _____ | 15d | |
| e | Other rental credits (see instructions)  Type ▶ _____ | 15e | |
| f | Other credits (see instructions)  Type ▶ | 15f | |
| | **International Transactions** | | |
| 16 | Attach Schedule K-2 (Form 1065), Partners' Distributive Share Items-International, and check this box to indicate that you are reporting items of international tax relevance . . . . . ☐ | | |
| | **Alternative Minimum Tax (AMT) Items** | | |
| 17a | Post-1986 depreciation adjustment . . . . . . . . . . . . | 17a | |
| b | Adjusted gain or loss . . . . . . . . . . . . . . | 17b | |
| c | Depletion (other than oil and gas) . . . . . . . . . . . | 17c | |
| d | Oil, gas, and geothermal properties—gross income . . . . . . . | 17d | |
| e | Oil, gas, and geothermal properties—deductions . . . . . . . . | 17e | |
| f | Other AMT items (attach statement) . . . . . . . . . . . | 17f | |
| | **Other Information** | | |
| 18a | Tax-exempt interest income . . . . . . . . . . . . . | 18a | |
| b | Other tax-exempt income . . . . . . . . . . . . . | 18b | |
| c | Nondeductible expenses . . . . . . . . . . . . . | 18c | 6,173 |
| 19a | Distributions of cash and marketable securities . . . . . . . . | 19a | 100,000 |
| b | Distributions of other property . . . . . . . . . . . . | 19b | |
| 20a | Investment income . . . . . . . . . . . . . . . | 20a | |
| b | Investment expenses . . . . . . . . . . . . . . | 20b | |
| c | Other items and amounts (attach statement) | | |
| 21 | Total foreign taxes paid or accrued . . . . . . . . . . . | 21 | |

Form **1065** (2021)

*(continued)*

**EXHIBIT 14-3**   *(concluded)*

Form 1065 (2021)                                                                                                             Page **5**

## Analysis of Net Income (Loss)

| | | | | | | |
|---|---|---|---|---|---|---|
| **1** | Net income (loss). Combine Schedule K, lines 1 through 11. From the result, subtract the sum of Schedule K, lines 12 through 13d, and 21 . . . . . . . . . . . . . . . . . . . **1** | | | | | 277,306 |

| **2** | Analysis by partner type: | **(i)** Corporate | **(ii)** Individual (active) | **(iii)** Individual (passive) | **(iv)** Partnership | **(v)** Exempt Organization | **(vi)** Nominee/Other |
|---|---|---|---|---|---|---|---|
| **a** | General partners | | 277,306 | | | | |
| **b** | Limited partners | | | | | | |

## Schedule L   Balance Sheets per Books

| | Assets | Beginning of tax year (a) | (b) | End of tax year (c) | (d) |
|---|---|---|---|---|---|
| **1** | Cash . . . . . . . . . . . . . | | 29,452 | | 35,452 |
| **2a** | Trade notes and accounts receivable . . | | | | |
| **b** | Less allowance for bad debts . . . . | | | | |
| **3** | Inventories . . . . . . . . . | | | | |
| **4** | U.S. government obligations . . . . | | | | |
| **5** | Tax-exempt securities . . . . . . | | | | |
| **6** | Other current assets (attach statement) . . | | | | |
| **7a** | Loans to partners (or persons related to partners) | | | | |
| **b** | Mortgage and real estate loans . . . | | | | |
| **8** | Other investments (attach statement) . . . | | 153,345 | | 105,480 |
| **9a** | Buildings and other depreciable assets . . | 368,600 | | 389,400 | |
| **b** | Less accumulated depreciation . . . | 87,496 | 281,104 | 96,765 | 292,635 |
| **10a** | Depletable assets . . . . . . . | | | | |
| **b** | Less accumulated depletion . . . . | | | | |
| **11** | Land (net of any amortization) . . . . | | | | |
| **12a** | Intangible assets (amortizable only) . . . | | | | |
| **b** | Less accumulated amortization . . . . | | | | |
| **13** | Other assets (attach statement) . . . . | | | | |
| **14** | Total assets . . . . . . . . . | | 463,901 | | 433,567 |
| | **Liabilities and Capital** | | | | |
| **15** | Accounts payable . . . . . . . | | | | |
| **16** | Mortgages, notes, bonds payable in less than 1 year | | 233,800 | | 228,333 |
| **17** | Other current liabilities (attach statement) . . . | | | | |
| **18** | All nonrecourse loans . . . . . . . | | | | |
| **19a** | Loans from partners (or persons related to partners) . | | | | |
| **b** | Mortgages, notes, bonds payable in 1 year or more . | | | | |
| **20** | Other liabilities (attach statement) . . . . | | | | |
| **21** | Partners' capital accounts . . . . . . | | 230,101 | | 205,234 |
| **22** | Total liabilities and capital . . . . . . . | | 463,901 | | 433,567 |

## Schedule M-1   Reconciliation of Income (Loss) per Books With Income (Loss) per Return

**Note:** The partnership may be required to file Schedule M-3. See instructions.

| | | | | | |
|---|---|---|---|---|---|
| **1** | Net income (loss) per books . . . . | 75,133 | **6** | Income recorded on books this year not included on Schedule K, lines 1 through 11 (itemize): | |
| **2** | Income included on Schedule K, lines 1, 2, 3c, 5, 6a, 7, 8, 9a, 10, and 11, not recorded on books this year (itemize): _____ | | **a** | Tax-exempt interest $ _____ | |
| **3** | Guaranteed payments (other than health insurance) . . . . . . . . . | 196,000 | **7** | Deductions included on Schedule K, lines 1 through 13d, and 21, not charged against book income this year (itemize): | |
| **4** | Expenses recorded on books this year not included on Schedule K, lines 1 through 13d, and 21 (itemize): | | **a** | Depreciation $ _____ | |
| **a** | Depreciation $ _____ | | | | |
| **b** | Travel and entertainment $  6,173 | 6,173 | **8** | Add lines 6 and 7 . . . . . . . . | |
| **5** | Add lines 1 through 4 . . . . . | 277,306 | **9** | Income (loss) (Analysis of Net Income (Loss), line 1). Subtract line 8 from line 5 | 277,306 |

## Schedule M-2   Analysis of Partners' Capital Accounts

| | | | | | |
|---|---|---|---|---|---|
| **1** | Balance at beginning of year . . . | 230,101 | **6** | Distributions: **a** Cash . . . . . . | 100,000 |
| **2** | Capital contributed: **a** Cash . . . | | | **b** Property . . . . . | |
| | **b** Property . . | | **7** | Other decreases (itemize): _____ | |
| **3** | Net income (loss) (see instructions) . | 75,133 | | | |
| **4** | Other increases (itemize): _____ | | **8** | Add lines 6 and 7 . . . . . . . . | 100,000 |
| **5** | Add lines 1 through 4 . . . . . . | 305,234 | **9** | Balance at end of year. Subtract line 8 from line 5 | 205,234 |

Form **1065** (2021)

**EXHIBIT 14-4**

651121

| | |
|---|---|
| ☐ Final K-1    ☐ Amended K-1 | OMB No. 1545-0123 |

**Schedule K-1**
**(Form 1065)**

2021

Department of the Treasury
Internal Revenue Service

For calendar year 2021, or tax year

beginning  /  / 2021   ending  /  /

**Partner's Share of Income, Deductions, Credits, etc.**   ► See back of form and separate instructions.

### Part I   Information About the Partnership

**A**   Partnership's employer identification number
92-1234567

**B**   Partnership's name, address, city, state, and ZIP code

Shafer and Jones Consulting, LLC
1842 Jones Business Center
Anywhere, NC  27858

**C**   IRS center where partnership filed return ► Kansas City, MO

**D**   ☐ Check if this is a publicly traded partnership (PTP)

### Part II   Information About the Partner

**E**   Partner's SSN or TIN (Do not use TIN of a disregarded entity. See instructions.)
412-34-5671

**F**   Name, address, city, state, and ZIP code for partner entered in E. See instructions.

Robert B. Jones
543 Bates Road
Anywhere, NC  27858

**G**   ☒ General partner or LLC member-manager   ☐ Limited partner or other LLC member

**H1**   ☒ Domestic partner   ☐ Foreign partner

**H2**   ☐ If the partner is a disregarded entity (DE), enter the partner's:
TIN _____   Name _____

**I1**   What type of entity is this partner?  Individual

**I2**   If this partner is a retirement plan (IRA/SEP/Keogh/etc.), check here ► ☐

**J**   Partner's share of profit, loss, and capital (see instructions):

| | Beginning | Ending |
|---|---|---|
| Profit | % | 40 % |
| Loss | % | 40 % |
| Capital | % | 40 % |

Check if decrease is due to sale or exchange of partnership interest . ► ☐

**K**   Partner's share of liabilities:

| | Beginning | Ending |
|---|---|---|
| Nonrecourse    . . | $ | $ |
| Qualified nonrecourse financing   . . . | $ | $ |
| Recourse   . . . | $ | $ 91,333 |

Check this box if Item K includes liability amounts from lower tier partnerships ► ☐

**L**   **Partner's Capital Account Analysis**

| | |
|---|---|
| **Beginning capital account** . . . $ | 92,040 |
| Capital contributed during the year . . $ | |
| Current year net income (loss) . . . $ | 30,053 |
| Other increase (decrease) (attach explanation) $ | |
| Withdrawals and distributions . . . $ ( | 40,000 ) |
| **Ending capital account** . . . . $ | 82,094 |

**M**   Did the partner contribute property with a built-in gain (loss)?
☐ Yes   ☒ No   If "Yes," attach statement. See instructions.

**N**   **Partner's Share of Net Unrecognized Section 704(c) Gain or (Loss)**
Beginning . . . . . . . . . $ _____
Ending . . . . . . . . . $ _____

### Part III   Partner's Share of Current Year Income, Deductions, Credits, and Other Items

| | | | | |
|---|---|---|---|---|
| 1 | Ordinary business income (loss)  38,310 | 14 | Self-employment earnings (loss)  A  132,310 |
| 2 | Net rental real estate income (loss) | | |
| 3 | Other net rental income (loss) | 15 | Credits |
| 4a | Guaranteed payments for services  96,000 | | |
| 4b | Guaranteed payments for capital | 16 | Schedule K-3 is attached if checked . . . . ► ☐ |
| 4c | Total guaranteed payments  96,000 | 17 | Alternative minimum tax (AMT) items |
| 5 | Interest income  492 | | |
| 6a | Ordinary dividends  1,294 | | |
| 6b | Qualified dividends  1,294 | 18 | Tax-exempt income and nondeductible expenses |
| 6c | Dividend equivalents | C | 2,469 |
| 7 | Royalties | | |
| 8 | Net short-term capital gain (loss) | | |
| 9a | Net long-term capital gain (loss)  (4,974) | 19 | Distributions  A  40,000 |
| 9b | Collectibles (28%) gain (loss) | | |
| 9c | Unrecaptured section 1250 gain | 20 | Other information |
| 10 | Net section 1231 gain (loss) | | |
| 11 | Other income (loss) | | |
| 12 | Section 179 deduction  2,000 | 21 | Foreign taxes paid or accrued |
| 13 | Other deductions  A  600 | | |
| 22 ☐ | More than one activity for at-risk purposes* | | |
| 23 ☐ | More than one activity for passive activity purposes* | | |

*See attached statement for additional information.

For IRS Use Only

For Paperwork Reduction Act Notice, see the Instructions for Form 1065.   www.irs.gov/Form1065   Cat. No. 11394R   **Schedule K-1 (Form 1065) 2021**

Source: U.S. Department of the Treasury, Internal Revenue Service, Schedule K-1 (Form 1065). Washington, DC: 2021.

*(continued)*

**EXHIBIT 14-4** *(concluded)*

651121

| | |
|---|---|
| **Schedule K-1 (Form 1065)** | **2021** |

☐ Final K-1   ☐ Amended K-1   OMB No. 1545-0123

Department of the Treasury
Internal Revenue Service

For calendar year 2021, or tax year

beginning ___ / ___ / 2021   ending ___ / ___ / ___

**Partner's Share of Income, Deductions, Credits, etc.**   ► See back of form and separate instructions.

*DRAFT AS OF August 6, 2021 DO NOT FILE*

### Part I   Information About the Partnership

**A** Partnership's employer identification number
92-1234567

**B** Partnership's name, address, city, state, and ZIP code

Shafer and Jones Consulting, LLC
1842 Jones Business Center
Anywhere, NC 27858

**C** IRS center where partnership filed return ► Kansas City, MO

**D** ☐ Check if this is a publicly traded partnership (PTP)

### Part II   Information About the Partner

**E** Partner's SSN or TIN (Do not use TIN of a disregarded entity. See instructions.)
412-34-5670

**F** Name, address, city, state, and ZIP code for partner entered in E. See instructions.

David A. Shafer
103 Flower Road
Anywhere, NC 27858

**G** ☒ General partner or LLC member-manager   ☐ Limited partner or other LLC member

**H1** ☒ Domestic partner   ☐ Foreign partner

**H2** ☐ If the partner is a disregarded entity (DE), enter the partner's:
TIN _____  Name _____

**I1** What type of entity is this partner?  Individual

**I2** If this partner is a retirement plan (IRA/SEP/Keogh/etc.), check here ► ☐

**J** Partner's share of profit, loss, and capital (see instructions):

| | Beginning | Ending |
|---|---|---|
| Profit | % | 60 % |
| Loss | % | 60 % |
| Capital | % | 60 % |

Check if decrease is due to sale or exchange of partnership interest ► ☐

**K** Partner's share of liabilities:

| | Beginning | Ending |
|---|---|---|
| Nonrecourse | $ | $ |
| Qualified nonrecourse financing | $ | $ |
| Recourse | $ | $ 137,000 |

Check this box if Item K includes liability amounts from lower tier partnerships ► ☐

**L** **Partner's Capital Account Analysis**

| | |
|---|---|
| Beginning capital account | $ 138,061 |
| Capital contributed during the year | $ |
| Current year net income (loss) | $ 45,080 |
| Other increase (decrease) (attach explanation) | $ |
| Withdrawals and distributions | $ ( 60,000 ) |
| Ending capital account | $ 123,140 |

**M** Did the partner contribute property with a built-in gain (loss)?
☐ Yes   ☒ No   If "Yes," attach statement. See instructions.

**N** Partner's Share of Net Unrecognized Section 704(c) Gain or (Loss)
Beginning . . . . . $ _____
Ending . . . . . $ _____

### Part III   Partner's Share of Current Year Income, Deductions, Credits, and Other Items

| # | Item | Amount | # | Item | Amount |
|---|---|---|---|---|---|
| 1 | Ordinary business income (loss) | 57,466 | 14 | Self-employment earnings (loss) | |
| | | | A | | 154,466 |
| 2 | Net rental real estate income (loss) | | | | |
| 3 | Other net rental income (loss) | | 15 | Credits | |
| 4a | Guaranteed payments for services | 100,000 | | | |
| 4b | Guaranteed payments for capital | | 16 | Schedule K-3 is attached if checked . . . . . ► ☐ | |
| 4c | Total guaranteed payments | 100,000 | 17 | Alternative minimum tax (AMT) items | |
| 5 | Interest income | 739 | | | |
| 6a | Ordinary dividends | 1,940 | | | |
| 6b | Qualified dividends | 1,940 | 18 | Tax-exempt income and nondeductible expenses | |
| 6c | Dividend equivalents | | C | | 3,704 |
| 7 | Royalties | | | | |
| 8 | Net short-term capital gain (loss) | | | | |
| 9a | Net long-term capital gain (loss) | (7,461) | 19 | Distributions | |
| | | | A | | 60,000 |
| 9b | Collectibles (28%) gain (loss) | | 20 | Other information | |
| 9c | Unrecaptured section 1250 gain | | | | |
| 10 | Net section 1231 gain (loss) | | | | |
| 11 | Other income (loss) | | | | |
| 12 | Section 179 deduction | 3,000 | 21 | Foreign taxes paid or accrued | |
| 13 | Other deductions | | | | |
| A | | 900 | | | |

22 ☐ More than one activity for at-risk purposes*
23 ☐ More than one activity for passive activity purposes*

*See attached statement for additional information.

*For IRS Use Only*

## Summary

| | |
|---|---|
| **LO 14-1:** Explain the rules dealing with the formation of a partnership. | <ul><li>Generally, there is no gain or loss on formation.</li><li>Basis determination is very important.</li><li>*Outside basis* is the tax basis of the partnership interest to the partner.</li><li>*Inside basis* is the partner's share of the basis of partnership assets.</li><li>The partnership holding period carries over from the contributing partner.</li><li>The FMV of services is income to the contributing partner.</li><li>Property contributed with liabilities may trigger a gain to the contributing partner.</li></ul> |
| **LO 14-2:** Be able to report partnership ordinary income or loss. | <ul><li>The partnership files an annual information return, Form 1065.</li><li>Partnership income is separated into ordinary income or loss and separately stated items.</li><li>Income or loss is reported to partners on Schedule K-1.</li><li>Ordinary income is calculated as for a Schedule C business.</li><li>Guaranteed payments are an expense to the partnership.</li><li>The § 179 depreciation expense deduction must be separately stated.</li><li>Partner health insurance premiums are treated as a guaranteed payment.</li></ul> |
| **LO 14-3:** Determine separately stated items. | <ul><li>Separately stated items are income or expense items that may be treated differently at the partner level.</li><li>Examples of separately stated items include interest, capital gains, charitable contributions, and self-employment income.</li></ul> |
| **LO 14-4:** Calculate partner basis. | <ul><li>In general, partner basis is equal to the basis of property contributed, plus or minus income or loss, plus or minus separately stated items, plus partner share of liabilities.</li></ul> |
| **LO 14-5:** Apply the rules for partnership distributions. | <ul><li>In general, no gain or loss is recorded on a nonliquidating distribution.</li><li>Distributions reduce basis.</li><li>Partner basis of property received generally equals the partnership basis.</li></ul> |
| **LO 14-6:** Correctly report partnership liquidations and dispositions. | <ul><li>Generally no gain or loss occurs on partnership liquidation.</li><li>Exceptions exist if amount in liquidation is less than basis and the distribution is only cash, receivables, or inventory.</li><li>Sale of partnership interest is sale of a capital asset.</li><li>If a partnership holds appreciated inventory or accounts receivable, part of the gain may be ordinary.</li></ul> |

## *EA Fast Fact*

ADMITTED TO PRACTICE BEFORE THE IRS **ENROLLED AGENT**

What kind of career opportunities available to Enrolled Agents? Here are but a few:

- Private practice—full or part time
- Small, medium, and large public accounting firms
- Law Firms
- Corporate Accounting Departments
- Investment Firms
- Banks
- IRS State Departments of Revenue

### IMPORTANT

You are eligible to receive absolutely free, the Surgent Enrolled Agent review program for Part I of the EA exam as a result of purchasing this text. To activate your free access, go to https://Surgent.com/McGrawHill/EA.

# Discussion Questions Mc Graw Hill **connect**

All applicable discussion questions are available with *Connect*©

LO 14-1    1. Discuss the formation of a partnership. Is any gain or loss recognized? Explain.

LO 14-1    2. What entity forms are considered partnerships for federal income tax purposes?

LO 14-1    3. How do taxation for the corporate form and taxation for the partnership form differ?

LO 14-1    4. What is the concept of *basis?* In your discussion, differentiate between outside basis and inside basis.

LO 14-1    5. Elaborate on the term *basis-in, basis-out.* What does that phrase mean in the context of a partnership formation?

LO 14-1    6. How can two partners, each with a 50% interest in a partnership, have different amounts of outside basis at the formation of a partnership? Shouldn't the two partners contribute the same amount to have the same interest?

LO 14-1    7. When a partnership receives an asset from a partner, does the partnership ever recognize a gain? What is the basis of the asset in the hands of the partnership after contribution?

LO 14-1    8. Discuss the concept of *steps into the shoes.* Does this concept pertain to the partnership, the partners, or both?

LO 14-2    9. Why would smaller partnerships (and other businesses for that matter) use only the tax basis of accounting, which does not follow GAAP?

LO 14-2    10. How is depreciation calculated by the partnership when a partner contributes a business asset?

_____

_____

_____

LO 14-2    11. Discuss the concepts of *ordinary income* and *separately stated items* concerning partnerships. When must a partnership item of income or loss be separately stated, and why?

_____

_____

_____

LO 14-2    12. Can a partner have a salary from a partnership? Why? What is a *guaranteed payment?*

_____

_____

_____

LO 14-2    13. Are guaranteed payments treated as ordinary items or as separately stated items?

_____

_____

_____

LO 14-2    14. Is the § 179 expense deduction allowed for partnerships? If so, is § 179 an ordinary income item or a separately stated item? Why?

_____

_____

_____

LO 14-3    15. If a partner owns a 20% interest, does that necessarily mean that the partner will receive 20% of the net income from the partnership? Explain.

_____

_____

_____

LO 14-3    16. Is partnership income considered self-employment income? If so, how is it calculated?

_____

_____

_____

LO 14-3    17. Why must some income and gain items be separately stated in a partnership?

_____

_____

_____

LO 14-4    18. Explain why nontaxable income and nondeductible expenses increase or reduce outside basis.

_____

_____

_____

LO 14-4    19. When is it mandatory that a partner calculate their partner interest basis (outside basis)? What items affect the outside basis of a partner?

_____

_____

_____

LO 14-4  20. How does a partner's share of partnership liabilities affect their outside basis?

_____

_____

_____

LO 14-5  21. The general rule is that partners do not recognize any gain when they receive a distribution. In what circumstances might a partner recognize a gain on a current distribution?

_____

_____

_____

LO 14-5  22. Define *precontribution gain*. What causes a partner to recognize it?

_____

_____

_____

LO 14-5  23. Describe the rules concerning the basis of property distributed to a partner. How does the concept of *basis-in, basis-out* apply to partnership distributions?

_____

_____

_____

LO 14-6  24. How can a partnership interest be disposed of? Which disposal method is more likely to produce a gain or loss? How is the gain or loss calculated?

_____

_____

_____

LO 14-6  25. How is the outside basis of a partner allocated to assets in a liquidation of the partnership interest? Include in your answer the effects of distributing cash, ordinary assets, § 1231 assets, and capital assets.

_____

_____

_____

## Multiple-Choice Questions  Mc Graw Hill **connect**

All applicable multiple-choice questions are available with **Connect**©

LO 14-1  26. Carmin performs services in exchange for a 25% interest in Real Estate Rental Partnership. The services were worth $15,000. The tax implications to Carmin are:

   *a.* No taxable income and a partnership interest with a basis of $0.

   *b.* No taxable income and a partnership interest with a basis of $15,000.

   *c.* $15,000 of taxable income and a partnership interest with a basis of $0.

   *d.* $15,000 of taxable income and a partnership interest with a basis of $15,000.

LO 14-1  27. Billy contributes land with an FMV of $7,000 and a basis of $3,000 to ABCD Partnership in return for a 5% partnership interest in the partnership. Billy's basis in the partnership:

   *a.* Is $0.

   *b.* Is $3,000.

   *c.* Is $7,000.

   *d.* Cannot be determined.

**LO 14-1**   28. Billy contributes land with an FMV of $7,000 and a basis of $3,000 to ABCD Partnership in return for a 5% partnership interest in the partnership. ABCD's basis in the land:

    *a.* Is $0.

    *b.* Is $3,000.

    *c.* Is $7,000.

    *d.* Cannot be determined.

**LO 14-1**   29. Jake has a Schedule C (that reports on the cash basis of accounting) with the following assets:

| | Basis | FMV |
|---|---|---|
| Cash | $ 4,500 | $ 4,500 |
| Accounts receivable (A/R) | –0– | 10,000 |
| Building | 95,000 | 155,000 |

Jake contributes these assets to form AJ Partnership and receives a 50% interest. His basis in the partnership interest is:

    *a.* $0.

    *b.* $99,500.

    *c.* $159,500.

    *d.* $169,500.

**LO 14-1**   30. Jake has a Schedule C with the following assets:

| | Basis | FMV |
|---|---|---|
| Cash | $ 4,500 | $ 4,500 |
| Accounts receivable (A/R) | –0– | 10,000 |
| Building | 95,000 | 155,000 |

Jake contributes these assets to form AJ Partnership and receives a 50% interest. AJ's basis in the assets is:

    *a.* Cash $4,500; A/R $0; building $155,000.

    *b.* Cash $4,500; A/R $10,000; building $155,000.

    *c.* Cash $4,500; A/R $0; building $95,000.

    *d.* Cash $4,500; A/R $10,000; building $95,000.

**LO 14-1**   31. Allie contributed the following business assets to ASW Partnership on August 1, 2021:

| | Basis | FMV | Date Purchased by Allie |
|---|---|---|---|
| Building | $175,000 | $300,000 | 07/01/08 |
| Inventory | 50,000 | 100,000 | 05/08/18 |

What is the holding period for the building and the inventory to ASW Partnership?

    *a.* Building—long-term capital or § 1231 asset.

    *b.* Building—short-term ordinary asset.

    *c.* Inventory—short-term ordinary asset.

    *d.* Both *a* and *c*.

**LO 14-1**   32. Sofia contributed the following business assets to S&S Partnership on March 3, 2021:

|  | Basis | FMV | Date Purchased by Shelly |
|---|---|---|---|
| Equipment | $75,000 | $ 45,000 | 07/01/20 |
| Accounts receivable | –0– | 100,000 | Various |

What is the basis in the equipment and the accounts receivable to S&S?

a. Equipment $0; accounts receivable $0.

b. Equipment $75,000; accounts receivable $0.

c. Equipment $45,000; accounts receivable $0.

d. Equipment $45,000; accounts receivable $100,000.

**LO 14-2**   33. Which of the following is considered when calculating ordinary income for a partnership?

a. Dividend income.

b. § 179 expense.

c. Guaranteed payments to partners.

d. Capital gains and losses.

**LO 14-3**   34. Styron is a partner in Styron, Lee, & Jane Partnership. Styron owned 25% from January 1, 2021, to June 30, 2021, when he bought Lee's 25% interest. He owned 50% for the rest of the year. The partnership had ordinary income of $88,000 and $12,000 in long-term capital gains. Barring any special allocations in a partnership agreement, Styron's share of ordinary income for the year is:

a. $11,000.

b. $33,000.

c. $88,000.

d. $100,000.

**LO 14-3**   35. All of the following are considered separately stated items to a partnership *except*

a. Charitable contributions.

b. § 179 expense.

c. Depreciation.

d. Capital gains and losses.

**LO 14-3**   36. Which of the following items from a partnership go into the calculation of a partner's self-employment income?

a. Rental income.

b. Dividend income.

c. Interest income.

d. § 179 expense.

**LO 14-3**   37. A partner's share of ordinary income or loss and separately stated items is reported to the partner via what form?

a. Form 1065.

b. Form 1040, Schedule SE.

c. Form 1065, Schedule K-1.

d. Form 1065, Schedule D.

**LO 14-3** 38. Retish is a 10% partner in a partnership. The partnership pays Retish a guaranteed payment of $45,000 per year. If the partnership's ordinary income is $38,000 before considering the guaranteed payment, the partnership will report ordinary income of how much?

    *a.* ($7,000).

    *b.* $ 0.

    *c.* $33,500.

    *d.* $38,000.

**LO 14-4** 39. The calculation of a partner's basis in their partnership interest is mandatory in which of the following situations?

    *a.* In a partnership loss year.

    *b.* At the liquidation or disposition of a partner's interest.

    *c.* When the partner receives nonliquidating distributions.

    *d.* All of the above.

**LO 14-4** 40. Maggie and Davis are equal partners in a partnership. When forming the partnership, Davis contributed a building with an FMV of $550,000 and a basis of $175,000. During the first year of operations, the partnership earned $170,000 in ordinary income and tax-exempt interest of $2,500. Assuming no special allocations, Davis's basis in the partnership interest at the end of the year is:

    *a.* $175,000.

    *b.* $261,250.

    *c.* $345,600.

    *d.* $347,500.

**LO 14-4** 41. All of the following items usually affect the basis of a partnership interest *except:*

    *a.* Cash or property contributed.

    *b.* Guaranteed payments.

    *c.* Partnership income or loss items.

    *d.* A partner's share of recourse liabilities.

**LO 14-4** 42. Partner Beth has a basis of $10,000 in a partnership at the beginning of the year. She receives $6,000 in cash distributions, her distributive share of income is $5,000, and she receives a land distribution with a basis of $8,000 (FMV $20,000). What is Beth's partnership interest basis at the end of the year?

    *a.* $0.

    *b.* $1,000.

    *c.* $9,000.

    *d.* $10,000.

**LO 14-5** 43. Molly, a 30% partner in XYZ Partnership, has a basis of $55,000 in her partnership interest. She receives a cash distribution of $54,000 at year-end. The distribution has what tax effect on Molly?

    *a.* No gain or loss is recognized, and she has a $55,000 basis in her partnership interest.

    *b.* No gain or loss is recognized, and she has a $1,000 basis in her partnership interest.

    *c.* She has a recognized gain of $37,500 and a basis of $0 in her partnership interest.

    *d.* She has a recognized gain of $55,000 and a basis of $0 in her partnership interest.

LO 14-5   44. A partner recognizes a gain on a current distribution in which of the following situations?

  *a.* When a partner receives a property distribution with a basis in excess of their basis.

  *b.* When money or marketable securities are distributed in excess of the partner's basis.

  *c.* When the current distribution triggers a precontribution gain.

  *d.* Both *b* and *c*.

LO 14-5   45. Katlin contributes land to a partnership with a basis of $44,000 and an FMV of $56,000 in 2019. In 2021, when the FMV of the land is $58,000, the partnership distributes the land to Bailey, another partner. Which of the following is true?

  *a.* Katlin recognizes no gain or loss.

  *b.* Bailey recognizes a gain of $14,000.

  *c.* Katlin recognizes a gain of $12,000.

  *d.* Bailey has a basis of $58,000 in the land.

LO 14-6   46. All of the following statements are correct concerning liquidating distributions of a partnership *except:*

  *a.* A loss can never be recognized.

  *b.* A distribution of money in excess of basis causes a gain to be recognized.

  *c.* Basis in a property distribution is allocated essentially the same as in a nonliquidating distribution.

  *d.* Generally no gain or loss is recognized when the liquidating distribution consists only of property.

LO 14-6   47. On November 1, Ashton sells her interest in XYZ Partnership to Skylar for $200,000 cash and a release of liability of $30,000. Ashton's basis at the beginning of the year was $125,000 (including the $30,000 of liability). Ashton's share of income through November 1 was $45,000, and she received a $15,000 cash distribution earlier in the year. What are the tax consequences to Ashton of the sale of her partnership interest?

  *a.* $0 tax effect.

  *b.* $45,000 capital gain.

  *c.* $75,000 capital gain.

  *d.* $105,000 capital gain.

## Problems  Mc Graw Hill **connect**

All applicable problems are available with **Connect**©

LO 14-1   48. Denise contributes the following assets to a partnership in exchange for a 25% partnership interest:

|  | FMV | Basis |
| --- | --- | --- |
| Cash | $20,000 | $20,000 |
| Office equipment | 12,000 | 5,000 |
| Auto | 20,000 | 6,000 |

What is Denise's beginning basis in her partnership interest?

**LO 14-1**   49. On June 1 of the current year, Patti contributes equipment with a $45,000 basis and a $35,000 FMV in exchange for a partnership interest. She purchased the equipment three years ago.

  *a.* What is Patti's basis in her partnership interest?

  *b.* What is Patti's holding period of her partnership interest?

  *c.* What is the basis of the equipment in the hands of the partnership?

  *d.* What is the holding period of the equipment in the hands of the partnership?

  *e.* How will the partnership depreciate the equipment in the year of contribution?

  _____

  _____

  _____

  _____

  _____

  _____

**LO 14-1, 14-4**   50. Luis, Gabi, and Katherine form a partnership. Luis and Gabi give equipment and a building, respectively. Katherine agrees to perform all of the accounting and office work in exchange for a 10% interest.

| | FMV | Basis | Partnership Percentage |
|---|---|---|---|
| Luis's equipment | $100,000 | $10,000 | 45% |
| Gabi's building | 100,000 | 45,000 | 45 |
| Katherine's services | –0– | –0– | 10 |

  *a.* Do any of the partners recognize any gain? If so, how much and why?

  *b.* What is the basis for each partner in their partnership interest?

  *c.* What is the basis to the partnership of each asset?

  _____

  _____

  _____

  _____

  _____

  _____

**LO 14-1, 14-4**   51. Moe, Johnny, and Raymond form a partnership and contribute the following assets:

| | FMV | Basis | Partnership Percentage |
|---|---|---|---|
| Moe's inventory | $ 50,000 | $10,000 | 33.3% |
| Johnny's building | 110,000 | 80,000 | 33.3 |
| Raymond's cash | 50,000 | 50,000 | 33.3 |

  Johnny's building has a mortgage of $60,000, which the partnership assumes.

  *a.* Do any of the partners recognize any gain? If so, how much and why?

  *b.* What is the basis for each partner in his partnership interest?

  *c.* What is the basis to the partnership in each asset?

  *d.* How would your answer change with respect to Johnny if the basis in the building were $45,000?

  _____

  _____

  _____

  _____

  _____

  _____

LO 14-2    52. Barry and Kurt are equal partners in the BK Partnership. Barry receives a guaranteed payment of $55,000. In addition to the guaranteed payment, Barry withdraws $10,000 from the partnership. The partnership has $24,000 in ordinary income during the year.

    *a.* How much income must Barry report from BK Partnership?

    *b.* What is the effect of the distribution on Barry's partnership basis?

_____

_____

_____

_____

_____

_____

LO 14-2    53. Kerry is a partner in the Kerry, Davis, Smith, & Jones Partnership. Kerry owned 25% from January 1, 2021 to June 30, 2021, when she bought Jones's 25% interest. She owned 50% for the rest of the year. The partnership had ordinary income of $146,000 and $15,000 in long-term capital gains. Barring any special allocations in a partnership agreement, what is Kerry's share of income?

_____

_____

_____

_____

_____

_____

LO 14-2, 14-3    54. Wade has a beginning basis in a partnership of $23,000. His share of income and expense from the partnership consists of the following amounts:

| | |
|---|---:|
| Ordinary income | $43,000 |
| Guaranteed payment | 12,000 |
| Long-term capital gain | 15,500 |
| § 1231 gain | 4,300 |
| Charitable contributions | 2,000 |
| § 179 expense | 18,000 |
| Cash distribution | 6,000 |

    *a.* What is Wade's self-employment income?

    *b.* Calculate Wade's basis at the end of the year.

_____

_____

_____

_____

_____

_____

LO 14-2, 14-3    55. Bryan and Eva are equal partners in BE Partnership. The partnership reports the following items of income and expense:

| | |
|---|---:|
| Ordinary income from operations | $13,000 |
| Interest income | 5,000 |
| Long-term capital gains | 23,000 |
| § 179 expense | 55,000 |
| Charitable contributions | 3,000 |

a. Which of these items are considered separately stated items? On what form will these items be reported to the partners?

b. Where will these amounts be reported by the partners?

_____

_____

_____

_____

_____

_____

**LO 14-4, 14-5** 56. Kim has a basis in her partnership interest of $12,000 when she receives a distribution from the partnership of $6,000 cash and equipment with a basis of $8,000 ($12,000 FMV).

a. How much gain or loss must Kim recognize on the distribution?

b. What is Kim's ending partnership basis?

c. What is Kim's basis in the equipment?

_____

_____

_____

_____

_____

_____

**LO 14-4, 14-5** 57. Zach contributed land with an FMV of $25,000 and a basis of $14,000 to a partnership on April 5, 2015. On June 6, 2021, the partnership distributed the land to Art, a partner in the same partnership. At distribution, the land had an FMV of $29,000.

a. What is the effect of the distribution to Zach, if any?

b. What is the effect of the distribution to Art?

_____

_____

_____

_____

_____

_____

**LO 14-5** 58. Roberto has a basis of $6,000 in a partnership at the beginning of the year. He receives $7,000 in cash distributions, his distributive share of income is $3,500, and he receives a land distribution with a basis of $6,000 (FMV $12,000).

a. Is Roberto required to recognize any gain? If so, how much is the gain?

b. What is Roberto's basis in the land?

c. What is Roberto's ending basis in his partnership interest?

_____

_____

_____

_____

_____

_____

LO 14-5   59. Rhonda has a basis of $8,000 in a partnership at the beginning of the year. She receives $12,000 in cash distributions, and her distributive share of income is $2,500.

     *a.* Is Rhonda required to recognize any gain? If so, how much?

     *b.* What is Rhonda's ending basis in her partnership interest?

_____

_____

_____

_____

_____

_____

LO 14-6   60. Rebecca has a $40,000 basis in her partnership interest when she receives liquidating distributions from the partnership. She receives cash of $24,000 and equipment with a $12,000 basis to the partnership. What are the tax consequences of the liquidating distributions to Rebecca?

_____

_____

_____

_____

_____

_____

LO 14-6   61. Calvin purchased a 40% partnership interest for $43,000 in February 2019. His share of partnership income in 2019 was $22,000, in 2020 was $25,000, and in 2021 was $12,000. He made no additional contributions to or withdrawals from the partnership. On December 18, 2021, Calvin sold his partnership interest for $103,000. What is his gain or loss on the sale of his partnership interest?

_____

_____

_____

_____

_____

_____

## Tax Return Problems

All applicable tax return problems are available with **Connect**©

**Tax Return Problem 1**   Paul and Wayne equally own PW Partnership. Paul's basis was $30,000 and Wayne's basis was $22,000 at the beginning of the year. PW Partnership had the following income and expense items:

| | |
|---|---:|
| Sales | $330,000 |
| Cost of goods sold | 220,000 |
| Guaranteed payment to Paul | 40,000 |
| Rent expense | 24,000 |
| Depreciation | 33,000 |
| Interest expense | 4,000 |
| Tax-exempt income | 3,000 |
| Health insurance premiums for Paul | 3,600 |
| Health insurance premiums for Wayne | 3,600 |

> *a.* Prepare pages 1 and 4 of Form 1065—ordinary income and separately stated items for the partnership.
>
> *b.* Calculate Paul's basis in his partnership interest.
>
> *c.* Calculate Wayne's basis in his partnership interest.

**Tax Return Problem 2**

Phil Williams and Liz Johnson are 60% and 40% partners, respectively, in Williams & Johnson Partnership. Their beginning basis is $33,000 for Phil and $31,000 for Liz. The partnership had the following activity during the year:

| | |
|---|---:|
| Income | $336,123 |
| Interest income | 1,259 |
| Dividend income (qualified) | 4,586 |
| Long-term capital gains | 13,458 |
| Total revenue | $355,426 |
| | |
| Expenses | |
| Salaries and wages (nonpartners) | $ 47,000 |
| Guaranteed payments | |
| Williams | 75,000 |
| Johnson | 50,000 |
| Depreciation (MACRS—includes $9,000 § 179 expense) | 41,888 |
| Interest expense | 5,220 |
| Taxes and licenses | 15,548 |
| Meals (100%) | 15,257 |
| Auto | 5,254 |
| Insurance (nonpartner health) | 6,000 |
| Accounting and legal | 2,800 |
| Repairs | 1,200 |
| Charitable contributions | 2,500 |
| Payroll penalties | 500 |
| Total expenses | $268,167 |
| Net income | $ 87,259 |

> *a.* Calculate the ordinary income for the partnership and prepare page 1 of Form 1065.
>
> *b.* Prepare page 4 of Form 1065.
>
> *c.* What is the ending basis for Phil Williams?
>
> *d.* What is the ending basis for Liz Johnson?

We have provided selected filled-in source documents that are available in *Connect.*

# Chapter **Fifteen**

# Corporate Taxation

One legal form under which a business can operate is the corporate form. From a tax perspective, a corporation can be a C corporation or an S corporation, both designations derived from the applicable Internal Revenue Code (IRC) subsection. In this chapter, we introduce the tax rules associated with both corporate forms.

### Learning Objectives

When you complete this chapter, you should understand the following learning objectives (LO):

**LO 15-1** Describe corporate formation and filing requirements.

**LO 15-2** Calculate corporate and shareholder basis.

**LO 15-3** Determine corporate taxable income and tax liability.

**LO 15-4** Explain the tax rules for transactions with shareholders.

**LO 15-5** Prepare Schedules L, M-1, and M-3.

**LO 15-6** Discuss other corporate issues.

**LO 15-7** Know the rules for tax treatment of Subchapter S corporations.

## INTRODUCTION

Businesses can choose to operate using a number of different legal structures, the most common of which are sole proprietorships, partnerships, regular corporations (called *C corporations*), and *Subchapter S corporations*. The *C* and *S* designations come from Subchapter C and Subchapter S of the Internal Revenue Code, where much of the tax law pertaining to these two entities is found.

The tax treatment of each of these structures differs, sometimes markedly so. We discussed sole proprietorships in Chapter 6 and partnerships in Chapter 14. In this chapter, we discuss C corporations and S corporations. In short, C corporations are taxed as a separate legal entity, and S corporations are taxed in a manner similar to a partnership.

## CORPORATE FORMATION AND FILING REQUIREMENTS
## LO 15-1

### Organization

An individual or group of individuals can choose to operate a business as a *corporation,* which is a legal entity. Although rules vary slightly from state to state, the general procedure is as follows. First, the individual(s) or other entities that form the corporation (called the *incorporators*) file articles of incorporation and bylaws with the appropriate agency in the state in which they want to become incorporated. Generally, the appropriate state agency is the Secretary of

State, the Corporation Commission, or something similar. The state agency then issues to the corporation a charter or comparable document indicating that the corporate entity exists and that it can operate in accordance with its corporate documents.

After incorporation, states require corporations to file an annual report and pay a fee. This report and fee indicate to the state that the corporation remains active. When corporations decide to terminate their activities, many states require the corporation to file a notification.

Large C corporations must use the accrual basis of accounting.[1] Corporations with average annual gross receipts over the last three years of $26 million or less can use the cash basis. Corporations that maintain inventory for sale to customers must use the accrual method of accounting at least for their sales and cost of goods sold unless their average annual gross receipts over the last three years are under $26 million, in which case the corporation can use the cash method.[2] Corporations must choose their method of accounting when they file their first return. If the corporation wishes to change its method of accounting subsequent to its first year of operation, it must file for permission to make the change.

C corporations can choose an accounting period when they file their first tax return without approval of the IRS. Corporations can choose a fiscal year that ends the last day of any month of the year. Often newly formed corporations do not give much thought to an appropriate fiscal year-end. Corporations should consider a fiscal year-end that occurs during a time of the year other than their busiest time. For example, the fiscal year of many retailers ends on January 31. Disney's fiscal year-end is September 30, right after its busy summer season.

## Filing Requirements

C corporations must file an annual Form 1120 (see Exhibit 15-1).[3] Filing is required even if the corporation did not have taxable income.

The due date for C corporation tax returns depends on the fiscal year of the corporation. For corporations operating a fiscal year that ends on June 30, the return is due on September 15, which is the 15th day of the third month after year-end. A seven-month extension is permitted from that date (to April 15) for a maximum period of 9.5 months.[4]

For all other C corporations, the initial filing date is the 15th day of the fourth month after the fiscal year-end. So, for example, a calendar-year corporate return is due on April 15 and a corporation with a fiscal year that ends on February 28 is required to file by June 15. A six-month extension is allowed from the original due date (for a total of 9.5 months).

---

**CONCEPT CHECK 15-1—**

**LO 15-1**

1. A corporation can use either the cash or accrual method of accounting. True or false?
2. Corporate tax returns are due _____ if no extension is requested.
3. The tax year of a corporation must end on December 31. True or false?

---

[1] IRC § 448.

[2] Using the accrual basis for cost of goods sold suggests the corporation will also use that method for inventories. Corporations that use the accrual basis for sales and cost of goods sold and the cash basis for other items are said to be using a hybrid method of accounting.

[3] IRC § 6012(a)(2).

[4] Reg. § 1.6081-3(a)(1).

**EXHIBIT 15-1**

| Form **1120** | **U.S. Corporation Income Tax Return** | OMB No. 1545-0123 |
|---|---|---|

Form **1120**
Department of the Treasury
Internal Revenue Service

**U.S. Corporation Income Tax Return**
For calendar year 2021 or tax year beginning _____ , 2021, ending _____ , 20 ____
▶ Go to *www.irs.gov/Form1120* for instructions and the latest information.

OMB No. 1545-0123

**2021**

**A** Check if:
1a Consolidated return (attach Form 851) ☐
b Life/nonlife consolidated return . . ☐
2 Personal holding co. (attach Sch. PH) . ☐
3 Personal service corp. (see instructions) . ☐
4 Schedule M-3 attached ☐

TYPE OR PRINT

Name

Number, street, and room or suite no. If a P.O. box, see instructions.

City or town, state or province, country, and ZIP or foreign postal code

**B** Employer identification number

**C** Date incorporated

**D** Total assets (see instructions)
$

**E** Check if: **(1)** ☐ Initial return   **(2)** ☐ Final return   **(3)** ☐ Name change   **(4)** ☐ Address change

DRAFT AS OF September 29, 2021 DO NOT FILE

**Income**

| | | |
|---|---|---|
| 1a | Gross receipts or sales . . . . . . . . . . . . . . . . | **1a** |
| b | Returns and allowances . . . . . . . . . . . . . . . | **1b** |
| c | Balance. Subtract line 1b from line 1a . . . . . . . . . . . . . . | **1c** |
| 2 | Cost of goods sold (attach Form 1125-A) . . . . . . . . . . . . . | **2** |
| 3 | Gross profit. Subtract line 2 from line 1c . . . . . . . . . . . . | **3** |
| 4 | Dividends and inclusions (Schedule C, line 23) . . . . . . . . . . . | **4** |
| 5 | Interest . . . . . . . . . . . . . . . . . . . . | **5** |
| 6 | Gross rents . . . . . . . . . . . . . . . . . . . | **6** |
| 7 | Gross royalties . . . . . . . . . . . . . . . . . . | **7** |
| 8 | Capital gain net income (attach Schedule D (Form 1120)) . . . . . . . | **8** |
| 9 | Net gain or (loss) from Form 4797, Part II, line 17 (attach Form 4797) . . . . | **9** |
| 10 | Other income (see instructions—attach statement) . . . . . . . . . | **10** |
| 11 | **Total income.** Add lines 3 through 10 . . . . . . . . . . . . ▶ | **11** |

**Deductions (See instructions for limitations on deductions.)**

| | | |
|---|---|---|
| 12 | Compensation of officers (see instructions—attach Form 1125-E) . . . . ▶ | **12** |
| 13 | Salaries and wages (less employment credits) . . . . . . . . . . | **13** |
| 14 | Repairs and maintenance . . . . . . . . . . . . . . . . | **14** |
| 15 | Bad debts . . . . . . . . . . . . . . . . . . . . | **15** |
| 16 | Rents . . . . . . . . . . . . . . . . . . . . . | **16** |
| 17 | Taxes and licenses . . . . . . . . . . . . . . . . . . | **17** |
| 18 | Interest (see instructions) . . . . . . . . . . . . . . . . | **18** |
| 19 | Charitable contributions . . . . . . . . . . . . . . . . | **19** |
| 20 | Depreciation from Form 4562 not claimed on Form 1125-A or elsewhere on return (attach Form 4562) . . . | **20** |
| 21 | Depletion . . . . . . . . . . . . . . . . . . . . | **21** |
| 22 | Advertising . . . . . . . . . . . . . . . . . . . . | **22** |
| 23 | Pension, profit-sharing, etc., plans . . . . . . . . . . . . . | **23** |
| 24 | Employee benefit programs . . . . . . . . . . . . . . . | **24** |
| 25 | Reserved for future use . . . . . . . . . . . . . . . . | **25** |
| 26 | Other deductions (attach statement) . . . . . . . . . . . . . | **26** |
| 27 | **Total deductions.** Add lines 12 through 26 . . . . . . . . . . ▶ | **27** |
| 28 | Taxable income before net operating loss deduction and special deductions. Subtract line 27 from line 11. . | **28** |
| 29a | Net operating loss deduction (see instructions) . . . . . . . . **29a** | |
| b | Special deductions (Schedule C, line 24) . . . . . . . . . . **29b** | |
| c | Add lines 29a and 29b . . . . . . . . . . . . . . . . | **29c** |

**Tax, Refundable Credits, and Payments**

| | | |
|---|---|---|
| 30 | **Taxable income.** Subtract line 29c from line 28. See instructions . . . . . | **30** |
| 31 | Total tax (Schedule J, Part I, line 11) . . . . . . . . . . . . . | **31** |
| 32 | Reserved for future use . . . . . . . . . . . . . . . . | **32** |
| 33 | Total payments and credits (Schedule J, Part III, line 23) . . . . . . . | **33** |
| 34 | Estimated tax penalty. See instructions. Check if Form 2220 is attached . . . . ▶ ☐ | **34** |
| 35 | **Amount owed.** If line 33 is smaller than the total of lines 31 and 34, enter amount owed . | **35** |
| 36 | **Overpayment.** If line 33 is larger than the total of lines 31 and 34, enter amount overpaid . | **36** |
| 37 | Enter amount from line 36 you want: **Credited to 2022 estimated tax** ▶ _____ Refunded ▶ | **37** |

**Sign Here**

Under penalties of perjury, I declare that I have examined this return, including accompanying schedules and statements, and to the best of my knowledge and belief, it is true, correct, and complete. Declaration of preparer (other than taxpayer) is based on all information of which preparer has any knowledge.

▶ _____  _____  ▶ _____
Signature of officer   Date   Title

May the IRS discuss this return with the preparer shown below? See instructions. ☐ Yes ☐ No

**Paid Preparer Use Only**

| Print/Type preparer's name | Preparer's signature | Date | Check ☐ if self-employed | PTIN |
|---|---|---|---|---|
| Firm's name ▶ | | | Firm's EIN ▶ | |
| Firm's address ▶ | | | Phone no. | |

For Paperwork Reduction Act Notice, see separate instructions.     Cat. No. 11450Q     Form **1120** (2021)

Source: U.S. Department of the Treasury, Internal Revenue Service, Form 1120. Washington, DC: 2021.

*(continued)*

**EXHIBIT 15-1** *(continued)*

Form 1120 (2021) Page **2**

| Schedule C | Dividends, Inclusions, and Special Deductions (see instructions) | (a) Dividends and inclusions | (b) % | (c) Special deductions (a) × (b) |
|---|---|---|---|---|
| 1 | Dividends from less-than-20%-owned domestic corporations (other than debt-financed stock) | | 50 | |
| 2 | Dividends from 20%-or-more-owned domestic corporations (other than debt-financed stock) | | 65 | |
| 3 | Dividends on certain debt-financed stock of domestic and foreign corporations | | See instructions | |
| 4 | Dividends on certain preferred stock of less-than-20%-owned public utilities | | 23.3 | |
| 5 | Dividends on certain preferred stock of 20%-or-more-owned public utilities | | 26.7 | |
| 6 | Dividends from less-than-20%-owned foreign corporations and certain FSCs | | 50 | |
| 7 | Dividends from 20%-or-more-owned foreign corporations and certain FSCs | | 65 | |
| 8 | Dividends from wholly owned foreign subsidiaries | | 100 | |
| 9 | **Subtotal.** Add lines 1 through 8. See instructions for limitations | | See instructions | |
| 10 | Dividends from domestic corporations received by a small business investment company operating under the Small Business Investment Act of 1958 | | 100 | |
| 11 | Dividends from affiliated group members | | 100 | |
| 12 | Dividends from certain FSCs | | 100 | |
| 13 | Foreign-source portion of dividends received from a specified 10%-owned foreign corporation (excluding hybrid dividends) (see instructions) | | 100 | |
| 14 | Dividends from foreign corporations not included on line 3, 6, 7, 8, 11, 12, or 13 (including any hybrid dividends) | | | |
| 15 | Reserved for future use | | | |
| 16a | Subpart F inclusions derived from the sale by a controlled foreign corporation (CFC) of the stock of a lower-tier foreign corporation treated as a dividend (attach Form(s) 5471) (see instructions) | | 100 | |
| b | Subpart F inclusions derived from hybrid dividends of tiered corporations (attach Form(s) 5471) (see instructions) | | | |
| c | Other inclusions from CFCs under subpart F not included on line 16a, 16b, or 17 (attach Form(s) 5471) (see instructions) | | | |
| 17 | Global Intangible Low-Taxed Income (GILTI) (attach Form(s) 5471 and Form 8992) | | | |
| 18 | Gross-up for foreign taxes deemed paid | | | |
| 19 | IC-DISC and former DISC dividends not included on line 1, 2, or 3 | | | |
| 20 | Other dividends | | | |
| 21 | Deduction for dividends paid on certain preferred stock of public utilities | | | |
| 22 | Section 250 deduction (attach Form 8993) | | | |
| 23 | **Total dividends and inclusions.** Add column (a), lines 9 through 20. Enter here and on page 1, line 4 | | | |
| 24 | **Total special deductions.** Add column (c), lines 9 through 22. Enter here and on page 1, line 29b | | | |

Form **1120** (2021)

**EXHIBIT 15-1**   *(continued)*

Form 1120 (2021)                                                                                              Page **3**

| Schedule J | Tax Computation and Payment (see instructions) | | |
|---|---|---|---|

**Part I—Tax Computation**

| 1 | Check if the corporation is a member of a controlled group (attach Schedule O (Form 1120)). See instructions ▶ ☐ | | |
|---|---|---|---|
| 2 | Income tax. See instructions | **2** | |
| 3 | Base erosion minimum tax amount (attach Form 8991) | **3** | |
| 4 | Add lines 2 and 3 | **4** | |
| 5a | Foreign tax credit (attach Form 1118) | **5a** | |
| b | Credit from Form 8834 (see instructions) | **5b** | |
| c | General business credit (attach Form 3800) | **5c** | |
| d | Credit for prior year minimum tax (attach Form 8827) | **5d** | |
| e | Bond credits from Form 8912 | **5e** | |
| 6 | **Total credits.** Add lines 5a through 5e | **6** | |
| 7 | Subtract line 6 from line 4 | **7** | |
| 8 | Personal holding company tax (attach Schedule PH (Form 1120)) | **8** | |
| 9a | Recapture of investment credit (attach Form 4255) | **9a** | |
| b | Recapture of low-income housing credit (attach Form 8611) | **9b** | |
| c | Interest due under the look-back method—completed long-term contracts (attach Form 8697) | **9c** | |
| d | Interest due under the look-back method—income forecast method (attach Form 8866) | **9d** | |
| e | Alternative tax on qualifying shipping activities (attach Form 8902) | **9e** | |
| f | Interest/tax due under section 453A(c) and/or section 453(l) | **9f** | |
| g | Other (see instructions—attach statement) | **9g** | |
| 10 | **Total.** Add lines 9a through 9g | **10** | |
| 11 | **Total tax.** Add lines 7, 8, and 10. Enter here and on page 1, line 31 | **11** | |

**Part II—Reserved For Future Use**

| 12 | Reserved for future use | **12** | |
|---|---|---|---|

**Part III—Payments and Refundable Credits**

| 13 | 2020 overpayment credited to 2021 | **13** | |
|---|---|---|---|
| 14 | 2021 estimated tax payments | **14** | |
| 15 | 2021 refund applied for on Form 4466 | **15** ( | ) |
| 16 | Combine lines 13, 14, and 15 | **16** | |
| 17 | Tax deposited with Form 7004 | **17** | |
| 18 | Withholding (see instructions) | **18** | |
| 19 | **Total payments.** Add lines 16, 17, and 18 | **19** | |
| 20 | Refundable credits from: | | |
| a | Form 2439 | **20a** | |
| b | Form 4136 | **20b** | |
| c | Reserved for future use | **20c** | |
| d | Other (attach statement—see instructions) | **20d** | |
| 21 | **Total credits.** Add lines 20a through 20d | **21** | |
| 22 | Reserved for future use | **22** | |
| 23 | **Total payments and credits.** Add lines 19 and 21. Enter here and on page 1, line 33 | **23** | |

Form **1120** (2021)

*(continued)*

DRAFT AS OF September 29, 2021 DO NOT FILE

**EXHIBIT 15-1** *(continued)*

Form 1120 (2021)      Page **4**

| **Schedule K** | **Other Information** (see instructions) | | | Yes | No |
|---|---|---|---|---|---|

**1**   Check accounting method:   **a** ☐ Cash     **b** ☐ Accrual     **c** ☐ Other (specify) ▶ _____

**2**   See the instructions and enter the:

**a**   Business activity code no. ▶ _____

**b**   Business activity ▶ _____

**c**   Product or service ▶ _____

**3**   Is the corporation a subsidiary in an affiliated group or a parent–subsidiary controlled group? . . . . . . .

If "Yes," enter name and EIN of the parent corporation ▶ _____

**4**   At the end of the tax year:

**a**   Did any foreign or domestic corporation, partnership (including any entity treated as a partnership), trust, or tax-exempt organization own directly 20% or more, or own, directly or indirectly, 50% or more of the total voting power of all classes of the corporation's stock entitled to vote? If "Yes," complete Part I of Schedule G (Form 1120) (attach Schedule G) . . .

**b**   Did any individual or estate own directly 20% or more, or own, directly or indirectly, 50% or more of the total voting power of all classes of the corporation's stock entitled to vote? If "Yes," complete Part II of Schedule G (Form 1120), (attach Schedule G)

**5**   At the end of the tax year, did the corporation:

**a**   Own directly 20% or more, or own, directly or indirectly, 50% or more of the total voting power of all classes of stock entitled to vote of any foreign or domestic corporation not included on **Form 851,** Affiliations Schedule? For rules of constructive ownership, see instructions.

If "Yes," complete (i) through (iv) below.

| **(i)** Name of Corporation | **(ii)** Employer Identification Number (if any) | **(iii)** Country of Incorporation | **(iv)** Percentage Owned in Voting Stock |
|---|---|---|---|
| | | | |
| | | | |
| | | | |

**b**   Own directly an interest of 20% or more, or own, directly or indirectly, an interest of 50% or more in any foreign or domestic partnership (including an entity treated as a partnership) or in the beneficial interest of a trust? For rules of constructive ownership, see instructions.

If "Yes," complete (i) through (iv) below.

| **(i)** Name of Entity | **(ii)** Employer Identification Number (if any) | **(iii)** Country of Organization | **(iv)** Maximum Percentage Owned in Profit, Loss, or Capital |
|---|---|---|---|
| | | | |
| | | | |
| | | | |

**6**   During this tax year, did the corporation pay dividends (other than stock dividends and distributions in exchange for stock) in excess of the corporation's current and accumulated earnings and profits? See sections 301 and 316 . . . . . . .

If "Yes," file **Form 5452,** Corporate Report of Nondividend Distributions. See the instructions for Form 5452.

If this is a consolidated return, answer here for the parent corporation and on Form 851 for each subsidiary.

**7**   At any time during the tax year, did one foreign person own, directly or indirectly, at least 25% of the total voting power of all classes of the corporation's stock entitled to vote or at least 25% of the total value of all classes of the corporation's stock? .

For rules of attribution, see section 318. If "Yes," enter:

**(a)** Percentage owned ▶ _____ and **(b)** Owner's country ▶ _____

**(c)** The corporation may have to file **Form 5472,** Information Return of a 25% Foreign-Owned U.S. Corporation or a Foreign Corporation Engaged in a U.S. Trade or Business. Enter the number of Forms 5472 attached ▶ _____

**8**   Check this box if the corporation issued publicly offered debt instruments with original issue discount . . . . . . . ▶ ☐

If checked, the corporation may have to file **Form 8281,** Information Return for Publicly Offered Original Issue Discount Instruments.

**9**   Enter the amount of tax-exempt interest received or accrued during the tax year ▶ $ _____

**10**   Enter the number of shareholders at the end of the tax year (if 100 or fewer) ▶ _____

**11**   If the corporation has an NOL for the tax year and is electing to forego the carryback period, check here (see instructions) ▶ ☐

If the corporation is filing a consolidated return, the statement required by Regulations section 1.1502-21(b)(3) must be attached or the election will not be valid.

**12**   Enter the available NOL carryover from prior tax years (do not reduce it by any deduction reported on page 1, line 29a.) . . . . . . . . . . . . . . . . . . . . . . . . ▶ $ _____

Form **1120** (2021)

**EXHIBIT 15-1**   *(continued)*

Form 1120 (2021)                                                                                                    Page **5**

| Schedule K | Other Information *(continued from page 4)* | Yes | No |
|---|---|---|---|

**13** Are the corporation's total receipts (page 1, line 1a, plus lines 4 through 10) for the tax year **and** its total assets at the end of the tax year less than $250,000? . . . . . . . . . . . . . . . . . . . . .

If "Yes," the corporation is not required to complete Schedules L, M-1, and M-2. Instead, enter the total amount of cash distributions and the book value of property distributions (other than cash) made during the tax year ▶ $ _____

**14** Is the corporation required to file Schedule UTP (Form 1120), Uncertain Tax Position Statement? See instructions . . . .

If "Yes," complete and attach Schedule UTP.

**15a** Did the corporation make any payments in 2021 that would require it to file Form(s) 1099? . . . . . . . . . . .

**b** If "Yes," did or will the corporation file required Form(s) 1099? . . . . . . . . . . . . . . . . .

**16** During this tax year, did the corporation have an 80%-or-more change in ownership, including a change due to redemption of its own stock? . . . . . . . . . . . . . . . . . . . . . . . . . . . . . .

**17** During or subsequent to this tax year, but before the filing of this return, did the corporation dispose of more than 65% (by value) of its assets in a taxable, non-taxable, or tax deferred transaction? . . . . . . . . . . . . . . .

**18** Did the corporation receive assets in a section 351 transfer in which any of the transferred assets had a fair market basis or fair market value of more than $1 million? . . . . . . . . . . . . . . . . . . . . . .

**19** During the corporation's tax year, did the corporation make any payments that would require it to file Forms 1042 and 1042-S under chapter 3 (sections 1441 through 1464) or chapter 4 (sections 1471 through 1474) of the Code? . . . . . . .

**20** Is the corporation operating on a cooperative basis? . . . . . . . . . . . . . . . . . . . . .

**21** During the tax year, did the corporation pay or accrue any interest or royalty for which the deduction is not allowed under section 267A? See instructions . . . . . . . . . . . . . . . . . . . . . . . . . .

If "Yes," enter the total amount of the disallowed deductions ▶ $ _____

**22** Does the corporation have gross receipts of at least $500 million in any of the 3 preceding tax years? (See sections 59A(e)(2) and (3)) . . . . . . . . . . . . . . . . . . . . . . . . . . . . . . .

If "Yes," complete and attach Form 8991.

**23** Did the corporation have an election under section 163(j) for any real property trade or business or any farming business in effect during the tax year? See instructions . . . . . . . . . . . . . . . . . . . . .

**24** Does the corporation satisfy one or more of the following? See instructions . . . . . . . . . . . . . .

**a** The corporation owns a pass-through entity with current, or prior year carryover, excess business interest expense.

**b** The corporation's aggregate average annual gross receipts (determined under section 448(c)) for the 3 tax years preceding the current tax year are more than $26 million and the corporation has business interest expense.

**c** The corporation is a tax shelter and the corporation has business interest expense.

If "Yes," complete and attach Form 8990.

**25** Is the corporation attaching Form 8996 to certify as a Qualified Opportunity Fund? . . . . . . . . . . . .

If "Yes," enter amount from Form 8996, line 15 . . . . . ▶ $

**26** Since December 22, 2017, did a foreign corporation directly or indirectly acquire substantially all of the properties held directly or indirectly by the corporation, and was the ownership percentage (by vote or value) for purposes of section 7874 greater than 50% (for example, the shareholders held more than 50% of the stock of the foreign corporation)? If "Yes," list the ownership percentage by vote and by value. See instructions . . . . . . . . . . . . . . . . . . . .

Percentage: By Vote _____                         By Value _____

Form **1120** (2021)

*(continued)*

**EXHIBIT 15-1** *(concluded)*

Form 1120 (2021)                                                                                          Page **6**

| Schedule L | Balance Sheets per Books | Beginning of tax year | | End of tax year | |
|---|---|---|---|---|---|
| | **Assets** | **(a)** | **(b)** | **(c)** | **(d)** |
| 1 | Cash | | | | |
| 2a | Trade notes and accounts receivable | | | | |
| b | Less allowance for bad debts | ( ) | | ( ) | |
| 3 | Inventories | | | | |
| 4 | U.S. government obligations | | | | |
| 5 | Tax-exempt securities (see instructions) | | | | |
| 6 | Other current assets (attach statement) | | | | |
| 7 | Loans to shareholders | | | | |
| 8 | Mortgage and real estate loans | | | | |
| 9 | Other investments (attach statement) | | | | |
| 10a | Buildings and other depreciable assets | | | | |
| b | Less accumulated depreciation | ( ) | | ( ) | |
| 11a | Depletable assets | | | | |
| b | Less accumulated depletion | ( ) | | ( ) | |
| 12 | Land (net of any amortization) | | | | |
| 13a | Intangible assets (amortizable only) | | | | |
| b | Less accumulated amortization | ( ) | | ( ) | |
| 14 | Other assets (attach statement) | | | | |
| 15 | Total assets | | | | |
| | **Liabilities and Shareholders' Equity** | | | | |
| 16 | Accounts payable | | | | |
| 17 | Mortgages, notes, bonds payable in less than 1 year | | | | |
| 18 | Other current liabilities (attach statement) | | | | |
| 19 | Loans from shareholders | | | | |
| 20 | Mortgages, notes, bonds payable in 1 year or more | | | | |
| 21 | Other liabilities (attach statement) | | | | |
| 22 | Capital stock: **a** Preferred stock | | | | |
| | **b** Common stock | | | | |
| 23 | Additional paid-in capital | | | | |
| 24 | Retained earnings—Appropriated (attach statement) | | | | |
| 25 | Retained earnings—Unappropriated | | | | |
| 26 | Adjustments to shareholders' equity (attach statement) | | | | |
| 27 | Less cost of treasury stock | | ( ) | | ( ) |
| 28 | Total liabilities and shareholders' equity | | | | |

| Schedule M-1 | Reconciliation of Income (Loss) per Books With Income per Return |
|---|---|

**Note:** The corporation may be required to file Schedule M-3. See instructions.

| 1 | Net income (loss) per books | | 7 | Income recorded on books this year not included on this return (itemize): | |
| 2 | Federal income tax per books | | | Tax-exempt interest   $ _____ | |
| 3 | Excess of capital losses over capital gains | | | _____ | |
| 4 | Income subject to tax not recorded on books this year (itemize): _____ | | 8 | Deductions on this return not charged against book income this year (itemize): | |
| | _____ | | a | Depreciation   $ _____ | |
| 5 | Expenses recorded on books this year not deducted on this return (itemize): | | b | Charitable contributions $ _____ | |
| a | Depreciation   $ _____ | | | _____ | |
| b | Charitable contributions   $ _____ | | | | |
| c | Travel and entertainment   $ _____ | | 9 | Add lines 7 and 8 | |
| 6 | Add lines 1 through 5 | | 10 | Income (page 1, line 28)—line 6 less line 9 | |

| Schedule M-2 | Analysis of Unappropriated Retained Earnings per Books (Schedule L, Line 25) |
|---|---|

| 1 | Balance at beginning of year | | 5 | Distributions: **a** Cash | |
| 2 | Net income (loss) per books | | | **b** Stock | |
| 3 | Other increases (itemize): _____ | | | **c** Property | |
| | _____ | | 6 | Other decreases (itemize): _____ | |
| | _____ | | 7 | Add lines 5 and 6 | |
| 4 | Add lines 1, 2, and 3 | | 8 | Balance at end of year (line 4 less line 7) | |

Form **1120** (2021)

# BASIS
## LO 15-2

As we noted when discussing partnership taxation in Chapter 14, basis involves two critical issues: (1) the basis of the ownership interest (stock in the case of a corporation) in the hands of the owner and (2) the basis to the corporation of property exchanged for the ownership interest.

When a C corporation or S corporation is formed, individuals purchase or otherwise acquire stock in the entity. The stock acquisition is, in effect, an exchange of cash or property for stock and can be a taxable transaction. If the transferors (i.e., the shareholders who are forming the corporation) control 80% or more of the corporation immediately after the exchange, the exchange is generally tax-free.[5]

| **EXAMPLE 15-1** | Marty and Sara decide to form Boone Company. Marty transfers $1,000 cash in exchange for 100 shares of stock, and Sara transfers a bond with a fair market value (FMV) of $1,000 (basis of $800) for 100 shares. They are the only two shareholders of Boone Company. Because they control 80% or more of Boone immediately after the exchange, the transaction is tax-free. |
|---|---|

Even when the 80% rule is met, a stockholder could be required to recognize a gain in two cases. The first is when the individual transfers property subject to a liability and the relief of liability is greater than the transferor's basis in the property. The gain is equal to the excess of liability over basis.

| **EXAMPLE 15-2** | Gina transfers an apartment building to GGG Company in exchange for all of the stock in the company. The building has a basis of $100,000, an FMV of $500,000, and debt (assumed by the company) of $300,000. Even though Gina controls more than 80% of the company immediately after the exchange, the transaction is taxable because she has debt relief in excess of basis. She has a gain of $200,000 (relief of debt of $300,000 minus building basis of $100,000). |
|---|---|

The second case involves an individual who contributes cash or property and receives, in return, stock plus other cash or property (this extra cash or property is called *boot*, discussed in an earlier chapter). In this case, the taxable gain is the lower of the FMV of the property received or the realized gain (the FMV of property contributed less the tax basis of the property contributed).

| **EXAMPLE 15-3** | Ernie receives all the stock of EBU Company in exchange for contributing a machine with a basis of $15,000 and an FMV of $25,000. Ernie also receives $3,000 cash from the company. The gain on transfer is $10,000 (the difference between the basis and FMV of the machine). The gain Ernie must report is $3,000, the lower of gain or cash received. |
|---|---|

To the corporate entity, the basis of the cash or property received is equal to the basis in the hands of the shareholder plus any gain recognized by the shareholder. The basis of the stock in the hands of the shareholder is equal to the basis of the property contributed plus any gain recognized, minus any boot received (boot includes relief of liability). The amounts of inside and outside basis for the stockholders in each of the three previous examples are as follows:

|  | Reported Gain | Stock Basis to Shareholder (Outside) | Property Basis to Corporation (Inside) |
|---|---|---|---|
| Marty | $ –0– | $ 1,000 | $ 1,000 |
| Sara | –0– | 800 | 800 |
| Gina | 200,000 | –0– | 300,000 |
| Ernie | 3,000 | 15,000 | 18,000 |

Shareholders do not recognize losses as a result of the formation of a corporation when the 80% test is met.

[5] IRC § 351.

If an individual provides services in exchange for stock upon the formation of a corporation, the individual will recognize ordinary income equal to the FMV of the services.

Unless a C corporation stockholder increases or decreases their proportionate ownership (buys or sells stock), there is generally no adjustment to the outside basis over time. This is not the case for Subchapter S corporations, as we will see later in this chapter.

**CONCEPT CHECK 15-2— LO 15-2**

1. When forming a corporation, if the transferors control at least 80% of the corporate entity, the formation is generally tax-free. True or false?
2. The basis to the corporation of property received is equal to _____.
3. Arturo contributed land with an FMV of $100,000 and basis of $40,000 to a newly formed corporation in exchange for 90% of the stock. Arturo's basis in the stock is _____.

# TAXABLE INCOME AND TAX LIABILITY
## LO 15-3

Corporate taxable income is generally determined using the same operating rules as a trade or business that we discussed in Chapter 6. The general formula to determine corporate taxable income and tax liability follows. The line numbers pertain to Form 1120 in Exhibit 15-1.

|  |
|---|
| Total gross receipts or sales (line 1c) |
| − Cost of goods sold (line 2) |
| Gross profit (line 3) |
| + Interest, dividends, capital gains, other income (lines 4–10) |
| Total income (line 11) |
| − Ordinary and necessary trade or business expenses (lines 12–27) |
| Taxable income before special deductions (line 28) |
| − Net operating loss deduction (line 29a) |
| − Dividends received deduction (line 29b) |
| = Taxable income (line 30) |
| × Applicable tax rates |
| = Tax liability (line 31) |
| − Tax payments during the tax year and tax credits (line 33) |
| = Tax due with return (line 35) or overpayment (line 36) |

In corporate taxation, the notion of Adjusted Gross Income (AGI) does not exist.

As mentioned, determination of corporate taxable income generally follows the trade or business rules discussed in Chapter 6. A few differences pertaining to corporations—capital gains and losses, charitable contributions, the dividends received deduction, and some miscellaneous differences—must be noted.

### Capital Gains and Losses (Form 1120, Line 8)

As we discussed in Chapter 7, individuals (or other noncorporate taxpayers) include capital gains and losses in income. If capital losses exceed capital gains, individuals recognize a net capital loss of up to $3,000 with any excess being carried forward indefinitely. C corporations are not permitted to report any net capital losses. Thus, capital losses can only offset capital gains.[6] In other words, the amount on Form 1120 line 8 must be either positive or zero; it cannot be negative.

[6] IRC § 1211(a).

Corporations are permitted to carry back excess capital losses three preceding years (starting with the earliest year) and then forward five years if any loss remains.[7] Corporations can use the carryback and carryforward amounts only against net capital gains in the years noted. Note that the rules are different for net *operating* losses. We discuss those rules later in this chapter.

**EXAMPLE 15-4**

ABC Company, a C corporation, was formed in 2016 and reported net income in each year of its operation. The company had net capital gains and losses as follows:

| | |
|---|---|
| 2017 | $ 7,000 gain |
| 2018 | 10,000 gain |
| 2019 | 1,000 gain |
| 2020 | 5,000 gain |
| 2021 | 21,000 loss |

The 2021 capital loss must be carried back three years starting with the earliest year. Thus, ABC Company will first apply the $21,000 loss from 2021 to tax year 2018, then to 2019, and finally to 2020. Because the total capital gains in those years were $16,000, ABC Company has a $5,000 capital loss to carry forward to tax years 2022 to 2026.

**TAX YOUR BRAIN**

Pirate Company was formed in 2016 and reported capital gains and losses, prior to any carryforwards and carrybacks, as follows:

| | |
|---|---|
| 2016 | $ 2,000 loss |
| 2017 | 7,000 gain |
| 2018 | 10,000 gain |
| 2019 | 16,000 loss |
| 2020 | 5,000 gain |
| 2021 | 14,000 loss |

What is the proper tax treatment of the capital gain carryforwards and carrybacks, and what is the resulting net capital gain or loss for each year indicated?

**ANSWER**

Work from the oldest date to the present. The 2016 loss is carried forward to 2017, resulting in a $5,000 gain in 2017. In 2018, the $10,000 gain will be reported. In 2019, the $16,000 loss will be carried back first to 2017, eliminating the remaining $5,000 gain, and then to 2018, eliminating the $10,000 gain. A $1,000 loss carryforward then remains from 2019. This carryforward will be applied to 2020 resulting in a $4,000 gain in 2020. Finally, the 2021 loss will be carried back to the remaining 2020 gain, giving Pirate Company a $10,000 loss carryforward to be used starting in 2022 and expiring in 2026.

If a corporation carries back a capital loss, it files an amended return for the prior year(s) and will receive a refund if tax was paid in the year.

The other major difference between individual and corporate taxation of capital gains pertains to tax rates. Individuals pay tax on net capital gains at a rate lower than for ordinary income. For corporations, net capital gains are included in income and are taxed at the regular corporate rate.

---

[7] IRC § 1212(a).

## Charitable Contributions

Corporations are permitted charitable contributions to qualified charitable organizations. The deduction is limited to 10% of taxable income before any of the following:

- Charitable contributions.
- Dividends received deduction (described next).
- Net operating loss carryback.
- Capital loss carryback.[8]

**NEW LAW**

Any contributions in excess of the permitted amount are carried forward for five years, are added to the charitable contributions in that year, and are subject to the 10% limitation. In future years, current contributions are deducted first.[9]

For 2020 and 2021 only, the limitation is increased from 10% to 25%.

---

**EXAMPLE 15-5**

In 2019, Szabo Company reported $50,000 of taxable income before charitable contributions. The company had charitable contributions of $8,000. Szabo's charitable contributions are limited to $5,000 ($50,000 × 10%). Thus, Szabo's taxable income will be $45,000, and its charitable contributions carryforward is $3,000. If the tax year was 2020 or 2021, Szabo Corporation would have a charitable contribution limit of $12,500 ($50,000 × 25%). In this case, the entire $8,000 charitable contribution would be deductible.

---

In general, if a corporation contributes ordinary income property, the deduction is limited to the corporation's basis in the property.[10] Ordinary income property is property that, if sold, would produce a gain other than a long-term capital gain. An example is inventory held by a corporation.

Taxpayers use carryforward information to determine any charitable contributions limitation but ignore carryback information. In effect, taxpayers use all information available when the return is filed but do not make changes for information that could become available in the future.

## Dividends Received Deduction

C corporations are permitted a tax deduction for a portion of the dividends they receive from other domestic corporations. The dividends received deduction (DRD) is a percentage of the dividend and varies depending on the percentage ownership in the dividend-paying corporation:[11]

| Ownership Percentage | Deduction Percentage |
|---|---|
| Less than 20% | 50% |
| 20% to less than 80% | 65% |
| 80% or more | 100% |

---

**EXAMPLE 15-6**

Duck Corporation owns 25% of Rose Company. Duck received a $10,000 dividend from Rose and is entitled to a $6,500 dividends received deduction. The deduction means that $3,500 of the dividend is included in Duck's taxable income. If Duck owned 15% of Rose, the DRD would have been $5,000, and only $5,000 of the dividend would have been taxable to Duck.

---

The DRD can be limited. If taxable income (before DRD or any capital loss carryback) is between 100% of the dividend and 50% (or 65% as appropriate) of the dividend, the DRD is limited to taxable income multiplied by the appropriate percentage.

---

[8] IRC § 170(b)(2).

[9] IRC § 170(d)(2).

[10] In IRC § 170(e). There are three limited cases in which the deduction can exceed basis.

[11] IRC § 246(b)(3)

**EXAMPLE 15-7**   Sylva Silverware owns 30% of Fredonia Flatware. Fredonia paid a $20,000 dividend to Sylva. Sylva's taxable income, before the DRD, was $50,000. Sylva's DRD is $13,000 ($20,000 × 65%).

**EXAMPLE 15-8**   Use the information from the previous example except that Sylva's taxable income, before the DRD, was $5,000. Sylva's taxable income is not between 65% of the dividend ($13,000) and 100% of the dividend ($20,000). Thus, the DRD is not limited.

**EXAMPLE 15-9**   Use the information from Example 15-7 except that Sylva's taxable income before the DRD was $18,000. In this case, Sylva's taxable income is in the limitation area (between $13,000 and $20,000). Thus, Sylva's DRD is limited to 65% of taxable income before the DRD, or $11,700 ($18,000 × 65%).

In Examples 15-7 through 15-9, if Sylva had owned less than 20% of Fredonia, the applicable percentage would have been 50% and the lower dollar limit for purposes of the limitation would have been $10,000 (the $20,000 dividend × 50%).

### Other Differences

Except for closely held C corporations, the passive loss rules (refer to Chapter 13) do not apply to corporations.[12] A *closely held C corporation* is one in which more than 50% of the value of its outstanding stock is owned, directly or indirectly, by not more than five individuals.[13]

Corporations normally incur various organizational expenses at the time of legal formation. These costs can include legal fees, incorporation fees, and filing fees. In general, capitalized costs are deductible over their useful life. Because the life of a corporation is theoretically indefinite, organizational expenses are recorded as a nonamortizable asset and are not deductible. However, the IRC permits corporations to elect to immediately deduct organizational expenses in an amount equal to the lower of (1) the amount of organizational expenses or (2) $5,000.[14] If total organizational expenses exceed $50,000, then the $5,000 amount is reduced to zero on a dollar-for-dollar basis. Thus, when organizational expenses exceed $55,000, no immediate deduction is permitted. Any remaining organizational expenses are deductible over a 180-month period beginning with the month the corporation begins business. Expenditures must be incurred before the end of the fiscal year in which the corporation begins business, and the election must be filed with the first tax return. Expenditures associated with issuing or selling stock are not deductible.

Organizational expenses are different from *start-up expenses,* which are incurred prior to the time the corporation begins to produce income. If the enterprise is operating as a business, the expenses would be deductible as ordinary and necessary business expenses. However, the business is not yet active and is not earning income; thus, the expenses are not deductible and must be capitalized. Corporations can elect to treat the expenses as deferred expenses and deduct them initially and/or over a 180-month period in a manner similar to that described for organizational expenses.[15] The 180-month period begins in the month in which the active trade or business begins. The election must be filed with the tax return for the corporation's first year. The calculations and limitations are determined separately for organizational expenses and for start-up expenses.

### Corporate Tax Rates

C corporations are separate taxable entities and pay tax. As we will see later in this chapter, S corporations are generally not taxed, but income, gains, losses, and other items are passed through to shareholders, similar to partnership taxation.

[12] IRC § 469(a)(2).
[13] IRC § 542(a)(2).
[14] IRC § 248(a).
[15] IRC § 195(b).

Once C corporation taxable income is determined, calculating the amount of tax liability is simple. Just multiply the taxable income by 21%.[16]

Previously, corporate tax liability was determined with reference to a tax table in a manner similar to individual taxes. The Tax Cuts and Jobs Act of 2017 changed corporate tax to a simple 21% flat tax.

**EXAMPLE 15-10**

Beaufort Company has taxable income of $1,200,000. Its tax liability is $252,000 (calculated as $1,200,000 × 21%).

## Estimated Payments

A C corporation must pay *estimated taxes*. The required annual payment is the lower of (1) 100% of the tax due for the year or (2) 100% of the tax due for the prior year.[17] Estimated payments can be made in four installments on the 15th day of the 4th, 6th, 9th, and 12th months of the corporation's fiscal year. For calendar-year corporations, the due dates are April 15, June 15, September 15, and December 15. Estimated payments are reported on Form 1120, line 33.

Large corporations (those with taxable income in excess of $1 million in any of the three preceding years) cannot use the prior-year tax safe harbor except for the first quarterly installment payment. These corporations must base the final three quarterly payments on their estimate of current-year tax due.

The corporate underpayment penalty is based on the same interest rate schedule used for individuals. The penalty is not deductible in any year.

## Net Operating Losses

In general, a net operating loss (NOL) occurs when the corporate entity has negative taxable income for the year.[18]

The 2017 Tax Cuts and Jobs Act and the 2020 CARES Act have both changed the tax accounting for NOLs. Now, NOLs fall into three categories.

NOLs that are generated in tax years beginning on or before December 31, 2017, can be carried back 2 years and forward 20 years.[19] Alternatively, the corporation can affirmatively elect to waive the carryback period and only carry the loss forward.[20] The election is irrevocable for the tax year.

NOLs that are generated in calendar years 2018, 2019, and 2020 can be carried back 5 years and then forward indefinitely. As was the case above, the corporation can affirmatively elect to waive the carryback period and only carry the loss forward. The election is irrevocable. These NOLs can offset up to 100% of taxable income in 2020 and before and offset up to 80% of taxable income after 2020.

NOLs that are generated in 2021 or later are not eligible for carryback and can be carried forward indefinitely. These NOLs can offset up to 80% of taxable income in the carryforward year.

In the case of NOL carrybacks, the carryback is first applied to the oldest year, then any remainder is applied to the second oldest year, and so forth.

The following examples illustrate the application of the three categories of NOL noted above.

**EXAMPLE 15-11**

Wilson Company was formed in 2015 and earned $10,000 in 2015 and $15,000 in 2016. In 2017, Wilson had an NOL of $12,000. If Wilson carried back the loss, the company would have zero income in 2015 and $13,000 income in 2016.

[16] IRC § 11(b).
[17] IRC § 6655.
[18] IRC § 172(c)
[19] IRC § 172, 172(b)(1).
[20] IRC § 172(b)(3).

**EXAMPLE 15-12**

Use the same information from Example 15-11. In this case, Wilson affirmatively elects to waive the carryback period. Prior to consideration of any NOL Wilson earned $8,000 in 2018 and earned $21,000 in 2019. Wilson would apply the 2017 NOL to 2018 income, would record zero net income in 2018, and would have a $4,000 carryforward for 2019. In 2019, Wilson would report net income of $17,000 (the pre-NOL net income of $21,000 minus the remaining $4,000 NOL carryforward).

**EXAMPLE 15-13**

Xavier Corporation was formed in 2017 and earned $50,000 in that year. Xavier earned $5,000 in 2018 and again in 2019. In 2020, Xavier recorded an NOL of $75,000. Xavier does not elect to waive the carryback period. In this case, the NOL would first be carried back to 2017 resulting in zero income for the year, with a $25,000 NOL remaining. The NOL would reduce the net income of 2018 and 2019 to zero and there would be a NOL carryforward of $15,000 for 2021 and beyond.

**EXAMPLE 15-14**

Use the same information from Example 15-13. Assume Xavier earned $16,000 in 2021. The NOL carryforward to 2021 is limited to 80% of 2021 taxable income, or $12,800. Xavier's 2021 taxable income after NOL carryforward is $3,200 ($16,000 − $12,800) and Xavier will have an NOL carryforward of $2,200 (initial $15,000 NOL carryforward minus $12,800 used in 2021).

**TAX YOUR BRAIN**

In tax year 2017, under what circumstances would a corporation choose to forgo the carryback period for a net operating loss and elect to only carry the loss forward?

**ANSWER**

If tax rates will be higher in the future and if the corporation expects to earn money in the future, it may make sense to only carry the NOL forward. For example, if tax rates in prior years were 30% and are expected to be 40% in the future, the corporation would receive an additional 10 cents for each dollar of NOL if the loss were only carried forward.

**CONCEPT CHECK 15-3—**
**LO 15-3**

1. Corporations follow the same tax rules for capital gains as do individuals. True or false?
2. The tax liability of a corporation with taxable income of $520,000 is _____.
3. In 2021, a corporation reported taxable income of $150,000 before charitable contributions. The corporation made charitable contributions of $50,000. Its permitted deduction for charitable contributions in the current tax year is _____.
4. Organizational expenses are automatically deductible over 180 months. True or false?
5. Corporate net operating losses from 2017 can be carried back _____ years and forward _____ years.

# TRANSACTIONS WITH SHAREHOLDERS
**LO 15-4**

### Dividends and Distributions

C corporations can pay cash or property (called *distributions*) to their shareholders. To the extent that distributions are from the earnings and profits of the corporation, the distribution is a *dividend*.[21] The corporation cannot deduct the cost of the dividend, and the shareholder reports taxable income in an amount equal to the fair market value of the property received.[22]

Earnings and profits (E&P) are conceptually similar to retained earnings except that they are calculated using tax law, not financial accounting standards.

Distributions paid in excess of E&P are nontaxable to the extent of the stockholder's basis in their stock. The excess of a distribution over the stockholder's basis is treated as a capital gain (assuming the stock is a capital asset in the hands of the stockholder).[23]

[21] IRC § 316.
[22] IRC § 301.
[23] IRC § 301(c)(2), (3).

If a corporation makes a distribution of property (not cash) that has a basis less than the fair market value (i.e., appreciated property), the corporation is treated as selling the property at its fair market value. Thus, the corporation recognizes a gain on the distribution of appreciated property.

**EXAMPLE 15-15**

Sasha received a $500 cash distribution from the E&P of Alpha Company. The dividend is fully taxable to Sasha.

**EXAMPLE 15-16**

Assume that Sasha's distribution was in the form of property with an FMV of $500 and a basis to Alpha Company of $400. Alpha will record a $100 gain. Sasha will report dividend income of $500.

**EXAMPLE 15-17**

Quad Company has E&P of $5,000. It makes a $6,000 cash distribution to Quincy, its sole shareholder. Assuming that Quincy has a basis in his stock of at least $1,000, he will report dividend income of $5,000 and a nontaxable distribution of $1,000. Quincy will reduce the basis of his stock by $1,000.

**EXAMPLE 15-18**

Use the information from Example 15-17. Assume that the basis of Quincy's stock is $200. In this case, he would report a dividend of $5,000, a nontaxable return of capital of $200, and a capital gain of $800. Quincy will also reduce the basis of his stock to zero.

The preceding discussion assumed that the distribution was made to shareholders on a pro rata basis. In other words, each shareholder receives a distribution proportionate to their ownership. Corporations can also make a non–pro rata distribution by which one or more stockholders receive a distribution that is not in proportion to their ownership percentage. If the distribution is in appreciated property, the corporation again has a deemed sale and gain based on FMV. The shareholder reports dividend income equal to the FMV of the cash or property received.

A shareholder may receive a distribution in full liquidation of their ownership interest. For example, a shareholder may sell all of their stock back to the corporation for cash or property. In such case, the shareholder will have a capital gain or loss equal to the difference between the FMV of the distribution and their basis in the stock.

## Liquidation

A *corporate liquidation* occurs when a corporation decides to cease doing business and wind up its business affairs. The corporation pays debts and distributes remaining assets to shareholders. In the case of a complete liquidation, the corporation records all assets and liabilities at fair market value (with associated write-ups or write-downs). The shareholder reports a capital gain or loss equal to the difference between their basis in the stock and the FMV of the property received.

**EXAMPLE 15-19**

Tara received cash of $5,000 and other assets with an FMV of $7,000 as a result of the complete liquidation of Blue Corporation. Tara's basis in the stock of Blue was $10,000. Tara will report a return of capital (nontaxable) of $10,000 and a capital gain of $2,000.

**CONCEPT CHECK 15-4— LO 15-4**

1. Dividends are always taxable to a shareholder. True or false?
2. If a corporation pays a dividend in property, the stockholder will have a dividend equal to the corporate basis in the property. True or false?
3. A corporation has earnings and profits of $10,000 and makes a cash distribution to its sole shareholder in the amount of $11,000. The amount of taxable dividend to the shareholder is _____.

# SCHEDULES L, M-1, AND M-3
## LO 15-5

Corporations must provide a beginning and ending balance sheet on Form 1120, Schedule L, as well as a reconciliation of book income to taxable income on Form 1120, Schedule M-1. See page 6 of Form 1120 in Exhibit 15-1 for both schedules. If a corporation's total receipts and total assets are both less than $250,000, the two schedules are not required.

Preparation of Schedule L is straightforward. It is prepared in accordance with the accounting method the corporation uses to keep its financial accounting records (accrual, cash, or mixed model).

Schedule M-1 can be more complex. It reconciles net income per books (line 1) with net income per the tax return (line 10). In effect, this schedule sets out all book/tax differences for the year regardless of whether they are permanent or temporary differences.

It is important to note that Schedule M-1 reconciles from net income per books (financial accounting net income) to net income per the tax law, *not* the other way around. Let's examine each of the lines individually.

*Line 2:* Federal income tax is an expense for book purposes but is not deductible for tax purposes. The amount of federal income tax expense must be added back to book income. This number is the federal income tax expense deduction on the income statement—*not* the tax expense on page 1 of the tax return.

*Line 3:* For book purposes, excess capital losses qualify as an expense. For tax purposes, recall that corporate capital losses are deductible only to the extent of capital gains. Thus, any excess of capital losses over capital gains must be added back to book income.

*Line 4:* Certain income may be taxable but may be properly excluded from book income. Examples include the last month's rent collected at lease signing by a landlord or the installment sale income reported in full on the books in a prior year. These items must be added to book income to arrive at taxable income.

 **NEW LAW**

*Line 5:* Certain expenses can be recorded on the books but are not deductible on the tax return. These items include the difference between accelerated depreciation taken on the books and straight-line depreciation for taxes in the early years of an asset's life; the difference between the book and tax deductions if charitable contributions are limited on the tax return; and 50% meal expenses that are not deductible on the tax return. For 2021 and 2022, business meals from a restaurant are fully deductible. These meals do not create a book/tax difference. All other business meals are subject to the 50% limitation.

*Line 7:* Some income is reported on the books but is not reported on the tax return. Examples include life insurance proceeds that can be excluded for taxes but must be included for book purposes; prepayment of the last month of rent that will be included on the tax return at the beginning of the lease but on the books at the end of the lease; and interest from tax-exempt bonds.

*Line 8:* Deductions can be taken on the tax return but are not deductible in the financial records. Tax return depreciation in excess of book depreciation is an example. Another is the tax deduction for previously disallowed charitable contributions. These were deducted on the financial statements in a prior year.

---

**EXAMPLE 15-20**

Martin Company had book income of $50,000 for the year. It also had the following differences between book income and tax income:

| | |
|---|---|
| Charitable contributions carryforward used in current year | $2,000 |
| Excess depreciation on tax return | 6,000 |

In addition, the company incurred $10,000 of nonrestaurant meal expense, only 50% of which is deductible for taxes. Martin Company's taxable income is $47,000 ($50,000 − $2,000 − $6,000 + [$10,000 × 50%]). A completed Schedule M-1 for Martin Company is shown in Exhibit 15-2.

**EXHIBIT 15-2**

| Schedule M-1 | Reconciliation of Income (Loss) per Books With Income per Return | | |
|---|---|---|---|
| | Note: Schedule M-3 required instead of Schedule M-1 if total assets are $10 million or more—see instructions | | |

| | | | | | | | |
|---|---|---|---|---|---|---|---|
| 1 | Net income (loss) per books | 50,000 | 7 | Income recorded on books this year not included on this return (itemize): | | | |
| 2 | Federal income tax per books | | | Tax-exempt interest  $ | | | |
| 3 | Excess of capital losses over capital gains | | | | | | |
| 4 | Income subject to tax not recorded on books this year (itemize): | | 8 | Deductions on this return not charged against book income this year (itemize): | | | |
| 5 | Expenses recorded on books this year not deducted on this return (itemize): | | a | Depreciation $ | 6,000 | | |
| a | Depreciation  $ | | b | Charitable contributions $ | 2,000 | | |
| b | Charitable contributions . $ | | | | | | |
| c | Travel and entertainment . $  5,000 | | | | | 8,000 | |
| | | 5,000 | 9 | Add lines 7 and 8 | | 8,000 | |
| 6 | Add lines 1 through 5 | 55,000 | 10 | Income (page 1, line 28)—line 6 less line 9 | | 47,000 | |

Source: U.S. Department of the Treasury, Internal Revenue Service, Form 1120. Washington, DC: 2021.

Corporations with total assets of $10 million or more must complete a separate Schedule M-3. This schedule is, in effect, an extremely detailed reconciliation of book income with taxable income. Thus, it is an expanded version of Schedule M-1 for large corporations. You can locate a Schedule M-3 on the IRS website (www.irs.gov).

**CONCEPT CHECK 15-5—**
**LO 15-5**

1. Completion of Schedule L is required of all corporations. True or false?
2. Schedule M-1 reconciles book income to taxable income. True or false?
3. A corporation's depreciation expense is lower on the financial statements than it is on the tax return. Would this difference be a negative or positive item on Schedule M-1?

# OTHER CORPORATE ISSUES
**LO 15-6**

Corporations can be part of a controlled group. The most common of these groups are parent–subsidiary groups or brother–sister groups, which we discuss here, in addition to corporate alternative minimum tax and the net business interest expense limitation.

## Parent–Subsidiary Groups
*Parent–subsidiary groups* are those for which a common parent corporation owns, directly or indirectly, at least 80% of one or more other corporations. The ownership can be one or more chains of corporations connected through stock ownership with the parent corporation.

**EXAMPLE 15-21**   Garcia Corporation owns 90% of Harnett Company. The two corporations are part of a parent–subsidiary group. The relationship holds as long as Garcia owns at least 80% of Harnett.

**EXAMPLE 15-22**   Garcia Corporation also owns 95% of Iona Company. Iona, in turn, owns 85% of Jasper Corporation. The entire Garcia/Iona/Jasper chain of corporations is part of a parent–subsidiary group.

Parent–subsidiary corporations can elect to file a consolidated tax return. Form 1122 is attached to the first consolidated return for each of the subsidiaries of the group.[24] An appropriate officer of the subsidiary signs the form, thereby consenting to be included in the group. All members of the parent–subsidiary group must be included. Subsidiaries no longer file

[24] Reg. § 1.1502-75(b).

separate returns. In subsequent years, Form 851, which is an affiliation schedule listing the corporations that are part of the consolidated return, is attached to the consolidated return.

Electing to file as a consolidated entity has certain advantages. For example, a consolidated return allows the entity to offset losses from one corporation against profits of another. In addition, profits from intercompany sales are deferred. There are potential disadvantages as well. The election is binding on future tax years, losses on intercompany sales cannot be immediately recognized, and elections made by the parent are binding on all subsidiaries.

## Brother–Sister Groups

A *brother–sister group* may exist if five or fewer persons own two or more corporations. The group exists if both of the following tests are met:

- **Total ownership test:** The shareholder group owns stock representing at least 80% of the voting shares of stock or at least 80% of the total value of all shares.
- **Common ownership test:** The shareholder group has common (identical) ownership of more than 50% of the voting power or more than 50% of the value of all shares.

At first glance, the tests seem to be the same with different percentages, but such is not the case. The 80% test examines ownership of an individual corporation. The 50% test, in effect, is based on the smallest common percentage across all of the corporations evaluated.

---

**EXAMPLE 15-23**

Three individuals have ownership interests in four different corporations as follows:

|  | Corporations | | | | Identical |
|---|---|---|---|---|---|
|  | A | B | C | D | Ownership |
| Reed | 60% | 20% | 30% | 30% | 20% |
| Smith | 30 | 65 | 30 | 40 | 30 |
| Thomas | 10 | 15 | 40 | 20 | 10 |
| Totals | 100% | 100% | 100% | 90% | 60% |

The Identical Ownership column represents the smallest number reading across the column. In other words, it is the identical ownership across all of the corporations. So, for example, Reed owns at least 20% of each of the corporations.

The total ownership test is met because the three individuals own at least 80% of each of the four corporations (in this example, for corporations A, B, and C, they actually own all the stock). The common ownership test is met because the common (identical) ownership is more than 50% (it is 60% in this example). Thus, the four corporations are all part of a brother–sister group.

---

**TAX YOUR BRAIN**

In Example 15-23, if Reed sold half of her ownership in Corporation B to an unrelated third party, would the corporations remain as a brother–sister group?

**ANSWER**

No. By reducing her ownership in Corporation B to 10% of the total, Reed now has an identical common ownership across the four corporations of 10%. Thus, the sum of the common ownership for all three individuals is exactly 50%. The common ownership test must be more than 50%. Thus, the entities are no longer a brother–sister group.

One way to think about the two tests is that the 80% test is a "vertical test" (does the group own at least 80% of a specific individual corporation?), whereas the 50% test is a "horizontal test" (what is the smallest percentage that an individual owns across the various corporations?).

Corporations within a brother–sister group continue to file individual tax returns. However, the IRS realizes that the common control within a brother–sister group can result in income or expense being inappropriately allocated between members of the group. Thus, the IRS has the authority to reallocate the income, deductions, and credits of the related corporations "in order to prevent the evasion of taxes or clearly reflect the income" of the individual corporations within the group.[25]

For purposes of determining corporate tax brackets, the accumulated earnings credit, and the minimum tax exemption, a controlled group is determined only with reference to the common ownership test. In all other cases, both tests are used.

## Corporate Alternative Minimum Tax

The Tax Cuts and Jobs Act of 2017 repealed the corporate Alternative Minimum Tax (AMT) beginning in 2018. Note that AMT continues to exist for taxpayers other than corporations.

For years prior to 2018, applying the old law for AMT may have resulted in the creation of AMT credits. In general, AMT credit carryovers to 2018 or later may be utilized to the extent of the taxpayer's regular tax liability. In 2018, if AMT credit carryovers exceed regular tax liability, 50% of the excess is refundable. The CARES Act permits a refundable credit equal to 100% of any excess in 2019. Alternatively, a taxpayer can elect to claim the entire credit in 2018 (in effect, the 50% limitation would be eliminated).

## Business Interest Expense Limitation

Business interest expense is only allowed to the extent it does not exceed the sum of (a) business interest income plus (b) 30% of Adjusted Taxable Income (ATI).[26] For 2019 and 2020, the CARES Act increased the 30% figure to 50%. ATI is taxable income before business interest income or expense, any NOL deduction, or any deduction for depreciation, amortization, or depletion.[27]

Interest expense that is disallowed in a year because of the limitation is carried forward indefinitely. In the carryforward year, the disallowed amount is treated as business interest expense paid or accrued in the carryforward year.[28]

The business interest expense limitation does not apply to any business with average annual gross receipts for the prior three years that is $26 million or less.

---

**EXAMPLE 15-24**

In 2021, Barcelona Corporation has ATI of $50,000, business interest expense of $10,000, and business interest income of $1,000. The limitation is equal to the sum of business interest income ($1,000) plus 30% of ATI ($15,000), for a total of $16,000. Because the business interest expense of $10,000 is less than the limitation amount, Barcelona can deduct all the business interest expense.

---

**EXAMPLE 15-25**

In 2021, Calgary Company has ATI of $20,000, business interest expense of $13,000, and business interest income of $1,000. The limitation is equal to the sum of business interest income ($1,000) plus 30% of ATI ($6,000), for a total of $7,000. The company can only deduct $7,000 of business interest expense. The remaining $6,000 can be carried forward to future years.

---

**CONCEPT CHECK 15-6— LO 15-6**

1. To be considered a parent–subsidiary group, the parent corporation must own, directly or indirectly, at least _____ percent of the subsidiary corporation.
2. A brother–sister group may exist if _____ or fewer persons own two or more corporations.

---

[25] IRC § 482.

[26] IRC § 163(j)(1).

[27] IRC § 163(j)(8)(A).

[28] IRC § 163(j)(2).

# SUBCHAPTER S CORPORATIONS
## LO 15-7

### General

A Subchapter S (Sub S) corporation is a "regular" corporation that has elected to be taxed under the provisions of Subchapter S of the IRC.[29] In effect, a Sub S corporation is a corporation for legal purposes but is taxed in a manner similar to a partnership. Thus, the shareholders (not the corporation) are taxed based on their proportionate share of net income and separately stated items.

A Sub S corporation is required to have the same year-end as its shareholders unless it receives permission from the IRS to have a different year-end. Sub S corporations file their annual tax returns on Form 1120S (see Exhibit 15-3). Tax returns for S corporations are due on the 15th day of the third month after the end of the fiscal year (March 15 for a calendar-year Sub S corporation). A six-month extension is permitted.

### Subchapter S Election

A corporation must affirmatively elect to be taxed as a Subchapter S corporation. The corporation must be a qualifying small business corporation that meets *all* of the following characteristics:[30]

- Be a domestic corporation.
- Have 100 or fewer shareholders who are all individuals, estates, and certain trusts.[31]
- Have only one class of stock.
- Have shareholders who are U.S. citizens or resident aliens.

For the election to be valid, it must be made on Form 2553, must be signed by all shareholders, and must be filed on a timely basis.[32] If the corporation wants the election to be valid for the current year, Form 2553 must be filed either in the prior fiscal year or before the 15th day of the third month of the current year. Thus, elections filed after the 2.5-month deadline are effective for the following year.

The Sub S election is valid until it is statutorily terminated or voluntarily revoked. The election is statutorily terminated if the corporation fails to meet the qualifications to be a Sub S corporation. For example, once the corporation has more than 100 shareholders, the election will be terminated. For statutorily terminated elections, the termination is effective on the day the terminating event occurs.

The corporation can choose to voluntarily revoke the election. If shareholders owning a majority of the voting stock consent, in writing, to revoke the election, the Sub S status will be terminated.[33] If the revocation is made (and filed) during the first 2.5 months of the tax year, the revocation will be effective as of the beginning of the year. If the revocation is made subsequent to that date, the Sub S status will be terminated as of the beginning of the following year. Shareholders can state a revocation date on or after the date the voluntary revocation is filed, and the revocation will be effective on the selected date.

In most circumstances, if an S corporation loses its status because of statutory or voluntary revocation, the corporation must wait five years before reelecting Sub S status.

### Taxable Income and Separately Stated Items

Generally items of income and expense are the same for a C corporation as for an S corporation.

As mentioned, a Sub S corporation is taxed as though it were a partnership. In other words, the shareholders, not the corporation, pay tax on the Subchapter S income. Unlike a partnership, a Sub S corporation can amortize organizational expenses and must recognize gains, but not losses, on distributions of property to shareholders. The dividends received deduction does not apply to a Sub S corporation.

---

[29] IRC § 1361.

[30] IRC § 1361(b).

[31] Members of a family are treated as one shareholder under IRC § 1361(c)(1). A family is defined as a common ancestor, the lineal descendants of that person, and the spouses or former spouses of the common ancestor or lineal descendants.

[32] IRC § 1362(a).

[33] IRC § 1362(d).

**EXHIBIT 15-3**

| Form **1120-S** | **U.S. Income Tax Return for an S Corporation** | OMB No. 1545-0123 |
|---|---|---|
| Department of the Treasury<br>Internal Revenue Service | ▶ Do not file this form unless the corporation has filed or<br>is attaching Form 2553 to elect to be an S corporation.<br>▶ Go to *www.irs.gov/Form1120S* for instructions and the latest information. | **2021** |

For calendar year 2021 or tax year beginning _____ , 2021, ending _____ , 20____

| **A** S election effective date | **TYPE OR PRINT** | Name | **D** Employer identification number |
|---|---|---|---|
| **B** Business activity code number (see instructions) | | Number, street, and room or suite no. If a P.O. box, see instructions. | **E** Date incorporated |
| **C** Check if Sch. M-3 attached ☐ | | City or town, state or province, country, and ZIP or foreign postal code | **F** Total assets (see instructions)<br>$ |

**G** Is the corporation electing to be an S corporation beginning with this tax year? See instructions. ☐ Yes ☐ No
**H** Check if: **(1)** ☐ Final return **(2)** ☐ Name change **(3)** ☐ Address change **(4)** ☐ Amended return **(5)** ☐ S election termination
**I** Enter the number of shareholders who were shareholders during any part of the tax year . . . . . . . . ▶ _____
**J** Check if corporation: **(1)** ☐ Aggregated activities for section 465 at-risk purposes **(2)** ☐ Grouped activities for section 469 passive activity purposes

**Caution:** Include **only** trade or business income and expenses on lines 1a through 21. See the instructions for more information.

**Income**

| | | | | |
|---|---|---|---|---|
| **1a** | Gross receipts or sales . . . . . . . . . . . . . . | **1a** | | |
| **b** | Returns and allowances . . . . . . . . . . . . . | **1b** | | |
| **c** | Balance. Subtract line 1b from line 1a . . . . . . . . . . . . . . . . . | | **1c** | |
| **2** | Cost of goods sold (attach Form 1125-A) . . . . . . . . . . . . . . . | | **2** | |
| **3** | Gross profit. Subtract line 2 from line 1c . . . . . . . . . . . . . . . | | **3** | |
| **4** | Net gain (loss) from Form 4797, line 17 (attach Form 4797) . . . . . . . . . | | **4** | |
| **5** | Other income (loss) (see instructions—attach statement) . . . . . . . . . . | | **5** | |
| **6** | **Total income (loss).** Add lines 3 through 5 . . . . . . . . . . . . . ▶ | | **6** | |

**Deductions** (see instructions for limitations)

| | | | |
|---|---|---|---|
| **7** | Compensation of officers (see instructions—attach Form 1125-E) . . . . . . . . | **7** | |
| **8** | Salaries and wages (less employment credits) . . . . . . . . . . . . . | **8** | |
| **9** | Repairs and maintenance . . . . . . . . . . . . . . . . . . | **9** | |
| **10** | Bad debts . . . . . . . . . . . . . . . . . . . . . | **10** | |
| **11** | Rents . . . . . . . . . . . . . . . . . . . . . . | **11** | |
| **12** | Taxes and licenses . . . . . . . . . . . . . . . . . . . | **12** | |
| **13** | Interest (see instructions) . . . . . . . . . . . . . . . . . | **13** | |
| **14** | Depreciation not claimed on Form 1125-A or elsewhere on return (attach Form 4562) . . . | **14** | |
| **15** | Depletion **(Do not deduct oil and gas depletion.)** . . . . . . . . . . . | **15** | |
| **16** | Advertising . . . . . . . . . . . . . . . . . . . . | **16** | |
| **17** | Pension, profit-sharing, etc., plans . . . . . . . . . . . . . . . | **17** | |
| **18** | Employee benefit programs . . . . . . . . . . . . . . . . . | **18** | |
| **19** | Other deductions (attach statement) . . . . . . . . . . . . . . . | **19** | |
| **20** | **Total deductions.** Add lines 7 through 19 . . . . . . . . . . . . . ▶ | **20** | |
| **21** | **Ordinary business income (loss).** Subtract line 20 from line 6 . . . . . . . . | **21** | |

**Tax and Payments**

| | | | | |
|---|---|---|---|---|
| **22a** | Excess net passive income or LIFO recapture tax (see instructions) . . . | **22a** | | |
| **b** | Tax from Schedule D (Form 1120-S) . . . . . . . . . | **22b** | | |
| **c** | Add lines 22a and 22b (see instructions for additional taxes) . . . . . . . . | | **22c** | |
| **23a** | 2021 estimated tax payments and 2020 overpayment credited to 2021 | **23a** | | |
| **b** | Tax deposited with Form 7004 . . . . . . . . . . | **23b** | | |
| **c** | Credit for federal tax paid on fuels (attach Form 4136) . . . . | **23c** | | |
| **d** | Add lines 23a through 23c . . . . . . . . . . . . . . . . . | | **23d** | |
| **24** | Estimated tax penalty (see instructions). Check if Form 2220 is attached . . . . . . ▶ ☐ | | **24** | |
| **25** | **Amount owed.** If line 23d is smaller than the total of lines 22c and 24, enter amount owed . . . | | **25** | |
| **26** | **Overpayment.** If line 23d is larger than the total of lines 22c and 24, enter amount overpaid . . . | | **26** | |
| **27** | Enter amount from line 26:   **Credited to 2022 estimated tax ▶**       Refunded ▶ | | **27** | |

**Sign Here**

Under penalties of perjury, I declare that I have examined this return, including accompanying schedules and statements, and to the best of my knowledge and belief, it is true, correct, and complete. Declaration of preparer (other than taxpayer) is based on all information of which preparer has any knowledge.

▶ _____   _____   ▶ _____
   Signature of officer              Date           Title

May the IRS discuss this return with the preparer shown below? See instructions. ☐ Yes ☐ No

**Paid Preparer Use Only**

| Print/Type preparer's name | Preparer's signature | Date | Check ☐ if self-employed | PTIN |
|---|---|---|---|---|
| Firm's name ▶ | | | Firm's EIN ▶ | |
| Firm's address ▶ | | | Phone no. | |

**For Paperwork Reduction Act Notice, see separate instructions.**      Cat. No. 11510H      Form **1120-S** (2021)

Source: U.S. Department of the Treasury, Internal Revenue Service, Form 1120S. Washington, DC: 2021.

**EXHIBIT 15-3**  *(continued)*

Form 1120-S (2021)                                                                                          Page **2**

| Schedule B | Other Information (see instructions) | Yes | No |
|---|---|---|---|

**1** Check accounting method:  **a** ☐ Cash   **b** ☐ Accrual
  **c** ☐ Other (specify) ▶ _____

**2** See the instructions and enter the:
  **a** Business activity ▶ _____   **b** Product or service ▶ _____

**3** At any time during the tax year, was any shareholder of the corporation a disregarded entity, a trust, an estate, or a nominee or similar person? If "Yes," attach Schedule B-1, Information on Certain Shareholders of an S Corporation .   .

**4** At the end of the tax year, did the corporation:

  **a** Own directly 20% or more, or own, directly or indirectly, 50% or more of the total stock issued and outstanding of any foreign or domestic corporation? For rules of constructive ownership, see instructions. If "Yes," complete (i) through (v) below  . . . . . . . . . .

| (i) Name of Corporation | (ii) Employer Identification Number (if any) | (iii) Country of Incorporation | (iv) Percentage of Stock Owned | (v) If Percentage in (iv) Is 100%, Enter the Date (if applicable) a Qualified Subchapter S Subsidiary Election Was Made |
|---|---|---|---|---|
| | | | | |
| | | | | |
| | | | | |

  **b** Own directly an interest of 20% or more, or own, directly or indirectly, an interest of 50% or more in the profit, loss, or capital in any foreign or domestic partnership (including an entity treated as a partnership) or in the beneficial interest of a trust? For rules of constructive ownership, see instructions. If "Yes," complete (i) through (v) below . . . . . . .

| (i) Name of Entity | (ii) Employer Identification Number (if any) | (iii) Type of Entity | (iv) Country of Organization | (v) Maximum Percentage Owned in Profit, Loss, or Capital |
|---|---|---|---|---|
| | | | | |
| | | | | |
| | | | | |

**5a** At the end of the tax year, did the corporation have any outstanding shares of restricted stock? . . . . . . . .
  If "Yes," complete lines (i) and (ii) below.
  **(i)** Total shares of restricted stock . . . . . . . . . ▶ _____
  **(ii)** Total shares of non-restricted stock . . . . . . . . ▶ _____

  **b** At the end of the tax year, did the corporation have any outstanding stock options, warrants, or similar instruments? .
  If "Yes," complete lines (i) and (ii) below.
  **(i)** Total shares of stock outstanding at the end of the tax year . ▶ _____
  **(ii)** Total shares of stock outstanding if all instruments were executed ▶ _____

**6** Has this corporation filed, or is it required to file, **Form 8918,** Material Advisor Disclosure Statement, to provide information on any reportable transaction? . . . . . . . . . . . . . . . . . .

**7** Check this box if the corporation issued publicly offered debt instruments with original issue discount . . . . ▶ ☐
  If checked, the corporation may have to file **Form 8281,** Information Return for Publicly Offered Original Issue Discount Instruments.

**8** If the corporation **(a)** was a C corporation before it elected to be an S corporation **or** the corporation acquired an asset with a basis determined by reference to the basis of the asset (or the basis of any other property) in the hands of a C corporation, **and (b)** has net unrealized built-in gain in excess of the net recognized built-in gain from prior years, enter the net unrealized built-in gain reduced by net recognized built-in gain from prior years. See instructions . . . . . ▶ $ _____

**9** Did the corporation have an election under section 163(j) for any real property trade or business or any farming business in effect during the tax year? See instructions . . . . . . . . . . . . . . . . .

**10** Does the corporation satisfy one or more of the following? See instructions . . . . . . . . . . . . .
  **a** The corporation owns a pass-through entity with current, or prior year carryover, excess business interest expense.
  **b** The corporation's aggregate average annual gross receipts (determined under section 448(c)) for the 3 tax years preceding the current tax year are more than $26 million and the corporation has business interest expense.
  **c** The corporation is a tax shelter and the corporation has business interest expense.
  If "Yes," complete and attach Form 8990.

**11** Does the corporation satisfy **both** of the following conditions? . . . . . . . . . . . . . .
  **a** The corporation's total receipts (see instructions) for the tax year were less than $250,000.
  **b** The corporation's total assets at the end of the tax year were less than $250,000.
  If "Yes," the corporation is not required to complete Schedules L and M-1.

Form **1120-S** (2021)

*(continued)*

**EXHIBIT 15-3** *(continued)*

Form 1120-S (2021)            Page **3**

### Schedule B   Other Information (see instructions) *(continued)*

| | | Yes | No |
|---|---|---|---|
| 12 | During the tax year, did the corporation have any non-shareholder debt that was canceled, was forgiven, or had the terms modified so as to reduce the principal amount of the debt? . . . . . . . . . . . . | | |
| | If "Yes," enter the amount of principal reduction . . . . . . . . . . ▶ $ _____ | | |
| 13 | During the tax year, was a qualified subchapter S subsidiary election terminated or revoked? If "Yes," see instructions . | | |
| 14a | Did the corporation make any payments in 2021 that would require it to file Form(s) 1099? . . . . . . | | |
| b | If "Yes," did the corporation file or will it file required Form(s) 1099? . . . . . . . . . . . | | |
| 15 | Is the corporation attaching Form 8996 to certify as a Qualified Opportunity Fund? . . . . . . . | | |
| | If "Yes," enter the amount from Form 8996, line 15 . . . . . . . . . ▶ $ _____ | | |

### Schedule K   Shareholders' Pro Rata Share Items

| | | | | | Total amount |
|---|---|---|---|---|---|
| **Income (Loss)** | 1 | Ordinary business income (loss) (page 1, line 21) . . . . . . . . . . . . . | | **1** | |
| | 2 | Net rental real estate income (loss) (attach Form 8825) . . . . . . . . . | | **2** | |
| | 3a | Other gross rental income (loss) . . . . . . | **3a** | | |
| | b | Expenses from other rental activities (attach statement) | **3b** | | |
| | c | Other net rental income (loss). Subtract line 3b from line 3a . . . . . | | **3c** | |
| | 4 | Interest income . . . . . . . . . . . . . . . . . . | | **4** | |
| | 5 | Dividends: **a** Ordinary dividends . . . . . . . . . . . . . | | **5a** | |
| | | **b** Qualified dividends . . . . . . | **5b** | | |
| | 6 | Royalties . . . . . . . . . . . . . . . . . . . . | | **6** | |
| | 7 | Net short-term capital gain (loss) (attach Schedule D (Form 1120-S)) . | | **7** | |
| | 8a | Net long-term capital gain (loss) (attach Schedule D (Form 1120-S)) . | | **8a** | |
| | b | Collectibles (28%) gain (loss) . . . . . . | **8b** | | |
| | c | Unrecaptured section 1250 gain (attach statement) . . . . | **8c** | | |
| | 9 | Net section 1231 gain (loss) (attach Form 4797) . . . . . . . | | **9** | |
| | 10 | Other income (loss) (see instructions) . . .   Type ▶ | | **10** | |
| **Deductions** | 11 | Section 179 deduction (attach Form 4562) . . . . . . . . . | | **11** | |
| | 12a | Charitable contributions . . . . . . . . . . . . . . | | **12a** | |
| | b | Investment interest expense . . . . . . . . . . . . | | **12b** | |
| | c | Section 59(e)(2) expenditures . . . . .   Type ▶ _____ | | **12c** | |
| | d | Other deductions (see instructions) . . . .   Type ▶ _____ | | **12d** | |
| **Credits** | 13a | Low-income housing credit (section 42(j)(5)) . . . . . . . | | **13a** | |
| | b | Low-income housing credit (other) . . . . . . . . . . . | | **13b** | |
| | c | Qualified rehabilitation expenditures (rental real estate) (attach Form 3468, if applicable) . . | | **13c** | |
| | d | Other rental real estate credits (see instructions)   Type ▶ _____ | | **13d** | |
| | e | Other rental credits (see instructions) . . .   Type ▶ _____ | | **13e** | |
| | f | Biofuel producer credit (attach Form 6478) . . . . . . . . | | **13f** | |
| | g | Other credits (see instructions) . . . . .   Type ▶ | | **13g** | |
| **International Transactions** | 14 | Attach Schedule K-2 (Form 1120-S), Shareholders' Pro Rata Share Items—International, and check this box to indicate you are reporting items of international tax relevance . . . . ▶ ☐ | | | |
| **Alternative Minimum Tax (AMT) Items** | 15a | Post-1986 depreciation adjustment . . . . . . . . . . . | | **15a** | |
| | b | Adjusted gain or loss . . . . . . . . . . . . . . | | **15b** | |
| | c | Depletion (other than oil and gas) . . . . . . . . . . | | **15c** | |
| | d | Oil, gas, and geothermal properties—gross income . . . . . | | **15d** | |
| | e | Oil, gas, and geothermal properties—deductions . . . . . | | **15e** | |
| | f | Other AMT items (attach statement) . . . . . . . . . . | | **15f** | |
| **Items Affecting Shareholder Basis** | 16a | Tax-exempt interest income . . . . . . . . . . . . | | **16a** | |
| | b | Other tax-exempt income . . . . . . . . . . . . . | | **16b** | |
| | c | Nondeductible expenses . . . . . . . . . . . . . | | **16c** | |
| | d | Distributions (attach statement if required) (see instructions) . . . | | **16d** | |
| | e | Repayment of loans from shareholders . . . . . . . . . | | **16e** | |
| | f | Foreign taxes paid or accrued . . . . . . . . . . . . | | **16f** | |

Form **1120-S** (2021)

**EXHIBIT 15-3**  *(continued)*

Form 1120-S (2021)                                                                                      Page **4**

| Schedule K | | Shareholders' Pro Rata Share Items *(continued)* | Total amount |
|---|---|---|---|
| Other Information | 17a | Investment income | 17a |
| | b | Investment expenses | 17b |
| | c | Dividend distributions paid from accumulated earnings and profits | 17c |
| | d | Other items and amounts (attach statement) | |
| Recon- ciliation | 18 | **Income (loss) reconciliation.** Combine the amounts on lines 1 through 10 in the far right column. From the result, subtract the sum of the amounts on lines 11 through 12d and 16f | 18 |

| Schedule L | | Balance Sheets per Books | Beginning of tax year | | End of tax year | |
|---|---|---|---|---|---|---|
| | | **Assets** | (a) | (b) | (c) | (d) |
| 1 | | Cash | | | | |
| 2a | | Trade notes and accounts receivable | | | | |
| b | | Less allowance for bad debts | ( ) | | ( ) | |
| 3 | | Inventories | | | | |
| 4 | | U.S. government obligations | | | | |
| 5 | | Tax-exempt securities (see instructions) | | | | |
| 6 | | Other current assets (attach statement) | | | | |
| 7 | | Loans to shareholders | | | | |
| 8 | | Mortgage and real estate loans | | | | |
| 9 | | Other investments (attach statement) | | | | |
| 10a | | Buildings and other depreciable assets | | | | |
| b | | Less accumulated depreciation | ( ) | | ( ) | |
| 11a | | Depletable assets | | | | |
| b | | Less accumulated depletion | ( ) | | ( ) | |
| 12 | | Land (net of any amortization) | | | | |
| 13a | | Intangible assets (amortizable only) | | | | |
| b | | Less accumulated amortization | ( ) | | ( ) | |
| 14 | | Other assets (attach statement) | | | | |
| 15 | | Total assets | | | | |
| | | **Liabilities and Shareholders' Equity** | | | | |
| 16 | | Accounts payable | | | | |
| 17 | | Mortgages, notes, bonds payable in less than 1 year | | | | |
| 18 | | Other current liabilities (attach statement) | | | | |
| 19 | | Loans from shareholders | | | | |
| 20 | | Mortgages, notes, bonds payable in 1 year or more | | | | |
| 21 | | Other liabilities (attach statement) | | | | |
| 22 | | Capital stock | | | | |
| 23 | | Additional paid-in capital | | | | |
| 24 | | Retained earnings | | | | |
| 25 | | Adjustments to shareholders' equity (attach statement) | | | | |
| 26 | | Less cost of treasury stock | ( ) | | ( ) | |
| 27 | | Total liabilities and shareholders' equity | | | | |

Form **1120-S** (2021)

*(continued)*

**EXHIBIT 15-3** *(concluded)*

Form 1120-S (2021) Page **5**

| **Schedule M-1** | **Reconciliation of Income (Loss) per Books With Income (Loss) per Return** |
|---|---|

**Note:** The corporation may be required to file Schedule M-3. See instructions.

| | | | |
|---|---|---|---|
| 1 | Net income (loss) per books . . . . | 5 | Income recorded on books this year not included on Schedule K, lines 1 through 10 (itemize): |
| 2 | Income included on Schedule K, lines 1, 2, 3c, 4, 5a, 6, 7, 8a, 9, and 10, not recorded on books this year (itemize) | a | Tax-exempt interest $ |
| 3 | Expenses recorded on books this year not included on Schedule K, lines 1 through 12 and 16f (itemize): | 6 | Deductions included on Schedule K, lines 1 through 12 and 16f, not charged against book income this year (itemize): |
| a | Depreciation $ | a | Depreciation $ |
| b | Travel and entertainment $ | 7 | Add lines 5 and 6 |
| 4 | Add lines 1 through 3 . . . . | 8 | Income (loss) (Schedule K, line 18). Subtract line 7 from line 4 . . . |

| **Schedule M-2** | **Analysis of Accumulated Adjustments Account, Shareholders' Undistributed Taxable Income Previously Taxed, Accumulated Earnings and Profits, and Other Adjustments Account** (see instructions) |
|---|---|

| | | (a) Accumulated adjustments account | (b) Shareholders' undistributed taxable income previously taxed | (c) Accumulated earnings and profits | (d) Other adjustments account |
|---|---|---|---|---|---|
| 1 | Balance at beginning of tax year . . . . . . | | | | |
| 2 | Ordinary income from page 1, line 21 . . . | | | | |
| 3 | Other additions . . . . . . . . . . | | | | |
| 4 | Loss from page 1, line 21 . . . . . . . | ( ) | | | |
| 5 | Other reductions . . . . . . . . . . | ( ) | | | ( ) |
| 6 | Combine lines 1 through 5 . . . . . . . | | | | |
| 7 | Distributions . . . . . . . . . . . | | | | |
| 8 | Balance at end of tax year. Subtract line 7 from line 6 . . . . . . . . . . . . | | | | |

Form **1120-S** (2021)

In a manner similar to partnership taxation, some items of income, expense, or credit are not included in income but are separately stated and allocated to shareholders on a per share, per day basis.[34] Separately stated items are on Schedule K (see pages 3 and 4 of Form 1120S in Exhibit 15-3). The Subchapter S Schedule K is similar to that for a partnership.

**EXAMPLE 15-26**

Pitt Company is a Subchapter S corporation with two shareholders, Tamar and Zeke, who own 60% and 40% of the corporation, respectively. During the year, Pitt has income of $50,000 that includes $3,000 of dividend income and $1,000 of charitable contributions. Pitt's Sub S taxable income is $48,000. The allocation of the income and separately stated items follows:

| | Tamar (60%) | Zeke (40%) | Total |
|---|---|---|---|
| Taxable income | $28,800 | $19,200 | $48,000 |
| Dividend income | 1,800 | 1,200 | 3,000 |
| Charitable contributions | 600 | 400 | 1,000 |

## Corporate and Shareholder Basis and Distributions

Upon formation, the basis rules for S corporations are the same as those for C corporations (noted previously). Significant differences, however, pertain to income and separately stated items and distributions. In effect, Sub S shareholders are taxed on their proportionate share of income and separately stated items but are not taxed when they receive a distribution. This treatment is similar to that for partners of a partnership.

[34] You might find it instructive to review the rules associated with separately stated items of a partnership in Chapter 14.

A Sub S shareholder who receives a K-1 from the corporation reports each item on their tax return in a manner similar to that done for a partnership (see Chapter 14). Each K-1 item increases or decreases the basis of the shareholder's stock. If the Sub S corporation reports a loss, the shareholder can take the loss only to the extent of their adjusted basis in the corporation's stock.

A shareholder's basis in the stock is increased or decreased by the following items:

---

Increases:

    Net income
    Separately stated income items (dividends, interest, capital gains, tax-
       exempt income, etc.)
    Capital contributions
    Loans from the shareholder to the corporation

Decreases:

    Net losses
    Separately stated expense items (charitable contributions, capital losses, etc.)
    Distributions from the corporation at fair market value

---

Decreases cannot reduce the shareholder's basis in stock below zero. Any excess first goes to reduce the basis of any loans from the shareholder to the corporation, and if any remains, it is suspended. When the corporation later recognizes items that increase basis (such as net income), the increases are allocated as follows: (1) increase the basis of shareholder loans, if any, to their original basis; (2) eliminate suspended losses; and (3) increase the basis of the stock for the remainder.

---

**EXAMPLE 15-27**

Thangam owns stock in a Subchapter S corporation. At the end of 2020, the tax basis of her stock was $2,000. She had previously made a $1,500 loan to the company. For year 2020, her share of the loss of the company was $4,500. To account for this loss, she would reduce the tax basis of her stock to $0, then would reduce the tax basis of her loan to $0, and would have a remaining $1,000 suspended loss ($4,500 − $2,000 − $1,500 = $1,000). In 2021, her share of corporate net income was $3,000. She would first increase the tax basis in the loan to its original $1,500. Then she would eliminate the $1,000 suspended loss. Finally, she would increase the tax basis of her stock by the remaining $500.

---

An S corporation differs from a partnership in that the shareholder does not increase their stock basis by their share of debt in the corporation.

---

**EXAMPLE 15-28**

Laurel owns stock in a Subchapter S corporation. At the end of 2020, her tax basis in the stock was $100. In 2021, her share of corporate net income was $150, and her share of a corporate charitable contribution was $300. At the end of 2021, a simple mathematical calculation would indicate that her stock basis is a negative $50 ($100 + $150 − $300 = [$50]). However, basis cannot be negative. Her basis is set to zero and the $50 shortfall is suspended to future years. If, in 2022, Laurel's share of corporate net income was $400, she would increase her stock basis by $400 and decrease her stock basis by the suspended $50, resulting in a December 2022 stock basis of $350.

---

## Schedule M-1

Schedule M-1 for Form 1120S is also a reconciliation between income for books and income for taxes. The substantive difference between an S corporation Schedule M-1 and a C corporation Schedule M-1 is that an S corporation has no line for federal income tax because the Subchapter S corporation does not pay federal income tax; the shareholders pay it.

| | |
|---|---|
| **CONCEPT CHECK 15-7— LO 15-7**  | 1. Corporations with fewer than 100 shareholders are automatically considered Subchapter S corporations. True or false? |
| | 2. A Subchapter S corporation is taxed in a manner similar to a partnership. True or false? |
| | 3. Subchapter S corporations file a Form _____. |
| | 4. Alyssa is a shareholder in a Subchapter S corporation and has a basis of $1,000 in her stock. The corporation gives her a $200 cash dividend. Is this dividend taxable to Alyssa? |
| | 5. Similar to a partnership, shareholders of a Subchapter S corporation increase the basis of their stock by their share of corporate debts. True or false? |

# Summary

**LO 15-1:** Describe corporate formation and filing requirements.

Corporations
- Are legal entities formed under the laws of a state.
- Can use cash basis of accounting if sales ≤$26 million or have no inventory.
- Can choose fiscal year-end in first year of corporate existence.
- File Form 1120.

**LO 15-2:** Calculate corporate and shareholder basis.
- No gain on formation of corporation if transferors control 80% or more.
- Relief of liability in excess of basis triggers gain equal to the excess.
- Boot received triggers gain.
- Basis to corporation is shareholder basis plus gain recognized by shareholder.
- Basis to shareholder is carryover basis plus gain recognized, minus boot received.

**LO 15-3:** Determine corporate taxable income and tax liability.
- Taxable income generally follows rules associated with trade or business (Chapter 6).
- Net capital losses are not permitted. Carry back three years and then forward five.
- Charitable contributions are limited to 10% of taxable income before considering charitable contributions. Excess is carried forward five years. For 2020 and 2021 only, the limitation is 25%.
- A deduction is permitted equal to 50%, 65%, or 100% of dividends received from other domestic corporations. DRD may be limited.
- Organizational expenditures and start-up expenses can be deducted over 180 months or more upon election.
- Taxable income is taxed at a rate of 21%.
- Estimated payments are required.
- Net operating losses are accounted for differently depending on the year the NOL is created. See text for details.

**LO 15-4:** Explain the tax rules for transactions with shareholders.
- Distributions from earnings and profits are dividends and are taxable to shareholders; not deductible by corporation.
- Distributions in excess of E&P are nontaxable to extent of stock basis and a capital gain in excess of basis.
- Distribution of property with FMV in excess of basis creates gain to corporation.
- Distribution in full liquidation of shareholder interest creates gain or loss equal to distribution compared to basis.

**LO 15-5:** Prepare Schedules L, M-1, and M-3.
- Schedule L is a beginning and ending balance sheet in accordance with financial accounting method.
- Schedule M-1 is a reconciliation from book income to taxable income.
- Schedule M-1 sets forth all book/tax differences, whether permanent or temporary.
- Schedule M-3, a comprehensive book/tax reconciliation, is for large corporations.

**LO 15-6:** Discuss other corporate issues.
- Parent–subsidiary groups are those in which a common parent owns, directly or indirectly, at least 80% of one or more other corporations.
- They can elect to file consolidated tax return.
- Brother–sister group may exist if five or fewer persons own two or more corporations.
- They must disclose to IRS.
- The corporate AMT was repealed in 2018.
- Deduction for business interest expense allowed to extent it does not exceed the sum of business interest income plus 30% of Adjusted Taxable Income. For 2020 only, the limitation is 50%.

**LO 15-7:** Know the rules for tax treatment of Subchapter S corporations.

Subchapter S corporations
- Are "regular" corporations that elect to be taxed in a manner similar to a partnership.
- File 1120S.
- Must meet four tests to elect Sub S status.
- Report taxable income and separately stated items similar to a partnership.
- Do not pay tax; shareholders do.
- Calculate shareholder basis similar to partnership except corporate debt does not affect basis.
- Can have distributions, which are not taxable to shareholders.

---

## *EA Fast Fact*

What are the key requirements for becoming an Enrolled Agent?

- **Education**–No specific degree requirement–but a significant amount of tax knowledge pertaining to the Enrolled Agent Exam.
- **Age**–Minimum 18
- **Citizenship/Residence**–Anywhere in the world, ***U.S. citizenship is not required.***
- **Compliance**–U.S. taxpayers must have filed all required tax returns for all years–and must have paid all their taxes–income, business, payroll, etc.
- **PTIN**–You must get a Preparer Tax Identification Number; *you cannot schedule an exam date without it.* Sign up online at https://rpr.irs.gov/datamart/mainMenuUSIRS.do
- **Form 2587**–Complete and submit your application for the EA Exam
- **EA Enrolled Agent Exam**–Pass all three parts of the Enrolled Agent.

**IMPORTANT**

You are eligible to receive absolutely free, the Surgent Enrolled Agent review program for Part I of the EA exam as a result of purchasing this text. To activate your free access, go to https://Surgent.com/McGrawHill/EA.

---

## Discussion Questions  Mc Graw Hill **connect**

All applicable discussion questions are available with *Connect*©

LO 15-1  1. Explain the circumstances in which a corporation can use the accrual basis or the cash basis of accounting.

_____

_____

_____

LO 15-1  2. When must a corporate tax return be filed? Can a corporation receive an extension of time to file a return, and if so, what is the length of the extension?

_____

_____

_____

LO 15-1  3. Without regard to any extensions of time to file, when is the income tax return due for a corporation with a May 31 year-end? An August 31 year-end? A February 28 year-end?

_____

_____

_____

LO 15-2    4. Explain the 80% rule as it pertains to the formation of a corporation.

_____
_____
_____

LO 15-2    5. In what instances could a gain be recorded associated with the issuance of stock upon formation of a corporation? Assume that the 80% test is met.

_____
_____
_____

LO 15-2    6. An individual contributes property with a fair market value in excess of basis to a corporation in exchange for stock. What is the basis of the stock in the hands of the shareholder, and what is the basis of the property contributed in the hands of the corporation?

_____
_____
_____

LO 15-3    7. What is the *dividends received deduction?* What is its purpose?

_____
_____
_____

LO 15-3    8. Explain the rules associated with capital loss carrybacks and carryforwards.

_____
_____
_____

LO 15-3    9. Explain the rules pertaining to the deductibility of charitable contributions for a C corporation.

_____
_____
_____

LO 15-3    10. Explain the difference between *organizational expenses* and *start-up expenditures.* In what circumstances are they deductible?

_____
_____
_____

LO 15-3    11. Explain the net operating loss rules for 2018 and later.

_____
_____
_____

LO 15-3    12. On what dates are estimated payments due for a calendar-year corporation? What are the dates for a corporation with a fiscal year ending August 31?

_____
_____
_____

**LO 15-3**    13. Explain the rules associated with the carryback and carryforward of net operating losses created in 2017.

_____

_____

_____

**LO 15-4**    14. A corporation may make a distribution to its shareholders. Depending on the circumstances, in the hands of the shareholder, the distribution can be classified as a dividend, a tax-free distribution, or a capital gain. Explain the circumstances in which each classification can occur.

_____

_____

_____

**LO 15-4**    15. In what circumstances does a corporation record a gain related to a distribution to a shareholder?

_____

_____

_____

**LO 15-5**    16. What is Schedule M-1, and what is its purpose?

_____

_____

_____

**LO 15-5**    17. What is Schedule L, and what is its purpose?

_____

_____

_____

**LO 15-6**    18. Explain the business interest expense limitation rules for 2021.

_____

_____

_____

**LO 15-6**    19. Under what circumstances can a parent–subsidiary group file a consolidated income tax return?

_____

_____

_____

**LO 15-6**    20. Why might a parent–subsidiary group choose to file, or not to file, a consolidated income tax return?

_____

_____

_____

**LO 15-6**    21. What are the two tests used to determine whether a group of corporations is a brother–sister group?

_____

_____

_____

**LO 15-7**   22. What criteria must a corporation meet to appropriately elect Subchapter S status?

_____

_____

_____

**LO 15-7**   23. A calendar-year corporation properly files a Subchapter S election on January 10, 2021. On what date is the election effective? What if the election were filed on June 1, 2021?

_____

_____

_____

**LO 15-7**   24. The Subchapter S status of a calendar-year corporation is statutorily terminated on August 12, 2021. The Subchapter S status is deemed to be terminated on what date? What is the answer if the status were voluntarily revoked on that date?

_____

_____

_____

## Multiple-Choice Questions

All applicable multiple-choice questions are available with *Connect*©

**LO 15-1**   25. Which of the following statements is correct?

    *a.* A calendar-year corporation must file its tax return no later than March 15 unless it requests an extension.

    *b.* A corporation is a legal entity that is taxed on its taxable income.

    *c.* Corporations choose their tax year in their first year of operation and can elect to change it in their third year of operation.

    *d.* Large corporations without inventory can choose to use either the cash or accrual method of accounting.

**LO 15-1**   26. A corporation has a fiscal year-end of June. If the corporation does not receive an automatic extension of time to file its return, the return will be due on the 15th of

    *a.* December.

    *b.* November.

    *c.* October.

    *d.* September.

**LO 15-2**   27. Two individuals form a corporation and own all of its stock. One individual contributes cash, and the other contributes property encumbered by a mortgage. The new corporation assumes the mortgage. Which of the following statements is true with respect to the individual who contributes the property?

    *a.* Because the 80% test is met, no gain or loss will be recognized.

    *b.* Gain is recognized to the extent of relief of liability.

    *c.* Gain is recognized to the extent of relief of liability in excess of the basis of property contributed.

    *d.* Gain is recognized to the extent that the fair market value of the stock exceeds the basis of the property contributed.

**LO 15-2**   28. Tameka and Janelle form a corporation in which each will own 50% of the stock. Tameka contributes $50,000 in cash. Janelle contributes property with a basis of $30,000 and an FMV of $60,000. She receives $10,000 of inventory from the corporation. Which of the following statements is true?

    *a.* Janelle will report a gain of $10,000.

    *b.* Janelle will report a gain of $30,000.

    *c.* Tameka will report a gain of $10,000.

    *d.* Neither Tameka nor Janelle will report a gain or loss as a result of these transactions.

**LO 15-2**   29. Svetlana forms a corporation in which she is the sole shareholder. She contributes a vehicle with a basis of $15,000 and an FMV of $8,000 in exchange for stock. She also contributes cash of $2,000. Svetlana will recognize

    *a.* A $5,000 loss.

    *b.* A $7,000 loss.

    *c.* A $10,000 loss.

    *d.* Neither a gain nor loss.

**LO 15-2**   30. Annabelle forms a corporation in which she is the sole shareholder. She transfers $20,000 cash plus land with a $100,000 adjusted basis and a $160,000 FMV in exchange for all the stock of the corporation. The corporation assumes the $140,000 mortgage on the land. What is her basis in the stock, and what is the gain she must report (if any)?

    *a.* No gain; stock basis is $120,000.

    *b.* Gain of $20,000; stock basis is $120,000.

    *c.* No gain; stock basis is $100,000.

    *d.* Gain of $20,000; stock basis is zero.

**LO 15-3**   31. Mountain Company owns 25% of Valley Company. Both are domestic corporations. Valley pays a $60,000 dividend to Mountain. What amount of dividend income will be included in the taxable income of Mountain Company?

    *a.* $15,000.

    *b.* $21,000.

    *c.* $39,000.

    *d.* $60,000.

**LO 15-3**   32. For Subchapter C corporations, which of the following statements is true?

    *a.* Capital losses can be carried back three years and then carried forward five years.

    *b.* Corporations can elect to forgo the carryback period for capital losses and only carry the losses forward.

    *c.* Capital losses can be carried back 2 years and then carried forward 20 years.

    *d.* Capital losses are permitted up to $3,000 per year.

**LO 15-1, 15-3**   33. Which of the following statements is false?

    *a.* A corporation with average sales in excess of $26,000,000 must use the accrual method of accounting.

    *b.* The charitable contributions of a corporation may be limited.

    *c.* A corporation may be entitled to a deduction for dividends received from other domestic corporations.

    *d.* Passive loss rules apply to all corporations.

LO 15-3    34. A calendar-year corporate taxpayer must make its final estimated tax payment on the 15th of which month?

    *a.* November.

    *b.* December.

    *c.* January.

    *d.* February.

LO 15-4    35. Which, if any, of the following statements concerning the shareholders of a Subchapter C corporation is correct?

    *a.* Shareholders are taxed on their proportionate share of earnings and profits as they are earned.

    *b.* Shareholders are taxed on distributions from corporate earnings and profits.

    *c.* Shareholders are never taxed on earnings and profits or distributions from the corporation.

    *d.* None of these statements is correct.

LO 15-4    36. Parker Company has earnings and profits of $8,000. It distributes capital gain property with a basis of $2,000 and FMV of $9,000 to Gertrude Parker, its sole shareholder. Gertrude has a basis of $10,000 in her stock. Which of the following statements is true with respect to this transaction?

    *a.* Gertrude will report dividend income of $2,000 and a capital gain of $7,000.

    *b.* Gertrude will report dividend income of $8,000.

    *c.* Gertrude will report dividend income of $8,000 and a nontaxable distribution of $1,000.

    *d.* Gertrude will report dividend income of $9,000.

LO 15-5    37. Which of the following is a negative adjustment on Schedule M-1?

    *a.* Federal income tax.

    *b.* Charitable contributions in excess of the limitation percentage.

    *c.* Depreciation for books in excess of depreciation for taxes.

    *d.* Tax-exempt interest income.

LO 15-5    38. Which of the following is a positive adjustment on Schedule M-1?

    *a.* Excess of capital losses over capital gains.

    *b.* Excess of capital gains over capital losses.

    *c.* Charitable contribution carryover to the current year.

    *d.* Depreciation for taxes in excess of depreciation for books.

LO 15-6    39. Banana Company is widely held. It owns 85% of Strawberry Corporation. Two individuals hold the remaining 15%. Which of the following statements is true?

    *a.* Banana and Strawberry must file a consolidated tax return.

    *b.* Banana and Strawberry can elect to file a consolidated tax return.

    *c.* Banana and Strawberry can file a consolidated tax return if the other owners of Strawberry agree.

    *d.* Banana and Strawberry are brother–sister corporations.

LO 15-6    40. Concerning the business interest expense deduction, which of the following statements is true?

     *a.* Disallowed interest expense can be carried forward indefinitely.

     *b.* The interest expense deduction cannot exceed 50% of adjusted taxable income.

     *c.* The interest expense limitation does not apply to a business with receipts under $26 million.

     *d.* Adjusted taxable income is equal to taxable income before business interest expense.

LO 15-7    41. Which of the following items increase basis for a stockholder of a Subchapter S corporation?

     *a.* Capital contributions.

     *b.* Charitable contributions.

     *c.* Net losses.

     *d.* Distributions from the corporation.

LO 15-7    42. Which of the following statements is incorrect?

     *a.* An S corporation can own stock of a C corporation.

     *b.* A C corporation can own stock of an S corporation.

     *c.* An S corporation can be a partner in a partnership.

     *d.* An estate can own stock of an S corporation.

LO 15-7    43. Which of the following statements concerning the shareholders of a Subchapter S corporation is correct?

     *a.* Shareholders are taxed on their proportionate share of earnings that are distributed.

     *b.* Shareholders are taxed on the distributions from the corporation.

     *c.* Shareholders are taxed on their proportionate share of earnings whether or not distributed.

     *d.* None of these statements is correct.

LO 15-4, 15-7    44. Chen received a $10,000 dividend from a Subchapter C corporation. He also owns a 50% interest in a Subchapter S corporation that reported $100,000 of taxable income. He received a distribution of $20,000 from the Subchapter S corporation. How much income will Chen report as a result of these events?

     *a.* $30,000.

     *b.* $40,000.

     *c.* $60,000.

     *d.* $80,000.

## Problems    **connect**

All applicable problems are available with *Connect*

LO 15-2    45. When a corporation is formed, in certain cases the transferor may report a gain. What are the instances in which a gain would be reported? In these cases, what is the basis of the stock held by the transferor?

_____

_____

_____

_____

_____

_____

LO 15-2    46. An individual contributes property with an FMV in excess of basis to a corporation in exchange for stock. The property is subject to a mortgage. In each of the following instances, determine the basis of the stock in the hands of the shareholder and the basis of the property contributed in the hands of the corporation. Assume that the 80% rule is met.

      *a.* The property is subject to a mortgage that is less than basis, and the corporation assumes the mortgage.

      *b.* The property is subject to a mortgage that is more than basis, and the corporation assumes the mortgage.

LO 15-2    47. Determine the basis of stock in the hands of the shareholder in each of the following instances. Assume that the 80% rule is met in all cases.

      *a.* Contribution of property with a basis of $1,000 and an FMV of $1,400.

      *b.* Contribution of property with a basis of $3,000 and an FMV of $3,800. The stockholder also received $500 cash from the corporation as part of the stock transaction.

      *c.* Contribution of property with a basis of $8,200 and an FMV of $12,500. The stockholder also received property with an FMV of $1,700 from the corporation as part of the stock transaction.

      *d.* Contribution of a building with an FMV of $200,000, a mortgage (assumed by the corporation) of $100,000, and a basis of $125,000.

      *e.* Contribution of a building with an FMV of $1,700,000, a mortgage (assumed by the corporation) of $1,000,000, and a basis of $635,000.

LO 15-2    48. Using the information from Problem 47, determine the basis of the property contributed in the hands of the corporation in each instance. Assume that the 80% rule is met in all cases.

**LO 15-3**    49. Explain the operation of the dividends received deduction.

_____

_____

_____

_____

_____

_____

**LO 15-3**    50. Determine the amount of the dividends received deduction in each of the following instances. In all cases, the net income figure includes the full dividend.

   *a.* Dividend of $10,000 from a 45% owned corporation; taxable income before DRD of $50,000.

   *b.* Dividend of $19,000 from a 15% owned corporation; taxable income before DRD of $75,000.

   *c.* Dividend of $22,000 from a 60% owned corporation; taxable income before DRD of $11,000.

   *d.* Dividend of $8,000 from a 10% owned corporation; taxable income before DRD of $7,000.

_____

_____

_____

_____

_____

_____

**LO 15-3**    51. For each of the following cases, determine the amount of capital gain or loss to report in each year (after taking into account any applicable carrybacks) and the capital loss carry-forward to 2021, if any. Assume that 2015 is the first year of operation for each corporation.

| | Capital Gain or Loss for Year Indicated | | | | | |
|---|---|---|---|---|---|---|
| Corporation | 2015 | 2016 | 2017 | 2018 | 2019 | 2020 |
| A | $ 4,000 | $7,000 | $(10,000) | $ 5,000 | $ 3,000 | $(1,000) |
| B | 5,000 | 3,000 | 3,000 | 4,000 | (20,000) | 2,000 |
| C | 5,000 | 9,000 | (3,000) | 2,000 | (20,000) | 8,000 |
| D | (50,000) | 7,000 | 3,000 | 11,000 | 10,000 | 2,000 |

_____

_____

_____

_____

_____

_____

**LO 15-3**    52. For 2021, determine the deductible charitable contribution in each of the following instances:

   *a.* Charitable contribution of $4,000 and taxable income before charitable contribution of $30,000.

   *b.* Charitable contribution of $8,000 and taxable income before charitable contribution of $30,000.

  *c.* Charitable contribution of $8,800 and taxable income before charitable contribution of $30,000. Taxable income includes a net operating loss carryforward of $5,000.

  *d.* Charitable contribution of $8,800 and taxable income before charitable contribution of $30,000. Taxable income includes a capital loss carryback of $5,000.

    _____

    _____

    _____

    _____

    _____

    _____

**LO 15-3** 53. Determine taxable income in each of the following independent cases. In all cases, the company was formed in 2012, was very profitable in all years prior to 2017, and had retained earnings of $1,000,000 at the end of 2017.

  *a.* In 2018, Company A has taxable income of $60,000 prior to consideration of any net operating loss. In 2017, the company incurred a net operating loss of $10,000. It did not elect to waive the carryback period. Determine 2018 taxable income.

  *b.* In 2018, Company B has taxable income of $50,000 prior to consideration of any net operating loss. In 2017, the company incurred a net operating loss of $20,000. It elected to waive the carryback period. Determine 2018 taxable income.

  *c.* In 2021, Company C has taxable income of $35,000 prior to consideration of any net operating loss. In 2020, the company incurred a net operating loss of $30,000 and elected to forgo the carryback period. Determine 2021 taxable income.

  *d.* In 2021, Company D has taxable income of $35,000 prior to consideration of any net operating loss. In 2017, the company incurred a net operating loss of $5,000. It elected to waive the carryback period. In 2018, the company incurred a net operating loss of $40,000. In 2019 and 2020 the company had net income of zero. Determine 2021 taxable income.

    _____

    _____

    _____

    _____

    _____

    _____

**LO 15-3** 54. Determine taxable income in each of the following instances. Assume that the corporation is a C corporation and that book income is before any income tax expense.

  *a.* Book income of $50,000 including capital gains of $2,000, a charitable contribution of $1,000, and nonrestaurant meals expenses of $3,000.

  *b.* Book income of $92,000 including capital losses of $3,000, a charitable contribution of $52,000, and restaurant meals expenses of $3,000.

  *c.* Book income of $76,000 including municipal bond interest of $2,000, a charitable contribution of $5,000, and dividends of $3,000 from a 10% owned domestic corporation. The corporation also has a $28,000 charitable contribution carryover.

  *d.* Book income of $129,000 including municipal bond interest of $2,000, a charitable contribution of $5,000, and dividends of $7,000 from a 70% owned domestic corporation. The corporation has a capital loss carryover of $6,000 and a capital gain of $2,500 in the current year.

_____
_____
_____
_____
_____
_____
_____

LO 15-3   55. LMNO Corporation was formed in 2011. It reported net income (loss) over the 2011 through 2017 tax years, before accounting for any net operating losses, as follows:

| | |
|---|---|
| 2011 | $ (4,000) |
| 2012 | 19,000 |
| 2013 | 23,000 |
| 2014 | (31,000) |
| 2015 | 11,000 |
| 2016 | (8,000) |
| 2017 | 3,000 |

  *a.* Determine annual taxable income after accounting for any net operating losses for 2011 to 2017 assuming the corporation does not waive the carryback period. Also determine any NOL carryforward to 2018.

  *b.* Determine annual taxable income after accounting for any net operating losses for 2011 to 2017 assuming the corporation waives the carryback period. Also determine any NOL carryforward to 2018.

_____
_____
_____
_____
_____
_____

LO 15-4   56. Determine the amount of taxable dividend, nontaxable distribution, and capital gain for the distributions made in each of the following cases:

  *a.* Corporate E&P of $10,000, shareholder stock basis of $12,000, distribution of $6,000.

  *b.* Corporate E&P of $7,500, shareholder stock basis of $7,000, distribution of $6,500.

  *c.* Corporate E&P of $16,000, shareholder stock basis of $5,000, distribution of $17,000.

  *d.* Corporate E&P of $14,000, shareholder stock basis of $11,000, distribution of $26,000.

_____
_____
_____
_____
_____
_____

LO 15-5   57. Go to the IRS website (www.irs.gov) and print page 6 of Form 1120. Complete Schedule M-1 for each of the following cases:

  *a.* Corporate financial statement: net income of $52,000 including tax expense of $15,000, charitable contributions of $3,000, and depreciation expense of $37,000. Depreciation expense for tax purposes is $46,000.

b. Corporate financial statement: net income of $59,000 including tax expense of $27,000, charitable contributions of $28,000, depreciation expense of $103,000, and nonrestaurant meals expenses of $31,000. Depreciation expense for tax purposes is $145,000.

c. Corporate financial statement: net income of $226,000 including tax expense of $111,000, charitable contributions of $16,000, municipal bond interest of $19,000, nonrestaurant meals expenses of $41,000, capital gains of $6,000, and depreciation expense of $142,000. Depreciation expense for tax purposes is $131,000, and the corporation has a $7,000 charitable contribution carryforward for the current year.

_____

_____

_____

_____

_____

_____

**LO 15-6** 58. In each of the following independent cases for tax year 2021, determine the amount of business interest expense deduction and disallowed interest expense carryforward, if any. Assume that average annual gross receipts exceed $26 million.

a. Company A has ATI of $70,000 and business interest expense of $20,000.

b. Company B has ATI of $90,000, business interest expense of $50,000, and business interest income of $2,000.

c. Company C has taxable income of $50,000 that includes business interest expense of $90,000 and depreciation of $20,000.

_____

_____

_____

_____

_____

_____

**LO 15-7** 59. Refer to Problem 54. Determine the amount of taxable income and separately stated items in each case, assuming the corporation is a Subchapter S corporation.

_____

_____

_____

_____

_____

_____

**LO 15-7** 60. Refer to Problem 57. Determine the amount of taxable income and separately stated items in each case, assuming the corporation is a Subchapter S corporation. Ignore any carryforward items.

_____

_____

_____

_____

_____

_____

## Tax Return Problems   Mc Graw Hill **connect**

All applicable tax return problems are available with **Connect**©

**Tax Return Problem 1**
Phil Williams and Liz Johnson are 60% and 40% shareholders, respectively, in WJ Corporation, a Subchapter S corporation. The corporation had the following activity during the year:

| | |
|---|---|
| Income | $336,123 |
| Interest income | 1,259 |
| Dividend income (qualified) | 4,586 |
| Long-term capital gains | 13,458 |
| Total revenue | $355,426 |
| Expenses | |
| Salaries and wages (nonofficers) | $ 47,000 |
| Salaries and wages, owners and officers | 125,000 |
| Depreciation (MACRS—includes $9,000 § 179 expense) | 41,888 |
| Interest expense | 5,220 |
| Taxes and licenses | 15,548 |
| Nonrestaurant meals (100%) | 15,257 |
| Auto | 5,254 |
| Insurance (nonofficer health) | 6,000 |
| Accounting and legal | 2,800 |
| Repairs | 1,200 |
| Charitable contributions | 2,500 |
| Payroll penalties | 500 |
| Total expenses | $268,167 |
| Net income | $ 87,259 |

During the year, the corporation made a distribution of $20,000, in total, to its shareholders. Complete page 1, Schedule K, and Schedule M-1 of Form 1120S.

**Tax Return Problem 2**
Harrell and Smith, Inc., 204 Ambulance Street, Anywhere, CA 92345, is a corporation (EIN 57-1234567) formed on January 1, 2015. Information concerning the corporation and its two shareholders follows. It uses tax/cash basis accounting, did not pay dividends in excess of earnings and profits, has no foreign shareholders, is not publicly traded, and has no NOL carrybacks.

Taye Harrell (SSN 412-34-5670), 1018 Lexington Downs, Anywhere, CA 92345, is a 60% shareholder. Della Smith (SSN 412-34-5671), 4564 Yates Road, Anywhere, CA 92345, is a 40% shareholder. Taye received a dividend of $60,000, and Della received a dividend of $40,000. Both of these dividends are in addition to their salaries.

### HARRELL AND SMITH, INC.
#### Comparative Balance Sheet
#### As of December 31, 2020, and December 31, 2021

| | 12/31/20 | 12/31/21 |
|---|---|---|
| Assets | | |
| Cash | $ 39,955 | $ 45,459 |
| Investments | 258,456 | 169,125 |
| Office equipment | 225,000 | 310,759 |
| Accumulated depreciation (equipment) | (156,000) | (165,379) |
| Building | 491,200 | 491,200 |
| Accumulated depreciation (building) | (37,232) | (49,826) |
| Total assets | $821,379 | $801,338 |

---

**HARRELL AND SMITH, INC.** *(concluded)*
**Comparative Balance Sheet**
**As of December 31, 2020, and December 31, 2021**

|  | 12/31/20 | 12/31/21 |
|---|---|---|
| Liabilities and equity |  |  |
| Notes payable | $353,600 | $335,458 |
| Common stock | 10,000 | 10,000 |
| Retained earnings | 457,779 | 455,880 |
| Total liabilities and equity | $821,379 | $801,338 |

---

**HARRELL AND SMITH, INC.**
**Income Statement**
**For the Year Ending December 31, 2021**

| Revenue |  |
|---|---|
| Consulting income | $866,689 |
| Interest income | 4,231 |
| Rental income | 9,000 |
| Dividend income (qualified) | 8,234 |
| Long-term capital losses | (8,200) |
| Total revenue | $879,954 |
| | |
| Expenses | |
| Salaries and wages (nonowners) | $253,000 |
| Officers' salaries | |
| Harrell | 225,000 |
| Smith | 150,000 |
| Depreciation | 21,973 |
| Interest expense | 20,127 |
| Taxes and licenses | 24,051 |
| Utilities | 15,500 |
| Travel | 11,850 |
| Nonrestaurant meals (100%) | 12,452 |
| Auto | 18,500 |
| Insurance (health) | 7,000 |
| Accounting and legal | 6,450 |
| Repairs | 3,200 |
| Charitable contributions | 12,000 |
| Payroll penalties | 750 |
| Total expenses | $781,853 |
| Net income | $ 98,101 |

---

Prepare Form 1120, pages 1–5, for Harrell and Smith, Inc. Schedule D and Form 4562 can be omitted (the information given is not sufficient to complete these forms).

We have provided selected filled-in source documents that are available in *Connect*.

# Appendix A

# Amended Tax Returns (Form 1040X)

Over 157 million individual income tax returns are filed each year. The vast majority of those returns are filed correctly. However, on occasion, the information on an already-filed tax return is determined to be incorrect.

There are literally hundreds of reasons why a previously filed return might be incorrect: a math error, a change of filing status, an additional or corrected informational tax form received, the basis or sales price on the sale of a capital asset initially reported incorrectly, a permitted itemized deduction omitted, and so on. There might be one error or multiple errors, and the changes might cause total tax liability to increase or decrease.

If a previously filed tax return is determined to be in error, the taxpayer must file an amended tax return on Form 1040X. On the amended return, the taxpayer provides numerical information concerning the tax return item(s) that is (are) being corrected plus a reconciliation between the original data and the correct data. The form also has a section where the taxpayer must explain the change.

Let us look at an example:

- Exhibit A-1 is the Form 1040 originally filed by Kim Watkins for tax year 2020. She had wage income and interest income, and she took the standard deduction. She originally received a refund of $396. After she had filed her return, she received a corrected Form 1099-INT from State Savings Bank. The corrected Form 1099-INT showed interest income in box 1 that was $250 more than originally reported.

- As a result of receiving this corrected Form 1099-INT, Kim must file an amended tax return. The completed Form 1040X amended tax return is shown in Exhibit A-2.

- Column A of the 1040X amended return provides tax information as it was originally filed. The information in column A comes from the data on the original Form 1040 in Exhibit A-1. Column B is used to indicate the numerical items that have changed. In this case, line 1, Adjusted Gross Income, must increase by $250 to properly report the information from the corrected Form 1099-INT received by Kim. Column C represents the corrected totals. The explanation for the change is provided in Part III on page 2.

- Note that we are preparing an amended return for tax year 2020. Thus, the amount of tax on line 6 of Form 1040X is determined using the 2020 tax tables. These tables can be found in the Form 1040 instructions for tax year 2020, available on the IRS website at www.irs.gov.

- Because Kim's income increased by $250, she will owe additional tax of $30. That amount is reflected on line 20. When Kim files her amended Form 1040X, she must include a check for $30. Kim is in the 12% tax bracket. The additional tax represents the 12% income tax that is due on the additional $250 of income ($250 × 12% = $30).

Only one item needed to be corrected in our example. If multiple changes are required, the taxpayer should clearly explain each item and provide a detailed summation and reconciliation.

Use the information from our previous example. Assume that Kim received two corrected 1099-INT forms, one from State Savings Bank that increased her interest income by $250 and another from State Bank and Trust that decreased her interest income by $100. In this case, the amount on line 1, column B, of Form 1040X would be $150, the net difference. The explanation in Part III on page 2 needs to clearly explain the change. Here is how Part III, Explanation of Changes, might appear in this case:

---

Taxpayer received two corrected Forms 1099-INT. One was from State Savings Bank. It showed corrected interest income $250 more than originally reported. The other was from State Bank and Trust. It showed corrected interest income $100 less than originally reported. The amount of Adjusted Gross Income on line 1 is increased by $150, determined as follows:

| | |
|---|---:|
| Change from corrected Form 1099-INT from State Savings Bank | $ 250 |
| Change from corrected Form 1099-INT from State Bank and Trust | (100) |
| Net change to Adjusted Gross Income | $ 150 |

---

It is extremely important to note that the amended return must be prepared using the tax rules in effect for the year of the original return. For example, if we were preparing an amended return for Kim Watkins for tax year 2019, the standard deduction on line 2 of Form 1040X would be $12,200 because that was the correct amount for tax year 2019. We would also use the tax tables or tax rate schedules for 2019.

Generally, an amended return must be filed within three years after the date the original return was filed or within two years after the date the taxpayer paid the tax due on the original return, whichever is later.

**EXHIBIT A-1**

**Form 1040** Department of the Treasury—Internal Revenue Service (99)
**U.S. Individual Income Tax Return** **2020** OMB No. 1545-0074 IRS Use Only—Do not write or staple in this space.

**Filing Status** ☑ Single ☐ Married filing jointly ☐ Married filing separately (MFS) ☐ Head of household (HOH) ☐ Qualifying widow(er) (QW)
Check only one box. If you checked the MFS box, enter the name of your spouse. If you checked the HOH or QW box, enter the child's name if the qualifying person is a child but not your dependent ▶

| Your first name and middle initial | Last name | Your social security number |
|---|---|---|
| Kim | Watkins | 4 1 2 3 4 5 6 7 0 |
| If joint return, spouse's first name and middle initial | Last name | Spouse's social security number |

Home address (number and street). If you have a P.O. box, see instructions. | Apt. no.
**123 Main Street**
City, town, or post office. If you have a foreign address, also complete spaces below. | State **TX** | ZIP code **77845**
**Bryan**
Foreign country name | Foreign province/state/county | Foreign postal code

**Presidential Election Campaign** Check here if you, or your spouse if filing jointly, want $3 to go to this fund. Checking a box below will not change your tax or refund. ☐ You ☐ Spouse

At any time during 2020, did you receive, sell, send, exchange, or otherwise acquire any financial interest in any virtual currency? ☐ Yes ☑ No

**Standard Deduction** **Someone can claim:** ☐ You as a dependent ☐ Your spouse as a dependent
☐ Spouse itemizes on a separate return or you were a dual-status alien

**Age/Blindness** **You:** ☐ Were born before January 2, 1956 ☐ Are blind **Spouse:** ☐ Was born before January 2, 1956 ☐ Is blind

**Dependents** (see instructions):
(1) First name Last name | (2) Social security number | (3) Relationship to you | (4) ✔ if qualifies for (see instructions): Child tax credit / Credit for other dependents

| | | |
|---|---|---|
| 1 | Wages, salaries, tips, etc. Attach Form(s) W-2 | **1** 45,491 |
| 2a | Tax-exempt interest | **2b** 1,173 |
| 3a | Qualified dividends | **3b** |
| 4a | IRA distributions | **4b** |
| 5a | Pensions and annuities | **5b** |
| 6a | Social security benefits | **6b** |
| 7 | Capital gain or (loss). Attach Schedule D if required. If not required, check here ▶ ☐ | **7** |
| 8 | Other income from Schedule 1, line 9 | **8** |
| 9 | Add lines 1, 2b, 3b, 4b, 5b, 6b, 7, and 8. This is your **total income** ▶ | **9** 46,664 |
| 10 | Adjustments to income: | |
| a | From Schedule 1, line 22 | 10a |
| b | Charitable contributions if you take the standard deduction. See instructions | 10b |
| c | Add lines 10a and 10b. These are your **total adjustments to income** ▶ | **10c** 0 |
| 11 | Subtract line 10c from line 9. This is your **adjusted gross income** ▶ | **11** 46,664 |
| 12 | Standard deduction or itemized deductions (from Schedule A) | **12** 12,400 |
| 13 | Qualified business income deduction. Attach Form 8995 or Form 8995-A | **13** |
| 14 | Add lines 12 and 13 | **14** 12,400 |
| 15 | **Taxable income.** Subtract line 14 from line 11. If zero or less, enter -0- | **15** 34,264 |

Attach Sch. B if required.

**Standard Deduction for—**
• Single or Married filing separately, $12,400
• Married filing jointly or Qualifying widow(er), $24,800
• Head of household, $18,650
• If you checked any box under *Standard Deduction,* see instructions.

For Disclosure, Privacy Act, and Paperwork Reduction Act Notice, see separate instructions. Cat. No. 11320B Form **1040** (2020)

Source: U.S. Department of the Treasury, Internal Revenue Service, Form 1040. Washington, DC: 2020. *(continued)*

## EXHIBIT A-1 *(concluded)*

Form 1040 (2020)                                                                                                                      Page **2**

| Line | Description | | Amount |
|---|---|---|---|
| 16 | **Tax** (see instructions). Check if any from Form(s): **1** ☐ 8814  **2** ☐ 4972  **3** ☐ _____ | 16 | 3,916 |
| 17 | Amount from Schedule 2, line 3 | 17 | |
| 18 | Add lines 16 and 17 | 18 | 3,916 |
| 19 | Child tax credit or credit for other dependents | 19 | |
| 20 | Amount from Schedule 3, line 7 | 20 | |
| 21 | Add lines 19 and 20 | 21 | 0 |
| 22 | Subtract line 21 from line 18. If zero or less, enter -0- | 22 | 3,916 |
| 23 | Other taxes, including self-employment tax, from Schedule 2, line 10 | 23 | |
| 24 | Add lines 22 and 23. This is your **total tax** ▶ | 24 | 3,916 |
| 25 | Federal income tax withheld from: | | |
| a | Form(s) W-2 ......... **25a** 4,312 | | |
| b | Form(s) 1099 ......... **25b** | | |
| c | Other forms (see instructions) ......... **25c** | | |
| d | Add lines 25a through 25c | 25d | 4,312 |
| 26 | 2020 estimated tax payments and amount applied from 2019 return | 26 | |
| 27 | Earned income credit (EIC) ......... **27** | | |
| 28 | Additional child tax credit. Attach Schedule 8812 ......... **28** | | |
| 29 | American opportunity credit from Form 8863, line 8 ......... **29** | | |
| 30 | Recovery rebate credit. See instructions ......... **30** | | |
| 31 | Amount from Schedule 3, line 13 ......... **31** | | |
| 32 | Add lines 27 through 31. These are your **total other payments and refundable credits** ▶ | 32 | 0 |
| 33 | Add lines 25d, 26, and 32. These are your **total payments** ▶ | 33 | 4,312 |

- If you have a qualifying child, attach Sch. EIC.
- If you have nontaxable combat pay, see instructions.

**Refund**

| 34 | If line 33 is more than line 24, subtract line 24 from line 33. This is the amount you **overpaid** | 34 | 396 |
|---|---|---|---|
| 35a | Amount of line 34 you want **refunded to you.** If Form 8888 is attached, check here ▶ ☐ | 35a | 396 |

Direct deposit? ▶ **b** Routing number _____  ▶ **c** Type: ☐ Checking  ☐ Savings
See instructions. ▶ **d** Account number _____

| 36 | Amount of line 34 you want **applied to your 2021 estimated tax** ▶ **36** | | |
|---|---|---|---|

**Amount You Owe**

For details on how to pay, see instructions.

| 37 | Subtract line 33 from line 24. This is the **amount you owe now** ▶ | 37 | |
|---|---|---|---|

**Note:** Schedule H and Schedule SE filers, line 37 may not represent all of the taxes you owe for 2020. See Schedule 3, line 12e, and its instructions for details.

| 38 | Estimated tax penalty (see instructions) ▶ **38** | | |
|---|---|---|---|

**Third Party Designee**

Do you want to allow another person to discuss this return with the IRS? See instructions ▶ ☐ **Yes.** Complete below.  ☐ **No**

Designee's name ▶ _____  Phone no. ▶ _____  Personal identification number (PIN) ▶ _____

**Sign Here**

Under penalties of perjury, I declare that I have examined this return and accompanying schedules and statements, and to the best of my knowledge and belief, they are true, correct, and complete. Declaration of preparer (other than taxpayer) is based on all information of which preparer has any knowledge.

Joint return? See instructions. Keep a copy for your records.

| Your signature | Date | Your occupation | If the IRS sent you an Identity Protection PIN, enter it here (see inst.) ▶ _____ |
|---|---|---|---|
| Spouse's signature. If a joint return, **both** must sign. | Date | Spouse's occupation | If the IRS sent your spouse an Identity Protection PIN, enter it here (see inst.) ▶ _____ |

Phone no. _____  Email address _____

**Paid Preparer Use Only**

| Preparer's name | Preparer's signature | Date | PTIN | Check if: ☐ Self-employed |
|---|---|---|---|---|
| Firm's name ▶ | | | Phone no. | |
| Firm's address ▶ | | | Firm's EIN ▶ | |

Go to *www.irs.gov/Form1040* for instructions and the latest information.                                        Form **1040** (2020)

**EXHIBIT A-2**

| Form **1040-X** (Rev. July 2021) | Department of the Treasury—Internal Revenue Service<br>**Amended U.S. Individual Income Tax Return**<br>▶ Use this revision to amend 2019 or later tax returns.<br>▶ Go to *www.irs.gov/Form1040X* for instructions and the latest information. | OMB No. 1545-0074 |
|---|---|---|

This return is for calendar year (enter year) **2020**   or fiscal year (enter month and year ended) _____

| Your first name and middle initial<br>**Kim** | Last name<br>**Watkins** | Your social security number<br>4 1 2 3 4 5 6 7 0 |
|---|---|---|
| If joint return, spouse's first name and middle initial | Last name | Spouse's social security number |

| Current home address (number and street). If you have a P.O. box, see instructions.<br>**123 Main Street** | Apt. no. | Your phone number |
|---|---|---|

City, town or post office, state, and ZIP code. If you have a foreign address, also complete spaces below. See instructions.
**Bryan, TX 77845**

| Foreign country name | Foreign province/state/county | Foreign postal code |
|---|---|---|

**Amended return filing status.** You **must** check one box even if you are not changing your filing status. **Caution:** In general, you can't change your filing status from married filing jointly to married filing separately after the return due date.

☑ Single   ☐ Married filing jointly   ☐ Married filing separately (MFS)   ☐ Head of household (HOH)   ☐ Qualifying widow(er) (QW)

If you checked the MFS box, enter the name of your spouse. If you checked the HOH or QW box, enter the child's name if the qualifying person is a child but not your dependent ▶

Use Part III on page 2 to explain any changes.
Enter on lines 1 through 23, columns A through C, the amounts for the return year entered above.

| | | | **A.** Original amount reported or as previously adjusted (see instructions) | **B.** Net change—amount of increase or (decrease)—explain in Part III | **C.** Correct amount |
|---|---|---|---|---|---|
| **Income and Deductions** | | | | | |
| 1 | Adjusted gross income. If a net operating loss (NOL) carryback is included, check here ▶ ☐ | 1 | 46,664 | 250 | 46,914 |
| 2 | Itemized deductions or standard deduction | 2 | 12,400 | | 12,400 |
| 3 | Subtract line 2 from line 1 | 3 | 34,264 | 250 | 34,514 |
| 4a | Reserved for future use | 4a | | | |
| b | Qualified business income deduction | 4b | | | |
| 5 | Taxable income. Subtract line 4b from line 3. If the result is zero or less, enter -0- | 5 | 34,264 | 250 | 34,514 |
| **Tax Liability** | | | | | |
| 6 | Tax. Enter method(s) used to figure tax (see instructions): **Tax Tables** | 6 | 3,916 | 30 | 3,946 |
| 7 | Nonrefundable credits. If a general business credit carryback is included, check here ▶ ☐ | 7 | | | |
| 8 | Subtract line 7 from line 6. If the result is zero or less, enter -0- | 8 | 3,916 | 30 | 3,946 |
| 9 | Reserved for future use | 9 | | | |
| 10 | Other taxes | 10 | | | |
| 11 | Total tax. Add lines 8 and 10 | 11 | 3,916 | 30 | 3,946 |
| **Payments** | | | | | |
| 12 | Federal income tax withheld and excess social security and tier 1 RRTA tax withheld. (**If changing,** see instructions.) | 12 | 4,312 | | 4,312 |
| 13 | Estimated tax payments, including amount applied from prior year's return | 13 | | | |
| 14 | Earned income credit (EIC) | 14 | | | |
| 15 | Refundable credits from: ☐ Schedule 8812  Form(s) ☐ 2439  ☐ 4136  ☐ 8863  ☐ 8885  ☐ 8962 or  ☐ other (specify): _____ | 15 | | | |
| 16 | Total amount paid with request for extension of time to file, tax paid with original return, and additional tax paid after return was filed | | | 16 | |
| 17 | Total payments. Add lines 12 through 15, column C, and line 16 | | | 17 | 4,312 |
| **Refund or Amount You Owe** | | | | | |
| 18 | Overpayment, if any, as shown on original return or as previously adjusted by the IRS | | | 18 | 396 |
| 19 | Subtract line 18 from line 17. (If less than zero, see instructions.) | | | 19 | 3,916 |
| 20 | **Amount you owe.** If line 11, column C, is more than line 19, enter the difference | | | 20 | 30 |
| 21 | If line 11, column C, is less than line 19, enter the difference. This is the amount **overpaid** on this return | | | 21 | |
| 22 | Amount of line 21 you want **refunded to you** | | | 22 | |
| 23 | Amount of line 21 you want **applied to your** (enter year): _____   estimated tax | 23 | | | |

Complete and sign this form on page 2.

**For Paperwork Reduction Act Notice, see separate instructions.**    Cat. No. 11360L    Form **1040-X** (Rev. 7-2021)

*(continued)*

Form 1040-X (Rev. 7-2021)

Page **2**

## Part I — Dependents

Complete this part to change any information relating to your dependents.
This would include a change in the number of dependents.
Enter the information for the return year entered at the top of page 1.

| | | A. Original number of dependents reported or as previously adjusted | B. Net change — amount of increase or (decrease) | C. Correct number |
|---|---|---|---|---|
| 24 | Reserved for future use . . . . . . . . . . | | | |
| 25 | Your dependent children who lived with you . . . . . . . | | | |
| 26 | Your dependent children who didn't live with you due to divorce or separation . . . . . . . . . . . . . . . . | | | |
| 27 | Other dependents . . . . . . . . . . . . . | | | |
| 28 | Reserved for future use . . . . . . . . . . | | | |
| 29 | Reserved for future use . . . . . . . . . . | | | |
| 30 | List **ALL** dependents (children and others) claimed on this amended return. | | | |

**Dependents** (see instructions):

If more than four dependents, see instructions and check here ▶ ☐

| (a) First name | Last name | (b) Social security number | (c) Relationship to you | (d) ✓ if qualifies for (see instructions): Child tax credit | Credit for other dependents |
|---|---|---|---|---|---|
| | | | | ☐ | ☐ |
| | | | | ☐ | ☐ |
| | | | | ☐ | ☐ |
| | | | | ☐ | ☐ |

## Part II — Presidential Election Campaign Fund (for the return year entered at the top of page 1)

Checking below won't increase your tax or reduce your refund.

☐ Check here if you didn't previously want $3 to go to the fund, but now do.

☐ Check here if this is a joint return and your spouse did not previously want $3 to go to the fund, but now does.

## Part III — Explanation of Changes. In the space provided below, tell us why you are filing Form 1040-X.

▶ Attach any supporting documents and new or changed forms and schedules.

Taxpayer received a corrected Form 1099-INT from State Savings Bank. The interest income shown in box 1 of the corrected Form 1099-INT was $250 greater than originally reported to the taxpayer. The $250 increase is reported on page 1 above, in line 1, box B.

**Sign Here**

Remember to keep a copy of this form for your records.

Under penalties of perjury, I declare that I have filed an original return, and that I have examined this amended return, including accompanying schedules and statements, and to the best of my knowledge and belief, this amended return is true, correct, and complete. Declaration of preparer (other than taxpayer) is based on all information about which the preparer has any knowledge.

▶ Your signature

Date

Your occupation

▶ Spouse's signature. If a joint return, **both** must sign.

Date

Spouse's occupation

**Paid Preparer Use Only**

| Print/Type preparer's name | Preparer's signature | Date | Check ☐ if self-employed | PTIN |
|---|---|---|---|---|
| Firm's name ▶ | | | Firm's EIN ▶ | |
| Firm's address ▶ | | | Phone no. | |

For forms and publications, visit *www.irs.gov*.

Form **1040-X** (Rev. 7-2021)

# Appendix B

# Comprehensive Problems

In this appendix, we provide a series of comprehensive tax return problems. In the text, the scope of the tax return problems is generally limited to the subject matter of the chapter. The comprehensive problems in this appendix require integration of tax materials across multiple chapters. Each problem does have a primary focus area—Schedule A, C, D, or E. We provide two problems for Schedules A, C, and D. In each case, the first problem is a bit easier than the second.

The problems can be completed using the TaxACT software provided with this text or using the tax forms found on the IRS website (www.irs.gov).

For all comprehensive problems, assume the taxpayer does NOT wish to contribute to the Presidential Election Fund, unless otherwise stated in the problem. In addition, the taxpayer did not receive, sell, send, exchange, or otherwise acquire any financial interest in any virtual currency during the year. For any Comprehensive Problem for which the taxpayers are entitled to a child tax credit, assume that the taxpayers did NOT receive any advance child tax credit payments during 2021. Thus, the entire child tax credit (if permitted) will be claimed on the 2021 tax return.

## COMPREHENSIVE PROBLEM 1

### With Emphasis on Schedule A

James and Esther Johnson live at 45678 S.W. 112th Street, Homestead, FL 33033. James, who is 67 years old (date of birth 12/14/1954), is retired and receiving social security benefits, and Esther, who is 66 years old (date of birth 6/11/1955), is also retired but working on a part-time basis. Their social security numbers are 412-34-5670 and 412-34-5671, respectively. The Johnsons had qualifying health care coverage at all times during the tax year.

Annual social security income for Jim is $22,000 (SSA-1099, box 5) and for Esther is $13,800 (SSA-1099, box 5).

Interest received by them from Central Bank is $2,545 (1099-INT, box 1). No income tax withholding was made.

Esther is an employee working part-time as an interior decorator for Decorating House, a corporation. Her Form W-2 shows the following information:

$$
\begin{aligned}
\text{Wages} &= \$25,000.00 \\
\text{Federal W/H} &= \$\ 2,000.00 \\
\text{Social security wages} &= \$25,000.00 \\
\text{Social security W/H} &= \$\ 1,550.00 \\
\text{Medicare wages} &= \$25,000.00 \\
\text{Medicare W/H} &= \$\ \ \ \ 362.50
\end{aligned}
$$

Their itemized deductions are as follows:

1. Mortgage interest on their main home, $11,950.
2. Real estate taxes, $7,900.
3. Personal property taxes, $185.

4. Doctors' expenses unreimbursed by insurance, $6,700.
5. Medical insurance premiums for the year, $2,900.
6. Prescribed medicine, $1,995.
7. Vitamins, $300.
8. Total cash contributions to their church, $675. The contributions were made over the course of the year, and no individual contribution was greater than $250.
9. Tax preparation fees for their 2020 return, $325, paid in 2021.
10. Lottery tickets bought by Esther during the year, $750. Winnings received, $940 (W-2G, box 1). Income tax withholding on winnings, $35 (W-2G, box 4).

Because the Johnsons live in Florida, where there is no state income tax, they will deduct the estimation of the general sales tax related to the area in which they live. The most efficient way to do this is by using the Sales Tax Calculator on the IRS website at http://apps.irs.gov/app/stdc/. A key point to remember in using the calculator is that "income" for this calculation also includes the nontaxable portion of social security benefits. For more information on using the IRS Sales Tax Calculator, refer to page 5-12 in the text.

*Required*

Prepare their individual income tax return using the appropriate forms and schedules. They do not want to contribute to the presidential election campaign and do not want anyone to be a third-party designee. For any missing information, make reasonable assumptions. They had qualifying health coverage at all times during the year.

# COMPREHENSIVE PROBLEM 2

## With Emphasis on Schedule A

Jamie and Cecilia Reyes are husband and wife and file a joint return. They live at 5677 Apple Cove Road, Boise, ID 83722. Jamie's social security number is 412-34-5670 (date of birth 6/15/1972) and Cecilia's is 412-34-5671 (date of birth 4/12/1974). They provide more than half of the support of their daughter, Carmen (age 23), social security number 412-34-5672 (date of birth 9/1/1998), who is a full-time veterinarian school student. Carmen received a $3,200 scholarship covering some of her tuition at college. She was not required to perform any services to receive the scholarship. Jamie and Cecilia furnish all of the support of Maria (Jamie's mother), social security number 412-34-5673 (date of birth 11/6/1951), who is age 70 and lives in a nursing home. They also have a son, Gustavo (age 4), social security number 412-34-5674 (date of birth 3/14/2017). The Reyes and all of their dependents had qualifying health care coverage at all times during the tax year.

Jamie's W-2 contained the following information:

Federal wages (box 1) = $145,625.00
Federal W/H (box 2) = $ 15,112.35
Social security wages (box 3) = $142,800.00
Social security W/H (box 4) = $ 8,853.60
Medicare wages (box 5) = $145,625.00
Medicare W/H (box 6) = $ 2,111.56
State wages (box 16) = $145,625.00
State W/H (box 17) = $ 5,435.00

Other receipts for the couple were as follows:

| | |
|---|---|
| Dividends (all qualified dividends) | $2,900 |
| Interest income: | |
| Union Bank | $1,320 |
| State of Idaho—interest on tax refund | 22 |
| City of Boise school bonds | 1,250 |
| Interest from U.S. savings bonds (not used for educational purposes) | 410 |
| 2020 federal income tax refund received in 2021 | 2,007 |
| 2020 state income tax refund received in 2021 | 218 |
| Idaho lottery winnings | 1,380 |
| Casino slot machine winnings | 2,250 |
| Gambling losses at casino | 6,500 |

Other information that the Reyeses provided for the 2021 tax year:

| | |
|---|---|
| Mortgage interest on personal residence | $10,081 |
| Loan interest on fully equipped motor home | 2,810 |
| Doctor's fee for a face-lift for Mrs. Reyes | 8,800 |
| Dentist's fee for a new dental bridge for Mr. Reyes | 3,250 |
| Vitamins for the entire family | 110 |
| Real estate property taxes paid | 5,025 |
| DMV fees on motor home (tax portion) | 1,044 |
| DMV fees on family autos (tax portion) | 436 |
| Doctors' bills for mother | 2,960 |
| Nursing home for mother | 11,375 |
| Wheelchair for mother | 1,030 |
| Property taxes on boat | 134 |
| Interest on personal credit card | 550 |
| Interest on loan to buy public school district bonds | 270 |
| Cash contributions to church (all the contributions were in cash and none more than $250 at any one time) | 5,100 |
| Cash contribution to man at bottom of freeway off-ramp | 25 |
| Contribution of furniture to Goodwill—cost basis | 4,000 |
| Contribution of same furniture listed above to Goodwill—fair market value | 410 |
| Tax return preparation fee for 2020 taxes | 625 |

### *Required*

Prepare a Form 1040 and appropriate schedules for the completion of the Reyes's tax return. They do not want to contribute to the presidential election campaign and do not want anyone to be a third-party designee. For any missing information, make reasonable assumptions. They had qualifying health coverage at all times during the year.

## COMPREHENSIVE PROBLEM 3

### With Emphasis on Schedule C

Christian Everland (SS# 412-34-5670) is single and resides at 3554 Arrival Road, Apt. 6E, Buckhead, GA 30625.

Last year Christian started his own landscaping business. He now has two employees and had the following business results in 2021:

| | |
|---|---|
| Revenue | $73,500 |
| Expenses | |
| Wages | $12,500 |
| Payroll taxes | 956 |
| Fuel | 3,500 |
| Repairs | 2,345 |
| Assets | |
| Truck, used 100% for business. Original cost of $22,000. Purchased on 03/01/21. | |
| Mower #1. Original cost of $4,500. Purchased new on 01/05/21. | |
| Mower #2. Leased for $200 per month for all of 2021. | |
| Other business equipment. Original cost of $4,000. Purchased new on 01/05/21. | |
| Section 179 depreciation is elected for all assets. | |

Christian has no other income, does not itemize, and has no dependents. He paid four quarterly federal tax estimates of $750 each.

### Required

Prepare Christian's Form 1040 and other appropriate forms and schedules. He wants to contribute to the presidential election campaign and does not want anyone to be a third-party designee. Christian had qualifying health care coverage at all times during the tax year. For any missing information, make reasonable assumptions.

## COMPREHENSIVE PROBLEM 4

### With Emphasis on Schedule C

Shelly Beaman (social security number 412-34-5670) is single and resides at 540 Front Street, Ashland, NC 27898.

| | |
|---|---|
| Shelly's W-2 wages | $55,800 |
| Federal withholding | 6,544 |
| Social security wages | 55,800 |
| Social security withholding | 3,460 |
| Medicare withholding | 809 |
| State withholding | 3,148 |
| 1099-INT New Bank | 977 |
| 1099-DIV XYZ, Inc. | |
| Ordinary dividends | 258 |
| Qualified dividends | 258 |

Shelly had the following itemized deductions:

| | |
|---|---|
| State income tax withholding (from W-2) | $ 3,348 |
| State income tax paid with 2020 return | 600 |
| Real estate tax | 4,200 |
| Mortgage interest | 11,800 |
| Charitable contributions | 3,050 |

Shelly also started her own home design consulting business in March 2021. The results of her business operations for 2021 follow:

| | | |
|---|---|---:|
| Gross receipts from clients | | $156,500 |
| Vehicle mileage | 21,000 business miles (2,100 per month) | |
| | 32,000 total miles during the year | |
| | 2014 Chevy Suburban | |
| | Placed in service 03/01/21 | |
| Postage | | (750) |
| Office supplies | | (1,500) |
| State license fees | | (155) |
| Supplies | | (5,300) |
| Professional fees | | (2,500) |
| Design software | | (1,000) |
| Professional education programs (registration) | | (550) |
| Travel to education program | | |
|   Airplane | | (350) |
|     Lodging $119/night × 3 nights | | |
|     Meals per diem 3 days | | |

| Business Assets | Date Purchased | Cost |
|---|---|---:|
| Laptop | 6/08/21 | $ 2,500 |
| Computer | 3/05/21 | 5,700 |
| Printer | 3/01/21 | 1,800 |
| Copier | 6/02/21 | 1,700 |
| Furniture | 4/01/21 | 5,000 |
| Building | 3/01/21 | 175,000 |

| | | |
|---|---|---:|
| Phone | | (600) |
| Internet service | | (450) |
| Rent | | (8,300) |
| Insurance | | (1,700) |

Shelly made a $30,000 estimated tax payment on April 10, 2021.

### Required

Prepare Shelly's Form 1040 including all appropriate schedules. Schedule A, Schedule B, Schedule C, Form 4562, and Schedule SE are required. Section 179 is elected on all eligible assets in 2021. She wants to contribute to the presidential election campaign and does not want anyone to be a third-party designee. Shelly had qualifying health care coverage at all times during the tax year. We have provided filled-in source documents that are available in *Connect*. For any missing information, make reasonable assumptions.

# COMPREHENSIVE PROBLEM 5

## With Emphasis on Schedule D

Casey Morgan is a single taxpayer, social security number 412-34-5670, who lives at 582 Brockton Lane, Columbus, OH 43081. Casey has income from a job as a manager, interest and dividend income, and stock investments. Some of these investments are in a mutual fund.

For the tax year 2021, Casey had the following income information:

| | |
|---|---|
| Wages | $128,796 |
| Social security tax withholding | 7,985 |
| Medicare tax withholding | 1,868 |
| Federal income tax withholding | 17,950 |
| State income tax withholding | 3,700 |

Casey had the following investment income:

| | |
|---|---|
| Foundation Bank 1099-INT | $ 1,000 |
| Great Return Mutual Fund 1099-INT | 2,105 |
| Great Return Mutual Fund 1099-DIV | 1,200 (ordinary dividends) ($0 qualified) |
| Great Return Mutual Fund 1099-DIV CGD | 4,380 (capital gain distribution) |

Casey had the following investment sales:

- A 1099-B from Great Return Mutual Fund for the sale of 100 shares of the fund. Casey had purchased 50 shares on September 21, 2020, for $650; 50 shares on October 1, 2020, for $500; and 50 shares on November 30, 2020, for $800. He sold 100 shares on June 13, 2021, for $700. She uses the average cost method to calculate the cost basis of fund shares.
- A 1099-B from XYZ Brokerage Company for $5,500 gross proceeds from the October 21, 2021, sale of 50 shares of Liquid Rhino Marketing. The shares were originally purchased on October 22, 2020, for $2,500.
- A 1099-B from ABC Brokerage Company for $2,000 gross proceeds from the November 2, 2021, sale of 60 shares of Crestwood Company. Casey originally inherited the shares from a relative on February 18, 2021. The shares had an FMV of $2,500 on the relative's date of death. The relative originally purchased the shares for $400 in 1993.

Other information:

- Casey had a capital loss carryover from 2020; $2,163 short-term.

Casey had the following itemized deductions:

| | |
|---|---|
| Medical insurance premiums | $ 5,000 |
| Real estate taxes | 6,210 |
| Home mortgage interest (Form 1098) | 24,891 |
| Cash charitable contributions | 2,000 |
| Tax preparation fee | 200 |

Casey does not want to contribute to the presidential election campaign and does not want anyone to be a third-party designee. Casey had qualifying health care coverage at all times during the tax year.

### *Required:*

Complete the tax return for Casey Morgan. For any missing information, make reasonable assumptions.

# COMPREHENSIVE PROBLEM 6

## With Emphasis on Schedule D

Debra Simon is a single taxpayer. She is employed as a corporate attorney and lives at 1400 Sand Dollar Circle, Sandville, FL 33868. Her social security number is 412-34-5670.

For tax year 2021, Debra had the following income information:

| | |
|---|---|
| Wages | $156,000 |
| Social security withholding | 8,853.60 |
| Medicare withholding | 2,262 |
| Federal income tax withheld | 31,850 |
| State income tax withheld | –0– |
| New Bank 1099-INT | 5,400 |
| Hope Bank 1099-INT | 3,875 |

Debra had the following stock transactions during 2021. A 1099-B was received for the proceeds of each sale:

| Transaction | Purchased | Sold | Proceeds | Cost | Sale Expenses |
|---|---|---|---|---|---|
| 300 sh. IBM | 01/05/13 | 5/11/21 | $ 16,500 | $14,100 | $    875 |
| 200 sh. SMI | 01/05/13 | 5/15/21 | 41,000 | 41,800 | 2,050 |
| 100 sh. BMI | 03/05/19 | 4/12/21 | 10,500 | 11,400 | 525 |
| 300 sh. ABC | 07/05/21 | 9/15/21 | 16,500 | 14,100 | 825 |
| 300 sh. DDC | 05/19/21 | 10/11/21 | 45,000 | 51,000 | 2,250 |
| 300 sh. PPC | 01/05/13 | 5/11/21 | 5,000 | 2,800 | 250 |
| 4,000 sh. LLP | Inherited | 12/11/21 | 436,000 | * | 21,800 |
| 1,500 sh. QQM | Inherited | 5/11/21 | 41,325 | * | 2,066 |

\* Debra inherited the LLP stock and the QQM stock when her father passed away on May 1, 2021. Debra's father purchased the LLP stock in 1970 for $35,000. The FMV of the LLP stock at the date of death was $415,500. The QQM stock was purchased by Debra's father on February 6, 2020, for $49,000. The FMV of the QQM stock at the date of death was $49,600.

Debra also sold her wine collection for $38,000. She had purchased the wine on January 5, 2016, for a total of $20,100.

Debra has a capital loss carryover from 2020 of $11,700: $3,000 short-term and $8,150 long-term.

Debra rents a condo (no mortgage interest) and lives in Florida (no state income tax). Thus, she claims the standard deduction.

### *Required*

Complete the 2021 tax return for Debra Simon. You do not need to complete the loss carryover worksheet but do need to enter the carryover amount in the appropriate place on Schedule D. She wants to contribute to the presidential election campaign and does not want anyone to be a third-party designee. Debra had qualifying health care coverage at all times during the tax year. For any missing information, make reasonable assumptions.

# COMPREHENSIVE PROBLEM 7

## With Emphasis on Schedule E

Chris and Stefani Watanabe live with their two boys at 1400 Victoria Lane, Riverside, CA 92501. Chris is an accountant who has his own accounting practice. Stefani is an elementary school teacher. Their sons, Justin and Jordan, are ages 13 and 10, respectively. Following is additional information regarding the Watanabes.

Social security numbers and birthdates for the Watanabe family:

| | | |
|---|---|---|
| Chris | 412-34-5670 | 05/23/1981 |
| Stefani | 412-34-5671 | 10/14/1982 |
| Justin | 412-34-5672 | 02/19/2008 |
| Jordan | 412-34-5673 | 07/02/2011 |

They paid $4,500 to Friendly Hills Child Care center for after-school care for both Justin and Jordan, allocated equally. The address is 2 River Dr, Riverside, CA 92501 and their ID number is 22-1234567.

Stefani's W-2 from the Riverside school district showed the following:

$$\text{Wages} = \$56,925.04$$
$$\text{Federal W/H} = \$6,935.90$$
$$\text{Social security wages} = \$56,925.04$$
$$\text{Social security W/H} = \$3,529.35$$
$$\text{Medicare wages} = \$56,925.04$$
$$\text{Medicare W/H} = \$\$825.41$$
$$\text{California W/H} = \$2,105.75$$

Chris's accounting business is located in downtown Riverside. His business had the following income and expense information for the year:

| | |
|---|---|
| Gross revenues | $168,000 |
| Expenses: | |
| Advertising | $ 2,100 |
| Insurance | 1,200 |
| Legal fees | 10,500 |
| Office supplies | 800 |
| Rent | 24,000 |
| Travel | 6,945 |
| Meals | 2,400 |
| Utilities | 2,800 |
| Wages | 34,000 |
| Dues | 650 |

Additionally, Chris and Stefani paid the following expenses during the year:

| | |
|---|---|
| Medical and dental expenses | $ 4,500 |
| Property tax (home on Victoria Lane) | 3,750 |
| State income taxes with the 2020 return | 3,900 |
| Donations to the church (cash) | 3,500 |
| Mortgage interest (home on Victoria Lane) | 17,550 |
| Stefani paid $950 in classroom expenses for her class | |

Chris and Stefani also earned $1,075 of interest income from California Bank during the year.

Lastly, Chris and Stefani own a three-bedroom cabin in Big Bear Lake (they bought it in January of 2009 for $300,000). The address is 3105 Stonehedge Road, Big Bear Lake, CA

92315. They did not use the property for personal use at any time during the year. The revenue and expenses for the Big Bear Lake rental property are as follows:

| | |
|---|---|
| Rental income | $18,000 |
| Expenses: | |
| Insurance | $ 1,200 |
| Property taxes | 2,500 |
| Auto (standard mileage) | 267 |
| Management fees | 1,600 |
| Repairs and maintenance | 1,100 |
| Mortgage interest | 9,000 |
| Depreciation | Calculate |
| Utilities | 450 |

The Watanabes also made $11,000 and $9,000 in federal and California estimated income tax payments, respectively, on 06/15/21.

## *Required*

Prepare the Watanabes' federal tax return. Use Form 1040, Schedule A, Schedule C, Schedule E, Schedule SE, and any additional schedules or forms they may need. The Watanabes had qualifying health care coverage at all times during the tax year. They do not want to contribute to the presidential election campaign, and they do not want anyone to be a third-party designee. For any missing information, make reasonable assumptions.

# Appendix C

# Concept Check Answers

## CHAPTER 1

### Concept Check 1-1

1. Progressive, proportional, regressive.
2. Proportional.
3. Progressive.

### Concept Check 1-2

1. True.
2. 22%. For a married couple, the marginal rate is 22% for taxable income between $81,050 and $172,750.
3. False. The average tax rate is the percentage that a taxpayer pays in tax given a certain amount of taxable income. The marginal tax rate represents the proportion of tax that he or she pays on the next dollar of taxable income.
4. False. All tax returns conform to the basic formula.

### Concept Check 1-3

1. Wages and interest. The category wages includes salary and tips.
2. Form 1099-G.

### Concept Check 1-4

1. True. Taxpayers must use the tax tables if their taxable income is under $100,000.
2. $11,578.
3. $11,574.64.

### Concept Check 1-5

1. False. Taxpayers pay an estimate of their tax liability during the year with income tax withholdings or quarterly estimated tax payments.
2. Required to pay, $392.

3. False. An Earned Income Credit is subtracted from the tax liability.

### Concept Check 1-6

1. Ways and Means.
2. The Internal Revenue Code.
3. True. For any action to become law, both houses of Congress and the president must agree.

### Concept Check 1-7

1. False. Statutory tax authority (the law) takes precedence over all other types of tax authority.
2. False. Revenue Procedures are issued by the IRS for use by all taxpayers.
3. IRS Treasury Regulations. See Table 1-6.

### Concept Check 1-8

1. False. Tax cases can be appealed to the U.S. Supreme Court.
2. False. The taxpayer can file a suit with the Tax Court, the district court, or the Court of Federal Claims.
3. Tax. The advantage of using the Tax Court is that the taxpayer does not need to pay the IRS's proposed assessment prior to trial.

## CHAPTER 2

### Concept Check 2-1

1. False. Only the very simplest returns will not use a Schedule.
2. True. Adjusted Gross Income (AGI) is an important concept because several deductions and credits depend upon the AGI amount. Some examples are the medical deduction and the Earned Income Credit.

## Concept Check 2-2

1. True. Yes, couples in the process of obtaining a divorce (where the divorce is not yet final) can file a joint return.

2. True. The social security number and full name of the spouse must be shown on the return.

3. False. The surviving spouse must also meet another rule that states the household needs to be the principal place of abode for the entire year (except for temporary absences) of both the taxpayer and a child, stepchild, or adopted child who can be claimed as a dependent by the taxpayer.

## Concept Check 2-3

1. In addition to the dependent taxpayer test, joint return test, and citizen or resident test, a qualifying child must meet the following five tests: relationship test, age test, residency test, support test, and special test for qualifying child of more than one taxpayer.

2. The child must be under 19 years of age, or under 24 years of age and a full-time student. For years after 2008, the child must be younger than the person claiming the dependency.

## Concept Check 2-4

1. False. A taxpayer must meet all of the four tests in order to be a qualifying relative.

2. False. A qualifying relative cannot earn an amount equal to or greater than $4,300.

## Concept Check 2-5

1. The amount of the standard deduction is
   a. Taxpayer is single, 42 years of age, and blind = $14,250 ($12,550 + $1,700).
   b. Taxpayer is head of household, 37 years of age, and not blind = $18,800.
   c. Taxpayers are married filing jointly, one spouse is 67 and the other one is 61 years of age, and neither is blind = $26,450 ($25,100 + $1,350).

## Concept Check 2-6

1. Tax for the single taxpayer is $3,956 and for the married taxpayers is $7,729.

2. The limitation for FICA (social security) for the year 2021 is $142,800.

## Concept Check 2-7

1. The failure to file a tax return penalty does not apply because the taxpayer filed an extension before his or her return was due. However, the failure to pay does apply. The amount is $30 [($3,000 × 0.5%) × 2 months].

2. True. The IRS can assess criminal penalties in addition to civil penalties. The former are applicable to tax evasion, willful failure to collect or pay tax, and willful failure to file a return.

# CHAPTER 3

## Concept Check 3-1

1. In general, an individual must recognize income on a tax return if a transaction meets all of the following three conditions: There must be an economic benefit; there must actually be a transaction that has reached a conclusion; and the income must not be tax-exempt income.

2. True. Certain income is statutorily excluded from taxation and will not be included in gross income even though the other two conditions are met. An example is tax-exempt interest.

## Concept Check 3-2

1. True. According to Reg. § 1.61-1(a), income may be realized in any form, whether in money, property, or services.

2. True. Receipt of property or services serves to trigger income recognition. Furthermore, taxpayers recognize income even if they receive it indirectly.

## Concept Check 3-3

1. False. Interest is taxable if received from state or local bonds issued for private activities, such as convention centers, industrial parks, or stadiums.

2. False. Schedule B is required if an individual receives *over* $1,500 of interest for the tax year.

## Concept Check 3-4

1. True. Qualified dividends (1) are made from the earnings and profits of the payer corporation and (2) are from domestic corporations or qualified foreign corporations.

2. False. Corporations normally pay dividends in the form of cash, but they may pay them in property or anything of economic value. The basis of the property received as a dividend in the hands of the shareholder is the property's fair market value at the date of distribution.

## Concept Check 3-5

1. The amount is $27,750 (22,000 + 4,500 + 1,250).

## Concept Check 3-6

1. Items such as jury duty and gambling winnings are listed under line 8 of Schedule 1.

## Concept Check 3-7

1. False. It is not taxable. This is an example of a *de minimis* benefit whose value is so small that keeping track of which employees received the benefit is administratively impractical.

2. True. It is not taxable. The individual must be a degree-seeking student at an educational institution and must use the proceeds for qualified tuition and related expenses (tuition, fees, books, supplies, and equipment). If the scholarship or fellowship payment exceeds permitted expenses, the excess is taxable income.

## Concept Check 3-8

1. True. The law limits the ability of taxpayers to create debt instruments with interest rates that materially vary from market rates on the date the instrument is created. Imputing interest will reallocate payments such that more of the payment will be interest and less principal.

2. True. If someone purchases a debt instrument (such as a bond) from an issuer for an amount less than par, the transaction creates original issue discount (OID). The initial OID is equal to the difference between the acquisition price and the maturity value.

# CHAPTER 4

## Concept Check 4-1

1. At least half-time at an eligible educational institution.
2. Tuition and fees.
3. $140,000.

## Concept Check 4-2

1. Self-employed.
2. Nontaxable.
3. Form 8889 and Form 1040.

## Concept Check 4-3

1. True.
2. True.

## Concept Check 4-4

1. Net.
2. For 2021, the employee's portion is calculated at 7.65%.
3. $200,000.

## Concept Check 4-5

1. False. For self-employed individuals, the deduction is 100% of the costs.

2. False. The limitation on this deduction is that taxpayers cannot deduct the cost of premiums that exceeds *net* earnings from self-employment.

3. True. If the taxpayer is entitled to participate in any subsidized health plan maintained by any employer of the taxpayer or of the taxpayer's spouse, a deduction is not allowed.

## Concept Check 4-6

1. As an *above-the-line* deduction.
2. Form 1099-INT.

## Concept Check 4-7

1. False. Alimony payments can be made only in cash. If the payment consists of property, it is a property settlement.

2. False. As long as the couple is legally separated and there is a written agreement requiring payments, it will be classified as alimony.

3. True. If alimony payments decrease sharply in the second or third year of payment, this is a signal that the nature of the payments might be a property settlement, not alimony.

## Concept Check 4-8

1. 900 hours.

2. $500.

3. Home schooling and nonathletic supplies for health or PE classes, except in the case of allowed Covid 19 supplies.

# CHAPTER 5

## Concept Check 5-1

1. 7.5% of AGI.

2. Actually paid. Payment by credit card meets this standard.

3. Insurance reimbursement.

4. Age.

## Concept Check 5-2

1. True. In addition, the two other criteria are that it must be on personal property and the property must be assessed, at a minimum, on an annual basis.

2. False. When property is sold during the year, both the buyer and the seller receive a deduction for a portion of the real estate tax paid according to the number of days each owner held the property.

3. False. The tax benefit rule states that if you receive a refund of that expense that was previously deducted on the tax return, you are required to include that refund in income when it is received.

4. False. The limit is $10,000.

## Concept Check 5-3

1. Acquire, construct, substantially improve.

2. $750,000.

3. Net investment.

4. 1%.

## Concept Check 5-4

1. True. Charitable contributions of cash can be taken as either a below-the-line deduction or as an itemized deduction.

2. False. The overall limitation on the deductibility of charitable contributions is 60% of AGI. The 30% limit relates to the contribution of appreciated capital gain property.

3. True. If noncash gifts are worth over $500, the taxpayer must file Form 8283.

## Concept Check 5-5

1. Sudden, unexpected, unusual.

2. Form 4684 and then carried to Schedule A.

3. Two; $100.

4. 10%.

## Concept Check 5-6

1. False. For Other Itemized Deductions there is no % of AGI limitation.

2. False. The amount of deductible gambling losses is limited to the extent of gambling winnings.

# CHAPTER 6

## Concept Check 6-1

1. False. Schedule C is used only for an activity in which the individual is self-employed, not an employee.

2. False. Any income received by the self-employed taxpayer is taxable and should be included on Schedule C. Not all individuals or organizations are required to send a 1099-NEC to the self-employed individual.

3. False. If gross receipts average less than $26 million, the cash method is allowed.

## Concept Check 6-2

1. Ordinary, necessary, reasonable.

2. Illegal bribes, kickbacks, and other such payments; payments for certain lobbying and political expenses; payments for fines and penalties.

## Concept Check 6-3

1. $1,300. When an asset is transferred from personal use to business use, the depreciable basis is the lesser of cost or FMV at transfer.
2. $17,600. The adjusted basis at the end of year 1 is the cost less the accumulated depreciation ($22,000 − $4,400).

## Concept Check 6-4

1. B. Autos are 5-year property under the MACRS rules.
2. C. An apartment complex is considered residential real property and thus has a 27.5-year life under the MACRS rules.
3. D. A warehouse is considered nonresidential real property and thus has a 39-year life under the MACRS rules.

## Concept Check 6-5

1. False. A taxpayer must use the half-year convention for personal property unless more than 40% of the basis is purchased in the last quarter of the year; then mid-quarter is required. The taxpayer must use the mid-month convention for real property.
2. True. If more than 40% of the basis of personal property is purchased in the fourth quarter, the taxpayer must use the mid-quarter convention.
3. True. The only time the half-year convention is not used is when more than 40% of the personal property is purchased in the fourth quarter.
4. False. Because an apartment complex is residential real property, the mid-month convention is required.
5. True. Once the convention is established, it never changes for an asset. Thus, if one-half year of depreciation is taken in the year of purchase, then one-half year of depreciation should be taken in the year of disposal. The same is true for mid-quarter and mid-month assets.

## Concept Check 6-6

1. $1,715. Equipment is a 7-year asset ($12,000 × 14.29%).
2. $1,049. 2023 would be the third year of depreciation, and the table percentage is 17.49% for year 3. But only one-half of a year of depreciation would be allowed ($12,000 × 17.49% × ½).
3. $9,501. An apartment complex is 27.5-year, mid-month property purchased in March. The appropriate percentage is the third column of Table 6A-6 ($330,000 × 2.879%).

## Concept Check 6-7

1. $12,000 in § 179 expense and $0 additional MACRS depreciation.
2. $1,050,000 in § 179 expense (up to the limit of $1,050,000 for 2021) and $715 in 7-year MACRS depreciation ($5,000 remaining basis × 14.29%).

## Concept Check 6-8

1. C. $26,200 in § 179 expense and $2,560 in MACRS depreciation [($39,000 − $26,200) × 20%] is allowed. The total is $28,760.
2. C. $26,200 × 80% business use = $20,960 in § 179 expense and $2,048 in regular depreciation ([$39,000 × 80%] − $20,960 § 179) × 20% (5-year MACRS percentage). The total is $23,008.

## Concept Check 6-9

1. False. The standard mileage rate incorporates depreciation into the mileage rate. A taxpayer uses either the standard mileage rate or the actual costs of operations including depreciation.
2. False. Transportation costs are deductible for all business travel except for commuting.
3. True. Once overnight rest is required with business travel, the taxpayer can then deduct meals and lodging.
4. True. A taxpayer can use the standard per diem of $55/day. The per diem is higher in high-cost areas.
5. False. The 2017 Tax Act eliminated entertainment costs as a deduction.

## Concept Check 6-10

1. D. The external painting is an indirect cost and is deductible based on the business use ratio ($3,000 × 20%). The office painting is a direct expense and is 100% deductible.
2. B. The home office expenses are deductible only to the extent of Schedule C income. Clients do not have to be seen at the home office, and § 179 is never allowed on real property. The home office can be depreciated over 27.5 years as residential real estate.
3. C. A business casualty loss when a property is partially destroyed is calculated using the lesser of the decrease in FMV or the adjusted basis of the property.

## Concept Check 6-11

1. True. Typically, if an activity has shown a profit for three of five consecutive years, the activity is not considered a hobby. The burden of proving the activity is a hobby shifts to the IRS.
2. True. Expenses are no longer allowed for hobbies.
3. False. Hobby expenses are no longer allowed.
4. False. If the educational costs help qualify the taxpayer for a new trade or business, the educational costs are not deductible.

## Concept Check 6-12

1. $7,489. $53,000 × 92.35% × 15.3%.
2. $1,419. $53,000 × 92.35% × 2.9%. Kia has already paid through her employer the maximum amount of wages subject to social security. Kia still must pay Medicare because there is no limit.
3. $6,106. $53,000 × 92.35% × 2.9% = $1,419 for Medicare. Additional self-employment tax of $5,207 must be paid. Kia has not reached the social security limit. She has $53,000 of non W-2 Income. Additional SS is $4,687 = .124 × $37,800 ($142,800 − $105,000).

# CHAPTER 7

## Concept Check 7-1

1. False. The gain or loss is the difference between the amount realized from the sale and the asset's adjusted basis.
2. False. Form 4797 is used to record the gain or loss from an asset used in a trade or business.
3. True.

## Concept Check 7-2

1. False. Inventory sold by a company appears on the income statement as the cost of goods sold and then on Schedule C for a sole proprietorship.
2. C. Property used in a trade or business.
3. False. Assets considered short-term are held for less than one year and are considered to be ordinary income assets.
4. True.
5. True.

## Concept Check 7-3

1. False. When an ordinary asset is sold, the gain or loss is termed an "ordinary gain or loss."

2. The distinction is important because of the preferential tax rate treatment on capital gains versus ordinary gains.
3. True.

## Concept Check 7-4

1. B. The tax treatment of a capital asset varies only if there is a gain. Losses are included for the netting process.
2. True.
3. False. Inherited property is always long-term property regardless of how long the asset belonged to the decedent or beneficiary.
4. False. The surtax is charged when MAGI is over the threshold amounts.
5.
   a. Collectible gains — 28%
   b. § 1202 gains — 28%
   c. Unrecaptured § 1250 gains — 25%
   d. Single taxpayer's regular taxable income is $40,350 — 0%
   e. Married filing jointly taxpayer's regular taxable income is $490,000 — 15%
   f. Married filing separately taxpayer's regular taxable income is $260,000 — 20%

## Concept Check 7-5

1. False. Losses are ordinary and fully deductible.
2. True.
3. Depreciation recapture rules transform some or all of a § 1231 gain into an ordinary gain.
4. § 1245 property is personal trade or business property subject to depreciation. § 1250 property includes depreciable real property used in a trade or business that has never been considered § 1245 property.
5. Unrecaptured gain is taxed at a 25% rate for all straight-line depreciation taken on the property. Recaptured gain is taxed at ordinary rates to the extent the depreciation taken exceeds straight-line depreciation.

## Concept Check 7-6

1. First in, first out—The first shares purchased are the first shares sold. This results in the largest gain when the value of the mutual fund units appreciates.
   Specific identification—The taxpayer specifies exactly which units are for sale from the fund.
   Average basis—The taxpayer takes the total cost basis and divides by the total number of units to get an average cost per unit (single category).

2. True.

3. False. The basis for property given as a gift depends on whether the FMV was higher or lower than the basis at the date of the gift.

4. False. The tax treatment of a gain on the sale of inherited property is always considered to be held long term regardless of the holding period of the deceased.

# CHAPTER 8

## Concept Check 8-1

1. True. Income and expenses associated with rental property are reported on Schedule E unless the taxpayer is a real estate professional and the rental activity is considered a trade or business.

2. False. All ordinary and necessary expenses related to a rental property are deductible in the current year, but capital improvements must be depreciated and deducted over the useful life of the asset category.

3. True. Rental property is depreciated over 27.5 years for residential and 39 years for nonresidential using the straight-line method.

4. False. The income and expenses associated with a rental property that is considered to be the taxpayer's trade or business are reported on Schedule C.

5. False. Expenses paid by the tenant or services provided in lieu of rent payments are components of rental income and must be reported at the fair market value.

## Concept Check 8-2

1. B. Primarily personal; rented less than 15 days.

2. A. Primarily rental; rented 15 days or more or personal use was less than 10% of rental days (i.e., less than 18 days).

3. A. Primarily rental; rented 15 days or more and personal use was no more than 14 days. Only 9 days of the 16 days are considered personal days because Darren worked for 7 days repairing the property.

4. C. Personal/rental; rented 15 days or more and personal use was more than 14 days.

## Concept Check 8-3

1. Personal/rental. The property was rented for 75 days and used for personal use for 30 days. Rental property used for personal use more than 14 days (or 10% of days rented) and rented for 15 days or more is categorized as personal/rental.

2. $6,000 × 75/105 = $4,286
   1,000 × 75/105 =    714
   1,400 × 75/105 =  1,000
     800 × 75/105 =    571
   2,000 × 75/105 =  1,429
   Allocated expenses $8,000

3. $6,000 × 75/365 = $1,233
   1,000 × 75/365 =    205
   1,400 × 75/105 =  1,000
     800 × 75/105 =    571
   2,000 × 75/105 =  1,429
   Allocated expenses $4,438

4. Rental income        $15,000
   Allocated expenses     8,000
   Net income           $ 7,000

## Concept Check 8-4

1. Schedule C. Royalty received as a result of a trade or business should be reported on Schedule C.

2. Schedule E. Royalty produced by an investment should be reported on Schedule E.

3. Schedule C. Readings based on books written are not royalties but payment for services performed and should be reported on Schedule C.

4. Schedule E. Royalties are payments received for the right to use intangible property. The payments are for the use of Jane's textbook.

## Concept Check 8-5

1. True. Flow-through entities supply each owner with a K-1 indicating their share of income, expenses, or losses.

2. False. Ordinary income from an S corporation is not considered self-employment income.

3. True. Partners, shareholders, or owners of flow-through entities must report their K-1 information on their individual tax returns on Form E.

4. True. A taxpayer is allowed up to $25,000 of rental losses against other nonpassive income subject to limitations and phaseouts.

# CHAPTER 9

## Concept Check 9-1

1. $1,080. ($4,500 × 24%)

2. $4,500
   $500 × 9 months = $4,500; although expenses of $6,000 do not exceed the maximum allowed, the amount used cannot be greater than $4,500 because Katie is a student.
3. $950
   $2,900 − $1,000 = $1,900 × 50% = $950

## Concept Check 9-2

1. $150

| | |
|---|---|
| Base amount | $7,500 |
| Less social security | 1,000 |
| Less ¹/₂ of AGI over $10,000 | 5,500 |
| Allowable base amount | 1,000 |
| Applicable % | × 15% |
| Credit | $  150 |

## Concept Check 9-3

1. $ 580
   $2,900 × 20% = $580
2. $1,113
   100% of first $2,000 and 25% of second $900 is the credit allowed of $2,225. However, the credit is partially phased out due to AGI.
   $2,225 × ($90,000 − $85,000/$10,000) = $1,113
3. $0
   Her AGI is greater than the maximum phaseout amount.
4. $740
   ($1,600 + $2,100) × 20% = $740

## Concept Check 9-4

1. $2,240
   ($8,000/$63,000) × $17,640 = $2,240 (less than foreign tax paid of $2,500)

## Concept Check 9-5

1. $6,000
   AGI limitations do not apply because their AGI is less than $150,000.
2. True. The child tax credit is not permitted if the child is age 18 or greater.
3. Yes. Glen meets all the requirements to be a qualifying relative.

## Concept Check 9-6

1. $150
   $1,500 × 10% = $150

2. $1,000
   $2,000 × 50% = $1,000 ($2,200 is over the maximum allowed)

## Concept Check 9-7

1. $0 in 2020.
   $14,440 in 2021.
   $10,800 + $3,950 = $14,750; however, the maximum allowed is $14,440.
2. $7,458
   $16,000 is more than the maximum of $14,440, so use $14,440. The credit must be phased out because of AGI as follows:
   [($256,660 − $236,000)/$40,000] × $14,440 = $7,458

## Concept Check 9-8

1. $3,618
2. $2,575
   $3,618 (maximum credit) − ([$32,000 − $25,470] × 15.98%) = $2,575
3a. $5,980
3b. $5,180 refund
   $5,980 credit − $800 tax liability = $5,180 refund; EIC is a refundable credit.

## Concept Check 9-9

1. False.  For 2021 and 2022, there is no upper income limitation for the premium tax credit.

# CHAPTER 10

## Concept Check 10-1

1. True.
2. True.

## Concept Check 10-2

1. False. They are also levied on noncash compensation as well as cash compensation other than through wages and salary.
2. False. Form W-4 is completed by the employee so the employer knows how much to withhold in federal income tax from the employee's compensation.
3. $129.14 using Table 4.
4. $8,853.60 (limit $142,800) in social security and $2,124.25 in Medicare taxes (no limit).
5. False. Only tips in excess of $20 per month are subject to tax withholding.

## Concept Check 10-3

1. False. New employers start as monthly schedule depositors. If in any one day tax liability equals $100,000, they become semiweekly schedule depositors.
2. False. The lookback period runs from the quarters starting July 1 of the current year through June 30 of the next year.
3. True.
4. False. A penalty is assessed only on the amount of tax that was not deposited on time.
5. True.

## Concept Check 10-4

1. True.
2. A.
3. Individuals who employ household workers and do not withhold any taxes during the year. The schedule is attached to the taxpayer's Form 1040.
4. They paid any one household employee wages of $2,300 or more in 2021, federal income taxes were withheld from employee wages, and household wages of at least $1,000 were paid to all household workers combined in any calendar quarter in 2020 or 2021.

## Concept Check 10-5

1. True.
2. Copy A is sent to the Social Security Administration along with Form W-3, which is the transmittal form. They are due January 31, 2022.
3. An employer who must correct an employee's W-2 must file Forms W-2C and W-3C as soon as possible.
4. The penalties for incorrectly preparing W-2s range from $50 per return to $280 per return with a maximum depending on the size of the business. Also a penalty of $570 per return (with no maximum) for intentional disregard for filing requirements.

## Concept Check 10-6

1. Method 1: Withhold at a flat rate of 22%. If taxes are withheld from regular wages, add the two amounts together, calculate the tax as if they are one payment, and subtract the amount of withholding already taken out of the employee's wages. Method 2: If taxes are not already withheld from regular wages, add the two amounts together, and calculate the tax as if they are one payment.
2. True.
3. Form W-9 is used for U.S. persons (including resident aliens) to document their taxpayer identification number (TIN). This form must be on file with the payer.

4. $50 for each failure unless the failure is due to reasonable cause, not to willful neglect. If the taxpayer makes false statements with no reasonable basis that result in backup withholding, a penalty of $500 is assessed. There can also be criminal penalties including fines and imprisonment.
5. False. There is no way of knowing whether the taxpayer will overpay and have a refund. The estimated payments contribute by having taxpayers pay additional taxes to limit the amount of possible underpayment.

# CHAPTER 11

## Concept Check 11-1

1. False. Tax is only delayed (deferred), not forgiven.
2. Distribution.
3. False. It is an example of an employer-sponsored plan.
4. Employer-sponsored plans include qualified pension and profit-sharing plans, 401(k) or 403(b) plans, Keogh plans, SEPs, and SIMPLE plans. Choose any two.
5. True.

## Concept Check 11-2

1. Defined benefit, defined contribution.
2. False. Some plans require employee contributions and some do not.
3. $19,500.
4. True. In fact, they can be used only by self-employed individuals.
5. True.

## Concept Check 11-3

1. Traditional IRA, Roth IRA.
2. $7,000.
3. False. As long as neither individual is an active participant in an employer plan, a deductible contribution is permitted regardless of the amount of AGI.
4. True.

## Concept Check 11-4

1. True.
2. $2,000.
3. $95,000. The phaseout is complete when AGI reaches $110,000.
4. True.

## Concept Check 11-5

1. True.
2. True.
3. 210.
4. 310.
5. True.

## Concept Check 11-6

1. True.
2. True.
3. True.
4. False. Coverdell distributions must be used for higher education expenses (subject to certain restrictions). If not, the distributions are taxable.

## Concept Check 11-7

1. Series, contract.
2. False. While payments are often the same amount per period, that is not a requirement.
3. True.

# CHAPTER 12

## Concept Check 12-1

1. True. A gain is never recognized with a nontaxable like-kind exchange unless the taxpayer receives boot. Then gain is recognized to the lesser of the realized gain or the FMV of the boot received.
2. True. Those are the three conditions necessary to execute a nontaxable like-kind exchange.
3. False. The taxpayer has 45 days to identify the replacement property and 180 days to actually receive the replacement property.
4. True. The basis in the replacement property is the adjusted basis of the property given up, plus the basis of boot given, plus gain recognized, less the FMV of boot received. This sum is typically the FMV of the property received less the postponed gain.

## Concept Check 12-2

1. $55,000. If the building is not replaced, the insurance proceeds are treated as sale proceeds and the gain is recognized in full.
2. Three years. The typical replacement period is two years. However, for real property held for use in a trade or business, the replacement period increases to three years.
3. $10,000 gain recognized. The realized gain of $55,000 is recognized to the lesser of the proceeds not used for replacement or the realized gain. In this case, the amount not used is the lesser of the two ($10,000).
4. $0 gain recognized. All of the proceeds were used to replace the property.
5. $60,000 is the adjusted basis. The basis is calculated as the cost of the new asset less the deferred gain ($115,000 − $55,000 deferred gain).

## Concept Check 12-3

1. A. The gross profit percentage is calculated by dividing the gross profit by the gross sales prices ($10,000/$30,000 = 33.3%).
2. B. The income recognized is $1,667 (the amount received in year 2 of $5,000 × 33.3% gross profit percentage).

## Concept Check 12-4

1. True. The maximum gain exclusion is $500,000 for married taxpayers who file a joint return.
2. False. If the move is caused by an employment change or for health reasons, a taxpayer is eligible for some reduced exclusion. The exclusion is calculated by taking a ratio of the number of days used as a personal residence and dividing it by 730 days.
3. False. Jogny would still be allowed to exclude his gain but only to the maximum exclusion of $250,000.

## Concept Check 12-5

1. $0. Because Leslie sold the stock to her brother, the related-party rules disallow any loss deduction on the sale by Leslie.
2. A. Leslie could deduct $2,000 in capital losses. In order for a corporation (or other entity) to be considered a related party, Leslie would have to have control of the corporation (greater than 50% ownership).

   B. $0. Because Leslie now has control of the corporation, she is considered a related party and the loss would be disallowed.
3. The purpose of the wash sale rules is to disallow a tax loss where the ownership of a company is not reduced. Thus, if a taxpayer buys similar stock within 30 days of a stock sale (before or after), any loss on the sale is disallowed.

# CHAPTER 13

## Concept Check 13-1

1. D. All of the above increase the at-risk of a taxpayer. See Table 13-1 for all of the increases and decreases of at-risk.

2. A. Nonrecourse debt does not increase the taxpayer's at-risk. Nonrecourse debt is debt that the taxpayer is not personally liable for.
3. C. The loss is indefinitely carried forward and can be deducted once the taxpayer gets additional at-risk.

## Concept Check 13-2

1. True. The only way a rental property is not a passive activity is when the taxpayer is a real estate professional. A rental business can qualify for nonpassive treatment if more than one-half of the personal services performed in a business during the year is performed in a real property trade or business and the taxpayer performs more than 750 hours of services in the activity.
2. True. Passive losses are allowed only to the extent of passive income. One exception is the $25,000 offset for rental properties.
3. False. The $25,000 offset is limited to $25,000 and is phased out after a taxpayer's AGI reaches $100,000.
4. True. Any suspended passive losses are allowed when the activity is sold.

## Concept Check 13-3

1. In order for a loss to be deducted, it must first be allowed under the at-risk rules. Once the loss is allowed under the at-risk rules, the passive loss rules are applied.
2. The main reason is that passive losses are allowed when an activity is sold or disposed of. Thus, if a taxpayer were considering the sale of a passive activity, he or she could lump all suspended passive losses on one activity and sell it. All of the losses would then be allowed. The allocation to all loss activities stops this potential abuse.
3. The taxpayer is eligible for the $25,000 offset for rental losses. However, the $25,000 limit is phased out once the taxpayer's AGI reaches $100,000 ([$105,000 − $100,000] × ¹/₂ = $2,500). Thus, only $22,500 of the rental loss would be allowed.

## Concept Check 13-4

1. True. Medical expenses are the same for AMT and regular tax.
2. True. No taxes are allowed as a deduction for AMT. Any taxes deducted on the regular return are added back as a positive adjustment for AMT.

3. True. Personal exemptions are not allowed for AMT or regular tax purposes in 2021.
4. True. If AMTI is greater than $199,900, the AMT rate is 28%.

# CHAPTER 14

## Concept Check 14-1

1. True. The only time gain is recognized by a contributing partner is when the partner receives an interest for services or when he or she is released of a liability in excess of basis.
2. True. The basis of the assets typically carries over from the partner to the partnership.
3. False. The basis is dependent on the basis of the assets the individual partners contributed to the partnership. One partner could have a $0 basis while the other partner might have $100,000, yet both share 50% in the profit and loss of the partnership.
4. False. Gain must be recognized to the extent of the FMV of the partnership interest received for services.
5. True. An increase or decrease in partnership liabilities is treated as a cash contribution or cash distribution and thus increases or decreases partnership basis.

## Concept Check 14-2

1. D. All of the above can be deducted from partnership income to determine the net income or loss from the partnership.
2. C. Any form of partnership files a Form 1065 informational return each year.
3. D. A guaranteed payment is a payment, usually for services, that is determined without regard to partnership income and is deductible by the partnership.

## Concept Check 14-3

1. All income and expense items of a partnership that may be treated differently at the partner level must be "separately stated." Rental income/loss, capital gains/losses, and charitable contributions all can be treated differently at the partner level. For example, an individual partner can take up to $3,000 of capital losses against ordinary income, while a corporate partner in the same partnership cannot.
2. A partner is not an employee of the partnership. Thus, income received by the partner from the partnership

has no social security or Medicare withheld by the partnership.

## Concept Check 14-4

1. True. These are two of the uses of basis. Basis is also used to determine the basis (or whether a gain is recognized) of property distributed.
2. False. If the basis is not increased by tax-exempt income, then the exempt income will eventually be taxed when the partnership interest is sold. The lower basis will cause a higher gain upon sale.
3. False. The basis is first reduced by all adjustments except for losses, then money distributed, and then the basis of any property distributed. After those items, any basis remaining is used to determine the deductibility of losses.
4. False. The basis is always increased by the partner's share of recourse debt.

## Concept Check 14-5

1. B. If a cash distribution or a release of liabilities exceeds basis, the partner will have a gain on a distribution from the partnership.
2. B. $12,000—the furniture would be reduced to the basis left in the partnership.
3. A. $8,000—the basis in the partnership is first reduced by the cash distribution. That leaves $8,000 for the furniture.

## Concept Check 14-6

1. A. Shelly's recognized gain would be $0. She did not receive cash in excess of her basis.

   B. Shelly's basis in the assets would be as follows:

   | | |
   |---|---|
   | Cash | $9,000 |
   | Inventory | $6,000 |
   | Equipment ($15,000 × $8,000/$20,000) | $6,000 |
   | Land ($15,000 × $12,000/$20,000) | $9,000 |

2. A. $99,000 ($55,000 beginning basis + $18,000 + $26,000)

   B. $8,000 ($107,000 sales price – $99,000 *basis*)

   C. Because the partnership interest is a capital asset and there was no mention of inventory or receivables in the partnership, the gain would be a long-term capital gain.

## CHAPTER 15

## Concept Check 15-1

1. False. Some corporations are prohibited from using the cash basis. Corporations with average annual revenues over $26 million must use the accrual basis. Corporations with inventory must use the accrual basis at least for sales and cost of goods sold unless its average annual gross receipts over the last three years is under $26 million.
2. The 15th day of the fourth month after the fiscal year-end.
3. False. In the first year of operation, a corporation establishes its tax year. Although many corporations choose December 31, that date is not required.

## Concept Check 15-2

1. True. Although an exchange of cash or property can be taxable, if the 80% rule is met, the formation activities are generally tax-free.
2. The basis in the hands of the shareholder plus any gain recognized by the shareholder.
3. $40,000, his carryover basis in the land.

## Concept Check 15-3

1. False. Corporations cannot report a net capital loss, whereas individuals can take up to $3,000 in capital losses in any tax year.
2. $109,200 ($520,000 × 21%).
3. $37,500. A corporation can take a charitable contribution in an amount not to exceed 25% of taxable income before charitable contribution.
4. False. Although organizational expenses are deductible over 180 months or more, the corporation must make an affirmative election in its first tax return in order to do so.
5. 2, 20.

## Concept Check 15-4

1. True. By definition, a dividend is a distribution from the earnings and profits of a corporation. Dividends are taxable to the shareholder. If a distribution is in excess of the earnings and profits of the corporation, it is not a dividend. It may or may not be taxable depending on the stockholder's basis in his or her stock.
2. False. Property dividends are taxed on the fair value of the property received by the stockholder.
3. $10,000. The amount of the dividend cannot exceed the earnings and profits of the corporation.

## Concept Check 15-5

1. False. Corporations with total receipts and total assets under $250,000 are not required to complete Schedule L.
2. True.
3. Negative. Schedule M-1 reconciles from book income to tax income. There is more depreciation on the tax return than on the books. That means book income needs to be reduced to arrive at taxable income.

## Concept Check 15-6

1. 80%.
2. Five.

## Concept Check 15-7

1. False. Not only must a corporation meet tests in addition to the 100-shareholder limit, the corporation also must affirmatively elect Subchapter S status.
2. True. While there are some differences, the tax treatments of a partnership and a Subchapter S corporation are similar.
3. 1120S.
4. Not taxable. Subchapter S dividends are not taxable to a shareholder.
5. False. Corporate debt does not affect shareholders' basis in their stock.

## 2021 Tax Table

See the instructions for line 16 to see if you must use the Tax Table below to figure your tax.

**Example.** Mr. and Mrs. Brown are filing a joint return. Their taxable income on Form 1040, line 15, is $25,300. First, they find the $25,300-25,350 taxable income line. Next, they find the column for married filing jointly and read down the column. The amount shown where the taxable income line and filing status column meet is $2,641. This is the tax amount they should enter in the entry space on Form 1040, line 16.

### Sample Table

| At Least | But Less Than | Single | Married filing jointly* | Married filing separately | Head of a household |
|---|---|---|---|---|---|
| | | | Your tax is— | | |
| 25,200 | 25,250 | 2,828 | 2,629 | 2,828 | 2,743 |
| 25,250 | 25,300 | 2,834 | 2,635 | 2,834 | 2,749 |
| 25,300 | 25,350 | 2,840 | (2,641) | 2,840 | 2,755 |
| 25,350 | 25,400 | 2,846 | 2,647 | 2,846 | 2,761 |

| If line 15 (taxable income) is— | | And you are— | | | |
|---|---|---|---|---|---|
| At least | But less than | Single | Married filing jointly* | Married filing separately | Head of a household |
| | | | Your tax is— | | |
| 0 | 5 | 0 | 0 | 0 | 0 |
| 5 | 15 | 1 | 1 | 1 | 1 |
| 15 | 25 | 2 | 2 | 2 | 2 |
| 25 | 50 | 4 | 4 | 4 | 4 |
| 50 | 75 | 6 | 6 | 6 | 6 |
| 75 | 100 | 9 | 9 | 9 | 9 |
| 100 | 125 | 11 | 11 | 11 | 11 |
| 125 | 150 | 14 | 14 | 14 | 14 |
| 150 | 175 | 16 | 16 | 16 | 16 |
| 175 | 200 | 19 | 19 | 19 | 19 |
| 200 | 225 | 21 | 21 | 21 | 21 |
| 225 | 250 | 24 | 24 | 24 | 24 |
| 250 | 275 | 26 | 26 | 26 | 26 |
| 275 | 300 | 29 | 29 | 29 | 29 |
| 300 | 325 | 31 | 31 | 31 | 31 |
| 325 | 350 | 34 | 34 | 34 | 34 |
| 350 | 375 | 36 | 36 | 36 | 36 |
| 375 | 400 | 39 | 39 | 39 | 39 |
| 400 | 425 | 41 | 41 | 41 | 41 |
| 425 | 450 | 44 | 44 | 44 | 44 |
| 450 | 475 | 46 | 46 | 46 | 46 |
| 475 | 500 | 49 | 49 | 49 | 49 |
| 500 | 525 | 51 | 51 | 51 | 51 |
| 525 | 550 | 54 | 54 | 54 | 54 |
| 550 | 575 | 56 | 56 | 56 | 56 |
| 575 | 600 | 59 | 59 | 59 | 59 |
| 600 | 625 | 61 | 61 | 61 | 61 |
| 625 | 650 | 64 | 64 | 64 | 64 |
| 650 | 675 | 66 | 66 | 66 | 66 |
| 675 | 700 | 69 | 69 | 69 | 69 |
| 700 | 725 | 71 | 71 | 71 | 71 |
| 725 | 750 | 74 | 74 | 74 | 74 |
| 750 | 775 | 76 | 76 | 76 | 76 |
| 775 | 800 | 79 | 79 | 79 | 79 |
| 800 | 825 | 81 | 81 | 81 | 81 |
| 825 | 850 | 84 | 84 | 84 | 84 |
| 850 | 875 | 86 | 86 | 86 | 86 |
| 875 | 900 | 89 | 89 | 89 | 89 |
| 900 | 925 | 91 | 91 | 91 | 91 |
| 925 | 950 | 94 | 94 | 94 | 94 |
| 950 | 975 | 96 | 96 | 96 | 96 |
| 975 | 1,000 | 99 | 99 | 99 | 99 |

### 1,000

| If line 15 (taxable income) is— | | And you are— | | | |
|---|---|---|---|---|---|
| At least | But less than | Single | Married filing jointly* | Married filing separately | Head of a household |
| | | | Your tax is— | | |
| 1,000 | 1,025 | 101 | 101 | 101 | 101 |
| 1,025 | 1,050 | 104 | 104 | 104 | 104 |
| 1,050 | 1,075 | 106 | 106 | 106 | 106 |
| 1,075 | 1,100 | 109 | 109 | 109 | 109 |
| 1,100 | 1,125 | 111 | 111 | 111 | 111 |
| 1,125 | 1,150 | 114 | 114 | 114 | 114 |
| 1,150 | 1,175 | 116 | 116 | 116 | 116 |
| 1,175 | 1,200 | 119 | 119 | 119 | 119 |
| 1,200 | 1,225 | 121 | 121 | 121 | 121 |
| 1,225 | 1,250 | 124 | 124 | 124 | 124 |
| 1,250 | 1,275 | 126 | 126 | 126 | 126 |
| 1,275 | 1,300 | 129 | 129 | 129 | 129 |
| 1,300 | 1,325 | 131 | 131 | 131 | 131 |
| 1,325 | 1,350 | 134 | 134 | 134 | 134 |
| 1,350 | 1,375 | 136 | 136 | 136 | 136 |
| 1,375 | 1,400 | 139 | 139 | 139 | 139 |
| 1,400 | 1,425 | 141 | 141 | 141 | 141 |
| 1,425 | 1,450 | 144 | 144 | 144 | 144 |
| 1,450 | 1,475 | 146 | 146 | 146 | 146 |
| 1,475 | 1,500 | 149 | 149 | 149 | 149 |
| 1,500 | 1,525 | 151 | 151 | 151 | 151 |
| 1,525 | 1,550 | 154 | 154 | 154 | 154 |
| 1,550 | 1,575 | 156 | 156 | 156 | 156 |
| 1,575 | 1,600 | 159 | 159 | 159 | 159 |
| 1,600 | 1,625 | 161 | 161 | 161 | 161 |
| 1,625 | 1,650 | 164 | 164 | 164 | 164 |
| 1,650 | 1,675 | 166 | 166 | 166 | 166 |
| 1,675 | 1,700 | 169 | 169 | 169 | 169 |
| 1,700 | 1,725 | 171 | 171 | 171 | 171 |
| 1,725 | 1,750 | 174 | 174 | 174 | 174 |
| 1,750 | 1,775 | 176 | 176 | 176 | 176 |
| 1,775 | 1,800 | 179 | 179 | 179 | 179 |
| 1,800 | 1,825 | 181 | 181 | 181 | 181 |
| 1,825 | 1,850 | 184 | 184 | 184 | 184 |
| 1,850 | 1,875 | 186 | 186 | 186 | 186 |
| 1,875 | 1,900 | 189 | 189 | 189 | 189 |
| 1,900 | 1,925 | 191 | 191 | 191 | 191 |
| 1,925 | 1,950 | 194 | 194 | 194 | 194 |
| 1,950 | 1,975 | 196 | 196 | 196 | 196 |
| 1,975 | 2,000 | 199 | 199 | 199 | 199 |

### 2,000

| If line 15 (taxable income) is— | | And you are— | | | |
|---|---|---|---|---|---|
| At least | But less than | Single | Married filing jointly* | Married filing separately | Head of a household |
| | | | Your tax is— | | |
| 2,000 | 2,025 | 201 | 201 | 201 | 201 |
| 2,025 | 2,050 | 204 | 204 | 204 | 204 |
| 2,050 | 2,075 | 206 | 206 | 206 | 206 |
| 2,075 | 2,100 | 209 | 209 | 209 | 209 |
| 2,100 | 2,125 | 211 | 211 | 211 | 211 |
| 2,125 | 2,150 | 214 | 214 | 214 | 214 |
| 2,150 | 2,175 | 216 | 216 | 216 | 216 |
| 2,175 | 2,200 | 219 | 219 | 219 | 219 |
| 2,200 | 2,225 | 221 | 221 | 221 | 221 |
| 2,225 | 2,250 | 224 | 224 | 224 | 224 |
| 2,250 | 2,275 | 226 | 226 | 226 | 226 |
| 2,275 | 2,300 | 229 | 229 | 229 | 229 |
| 2,300 | 2,325 | 231 | 231 | 231 | 231 |
| 2,325 | 2,350 | 234 | 234 | 234 | 234 |
| 2,350 | 2,375 | 236 | 236 | 236 | 236 |
| 2,375 | 2,400 | 239 | 239 | 239 | 239 |
| 2,400 | 2,425 | 241 | 241 | 241 | 241 |
| 2,425 | 2,450 | 244 | 244 | 244 | 244 |
| 2,450 | 2,475 | 246 | 246 | 246 | 246 |
| 2,475 | 2,500 | 249 | 249 | 249 | 249 |
| 2,500 | 2,525 | 251 | 251 | 251 | 251 |
| 2,525 | 2,550 | 254 | 254 | 254 | 254 |
| 2,550 | 2,575 | 256 | 256 | 256 | 256 |
| 2,575 | 2,600 | 259 | 259 | 259 | 259 |
| 2,600 | 2,625 | 261 | 261 | 261 | 261 |
| 2,625 | 2,650 | 264 | 264 | 264 | 264 |
| 2,650 | 2,675 | 266 | 266 | 266 | 266 |
| 2,675 | 2,700 | 269 | 269 | 269 | 269 |
| 2,700 | 2,725 | 271 | 271 | 271 | 271 |
| 2,725 | 2,750 | 274 | 274 | 274 | 274 |
| 2,750 | 2,775 | 276 | 276 | 276 | 276 |
| 2,775 | 2,800 | 279 | 279 | 279 | 279 |
| 2,800 | 2,825 | 281 | 281 | 281 | 281 |
| 2,825 | 2,850 | 284 | 284 | 284 | 284 |
| 2,850 | 2,875 | 286 | 286 | 286 | 286 |
| 2,875 | 2,900 | 289 | 289 | 289 | 289 |
| 2,900 | 2,925 | 291 | 291 | 291 | 291 |
| 2,925 | 2,950 | 294 | 294 | 294 | 294 |
| 2,950 | 2,975 | 296 | 296 | 296 | 296 |
| 2,975 | 3,000 | 299 | 299 | 299 | 299 |

Source: U.S. Department of the Treasury, Internal Revenue Service, Form 1040, 2020 Tax Table. Washington, DC: 2021.

DRAFT AS OF September 1, 2021

## 3,000

| If line 15 (taxable income) is— At least | But less than | Single | Married filing jointly * | Married filing separately | Head of a household |
|---|---|---|---|---|---|
| 3,000 | 3,050 | 303 | 303 | 303 | 303 |
| 3,050 | 3,100 | 308 | 308 | 308 | 308 |
| 3,100 | 3,150 | 313 | 313 | 313 | 313 |
| 3,150 | 3,200 | 318 | 318 | 318 | 318 |
| 3,200 | 3,250 | 323 | 323 | 323 | 323 |
| 3,250 | 3,300 | 328 | 328 | 328 | 328 |
| 3,300 | 3,350 | 333 | 333 | 333 | 333 |
| 3,350 | 3,400 | 338 | 338 | 338 | 338 |
| 3,400 | 3,450 | 343 | 343 | 343 | 343 |
| 3,450 | 3,500 | 348 | 348 | 348 | 348 |
| 3,500 | 3,550 | 353 | 353 | 353 | 353 |
| 3,550 | 3,600 | 358 | 358 | 358 | 358 |
| 3,600 | 3,650 | 363 | 363 | 363 | 363 |
| 3,650 | 3,700 | 368 | 368 | 368 | 368 |
| 3,700 | 3,750 | 373 | 373 | 373 | 373 |
| 3,750 | 3,800 | 378 | 378 | 378 | 378 |
| 3,800 | 3,850 | 383 | 383 | 383 | 383 |
| 3,850 | 3,900 | 388 | 388 | 388 | 388 |
| 3,900 | 3,950 | 393 | 393 | 393 | 393 |
| 3,950 | 4,000 | 398 | 398 | 398 | 398 |

## 4,000

| At least | But less than | Single | Married filing jointly * | Married filing separately | Head of a household |
|---|---|---|---|---|---|
| 4,000 | 4,050 | 403 | 403 | 403 | 403 |
| 4,050 | 4,100 | 408 | 408 | 408 | 408 |
| 4,100 | 4,150 | 413 | 413 | 413 | 413 |
| 4,150 | 4,200 | 418 | 418 | 418 | 418 |
| 4,200 | 4,250 | 423 | 423 | 423 | 423 |
| 4,250 | 4,300 | 428 | 428 | 428 | 428 |
| 4,300 | 4,350 | 433 | 433 | 433 | 433 |
| 4,350 | 4,400 | 438 | 438 | 438 | 438 |
| 4,400 | 4,450 | 443 | 443 | 443 | 443 |
| 4,450 | 4,500 | 448 | 448 | 448 | 448 |
| 4,500 | 4,550 | 453 | 453 | 453 | 453 |
| 4,550 | 4,600 | 458 | 458 | 458 | 458 |
| 4,600 | 4,650 | 463 | 463 | 463 | 463 |
| 4,650 | 4,700 | 468 | 468 | 468 | 468 |
| 4,700 | 4,750 | 473 | 473 | 473 | 473 |
| 4,750 | 4,800 | 478 | 478 | 478 | 478 |
| 4,800 | 4,850 | 483 | 483 | 483 | 483 |
| 4,850 | 4,900 | 488 | 488 | 488 | 488 |
| 4,900 | 4,950 | 493 | 493 | 493 | 493 |
| 4,950 | 5,000 | 498 | 498 | 498 | 498 |

## 5,000

| At least | But less than | Single | Married filing jointly * | Married filing separately | Head of a household |
|---|---|---|---|---|---|
| 5,000 | 5,050 | 503 | 503 | 503 | 503 |
| 5,050 | 5,100 | 508 | 508 | 508 | 508 |
| 5,100 | 5,150 | 513 | 513 | 513 | 513 |
| 5,150 | 5,200 | 518 | 518 | 518 | 518 |
| 5,200 | 5,250 | 523 | 523 | 523 | 523 |
| 5,250 | 5,300 | 528 | 528 | 528 | 528 |
| 5,300 | 5,350 | 533 | 533 | 533 | 533 |
| 5,350 | 5,400 | 538 | 538 | 538 | 538 |
| 5,400 | 5,450 | 543 | 543 | 543 | 543 |
| 5,450 | 5,500 | 548 | 548 | 548 | 548 |
| 5,500 | 5,550 | 553 | 553 | 553 | 553 |
| 5,550 | 5,600 | 558 | 558 | 558 | 558 |
| 5,600 | 5,650 | 563 | 563 | 563 | 563 |
| 5,650 | 5,700 | 568 | 568 | 568 | 568 |
| 5,700 | 5,750 | 573 | 573 | 573 | 573 |
| 5,750 | 5,800 | 578 | 578 | 578 | 578 |
| 5,800 | 5,850 | 583 | 583 | 583 | 583 |
| 5,850 | 5,900 | 588 | 588 | 588 | 588 |
| 5,900 | 5,950 | 593 | 593 | 593 | 593 |
| 5,950 | 6,000 | 598 | 598 | 598 | 598 |

## 6,000

| At least | But less than | Single | Married filing jointly * | Married filing separately | Head of a household |
|---|---|---|---|---|---|
| 6,000 | 6,050 | 603 | 603 | 603 | 603 |
| 6,050 | 6,100 | 608 | 608 | 608 | 608 |
| 6,100 | 6,150 | 613 | 613 | 613 | 613 |
| 6,150 | 6,200 | 618 | 618 | 618 | 618 |
| 6,200 | 6,250 | 623 | 623 | 623 | 623 |
| 6,250 | 6,300 | 628 | 628 | 628 | 628 |
| 6,300 | 6,350 | 633 | 633 | 633 | 633 |
| 6,350 | 6,400 | 638 | 638 | 638 | 638 |
| 6,400 | 6,450 | 643 | 643 | 643 | 643 |
| 6,450 | 6,500 | 648 | 648 | 648 | 648 |
| 6,500 | 6,550 | 653 | 653 | 653 | 653 |
| 6,550 | 6,600 | 658 | 658 | 658 | 658 |
| 6,600 | 6,650 | 663 | 663 | 663 | 663 |
| 6,650 | 6,700 | 668 | 668 | 668 | 668 |
| 6,700 | 6,750 | 673 | 673 | 673 | 673 |
| 6,750 | 6,800 | 678 | 678 | 678 | 678 |
| 6,800 | 6,850 | 683 | 683 | 683 | 683 |
| 6,850 | 6,900 | 688 | 688 | 688 | 688 |
| 6,900 | 6,950 | 693 | 693 | 693 | 693 |
| 6,950 | 7,000 | 698 | 698 | 698 | 698 |

## 7,000

| At least | But less than | Single | Married filing jointly * | Married filing separately | Head of a household |
|---|---|---|---|---|---|
| 7,000 | 7,050 | 703 | 703 | 703 | 703 |
| 7,050 | 7,100 | 708 | 708 | 708 | 708 |
| 7,100 | 7,150 | 713 | 713 | 713 | 713 |
| 7,150 | 7,200 | 718 | 718 | 718 | 718 |
| 7,200 | 7,250 | 723 | 723 | 723 | 723 |
| 7,250 | 7,300 | 728 | 728 | 728 | 728 |
| 7,300 | 7,350 | 733 | 733 | 733 | 733 |
| 7,350 | 7,400 | 738 | 738 | 738 | 738 |
| 7,400 | 7,450 | 743 | 743 | 743 | 743 |
| 7,450 | 7,500 | 748 | 748 | 748 | 748 |
| 7,500 | 7,550 | 753 | 753 | 753 | 753 |
| 7,550 | 7,600 | 758 | 758 | 758 | 758 |
| 7,600 | 7,650 | 763 | 763 | 763 | 763 |
| 7,650 | 7,700 | 768 | 768 | 768 | 768 |
| 7,700 | 7,750 | 773 | 773 | 773 | 773 |
| 7,750 | 7,800 | 778 | 778 | 778 | 778 |
| 7,800 | 7,850 | 783 | 783 | 783 | 783 |
| 7,850 | 7,900 | 788 | 788 | 788 | 788 |
| 7,900 | 7,950 | 793 | 793 | 793 | 793 |
| 7,950 | 8,000 | 798 | 798 | 798 | 798 |

## 8,000

| At least | But less than | Single | Married filing jointly * | Married filing separately | Head of a household |
|---|---|---|---|---|---|
| 8,000 | 8,050 | 803 | 803 | 803 | 803 |
| 8,050 | 8,100 | 808 | 808 | 808 | 808 |
| 8,100 | 8,150 | 813 | 813 | 813 | 813 |
| 8,150 | 8,200 | 818 | 818 | 818 | 818 |
| 8,200 | 8,250 | 823 | 823 | 823 | 823 |
| 8,250 | 8,300 | 828 | 828 | 828 | 828 |
| 8,300 | 8,350 | 833 | 833 | 833 | 833 |
| 8,350 | 8,400 | 838 | 838 | 838 | 838 |
| 8,400 | 8,450 | 843 | 843 | 843 | 843 |
| 8,450 | 8,500 | 848 | 848 | 848 | 848 |
| 8,500 | 8,550 | 853 | 853 | 853 | 853 |
| 8,550 | 8,600 | 858 | 858 | 858 | 858 |
| 8,600 | 8,650 | 863 | 863 | 863 | 863 |
| 8,650 | 8,700 | 868 | 868 | 868 | 868 |
| 8,700 | 8,750 | 873 | 873 | 873 | 873 |
| 8,750 | 8,800 | 878 | 878 | 878 | 878 |
| 8,800 | 8,850 | 883 | 883 | 883 | 883 |
| 8,850 | 8,900 | 888 | 888 | 888 | 888 |
| 8,900 | 8,950 | 893 | 893 | 893 | 893 |
| 8,950 | 9,000 | 898 | 898 | 898 | 898 |

## 9,000

| At least | But less than | Single | Married filing jointly * | Married filing separately | Head of a household |
|---|---|---|---|---|---|
| 9,000 | 9,050 | 903 | 903 | 903 | 903 |
| 9,050 | 9,100 | 908 | 908 | 908 | 908 |
| 9,100 | 9,150 | 913 | 913 | 913 | 913 |
| 9,150 | 9,200 | 918 | 918 | 918 | 918 |
| 9,200 | 9,250 | 923 | 923 | 923 | 923 |
| 9,250 | 9,300 | 928 | 928 | 928 | 928 |
| 9,300 | 9,350 | 933 | 933 | 933 | 933 |
| 9,350 | 9,400 | 938 | 938 | 938 | 938 |
| 9,400 | 9,450 | 943 | 943 | 943 | 943 |
| 9,450 | 9,500 | 948 | 948 | 948 | 948 |
| 9,500 | 9,550 | 953 | 953 | 953 | 953 |
| 9,550 | 9,600 | 958 | 958 | 958 | 958 |
| 9,600 | 9,650 | 963 | 963 | 963 | 963 |
| 9,650 | 9,700 | 968 | 968 | 968 | 968 |
| 9,700 | 9,750 | 973 | 973 | 973 | 973 |
| 9,750 | 9,800 | 978 | 978 | 978 | 978 |
| 9,800 | 9,850 | 983 | 983 | 983 | 983 |
| 9,850 | 9,900 | 988 | 988 | 988 | 988 |
| 9,900 | 9,950 | 993 | 993 | 993 | 993 |
| 9,950 | 10,000 | 998 | 998 | 998 | 998 |

## 10,000

| At least | But less than | Single | Married filing jointly * | Married filing separately | Head of a household |
|---|---|---|---|---|---|
| 10,000 | 10,050 | 1,004 | 1,003 | 1,004 | 1,003 |
| 10,050 | 10,100 | 1,010 | 1,008 | 1,010 | 1,008 |
| 10,100 | 10,150 | 1,016 | 1,013 | 1,016 | 1,013 |
| 10,150 | 10,200 | 1,022 | 1,018 | 1,022 | 1,018 |
| 10,200 | 10,250 | 1,028 | 1,023 | 1,028 | 1,023 |
| 10,250 | 10,300 | 1,034 | 1,028 | 1,034 | 1,028 |
| 10,300 | 10,350 | 1,040 | 1,033 | 1,040 | 1,033 |
| 10,350 | 10,400 | 1,046 | 1,038 | 1,046 | 1,038 |
| 10,400 | 10,450 | 1,052 | 1,043 | 1,052 | 1,043 |
| 10,450 | 10,500 | 1,058 | 1,048 | 1,058 | 1,048 |
| 10,500 | 10,550 | 1,064 | 1,053 | 1,064 | 1,053 |
| 10,550 | 10,600 | 1,070 | 1,058 | 1,070 | 1,058 |
| 10,600 | 10,650 | 1,076 | 1,063 | 1,076 | 1,063 |
| 10,650 | 10,700 | 1,082 | 1,068 | 1,082 | 1,068 |
| 10,700 | 10,750 | 1,088 | 1,073 | 1,088 | 1,073 |
| 10,750 | 10,800 | 1,094 | 1,078 | 1,094 | 1,078 |
| 10,800 | 10,850 | 1,100 | 1,083 | 1,100 | 1,083 |
| 10,850 | 10,900 | 1,106 | 1,088 | 1,106 | 1,088 |
| 10,900 | 10,950 | 1,112 | 1,093 | 1,112 | 1,093 |
| 10,950 | 11,000 | 1,118 | 1,098 | 1,118 | 1,098 |

## 11,000

| At least | But less than | Single | Married filing jointly * | Married filing separately | Head of a household |
|---|---|---|---|---|---|
| 11,000 | 11,050 | 1,124 | 1,103 | 1,124 | 1,103 |
| 11,050 | 11,100 | 1,130 | 1,108 | 1,130 | 1,108 |
| 11,100 | 11,150 | 1,136 | 1,113 | 1,136 | 1,113 |
| 11,150 | 11,200 | 1,142 | 1,118 | 1,142 | 1,118 |
| 11,200 | 11,250 | 1,148 | 1,123 | 1,148 | 1,123 |
| 11,250 | 11,300 | 1,154 | 1,128 | 1,154 | 1,128 |
| 11,300 | 11,350 | 1,160 | 1,133 | 1,160 | 1,133 |
| 11,350 | 11,400 | 1,166 | 1,138 | 1,166 | 1,138 |
| 11,400 | 11,450 | 1,172 | 1,143 | 1,172 | 1,143 |
| 11,450 | 11,500 | 1,178 | 1,148 | 1,178 | 1,148 |
| 11,500 | 11,550 | 1,184 | 1,153 | 1,184 | 1,153 |
| 11,550 | 11,600 | 1,190 | 1,158 | 1,190 | 1,158 |
| 11,600 | 11,650 | 1,196 | 1,163 | 1,196 | 1,163 |
| 11,650 | 11,700 | 1,202 | 1,168 | 1,202 | 1,168 |
| 11,700 | 11,750 | 1,208 | 1,173 | 1,208 | 1,173 |
| 11,750 | 11,800 | 1,214 | 1,178 | 1,214 | 1,178 |
| 11,800 | 11,850 | 1,220 | 1,183 | 1,220 | 1,183 |
| 11,850 | 11,900 | 1,226 | 1,188 | 1,226 | 1,188 |
| 11,900 | 11,950 | 1,232 | 1,193 | 1,232 | 1,193 |
| 11,950 | 12,000 | 1,238 | 1,198 | 1,238 | 1,198 |

## 12,000

| At least | But less than | Single | Married filing jointly * | Married filing separately | Head of a household |
|---|---|---|---|---|---|
| 12,000 | 12,050 | 1,244 | 1,203 | 1,244 | 1,203 |
| 12,050 | 12,100 | 1,250 | 1,208 | 1,250 | 1,208 |
| 12,100 | 12,150 | 1,256 | 1,213 | 1,256 | 1,213 |
| 12,150 | 12,200 | 1,262 | 1,218 | 1,262 | 1,218 |
| 12,200 | 12,250 | 1,268 | 1,223 | 1,268 | 1,223 |
| 12,250 | 12,300 | 1,274 | 1,228 | 1,274 | 1,228 |
| 12,300 | 12,350 | 1,280 | 1,233 | 1,280 | 1,233 |
| 12,350 | 12,400 | 1,286 | 1,238 | 1,286 | 1,238 |
| 12,400 | 12,450 | 1,292 | 1,243 | 1,292 | 1,243 |
| 12,450 | 12,500 | 1,298 | 1,248 | 1,298 | 1,248 |
| 12,500 | 12,550 | 1,304 | 1,253 | 1,304 | 1,253 |
| 12,550 | 12,600 | 1,310 | 1,258 | 1,310 | 1,258 |
| 12,600 | 12,650 | 1,316 | 1,263 | 1,316 | 1,263 |
| 12,650 | 12,700 | 1,322 | 1,268 | 1,322 | 1,268 |
| 12,700 | 12,750 | 1,328 | 1,273 | 1,328 | 1,273 |
| 12,750 | 12,800 | 1,334 | 1,278 | 1,334 | 1,278 |
| 12,800 | 12,850 | 1,340 | 1,283 | 1,340 | 1,283 |
| 12,850 | 12,900 | 1,346 | 1,288 | 1,346 | 1,288 |
| 12,900 | 12,950 | 1,352 | 1,293 | 1,352 | 1,293 |
| 12,950 | 13,000 | 1,358 | 1,298 | 1,358 | 1,298 |

## 13,000

| At least | But less than | Single | Married filing jointly * | Married filing separately | Head of a household |
|---|---|---|---|---|---|
| 13,000 | 13,050 | 1,364 | 1,303 | 1,364 | 1,303 |
| 13,050 | 13,100 | 1,370 | 1,308 | 1,370 | 1,308 |
| 13,100 | 13,150 | 1,376 | 1,313 | 1,376 | 1,313 |
| 13,150 | 13,200 | 1,382 | 1,318 | 1,382 | 1,318 |
| 13,200 | 13,250 | 1,388 | 1,323 | 1,388 | 1,323 |
| 13,250 | 13,300 | 1,394 | 1,328 | 1,394 | 1,328 |
| 13,300 | 13,350 | 1,400 | 1,333 | 1,400 | 1,333 |
| 13,350 | 13,400 | 1,406 | 1,338 | 1,406 | 1,338 |
| 13,400 | 13,450 | 1,412 | 1,343 | 1,412 | 1,343 |
| 13,450 | 13,500 | 1,418 | 1,348 | 1,418 | 1,348 |
| 13,500 | 13,550 | 1,424 | 1,353 | 1,424 | 1,353 |
| 13,550 | 13,600 | 1,430 | 1,358 | 1,430 | 1,358 |
| 13,600 | 13,650 | 1,436 | 1,363 | 1,436 | 1,363 |
| 13,650 | 13,700 | 1,442 | 1,368 | 1,442 | 1,368 |
| 13,700 | 13,750 | 1,448 | 1,373 | 1,448 | 1,373 |
| 13,750 | 13,800 | 1,454 | 1,378 | 1,454 | 1,378 |
| 13,800 | 13,850 | 1,460 | 1,383 | 1,460 | 1,383 |
| 13,850 | 13,900 | 1,466 | 1,388 | 1,466 | 1,388 |
| 13,900 | 13,950 | 1,472 | 1,393 | 1,472 | 1,393 |
| 13,950 | 14,000 | 1,478 | 1,398 | 1,478 | 1,398 |

## 14,000

| At least | But less than | Single | Married filing jointly * | Married filing separately | Head of a household |
|---|---|---|---|---|---|
| 14,000 | 14,050 | 1,484 | 1,403 | 1,484 | 1,403 |
| 14,050 | 14,100 | 1,490 | 1,408 | 1,490 | 1,408 |
| 14,100 | 14,150 | 1,496 | 1,413 | 1,496 | 1,413 |
| 14,150 | 14,200 | 1,502 | 1,418 | 1,502 | 1,418 |
| 14,200 | 14,250 | 1,508 | 1,423 | 1,508 | 1,423 |
| 14,250 | 14,300 | 1,514 | 1,428 | 1,514 | 1,429 |
| 14,300 | 14,350 | 1,520 | 1,433 | 1,520 | 1,435 |
| 14,350 | 14,400 | 1,526 | 1,438 | 1,526 | 1,441 |
| 14,400 | 14,450 | 1,532 | 1,443 | 1,532 | 1,447 |
| 14,450 | 14,500 | 1,538 | 1,448 | 1,538 | 1,453 |
| 14,500 | 14,550 | 1,544 | 1,453 | 1,544 | 1,459 |
| 14,550 | 14,600 | 1,550 | 1,458 | 1,550 | 1,465 |
| 14,600 | 14,650 | 1,556 | 1,463 | 1,556 | 1,471 |
| 14,650 | 14,700 | 1,562 | 1,468 | 1,562 | 1,477 |
| 14,700 | 14,750 | 1,568 | 1,473 | 1,568 | 1,483 |
| 14,750 | 14,800 | 1,574 | 1,478 | 1,574 | 1,489 |
| 14,800 | 14,850 | 1,580 | 1,483 | 1,580 | 1,495 |
| 14,850 | 14,900 | 1,586 | 1,488 | 1,586 | 1,501 |
| 14,900 | 14,950 | 1,592 | 1,493 | 1,592 | 1,507 |
| 14,950 | 15,000 | 1,598 | 1,498 | 1,598 | 1,513 |

## 15,000

| At least | But less than | Single | Married filing jointly * | Married filing separately | Head of a household |
|---|---|---|---|---|---|
| 15,000 | 15,050 | 1,604 | 1,503 | 1,604 | 1,519 |
| 15,050 | 15,100 | 1,610 | 1,508 | 1,610 | 1,525 |
| 15,100 | 15,150 | 1,616 | 1,513 | 1,616 | 1,531 |
| 15,150 | 15,200 | 1,622 | 1,518 | 1,622 | 1,537 |
| 15,200 | 15,250 | 1,628 | 1,523 | 1,628 | 1,543 |
| 15,250 | 15,300 | 1,634 | 1,528 | 1,634 | 1,549 |
| 15,300 | 15,350 | 1,640 | 1,533 | 1,640 | 1,555 |
| 15,350 | 15,400 | 1,646 | 1,538 | 1,646 | 1,561 |
| 15,400 | 15,450 | 1,652 | 1,543 | 1,652 | 1,567 |
| 15,450 | 15,500 | 1,658 | 1,548 | 1,658 | 1,573 |
| 15,500 | 15,550 | 1,664 | 1,553 | 1,664 | 1,579 |
| 15,550 | 15,600 | 1,670 | 1,558 | 1,670 | 1,585 |
| 15,600 | 15,650 | 1,676 | 1,563 | 1,676 | 1,591 |
| 15,650 | 15,700 | 1,682 | 1,568 | 1,682 | 1,597 |
| 15,700 | 15,750 | 1,688 | 1,573 | 1,688 | 1,603 |
| 15,750 | 15,800 | 1,694 | 1,578 | 1,694 | 1,609 |
| 15,800 | 15,850 | 1,700 | 1,583 | 1,700 | 1,615 |
| 15,850 | 15,900 | 1,706 | 1,588 | 1,706 | 1,621 |
| 15,900 | 15,950 | 1,712 | 1,593 | 1,712 | 1,627 |
| 15,950 | 16,000 | 1,718 | 1,598 | 1,718 | 1,633 |

## 16,000

| At least | But less than | Single | Married filing jointly * | Married filing separately | Head of a household |
|---|---|---|---|---|---|
| 16,000 | 16,050 | 1,724 | 1,603 | 1,724 | 1,639 |
| 16,050 | 16,100 | 1,730 | 1,608 | 1,730 | 1,645 |
| 16,100 | 16,150 | 1,736 | 1,613 | 1,736 | 1,651 |
| 16,150 | 16,200 | 1,742 | 1,618 | 1,742 | 1,657 |
| 16,200 | 16,250 | 1,748 | 1,623 | 1,748 | 1,663 |
| 16,250 | 16,300 | 1,754 | 1,628 | 1,754 | 1,669 |
| 16,300 | 16,350 | 1,760 | 1,633 | 1,760 | 1,675 |
| 16,350 | 16,400 | 1,766 | 1,638 | 1,766 | 1,681 |
| 16,400 | 16,450 | 1,772 | 1,643 | 1,772 | 1,687 |
| 16,450 | 16,500 | 1,778 | 1,648 | 1,778 | 1,693 |
| 16,500 | 16,550 | 1,784 | 1,653 | 1,784 | 1,699 |
| 16,550 | 16,600 | 1,790 | 1,658 | 1,790 | 1,705 |
| 16,600 | 16,650 | 1,796 | 1,663 | 1,796 | 1,711 |
| 16,650 | 16,700 | 1,802 | 1,668 | 1,802 | 1,717 |
| 16,700 | 16,750 | 1,808 | 1,673 | 1,808 | 1,723 |
| 16,750 | 16,800 | 1,814 | 1,678 | 1,814 | 1,729 |
| 16,800 | 16,850 | 1,820 | 1,683 | 1,820 | 1,735 |
| 16,850 | 16,900 | 1,826 | 1,688 | 1,826 | 1,741 |
| 16,900 | 16,950 | 1,832 | 1,693 | 1,832 | 1,747 |
| 16,950 | 17,000 | 1,838 | 1,698 | 1,838 | 1,753 |

## 17,000

| At least | But less than | Single | Married filing jointly * | Married filing separately | Head of a household |
|---|---|---|---|---|---|
| 17,000 | 17,050 | 1,844 | 1,703 | 1,844 | 1,759 |
| 17,050 | 17,100 | 1,850 | 1,708 | 1,850 | 1,765 |
| 17,100 | 17,150 | 1,856 | 1,713 | 1,856 | 1,771 |
| 17,150 | 17,200 | 1,862 | 1,718 | 1,862 | 1,777 |
| 17,200 | 17,250 | 1,868 | 1,723 | 1,868 | 1,783 |
| 17,250 | 17,300 | 1,874 | 1,728 | 1,874 | 1,789 |
| 17,300 | 17,350 | 1,880 | 1,733 | 1,880 | 1,795 |
| 17,350 | 17,400 | 1,886 | 1,738 | 1,886 | 1,801 |
| 17,400 | 17,450 | 1,892 | 1,743 | 1,892 | 1,807 |
| 17,450 | 17,500 | 1,898 | 1,748 | 1,898 | 1,813 |
| 17,500 | 17,550 | 1,904 | 1,753 | 1,904 | 1,819 |
| 17,550 | 17,600 | 1,910 | 1,758 | 1,910 | 1,825 |
| 17,600 | 17,650 | 1,916 | 1,763 | 1,916 | 1,831 |
| 17,650 | 17,700 | 1,922 | 1,768 | 1,922 | 1,837 |
| 17,700 | 17,750 | 1,928 | 1,773 | 1,928 | 1,843 |
| 17,750 | 17,800 | 1,934 | 1,778 | 1,934 | 1,849 |
| 17,800 | 17,850 | 1,940 | 1,783 | 1,940 | 1,855 |
| 17,850 | 17,900 | 1,946 | 1,788 | 1,946 | 1,861 |
| 17,900 | 17,950 | 1,952 | 1,793 | 1,952 | 1,867 |
| 17,950 | 18,000 | 1,958 | 1,798 | 1,958 | 1,873 |

## 18,000

| At least | But less than | Single | Married filing jointly * | Married filing separately | Head of a household |
|---|---|---|---|---|---|
| 18,000 | 18,050 | 1,964 | 1,803 | 1,964 | 1,879 |
| 18,050 | 18,100 | 1,970 | 1,808 | 1,970 | 1,885 |
| 18,100 | 18,150 | 1,976 | 1,813 | 1,976 | 1,891 |
| 18,150 | 18,200 | 1,982 | 1,818 | 1,982 | 1,897 |
| 18,200 | 18,250 | 1,988 | 1,823 | 1,988 | 1,903 |
| 18,250 | 18,300 | 1,994 | 1,828 | 1,994 | 1,909 |
| 18,300 | 18,350 | 2,000 | 1,833 | 2,000 | 1,915 |
| 18,350 | 18,400 | 2,006 | 1,838 | 2,006 | 1,921 |
| 18,400 | 18,450 | 2,012 | 1,843 | 2,012 | 1,927 |
| 18,450 | 18,500 | 2,018 | 1,848 | 2,018 | 1,933 |
| 18,500 | 18,550 | 2,024 | 1,853 | 2,024 | 1,939 |
| 18,550 | 18,600 | 2,030 | 1,858 | 2,030 | 1,945 |
| 18,600 | 18,650 | 2,036 | 1,863 | 2,036 | 1,951 |
| 18,650 | 18,700 | 2,042 | 1,868 | 2,042 | 1,957 |
| 18,700 | 18,750 | 2,048 | 1,873 | 2,048 | 1,963 |
| 18,750 | 18,800 | 2,054 | 1,878 | 2,054 | 1,969 |
| 18,800 | 18,850 | 2,060 | 1,883 | 2,060 | 1,975 |
| 18,850 | 18,900 | 2,066 | 1,888 | 2,066 | 1,981 |
| 18,900 | 18,950 | 2,072 | 1,893 | 2,072 | 1,987 |
| 18,950 | 19,000 | 2,078 | 1,898 | 2,078 | 1,993 |

## 19,000

| At least | But less than | Single | Married filing jointly * | Married filing separately | Head of a household |
|---|---|---|---|---|---|
| 19,000 | 19,050 | 2,084 | 1,903 | 2,084 | 1,999 |
| 19,050 | 19,100 | 2,090 | 1,908 | 2,090 | 2,005 |
| 19,100 | 19,150 | 2,096 | 1,913 | 2,096 | 2,011 |
| 19,150 | 19,200 | 2,102 | 1,918 | 2,102 | 2,017 |
| 19,200 | 19,250 | 2,108 | 1,923 | 2,108 | 2,023 |
| 19,250 | 19,300 | 2,114 | 1,928 | 2,114 | 2,029 |
| 19,300 | 19,350 | 2,120 | 1,933 | 2,120 | 2,035 |
| 19,350 | 19,400 | 2,126 | 1,938 | 2,126 | 2,041 |
| 19,400 | 19,450 | 2,132 | 1,943 | 2,132 | 2,047 |
| 19,450 | 19,500 | 2,138 | 1,948 | 2,138 | 2,053 |
| 19,500 | 19,550 | 2,144 | 1,953 | 2,144 | 2,059 |
| 19,550 | 19,600 | 2,150 | 1,958 | 2,150 | 2,065 |
| 19,600 | 19,650 | 2,156 | 1,963 | 2,156 | 2,071 |
| 19,650 | 19,700 | 2,162 | 1,968 | 2,162 | 2,077 |
| 19,700 | 19,750 | 2,168 | 1,973 | 2,168 | 2,083 |
| 19,750 | 19,800 | 2,174 | 1,978 | 2,174 | 2,089 |
| 19,800 | 19,850 | 2,180 | 1,983 | 2,180 | 2,095 |
| 19,850 | 19,900 | 2,186 | 1,988 | 2,186 | 2,101 |
| 19,900 | 19,950 | 2,192 | 1,993 | 2,192 | 2,107 |
| 19,950 | 20,000 | 2,198 | 1,999 | 2,198 | 2,113 |

## 20,000

| At least | But less than | Single | Married filing jointly * | Married filing separately | Head of a household |
|---|---|---|---|---|---|
| 20,000 | 20,050 | 2,204 | 2,005 | 2,204 | 2,119 |
| 20,050 | 20,100 | 2,210 | 2,011 | 2,210 | 2,125 |
| 20,100 | 20,150 | 2,216 | 2,017 | 2,216 | 2,131 |
| 20,150 | 20,200 | 2,222 | 2,023 | 2,222 | 2,137 |
| 20,200 | 20,250 | 2,228 | 2,029 | 2,228 | 2,143 |
| 20,250 | 20,300 | 2,234 | 2,035 | 2,234 | 2,149 |
| 20,300 | 20,350 | 2,240 | 2,041 | 2,240 | 2,155 |
| 20,350 | 20,400 | 2,246 | 2,047 | 2,246 | 2,161 |
| 20,400 | 20,450 | 2,252 | 2,053 | 2,252 | 2,167 |
| 20,450 | 20,500 | 2,258 | 2,059 | 2,258 | 2,173 |
| 20,500 | 20,550 | 2,264 | 2,065 | 2,264 | 2,179 |
| 20,550 | 20,600 | 2,270 | 2,071 | 2,270 | 2,185 |
| 20,600 | 20,650 | 2,276 | 2,077 | 2,276 | 2,191 |
| 20,650 | 20,700 | 2,282 | 2,083 | 2,282 | 2,197 |
| 20,700 | 20,750 | 2,288 | 2,089 | 2,288 | 2,203 |
| 20,750 | 20,800 | 2,294 | 2,095 | 2,294 | 2,209 |
| 20,800 | 20,850 | 2,300 | 2,101 | 2,300 | 2,215 |
| 20,850 | 20,900 | 2,306 | 2,107 | 2,306 | 2,221 |
| 20,900 | 20,950 | 2,312 | 2,113 | 2,312 | 2,227 |
| 20,950 | 21,000 | 2,318 | 2,119 | 2,318 | 2,233 |

| If line 15 (taxable income) is— | | And you are— | | | |
|---|---|---|---|---|---|
| At least | But less than | Single | Married filing jointly * | Married filing separately | Head of a household |
| | | Your tax is— | | | |
| **21,000** | | | | | |
| 21,000 | 21,050 | 2,324 | 2,125 | 2,324 | 2,239 |
| 21,050 | 21,100 | 2,330 | 2,131 | 2,330 | 2,245 |
| 21,100 | 21,150 | 2,336 | 2,137 | 2,336 | 2,251 |
| 21,150 | 21,200 | 2,342 | 2,143 | 2,342 | 2,257 |
| 21,200 | 21,250 | 2,348 | 2,149 | 2,348 | 2,263 |
| 21,250 | 21,300 | 2,354 | 2,155 | 2,354 | 2,269 |
| 21,300 | 21,350 | 2,360 | 2,161 | 2,360 | 2,275 |
| 21,350 | 21,400 | 2,366 | 2,167 | 2,366 | 2,281 |
| 21,400 | 21,450 | 2,372 | 2,173 | 2,372 | 2,287 |
| 21,450 | 21,500 | 2,378 | 2,179 | 2,378 | 2,293 |
| 21,500 | 21,550 | 2,384 | 2,185 | 2,384 | 2,299 |
| 21,550 | 21,600 | 2,390 | 2,191 | 2,390 | 2,305 |
| 21,600 | 21,650 | 2,396 | 2,197 | 2,396 | 2,311 |
| 21,650 | 21,700 | 2,402 | 2,203 | 2,402 | 2,317 |
| 21,700 | 21,750 | 2,408 | 2,209 | 2,408 | 2,323 |
| 21,750 | 21,800 | 2,414 | 2,215 | 2,414 | 2,329 |
| 21,800 | 21,850 | 2,420 | 2,221 | 2,420 | 2,335 |
| 21,850 | 21,900 | 2,426 | 2,227 | 2,426 | 2,341 |
| 21,900 | 21,950 | 2,432 | 2,233 | 2,432 | 2,347 |
| 21,950 | 22,000 | 2,438 | 2,239 | 2,438 | 2,353 |
| **22,000** | | | | | |
| 22,000 | 22,050 | 2,444 | 2,245 | 2,444 | 2,359 |
| 22,050 | 22,100 | 2,450 | 2,251 | 2,450 | 2,365 |
| 22,100 | 22,150 | 2,456 | 2,257 | 2,456 | 2,371 |
| 22,150 | 22,200 | 2,462 | 2,263 | 2,462 | 2,377 |
| 22,200 | 22,250 | 2,468 | 2,269 | 2,468 | 2,383 |
| 22,250 | 22,300 | 2,474 | 2,275 | 2,474 | 2,389 |
| 22,300 | 22,350 | 2,480 | 2,281 | 2,480 | 2,395 |
| 22,350 | 22,400 | 2,486 | 2,287 | 2,486 | 2,401 |
| 22,400 | 22,450 | 2,492 | 2,293 | 2,492 | 2,407 |
| 22,450 | 22,500 | 2,498 | 2,299 | 2,498 | 2,413 |
| 22,500 | 22,550 | 2,504 | 2,305 | 2,504 | 2,419 |
| 22,550 | 22,600 | 2,510 | 2,311 | 2,510 | 2,425 |
| 22,600 | 22,650 | 2,516 | 2,317 | 2,516 | 2,431 |
| 22,650 | 22,700 | 2,522 | 2,323 | 2,522 | 2,437 |
| 22,700 | 22,750 | 2,528 | 2,329 | 2,528 | 2,443 |
| 22,750 | 22,800 | 2,534 | 2,335 | 2,534 | 2,449 |
| 22,800 | 22,850 | 2,540 | 2,341 | 2,540 | 2,455 |
| 22,850 | 22,900 | 2,546 | 2,347 | 2,546 | 2,461 |
| 22,900 | 22,950 | 2,552 | 2,353 | 2,552 | 2,467 |
| 22,950 | 23,000 | 2,558 | 2,359 | 2,558 | 2,473 |
| **23,000** | | | | | |
| 23,000 | 23,050 | 2,564 | 2,365 | 2,564 | 2,479 |
| 23,050 | 23,100 | 2,570 | 2,371 | 2,570 | 2,485 |
| 23,100 | 23,150 | 2,576 | 2,377 | 2,576 | 2,491 |
| 23,150 | 23,200 | 2,582 | 2,383 | 2,582 | 2,497 |
| 23,200 | 23,250 | 2,588 | 2,389 | 2,588 | 2,503 |
| 23,250 | 23,300 | 2,594 | 2,395 | 2,594 | 2,509 |
| 23,300 | 23,350 | 2,600 | 2,401 | 2,600 | 2,515 |
| 23,350 | 23,400 | 2,606 | 2,407 | 2,606 | 2,521 |
| 23,400 | 23,450 | 2,612 | 2,413 | 2,612 | 2,527 |
| 23,450 | 23,500 | 2,618 | 2,419 | 2,618 | 2,533 |
| 23,500 | 23,550 | 2,624 | 2,425 | 2,624 | 2,539 |
| 23,550 | 23,600 | 2,630 | 2,431 | 2,630 | 2,545 |
| 23,600 | 23,650 | 2,636 | 2,437 | 2,636 | 2,551 |
| 23,650 | 23,700 | 2,642 | 2,443 | 2,642 | 2,557 |
| 23,700 | 23,750 | 2,648 | 2,449 | 2,648 | 2,563 |
| 23,750 | 23,800 | 2,654 | 2,455 | 2,654 | 2,569 |
| 23,800 | 23,850 | 2,660 | 2,461 | 2,660 | 2,575 |
| 23,850 | 23,900 | 2,666 | 2,467 | 2,666 | 2,581 |
| 23,900 | 23,950 | 2,672 | 2,473 | 2,672 | 2,587 |
| 23,950 | 24,000 | 2,678 | 2,479 | 2,678 | 2,593 |
| **24,000** | | | | | |
| 24,000 | 24,050 | 2,684 | 2,485 | 2,684 | 2,599 |
| 24,050 | 24,100 | 2,690 | 2,491 | 2,690 | 2,605 |
| 24,100 | 24,150 | 2,696 | 2,497 | 2,696 | 2,611 |
| 24,150 | 24,200 | 2,702 | 2,503 | 2,702 | 2,617 |
| 24,200 | 24,250 | 2,708 | 2,509 | 2,708 | 2,623 |
| 24,250 | 24,300 | 2,714 | 2,515 | 2,714 | 2,629 |
| 24,300 | 24,350 | 2,720 | 2,521 | 2,720 | 2,635 |
| 24,350 | 24,400 | 2,726 | 2,527 | 2,726 | 2,641 |
| 24,400 | 24,450 | 2,732 | 2,533 | 2,732 | 2,647 |
| 24,450 | 24,500 | 2,738 | 2,539 | 2,738 | 2,653 |
| 24,500 | 24,550 | 2,744 | 2,545 | 2,744 | 2,659 |
| 24,550 | 24,600 | 2,750 | 2,551 | 2,750 | 2,665 |
| 24,600 | 24,650 | 2,756 | 2,557 | 2,756 | 2,671 |
| 24,650 | 24,700 | 2,762 | 2,563 | 2,762 | 2,677 |
| 24,700 | 24,750 | 2,768 | 2,569 | 2,768 | 2,683 |
| 24,750 | 24,800 | 2,774 | 2,575 | 2,774 | 2,689 |
| 24,800 | 24,850 | 2,780 | 2,581 | 2,780 | 2,695 |
| 24,850 | 24,900 | 2,786 | 2,587 | 2,786 | 2,701 |
| 24,900 | 24,950 | 2,792 | 2,593 | 2,792 | 2,707 |
| 24,950 | 25,000 | 2,798 | 2,599 | 2,798 | 2,713 |
| **25,000** | | | | | |
| 25,000 | 25,050 | 2,804 | 2,605 | 2,804 | 2,719 |
| 25,050 | 25,100 | 2,810 | 2,611 | 2,810 | 2,725 |
| 25,100 | 25,150 | 2,816 | 2,617 | 2,816 | 2,731 |
| 25,150 | 25,200 | 2,822 | 2,623 | 2,822 | 2,737 |
| 25,200 | 25,250 | 2,828 | 2,629 | 2,828 | 2,743 |
| 25,250 | 25,300 | 2,834 | 2,635 | 2,834 | 2,749 |
| 25,300 | 25,350 | 2,840 | 2,641 | 2,840 | 2,755 |
| 25,350 | 25,400 | 2,846 | 2,647 | 2,846 | 2,761 |
| 25,400 | 25,450 | 2,852 | 2,653 | 2,852 | 2,767 |
| 25,450 | 25,500 | 2,858 | 2,659 | 2,858 | 2,773 |
| 25,500 | 25,550 | 2,864 | 2,665 | 2,864 | 2,779 |
| 25,550 | 25,600 | 2,870 | 2,671 | 2,870 | 2,785 |
| 25,600 | 25,650 | 2,876 | 2,677 | 2,876 | 2,791 |
| 25,650 | 25,700 | 2,882 | 2,683 | 2,882 | 2,797 |
| 25,700 | 25,750 | 2,888 | 2,689 | 2,888 | 2,803 |
| 25,750 | 25,800 | 2,894 | 2,695 | 2,894 | 2,809 |
| 25,800 | 25,850 | 2,900 | 2,701 | 2,900 | 2,815 |
| 25,850 | 25,900 | 2,906 | 2,707 | 2,906 | 2,821 |
| 25,900 | 25,950 | 2,912 | 2,713 | 2,912 | 2,827 |
| 25,950 | 26,000 | 2,918 | 2,719 | 2,918 | 2,833 |
| **26,000** | | | | | |
| 26,000 | 26,050 | 2,924 | 2,725 | 2,924 | 2,839 |
| 26,050 | 26,100 | 2,930 | 2,731 | 2,930 | 2,845 |
| 26,100 | 26,150 | 2,936 | 2,737 | 2,936 | 2,851 |
| 26,150 | 26,200 | 2,942 | 2,743 | 2,942 | 2,857 |
| 26,200 | 26,250 | 2,948 | 2,749 | 2,948 | 2,863 |
| 26,250 | 26,300 | 2,954 | 2,755 | 2,954 | 2,869 |
| 26,300 | 26,350 | 2,960 | 2,761 | 2,960 | 2,875 |
| 26,350 | 26,400 | 2,966 | 2,767 | 2,966 | 2,881 |
| 26,400 | 26,450 | 2,972 | 2,773 | 2,972 | 2,887 |
| 26,450 | 26,500 | 2,978 | 2,779 | 2,978 | 2,893 |
| 26,500 | 26,550 | 2,984 | 2,785 | 2,984 | 2,899 |
| 26,550 | 26,600 | 2,990 | 2,791 | 2,990 | 2,905 |
| 26,600 | 26,650 | 2,996 | 2,797 | 2,996 | 2,911 |
| 26,650 | 26,700 | 3,002 | 2,803 | 3,002 | 2,917 |
| 26,700 | 26,750 | 3,008 | 2,809 | 3,008 | 2,923 |
| 26,750 | 26,800 | 3,014 | 2,815 | 3,014 | 2,929 |
| 26,800 | 26,850 | 3,020 | 2,821 | 3,020 | 2,935 |
| 26,850 | 26,900 | 3,026 | 2,827 | 3,026 | 2,941 |
| 26,900 | 26,950 | 3,032 | 2,833 | 3,032 | 2,947 |
| 26,950 | 27,000 | 3,038 | 2,839 | 3,038 | 2,953 |
| **27,000** | | | | | |
| 27,000 | 27,050 | 3,044 | 2,845 | 3,044 | 2,959 |
| 27,050 | 27,100 | 3,050 | 2,851 | 3,050 | 2,965 |
| 27,100 | 27,150 | 3,056 | 2,857 | 3,056 | 2,971 |
| 27,150 | 27,200 | 3,062 | 2,863 | 3,062 | 2,977 |
| 27,200 | 27,250 | 3,068 | 2,869 | 3,068 | 2,983 |
| 27,250 | 27,300 | 3,074 | 2,875 | 3,074 | 2,989 |
| 27,300 | 27,350 | 3,080 | 2,881 | 3,080 | 2,995 |
| 27,350 | 27,400 | 3,086 | 2,887 | 3,086 | 3,001 |
| 27,400 | 27,450 | 3,092 | 2,893 | 3,092 | 3,007 |
| 27,450 | 27,500 | 3,098 | 2,899 | 3,098 | 3,013 |
| 27,500 | 27,550 | 3,104 | 2,905 | 3,104 | 3,019 |
| 27,550 | 27,600 | 3,110 | 2,911 | 3,110 | 3,025 |
| 27,600 | 27,650 | 3,116 | 2,917 | 3,116 | 3,031 |
| 27,650 | 27,700 | 3,122 | 2,923 | 3,122 | 3,037 |
| 27,700 | 27,750 | 3,128 | 2,929 | 3,128 | 3,043 |
| 27,750 | 27,800 | 3,134 | 2,935 | 3,134 | 3,049 |
| 27,800 | 27,850 | 3,140 | 2,941 | 3,140 | 3,055 |
| 27,850 | 27,900 | 3,146 | 2,947 | 3,146 | 3,061 |
| 27,900 | 27,950 | 3,152 | 2,953 | 3,152 | 3,067 |
| 27,950 | 28,000 | 3,158 | 2,959 | 3,158 | 3,073 |
| **28,000** | | | | | |
| 28,000 | 28,050 | 3,164 | 2,965 | 3,164 | 3,079 |
| 28,050 | 28,100 | 3,170 | 2,971 | 3,170 | 3,085 |
| 28,100 | 28,150 | 3,176 | 2,977 | 3,176 | 3,091 |
| 28,150 | 28,200 | 3,182 | 2,983 | 3,182 | 3,097 |
| 28,200 | 28,250 | 3,188 | 2,989 | 3,188 | 3,103 |
| 28,250 | 28,300 | 3,194 | 2,995 | 3,194 | 3,109 |
| 28,300 | 28,350 | 3,200 | 3,001 | 3,200 | 3,115 |
| 28,350 | 28,400 | 3,206 | 3,007 | 3,206 | 3,121 |
| 28,400 | 28,450 | 3,212 | 3,013 | 3,212 | 3,127 |
| 28,450 | 28,500 | 3,218 | 3,019 | 3,218 | 3,133 |
| 28,500 | 28,550 | 3,224 | 3,025 | 3,224 | 3,139 |
| 28,550 | 28,600 | 3,230 | 3,031 | 3,230 | 3,145 |
| 28,600 | 28,650 | 3,236 | 3,037 | 3,236 | 3,151 |
| 28,650 | 28,700 | 3,242 | 3,043 | 3,242 | 3,157 |
| 28,700 | 28,750 | 3,248 | 3,049 | 3,248 | 3,163 |
| 28,750 | 28,800 | 3,254 | 3,055 | 3,254 | 3,169 |
| 28,800 | 28,850 | 3,260 | 3,061 | 3,260 | 3,175 |
| 28,850 | 28,900 | 3,266 | 3,067 | 3,266 | 3,181 |
| 28,900 | 28,950 | 3,272 | 3,073 | 3,272 | 3,187 |
| 28,950 | 29,000 | 3,278 | 3,079 | 3,278 | 3,193 |
| **29,000** | | | | | |
| 29,000 | 29,050 | 3,284 | 3,085 | 3,284 | 3,199 |
| 29,050 | 29,100 | 3,290 | 3,091 | 3,290 | 3,205 |
| 29,100 | 29,150 | 3,296 | 3,097 | 3,296 | 3,211 |
| 29,150 | 29,200 | 3,302 | 3,103 | 3,302 | 3,217 |
| 29,200 | 29,250 | 3,308 | 3,109 | 3,308 | 3,223 |
| 29,250 | 29,300 | 3,314 | 3,115 | 3,314 | 3,229 |
| 29,300 | 29,350 | 3,320 | 3,121 | 3,320 | 3,235 |
| 29,350 | 29,400 | 3,326 | 3,127 | 3,326 | 3,241 |
| 29,400 | 29,450 | 3,332 | 3,133 | 3,332 | 3,247 |
| 29,450 | 29,500 | 3,338 | 3,139 | 3,338 | 3,253 |
| 29,500 | 29,550 | 3,344 | 3,145 | 3,344 | 3,259 |
| 29,550 | 29,600 | 3,350 | 3,151 | 3,350 | 3,265 |
| 29,600 | 29,650 | 3,356 | 3,157 | 3,356 | 3,271 |
| 29,650 | 29,700 | 3,362 | 3,163 | 3,362 | 3,277 |
| 29,700 | 29,750 | 3,368 | 3,169 | 3,368 | 3,283 |
| 29,750 | 29,800 | 3,374 | 3,175 | 3,374 | 3,289 |
| 29,800 | 29,850 | 3,380 | 3,181 | 3,380 | 3,295 |
| 29,850 | 29,900 | 3,386 | 3,187 | 3,386 | 3,301 |
| 29,900 | 29,950 | 3,392 | 3,193 | 3,392 | 3,307 |
| 29,950 | 30,000 | 3,398 | 3,199 | 3,398 | 3,313 |

## 30,000

| If line 15 (taxable income) is— | | And you are— | | | |
|---|---|---|---|---|---|
| At least | But less than | Single | Married filing jointly * | Married filing separately | Head of a household |
| | | Your tax is— | | | |
| 30,000 | 30,050 | 3,404 | 3,205 | 3,404 | 3,319 |
| 30,050 | 30,100 | 3,410 | 3,211 | 3,410 | 3,325 |
| 30,100 | 30,150 | 3,416 | 3,217 | 3,416 | 3,331 |
| 30,150 | 30,200 | 3,422 | 3,223 | 3,422 | 3,337 |
| 30,200 | 30,250 | 3,428 | 3,229 | 3,428 | 3,343 |
| 30,250 | 30,300 | 3,434 | 3,235 | 3,434 | 3,349 |
| 30,300 | 30,350 | 3,440 | 3,241 | 3,440 | 3,355 |
| 30,350 | 30,400 | 3,446 | 3,247 | 3,446 | 3,361 |
| 30,400 | 30,450 | 3,452 | 3,253 | 3,452 | 3,367 |
| 30,450 | 30,500 | 3,458 | 3,259 | 3,458 | 3,373 |
| 30,500 | 30,550 | 3,464 | 3,265 | 3,464 | 3,379 |
| 30,550 | 30,600 | 3,470 | 3,271 | 3,470 | 3,385 |
| 30,600 | 30,650 | 3,476 | 3,277 | 3,476 | 3,391 |
| 30,650 | 30,700 | 3,482 | 3,283 | 3,482 | 3,397 |
| 30,700 | 30,750 | 3,488 | 3,289 | 3,488 | 3,403 |
| 30,750 | 30,800 | 3,494 | 3,295 | 3,494 | 3,409 |
| 30,800 | 30,850 | 3,500 | 3,301 | 3,500 | 3,415 |
| 30,850 | 30,900 | 3,506 | 3,307 | 3,506 | 3,421 |
| 30,900 | 30,950 | 3,512 | 3,313 | 3,512 | 3,427 |
| 30,950 | 31,000 | 3,518 | 3,319 | 3,518 | 3,433 |

## 31,000

| At least | But less than | Single | Married filing jointly * | Married filing separately | Head of a household |
|---|---|---|---|---|---|
| 31,000 | 31,050 | 3,524 | 3,325 | 3,524 | 3,439 |
| 31,050 | 31,100 | 3,530 | 3,331 | 3,530 | 3,445 |
| 31,100 | 31,150 | 3,536 | 3,337 | 3,536 | 3,451 |
| 31,150 | 31,200 | 3,542 | 3,343 | 3,542 | 3,457 |
| 31,200 | 31,250 | 3,548 | 3,349 | 3,548 | 3,463 |
| 31,250 | 31,300 | 3,554 | 3,355 | 3,554 | 3,469 |
| 31,300 | 31,350 | 3,560 | 3,361 | 3,560 | 3,475 |
| 31,350 | 31,400 | 3,566 | 3,367 | 3,566 | 3,481 |
| 31,400 | 31,450 | 3,572 | 3,373 | 3,572 | 3,487 |
| 31,450 | 31,500 | 3,578 | 3,379 | 3,578 | 3,493 |
| 31,500 | 31,550 | 3,584 | 3,385 | 3,584 | 3,499 |
| 31,550 | 31,600 | 3,590 | 3,391 | 3,590 | 3,505 |
| 31,600 | 31,650 | 3,596 | 3,397 | 3,596 | 3,511 |
| 31,650 | 31,700 | 3,602 | 3,403 | 3,602 | 3,517 |
| 31,700 | 31,750 | 3,608 | 3,409 | 3,608 | 3,523 |
| 31,750 | 31,800 | 3,614 | 3,415 | 3,614 | 3,529 |
| 31,800 | 31,850 | 3,620 | 3,421 | 3,620 | 3,535 |
| 31,850 | 31,900 | 3,626 | 3,427 | 3,626 | 3,541 |
| 31,900 | 31,950 | 3,632 | 3,433 | 3,632 | 3,547 |
| 31,950 | 32,000 | 3,638 | 3,439 | 3,638 | 3,553 |

## 32,000

| At least | But less than | Single | Married filing jointly * | Married filing separately | Head of a household |
|---|---|---|---|---|---|
| 32,000 | 32,050 | 3,644 | 3,445 | 3,644 | 3,559 |
| 32,050 | 32,100 | 3,650 | 3,451 | 3,650 | 3,565 |
| 32,100 | 32,150 | 3,656 | 3,457 | 3,656 | 3,571 |
| 32,150 | 32,200 | 3,662 | 3,463 | 3,662 | 3,577 |
| 32,200 | 32,250 | 3,668 | 3,469 | 3,668 | 3,583 |
| 32,250 | 32,300 | 3,674 | 3,475 | 3,674 | 3,589 |
| 32,300 | 32,350 | 3,680 | 3,481 | 3,680 | 3,595 |
| 32,350 | 32,400 | 3,686 | 3,487 | 3,686 | 3,601 |
| 32,400 | 32,450 | 3,692 | 3,493 | 3,692 | 3,607 |
| 32,450 | 32,500 | 3,698 | 3,499 | 3,698 | 3,613 |
| 32,500 | 32,550 | 3,704 | 3,505 | 3,704 | 3,619 |
| 32,550 | 32,600 | 3,710 | 3,511 | 3,710 | 3,625 |
| 32,600 | 32,650 | 3,716 | 3,517 | 3,716 | 3,631 |
| 32,650 | 32,700 | 3,722 | 3,523 | 3,722 | 3,637 |
| 32,700 | 32,750 | 3,728 | 3,529 | 3,728 | 3,643 |
| 32,750 | 32,800 | 3,734 | 3,535 | 3,734 | 3,649 |
| 32,800 | 32,850 | 3,740 | 3,541 | 3,740 | 3,655 |
| 32,850 | 32,900 | 3,746 | 3,547 | 3,746 | 3,661 |
| 32,900 | 32,950 | 3,752 | 3,553 | 3,752 | 3,667 |
| 32,950 | 33,000 | 3,758 | 3,559 | 3,758 | 3,673 |

## 33,000

| At least | But less than | Single | Married filing jointly * | Married filing separately | Head of a household |
|---|---|---|---|---|---|
| 33,000 | 33,050 | 3,764 | 3,565 | 3,764 | 3,679 |
| 33,050 | 33,100 | 3,770 | 3,571 | 3,770 | 3,685 |
| 33,100 | 33,150 | 3,776 | 3,577 | 3,776 | 3,691 |
| 33,150 | 33,200 | 3,782 | 3,583 | 3,782 | 3,697 |
| 33,200 | 33,250 | 3,788 | 3,589 | 3,788 | 3,703 |
| 33,250 | 33,300 | 3,794 | 3,595 | 3,794 | 3,709 |
| 33,300 | 33,350 | 3,800 | 3,601 | 3,800 | 3,715 |
| 33,350 | 33,400 | 3,806 | 3,607 | 3,806 | 3,721 |
| 33,400 | 33,450 | 3,812 | 3,613 | 3,812 | 3,727 |
| 33,450 | 33,500 | 3,818 | 3,619 | 3,818 | 3,733 |
| 33,500 | 33,550 | 3,824 | 3,625 | 3,824 | 3,739 |
| 33,550 | 33,600 | 3,830 | 3,631 | 3,830 | 3,745 |
| 33,600 | 33,650 | 3,836 | 3,637 | 3,836 | 3,751 |
| 33,650 | 33,700 | 3,842 | 3,643 | 3,842 | 3,757 |
| 33,700 | 33,750 | 3,848 | 3,649 | 3,848 | 3,763 |
| 33,750 | 33,800 | 3,854 | 3,655 | 3,854 | 3,769 |
| 33,800 | 33,850 | 3,860 | 3,661 | 3,860 | 3,775 |
| 33,850 | 33,900 | 3,866 | 3,667 | 3,866 | 3,781 |
| 33,900 | 33,950 | 3,872 | 3,673 | 3,872 | 3,787 |
| 33,950 | 34,000 | 3,878 | 3,679 | 3,878 | 3,793 |

## 34,000

| At least | But less than | Single | Married filing jointly * | Married filing separately | Head of a household |
|---|---|---|---|---|---|
| 34,000 | 34,050 | 3,884 | 3,685 | 3,884 | 3,799 |
| 34,050 | 34,100 | 3,890 | 3,691 | 3,890 | 3,805 |
| 34,100 | 34,150 | 3,896 | 3,697 | 3,896 | 3,811 |
| 34,150 | 34,200 | 3,902 | 3,703 | 3,902 | 3,817 |
| 34,200 | 34,250 | 3,908 | 3,709 | 3,908 | 3,823 |
| 34,250 | 34,300 | 3,914 | 3,715 | 3,914 | 3,829 |
| 34,300 | 34,350 | 3,920 | 3,721 | 3,920 | 3,835 |
| 34,350 | 34,400 | 3,926 | 3,727 | 3,926 | 3,841 |
| 34,400 | 34,450 | 3,932 | 3,733 | 3,932 | 3,847 |
| 34,450 | 34,500 | 3,938 | 3,739 | 3,938 | 3,853 |
| 34,500 | 34,550 | 3,944 | 3,745 | 3,944 | 3,859 |
| 34,550 | 34,600 | 3,950 | 3,751 | 3,950 | 3,865 |
| 34,600 | 34,650 | 3,956 | 3,757 | 3,956 | 3,871 |
| 34,650 | 34,700 | 3,962 | 3,763 | 3,962 | 3,877 |
| 34,700 | 34,750 | 3,968 | 3,769 | 3,968 | 3,883 |
| 34,750 | 34,800 | 3,974 | 3,775 | 3,974 | 3,889 |
| 34,800 | 34,850 | 3,980 | 3,781 | 3,980 | 3,895 |
| 34,850 | 34,900 | 3,986 | 3,787 | 3,986 | 3,901 |
| 34,900 | 34,950 | 3,992 | 3,793 | 3,992 | 3,907 |
| 34,950 | 35,000 | 3,998 | 3,799 | 3,998 | 3,913 |

## 35,000

| At least | But less than | Single | Married filing jointly * | Married filing separately | Head of a household |
|---|---|---|---|---|---|
| 35,000 | 35,050 | 4,004 | 3,805 | 4,004 | 3,919 |
| 35,050 | 35,100 | 4,010 | 3,811 | 4,010 | 3,925 |
| 35,100 | 35,150 | 4,016 | 3,817 | 4,016 | 3,931 |
| 35,150 | 35,200 | 4,022 | 3,823 | 4,022 | 3,937 |
| 35,200 | 35,250 | 4,028 | 3,829 | 4,028 | 3,943 |
| 35,250 | 35,300 | 4,034 | 3,835 | 4,034 | 3,949 |
| 35,300 | 35,350 | 4,040 | 3,841 | 4,040 | 3,955 |
| 35,350 | 35,400 | 4,046 | 3,847 | 4,046 | 3,961 |
| 35,400 | 35,450 | 4,052 | 3,853 | 4,052 | 3,967 |
| 35,450 | 35,500 | 4,058 | 3,859 | 4,058 | 3,973 |
| 35,500 | 35,550 | 4,064 | 3,865 | 4,064 | 3,979 |
| 35,550 | 35,600 | 4,070 | 3,871 | 4,070 | 3,985 |
| 35,600 | 35,650 | 4,076 | 3,877 | 4,076 | 3,991 |
| 35,650 | 35,700 | 4,082 | 3,883 | 4,082 | 3,997 |
| 35,700 | 35,750 | 4,088 | 3,889 | 4,088 | 4,003 |
| 35,750 | 35,800 | 4,094 | 3,895 | 4,094 | 4,009 |
| 35,800 | 35,850 | 4,100 | 3,901 | 4,100 | 4,015 |
| 35,850 | 35,900 | 4,106 | 3,907 | 4,106 | 4,021 |
| 35,900 | 35,950 | 4,112 | 3,913 | 4,112 | 4,027 |
| 35,950 | 36,000 | 4,118 | 3,919 | 4,118 | 4,033 |

## 36,000

| At least | But less than | Single | Married filing jointly * | Married filing separately | Head of a household |
|---|---|---|---|---|---|
| 36,000 | 36,050 | 4,124 | 3,925 | 4,124 | 4,039 |
| 36,050 | 36,100 | 4,130 | 3,931 | 4,130 | 4,045 |
| 36,100 | 36,150 | 4,136 | 3,937 | 4,136 | 4,051 |
| 36,150 | 36,200 | 4,142 | 3,943 | 4,142 | 4,057 |
| 36,200 | 36,250 | 4,148 | 3,949 | 4,148 | 4,063 |
| 36,250 | 36,300 | 4,154 | 3,955 | 4,154 | 4,069 |
| 36,300 | 36,350 | 4,160 | 3,961 | 4,160 | 4,075 |
| 36,350 | 36,400 | 4,166 | 3,967 | 4,166 | 4,081 |
| 36,400 | 36,450 | 4,172 | 3,973 | 4,172 | 4,087 |
| 36,450 | 36,500 | 4,178 | 3,979 | 4,178 | 4,093 |
| 36,500 | 36,550 | 4,184 | 3,985 | 4,184 | 4,099 |
| 36,550 | 36,600 | 4,190 | 3,991 | 4,190 | 4,105 |
| 36,600 | 36,650 | 4,196 | 3,997 | 4,196 | 4,111 |
| 36,650 | 36,700 | 4,202 | 4,003 | 4,202 | 4,117 |
| 36,700 | 36,750 | 4,208 | 4,009 | 4,208 | 4,123 |
| 36,750 | 36,800 | 4,214 | 4,015 | 4,214 | 4,129 |
| 36,800 | 36,850 | 4,220 | 4,021 | 4,220 | 4,135 |
| 36,850 | 36,900 | 4,226 | 4,027 | 4,226 | 4,141 |
| 36,900 | 36,950 | 4,232 | 4,033 | 4,232 | 4,147 |
| 36,950 | 37,000 | 4,238 | 4,039 | 4,238 | 4,153 |

## 37,000

| At least | But less than | Single | Married filing jointly * | Married filing separately | Head of a household |
|---|---|---|---|---|---|
| 37,000 | 37,050 | 4,244 | 4,045 | 4,244 | 4,159 |
| 37,050 | 37,100 | 4,250 | 4,051 | 4,250 | 4,165 |
| 37,100 | 37,150 | 4,256 | 4,057 | 4,256 | 4,171 |
| 37,150 | 37,200 | 4,262 | 4,063 | 4,262 | 4,177 |
| 37,200 | 37,250 | 4,268 | 4,069 | 4,268 | 4,183 |
| 37,250 | 37,300 | 4,274 | 4,075 | 4,274 | 4,189 |
| 37,300 | 37,350 | 4,280 | 4,081 | 4,280 | 4,195 |
| 37,350 | 37,400 | 4,286 | 4,087 | 4,286 | 4,201 |
| 37,400 | 37,450 | 4,292 | 4,093 | 4,292 | 4,207 |
| 37,450 | 37,500 | 4,298 | 4,099 | 4,298 | 4,213 |
| 37,500 | 37,550 | 4,304 | 4,105 | 4,304 | 4,219 |
| 37,550 | 37,600 | 4,310 | 4,111 | 4,310 | 4,225 |
| 37,600 | 37,650 | 4,316 | 4,117 | 4,316 | 4,231 |
| 37,650 | 37,700 | 4,322 | 4,123 | 4,322 | 4,237 |
| 37,700 | 37,750 | 4,328 | 4,129 | 4,328 | 4,243 |
| 37,750 | 37,800 | 4,334 | 4,135 | 4,334 | 4,249 |
| 37,800 | 37,850 | 4,340 | 4,141 | 4,340 | 4,255 |
| 37,850 | 37,900 | 4,346 | 4,147 | 4,346 | 4,261 |
| 37,900 | 37,950 | 4,352 | 4,153 | 4,352 | 4,267 |
| 37,950 | 38,000 | 4,358 | 4,159 | 4,358 | 4,273 |

## 38,000

| At least | But less than | Single | Married filing jointly * | Married filing separately | Head of a household |
|---|---|---|---|---|---|
| 38,000 | 38,050 | 4,364 | 4,165 | 4,364 | 4,279 |
| 38,050 | 38,100 | 4,370 | 4,171 | 4,370 | 4,285 |
| 38,100 | 38,150 | 4,376 | 4,177 | 4,376 | 4,291 |
| 38,150 | 38,200 | 4,382 | 4,183 | 4,382 | 4,297 |
| 38,200 | 38,250 | 4,388 | 4,189 | 4,388 | 4,303 |
| 38,250 | 38,300 | 4,394 | 4,195 | 4,394 | 4,309 |
| 38,300 | 38,350 | 4,400 | 4,201 | 4,400 | 4,315 |
| 38,350 | 38,400 | 4,406 | 4,207 | 4,406 | 4,321 |
| 38,400 | 38,450 | 4,412 | 4,213 | 4,412 | 4,327 |
| 38,450 | 38,500 | 4,418 | 4,219 | 4,418 | 4,333 |
| 38,500 | 38,550 | 4,424 | 4,225 | 4,424 | 4,339 |
| 38,550 | 38,600 | 4,430 | 4,231 | 4,430 | 4,345 |
| 38,600 | 38,650 | 4,436 | 4,237 | 4,436 | 4,351 |
| 38,650 | 38,700 | 4,442 | 4,243 | 4,442 | 4,357 |
| 38,700 | 38,750 | 4,448 | 4,249 | 4,448 | 4,363 |
| 38,750 | 38,800 | 4,454 | 4,255 | 4,454 | 4,369 |
| 38,800 | 38,850 | 4,460 | 4,261 | 4,460 | 4,375 |
| 38,850 | 38,900 | 4,466 | 4,267 | 4,466 | 4,381 |
| 38,900 | 38,950 | 4,472 | 4,273 | 4,472 | 4,387 |
| 38,950 | 39,000 | 4,478 | 4,279 | 4,478 | 4,393 |

## 39,000

| If line 15 (taxable income) is— | | And you are— | | | |
| --- | --- | --- | --- | --- | --- |
| At least | But less than | Single | Married filing jointly * | Married filing separately | Head of a household |
| | | Your tax is— | | | |
| 39,000 | 39,050 | 4,484 | 4,285 | 4,484 | 4,399 |
| 39,050 | 39,100 | 4,490 | 4,291 | 4,490 | 4,405 |
| 39,100 | 39,150 | 4,496 | 4,297 | 4,496 | 4,411 |
| 39,150 | 39,200 | 4,502 | 4,303 | 4,502 | 4,417 |
| 39,200 | 39,250 | 4,508 | 4,309 | 4,508 | 4,423 |
| 39,250 | 39,300 | 4,514 | 4,315 | 4,514 | 4,429 |
| 39,300 | 39,350 | 4,520 | 4,321 | 4,520 | 4,435 |
| 39,350 | 39,400 | 4,526 | 4,327 | 4,526 | 4,441 |
| 39,400 | 39,450 | 4,532 | 4,333 | 4,532 | 4,447 |
| 39,450 | 39,500 | 4,538 | 4,339 | 4,538 | 4,453 |
| 39,500 | 39,550 | 4,544 | 4,345 | 4,544 | 4,459 |
| 39,550 | 39,600 | 4,550 | 4,351 | 4,550 | 4,465 |
| 39,600 | 39,650 | 4,556 | 4,357 | 4,556 | 4,471 |
| 39,650 | 39,700 | 4,562 | 4,363 | 4,562 | 4,477 |
| 39,700 | 39,750 | 4,568 | 4,369 | 4,568 | 4,483 |
| 39,750 | 39,800 | 4,574 | 4,375 | 4,574 | 4,489 |
| 39,800 | 39,850 | 4,580 | 4,381 | 4,580 | 4,495 |
| 39,850 | 39,900 | 4,586 | 4,387 | 4,586 | 4,501 |
| 39,900 | 39,950 | 4,592 | 4,393 | 4,592 | 4,507 |
| 39,950 | 40,000 | 4,598 | 4,399 | 4,598 | 4,513 |

## 40,000

| At least | But less than | Single | Married filing jointly * | Married filing separately | Head of a household |
| --- | --- | --- | --- | --- | --- |
| 40,000 | 40,050 | 4,604 | 4,405 | 4,604 | 4,519 |
| 40,050 | 40,100 | 4,610 | 4,411 | 4,610 | 4,525 |
| 40,100 | 40,150 | 4,616 | 4,417 | 4,616 | 4,531 |
| 40,150 | 40,200 | 4,622 | 4,423 | 4,622 | 4,537 |
| 40,200 | 40,250 | 4,628 | 4,429 | 4,628 | 4,543 |
| 40,250 | 40,300 | 4,634 | 4,435 | 4,634 | 4,549 |
| 40,300 | 40,350 | 4,640 | 4,441 | 4,640 | 4,555 |
| 40,350 | 40,400 | 4,646 | 4,447 | 4,646 | 4,561 |
| 40,400 | 40,450 | 4,652 | 4,453 | 4,652 | 4,567 |
| 40,450 | 40,500 | 4,658 | 4,459 | 4,658 | 4,573 |
| 40,500 | 40,550 | 4,664 | 4,465 | 4,664 | 4,579 |
| 40,550 | 40,600 | 4,675 | 4,471 | 4,675 | 4,585 |
| 40,600 | 40,650 | 4,686 | 4,477 | 4,686 | 4,591 |
| 40,650 | 40,700 | 4,697 | 4,483 | 4,697 | 4,597 |
| 40,700 | 40,750 | 4,708 | 4,489 | 4,708 | 4,603 |
| 40,750 | 40,800 | 4,719 | 4,495 | 4,719 | 4,609 |
| 40,800 | 40,850 | 4,730 | 4,501 | 4,730 | 4,615 |
| 40,850 | 40,900 | 4,741 | 4,507 | 4,741 | 4,621 |
| 40,900 | 40,950 | 4,752 | 4,513 | 4,752 | 4,627 |
| 40,950 | 41,000 | 4,763 | 4,519 | 4,763 | 4,633 |

## 41,000

| At least | But less than | Single | Married filing jointly * | Married filing separately | Head of a household |
| --- | --- | --- | --- | --- | --- |
| 41,000 | 41,050 | 4,774 | 4,525 | 4,774 | 4,639 |
| 41,050 | 41,100 | 4,785 | 4,531 | 4,785 | 4,645 |
| 41,100 | 41,150 | 4,796 | 4,537 | 4,796 | 4,651 |
| 41,150 | 41,200 | 4,807 | 4,543 | 4,807 | 4,657 |
| 41,200 | 41,250 | 4,818 | 4,549 | 4,818 | 4,663 |
| 41,250 | 41,300 | 4,829 | 4,555 | 4,829 | 4,669 |
| 41,300 | 41,350 | 4,840 | 4,561 | 4,840 | 4,675 |
| 41,350 | 41,400 | 4,851 | 4,567 | 4,851 | 4,681 |
| 41,400 | 41,450 | 4,862 | 4,573 | 4,862 | 4,687 |
| 41,450 | 41,500 | 4,873 | 4,579 | 4,873 | 4,693 |
| 41,500 | 41,550 | 4,884 | 4,585 | 4,884 | 4,699 |
| 41,550 | 41,600 | 4,895 | 4,591 | 4,895 | 4,705 |
| 41,600 | 41,650 | 4,906 | 4,597 | 4,906 | 4,711 |
| 41,650 | 41,700 | 4,917 | 4,603 | 4,917 | 4,717 |
| 41,700 | 41,750 | 4,928 | 4,609 | 4,928 | 4,723 |
| 41,750 | 41,800 | 4,939 | 4,615 | 4,939 | 4,729 |
| 41,800 | 41,850 | 4,950 | 4,621 | 4,950 | 4,735 |
| 41,850 | 41,900 | 4,961 | 4,627 | 4,961 | 4,741 |
| 41,900 | 41,950 | 4,972 | 4,633 | 4,972 | 4,747 |
| 41,950 | 42,000 | 4,983 | 4,639 | 4,983 | 4,753 |

## 42,000

| If line 15 (taxable income) is— | | And you are— | | | |
| --- | --- | --- | --- | --- | --- |
| At least | But less than | Single | Married filing jointly * | Married filing separately | Head of a household |
| | | Your tax is— | | | |
| 42,000 | 42,050 | 4,994 | 4,645 | 4,994 | 4,759 |
| 42,050 | 42,100 | 5,005 | 4,651 | 5,005 | 4,765 |
| 42,100 | 42,150 | 5,016 | 4,657 | 5,016 | 4,771 |
| 42,150 | 42,200 | 5,027 | 4,663 | 5,027 | 4,777 |
| 42,200 | 42,250 | 5,038 | 4,669 | 5,038 | 4,783 |
| 42,250 | 42,300 | 5,049 | 4,675 | 5,049 | 4,789 |
| 42,300 | 42,350 | 5,060 | 4,681 | 5,060 | 4,795 |
| 42,350 | 42,400 | 5,071 | 4,687 | 5,071 | 4,801 |
| 42,400 | 42,450 | 5,082 | 4,693 | 5,082 | 4,807 |
| 42,450 | 42,500 | 5,093 | 4,699 | 5,093 | 4,813 |
| 42,500 | 42,550 | 5,104 | 4,705 | 5,104 | 4,819 |
| 42,550 | 42,600 | 5,115 | 4,711 | 5,115 | 4,825 |
| 42,600 | 42,650 | 5,126 | 4,717 | 5,126 | 4,831 |
| 42,650 | 42,700 | 5,137 | 4,723 | 5,137 | 4,837 |
| 42,700 | 42,750 | 5,148 | 4,729 | 5,148 | 4,843 |
| 42,750 | 42,800 | 5,159 | 4,735 | 5,159 | 4,849 |
| 42,800 | 42,850 | 5,170 | 4,741 | 5,170 | 4,855 |
| 42,850 | 42,900 | 5,181 | 4,747 | 5,181 | 4,861 |
| 42,900 | 42,950 | 5,192 | 4,753 | 5,192 | 4,867 |
| 42,950 | 43,000 | 5,203 | 4,759 | 5,203 | 4,873 |

## 43,000

| At least | But less than | Single | Married filing jointly * | Married filing separately | Head of a household |
| --- | --- | --- | --- | --- | --- |
| 43,000 | 43,050 | 5,214 | 4,765 | 5,214 | 4,879 |
| 43,050 | 43,100 | 5,225 | 4,771 | 5,225 | 4,885 |
| 43,100 | 43,150 | 5,236 | 4,777 | 5,236 | 4,891 |
| 43,150 | 43,200 | 5,247 | 4,783 | 5,247 | 4,897 |
| 43,200 | 43,250 | 5,258 | 4,789 | 5,258 | 4,903 |
| 43,250 | 43,300 | 5,269 | 4,795 | 5,269 | 4,909 |
| 43,300 | 43,350 | 5,280 | 4,801 | 5,280 | 4,915 |
| 43,350 | 43,400 | 5,291 | 4,807 | 5,291 | 4,921 |
| 43,400 | 43,450 | 5,302 | 4,813 | 5,302 | 4,927 |
| 43,450 | 43,500 | 5,313 | 4,819 | 5,313 | 4,933 |
| 43,500 | 43,550 | 5,324 | 4,825 | 5,324 | 4,939 |
| 43,550 | 43,600 | 5,335 | 4,831 | 5,335 | 4,945 |
| 43,600 | 43,650 | 5,346 | 4,837 | 5,346 | 4,951 |
| 43,650 | 43,700 | 5,357 | 4,843 | 5,357 | 4,957 |
| 43,700 | 43,750 | 5,368 | 4,849 | 5,368 | 4,963 |
| 43,750 | 43,800 | 5,379 | 4,855 | 5,379 | 4,969 |
| 43,800 | 43,850 | 5,390 | 4,861 | 5,390 | 4,975 |
| 43,850 | 43,900 | 5,401 | 4,867 | 5,401 | 4,981 |
| 43,900 | 43,950 | 5,412 | 4,873 | 5,412 | 4,987 |
| 43,950 | 44,000 | 5,423 | 4,879 | 5,423 | 4,993 |

## 44,000

| At least | But less than | Single | Married filing jointly * | Married filing separately | Head of a household |
| --- | --- | --- | --- | --- | --- |
| 44,000 | 44,050 | 5,434 | 4,885 | 5,434 | 4,999 |
| 44,050 | 44,100 | 5,445 | 4,891 | 5,445 | 5,005 |
| 44,100 | 44,150 | 5,456 | 4,897 | 5,456 | 5,011 |
| 44,150 | 44,200 | 5,467 | 4,903 | 5,467 | 5,017 |
| 44,200 | 44,250 | 5,478 | 4,909 | 5,478 | 5,023 |
| 44,250 | 44,300 | 5,489 | 4,915 | 5,489 | 5,029 |
| 44,300 | 44,350 | 5,500 | 4,921 | 5,500 | 5,035 |
| 44,350 | 44,400 | 5,511 | 4,927 | 5,511 | 5,041 |
| 44,400 | 44,450 | 5,522 | 4,933 | 5,522 | 5,047 |
| 44,450 | 44,500 | 5,533 | 4,939 | 5,533 | 5,053 |
| 44,500 | 44,550 | 5,544 | 4,945 | 5,544 | 5,059 |
| 44,550 | 44,600 | 5,555 | 4,951 | 5,555 | 5,065 |
| 44,600 | 44,650 | 5,566 | 4,957 | 5,566 | 5,071 |
| 44,650 | 44,700 | 5,577 | 4,963 | 5,577 | 5,077 |
| 44,700 | 44,750 | 5,588 | 4,969 | 5,588 | 5,083 |
| 44,750 | 44,800 | 5,599 | 4,975 | 5,599 | 5,089 |
| 44,800 | 44,850 | 5,610 | 4,981 | 5,610 | 5,095 |
| 44,850 | 44,900 | 5,621 | 4,987 | 5,621 | 5,101 |
| 44,900 | 44,950 | 5,632 | 4,993 | 5,632 | 5,107 |
| 44,950 | 45,000 | 5,643 | 4,999 | 5,643 | 5,113 |

## 45,000

| If line 15 (taxable income) is— | | And you are— | | | |
| --- | --- | --- | --- | --- | --- |
| At least | But less than | Single | Married filing jointly * | Married filing separately | Head of a household |
| | | Your tax is— | | | |
| 45,000 | 45,050 | 5,654 | 5,005 | 5,654 | 5,119 |
| 45,050 | 45,100 | 5,665 | 5,011 | 5,665 | 5,125 |
| 45,100 | 45,150 | 5,676 | 5,017 | 5,676 | 5,131 |
| 45,150 | 45,200 | 5,687 | 5,023 | 5,687 | 5,137 |
| 45,200 | 45,250 | 5,698 | 5,029 | 5,698 | 5,143 |
| 45,250 | 45,300 | 5,709 | 5,035 | 5,709 | 5,149 |
| 45,300 | 45,350 | 5,720 | 5,041 | 5,720 | 5,155 |
| 45,350 | 45,400 | 5,731 | 5,047 | 5,731 | 5,161 |
| 45,400 | 45,450 | 5,742 | 5,053 | 5,742 | 5,167 |
| 45,450 | 45,500 | 5,753 | 5,059 | 5,753 | 5,173 |
| 45,500 | 45,550 | 5,764 | 5,065 | 5,764 | 5,179 |
| 45,550 | 45,600 | 5,775 | 5,071 | 5,775 | 5,185 |
| 45,600 | 45,650 | 5,786 | 5,077 | 5,786 | 5,191 |
| 45,650 | 45,700 | 5,797 | 5,083 | 5,797 | 5,197 |
| 45,700 | 45,750 | 5,808 | 5,089 | 5,808 | 5,203 |
| 45,750 | 45,800 | 5,819 | 5,095 | 5,819 | 5,209 |
| 45,800 | 45,850 | 5,830 | 5,101 | 5,830 | 5,215 |
| 45,850 | 45,900 | 5,841 | 5,107 | 5,841 | 5,221 |
| 45,900 | 45,950 | 5,852 | 5,113 | 5,852 | 5,227 |
| 45,950 | 46,000 | 5,863 | 5,119 | 5,863 | 5,233 |

## 46,000

| At least | But less than | Single | Married filing jointly * | Married filing separately | Head of a household |
| --- | --- | --- | --- | --- | --- |
| 46,000 | 46,050 | 5,874 | 5,125 | 5,874 | 5,239 |
| 46,050 | 46,100 | 5,885 | 5,131 | 5,885 | 5,245 |
| 46,100 | 46,150 | 5,896 | 5,137 | 5,896 | 5,251 |
| 46,150 | 46,200 | 5,907 | 5,143 | 5,907 | 5,257 |
| 46,200 | 46,250 | 5,918 | 5,149 | 5,918 | 5,263 |
| 46,250 | 46,300 | 5,929 | 5,155 | 5,929 | 5,269 |
| 46,300 | 46,350 | 5,940 | 5,161 | 5,940 | 5,275 |
| 46,350 | 46,400 | 5,951 | 5,167 | 5,951 | 5,281 |
| 46,400 | 46,450 | 5,962 | 5,173 | 5,962 | 5,287 |
| 46,450 | 46,500 | 5,973 | 5,179 | 5,973 | 5,293 |
| 46,500 | 46,550 | 5,984 | 5,185 | 5,984 | 5,299 |
| 46,550 | 46,600 | 5,995 | 5,191 | 5,995 | 5,305 |
| 46,600 | 46,650 | 6,006 | 5,197 | 6,006 | 5,311 |
| 46,650 | 46,700 | 6,017 | 5,203 | 6,017 | 5,317 |
| 46,700 | 46,750 | 6,028 | 5,209 | 6,028 | 5,323 |
| 46,750 | 46,800 | 6,039 | 5,215 | 6,039 | 5,329 |
| 46,800 | 46,850 | 6,050 | 5,221 | 6,050 | 5,335 |
| 46,850 | 46,900 | 6,061 | 5,227 | 6,061 | 5,341 |
| 46,900 | 46,950 | 6,072 | 5,233 | 6,072 | 5,347 |
| 46,950 | 47,000 | 6,083 | 5,239 | 6,083 | 5,353 |

## 47,000

| At least | But less than | Single | Married filing jointly * | Married filing separately | Head of a household |
| --- | --- | --- | --- | --- | --- |
| 47,000 | 47,050 | 6,094 | 5,245 | 6,094 | 5,359 |
| 47,050 | 47,100 | 6,105 | 5,251 | 6,105 | 5,365 |
| 47,100 | 47,150 | 6,116 | 5,257 | 6,116 | 5,371 |
| 47,150 | 47,200 | 6,127 | 5,263 | 6,127 | 5,377 |
| 47,200 | 47,250 | 6,138 | 5,269 | 6,138 | 5,383 |
| 47,250 | 47,300 | 6,149 | 5,275 | 6,149 | 5,389 |
| 47,300 | 47,350 | 6,160 | 5,281 | 6,160 | 5,395 |
| 47,350 | 47,400 | 6,171 | 5,287 | 6,171 | 5,401 |
| 47,400 | 47,450 | 6,182 | 5,293 | 6,182 | 5,407 |
| 47,450 | 47,500 | 6,193 | 5,299 | 6,193 | 5,413 |
| 47,500 | 47,550 | 6,204 | 5,305 | 6,204 | 5,419 |
| 47,550 | 47,600 | 6,215 | 5,311 | 6,215 | 5,425 |
| 47,600 | 47,650 | 6,226 | 5,317 | 6,226 | 5,431 |
| 47,650 | 47,700 | 6,237 | 5,323 | 6,237 | 5,437 |
| 47,700 | 47,750 | 6,248 | 5,329 | 6,248 | 5,443 |
| 47,750 | 47,800 | 6,259 | 5,335 | 6,259 | 5,449 |
| 47,800 | 47,850 | 6,270 | 5,341 | 6,270 | 5,455 |
| 47,850 | 47,900 | 6,281 | 5,347 | 6,281 | 5,461 |
| 47,900 | 47,950 | 6,292 | 5,353 | 6,292 | 5,467 |
| 47,950 | 48,000 | 6,303 | 5,359 | 6,303 | 5,473 |

## 48,000 / 49,000 / 50,000

| If line 15 (taxable income) is— At least | But less than | And you are— Single | Married filing jointly * | Married filing separately | Head of a household |
|---|---|---|---|---|---|
| **48,000** | | | | | |
| 48,000 | 48,050 | 6,314 | 5,365 | 6,314 | 5,479 |
| 48,050 | 48,100 | 6,325 | 5,371 | 6,325 | 5,485 |
| 48,100 | 48,150 | 6,336 | 5,377 | 6,336 | 5,491 |
| 48,150 | 48,200 | 6,347 | 5,383 | 6,347 | 5,497 |
| 48,200 | 48,250 | 6,358 | 5,389 | 6,358 | 5,503 |
| 48,250 | 48,300 | 6,369 | 5,395 | 6,369 | 5,509 |
| 48,300 | 48,350 | 6,380 | 5,401 | 6,380 | 5,515 |
| 48,350 | 48,400 | 6,391 | 5,407 | 6,391 | 5,521 |
| 48,400 | 48,450 | 6,402 | 5,413 | 6,402 | 5,527 |
| 48,450 | 48,500 | 6,413 | 5,419 | 6,413 | 5,533 |
| 48,500 | 48,550 | 6,424 | 5,425 | 6,424 | 5,539 |
| 48,550 | 48,600 | 6,435 | 5,431 | 6,435 | 5,545 |
| 48,600 | 48,650 | 6,446 | 5,437 | 6,446 | 5,551 |
| 48,650 | 48,700 | 6,457 | 5,443 | 6,457 | 5,557 |
| 48,700 | 48,750 | 6,468 | 5,449 | 6,468 | 5,563 |
| 48,750 | 48,800 | 6,479 | 5,455 | 6,479 | 5,569 |
| 48,800 | 48,850 | 6,490 | 5,461 | 6,490 | 5,575 |
| 48,850 | 48,900 | 6,501 | 5,467 | 6,501 | 5,581 |
| 48,900 | 48,950 | 6,512 | 5,473 | 6,512 | 5,587 |
| 48,950 | 49,000 | 6,523 | 5,479 | 6,523 | 5,593 |
| **49,000** | | | | | |
| 49,000 | 49,050 | 6,534 | 5,485 | 6,534 | 5,599 |
| 49,050 | 49,100 | 6,545 | 5,491 | 6,545 | 5,605 |
| 49,100 | 49,150 | 6,556 | 5,497 | 6,556 | 5,611 |
| 49,150 | 49,200 | 6,567 | 5,503 | 6,567 | 5,617 |
| 49,200 | 49,250 | 6,578 | 5,509 | 6,578 | 5,623 |
| 49,250 | 49,300 | 6,589 | 5,515 | 6,589 | 5,629 |
| 49,300 | 49,350 | 6,600 | 5,521 | 6,600 | 5,635 |
| 49,350 | 49,400 | 6,611 | 5,527 | 6,611 | 5,641 |
| 49,400 | 49,450 | 6,622 | 5,533 | 6,622 | 5,647 |
| 49,450 | 49,500 | 6,633 | 5,539 | 6,633 | 5,653 |
| 49,500 | 49,550 | 6,644 | 5,545 | 6,644 | 5,659 |
| 49,550 | 49,600 | 6,655 | 5,551 | 6,655 | 5,665 |
| 49,600 | 49,650 | 6,666 | 5,557 | 6,666 | 5,671 |
| 49,650 | 49,700 | 6,677 | 5,563 | 6,677 | 5,677 |
| 49,700 | 49,750 | 6,688 | 5,569 | 6,688 | 5,683 |
| 49,750 | 49,800 | 6,699 | 5,575 | 6,699 | 5,689 |
| 49,800 | 49,850 | 6,710 | 5,581 | 6,710 | 5,695 |
| 49,850 | 49,900 | 6,721 | 5,587 | 6,721 | 5,701 |
| 49,900 | 49,950 | 6,732 | 5,593 | 6,732 | 5,707 |
| 49,950 | 50,000 | 6,743 | 5,599 | 6,743 | 5,713 |
| **50,000** | | | | | |
| 50,000 | 50,050 | 6,754 | 5,605 | 6,754 | 5,719 |
| 50,050 | 50,100 | 6,765 | 5,611 | 6,765 | 5,725 |
| 50,100 | 50,150 | 6,776 | 5,617 | 6,776 | 5,731 |
| 50,150 | 50,200 | 6,787 | 5,623 | 6,787 | 5,737 |
| 50,200 | 50,250 | 6,798 | 5,629 | 6,798 | 5,743 |
| 50,250 | 50,300 | 6,809 | 5,635 | 6,809 | 5,749 |
| 50,300 | 50,350 | 6,820 | 5,641 | 6,820 | 5,755 |
| 50,350 | 50,400 | 6,831 | 5,647 | 6,831 | 5,761 |
| 50,400 | 50,450 | 6,842 | 5,653 | 6,842 | 5,767 |
| 50,450 | 50,500 | 6,853 | 5,659 | 6,853 | 5,773 |
| 50,500 | 50,550 | 6,864 | 5,665 | 6,864 | 5,779 |
| 50,550 | 50,600 | 6,875 | 5,671 | 6,875 | 5,785 |
| 50,600 | 50,650 | 6,886 | 5,677 | 6,886 | 5,791 |
| 50,650 | 50,700 | 6,897 | 5,683 | 6,897 | 5,797 |
| 50,700 | 50,750 | 6,908 | 5,689 | 6,908 | 5,803 |
| 50,750 | 50,800 | 6,919 | 5,695 | 6,919 | 5,809 |
| 50,800 | 50,850 | 6,930 | 5,701 | 6,930 | 5,815 |
| 50,850 | 50,900 | 6,941 | 5,707 | 6,941 | 5,821 |
| 50,900 | 50,950 | 6,952 | 5,713 | 6,952 | 5,827 |
| 50,950 | 51,000 | 6,963 | 5,719 | 6,963 | 5,833 |

## 51,000 / 52,000 / 53,000

| If line 15 (taxable income) is— At least | But less than | And you are— Single | Married filing jointly * | Married filing separately | Head of a household |
|---|---|---|---|---|---|
| **51,000** | | | | | |
| 51,000 | 51,050 | 6,974 | 5,725 | 6,974 | 5,839 |
| 51,050 | 51,100 | 6,985 | 5,731 | 6,985 | 5,845 |
| 51,100 | 51,150 | 6,996 | 5,737 | 6,996 | 5,851 |
| 51,150 | 51,200 | 7,007 | 5,743 | 7,007 | 5,857 |
| 51,200 | 51,250 | 7,018 | 5,749 | 7,018 | 5,863 |
| 51,250 | 51,300 | 7,029 | 5,755 | 7,029 | 5,869 |
| 51,300 | 51,350 | 7,040 | 5,761 | 7,040 | 5,875 |
| 51,350 | 51,400 | 7,051 | 5,767 | 7,051 | 5,881 |
| 51,400 | 51,450 | 7,062 | 5,773 | 7,062 | 5,887 |
| 51,450 | 51,500 | 7,073 | 5,779 | 7,073 | 5,893 |
| 51,500 | 51,550 | 7,084 | 5,785 | 7,084 | 5,899 |
| 51,550 | 51,600 | 7,095 | 5,791 | 7,095 | 5,905 |
| 51,600 | 51,650 | 7,106 | 5,797 | 7,106 | 5,911 |
| 51,650 | 51,700 | 7,117 | 5,803 | 7,117 | 5,917 |
| 51,700 | 51,750 | 7,128 | 5,809 | 7,128 | 5,923 |
| 51,750 | 51,800 | 7,139 | 5,815 | 7,139 | 5,929 |
| 51,800 | 51,850 | 7,150 | 5,821 | 7,150 | 5,935 |
| 51,850 | 51,900 | 7,161 | 5,827 | 7,161 | 5,941 |
| 51,900 | 51,950 | 7,172 | 5,833 | 7,172 | 5,947 |
| 51,950 | 52,000 | 7,183 | 5,839 | 7,183 | 5,953 |
| **52,000** | | | | | |
| 52,000 | 52,050 | 7,194 | 5,845 | 7,194 | 5,959 |
| 52,050 | 52,100 | 7,205 | 5,851 | 7,205 | 5,965 |
| 52,100 | 52,150 | 7,216 | 5,857 | 7,216 | 5,971 |
| 52,150 | 52,200 | 7,227 | 5,863 | 7,227 | 5,977 |
| 52,200 | 52,250 | 7,238 | 5,869 | 7,238 | 5,983 |
| 52,250 | 52,300 | 7,249 | 5,875 | 7,249 | 5,989 |
| 52,300 | 52,350 | 7,260 | 5,881 | 7,260 | 5,995 |
| 52,350 | 52,400 | 7,271 | 5,887 | 7,271 | 6,001 |
| 52,400 | 52,450 | 7,282 | 5,893 | 7,282 | 6,007 |
| 52,450 | 52,500 | 7,293 | 5,899 | 7,293 | 6,013 |
| 52,500 | 52,550 | 7,304 | 5,905 | 7,304 | 6,019 |
| 52,550 | 52,600 | 7,315 | 5,911 | 7,315 | 6,025 |
| 52,600 | 52,650 | 7,326 | 5,917 | 7,326 | 6,031 |
| 52,650 | 52,700 | 7,337 | 5,923 | 7,337 | 6,037 |
| 52,700 | 52,750 | 7,348 | 5,929 | 7,348 | 6,043 |
| 52,750 | 52,800 | 7,359 | 5,935 | 7,359 | 6,049 |
| 52,800 | 52,850 | 7,370 | 5,941 | 7,370 | 6,055 |
| 52,850 | 52,900 | 7,381 | 5,947 | 7,381 | 6,061 |
| 52,900 | 52,950 | 7,392 | 5,953 | 7,392 | 6,067 |
| 52,950 | 53,000 | 7,403 | 5,959 | 7,403 | 6,073 |
| **53,000** | | | | | |
| 53,000 | 53,050 | 7,414 | 5,965 | 7,414 | 6,079 |
| 53,050 | 53,100 | 7,425 | 5,971 | 7,425 | 6,085 |
| 53,100 | 53,150 | 7,436 | 5,977 | 7,436 | 6,091 |
| 53,150 | 53,200 | 7,447 | 5,983 | 7,447 | 6,097 |
| 53,200 | 53,250 | 7,458 | 5,989 | 7,458 | 6,103 |
| 53,250 | 53,300 | 7,469 | 5,995 | 7,469 | 6,109 |
| 53,300 | 53,350 | 7,480 | 6,001 | 7,480 | 6,115 |
| 53,350 | 53,400 | 7,491 | 6,007 | 7,491 | 6,121 |
| 53,400 | 53,450 | 7,502 | 6,013 | 7,502 | 6,127 |
| 53,450 | 53,500 | 7,513 | 6,019 | 7,513 | 6,133 |
| 53,500 | 53,550 | 7,524 | 6,025 | 7,524 | 6,139 |
| 53,550 | 53,600 | 7,535 | 6,031 | 7,535 | 6,145 |
| 53,600 | 53,650 | 7,546 | 6,037 | 7,546 | 6,151 |
| 53,650 | 53,700 | 7,557 | 6,043 | 7,557 | 6,157 |
| 53,700 | 53,750 | 7,568 | 6,049 | 7,568 | 6,163 |
| 53,750 | 53,800 | 7,579 | 6,055 | 7,579 | 6,169 |
| 53,800 | 53,850 | 7,590 | 6,061 | 7,590 | 6,175 |
| 53,850 | 53,900 | 7,601 | 6,067 | 7,601 | 6,181 |
| 53,900 | 53,950 | 7,612 | 6,073 | 7,612 | 6,187 |
| 53,950 | 54,000 | 7,623 | 6,079 | 7,623 | 6,193 |

## 54,000 / 55,000 / 56,000

| If line 15 (taxable income) is— At least | But less than | And you are— Single | Married filing jointly * | Married filing separately | Head of a household |
|---|---|---|---|---|---|
| **54,000** | | | | | |
| 54,000 | 54,050 | 7,634 | 6,085 | 7,634 | 6,199 |
| 54,050 | 54,100 | 7,645 | 6,091 | 7,645 | 6,205 |
| 54,100 | 54,150 | 7,656 | 6,097 | 7,656 | 6,211 |
| 54,150 | 54,200 | 7,667 | 6,103 | 7,667 | 6,217 |
| 54,200 | 54,250 | 7,678 | 6,109 | 7,678 | 6,226 |
| 54,250 | 54,300 | 7,689 | 6,115 | 7,689 | 6,237 |
| 54,300 | 54,350 | 7,700 | 6,121 | 7,700 | 6,248 |
| 54,350 | 54,400 | 7,711 | 6,127 | 7,711 | 6,259 |
| 54,400 | 54,450 | 7,722 | 6,133 | 7,722 | 6,270 |
| 54,450 | 54,500 | 7,733 | 6,139 | 7,733 | 6,281 |
| 54,500 | 54,550 | 7,744 | 6,145 | 7,744 | 6,292 |
| 54,550 | 54,600 | 7,755 | 6,151 | 7,755 | 6,303 |
| 54,600 | 54,650 | 7,766 | 6,157 | 7,766 | 6,314 |
| 54,650 | 54,700 | 7,777 | 6,163 | 7,777 | 6,325 |
| 54,700 | 54,750 | 7,788 | 6,169 | 7,788 | 6,336 |
| 54,750 | 54,800 | 7,799 | 6,175 | 7,799 | 6,347 |
| 54,800 | 54,850 | 7,810 | 6,181 | 7,810 | 6,358 |
| 54,850 | 54,900 | 7,821 | 6,187 | 7,821 | 6,369 |
| 54,900 | 54,950 | 7,832 | 6,193 | 7,832 | 6,380 |
| 54,950 | 55,000 | 7,843 | 6,199 | 7,843 | 6,391 |
| **55,000** | | | | | |
| 55,000 | 55,050 | 7,854 | 6,205 | 7,854 | 6,402 |
| 55,050 | 55,100 | 7,865 | 6,211 | 7,865 | 6,413 |
| 55,100 | 55,150 | 7,876 | 6,217 | 7,876 | 6,424 |
| 55,150 | 55,200 | 7,887 | 6,223 | 7,887 | 6,435 |
| 55,200 | 55,250 | 7,898 | 6,229 | 7,898 | 6,446 |
| 55,250 | 55,300 | 7,909 | 6,235 | 7,909 | 6,457 |
| 55,300 | 55,350 | 7,920 | 6,241 | 7,920 | 6,468 |
| 55,350 | 55,400 | 7,931 | 6,247 | 7,931 | 6,479 |
| 55,400 | 55,450 | 7,942 | 6,253 | 7,942 | 6,490 |
| 55,450 | 55,500 | 7,953 | 6,259 | 7,953 | 6,501 |
| 55,500 | 55,550 | 7,964 | 6,265 | 7,964 | 6,512 |
| 55,550 | 55,600 | 7,975 | 6,271 | 7,975 | 6,523 |
| 55,600 | 55,650 | 7,986 | 6,277 | 7,986 | 6,534 |
| 55,650 | 55,700 | 7,997 | 6,283 | 7,997 | 6,545 |
| 55,700 | 55,750 | 8,008 | 6,289 | 8,008 | 6,556 |
| 55,750 | 55,800 | 8,019 | 6,295 | 8,019 | 6,567 |
| 55,800 | 55,850 | 8,030 | 6,301 | 8,030 | 6,578 |
| 55,850 | 55,900 | 8,041 | 6,307 | 8,041 | 6,589 |
| 55,900 | 55,950 | 8,052 | 6,313 | 8,052 | 6,600 |
| 55,950 | 56,000 | 8,063 | 6,319 | 8,063 | 6,611 |
| **56,000** | | | | | |
| 56,000 | 56,050 | 8,074 | 6,325 | 8,074 | 6,622 |
| 56,050 | 56,100 | 8,085 | 6,331 | 8,085 | 6,633 |
| 56,100 | 56,150 | 8,096 | 6,337 | 8,096 | 6,644 |
| 56,150 | 56,200 | 8,107 | 6,343 | 8,107 | 6,655 |
| 56,200 | 56,250 | 8,118 | 6,349 | 8,118 | 6,666 |
| 56,250 | 56,300 | 8,129 | 6,355 | 8,129 | 6,677 |
| 56,300 | 56,350 | 8,140 | 6,361 | 8,140 | 6,688 |
| 56,350 | 56,400 | 8,151 | 6,367 | 8,151 | 6,699 |
| 56,400 | 56,450 | 8,162 | 6,373 | 8,162 | 6,710 |
| 56,450 | 56,500 | 8,173 | 6,379 | 8,173 | 6,721 |
| 56,500 | 56,550 | 8,184 | 6,385 | 8,184 | 6,732 |
| 56,550 | 56,600 | 8,195 | 6,391 | 8,195 | 6,743 |
| 56,600 | 56,650 | 8,206 | 6,397 | 8,206 | 6,754 |
| 56,650 | 56,700 | 8,217 | 6,403 | 8,217 | 6,765 |
| 56,700 | 56,750 | 8,228 | 6,409 | 8,228 | 6,776 |
| 56,750 | 56,800 | 8,239 | 6,415 | 8,239 | 6,787 |
| 56,800 | 56,850 | 8,250 | 6,421 | 8,250 | 6,798 |
| 56,850 | 56,900 | 8,261 | 6,427 | 8,261 | 6,809 |
| 56,900 | 56,950 | 8,272 | 6,433 | 8,272 | 6,820 |
| 56,950 | 57,000 | 8,283 | 6,439 | 8,283 | 6,831 |

## 57,000

| At least | But less than | Single | Married filing jointly * | Married filing separately | Head of a household |
|---|---|---|---|---|---|
| 57,000 | 57,050 | 8,294 | 6,445 | 8,294 | 6,842 |
| 57,050 | 57,100 | 8,305 | 6,451 | 8,305 | 6,853 |
| 57,100 | 57,150 | 8,316 | 6,457 | 8,316 | 6,864 |
| 57,150 | 57,200 | 8,327 | 6,463 | 8,327 | 6,875 |
| 57,200 | 57,250 | 8,338 | 6,469 | 8,338 | 6,886 |
| 57,250 | 57,300 | 8,349 | 6,475 | 8,349 | 6,897 |
| 57,300 | 57,350 | 8,360 | 6,481 | 8,360 | 6,908 |
| 57,350 | 57,400 | 8,371 | 6,487 | 8,371 | 6,919 |
| 57,400 | 57,450 | 8,382 | 6,493 | 8,382 | 6,930 |
| 57,450 | 57,500 | 8,393 | 6,499 | 8,393 | 6,941 |
| 57,500 | 57,550 | 8,404 | 6,505 | 8,404 | 6,952 |
| 57,550 | 57,600 | 8,415 | 6,511 | 8,415 | 6,963 |
| 57,600 | 57,650 | 8,426 | 6,517 | 8,426 | 6,974 |
| 57,650 | 57,700 | 8,437 | 6,523 | 8,437 | 6,985 |
| 57,700 | 57,750 | 8,448 | 6,529 | 8,448 | 6,996 |
| 57,750 | 57,800 | 8,459 | 6,535 | 8,459 | 7,007 |
| 57,800 | 57,850 | 8,470 | 6,541 | 8,470 | 7,018 |
| 57,850 | 57,900 | 8,481 | 6,547 | 8,481 | 7,029 |
| 57,900 | 57,950 | 8,492 | 6,553 | 8,492 | 7,040 |
| 57,950 | 58,000 | 8,503 | 6,559 | 8,503 | 7,051 |

## 58,000

| At least | But less than | Single | Married filing jointly * | Married filing separately | Head of a household |
|---|---|---|---|---|---|
| 58,000 | 58,050 | 8,514 | 6,565 | 8,514 | 7,062 |
| 58,050 | 58,100 | 8,525 | 6,571 | 8,525 | 7,073 |
| 58,100 | 58,150 | 8,536 | 6,577 | 8,536 | 7,084 |
| 58,150 | 58,200 | 8,547 | 6,583 | 8,547 | 7,095 |
| 58,200 | 58,250 | 8,558 | 6,589 | 8,558 | 7,106 |
| 58,250 | 58,300 | 8,569 | 6,595 | 8,569 | 7,117 |
| 58,300 | 58,350 | 8,580 | 6,601 | 8,580 | 7,128 |
| 58,350 | 58,400 | 8,591 | 6,607 | 8,591 | 7,139 |
| 58,400 | 58,450 | 8,602 | 6,613 | 8,602 | 7,150 |
| 58,450 | 58,500 | 8,613 | 6,619 | 8,613 | 7,161 |
| 58,500 | 58,550 | 8,624 | 6,625 | 8,624 | 7,172 |
| 58,550 | 58,600 | 8,635 | 6,631 | 8,635 | 7,183 |
| 58,600 | 58,650 | 8,646 | 6,637 | 8,646 | 7,194 |
| 58,650 | 58,700 | 8,657 | 6,643 | 8,657 | 7,205 |
| 58,700 | 58,750 | 8,668 | 6,649 | 8,668 | 7,216 |
| 58,750 | 58,800 | 8,679 | 6,655 | 8,679 | 7,227 |
| 58,800 | 58,850 | 8,690 | 6,661 | 8,690 | 7,238 |
| 58,850 | 58,900 | 8,701 | 6,667 | 8,701 | 7,249 |
| 58,900 | 58,950 | 8,712 | 6,673 | 8,712 | 7,260 |
| 58,950 | 59,000 | 8,723 | 6,679 | 8,723 | 7,271 |

## 59,000

| At least | But less than | Single | Married filing jointly * | Married filing separately | Head of a household |
|---|---|---|---|---|---|
| 59,000 | 59,050 | 8,734 | 6,685 | 8,734 | 7,282 |
| 59,050 | 59,100 | 8,745 | 6,691 | 8,745 | 7,293 |
| 59,100 | 59,150 | 8,756 | 6,697 | 8,756 | 7,304 |
| 59,150 | 59,200 | 8,767 | 6,703 | 8,767 | 7,315 |
| 59,200 | 59,250 | 8,778 | 6,709 | 8,778 | 7,326 |
| 59,250 | 59,300 | 8,789 | 6,715 | 8,789 | 7,337 |
| 59,300 | 59,350 | 8,800 | 6,721 | 8,800 | 7,348 |
| 59,350 | 59,400 | 8,811 | 6,727 | 8,811 | 7,359 |
| 59,400 | 59,450 | 8,822 | 6,733 | 8,822 | 7,370 |
| 59,450 | 59,500 | 8,833 | 6,739 | 8,833 | 7,381 |
| 59,500 | 59,550 | 8,844 | 6,745 | 8,844 | 7,392 |
| 59,550 | 59,600 | 8,855 | 6,751 | 8,855 | 7,403 |
| 59,600 | 59,650 | 8,866 | 6,757 | 8,866 | 7,414 |
| 59,650 | 59,700 | 8,877 | 6,763 | 8,877 | 7,425 |
| 59,700 | 59,750 | 8,888 | 6,769 | 8,888 | 7,436 |
| 59,750 | 59,800 | 8,899 | 6,775 | 8,899 | 7,447 |
| 59,800 | 59,850 | 8,910 | 6,781 | 8,910 | 7,458 |
| 59,850 | 59,900 | 8,921 | 6,787 | 8,921 | 7,469 |
| 59,900 | 59,950 | 8,932 | 6,793 | 8,932 | 7,480 |
| 59,950 | 60,000 | 8,943 | 6,799 | 8,943 | 7,491 |

## 60,000

| At least | But less than | Single | Married filing jointly * | Married filing separately | Head of a household |
|---|---|---|---|---|---|
| 60,000 | 60,050 | 8,954 | 6,805 | 8,954 | 7,502 |
| 60,050 | 60,100 | 8,965 | 6,811 | 8,965 | 7,513 |
| 60,100 | 60,150 | 8,976 | 6,817 | 8,976 | 7,524 |
| 60,150 | 60,200 | 8,987 | 6,823 | 8,987 | 7,535 |
| 60,200 | 60,250 | 8,998 | 6,829 | 8,998 | 7,546 |
| 60,250 | 60,300 | 9,009 | 6,835 | 9,009 | 7,557 |
| 60,300 | 60,350 | 9,020 | 6,841 | 9,020 | 7,568 |
| 60,350 | 60,400 | 9,031 | 6,847 | 9,031 | 7,579 |
| 60,400 | 60,450 | 9,042 | 6,853 | 9,042 | 7,590 |
| 60,450 | 60,500 | 9,053 | 6,859 | 9,053 | 7,601 |
| 60,500 | 60,550 | 9,064 | 6,865 | 9,064 | 7,612 |
| 60,550 | 60,600 | 9,075 | 6,871 | 9,075 | 7,623 |
| 60,600 | 60,650 | 9,086 | 6,877 | 9,086 | 7,634 |
| 60,650 | 60,700 | 9,097 | 6,883 | 9,097 | 7,645 |
| 60,700 | 60,750 | 9,108 | 6,889 | 9,108 | 7,656 |
| 60,750 | 60,800 | 9,119 | 6,895 | 9,119 | 7,667 |
| 60,800 | 60,850 | 9,130 | 6,901 | 9,130 | 7,678 |
| 60,850 | 60,900 | 9,141 | 6,907 | 9,141 | 7,689 |
| 60,900 | 60,950 | 9,152 | 6,913 | 9,152 | 7,700 |
| 60,950 | 61,000 | 9,163 | 6,919 | 9,163 | 7,711 |

## 61,000

| At least | But less than | Single | Married filing jointly * | Married filing separately | Head of a household |
|---|---|---|---|---|---|
| 61,000 | 61,050 | 9,174 | 6,925 | 9,174 | 7,722 |
| 61,050 | 61,100 | 9,185 | 6,931 | 9,185 | 7,733 |
| 61,100 | 61,150 | 9,196 | 6,937 | 9,196 | 7,744 |
| 61,150 | 61,200 | 9,207 | 6,943 | 9,207 | 7,755 |
| 61,200 | 61,250 | 9,218 | 6,949 | 9,218 | 7,766 |
| 61,250 | 61,300 | 9,229 | 6,955 | 9,229 | 7,777 |
| 61,300 | 61,350 | 9,240 | 6,961 | 9,240 | 7,788 |
| 61,350 | 61,400 | 9,251 | 6,967 | 9,251 | 7,799 |
| 61,400 | 61,450 | 9,262 | 6,973 | 9,262 | 7,810 |
| 61,450 | 61,500 | 9,273 | 6,979 | 9,273 | 7,821 |
| 61,500 | 61,550 | 9,284 | 6,985 | 9,284 | 7,832 |
| 61,550 | 61,600 | 9,295 | 6,991 | 9,295 | 7,843 |
| 61,600 | 61,650 | 9,306 | 6,997 | 9,306 | 7,854 |
| 61,650 | 61,700 | 9,317 | 7,003 | 9,317 | 7,865 |
| 61,700 | 61,750 | 9,328 | 7,009 | 9,328 | 7,876 |
| 61,750 | 61,800 | 9,339 | 7,015 | 9,339 | 7,887 |
| 61,800 | 61,850 | 9,350 | 7,021 | 9,350 | 7,898 |
| 61,850 | 61,900 | 9,361 | 7,027 | 9,361 | 7,909 |
| 61,900 | 61,950 | 9,372 | 7,033 | 9,372 | 7,920 |
| 61,950 | 62,000 | 9,383 | 7,039 | 9,383 | 7,931 |

## 62,000

| At least | But less than | Single | Married filing jointly * | Married filing separately | Head of a household |
|---|---|---|---|---|---|
| 62,000 | 62,050 | 9,394 | 7,045 | 9,394 | 7,942 |
| 62,050 | 62,100 | 9,405 | 7,051 | 9,405 | 7,953 |
| 62,100 | 62,150 | 9,416 | 7,057 | 9,416 | 7,964 |
| 62,150 | 62,200 | 9,427 | 7,063 | 9,427 | 7,975 |
| 62,200 | 62,250 | 9,438 | 7,069 | 9,438 | 7,986 |
| 62,250 | 62,300 | 9,449 | 7,075 | 9,449 | 7,997 |
| 62,300 | 62,350 | 9,460 | 7,081 | 9,460 | 8,008 |
| 62,350 | 62,400 | 9,471 | 7,087 | 9,471 | 8,019 |
| 62,400 | 62,450 | 9,482 | 7,093 | 9,482 | 8,030 |
| 62,450 | 62,500 | 9,493 | 7,099 | 9,493 | 8,041 |
| 62,500 | 62,550 | 9,504 | 7,105 | 9,504 | 8,052 |
| 62,550 | 62,600 | 9,515 | 7,111 | 9,515 | 8,063 |
| 62,600 | 62,650 | 9,526 | 7,117 | 9,526 | 8,074 |
| 62,650 | 62,700 | 9,537 | 7,123 | 9,537 | 8,085 |
| 62,700 | 62,750 | 9,548 | 7,129 | 9,548 | 8,096 |
| 62,750 | 62,800 | 9,559 | 7,135 | 9,559 | 8,107 |
| 62,800 | 62,850 | 9,570 | 7,141 | 9,570 | 8,118 |
| 62,850 | 62,900 | 9,581 | 7,147 | 9,581 | 8,129 |
| 62,900 | 62,950 | 9,592 | 7,153 | 9,592 | 8,140 |
| 62,950 | 63,000 | 9,603 | 7,159 | 9,603 | 8,151 |

## 63,000

| At least | But less than | Single | Married filing jointly * | Married filing separately | Head of a household |
|---|---|---|---|---|---|
| 63,000 | 63,050 | 9,614 | 7,165 | 9,614 | 8,162 |
| 63,050 | 63,100 | 9,625 | 7,171 | 9,625 | 8,173 |
| 63,100 | 63,150 | 9,636 | 7,177 | 9,636 | 8,184 |
| 63,150 | 63,200 | 9,647 | 7,183 | 9,647 | 8,195 |
| 63,200 | 63,250 | 9,658 | 7,189 | 9,658 | 8,206 |
| 63,250 | 63,300 | 9,669 | 7,195 | 9,669 | 8,217 |
| 63,300 | 63,350 | 9,680 | 7,201 | 9,680 | 8,228 |
| 63,350 | 63,400 | 9,691 | 7,207 | 9,691 | 8,239 |
| 63,400 | 63,450 | 9,702 | 7,213 | 9,702 | 8,250 |
| 63,450 | 63,500 | 9,713 | 7,219 | 9,713 | 8,261 |
| 63,500 | 63,550 | 9,724 | 7,225 | 9,724 | 8,272 |
| 63,550 | 63,600 | 9,735 | 7,231 | 9,735 | 8,283 |
| 63,600 | 63,650 | 9,746 | 7,237 | 9,746 | 8,294 |
| 63,650 | 63,700 | 9,757 | 7,243 | 9,757 | 8,305 |
| 63,700 | 63,750 | 9,768 | 7,249 | 9,768 | 8,316 |
| 63,750 | 63,800 | 9,779 | 7,255 | 9,779 | 8,327 |
| 63,800 | 63,850 | 9,790 | 7,261 | 9,790 | 8,338 |
| 63,850 | 63,900 | 9,801 | 7,267 | 9,801 | 8,349 |
| 63,900 | 63,950 | 9,812 | 7,273 | 9,812 | 8,360 |
| 63,950 | 64,000 | 9,823 | 7,279 | 9,823 | 8,371 |

## 64,000

| At least | But less than | Single | Married filing jointly * | Married filing separately | Head of a household |
|---|---|---|---|---|---|
| 64,000 | 64,050 | 9,834 | 7,285 | 9,834 | 8,382 |
| 64,050 | 64,100 | 9,845 | 7,291 | 9,845 | 8,393 |
| 64,100 | 64,150 | 9,856 | 7,297 | 9,856 | 8,404 |
| 64,150 | 64,200 | 9,867 | 7,303 | 9,867 | 8,415 |
| 64,200 | 64,250 | 9,878 | 7,309 | 9,878 | 8,426 |
| 64,250 | 64,300 | 9,889 | 7,315 | 9,889 | 8,437 |
| 64,300 | 64,350 | 9,900 | 7,321 | 9,900 | 8,448 |
| 64,350 | 64,400 | 9,911 | 7,327 | 9,911 | 8,459 |
| 64,400 | 64,450 | 9,922 | 7,333 | 9,922 | 8,470 |
| 64,450 | 64,500 | 9,933 | 7,339 | 9,933 | 8,481 |
| 64,500 | 64,550 | 9,944 | 7,345 | 9,944 | 8,492 |
| 64,550 | 64,600 | 9,955 | 7,351 | 9,955 | 8,503 |
| 64,600 | 64,650 | 9,966 | 7,357 | 9,966 | 8,514 |
| 64,650 | 64,700 | 9,977 | 7,363 | 9,977 | 8,525 |
| 64,700 | 64,750 | 9,988 | 7,369 | 9,988 | 8,536 |
| 64,750 | 64,800 | 9,999 | 7,375 | 9,999 | 8,547 |
| 64,800 | 64,850 | 10,010 | 7,381 | 10,010 | 8,558 |
| 64,850 | 64,900 | 10,021 | 7,387 | 10,021 | 8,569 |
| 64,900 | 64,950 | 10,032 | 7,393 | 10,032 | 8,580 |
| 64,950 | 65,000 | 10,043 | 7,399 | 10,043 | 8,591 |

## 65,000

| At least | But less than | Single | Married filing jointly * | Married filing separately | Head of a household |
|---|---|---|---|---|---|
| 65,000 | 65,050 | 10,054 | 7,405 | 10,054 | 8,602 |
| 65,050 | 65,100 | 10,065 | 7,411 | 10,065 | 8,613 |
| 65,100 | 65,150 | 10,076 | 7,417 | 10,076 | 8,624 |
| 65,150 | 65,200 | 10,087 | 7,423 | 10,087 | 8,635 |
| 65,200 | 65,250 | 10,098 | 7,429 | 10,098 | 8,646 |
| 65,250 | 65,300 | 10,109 | 7,435 | 10,109 | 8,657 |
| 65,300 | 65,350 | 10,120 | 7,441 | 10,120 | 8,668 |
| 65,350 | 65,400 | 10,131 | 7,447 | 10,131 | 8,679 |
| 65,400 | 65,450 | 10,142 | 7,453 | 10,142 | 8,690 |
| 65,450 | 65,500 | 10,153 | 7,459 | 10,153 | 8,701 |
| 65,500 | 65,550 | 10,164 | 7,465 | 10,164 | 8,712 |
| 65,550 | 65,600 | 10,175 | 7,471 | 10,175 | 8,723 |
| 65,600 | 65,650 | 10,186 | 7,477 | 10,186 | 8,734 |
| 65,650 | 65,700 | 10,197 | 7,483 | 10,197 | 8,745 |
| 65,700 | 65,750 | 10,208 | 7,489 | 10,208 | 8,756 |
| 65,750 | 65,800 | 10,219 | 7,495 | 10,219 | 8,767 |
| 65,800 | 65,850 | 10,230 | 7,501 | 10,230 | 8,778 |
| 65,850 | 65,900 | 10,241 | 7,507 | 10,241 | 8,789 |
| 65,900 | 65,950 | 10,252 | 7,513 | 10,252 | 8,800 |
| 65,950 | 66,000 | 10,263 | 7,519 | 10,263 | 8,811 |

**If line 15 (taxable income) is— / And you are—**

Columns: At least | But less than | Single | Married filing jointly* | Married filing separately | Head of a household — Your tax is—

## 66,000

| At least | But less than | Single | Married filing jointly* | Married filing separately | Head of a household |
|---|---|---|---|---|---|
| 66,000 | 66,050 | 10,274 | 7,525 | 10,274 | 8,822 |
| 66,050 | 66,100 | 10,285 | 7,531 | 10,285 | 8,833 |
| 66,100 | 66,150 | 10,296 | 7,537 | 10,296 | 8,844 |
| 66,150 | 66,200 | 10,307 | 7,543 | 10,307 | 8,855 |
| 66,200 | 66,250 | 10,318 | 7,549 | 10,318 | 8,866 |
| 66,250 | 66,300 | 10,329 | 7,555 | 10,329 | 8,877 |
| 66,300 | 66,350 | 10,340 | 7,561 | 10,340 | 8,888 |
| 66,350 | 66,400 | 10,351 | 7,567 | 10,351 | 8,899 |
| 66,400 | 66,450 | 10,362 | 7,573 | 10,362 | 8,910 |
| 66,450 | 66,500 | 10,373 | 7,579 | 10,373 | 8,921 |
| 66,500 | 66,550 | 10,384 | 7,585 | 10,384 | 8,932 |
| 66,550 | 66,600 | 10,395 | 7,591 | 10,395 | 8,943 |
| 66,600 | 66,650 | 10,406 | 7,597 | 10,406 | 8,954 |
| 66,650 | 66,700 | 10,417 | 7,603 | 10,417 | 8,965 |
| 66,700 | 66,750 | 10,428 | 7,609 | 10,428 | 8,976 |
| 66,750 | 66,800 | 10,439 | 7,615 | 10,439 | 8,987 |
| 66,800 | 66,850 | 10,450 | 7,621 | 10,450 | 8,998 |
| 66,850 | 66,900 | 10,461 | 7,627 | 10,461 | 9,009 |
| 66,900 | 66,950 | 10,472 | 7,633 | 10,472 | 9,020 |
| 66,950 | 67,000 | 10,483 | 7,639 | 10,483 | 9,031 |

## 67,000

| At least | But less than | Single | Married filing jointly* | Married filing separately | Head of a household |
|---|---|---|---|---|---|
| 67,000 | 67,050 | 10,494 | 7,645 | 10,494 | 9,042 |
| 67,050 | 67,100 | 10,505 | 7,651 | 10,505 | 9,053 |
| 67,100 | 67,150 | 10,516 | 7,657 | 10,516 | 9,064 |
| 67,150 | 67,200 | 10,527 | 7,663 | 10,527 | 9,075 |
| 67,200 | 67,250 | 10,538 | 7,669 | 10,538 | 9,086 |
| 67,250 | 67,300 | 10,549 | 7,675 | 10,549 | 9,097 |
| 67,300 | 67,350 | 10,560 | 7,681 | 10,560 | 9,108 |
| 67,350 | 67,400 | 10,571 | 7,687 | 10,571 | 9,119 |
| 67,400 | 67,450 | 10,582 | 7,693 | 10,582 | 9,130 |
| 67,450 | 67,500 | 10,593 | 7,699 | 10,593 | 9,141 |
| 67,500 | 67,550 | 10,604 | 7,705 | 10,604 | 9,152 |
| 67,550 | 67,600 | 10,615 | 7,711 | 10,615 | 9,163 |
| 67,600 | 67,650 | 10,626 | 7,717 | 10,626 | 9,174 |
| 67,650 | 67,700 | 10,637 | 7,723 | 10,637 | 9,185 |
| 67,700 | 67,750 | 10,648 | 7,729 | 10,648 | 9,196 |
| 67,750 | 67,800 | 10,659 | 7,735 | 10,659 | 9,207 |
| 67,800 | 67,850 | 10,670 | 7,741 | 10,670 | 9,218 |
| 67,850 | 67,900 | 10,681 | 7,747 | 10,681 | 9,229 |
| 67,900 | 67,950 | 10,692 | 7,753 | 10,692 | 9,240 |
| 67,950 | 68,000 | 10,703 | 7,759 | 10,703 | 9,251 |

## 68,000

| At least | But less than | Single | Married filing jointly* | Married filing separately | Head of a household |
|---|---|---|---|---|---|
| 68,000 | 68,050 | 10,714 | 7,765 | 10,714 | 9,262 |
| 68,050 | 68,100 | 10,725 | 7,771 | 10,725 | 9,273 |
| 68,100 | 68,150 | 10,736 | 7,777 | 10,736 | 9,284 |
| 68,150 | 68,200 | 10,747 | 7,783 | 10,747 | 9,295 |
| 68,200 | 68,250 | 10,758 | 7,789 | 10,758 | 9,306 |
| 68,250 | 68,300 | 10,769 | 7,795 | 10,769 | 9,317 |
| 68,300 | 68,350 | 10,780 | 7,801 | 10,780 | 9,328 |
| 68,350 | 68,400 | 10,791 | 7,807 | 10,791 | 9,339 |
| 68,400 | 68,450 | 10,802 | 7,813 | 10,802 | 9,350 |
| 68,450 | 68,500 | 10,813 | 7,819 | 10,813 | 9,361 |
| 68,500 | 68,550 | 10,824 | 7,825 | 10,824 | 9,372 |
| 68,550 | 68,600 | 10,835 | 7,831 | 10,835 | 9,383 |
| 68,600 | 68,650 | 10,846 | 7,837 | 10,846 | 9,394 |
| 68,650 | 68,700 | 10,857 | 7,843 | 10,857 | 9,405 |
| 68,700 | 68,750 | 10,868 | 7,849 | 10,868 | 9,416 |
| 68,750 | 68,800 | 10,879 | 7,855 | 10,879 | 9,427 |
| 68,800 | 68,850 | 10,890 | 7,861 | 10,890 | 9,438 |
| 68,850 | 68,900 | 10,901 | 7,867 | 10,901 | 9,449 |
| 68,900 | 68,950 | 10,912 | 7,873 | 10,912 | 9,460 |
| 68,950 | 69,000 | 10,923 | 7,879 | 10,923 | 9,471 |

## 69,000

| At least | But less than | Single | Married filing jointly* | Married filing separately | Head of a household |
|---|---|---|---|---|---|
| 69,000 | 69,050 | 10,934 | 7,885 | 10,934 | 9,482 |
| 69,050 | 69,100 | 10,945 | 7,891 | 10,945 | 9,493 |
| 69,100 | 69,150 | 10,956 | 7,897 | 10,956 | 9,504 |
| 69,150 | 69,200 | 10,967 | 7,903 | 10,967 | 9,515 |
| 69,200 | 69,250 | 10,978 | 7,909 | 10,978 | 9,526 |
| 69,250 | 69,300 | 10,989 | 7,915 | 10,989 | 9,537 |
| 69,300 | 69,350 | 11,000 | 7,921 | 11,000 | 9,548 |
| 69,350 | 69,400 | 11,011 | 7,927 | 11,011 | 9,559 |
| 69,400 | 69,450 | 11,022 | 7,933 | 11,022 | 9,570 |
| 69,450 | 69,500 | 11,033 | 7,939 | 11,033 | 9,581 |
| 69,500 | 69,550 | 11,044 | 7,945 | 11,044 | 9,592 |
| 69,550 | 69,600 | 11,055 | 7,951 | 11,055 | 9,603 |
| 69,600 | 69,650 | 11,066 | 7,957 | 11,066 | 9,614 |
| 69,650 | 69,700 | 11,077 | 7,963 | 11,077 | 9,625 |
| 69,700 | 69,750 | 11,088 | 7,969 | 11,088 | 9,636 |
| 69,750 | 69,800 | 11,099 | 7,975 | 11,099 | 9,647 |
| 69,800 | 69,850 | 11,110 | 7,981 | 11,110 | 9,658 |
| 69,850 | 69,900 | 11,121 | 7,987 | 11,121 | 9,669 |
| 69,900 | 69,950 | 11,132 | 7,993 | 11,132 | 9,680 |
| 69,950 | 70,000 | 11,143 | 7,999 | 11,143 | 9,691 |

## 70,000

| At least | But less than | Single | Married filing jointly* | Married filing separately | Head of a household |
|---|---|---|---|---|---|
| 70,000 | 70,050 | 11,154 | 8,005 | 11,154 | 9,702 |
| 70,050 | 70,100 | 11,165 | 8,011 | 11,165 | 9,713 |
| 70,100 | 70,150 | 11,176 | 8,017 | 11,176 | 9,724 |
| 70,150 | 70,200 | 11,187 | 8,023 | 11,187 | 9,735 |
| 70,200 | 70,250 | 11,198 | 8,029 | 11,198 | 9,746 |
| 70,250 | 70,300 | 11,209 | 8,035 | 11,209 | 9,757 |
| 70,300 | 70,350 | 11,220 | 8,041 | 11,220 | 9,768 |
| 70,350 | 70,400 | 11,231 | 8,047 | 11,231 | 9,779 |
| 70,400 | 70,450 | 11,242 | 8,053 | 11,242 | 9,790 |
| 70,450 | 70,500 | 11,253 | 8,059 | 11,253 | 9,801 |
| 70,500 | 70,550 | 11,264 | 8,065 | 11,264 | 9,812 |
| 70,550 | 70,600 | 11,275 | 8,071 | 11,275 | 9,823 |
| 70,600 | 70,650 | 11,286 | 8,077 | 11,286 | 9,834 |
| 70,650 | 70,700 | 11,297 | 8,083 | 11,297 | 9,845 |
| 70,700 | 70,750 | 11,308 | 8,089 | 11,308 | 9,856 |
| 70,750 | 70,800 | 11,319 | 8,095 | 11,319 | 9,867 |
| 70,800 | 70,850 | 11,330 | 8,101 | 11,330 | 9,878 |
| 70,850 | 70,900 | 11,341 | 8,107 | 11,341 | 9,889 |
| 70,900 | 70,950 | 11,352 | 8,113 | 11,352 | 9,900 |
| 70,950 | 71,000 | 11,363 | 8,119 | 11,363 | 9,911 |

## 71,000

| At least | But less than | Single | Married filing jointly* | Married filing separately | Head of a household |
|---|---|---|---|---|---|
| 71,000 | 71,050 | 11,374 | 8,125 | 11,374 | 9,922 |
| 71,050 | 71,100 | 11,385 | 8,131 | 11,385 | 9,933 |
| 71,100 | 71,150 | 11,396 | 8,137 | 11,396 | 9,944 |
| 71,150 | 71,200 | 11,407 | 8,143 | 11,407 | 9,955 |
| 71,200 | 71,250 | 11,418 | 8,149 | 11,418 | 9,966 |
| 71,250 | 71,300 | 11,429 | 8,155 | 11,429 | 9,977 |
| 71,300 | 71,350 | 11,440 | 8,161 | 11,440 | 9,988 |
| 71,350 | 71,400 | 11,451 | 8,167 | 11,451 | 9,999 |
| 71,400 | 71,450 | 11,462 | 8,173 | 11,462 | 10,010 |
| 71,450 | 71,500 | 11,473 | 8,179 | 11,473 | 10,021 |
| 71,500 | 71,550 | 11,484 | 8,185 | 11,484 | 10,032 |
| 71,550 | 71,600 | 11,495 | 8,191 | 11,495 | 10,043 |
| 71,600 | 71,650 | 11,506 | 8,197 | 11,506 | 10,054 |
| 71,650 | 71,700 | 11,517 | 8,203 | 11,517 | 10,065 |
| 71,700 | 71,750 | 11,528 | 8,209 | 11,528 | 10,076 |
| 71,750 | 71,800 | 11,539 | 8,215 | 11,539 | 10,087 |
| 71,800 | 71,850 | 11,550 | 8,221 | 11,550 | 10,098 |
| 71,850 | 71,900 | 11,561 | 8,227 | 11,561 | 10,109 |
| 71,900 | 71,950 | 11,572 | 8,233 | 11,572 | 10,120 |
| 71,950 | 72,000 | 11,583 | 8,239 | 11,583 | 10,131 |

## 72,000

| At least | But less than | Single | Married filing jointly* | Married filing separately | Head of a household |
|---|---|---|---|---|---|
| 72,000 | 72,050 | 11,594 | 8,245 | 11,594 | 10,142 |
| 72,050 | 72,100 | 11,605 | 8,251 | 11,605 | 10,153 |
| 72,100 | 72,150 | 11,616 | 8,257 | 11,616 | 10,164 |
| 72,150 | 72,200 | 11,627 | 8,263 | 11,627 | 10,175 |
| 72,200 | 72,250 | 11,638 | 8,269 | 11,638 | 10,186 |
| 72,250 | 72,300 | 11,649 | 8,275 | 11,649 | 10,197 |
| 72,300 | 72,350 | 11,660 | 8,281 | 11,660 | 10,208 |
| 72,350 | 72,400 | 11,671 | 8,287 | 11,671 | 10,219 |
| 72,400 | 72,450 | 11,682 | 8,293 | 11,682 | 10,230 |
| 72,450 | 72,500 | 11,693 | 8,299 | 11,693 | 10,241 |
| 72,500 | 72,550 | 11,704 | 8,305 | 11,704 | 10,252 |
| 72,550 | 72,600 | 11,715 | 8,311 | 11,715 | 10,263 |
| 72,600 | 72,650 | 11,726 | 8,317 | 11,726 | 10,274 |
| 72,650 | 72,700 | 11,737 | 8,323 | 11,737 | 10,285 |
| 72,700 | 72,750 | 11,748 | 8,329 | 11,748 | 10,296 |
| 72,750 | 72,800 | 11,759 | 8,335 | 11,759 | 10,307 |
| 72,800 | 72,850 | 11,770 | 8,341 | 11,770 | 10,318 |
| 72,850 | 72,900 | 11,781 | 8,347 | 11,781 | 10,329 |
| 72,900 | 72,950 | 11,792 | 8,353 | 11,792 | 10,340 |
| 72,950 | 73,000 | 11,803 | 8,359 | 11,803 | 10,351 |

## 73,000

| At least | But less than | Single | Married filing jointly* | Married filing separately | Head of a household |
|---|---|---|---|---|---|
| 73,000 | 73,050 | 11,814 | 8,365 | 11,814 | 10,362 |
| 73,050 | 73,100 | 11,825 | 8,371 | 11,825 | 10,373 |
| 73,100 | 73,150 | 11,836 | 8,377 | 11,836 | 10,384 |
| 73,150 | 73,200 | 11,847 | 8,383 | 11,847 | 10,395 |
| 73,200 | 73,250 | 11,858 | 8,389 | 11,858 | 10,406 |
| 73,250 | 73,300 | 11,869 | 8,395 | 11,869 | 10,417 |
| 73,300 | 73,350 | 11,880 | 8,401 | 11,880 | 10,428 |
| 73,350 | 73,400 | 11,891 | 8,407 | 11,891 | 10,439 |
| 73,400 | 73,450 | 11,902 | 8,413 | 11,902 | 10,450 |
| 73,450 | 73,500 | 11,913 | 8,419 | 11,913 | 10,461 |
| 73,500 | 73,550 | 11,924 | 8,425 | 11,924 | 10,472 |
| 73,550 | 73,600 | 11,935 | 8,431 | 11,935 | 10,483 |
| 73,600 | 73,650 | 11,946 | 8,437 | 11,946 | 10,494 |
| 73,650 | 73,700 | 11,957 | 8,443 | 11,957 | 10,505 |
| 73,700 | 73,750 | 11,968 | 8,449 | 11,968 | 10,516 |
| 73,750 | 73,800 | 11,979 | 8,455 | 11,979 | 10,527 |
| 73,800 | 73,850 | 11,990 | 8,461 | 11,990 | 10,538 |
| 73,850 | 73,900 | 12,001 | 8,467 | 12,001 | 10,549 |
| 73,900 | 73,950 | 12,012 | 8,473 | 12,012 | 10,560 |
| 73,950 | 74,000 | 12,023 | 8,479 | 12,023 | 10,571 |

## 74,000

| At least | But less than | Single | Married filing jointly* | Married filing separately | Head of a household |
|---|---|---|---|---|---|
| 74,000 | 74,050 | 12,034 | 8,485 | 12,034 | 10,582 |
| 74,050 | 74,100 | 12,045 | 8,491 | 12,045 | 10,593 |
| 74,100 | 74,150 | 12,056 | 8,497 | 12,056 | 10,604 |
| 74,150 | 74,200 | 12,067 | 8,503 | 12,067 | 10,615 |
| 74,200 | 74,250 | 12,078 | 8,509 | 12,078 | 10,626 |
| 74,250 | 74,300 | 12,089 | 8,515 | 12,089 | 10,637 |
| 74,300 | 74,350 | 12,100 | 8,521 | 12,100 | 10,648 |
| 74,350 | 74,400 | 12,111 | 8,527 | 12,111 | 10,659 |
| 74,400 | 74,450 | 12,122 | 8,533 | 12,122 | 10,670 |
| 74,450 | 74,500 | 12,133 | 8,539 | 12,133 | 10,681 |
| 74,500 | 74,550 | 12,144 | 8,545 | 12,144 | 10,692 |
| 74,550 | 74,600 | 12,155 | 8,551 | 12,155 | 10,703 |
| 74,600 | 74,650 | 12,166 | 8,557 | 12,166 | 10,714 |
| 74,650 | 74,700 | 12,177 | 8,563 | 12,177 | 10,725 |
| 74,700 | 74,750 | 12,188 | 8,569 | 12,188 | 10,736 |
| 74,750 | 74,800 | 12,199 | 8,575 | 12,199 | 10,747 |
| 74,800 | 74,850 | 12,210 | 8,581 | 12,210 | 10,758 |
| 74,850 | 74,900 | 12,221 | 8,587 | 12,221 | 10,769 |
| 74,900 | 74,950 | 12,232 | 8,593 | 12,232 | 10,780 |
| 74,950 | 75,000 | 12,243 | 8,599 | 12,243 | 10,791 |

| If line 15 (taxable income) is— | | And you are— | | | |
|---|---|---|---|---|---|
| At least | But less than | Single | Married filing jointly * | Married filing separately | Head of a household |
| | | Your tax is— | | | |

## 75,000

| At least | But less than | Single | MFJ | MFS | HoH |
|---|---|---|---|---|---|
| 75,000 | 75,050 | 12,254 | 8,605 | 12,254 | 10,802 |
| 75,050 | 75,100 | 12,265 | 8,611 | 12,265 | 10,813 |
| 75,100 | 75,150 | 12,276 | 8,617 | 12,276 | 10,824 |
| 75,150 | 75,200 | 12,287 | 8,623 | 12,287 | 10,835 |
| 75,200 | 75,250 | 12,298 | 8,629 | 12,298 | 10,846 |
| 75,250 | 75,300 | 12,309 | 8,635 | 12,309 | 10,857 |
| 75,300 | 75,350 | 12,320 | 8,641 | 12,320 | 10,868 |
| 75,350 | 75,400 | 12,331 | 8,647 | 12,331 | 10,879 |
| 75,400 | 75,450 | 12,342 | 8,653 | 12,342 | 10,890 |
| 75,450 | 75,500 | 12,353 | 8,659 | 12,353 | 10,901 |
| 75,500 | 75,550 | 12,364 | 8,665 | 12,364 | 10,912 |
| 75,550 | 75,600 | 12,375 | 8,671 | 12,375 | 10,923 |
| 75,600 | 75,650 | 12,386 | 8,677 | 12,386 | 10,934 |
| 75,650 | 75,700 | 12,397 | 8,683 | 12,397 | 10,945 |
| 75,700 | 75,750 | 12,408 | 8,689 | 12,408 | 10,956 |
| 75,750 | 75,800 | 12,419 | 8,695 | 12,419 | 10,967 |
| 75,800 | 75,850 | 12,430 | 8,701 | 12,430 | 10,978 |
| 75,850 | 75,900 | 12,441 | 8,707 | 12,441 | 10,989 |
| 75,900 | 75,950 | 12,452 | 8,713 | 12,452 | 11,000 |
| 75,950 | 76,000 | 12,463 | 8,719 | 12,463 | 11,011 |

## 76,000

| At least | But less than | Single | MFJ | MFS | HoH |
|---|---|---|---|---|---|
| 76,000 | 76,050 | 12,474 | 8,725 | 12,474 | 11,022 |
| 76,050 | 76,100 | 12,485 | 8,731 | 12,485 | 11,033 |
| 76,100 | 76,150 | 12,496 | 8,737 | 12,496 | 11,044 |
| 76,150 | 76,200 | 12,507 | 8,743 | 12,507 | 11,055 |
| 76,200 | 76,250 | 12,518 | 8,749 | 12,518 | 11,066 |
| 76,250 | 76,300 | 12,529 | 8,755 | 12,529 | 11,077 |
| 76,300 | 76,350 | 12,540 | 8,761 | 12,540 | 11,088 |
| 76,350 | 76,400 | 12,551 | 8,767 | 12,551 | 11,099 |
| 76,400 | 76,450 | 12,562 | 8,773 | 12,562 | 11,110 |
| 76,450 | 76,500 | 12,573 | 8,779 | 12,573 | 11,121 |
| 76,500 | 76,550 | 12,584 | 8,785 | 12,584 | 11,132 |
| 76,550 | 76,600 | 12,595 | 8,791 | 12,595 | 11,143 |
| 76,600 | 76,650 | 12,606 | 8,797 | 12,606 | 11,154 |
| 76,650 | 76,700 | 12,617 | 8,803 | 12,617 | 11,165 |
| 76,700 | 76,750 | 12,628 | 8,809 | 12,628 | 11,176 |
| 76,750 | 76,800 | 12,639 | 8,815 | 12,639 | 11,187 |
| 76,800 | 76,850 | 12,650 | 8,821 | 12,650 | 11,198 |
| 76,850 | 76,900 | 12,661 | 8,827 | 12,661 | 11,209 |
| 76,900 | 76,950 | 12,672 | 8,833 | 12,672 | 11,220 |
| 76,950 | 77,000 | 12,683 | 8,839 | 12,683 | 11,231 |

## 77,000

| At least | But less than | Single | MFJ | MFS | HoH |
|---|---|---|---|---|---|
| 77,000 | 77,050 | 12,694 | 8,845 | 12,694 | 11,242 |
| 77,050 | 77,100 | 12,705 | 8,851 | 12,705 | 11,253 |
| 77,100 | 77,150 | 12,716 | 8,857 | 12,716 | 11,264 |
| 77,150 | 77,200 | 12,727 | 8,863 | 12,727 | 11,275 |
| 77,200 | 77,250 | 12,738 | 8,869 | 12,738 | 11,286 |
| 77,250 | 77,300 | 12,749 | 8,875 | 12,749 | 11,297 |
| 77,300 | 77,350 | 12,760 | 8,881 | 12,760 | 11,308 |
| 77,350 | 77,400 | 12,771 | 8,887 | 12,771 | 11,319 |
| 77,400 | 77,450 | 12,782 | 8,893 | 12,782 | 11,330 |
| 77,450 | 77,500 | 12,793 | 8,899 | 12,793 | 11,341 |
| 77,500 | 77,550 | 12,804 | 8,905 | 12,804 | 11,352 |
| 77,550 | 77,600 | 12,815 | 8,911 | 12,815 | 11,363 |
| 77,600 | 77,650 | 12,826 | 8,917 | 12,826 | 11,374 |
| 77,650 | 77,700 | 12,837 | 8,923 | 12,837 | 11,385 |
| 77,700 | 77,750 | 12,848 | 8,929 | 12,848 | 11,396 |
| 77,750 | 77,800 | 12,859 | 8,935 | 12,859 | 11,407 |
| 77,800 | 77,850 | 12,870 | 8,941 | 12,870 | 11,418 |
| 77,850 | 77,900 | 12,881 | 8,947 | 12,881 | 11,429 |
| 77,900 | 77,950 | 12,892 | 8,953 | 12,892 | 11,440 |
| 77,950 | 78,000 | 12,903 | 8,959 | 12,903 | 11,451 |

## 78,000

| At least | But less than | Single | MFJ | MFS | HoH |
|---|---|---|---|---|---|
| 78,000 | 78,050 | 12,914 | 8,965 | 12,914 | 11,462 |
| 78,050 | 78,100 | 12,925 | 8,971 | 12,925 | 11,473 |
| 78,100 | 78,150 | 12,936 | 8,977 | 12,936 | 11,484 |
| 78,150 | 78,200 | 12,947 | 8,983 | 12,947 | 11,495 |
| 78,200 | 78,250 | 12,958 | 8,989 | 12,958 | 11,506 |
| 78,250 | 78,300 | 12,969 | 8,995 | 12,969 | 11,517 |
| 78,300 | 78,350 | 12,980 | 9,001 | 12,980 | 11,528 |
| 78,350 | 78,400 | 12,991 | 9,007 | 12,991 | 11,539 |
| 78,400 | 78,450 | 13,002 | 9,013 | 13,002 | 11,550 |
| 78,450 | 78,500 | 13,013 | 9,019 | 13,013 | 11,561 |
| 78,500 | 78,550 | 13,024 | 9,025 | 13,024 | 11,572 |
| 78,550 | 78,600 | 13,035 | 9,031 | 13,035 | 11,583 |
| 78,600 | 78,650 | 13,046 | 9,037 | 13,046 | 11,594 |
| 78,650 | 78,700 | 13,057 | 9,043 | 13,057 | 11,605 |
| 78,700 | 78,750 | 13,068 | 9,049 | 13,068 | 11,616 |
| 78,750 | 78,800 | 13,079 | 9,055 | 13,079 | 11,627 |
| 78,800 | 78,850 | 13,090 | 9,061 | 13,090 | 11,638 |
| 78,850 | 78,900 | 13,101 | 9,067 | 13,101 | 11,649 |
| 78,900 | 78,950 | 13,112 | 9,073 | 13,112 | 11,660 |
| 78,950 | 79,000 | 13,123 | 9,079 | 13,123 | 11,671 |

## 79,000

| At least | But less than | Single | MFJ | MFS | HoH |
|---|---|---|---|---|---|
| 79,000 | 79,050 | 13,134 | 9,085 | 13,134 | 11,682 |
| 79,050 | 79,100 | 13,145 | 9,091 | 13,145 | 11,693 |
| 79,100 | 79,150 | 13,156 | 9,097 | 13,156 | 11,704 |
| 79,150 | 79,200 | 13,167 | 9,103 | 13,167 | 11,715 |
| 79,200 | 79,250 | 13,178 | 9,109 | 13,178 | 11,726 |
| 79,250 | 79,300 | 13,189 | 9,115 | 13,189 | 11,737 |
| 79,300 | 79,350 | 13,200 | 9,121 | 13,200 | 11,748 |
| 79,350 | 79,400 | 13,211 | 9,127 | 13,211 | 11,759 |
| 79,400 | 79,450 | 13,222 | 9,133 | 13,222 | 11,770 |
| 79,450 | 79,500 | 13,233 | 9,139 | 13,233 | 11,781 |
| 79,500 | 79,550 | 13,244 | 9,145 | 13,244 | 11,792 |
| 79,550 | 79,600 | 13,255 | 9,151 | 13,255 | 11,803 |
| 79,600 | 79,650 | 13,266 | 9,157 | 13,266 | 11,814 |
| 79,650 | 79,700 | 13,277 | 9,163 | 13,277 | 11,825 |
| 79,700 | 79,750 | 13,288 | 9,169 | 13,288 | 11,836 |
| 79,750 | 79,800 | 13,299 | 9,175 | 13,299 | 11,847 |
| 79,800 | 79,850 | 13,310 | 9,181 | 13,310 | 11,858 |
| 79,850 | 79,900 | 13,321 | 9,187 | 13,321 | 11,869 |
| 79,900 | 79,950 | 13,332 | 9,193 | 13,332 | 11,880 |
| 79,950 | 80,000 | 13,343 | 9,199 | 13,343 | 11,891 |

## 80,000

| At least | But less than | Single | MFJ | MFS | HoH |
|---|---|---|---|---|---|
| 80,000 | 80,050 | 13,354 | 9,205 | 13,354 | 11,902 |
| 80,050 | 80,100 | 13,365 | 9,211 | 13,365 | 11,913 |
| 80,100 | 80,150 | 13,376 | 9,217 | 13,376 | 11,924 |
| 80,150 | 80,200 | 13,387 | 9,223 | 13,387 | 11,935 |
| 80,200 | 80,250 | 13,398 | 9,229 | 13,398 | 11,946 |
| 80,250 | 80,300 | 13,409 | 9,235 | 13,409 | 11,957 |
| 80,300 | 80,350 | 13,420 | 9,241 | 13,420 | 11,968 |
| 80,350 | 80,400 | 13,431 | 9,247 | 13,431 | 11,979 |
| 80,400 | 80,450 | 13,442 | 9,253 | 13,442 | 11,990 |
| 80,450 | 80,500 | 13,453 | 9,259 | 13,453 | 12,001 |
| 80,500 | 80,550 | 13,464 | 9,265 | 13,464 | 12,012 |
| 80,550 | 80,600 | 13,475 | 9,271 | 13,475 | 12,023 |
| 80,600 | 80,650 | 13,486 | 9,277 | 13,486 | 12,034 |
| 80,650 | 80,700 | 13,497 | 9,283 | 13,497 | 12,045 |
| 80,700 | 80,750 | 13,508 | 9,289 | 13,508 | 12,056 |
| 80,750 | 80,800 | 13,519 | 9,295 | 13,519 | 12,067 |
| 80,800 | 80,850 | 13,530 | 9,301 | 13,530 | 12,078 |
| 80,850 | 80,900 | 13,541 | 9,307 | 13,541 | 12,089 |
| 80,900 | 80,950 | 13,552 | 9,313 | 13,552 | 12,100 |
| 80,950 | 81,000 | 13,563 | 9,319 | 13,563 | 12,111 |

## 81,000

| At least | But less than | Single | MFJ | MFS | HoH |
|---|---|---|---|---|---|
| 81,000 | 81,050 | 13,574 | 9,325 | 13,574 | 12,122 |
| 81,050 | 81,100 | 13,585 | 9,334 | 13,585 | 12,133 |
| 81,100 | 81,150 | 13,596 | 9,345 | 13,596 | 12,144 |
| 81,150 | 81,200 | 13,607 | 9,356 | 13,607 | 12,155 |
| 81,200 | 81,250 | 13,618 | 9,367 | 13,618 | 12,166 |
| 81,250 | 81,300 | 13,629 | 9,378 | 13,629 | 12,177 |
| 81,300 | 81,350 | 13,640 | 9,389 | 13,640 | 12,188 |
| 81,350 | 81,400 | 13,651 | 9,400 | 13,651 | 12,199 |
| 81,400 | 81,450 | 13,662 | 9,411 | 13,662 | 12,210 |
| 81,450 | 81,500 | 13,673 | 9,422 | 13,673 | 12,221 |
| 81,500 | 81,550 | 13,684 | 9,433 | 13,684 | 12,232 |
| 81,550 | 81,600 | 13,695 | 9,444 | 13,695 | 12,243 |
| 81,600 | 81,650 | 13,706 | 9,455 | 13,706 | 12,254 |
| 81,650 | 81,700 | 13,717 | 9,466 | 13,717 | 12,265 |
| 81,700 | 81,750 | 13,728 | 9,477 | 13,728 | 12,276 |
| 81,750 | 81,800 | 13,739 | 9,488 | 13,739 | 12,287 |
| 81,800 | 81,850 | 13,750 | 9,499 | 13,750 | 12,298 |
| 81,850 | 81,900 | 13,761 | 9,510 | 13,761 | 12,309 |
| 81,900 | 81,950 | 13,772 | 9,521 | 13,772 | 12,320 |
| 81,950 | 82,000 | 13,783 | 9,532 | 13,783 | 12,331 |

## 82,000

| At least | But less than | Single | MFJ | MFS | HoH |
|---|---|---|---|---|---|
| 82,000 | 82,050 | 13,794 | 9,543 | 13,794 | 12,342 |
| 82,050 | 82,100 | 13,805 | 9,554 | 13,805 | 12,353 |
| 82,100 | 82,150 | 13,816 | 9,565 | 13,816 | 12,364 |
| 82,150 | 82,200 | 13,827 | 9,576 | 13,827 | 12,375 |
| 82,200 | 82,250 | 13,838 | 9,587 | 13,838 | 12,386 |
| 82,250 | 82,300 | 13,849 | 9,598 | 13,849 | 12,397 |
| 82,300 | 82,350 | 13,860 | 9,609 | 13,860 | 12,408 |
| 82,350 | 82,400 | 13,871 | 9,620 | 13,871 | 12,419 |
| 82,400 | 82,450 | 13,882 | 9,631 | 13,882 | 12,430 |
| 82,450 | 82,500 | 13,893 | 9,642 | 13,893 | 12,441 |
| 82,500 | 82,550 | 13,904 | 9,653 | 13,904 | 12,452 |
| 82,550 | 82,600 | 13,915 | 9,664 | 13,915 | 12,463 |
| 82,600 | 82,650 | 13,926 | 9,675 | 13,926 | 12,474 |
| 82,650 | 82,700 | 13,937 | 9,686 | 13,937 | 12,485 |
| 82,700 | 82,750 | 13,948 | 9,697 | 13,948 | 12,496 |
| 82,750 | 82,800 | 13,959 | 9,708 | 13,959 | 12,507 |
| 82,800 | 82,850 | 13,970 | 9,719 | 13,970 | 12,518 |
| 82,850 | 82,900 | 13,981 | 9,730 | 13,981 | 12,529 |
| 82,900 | 82,950 | 13,992 | 9,741 | 13,992 | 12,540 |
| 82,950 | 83,000 | 14,003 | 9,752 | 14,003 | 12,551 |

## 83,000

| At least | But less than | Single | MFJ | MFS | HoH |
|---|---|---|---|---|---|
| 83,000 | 83,050 | 14,014 | 9,763 | 14,014 | 12,562 |
| 83,050 | 83,100 | 14,025 | 9,774 | 14,025 | 12,573 |
| 83,100 | 83,150 | 14,036 | 9,785 | 14,036 | 12,584 |
| 83,150 | 83,200 | 14,047 | 9,796 | 14,047 | 12,595 |
| 83,200 | 83,250 | 14,058 | 9,807 | 14,058 | 12,606 |
| 83,250 | 83,300 | 14,069 | 9,818 | 14,069 | 12,617 |
| 83,300 | 83,350 | 14,080 | 9,829 | 14,080 | 12,628 |
| 83,350 | 83,400 | 14,091 | 9,840 | 14,091 | 12,639 |
| 83,400 | 83,450 | 14,102 | 9,851 | 14,102 | 12,650 |
| 83,450 | 83,500 | 14,113 | 9,862 | 14,113 | 12,661 |
| 83,500 | 83,550 | 14,124 | 9,873 | 14,124 | 12,672 |
| 83,550 | 83,600 | 14,135 | 9,884 | 14,135 | 12,683 |
| 83,600 | 83,650 | 14,146 | 9,895 | 14,146 | 12,694 |
| 83,650 | 83,700 | 14,157 | 9,906 | 14,157 | 12,705 |
| 83,700 | 83,750 | 14,168 | 9,917 | 14,168 | 12,716 |
| 83,750 | 83,800 | 14,179 | 9,928 | 14,179 | 12,727 |
| 83,800 | 83,850 | 14,190 | 9,939 | 14,190 | 12,738 |
| 83,850 | 83,900 | 14,201 | 9,950 | 14,201 | 12,749 |
| 83,900 | 83,950 | 14,212 | 9,961 | 14,212 | 12,760 |
| 83,950 | 84,000 | 14,223 | 9,972 | 14,223 | 12,771 |

| If line 15 (taxable income) is— | | And you are— | | | |
|---|---|---|---|---|---|
| At least | But less than | Single | Married filing jointly * | Married filing separately | Head of a house-hold |
| | | Your tax is— | | | |

## 84,000

| At least | But less than | Single | MFJ | MFS | HoH |
|---|---|---|---|---|---|
| 84,000 | 84,050 | 14,234 | 9,983 | 14,234 | 12,782 |
| 84,050 | 84,100 | 14,245 | 9,994 | 14,245 | 12,793 |
| 84,100 | 84,150 | 14,256 | 10,005 | 14,256 | 12,804 |
| 84,150 | 84,200 | 14,267 | 10,016 | 14,267 | 12,815 |
| 84,200 | 84,250 | 14,278 | 10,027 | 14,278 | 12,826 |
| 84,250 | 84,300 | 14,289 | 10,038 | 14,289 | 12,837 |
| 84,300 | 84,350 | 14,300 | 10,049 | 14,300 | 12,848 |
| 84,350 | 84,400 | 14,311 | 10,060 | 14,311 | 12,859 |
| 84,400 | 84,450 | 14,322 | 10,071 | 14,322 | 12,870 |
| 84,450 | 84,500 | 14,333 | 10,082 | 14,333 | 12,881 |
| 84,500 | 84,550 | 14,344 | 10,093 | 14,344 | 12,892 |
| 84,550 | 84,600 | 14,355 | 10,104 | 14,355 | 12,903 |
| 84,600 | 84,650 | 14,366 | 10,115 | 14,366 | 12,914 |
| 84,650 | 84,700 | 14,377 | 10,126 | 14,377 | 12,925 |
| 84,700 | 84,750 | 14,388 | 10,137 | 14,388 | 12,936 |
| 84,750 | 84,800 | 14,399 | 10,148 | 14,399 | 12,947 |
| 84,800 | 84,850 | 14,410 | 10,159 | 14,410 | 12,958 |
| 84,850 | 84,900 | 14,421 | 10,170 | 14,421 | 12,969 |
| 84,900 | 84,950 | 14,432 | 10,181 | 14,432 | 12,980 |
| 84,950 | 85,000 | 14,443 | 10,192 | 14,443 | 12,991 |

## 85,000

| At least | But less than | Single | MFJ | MFS | HoH |
|---|---|---|---|---|---|
| 85,000 | 85,050 | 14,454 | 10,203 | 14,454 | 13,002 |
| 85,050 | 85,100 | 14,465 | 10,214 | 14,465 | 13,013 |
| 85,100 | 85,150 | 14,476 | 10,225 | 14,476 | 13,024 |
| 85,150 | 85,200 | 14,487 | 10,236 | 14,487 | 13,035 |
| 85,200 | 85,250 | 14,498 | 10,247 | 14,498 | 13,046 |
| 85,250 | 85,300 | 14,509 | 10,258 | 14,509 | 13,057 |
| 85,300 | 85,350 | 14,520 | 10,269 | 14,520 | 13,068 |
| 85,350 | 85,400 | 14,531 | 10,280 | 14,531 | 13,079 |
| 85,400 | 85,450 | 14,542 | 10,291 | 14,542 | 13,090 |
| 85,450 | 85,500 | 14,553 | 10,302 | 14,553 | 13,101 |
| 85,500 | 85,550 | 14,564 | 10,313 | 14,564 | 13,112 |
| 85,550 | 85,600 | 14,575 | 10,324 | 14,575 | 13,123 |
| 85,600 | 85,650 | 14,586 | 10,335 | 14,586 | 13,134 |
| 85,650 | 85,700 | 14,597 | 10,346 | 14,597 | 13,145 |
| 85,700 | 85,750 | 14,608 | 10,357 | 14,608 | 13,156 |
| 85,750 | 85,800 | 14,619 | 10,368 | 14,619 | 13,167 |
| 85,800 | 85,850 | 14,630 | 10,379 | 14,630 | 13,178 |
| 85,850 | 85,900 | 14,641 | 10,390 | 14,641 | 13,189 |
| 85,900 | 85,950 | 14,652 | 10,401 | 14,652 | 13,200 |
| 85,950 | 86,000 | 14,663 | 10,412 | 14,663 | 13,211 |

## 86,000

| At least | But less than | Single | MFJ | MFS | HoH |
|---|---|---|---|---|---|
| 86,000 | 86,050 | 14,674 | 10,423 | 14,674 | 13,222 |
| 86,050 | 86,100 | 14,685 | 10,434 | 14,685 | 13,233 |
| 86,100 | 86,150 | 14,696 | 10,445 | 14,696 | 13,244 |
| 86,150 | 86,200 | 14,707 | 10,456 | 14,707 | 13,255 |
| 86,200 | 86,250 | 14,718 | 10,467 | 14,718 | 13,266 |
| 86,250 | 86,300 | 14,729 | 10,478 | 14,729 | 13,277 |
| 86,300 | 86,350 | 14,740 | 10,489 | 14,740 | 13,288 |
| 86,350 | 86,400 | 14,751 | 10,500 | 14,751 | 13,299 |
| 86,400 | 86,450 | 14,763 | 10,511 | 14,763 | 13,311 |
| 86,450 | 86,500 | 14,775 | 10,522 | 14,775 | 13,323 |
| 86,500 | 86,550 | 14,787 | 10,533 | 14,787 | 13,335 |
| 86,550 | 86,600 | 14,799 | 10,544 | 14,799 | 13,347 |
| 86,600 | 86,650 | 14,811 | 10,555 | 14,811 | 13,359 |
| 86,650 | 86,700 | 14,823 | 10,566 | 14,823 | 13,371 |
| 86,700 | 86,750 | 14,835 | 10,577 | 14,835 | 13,383 |
| 86,750 | 86,800 | 14,847 | 10,588 | 14,847 | 13,395 |
| 86,800 | 86,850 | 14,859 | 10,599 | 14,859 | 13,407 |
| 86,850 | 86,900 | 14,871 | 10,610 | 14,871 | 13,419 |
| 86,900 | 86,950 | 14,883 | 10,621 | 14,883 | 13,431 |
| 86,950 | 87,000 | 14,895 | 10,632 | 14,895 | 13,443 |

## 87,000

| At least | But less than | Single | MFJ | MFS | HoH |
|---|---|---|---|---|---|
| 87,000 | 87,050 | 14,907 | 10,643 | 14,907 | 13,455 |
| 87,050 | 87,100 | 14,919 | 10,654 | 14,919 | 13,467 |
| 87,100 | 87,150 | 14,931 | 10,665 | 14,931 | 13,479 |
| 87,150 | 87,200 | 14,943 | 10,676 | 14,943 | 13,491 |
| 87,200 | 87,250 | 14,955 | 10,687 | 14,955 | 13,503 |
| 87,250 | 87,300 | 14,967 | 10,698 | 14,967 | 13,515 |
| 87,300 | 87,350 | 14,979 | 10,709 | 14,979 | 13,527 |
| 87,350 | 87,400 | 14,991 | 10,720 | 14,991 | 13,539 |
| 87,400 | 87,450 | 15,003 | 10,731 | 15,003 | 13,551 |
| 87,450 | 87,500 | 15,015 | 10,742 | 15,015 | 13,563 |
| 87,500 | 87,550 | 15,027 | 10,753 | 15,027 | 13,575 |
| 87,550 | 87,600 | 15,039 | 10,764 | 15,039 | 13,587 |
| 87,600 | 87,650 | 15,051 | 10,775 | 15,051 | 13,599 |
| 87,650 | 87,700 | 15,063 | 10,786 | 15,063 | 13,611 |
| 87,700 | 87,750 | 15,075 | 10,797 | 15,075 | 13,623 |
| 87,750 | 87,800 | 15,087 | 10,808 | 15,087 | 13,635 |
| 87,800 | 87,850 | 15,099 | 10,819 | 15,099 | 13,647 |
| 87,850 | 87,900 | 15,111 | 10,830 | 15,111 | 13,659 |
| 87,900 | 87,950 | 15,123 | 10,841 | 15,123 | 13,671 |
| 87,950 | 88,000 | 15,135 | 10,852 | 15,135 | 13,683 |

## 88,000

| At least | But less than | Single | MFJ | MFS | HoH |
|---|---|---|---|---|---|
| 88,000 | 88,050 | 15,147 | 10,863 | 15,147 | 13,695 |
| 88,050 | 88,100 | 15,159 | 10,874 | 15,159 | 13,707 |
| 88,100 | 88,150 | 15,171 | 10,885 | 15,171 | 13,719 |
| 88,150 | 88,200 | 15,183 | 10,896 | 15,183 | 13,731 |
| 88,200 | 88,250 | 15,195 | 10,907 | 15,195 | 13,743 |
| 88,250 | 88,300 | 15,207 | 10,918 | 15,207 | 13,755 |
| 88,300 | 88,350 | 15,219 | 10,929 | 15,219 | 13,767 |
| 88,350 | 88,400 | 15,231 | 10,940 | 15,231 | 13,779 |
| 88,400 | 88,450 | 15,243 | 10,951 | 15,243 | 13,791 |
| 88,450 | 88,500 | 15,255 | 10,962 | 15,255 | 13,803 |
| 88,500 | 88,550 | 15,267 | 10,973 | 15,267 | 13,815 |
| 88,550 | 88,600 | 15,279 | 10,984 | 15,279 | 13,827 |
| 88,600 | 88,650 | 15,291 | 10,995 | 15,291 | 13,839 |
| 88,650 | 88,700 | 15,303 | 11,006 | 15,303 | 13,851 |
| 88,700 | 88,750 | 15,315 | 11,017 | 15,315 | 13,863 |
| 88,750 | 88,800 | 15,327 | 11,028 | 15,327 | 13,875 |
| 88,800 | 88,850 | 15,339 | 11,039 | 15,339 | 13,887 |
| 88,850 | 88,900 | 15,351 | 11,050 | 15,351 | 13,899 |
| 88,900 | 88,950 | 15,363 | 11,061 | 15,363 | 13,911 |
| 88,950 | 89,000 | 15,375 | 11,072 | 15,375 | 13,923 |

## 89,000

| At least | But less than | Single | MFJ | MFS | HoH |
|---|---|---|---|---|---|
| 89,000 | 89,050 | 15,387 | 11,083 | 15,387 | 13,935 |
| 89,050 | 89,100 | 15,399 | 11,094 | 15,399 | 13,947 |
| 89,100 | 89,150 | 15,411 | 11,105 | 15,411 | 13,959 |
| 89,150 | 89,200 | 15,423 | 11,116 | 15,423 | 13,971 |
| 89,200 | 89,250 | 15,435 | 11,127 | 15,435 | 13,983 |
| 89,250 | 89,300 | 15,447 | 11,138 | 15,447 | 13,995 |
| 89,300 | 89,350 | 15,459 | 11,149 | 15,459 | 14,007 |
| 89,350 | 89,400 | 15,471 | 11,160 | 15,471 | 14,019 |
| 89,400 | 89,450 | 15,483 | 11,171 | 15,483 | 14,031 |
| 89,450 | 89,500 | 15,495 | 11,182 | 15,495 | 14,043 |
| 89,500 | 89,550 | 15,507 | 11,193 | 15,507 | 14,055 |
| 89,550 | 89,600 | 15,519 | 11,204 | 15,519 | 14,067 |
| 89,600 | 89,650 | 15,531 | 11,215 | 15,531 | 14,079 |
| 89,650 | 89,700 | 15,543 | 11,226 | 15,543 | 14,091 |
| 89,700 | 89,750 | 15,555 | 11,237 | 15,555 | 14,103 |
| 89,750 | 89,800 | 15,567 | 11,248 | 15,567 | 14,115 |
| 89,800 | 89,850 | 15,579 | 11,259 | 15,579 | 14,127 |
| 89,850 | 89,900 | 15,591 | 11,270 | 15,591 | 14,139 |
| 89,900 | 89,950 | 15,603 | 11,281 | 15,603 | 14,151 |
| 89,950 | 90,000 | 15,615 | 11,292 | 15,615 | 14,163 |

## 90,000

| At least | But less than | Single | MFJ | MFS | HoH |
|---|---|---|---|---|---|
| 90,000 | 90,050 | 15,627 | 11,303 | 15,627 | 14,175 |
| 90,050 | 90,100 | 15,639 | 11,314 | 15,639 | 14,187 |
| 90,100 | 90,150 | 15,651 | 11,325 | 15,651 | 14,199 |
| 90,150 | 90,200 | 15,663 | 11,336 | 15,663 | 14,211 |
| 90,200 | 90,250 | 15,675 | 11,347 | 15,675 | 14,223 |
| 90,250 | 90,300 | 15,687 | 11,358 | 15,687 | 14,235 |
| 90,300 | 90,350 | 15,699 | 11,369 | 15,699 | 14,247 |
| 90,350 | 90,400 | 15,711 | 11,380 | 15,711 | 14,259 |
| 90,400 | 90,450 | 15,723 | 11,391 | 15,723 | 14,271 |
| 90,450 | 90,500 | 15,735 | 11,402 | 15,735 | 14,283 |
| 90,500 | 90,550 | 15,747 | 11,413 | 15,747 | 14,295 |
| 90,550 | 90,600 | 15,759 | 11,424 | 15,759 | 14,307 |
| 90,600 | 90,650 | 15,771 | 11,435 | 15,771 | 14,319 |
| 90,650 | 90,700 | 15,783 | 11,446 | 15,783 | 14,331 |
| 90,700 | 90,750 | 15,795 | 11,457 | 15,795 | 14,343 |
| 90,750 | 90,800 | 15,807 | 11,468 | 15,807 | 14,355 |
| 90,800 | 90,850 | 15,819 | 11,479 | 15,819 | 14,367 |
| 90,850 | 90,900 | 15,831 | 11,490 | 15,831 | 14,379 |
| 90,900 | 90,950 | 15,843 | 11,501 | 15,843 | 14,391 |
| 90,950 | 91,000 | 15,855 | 11,512 | 15,855 | 14,403 |

## 91,000

| At least | But less than | Single | MFJ | MFS | HoH |
|---|---|---|---|---|---|
| 91,000 | 91,050 | 15,867 | 11,523 | 15,867 | 14,415 |
| 91,050 | 91,100 | 15,879 | 11,534 | 15,879 | 14,427 |
| 91,100 | 91,150 | 15,891 | 11,545 | 15,891 | 14,439 |
| 91,150 | 91,200 | 15,903 | 11,556 | 15,903 | 14,451 |
| 91,200 | 91,250 | 15,915 | 11,567 | 15,915 | 14,463 |
| 91,250 | 91,300 | 15,927 | 11,578 | 15,927 | 14,475 |
| 91,300 | 91,350 | 15,939 | 11,589 | 15,939 | 14,487 |
| 91,350 | 91,400 | 15,951 | 11,600 | 15,951 | 14,499 |
| 91,400 | 91,450 | 15,963 | 11,611 | 15,963 | 14,511 |
| 91,450 | 91,500 | 15,975 | 11,622 | 15,975 | 14,523 |
| 91,500 | 91,550 | 15,987 | 11,633 | 15,987 | 14,535 |
| 91,550 | 91,600 | 15,999 | 11,644 | 15,999 | 14,547 |
| 91,600 | 91,650 | 16,011 | 11,655 | 16,011 | 14,559 |
| 91,650 | 91,700 | 16,023 | 11,666 | 16,023 | 14,571 |
| 91,700 | 91,750 | 16,035 | 11,677 | 16,035 | 14,583 |
| 91,750 | 91,800 | 16,047 | 11,688 | 16,047 | 14,595 |
| 91,800 | 91,850 | 16,059 | 11,699 | 16,059 | 14,607 |
| 91,850 | 91,900 | 16,071 | 11,710 | 16,071 | 14,619 |
| 91,900 | 91,950 | 16,083 | 11,721 | 16,083 | 14,631 |
| 91,950 | 92,000 | 16,095 | 11,732 | 16,095 | 14,643 |

## 92,000

| At least | But less than | Single | MFJ | MFS | HoH |
|---|---|---|---|---|---|
| 92,000 | 92,050 | 16,107 | 11,743 | 16,107 | 14,655 |
| 92,050 | 92,100 | 16,119 | 11,754 | 16,119 | 14,667 |
| 92,100 | 92,150 | 16,131 | 11,765 | 16,131 | 14,679 |
| 92,150 | 92,200 | 16,143 | 11,776 | 16,143 | 14,691 |
| 92,200 | 92,250 | 16,155 | 11,787 | 16,155 | 14,703 |
| 92,250 | 92,300 | 16,167 | 11,798 | 16,167 | 14,715 |
| 92,300 | 92,350 | 16,179 | 11,809 | 16,179 | 14,727 |
| 92,350 | 92,400 | 16,191 | 11,820 | 16,191 | 14,739 |
| 92,400 | 92,450 | 16,203 | 11,831 | 16,203 | 14,751 |
| 92,450 | 92,500 | 16,215 | 11,842 | 16,215 | 14,763 |
| 92,500 | 92,550 | 16,227 | 11,853 | 16,227 | 14,775 |
| 92,550 | 92,600 | 16,239 | 11,864 | 16,239 | 14,787 |
| 92,600 | 92,650 | 16,251 | 11,875 | 16,251 | 14,799 |
| 92,650 | 92,700 | 16,263 | 11,886 | 16,263 | 14,811 |
| 92,700 | 92,750 | 16,275 | 11,897 | 16,275 | 14,823 |
| 92,750 | 92,800 | 16,287 | 11,908 | 16,287 | 14,835 |
| 92,800 | 92,850 | 16,299 | 11,919 | 16,299 | 14,847 |
| 92,850 | 92,900 | 16,311 | 11,930 | 16,311 | 14,859 |
| 92,900 | 92,950 | 16,323 | 11,941 | 16,323 | 14,871 |
| 92,950 | 93,000 | 16,335 | 11,952 | 16,335 | 14,883 |

| If line 15 (taxable income) is— | | And you are— | | | |
|---|---|---|---|---|---|
| At least | But less than | Single | Married filing jointly * | Married filing separately | Head of a household |
| | | | Your tax is— | | |

## 93,000

| At least | But less than | Single | Married filing jointly * | Married filing separately | Head of a household |
|---|---|---|---|---|---|
| 93,000 | 93,050 | 16,347 | 11,963 | 16,347 | 14,895 |
| 93,050 | 93,100 | 16,359 | 11,974 | 16,359 | 14,907 |
| 93,100 | 93,150 | 16,371 | 11,985 | 16,371 | 14,919 |
| 93,150 | 93,200 | 16,383 | 11,996 | 16,383 | 14,931 |
| 93,200 | 93,250 | 16,395 | 12,007 | 16,395 | 14,943 |
| 93,250 | 93,300 | 16,407 | 12,018 | 16,407 | 14,955 |
| 93,300 | 93,350 | 16,419 | 12,029 | 16,419 | 14,967 |
| 93,350 | 93,400 | 16,431 | 12,040 | 16,431 | 14,979 |
| 93,400 | 93,450 | 16,443 | 12,051 | 16,443 | 14,991 |
| 93,450 | 93,500 | 16,455 | 12,062 | 16,455 | 15,003 |
| 93,500 | 93,550 | 16,467 | 12,073 | 16,467 | 15,015 |
| 93,550 | 93,600 | 16,479 | 12,084 | 16,479 | 15,027 |
| 93,600 | 93,650 | 16,491 | 12,095 | 16,491 | 15,039 |
| 93,650 | 93,700 | 16,503 | 12,106 | 16,503 | 15,051 |
| 93,700 | 93,750 | 16,515 | 12,117 | 16,515 | 15,063 |
| 93,750 | 93,800 | 16,527 | 12,128 | 16,527 | 15,075 |
| 93,800 | 93,850 | 16,539 | 12,139 | 16,539 | 15,087 |
| 93,850 | 93,900 | 16,551 | 12,150 | 16,551 | 15,099 |
| 93,900 | 93,950 | 16,563 | 12,161 | 16,563 | 15,111 |
| 93,950 | 94,000 | 16,575 | 12,172 | 16,575 | 15,123 |

## 94,000

| At least | But less than | Single | Married filing jointly * | Married filing separately | Head of a household |
|---|---|---|---|---|---|
| 94,000 | 94,050 | 16,587 | 12,183 | 16,587 | 15,135 |
| 94,050 | 94,100 | 16,599 | 12,194 | 16,599 | 15,147 |
| 94,100 | 94,150 | 16,611 | 12,205 | 16,611 | 15,159 |
| 94,150 | 94,200 | 16,623 | 12,216 | 16,623 | 15,171 |
| 94,200 | 94,250 | 16,635 | 12,227 | 16,635 | 15,183 |
| 94,250 | 94,300 | 16,647 | 12,238 | 16,647 | 15,195 |
| 94,300 | 94,350 | 16,659 | 12,249 | 16,659 | 15,207 |
| 94,350 | 94,400 | 16,671 | 12,260 | 16,671 | 15,219 |
| 94,400 | 94,450 | 16,683 | 12,271 | 16,683 | 15,231 |
| 94,450 | 94,500 | 16,695 | 12,282 | 16,695 | 15,243 |
| 94,500 | 94,550 | 16,707 | 12,293 | 16,707 | 15,255 |
| 94,550 | 94,600 | 16,719 | 12,304 | 16,719 | 15,267 |
| 94,600 | 94,650 | 16,731 | 12,315 | 16,731 | 15,279 |
| 94,650 | 94,700 | 16,743 | 12,326 | 16,743 | 15,291 |
| 94,700 | 94,750 | 16,755 | 12,337 | 16,755 | 15,303 |
| 94,750 | 94,800 | 16,767 | 12,348 | 16,767 | 15,315 |
| 94,800 | 94,850 | 16,779 | 12,359 | 16,779 | 15,327 |
| 94,850 | 94,900 | 16,791 | 12,370 | 16,791 | 15,339 |
| 94,900 | 94,950 | 16,803 | 12,381 | 16,803 | 15,351 |
| 94,950 | 95,000 | 16,815 | 12,392 | 16,815 | 15,363 |

## 95,000

| At least | But less than | Single | Married filing jointly * | Married filing separately | Head of a household |
|---|---|---|---|---|---|
| 95,000 | 95,050 | 16,827 | 12,403 | 16,827 | 15,375 |
| 95,050 | 95,100 | 16,839 | 12,414 | 16,839 | 15,387 |
| 95,100 | 95,150 | 16,851 | 12,425 | 16,851 | 15,399 |
| 95,150 | 95,200 | 16,863 | 12,436 | 16,863 | 15,411 |
| 95,200 | 95,250 | 16,875 | 12,447 | 16,875 | 15,423 |
| 95,250 | 95,300 | 16,887 | 12,458 | 16,887 | 15,435 |
| 95,300 | 95,350 | 16,899 | 12,469 | 16,899 | 15,447 |
| 95,350 | 95,400 | 16,911 | 12,480 | 16,911 | 15,459 |
| 95,400 | 95,450 | 16,923 | 12,491 | 16,923 | 15,471 |
| 95,450 | 95,500 | 16,935 | 12,502 | 16,935 | 15,483 |
| 95,500 | 95,550 | 16,947 | 12,513 | 16,947 | 15,495 |
| 95,550 | 95,600 | 16,959 | 12,524 | 16,959 | 15,507 |
| 95,600 | 95,650 | 16,971 | 12,535 | 16,971 | 15,519 |
| 95,650 | 95,700 | 16,983 | 12,546 | 16,983 | 15,531 |
| 95,700 | 95,750 | 16,995 | 12,557 | 16,995 | 15,543 |
| 95,750 | 95,800 | 17,007 | 12,568 | 17,007 | 15,555 |
| 95,800 | 95,850 | 17,019 | 12,579 | 17,019 | 15,567 |
| 95,850 | 95,900 | 17,031 | 12,590 | 17,031 | 15,579 |
| 95,900 | 95,950 | 17,043 | 12,601 | 17,043 | 15,591 |
| 95,950 | 96,000 | 17,055 | 12,612 | 17,055 | 15,603 |

| If line 15 (taxable income) is— | | And you are— | | | |
|---|---|---|---|---|---|
| At least | But less than | Single | Married filing jointly * | Married filing separately | Head of a household |
| | | | Your tax is— | | |

## 96,000

| At least | But less than | Single | Married filing jointly * | Married filing separately | Head of a household |
|---|---|---|---|---|---|
| 96,000 | 96,050 | 17,067 | 12,623 | 17,067 | 15,615 |
| 96,050 | 96,100 | 17,079 | 12,634 | 17,079 | 15,627 |
| 96,100 | 96,150 | 17,091 | 12,645 | 17,091 | 15,639 |
| 96,150 | 96,200 | 17,103 | 12,656 | 17,103 | 15,651 |
| 96,200 | 96,250 | 17,115 | 12,667 | 17,115 | 15,663 |
| 96,250 | 96,300 | 17,127 | 12,678 | 17,127 | 15,675 |
| 96,300 | 96,350 | 17,139 | 12,689 | 17,139 | 15,687 |
| 96,350 | 96,400 | 17,151 | 12,700 | 17,151 | 15,699 |
| 96,400 | 96,450 | 17,163 | 12,711 | 17,163 | 15,711 |
| 96,450 | 96,500 | 17,175 | 12,722 | 17,175 | 15,723 |
| 96,500 | 96,550 | 17,187 | 12,733 | 17,187 | 15,735 |
| 96,550 | 96,600 | 17,199 | 12,744 | 17,199 | 15,747 |
| 96,600 | 96,650 | 17,211 | 12,755 | 17,211 | 15,759 |
| 96,650 | 96,700 | 17,223 | 12,766 | 17,223 | 15,771 |
| 96,700 | 96,750 | 17,235 | 12,777 | 17,235 | 15,783 |
| 96,750 | 96,800 | 17,247 | 12,788 | 17,247 | 15,795 |
| 96,800 | 96,850 | 17,259 | 12,799 | 17,259 | 15,807 |
| 96,850 | 96,900 | 17,271 | 12,810 | 17,271 | 15,819 |
| 96,900 | 96,950 | 17,283 | 12,821 | 17,283 | 15,831 |
| 96,950 | 97,000 | 17,295 | 12,832 | 17,295 | 15,843 |

## 97,000

| At least | But less than | Single | Married filing jointly * | Married filing separately | Head of a household |
|---|---|---|---|---|---|
| 97,000 | 97,050 | 17,307 | 12,843 | 17,307 | 15,855 |
| 97,050 | 97,100 | 17,319 | 12,854 | 17,319 | 15,867 |
| 97,100 | 97,150 | 17,331 | 12,865 | 17,331 | 15,879 |
| 97,150 | 97,200 | 17,343 | 12,876 | 17,343 | 15,891 |
| 97,200 | 97,250 | 17,355 | 12,887 | 17,355 | 15,903 |
| 97,250 | 97,300 | 17,367 | 12,898 | 17,367 | 15,915 |
| 97,300 | 97,350 | 17,379 | 12,909 | 17,379 | 15,927 |
| 97,350 | 97,400 | 17,391 | 12,920 | 17,391 | 15,939 |
| 97,400 | 97,450 | 17,403 | 12,931 | 17,403 | 15,951 |
| 97,450 | 97,500 | 17,415 | 12,942 | 17,415 | 15,963 |
| 97,500 | 97,550 | 17,427 | 12,953 | 17,427 | 15,975 |
| 97,550 | 97,600 | 17,439 | 12,964 | 17,439 | 15,987 |
| 97,600 | 97,650 | 17,451 | 12,975 | 17,451 | 15,999 |
| 97,650 | 97,700 | 17,463 | 12,986 | 17,463 | 16,011 |
| 97,700 | 97,750 | 17,475 | 12,997 | 17,475 | 16,023 |
| 97,750 | 97,800 | 17,487 | 13,008 | 17,487 | 16,035 |
| 97,800 | 97,850 | 17,499 | 13,019 | 17,499 | 16,047 |
| 97,850 | 97,900 | 17,511 | 13,030 | 17,511 | 16,059 |
| 97,900 | 97,950 | 17,523 | 13,041 | 17,523 | 16,071 |
| 97,950 | 98,000 | 17,535 | 13,052 | 17,535 | 16,083 |

## 98,000

| At least | But less than | Single | Married filing jointly * | Married filing separately | Head of a household |
|---|---|---|---|---|---|
| 98,000 | 98,050 | 17,547 | 13,063 | 17,547 | 16,095 |
| 98,050 | 98,100 | 17,559 | 13,074 | 17,559 | 16,107 |
| 98,100 | 98,150 | 17,571 | 13,085 | 17,571 | 16,119 |
| 98,150 | 98,200 | 17,583 | 13,096 | 17,583 | 16,131 |
| 98,200 | 98,250 | 17,595 | 13,107 | 17,595 | 16,143 |
| 98,250 | 98,300 | 17,607 | 13,118 | 17,607 | 16,155 |
| 98,300 | 98,350 | 17,619 | 13,129 | 17,619 | 16,167 |
| 98,350 | 98,400 | 17,631 | 13,140 | 17,631 | 16,179 |
| 98,400 | 98,450 | 17,643 | 13,151 | 17,643 | 16,191 |
| 98,450 | 98,500 | 17,655 | 13,162 | 17,655 | 16,203 |
| 98,500 | 98,550 | 17,667 | 13,173 | 17,667 | 16,215 |
| 98,550 | 98,600 | 17,679 | 13,184 | 17,679 | 16,227 |
| 98,600 | 98,650 | 17,691 | 13,195 | 17,691 | 16,239 |
| 98,650 | 98,700 | 17,703 | 13,206 | 17,703 | 16,251 |
| 98,700 | 98,750 | 17,715 | 13,217 | 17,715 | 16,263 |
| 98,750 | 98,800 | 17,727 | 13,228 | 17,727 | 16,275 |
| 98,800 | 98,850 | 17,739 | 13,239 | 17,739 | 16,287 |
| 98,850 | 98,900 | 17,751 | 13,250 | 17,751 | 16,299 |
| 98,900 | 98,950 | 17,763 | 13,261 | 17,763 | 16,311 |
| 98,950 | 99,000 | 17,775 | 13,272 | 17,775 | 16,323 |

| If line 15 (taxable income) is— | | And you are— | | | |
|---|---|---|---|---|---|
| At least | But less than | Single | Married filing jointly * | Married filing separately | Head of a household |
| | | | Your tax is— | | |

## 99,000

| At least | But less than | Single | Married filing jointly * | Married filing separately | Head of a household |
|---|---|---|---|---|---|
| 99,000 | 99,050 | 17,787 | 13,283 | 17,787 | 16,335 |
| 99,050 | 99,100 | 17,799 | 13,294 | 17,799 | 16,347 |
| 99,100 | 99,150 | 17,811 | 13,305 | 17,811 | 16,359 |
| 99,150 | 99,200 | 17,823 | 13,316 | 17,823 | 16,371 |
| 99,200 | 99,250 | 17,835 | 13,327 | 17,835 | 16,383 |
| 99,250 | 99,300 | 17,847 | 13,338 | 17,847 | 16,395 |
| 99,300 | 99,350 | 17,859 | 13,349 | 17,859 | 16,407 |
| 99,350 | 99,400 | 17,871 | 13,360 | 17,871 | 16,419 |
| 99,400 | 99,450 | 17,883 | 13,371 | 17,883 | 16,431 |
| 99,450 | 99,500 | 17,895 | 13,382 | 17,895 | 16,443 |
| 99,500 | 99,550 | 17,907 | 13,393 | 17,907 | 16,455 |
| 99,550 | 99,600 | 17,919 | 13,404 | 17,919 | 16,467 |
| 99,600 | 99,650 | 17,931 | 13,415 | 17,931 | 16,479 |
| 99,650 | 99,700 | 17,943 | 13,426 | 17,943 | 16,491 |
| 99,700 | 99,750 | 17,955 | 13,437 | 17,955 | 16,503 |
| 99,750 | 99,800 | 17,967 | 13,448 | 17,967 | 16,515 |
| 99,800 | 99,850 | 17,979 | 13,459 | 17,979 | 16,527 |
| 99,850 | 99,900 | 17,991 | 13,470 | 17,991 | 16,539 |
| 99,900 | 99,950 | 18,003 | 13,481 | 18,003 | 16,551 |
| 99,950 | 100,000 | 18,015 | 13,492 | 18,015 | 16,563 |

**$100,000 or over use the Tax Computation Worksheet**

# Appendix E

# IRS Tax Forms

Included in this Appendix are copies of select IRS tax forms that are used throughout *Fundamentals of Taxation*. All of these forms are also available for download from the IRS website: www.irs.gov.

Form **1040**
Department of the Treasury—Internal Revenue Service (99)
**U.S. Individual Income Tax Return** 2021 OMB No. 1545-0074 | IRS Use Only—Do not write or staple in this space.

**Filing Status**
Check only one box.
☐ Single ☐ Married filing jointly ☐ Married filing separately (MFS) ☐ Head of household (HOH) ☐ Qualifying widow(er) (QW)

If you checked the MFS box, enter the name of your spouse. If you checked the HOH or QW box, enter the child's name if the qualifying person is a child but not your dependent ▶

| Your first name and middle initial | Last name | Your social security number |
|---|---|---|
| If joint return, spouse's first name and middle initial | Last name | Spouse's social security number |

Home address (number and street). If you have a P.O. box, see instructions. | Apt. no.

City, town, or post office. If you have a foreign address, also complete spaces below. | State | ZIP code

Foreign country name | Foreign province/state/county | Foreign postal code

**Presidential Election Campaign**
Check here if you, or your spouse if filing jointly, want $3 to go to this fund. Checking a box below will not change your tax or refund.
☐ You ☐ Spouse

At any time during 2021, did you receive, sell, exchange, or otherwise dispose of any financial interest in any virtual currency? ☐ Yes ☐ No

**Standard Deduction**
Someone can claim: ☐ You as a dependent ☐ Your spouse as a dependent
☐ Spouse itemizes on a separate return or you were a dual-status alien

**Age/Blindness** You: ☐ Were born before January 2, 1957 ☐ Are blind **Spouse:** ☐ Was born before January 2, 1957 ☐ Is blind

**Dependents** (see instructions):
If more than four dependents, see instructions and check here ▶ ☐

| (1) First name    Last name | (2) Social security number | (3) Relationship to you | (4) ✔ if qualifies for (see instructions): Child tax credit | Credit for other dependents |
|---|---|---|---|---|
| | | | ☐ | ☐ |
| | | | ☐ | ☐ |
| | | | ☐ | ☐ |
| | | | ☐ | ☐ |

Attach Sch. B if required.

**Standard Deduction for—**
• Single or Married filing separately, $12,550
• Married filing jointly or Qualifying widow(er), $25,100
• Head of household, $18,800
• If you checked any box under *Standard Deduction,* see instructions.

| | | | |
|---|---|---|---|
| 1 | Wages, salaries, tips, etc. Attach Form(s) W-2 | | 1 |
| 2a | Tax-exempt interest . . . 2a | **b** Taxable interest . . . . . | 2b |
| 3a | Qualified dividends . . . 3a | **b** Ordinary dividends . . . . | 3b |
| 4a | IRA distributions . . . . 4a | **b** Taxable amount . . . . . | 4b |
| 5a | Pensions and annuities . . 5a | **b** Taxable amount . . . . . | 5b |
| 6a | Social security benefits . . 6a | **b** Taxable amount . . . . . | 6b |
| 7 | Capital gain or (loss). Attach Schedule D if required. If not required, check here . . . ▶ ☐ | | 7 |
| 8 | Other income from Schedule 1, line 10 . . . . . . . . . . . . . . . | | 8 |
| 9 | Add lines 1, 2b, 3b, 4b, 5b, 6b, 7, and 8. This is your **total income** . . . . . ▶ | | 9 |
| 10 | Adjustments to income from Schedule 1, line 26 . . . . . . . . . . . . | | 10 |
| 11 | Subtract line 10 from line 9. This is your **adjusted gross income** . . . . . . . ▶ | | 11 |
| 12a | **Standard deduction or itemized deductions** (from Schedule A) . . . 12a | | |
| b | Charitable contributions if you take the standard deduction (see instructions) 12b | | |
| c | Add lines 12a and 12b . . . . . . . . . . . . . . . . . . . | | 12c |
| 13 | Qualified business income deduction from Form 8995 or Form 8995-A . . . . . | | 13 |
| 14 | Add lines 12c and 13 . . . . . . . . . . . . . . . . . . . . | | 14 |
| 15 | **Taxable income.** Subtract line 14 from line 11. If zero or less, enter -0- . . . . . . | | 15 |

For Disclosure, Privacy Act, and Paperwork Reduction Act Notice, see separate instructions. | Cat. No. 11320B | Form **1040** (2021)

Source: U.S. Department of the Treasury, Internal Revenue Service, Form 1040. Washington, DC: 2021.

Form 1040 (2021)                                                                 Page **2**

| | | | | |
|---|---|---|---|---|
| 16 | **Tax** (see instructions). Check if any from Form(s): **1** ☐ 8814 **2** ☐ 4972 **3** ☐ _____ | | 16 | |
| 17 | Amount from Schedule 2, line 3 | | 17 | |
| 18 | Add lines 16 and 17 | | 18 | |
| 19 | Nonrefundable child tax credit or credit for other dependents from Schedule 8812 | | 19 | |
| 20 | Amount from Schedule 3, line 8 | | 20 | |
| 21 | Add lines 19 and 20 | | 21 | |
| 22 | Subtract line 21 from line 18. If zero or less, enter -0- | | 22 | |
| 23 | Other taxes, including self-employment tax, from Schedule 2, line 21 | | 23 | |
| 24 | Add lines 22 and 23. This is your **total tax** ▶ | | 24 | |

| | | | |
|---|---|---|---|
| 25 | Federal income tax withheld from: | | |
| a | Form(s) W-2 | 25a | |
| b | Form(s) 1099 | 25b | |
| c | Other forms (see instructions) | 25c | |
| d | Add lines 25a through 25c | | 25d |

*If you have a qualifying child, attach Sch. EIC.*

| | | | | |
|---|---|---|---|---|
| 26 | 2021 estimated tax payments and amount applied from 2020 return | | 26 | |
| 27a | Earned income credit (EIC) | 27a | | |
| | Check here if you had not reached the age of 19 by December 31, 2021, and satisfy all other requirements for claiming the EIC. See instructions ▶ ☐ | | | |
| b | Nontaxable combat pay election | 27b | | |
| c | Prior year (2019) earned income | 27c | | |
| 28 | Refundable child tax credit or additional child tax credit from Schedule 8812 | 28 | | |
| 29 | American opportunity credit from Form 8863, line 8 | 29 | | |
| 30 | Recovery rebate credit. See instructions | 30 | | |
| 31 | Amount from Schedule 3, line 15 | 31 | | |
| 32 | Add lines 27a and 28 through 31. These are your **total other payments and refundable credits** ▶ | | 32 | |
| 33 | Add lines 25d, 26, and 32. These are your **total payments** ▶ | | 33 | |

**Refund**

Direct deposit?
See instructions.

| | | | |
|---|---|---|---|
| 34 | If line 33 is more than line 24, subtract line 24 from line 33. This is the amount you **overpaid** | 34 | |
| 35a | Amount of line 34 you want **refunded to you.** If Form 8888 is attached, check here ▶ ☐ | 35a | |
| ▶ b | Routing number _____ ▶ c Type: ☐ Checking ☐ Savings | | |
| ▶ d | Account number _____ | | |
| 36 | Amount of line 34 you want **applied to your 2022 estimated tax** ▶ 36 | | |

**Amount You Owe**

| | | | |
|---|---|---|---|
| 37 | **Amount you owe.** Subtract line 33 from line 24. For details on how to pay, see instructions ▶ | 37 | |
| 38 | Estimated tax penalty (see instructions) ▶ 38 | | |

**Third Party Designee**

Do you want to allow another person to discuss this return with the IRS? See instructions ▶ ☐ **Yes.** Complete below.  ☐ **No**

| Designee's name ▶ | Phone no. ▶ | Personal identification number (PIN) ▶ | |
|---|---|---|---|

**Sign Here**

Joint return?
See instructions.
Keep a copy for your records.

Under penalties of perjury, I declare that I have examined this return and accompanying schedules and statements, and to the best of my knowledge and belief, they are true, correct, and complete. Declaration of preparer (other than taxpayer) is based on all information of which preparer has any knowledge.

| Your signature | Date | Your occupation | If the IRS sent you an Identity Protection PIN, enter it here (see inst.) ▶ |
|---|---|---|---|
| Spouse's signature. If a joint return, **both** must sign. | Date | Spouse's occupation | If the IRS sent your spouse an Identity Protection PIN, enter it here (see inst.) ▶ |
| Phone no. | | Email address | |

**Paid Preparer Use Only**

| Preparer's name | Preparer's signature | Date | PTIN | Check if: ☐ Self-employed |
|---|---|---|---|---|
| Firm's name ▶ | | | Phone no. | |
| Firm's address ▶ | | | Firm's EIN ▶ | |

Go to *www.irs.gov/Form1040* for instructions and the latest information.                    Form **1040** (2021)

| SCHEDULE 1<br>(Form 1040)<br><br>Department of the Treasury<br>Internal Revenue Service | **Additional Income and Adjustments to Income**<br>▶ Attach to Form 1040, 1040-SR, or 1040-NR.<br>▶ Go to *www.irs.gov/Form1040* for instructions and the latest information. | OMB No. 1545-0074<br>**2021**<br>Attachment<br>Sequence No. **01** |
|---|---|---|
| Name(s) shown on Form 1040, 1040-SR, or 1040-NR | | **Your social security number** |

### Part I    Additional Income

| | | | |
|---|---|---|---|
| 1 | Taxable refunds, credits, or offsets of state and local income taxes . . . . . . | **1** | |
| 2a | Alimony received . . . . . . . . . . . . . . . . . . . | **2a** | |
| b | Date of original divorce or separation agreement (see instructions) ▶ _____ | | |
| 3 | Business income or (loss). Attach Schedule C . . . . . . . . . . | **3** | |
| 4 | Other gains or (losses). Attach Form 4797 . . . . . . . . . . . | **4** | |
| 5 | Rental real estate, royalties, partnerships, S corporations, trusts, etc. Attach Schedule E . . . . . . . . . . . . . . . . . . . . | **5** | |
| 6 | Farm income or (loss). Attach Schedule F . . . . . . . . . . . | **6** | |
| 7 | Unemployment compensation . . . . . . . . . . . . . . . | **7** | |
| 8 | Other income: | | |
| a | Net operating loss . . . . . . . . . | **8a** ( ) | |
| b | Gambling income . . . . . . . . . . | **8b** | |
| c | Cancellation of debt . . . . . . . . . | **8c** | |
| d | Foreign earned income exclusion from Form 2555 . . . . . | **8d** ( ) | |
| e | Taxable Health Savings Account distribution . . . . . . . | **8e** | |
| f | Alaska Permanent Fund dividends . . . . . . . . . | **8f** | |
| g | Jury duty pay . . . . . . . . . . . | **8g** | |
| h | Prizes and awards . . . . . . . . . | **8h** | |
| i | Activity not engaged in for profit income . . . . . . . | **8i** | |
| j | Stock options . . . . . . . . . . . | **8j** | |
| k | Income from the rental of personal property if you engaged in the rental for profit but were not in the business of renting such property . . . . . . . . . . | **8k** | |
| l | Olympic and Paralympic medals and USOC prize money (see instructions) . . . . . . . . . | **8l** | |
| m | Section 951(a) inclusion (see instructions) . . . . . . . | **8m** | |
| n | Section 951A(a) inclusion (see instructions) . . . . . . . | **8n** | |
| o | Section 461(l) excess business loss adjustment . . . . . . | **8o** | |
| p | Taxable distributions from an ABLE account (see instructions) . | **8p** | |
| z | Other income. List type and amount ▶ _____ _____ | **8z** | |
| 9 | Total other income. Add lines 8a through 8z . . . . . . . . . . | **9** | |
| 10 | Combine lines 1 through 7 and 9. Enter here and on Form 1040, 1040-SR, or 1040-NR, line 8 . . . . . . . . . . . . . . . . . . | **10** | |

For Paperwork Reduction Act Notice, see your tax return instructions.          Cat. No. 71479F          Schedule 1 (Form 1040) 2021

Schedule 1 (Form 1040) 2021 | Page **2**

## Part II    Adjustments to Income

| | | |
|---|---|---|
| **11** | Educator expenses . . . . . . . . . . . . . . . . . . . . | **11** |
| **12** | Certain business expenses of reservists, performing artists, and fee-basis government officials. Attach Form 2106 . . . . . . . . . . | **12** |
| **13** | Health savings account deduction. Attach Form 8889 . . . . . . . . . | **13** |
| **14** | Moving expenses for members of the Armed Forces. Attach Form 3903 . . . . | **14** |
| **15** | Deductible part of self-employment tax. Attach Schedule SE . . . . . . . | **15** |
| **16** | Self-employed SEP, SIMPLE, and qualified plans . . . . . . . . . . | **16** |
| **17** | Self-employed health insurance deduction . . . . . . . . . . . . | **17** |
| **18** | Penalty on early withdrawal of savings . . . . . . . . . . . . . | **18** |
| **19a** | Alimony paid . . . . . . . . . . . . . . . . . . . . . | **19a** |
| **b** | Recipient's SSN . . . . . . . . . . . . . . . . . ▶ | |
| **c** | Date of original divorce or separation agreement (see instructions) ▶ | |
| **20** | IRA deduction . . . . . . . . . . . . . . . . . . . . | **20** |
| **21** | Student loan interest deduction . . . . . . . . . . . . . . . | **21** |
| **22** | Reserved for future use . . . . . . . . . . . . . . . . . | **22** |
| **23** | Archer MSA deduction . . . . . . . . . . . . . . . . . . | **23** |
| **24** | Other adjustments: | |

| | | | |
|---|---|---|---|
| **a** | Jury duty pay (see instructions) . . . . . . . . . . . | **24a** | |
| **b** | Deductible expenses related to income reported on line 8k from the rental of personal property engaged in for profit . . . . . | **24b** | |
| **c** | Nontaxable amount of the value of Olympic and Paralympic medals and USOC prize money reported on line 8l . . . . . | **24c** | |
| **d** | Reforestation amortization and expenses . . . . . . . . | **24d** | |
| **e** | Repayment of supplemental unemployment benefits under the Trade Act of 1974 . . . . . . . . . . . . . . | **24e** | |
| **f** | Contributions to section 501(c)(18)(D) pension plans . . . . . | **24f** | |
| **g** | Contributions by certain chaplains to section 403(b) plans . . | **24g** | |
| **h** | Attorney fees and court costs for actions involving certain unlawful discrimination claims (see instructions) . . . . . | **24h** | |
| **i** | Attorney fees and court costs you paid in connection with an award from the IRS for information you provided that helped the IRS detect tax law violations . . . . . . . . . . . . | **24i** | |
| **j** | Housing deduction from Form 2555 . . . . . . . . . | **24j** | |
| **k** | Excess deductions of section 67(e) expenses from Schedule K-1 (Form 1041) . . . . . . . . . . . . . . . . | **24k** | |
| **z** | Other adjustments. List type and amount ▶ _____ | **24z** | |

| | | |
|---|---|---|
| **25** | Total other adjustments. Add lines 24a through 24z . . . . . . . . . | **25** |
| **26** | Add lines 11 through 23 and 25. These are your **adjustments to income.** Enter here and on Form 1040 or 1040-SR, line 10, or Form 1040-NR, line 10a . . . . . | **26** |

Schedule 1 (Form 1040) 2021

**SCHEDULE 2**
**(Form 1040)**

Department of the Treasury
Internal Revenue Service

**Additional Taxes**

▶ Attach to Form 1040, 1040-SR, or 1040-NR.
▶ Go to *www.irs.gov/Form1040* for instructions and the latest information.

OMB No. 1545-0074

2021

Attachment
Sequence No. 02

Name(s) shown on Form 1040, 1040-SR, or 1040-NR

Your social security number

## Part I   Tax

| | | |
|---|---|---|
| 1 | Alternative minimum tax. Attach Form 6251 | 1 |
| 2 | Excess advance premium tax credit repayment. Attach Form 8962 | 2 |
| 3 | Add lines 1 and 2. Enter here and on Form 1040, 1040-SR, or 1040-NR, line 17 | 3 |

## Part II   Other Taxes

| | | |
|---|---|---|
| 4 | Self-employment tax. Attach Schedule SE | 4 |
| 5 | Social security and Medicare tax on unreported tip income. Attach Form 4137 | 5 |
| 6 | Uncollected social security and Medicare tax on wages. Attach Form 8919 | 6 |
| 7 | Total additional social security and Medicare tax. Add lines 5 and 6 | 7 |
| 8 | Additional tax on IRAs or other tax-favored accounts. Attach Form 5329 if required | 8 |
| 9 | Household employment taxes. Attach Schedule H | 9 |
| 10 | Repayment of first-time homebuyer credit. Attach Form 5405 if required | 10 |
| 11 | Additional Medicare Tax. Attach Form 8959 | 11 |
| 12 | Net investment income tax. Attach Form 8960 | 12 |
| 13 | Uncollected social security and Medicare or RRTA tax on tips or group-term life insurance from Form W-2, box 12 | 13 |
| 14 | Interest on tax due on installment income from the sale of certain residential lots and timeshares | 14 |
| 15 | Interest on the deferred tax on gain from certain installment sales with a sales price over $150,000 | 15 |
| 16 | Recapture of low-income housing credit. Attach Form 8611 | 16 |

*(continued on page 2)*

For Paperwork Reduction Act Notice, see your tax return instructions.   Cat. No. 71478U   Schedule 2 (Form 1040) 2021

Schedule 2 (Form 1040) 2021

Page **2**

## Part II   Other Taxes *(continued)*

| | | | |
|---|---|---|---|
| **17** | Other additional taxes: | | |
| **a** | Recapture of other credits. List type, form number, and amount ▶ _____ | **17a** | |
| **b** | Recapture of federal mortgage subsidy. If you sold your home in 2021, see instructions . . . . . . . . . . . | **17b** | |
| **c** | Additional tax on HSA distributions. Attach Form 8889 . . . | **17c** | |
| **d** | Additional tax on an HSA because you didn't remain an eligible individual. Attach Form 8889 . . . . . . . . . . | **17d** | |
| **e** | Additional tax on Archer MSA distributions. Attach Form 8853 . | **17e** | |
| **f** | Additional tax on Medicare Advantage MSA distributions. Attach Form 8853 . . . . . . . . . . . . . . | **17f** | |
| **g** | Recapture of a charitable contribution deduction related to a fractional interest in tangible personal property . . . . | **17g** | |
| **h** | Income you received from a nonqualified deferred compensation plan that fails to meet the requirements of section 409A . . . | **17h** | |
| **i** | Compensation you received from a nonqualified deferred compensation plan described in section 457A . . . . . . | **17i** | |
| **j** | Section 72(m)(5) excess benefits tax . . . . . . . . . | **17j** | |
| **k** | Golden parachute payments . . . . . . . . . . | **17k** | |
| **l** | Tax on accumulation distribution of trusts . . . . . . . | **17l** | |
| **m** | Excise tax on insider stock compensation from an expatriated corporation . . . . . . . . . . . . . . . . | **17m** | |
| **n** | Look-back interest under section 167(g) or 460(b) from Form 8697 or 8866 . . . . . . . . . . . . . . . | **17n** | |
| **o** | Tax on non-effectively connected income for any part of the year you were a nonresident alien from Form 1040-NR . . . . | **17o** | |
| **p** | Any interest from Form 8621, line 16f, relating to distributions from, and dispositions of, stock of a section 1291 fund . . . . | **17p** | |
| **q** | Any interest from Form 8621, line 24 . . . . . . . . . | **17q** | |
| **z** | Any other taxes. List type and amount ▶ _____ | **17z** | |
| **18** | Total additional taxes. Add lines 17a through 17z . . . . . . . . . . . . . . | **18** | |
| **19** | Additional tax from Schedule 8812 . . . . . . . . . . . . . . . . . . | **19** | |
| **20** | Section 965 net tax liability installment from Form 965-A . . . | **20** | |
| **21** | Add lines 4, 7 through 16, 18, and 19. These are your **total other taxes.** Enter here and on Form 1040 or 1040-SR, line 23, or Form 1040-NR, line 23b . . . . . . . | **21** | |

Schedule 2 (Form 1040) 2021

| SCHEDULE 3 (Form 1040) | Additional Credits and Payments | OMB No. 1545-0074 |
|---|---|---|
| Department of the Treasury<br>Internal Revenue Service | ▶ Attach to Form 1040, 1040-SR, or 1040-NR.<br>▶ Go to *www.irs.gov/Form1040* for instructions and the latest information. | 2021<br>Attachment<br>Sequence No. 03 |

Name(s) shown on Form 1040, 1040-SR, or 1040-NR | Your social security number

### Part I   Nonrefundable Credits

| | | |
|---|---|---|
| 1 | Foreign tax credit. Attach Form 1116 if required . . . . . . . | 1 |
| 2 | Credit for child and dependent care expenses from Form 2441, line 11. Attach Form 2441 | 2 |
| 3 | Education credits from Form 8863, line 19 . . . . . . . | 3 |
| 4 | Retirement savings contributions credit. Attach Form 8880 . . | 4 |
| 5 | Residential energy credits. Attach Form 5695 . . . . . . | 5 |
| 6 | Other nonrefundable credits: | |
| a | General business credit. Attach Form 3800 . . . . . | 6a |
| b | Credit for prior year minimum tax. Attach Form 8801 . . . | 6b |
| c | Adoption credit. Attach Form 8839 . . . . . . . . | 6c |
| d | Credit for the elderly or disabled. Attach Schedule R . . . . | 6d |
| e | Alternative motor vehicle credit. Attach Form 8910 . . . . | 6e |
| f | Qualified plug-in motor vehicle credit. Attach Form 8936 . . . | 6f |
| g | Mortgage interest credit. Attach Form 8396 . . . . . . | 6g |
| h | District of Columbia first-time homebuyer credit. Attach Form 8859 | 6h |
| i | Qualified electric vehicle credit. Attach Form 8834 . . . . . | 6i |
| j | Alternative fuel vehicle refueling property credit. Attach Form 8911 | 6j |
| k | Credit to holders of tax credit bonds. Attach Form 8912 . . . | 6k |
| l | Amount on Form 8978, line 14. See instructions . . . . . | 6l |
| z | Other nonrefundable credits. List type and amount ▶ _____ | 6z |
| 7 | Total other nonrefundable credits. Add lines 6a through 6z . . . . . . . . . | 7 |
| 8 | Add lines 1 through 5 and 7. Enter here and on Form 1040, 1040-SR, or 1040-NR, line 20 . . . . . . . . . . . . . . . . . . . . . . . . | 8 |

*(continued on page 2)*

For Paperwork Reduction Act Notice, see your tax return instructions. | Cat. No. 71480G | Schedule 3 (Form 1040) 2021

---

Schedule 3 (Form 1040) 2021 | | Page **2**

### Part II   Other Payments and Refundable Credits

| | | |
|---|---|---|
| 9 | Net premium tax credit. Attach Form 8962 . . . . . . | 9 |
| 10 | Amount paid with request for extension to file (see instructions) . . . . . . . | 10 |
| 11 | Excess social security and tier 1 RRTA tax withheld . . . . . . . . . | 11 |
| 12 | Credit for federal tax on fuels. Attach Form 4136 . . . . . . . | 12 |
| 13 | Other payments or refundable credits: | |
| a | Form 2439 . . . . . . . . . . . . | 13a |
| b | Qualified sick and family leave credits from Schedule(s) H and Form(s) 7202 for leave taken before April 1, 2021 . . . . | 13b |
| c | Health coverage tax credit from Form 8885 . . . . | 13c |
| d | Credit for repayment of amounts included in income from earlier years . . . . . . . . . . . . | 13d |
| e | Reserved for future use . . . . . . . . . | 13e |
| f | Net section 965 inclusions . . . . . . . . | 13f |
| g | Credit for child and dependent care expenses from Form 2441, line 10. Attach Form 2441 . . . . . . . . . . | 13g |
| h | Qualified sick and family leave credits from Schedule(s) H and Form(s) 7202 for leave taken after March 31, 2021 . . . . . | 13h |
| z | Other payments or refundable credits. List type and amount ▶ _____ | 13z |
| 14 | Total other payments or refundable credits. Add lines 13a through 13z . . . . . | 14 |
| 15 | Add lines 9 through 12 and 14. Enter here and on Form 1040, 1040-SR, or 1040-NR, line 31 . . . . . . . . . . . . . . . . . . . . . . | 15 |

Schedule 3 (Form 1040) 2021

| SCHEDULE A<br>(Form 1040)<br><br>Department of the Treasury<br>Internal Revenue Service (99) | **Itemized Deductions**<br>► Go to *www.irs.gov/ScheduleA* for instructions and the latest information.<br>► Attach to Form 1040 or 1040-SR.<br>**Caution:** If you are claiming a net qualified disaster loss on Form 4684, see the instructions for line 16. | OMB No. 1545-0074<br><br>2021<br><br>Attachment<br>Sequence No. **07** |
|---|---|---|

Name(s) shown on Form 1040 or 1040-SR | Your social security number

| **Medical and Dental Expenses** | | **Caution:** Do not include expenses reimbursed or paid by others. | |
|---|---|---|---|
| | 1 | Medical and dental expenses (see instructions) . . . . . . | 1 |
| | 2 | Enter amount from Form 1040 or 1040-SR, line 11 ☐ 2 | |
| | 3 | Multiply line 2 by 7.5% (0.075) . . . . . . . . . . | 3 |
| | 4 | Subtract line 3 from line 1. If line 3 is more than line 1, enter -0- . . . . . . . . . | 4 |
| **Taxes You Paid** | 5 | State and local taxes. | |
| | a | State and local income taxes or general sales taxes. You may include either income taxes or general sales taxes on line 5a, but not both. If you elect to include general sales taxes instead of income taxes, check this box . . . . . . . . . . . . . . . . ► ☐ | 5a |
| | b | State and local real estate taxes (see instructions) . . . . . . | 5b |
| | c | State and local personal property taxes . . . . . . . . | 5c |
| | d | Add lines 5a through 5c . . . . . . . . . . . . . | 5d |
| | e | Enter the smaller of line 5d or $10,000 ($5,000 if married filing separately) . . . . . . . . . . . . . . . . . . | 5e |
| | 6 | Other taxes. List type and amount ► _____ | 6 |
| | 7 | Add lines 5e and 6 . . . . . . . . . . . . . . . | 7 |
| **Interest You Paid**<br><br>**Caution:** Your mortgage interest deduction may be limited (see instructions). | 8 | Home mortgage interest and points. If you didn't use all of your home mortgage loan(s) to buy, build, or improve your home, see instructions and check this box . . . . . . . . . . ► ☐ | |
| | a | Home mortgage interest and points reported to you on Form 1098. See instructions if limited . . . . . . . . . . . . | 8a |
| | b | Home mortgage interest not reported to you on Form 1098. See instructions if limited. If paid to the person from whom you bought the home, see instructions and show that person's name, identifying no., and address . . . . . . . . . . . . . . . . . .<br>► _____ | 8b |
| | c | Points not reported to you on Form 1098. See instructions for special rules . . . . . . . . . . . . . . . . . . . | 8c |
| | d | Mortgage insurance premiums (see instructions) . . . . . . | 8d |
| | e | Add lines 8a through 8d . . . . . . . . . . . . . | 8e |
| | 9 | Investment interest. Attach Form 4952 if required. See instructions . | 9 |
| | 10 | Add lines 8e and 9 . . . . . . . . . . . . . . . | 10 |
| **Gifts to Charity**<br><br>**Caution:** If you made a gift and got a benefit for it, see instructions. | 11 | Gifts by cash or check. If you made any gift of $250 or more, see instructions . . . . . . . . . . . . . . . . | 11 |
| | 12 | Other than by cash or check. If you made any gift of $250 or more, see instructions. You **must** attach Form 8283 if over $500. . . . | 12 |
| | 13 | Carryover from prior year . . . . . . . . . . . . . | 13 |
| | 14 | Add lines 11 through 13 . . . . . . . . . . . . . | 14 |
| **Casualty and Theft Losses** | 15 | Casualty and theft loss(es) from a federally declared disaster (other than net qualified disaster losses). Attach Form 4684 and enter the amount from line 18 of that form. See instructions . . . . . . . . . . . | 15 |
| **Other Itemized Deductions** | 16 | Other—from list in instructions. List type and amount ► _____ _____ | 16 |
| **Total Itemized Deductions** | 17 | Add the amounts in the far right column for lines 4 through 16. Also, enter this amount on Form 1040 or 1040-SR, line 12a . . . . . . . . . . | 17 |
| | 18 | If you elect to itemize deductions even though they are less than your standard deduction, check this box . . . . . . . . . . . . . . . . . ► ☐ | |

For Paperwork Reduction Act Notice, see the Instructions for Forms 1040 and 1040-SR. | Cat. No. 17145C | **Schedule A (Form 1040) 2021**

| SCHEDULE B<br>(Form 1040)<br><br>Department of the Treasury<br>Internal Revenue Service (99) | **Interest and Ordinary Dividends**<br><br>▶ Go to *www.irs.gov/ScheduleB* for instructions and the latest information.<br>▶ Attach to Form 1040 or 1040-SR. | OMB No. 1545-0074<br><br>**2021**<br>Attachment<br>Sequence No. **08** |
|---|---|---|

Name(s) shown on return | Your social security number

### Part I

**Interest**

(See instructions and the instructions for Forms 1040 and 1040-SR, line 2b.)

**Note:** If you received a Form 1099-INT, Form 1099-OID, or substitute statement from a brokerage firm, list the firm's name as the payer and enter the total interest shown on that form.

| | | | **Amount** |
|---|---|---|---|
| **1** | List name of payer. If any interest is from a seller-financed mortgage and the buyer used the property as a personal residence, see the instructions and list this interest first. Also, show that buyer's social security number and address ▶ | **1** | |
| **2** | Add the amounts on line 1 . . . . . . . . . . . . . . . . | **2** | |
| **3** | Excludable interest on series EE and I U.S. savings bonds issued after 1989. Attach Form 8815 . . . . . . . . . . . . . . . . . | **3** | |
| **4** | Subtract line 3 from line 2. Enter the result here and on Form 1040 or 1040-SR, line 2b . . . . . . . . . . . . . . . . . . . . . ▶ | **4** | |

**Note:** If line 4 is over $1,500, you must complete Part III.

### Part II

**Ordinary Dividends**

(See instructions and the instructions for Forms 1040 and 1040-SR, line 3b.)

**Note:** If you received a Form 1099-DIV or substitute statement from a brokerage firm, list the firm's name as the payer and enter the ordinary dividends shown on that form.

| | | | **Amount** |
|---|---|---|---|
| **5** | List name of payer ▶ | **5** | |
| **6** | Add the amounts on line 5. Enter the total here and on Form 1040 or 1040-SR, line 3b . . . . . . . . . . . . . . . . . . . . . ▶ | **6** | |

**Note:** If line 6 is over $1,500, you must complete Part III.

### Part III

**Foreign Accounts and Trusts**

**Caution:** If required, failure to file FinCEN Form 114 may result in substantial penalties. See instructions.

You must complete this part if you **(a)** had over $1,500 of taxable interest or ordinary dividends; **(b)** had a foreign account; or **(c)** received a distribution from, or were a grantor of, or a transferor to, a foreign trust.

| | | Yes | No |
|---|---|---|---|
| **7a** | At any time during 2021, did you have a financial interest in or signature authority over a financial account (such as a bank account, securities account, or brokerage account) located in a foreign country? See instructions . . . . . . . . . . . | | |
| | If "Yes," are you required to file FinCEN Form 114, Report of Foreign Bank and Financial Accounts (FBAR), to report that financial interest or signature authority? See FinCEN Form 114 and its instructions for filing requirements and exceptions to those requirements . . . . . . | | |
| **b** | If you are required to file FinCEN Form 114, enter the name of the foreign country where the financial account is located ▶ | | |
| **8** | During 2021, did you receive a distribution from, or were you the grantor of, or transferor to, a foreign trust? If "Yes," you may have to file Form 3520. See instructions . . . . . . . . . | | |

For Paperwork Reduction Act Notice, see your tax return instructions. | Cat. No. 17146N | Schedule B (Form 1040) 2021

# SCHEDULE C
# (Form 1040)

Department of the Treasury
Internal Revenue Service (99)

# Profit or Loss From Business
### (Sole Proprietorship)
► Go to *www.irs.gov/ScheduleC* for instructions and the latest information.
► **Attach to Form 1040, 1040-SR, 1040-NR, or 1041; partnerships must generally file Form 1065.**

OMB No. 1545-0074

**2021**

Attachment
Sequence No. **09**

Name of proprietor | Social security number (SSN)

**A** Principal business or profession, including product or service (see instructions) | **B** Enter code from instructions ►

**C** Business name. If no separate business name, leave blank. | **D** Employer ID number (EIN) (see instr.)

**E** Business address (including suite or room no.) ►
City, town or post office, state, and ZIP code

**F** Accounting method: **(1)** ☐ Cash   **(2)** ☐ Accrual   **(3)** ☐ Other (specify) ►

**G** Did you "materially participate" in the operation of this business during 2021? If "No," see instructions for limit on losses   ☐ Yes ☐ No

**H** If you started or acquired this business during 2021, check here ► ☐

**I** Did you make any payments in 2021 that would require you to file Form(s) 1099? See instructions   ☐ Yes ☐ No

**J** If "Yes," did you or will you file required Form(s) 1099?   ☐ Yes ☐ No

## Part I   Income

| | | | |
|---|---|---|---|
| 1 | Gross receipts or sales. See instructions for line 1 and check the box if this income was reported to you on Form W-2 and the "Statutory employee" box on that form was checked ► ☐ | **1** | |
| 2 | Returns and allowances | **2** | |
| 3 | Subtract line 2 from line 1 | **3** | |
| 4 | Cost of goods sold (from line 42) | **4** | |
| 5 | **Gross profit.** Subtract line 4 from line 3 | **5** | |
| 6 | Other income, including federal and state gasoline or fuel tax credit or refund (see instructions) | **6** | |
| 7 | **Gross income.** Add lines 5 and 6 ► | **7** | |

## Part II   Expenses. Enter expenses for business use of your home **only** on line 30.

| | | | | | | |
|---|---|---|---|---|---|---|
| 8 | Advertising | **8** | | 18 | Office expense (see instructions) | **18** |
| 9 | Car and truck expenses (see instructions) | **9** | | 19 | Pension and profit-sharing plans | **19** |
| 10 | Commissions and fees | **10** | | 20 | Rent or lease (see instructions): | |
| 11 | Contract labor (see instructions) | **11** | | a | Vehicles, machinery, and equipment | **20a** |
| 12 | Depletion | **12** | | b | Other business property | **20b** |
| 13 | Depreciation and section 179 expense deduction (not included in Part III) (see instructions) | **13** | | 21 | Repairs and maintenance | **21** |
| | | | | 22 | Supplies (not included in Part III) | **22** |
| | | | | 23 | Taxes and licenses | **23** |
| | | | | 24 | Travel and meals: | |
| 14 | Employee benefit programs (other than on line 19) | **14** | | a | Travel | **24a** |
| 15 | Insurance (other than health) | **15** | | b | Deductible meals (see instructions) | **24b** |
| 16 | Interest (see instructions): | | | 25 | Utilities | **25** |
| a | Mortgage (paid to banks, etc.) | **16a** | | 26 | Wages (less employment credits) | **26** |
| b | Other | **16b** | | 27a | Other expenses (from line 48) | **27a** |
| 17 | Legal and professional services | **17** | | b | **Reserved for future use** | **27b** |

| | | | |
|---|---|---|---|
| 28 | **Total expenses** before expenses for business use of home. Add lines 8 through 27a ► | **28** | |
| 29 | Tentative profit or (loss). Subtract line 28 from line 7 | **29** | |
| 30 | Expenses for business use of your home. Do not report these expenses elsewhere. Attach Form 8829 unless using the simplified method. See instructions. | | |
| | **Simplified method filers only:** Enter the total square footage of (a) your home: _____ and (b) the part of your home used for business: _____ . Use the Simplified Method Worksheet in the instructions to figure the amount to enter on line 30 | **30** | |
| 31 | **Net profit or (loss).** Subtract line 30 from line 29. | | |
| | • If a profit, enter on both **Schedule 1 (Form 1040), line 3,** and on **Schedule SE, line 2.** (If you checked the box on line 1, see instructions). Estates and trusts, enter on **Form 1041, line 3.** | **31** | |
| | • If a loss, you **must** go to line 32. | | |
| 32 | If you have a loss, check the box that describes your investment in this activity. See instructions. | | |
| | • If you checked 32a, enter the loss on both **Schedule 1 (Form 1040), line 3,** and on **Schedule SE, line 2.** (If you checked the box on line 1, see the line 31 instructions.) Estates and trusts, enter on **Form 1041, line 3.** | 32a ☐ All investment is at risk. | |
| | • If you checked 32b, you **must** attach **Form 6198.** Your loss may be limited. | 32b ☐ Some investment is not at risk. | |

**For Paperwork Reduction Act Notice, see the separate instructions.**   Cat. No. 11334P   Schedule C (Form 1040) 2021

Schedule C (Form 1040) 2021 | Page **2**

**Part III** **Cost of Goods Sold** (see instructions)

33 Method(s) used to value closing inventory: **a** ☐ Cost **b** ☐ Lower of cost or market **c** ☐ Other (attach explanation)

34 Was there any change in determining quantities, costs, or valuations between opening and closing inventory? If "Yes," attach explanation . . . ☐ Yes ☐ No

35 Inventory at beginning of year. If different from last year's closing inventory, attach explanation | 35
36 Purchases less cost of items withdrawn for personal use | 36
37 Cost of labor. Do not include any amounts paid to yourself | 37
38 Materials and supplies | 38
39 Other costs | 39
40 Add lines 35 through 39 | 40
41 Inventory at end of year | 41
42 **Cost of goods sold.** Subtract line 41 from line 40. Enter the result here and on line 4 | 42

**Part IV** **Information on Your Vehicle.** Complete this part **only** if you are claiming car or truck expenses on line 9 and are not required to file Form 4562 for this business. See the instructions for line 13 to find out if you must file Form 4562.

43 When did you place your vehicle in service for business purposes? (month/day/year) ▶ ___/___/___

44 Of the total number of miles you drove your vehicle during 2021, enter the number of miles you used your vehicle for:

**a** Business _____ **b** Commuting (see instructions) _____ **c** Other _____

45 Was your vehicle available for personal use during off-duty hours? ☐ Yes ☐ No

46 Do you (or your spouse) have another vehicle available for personal use? ☐ Yes ☐ No

47a Do you have evidence to support your deduction? ☐ Yes ☐ No

**b** If "Yes," is the evidence written? ☐ Yes ☐ No

**Part V** **Other Expenses.** List below business expenses not included on lines 8–26 or line 30.

48 **Total other expenses.** Enter here and on line 27a | 48

Schedule C (Form 1040) 2021

| **SCHEDULE D**<br>(Form 1040)<br><br>Department of the Treasury<br>Internal Revenue Service (99) | **Capital Gains and Losses**<br><br>▶ Attach to Form 1040, 1040-SR, or 1040-NR.<br>▶ Go to *www.irs.gov/ScheduleD* for instructions and the latest information.<br>▶ Use Form 8949 to list your transactions for lines 1b, 2, 3, 8b, 9, and 10. | OMB No. 1545-0074<br><br>**2021**<br><br>Attachment<br>Sequence No. **12** |
|---|---|---|

| Name(s) shown on return | Your social security number |
|---|---|

Did you dispose of any investment(s) in a qualified opportunity fund during the tax year? ☐ **Yes** ☐ **No**
If "Yes," attach Form 8949 and see its instructions for additional requirements for reporting your gain or loss.

**Part I   Short-Term Capital Gains and Losses—Generally Assets Held One Year or Less** (see instructions)

| See instructions for how to figure the amounts to enter on the lines below.<br><br>This form may be easier to complete if you round off cents to whole dollars. | **(d)**<br>Proceeds<br>(sales price) | **(e)**<br>Cost<br>(or other basis) | **(g)**<br>Adjustments<br>to gain or loss from<br>Form(s) 8949, Part I,<br>line 2, column (g) | **(h) Gain or (loss)**<br>Subtract column (e)<br>from column (d) and<br>combine the result<br>with column (g) |
|---|---|---|---|---|
| **1a** Totals for all short-term transactions reported on Form 1099-B for which basis was reported to the IRS and for which you have no adjustments (see instructions). However, if you choose to report all these transactions on Form 8949, leave this line blank and go to line 1b | | | | |
| **1b** Totals for all transactions reported on Form(s) 8949 with **Box A** checked . . . . . . . . . | | | | |
| **2** Totals for all transactions reported on Form(s) 8949 with **Box B** checked . . . . . . . . . | | | | |
| **3** Totals for all transactions reported on Form(s) 8949 with **Box C** checked . . . . . . . . . | | | | |

| | | |
|---|---|---|
| **4** Short-term gain from Form 6252 and short-term gain or (loss) from Forms 4684, 6781, and 8824 . . | **4** | |
| **5** Net short-term gain or (loss) from partnerships, S corporations, estates, and trusts from Schedule(s) K-1 . . . . . . . . . . . . . . . . . . . . . . . . | **5** | |
| **6** Short-term capital loss carryover. Enter the amount, if any, from line 8 of your **Capital Loss Carryover Worksheet** in the instructions . . . . . . . . . . . . . . . . . | **6** ( ) |
| **7** **Net short-term capital gain or (loss).** Combine lines 1a through 6 in column (h). If you have any long-term capital gains or losses, go to Part II below. Otherwise, go to Part III on the back . . . . . . | **7** | |

**Part II   Long-Term Capital Gains and Losses—Generally Assets Held More Than One Year** (see instructions)

| See instructions for how to figure the amounts to enter on the lines below.<br><br>This form may be easier to complete if you round off cents to whole dollars. | **(d)**<br>Proceeds<br>(sales price) | **(e)**<br>Cost<br>(or other basis) | **(g)**<br>Adjustments<br>to gain or loss from<br>Form(s) 8949, Part II,<br>line 2, column (g) | **(h) Gain or (loss)**<br>Subtract column (e)<br>from column (d) and<br>combine the result<br>with column (g) |
|---|---|---|---|---|
| **8a** Totals for all long-term transactions reported on Form 1099-B for which basis was reported to the IRS and for which you have no adjustments (see instructions). However, if you choose to report all these transactions on Form 8949, leave this line blank and go to line 8b . | | | | |
| **8b** Totals for all transactions reported on Form(s) 8949 with **Box D** checked . . . . . . . . . | | | | |
| **9** Totals for all transactions reported on Form(s) 8949 with **Box E** checked . . . . . . . . . | | | | |
| **10** Totals for all transactions reported on Form(s) 8949 with **Box F** checked. . . . . . . . . | | | | |

| | | |
|---|---|---|
| **11** Gain from Form 4797, Part I; long-term gain from Forms 2439 and 6252; and long-term gain or (loss) from Forms 4684, 6781, and 8824 . . . . . . . . . . . . . . . . | **11** | |
| **12** Net long-term gain or (loss) from partnerships, S corporations, estates, and trusts from Schedule(s) K-1 | **12** | |
| **13** Capital gain distributions. See the instructions . . . . . . . . . . . . . . . | **13** | |
| **14** Long-term capital loss carryover. Enter the amount, if any, from line 13 of your **Capital Loss Carryover Worksheet** in the instructions . . . . . . . . . . . . . . . | **14** ( ) |
| **15** **Net long-term capital gain or (loss).** Combine lines 8a through 14 in column (h). Then, go to Part III on the back . . . . . . . . . . . . . . . . . . . . . . . . | **15** | |

| For Paperwork Reduction Act Notice, see your tax return instructions. | Cat. No. 11338H | Schedule D (Form 1040) 2021 |
|---|---|---|

Source: U.S. Department of the Treasury, Internal Revenue Service, SCHEDULE D (Form 1040). Washington, DC: 2021.

**Part III**   **Summary**

**16**   Combine lines 7 and 15 and enter the result . . . . . . . . . . . . . . . . .    **16**

- If line 16 is a **gain,** enter the amount from line 16 on Form 1040, 1040-SR, or 1040-NR, line 7. Then, go to line 17 below.
- If line 16 is a **loss,** skip lines 17 through 20 below. Then, go to line 21. Also be sure to complete line 22.
- If line 16 is **zero,** skip lines 17 through 21 below and enter -0- on Form 1040, 1040-SR, or 1040-NR, line 7. Then, go to line 22.

**17**   Are lines 15 and 16 **both** gains?
☐ **Yes.** Go to line 18.
☐ **No.** Skip lines 18 through 21, and go to line 22.

**18**   If you are required to complete the **28% Rate Gain Worksheet** (see instructions), enter the amount, if any, from line 7 of that worksheet . . . . . . . . . . . . ▶   **18**

**19**   If you are required to complete the **Unrecaptured Section 1250 Gain Worksheet** (see instructions), enter the amount, if any, from line 18 of that worksheet . . . . . . . . ▶   **19**

**20**   Are lines 18 and 19 both zero or blank and are you not filing Form 4952?
☐ **Yes.** Complete the **Qualified Dividends and Capital Gain Tax Worksheet** in the instructions for Forms 1040 and 1040-SR, line 16. **Don't** complete lines 21 and 22 below.

☐ **No.** Complete the **Schedule D Tax Worksheet** in the instructions. **Don't** complete lines 21 and 22 below.

**21**   If line 16 is a loss, enter here and on Form 1040, 1040-SR, or 1040-NR, line 7, the **smaller** of:

- The loss on line 16; or
- ($3,000), or if married filing separately, ($1,500) . . . . . . . . . . . .    **21** ( )

**Note:** When figuring which amount is smaller, treat both amounts as positive numbers.

**22**   Do you have qualified dividends on Form 1040, 1040-SR, or 1040-NR, line 3a?

☐ **Yes.** Complete the **Qualified Dividends and Capital Gain Tax Worksheet** in the instructions for Forms 1040 and 1040-SR, line 16.

☐ **No.** Complete the rest of Form 1040, 1040-SR, or 1040-NR.

DRAFT AS OF August 18, 2021 DO NOT FILE

| SCHEDULE E<br>(Form 1040)<br><br>Department of the Treasury<br>Internal Revenue Service (99) | **Supplemental Income and Loss**<br>(From rental real estate, royalties, partnerships, S corporations, estates, trusts, REMICs, etc.)<br>▶ Attach to Form 1040, 1040-SR, 1040-NR, or 1041.<br>▶ Go to *www.irs.gov/ScheduleE* for instructions and the latest information. | OMB No. 1545-0074<br><br>2021<br><br>Attachment<br>Sequence No. **13** |
|---|---|---|

Name(s) shown on return | Your social security number

### Part I   Income or Loss From Rental Real Estate and Royalties   Note: If you are in the business of renting personal property, use Schedule C. See instructions. If you are an individual, report farm rental income or loss from **Form 4835** on page 2, line 40.

**A** Did you make any payments in 2021 that would require you to file Form(s) 1099? See instructions . . . . . . ☐ Yes ☐ No
**B** If "Yes," did you or will you file required Form(s) 1099? . . . . . . . . . . . . . . . . . ☐ Yes ☐ No

**1a** Physical address of each property (street, city, state, ZIP code)

A
B
C

| 1b | Type of Property<br>(from list below) | 2 | For each rental real estate property listed above, report the number of fair rental and personal use days. Check the **QJV** box only if you meet the requirements to file as a qualified joint venture. See instructions. | | Fair Rental Days | Personal Use Days | QJV |
|---|---|---|---|---|---|---|---|
| A | | | | A | | | ☐ |
| B | | | | B | | | ☐ |
| C | | | | C | | | ☐ |

**Type of Property:**
1  Single Family Residence   3  Vacation/Short-Term Rental   5  Land   7  Self-Rental
2  Multi-Family Residence   4  Commercial   6  Royalties   8  Other (describe)

| Income: | Properties: | | A | B | C |
|---|---|---|---|---|---|
| **3** Rents received . . . . . . . . . . . . | 3 | | | | |
| **4** Royalties received . . . . . . . . . . | 4 | | | | |
| **Expenses:** | | | | | |
| **5** Advertising . . . . . . . . . . . | 5 | | | | |
| **6** Auto and travel (see instructions) . . . . . | 6 | | | | |
| **7** Cleaning and maintenance . . . . . . . | 7 | | | | |
| **8** Commissions. . . . . . . . . . . | 8 | | | | |
| **9** Insurance . . . . . . . . . . . | 9 | | | | |
| **10** Legal and other professional fees . . . . . | 10 | | | | |
| **11** Management fees . . . . . . . . . | 11 | | | | |
| **12** Mortgage interest paid to banks, etc. (see instructions) | 12 | | | | |
| **13** Other interest. . . . . . . . . . | 13 | | | | |
| **14** Repairs. . . . . . . . . . . | 14 | | | | |
| **15** Supplies . . . . . . . . . . . | 15 | | | | |
| **16** Taxes . . . . . . . . . . . | 16 | | | | |
| **17** Utilities . . . . . . . . . . . | 17 | | | | |
| **18** Depreciation expense or depletion . . . . . | 18 | | | | |
| **19** Other (list) ▶ _____ | 19 | | | | |
| **20** Total expenses. Add lines 5 through 19 . . . . | 20 | | | | |
| **21** Subtract line 20 from line 3 (rents) and/or 4 (royalties). If result is a (loss), see instructions to find out if you must file **Form 6198** . . . . . . . . . . | 21 | | | | |
| **22** Deductible rental real estate loss after limitation, if any, on **Form 8582** (see instructions) . . . . . . | 22 | ( ) | ( ) | ( ) | ( ) |

| 23a | Total of all amounts reported on line 3 for all rental properties . . . . | 23a | |
|---|---|---|---|
| **b** | Total of all amounts reported on line 4 for all royalty properties . . . . | 23b | |
| **c** | Total of all amounts reported on line 12 for all properties . . . . . | 23c | |
| **d** | Total of all amounts reported on line 18 for all properties . . . . . | 23d | |
| **e** | Total of all amounts reported on line 20 for all properties . . . . . | 23e | |

| **24** | **Income.** Add positive amounts shown on line 21. **Do not** include any losses . . . . . . . | 24 | |
|---|---|---|---|
| **25** | **Losses.** Add royalty losses from line 21 and rental real estate losses from line 22. Enter total losses here . | 25 | ( ) |
| **26** | **Total rental real estate and royalty income or (loss).** Combine lines 24 and 25. Enter the result here. If Parts II, III, IV, and line 40 on page 2 do not apply to you, also enter this amount on Schedule 1 (Form 1040), line 5. Otherwise, include this amount in the total on line 41 on page 2 . | 26 | |

For Paperwork Reduction Act Notice, see the separate instructions.       Cat. No. 11344L       Schedule E (Form 1040) 2021

Source: U.S. Department of the Treasury, Internal Revenue Service, SCHEDULE E (Form 1040). Washington, DC: 2021.

Schedule E (Form 1040) 2021      Attachment Sequence No. **13**      Page **2**

| Name(s) shown on return. Do not enter name and social security number if shown on other side. | Your social security number |
|---|---|

**Caution:** The IRS compares amounts reported on your tax return with amounts shown on Schedule(s) K-1.

**Part II**   **Income or Loss From Partnerships and S Corporations** — **Note:** If you report a loss, receive a distribution, dispose of stock, or receive a loan repayment from an S corporation, you **must** check the box in column **(e)** on line 28 and attach the required basis computation. If you report a loss from an at-risk activity for which **any** amount is **not** at risk, you **must** check the box in column **(f)** on line 28 and attach **Form 6198**. See instructions.

27  Are you reporting any loss not allowed in a prior year due to the at-risk or basis limitations, a prior year unallowed loss from a passive activity (if that loss was not reported on Form 8582), or unreimbursed partnership expenses? If you answered "Yes," see instructions before completing this section . . . . . . . . . . . . . . . . .  ☐ Yes ☐ No

| 28 | (a) Name | (b) Enter P for partnership; S for S corporation | (c) Check if foreign partnership | (d) Employer identification number | (e) Check if basis computation is required | (f) Check if any amount is not at risk |
|---|---|---|---|---|---|---|
| **A** | | | ☐ | | ☐ | ☐ |
| **B** | | | ☐ | | ☐ | ☐ |
| **C** | | | ☐ | | ☐ | ☐ |
| **D** | | | ☐ | | ☐ | ☐ |

| | Passive Income and Loss | | Nonpassive Income and Loss | | |
|---|---|---|---|---|---|
| | (g) Passive loss allowed (attach **Form 8582** if required) | (h) Passive income from **Schedule K-1** | (i) Nonpassive loss allowed (see **Schedule K-1**) | (j) Section 179 expense deduction from **Form 4562** | (k) Nonpassive income from **Schedule K-1** |
| **A** | | | | | |
| **B** | | | | | |
| **C** | | | | | |
| **D** | | | | | |
| **29a** Totals | | | | | |
| **b** Totals | | | | | |

| 30 | Add columns (h) and (k) of line 29a. . . . . . . . . . | 30 | |
|---|---|---|---|
| 31 | Add columns (g), (i), and (j) of line 29b. . . . . . . . . | 31 ( | ) |
| 32 | **Total partnership and S corporation income or (loss).** Combine lines 30 and 31 . . . . | 32 | |

**Part III**   **Income or Loss From Estates and Trusts**

| 33 | (a) Name | (b) Employer identification number |
|---|---|---|
| **A** | | |
| **B** | | |

| | Passive Income and Loss | | Nonpassive Income and Loss | |
|---|---|---|---|---|
| | (c) Passive deduction or loss allowed (attach **Form 8582** if required) | (d) Passive income from **Schedule K-1** | (e) Deduction or loss from **Schedule K-1** | (f) Other income from **Schedule K-1** |
| **A** | | | | |
| **B** | | | | |
| **34a** Totals | | | | |
| **b** Totals | | | | |

| 35 | Add columns (d) and (f) of line 34a . . . . . . . . . . . | 35 | |
|---|---|---|---|
| 36 | Add columns (c) and (e) of line 34b . . . . . . . . . . . | 36 ( | ) |
| 37 | **Total estate and trust income or (loss).** Combine lines 35 and 36 . . . . . . . . . | 37 | |

**Part IV**   **Income or Loss From Real Estate Mortgage Investment Conduits (REMICs)—Residual Holder**

| 38 | (a) Name | (b) Employer identification number | (c) Excess inclusion from **Schedules Q**, line 2c (see instructions) | (d) Taxable income (net loss) from **Schedules Q**, line 1b | (e) Income from **Schedules Q**, line 3b |
|---|---|---|---|---|---|
| | | | | | |

| 39 | Combine columns (d) and (e) only. Enter the result here and include in the total on line 41 below | 39 | |
|---|---|---|---|

**Part V**   **Summary**

| 40 | Net farm rental income or (loss) from **Form 4835**. Also, complete line 42 below . . . . . . | 40 | |
|---|---|---|---|
| 41 | **Total income or (loss).** Combine lines 26, 32, 37, 39, and 40. Enter the result here and on Schedule 1 (Form 1040), line 5 ▶ | 41 | |
| 42 | **Reconciliation of farming and fishing income.** Enter your **gross** farming and fishing income reported on Form 4835, line 7; Schedule K-1 (Form 1065), box 14, code B; Schedule K-1 (Form 1120-S), box 17, code AD; and Schedule K-1 (Form 1041), box 14, code F. See instructions . . | 42 | |
| 43 | **Reconciliation for real estate professionals.** If you were a real estate professional (see instructions), enter the net income or (loss) you reported anywhere on Form 1040, Form 1040-SR, or Form 1040-NR from all rental real estate activities in which you materially participated under the passive activity loss rules . . . . . . | 43 | |

Schedule E (Form 1040) 2021

| SCHEDULE EIC<br>(Form 1040)<br><br>Department of the Treasury<br>Internal Revenue Service (99) | **Earned Income Credit**<br>Qualifying Child Information<br><br>► **Complete and attach to Form 1040 or 1040-SR only if you have a qualifying child.**<br>► **Go to** *www.irs.gov/ScheduleEIC* **for the latest information.** | 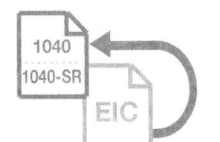 | OMB No. 1545-0074<br><br>2021<br><br>Attachment<br>Sequence No. **43** |
|---|---|---|---|

| Name(s) shown on return | Your social security number |
|---|---|

If you are separated from your spouse, filing a separate return and meet the requirements to claim the EIC (see instructions), check here ☐

***Before you begin:***
- See the instructions for Form 1040, lines 27a, 27b, and 27c, to make sure that **(a)** you can take the EIC, and **(b)** you have a qualifying child.
- Be sure the child's name on line 1 and social security number (SSN) on line 2 agree with the child's social security card. Otherwise, at the time we process your return, we may reduce your EIC. If the name or SSN on the child's social security card is not correct, call the Social Security Administration at 1-800-772-1213.

⚠️ **CAUTION**
- *You can't claim the EIC for a child who didn't live with you for more than half of the year.*
- *If you take the EIC even though you are not eligible, you may not be allowed to take the credit for up to 10 years. See the instructions for details.*
- *It will take us longer to process your return and issue your refund if you do not fill in all lines that apply for each qualifying child.*

| Qualifying Child Information | Child 1 | Child 2 | Child 3 |
|---|---|---|---|
| **1   Child's name**<br>If you have more than three qualifying children, you have to list only three to get the maximum credit. | First name          Last name | First name          Last name | First name          Last name |
| **2   Child's SSN**<br>The child must have an SSN as defined in the instructions for Form 1040, lines 27a, 27b, and 27c, unless the child was born and died in 2021. If your child was born and died in 2021 and did not have an SSN, enter "Died" on this line and attach a copy of the child's birth certificate, death certificate, or hospital medical records showing a live birth. | | | |
| **3   Child's year of birth** | Year ___ ___ ___ ___<br>*If born after 2002 and the child is younger than you (or your spouse, if filing jointly), skip lines 4a and 4b; go to line 5.* | Year ___ ___ ___ ___<br>*If born after 2002 and the child is younger than you (or your spouse, if filing jointly), skip lines 4a and 4b; go to line 5.* | Year ___ ___ ___ ___<br>*If born after 2002 and the child is younger than you (or your spouse, if filing jointly), skip lines 4a and 4b; go to line 5.* |
| **4 a** Was the child under age 24 at the end of 2021, a student, and younger than you (or your spouse, if filing jointly)? | ☐ **Yes.**     ☐ **No.**<br>*Go to line 5.*     *Go to line 4b.* | ☐ **Yes.**     ☐ **No.**<br>*Go to line 5.*     *Go to line 4b.* | ☐ **Yes.**     ☐ **No.**<br>*Go to line 5.*     *Go to line 4b.* |
| **b** Was the child permanently and totally disabled during any part of 2021? | ☐ **Yes.**     ☐ **No.**<br>*Go to line 5.*     The child is not a qualifying child. | ☐ **Yes.**     ☐ **No.**<br>*Go to line 5.*     The child is not a qualifying child. | ☐ **Yes.**     ☐ **No.**<br>*Go to line 5.*     The child is not a qualifying child. |
| **5   Child's relationship to you**<br>(for example, son, daughter, grandchild, niece, nephew, eligible foster child, etc.) | | | |
| **6   Number of months child lived with you in the United States during 2021**<br>• If the child lived with you for more than half of 2021 but less than 7 months, enter "7."<br>• If the child was born or died in 2021 and your home was the child's home for more than half the time he or she was alive during 2021, enter "12." | _____ months<br>*Do not enter more than 12 months.* | _____ months<br>*Do not enter more than 12 months.* | _____ months<br>*Do not enter more than 12 months.* |

| **For Paperwork Reduction Act Notice, see your tax return instructions.** | Cat. No. 13339M | Schedule EIC (Form 1040) 2021 |
|---|---|---|

| SCHEDULE SE | Self-Employment Tax | OMB No. 1545-0074 |
|---|---|---|
| (Form 1040) | ▶ **Go to** *www.irs.gov/ScheduleSE* for instructions and the latest information. | **2021** |
| Department of the Treasury<br>Internal Revenue Service (99) | ▶ **Attach to** Form 1040, 1040-SR, or 1040-NR. | Attachment<br>Sequence No. **17** |

| Name of person with self-employment income (as shown on Form 1040, 1040-SR, or 1040-NR) | Social security number of person<br>with **self-employment** income ▶ |
|---|---|

### Part I   Self-Employment Tax

**Note:** If your only income subject to self-employment tax is **church employee income,** see instructions for how to report your income and the definition of church employee income.

**A**  If you are a minister, member of a religious order, or Christian Science practitioner **and** you filed Form 4361, but you had $400 or more of **other** net earnings from self-employment, check here and continue with Part I . . . . . . . . ▶ ☐

Skip lines 1a and 1b if you use the farm optional method in Part II. See instructions.

| | | | |
|---|---|---|---|
| **1a** | Net farm profit or (loss) from Schedule F, line 34, and farm partnerships, Schedule K-1 (Form 1065), box 14, code A . . . . . . . . . . . . . . . . . . . . . . . | **1a** | |
| **b** | If you received social security retirement or disability benefits, enter the amount of Conservation Reserve Program payments included on Schedule F, line 4b, or listed on Schedule K-1 (Form 1065), box 20, code AH | **1b** ( ) | |

Skip line 2 if you use the nonfarm optional method in Part II. See instructions.

| | | | |
|---|---|---|---|
| **2** | Net profit or (loss) from Schedule C, line 31; and Schedule K-1 (Form 1065), box 14, code A (other than farming). See instructions for other income to report or if you are a minister or member of a religious order | **2** | |
| **3** | Combine lines 1a, 1b, and 2 . . . . . . . . . . . . . . . . . . . . . . . . | **3** | |
| **4a** | If line 3 is more than zero, multiply line 3 by 92.35% (0.9235). Otherwise, enter amount from line 3 | **4a** | |
| | **Note:** If line 4a is less than $400 due to Conservation Reserve Program payments on line 1b, see instructions. | | |
| **b** | If you elect one or both of the optional methods, enter the total of lines 15 and 17 here . . . . | **4b** | |
| **c** | Combine lines 4a and 4b. If less than $400, **stop;** you don't owe self-employment tax. **Exception:** If less than $400 and you had **church employee income,** enter -0- and continue . . . . . . . ▶ | **4c** | |
| **5a** | Enter your **church employee income** from Form W-2. See instructions for definition of church employee income . . . . . . . . . . . | **5a** | **5b** | |
| **b** | Multiply line 5a by 92.35% (0.9235). If less than $100, enter -0- . . . . . . . . . | **5b** | |
| **6** | Add lines 4c and 5b . . . . . . . . . . . . . . . . . . . . . . . . . . | **6** | |
| **7** | Maximum amount of combined wages and self-employment earnings subject to social security tax or the 6.2% portion of the 7.65% railroad retirement (tier 1) tax for 2021 . . . . . . . . . | **7** | 142,800 |
| **8a** | Total social security wages and tips (total of boxes 3 and 7 on Form(s) W-2) and railroad retirement (tier 1) compensation. If $142,800 or more, skip lines 8b through 10, and go to line 11 . . . . . . . . . . | **8a** | | |
| **b** | Unreported tips subject to social security tax from Form 4137, line 10 . . . | **8b** | | |
| **c** | Wages subject to social security tax from Form 8919, line 10 . . . . . . | **8c** | | |
| **d** | Add lines 8a, 8b, and 8c . . . . . . . . . . . . . . . . . . . . . . . . | **8d** | |
| **9** | Subtract line 8d from line 7. If zero or less, enter -0- here and on line 10 and go to line 11 . . ▶ | **9** | |
| **10** | Multiply the **smaller** of line 6 or line 9 by 12.4% (0.124) . . . . . . . . . . . . . | **10** | |
| **11** | Multiply line 6 by 2.9% (0.029) . . . . . . . . . . . . . . . . . . . . . . | **11** | |
| **12** | **Self-employment tax.** Add lines 10 and 11. Enter here and on **Schedule 2 (Form 1040), line 4** . . | **12** | |
| **13** | **Deduction for one-half of self-employment tax.** Multiply line 12 by 50% (0.50). Enter here and on **Schedule 1 (Form 1040), line 15** . . . . . . . . . . . . . . . . . . . . . . | **13** | |

### Part II   Optional Methods To Figure Net Earnings (see instructions)

**Farm Optional Method.** You may use this method **only** if (a) your gross farm income¹ wasn't more than $8,820, **or** (b) your net farm profits² were less than $6,367.

| | | | |
|---|---|---|---|
| **14** | Maximum income for optional methods . . . . . . . . . . . . . . . . . . . . | **14** | 5,880 |
| **15** | Enter the **smaller** of: two-thirds (²/₃) of gross farm income¹ (not less than zero) **or** $5,880. Also, include this amount on line 4b above . . . . . . . . . . . . . . . . . . . . . . . . | **15** | |

**Nonfarm Optional Method.** You may use this method **only** if (a) your net nonfarm profits³ were less than $6,367 and also less than 72.189% of your gross nonfarm income,⁴ **and** (b) you had net earnings from self-employment of at least $400 in 2 of the prior 3 years. **Caution:** You may use this method no more than five times.

| | | | |
|---|---|---|---|
| **16** | Subtract line 15 from line 14 . . . . . . . . . . . . . . . . . . . . . . . | **16** | |
| **17** | Enter the **smaller** of: two-thirds (²/₃) of gross nonfarm income⁴ (not less than zero) **or** the amount on line 16. Also, include this amount on line 4b above . . . . . . . . . . . . . . . . . | **17** | |

¹ From Sch. F, line 9; and Sch. K-1 (Form 1065), box 14, code B.
² From Sch. F, line 34; and Sch. K-1 (Form 1065), box 14, code A—minus the amount you would have entered on line 1b had you not used the optional method.
³ From Sch. C, line 31; and Sch. K-1 (Form 1065), box 14, code A.
⁴ From Sch. C, line 7; and Sch. K-1 (Form 1065), box 14, code C.

**For Paperwork Reduction Act Notice, see your tax return instructions.**      Cat. No. 11358Z      **Schedule SE (Form 1040) 2021**

Source: U.S. Department of the Treasury, Internal Revenue Service, SCHEDULE SE (Form 1040). Washington, DC: 2021.

| Form **4562** | **Depreciation and Amortization** | OMB No. 1545-0172 |
|---|---|---|

Form **4562**

Department of the Treasury
Internal Revenue Service   (99)

**Depreciation and Amortization**
**(Including Information on Listed Property)**
► Attach to your tax return.
► Go to *www.irs.gov/Form4562* for instructions and the latest information.

OMB No. 1545-0172
**2021**
Attachment
Sequence No. **179**

| Name(s) shown on return | Business or activity to which this form relates | Identifying number |
|---|---|---|

**Part I** | **Election To Expense Certain Property Under Section 179**
**Note:** If you have any listed property, complete Part V before you complete Part I.

| | | |
|---|---|---|
| 1 | Maximum amount (see instructions) | **1** |
| 2 | Total cost of section 179 property placed in service (see instructions) | **2** |
| 3 | Threshold cost of section 179 property before reduction in limitation (see instructions) | **3** |
| 4 | Reduction in limitation. Subtract line 3 from line 2. If zero or less, enter -0- | **4** |
| 5 | Dollar limitation for tax year. Subtract line 4 from line 1. If zero or less, enter -0-. If married filing separately, see instructions | **5** |

| 6 | (a) Description of property | (b) Cost (business use only) | (c) Elected cost |
|---|---|---|---|
| | | | |

| | | | |
|---|---|---|---|
| 7 | Listed property. Enter the amount from line 29 . . . . . . . | 7 | |
| 8 | Total elected cost of section 179 property. Add amounts in column (c), lines 6 and 7 | | **8** |
| 9 | Tentative deduction. Enter the **smaller** of line 5 or line 8 | | **9** |
| 10 | Carryover of disallowed deduction from line 13 of your 2020 Form 4562 | | **10** |
| 11 | Business income limitation. Enter the smaller of business income (not less than zero) or line 5. See instructions | | **11** |
| 12 | Section 179 expense deduction. Add lines 9 and 10, but don't enter more than line 11 | | **12** |
| 13 | Carryover of disallowed deduction to 2022. Add lines 9 and 10, less line 12 ► | **13** | |

**Note:** Don't use Part II or Part III below for listed property. Instead, use Part V.

**Part II** | **Special Depreciation Allowance and Other Depreciation (Don't** include listed property. See instructions.**)**

| | | |
|---|---|---|
| 14 | Special depreciation allowance for qualified property (other than listed property) placed in service during the tax year. See instructions . . . . . . . . . . . . . . . | **14** |
| 15 | Property subject to section 168(f)(1) election | **15** |
| 16 | Other depreciation (including ACRS) . . . . . . . . . . . . . . . . . . | **16** |

**Part III** | **MACRS Depreciation (Don't** include listed property. See instructions.**)**

**Section A**

| | | |
|---|---|---|
| 17 | MACRS deductions for assets placed in service in tax years beginning before 2021 . . . . . . | **17** |
| 18 | If you are electing to group any assets placed in service during the tax year into one or more general asset accounts, check here . . . . . . . . . . . . . . . . . . . ► ☐ | |

**Section B—Assets Placed in Service During 2021 Tax Year Using the General Depreciation System**

| (a) Classification of property | (b) Month and year placed in service | (c) Basis for depreciation (business/investment use only—see instructions) | (d) Recovery period | (e) Convention | (f) Method | (g) Depreciation deduction |
|---|---|---|---|---|---|---|
| 19a  3-year property | | | | | | |
| b  5-year property | | | | | | |
| c  7-year property | | | | | | |
| d  10-year property | | | | | | |
| e  15-year property | | | | | | |
| f  20-year property | | | | | | |
| g  25-year property | | | 25 yrs. | | S/L | |
| h  Residential rental property | | | 27.5 yrs. | MM | S/L | |
| | | | 27.5 yrs. | MM | S/L | |
| i  Nonresidential real property | | | 39 yrs. | MM | S/L | |
| | | | | MM | S/L | |

**Section C—Assets Placed in Service During 2021 Tax Year Using the Alternative Depreciation System**

| | | | | | | |
|---|---|---|---|---|---|---|
| 20a  Class life | | | | | S/L | |
| b  12-year | | | 12 yrs. | | S/L | |
| c  30-year | | | 30 yrs. | MM | S/L | |
| d  40-year | | | 40 yrs. | MM | S/L | |

**Part IV** | **Summary** (See instructions.)

| | | |
|---|---|---|
| 21 | Listed property. Enter amount from line 28 . . . . . . . . . . . . . . . . | **21** |
| 22 | **Total.** Add amounts from line 12, lines 14 through 17, lines 19 and 20 in column (g), and line 21. Enter here and on the appropriate lines of your return. Partnerships and S corporations—see instructions . | **22** |
| 23 | For assets shown above and placed in service during the current year, enter the portion of the basis attributable to section 263A costs . . . . . . . . . | 23 |

For Paperwork Reduction Act Notice, see separate instructions.   Cat. No. 12906N   Form **4562** (2021)

Form 4562 (2021) Page **2**

## Part V — Listed Property (Include automobiles, certain other vehicles, certain aircraft, and property used for entertainment, recreation, or amusement.)

**Note:** For any vehicle for which you are using the standard mileage rate or deducting lease expense, complete **only** 24a, 24b, columns (a) through (c) of Section A, all of Section B, and Section C if applicable.

### Section A—Depreciation and Other Information (Caution: See the instructions for limits for passenger automobiles.)

**24a** Do you have evidence to support the business/investment use claimed? ☐ Yes ☐ No   **24b** If "Yes," is the evidence written? ☐ Yes ☐ No

| (a) Type of property (list vehicles first) | (b) Date placed in service | (c) Business/ investment use percentage | (d) Cost or other basis | (e) Basis for depreciation (business/investment use only) | (f) Recovery period | (g) Method/ Convention | (h) Depreciation deduction | (i) Elected section 179 cost |
|---|---|---|---|---|---|---|---|---|
| **25** Special depreciation allowance for qualified listed property placed in service during the tax year and used more than 50% in a qualified business use. See instructions . **25** | | | | | | | | |
| **26** Property used more than 50% in a qualified business use: | | | | | | | | |
| | | % | | | | | | |
| | | % | | | | | | |
| | | % | | | | | | |
| **27** Property used 50% or less in a qualified business use: | | | | | | | | |
| | | % | | | S/L – | | | |
| | | % | | | S/L – | | | |
| | | % | | | S/L – | | | |
| **28** Add amounts in column (h), lines 25 through 27. Enter here and on line 21, page 1 . **28** | | | | | | | | |
| **29** Add amounts in column (i), line 26. Enter here and on line 7, page 1 . . . . . . . . . . **29** | | | | | | | | |

### Section B—Information on Use of Vehicles

Complete this section for vehicles used by a sole proprietor, partner, or other "more than 5% owner," or related person. If you provided vehicles to your employees, first answer the questions in Section C to see if you meet an exception to completing this section for those vehicles.

| | (a) Vehicle 1 | (b) Vehicle 2 | (c) Vehicle 3 | (d) Vehicle 4 | (e) Vehicle 5 | (f) Vehicle 6 |
|---|---|---|---|---|---|---|
| **30** Total business/investment miles driven during the year (**don't** include commuting miles) . | | | | | | |
| **31** Total commuting miles driven during the year | | | | | | |
| **32** Total other personal (noncommuting) miles driven . . . . . . . . . | | | | | | |
| **33** Total miles driven during the year. Add lines 30 through 32 . . . . . . . | | | | | | |
| **34** Was the vehicle available for personal use during off-duty hours? . . . . . | Yes   No | Yes   No | Yes   No | Yes   No | Yes   No | Yes   No |
| **35** Was the vehicle used primarily by a more than 5% owner or related person? . . | | | | | | |
| **36** Is another vehicle available for personal use? | | | | | | |

### Section C—Questions for Employers Who Provide Vehicles for Use by Their Employees

Answer these questions to determine if you meet an exception to completing Section B for vehicles used by employees who **aren't** more than 5% owners or related persons. See instructions.

| | | Yes | No |
|---|---|---|---|
| **37** | Do you maintain a written policy statement that prohibits all personal use of vehicles, including commuting, by your employees? . . . . . . . . . . . . . . . . | | |
| **38** | Do you maintain a written policy statement that prohibits personal use of vehicles, except commuting, by your employees?  See the instructions for vehicles used by corporate officers, directors, or 1% or more owners . . | | |
| **39** | Do you treat all use of vehicles by employees as personal use? . . . . . . . . . . . . . | | |
| **40** | Do you provide more than five vehicles to your employees, obtain information from your employees about the use of the vehicles, and retain the information received? . . . . . . . . . . . . . . | | |
| **41** | Do you meet the requirements concerning qualified automobile demonstration use? See instructions. . . . . . | | |

**Note:** If your answer to 37, 38, 39, 40, or 41 is "Yes," don't complete Section B for the covered vehicles.

## Part VI — Amortization

| (a) Description of costs | (b) Date amortization begins | (c) Amortizable amount | (d) Code section | (e) Amortization period or percentage | (f) Amortization for this year |
|---|---|---|---|---|---|
| **42** Amortization of costs that begins during your 2021 tax year (see instructions): | | | | | |
| | | | | | |
| | | | | | |
| **43** Amortization of costs that began before your 2021 tax year . . . . . . . . . . . . **43** | | | | | |
| **44** **Total.** Add amounts in column (f). See the instructions for where to report . . . . . . . . **44** | | | | | |

Form **4562** (2021)

| Form **4797** | **Sales of Business Property**<br>(Also Involuntary Conversions and Recapture Amounts<br>Under Sections 179 and 280F(b)(2))<br>▶ **Attach to your tax return.**<br>▶ **Go to** *www.irs.gov/Form4797* **for instructions and the latest information.** | OMB No. 1545-0184<br>**2021**<br>Attachment<br>Sequence No. **27** |
|---|---|---|

Department of the Treasury
Internal Revenue Service

Name(s) shown on return | Identifying number

**1a** Enter the gross proceeds from sales or exchanges reported to you for 2021 on Form(s) 1099-B or 1099-S (or substitute statement) that you are including on line 2, 10, or 20. See instructions ........... | **1a**

**b** Enter the total amount of gain that you are including on lines 2, 10, and 24 due to the partial dispositions of MACRS assets ........................................... | **1b**

**c** Enter the total amount of loss that you are including on lines 2 and 10 due to the partial dispositions of MACRS assets ........................................... | **1c**

**Part I** **Sales or Exchanges of Property Used in a Trade or Business and Involuntary Conversions From Other Than Casualty or Theft—Most Property Held More Than 1 Year** (see instructions)

| **2** | **(a)** Description of property | **(b)** Date acquired (mo., day, yr.) | **(c)** Date sold (mo., day, yr.) | **(d)** Gross sales price | **(e)** Depreciation allowed or allowable since acquisition | **(f)** Cost or other basis, plus improvements and expense of sale | **(g)** Gain or (loss) Subtract (f) from the sum of (d) and (e) |
|---|---|---|---|---|---|---|---|
| | | | | | | | |
| | | | | | | | |
| | | | | | | | |

**3** Gain, if any, from Form 4684, line 39 ........................ | **3**

**4** Section 1231 gain from installment sales from Form 6252, line 26 or 37 ......... | **4**

**5** Section 1231 gain or (loss) from like-kind exchanges from Form 8824 ........... | **5**

**6** Gain, if any, from line 32, from other than casualty or theft .............. | **6**

**7** Combine lines 2 through 6. Enter the gain or (loss) here and on the appropriate line as follows ...... | **7**

**Partnerships and S corporations.** Report the gain or (loss) following the instructions for Form 1065, Schedule K, line 10, or Form 1120-S, Schedule K, line 9. Skip lines 8, 9, 11, and 12 below.

**Individuals, partners, S corporation shareholders, and all others.** If line 7 is zero or a loss, enter the amount from line 7 on line 11 below and skip lines 8 and 9. If line 7 is a gain and you didn't have any prior year section 1231 losses, or they were recaptured in an earlier year, enter the gain from line 7 as a long-term capital gain on the Schedule D filed with your return and skip lines 8, 9, 11, and 12 below.

**8** Nonrecaptured net section 1231 losses from prior years. See instructions ......... | **8**

**9** Subtract line 8 from line 7. If zero or less, enter -0-. If line 9 is zero, enter the gain from line 7 on line 12 below. If line 9 is more than zero, enter the amount from line 8 on line 12 below and enter the gain from line 9 as a long-term capital gain on the Schedule D filed with your return. See instructions. ................. | **9**

**Part II** **Ordinary Gains and Losses** (see instructions)

**10** Ordinary gains and losses not included on lines 11 through 16 (include property held 1 year or less):

| | | | | | | | |
|---|---|---|---|---|---|---|---|
| | | | | | | | |
| | | | | | | | |
| | | | | | | | |

**11** Loss, if any, from line 7 ............................. | **11** ( )

**12** Gain, if any, from line 7 or amount from line 8, if applicable ............. | **12**

**13** Gain, if any, from line 31 ............................ | **13**

**14** Net gain or (loss) from Form 4684, lines 31 and 38a ................. | **14**

**15** Ordinary gain from installment sales from Form 6252, line 25 or 36 .......... | **15**

**16** Ordinary gain or (loss) from like-kind exchanges from Form 8824 ........... | **16**

**17** Combine lines 10 through 16. ......................... | **17**

**18** For all except individual returns, enter the amount from line 17 on the appropriate line of your return and skip lines a and b below. For individual returns, complete lines a and b below.

**a** If the loss on line 11 includes a loss from Form 4684, line 35, column (b)(ii), enter that part of the loss here. Enter the loss from income-producing property on Schedule A (Form 1040), line 16. (Do not include any loss on property used as an employee.) Identify as from "Form 4797, line 18a." See instructions ............ | **18a**

**b** Redetermine the gain or (loss) on line 17 excluding the loss, if any, on line 18a. Enter here and on Schedule 1 (Form 1040), Part I, line 4 ......................... | **18b**

**For Paperwork Reduction Act Notice, see separate instructions.** | Cat. No. 13086I | Form **4797** (2021)

Form 4797 (2021)                                                                                                   Page **2**

## Part III   Gain From Disposition of Property Under Sections 1245, 1250, 1252, 1254, and 1255
(see instructions)

| 19 | (a) Description of section 1245, 1250, 1252, 1254, or 1255 property: | (b) Date acquired (mo., day, yr.) | (c) Date sold (mo., day, yr.) |
|----|----------------------------------------------------------------------|-----------------------------------|-------------------------------|
| A  | | | |
| B  | | | |
| C  | | | |
| D  | | | |

These columns relate to the properties on lines 19A through 19D. ▶

| | | | Property A | Property B | Property C | Property D |
|---|---|---|---|---|---|---|
| 20 | Gross sales price (**Note:** *See line 1a before completing.*) . | 20 | | | | |
| 21 | Cost or other basis plus expense of sale . . . . . | 21 | | | | |
| 22 | Depreciation (or depletion) allowed or allowable . . | 22 | | | | |
| 23 | Adjusted basis. Subtract line 22 from line 21 . . . | 23 | | | | |
| 24 | Total gain. Subtract line 23 from line 20 . . . . . | 24 | | | | |
| 25 | **If section 1245 property:** | | | | | |
| a | Depreciation allowed or allowable from line 22 . . | 25a | | | | |
| b | Enter the **smaller** of line 24 or 25a. . . . . | 25b | | | | |
| 26 | **If section 1250 property:** If straight line depreciation was used, enter -0- on line 26g, except for a corporation subject to section 291. | | | | | |
| a | Additional depreciation after 1975. See instructions . | 26a | | | | |
| b | Applicable percentage multiplied by the **smaller** of line 24 or line 26a. See instructions. . . . . . . . | 26b | | | | |
| c | Subtract line 26a from line 24. If residential rental property **or** line 24 isn't more than line 26a, skip lines 26d and 26e | 26c | | | | |
| d | Additional depreciation after 1969 and before 1976. . | 26d | | | | |
| e | Enter the **smaller** of line 26c or 26d . . . . . | 26e | | | | |
| f | Section 291 amount (corporations only) . . . . . | 26f | | | | |
| g | Add lines 26b, 26e, and 26f . . . . . . . . | 26g | | | | |
| 27 | **If section 1252 property:** Skip this section if you didn't dispose of farmland or if this form is being completed for a partnership. | | | | | |
| a | Soil, water, and land clearing expenses . . . . . | 27a | | | | |
| b | Line 27a multiplied by applicable percentage. See instructions | 27b | | | | |
| c | Enter the **smaller** of line 24 or 27b . . . . . . | 27c | | | | |
| 28 | **If section 1254 property:** | | | | | |
| a | Intangible drilling and development costs, expenditures for development of mines and other natural deposits, mining exploration costs, and depletion. See instructions | 28a | | | | |
| b | Enter the **smaller** of line 24 or 28a. . . . . . . | 28b | | | | |
| 29 | **If section 1255 property:** | | | | | |
| a | Applicable percentage of payments excluded from income under section 126. See instructions . . . . | 29a | | | | |
| b | Enter the **smaller** of line 24 or 29a. See instructions | 29b | | | | |

**Summary of Part III Gains.** Complete property columns A through D through line 29b before going to line 30.

| 30 | Total gains for all properties. Add property columns A through D, line 24 . . . . . . . . . . . | 30 | |
|----|--------------------------------------------------------------------------------------------------|----|--|
| 31 | Add property columns A through D, lines 25b, 26g, 27c, 28b, and 29b. Enter here and on line 13 . . . . . . . | 31 | |
| 32 | Subtract line 31 from line 30. Enter the portion from casualty or theft on Form 4684, line 33. Enter the portion from other than casualty or theft on Form 4797, line 6 . . . . . . . . . . . . . . . . . . . . . . . | 32 | |

## Part IV   Recapture Amounts Under Sections 179 and 280F(b)(2) When Business Use Drops to 50% or Less
(see instructions)

| | | | (a) Section 179 | (b) Section 280F(b)(2) |
|---|---|---|-----------------|------------------------|
| 33 | Section 179 expense deduction or depreciation allowable in prior years. . . . . . . . . | 33 | | |
| 34 | Recomputed depreciation. See instructions . . . . . . . . . . . . . . . . . | 34 | | |
| 35 | Recapture amount. Subtract line 34 from line 33. See the instructions for where to report . . | 35 | | |

Form **4797** (2021)

Form **8949**

Department of the Treasury
Internal Revenue Service

## Sales and Other Dispositions of Capital Assets

▶ Go to *www.irs.gov/Form8949* for instructions and the latest information.
▶ File with your Schedule D to list your transactions for lines 1b, 2, 3, 8b, 9, and 10 of Schedule D.

OMB No. 1545-0074

2021

Attachment
Sequence No. **12A**

| Name(s) shown on return | Social security number or taxpayer identification number |
|---|---|

*Before you check Box A, B, or C below, see whether you received any Form(s) 1099-B or substitute statement(s) from your broker. A substitute statement will have the same information as Form 1099-B. Either will show whether your basis (usually your cost) was reported to the IRS by your broker and may even tell you which box to check.*

**Part I** | **Short-Term.** Transactions involving capital assets you held 1 year or less are generally short-term (see instructions). For long-term transactions, see page 2.

**Note:** You may aggregate all short-term transactions reported on Form(s) 1099-B showing basis was reported to the IRS and for which no adjustments or codes are required. Enter the totals directly on Schedule D, line 1a; you aren't required to report these transactions on Form 8949 (see instructions).

**You *must* check Box A, B, *or* C below. Check only one box.** If more than one box applies for your short-term transactions, complete a separate Form 8949, page 1, for each applicable box. If you have more short-term transactions than will fit on this page for one or more of the boxes, complete as many forms with the same box checked as you need.

☐ **(A)** Short-term transactions reported on Form(s) 1099-B showing basis was reported to the IRS (see **Note** above)
☐ **(B)** Short-term transactions reported on Form(s) 1099-B showing basis **wasn't** reported to the IRS
☐ **(C)** Short-term transactions not reported to you on Form 1099-B

| 1 | | | | | | Adjustment, if any, to gain or loss. If you enter an amount in column (g), enter a code in column (f). See the separate instructions. | | |
|---|---|---|---|---|---|---|---|---|
| | **(a)** Description of property (Example: 100 sh. XYZ Co.) | **(b)** Date acquired (Mo., day, yr.) | **(c)** Date sold or disposed of (Mo., day, yr.) | **(d)** Proceeds (sales price) (see instructions) | **(e)** Cost or other basis. See the **Note** below and see *Column (e)* in the separate instructions | **(f)** Code(s) from instructions | **(g)** Amount of adjustment | **(h)** Gain or (loss). Subtract column (e) from column (d) and combine the result with column (g) |
| | | | | | | | | |
| | | | | | | | | |
| | | | | | | | | |
| | | | | | | | | |
| | | | | | | | | |
| | | | | | | | | |
| | | | | | | | | |
| | | | | | | | | |
| | | | | | | | | |
| | | | | | | | | |
| | | | | | | | | |
| | | | | | | | | |
| | | | | | | | | |
| | | | | | | | | |

**2 Totals.** Add the amounts in columns (d), (e), (g), and (h) (subtract negative amounts). Enter each total here and include on your Schedule D, **line 1b** (if **Box A** above is checked), **line 2** (if **Box B** above is checked), or **line 3** (if **Box C** above is checked) ▶

**Note:** If you checked Box A above but the basis reported to the IRS was incorrect, enter in column (e) the basis as reported to the IRS, and enter an adjustment in column (g) to correct the basis. See *Column (g)* in the separate instructions for how to figure the amount of the adjustment.

**For Paperwork Reduction Act Notice, see your tax return instructions.** | Cat. No. 37768Z | Form **8949** (2021)

Form 8949 (2021)

| Name(s) shown on return. Name and SSN or taxpayer identification no. not required if shown on other side | Social security number or taxpayer identification number |
|---|---|

*Before you check Box D, E, or F below, see whether you received any Form(s) 1099-B or substitute statement(s) from your broker. A substitute statement will have the same information as Form 1099-B. Either will show whether your basis (usually your cost) was reported to the IRS by your broker and may even tell you which box to check.*

**Part II** **Long-Term.** Transactions involving capital assets you held more than 1 year are generally long-term (see instructions). For short-term transactions, see page 1.

**Note:** You may aggregate all long-term transactions reported on Form(s) 1099-B showing basis was reported to the IRS and for which no adjustments or codes are required. Enter the totals directly on Schedule D, line 8a; you aren't required to report these transactions on Form 8949 (see instructions).

**You *must* check Box D, E, *or* F below. Check only one box.** If more than one box applies for your long-term transactions, complete a separate Form 8949, page 2, for each applicable box. If you have more long-term transactions than will fit on this page for one or more of the boxes, complete as many forms with the same box checked as you need.

- ☐ **(D)** Long-term transactions reported on Form(s) 1099-B showing basis was reported to the IRS (see **Note** above)
- ☐ **(E)** Long-term transactions reported on Form(s) 1099-B showing basis **wasn't** reported to the IRS
- ☐ **(F)** Long-term transactions not reported to you on Form 1099-B

| 1 (a) Description of property (Example: 100 sh. XYZ Co.) | (b) Date acquired (Mo., day, yr.) | (c) Date sold or disposed of (Mo., day, yr.) | (d) Proceeds (sales price) (see instructions) | (e) Cost or other basis. See the Note below and see Column (e) in the separate instructions | (f) Code(s) from instructions | (g) Amount of adjustment | (h) Gain or (loss). Subtract column (e) from column (d) and combine the result with column (g) |
|---|---|---|---|---|---|---|---|
| | | | | | | | |
| | | | | | | | |
| | | | | | | | |
| | | | | | | | |
| | | | | | | | |
| | | | | | | | |
| | | | | | | | |
| | | | | | | | |
| | | | | | | | |
| | | | | | | | |
| | | | | | | | |
| | | | | | | | |
| | | | | | | | |
| | | | | | | | |

**2 Totals.** Add the amounts in columns (d), (e), (g), and (h) (subtract negative amounts). Enter each total here and include on your Schedule D, **line 8b** (if **Box D** above is checked), **line 9** (if **Box E** above is checked), or **line 10** (if **Box F** above is checked) ▶

**Note:** If you checked Box D above but the basis reported to the IRS was incorrect, enter in column (e) the basis as reported to the IRS, and enter an adjustment in column (g) to correct the basis. See *Column (g)* in the separate instructions for how to figure the amount of the adjustment.

Form **8949** (2021)

# 2021 Federal Income Tax Information

## 2021 Federal Tax Rate Schedules

### Schedule X-Single

| If taxable income is over: | But not over: | The tax is: |
|---|---|---|
| $0 | $9,950 | 10% of taxable income |
| $9,950 | $40,525 | $995.00 plus 12% of the excess over $9,950 |
| $40,525 | $86,375 | $4,664.00 plus 22% of the excess over $40,525 |
| $86,375 | $164,925 | $14,751.00 plus 24% of the excess over $86,375 |
| $164,925 | $209,425 | $33,603.00 plus 32% of the excess over $164,925 |
| $209,425 | $523,600 | $47,843.00 plus 35% of the excess over $209,425 |
| $523,600 | — | $157,804.25 plus 37% of the excess over $523,600 |

### Schedule Y-1-Married Filing Jointly or Qualifying Widow(er)

| If taxable income is over: | But not over: | The tax is: |
|---|---|---|
| $0 | $19,900 | 10% of taxable income |
| $19,900 | $81,050 | $1,990.00 plus 12% of the excess over $19,990 |
| $81,050 | $172,750 | $9,328.00 plus 22% of the excess over $81,050 |
| $172,750 | $329,850 | $29,502.00 plus 24% of the excess over $172,750 |
| $329,850 | $418,850 | $67,206.00 plus 32% of the excess over $329,850 |
| $418,850 | $628,300 | $95,686.00 plus 35% of the excess over $418,850 |
| $628,300 | — | $168,993.50 plus 37% of the excess over $628,300 |

### Schedule Y-2-Married Filing Separately

| If taxable income is over: | But not over: | The tax is: |
|---|---|---|
| $0 | $9,950 | 10% of taxable income |
| $9,950 | $40,525 | $995.00 plus 12% of the excess over $9,950 |
| $40,525 | $86,375 | $4,664.00 plus 22% of the excess over $40,525 |
| $86,375 | $164,925 | $14,751.00 plus 24% of the excess over $86,375 |
| $164,925 | $209,425 | $33,603.00 plus 32% of the excess over $164,925 |
| $209,425 | $314,150 | $47,843.00 plus 35% of the excess over $209,425 |
| $314,150 | — | $84,496.75 plus 37% of the excess over $314,150 |

### Schedule Z-Head of Household

| If taxable income is over: | But not over: | The tax is: |
|---|---|---|
| $0 | $14,200 | 10% of taxable income |
| $14,200 | $54,200 | $1,420.00 plus 12% of the excess over $14,200 |
| $54,200 | $86,350 | $6,220.00 plus 22% of the excess over $54,200 |
| $86,350 | $164,900 | $13,293.00 plus 24% of the excess over $86,350 |
| $164,900 | $209,400 | $32,145.00 plus 32% of the excess over $164,900 |
| $209,400 | $523,600 | $46,385.00 plus 35% of the excess over $209,400 |
| $523,600 | — | $156,355.00 plus 37% of the excess over $523,600 |

## Qualified Dividends & Capital Gains Tax Rates

| | |
|---|---|
| Collectible gain | 28% |
| Section 1202 gain | 28% |
| Unrecaptured Section 1250 gain | 25% |

Other capital gains and qualified dividends based on taxable income:

Zero tax rate:
Single & Married filing separately: taxable income of $0–$40,400
Married filing jointly: taxable income of $0–$80,800
Head of household: taxable income of $0–$54,100

15% tax rate:
Single: taxable income of $40,401–$445,850
Married filing jointly: taxable income of $80,801–$501,600
Married filing separately: taxable income of $40,401–$250,800
Head of household: taxable income of $54,101–$473,750

20% tax rate:
Single: taxable income over $445,850
Married filing jointly: taxable income over $501,600
Married filing separately: taxable income over $250,800
Head of household: taxable income over $473,750

Short-term capital gains (held 1 year or less) are taxed at ordinary tax rates

## Standard Deduction

| Filing Status | Basic Standard Deduction |
|---|---|
| Single | $12,550 |
| Married filing jointly | $25,100 |
| Married filing separately | $12,550 |
| Head of household | $18,800 |
| Qualifying widow(er) | $25,100 |
| Additional over 65 or blind | |
| Married, qual. widow(er) | $1,350 |
| Single/Head of household | $1,700 |

## Social Security, Medicare, & Self-Employment Taxes

| Employee | Rate | Income Limit |
|---|---|---|
| • Social Security | 6.2% | $142,800 |
| • Medicare | 1.45% | Unlimited |
| • Total | 7.65% | |

| Self-employed | Rate | Income Limit |
|---|---|---|
| • Social Security | 12.4% | $142,800 |
| • Medicare | 2.9% | Unlimited |
| • Total | 15.3% | |

An additional Medicare tax of 0.9% is assessed on wages and self-employment income in excess of $250,000 (married filing jointly), $125,000 (married filing separately), or $200,000 (all others).

## Standard Mileage Rates

| | |
|---|---|
| Business miles | $0.56 |
| Charity miles | $0.14 |
| Medical miles | $0.16 |
| Moving miles | $0.16 |

## Child Tax Credit

| | |
|---|---|
| Amount per child under age 6 | $3,600 |
| Amount per child age 6 to 17 | $3,000 |

Credit reduction of 5% of AGI over the following thresholds until total credit is reduced to $2,000 per qualifying child.

Single=$75,000; head of household=$112,500; Married filing jointly=$150,000

Further credit reduction of $5 for each $1,000, or fraction thereof, for AGI in excess of $400,000 (MFJ) or $200,000 (all other taxpayers).

## Coverdell Educational Savings Accounts

Contributions limit—$2,000 per year per beneficiary, must be in cash, and must be made before the beneficiary turns 18.

| Phase-out Thresholds | |
|---|---|
| Married filing jointly—AGI | $190,000–$220,000 |
| Single—AGI | $95,000–$110,000 |

## Traditional IRA Contribution Deduction

IRA contributions—Lower of $6,000 or the amount of compensation

Individuals who are age 50 or older—Lower of $7,000 or compensation.

Phase-outs if the individual is a participant in another retirement plan:

| | | |
|---|---|---|
| Married | $105,000–$125,000 | Phase-out range |
| | Greater than $125,000—no deduction | |
| Single | $66,000–$76,000 | Phase-out range |
| | Greater than $76,000—no deduction | |

## Roth IRA Contribution

| | |
|---|---|
| Roth contribution | $6,000 or compensation |
| 50 or older | $7,000 or compensation |

All Roth contributions are not tax deductible

Joint Returns—$198,000–$208,000 phase-out range

Single or head of household—$125,000–$140,000 phase-out range

## Health Savings Account Contribution

| | |
|---|---|
| Individual | $3,600 |
| Family | $7,200 |

Taxpayers who are age 55 or older may contribute an additional $1,000 ($4,600 individual or $8,200 family)

# Index

# R

Real estate taxes, 5-11
Realization of income, 3-1–3-3
Realized gains or losses from sales of property, 7-3
Recapture rules
for alimony paid, 4-17–4-18
in installment sales, 12-15
for sales of business property, 7-21–7-26
Recognition of gains or losses from sales of property, 7-3, 7-7–7-8
Recording gross income, 3-1–3-2
Recourse liabilities, for at-risk purposes, 13-5, 13-7
Recovery Rebate Credit (RRC), 1-21–1-22
Reduced maximum exclusion, 12-16, 12-18
Refunds of state and local taxes, 3-10
Regressive structure for tax rates, 1-4
Regulated investment companies, 3-8
Related parties
installment sales and, 12-15
in like-kind exchanges, 12-6
losses of, 12-21–12-22
Relationship or member of household test for qualifying relatives, 2-17
Relationship test for dependent children, 2-15
Rental property
expenses of, 8-3–8-5, 8-9
farm, 8-2
Form 4562 for, 8-7–8-8
income from, 8-2–8-3
passive activity loss rules and, 13-11–13-15
Schedule E for, 8-6, 8-14–8-15
vacation homes as, 8-9–8-13, 8-16
Replacement property, in involuntary conversions, 12-10–12-13
Required minimum distribution (RMD), from retirement plans, 11-17
Research Institute of America (RIA), 1-24
Residency test for dependent children, 2-15
Retirement plans, 11-1–11-41
Coverdell Education Savings Account distributions, 11-20, 11-22
distributions from qualified pension plans, 11-16–11-19
401(k) plans sponsored by employers, 11-6
income from, 1-9
individual-sponsored, 11-9–11-12
Keogh plans, 11-6–11-7
qualified pension plans sponsored by employers, 11-3–11-5
SIMPLE plans, 11-7–11-9
Simplified Employee Pensions (SEP), 11-7
taxation of annuity contracts, 11-23–11-26
taxation of Roth IRA distributions, 11-20–11-21
taxation of traditional IRA distributions, 11-20
tax-deferred nonretirement plans, 11-12–11-15
tax-deferred plans and annuities, 11-1–11-3
Retirement savings contribution tax credit, 9-18–9-20
Revenue Procedure, AMT, 13-25
Revenue rulings and procedures, 1-25–1-26
Revised Form 941, payroll taxes, 10-40
RIA (Research Institute of America), 1-24
RMD (required minimum distribution), from retirement plans, 11-17
Rollovers to retirement plans, 11-22
Roth Individual Retirement Accounts (IRAs)
conversions of traditional IRAs to, 11-22, 11-23
distributions from, 11-20–11-21
401(k) retirement plans as, 11-11
overview, 9-18
Royalty income, 8-16–8-17
RRC (Recovery Rebate Credit), 1-21–1-22

# S

Safe harbor rule, 10-37
Sales, installment, 12-13–12-17
Sales of block stock, 7-26, 7-31–7-32
Sales of business property. *See also* Special property transactions
Form 4797 for, 7-27–7-28

overview, 7-20, 7-39
recapture provisions for, 7-21–7-26
Schedule D for, 7-29–7-30
Sales of capital assets. *See also* Special property transactions
Form 8949 for, 7-14, 7-17
holding period for, 7-9–7-10
netting capital gains and losses, 7-12–7-13
overview, 7-39
Schedule D for, 7-15–7-16, 7-18–7-19
tax rates for, 7-10–7-12
Sales of inherited property, 7-38
Sales of mutual funds, 7-26, 7-32–7-37
Sales of ordinary assets, 7-7–7-8, 7-39
Sales of partnership interest, 14-21–14-22
Sales of personal residences, 12-16, 12-18–12-20
Sales of property received as gift, 7-38
Sales of worthless securities, 7-33, 7-37–7-38
Sales taxes, as proportional tax, 1-4
Savings bonds
interest exclusion on, 3-24–3-25
interest taxability of, 3-4
Schedule 1 of Form 1040
additional income reported on, 1-9
example of, 1-11–1-13, 2-4–2-5
line-by-line, 2-9
Schedule 2 of Form 1040
example of, 2-6–2-7
line-by-line, 2-10
premium credits reported on, 9-28
Schedule 3 of Form 1040
adoption credits reported on, 9-19–9-21
child and dependent care expenses reported on, 9-2
education tax credits reported on, 9-7
elderly or disabled credit reported on, 9-6
example of, 2-8
foreign tax credits reported on, 9-13
line-by-line, 2-10
premium credits reported on, 9-28
retirement savings contribution tax credits reported on, 9-18–9-19
Schedule A
comprehensive tax return problems on, B-1–B-3
itemized deductions reported on, 5-13, 5-18
Schedule B, interest and ordinary dividends, 3-5–3-7, 10-22
Schedule B, payroll tax liability, 10-22
Schedule C
comprehensive tax return problems on, B-3–B-5
example of, 6-37–6-42
income types reported on, 6-5–6-6
self-employed business income reported on, 1-6, 6-2–6-4
Schedule D
comprehensive tax return problems on, B-5–B-7
for property sale gains or losses, 7-12
for sales of business property, 7-29–7-30
for sales of capital assets, 7-15–7-16, 7-18–7-19
Schedule EIC (earned income credit), 2-23, 9-25–9-27
Schedule E, rental property
comprehensive tax return problem on, B-7–B-9
examples of, 8-6, 8-14–8-15
Schedule H, household employment taxes, 10-26, 10-29–10-30
Schedule K-1, flow-through entities, 8-18–8-21, 13-4, 13-13, 13-29, 14-13–14-15, 14-29–14-30
Schedule L, corporate balance sheet, 15-17
Schedule M-1, book to taxable income reconciliation for corporations, 15-17–15-18, 15-27
Schedule M-3, book to taxable income reconciliation for large corporations, 15-18
Schedule R, elderly or disabled credit, 9-7
Scholarships and fellowships, 3-17
S corporations. *See* Subchapter S corporations
SDI (state disability insurance), 5-12
2nd Story Software, 1-16
Self-employment business income, 6-1–6-61. *See also* Self-employment tax
bad debts, 6-30
casualty losses, 6-30–6-32
cost of goods sold in, 6-6

depreciation in
basis of, 6-9–6-10
conventions for, 6-10–6-14
IRC § 179 expense election, 6-14–6-15
limitations on, 6-17–6-18
methods of, 6-13–6-14
100% bonus, 6-15–6-16
overview, 6-8
education expenses, 6-34
health insurance deduction, 4-13–4-14
hobby loss rules, 6-33
home office, 6-27–6-29
Keogh retirement plans for, 11-6–11-7
ordinary and necessary trade or business expenses in, 6-7–6-8
overview, 6-1–6-2
partnership income as, 14-15
qualified business income deduction, 6-43–6-44
return example of, 6-37–6-42
Schedule C for reporting, 1-6, 6-2–6-4
transportation expenses, 6-18–6-24
travel expenses, 6-24–6-26
Self-employment tax
components of, 6-34–6-36
deduction for half of, 4-12–4-13
reporting, 10-22–10-23
Separated parents, dependent children and, 2-16
Separately stated items
in partnerships taxation, 14-13–14-15
of Subchapter S corporations, 15-21
SEP retirement plans, 9-18, 11-7
Service contribution to partnerships, 14-4–14-5
Shareholder loans, 3-27
Shoebox to Software feature
alimony paid, 4-17
alternative minimum tax, 13-33
casualty and theft losses, 5-28
charitable deductions, 5-23–5-24
child tax credits, 9-18–9-19
deductible interest, 5-15
depreciation, 6-19
dividends, 3-9
early withdrawal penalties, 4-7, 4-15
flow-through entities, 8-19
Form 1099-R, reporting contributions and distributions, 11-24
Form 1116, foreign tax credits, 9-14
Form 2441, child and dependent care expenses, 9-4
Form 8824, reports the FMV, 12-7
Form 8839, adoption tax credits, 9-21
Form 8863, report education credit, 9-11
health savings account, 4-7
installment sales, 12-16–12-18
interest expense deduction, 5-19
involuntary conversions, 12-12
like-kind exchanges, 12-7
material participation tests, 13-12
medical expense deductions, 5-8
ordinary income or loss, 7-7
rental property, 8-5, 8-13
residential property sales, 12-19
retirement plan contribution deduction, 11-8, 11-12
retirement savings contribution tax credits, 9-19
return examples, 3-19, 4-19, 5-31, 6-37, 9-25
Schedule D, 7-12
Schedule EIC, 9-25
Schedule R, elderly or disabled credit, 9-7
social security benefits, 3-12
source documents, 1-16–1-18
student loan interest, 4-5
taxable interest, 3-5
tax payment calculation, 2-25
§ 1250 recapture of depreciation deduction previously taken, 7-26
§ 1245 recapture of depreciation on personal trade or business property, 7-21
Short-term capital assets, 7-9
Sickness and injury compensation, 3-18
SIMPLE employer-sponsored retirement plans, 9-18–9-19, 11-7–11-9
Simplified Employee Pensions (SEP), 9-18, 11-7
Single, filing status as, 2-11
Sixteenth Amendment to U.S. Constitution, 1-1–1-2